# CALIFORNIA
# HIKING

# FOGHORN OUTDOORS CALIFORNIA HIKING

## Seventh Edition

## Tom Stienstra • Ann Marie Brown

Printing History
1st edition—1994
7th edition—March 2005
5 4 3 2 1

Avalon Travel Publishing
An Imprint of
Avalon Publishing Group, Inc.

AVALON
publishing group incorporated

Text © 2005 by Tom Stienstra, Ann Marie Brown.
All rights reserved.
Illustrations and maps © 2005 by Avalon Travel Publishing.
All rights reserved.

Some photos and illustrations are used by permission
and are the property of the original copyright owners.

ISBN: 1-56691-688-7
ISSN: 1078-960X

Editors: Amy Scott, Ellie Behrstock
Series Manager: Grace Fujimoto
Acquisitions Editor: Rebecca K. Browning
Copy Editor: Wendy Taylor
Proofreader: Erika Howsare
Graphics Coordinator: Susan Snyder
Production Coordinator: Darren Alessi
Cover and Interior Designer: Darren Alessi
Map Editor: Olivia Solís
Cartographers: CHK America, Kat Kalamaras, Suzanne Service, Mike Morgenfeld
Indexer: Ellie Behrstock

Front cover photo: Patrick's Point near Wedding Rock © Gary Todoroff

Printed in the United States of America by Worzalla

Foghorn Outdoors and the Foghorn Outdoors logo are the property of Avalon Travel Publishing, an imprint of Avalon Publishing Group, Inc. All other marks and logos depicted are the property of the original owners.

All rights reserved. No part of this book may be translated or reproduced in any form, except brief extracts by a reviewer for the purpose of a review, without written permission of the copyright owner.

Although every effort was made to ensure that the information was correct at the time of going to press, the author and publisher do not assume and hereby disclaim any liability to any party for any loss or damage caused by errors, omissions, or any potential travel disruption due to labor or financial difficulty, whether such errors or omissions result from negligence, accident, or any other cause.

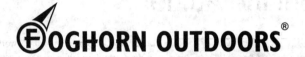

# CALIFORNIA
# HIKING

The Complete Guide to More Than 1,000 Hikes

Seventh Edition

Tom Stienstra • Ann Marie Brown

AVALON
TRAVEL

# About the Author

Tom Stienstra has made it his life's work to explore the West, traveling 200 days a year—camping, hiking, fishing, biking, boating, and flying—searching for the best of the outdoors and then writing about it. Tom is the nation's top-selling author of outdoors guidebooks. He has been named California Outdoor Writer of the Year four times and has twice been awarded National Outdoor Writer of the Year, newspaper division, by the Outdoor Writers Association of America. Tom is the outdoors columnist for the *San Francisco Chronicle,* and his articles also have appeared on www.SFGate.com and in newspapers around the country.

His wife, Stephani, has co-authored two books with him. They live with their sons in Northern California.

In this edition of *Foghorn Outdoors California Hiking,* Tom made revisions to Lassen and Modoc, Mendocino and Wine Country, Redwood Empire, Sacramento and Gold Country, San Francisco Bay Area, Shasta and Trinity, and Tahoe and the Northern Sierra chapters.

You can contact Tom directly via his website: www.TomStienstra.com. There you'll also find his other books, including:

*Foghorn Outdoors California Camping*
*Foghorn Outdoors California Fishing*
*Foghorn Outdoors California Recreational Lakes & Rivers*
*Foghorn Outdoors California Wildlife* (with illustrator Paul Johnson)
*Foghorn Outdoors Northern California Cabins & Cottages* (with Stephani Stienstra)
*Foghorn Outdoors Oregon Camping*
*Foghorn Outdoors Pacific Northwest Camping*
*Foghorn Outdoors Washington Camping* (with Stephani Stienstra)

# About the Author

© BILL RHOADES

The author of 12 outdoors guidebooks, Ann Marie Brown is a dedicated California outdoorswoman. She hikes, bikes, and camps more than 150 days each year in a dedicated effort to avoid routine, complacency, and getting a real job.

Ann Marie's work has appeared in *Sunset, VIA,* and *Backpacker* magazines. As a way of giving back a little of what she gets from her experiences in nature, she writes and edits for several environmental groups, including the Sierra Club and Natural Resources Defense Council. When not traipsing along a California trail, Ann Marie can be found at her home near Yosemite National Park.

In this edition of *Foghorn Outdoors California Hiking,* Ann Marie was responsible for updates to Death Valley, Los Angeles and Vicinity, Monterey and Big Sur, San Diego and Vicinity, San Joaquin Valley, Santa Barbara and Vicinity, Sequoia and Kings Canyon, The Southern Deserts, and Yosemite and Mammoth Lakes chapters.

Ann Marie's other guidebooks include:

*Foghorn Outdoors 101 Great Hikes of the San Francisco Bay Area*
*Foghorn Outdoors 250 Great Hikes in California's National Parks*
*Foghorn Outdoors Bay Area Biking*
*Foghorn Outdoors California Waterfalls*
*Foghorn Outdoors Easy Biking in Northern California*
*Foghorn Outdoors Easy Camping in Southern California*
*Foghorn Outdoors Easy Hiking in Northern California*
*Foghorn Outdoors Easy Hiking in Southern California*
*Foghorn Outdoors Northern California Biking*
*Foghorn Outdoors Southern California Cabins & Cottages*
*Moon Handbooks Yosemite*

For more information on these titles, visit Ann Marie's website: www.annmariebrown.com.

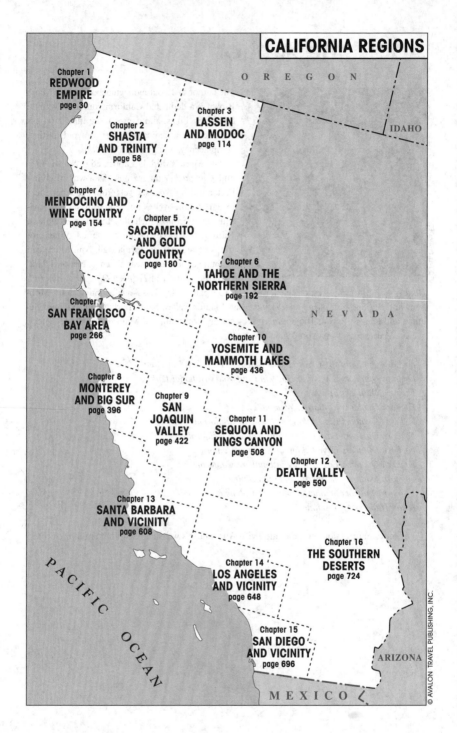

# CALIFORNIA REGIONS

**Chapter 1**
**REDWOOD EMPIRE**
page 30

**Chapter 2**
**SHASTA AND TRINITY**
page 58

**Chapter 3**
**LASSEN AND MODOC**
page 114

**Chapter 4**
**MENDOCINO AND WINE COUNTRY**
page 154

**Chapter 5**
**SACRAMENTO AND GOLD COUNTRY**
page 180

**Chapter 6**
**TAHOE AND THE NORTHERN SIERRA**
page 192

**Chapter 7**
**SAN FRANCISCO BAY AREA**
page 266

**Chapter 10**
**YOSEMITE AND MAMMOTH LAKES**
page 436

**Chapter 8**
**MONTEREY AND BIG SUR**
page 396

**Chapter 9**
**SAN JOAQUIN VALLEY**
page 422

**Chapter 11**
**SEQUOIA AND KINGS CANYON**
page 508

**Chapter 12**
**DEATH VALLEY**
page 590

**Chapter 13**
**SANTA BARBARA AND VICINITY**
page 608

**Chapter 16**
**THE SOUTHERN DESERTS**
page 724

**Chapter 14**
**LOS ANGELES AND VICINITY**
page 648

**Chapter 15**
**SAN DIEGO AND VICINITY**
page 696

OREGON

IDAHO

NEVADA

ARIZONA

MEXICO

PACIFIC OCEAN

© AVALON TRAVEL PUBLISHING, INC.

© TOM STIENSTRA

# Contents

## SPECIAL TOPICS

*Fun Stuff 10* • *Adding to the Pack 13* • *Facts about Mountain Lions 15* • *Making Long-Distance Trips Work 24*

**Including:**
- Arcata Marsh and Wildlife Sanctuary
- Arcata Redwood Park
- Benbow Lake State Recreation Area
- Del Norte Redwoods State Park
- Grizzly Creek Redwoods State Park
- Humboldt Redwoods State Park
- Jedediah Smith Redwoods State Park
- King Range National Conservation Area
- Patrick's Point State Park
- Prairie Creek Redwoods State Park
- Redwood National and State Parks
- Richardson Grove State Park
- Russ City Park
- Siskiyou Wilderness
- Smith River National Recreation Area

**Including:**
- Castle Crags State Park
- Castle Lake
- Klamath National Forest
- Klamath River
- Lake Siskiyou
- Marble Mountain Wilderness
- McCloud River
- Mount Shasta
- Russian Wilderness
- Ruth Lake
- Shasta Lake
- Shasta-Trinity National Forest
- Siskiyou Mountains
- Siskiyou Wilderness
- Six Rivers National Forest
- Smith River National Recreation Area
- Trinity Alps Wilderness
- Trinity Lake
- Whiskeytown Lake National Recreation Area
- Yolla Bolly Wilderness

- Clark Fork Stanislaus River
- D. L. Bliss State Park
- Desolation Wilderness
- Echo Lake
- Eldorado National Forest
- Emerald Bay State Park
- Emigrant Wilderness
- Fallen Leaf Lake
- French Meadows Reservoir
- Gold Lakes Basin
- Granite Chief Wilderness
- Grover Hot Springs State Park
- Hell Hole Reservoir
- Humboldt-Toiyabe National Forest
- Kirkwood Lake
- Lake Alpine
- Lake Spaulding
- Lake Tahoe
- Little Grass Valley Reservoir
- Mokelumne Wilderness
- North Fork American River
- Packer Lake
- Pinecrest Lake
- Plumas National Forest
- Plumas-Eureka State Park
- Silver Lake
- Smith Lake
- Squaw Valley
- Sugar Pine Point State Park
- Sugar Pine Reservoir
- Tahoe National Forest

**Including:**

- Alameda Creek
- Alcatraz Island
- Almaden Quicksilver County Park
- Alpine Lake Dam
- Alum Rock City Park
- Anderson Dam
- Angel Island State Park
- Año Nuevo State Reserve
- Anthony Chabot Regional Park
- Big Basin Redwoods State Park
- Black Diamond Mines Regional Preserve
- Bolinas Lagoon
- Boulder Creek
- Briones Regional Park
- Butano State Park
- Calero Reservoir County Park
- Carquinez Strait Regional Shoreline
- Castle Rock State Park
- China Camp State Park
- Coal Creek Open Space Preserve
- Contra Loma Regional Park
- Coyote Hills Regional Park
- Coyote Point County Park
- Coyote-Hellyer County Park
- Crown Memorial State Beach
- Crystal Springs Reservoir
- Cull Canyon Regional Recreation Area
- Del Valle Regional Park
- Diablo Foothills Regional Park
- Don Castro Regional Recreation Area
- Ed R. Levin County Park
- El Sereno Open Space Preserve
- Garin Regional Park
- Half Moon Bay
- Hayward Regional Shoreline
- Henry Cowell Redwoods State Park
- Henry W. Coe State Park
- Huckleberry Botanic Regional Preserve
- Joseph D. Grant County Park
- Kennedy Grove Regional Recreation Area
- Lagunitas Lake
- Las Trampas Regional Wilderness
- Lexington Reservoir County Park
- Loch Lomond Recreation Area
- Long Ridge Open Space Preserve
- Los Trancos Open Space Preserve
- Madera Open Space Preserve
- Marin Headlands
- Martin Luther King Regional Shoreline
- Martinez Regional Shoreline

## Chapter 8—Monterey and Big Sur . . . . . . . . . . . . . . . . . . . 393

## Chapter 9—San Joaquin Valley . . . . . . . . . . . . . . . . . . . . 419

# Our Commitment

We are committed to making *Foghorn Outdoors California Hiking* the most accurate, thorough, and enjoyable hiking guide to the state. With this seventh edition you can rest assured that every hiking trail in this book has been carefully reviewed and accompanied by the most up-to-date information. Be aware that with the passing of time some of the fees listed herein may have changed, and trails may have closed unexpectedly. If you have a specific need or concern, it's best to call the location ahead of time.

If you would like to comment on the book, whether it's to suggest a trail we overlooked, or to let us know about any noteworthy experience—good or bad—that occurred while using *Foghorn Outdoors California Hiking* as your guide, we would appreciate hearing from you. Please address correspondence to:

*Foghorn Outdoors California Hiking,* seventh edition
Avalon Travel Publishing
1400 65th Street, Suite 250
Emeryville, CA 94608

email: atpfeedback@avalonpub.com
If you send us an email, please put "California Hiking" in the subject line.

# How to Use this Book

*Foghorn Outdoors California Hiking* is divided into 16 chapters based on major geographic regions in the state. Each chapter begins with a map of the region, which is further broken down into detail maps. These detail maps show the location of all the hikes in that chapter.

This guide can be navigated easily in two ways:

1. If you know the name of the specific trail you want to hike, or the name of the surrounding geographical area or nearby feature (town, national or state park, forest, mountain, lake, river, etc.), look it up in the index and turn to the corresponding page.

2. If you know the general area you want to visit, turn to the map at the beginning of the chapter that covers the area. Each chapter map is broken down into detail maps, which show by number all the hikes in that chapter. You can then determine which trails are in or near your destination by their corresponding numbers. Hikes are listed sequentially in each chapter so you can turn to the page with the corresponding map number for the hike you're interested in.

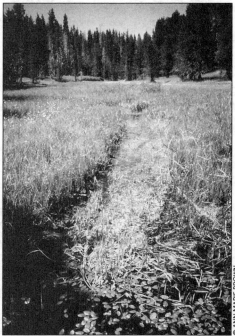

Ringed by tall conifers, McGurk Meadow is one of Yosemite's less-visited jewels—and it's an easy hike off Glacier Point Road.

# About the Trail Profiles

Each hike in this book is listed in a consistent, easy-to-read format to help you choose the ideal hike. From a general overview of the setting to detailed driving directions, the profile will provide all the information you need. Here is an example:

Map number and hike number →

Round-trip mileage (unless otherwise noted) and the approximate amount of time needed to complete the hike (actual times can vary widely, especially on longer hikes) →

Map on which the trailhead can be found and page number on which the map can be found →

Symbol indicating that the hike is listed among the author's top picks →

The difficulty rating (boot—rated 1–5) is based on the steepness of the trail and how difficult it is to traverse; the quality rating (mountain—rated 1–10) is based largely on scenic beauty, but it also takes into account how crowded the trail is and whether noise of nearby civilization is audible →

General location of the trail, named by its proximity to the nearest major town or landmark →

## ■ SOMEWHERE USA HIKE
### 9.0 mi/5.0 hrs                       4 ◄8
### At the mouth of the Somewhere River on Lake Someplace
### Map 1.2, page 24

Ⓕ Each hike in this book begins with a brief overview of its setting. The description typically covers what kind of terrain to expect, what might be seen, and any conditions that may make the hike difficult to navigate. Side trips, such as to waterfalls or panoramic vistas, in addition to ways to combine the trail with others nearby for a longer outing, are also noted here. In many cases, mile-by-mile trail directions are included.

**User Groups:** This section notes the types of users that are permitted on the trail, including hikers, mountain bikers, horseback riders, and dogs. Wheelchair access is also noted here.

**Permits:** This section notes whether a permit is required for hiking, or, if the hike spans more than one day, whether one is required for camping. Any fees, such as for parking, day use, or entrance, are also noted here.

**Maps:** This section provides information on how to obtain detailed trail maps of the hike and its environs. Whenever applicable, names of U.S. Geologic Survey (USGS) topographic maps and national forest maps are also included; contact information for these and other map sources are noted in the Resources secttion at the back of this book.

**Directions:** This section provides mile-by-mile driving directions to the trailhead from the nearest major town.

**Contact:** This section provides an address and phone number for each hike. The contact is usually the agency maintaining the trail but may also be a trail club or other organization.

## About the Maps

This book is divided into chapters based on regions; an overview map of these regions precedes the table of contents and is printed on the inside of the back cover. At the start of each chapter, you'll find a map of the entire region, enhanced by a grid that divides the region into smaller sections. These sections are then enlarged into individual detail maps. Trailheads are noted on the detail maps by number.

Reference to adjacent regions

Detail map number and page number

Detail area does not contain any hikes (map not included in chapter)

Grid line divides region into detail maps

Region border

REGION/CHAPTER MAP EXAMPLE

MAP 11.1 page 497

MAP 11.2 page 498

No Hikes

MAP 11.3 page 499

MAP 11.4 page 500

Locates region within state

Detail map 11.4 shown on next page

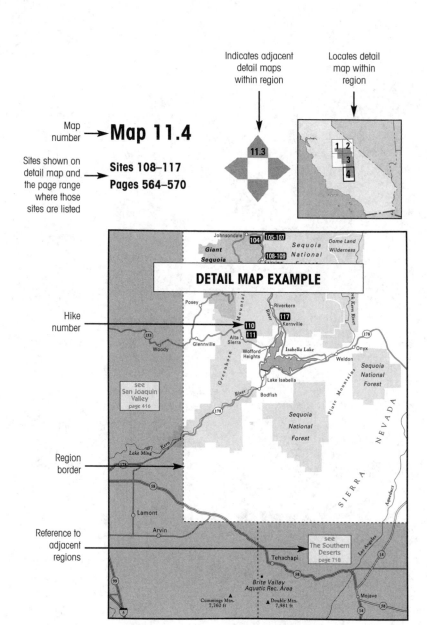

Map
number → **Map 11.4**

Sites shown on
detail map and → **Sites 108–117**
the page range      **Pages 564–570**
where those
sites are listed

Indicates adjacent
detail maps
within region

11.3

Locates detail
map within
region

1 2
3
4

**DETAIL MAP EXAMPLE**

Johnsondale   105-107   Sequoia   Dome Land
104                     National   Wilderness
Giant                   108-109
Sequoia        Fairview

Hike
number →   Posey          Riverkern   117
                                       Kernville   110
           155   Glennville   Alta   111
           Woody          Sierra
                          Wofford-   Isabella Lake   178   Onyx
                          Heights                    Weldon   Sequoia
                                                              National
           see                      Lake Isabella            Forest
           San Joaquin   River   Bodfish
           Valley
           page 416     178
                                    Sequoia
           Lake Ming   Kern        National
                                   Forest
Region
border →            178
                                                    SIERRA   NEVADA
           58
           Lamont
           Arvin                              see
Reference to                                  The Southern
adjacent                                      Deserts
regions →                        Tehachapi    page 718   14
           99                    58
                          Brite Valley
                          Aquatic Rec. Area
           5   Cummings Mtn.   Double Mtn.   Mojave
               7,760 ft        7,981 ft      14   58

# Introduction

© ROBERT HOLMES/CALTOUR

# Best Hikes

Can't decide where to hike this weekend? Here are our picks for the best hikes in California, listed alphabetically, in 19 different categories:

## Best Hikes to (F) Waterfalls

**Bridalveil Fall,** Yosemite National Park, Yosemite and Mammoth Lakes, page 471.
**Burney Falls Loop Trail,** McArthur-Burney Falls Memorial State Park, Lassen and Modoc, page 123.
**Chilnualna Fall,** Yosemite National Park, Yosemite and Mammoth Lakes, page 479.
**Devils Postpile and Rainbow Falls,** Devils Postpile National Monument, Yosemite and Mammoth Lakes, page 494.
**Feather Falls National Recreation Trail,** Plumas National Forest, Sacramento and Gold Country, page 184.
**Grouse Falls,** Tahoe National Forest, Tahoe and the Northern Sierra, page 217.
**Hetch Hetchy Reservoir,** Yosemite National Park, Yosemite and Mammoth Lakes, page 447.
**Illilouette Fall,** Yosemite National Park, Yosemite and Mammoth Lakes, page 477.
**McWay Falls Overlook,** Julia Pfeiffer Burns State Park, Monterey and Big Sur, page 415.

Chilnualna Fall

© ANN MARIE BROWN

**Mist and John Muir Loop to Nevada Fall,** Yosemite National Park, Yosemite and Mammoth Lakes, page 469.
**Tokopah Falls,** Sequoia National Park, Sequoia and Kings Canyon, page 544.
**Upper Yosemite Fall,** Yosemite National Park, Yosemite and Mammoth Lakes, page 465.
**Waterwheel Falls,** Yosemite National Park, Yosemite and Mammoth Lakes, page 460.

## (F) Best Hikes to See Wildflowers

**Antelope Valley Poppy Reserve Loop,** west of Lancaster, The Southern Deserts, page 738.
**Chimney Rock Trail,** Point Reyes National Seashore, San Francisco Bay Area, page 275.
**Grass Valley Loop,** Anthony Chabot Regional Park, San Francisco Bay Area, page 347.
**Hites Cove Trail,** Sierra National Forest, Yosemite and Mammoth Lakes, page 465.
**Lundy Canyon Trail,** Hoover Wilderness, Yosemite and Mammoth Lakes, page 444.
**Montaña de Oro Bluffs Trail,** Montaña de Oro State Park, Santa Barbara and Vicinity, page 617.
**Path of the Padres,** San Luis Reservoir State Recreation Area, San Joaquin Valley, page 428.
**Rocky Ridge and Soberanes Canyon Loop,** Garrapata State Park, Monterey and Big Sur, page 405.

**Whitney Portal to Lake Thomas Edison (JMT/PCT),** John Muir Wilderness, Sequoia and Kings Canyon, page 573.

 ## ⓕ Best Butt-Kickers

**Alta Peak,** Sequoia National Park, Sequoia and Kings Canyon, page 542.

**Beacroft Trail,** Tahoe National Forest, Tahoe and the Northern Sierra, page 214.

**Devils Punchbowl,** Siskiyou Wilderness, Shasta and Trinity, page 66.

**Half Dome,** Yosemite National Park, Yosemite and Mammoth Lakes, page 470.

**Lookout Peak,** Kings Canyon National Park, Sequoia and Kings Canyon, page 532.

**Mount Baldy,** Angeles National Forest, Los Angeles and Vicinity, page 676.

**Mount Whitney Trail,** John Muir Wilderness, Sequoia and Kings Canyon, page 571.

**Whitney Portal to Lake Thomas Edison (JMT/PCT),** John Muir Wilderness, Sequoia and Kings Canyon, page 573.

**Rooster Comb Loop,** Henry W. Coe State Park, San Francisco Bay Area, page 384.

**Shasta Summit Trail,** Mount Shasta Wilderness, Shasta and Trinity, page 88.

**Vivian Creek Trail to Mount San Gorgonio,** San Gorgonio Wilderness, Los Angeles and Vicinity, page 689.

## ⓕ Best Hikes with a View

**Aerial Tramway to San Jacinto Peak,** Mount San Jacinto State Park and Wilderness, The Southern Deserts, page 745.

**Clouds Rest,** Yosemite National Park, Yosemite and Mammoth Lakes, page 454.

**Deadfall Lakes Trail (to Mount Eddy),** Shasta-Trinity National Forest, Shasta and Trinity, page 85.

**Devils Slide Trail to Tahquitz Peak,** San Jacinto Wilderness, Los Angeles and Vicinity, page 692.

**Fresno Dome,** Sierra National Forest, Yosemite and Mammoth Lakes, page 482.

**High Sierra Trail to Hamilton Lake,** Sequoia National Park, Sequoia and Kings Canyon, page 546.

**Lassen Peak Trail,** Lassen Volcanic National Park, Lassen and Modoc, page 137.

**Little Baldy,** Sequoia National Park, Sequoia and Kings Canyon, page 540.

**Moro Rock,** Sequoia National Park, Sequoia and Kings Canyon, page 548.

**Mount Baldy,** Angeles National Forest, Los Angeles and Vicinity, page 676.

**Mount Whitney Trail,** John Muir Wilderness, Sequoia and Kings Canyon, page 571.

**Needles Lookout,** Sequoia National Forest, Sequoia and Kings Canyon, page 566.

**Perimeter/Summit Trail,** Angel Island State Park, San Francisco Bay Area, page 305.

**Panorama Trail,** Yosemite National Park, Yosemite and Mammoth Lakes, page 476.

**Rubicon Trail,** D. L. Bliss State Park, Tahoe and the Northern Sierra, page 225.

**Sentinel Dome,** Yosemite National Park, Yosemite and Mammoth Lakes, page 475.

**Whitney Portal to Lake Thomas Edison (JMT/PCT),** John Muir Wilderness, Sequoia and Kings Canyon, page 573.

 ## ⓕ Best Meadow Hikes

**Casa Vieja Meadow,** Golden Trout Wilderness, Sequoia and Kings Canyon, page 576.

**Grass Valley Loop,** Anthony Chabot Regional Park, San Francisco Bay Area, page 347.

**Manter Meadow Loop,** Dome Land Wilderness, Sequoia and Kings Canyon, page 584.

**McGurk Meadow & Dewey Point,** Yosemite National Park, Yosemite and Mammoth Lakes, page 473.

**Panther Meadows,** Mount Shasta Wilderness, Shasta and Trinity, page 89.

**Whitney Portal to Lake Thomas Edison (JMT/PCT),** John Muir Wilderness, Sequoia and Kings Canyon, page 573.

**Zumwalt Meadow Loop,** Kings Canyon National Park, Sequoia and Kings Canyon, page 533.

## Ⓕ Best Hikes to Swimming Holes

**Alder Creek Trail,** Sequoia National Forest, Sequoia and Kings Canyon, page 568.

**Big Falls,** Santa Lucia Wilderness, Santa Barbara and Vicinity, page 619.

**Cedar Creek and the Fishbowls,** Sespe Wilderness, Santa Barbara and Vicinity, page 634.

**Green Valley Falls,** Cuyamaca Rancho State Park, San Diego and Vicinity, page 714.

**Little Falls,** Santa Lucia Wilderness, Santa Barbara and Vicinity, page 620.

**Paradise Creek Trail,** Sequoia National Park, Sequoia and Kings Canyon, page 549.

**Santa Paula Canyon to Big Cone Camp,** Los Padres National Forest, Santa Barbara and Vicinity, page 637.

**Toad Lake Trail,** Shasta-Trinity National Forest, Shasta and Trinity, page 86.

## Ⓕ Best Self-Guided Nature Walks

**Elephant Tree Trail,** Anza-Borrego Desert State Park, San Diego and Vicinity, page 712.

**Inaja Memorial Trail,** Cleveland National Forest, San Diego and Vicinity, page 709.

**McCloud Nature Trail,** Shasta-Trinity National Forest, Shasta and Trinity, page 100.

**McGrath State Beach Nature Trail,** McGrath State Beach, Santa Barbara and Vicinity, page 638.

**Methuselah Trail,** Inyo National Forest, Yosemite and Mammoth Lakes, page 503.

**Piño Alto Trail,** Los Padres National Forest, Santa Barbara and Vicinity, page 626.

**Ponderosa Vista Nature Trail,** San Bernardino National Forest, Los Angeles and Vicinity, page 686.

**Rainbow and Lake of the Sky Trails,** Tahoe National Forest, Tahoe and the Northern Sierra, page 230.

**Shadow of the Giants,** Sierra National Forest, Yosemite and Mammoth Lakes, page 481.

**Trail of the Gargoyles,** Stanislaus National Forest, Tahoe and the Northern Sierra, page 258.

**Unal Trail,** Sequoia National Forest, Sequoia and Kings Canyon, page 582.

## Ⓕ Best Hikes Among Redwoods or Sequoias

**Boy Scout Tree Trail,** Jedediah Smith Redwoods State Park, Redwood Empire, page 35.

**Bull Creek Flats,** Humboldt Redwoods State Park, Redwood Empire, page 48.

**Congress Trail Loop,** Sequoia National Park, Sequoia and Kings Canyon, page 545.

**General Grant Tree Trail,** Kings Canyon National Park, Sequoia and Kings Canyon, page 528.

**Main Trail,** Muir Woods National Monument, San Francisco Bay Area, page 296.

**Redwood Canyon,** Kings Canyon National Park, Sequoia and Kings Canyon, page 535.

**Redwood Creek Trail,** Redwood National Park, Redwood Empire, page 44.

**Shadow of the Giants,** Sierra National Forest, Yosemite and Mammoth Lakes, page 481.

**Tall Trees Trail,** Redwood National Park, Redwood Empire, page 41.

**Trail of 100 Giants,** Sequoia National Forest, Sequoia and Kings Canyon, page 567.

## Ⓕ Best Short Backpack Trips

**Coast Trail,** Point Reyes National Seashore, San Francisco Bay Area, page 277.

**Gabrielino Trail to Bear Canyon,** Angeles National Forest, Los Angeles and Vicinity, page 656.

**Glen Aulin and Tuolumne Falls,** Yosemite National Park, Yosemite and Mammoth Lakes, page 461.

**Ladybug Trail,** Sequoia National Park, Sequoia and Kings Canyon, page 560.

May Lake and Mount Hoffman, Yosemite National Park, Yosemite and Mammoth Lakes, page 453.

Taylor Lake Trail, Russian Wilderness, Shasta and Trinity, page 81.

Toad Lake Trail, Shasta-Trinity National Forest, Shasta and Trinity, page 86.

Winnemucca Lake from Woods Lake, Mokelumne Wilderness, Tahoe and the Northern Sierra, page 248.

## ✔ Best One-Way
ⓕ Hikes with Shuttle

Lost Coast Trail, Sinkyone Wilderness State Park, Mendocino and Wine Country, page 159.

Panorama Trail, Yosemite National Park, Yosemite and Mammoth Lakes, page 476.

Pohono Trail, Yosemite National Park, Yosemite and Mammoth Lakes, page 476.

Skyline-to-the-Sea Trail, Big Basin Redwoods State Park, San Francisco Bay Area, page 368.

Whitney Portal to Lake Thomas Edison (JMT/PCT), John Muir Wilderness, Sequoia and Kings Canyon, page 573.

Winnemucca Lake from Woods Lake, Mokelumne Wilderness

© ANN MARIE BROWN

## ⓕ Best Beach and Coastal Walks

Bayside Trail, Cabrillo National Monument, San Diego and Vicinity, page 704.

Cabrillo Tidepools, Cabrillo National Monument, San Diego and Vicinity, page 705.

Coast Trail, Point Reyes National Seashore, San Francisco Bay Area, page 277.

Lost Coast Trail, King Range National Conservation Area, Redwood Empire, page 50.

Lost Coast Trail, Sinkyone Wilderness State Park, Mendocino and Wine Country, page 159.

Montaña de Oro Bluffs Trail, Montaña de Oro State Park, Santa Barbara and Vicinity, page 617.

Old Landing Cove Trail, Wilder Ranch State Park, Monterey and Big Sur, page 398.

Point Lobos Perimeter, Point Lobos State Reserve, Monterey and Big Sur, page 404.

Razor Point and Beach Trail Loop, Torrey Pines State Reserve, San Diego and Vicinity, page 702.

Rim Loop Trail, Patrick's Point State Park, Redwood Empire, page 44.

## ⓕ Best Hikes to See Wildlife

*Note: Seeing wildlife is not guaranteed and is often seasonally influenced.*

Año Nuevo Trail, Año Nuevo State Reserve, San Francisco Bay Area, page 371.

Captain Jack's Stronghold, Lava Beds National Monument, Lassen and Modoc, page 119.

Coastal Trail (Fern Canyon/Ossagon Section), Prairie Creek Redwoods State Park, Redwood Empire, page 42.

**Desert Tortoise Discovery Loop,** Desert Tortoise Natural Area, The Southern Deserts, page 735.

**Pescadero Marsh,** south of Pescadero, San Francisco Bay Area, page 334.

**Spirit Lake Trail,** Marble Mountain Wilderness, Shasta and Trinity, page 69.

**Tomales Point Trail,** Point Reyes National Seashore, San Francisco Bay Area, page 271.

**Tule Elk State Reserve,** west of Bakersfield, San Joaquin Valley, page 431.

## Ⓕ Best Hikes for Bird-Watching

**Abbotts Lagoon Trail,** Point Reyes National Seashore, San Francisco Bay Area, page 272.

**Arcata Marsh Trail,** Arcata Marsh and Wildlife Sanctuary, Redwood Empire, page 45.

**Arrowhead Marsh,** Martin Luther King Regional Shoreline, San Francisco Bay Area, page 345.

**Audubon Canyon Ranch Trail,** near Bolinas Lagoon, San Francisco Bay Area, page 286.

**Carrizo Plain and Painted Rock,** Carrizo Plains Natural Area, San Joaquin Valley, page 430.

**Chester, Sousa, and Winton Marsh Trails,** San Luis National Wildlife Refuge, San Joaquin Valley, page 427.

**Elkhorn Slough South Marsh Loop,** Elkhorn Slough National Estuarine Reserve, Monterey and Big Sur, page 401.

**Mono Lake South Tufa Trail,** Mono Lake Tufa State Reserve, Yosemite and Mammoth Lakes, page 487.

**Silverwood Wildlife Sanctuary,** near Lakeside, San Diego and Vicinity, page 713.

## Ⓕ Best Summit Hikes

**Aerial Tramway to San Jacinto Peak,** Mount San Jacinto State Park, The Southern Deserts, page 745.

**East Peak Mount Tamalpais,** Mount Tamalpais State Park, San Francisco Bay Area, page 292.

**Grizzly Lake (Thompson Peak),** Trinity Alps Wilderness, Shasta and Trinity, page 76.

**Lassen Peak Trail,** Lassen Volcanic National Park, Lassen and Modoc, page 137.

**Mount Baldy,** Angeles National Forest, Los Angeles and Vicinity, page 676.

**Mount Whitney Trail,** John Muir Wilderness, Sequoia and Kings Canyon, page 571.

**Preston Peak,** Siskiyou Wilderness, Shasta and Trinity, page 64.

**Shasta Summit Trail,** Shasta-Trinity National Forest, Shasta and Trinity, page 88.

**Vivian Creek Trail to Mount San Gorgonio,** San Gorgonio Wilderness, Los Angeles and Vicinity, page 689.

**White Mountain Peak Trail,** Inyo National Forest, Yosemite and Mammoth Lakes, page 503.

## Ⓕ Best Island Walks

**Caliche Forest and Point Bennett,** Channel Islands National Park, Santa Barbara and Vicinity, page 640.

**East Anacapa Island Loop Trail,** Channel Islands National Park, Santa Barbara and Vicinity, page 643.

**Empire Landing Road Trail,** Catalina Island, Los Angeles and Vicinity, page 671.

**Perimeter/Summit Trail,** Angel Island State Park, San Francisco Bay Area, page 305.

**Two Harbors to Emerald Bay,** Catalina Island, Los Angeles and Vicinity, page 670.

## Ⓕ Best Wheelchair-Accessible Trails

**Abbotts Lagoon Trail,** Point Reyes National Seashore, San Francisco Bay Area, page 272.

**Kangaroo Lake Trailhead,** Klamath National Forest, Shasta and Trinity, page 84.

Mastodon Peak Trail in Joshua Tree National Park

**Lake Cleone Trail,** MacKerricher State Park, Mendocino and Wine Country, page 161.
**Lower Yosemite Fall,** Yosemite National Park, Yosemite and Mammoth Lakes, page 467.
**McWay Falls Overlook,** Julia Pfeiffer Burns State Park, Monterey and Big Sur, page 415.
**Roaring River Falls,** Kings Canyon National Park, Sequoia and Kings Canyon, page 533.
**Salt Creek Interpretive Trail,** Death Valley National Park, Death Valley, page 600.
**Sierra Discovery Trail,** PG&E Bear Valley Recreation Area, Tahoe and the Northern Sierra, page 208.
**South Yuba Independence Trail,** near Nevada City, Sacramento and Gold Country, page 185.
**Taylor Lake Trail,** Russian Wilderness, Shasta and Trinity, page 81.

##  Best Hikes in Desert Terrain
**Borrego Palm Canyon Falls,** Anza-Borrego Desert State Park, San Diego and Vicinity, page 708.
**Kelso Dunes,** Mojave National Preserve, The Southern Deserts, page 743.
**Lost Palms Oasis,** Joshua Tree National Park, The Southern Deserts, page 750.
**Mastodon Peak,** Joshua Tree National Park, The Southern Deserts, page 749.
**Mosaic Canyon,** Death Valley National Park, Death Valley, page 597.
**Ryan Mountain Trail,** Joshua Tree National Park, The Southern Deserts, page 748.
**Tahquitz Canyon,** Aqua Caliente Indian Reservation, The Southern Deserts, page 747.
**Ubehebe Peak,** Death Valley National Park, Death Valley, page 596.
**Wildrose Peak Trail,** Death Valley National Park, Death Valley, page 598.

## Best Hikes for Kids
**Angora Lakes Trail,** Tahoe National Forest, Tahoe and the Northern Sierra, page 233.
**Año Nuevo Trail,** Año Nuevo State Reserve, San Francisco Bay Area, page 371.
**Cabrillo Tidepools,** Cabrillo National Monument, San Diego and Vicinity, page 705.

© ANN MARIE BROWN

Massive Roosevelt elk are your companions on the Coastal Trail in Prairie Creek State Park.

**Desert Tortoise Discovery Loop,** Desert Tortoise Natural Area, The Southern Deserts, page 735.
**Devils Postpile and Rainbow Falls,** Devils Postpile National Monument, Yosemite and Mammoth Lakes, page 494.
**Fitzgerald Marine Reserve,** Moss Beach, San Francisco Bay Area, page 319.
**Pinecrest Lake National Recreation Trail,** Stanislaus National Forest, Yosemite and Mammoth Lakes, page 440.
**Rainbow and Lake of the Sky Trails,** Tahoe National Forest, Tahoe and the Northern Sierra, page 230.
**Tokopah Falls,** Sequoia National Park, Sequoia and Kings Canyon, page 544.
**Tomales Point Trail,** Point Reyes National Seashore, San Francisco Bay Area, page 271.

## Ⓕ Best Hikes to See Fall Colors

**Boucher Trail and Scott's Cabin Loop,** Palomar Mountain State Park, San Diego and Vicinity, page 706.
**Carlon Falls,** Stanislaus National Forest, Yosemite and Mammoth Lakes, page 449.
**Convict Canyon to Lake Dorothy,** Inyo National Forest, Yosemite and Mammoth Lakes, page 499.
**Desert View and Canyon Oak Loop,** William Heise County Park, San Diego and Vicinity, page 710.
**Fallen Leaf Lake Trail,** Tahoe National Forest, Tahoe and the Northern Sierra, page 232.
**Farewell Gap Trail to Aspen Flat,** Sequoia National Park, Sequoia and Kings Canyon, page 553.
**Lundy Canyon Trail,** Hoover Wilderness, Yosemite and Mammoth Lakes, page 444.
**McGee Creek to Steelhead Lake,** John Muir Wilderness, Yosemite and Mammoth Lakes, page 500.
**Stonewall Peak Trail,** Cuyamaca Rancho State Park, San Diego and Vicinity, page 714.

# Hiking Tips

## Day Hiker's Equipment List

Aside from the shoes on your feet (see Selecting the Right Boots), it doesn't take much equipment to go day hiking. Whereas backpackers must concern themselves with tents, sleeping pads, pots and pans, and the like, day hikers have an easier time of it. Still, too many day hikers set out carrying too little and get into trouble as a result. Here's our list of essentials:

### 1. Food and Water

Water is even more important than food, although it's unwise to get caught without a picnic, or at least some edible supplies for emergencies. If you don't want to carry the weight of a couple water bottles, at least carry a purifier or filtering device so you can get water from streams, rivers, or lakes. It goes without saying, but never, ever drink water from a natural source without purifying it. The microscopic organisms *Giardia lamblia* and *Cryptosporidium* are found in backcountry water sources and can cause a litany of terrible gastrointestinal problems. Only purifying or boiling water from natural sources will eliminate giardiasis.

> The only sure way to beat giardiasis and other water-borne diseases is to filter or boil water before drinking from natural sources.

The new water bottle–style purifiers, such as those made by Bota or Exstream, are as light as an empty plastic bottle and eliminate the need to carry both a filter and a bottle. You simply dip the bottle in the stream, screw on the top (which has a filter inside it), and squeeze the bottle to drink. The water is filtered on its way out of the squeeze top.

Of course, in many areas, you won't find a natural water source to filter from, so carrying water is still necessary. Remember that trails that cross running streams in the winter and spring months may cross dry streams in the summer and autumn months.

What you carry for food is up to you. Some people go gourmet and carry the complete inventory of a fancy grocery store. If you don't want to bother with much weight, stick with high-energy snacks like nutrition bars, nuts, dried fruit, turkey or beef jerky, and crackers. Our rule is always to bring more than you think you can eat. You can always carry it back out with you, or give it to somebody else on the trail who needs it.

If you're hiking in a group, each of you should carry your own food and water just in case someone gets too far ahead or behind.

### 2. Trail Map

A map of the park or public land you're visiting is essential. Never count on trail signs to get you where you want to go. Signs get knocked down or disappear with alarming frequency, due to rain, wind, or park visitors looking for souvenirs.

Always obtain a map from the managing agency of the place you're visiting. Their names and phone numbers are listed in this book. For national forest maps, USGS topographical maps, and maps from commercial services, such as Tom Harrison Maps, see the Map Sources section in the Resource Guide at the back of this book.

### 3. Extra Clothing

On the trail, conditions can change at any time. Not only can the weather suddenly turn windy,

## Fun Stuff

These items aren't necessary, but they can make your trip a lot more fun:
- wildflower and/or bird identification book
- small pair of binoculars
- fishing license and lightweight fishing equipment
- deck of cards
- paperback book
- picnic gear

foggy, or rainy, but your own body conditions also change: You'll perspire as you hike up a sunny hill and then get chilled at the top of a windy ridge or when you head into shade. Because of this, cotton fabrics don't function well in the outdoors. Once cotton gets wet, it stays wet. Generally, polyester-blend fabrics dry faster. Some high-tech fabrics will actually wick moisture away from your skin. Invest in a few items of clothing made from these fabrics and you'll be more comfortable when you hike.

Always carry a lightweight jacket with you, preferably one that is waterproof and also wind-resistant. If your jacket isn't waterproof, pack along one of the $2, single-use rain ponchos that come in a package the size of a deck of cards (available at outdoors stores and drug stores). If you can't part with two bucks, carry an extra-large garbage bag, which can be converted into a waterproof vest. In cooler temperatures, or when heading to a mountain summit (even on a hot day), carry gloves and a hat as well.

### 4. Flashlight

Just in case your hike takes a little longer than you planned, bring at least one flashlight. Mini-flashlights are available everywhere, weigh almost nothing, and can save the day—or night. We especially like the tiny squeeze flashlights, about the size and shape of a quarter, that you can clip on to any key ring. Some turn on and off with a small switch, so you don't have to squeeze them for extended periods. (The Photon Micro-Light is a popular brand.) Whatever kind of flashlight you carry, make sure the batteries work before you set out on the trail. Always take along an extra set of batteries and an extra bulb, or simply an extra flashlight or two. You never know when the darn things will run out of juice.

### 5. Sunglasses and Sunscreen

You know the dangers of the sun. Wear sunglasses to protect your eyes and sunscreen with a high SPF on any exposed skin. Put on your sunscreen 30 minutes before you go outdoors so it has time to take effect. If you spend a lot of time outdoors, invest in a good wide-brimmed hat. Wearing lip balm with a high SPF is also a smart idea.

### 6. Insect Repellent

Several kinds of insect repellent now come with sunscreen, so you can put on one lotion instead of two. Many types of insect repellent have an ingredient called DEET, which is extremely effective but also quite toxic. Children should not use repellent with high levels of DEET, although it seems to be safe for adults. Many other types of repellent are made of natural substances, such as lemon oil. What works best? Everybody has his or her opinion. If you visit the High Sierra in the middle of a major mosquito hatch, it often seems like nothing works except covering your entire body in mosquito netting. For typical summer days outside of a hatch period, find a repellent you like and carry it with you.

## 7. First-Aid Kit
Nothing major is required here unless you're fully trained in first aid, but a few supplies for treating blisters, an antibiotic ointment, and an anti-inflammatory medicine (such as ibuprofen) can be valuable tools in minor and major emergencies. (For details on taking care of and preventing blisters, see Foot Care and Footwear.) If anyone in your party is allergic to bee stings or anything else in the outdoors, carry their medication.

## 8. Swiss Army–Style Pocket Knife
Be sure to carry one with several blades, a can opener, a scissors, and a tweezers. The latter is useful for removing slivers or ticks.

## 9. Compass
A compass can be a real lifesaver. Just be sure that you know how to use it. See Maps, Compasses, and Altimeters for more details.

## 10. Emergency Supplies
Ask yourself this question, "What would I need to have if I had to spend the night out here?" Aside from food, water, and other items previously listed, here are some basic emergency supplies that will get you through an unplanned night in the wilderness:
• Lightweight space blanket or sleeping bag made of foil-like mylar film, designed to reflect radiating body heat. These make a great emergency shelter and weigh and cost almost nothing.
• A lighter or a couple packs of matches in a waterproof container (or sealable plastic bag) and a candle, just in case you ever need to build a fire in a serious emergency.
• Whistle. If you ever need help, you can blow a whistle for a lot longer than you can shout.
• Small signal mirror. It could be just what you need to get found if you ever get lost.

# Foot Care and Footwear
Every hiker eventually conducts a search for the perfect boot. This means looking for something that will provide ideal foot and ankle support and won't cause blisters. Although there are dozens of possibilities—in fact so many that it can be confusing—you *can* find the perfect boot.

For advice on selecting boots, two of the nation's preeminent long-distance hikers, Brian Robinson of Mountain View (7,200 miles in 2001) and Ray Jardine of Oregon (2,700 miles of Pacific Crest Trail in three months), weighed in on the discussion. Both believe that the weight of a boot is the defining factor when selecting hiking footwear. They both go as light as possible, believing that heavy boots will eventually tire you out. Arch support is also vital, especially to people who hike less frequently and thus have not developed great foot strength.

To stay blister-free, the most important factors are clean feet,

One way to avoid blisters and muscle soreness is to rotate several pairs of different-style boots and shoes according to the terrain. Use heavy boots for steep trails with loose footing, and lightweight models for flat routes with a hard surface.

good socks, and the flexibility of a boot. If there is any foot slippage from a too-thin or compressed sock, accumulated dirt, or a stiff boot, you can rub up a blister in minutes. Wearing two pairs of socks can sometimes do the trick—try two fresh sets of SmartWool socks ($14 a pop), or try one pair over the top of a lightweight wicking liner sock. If you still get a blister or two, know how to treat them fast so they don't turn your walk into a sore-footed endurance test.

## Selecting the Right Boots

In addition to finding boots with the proper flexibility, comfort, and arch support, you'll need to consider the types of terrain you'll be covering and the number of miles (or number of days) you'll be hiking. Investing in the correct shoes will take some time and research, but your feet will thank you for it.

> It is an unforgiving error to wear thin cotton socks when trying on boots. Later, when you try to stuff a foot pad, two socks, and your feet into the boots, there just won't be enough room.

There are three basic kinds of hiking footwear, ranging from lightweight to midweight to heavyweight. Select the right one for you or pay the consequences. One great trick when on a hiking vacation is to bring a couple different pairs, and then for each hike, wear different footwear. By changing boots, you change the points of stress on your feet and legs, greatly reducing soreness and the chance of creating a hot spot on a foot. This also allows you to go lightweight on flat trails with a hard surface, and heavyweight on steep trails with loose footing, where additional boot weight can help traction in downhill stretches.

### Lightweight Hiking Boots

In the first category, lightweight hiking boots (or even very sturdy athletic shoes) are designed for day-hiking and short and easy backpacking trips. For those with strong feet and arches, they are popular even on multiday trips. Some of the newer models are like rugged athletic shoes, designed with a Gore-Tex top for lightness and a Vibram sole for traction. These are perfect for people who like to hike but rarely carry a heavy backpack. Because these boots are flexible, they are easy to break in, and with fresh socks they rarely cause blister problems. Because they are lightweight and usually made of a breathable fabric, hiking fatigue is greatly reduced. For day-hiking, they are the footwear of choice for most.

On the negative side, because these boots are so light, traction is not always good on steep, slippery surfaces, and you can lose your footing and fall. In addition, lightweight boots provide less than ideal ankle and arch support, which can be a problem on rocky or steep trails. Turn your ankle and your trip can be ruined. Lightweight hiking boots often are not very durable, either. If you hike a lot, you may wear a pair out in one summer.

### Midweight Hiking Boots or Backpacking Boots

These boots are designed for both on- and off-trail hiking, and are constructed to meet the demands of carrying a light to moderately heavy pack. They usually feature high ankle support, a deep Vibram lug sole, built-in orthotics, arch support, and often a waterproof exterior. They can stand up to hundreds of miles of wilderness use, even if they are banged against rocks and walked through streams.

On the negative side, midweight or backpacking boots can be quite hot, as they are often made of leather and are not breathable. If the boots get wet, they can take days to dry. They weigh a fair amount and can tire you out, especially if you are not accustomed to having weight on your feet. This may reduce the number of miles you are capable of hiking in a day.

## Ⓕ Adding to the Pack

If you're setting out on a long-distance adventure, it pays to add these two lightweight items to your backpack: an Ace elastic bandage and a pair of gaiters.

For sprained ankles and twisted knees, an Ace bandage can be like an insurance policy to get you back on the trail and out of trouble. There have been many cases where hikers with a twisted ankle or a sprained knee have relied on a good wrap with a four-inch bandage for the added support to get them home. Always buy the Ace bandage that comes with the clips permanently attached, so you don't have to worry about losing them.

Gaiters are leggings made of water-repellent fabric (Gore-Tex is a popular brand) that fit from just below your knees, over your calves, and attach under your boots. They are of particular help when walking in damp areas or in places where rain is common. As your legs brush against ferns or low-lying plants, gaiters will deflect the moisture. Without them, your pants will be soaking wet in short order.

Should your boots become wet, never to try to force them to dry. Some well-meaning folks will try to dry them quickly at the edge of a campfire or actually put the boots in an oven. Although this may dry the boots, it can also loosen the glue that holds them together, ultimately weakening them until one day they fall apart in a heap. A better bet is to treat the leather so the boots become water repellent. Silicone-based liquids are the easiest to use and the least greasy of the treatments available.

A final tip is to have another pair of lightweight shoes or moccasins that you can wear around after a trip. This will give your feet the rest they deserve.

### Mountaineering Boots or Heavyweight Backpacking Boots

Like midweight boots, these shoes are designed for both on- and off-trail hiking, but they can stand up to the rigors of carrying a much heavier load. They are designed to be worn on multi-day backpacking trips (four days or more with substantial miles hiked each day). Mountaineering boots are identified by midrange tops, laces that extend almost as far as the toes, and ankle areas that are as stiff as a board. The lack of "give" is what endears them to mountaineers. Their stiffness is preferred when rock climbing, walking off-trail on craggy surfaces, or hiking down the edge of streambeds. Because these boots don't yield on rugged terrain, they can reduce ankle and foot injuries and provide better traction. Some are made so that they can accept crampons for travel on snow and ice.

The drawback to stiff boots is that if you don't have the proper socks and your foot starts slipping around in the boot, you will get a set of blisters that require so much tape and moleskin you will end up looking like a mummy. Also, heavyweight boots must be broken in for weeks or even months before taking them out on the trail.

### At the Store

There are many styles, brands, and price ranges to choose from. If you wander about comparing all their many features, you will get as confused as a kid in a toy store. Instead, go into the store with your mind clear about what you want. For the best quality, expect to spend $60-150 for lightweight hiking boots, $100-200 for midweight boots, and $150-250 for mountaineering boots. If you go much cheaper, the quality of the boot—and the health of your feet—will likely suffer. This is one area where you don't want to scrimp.

If you plan on using the advice of a shoe salesperson, first look at what kind of boots he or she is wearing. If the salesperson isn't even wearing boots, then take whatever he or she says with a grain of salt. Most people who own quality boots, including salespeople, will wear them almost daily if their job allows, since boots are the best footwear available.

Enter the store with a precise use and style in mind. Rather than fish for suggestions, tell the salesperson exactly what type of hiking you plan to do. Try two or three brands of the same category of shoe (lightweight, midweight, or heavyweight/mountaineering). Try on both boots in a pair simultaneously so you know exactly how they'll feel. Always try them on over a good pair of hiking socks (see Socks, below), not regular everyday socks. If possible, walk up and down a set of stairs, or up and down an incline, while wearing the boots. Your feet should not slide forward easily, and your heel should not move from side to side. Are the boots too stiff? Are your feet snug yet comfortable, or do they slip? Do they have that "right" kind of feel when you walk?

## Socks

People can spend so much energy selecting the right kind of boot that they virtually overlook wearing the right kind of socks. One goes with the other.

Your socks should be thick enough to cushion your feet and should fit snugly. Without good socks you might fasten the bootlaces too tight, and that's like putting a tourniquet on your feet. On long trips of a week or more, you should have plenty of clean socks on hand, or plan on washing what you have during your trip. As socks become worn, they also become compressed, dirty, and damp. If they fold over, you'll get a blister.

Do not wear cotton socks. Your foot can get damp and mix with dirt, which can cause a hot spot to start on your foot. Instead, start with a sock made of a synthetic composite, such as those made by SmartWool. These will partially wick moisture away from the skin.

If you choose to wear two pairs, or a pair of socks over a sock liner, the exterior sock should be wool or its synthetic equivalent. This will cushion your feet, create a snug fit in your boot, and provide some additional warmth and insulation in cold weather. It is critical to keep socks clean. If you wear multiple socks, you may need to go up a boot size to accommodate the extra layers around your feet.

## Blisters

In almost all cases, blisters are caused by the simple rubbing of skin against the rugged interior of a boot. It can be worsened by several factors:

- a very stiff boot or one that allows your foot to move independently inside it as you walk, instead of it flexing along with your foot.
- thin, ragged, or dirty socks, which are the fastest route to blisters. Thin socks allow your feet to move inside of your boots, ragged socks allow your skin to chafe directly against the boot's interior, and dirty socks wrinkle and fold, also rubbing against your feet instead of cushioning them.
- soft feet. By themselves, soft feet will not cause blisters, but in combination with a stiff boot or thin socks, they can cause terrible problems. One way to cushion your soles is to keep a fresh foot pad made of sponge rubber in your boot. But note that brand-new foot pads are often slippery for a few days, and that can cause blisters. The pads need to be broken in before an expedition, just as with a new boot. Another cure for soft feet is to get out and walk or jog on a

regular basis prior to your hiking trip. In addition, going barefoot regularly can be the best way to build up foot strength and arch support, and to toughen up the bottom of your feet.

The key to treating blisters is to work fast at the first sign of a hot spot. If you feel a hot spot, never keep walking, figuring the problem will go away. Stop immediately and remedy the situation. Before you remove your socks, check to see if the sock is wrinkled—a likely cause of the problem. If so, either change socks or pull them tight, removing the tiny folds, after taking care of the blister.

To take care of the blister, cut a piece of moleskin to cover the offending spot, securing the moleskin with white medical tape. If moleskin is not available, small Band-Aids can do the job, but these have to be replaced daily, and sometimes with even more frequency. At night, clean your feet and sleep without socks. That will allow your feet to dry and heal.

## Snakes, Mountain Lions, and Bears

All three of these creatures deserve your respect, and you should understand a little bit about them.

### Rattlesnakes

California has six poisonous snake species, and all are types of rattlesnakes: speckled, sidewinder, red diamond, Mojave, western, and western diamondback. These members of the pit viper family have wide triangular heads, narrow necks, and rattles on their tails. Rattlesnakes generally live in lower-elevation areas and are rarely seen above 6,500 feet.

The standard advice for dealing with rattlesnakes is to give them lots of room. If you're hiking on a warm day when they might be out and about (they particularly favor temperatures in the 70- to 90-degree range), keep your eyes open so you don't step on one. Rattlesnakes often blend in very well with the brown and tan colors of an earthen trail. Also, watch where you put your hands, especially if you are scrambling over rocks. Be particularly wary of rattlesnakes in the spring months; most bites occur then, when the snakes come out of their winter hibernation and are particularly active.

Most snakes will slither off at the sound of your footsteps; if you encounter one, freeze or

 **Facts about Mountain Lions**

Mountain lion expert Steve Torres of the Department of Fish and Game (DFG) provided the following list of truths regarding mountain lions:

1. Mountain lions are very shy and wary of humans. Attacks on people are extremely rare. That is why any threatening encounter can make the news, because it is an anomaly.

2. Mountain lions are rarely seen. They are masters of stealth. That is why repeat sightings are alarming and should be reported to the DFG headquarters, in Sacramento, at 916/445-0411.

3. Mountain lions are known for their silence and are rarely vocal. If you hear the cry or roar of a lion, your experience is likely a once-in-a-lifetime event.

4. Mountain lions are not threatened or endangered in any way. Populations are stable to increasing. The biggest threat to mountain lions is loss of habitat to development.

5. Mountain lions are not afraid of dogs. Whereas packs of trained hounds are capable of putting a lion in a tree, solitary pets of all kinds, including dogs, are fair game for mountain lions. In areas with documented mountain lion habitat, dogs should be kept inside at night.

move back slowly so that it can get away. They will almost always shake their tails and produce a rattling or buzzing noise to warn you off. The sound is unmistakable, even if you've never heard it before.

Although rattlesnake bites sting and are quite frightening, they are only rarely fatal. Rattlesnakes will sometimes strike without biting, and even when they do bite, their bites do not always release venom. If you should get bitten by a rattlesnake, snake bite kits (or venom extractors) are basically useless. Instead, your car key is your best first aid. Don't panic or run. Walk slowly back to your car, then drive yourself to the nearest hospital. Avoid running or unnecessary movement, because this helps circulate the venom through your system. The bitten area will probably start to swell, so remove any jewelry or constricting clothing from the area. Do not apply ice to the wound, and keep the bite area below the level of your heart. This is usually not a problem, since most bites are on ankles or hands. Most importantly, stay calm and move slowly.

## Mountain Lions

The mountain lion (also called cougar or puma) lives in almost every region of California but is rarely seen. Most habitat that is wild enough to support deer will support mountain lions, which typically eat about one deer per week. When the magnificent cats do show themselves, they receive a lot of media attention. The few mountain lion attacks on California hikers have been widely publicized. Still, the vast majority of hikers never see a mountain lion, and those who do usually report that the cat vanished into the brush at the first sign of nearby humans.

Many parks now have posted warning signs at trailheads about mountain lions—a red light for hikers that is repeated over and over. In addition, the Department of Fish and Game (DFG) printed a widely circulated pamphlet on mountain lions, and while well meaning, it sends the same signal: Trouble ahead!

> When it comes to danger, a daily commute in California is a lot riskier than meeting up with a mountain lion. The facts show that the most dangerous part of a hiking trip by far is the drive to the trailhead.

The public has been unnecessarily rendered nervous about mountain lions. The true dangers in California are driving and crime. Mountain lions? Not even on the radar scope.

If you're hiking in an area where mountain lions or their tracks have been spotted, remember to keep children close to you on the trail, and your dog leashed. If you see a mountain lion and it doesn't run away immediately, make yourself appear as large as possible (raise your arms, open your jacket, wave a big stick) and speak loudly and firmly or shout. If you have children with you, pick them up off the ground, but try to do it without crouching down or leaning over. (Crouching makes you appear smaller and less aggressive, more like prey.) Don't turn your back on the cat or run from it, but rather back away slowly and deliberately, always retaining your aggressive pose and continuing to speak loudly. Mountain lions are far more likely to attack a fleeing mammal than one that stands its ground. Even after attacking, they have been successfully fought off by adult hikers and even children who used rocks and sticks to defend themselves.

## Bears

The only bears found in California are black bears (even though they are usually brown in color). A century ago, our state bear, the grizzly, roamed here as well, but the last one was shot and killed in the 1930s. Black bears almost never harm human beings—although you should never approach or feed a bear, or get between a bear and its cubs or its food. Black bears weigh between 250 and 400 pounds, can run up to 30 miles per hour, and are powerful swimmers and

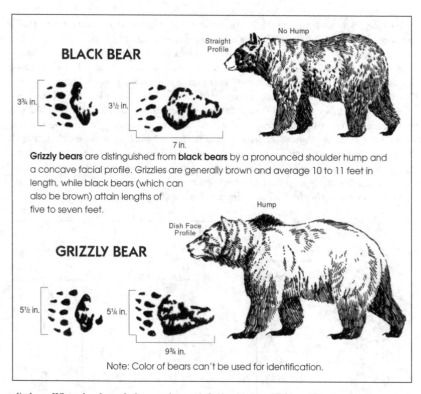

**BLACK BEAR**

Straight Profile

No Hump

3¾ in.

3½ in.

7 in.

Grizzly bears are distinguished from **black bears** by a pronounced shoulder hump and a concave facial profile. Grizzlies are generally brown and average 10 to 11 feet in length, while black bears (which can also be brown) attain lengths of five to seven feet.

Hump

Dish Face Profile

**GRIZZLY BEAR**

5½ in.

5¼ in.

9¾ in.

Note: Color of bears can't be used for identification.

climbers. When they bound, the muscles on their shoulders roll like ocean breakers. If provoked, a bear could cause serious injury.

There's only one important fact to remember about bears: They love snacks. The average black bear has to eat as much as 30,000 calories a day, and since their natural diet is made up of berries, fruits, plants, fish, insects, and the like, the high-calorie food of human beings is very appealing to them. Unfortunately, too many California campers have trained our state's bears to crave the taste of corn chips, hot dogs, and soda pop.

Any time you see a bear, it's almost a given that it is looking for food, preferably something sweet. Bears have become specialists in the food-raiding business. As a result, you must be absolutely certain that you keep your food away from them. This is best accomplished with a bear-proof food canister, required equipment when backpacking in parts of Yosemite National Park, Sequoia and Kings Canyon National Parks, Mount Whitney Wilderness, and associate trailheads in Inyo National Forest. At campgrounds at these areas, metal bear-proof food storage lockers must be used. Never leave your food unattended or in your vehicle. Tickets are commonly issued for either of these violations. In addition, get an update from the rangers in your park about suitable bear precautions.

Bears are sometimes encountered on trails, although not as frequently as in campgrounds. If you're hiking, bears will most likely hear you coming and avoid you. If one approaches you, either on the trail or in camp, yell loudly, throw small rocks or pine cones in the vicinity, and try to frighten the bear away. A bear that is afraid of humans is a bear that will stay wild and stay alive.

Backpackers should always use plastic bear canisters to store their food for overnight trips. Hanging food from a tree is largely ineffective when done improperly, and the practice is now banned in parts of Yosemite and Sequoia and Kings Canyon National Parks, as well as at the Mount Whitney trailheads; in these places, bear-proof food canisters are required. You can rent or buy a bear canister from most outdoor stores, or from many ranger stations in national parks and national forests. For more information, or to rent a canister, contact Yosemite National Park at 209/372-0200, Sequoia and Kings Canyon National Parks at 559/565-3341, or Inyo National Forest at 760/873-2400.

If you are backpacking in an area where bear canisters are not required, or where bears aren't as bold as they are in the heavily visited areas of the Sierra Nevada, you can substitute a food hang for a bear canister. This is where you place place your food in a plastic or canvas garbage bag (always double bag your food), then suspend it from a rope in midair, 10 feet from the trunk of a tree and 20 feet off the ground. Counterbalancing two bags with a rope thrown over a tree limb is very effective, but finding an appropriate limb can be difficult.

In an area frequented by bears, a good **bear-proof food hang** is a must. Food should be stored in a plastic bag 10 feet from the trunk of the tree and at least 20 feet from the ground.

This is most easily accomplished by tying a rock to a rope, then throwing it over a high but sturdy tree limb. Next, tie your food bag to the rope and hoist it in the air. When you are satisfied with the position of the food bag, tie off the end of the rope to another tree.

Once a bear gets his mitts on your food, he considers it his. There is nothing you can do. If this happens to you once, you will learn never to let food sit unattended.

## Ticks, Poison Oak, and Stinging Nettles

These three things are far worse than a whole convention of snakes, mountain lions, and bears. But you can avoid them with a little common sense, and here's how:

### Ticks

The easiest way to stay clear of ticks is to wear long pants and long sleeves, and to check your clothes when you take them off. If it's too hot to be covered up in long sleeves, just make sure you look yourself over thoroughly when you leave the trail and remove anything that's crawling on you. (A good friend can assist you in this pursuit.) Be especially wary of ticks in the winter and spring months, when they are most prevalent.

Remember that if you find a tick on your skin, the larger brown ones are harmless. Of the nearly 50 varieties of ticks present in California, only the tiny brown-black ones, called the western black-legged tick, can carry Lyme disease. If you find a tick on you and he's actually biting into your skin (not just crawling around), you should remove the tick, put it in a plastic bag, and take it to your doctor for examination to see if it is carrying Lyme disease.

The best way to remove a tick is by grasping it as close to your skin as possible, then pulling it gently and slowly straight out, without twisting or jerking it. Tweezers work well for the job, and many Swiss Army knives include tweezers.

Rangers also warn people that if they've been in the outdoors, and then a few days or a week later start to experience headaches, fever, nausea, or rashes, they should see a doctor immediately and tell him or her that they are concerned about possible exposure to ticks and Lyme disease. Caught in its early stages, Lyme disease is easily treated with antibiotics.

### Poison Oak

That old Boy Scout motto holds true: Leaves of three, let them be. Learn to recognize and avoid *Toxicodendron diversilobum,* which produces an itching rash that can last for weeks. The shiny-leaved shrub grows with maddening exuberance in California coastal and mountain canyons below 5,000 feet. If you can't readily identify poison oak, stay away from vinelike plants that have three leaves. Remember that in spring and summer, poison oak looks a little like wild blackberry bushes and often has red colors in its leaves, as well as green. In late fall and winter, poison oak goes dormant and loses its leaves, but it's still potent.

Avoid poison oak by staying on the trail and wearing long pants and long sleeves in areas that are

Avoiding
**Poison Oak:**
Remember
the old Boy Scout
saying:
"Leaves of three,
let them be."

encroached by it. If you prefer to wear shorts when you hike, try a pair of the convertible pants that are found at most outdoor stores. These are lightweight pants with legs that zip off to convert to shorts. Put the pant legs on when you come to an area that is rife with poison oak. If you accidentally touch the plant with your bare skin, wash off the area as soon as possible. Waiting until you get home five hours later may be too late, so wash as best as you can, using stream water or whatever is available. Hikers who are highly allergic to poison oak should consider carrying packages of Technu, a poison oak wash-off treatment that is sold in bottles or individual foil packs. Carrying one little package could save you weeks of scratching.

Remember that if poison oak touches your clothes, your pack, or even your dog, and then you handle any of those items, the oils can rub off onto your skin. Wash everything thoroughly as soon as you get home.

## Stinging Nettles

Ouch! This member of the nettle family is bright green, can grow to six feet tall, and is covered with tiny stinging hairs. When you brush against one, it zaps you with its poison, which feels like a mild bee sting. The sting can last for up to 24 hours. Stinging nettles grow near creeks or streams, and they're usually found in tandem with deer ferns and sword ferns. If the nettles zing you, grab a nearby fern leaf and rub the underside of it against the stinging area. It sounds odd, but it sometimes helps to take the sting out. If it doesn't help, you're out of luck, and you just have to wait for the sting to go away.

# Other Hazards on the Trail

## Hypothermia

A leading cause of death in the outdoors is hypothermia, which occurs when your body's core temperature drops low enough that your vital organs can no longer function. Most cases of hypothermia occur at temperatures in the 50s, not below freezing, as you might expect. Often the victim has gotten wet, and/or is fatigued from physical exertion.

Initial symptoms of hypothermia include uncontrollable shivering, often followed by a complete stop in shivering, extreme lethargy, and an inability to reason. A hypothermic person will often want to lay down and rest or sleep. His or her hiking partners must jump into action to get the victim warm and dry immediately. Remove all wet clothes and put on dry ones. Cover his or her head with a warm hat. If someone in the group has an emergency space blanket (see Day Hiker's Equipment List), wrap it around the victim. Get the hypothermic person to eat some quick-energy food, even candy, and drink warm beverages—this helps the body produce heat. Do not give the person alcohol, as this encourages heat loss.

## Heat Stroke

Usually the result of overexposure to the sun and dehydration, symptoms of heat stroke include headache, mental confusion, and cramps throughout the body. Immediate action must be taken to reduce the body's core temperature. Pour water on the victim's head. Have him or her sit in a cool stream if possible. Make the person drink as much liquid as possible. Heat stroke is easily avoided by staying adequately hydrated and wearing a large-brimmed hat for protection from the sun.

## Altitude Sickness and Adjusting to Altitude

Many hikers experience a shortness of breath when hiking only a few thousand feet higher than the elevation where they live. If you live on the California coast, you may notice slightly labored breathing while hiking at an elevation as low as 5,000 feet. As you go higher, it gets worse, sometimes leading to headaches and nausea. It takes a full 72 hours to acclimate to major elevation changes, although most people acclimatize after only 24 to 48 hours. The best preparation for hiking at a high elevation is to sleep at that elevation, or as close to it as possible, the night before. If you are planning a strenuous hike at 7,000 feet or above, spend a day or two before doing easier hikes at the same elevation. Also, get plenty of rest and drink plenty of fluids. Lack of sleep, and alcohol, can contribute to your susceptibility to "feeling the altitude."

Serious altitude sickness typically occurs above 10,000 feet. It is generally preventable by simply allowing enough time for acclimation. But how do you acclimate for a climb to the top of Mount Whitney or Shasta, at more than 14,000 feet? The answer is you can't, at least not completely. Spending a few days beforehand hiking at 10,000 feet and above will help tremendously. Staying fueled with food and fully hydrated will also help. But if you've never hiked above a certain elevation—say 13,000 feet—you don't know how you are going to feel until you get there. If you start to feel ill (nausea, vomiting, severe headache), you are experiencing altitude sickness. Some people can get by with taking aspirin and trudging onward, but if you are seriously ill, the only cure is to descend as soon as possible. If the altitude has gotten to you badly enough, you may need someone to help you walk. Fatigue and elevation sickness can cloud your judgment in the same manner than hypothermia does, so take action before your symptoms become too severe.

## Lightning

If you see or hear a thunderstorm approaching, avoid exposed ridges and peaks. This is disheartening advice when you're only a mile from the summit of Half Dome, but follow it anyway. If you're already on a mountain top, stay out of enclosed places, such as rock caves or recesses. Confined areas are deadly in lightning storms; hikers seeking refuge from lightning have been killed inside the stone hut on top of Mount Whitney. Do not lean against rock slopes or trees; try to keep a few feet of air space around you. Squat low on your boot soles, or sit on your day pack, jacket, or anything that will insulate you in case lightning strikes the ground.

# Maps, Compasses, and Altimeters

For some hikers, it is quite easy to become lost. If you don't get your bearings, getting found is the difficult part. If you're hiking with a family or group, make sure everybody stays together. If anyone decides to split off from the group for any reason, make sure they have a trail map with them and that they know how to read it. Also, ensure that everyone in your group knows the rules regarding what to do if they get lost:

• Whistle or shout loudly at regular intervals.

• "Hug" a tree. Or a big rock or a bush. That means find a noticeable landmark, sit down next to it, and don't move. Continue to whistle or shout loudly. A lost person is easier to find if they stay in one place.

In areas above tree line or where the trail becomes faint, some hikers will mark the route with piles of small rocks to act as directional signs for the return trip. But if an unexpected snow buries these piles of rocks, or if you get well off the track, all you are left with is a moonscape. That is why every hiker should understand the concept of orienteering. In the process, you become a mountaineer.

When lost, the first step is to secure your present situation—that is, to make sure it does not get any worse. Take stock of your food, foul-weather gear, camp fuel, clothes, and your readiness to spend the night. Keep in mind that this is an adventure, not a crisis.

The **topographical map** is easier to read than many believe. Lines close together mean steep gradients; lines farther apart mean gentle gradients; V-shaped sets of lines pointing to higher elevations mean gulleys or stream-beds; V-shaped sets of lines pointing to lower elevations mean ridges.

Then take out your topographic map, compass, and altimeter. What? Right: Never go into the unknown without them. Place the map on the ground, then set the compass atop the map and orient it north. In most cases, you will easily be able to spot landmarks, such as prominent mountaintops. In cases with a low overcast, where mountains are obscured in clouds, you can take this adventure one step further by checking your altimeter. By scanning the elevation lines on the map, you will be able to trace your near-exact position.

Always be prepared to rely on yourself, but also file a trip plan with the local ranger station, especially if hiking in remote wilderness areas. Carry plenty of food, fuel, and a camp stove. Make sure your clothes, weather gear, sleeping bag, and tent will keep you dry and warm. Always carry a compass, altimeter, and map with elevation lines, and know how to use them, practicing in good weather to get the feel of it.

With enough experience, you will discover that you can "read" the land so well that you will hardly even need to reference a map to find your way.

## Tips For Avoiding the Crowds

Although many regions of California exist where you can hike without seeing another soul, even on holiday weekends, some of our better-known parks and public lands are notorious for crowds. No matter where in California you want to hike, there's no reason to subject yourself to packed parking lots, long lines of people snaking up and down switchbacks, and trail destinations that look like Times Square on New Year's Eve. If you take a few simple steps, you can avoid the crowds almost anywhere, even in well-traveled parks near urban areas and in our famous national parks.

• Hike in the off-season. For most public lands, the off-season is any time other than summer, or any time when school is in session. Late September through mid-May is an excellent period of time for hiking trips (except during the week between Christmas and New

Year's and Easter week). Try to avoid periods near holidays; many people try to beat the crowds by traveling right before or after a holiday, and the result is more crowds.

- Time your trip for midweek. Tuesday, Wednesday, and Thursday are always the quietest days of the week in any park or public land.
- Get up early. Even Yosemite Valley is serene and peaceful until 8 or 9 A.M.. In most parks, if you arrive at the trailhead before 9 A.M., you'll have the first few hours on the trail all to yourself. As an insurance policy, get to the trailhead even earlier.
- If you can't get up early, stay out late. When the days are long in summer, you can hike shorter trails from 4 P.M. to 7:30 P.M. or even later. You may see other hikers in the first hour or so, but they'll soon disperse. Trailhead parking lots are often packed at 1 P.M., then nearly empty at 5 P.M. Note that if you hike in the late afternoon or evening, you should always carry a flashlight with you (at least one per person), just in case it gets dark sooner than you planned.
- Get out and hike in foul weather. Don your favorite impermeable layer, and go where fair-weather hikers dare not go. Some of the best memories are made on rainy days, cloudy days, foggy days, and days when the wind blows at gale force. The fact is, the vast majority of hikers only hike when the sun is out. Witness nature in all its varied moods, and you may be surprised at how much fun you have.

## The John Muir Trail and the Pacific Crest Trail

You can have a foothold in the sky with every step on the John Muir Trail (JMT). The trail starts at practically the tip-top of North America—Mount Whitney—and takes you northward across a land of 12,000-foot passes and Ansel Adams–style vistas, then eventually pours you into nature's showpiece of the world, Yosemite Valley.

How could you top that? There is only one way: to hike the Pacific Crest Trail (PCT), of which the JMT partially overlaps. The PCT extends from the Mexico border for 1,700 miles north to Oregon, and then beyond all the way to its end, at the Canadian border—a total distance of 2,650 miles.

The JMT and the PCT are the two premier expeditions in North America. The JMT usually takes about three weeks to complete, covering about 250 miles, including side trips for food drops and other forays. Some swear that the trip should be hiked from north to south, but most prefer south to north, starting with the awesome climb from Whitney Portal to the Whitney Summit, a climb of more than 5,000 feet. Three weeks later, the trip ends with a spectacular descent into Yosemite Valley, past hundreds of gawking tourists on the final three miles on the Mist Trail. Some cheat by starting at Tuolumne Meadows, thus

> The Pacific Crest Trail extends from Mexico to Canada—a total distance of 2,650 miles—1,700 of which are in California.

avoiding a 4,000-foot climb out of Yosemite Valley, then heading south, but that is a hollow victory, having technically not completed the trip.

John Muir called the Sierra Nevada the "Range of Light." The trail that traverses it has become America's greatest hike—officially 211 miles from the Whitney Summit to Happy Isles in Yosemite Valley. It is a land spiked by 13,000-foot granite spires, untouched sapphire lakes loaded with trout, and canyons that drop as if they were the edge of the earth. There are many highlights, including the Mount Whitney Wilderness, John Muir Wilderness, Kings Canyon National Park, crossing the ice cut at Forester Pass, topping Muir Pass at Muir Hut, the incredible pyramidlike ridgeline near Selden Pass, catching golden trout where a cast can be like tossing a dog a bone, crossing the headwaters of Rush Creek, and finally dropping over Donohue Pass down to Lyell Fork and Tuolumne Meadows.

## Making Long-Distance Trips Work

When hiking with others, and especially over several days, it pays to do a little planning and a lot of communicating. Here are some tips to having a successful trip:

1. The destination and activities must be agreed upon. A meeting of the minds gives everybody an equal stake in the trip.
2. If backpacking, guarantee yourself refreshing sleep. Make certain that your sleeping bag, pillow, pad, and tent are clean, dry, warm, and comfortable.
3. Develop technical expertise. Test all gear at home before putting it to use on the trail.
4. Guarantee yourself action. Pick a destination with your favorite activity: adventuring, wildlife watching, swimming, fishing. . . .
5. Guarantee yourself quiet time. Savor the views and the sound of a stream running free, and reserve time with people you care for, and your soul will be recharged.
6. Accordance on food. Always have complete agreement on the selections for each meal, and check for allergies.
7. Agree on a wake-up time. Then when morning comes, you will be on course from the start.
8. Equal chances at the fun stuff. Many duties can be shared over the course of a trip, such as navigating and preparing meals.
9. Be aware, not self-absorbed. Live so there can be magic in every moment, with an awareness of the senses: sight, sound, smell, touch, taste, and how you feel inside. Have an outlook that alone can promote great satisfaction.
10. No whining. You can't always control your surroundings, only your state of mind.

Yet the PCT goes far beyond this scope. It crosses through 37 wilderness areas, 20 national forests, and seven national parks, topping out at 13,180 feet at Forester Pass in the south Sierra. It also features the worst parts of the entire 2,700-mile route, the Hat Creek Rim (30 miles without water) and across the Mojave, where a siege of hot weather can have you praying for a sip of water out of a cow's hoof print.

All of the JMT and many of the PCT routes are detailed in this book, including how to get wilderness permits, directions to trailheads, maps, contacts, and trail highlights. Many hikers choose not to hike the entire JMT or PCT in one shot. Rather, they use a PCT trailhead, then head up to the crest, taking off on side trips as they choose.

## Hiking with Dogs

Dogs are wonderful friends and great companions. But dogs and nature do not mix well. Bless their furry little hearts, most dogs can't help but disturb wildlife, given half a chance. Even if they don't chase or bark at wildlife, dogs leave droppings that may intimidate other mammals into changing their normal routine. Kept on a leash, a dog can be the best hiking companion you could ask for.

Dogs are allowed on some trails in California and not on others. For many dog owners, it's confusing. When using this book, check the "User Groups" listing under each trail listing to see whether or not dogs are permitted. Always call the park or public land in advance if you are traveling some distance with your dog.

Here's a general guideline to park rules about dogs:

© ANN MARIE BROWN

If you are visiting a national or state park, 99 percent of the time, your dog will not be allowed to hike with you. There are only a few exceptions to this rule within the national and state park systems. Dogs are usually allowed in campgrounds or picnic areas, but they are not allowed on trails in these parks. If you are planning to visit a national or state park, consider leaving your dog at home.

At other types of parks (county parks, regional parks, and so on), dogs may or may not be allowed on trails. Always follow and obey a park's specific rules about dogs. Oftentimes, if dogs are allowed, they must be on a six-foot or shorter leash. Don't try to get away with carrying the leash in your hand while your dog runs free; rangers may give you a ticket.

In national forest or wilderness lands, dogs are usually permitted off leash, except in special wildlife management areas or other special-use areas. Understand that your dog should still be under voice control—for his or her safety more than anything. The outdoors presents many hazards for dogs, including mountain lions, porcupines, black bears, ticks, and a host of other potential problems. Dogs are frequently lost in national forest areas. Keeping your dog close to your side or on a leash in the national forests will help you both have a worry-free trip and a great time.

## Protecting the Outdoors

Take good care of this beautiful land you're hiking on. The basics are simple: Leave no trace of your visit. Pack out all your trash. Do your best not to disturb animal or plant life. Don't collect specimens of plants, wildlife, or even pine cones. Never, ever carve anything into the trunks of trees. If you're following a trail, don't cut the switchbacks. Leave everything in nature exactly as you found it, because each tiny piece has its place in the great scheme of things.

You can go the extra mile, too. Pick up any litter that you see on the trail. Teach your children to do this as well. Carry an extra bag to hold picked-up litter until you get to a trash receptacle, or just keep an empty pocket for that purpose in your day pack or fanny sack.

If you have the extra time or energy, join a trail organization in your area or spend some time volunteering in your local park. Anything you do to help this beautiful planet will be repaid to you, many times over.

## Chapter 1

© ANN MARIE BROWN

# Redwood Empire

# Redwood Empire

Visitors come from around the world to the Redwood Empire for one reason: to see the groves of giant redwoods, the tallest trees in the world. On a perfect day in the redwoods here, refracted sunlight beams through the forest canopy, creating a solemn, cathedral-like effect. It feels as if you are standing in the center of the earth's pure magic.

But the redwood forests are only one of the attractions in this area. The Smith River Canyon, Del Norte and Humboldt coasts, and the remote edge of the Siskiyou Wilderness in Six Rivers National Forest all make this region like none other in the world.

On sunny days in late summer, some first-time visitors are incredulous that so few people live in the Redwood Empire. The reason it's not very populated also happens to explain why the trees grow so tall: With few exceptions, the weather consists of rain in the winter—often for weeks at a time—and fog in the summer. If the sun does manage to appear, it's an event almost strange enough to warrant calling the police to say you've spotted a round, yellow UFO. So most folks are content to just visit.

For outstanding days of adventure, three stellar areas should be on your must-see list: the redwood parks from Trinidad to Klamath River, the Smith River National Recreation Area, and the Lost Coast.

The hikes from Trinidad to the Klamath River feature some of the best adventuring day trips in Northern California. A good place to start is Prairie Creek Redwoods State Park, where you can see fantastic herds of Roosevelt elk. Then head over to the beach by hiking Fern Canyon for 20 minutes along the bottom of a canyon, past vertical walls covered with ferns. Then continue north on Coastal Trail, where pristine woodlands and fantastic expanses of untouched beaches await. All the trails through the redwoods north of the Klamath River are winners; it's just a matter of matching up your level of ambition to the right hike.

The Smith River National Recreation Area is equally gorgeous. The

Smith is one of the last major free-flowing rivers in America. Wild, unsullied, and beautiful, it's set in a series of gorges and bordered by national forest. The centerpiece is Jedediah Smith Redwoods State Park and its grove of monster-sized redwoods. South Fork Road provides an extended tour into Six Rivers National Forest along the South Fork Smith River, with the option of visiting many of the largest trees in Jedediah Smith Redwoods State Park. The best turnoff is located on U.S. 199 just northeast of the town of Hiouchi. Turn right, cross two bridges, and you will arrive at a fork in the road. Turning left at the fork will take you along the South Fork Smith River and deep into Six Rivers National Forest. Turning right at the fork will take you to a series of trailheads for hikes into redwoods—of these, the best is Boy Scout Tree Trail.

The Lost Coast is often overlooked by visitors because it's difficult to reach. Access is only via a slow, curvy road through the Mattole River Valley, past Petrolia, and out to a piece of coast. The experience is like being in suspended animation—peaceful surroundings with a striking lack of people. One of the best ways to capture the sensation is to drive out near the mouth of the Mattole, then hike south on Coastal Trail long enough to get a feel for the area.

Compared to other regions in California, this corner of the state is somewhat one dimensional. The emphasis here is primarily on exploring the redwoods and the coast, and to some extent, the Smith River. Most of the campgrounds here are designed with those things in mind. There are many private campgrounds set on U.S. 101, as well as near the mouths of the Smith and Klamath Rivers. These make fine base camps for fishing trips when the salmon are running. The state and national park campgrounds in the redwoods are in high demand, and reservations are often necessary during the peak summer vacation season. On the opposite end of the spectrum are primitive and remote settings in Six Rivers National Forest and the Lost Coast—and there are even a few surprise nuggets in Redwood National Park.

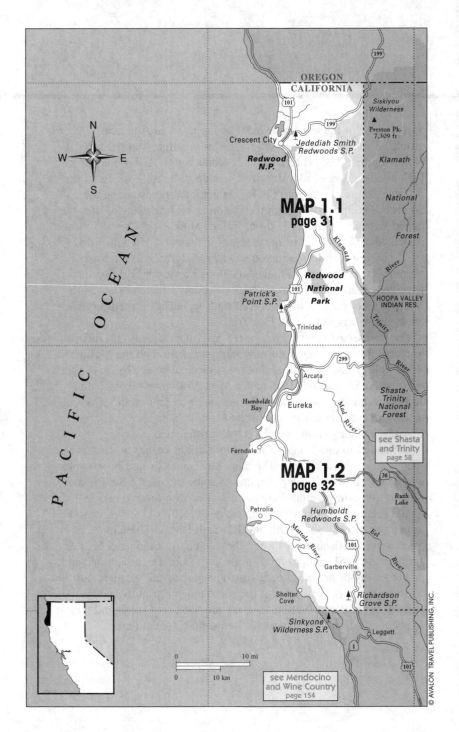

# Map 1.1

## Hikes 1–24
## Pages 33–45

© AVALON TRAVEL PUBLISHING, INC.

# Map 1.2

## Hikes 25–40
## Pages 45–54

# 1 WILDLIFE DUNE AREA
## 2.5 mi / 1.0 hr

**on the coast of Del Norte County north of Crescent City**

Map 1.1, page 31

The Pelican Bay Sand Dunes seem to sweep on forever, spanning more than 10 miles from the mouth of the Smith River south along the Pacific Ocean, nearly reaching Crescent City. After parking at Kellogg Beach, walk north or south for five minutes or five hours—take your pick. Either way, you will feel like a solitary speck against the enormous backdrop of untouched sand dunes and ocean. Only rarely will you see other people. The area is known by several names, including Fort Dick Beach, Kellogg Beach, and Pelican Bay Sand Dunes, but by any name, it's a good place to escape to nothing but wide-open beach for miles.

**User Groups:** Hikers, dogs, and horses. Mountain bikes permitted but not recommended. No wheelchair facilities.

**Permits:** No permits are required. Parking and access are free.

**Maps:** For a free brochure and map, write to Tolowa Dunes State Park at the address below. For topographic maps, ask the USGS for Crescent City and Smith River.

**Directions:** On U.S. 101 in Crescent City, turn northwest on Northcrest Drive and drive 1.5 miles to Old Mill Road. Turn left on Old Mill Road and drive 1.25 miles to the end of Old Mill Road and the junction with Sand Hill Road. Turn left on Sand Hill Road (at the Department of Fish and Game office) and drive .25 mile to the parking lot and the trailhead.

For trail and walk-in beach access: On U.S. 101 in Crescent City, turn northwest on Northcrest Drive and drive six miles (it becomes Lake Earl Drive) to Lower Lake Road. Turn left on Lower Lake Road and drive 2.5 miles to Kellogg Road. Turn left and drive .5 mile to the trailhead.

Alternative access: Follow the above access directions, but after turning left on Lower Lake Road, drive five miles to Pala Road. Turn left and drive .5 mile to the trailhead.

**Contact:** Tolowa Dunes State Park, 1375 Elk Valley Road, Crescent City, CA 95531, 707/464-6101, ext. 5151, website: www.parks.ca.gov (click on Find A Park).

# 2 STONY CREEK TRAIL
## 1.2 mi / 0.75 hr

**in Smith River National Recreation Area northeast of Crescent City**

Map 1.1, page 31

This easy walk in an unblemished river setting will take hikers to the mouth of Stony Creek, right where it pours into the North Fork Smith River. It's the kind of special place where you just sit and listen to the flow of moving water as it gurgles and pops its way over stones smoothed by years of river flows. The hike is easy, with a few ups and downs as it follows a bluff adjacent to the North Fork Smith (a designated Wild and Scenic River), then is routed right out to the mouth of Stony Creek. You're surrounded by woods, water, and in the spring, wildflowers. Note: For years this was spelled Stoney Creek, but it has since been changed.

**User Groups:** Hikers and dogs. No horses or mountain bikes. No wheelchair facilities.

**Permits:** Campfire permits (free) are required. Parking and access are free, but parking space is very limited.

**Maps:** For a free brochure and hiking guide, write to Smith River National Recreation Area at the address below. For a map, ask the U.S. Forest Service for Six Rivers National Forest. For a topographic map, ask the USGS for Gasquet.

**Directions:** From Crescent City, drive north on U.S. 101 for three miles, turn east onto U.S. 199, and drive 14 miles to Gasquet. Turn left on Middle Fork/Gasquet Road and drive about 100 feet to North Fork Road. Turn right and drive another mile. Then turn right on Stony Creek Road and drive a short distance to the trailhead.

**Contact:** Smith River National Recreation Area,

P.O. Box 228, Gasquet, CA 95543, 707/457-3131, website: www.fs.fed.us/r5 (click on Forest Offices).

## ❸ ELK CAMP RIDGE TRAIL
### 7.5–16.4 mi /
### 3.5 hrs–2.0 days

**in Smith River National Recreation Area northeast of Crescent City**

Map 1.1, page 31

This trail is like a walk through history. It was originally part of a pack trail between Crescent City and the gold mines in southern Oregon, and the memories of the old days can shadow your hike much of the way. The trailhead is at 1,200 feet, but the route climbs right up to the ridge, reaching more than 3,000 feet. Once you reach the ridge, you have excellent views of surrounding peaks (Preston Peak is the big one) and the Smith River Canyon. Hikers may also notice that much of the vegetation along the trail is stunted, a result of the high mineral content in the serpentine rocks. The trail keeps climbing and ends at 3,400 feet. From start to finish, the trail covers 8.2 miles, although most hikers only make it halfway before they return. Since most of the route traces a ridgeline, there are no suitable camping areas.

**User Groups:** Hikers, dogs, horses, and mountain bikes. No wheelchair facilities.

**Permits:** Campfire permits (free) are required. Parking and access are free.

**Maps:** For a free brochure and hiking guide, write to the Smith River National Recreation Area at the address below. For a map, ask the U.S. Forest Service for Six Rivers National Forest. For topographic maps, ask the USGS for Gasquet and High Plateau Mountain.

**Directions:** From Crescent City, drive north on U.S. 101 for three miles, turn east on U.S. 199, and drive 14 miles to Gasquet. Turn left on Middle Fork/Gasquet Road and drive 100 feet; bear right as the road forks. Drive .5 mile, turn right on Old Gasquet Toll Road (County Road 314), and drive 2.3 miles. Turn left at

the sign for the trailhead, and drive 1.4 steep and rough miles to the trailhead.

**Contact:** Smith River National Recreation Area, P.O. Box 228, Gasquet, CA 95543, 707/457-3131, website: www.fs.fed.us/r5 (click on Forest Offices).

## ❹ MYRTLE CREEK TRAIL
### 2.0 mi / 0.75 hr

**in the Smith River National Recreation Area**

Map 1.1, page 31

This interpretive trail follows year-round Myrtle Creek. The stream drainage runs along a geological boundary between typical local soils (which support redwood and Douglas fir forests) and dry, reddish, iron- and magnesium-rich serpentine soil (where rarer native species grow, such as Bolander's and Vollmer's lilies). It's an easy hike with a lot to look at and learn about, including the remains of an extensive hydraulic mining operation, dating back to 1853, when gold was discovered here. Hikers are asked to respect this vulnerable habitat by keeping to the trail. Collecting artifacts or plants is prohibited.

**User Groups:** Hikers and dogs. No horses or mountain bikes.

**Permits:** Campfire permits (free) are required for overnight use. Parking and access are free.

**Maps:** For a free brochure and hiking guide, write to Smith River National Recreation Area at the address below. For a topographic map, ask the USGS for Hiouchi.

**Directions:** From Crescent City, drive three miles north on U.S. 101, then east on U.S. 199. Drive seven miles to the parking area and trailhead. Park on the south side of U.S. 199 and cross the road to access the trailhead.

**Contact:** Smith River National Recreation Area, P.O. Box 228, Gasquet, CA 95543, 707/457-3131, website: www.fs.fed.us/r5 (click on Forest Offices).

## 5 BOY SCOUT TREE TRAIL
### 7.0 mi / 3.5 hrs

**in Jedediah Smith Redwoods State Park northeast of Crescent City**

Map 1.1, page 31

This is the kind of place where a nature lover can find religion; where the beauty is pure and untouched. The trail is a soft dirt path—often sprinkled with redwood needles—that allows hikers to penetrate deep into an old-growth redwood forest, complete with a giant fern understory and high-limbed canopy. The centerpiece is the Boy Scout Tree, the largest tree on the trail, but what you will remember the most is the serenity of a forest of old redwoods.

This is an easy hike, nearly flat and with only small hills—yet it's extremely rewarding. Just walk into the forest, and a few hours later, walk out. Those few hours can change how you feel about the world. A bonus known to relatively few is Fern Falls, a 40-foot waterfall. Reaching it requires a 3.5-mile hike one-way, making it a 7-mile round-trip hike.

**User Groups:** Hikers only. No dogs, horses, or mountain bikes. No wheelchair facilities.

**Permits:** No permits are required. Parking and access are free.

**Maps:** A trail map is available for a fee from Jedediah Smith Redwoods State Park at the address below. For a topographic map, ask the USGS for Hiouchi.

**Directions:** From U.S. 101 in Crescent City, turn east on Elk Valley Road and drive one mile to Howland Hill Road. Turn right and drive 3.5 miles to the trailhead, on the left. The last two miles are unpaved.

Note: If you plan to camp at Jedediah Smith Redwoods State Park, use these directions: On U.S. 199, drive east just past Hiouchi to South Fork Road. Turn right on South Fork Road (County Road 427) and cross two bridges. At the junction, turn right on Howland Hill Road and drive about five miles to a small parking area and the signed trailhead, on the right side of the road.

**Contact:** Jedediah Smith Redwoods State Park, 1375 Elk Valley Road, Crescent City, CA 95531, 707/464-6101, ext. 5112, website: www.parks .ca.gov (click on Find A Park).

## 6 STOUT GROVE TRAIL
### 0.6 mi / 0.5 hr

**in Jedediah Smith Redwoods State Park northeast of Crescent City**

Map 1.1, page 31

Visiting giant old redwood trees can affect people for a long time. The Stout Tree, the largest redwood in Jedediah Smith Redwoods State Park, is the attraction on this hike. It is so old that it can make your stay on earth seem mighty brief. The wide, level trail is a 10-minute walk that takes an easy course to the Stout Grove and then on to the Stout Tree. Most people take longer than 10 minutes, of course, because they're not used to seeing anything this size, and they take their time, absorbing the surroundings. The Stout Tree is being "loved to death" by people who touch it or trample the undergrowth, and rangers make a special request that you take a picture and leave it at that. Most everybody makes the mandatory stroll to the nearby Smith River, located a few minutes' walk beyond the Stout Tree. A trail that ran alongside the river once started here, but it was washed out by erosion from floodwaters.

**User Groups:** Hikers and wheelchairs. No dogs, horses, or mountain bikes. Those who want closer vehicular access can call the park at 707/464-6101, ext. 5112, to get the key to the gate.

**Permits:** No permits are required. Parking and access are free.

**Maps:** A trail map is available for a fee from Jedediah Smith Redwoods State Park at the address below. For a topographic map, ask the USGS for Hiouchi.

**Directions:** From Crescent City, drive about three miles north on U.S. 101, then turn east on U.S. 199. Drive about 10 miles (past the formal entrance to Jedediah Smith Redwoods State Park) to Hiouchi. Just past Hiouchi turn right on South Fork Road (County Road 427)

and cross two bridges. At the junction, turn right onto Howland Hill Road and drive about two miles to a small parking area (on the right) and the signed trailhead.

**Contact:** Jedediah Smith Redwoods State Park, 1375 Elk Valley Road, Crescent City, CA 95531, 707/464-6101, ext. 5112, website: www.parks.ca .gov (click on Find A Park).

## 7 CRAIG'S CREEK TRAIL
### 7.4 mi / 4.25 hrs

**in Smith River National Recreation Area northeast of Crescent City**

Map 1.1, page 31

An old miners' pack route, vintage 1800s, has been converted into this hiking trail, an obscure path that is overlooked by most visitors. It starts along the South Fork Smith River, loops up the slopes of Craig's Creek Mountain and back down to the river, and ends where Craig's Creek enters the South Fork. In the process, it rises above the river and passes through forest, including old-growth redwoods and Douglas fir. Because of the contour of the mountain, the hike includes a good climb. The starting and ending elevations are the same (200 feet). Most of the time, you can have the entire trail to yourself. The South Fork Smith is very pretty here—a clear, free-flowing stream that drains a huge expanse of the Siskiyou Wilderness.

**User Groups:** Hikers, dogs, horses, and mountain bikes. No wheelchair facilities.

**Permits:** For overnight use, a campfire permit (free) is required. Parking and access are free.

**Maps:** For a free brochure and hiking guide, write to Smith River National Recreation Area at the address below. For a map, ask the U.S. Forest Service for Six Rivers National Forest. For a topographic map, ask the USGS for Hiouchi.

**Directions:** From Crescent City, drive north on U.S. 101 for three miles, turn east on U.S. 199, and drive seven miles. Just past Hiouchi turn right on South Fork Road (County Road 427) and drive approximately one-third mile. Park in the boat access facility area.

**Contact:** Smith River National Recreation Area, P.O. Box 228, Gasquet, CA 95543, 707/457-3131, website: www.fs.fed.us/r5 (click on Forest Offices).

## 8 FRENCH HILL TRAIL
### 5.6 mi / 3.25 hrs

**in Smith River National Recreation Area northeast of Crescent City**

Map 1.1, page 31

This trail was created originally as part of the route to transport supplies to build the Camp Six fire lookout station. It is fairly steep, and some use it for an aerobic workout. It passes through old-growth Douglas fir and sugar pines, a forest that has thrived from so much moisture. The beauty and quality of the trail are poor to fair compared to that of other nearby areas. The significance that rates making this book is that the while the lookout has long been retired, a high-tech automatic rain gauge was positioned in its place. In 1983, this rain gauge documented the most rain ever recorded in the continental United States for one season: 257 inches. You can drive right to this site.

**User Groups:** Hikers, dogs, horses, and mountain bikes. No wheelchair facilities.

**Permits:** No permits are required. Parking and access are free.

**Maps:** For a free brochure and hiking guide, write to Smith River National Recreation Area at the address below. For a map, ask the U.S. Forest Service for Six Rivers National Forest. For a topographic map, ask the USGS for Gasquet.

**Directions:** From Crescent City, drive north on U.S. 101 for three miles, turn east on U.S. 199, and drive 14 miles to Gasquet. Park at the Smith River National Recreation Area Visitor Center (on the left). The trail is located directly across the highway.

**Contact:** Smith River National Recreation Area, P.O. Box 228, Gasquet, CA 95543, 707/457-3131, website: www.fs.fed.us/r5 (click on Forest Offices).

## 9 COASTAL TRAIL (LAST CHANCE SECTION)
### 14.0 mi / 8.0 hrs

**in Del Norte Redwoods State Park south of Crescent City**

Map 1.1, page 31

You get a little bit of heaven and a little bit of hell on this hike. It's one of the feature trips on the Del Norte coast, coursing through virgin forest and meadows (with beautiful wildflowers in the spring) and granting great coastal views in several spots. The trail starts along the coast, veers up sharply into coastal spruce and fir, and then dips into dense, old-growth forest. That's the heaven. The hell starts when you begin the difficult and steep climb, a gain of 1,400 feet. Ever wonder why the trees are so big? It's because with heavy rain in the winter and ponderous fog in summer, they are dripping with moisture. Like many coastal hikes, hitting good weather is the key. Note that when you're crossing meadows, ticks can be a common problem.

**User Groups:** Hikers and mountain bikes (restricted to first six miles only). No dogs or horses. No wheelchair facilities.

**Permits:** No permits are required. Parking and access are free.

**Maps:** A trail guide is available for a fee from Redwood National and State Parks, 1111 2nd Street, Crescent City, CA 95531, 707/464-6101. For a topographic map, ask the USGS for Sister Rocks.

**Directions:** From Crescent City, drive south on U.S. 101 for about 2.5 miles. At milepost 23.03, turn west onto Enderts Beach Road. Continue for 2.5 miles to the trailhead at the end of the road.

**Contact:** California State Parks, North Coast Redwoods District, 1375 Elk Valley Road, Crescent City, CA 95531, 707/464-6101, website: www.parks.ca.gov (click on Find A Park).

## 10 GUNBARREL TRAIL
### 2.6 mi / 1.75 hrs

**in Smith River National Recreation Area east of Crescent City**

Map 1.1, page 31

Now just a minute here. Do you really want to try this hike? If so, get your ambitions in clear focus, and if you like what you see, go for it, because your reward will be complete peace and solitude. But it comes with a price: a terrible, long, and circuitous drive to reach the trailhead, which is two hours from the Gasquet Ranger Station. Then the hike itself demands a steep climb on the return trip, a 1,200-foot elevation gain within little more than a mile.

This trail starts at a ridgeline at 2,500 feet, then dives down the canyon all the way to the South Fork Smith River, where it junctions with South Kelsey Trail. This is a beautiful spot; the water is pure and the people nil. Alas, the return is the killer (a demanding climb), and that is why few people make this round-trip.

**User Groups:** Hikers, dogs, horses, and mountain bikes. No wheelchair facilities.

**Permits:** No permits are required. Parking and access are free.

**Maps:** For a free brochure and hiking guide, contact the Smith River National Recreation Area at the address below. For a map, ask the U.S. Forest Service for Six Rivers National Forest. For a topographic map, ask the USGS for Ship Mountain.

**Directions:** From Crescent City, turn east on U.S. 199 and drive 25 miles. Turn right on Little Jones Creek Road (Forest Service Highway 16) and drive south 9.6 miles. When the road forks, bear right on Forest Road 16N02 for 4.8 miles, turn left onto Forest Road 16N18 (gated and closed from October through January), and drive six miles. Bear left on Forest Road 15N34 and continue on this road for approximately two miles. Park at the end of the road. The trailhead is on the left.

Contact: Smith River National Recreation Area, P.O. Box 228, Gasquet, CA 95543, 707/457-3131, website: www.fs.fed.us/r5 (click on Forest Offices).

## 11 McCLENDON FORD TRAIL
2.0 mi / 1.5 hrs

**in Smith River National Recreation Area east of Crescent City**

Map 1.1, page 31

This is a perfect trail for a hot summer day, complete with a swimming hole. It's an easy hike through a large forest of Douglas fir. The trail crosses Horse Creek, a small tributary, and then leads to a pretty beach on the South Fork Smith River. The starting elevation is 1,000 feet, and the ending elevation is 200 feet. Get the idea? Right, this trail follows an easy descent to the river, taking about 45 minutes to get there. The swimming hole on the river is secluded and out of the way of most vacationers, so most often, you have the place completely to yourself. Note: This is also the trailhead for South Kelsey Trail. If you are unfamiliar with the area, be sure to have a map of Six Rivers National Forest to reach the trailhead.

**User Groups:** Hikers, dogs, horses, and mountain bikes. No wheelchair facilities.

**Permits:** No permits are required. Parking and access are free.

**Maps:** For a free brochure and hiking guide, write to Smith River National Recreation Area at the address below. For a map, ask the U.S. Forest Service for Six Rivers National Forest. For a topographic map, ask the USGS for Ship Mountain.

**Directions:** From Crescent City, drive north on U.S. 101 for three miles, turn east on U.S. 199, and drive seven miles. Just past Hiouchi, turn right on South Fork Road (County Road 427) and drive 14 miles. Turn right on Forest Road 15 and drive 3.5 more miles to a sign indicating the South Kelsey Trailhead. Turn left and drive two miles. Hike on South Kelsey Trail for .5 mile before connecting with McClendon Ford Trail.

Contact: Smith River National Recreation Area, P.O. Box 228, Gasquet, CA 95543, 707/457-3131, website: www.fs.fed.us/r5 (click on Forest Offices).

## 12 SOUTH KELSEY TRAIL
34.0 mi / 3.0 days

**in Smith River National Recreation Area east of Crescent City**

Map 1.1, page 31

Back before cars, trains, and planes, Kelsey Trail spanned 200 miles from Crescent City eastward to Fort Jones near Yreka. It was built in the mid-19th century by Chinese laborers as a mule-train route. Today it has a different purpose, with different sections providing excellent backpacking circuits. The trailhead is near Horse Creek, on the South Fork Smith River, at a 1,200-foot elevation. The trail initially drops down along the South Fork and continues south for seven miles. A few camps are here along the river, including the Buck Creek shelter (rebuilt in 2001), which is heaven during a heavy rainstorm. The trail then rises above the river, climbing for six miles all the way to Baldy Peak and spectacular views. Another 3.1 miles will get you to your destination, Harrington Lake, set at 5,775 feet. With so much "up" going in, take heart that at least the return trip will be mainly downhill. The trailhead also provides access to McClendon Ford Trail. Other maintained sections of Kelsey Trail are noted in the Marble Mountain Wilderness (see listing in Shasta and Trinity chapter).

**User Groups:** Hikers, dogs, and horses. Mountain bikes are permitted only to the wilderness boundary. No wheelchair facilities.

**Permits:** A campfire permit (free) is required. Parking and access are free.

**Maps:** For a free brochure and hiking guide, write to Smith River National Recreation Area at the address below. For a map, ask the U.S. Forest Service for Six Rivers National Forest. For a topographic map, ask the USGS for Summit Valley.

**Directions:** From Crescent City, drive north

on U.S. 101 for three miles, turn east on U.S. 199, and drive seven miles. Just past Hiouchi, turn right on South Fork Road (County Road 427) and drive 14 miles. Turn right on Forest Road 15 and drive 3.5 more miles to a sign indicating the South Kelsey Trailhead. Turn left and drive two miles.

**Contact:** Smith River National Recreation Area, P.O. Box 228, Gasquet, CA 95543, 707/457-3131, website: www.fs.fed.us/r5 (click on Forest Offices).

## 13 SUMMIT VALLEY TRAIL
### 16.2 mi / 2.0 days

**in Smith River National Recreation Area east of Crescent City**

Map 1.1, page 31

This hike is best taken in the early summer—when the wildflowers are blooming; the Smith River is running with a fresh, ample flow; and the temperature is not too warm. The latter becomes a factor on the return trip, which is a killer climb. The trailhead is set on a ridge at 4,600 feet, and the first mile of the hike is on an old jeep road. It then becomes a hiking path as it travels through meadows, where the wildflowers are spectacular in early summer. But then the trail drops, plunging into a canyon and landing hikers along the South Fork Smith River at Elkhorn Bar, a beautiful spot at an elevation of 1,160 feet. Here it junctions with South Kelsey Trail, where you'll find a few primitive campsites along the river. Well, when it comes to hiking, what goes down must come up, and you got it: The return trip is a death march—a 3,500-foot climb over the span of eight miles. Your car waiting at the trailhead will never look so good. This trip can be lengthened easily by joining South Kelsey Trail.

**User Groups:** Hikers, dogs, and horses. Mountain bikes are permitted only to the wilderness boundary. No wheelchair facilities.

**Permits:** A campfire permit (free) is required. Parking and access are free.

**Maps:** Write to Smith River National Recreation Area at the address below for a free brochure and hiking guide. For a map, ask the U.S. Forest Service for Six Rivers National Forest. For a topographic map, ask the USGS for Summit Valley.

**Directions:** From Crescent City, drive north on U.S. 101 for three miles, turn east on U.S. 199, and drive seven miles. Just past Hiouchi, turn right on South Fork Road (County Road 427) and drive 14 miles. Turn right on Forest Road 15 and drive 15 miles to the trailhead, on the left. Park on the side of the road.

**Contact:** Smith River National Recreation Area, P.O. Box 228, Gasquet, CA 95543, 707/457-3131, website: www.fs.fed.us/r5 (click on Forest Offices).

## 14 BALDY PEAK TRAIL
### 10.4 mi / 2.0 days

**in the Siskiyou Wilderness east of Crescent City**

Map 1.1, page 31

The route to Baldy Peak is actually a section of South Kelsey Trail (see listing in this chapter), the historic route that once went east from Crescent City all the way through the Marble Mountain Wilderness to Fort Jones. This part of it is an excellent trip, and if you get caught in the rain, a bonus is that the Bear Wallow Shelter (not much more than a roof) is available just beyond the summit. The trip starts on Gunbarrel Trail, which extends for 1.25 miles to the junction with Kelsey Trail. From there, it's four miles to Baldy Peak, at 5,775 feet. The views are outstanding, especially to the north, where you'll see 7,309-foot Preston Peak, the most impressive feature in this wild landscape.

An option for those with plenty of time and endurance is to continue east on Kelsey Trail, which extends about 12 miles farther to Red Hill (5,642 feet), Bear Peak (5,740 feet), and nearby Bear Lake. The latter has an excellent campsite.

**User Groups:** Hikers, dogs, and horses. No mountain bikes. No wheelchair facilities.

**Permits:** A campfire permit is required. Parking and access are free.

**Maps:** For a free brochure and hiking guide, write to Smith River National Recreation Area at the address below. For a map, ask the U.S. Forest Service for Klamath National Forest. For a topographic map, ask the USGS for Prescott Mountain.

**Directions:** This recommended trailhead can be reached only by hiking Gunbarrel Trail (see listing in this chapter): From Crescent City, drive north on U.S. 101 for three miles to U.S. 199. Bear right (east) on U.S. 199, and drive 25 miles to Little Jones Creek Road/Jawbone Road (Forest Road 16). Turn right and drive 14.4 miles. When the road forks, bear sharply left (to stay on Forest Road 16), and continue to Forest Road 16N18. Turn left and drive five miles to Forest Road 15N34. Bear left on Forest Road 15N34 and drive 1.2 miles to the end of the road. The trailhead is on the left. Hike Gunbarrel Trail for 1.2 miles to reach the Baldy Peak section of South Kelsey Trail.

Note: The trailhead suggested here is fine if your planned adventure is to Baldy Peak and back. Many people have longer backpacking adventures planned and prefer the trailhead for South Kelsey Trail (see listing in this chapter).

**Contact:** Smith River National Recreation Area, P.O. Box 228, Gasquet, CA 95543, 707/457-3131, website: www.fs.fed.us/r5 (click on Forest Offices); Klamath National Forest, Happy Camp Ranger District, P.O. Box 377, 63822 Highway 96, Happy Camp, CA 96039-0377, 530/493-2243, website: www.fs.fed.us/r5 (click on Forest Offices).

## 15 YUROK LOOP
### 1.0 mi / 0.5 hr

**in Redwood National and State Parks south of Crescent City**

Map 1.1, page 31

The Yurok Loop is a great short loop hike that starts right next to pretty Lagoon Creek Pond in Redwood National and State Parks. Here's the deal: From the trailhead, it's a 10-minute walk above a beautiful beach with lots of driftwood, and a gentle climb to a great coastal

overlook. From here you can scan miles of ocean and many rocky stacks. After enjoying the view, head south, and when you reach a junction, turn left and enter a forest where the trail burrows almost like a tunnel, heading gently downhill. It then emerges from the forest and leads back to the parking lot, making it a delightful and easy walk that is a perfect break for highway drivers.

Special note: The Hidden Beach section of Coastal Trail (see the following listing) junctions with this trail.

**User Groups:** Hikers only. No dogs, horses, or mountain bikes.

**Permits:** No permits are required. Parking and access are free.

**Maps:** A trail guide is available for a fee from Redwood National and State Parks Headquarters at the address below. For a topographic map, ask the USGS for Requa.

**Directions:** From Crescent City, drive south on U.S. 101 for approximately 14 miles. Turn right at the sign for the Lagoon Creek Parking Area. The trailhead is adjacent to the parking lot (on the ocean/north side).

**Contact:** Redwood National and State Parks, 1111 2nd Street, Crescent City, CA 95531, 707/464-6101, website: www.nps.gov/redw/.

## 16 COASTAL TRAIL (HIDDEN BEACH SECTION)
### 8.0 mi / 5.0 hrs

**in Redwood National Park south of Crescent City**

Map 1.1, page 31

One of the greatest lookouts anywhere in the hemisphere is available at the Klamath Overlook, where you can scan the vast ocean-blue horizon and actually see the curvature of the earth. This is also an excellent place to see the spouts of passing whales in winter and early spring. After parking, enjoy the view and then head off. It's only a three-mile round-trip to Hidden Beach and back. But you can continue near False Klamath Rock, making it an eight-miler. The trail runs along coastal bluffs and rocky cliffs, with sweeping views of the ocean. Pray for a clear day.

**User Groups:** Hikers only. No dogs, horses, or mountain bikes.

**Permits:** No permits are required. Parking and access are free.

**Maps:** A trail guide is available for a fee from Redwood National and State Parks Headquarters at the address below. For a topographic map, ask the USGS for Requa.

**Directions:** From Eureka, drive north on U.S. 101 for about 60 miles to the Klamath River. Continue two miles north of the Klamath River Bridge to Requa Road. Turn west on Requa Road and drive 2.5 miles to the Klamath Overlook, at the end of the road. The trailhead is at the south end of the parking area. Head north on Coastal Trail.

**Contact:** Redwood National and State Parks, 1111 2nd Street, Crescent City, CA 95531, 707/464-6101, website: www.nps.gov/redw/.

## 17 LOST MAN CREEK TRAIL
### 2.0 mi / 1.0 hr

in Redwood National Park south of Klamath

**Map 1.1, page 31**

Lost Man Creek is very pretty, with many rock pools and lots of lush vegetation. It's also a destination that is easy to reach. The trail heads southeast, the first 1.5 miles nearly flat, then starts to climb moderately, and then nearly levels out along the creek. Bring your camera, because it is rare to reach such a pristine setting with such a short walk. The trail is actually a wide gravel roadbed—an old logging road that the park service plans on reclaiming and turning into a more low-key setting. Although the two-mile round-trip is as far as most hikers take it, the trail actually continues for 10 miles, all the way back down to Bald Hills Road. But only the deranged make the 20-mile round-trip—it's so steep that you'll be howling at the moon like a lone wolf.

**User Groups:** Hikers only. No dogs, horses, or mountain bikes.

**Permits:** No permits are required. Parking and access are free.

**Maps:** A trail guide is available for a fee from Redwood National and State Parks Headquarters at the address below. For a topographic map, ask the USGS for Orick.

**Directions:** From Eureka, drive north on U.S. 101 for 41 miles to Orick. Continue north for 3.5 miles just past Davison Road to Lost Man Creek Road. Turn right and drive .75 mile to the parking area and trailhead. Trailers and RVs are not permitted on Lost Man Creek Road.

**Contact:** Redwood National and State Parks, 1111 2nd Street, Crescent City, CA 95531, 707/464-6101, website: www.nps.gov/redw/.

## 18 TALL TREES TRAIL
### 3.2 mi / 1.5 hrs

in Redwood National Park south of Klamath

**Map 1.1, page 31**

This hike is routed into a grove of tall and ancient redwoods of cathedral-like beauty, with the trail shaded and surrounded by a lush fern understory. Your mission here is to reach Tall Trees Grove, home of a 357-foot-high redwood estimated to be 600 years old. According to rangers, this tree has lost about 10 feet of height because of drying and is no longer considered the world's tallest tree. In the summer, Tall Trees Trail is popular, with visitors from all over the United States arriving to see the giant old-growth redwoods. The hike to the grove is just over a mile, and if you want to extend the adventure, you can return cross-country along Redwood Creek or head off toward Emerald Ridge (which is more of a cross-country route, not a designated trail). Warning: There is poison oak off the trail in this area.

**User Groups:** Hikers only. No dogs, horses, or mountain bikes. No wheelchair facilities.

**Permits:** A permit is required if you want to drive to the trailhead, with only a limited number of cars allowed per day. Permits are free and can be obtained at the Redwood Information Center starting at 9 A.M. In the summer months it's advisable to arrive as early as possible.

**Maps:** A trail guide is available for a fee from Redwood National and State Parks Headquarters at the address below. For a topographic map, ask the USGS for Orick.

**Directions:** From Eureka, drive north on U.S. 101 for 40 miles. About a mile before reaching Orick, stop at the Redwood Information Center, at the west side of the highway. Here you secure a permit number, which is actually a gate combination number you'll need. Drive north on U.S. 101 through Orick. About .25 mile north of Orick, turn right on Bald Hills Road. Look for the Tall Tree Access sign and drive seven miles to a locked gate, on the right. Open the gate using your permit/combination number, drive through, close and lock the gate, and then drive six miles down the gravel road (C-Line Road) to the trailhead. No RVs or trailers are permitted.

**Contact:** Redwood National and State Parks, 1111 2nd Street, Crescent City, CA 95531, 707/464-6101, website: www.nps.gov/redw/.

## 19 COASTAL TRAIL (FERN CANYON/ OSSAGON SECTION)

**5.4 mi / 3.0 hrs**

**in Prairie Creek Redwoods State Park south of Klamath**

Map 1.1, page 31

This is a great hike, once one of the best coastal hikes anywhere. There is a good chance of seeing Roosevelt elk (Prairie Creek Redwoods State Park is loaded with them), Fern Canyon (see the following hike), a dense forest (quiet and pretty), and a series of hidden waterfalls. In addition, there is a huge beach that's spotless—that's right, not even a single piece of litter. Start from the parking area by crossing a shallow stream, and then take the near-level walk on the trail north as far as your heart desires. Most visitors enjoy the waterfalls and the beach, stopping for a picnic before returning. Elk are common here, and while they are accustomed to seeing people, be sure to give them plenty of room anyway. The only downer here is the mountain bikes. This trail is often wet and soft, so bike tires damage the trail by leaving tire furrows, and bikers often go too fast for such an unblemished spot. Note that there is a great trail camp about three miles in, but because overnight parking is forbidden at the trailhead, access is best from the east side of Prairie Creek Redwoods State Park, with a one-way hike of 7.5 miles.

**User Groups:** Hikers and mountain bikes. No dogs or horses. No wheelchair facilities.

**Permits:** No permits are required. There is a state park day-use fee of $6 per vehicle. Overnight parking is not permitted.

**Maps:** Trail maps are available at the park visitors center for a fee. For a topographic map, ask the USGS for Fern Canyon.

**Directions:** From Eureka, drive north on U.S. 101 for 41 miles to Orick. Continue north for 2.5 miles to Davison Road. Turn west on Davison Road and drive eight miles to Fern Canyon Trail. No trailers or RVs are permitted.

**Contact:** Prairie Creek Redwoods State Park, 127011 Newton B. Drury Scenic Parkway, Orick, CA 95555, 707/464-6101, ext. 5300, website: www.parks.ca.gov (click on Find A Park).

## 20 FERN CANYON LOOP TRAIL

**0.8 mi / 0.5 hr**

**in Prairie Creek Redwoods State Park south of Klamath**

Map 1.1, page 31

The Fern Canyon Loop might just be the most inspiring short hike in California. When you walk along the bottom of Fern Canyon, you'll be surrounded by 50-foot-high walls covered with giant ferns—a dramatic setting that isn't duplicated anywhere in the state. Also adding to the beauty is a small waterfall, pouring in through a chasm in the canyon wall and gushing into Home Creek. But it is Home Creek, which runs through the bottom of the canyon, that can cause the one serious problem here. In winter this creek can flood, making the trail impassable. Although bridges are provided from June through September, wear waterproof footwear—hikers often have to hop back and forth across the stream in order to reach the back of the canyon. At the end of the canyon, turn left and climb the trail to the canyon rim, and then continue through the forest back to the trailhead. A bonus is the adjacent beach, which is wide open and spans for miles. It is also common to see Roosevelt elk on the drive in. Note that this trail is recommended and well known by many, so it can get a lot of use during the summer months.

**User Groups:** Hikers only. No dogs, horses, or mountain bikes. No wheelchair facilities.

**Permits:** No permits are required. There is a state park day-use fee of $6 per vehicle.

**Maps:** Trail maps are available at the park visitors center for a fee. For a topographic map, ask the USGS for Fern Canyon.

**Directions:** From Eureka, drive north on U.S. 101 for 41 miles to Orick. Continue north for 2.5 miles to Davison Road. Turn west on Davison Road and drive eight miles to Fern Canyon Trail. No trailers or RVs are permitted.

**Contact:** Prairie Creek Redwoods State Park, 127011 Newton B. Drury Scenic Parkway, Orick, CA 95555, 707/464-6101, ext. 5300, website: www.parks.ca.gov (click on Find A Park).

## 21 SKUNK CABBAGE TRAIL
**7.0 mi / 3.0 hrs**

**in Redwood National Park south of Klamath**

Map 1.1, page 31

Hidden in the Redwood Empire is a rainforest jungle that looks like it's right out of *Jurassic Park*. You might even swear that a T-Rex must be lurking amid the massive vegetation, spruce, and redwoods. Few places anywhere cast such an aura as that found here on the Skunk Cabbage Trail in Redwood National Park, set near the little town of Orick. This trail is routed 3.5 miles amid a stunning forest understory out to a coastal bluff edged by the Pacific Ocean. Instead of dinosaurs, you might see black bear, endangered northern spotted owls, or marbled murrelets. Every step is filled with the sense that this is an ancient place for old souls and youthful spirits.

From the parking area, the trail quickly enters a dense redwood and spruce forest, where the canopy is often completely enclosed by towering tree limbs. The trail meanders along a small watershed, Skunk Cabbage Creek; set beneath is a luxuriant forest floor filled with huge sword ferns, sorrel, and the giant skunk cabbage. The latter is a herbaceous plant with massive stalks, a perennial that reaches its full growth from May through June. It is called skunk cabbage because of its strong scent when taken in up close and personal; it's even considered by some to be rank. But the smell isn't a factor in this trip, rather, it's about how the lavish growth of the plant adds a sense of age-old mystery of this quiet jungle. The trail eventually winds its way through redwoods as you near the coastal bluffs, which is a good picnic site and turnaround spot.

Note that in fall and winter, the skunk cabbage die off, and this hike becomes just another pretty hike in the redwoods.

**User Groups:** Hikers only. No mountain bikes, dogs, or horses. No wheelchair facilities.

**Permits:** Parking and access are free.

**Maps:** Trail maps are available at the park visitors center for a fee. For a topographic map, ask the USGS for Fern Canyon.

**Directions:** From Eureka, take U.S. 101 north for 41 miles to the signed exit for Redwood Information Center (if you reach Orick, you have gone one mile too far) and get in left turn lane. Turn left and go 150 yards to the parking area. After obtaining trail and park materials at the center, then turn left (north) on U.S. 101 and drive two miles (through Orick) to the trailhead entrance road on the left (comes up suddenly), signed Skunk Cabbage Trail. Turn left and drive one-quarter mile to a parking area.

**Contact:** Redwood Visitor Center, Orick, 707/464-6101, ext. 5265; Redwood National and State Parks, 1111 2nd Street, Crescent City, CA 95531, website: www.nps.gov/redw/.

## 22 REDWOOD CREEK TRAIL
16.0 mi / 1.0 day

**in Redwood National Park south of Klamath**

Map 1.1, page 31

The Redwood Creek Trail has become a feature hike in Redwood National Park. Though most visitors cut the trip short, it still provides exceptional beauty even in short pieces, with a chance to see elk near the parking area. The trail is routed along Redwood Creek, a pretty stream that flows out to sea near Orick. As you hike into the interior, you'll notice the diversity of the forest, with spruce, alder, redwoods, and maples, as well lush fern beds in some areas. Stinging nettle is also abundant here, so stay on the trail. The stream attracts a diversity of wildlife, with ducks, herons, and hawks the most common sightings, and ruffed grouse and eagles are occasionally seen. In the summer, the first mile or two of the trail can be quite crowded, but just keep on going. The farther you go, the fewer people you'll see. Note that during the winter, the creek can flood the trail in some areas, making it impassable.

**User Groups:** Hikers only. No dogs, horses, or mountain bikes. No wheelchair facilities.

**Permits:** No permits are required. Parking and access are free.

**Maps:** A trail guide is available for a fee from Redwood National and State Parks Headquarters at the address below. For a topographic map, ask the USGS for Orick.

**Directions:** From Eureka, drive north on U.S. 101 for approximately 41 miles to Orick and then about .25 mile north of Orick to Bald Hills Road. Turn right on Bald Hills Road and drive .25 mile to the access road. Turn right and drive one-half mile to the parking area and trailhead.

**Contact:** Redwood National and State Parks, 1111 2nd Street, Crescent City, CA 95531, 707/464-6101, website: www.nps.gov/redw/; California State Parks, North Coast Redwoods District, 707/445-6547, website: www.parks.ca.gov (click on Find A Park).

## 23 RIM LOOP TRAIL
5.0 mi / 2.5 hrs

**at Patrick's Point State Park north of Eureka**

Map 1.1, page 31

Patrick's Point State Park is set on a coastal headland lush with ferns, spruce, and wildflowers. It's bordered by the Pacific, which means visitors can go tidepool hopping or whale-watching. That means that with this trail, you get the best of two worlds. At times it tunnels through thick vegetation, and at other times it opens up to sweeping ocean views. Along the way, several spur trails provide access to many features, including Mussel Rocks, Wedding Rock, Agate Beach, Rocky Point, Patrick's Point, Abalone Point, and Palmer's Point. The views are sensational at every one of these spots. The elevation of the trail is 200 feet and is nearly level its entire length. Each of the spur trails thus drops 200 feet to the beach. The spur trails, while short (they add just 1.5 miles to the hike), will make this a two- to three-hour trip, since you just won't want to rush through it. In addition, Octopus Tree Trail offers a short hike that starts just across from the northern end of Rim Loop Trail. This bonus trail provides a chance to see many spruce trees with roots that have straddled downed logs (hence the name Octopus Trees).

The only downers here are the fog and the heavy tourist traffic, both of which are common during the summer.

**User Groups:** Hikers only. No dogs, horses, or mountain bikes. The best wheelchair-accessible hiking trail in this park is from the visitors center to the Sumeg Village.

**Permits:** No permits are required. A state park day-use fee of $6 per vehicle is charged.

**Maps:** A park map and brochure are available for a fee from Patrick's Point State Park at the address below. For a topographic map, ask the USGS for Trinidad.

**Directions:** From Eureka, drive north on U.S. 101 for 22 miles to Trinidad and continue north for 5.5 miles. Take the Patrick's Point Drive exit. At the stop sign, turn left and drive .5 mile to the entrance station. Continue to the Agate Beach parking area.

**Contact:** Patrick's Point State Park, 4150 Patrick's Point Drive, Trinidad, CA 95570, 707/677-3570, website: www.parks.ca.gov (click on Find A Park).

## 24 TSURAI LOOP
### 1.5 mi / 1.0 hr

**on Trinidad Head on the Humboldt coast north of Eureka**

Map 1.1, page 31

The Tsurai Loop is a great, easy walk with coastal vistas, unique terrain, and a nearby restaurant. The terrain includes the 300-foot miniature mountain at Trinidad Head, the pretty beachfront to the north of the Trinidad Head area, and the Trinidad Pier. The trip is best done in a counterclockwise loop. It starts by hiking up for beautiful views to the north, eventually reaching this perfectly situated rock lookout of the ocean. On clear days it can be an ideal spot to watch for the puff-of-smoke spouts on the ocean surface (made by migrating whales). The trail circles the mountain and then climbs to the top, a flat summit, where the views are only fair. The views are actually a lot better just 50 yards to the south, looking south toward Eureka and Humboldt Bay. As you head back down, you get more views of the rocky Trinidad Harbor and coast. The restaurant? It's called Seascape, and you can get a crab or shrimp omelet (in season) for breakfast that'll have your mouth watering every time you start driving north of Eureka on U.S. 101. If there's a wait at the restaurant, don't hesitate to line up anyway.

**User Groups:** Hikers and dogs. Mountain bikes permitted but not recommended. No horses. No wheelchair facilities.

**Permits:** No permits are required. Parking and access are free.

**Maps:** For a topographic map, ask the USGS for Trinidad.

**Directions:** From Eureka, drive north on U.S.

101 for 28 miles to Trinidad. Take the Trinidad exit, turn left at the stop sign, and drive under the U.S. 101 overpass to Main Street. Continue on Main Street to Trinity Street. Turn left and drive a short distance to Edwards Street. Turn right on Edwards Street and drive to the parking area at the foot of the harbor.

**Contact:** There is no managing agency for information.

## 25 ARCATA MARSH TRAIL
### 2.0–4.5 mi / 1.0–2.0 hrs

**in Arcata Marsh and Wildlife Sanctuary on the northern edge of Humboldt Bay**

Map 1.2, page 32

The 236-acre Arcata Marsh is the most popular bird-watching area in Northern California, and it's best explored by walking the loop. It is set on a levee above the marsh; the trail is short, flat, and routed in a loop for perfect viewing possibilities. The loop is two miles, but it can be extended on other trails for a longer trip. Several wooden photography blinds are available on the route, where you can hide yourself to view the ponds up close and take pictures of the birds. The setting is unique, with the coast, saltwater bay, brackish-water marsh, pond, foothills, and streams all nearby. This diversity means that an outstanding variety of species (more than 250) are attracted to the area, with sightings often including belted kingfishers, ospreys, peregrine falcons, black phoebes, and song and savannah sparrows. In other words, birds from nearly all habitats are represented, which explains why the Audubon Society gives guided tours every Saturday at 8:30 A.M. A lot of people drive here to eat a picnic lunch, and just like Pavlov's dogs, tons of birds show up in the parking lot daily at noon for handouts. The rangers request that you don't feed the birds.

Also of interest is the Arcata Marsh Interpretive Center, located at the southwest corner of the parking area, where activities for children are held. The interpretive center is open from 9 A.M. to 5 P.M. daily and has free maps, literature, and a posted list of recent bird sightings.

**User Groups:** Hikers, dogs, and mountain bikes. No horses.

**Permits:** No permits are required. Parking and access are free.

**Maps:** For a free, detailed trail map, contact the City of Arcata at the address below and ask for the Marsh and Wildlife Trail map. For a topographic map, ask the USGS for Arcata South.

**Directions:** From Eureka, drive north on U.S. 101 for five miles to Arcata and the Samoa Boulevard exit. Take that exit and turn west onto Samoa Boulevard; drive to I Street. Turn left (south) and continue to the parking area.

**Contact:** Arcata Marsh Interpretive Center, 707/826-2359; City of Arcata, Environmental Services Department, 736 F Street, Arcata, CA 95521, 707/822-8184, website: www.arcatacityhall.org/arcata_marsh.html.

## 26 REDWOOD LOOP
### 6.2 mi / 3.0 hrs

**in Arcata Redwood Park in the Arcata foothills**

Map 1.2, page 32

Arcata Redwoods Park provides a respite for students at nearby Humboldt State and for locals who want to wander amid a beautiful second-growth forest. A network of 18 trails covering about 10 miles in all is here, and the Redwood Loop connects several of them. For newcomers a map is an absolute necessity. Mountain bikes are prohibited at about 50 percent of the trails in the Arcata redwoods, although these rules are occasionally broken.

Start at the sign noting Redwood Park Trail (mountain bikes are not allowed at this trailhead) and take Nature Trail, which will take you by many huge stumps, a small creek, and a forest of redwoods and spruce. The complete route features a 1,200-foot elevation gain and then loss, making it a steep trail both on the way up and on the way down. On weekends, kamikaze mountain bikers tearing downhill

can turn this hike into an extremely unpleasant experience.

**User Groups:** Hikers, dogs, horses, and mountain bikes. Certain sections of the trail are off-limits to horses and mountain bikes; check the trail map for details. No wheelchair facilities.

**Permits:** No permits are required. Parking and access are free.

**Maps:** For a free, detailed trail map, contact the City of Arcata at the address below and ask for the Community Forest Trail map. A free mountain bike trail map is also available. For topographic maps, ask the USGS for Arcata North and Arcata South.

**Directions:** From Eureka, drive north on U.S. 101 to Arcata and the 14th Street exit. Take the 14th Street exit and drive east for about one mile into the parking area (look for the Redwood Park Trails sign). No mountain bikes are permitted here. Bikers and equestrians should use the Meadow trailhead, located where 14th Street enters the park.

**Contact:** City of Arcata, Environmental Services Department, 736 F Street, Arcata, CA 95521, 707/822-8184, website: www.arcata-parksandrec.com.

## 27 RUSS CITY PARK DOUBLE LOOP
### 2.2 mi / 2.0 hrs

**in Russ City Park in Ferndale south of Eureka**

Map 1.2, page 32

Russ City Park is Humboldt County's backyard wilderness. Covering just 105 acres, the park has been retained in its primitive state for wildlife, birds, and hikers. Though there's no posted, official name to this recommended route, we call the trail Double Loop, because it's set in the shape of a figure eight, which is quite rare. The trail includes a climb up Lytel Ridge, passing Francis Creek, with sections routed through heavy fern beds and large firs, and offering views of a small pond and the Eel River floodplain. Although the trip is relatively short and easy enough, the terrain is steep in spots, and the trail is challenging, complete with switchbacks. Heavy fog or rain can make it slippery here. Since it's a city park, Russ is little known by outsiders and can provide quiet, secluded hiking.

**User Groups:** Hikers and dogs. No horses or mountain bikes. No wheelchair facilities.

**Permits:** No permits are required. Parking and access are free.

**Maps:** A free map and brochure can be obtained by contacting the City of Ferndale at the address below. For a topographic map, ask the USGS for Ferndale.

**Directions:** From Eureka, drive south on U.S. 101 for 11 miles to the Ferndale/Fernbridge exit. Take that exit and drive straight about .75 mile. Turn right and drive west five miles through town to Ocean Avenue. Turn left on Ocean Avenue and drive .75 mile to the park, on the right.

**Contact:** City of Ferndale, P.O. Box 1095, Ferndale, CA 95536, 707/786-4224, website: www.ferndale-ca-gov.org.

## 28 RATHERT GROVE/ GRIZZLY CREEK TRAIL

**1.8 mi / 1.0 hr**

**at Grizzly Creek Redwoods State Park near Bridgeville**

Map 1.2, page 32

This pretty hike is an easy walk through the redwoods. It crosses a small bridge at Grizzly Creek and tunnels under the redwood forest canopy into Rathert Grove, one of four relatively small yet pristine old-growth redwood groves protected in this park. There is nothing difficult about this or the other hikes in the park. In fact, stairs are provided in many of the few, short, steeper spots. What makes this hike special is that on a weekday, you can have an entire old-growth redwood grove all to yourself. Where else can you do that?

Grizzly Creek Redwoods State Park is one of the most overlooked redwood state parks in California, receiving fewer than 25,000 visitors per year—and most of those in July and

August. It is often overlooked because it is not located on U.S. 101, but rather Highway 36, a curvy two-laner that provides access to some of the state's most remote areas. Many discover the park by accident, usually heading up to fish, canoe, or kayak the Van Duzen River; the state park provides an excellent river access point, as well as a campground.

The park covers 390 acres. It was spared the chainsaws of loggers by the Georgia-Pacific Corporation, and in return, founder Owen R. Cheatham had one of the park's magnificent old-growth groves named for him.

**User Groups:** Hikers only. No dogs, horses, or mountain bikes are permitted. Some facilities are wheelchair accessible, but there is no trail access for wheelchairs.

**Permits:** No permits are required. A fee of $6 per vehicle is charged for parking.

**Maps:** For a free brochure and map, write Grizzly Creek Redwoods at the address below. For a topographic map, ask the USGS for Redcrest Quad.

**Directions:** From Eureka, drive south on U.S. 101 to the junction of Highway 36 at Alton. Turn east on Highway 36 and drive 17.2 miles to the park entrance, on the right.

**Contact:** Grizzly Creek Redwoods State Park, 707/777-3683, website: www.parks.ca.gov (click on Find A Park).

## 29 5 ALLENS' TRAIL

**1.5 mi / 1.5 hrs**

**in Humboldt Redwoods State Park south of Eureka**

Map 1.2, page 32

The 5 Allens' Trail will provide a lasting impression of Humboldt Redwoods State Park for one reason: If you're unprepared, the trail is something of a butt-kicker. Ah, but it's also very short and is well worth the effort in exchange for quiet wonders.

From the trailhead near the Eel River, walk under the highway and then start the climb. Up, up, and up it goes, ascending 1,200 feet over the course of just .75 mile. The trail passes through a forest of mixed conifers; the tree canopy provides needed shade in the summer. Even though the hike is quite short, few people make it to the end. But if you want a quiet, peaceful spot—and are willing to pay to get it—you'll find it at the end.

A great short side trip from the trailhead is to instead hike north, along the Eel River to High Rock, one of the better shoreline fishing spots for steelhead during the winter migrations.
**User Groups:** Hikers only. No dogs, horses, or mountain bikes. No wheelchair facilities.
**Permits:** No permits are required. Parking and access are free.
**Maps:** A map can be obtained for a fee from Humboldt Redwoods State Park at the address below. For a topographic map, ask the USGS for Weott.
**Directions:** From Eureka, drive south on U.S. 101 to the Redcrest exit. Take that exit and turn left, drive under the overpass, and continue a short distance to Avenue of the Giants. Turn right on Avenue of the Giants and drive south three miles (past High Rock Conservation Camp) to the 5 Allens' trailhead parking lot, on the left.

For an alternate route from Garberville, drive north on U.S. 101 to the Founders Tree/Rockefeller Forest exit. Take that exit (north), turn right, and drive about 200 yards to Avenue of the Giants. Turn left on Avenue of the Giants, cross over the South Fork Eel River, and then bear right at the intersection in order to stay on Avenue of the Giants. Drive a short distance to the 5 Allens' trailhead parking lot, on the right.
**Contact:** Humboldt Redwoods State Park, Box 100, Weott, CA 95571, 707/946-2409, website: www.parks.ca.gov (click on Find A Park).

## 30 FOUNDERS GROVE NATURE TRAIL
**0.5 mi / 0.5 hr**

**in Humboldt Redwoods State Park south of Eureka**

Map 1.2, page 32

There's some irony on this hike. What was once the tallest redwood tree in the park is now the longest redwood tree in the park. What? That's because the Dyerville Giant fell, so this massive redwood is now in prone position. It still is an attraction among the 100 miles of trails at Humboldt Redwoods State Park. Little .5-mile Founders Grove Nature Trail provides the shortest and most easily accessible walk in the park. The trail also gives the quickest payoff, which explains why it's the park's most popular hike. The trail's location, near U.S. 101, makes it easy to reach. At the trailhead you'll find a small box with brochures describing each element of the self-guided nature trail. All the while you'll be surrounded by old-growth redwoods—a great reward for such a small physical investment.
**User Groups:** Hikers only. There is wheelchair access, although the trail is a bit uneven. No dogs, horses, or mountain bikes.
**Permits:** No permits are required. There is a fee of $6 per vehicle.
**Maps:** A map is available for a fee from Humboldt Redwoods State Park at the address below. For a topographic map, ask the USGS for Weott.
**Directions:** From Garberville, drive north on U.S. 101 about 20 miles to the Founder Tree/Rockefeller Forest exit. Take that exit and drive a short distance to Avenue of the Giants. Drive 100 yards (crossing Avenue of the Giants) to the Founders Grove Parking Area/Trailhead (it's well signed).
**Contact:** Humboldt Redwoods State Park, Box 100, Weott, CA 95571, 707/946-2409, website: www.parks.ca.gov (click on Find A Park).

## 31 BULL CREEK FLATS
**9.0 mi / 5.25 hrs**

**in Humboldt Redwoods State Park south of Eureka**

Map 1.2, page 32

This trail offers a streamside walk complete with giant redwoods and a babbling brook. Starting at the trailhead at Bull Creek Flats (a short walk to the Federation Grove), the trail heads west along Bull Creek, an easy but steady grade as you hike upstream. All the while you're surrounded by forest, both redwoods and fir in a variety of mixes. Most people cross the seasonal bridge at the Big Tree and head back toward the beginning of the trail, at Bull Creek Flats, to make a loop. The feature hike of the route is the Big Tree Area and the giant tree, which you'll reach after four miles of hiking. There are many redwoods here that range from 5 to 10 feet in diameter. The big attraction for years was the Flat Iron Tree, a huge leaning redwood that grew in strange dimensions in order to support itself. Well, it's not leaning anymore, because it fell down and went boom. On the broad side, the Flat Iron Tree measures more than 15 feet. After the trail passes the Big Tree Area, it's routed to the mouth of Albee Creek, ending at Mattole Road. The trailhead here (at Mattole Road), by the way, provides a shorter hike of about a mile to the seasonal bridge at the Big Tree Area.

**User Groups:** Hikers only. No dogs, horses, or mountain bikes. No wheelchair facilities.

**Permits:** No permits are required. Parking and access are free.

**Maps:** A map is available for a fee from Humboldt Redwoods State Park at the address below. For a topographic map, ask the USGS for Weott.

**Directions:** From Garberville, drive north on U.S. 101 about 20 miles to the Founder Tree/Rockefeller Forest exit. Take that exit and turn left and drive a short distance to Avenue of the Giants. Turn left and drive a short distance to Mattole Road (the sign will say Rockefeller Forest/Honeydew, not Mattole Road). Turn left and drive 1.3 miles to the Lower Bull Creek Flats trailhead.

**Contact:** Humboldt Redwoods State Park, Box 100, Weott, CA 95571, 707/946-2409, website: www.parks.ca.gov (click on Find A Park).

## 32 WILLIAMS GROVE TRAIL
### 3.5 mi / 2.0 hrs

in Humboldt Redwoods State Park south of Eureka

**Map 1.2, page 32**

This trail makes an ideal, easy trip for campers staying at the Hidden Springs Campground in Humboldt Redwoods State Park. The camp is set in forest just above a big bend in the South Fork Eel River, with the trailhead on the southwest side of the camp. The trail starts out nearly flat, then turns right and parallels the highway. It's easy walking all the way, amid redwoods both young and old. Then the trail crosses under the highway and down the hill to Williams Grove, which has a picnic area and restrooms. Williams Grove Picnic Area can also be reached by car and then used as a trailhead to hike this route in reverse.

**User Groups:** Hikers only. No dogs, horses, or mountain bikes. No wheelchair facilities.

**Permits:** No permits are required. A parking fee of $6 is charged per vehicle; parking is free for campers.

**Maps:** A map is available for a fee from Humboldt Redwoods State Park at the address below. For topographic maps, ask the USGS for Weott and Myers Flat.

**Directions:** From Garberville on U.S. 101, drive to the Myers Flat exit (north of Garberville). Take that exit to Avenue of the Giants. Turn right and drive one mile northwest to Williams Grove parking area. Note: Hidden Springs Campground (open only during the summer) is located one mile south from the U.S. 101 turnoff.

**Contact:** Humboldt Redwoods State Park, Box 100, Weott, CA 95571, 707/946-2409, website: www.parks.ca.gov (click on Find A Park).

## 33 LOST COAST TRAIL/ MATTOLE TRAILHEAD

**25.0 mi one-way / 3.0 days**

**on the Humboldt coast south of Eureka in King Range National Conservation Area**

Map 1.2, page 32

The Lost Coast and the people who live there seem to be in a different orbit from the rest of California, and that's exactly why visitors make the trip up here. It's called the Lost Coast because of the isolation of the area, which is shielded on all sides by natural boundaries. For a first visit and a great day hike, take the abandoned jeep trail from the campground at Lighthouse Road and head south three miles to the Punta Gorda Lighthouse. You'll get a glimpse of the greatness here, and you'll probably get the inspiration to continue on Lost Coast Trail, one of California's greatest weekend trips. Set primarily on bluffs and beaches, the trail spans 25 miles from the mouth of the Mattole River south to Shelter Cove. Along the way it traces some of California's most remote portions of coastline. With two vehicles, one parked at each end of the trail, hikers can set up their own shuttle, then hike the trail one-way. A paid shuttle service is available as well (see the Contact section, below). This hike is best done from north to south because of winds out of the north; you want them at your back, not in your face. Firm-fitting waterproof boots with good, gripping soles are a necessity: they should be firm fitting because some of the walking is in soft sand, waterproof because there are several small creek crossings, and good gripping because some scrambling over wet boulders is required.

Special note: Some parts of Lost Coast Trail are impassable during high tides. Watch for ticks, and take a tide table. Be cautious: This is an extremely isolated area. In many parts, there is no trail, and there is a lot of boulder hopping, where it is possible to twist an ankle. Also note that in the winter, the beach can be angled quite steeply toward the water, making it perfect for a person with legs of different length. Also note that bears along this trail are experts at raiding food packs at night. Finally, this trip, while remote, has become a popular one-way romp. This means that if you have hikers 200 yards in front of you, you may be seeing them all day. Note that the deli at Shelter Cove is considered a must for many hikers doing this trip; it has the best fish-and-chips around, great with plenty of malt vinegar.

**User Groups:** Hikers, dogs, horses, and mountain bikes. No wheelchair facilities.

**Permits:** Day-use permits are required for organized groups only. A campfire permit (free) is required for overnight use. Parking and access are free.

**Maps:** A detailed trail map is available for a fee, and a free map and brochure can be obtained from the Bureau of Land Management at the address below. Specify the King Range Conservation Area map. For topographic maps, ask the USGS for Petrolia, Cooskie Creek, Shubrick Peak, and Shelter Cove.

**Directions:** From U.S. 101 in Garberville, drive north to the South Fork-Honeydew exit. Take that exit, drive west on Bull Creek Road, and continue 23 miles to Honeydew and Mattole Road. Turn right on Mattole Road and drive 14 miles (toward Petrolia). At the second bridge over the Mattole Road (one mile before Petrolia), turn left on Lighthouse Road. Drive west on Lighthouse Road to its end. The trailhead is just past Mattole Campground.

**Contact:** Bureau of Land Management, Arcata Resource Area, 1695 Heindon Road, Arcata, CA 95521-4573, 707/825-2300, website: www.ca.blm.gov/arcata/king_range.html; Lost Coast Trail Transport Service, 707/986-9909, website: www.lostcoasttrail.com; Shelter Cove Campground, 707/986-7474.

## 34 KING CREST TRAIL

**10.6 mi / 6.5 hrs**

**in King Range National Conservation Area south of Eureka**

Map 1.2, page 32

King's Peak is one of the most prized destinations in the King Range. At 4,087 feet it's the highest point on the Northern California coast, and from it you get a view that can make you feel that you're perched on top of the world. The ocean seems to stretch on forever to the west, and on a perfect day you can make out the top of Mount Lassen behind the ridgeline of the Yolla Bolly Wilderness, to the east.

Reaching King's Peak requires a 5.3-mile hike from the Northslide Peak trailhead on Smith-Etter Road, and in the process, you climb about 700 feet. Making the trip on a clear day is an absolute necessity, since the climb is buffered by the reward of the sweeping views. Trail signs are very poor, and water supplies at trail camps are from dubious sources, so it's also essential to have a good map and a double-canteen water supply. The entire King Crest Trail extends 10 miles one-way, starting from the trailhead listed in this hike to Saddle Mountain trailhead; then it descends four miles to the beach. That makes a one-way overnight trip with a shuttle vehicle at the end of the trail an ideal alternative. Note that the portion that heads down to the beach is called Buck Creek Trail and that it is very steep, with portions difficult to follow—this is considered an advanced hike; for some hikers, orienteering with a map and compass may be required.

**User Groups:** Hikers, dogs, horses, and mountain bikes. No wheelchair facilities.

**Permits:** A campfire permit (free) is required for overnight use. Parking and access are free.

**Maps:** A detailed trail map is available for a fee, and a free map and brochure can be obtained from the Bureau of Land Management at the address below; ask for the King Range Conservation Area map. For a topographic map, ask the USGS for Shubrick Peak.

**Directions:** On U.S. 101, drive to the South Fork-Honeydew exit (just north of Garberville). Take that exit to Wilder Ridge Road and turn southwest. Drive one mile to Smith-Etter Road and turn west. Drive six miles to the trailhead (this is a primitive, four-wheel-drive road and is closed from November 1 to March 31).

**Contact:** Bureau of Land Management, Arcata Resource Area, 1695 Heindon Road, Arcata, CA 95521-4573, 707/825-2300, website: www.ca.blm.gov/arcata/king_range.html; Lost Coast Trail Transport Service, 707/986-9909, website: www.lostcoasttrail.com.

## 35 SPANISH RIDGE TRAIL
**9.6 mi / 1.0 day**

**in King Range National Conservation Area south of Eureka**

Map 1.2, page 32

In just a few miles, you can gain access to some of the most remote sections of the California coast. Alas, there's a price (and we'll get to that).

From the Spanish Ridge trailhead, hike 1.8 miles along Cooskie Creek Trail and climb an easy 200 feet before reaching the junction with Spanish Ridge Trail. You then descend 2,300 feet in three miles en route to the coast. Know what that means? Right. Going back, you'll climb 2,300 feet in three miles, and unless you can get a helicopter ride back, you're looking at some serious grunt work—but it's worth it.

The King Range is very rugged, primitive, and isolated. Thanks to that bumpy access road and the climb on the return trip, it's rare to see other people here. And because there are no water sources along this trail, each hiker should carry two canteens of water. This trail is for experienced hikers only, and as with several of the hikes in the King Range, you should bring a map and a compass.

**User Groups:** Hikers, dogs, mountain bikes, and horses. No wheelchair facilities.

**Permits:** A campfire permit (free) is required for overnight use. Parking and access are free.

**Maps:** A detailed trail map is available for a fee, and a free map and brochure can be obtained from the Bureau of Land Management at the address below; ask for the King Range Conservation Area map. For topographic maps, ask the USGS for Cooskie Creek and Shubrick Peak.

**Directions:** On U.S. 101, drive to the South Fork-Honeydew exit (just north of Garberville). Take that exit to Wilder Ridge Road and turn southwest. Drive one mile to Smith-Etter Road and turn west. Drive 10 miles (this is a primitive, four-wheel-drive road and is closed from November 1 to March 31) to Telegraph Ridge Road. Turn northwest on Telegraph Ridge Road and drive eight miles to the trailhead gate. In summer, continue driving two miles to the trailhead. When the gate is locked, the trailhead is accessible only by a two-mile walk.

**Contact:** Bureau of Land Management, Arcata Resource Area, 1695 Heindon Road, Arcata, CA 95521-4573, 707/825-2300, website: www.ca.blm.gov/arcata/king_range.html.

## 36 PIONEER TRAIL LOOP
**2.8 mi / 2.0 hrs**

**in Benbow Lake State Recreation Area south of Garberville**

Map 1.2, page 32

You can scan map after map and never find Benbow Lake. In fact, in the future, you might be able to scan the landscape here and not find it either. That is because for many years, Benbow Lake has been a seasonal lake, created each summer only by a temporary dam on the Eel River. This dam blocks the downstream migration of juvenile steelhead, and because of the depleted status of the species, the decision over whether or not to install the dam is reviewed each year. For instance, there was no lake in 2000, 2001, and 2002. And it may never go in again if the steelhead are listed as endangered. When the Eel is dammed, Benbow Lake becomes a popular recreation site for sunbathing, swimming, boating (without motors), and camping. Hiking is a popular alternative, especially on this loop trail.

Start on Pratt Mill Trail near campsite No. 57, at an elevation of 400 feet. You can create a 3.5-mile loop by connecting to Lost Coast Trail; this is best hiked north to south to keep the north winds out of one's face. Lost Coast Trail Transport does a paid shuttle service here. This route features some river frontage, a sprinkling of giant redwoods, a meadow, and a portion of trail along the Eel River drainage (Benbow Lake).

**User Groups:** Hikers only. No dogs, horses, or mountain bikes. No wheelchair facilities.

**Permits:** No permits are required. A fee of $6 per vehicle is charged for parking.

**Maps:** A map and brochure can be obtained by contacting Benbow Lake State Recreation Area at the address below. For a topographic map, ask the USGS for Garberville.

**Directions:** From Santa Rosa, drive north on U.S. 101 to Leggett and continue for 22 miles to the Benbow exit. Take the Benbow exit, turn right on Benbow Drive, and drive one mile to the Benbow Lake State Recreation Area Campground. The trailhead is located next to campsite No. 57.

**Contact:** Benbow Lake State Recreation Area, c/o California State Parks, North Coast Redwoods District, Piercy Sector, 1600 U.S. Highway 101, No. 8, Garberville, CA 95542, 707/247-3319; Benbow Lake, 707/923-3238, website: www.parks.ca.gov (click on Find A Park); Lost Coast Trail Transport Service, 707/986-9909, website: www.lostcoasttrail.com.

## 37 LOOKOUT POINT LOOP TRAIL
**1.7 mi / 1.0 hr**

**in Richardson Grove State Park south of Garberville**

Map 1.2, page 32

Big woods. Big water. That's what Lookout Point Loop Trail supplies, with a tour through giant redwoods culminating at the canyon rim over the South Fork Eel River. Giant redwoods approaching 300 feet tall and estimated to be 1,000 years old are the highlight of Richardson Grove, while younger redwoods, fir, and tan oak fill out the forest. To be honest, if you look close, there's actually more tan oak and fir than redwoods. The trail passes through forest and rises to Lookout Point, where there's an excellent view of the South Fork. You can also see the Oak Flat Campground from here. As a free-flowing river, the South Fork Eel River can seem like a small trickle in late summer or a howling torrent during peak flows in winter. When looking down from Lookout

Point during summer, it may seem hard to imagine how high the Eel has risen in high-water years. In 1955, 1963, 1986, 1997, and 1998, the river actually flooded its banks and wiped out several campgrounds in the state park. This is an easy and popular hike, both for daytime park visitors and for overnighters at Madrone Campground.

**User Groups:** Hikers only. No dogs, horses, or mountain bikes. No wheelchair facilities.

**Permits:** No permits are required. A state park entrance fee of $6 is charged per vehicle.

**Maps:** For a trail guide and brochure (free), write Richardson Grove State Park at the address below. For a topographic map, ask the USGS for Garberville.

**Directions:** From Santa Rosa, drive north on U.S. 101 to Leggett. Continue north on U.S. 101 about 17 miles to the park entrance, on the west side of the highway. Follow the signs to the Redwood Day-Use Parking Area. Access to the trailhead is at the parking area and also out of Madrone Campground.

**Contact:** Richardson Grove State Park, c/o California State Parks, North Coast Redwoods District, Piercy Sector, 1600 U.S. Highway 101, No. 8, Garberville, CA 95542, 707/247-3319, ranger 707/247-3318, website: www.parks.ca.gov (click on Find A Park).

## 38 DURPHY CREEK LOOP
### 4.0 mi / 3.0 hrs

**in Richardson Grove State Park south of Garberville**

Map 1.2, page 32

Be ready for a good climb, have a full canteen of water, and note that no whiners are allowed. Why? Because this loop trail is the most challenging hike in Richardson Grove State Park. It starts easily enough, routed right along the left side of Durphy Creek at a tolerable grade. But when the trail turns left and starts to climb up the canyon, all tolerance is forgotten. The trail climbs 800 feet in less than .5 mile, with a short cutoff to Tan Oak Springs, then onward to the ridge at 1,400 feet. On the way back

down, the route descends through a dense forest of tan oak and is quite steep in the last .5 mile, which includes some switchbacks. To complete the loop, turn left at Lookout Point Trail and hike back toward Madrone Campground.

**User Groups:** Hikers only. No dogs, horses, or mountain bikes. No wheelchair facilities.

**Permits:** No permits are required. A fee of $6 per vehicle is charged for parking.

**Maps:** For a trail guide and brochure (free), write Richardson Grove State Park at the address below. For a topographic map, ask the USGS for Garberville.

**Directions:** From Santa Rosa, drive north on U.S. 101 to Leggett. Continue north on U.S. 101 about 17 miles to the park entrance, on the west side of the highway. Follow the signs to the Redwood Day-Use Parking Area. Walk .25 mile to Madrone Campground and to the trailhead.

**Contact:** Richardson Grove State Park, c/o California State Parks, North Coast Redwoods District, Piercy Sector, 1600 U.S. Highway 101, No. 8, Garberville, CA 95542, 707/247-3319, ranger 707/247-3318, website: www.parks.ca.gov (click on Find A Park).

## 39 WOODLANDS LOOP TRAIL
### 1.6 mi / 1.0 hr

**in Richardson Grove State Park south of Garberville**

Map 1.2, page 32

You want easy? You get easy. You want forest? You get forest. You want a campground trailhead? You get a campground trailhead. The Woodlands Loop, an easy, pretty trail that starts at the Huckleberry Campground, does all that and more. The trail crosses North Creek and then goes through both redwoods and tan oak that are dense at times. It also includes a gentle uphill portion, rising about 250 feet. The trail and camp are set on the west side of U.S. 101, and with the South Fork Eel River on the east side of the highway, there's no direct river access from this trail or the nearby campground.

**User Groups:** Hikers only. No dogs, horses, or mountain bikes. No wheelchair facilities.

**Permits:** No permits are required. A fee of $6 per vehicle is charged for parking.

**Maps:** For a trail guide and brochure (free), write Richardson Grove State Park at the address below. For a topographic map, ask the USGS for Garberville.

**Directions:** From Santa Rosa, drive north on U.S. 101 to Leggett. Continue north on U.S. 101 about 17 miles to the park entrance, on the west side of the highway. The trailhead is accessible from the parking lot just inside the entrance.

**Contact:** Richardson Grove State Park, c/o California State Parks, North Coast Redwoods District, Piercy Sector, 1600 U.S. Highway 101, No. 8, Garberville, CA 95542, 707/247-3319, ranger 707/247-3318, website: www.parks.ca.gov (click on Find A Park).

## 40 TOUMEY GROVE TRAIL
**3.8 mi / 2.75 hrs**

in Richardson Grove State Park south of Garberville

Map 1.2, page 32

The Toumey Trail is one of Richardson Grove State Park's feature summer hikes. It includes walking over the South Fork Eel River on the summer bridge, through a majestic stand of old redwoods, up to Kauffman Springs, and beyond to the Panorama Point Lookout. The trailhead is located between campsite Nos. 123 and 126 at Oak Flat Campground. The trail crosses the river and enters the redwoods; take your time and enjoy the surroundings. The trail climbs 300 feet, rising quickly with a few switchbacks, and arrives at Panorama Point, with excellent views of the Eel River Canyon and Richardson Grove redwoods.

Special note: This trail can be accessed only in the summer months.

**User Groups:** Hikers only. No dogs, horses, or mountain bikes. No wheelchair facilities.

**Permits:** No permits are required. A fee of $6 per vehicle is charged for parking.

**Maps:** For a trail guide and brochure (free), write Richardson Grove State Park at the address below. For a topographic map, ask the USGS for Garberville.

**Directions:** From Santa Rosa, drive north on U.S. 101 to Leggett. Continue north on U.S. 101 about 17 miles to the park entrance, on the west side of the highway. Follow the signs to Oak Flat Campground. The trailhead is located between campsite Nos. 123 and 126. This trail is open only in the summer months.

**Contact:** Richardson Grove State Park, c/o California State Parks, North Coast Redwoods District, Piercy Sector, 1600 U.S. Highway 101, No. 8, Garberville, CA 95542, 707/247-3319, ranger 707/247-3318, website: www.parks.ca.gov (click on Find A Park).

© ROBERT HOLMES/CALTOUR

# Shasta and Trinity

# Shasta and Trinity

**A**t 14,162 feet, Mount Shasta rises like a diamond in a field of coal. Its sphere of influence spans a radius of 125 miles, and its shadow is felt everywhere in the region. Not surprisingly, climbing its mammoth face is the No. 1 activity in the region. It is a truly awe-inspiring half-hike, half-climb on California's most beautiful mountain.

In addition, there are several remarkable backpacking destinations hidden in the western sector of this region: Preston Peak, Clear Creek, Wilderness Falls, and Devils Punchbowl.

But to focus solely on hiking would be a disservice. In fact, this is one of the best areas in North America for an outdoor adventure—especially one involving fishing, powerboating, rafting, and exploring. The region offers giant Shasta Lake, the Sacramento River above and below the lake, the McCloud River, the Trinity Alps, Marble Mountain Wilderness, Russian Wilderness, Castle Crags State Park, Shasta Lake and Whiskeytown National Recreation Areas, and the Klamath Mountains. There are also several hundred miles of Pacific Crest Trail (PCT) that are routed across the best of it.

At the charmed center of this beautiful region is the Trinity Alps, where lakes are sprinkled everywhere. It's also home to the headwaters for feeder streams to the Trinity River, Klamath River, New River, Wooley Creek, and others.

The neighboring Klamath Mountains are well known as Bigfoot

Country by locals. If you drive up the Forest Service road at Bluff Creek, just off Highway 96 upstream of Weitchpec, you can even find the spot where the famous Bigfoot film clip, once believed to be genuine, was shot with an 8mm camera in the 1960s by a hiker. Well, we haven't seen Bigfoot, but we have discovered tons of outdoor recreation. This remote region features miles of the Klamath and Salmon Rivers, as well as the Marble Mountain Wilderness. Options include canoeing, rafting, and fishing for steelhead on the Klamath River, or hiking into your choice of more than 100 wilderness lakes.

Castle Crags and the Trinity Divide feature hikes to Mount Eddy, the Crags, Grey Rocks, and dozens of pristine lakes, many with fantastic campsites. There are also hikes along portions of rivers, including stellar easy walks along the McCloud River.

Shasta Lake is one of America's top recreation lakes. It is the one destination that is big enough to handle all who love it. The massive reservoir boasts 370 miles of shoreline, 1,200 campsites, 21 boat launches, 11 marinas, 35 resorts, and numerous houseboat and cabin rentals. A remarkable 22 species of fish live in the lake. Many of the campgrounds feature lake views. In addition, getting here is easy—it's a straight shot off of I-5. Hidden here is the boat-in Greens Creek trailhead, as well as several others that offer pretty spots with lake views.

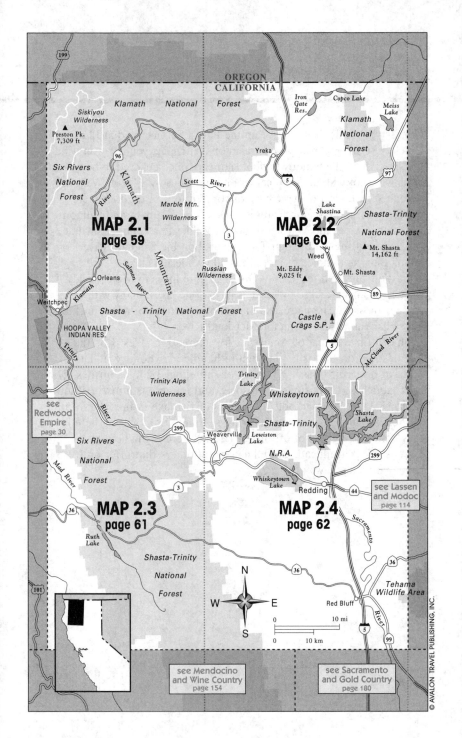

# Map 2.1

## Hikes 1–22
## Pages 63–76

# Map 2.2

**Hikes 23–59**
**Pages 77–100**

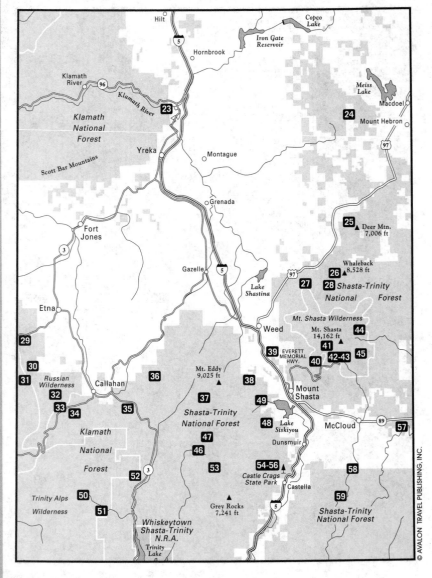

# Map 2.3

## Hikes 60–66
## Pages 101–104

© AVALON TRAVEL PUBLISHING, INC.

# Map 2.4

**Hikes 67–75**
**Pages 105–109**

# 1 YOUNGS VALLEY TRAIL
## 13.0 mi / 1.0 day

in the Siskiyou Wilderness east of
Crescent City

**Map 2.1, page 59**

The 6.5-mile trip from Youngs Valley down
Clear Creek to Youngs Meadow is a beautiful
and rewarding trip. Youngs Meadow, set at an
elevation of 4,500 feet on the western slope of
Preston Peak, is very pretty and makes an excellent picnic area and campsite.

The hike features a 600-foot descent into the
canyon and to Clear Creek. From here the ambitious can take this trip farther—much farther.
The Youngs Valley Trail is a great first leg of
a multiday trip, ultimately heading either farther down Clear Creek to Wilderness Falls,
which is an awesome setting (see the following
hike), or to Rattlesnake Meadows, on the slopes
of Preston Peak—a short but rugged climb.

Note that this trail was once much shorter,
but the access road has since been gated. So
when you start the hike, you will be on the old
Forest Road. It eventually turns to trail then
drops down into Youngs Valley.

**User Groups:** Hikers, dogs, and horses. No
mountain bikes. No wheelchair facilities.

**Permits:** No permits are required. A campfire
permit (free) is required for overnight use.
Parking and access are free.

**Maps:** For a free brochure and hiking guide,
write to Smith River National Recreation Area
at the address below. For a map, ask the U.S.
Forest Service for Klamath National Forest.
For a topographic map, ask the USGS for
Devils Punchbowl.

**Directions:** From Crescent City, drive north
on U.S. 101 for three miles to U.S. 199. Bear
right (east) on U.S. 199 and drive 32 miles to
Forest Road 18N07. Turn right and drive five
miles to Forest Road 18N07. Continue on Forest Road 18N07 for 10 miles (twisty) toward
Sanger Lake. Just before Sanger Lake, bear
right on Forest Road 4803 (signed Youngs Valley Trail) and drive one mile to the end of the
road and the trailhead.

**Contact:** Smith River National Recreation Area,
P.O. Box 228, Gasquet, CA 95543, 707/457-
3131, website: www.fs.fed.us/r5 (click on Forest Offices); Klamath National Forest, Happy
Camp Ranger District, P.O. Box 377, 63822
Highway 96, Happy Camp, CA 96039-0377,
530/493-2243, fax 530/493-1796, website:
www.fs.fed.us/r5 (click on Forest Offices).

# 2 DOE FLAT TRAIL
## 3.0 mi / 1.5 hrs

in Smith River National Recreation Area east
of Crescent City

**Map 2.1, page 59**

Doe Flat is the best backpacking jump-off point
for the Siskiyou Wilderness, and as long as you
know that, you'll have all the motivation you
need for the trip. There are several excellent
destinations from Doe Flat, including Buck
Lake, Devils Punchbowl, and Wilderness Falls.
After parking, the first .75 mile of this easy
hike is on a closed forest service road. After
that, a trail is routed through forest and then
intersects with Buck Lake Trail. To reach Doe
Flat and its campsite, turn left. To reach Buck
Lake, turn right (it's only .1 mile to the lake).
The area is well wooded, with some huge Jeffrey pines and cedars. For late arrivals, a bonus
at the trailhead is a small, primitive camping
area with three sites and a vault toilet.

**User Groups:** Hikers, dogs, and horses. No
mountain bikes. No wheelchair facilities.

**Permits:** No permits are required. A campfire
permit (free) is required for overnight use.
Parking and access are free.

**Maps:** For a free brochure and hiking guide,
write to Smith River National Recreation Area
at the address below. For a map, ask the U.S.
Forest Service for Klamath National Forest.
For a topographic map, ask the USGS for
Devils Punchbowl.

**Directions:** From Crescent City, drive north
on U.S. 101 for three miles. Turn east on U.S.
199 and drive 25 miles. Turn right on Little
Jones Creek Road/Jawbone Road (Forest Road
16) and drive south 9.6 miles to a fork with

Forest Road 16N02. When the road forks, bear sharply left on Forest Road 16N02 and drive four miles to the trailhead, at the end of the road.

**Contact:** Smith River National Recreation Area, P.O. Box 228, Gasquet, CA 95543, 707/457-3131, website: www.fs.fed.us/r5 (click on Forest Offices).

## 3 PRESTON PEAK
**19.0 mi / 2.0 days**

**in the Siskiyou Wilderness east of Crescent City**

Map 2.1, page 59

Only mountaineers need sign up for this trip. The last mile to reach the summit of Preston Peak is steep, rough, and primitive; it can be scary and dangerous for newcomers to mountaineering. With no marked trail on top, hikers must have the ability to scramble cross-country and recognize any dangerous spots—and then avoid them. That done, you'll gain the top—7,309 feet and by far the highest spot in the region, with wondrous surrounding views. Even Mount Shasta, way off to the southeast, comes clearly into view, along with the famous peaks in the Trinity Alps and Marble Mountain Wilderness. A favorite route to climb Preston Peak is to hike Youngs Valley Trail to Youngs Meadow (an easy five miles), head down Clear Creek Trail (another easy mile), and then turn east on Rattlesnake Meadow Trail (two very steep, rough, and primitive miles). At the end of Rattlesnake Meadow Trail, hikers must go cross-country for another mile or so to Preston Peak. The last mile is a scramble. Pick your route very carefully and make no climbing mistakes. Although this is a nontechnical climb, there is one difficult spot that can be dangerous—it's a mix of shale, loose gravel, and boulders, with no discernible trail. Take your time and pick your way up one step at a time.

Special note: Always stay off this mountain in wet weather, because the route is very slippery. Always avoid routes that cross through loose shale, which can be extremely dangerous. A fall here can be life threatening.

**User Groups:** Hikers only. Dogs are permitted but are strongly not recommended on the nonforested slopes of Preston Peak. No horses or mountain bikes. No wheelchair facilities.

**Permits:** A campfire permit is required for overnight use. Parking and access are free.

**Maps:** For a map, ask the U.S. Forest Service for Six Rivers and Klamath National Forest. For a topographic map, ask the USGS for Devils Punchbowl.

**Directions:** From Crescent City, drive north on U.S. 101 for three miles to U.S. 199. Bear right (east) on U.S. 199 and drive 32 miles to Forest Road 18N07. Turn right and drive five miles to Forest Road 18N07. Continue on Forest Road 18N07 for 10 miles (twisty) toward Sanger Lake. Just before Sanger Lake, bear right on Forest Road 4803 (signed Youngs Valley Trail) and drive one mile to the trailhead, at the end of the road.

**Contact:** Klamath National Forest, Happy Camp Ranger District, P.O. Box 377, 63822 Highway 96, Happy Camp, CA 96039-0377, 530/493-2243, website: www.fs.fed.us/r5 (click on Forest Offices); Smith River National Recreation Area, P.O. Box 228, Gasquet, CA 95543, 707/457-3131, website: www.fs.fed.us/r5 (click on Forest Offices).

## 4 ISLAND LAKE TRAIL
**12.0 mi / 2.0 days**

**in Smith River National Recreation Area east of Crescent City**

Map 2.1, page 59

Island Lake is a mountain bowl framed by the back wall of Jedediah Mountain, a wild, primitive area where threatened spotted owls are more common than hikers. The trailhead is at the Bear Basin area. The trip starts with a walk on a portion of trail that is routed down to the South Fork Smith River, where you'll enter the untouched Siskiyou Wilderness. Enjoy the stream; the hike that follows can have some begging for the memory. The trail intersects with the old route and then rises along a mountain spine, climbing up, up, and up for what seems like an endless three miles. It finally tops a ridge and turns around a bend, where little Island Lake comes into view. A great sense of relief will wash over you.

There are two excellent camps at the lake, set in trees near the lake's shore. The trout are eager to bite, but most are very small, dinker-sized brook trout. A great afternoon side trip is to hike the rim around the lake, which is most easily done in a counterclockwise direction to the top of Jedediah Mountain—a perfect picnic site and a great lookout.

If you hiked to Island Lake in years prior to 2003, you will note that the trailhead has been moved a few miles, lengthening the distance to the lake from four miles to six miles. The purpose of this trailhead change is to keep vehicles away from the wilderness, because a fungus that is most commonly introduced from tires on vehicles threatens Port Orford cedars.

**User Groups:** Hikers, dogs, and horses. No mountain bikes. No wheelchair facilities.

**Permits:** A campfire permit is required. Parking and access are free.

**Maps:** For a free brochure and hiking guide, write to Smith River National Recreation Area at the address below. For a map, ask the U.S. Forest Service for Six Rivers and Klamath National Forest. For a topographic map, ask the USGS for Devils Punchbowl.

**Directions:** From Crescent City, drive north on U.S. 101 for three miles to U.S. 199. Bear right (east) on U.S. 199 and drive 25 miles to Little Jones Creek Road/Jawbone Road (Forest Road 16). Turn right and drive eight miles to Forest Road 16N02. Turn left and drive 2.5 miles to Forest Road 16N10. Turn right. The trailhead is located on your immediate right.

**Contact:** Smith River National Recreation Area, P.O. Box 228, Gasquet, CA 95543, 707/457-3131, website: www.fs.fed.us/r5 (click on Forest Offices); Klamath National Forest, Happy Camp Ranger District, P.O. Box 377, 63822 Highway 96, Happy Camp, CA 96039-0377,

530/493-2243, website: www.fs.fed.us/r5 (click on Forest Offices).

# ⑤ BUCK LAKE TRAIL (VIA DOE FLAT TRAIL)

**6.2 mi / 3.0 hrs**

in the Siskiyou Wilderness east of Crescent City

Map 2.1, page 59

The first time we saw Buck Lake was a Memorial Day weekend, as well as the opening day of trout season here, and there were so many rising brook trout that all the dimples on the lake surface looked like rain drops. Set in the heart of a wilderness forest at an elevation of 4,300 feet, Buck Lake is a little crystal lake surrounded by old-growth firs. After parking, the first .75 mile of this easy hike is on a closed forest service road. After that, a trail is routed through forest and then intersects with Buck Lake Trail. Turn right on Buck Lake Trail and hike .1 mile to the lake. There are plenty of deer and bear in the area, and the brook trout at the lake are abundant, though small. From Doe Flat to Buck Lake, you'll cross through beautiful meadows and forest—including Douglas, white, and red firs, along with some maples. In the fall, the changing colors of the maples add a pretty touch to the trip. There is an excellent backpacker's campsite at Doe Flat.

**User Groups:** Hikers, dogs, and horses. No mountain bikes. No wheelchair facilities.

**Permits:** No permits are required. A campfire permit (free) is required for overnight use. Parking and access are free.

**Maps:** For a free brochure and hiking guide, write to Smith River National Recreation Area at the address below. For a map, ask the U.S. Forest Service for Six Rivers and Klamath National Forest. For a topographic map, ask the USGS for Devils Punchbowl.

**Directions:** From Crescent City, drive north on U.S. 101 for three miles. Turn east on U.S. 199 and drive 25 miles. Turn right on Little Jones Creek Road/Jawbone Road (Forest Road 16) and drive south 9.6 miles to a fork with

Forest Road 16N02. When the road forks, bear sharply left on Forest Road 16N02 and drive four miles to the trailhead, at the end of the road. Take Doe Flat trailhead.

**Contact:** Smith River National Recreation Area, P.O. Box 228, Gasquet, CA 95543, 707/457-3131, website: www.fs.fed.us/r5 (click on Forest Offices).

## 6 DEVILS PUNCHBOWL (VIA DOE FLAT TRAIL)
### 12.2 mi / 1.5 days

**in the Siskiyou Wilderness east of Crescent City**

Map 2.1, page 59

You'll be wondering if you're afflicted with a hex or a charm when you take the trip to Devils Punchbowl, set at an elevation of 4,800 feet. The hex? The trail includes a climb of 1,500 feet in two miles that'll have you wheezing like a donkey low on hay. The charm? The first view of Devils Punchbowl is not only drop-dead gorgeous but is a sight you will never forget. It's small but pristine, set in a mountain granite bowl, framed by an imposing back wall—a shrine. After parking, the first .75 mile of this easy hike is on a closed forest service road. After that, a trail is routed through forest and then intersects with Buck Lake Trail (Buck Lake is only .1 mile off to the right). Turn left, staying on Doe Flat Trail, and you will quickly reach Doe Flat and its campsite. Continue past Doe Flat and a short way along Doe Creek. Just after the trail passes a little dirt mound, look for a right turn across Doe Creek. The turn is signed Devils Punchbowl, but the sign is occasionally stolen, so be alert for the trail on the right side of Doe Creek. From here hikers start the first of several switchbacks up Bear Mountain—a long, forbidding butt-kicker. When you finally top the ridge, the route crosses Devils Creek and leaves the forest behind, crossing bare granite domes; the trail is marked only by small stacks of rocks. You pass a smaller lake, cross a rise, and then the beautiful, gemlike lake awaits. This place is something of a leg-

end but is visited only by those willing to pay the price of the terrible climb to reach it.

Special note: The entire region surrounding Devils Punchbowl consists of sheets of bare granite. The few campsites here are merely small, flat sleeping spaces on rock. There is no firewood available, so bring a backpacking stove for cooking. Bring sealable plastic bags to carry out waste.

**User Groups:** Hikers and dogs. No horses or mountain bikes. No wheelchair facilities.

**Permits:** No permits are required. A campfire permit (free) is required for overnight use. Parking and access are free.

**Maps:** For a free brochure and hiking guide, write to Smith River National Recreation Area at the address below. For a map, ask the U.S. Forest Service for Six Rivers and Klamath National Forest. For a topographic map, ask the USGS for Devils Punchbowl.

**Directions:** From Crescent City, drive north on U.S. 101 for three miles to U.S. 199. Turn east on U.S. 199 and drive 25 miles to Little Jones Creek Road/Jawbone Road (Forest Road 16). Turn right on Little Jones Creek Road (Forest Road 16) and drive south 9.6 miles. When the road forks, bear sharply left on Forest Road 16N02 and drive five miles to the trailhead, at the end of the road. Hike Doe Flat Trail for 2.5 miles to reach the trailhead for Devils Punchbowl.

**Contact:** Smith River National Recreation Area, P.O. Box 228, Gasquet, CA 95543, 707/457-3131, website: www.fs.fed.us/r5 (click on Forest Offices); Klamath National Forest, Happy Camp Ranger District, P.O. Box 377, 63822 Highway 96, Happy Camp, CA 96039-0377, 530/493-2243, website: www.fs.fed.us/r5 (click on Forest Offices).

## 7 WILDERNESS FALLS
### 18.0 mi / 2.0 days

**in the Siskiyou Wilderness east of Crescent City**

Map 2.1, page 59

Wilderness Falls is one of the great secrets of northwestern California. It's a true hidden jewel—dramatic and pure, and not only untouched, but largely unseen. This bubbling tower of water, created by Clear Creek, crashes down about 35 feet into a boulder then pounds its way down into a foaming pool that's 100 feet across.

The recommended route is to start on Clear Creek National Recreation Trail out of Youngs Valley (see Youngs Valley Trail in this chapter). Follow Clear Creek Trail for about nine miles to the waterfall. The trail features a 600-foot descent to the stream, then a gentle descent the rest of the way. There is an excellent campsite about a quarter of a mile upstream from the falls. It's an easy hike to the waterfall, but the trip back is up all the way and is best started very early in the morning, when the temperature is the coolest.

Wilderness Falls can also be accessed out of Doe Flat (see Doe Flat Trail), but in late May and June, this route includes a wet, cold, and slippery ford of Clear Creek. In summer, it is a much easier crossing.

**User Groups:** Hikers, dogs, and horses. No mountain bikes. No wheelchair facilities.

**Permits:** A campfire permit (free) is required for overnight use. Parking and access are free.

**Maps:** For a map, ask the U.S. Forest Service for Six Rivers and Klamath National Forest. For a topographic map, ask the USGS for Devils Punchbowl.

**Directions:** From Crescent City, drive north on U.S. 101 for three miles to U.S. 199. Bear right (east) on U.S. 199 and drive 32 miles to Forest Road 18N07. Turn right and drive five miles to Forest Road 18N07. Continue on Forest Road 18N07 for 10 miles (twisty) toward Sanger Lake. Just before Sanger Lake, bear right on Forest Road 4803 (signed Youngs Valley Trail) and drive one mile to the trailhead, at the end of the road.

**Contact:** Klamath National Forest, Happy Camp Ranger District, P.O. Box 377, 63822 Highway 96, Happy Camp, CA 96039-0377, 530/493-2243, website: www.fs.fed.us/r5 (click on Forest Offices); Smith River National Recreation Area, P.O. Box 228, Gasquet, CA 95543, 707/457-3131, website: www.fs.fed.us/r5 (click on Forest Offices).

## 8 SEIAD VALLEY TO OREGON BORDER (PCT)
### 36.0 mi one-way / 3.0 days
in Klamath National Forest from Seiad Valley to the Siskiyou Mountains

**Map 2.1, page 59**

Not many people hike this section of the Pacific Crest Trail, the northernmost segment in California. But it's a great chunk of trail, whether for a day hike or for the whole duration—all the way to Wards Fork Gap, on the edge of the Rogue Wilderness, in southern Oregon. The ambitious few will head up from the trailhead to the junction of the Boundary National Recreation Trail, a seven-mile trip one-way. The first five miles are a steep climb out of the Klamath River Valley, rising to Upper Devils Peak, which has an elevation of 6,040 feet.

This hike marks the final steps of the 1,700-mile Pacific Crest Trail in California, an epic journey for all, but always classic, even if only sections are enjoyed. If you decide to attempt the south-to-north route, see the Grider Creek to Seiad Valley (PCT) hike in this chapter.

**User Groups:** Hikers, dogs, and horses. No mountain bikes. No wheelchair facilities.

**Permits:** No permits are required. Parking and access are free.

**Maps:** A trail information sheet can be obtained by contacting the Happy Camp Ranger District at the address below. For a map, ask the U.S. Forest Service for Klamath National Forest. For a topographic map, ask the USGS for Seiad Valley.

**Directions:** From I-5 north of Yreka, turn west on Highway 96 and drive approximately 50 miles to the town of Seiad Valley. Continue another mile west on Highway 96 to the trailhead, on the north (right) side. Parking is minimal; park across the highway.

**Contact:** Klamath National Forest, Happy Camp Ranger District, P.O. Box 377, 63822

Highway 96, Happy Camp, CA 96039-0377, 530/493-2243, website: www.fs.fed.us/r5 (click on Forest Offices).

## 9 GRIDER CREEK TO SEIAD VALLEY (PCT)

**7.0 mi one-way / 1.0 day**

in Klamath National Forest, southeast of Happy Camp to the Grider Creek Trailhead

Map 2.1, page 59

The Pacific Crest Trail provides a good access point at the headwaters of Grider Creek, although most hikers use it to head south into the Marble Mountain Wilderness, not north. The trail is seven miles one-way, with an additional five miles of road to the town of Seiad Valley on Highway 96, an excellent place for PCT hikers to pick up a food stash and dump garbage (you could walk the road, but most try to hitch a ride). The trail here follows Grider Creek, an easy descent northward as the stream pours toward the Klamath River. The only downer is that the last three miles are on a dirt Forest Service road, but for PCT hikers, it's a sign that the next restaurant is not far off. The area features magnificent stands of virgin timber—a mixed conifer forest of cedar, pine, and fir. A good Forest Service campground (Grider Creek Camp) is available about three miles before reaching Seiad Valley.

To pick up the next trail heading for the Oregon border, see the Seiad Valley to Oregon Border (PCT) hike in this chapter. If you are hiking this trail in reverse, see the Etna Summit to Grider Creek (PCT) hike in this chapter to continue south.

**User Groups:** Hikers, dogs, and horses. No mountain bikes. No wheelchair facilities.

**Permits:** A campfire permit (free) is required. Parking and access are free.

**Maps:** A trail information sheet can be obtained by contacting the Happy Camp Ranger District at the address below. For a map, ask the U.S. Forest Service for Klamath National Forest. For a topographic map, ask the USGS for Seiad Valley.

**Directions:** From I-5 north of Yreka, turn west on Highway 96 and drive approximately 40 miles to Walker Creek/Grider Creek Road (Forest Road 46N64), located one mile before Seiad Valley. Turn left on Walker Creek Road and drive about 50 feet (staying to the left as it runs adjacent to the Klamath River) to Grider Creek Road. Turn right and drive two miles to the trailhead.

**Contact:** Klamath National Forest, Happy Camp Ranger District, P.O. Box 377, 63822 Highway 96, Happy Camp, CA 96039-0377, 530/493-2243, website: www.fs.fed.us/r5 (click on Forest Offices).

## 10 HAYPRESS MEADOWS TRAILHEAD

**29.0 mi / 3.0 days**

in the Marble Mountain Wilderness near Somes Bar

Map 2.1, page 59

The Cuddihy Lakes basin is one of the prettiest sections of the Marble Mountain Wilderness. It also is home to one of the largest concentrations of bears anywhere in California, according to the Department of Fish and Game. But this is a great trip, leading out to One Mile Lake and the Cuddihy Lakes. This area is perfect for backpacking, with beauty, lookouts, and good trail access. Park at the trailhead (at 4,500 feet), then begin the first two miles of trail up and across a fir-covered slope of a small peak (a little butt-kicker of a climb). Then the trail descends into Haypress Meadows, a major junction. Turn right and head up Sandy Ridge, which is a long, steady climb; plan to top the ridge and then camp at Monument Lake, Meteor Lake, One Mile Lake, or Cuddihy Lakes. The view from Sandy Ridge is a sweeping lookout of the Marble Mountains to the east and the Siskiyous to the west, with mountaintop glimpses of Mount Shasta and the Marble Rim.

**User Groups:** Hikers, dogs, and horses. No mountain bikes. No wheelchair facilities.

**Permits:** A campfire permit (free) is required for overnight use. Parking and access are free.

**Maps:** A trail information sheet can be obtained by contacting the Ukonom Ranger District at the address below. For a map, ask the U.S. Forest Service for Klamath National Forest or Marble Mountain Wilderness. For a topographic map, ask the USGS for Somes Bar.

**Directions:** From Highway 299 at Willow Creek, turn north on Highway 96 and drive 42 miles to Orleans. Continue eight miles to Somes Bar and Salmon River Road. Turn right on Salmon River Road (Highway 93) and drive 100 feet to a sign that says Camp 3/Haypress Trailhead and Forest Road 15N17 (Offield Mountain Road). Turn left and drive 14.6 miles to Forest Road 15N17E. Turn left and drive 1.5 miles to the access road for Haypress trailhead. Turn left and drive one mile to the trailhead.

**Contact:** Klamath National Forest, Ukonom Ranger District, Highway 96 and Ishi Pishi Road, P.O. Box 410, Orleans, CA 95556-0410, 530/627-3291, website: www.fs.fed.us/r5 (click on Forest Offices).

## **11** SPIRIT LAKE TRAIL
### 34.0 mi / 4.0 days

**in the Marble Mountain Wilderness near Somes Bar**

Map 2.1, page 59

 We've hiked to hundreds and hundreds of mountain lakes, and Spirit Lake is one of the prettiest we've ever seen. It sits at the bottom of a mountain bowl encircled by old-growth trees, with a few campsites set at the side of the lake. The Karuk tribe considers this a sacred place. The abundance of wildlife can be remarkable. The far side of the lake is a major deer migration route, an osprey makes regular trips to pluck trout out of the lake for dinner, and the fishing is quite good, especially early in the summer.

Spirit Lake can be the feature destination for a week-long backpack loop, beginning on Haypress Meadows Trail and leading up to Sandy Ridge and then out to the lake, about 17 miles one-way. Most hikers will stop for the night at One Mile or the Cuddihy Lakes on the way out, and that is why those two areas get so much use. Spirit Lake is best visited during the first week of June, when the nights are still cold, the people are few, and the area abounds with fish and deer.

**User Groups:** Hikers, dogs, and horses. No mountain bikes. No wheelchair facilities.

**Permits:** A campfire permit (free) is required for overnight use. Parking and access are free.

**Maps:** A trail information sheet can be obtained by contacting the Ukonom Ranger District at the address below. For a map, ask the U.S. Forest Service for Klamath National Forest or Marble Mountain Wilderness. For a topographic map, ask the USGS for Somes Bar.

**Directions:** From Highway 299 at Willow Creek, turn north on Highway 96 and drive 42 miles to Orleans. Continue eight miles to Somes Bar and Salmon River Road. Turn right on Salmon River Road (Highway 93) and drive 100 feet to a sign that says Camp 3/Haypress Trailhead and Forest Road 15N17 (Offield Mountain Road). Turn left and drive 14.6 miles to Forest Road 15N17E. Turn left and drive 1.5 miles to the access road for Haypress trailhead. Turn left and drive one mile to the trailhead.

**Contact:** Klamath National Forest, Ukonom Ranger District, Highway 96 and Ishi Pishi Road, P.O. Box 410, Orleans, CA 95556-0410, 530/627-3291, website: www.fs.fed.us/r5 (click on Forest Offices).

## **12** KELSEY CREEK TRAIL
### 18.0 mi / 2.0 days

**in the Marble Mountain Wilderness west of Yreka**

Map 2.1, page 59

The Kelsey Creek Trail offers many miles of beautiful streamside travel, with Paradise Lake basin as the intended destination for most hikers on this route. The trailhead is set near the confluence of Kelsey Creek and the Scott River, and from there, the trail follows Kelsey Creek upstream. Wildflowers are abundant in the meadows. After four miles and two creek crossings, you'll reach Maple Falls, the prettiest waterfall in the region. The trail continues up the canyon, finally rising to intersect with the Pacific Crest Trail, just below Red Rock. From this junction, hikers have many options. The closest lake is secluded Bear Lake, a pretty spot but, alas, with some tules and mosquitoes. To reach it from the junction requires a short but steep drop into the basin to the immediate west.

**User Groups:** Hikers, dogs, and horses. No mountain bikes. No wheelchair facilities.

**Permits:** A campfire permit (free) is required for overnight use. Parking and access are free.

**Maps:** A trail information sheet can be obtained by contacting the Scott River Ranger District at the address below. For a map, ask the U.S. Forest Service for Klamath National Forest or Marble Mountain Wilderness. For topographic maps, ask the USGS for Scott Bar and Grider Valley.

**Directions:** From I-5 at Yreka, take the Highway 3/Fort Jones exit and drive 16.5 miles to Fort Jones and Scott River Road. Turn right on Scott River Road and drive 16.8 miles to the Scott River Bridge. Cross it and then turn left immediately, following the road for .3 mile. Bear right on another dirt road (do not continue to a second bridge) and drive .25 mile to the trailhead.

**Contact:** Klamath National Forest, Salmon River & Scott River Ranger Districts, 11263 North Highway 3, Fort Jones, CA 96032-9702, 530/468-5351, website: www.fs.fed.us/r5 (click on Forest Offices).

## ⓭ PARADISE LAKE TRAIL
**4.0 mi / 2.75 hrs**   🥾  ◄⑧

**in the Marble Mountain Wilderness west of Yreka**

Map 2.1, page 59

Paradise Lake, set at an elevation of 5,920 feet, is the easiest lake to reach of the 79 lakes in the Marble Mountain Wilderness. The pretty hike is short enough for a day trip, and it has good lakeside campgrounds if you want to turn your trip into an overnighter. There are also some excellent side trips, including

climbing Kings Castle (see the following hike), which tops the mountain rim on the back side of the lake.

From the trailhead (at 4,880 feet), the route quickly enters a designated wilderness, then climbs for nearly two miles (steeply in some areas) and switches back and forth through an old, untouched forest. It then emerges from the trees and rises to a saddle; on the other side is Paradise Lake, sitting in a mountain pocket, emerald green and peaceful. Paradise is a mostly shallow lake with few trout, but it does have one deep area. Because the hike to the lake takes only two hours, there are usually campers here all summer long.

**User Groups:** Hikers, dogs, and horses. No mountain bikes. No wheelchair facilities.

**Permits:** No permits are required. A campfire permit (free) is required for overnight use. Parking and access are free.

**Maps:** A trail information sheet can be obtained by contacting the Scott River Ranger District at the address below. For a map, ask the U.S. Forest Service for Klamath National Forest or Marble Mountain Wilderness. For topographic maps, ask the USGS for Scott Bar and Marble Mountain.

**Directions:** From I-5 at Yreka, take the Highway 3/Fort Jones exit and drive 16.5 miles to Fort Jones. Turn right on Scott River Road and drive 16.8 miles to the turnoff for Indian Scotty Campground. Cross the concrete bridge, bear left on Forest Road 44N45, and drive about five miles. Turn right on an unmarked forest road and drive six miles (signed Paradise Lake) to the trailhead, near the wilderness border.

**Contact:** Klamath National Forest, Salmon River & Scott River Ranger Districts, 11263 North Highway 3, Fort Jones, CA 96032-9702, 530/468-5351, website: www.fs.fed.us/r5 (click on Forest Offices).

## 14 KINGS CASTLE TRAIL
**5.5 mi / 5.0 hrs**

**in the Marble Mountain Wilderness west of Yreka**

Map 2.1, page 59

Kings Castle is the imposing perch that sits on the back side of Paradise Lake, a .5-mile climb that tops out at the summit at 7,405 feet. It's a great hike with unforgettable views, looking down at little Paradise Lake as well as far beyond to Northern California's most famous mountain peaks. From the trailhead of Paradise Lake Trail, you make the 1,040-foot climb up to Paradise Lake. From the foot of Paradise Lake, bear to the left and cross the lake's inlet, on the left side. Here you will pick up the route. It climbs up out of the basin to a ridge (great views start here), and then you gain the peak of Kings Castle by climbing a series of switchbacks up the back side. It is a special trip every step of the way—a climb of 2,525 feet from the trailhead. Although not a maintained trail, the route is worn well enough to follow. On the first trip here, this guy didn't see the trail and instead scrambled up the face, bushwhacking it—a difficult ascent, steep all the way. On the top, he was congratulating himself for being such a wonderful mountaineer, when right then, these two Girl Scouts came bounding up the back side, easy and happy. "How'd you get here?" he asked. "We just took the trail," one answered. "Trail? What trail?"

**User Groups:** Hikers only. No dogs, horses, or mountain bikes. No wheelchair facilities.

**Permits:** No permits are required. A campfire permit (free) is required for overnight use. Parking and access are free.

**Maps:** A trail information sheet can be obtained by contacting the Scott River Ranger District at the address below. For a map, ask the U.S. Forest Service for Klamath National Forest or Marble Mountain Wilderness. For topographic maps, ask the USGS for Scott Bar and Marble Mountain.

**Directions:** From I-5 at Yreka, take the Highway 3/Fort Jones exit and drive 16.5 miles to Fort Jones. Turn right on Scott River Road and drive 16.8 miles to the turnoff for Indian Scotty Campground. Cross the concrete bridge, bear left on forest road 44N45, and drive about five miles. Turn right on an unmarked forest road and drive six miles (signed Paradise Lake) to the trailhead near the wilderness border. Hike 1.9 miles to Paradise Lake; bear right and continue another .5 mile to Kings Castle.

**Contact:** Klamath National Forest, Salmon River & Scott River Ranger Districts, 11263 North Highway 3, Fort Jones, CA 96032-9702, 530/468-5351, website: www.fs.fed.us/r5 (click on Forest Offices).

## 15 MARBLE MOUNTAIN RIM
**16.0 mi / 2.0 days**

**in the Marble Mountain Wilderness west of Yreka**

Map 2.1, page 59

Marble isn't usually thought of as a precious stone, but it's gemlike for hikers on this trail. With Marble Valley nearby, climbing the Marble Mountain Rim can be a perfect weekend trip and is easily extended into a longer one. The trailhead at Lovers Camp is probably the most popular in the entire wilderness, especially for packers going by horse into Marble Mountain Wilderness (horses aren't allowed on this trail; corrals are available at the trailhead). The route heads up Canyon Creek, a moderate climb, then intersects the Pacific Crest Trail at Marble Valley. This area is very scenic, with lots of deer and wild orchids. Turn left, and the trail crosses Marble Mountain itself, and once you've arrived, a side trip to the Marble Rim is mandatory. The views are stunning, sweeping in both directions, with steep drop-offs adding to the quiet drama. The rock itself is unlike anything else in Northern California—a mix of black, red, and tan marble, something you'll never forget.

**User Groups:** Hikers only. No dogs, horses, or mountain bikes. No wheelchair facilities.

**Permits:** A campfire permit (free) is required for overnight use. Parking and access are free.

**Maps:** A trail information sheet can be obtained by contacting the Scott River Ranger District at the address below. For a map, ask the U.S. Forest Service for Klamath National Forest or Marble Mountain Wilderness. For topographic maps, ask the USGS for Scott Bar and Marble Mountain.

**Directions:** From I-5 at Yreka, take the Highway 3/Fort Jones exit and drive 16.5 miles to Fort Jones. Turn right on Scott River Road and drive 16.8 miles to the turnoff for Indian Scotty Campground. Cross the concrete bridge, bear left on Forest Road 44N45, and drive 5.4 miles to Forest Road 43N45. Turn left and drive 1.7 miles to Lovers Camp. Bear right and drive .1 mile to the trailhead.

**Contact:** Klamath National Forest, Salmon River & Scott River Ranger Districts, 11263 North Highway 3, Fort Jones, CA 96032-9702, 530/468-5351, website: www.fs.fed.us/r5 (click on Forest Offices).

## 16 SKY HIGH LAKES
### 14.0 mi / 2.0 days

**in the Marble Mountain Wilderness west of Yreka**

Map 2.1, page 59

The Sky High Lakes make for a great overnighter, a seven-mile hike each day, or an inspired one-day in-and-outer. The trip starts at the Canyon Creek trailhead near Lovers Camp. For this trip, take Canyon Creek Trail for about a mile up to a fork, and continue straight (do not turn left and cross Canyon Creek). From here the trail continues to climb, skirting below Marble Mountain, and eventually to Lower Sky High Lake. This is your destination, set below a monster of a rock, Peak 6817. Nearby, little Frying Pan Lake and Upper Sky High Lake provide side jaunts. Note that the trail continues to climb up to the rim and hooks up with the Pacific Crest Trail, making an 18-mile loop trip possible.

**User Groups:** Hikers, dogs, and horses. No mountain bikes. No wheelchair facilities.

**Permits:** A campfire permit is required only

for hikers planning to camp in the wilderness. Parking and access are free.

**Maps:** A trail information sheet can be obtained by contacting the Scott River Ranger District at the address below. For a map, ask the U.S. Forest Service for Klamath National Forest or Marble Mountain Wilderness. For a topographic map, ask the USGS for Marble Mountain.

**Directions:** From I-5 at Yreka, take the Highway 3/Fort Jones exit and drive 16.5 miles to Fort Jones. Turn right on Scott River Road and drive 16.8 miles to the turnoff for Indian Scotty Campground. Cross the concrete bridge, bear left on Forest Road 44N45, and drive 5.4 miles to Forest Road 43N45. Turn left and drive 1.7 miles to Lovers Camp. Bear right and drive .1 mile to the Canyon Creek trailhead.

**Contact:** Klamath National Forest, Salmon River & Scott River Ranger Districts, 11263 North Highway 3, Fort Jones, CA 96032-9702, 530/468-5351, website: www.fs.fed.us/r5 (click on Forest Offices).

## 17 SHACKLEFORD CREEK TRAIL
### 13.0 mi / 2.0 days

**in the Marble Mountain Wilderness west of Yreka**

Map 2.1, page 59

Campbell, Cliff, and Summit Lakes are three of the prettiest lakes in the Marble Mountain Wilderness. The ease of reaching them on the Shackleford Trail (only 5.5 miles to Campbell Lake) makes them a popular destination all summer long. The trail is routed up Shackleford Creek to a basin set just below the Pacific Crest Trail. Here you'll find a series of small mountain lakes. Note that ambitious trekkers traveling off-trail, cross-country style, can create routes to little Gem, Jewel, and Angel Lakes. A bonus is that the trip can be extended by hiking up the rim to the Pacific Crest Trail, then turning right and going three miles to the Sky High Lakes.

**User Groups:** Hikers, dogs, and horses. No mountain bikes. No wheelchair facilities.

**Permits:** A campfire permit is required only

for hikers planning to camp in the wilderness. Parking and access are free.

**Maps:** A trail information sheet can be obtained by contacting the Scott River Ranger District at the address below. For a map, ask the U.S. Forest Service for Klamath National Forest or Marble Mountain Wilderness. For a topographic map, ask the USGS for Boulder Peak.

**Directions:** From I-5 at Yreka, take the Highway 3/Fort Jones exit and drive 16.5 miles to Fort Jones and Scott River Road. Turn right on Scott River Road and drive seven miles to Quartz Valley Road. Turn left on Quartz Valley Road and drive about four miles to the sign for Shackleford trailhead and Forest Road 43N21. Turn right and drive 6.5 miles to the trailhead, at the end of the road.

**Contact:** Klamath National Forest, Salmon River & Scott River Ranger Districts, 11263 North Highway 3, Fort Jones, CA 96032-9702, 530/468-5351, website: www.fs.fed.us/r5 (click on Forest Offices).

## 18 MULE BRIDGE TRAILHEAD
**28.0 mi / 3.0 days**

**in the Marble Mountain Wilderness west of Etna**

Map 2.1, page 59

The trailhead at Mule Bridge is set alongside the Salmon River, and once you've tightened your backpack, get ready for a long climb up the river drainage. The trail follows the Salmon River all the way up to its headwaters, gaining about 3,500 feet in the process. Plan on climbing for 14 or 15 miles along the river until you start reaching the higher country, where there are many lakeside camps. The trail forks eight miles from the trailhead, with the right-hand fork leading to Shelly Meadows and the Pacific Crest Trail. The main trail continues north for access to Upper Abbotts Camp and many lakes in the upper drainage. This trail ties in with Little North Fork Trail near Hancock Lake. The prettiest glacial-formed lakes in this region are Lake of the Island (12-mile hike), Abbott Lake (13-mile hike), and Lake Ethel (14-mile hike). Even more re-

mote lakes are Wooley Lake, Milne Lake, and Osprey Lake; these require cross-country travel. The best way to get there is by taking Big Gulch Trail northeast from Upper Abbotts Camp and continuing to Grants Meadows. From here it's up and over a ridge to the lakes. This route is the gentler way to reach this area. Another picturesque lake is Cabin Gulch Lake, which is best reached by taking the right-hand fork to meet the east end of Bug Gulch Trail. Good campsites are available at Cabin Gulch (12-mile hike, elevation 6,000 feet), Grants Meadows (13.5-mile hike, elevation 6,200 feet), and Shelly Meadows (15-mile hike, elevation 6,300 feet).

**User Groups:** Hikers, dogs, and horses. No mountain bikes. No wheelchair facilities.

**Permits:** A campfire permit (free) is required for campfires and stoves. Parking and access are free.

**Maps:** A trail information sheet can be obtained by contacting the Salmon Ranger District at the address below. For a map, ask the U.S. Forest Service for Klamath National Forest or Marble Mountain Wilderness. For a topographic map, ask the USGS for Sawyers Bar.

**Directions:** From I-5 at Yreka, take the Highway 3/Fort Jones exit and drive southwest 28 miles to Etna. Turn west on Etna-Somes Bar Road (which is Main Street in town) and drive 21 miles to Idlewild Campground. As you enter the campground, take the left fork in the road and continue two miles to the trailhead.

**Contact:** Klamath National Forest, Salmon River & Scott River Ranger Districts, 11263 North Highway 3, Fort Jones, CA 96032-9702, 530/468-5351, website: www.fs.fed.us/r5 (click on Forest Offices).

## 19 LITTLE NORTH FORK TRAILHEAD
**16.0 mi / 2.0 days**

**in the Marble Mountain Wilderness near Sawyers Bar**

Map 2.1, page 59

Your destination options from this trailhead? There are many: Chimney Rock, Clear Lake,

Lily Lake, and Chimney Rock Lake. This trail provides an excellent trip—as long as you don't mind the long grind of a climb to reach the lakes. Like a lot of trails on the edge of the wilderness, this one starts with a long haul out of a river canyon. From the Little North Fork trailhead, start by climbing out toward Chimney Rock, grunting out a rise of about 4,000 feet as you leave the river lowlands and reach the Marble Mountain Wilderness. It's about an eight-mile trip to Clear Lake, a good first day's destination. Although you can simply return the next day, most people will take several days to venture deeper into the wilderness, with 13 lakes and 20 miles of stream in the Upper Abbotts Camp and English Peak areas.

**User Groups:** Hikers, dogs, and horses. No mountain bikes. No wheelchair facilities.

**Permits:** A campfire permit (free) is required for campfires and stove. Parking and access are free.

**Maps:** A trail information sheet can be obtained by contacting the Salmon Ranger District at the address below. For a map, ask the U.S. Forest Service for Klamath National Forest or Marble Mountain Wilderness. For a topographic map, ask the USGS for Sawyers Bar.

**Directions:** From I-5 at Yreka, take the Highway 3/Fort Jones exit and drive southwest 28 miles to Etna at Sawyers Bar Road. Turn west on Sawyers Bar Road and drive about 25 miles to the town of Sawyers Bar. Continue west on the same road for four miles to Little North Fork Road (Forest Road 40N51). Turn right (north) and drive two miles to the trailhead, at the end of the road.

**Contact:** Klamath National Forest, Salmon River & Scott River Ranger Districts, 11263 North Highway 3, Fort Jones, CA 96032-9702, 530/468-5351, website: www.fs.fed.us/r5 (click on Forest Offices).

## 20 HORSE TRAIL RIDGE NATIONAL RECREATION TRAIL

**13.0 mi one-way / 2.0 days**

in Six Rivers National Forest on the western edge of the Trinity Alps Wilderness east of Hoopa

**Map 2.1, page 59**

This is one of the lesser-known national recreation trails in the western United States, but it has many excellent features, and, alas, a few negative ones as well. Leaving a shuttle vehicle at both trailheads allows hikers to access Horse Trail Ridge from one end to the other in a weekend, but it's best to make the six-mile trip to Mill Creek Lakes, set in the least explored western sector of the Trinity Alps. Although some of the region has been burned severely by wildfire, the Mill Creek Lakes area remains untouched by fire, like an island of green.

This is a good overnighter and will provide you with a feel for the area. From the trailhead (at 4,800 feet), the grades are gradual, with relatively easy elevation climbs and descents. A majority of the forest along the trail was burned in the 1999 Megram fire; in all, the fire affects 10 miles of this route. If you want to add to your trip, take the Devils Backbone east. Though there is no water available on this route, it peaks at Trinity Summit, at about 5,800 feet, where there's a historic cabin. Other hikers are rare in this area, and most of the time, you'll feel as if you have the universe to yourself.

Special note: Do not drink the water available here without first treating it with the best filtration system you can afford.

**User Groups:** Hikers, dogs, and horses. No mountain bikes. No wheelchair facilities.

**Permits:** A wilderness permit is required for hikers planning on camping. Parking and access are free.

**Maps:** For a map, ask the U.S. Forest Service for Six Rivers National Forest. For topographic maps, ask the USGS for Tish Tang Point and Trinity Mountain.

**Directions:** From Arcata, go east on Highway 299 to Willow Creek. Turn north on Highway

96 and drive about 12 miles into Hoopa Valley to Big Hill Road. Turn right (east) on Big Hill Road and drive 11 miles to the Six Rivers National Forest border (the road becomes Forest Road 8N01). Continue for 4.5 miles (the road becomes Forest Road 10N02) to the Redcap trailhead (once off Hoopa reservation land, stay on the chip-seal road).

**Contact:** Six Rivers National Forest, Lower Trinity Ranger District, P.O. Box 68, Willow Creek, CA 95573, 530/629-2118, website: www.fs.fed.us/r5 (click on Forest Offices).

## 21 LITTLE SOUTH FORK LAKE TRAIL
### 13.0 mi / 2.0 days

in the Trinity Alps Wilderness near Cecilville

**Map 2.1, page 59**

You have to be a little bit crazy to try this trip, and that's why we signed up. There's just no easy way to get to Little South Fork Lake and its two idyllic campsites, excellent swimming, and large trout. It's the toughest lake to reach in Northern California. This route is largely off trail and requires skirting a big waterfall, but there's no better way in—we've tried three different routes.

From the South Fork trailhead, the trip starts out easy enough, with four miles along the Salmon River; then it bears up along Little South Fork Creek. For most of this route, there is something of a trail. The trail dead-ends into Little South Fork Creek. (A faint route on the other side of the creek, the north side, climbs through brush and up the canyon, and should be avoided.) From here, there is no trail available; the best route, though still steep and very difficult, is to lateral across the slope on the right side of the stream. After leaving the trail, it's 1.25 miles to a beautiful, pristine waterfall. To get around the waterfall, loop back and circle it to the right; if you go to the left, you'll add several dreadful hours to the trip (we tried that, too). Remember that there is no trail and no marked route. It is a cross-country scram-

ble and very slow going. (If you want a trail, this is not the hike for you.) It's another 1.25 miles to the lake, which can take hours of hiking up and across the wooded slope until you emerge from the forest onto granite plates. Ahead is the lake, beautifully set in a rock bowl framed by a high back wall. There are excellent campsites at each end of the lake.

We hiked into this lake once from Caribou Lakes by climbing the Sawtooth Ridge and dropping down into the basin—the entire route, also off trail, creates a potentially hazardous proposition, with some rock climbing and descents. On another trip from Caribou Lakes, we dropped down into Little South Fork Canyon, losing thousands of feet in altitude and in the process getting caught in a brush field like bugs in a spider web. Neither of these other two routes is recommended. In fact, the suggested route is not recommended either. One ranger said we were crazy to include it in the book. He was right, of course.

**User Groups:** Hikers only. Dogs are permitted but strongly advised against. No horses or mountain bikes. No wheelchair facilities.

**Permits:** A free wilderness permit is required for hikers planning to camp.

**Maps:** For a map, ask the U.S. Forest Service for Klamath National Forest or Trinity Alps Wilderness. For a topographic map, ask the USGS for Thompson Peak.

**Directions:** From Redding, drive north on I-5 for 70 miles. Just past Weed, take the Edgewood exit. At the stop sign, turn left and drive through the underpass to another stop sign. Turn right on Old Highway 99 and drive about six miles to Gazelle. Turn left on Gazelle-Callahan Road and drive 27 miles to Callahan. From Callahan on Highway 3, turn west on Cecilville Road and drive 28 miles to Caribou Road/County Road 1E003 (across from East Fork Campground). Turn left (south) on Caribou Road and drive 3.5 miles to a fork. Bear left at the fork and drive 2.5 miles to the South Fork trailhead.

**Contact:** Klamath National Forest, Salmon

River & Scott River Ranger Districts, 11263 North Highway 3, Fort Jones, CA 96032-9702, 530/468-5351, website: www.fs.fed.us/r5 (click on Forest Offices).

## 22 GRIZZLY LAKE
### 12.0 mi / 2.0 days or
### 38.0 mi / 5.0 days

**in the Trinity Alps Wilderness north of Junction City**

Map 2.1, page 59

Take your pick: From the China Creek trailhead, a butt-kicking six-mile climb with a 5,000-foot elevation gain (with a 1,500-foot canyon descent included on the way); or from the Hobo Gulch trailhead, a moderate grade over the course of 19 miles to make the lake. Despite this difficulty, Grizzly Lake can be crowded, because it is the preeminent destination in the Trinity Alps. It is set below awesome Thompson Peak (8,863 feet), with one of the most beautiful wilderness waterfalls anywhere, 80-foot Grizzly Falls, set at the lake's cliff outfall. The lake is so pristine that you can spend hours just looking at it.

Given a choice, most people take the short, butt-kicker route, then cuss at themselves on the way in for doing so. There is almost nothing rewarding about it, and most complete the trip with head down, trying to think about something else. Before you race off to this destination, think long and hard if you really are ready to pay a terrible physical toll to get there. Surprisingly, many do this regardless of the price, and the place gets fairly heavy use.

Or, on the other hand, take the longer but more gradual climb. That is from the Hobo Gulch trailhead, set deep in the national forest along Backbone Ridge. On this route, Grizzly Lake is 19 miles away. So instead of camping along lakes, hikers camp along pretty streams and flats, taking days to reach the promised land at Grizzly Lake.

The trail from Hobo Gulch starts by heading straight north about five miles along the North Fork Trinity River to Rattlesnake Camp,

climbing very gently. Cross Rattlesnake Creek, and continue another three miles past the old Morrison Cabin (from the mining days) and on to Pfeiffer Flat. Here the North Fork Trinity is joined by Grizzly Creek, an attractive backpacking destination. From Pfeiffer Flat, the trail follows Grizzly Creek, rising high toward the Trinity Sawtooth Ridge and requiring an uphill pull to beautiful Grizzly Meadows and then to Grizzly Lake; the final mile is a scramble over a clear hiking route amid rock.

For rock climbers, climbing the lake bowl in a clockwise direction makes for an exciting scramble to Thompson Peak and a perch just below the rock summit; to reach the tip-top of the mountain requires a technical climb.

**User Groups:** Hikers, dogs, and horses. No mountain bikes. No wheelchair facilities.

**Permits:** A wilderness permit is required for hikers planning to camp.

**Maps:** For a map, ask the U.S. Forest Service for Shasta-Trinity National Forest or Trinity Alps Wilderness. For a topographic map, ask the USGS for Thurston Peaks.

**Directions:** To Hobo Gulch trailhead from Weaverville, drive 13 miles west on Highway 299 to Helena and East Fork Road. Turn north on East Fork Road (County Road 421) and drive 3.9 miles to Hobo Gulch Road. Turn left on Hobo Gulch Road (Forest Road 34N07Y) and drive 12 miles to the Hobo Gulch trailhead, located at Hobo Gulch Campground, at the end of the road.

To China Creek trailhead from Redding, drive north on I-5 for 70 miles. Just past Weed, take the Edgewood exit. At the stop sign, turn left and drive through the underpass to another stop sign. Turn right on Old Highway 99 and drive about six miles to Gazelle. Turn left on Gazelle-Callahan Road and drive 27 miles to Callahan. From Callahan on Highway 3, turn west on Cecilville Road and drive 27 miles to Forest Road 37N24. Turn south and drive 3.8 miles to Forest Road 37N07 (it's well signed). Take Forest 37N07 and drive six miles to the trailhead.

Contact: Shasta-Trinity National Forest, Weaverville Ranger Station, P.O. Box 1190, 210 Main Street, Weaverville, CA 96093, 530/623-2121, website: www.fs.fed.us/r5 (click on Forest Offices).

## 23 TREE OF HEAVEN TRAIL
### 3.5 mi / 2.0 hrs

**on the Klamath River in Klamath National Forest northwest of Yreka**

**Map 2.2, page 60**

The trail out of the Tree of Heaven Campground is one of the best streamside trails anywhere along the Klamath River. Heading downstream along the Klamath, it's a level path that sometimes probes through heavy vegetation and other times offers direct river access. The fall is an excellent time for berry picking. The trail ends at a good fishing access spot, but the fishing is poor during the prime camping/hiking/vacation season. Salmon start arriving in September; steelhead, in November and December. The Tree of Heaven River access is also a good take-out point for rafters and drift boaters making the all-day run down from Iron Canyon Dam.

**User Groups:** Hikers, dogs, horses, and mountain bikes. No wheelchair facilities.

**Permits:** No permits are required. Parking and access are free.

**Maps:** For a map, ask the U.S. Forest Service for Klamath National Forest. For a topographic map, ask the USGS for Badger Mountain.

**Directions:** From Yreka, drive 10 miles north on I-5 to the Highway 96 exit. Turn west on Highway 96 and drive about five miles. Look for the Tree of Heaven Campground, on the left. The trailhead is located at the west end of the campground.

**Contact:** Klamath National Forest, Salmon River & Scott River Ranger Districts, 11263 North Highway 3, Fort Jones, CA 96032-9702, 530/468-5351, website: www.fs.fed.us/r5 (click on Forest Offices).

## 24 JUANITA LAKE TRAIL
### 1.75 mi / 1.0 hr

**in Klamath National Forest east of Yreka**

**Map 2.2, page 60**

Not many people know about Juanita Lake, including many Siskiyou County residents, but once they find out, on their first visit, they often will take this easy loop trail around the lake to get a feel for the place. The lake is set in a mixed conifer forest, though few trees here are large. Wildlife in the area includes osprey and bald eagles. In the last hour of light during summer, both osprey and eagles occasionally make a fishing trip to the lake. Juanita Lake is a small lake that provides lakeside camping and fishing for brook trout—it's stocked with 2,000 per year. The small fishing piers are wheelchair accessible.

A good side trip is driving on the forest road up to Ball Mountain, about two miles southwest of the lake, for great views of Mount Shasta from the 7,786-foot summit.

**User Groups:** Hikers and leashed dogs. No mountain bikes or horses. The fishing piers are wheelchair accessible.

**Permits:** No permits are required. Parking and access are free.

**Maps:** For a map, ask the U.S. Forest Service for Klamath National Forest. For a topographic map, ask the USGS for Panther Rock.

**Directions:** From northbound I-5 at Weed, take the Central Weed/Klamath Falls (Highway 97) exit. Bear north (right) through Weed to Highway 97. Turn north on Highway 97 and drive 35 miles to Ball Mountain Road. Turn left and drive two miles to a signed turnoff for Juanita Lake. Turn right and drive about three miles to the lake (it's well signed). The trailhead is near the boat dock at the campground.

**Contact:** Klamath National Forest, Goosenest Ranger District, 37805 Highway 97, Macdoel, CA 96058, 530/398-4391, fax 530/398-4599, website: www.fs.fed.us/r5 (click on Forest Offices).

## 25 DEER MOUNTAIN
### 4.0 mi / 2.25 hrs

**in Klamath National Forest north of Mount Shasta**

Map 2.2, page 60

Deer Mountain is the second in a line of small peaks set on the north side of Mount Shasta that extend all the way to the Medicine Lake wildlands. North from Shasta, the first peak is the Whaleback, at an elevation of 8,528 feet, and the second is Deer Mountain, at 7,006 feet. Starting elevation at the parking area is 6,200 feet, and from here you climb 800 feet through forest consisting of various pines and firs to gain the summit. This route gets very little use, even though it's easy to reach and the destination is a mountaintop. Most out-of-towners visiting this area are attracted to the trails on Mount Shasta instead, and most locals just plain overlook it.

**User Groups:** Hikers, dogs, horses, and mountain bikes. No wheelchair facilities.

**Permits:** No permits are required. Parking and access are free.

**Maps:** For a map, ask the U.S. Forest Service for Klamath National Forest. For a topographic map, ask the USGS for Whaleback.

**Directions:** From northbound I-5 at Weed, take the Central Weed/Klamath Falls (Highway 97) exit. Bear north (right) through Weed to Highway 97. Turn north (right) on Highway 97 and drive about 15 miles to Deer Mountain Road/Forest Road 19 (Forest Road 42N12). Turn right and drive four miles to Deer Mountain Snowmobile Park and Forest Road 44N23. Turn left on Forest Road 44N23 and drive about two miles. There is no designated trailhead; park off the road and hike cross-country to the top of the mountain. Forest Road 43N69 loops around the base of the mountain; you may also hike from anywhere along that road.

**Contact:** Klamath National Forest, Goosenest Ranger District, 37805 Highway 97, Macdoel, CA 96058, 530/398-4391, fax 530/398-4599, website: www.fs.fed.us/r5 (click on Forest Offices).

## 26 THE WHALEBACK
### 3.0 mi / 2.5 hrs

**in Klamath National Forest north of Mount Shasta**

Map 2.2, page 60

Driving north on I-5, you'll see a large, hump-like mountain that sits directly north of Shasta. It looks like a huge volcanic bump that was born when Shasta was active; that's because it is. This is the Whaleback, 8,528 feet high, providing an excellent hike with a surprise reward at the top. That surprise is a large crater. The Whaleback Summit is actually a volcanic cinder cone with a collapsed center. This interesting geology, along with the unsurpassed view of Mount Shasta to the south, makes this a first-rate hike. Yet almost nobody tries it, most likely because they don't realize how near you can drive to the top, or because there is no formal trail. After parking at the gate, you just hike cross-country style up to the rim; it's steep all the way. The 1.5-mile hike is a scramble only in a few places. In the process, you'll climb 1,100 feet, from a starting elevation of 7,400 feet, to Whaleback Rim.

**User Groups:** Hikers, dogs, horses, and mountain bikes. No wheelchair facilities.

**Permits:** No permits are required. Parking and access are free.

**Maps:** For a map, ask the U.S. Forest Service for Klamath National Forest. For a topographic map, ask the USGS for Whaleback.

**Directions:** From northbound I-5 at Weed, take the Central Weed/Klamath Falls (Highway 97) exit. Bear north (right) through Weed to Highway 97. Turn north (right) on Highway 97 and drive 15 miles to Deer Mountain Road. Turn right on Deer Mountain Road and drive four miles to Deer Mountain Snowmobile Park. Drive east on Deer Mountain Road/Forest Road 19 (Forest Road 42N12) for three miles to Forest Road 42N24. Turn right on Forest Road 42N24 and drive three miles to a gate. Park and hike in. There is no designated trail; you must hike cross-country from the road. The peak is about 1.5 miles from the gate.

**Contact:** Klamath National Forest, Goosenest Ranger District, 37805 Highway 97, Macdoel, CA 96058, 530/398-4391, fax 530/398-4599, website: www.fs.fed.us/r5 (click on Forest Offices).

## 27 WHITNEY FALLS TRAILHEAD
### 3.4 mi / 2.5 hrs

**on the northwest slope of Mount Shasta**

**Map 2.2, page 60**

Mount Shasta, at 14,162 feet, is the most prominent landmark in Northern California, and it's well known for its outstanding summit routes on its southern slopes. What is less known, however, is that there are four trailheads set on Shasta's northern and eastern foothills that grant hikers choice day walks and mountaineers a starting point for difficult climbs over glaciers to the top. Those four forgotten trailheads are at Whitney Falls, North Gate, Brewer Creek, and Clear Creek. The Whitney Falls trailhead is at about 5,600 feet, and from it, the trail heads uphill (for the most part, something of a nightmare). This trailhead and first mile were buried under a flow of mud and debris from a flash flood. Although interesting to geologists, it requires hikers to negotiate rocks, boulders, logs, and deep erosion channels. Look for the faint trail on the right side of the flow. Follow this trail uphill until you pass through a small gorge, then look for the trail heading out of the drainage. The trail spans 1.6 miles to a fork at 6,400 feet, and for day hikers the best bet is turning right and climbing partially up the treeless slope for a fantastic lookout and picnic site. Here you'll discover hidden Whitney Falls, a 250-foot waterfall, with its thin, silvery wisp tumbling through a narrow chute in a dramatic ashen gorge. It takes perfect timing to see this waterfall at anything more than a trickle. The view to the north of Shasta Valley is outstanding, highlighted by the series of hummocks, which are actually chunks of Shasta's former summit that were carried here like miniature hilltops in a massive lava flow after Shasta's last eruption, 600 years ago.

Special notes: If you turn left at the fork instead, you'll venture through forest, then up through another gutted stream drainage. The trail ends, and mountaineers will have to pass Coquette Falls, and then near the peak at the Bolam Glacier, in order to make the summit. Safety gear and expert climbing skills are required. Also note that this trailhead was long called the Bolam Creek trailhead. That was changed in 2002. A new Bolam Creek Trail and route up the north flank of Shasta is planned when funds and manpower become available.

**User Groups:** Hikers only. No dogs, horses, or mountain bikes. No wheelchair facilities.

**Permits:** Parking and access are free. A free wilderness permit is required for both day use and overnight use; a $15 permit is required for hikers climbing over 10,000 feet in elevation, or you can buy an annual pass for $25. All climbers are required to pack out waste and must bring a pack-out bag.

**Maps:** For a map, ask the U.S. Forest Service for Shasta-Trinity National Forest or Mount Shasta Wilderness. For a topographic map, ask the USGS for Mount Shasta.

**Directions:** From I-5, drive to the Central Weed/Klamath Falls (Highway 97) exit. Take that exit and drive through Weed to Highway 97. Turn right and drive 11 miles to Bolam Road (Forest Road 43N21), which is usually unsigned. (If you reach County Road A12 on the left, you have gone .25 mile too far.) Drive on Bolam Road for four miles toward the mountain (Mount Shasta), crossing the railroad tracks and continuing to the trailhead, at the end of the road. A high-clearance vehicle is required.

**Contact:** Shasta-Trinity National Forest, Mount Shasta Ranger District, 204 West Alma, Mount Shasta, CA 96067, 530/926-4511, website: www.fs.fed.us/r5 (click on Forest Offices).

## 28 NORTH GATE TRAILHEAD
4.0 mi / 2.75 hrs

**on the north slope of Mount Shasta**

Map 2.2, page 60

The North Gate trailhead, set at about 7,000 feet, is one of Mount Shasta's most obscure and least used trails. It sits on the north flank of Shasta, just below a mountain mound called North Gate. The route skirts this mound, following a small stream uphill for 1.6 miles; then farther along, the trail deteriorates and disappears as it nears tree line at 8,400 feet. From here, most day hikers will climb another 400 feet to the source of the creek, a small spring, and have lunch while enjoying the view to the north.

Special note: Mountain climbers who use this route to climb to the Shasta Summit will discover the going is quite easy at first after leaving tree line. The trip then becomes very steep, difficult, and dangerous, whether via Bolam or Hotlum Glacier. This route is only for experienced mountain climbers who are aware of the extreme risks of crossing steep, sheer glaciers.

**User Groups:** Hikers only. No dogs, horses, or mountain bikes. No wheelchair facilities.

**Permits:** Parking and access are free. A free wilderness permit is required for both day use and overnight use; a $15 permit is required for hikers climbing over 10,000 feet in elevation, or you can buy an annual pass for $25. All climbers are required to pack out waste and must bring a pack-out bag.

**Maps:** For a map, ask the U.S. Forest Service for Shasta-Trinity National Forest or Mount Shasta Wilderness. For a topographic map, ask the USGS for Mount Shasta.

**Directions:** From I-5, drive to the Central Weed/Klamath Falls (Highway 97) exit. Take that exit and drive through Weed to Highway 97. Turn right and drive 13.5 miles to Military Pass Road (Forest Road 19). Turn right and drive 4.5 miles to a fork with Forest Road 42N16 (Andesite Logging Road). Bear right and drive four miles to the parking area, at the end of the road.

**Contact:** Shasta-Trinity National Forest, Mount Shasta Ranger District, 204 West Alma, Mount Shasta, CA 96067, 530/926-4511, website: www.fs.fed.us/r5 (click on Forest Offices). A 24-hour climbing report is available by calling 530/926-5555.

## 29 ETNA SUMMIT TO GRIDER CREEK (PCT)
49.0 mi one-way / 4.0 days

**from Etna Summit north into the Marble Mountain Wilderness west of Etna**

Map 2.2, page 60

The Etna Summit is one of the major access points for the Pacific Crest Trail in Northern California. There is a good, safe parking area (with a nice view), and at an elevation of 5,492 feet, you don't have to start your hike with a wicked climb that is demanded at so many other wilderness trailheads. From Etna Summit, the trail starts by crossing rugged, dry, and often hot terrain that is best dealt with in the morning; you'll reach Shelly Lake about eight miles in. Note that there is no water available along this route until Shelly Lake. The campground at Shelly Meadows is a good first-night stopover. From there, an excellent second-day destination is the Marble Valley, about another 10 miles north, with camping in the nearby Sky High Lakes Basin. The next 20 miles of trail cross through and out of the Marble Mountains. You'll pass Marble Mountain (a side trip to Marble Rim is mandatory), Paradise Lake (many visitors will make camp here), and Kings Castle. Most of the trail here is above tree line, with outstanding lookouts at several points, including a great vista from Marble Rim. Moving onward, the trail follows Big Ridge to Buckhorn Mountain (6,908 feet), continues past Huckleberry Mountain (6,303 feet), and then drops down to the headwaters of Grider Creek, the next major trailhead-access point. As you head north, the trail becomes less and less traveled.

To pick up the next trail heading north, see the Grider Creek to Seiad Valley (PCT) hike in this chapter. If you are walking this trail in reverse, see the Cecilville Road to Russian Wilderness (PCT) hike in this chapter to continue south.

**User Groups:** Hikers, dogs, and horses. No mountain bikes. No wheelchair facilities.

**Permits:** Campfire permits (free) are required for campfires and stoves. Parking and access are free.

**Maps:** A trail information sheet can be obtained by contacting the Salmon River Ranger District at the address below. For a map, ask the U.S. Forest Service for Klamath National Forest or Marble Mountain Wilderness. For a topographic map, ask the USGS for Eaton Peak.

**Directions:** From I-5 at Yreka, take the Highway 3/Fort Jones exit and drive 28 miles to Etna. Turn west on Etna-Somes Bar Road (called Main Street in town) and drive 10.5 miles to Etna Summit. The parking area is along the road.

**Contact:** Klamath National Forest, Salmon River & Scott River Ranger Districts, 11263 North Highway 3, Fort Jones, CA 96032-9702, 530/468-5351, website: www.fs.fed.us/r5 (click on Forest Offices).

## 30 TAYLOR LAKE TRAIL
### 1.0 mi / 0.5 hr

**from Etna Summit into the Russian Wilderness west of Etna**

Map 2.2, page 60

Taylor Lake is proof that wilderness-like lakes can be accessible by wheelchair. The trail is made of hard-packed dirt and is wheelchair accessible, though wheelchairs with wide wheels are recommended. For those with boots instead of wheels, it's about a 10-minute walk to Taylor Lake, a long, narrow lake set on the northern end of the Russian Wilderness. Trout fishing is often very good here, and the walk is short enough for hikers to bring along a small raft or float tube. The only downer here

is that the Forest Service occasionally permits cows to graze, and they stomp the grass at the far end of the lake—and sometimes even walk in the shallows. Although cows are still permitted, the Forest Service has rerouted the trail so that hikers won't be walking amid them at the meadow.

For a side-trip option, the Pacific Crest Trail runs east just above the lake, although the most direct access in the area for the PCT is at nearby Etna Summit.

**User Groups:** Hikers, wheelchairs, dogs, and horses. No mountain bikes.

**Permits:** No permits are required for day use. A campfire permit (free) is required for campfires and stoves. Parking and access are free.

**Maps:** A trail information sheet can be obtained by contacting the Salmon Ranger District at the address below. For a map, ask the U.S. Forest Service for Klamath National Forest or Marble Mountain Wilderness. For a topographic map, ask the USGS for Eaton Peak.

**Directions:** From I-5 at Yreka, take the Highway 3/Fort Jones exit and drive 28 miles southwest to Etna. Turn west on Etna-Somes Bar Road (called Main Street in town) and drive 10.25 miles just past Etna Summit to Forest Road 41N18 (a signed access road). Turn left and continue to the trailhead.

**Contact:** Klamath National Forest, Salmon River & Scott River Ranger Districts, 11263 North Highway 3, Fort Jones, CA 96032-9702, 530/468-5351, website: www.fs.fed.us/r5 (click on Forest Offices).

## 31 STATUE LAKE
### 6.0 mi / 4.0 hrs

**in the Russian Wilderness west of Etna**

Map 2.2, page 60

Statue Lake earned its name from the unique granite sculptures that frame the back wall of the lake. When you first arrive at the small lake, it's a wondrous yet solemn sight, one of nature's mountain temples. Some of the granite outcrops look like fingers sculpted with a giant chisel. There is a small primitive campsite on a granite bluff, from which you can often see small brook trout rising to feed in the lake.

After parking at the Music Creek trailhead, start the trip by hiking up a moderate grade and climbing about a mile to the Pacific Crest Trail. Turn right and hike on the PCT for about 1.5 miles, an easy walk in the forest. When you reach a small spring creek, stop and fill your canteens, then leave the trail and head uphill. It's about a 30-minute, cross-country hike to the lake, and the last 10 minutes is over a large field of boulders.

**User Groups:** Hikers only. Dogs are permitted but not advised because of the route crossing a boulder field. No horses or mountain bikes. No wheelchair facilities.

**Permits:** No permits are required for day use. A campfire permit (free) is required for campfires and stoves. Parking and access are free.

**Maps:** A trail information sheet can be obtained by contacting the Salmon Ranger District at the address below. For a map, ask the U.S. Forest Service for Klamath National Forest or Marble Mountain Wilderness. For a topographic map, ask the USGS for Sawyers Bar.

**Directions:** From I-5 at Yreka, take the Highway 3/Fort Jones exit and drive 28 miles southwest to Etna. Turn west on Etna-Somes Bar Road (called Main Street in town), drive over Etna Summit, and continue down the other side to Forest Road 40N54 (just before the Salmon River Bridge). Turn left on Forest Road 40N54 and drive eight miles to the Music Creek trailhead. (A sign that says Pacific Crest Trail is usually posted. The sign for Music Creek trailhead is repeatedly stolen.)

**Contact:** Klamath National Forest, Salmon River & Scott River Ranger Districts, 11263 North Highway 3, Fort Jones, CA 96032-9702, 530/468-5351, website: www.fs.fed.us/r5 (click on Forest Offices).

## 32 TRAIL CREEK TRAIL
**7.0 mi / 2.0 days**

**in the Russian Wilderness west of Callahan**

Map 2.2, page 60

Because few (other than me, apparently) people use this trail, it has largely been decommissioned by the Forest Service—that is, no trail maintenance is performed.

For most hikers, the trailhead for the Pacific Crest Trail off the Cecilville-Callahan Road is by far preferable. This provides a much easier route into the southern portion of the Russian Wilderness, but it will add 10 miles to your round-trip.

The Russian Wilderness is a place so pristine and so small that it just can't handle many visitors. If you go, walk softly, and treat the fragile area with care. The route into the Russian Wilderness—the Trail Creek Trail—is more of an old jeep road, involving a steep climb and drop, then a short cross-country jaunt. When you finish, you could always write the book, *My Life as a Jeep*. From Trail Creek Camp to the PCT, you are unlikely to see anybody but your companions, and that's a plus. This is also a good route with dogs, because you won't see a soul.

The trailhead is located a short distance up a gravel road across from Trail Creek Campground, which is on Cecilville-Callahan Road. For the first 1.5 miles, the trail heads steeply up on an old fire lane. It continues to climb, and as you near the crest, you'll junction with the Pacific Crest Trail; turn left, then just five minutes later, turn at a signed junction to Syphon Lake. This is a good first night's camp, with Russian or Waterdog Lakes as good second-day destinations.

Once you hit the high country, the lakes are very beautiful, especially Russian Lake, which is excellent for swimming. Because the wilderness here is small, it does not take many people hiking in to take up the campsites. Expect occasional cow sightings in midsummer near Syphon Lake.

**User Groups:** Hikers, dogs, and horses. Mountain bikes allowed only outside of the wilderness border. No wheelchair facilities.

**Permits:** A wilderness permit is required for hikers planning to camp. Parking and access are free.

**Maps:** For a map, ask the U.S. Forest Service for Klamath National Forest. For topographic maps, ask the USGS for Deadman Peak and Eaton Peak.

**Directions:** From Redding, drive north on I-5 for 70 miles. Just past Weed, take the Edgewood exit. At the stop sign, turn left and drive through the underpass to another stop sign. Turn right on Old Highway 99 and drive six miles to Gazelle. Turn left at Gazelle on Gazelle-Callahan Road and drive about 20 miles to Callahan. From Callahan on Highway 3, turn west on County Road 402 (Cecilville Road) and drive 17 miles to Trail Creek Campground. The trail heads north from a gravel road located across from the campground.

**Contact:** Klamath National Forest, Salmon River & Scott River Ranger Districts, 11263 North Highway 3, Fort Jones, CA 96032-9702, 530/468-5351, website: www.fs.fed.us/r5 (click on Forest Offices).

## **33** CECILVILLE ROAD TO RUSSIAN WILDERNESS (PCT)
**3.0 mi one-way / 1.0 day**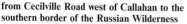

**from Cecilville Road west of Callahan to the southern border of the Russian Wilderness**

Map 2.2, page 60

The long, steady climb up to the southern border of the Russian Wilderness starts from the bottom of the canyon at the North Fork Scott River. From the trailhead, a good side trip (to the south) is the short hike to Hidden Lake or South Fork Lakes. Those venturing onward along the PCT enter a complex habitat web that includes the headwaters of the Scott, Salmon, and Trinity Rivers, along with the beautiful scenery that such diversity creates. This section of the trail is rarely used—it's estimated that less than 1,000 people a year hike here.

Most of them use this as a jump-off spot to the Russian Wilderness.

To pick up the next trail heading north (actually, in this case, heading west), see the Etna Summit to Grider Creek (PCT) hike in this chapter. If you are walking this trail in reverse, see the Scott Mountain to Cecilville Road (PCT) hike in this chapter to continue east.

**User Groups:** Hikers, dogs, and horses. No mountain bikes. No wheelchair facilities.

**Permits:** No permits are required for this section. Parking and access are free.

**Maps:** For topographic maps, ask the USGS for Deadman Peak and Eaton Peak.

**Directions:** From Callahan on Highway 3, turn west on Cecilville Road (County Road 402) and drive 11.5 miles to the Cecilville Summit. Parking is limited here; a larger parking area is located just past Cecilville Summit at the Carter Meadows trailhead (it will add .25 mile to your hike).

**Contact:** Klamath National Forest, Salmon River & Scott River Ranger Districts, 11263 North Highway 3, Fort Jones, CA 96032-9702, 530/468-5351, website: www.fs.fed.us/r5 (click on Forest Offices).

## **34** TRAIL GULCH
**4.5 mi / 3.25 hrs**

**in the Trinity Alps Wilderness west of Callahan**

Map 2.2, page 60

The Trail Gulch Trail rises along Trail Gulch Creek, steeply at times, but in just 2.25 miles, you'll arrive at Trail Gulch Lake. That makes it close enough to go in and out in a day, or better yet, you can make it a good weekend overnighter without tremendous strain. Set northeast of Deadman Peak (7,741 feet) in the Trinity Alps Wilderness, the round, pretty lake is stocked by airplane every year with small trout (a nice bonus). Another bonus is how simple it is to extend your trip either to other mountain lakes or deep into the Trinity Alps Wilderness. Long Gulch Lake is just another three miles from Trail Gulch Lake, making it a good side trip. If you choose to extend into the Trinity Alps instead, the trail is routed along North Fork Coffee Creek to Kickapoo Waterfall, about nine miles from Trail Gulch Lake. This trip is crowded on summer weekends. Experienced hikers may note that on many maps, Trail Gulch Lake is misidentified as Long Gulch Lake, and vice versa.

**User Groups:** Hikers, dogs, and horses. No mountain bikes. No wheelchair facilities.

**Permits:** A wilderness permit is required for hikers planning to camp. Parking and access are free.

**Maps:** For a map, ask the U.S. Forest Service for Klamath National Forest or Trinity Alps Wilderness. For topographic maps, ask the USGS for Deadman Peak and Billys Peak.

**Directions:** From Redding, drive north on I-5 for 70 miles. Just past Weed, take the Edgewood exit. At the stop sign, turn left and drive through the underpass to another stop sign. Turn right on Old Highway 99 and drive about six miles to Gazelle. Turn left on Gazelle-Callahan Road and drive about 20 miles to Callahan. From Callahan on Highway 3, turn west on County Road 402 (Cecilville Road) and drive 11 miles. Turn left on Forest Road 39N08 and drive 1.5 miles to the trailhead.

**Contact:** Klamath National Forest, Salmon River & Scott River Ranger Districts, 11263 North Highway 3, Fort Jones, CA 96032-9702, 530/468-5351, website: www.fs.fed.us/r5 (click on Forest Offices).

## 35 SCOTT MOUNTAIN TO CECILVILLE ROAD (PCT)

**18.0 mi one-way / 2.0 days**

from Highway 3 at Scott Mountain Campground to Cecilville Road near the northern border of the Trinity Alps Wilderness

Map 2.2, page 60

Short hikes on spur trails to a number of wilderness lakes are the highlight of this section of the Pacific Crest Trail. From the camp at Scott Mountain, the trail is routed west for five miles, where the first of a series of lakes is within .5

mile of the trail. They include Upper Boulder, East Boulder, Mid Boulder, and Telephone Lakes—all quite pretty and accessible from the main trail. After hiking past Eagle Peak, set at 7,789 feet, you'll pass additional short cutoffs that are routed to West Boulder, Mavis, and Fox Creek Lakes. Hikers often camp at one of these lakes before dropping to the South Fork Scott River and heading north into the Russian Wilderness.

To pick up the next trail heading north (actually, in this case, heading west), see the Cecilville Road to Russian Wilderness (PCT) hike in this chapter. If you are walking this trail in reverse, see the Mumbo Basin to Scott Mountain (PCT) hike in this chapter to continue south.

**User Groups:** Hikers, dogs, and horses. No mountain bikes. No wheelchair facilities.

**Permits:** A wilderness permit is required for camping in the Trinity Alps Wilderness. Contact the Weaverville Ranger District at the address below for information.

**Maps:** For topographic maps, ask the USGS for Scott Mountain, Tangle Blue Lake, Billys Peak, and Deadman Peak.

**Directions:** From Callahan, drive south on Highway 3 about seven miles to the trailhead, at Scott Mountain Campground.

**Contact:** Shasta-Trinity National Forest, Weaverville Ranger Station, P.O. Box 1190, 210 Main Street, Weaverville, CA 96093, 530/623-2121, website: www.fs.fed.us/r5 (click on Forest Offices).

## 36 KANGAROO LAKE TRAILHEAD

**3.0 mi / 2.25 hrs**

in Klamath National Forest east of Callahan

Map 2.2, page 60

Ⓕ A remote paved road leads right to Kangaroo Lake, set at 6,050 feet, providing one of the most easily reached pristine mountain lakes, with a campground, wheelchair-accessible fishing, and a great trailhead located out of the campground. Here the trail rises steeply, and it quickly connects with the Pacific Crest Trail. From the Pacific Crest Trail, hikers can make the scramble to Cory Peak, at 7,737 feet, for a 360-degree view. This is a great picnic site. All of Northern California's prominent mountain peaks are in view here, and immediately below you, to the west, is Kangaroo Lake, like a large sapphire. The lake covers only 21 acres but often produces large brook trout, most of them 12- to 14-inchers. Backpackers can extend this trip eastward four miles on the Pacific Crest Trail past Robbers Meadow to Bull Lake, a small lake in a relatively sparse setting. In an unsolved conflict, most hikers call this the Kangaroo Lake trailhead, while Forest Service rangers refer to it as the Fen trailhead.

**User Groups:** Hikers, dogs, horses, and mountain bikes. Fishing is wheelchair accessible.

**Permits:** No permits are required. Parking and access are free.

**Maps:** A trail guide can be obtained by contacting Klamath National Forest at the address below. For a map, ask the U.S. Forest Service for Klamath National Forest. For a topographic map, ask the USGS for Scott Mountain.

**Directions:** On I-5, drive north of Weed to the Edgewood exit. Take that exit, turn left at the stop sign, and drive a short distance (under the freeway) to Old Highway 99. Turn right and drive six miles to Gazelle and Gazelle-Callahan Road. Turn left on Gazelle-Callahan Road and drive over the summit. Drive down the other side of the mountain about five miles to Rail Creek Road. Turn left on Rail Creek Road and drive seven miles to where the road dead-ends, at the parking area for Kangaroo Lake. The trail starts to the right, down the road from the campground.

**Contact:** Klamath National Forest, Salmon River & Scott River Ranger Districts, 11263 North Highway 3, Fort Jones, CA 96032-9702, 530/468-5351, website: www.fs.fed.us/r5 (click on Forest Offices).

## 37 DEADFALL LAKES TRAIL
**5.0 mi / 3.0 hrs**

**in Shasta-Trinity National Forest west of Mount Shasta**

**Map 2.2, page 60**

The sight of Middle Deadfall Lake is always a happy shock to newcomers. Here, tucked away on the west side of Mount Eddy, are three wilderness lakes, the prize being Middle Deadfall. At 25 acres, it's far larger than one might expect—and far prettier, too. Because the parking area and trailhead are at the ridgeline, the hike to this lake is much easier than to other wilderness lakes, making it an excellent day hike.

Start the trip by taking the Pacific Crest trailhead at the south end of the parking lot. The trail is routed through a mixed conifer forest, with views of the Trinity Alps off to the west and with a very gentle rising grade most of the way. As you near the lake, you'll cross a shallow stream (protruding rocks will keep you dry) and come to a junction (the Pacific Crest Trail bears to the right; the Mount Eddy Summit Trail turns to the left). Continue straight ahead (many people walk past a winter-snow survey marker) up a short rise, and then suddenly below you is Middle Deadfall Lake, at 7,300 feet—one of the highlights along the Pacific Crest Trail. The best and most secluded campsite here is around the back side of the lake. There are two other lakes nearby: tiny and rarely visited Upper Deadfall, at 7,800 feet, and even smaller Lower Deadfall, at 7,150 feet, which covers five acres and is overlooked in the shadow of its nearby big brother. A great side trip for campers at Middle Deadfall Lake is making the 3.5-mile hike to the top of Mount Eddy, at 9,025 feet (a 1,700-foot climb). It's one of Northern California's greatest lookouts—there's no better view of the western slopes of Mount Shasta.

There is one continuing problem on this route. On a regular basis, mountain bikers illegally ride the Pacific Crest Trail here (which overlaps this route for three miles) between the trailhead above Gumboot Lake, to the north, and the Parks Creek trailhead, to the south. Bikes are banned from the entire length of the PCT, of course.

**User Groups:** Hikers, dogs, and horses. No mountain bikes. No wheelchair facilities.

**Permits:** A campfire permit (free) is required for overnight use. Parking and access are free.

**Maps:** For a map, ask the U.S. Forest Service for Shasta-Trinity National Forest. For a topographic map, ask the USGS for Mount Eddy.

**Directions:** On I-5, drive north of Weed to the Edgewood exit. Take that exit, turn left at the stop sign, and drive a short distance (under the freeway) to Old Highway 99. Turn right and drive .5 mile to Stewart Springs Road. Turn left on Stewart Springs Road and drive to the road's end, at Stewart Springs Resort. Bear right on Forest Road 17 (Parks Creek Road) and drive nine miles to the Deadfall Lakes parking area, at the summit. The trailhead is at the south side of the parking area. Take the Pacific Crest Trail, heading south.

**Contact:** Shasta-Trinity National Forest, Mount Shasta Ranger District, 204 West Alma, Mount Shasta, CA 96067, 530/926-4511, website: www.fs.fed.us/r5 (click on Forest Offices).

## 38 TOAD LAKE TRAIL
**1.5 mi / 2.0 days**

in Shasta-Trinity National Forest west of Mount Shasta

Map 2.2, page 60

You might be wondering why a 1.5-mile round-trip hike, with a difficulty rating of only one, is projected as a two-day trip. The reason is the drive to the trailhead. It's an endless, twisting road that winds its way up the Middle Fork drainage of the Sacramento River, rising up along the west flank of Mount Eddy. No one should go up and back in a day. (And keep your tongue in your mouth, because the ride is so jarring that you might bite off the end of it when you hit a big pothole.) But once parked, you'll immediately notice the perfect calm, and then, with a 15-minute walk to the

lake (at 6,950 feet), you'll be furnished with a picture-perfect lakeside campsite.

The lake covers 23 acres, provides excellent swimming, fair fishing for small trout, and great side trips. The best is the one-mile hike from Toad Lake to Porcupine Lake, an idyllic spot for a picnic or a walk along the shore. To get there from Toad Lake, take the trail that's routed behind the lake up to the Pacific Crest Trail, and then walk south for .25 mile on the PCT to the Porcupine Lake cutoff, on the right.

**User Groups:** Hikers, dogs, and horses. No mountain bikes allowed on the Pacific Crest Trail. No wheelchair facilities.

**Permits:** No permits are required. Parking and access are free.

**Maps:** For a map, ask the U.S. Forest Service for Shasta-Trinity National Forest. For a topographic map, ask the USGS for Mount Eddy.

**Directions:** From I-5 at Mount Shasta city, take the Central Mount Shasta exit. At the stop sign, turn west and drive .5 mile to Old Stage Road. Turn left on Old Stage Road and drive .25 mile to a fork with W. A. Barr Road. Stay to the right at the fork and drive two miles, cross Box Canyon Dam at Lake Siskiyou, and continue around the lake on W. A. Barr Road (which becomes Forest Road 26/South Fork Road). Continue four miles past the Lake Siskiyou Camp resort, cross an unnamed concrete bridge, and turn right at the next dirt road (signed Toad Lake/Morgan Meadows). Drive .2 mile to the first fork, bear left, and drive 11 miles to the lake trailhead parking area. The road is very rough and twisting, and for the last .5 mile, a high-clearance, four-wheel-drive vehicle is recommended. It is a .5-mile walk from the parking area to the lake.

**Contact:** Shasta-Trinity National Forest, Mount Shasta Ranger District, 204 West Alma, Mount Shasta, CA 96067, 530/926-4511, website: www.fs.fed.us/r5 (click on Forest Offices).

## 39 BLACK BUTTE TRAIL
**5.0 mi / 3.5 hrs**

**in Shasta-Trinity National Forest between I-5 and Mount Shasta**

Map 2.2, page 60

Anybody who has cruised I-5 north to Oregon and gawked in astonishment at Mount Shasta has inevitably seen Black Butte right alongside the highway. That's right, it's that barren cinder cone set between the highway and Mount Shasta, and it can pique a traveler's curiosity. The trail is routed right to the top and can answer all of your questions. But you may not like all of the answers. Over the course of 2.5 miles, you'll climb 1,845 feet—much of it steep, most of it rocky, and in the summer, all of it hot and dry. Shade is nonexistent. There are only two rewards. One is claiming the summit, at 6,325 feet, where you'll find the foundation of an old U.S. Forest Service lookout and great 360-degree views; the other is that the hike is an excellent warm-up for people who are planning to climb Mount Shasta. (That is, providing you don't need a week to recover.)

**User Groups:** Hikers and dogs. No horses or mountain bikes. No wheelchair facilities.

**Permits:** No permits are required.

**Maps:** A trail information sheet is available by contacting the Mount Shasta Ranger District at the address below. For a map, ask the U.S. Forest Service for Shasta-Trinity National Forest. For a topographic map, ask the USGS for Mount Shasta city.

**Directions:** From I-5 at Mount Shasta city, take the Central Mount Shasta exit, drive east on Lake Street for one mile, and bear left on Washington Drive. (Washington Drive becomes Everitt Memorial Highway.) Continue on Washington/Everitt Memorial Highway (past the high school) for about two miles, and look for the sign for Spring Hill Plantation (on the right) and Forest Road 41N18 (on the left). Turn left on Forest Road 41N18/Ash Flat (a gravel road), drive about 200 yards, and bear right, continuing on Forest Road 41N18 for 2.5 miles. After the road crosses under the overhead power line, turn left on Forest Road 41N18A (Black Butte Road) and drive .75 mile to the trailhead. Parking is very limited; be sure to park off the road.

**Contact:** Shasta-Trinity National Forest, Mount Shasta Ranger District, 204 West Alma, Mount Shasta, CA 96067, 530/926-4511, website: www.fs.fed.us/r5 (click on Forest Offices).

## 40 SAND FLAT TRAILHEAD
**3.4 mi / 2.75 hrs**

**on the southern slope of Mount Shasta**

Map 2.2, page 60

The hike from Sand Flat to Horse Camp, a distance of 1.7 miles, will give you a good taste of the Mount Shasta experience, and you're likely to savor the flavors. Many who make this day hike are compelled to return to climb all the way to the top. We were!

Sand Flat provides a good shaded parking area to start from, at a 6,800-foot elevation. The trail immediately takes off uphill—gradually at first, but then it becomes quite steep. At 7,360 feet, it intersects with Bunny Flat Trail and then continues rising through the forest. Along the way are amazing examples of how avalanches have knocked down entire sections of forest. When you reach Horse Camp, at 7,800 feet, nearing timberline, you'll find many rewards. The first is springwater flowing continuously out of a piped fountain near the Sierra Hut; it's perhaps the best-tasting water in the world. The second is the foreboding view of Red Bank, which forms the mountain rim above Horse Camp. The third is the opportunity to hike up a short way above tree line for the sweeping views to the south of Castle Crags and Lake Siskiyou. After taking the first steps on Summit Trail, you'll likely yearn to keep going all the way to the very top of this magic mountain. If you wish to hike Summit Trail, see the following hike out of Bunny Flat trailhead.

**User Groups:** Hikers only. No dogs, horses, or mountain bikes. No wheelchair facilities.

**Permits:** Parking and access are free. A free

wilderness permit is required for both day use and overnight use; a $15 permit is required for hikers climbing over 10,000 feet in elevation, or you can buy an annual pass for $25. All climbers are required to pack out waste and must bring a pack-out bag.

**Maps:** For a map, ask the U.S. Forest Service for Shasta-Trinity National Forest or Mount Shasta Wilderness. For a topographic map, ask the USGS for Mount Shasta.

**Directions:** From I-5 at Mount Shasta city, take the Central Mount Shasta exit, drive east on Lake Street for one mile, and bear left on Washington Drive (which becomes Everitt Memorial Highway). Continue on Everitt Memorial Highway for eight miles to Sand Flat Loop (Forest Road 41N60). Turn left and drive to the trailhead.

**Contact:** Shasta-Trinity National Forest, Mount Shasta Ranger District, 204 West Alma, Mount Shasta, CA 96067, 530/926-4511, website: www.fs.fed.us/r5 (click on Forest Offices). A 24-hour climbing report is available by calling 530/926-5555.

## 41 SHASTA SUMMIT TRAIL
**14 mi / 1.5 days**    🥾5  ◁10

### on the southern slope of Mount Shasta

Map 2.2, page 60

The hike to the top of Mount Shasta is a great challenge, an ascent of 7,000 feet over ice, snow, and rock while trying to suck what little oxygen you can out of the thin air. It may be the greatest adventure in the West that most people have an honest chance of achieving. The primary dangers are from tumbling boulders and bad weather (which stops half the people who try the climb), including high winds on top in May and June. Yet most hikers in good condition who start the trip very early and have the proper equipment can summit, especially from mid-July through August, when the weather is benign. Early? You should depart from Bunny Flat by 3 A.M., or hike in a day early, set up a base camp at Horse Camp

(at tree line), and start no later than 4 A.M. Equipment? A day pack with warm clothes, a windbreaker, two canteens of water, food, and an ice ax and crampons are mandatory. Refill your canteen wherever you find a rivulet of water (it's occasionally possible at Red Bank); rangers recommend using a water filter.

It's an absolute must to make an early start. In the hot summer months, towering cumulus clouds sometimes form on Mount Shasta during the afternoon, and by then you'll want to be making the trip down. If towering cumuli begin forming by noon, intense thunderstorms are possible by midafternoon.

The trip starts out of Bunny Flat at 6,900 feet, leads through a forest of Shasta red firs, climbs to where the trail intersects with the route out of Sand Flat, then turns right and rises to Horse Camp, at an elevation of 7,800 feet and a distance of 1.8 miles. It is a must to fill your canteens here. After filling your canteens at the spring, start hiking Summit Trail. Make your first steps across a series of large stones called Olberman's Causeway. From here, the trail quickly rises above timberline, gaining 1,000 feet per mile for six miles, and after a short time, it becomes a faint path. Often this is where the snow and ice start, and you must stop and strap your crampons onto your boots. The walking is easy with crampons. The trail climbs up Avalanche Gulch, and some people stop to make trail camps at a flat spot called Helen Lake, at 10,440 feet. Hikers not acclimated to high altitudes may begin experiencing some dizziness, but there's no relief in sight. At this point, the hike gets steeper (about a 35-degree slope), and many give up before reaching Red Bank—a huge, red, volcanic outcrop at about 12,500 feet. At Red Bank you'll need your ice ax in order to pull your way through a narrow and steep rock/ice chute, where a slip is certain without crampons.

When you emerge atop Red Bank, you are nearly 13,000 feet high, at the foot of a glacier field and Misery Hill, named so because it's a long, slow climb—through snow in spring, scree in summer, and hey, because some people actually mistake it for the peak. Once atop Misery Hill, though, you'll see the true Shasta Summit, a massive pinnacle of lava that seems to jut straight up into the air. With a final push, follow the trail, grabbing rocks to help pull you up and sucking the thin air, and with a few last steps, you'll be on top, at 14,162 feet. On clear days you can see hundreds of miles in all directions, and the sky is a deeper cobalt blue than you ever imagined. On top, you'll sign your name in a logbook in an old rusted metal box, then take in the grand wonders surrounding you. It's a remarkable trip, one that can inspire some people to keep their bodies in good enough shape to make the trip every year.

All hikers must pack out their waste. Special waste pack-out bags are available at no charge at the trailhead and at the Mount Shasta Ranger Station in Mount Shasta.

The biggest danger and largest number of injuries on Mount Shasta come not from falling, but from being hit by tumbling boulders. In fact, our former research assistant, Robyn Brewer, was struck in the foot by a boulder in her first attempt at climbing Shasta. She was hit so hard that it knocked her hiking boot off, breaking her foot and requiring an emergency helicopter airlift out for medical treatment. Always keep a good distance between you and your hiking partners, don't hike in a vertical line, and if a rock comes bouncing down, always shout, "Rock! Rock!" Some guides recommend wearing helmets. By the way, Robyn returned to Mount Shasta the following two years and made it to the top on both trips.

The mountain is best hiked when it still has a good coating of snow and ice, which provide excellent footing with crampons. When the snow and ice melt off in late fall, tromping through the small volcanic rocks is like slogging in mushy sand.

Drink lots of water. In high altitudes, dehydration is a common problem and can result in early exhaustion and extreme vulnerability to mountain sickness.

**User Groups:** Hikers only. No dogs, horses, or mountain bikes. No wheelchair facilities.

**Permits:** Parking and access are free. A free wilderness permit is required for both day use and overnight use; a $15 permit is required for hikers climbing over 10,000 feet in elevation, or you can buy an annual pass for $25. All climbers are required to pack out waste and must bring a pack-out bag.

**Maps:** For a map, ask the U.S. Forest Service for Shasta-Trinity National Forest or Mount Shasta Wilderness. For a topographic map, ask the USGS for Mount Shasta.

**Directions:** From I-5 at Mount Shasta city, take the Central Mount Shasta exit, drive east on Lake Street for one mile, and bear left on Washington Drive (which becomes Everitt Memorial Highway). Continue on Everitt Memorial Highway for 10 miles to Bunny Flat. As you drive in, the trailhead is on the left.

**Contact:** Shasta-Trinity National Forest, Mount Shasta Ranger District, 204 West Alma, Mount Shasta, CA 96067, 530/926-4511, website: www.fs.fed.us/r5 (click on Forest Offices); 24-hour climbing report: 530/926-5555 or 530/926-9613; rental equipment: Fifth Season, Mount Shasta, 530/926-3606; House of Board & Ski, 530/926-2359; climbing guides: Shasta Mountain Guides, 530/926-3117; Alpine Skills, 530/426-9108; or Sierra Wilderness, 707/455-9358.

## 42 PANTHER MEADOWS
**2.8 mi / 1.75 hrs**

**on the southern slope of Mount Shasta**

Map 2.2, page 60

Panther Meadows is considered a sacred Native American site. Even those who are unaware of it seem to realize intuitively that this is a special place and find themselves walking softly and talking quietly when visiting. The trail is easy to reach, located just off to the right of the wide, paved, two-lane Everitt Memorial Highway. This hike is a short one, from Panther Meadows to Gray Butte and back.

From the parking area, the trail starts by heading east past meadow and forest, and after .6 mile, it turns right and begins a steady climb for .8 mile to Gray Butte. To reach the top (at 8,119 feet), it is a scramble over sharp-edged volcanic rock. But it is well worth it: There is a perfect lookout to the south, with Castle Crags, Mount Lassen, and the drop-off in the Sacramento Valley all prominent. Note that the northeast flank of Gray Butte is a sculpted volcanic valley that is called The Gate. Some mountain visitors consider this to be the mountain's sacred portal to the spiritual dimension. Gray Butte can also be reached easily from the Squaw Valley trailhead, which is located another mile up the access road; look for the signed trailhead and the small parking area on the right.

**User Groups:** Hikers only. Dogs are allowed at Gray Butte, but not beyond. No horses or mountain bikes. No wheelchair facilities.

**Permits:** Parking and access are free. A free wilderness permit is required for both day use and overnight use; a $15 permit is required for hikers climbing over 10,000 feet in elevation, or you can buy an annual pass for $25. All climbers are required to pack out waste and must bring a pack-out bag.

**Maps:** For a map, ask the U.S. Forest Service for Shasta-Trinity National Forest or Mount Shasta Wilderness. For a topographic map, ask the USGS for Mount Shasta.

**Directions:** From I-5 at Mount Shasta city, take the Central Mount Shasta exit, drive east on Lake Street for one mile, and bear left on Washington Drive (which becomes Everitt Memorial Highway). Continue on Everitt Memorial Highway for 13 miles (past Bunny Flat) to Panther Meadows Campground, on the right. Turn right and drive to the parking area.

**Contact:** Shasta-Trinity National Forest, Mount Shasta Ranger District, 204 West Alma, Mount Shasta, CA 96067, 530/926-4511, website: www.fs.fed.us/r5 (click on Forest Offices). A 24-hour climbing report is available by calling 530/926-5555 or 530/926-9613.

## 43 OLD SKI BOWL TRAILHEAD
### 2.5 mi / 2.0 hrs

**on the southern slope of Mount Shasta**

Map 2.2, page 60

One of the great hikes on Mount Shasta is climbing from the Old Ski Bowl lodge site up to Green Butte. At 7,800 feet and set just above timberline, it's the highest drive-to trailhead on Mount Shasta. That means the entire route crosses a volcanic slope, with great views every step of the way and leading to a unique destination as well. Green Butte, a huge rock outcrop set at 9,193 feet, is a perfect perch.

At the parking area, there's an obvious trail (though it's unsigned) that leads up toward Green Butte, which is also clearly obvious just a mile away. But while the trip is short, it's very steep, with a 1,300-foot elevation gain. Along the way, a great bonus is a natural spring set about halfway up the butte; be sure to find it and fill your canteen with this sweet-tasting spring water. Although Green Butte is the destination of most visitors here, the hiking route continues to 9,600 feet before disintegrating in the lava rubble and snow. The Old Ski Bowl is one of the legendary spots on Shasta. It was here that a developer desecrated Shasta wildlands by building a ski area above tree line. Well, nature gives, and nature takes back. With no trees to hold snow in place, the old mountain wiped out the ski lifts with an avalanche. Ironically, in the mid-1990s, a new ski area was proposed at the same spot. The week before the decision was made, another avalanche pounded through, clearing a giant swath of trees and wiping out an area right where the lodge had been proposed. Now again, the Shasta Wilderness is untouched by the hand of mankind, rising like a diamond in a field of coal.

**User Groups:** Hikers only. Dogs are permitted in Old Ski Bowl, but not beyond into Mount Shasta Wilderness. No horses or mountain bikes. No wheelchair facilities.

**Permits:** Parking and access are free. A free wilderness permit is required for both day use and overnight use; a $15 permit is required for hikers climbing over 10,000 feet in elevation, or you can buy an annual pass for $25. All climbers are required to pack out waste and must bring a pack-out bag.

**Maps:** For a map, ask the U.S. Forest Service for Shasta-Trinity National Forest or Mount Shasta Wilderness. For a topographic map, ask the USGS for Mount Shasta.

**Directions:** From I-5 at Mount Shasta city, take the Central Mount Shasta exit, drive east on Lake Street for one mile, and bear left on Washington Drive (which becomes Everitt Memorial Highway). Continue on Everitt Memorial Highway for 13.5 miles (past Panther Meadows Campground, on the right) to the parking area for the Old Ski Bowl site, at the end of the road.

**Contact:** Shasta-Trinity National Forest, Mount Shasta Ranger District, 204 West Alma, Mount Shasta, CA 96067, 530/926-4511, website: www.fs.fed.us/r5 (click on Forest Offices). A 24-hour climbing report is available by calling 530/926-5555 or 530/926-9613.

## 44 BREWER CREEK TRAILHEAD
### 4.2 mi / 3.0 hrs

**on the northeast slope of Mount Shasta**

**Map 2.2, page 60**

It's so quiet here that you can practically hear the wildflowers bloom. We've hiked the north slope of Shasta out of the Brewer Creek trailhead several times and have never seen another person. The trip is a perfect day hike. The trailhead is set near Brewer Creek (at 7,200 feet), hence the name. After a short walk through a section of forest that was selectively logged many years ago, you'll enter the Shasta Wilderness and be surrounded by old-growth firs, many quite scraggly from enduring harsh winters and the short growing season. Here the trail gets more steep—a steady climb up through forest, with gradual switchbacks as it goes. When you near tree line, at 7,700 feet, the trail turns to the left and begins to lateral across

the mountain. It's 2.1 miles to timberline from the trailhead, and most people hike to this point, then turn back. However, you can add an easy mile or two by climbing a wide, volcanic slope with good footing all the way and rising to 9,500 feet. This is a great spot for a picnic, providing nice views to the north and also perhaps inspiring dreams of the day you'll next climb all the way to the top of Shasta.

Special note: Mountaineers who try to climb Shasta from this trailhead have only one good route from the point where the trail meets tree line, which is to head to the right up and over Hotlum Glacier. This route is extremely difficult, very steep, and dangerous.

**User Groups:** Hikers only. No dogs, horses, or mountain bikes. No wheelchair facilities.

**Permits:** Parking and access are free. A free wilderness permit is required for both day use and overnight use; a $15 permit is required for hikers climbing over 10,000 feet in elevation, or you can buy an annual pass for $25. All climbers are required to pack out waste and must bring a pack-out bag.

**Maps:** For a map, ask the U.S. Forest Service for Shasta-Trinity National Forest or Mount Shasta Wilderness. For a topographic map, ask the USGS for Mount Shasta.

**Directions:** From I-5 in Redding, drive north for 47 miles to the Highway 89/McCloud-Reno exit. Bear right on Highway 89 and drive nine miles to McCloud, then continue for another 2.8 miles to Pilgrim Creek Road. Turn left on Pilgrim Creek Road (Forest Road 13) and drive 7.1 miles to Forest Road 19 (Sugar Pine Butte Road). Turn left and drive .9 mile to Forest Road 42N02. Turn left and drive two miles to Forest Road 42N10. Turn left and drive two miles to the trailhead parking area.

**Contact:** Shasta-Trinity National Forest, Mount Shasta Ranger District, 204 West Alma, Mount Shasta, CA 96067, 530/926-4511, website: www.fs.fed.us/r5 (click on Forest Offices); McCloud Ranger District, 530/964-2184. A 24-hour climbing report is available by calling 530/926-5555 or 530/926-9613.

## 45 MUD CREEK FALLS
**2.0 mi / 1.5 hrs**

**on the southeast slope of Mount Shasta**

Map 2.2, page 60

A short walk on the remote southeast flank of Mount Shasta can provide entry to a land of enchantment that features deep canyons and views of glaciers and Mount Shasta's prettiest waterfall. The drive in is circuitous but well signed, and it's a surprise to find other cars parked at the trailhead. The hike starts on an old overgrown jeep road, slowly emerging from a sparse forest of Shasta red fir and climbing to the eastern edge of the dramatic Mud Creek Canyon, at about 7,000 feet in elevation. From here, most hikers climb on for another 15 minutes, arriving at a perfect view of the waterfall at the bottom of the canyon. The waterfall, best viewed with binoculars, is perhaps 125 feet high. It's wide, and silver, but distant. This area is rich in natural history—the canyon was carved by a glacier and is still fed with water from the towering, fractured Konwakiton Glacier, which runs the color of volcanic silt.

**User Groups:** Hikers only. No dogs, horses, or mountain bikes. No wheelchair facilities.

**Permits:** Parking and access are free. A free wilderness permit is required for both day use and overnight use; a $15 permit is required for hikers climbing over 10,000 feet in elevation, or you can buy an annual pass for $25. All climbers are required to pack out waste and must bring a pack-out bag.

**Maps:** For a map, ask the U.S. Forest Service for Shasta-Trinity National Forest or Mount Shasta Wilderness. For a topographic map, ask the USGS for Mount Shasta.

**Directions:** From I-5 in Redding, drive north for 47 miles to the Highway 89/McCloud-Reno exit. Bear right on Highway 89 and drive nine miles to McCloud, then continue for another 2.8 miles to Pilgrim Creek Road. Turn left on Pilgrim Creek Road (Forest Road 13) and drive five miles (paved) to Forest Road 41N15 (Widow Springs Road). Turn left and drive about five

miles to Forest Road 31 (McKenzie Butte). Cross this road and drive straight on Forest Road 41N61 (Cold Creek Road), a dirt and gravel road, for about a mile. Turn left on Forest Road 41N25Y (Clear Creek Road) and drive about three miles to the parking area for the Clear Creek trailhead. The road is well signed.

**Contact:** Shasta-Trinity National Forest, Mount Shasta Ranger District, 204 West Alma, Mount Shasta, CA 96067, 530/926-4511, website: www.fs.fed.us/r5 (click on Forest Offices); McCloud Ranger District, 530/964-2184. A 24-hour climbing report is available by calling 530/926-5555 or 530/926-9613.

## 46 MUMBO BASIN TO SCOTT MOUNTAIN (PCT)
**35.0 mi one-way / 4.0 days**

**in Shasta-Trinity National Forest from Gumboot trailhead to Scott Mountain**

Map 2.2, page 60

The PCT starts at a popular trailhead but quickly jumps northward into remote, beautiful country. The first highlight, only a mile up the trail, is the view below, to the left of secluded Picayune Lake. The trail heads on, passing little Porcupine Lake (well below, and out of reach), an idyllic setting which requires a side trip. Then it heads over the rim and down to Deadfall Lakes, an excellent camping spot. From the ridge, an irresistible side trip is the one-mile trek to the top of Mount Eddy (at 9,025 feet), with its incomparable view of Mount Shasta. From Deadfall Lakes, the trail continues down, rounds the headwaters of the Trinity River, then climbs back up Chilcoot Pass and Bull Lake. From here, it's a 10-mile pull to the Scott Mountain Summit trailhead (see the Cecilville Road to Russian Wilderness [PCT] hike in this chapter).

If you are walking this trail in reverse, see the Castle Crags to Mumbo Basin (PCT) hike in this chapter to continue south.

**User Groups:** Hikers, dogs, and horses. No mountain bikes. No wheelchair facilities.

**Permits:** No permits are required. Parking and access are free.

**Maps:** For topographic maps, ask the USGS for Mumbo Basin, South China Mountain, and Scott Mountain.

**Directions:** From I-5 at Mount Shasta city, take the Central Mount Shasta exit. At the stop sign, turn west and drive .5 mile to Old Stage Road. Turn left on Old Stage Road and drive .25 mile to a fork with W. A. Barr Road. Stay to the right at the fork and drive two miles, cross Box Canyon Dam at Lake Siskiyou, and continue around the lake on W. A. Barr Road (which becomes Forest Road 26/South Fork Road). Continue four miles past the Lake Siskiyou Camp resort and continue up the canyon for 12.5 miles to Gumboot Lake Road. Bear right, staying on Forest Road 26, and continue 2.5 miles to the ridge and the parking area and trailhead.

**Contact:** Shasta-Trinity National Forest, Mount Shasta Ranger District, 204 West Alma, Mount Shasta, CA 96067, 530/926-4511, website: www.fs.fed.us/r5 (click on Forest Offices).

## 47 GUMBOOT LAKE TRAILHEAD
**1.5 mi / 1.5 hrs**

**in Shasta-Trinity National Forest west of Mount Shasta**

**Map 2.2, page 60**

If you must always have a trail to hike on, well, this trip is not for you. But if you don't mind a little cross-country scramble to a mountain rim then a short cutoff to a peak, with spectacular views of Gumboot Lake and Mount Shasta beyond, then sign up for this hike. Starting at an elevation of 6,050 feet at Gumboot Lake, which is pretty and has good trout fishing, you circle the lake on the right side, where there's a good trail. At the back of the lake, break off to the right the trail and start climbing the slope, heading up toward the ridge that circles the back of the lake. A little less than halfway to the top, you'll pass Little Gumboot Lake and then scramble your way to the ridge, where you'll intersect with the Pacific Crest Trail. Head to the left for a short distance, then again break off the trail, this time to the left,

heading on the mountain spine toward the peak that towers over Gumboot Lake, with Mount Shasta as the backdrop off to the east. This peak is your destination. The world may not be perfect, but from this lookout, it comes close.

**User Groups:** Hikers and dogs only. No horses or mountain bikes. No wheelchair facilities.

**Permits:** No permits are required. Parking and access are free.

**Maps:** For a map, ask the U.S. Forest Service for Shasta-Trinity National Forest. For a topographic map, ask the USGS for Mumbo Basin.

**Directions:** From I-5 at Mount Shasta city, take the Central Mount Shasta exit. At the stop sign, turn west and drive .5 mile to Old Stage Road. Turn left on Old Stage Road and drive .25 mile to a fork with W. A. Barr Road. Stay to the right at the fork and drive two miles, cross Box Canyon Dam at Lake Siskiyou, and continue around the lake on W. A. Barr Road (which becomes Forest Road 26/South Fork Road). Continue four miles past the Lake Siskiyou Camp resort and continue up the canyon to Gumboot Lake Road (Forest Road 40N37). Bear left on Gumboot Lake Road and drive .5 mile to the parking area near the shore of the lake.

**Contact:** Shasta-Trinity National Forest, Mount Shasta Ranger District, 204 West Alma, Mount Shasta, CA 96067, 530/926-4511, website: www.fs.fed.us/r5 (click on Forest Offices).

## 48 HEART LAKE TRAIL
**3.0 mi / 2.25 hrs**

**at Castle Lake in Shasta-Trinity National Forest west of Mount Shasta**

**Map 2.2, page 60**

The tale of Castle Lake, set at an elevation of 5,450 feet, is that the water is like none other in the world, which has led some people to jump into the lake for complete renewal. In reality, the water is so pure, containing few nutrients of any kind, that U.C. Davis has a water sampling station here in an ongoing comparison study with Lake Tahoe.

The trailhead is on the left side of the lake,

just across the outlet stream. From there, the trail rises up along the slope just left of the lake. Below is Castle Lake, a pretty sight that's set in a rock bowl with a high back wall. The trail rises up to a saddle at 5,900 feet. At the saddle, bear uphill to the right on the faint trail. It's an easy scramble up over a lip at 6,050 feet, where little Heart Lake is tucked away. Because the lake is small, the water warms up by midsummer, making it great for swimming. In addition, if you scramble up the back wall of the little lake, you'll get a breathtaking view of Mount Shasta. Also note that the best drive-to spot anywhere for photographs of Mount Shasta is on Castle Lake Road at a turnout about one mile downhill from the Castle Lake parking area.

**User Groups:** Hikers and dogs. Not suitable for horses or mountain bikes. No wheelchair facilities.

**Permits:** No permits are required. Parking and access is free.

**Maps:** For a map, ask the U.S. Forest Service for Shasta-Trinity National Forest or Castle Crags Wilderness. For a topographic map, ask the USGS for Mount Shasta city.

**Directions:** From I-5 at Mount Shasta city, take the Central Mount Shasta exit. At the stop sign, turn west and drive .5 mile to Old Stage Road. Turn left on Old Stage Road and drive .25 mile to a fork with W. A. Barr Road. Stay to the right at the fork and drive two miles, cross Box Canyon Dam at Lake Siskiyou, and continue .5 mile to Castle Lake Road. Turn left and drive 7.5 miles to the parking area at the end of the road, at Castle Lake. The trailhead begins on the eastern end of the parking lot.

**Contact:** Shasta-Trinity National Forest, Mount Shasta Ranger District, 204 West Alma, Mount Shasta, CA 96067, 530/926-4511, website: www.fs.fed.us/r5 (click on Forest Offices).

## 49 SISSON-CALLAHAN

**14.0 mi one-way / 2.0 days**

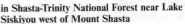

in Shasta-Trinity National Forest near Lake Siskiyou west of Mount Shasta

**Map 2.2, page 60**

The Sisson-Callahan Trail is something of a legend in the Mount Shasta area, yet it is little traveled these days. It was long ago a well-known, well-traveled route up the east flank of Mount Eddy, over the top (through a saddle below the summit) and down to Deadfall Lakes. But with a much easier route long available from the Deadfall Lakes trailhead, this trail is passed over. Why? The route is long, steep, and hot, climbing 5,000 feet over the course of nine miles to the top of Mount Eddy (at 9,025 feet), then down nearly 2,000 feet in two miles to Deadfall Lakes for the nearest campsite. In addition, the great scenic beauty doesn't start until you've climbed several thousand feet, and by then you'll care more about how much water is left in your canteen than about the incredible sweeping view of Mount Shasta to the east. Alas, you'll then face killer switchbacks to reach the Eddy Ridge. As you reach the Eddy crest, look close and you will find an old sign for a former route for the Pacific Crest Trail; it might be 50 or 60 years old. From here it is mandatory to hike the switchbacks up to the Mount Eddy Summit. After that, it's a 2,000-foot descent to Middle Deadfall Lake, where you make camp. Your hiking reward comes the next morning, when after lounging around at Lower Deadfall Lake, you walk out three nearly level miles to the Park Creek/PCT trailhead, then catch your shuttle ride back to the town of Mount Shasta. All in all, this is a genuine butt-kicker of a trail. Unless you want to do a hike that no one else does, a much better route to the Deadfall Lakes and Mount Eddy is from the Parks Creek trailhead, listed in this chapter as Deadfall Lakes Trail.

**User Groups:** Hikers, dogs, and horses. No mountain bikes. No wheelchair facilities.

**Permits:** No permits are required. Parking and access are free.

**Maps:** For a map, ask the U.S. Forest Service for Shasta-Trinity National Forest. For topographic maps, ask the USGS for Mount Shasta city and Mount Eddy.

**Directions:** From I-5 at Mount Shasta city, take the Central Mount Shasta exit. At the stop sign, turn west and drive .5 mile to Old Stage Road. Turn left on Old Stage Road and drive .25 mile to a fork with W. A. Barr Road. Stay to the right at the fork and drive two miles to North Shore Road (if you cross the dam at Lake Siskiyou, you have gone too far). Turn right on North Shore (which becomes Forest Road 40N27/Deer Creek Road) and drive four miles, across the bridge on Deer Creek to the next major junction, Forest Road 40N27C. Turn left on Forest Road 40N27C and park along the edge of the road before the ford on the North Fork Sacramento. (The water here is sometimes deeper than it looks; don't be tempted to drive it.) The Sisson-Callahan Trail (which first appears as a road) starts on the other side of the ford, on an old logging skid road that goes to the right. Within .5 mile, it turns into a trail.

**Contact:** Shasta-Trinity National Forest, Mount Shasta Ranger District, 204 West Alma, Mount Shasta, CA 96067, 530/926-4511, website: www.fs.fed.us/r5 (click on Forest Offices).

## 50 CARIBOU LAKES TRAIL
**18.0 mi / 2.0 days**

**in the Trinity Alps Wilderness northwest of Trinity Lake**

Map 2.2, page 60

The Caribou Lakes Basin provides the classic Trinity Alps scene: three high mountain lakes, beautiful and serene, with the back wall of the Sawtooth Ridge casting a monumental backdrop on one side, and on the other side, a drop-off and great views of a series of mountain peaks and ridgelines. Sunsets are absolutely remarkable when viewed from here. The centerpiece is Caribou Lake, the largest lake in the Trinity Alps Wilderness. Because it's a nine-mile hike to the Caribou

Lakes Basin, this makes an excellent first-day destination for backpackers exploring this section of the Trinity Alps Wilderness. The trail starts at the bottom of the Salmon River, however, and like all trails that start at the bottom of canyons, it means you begin the trip with a terrible climb that never seems to end. Plan on drinking a full canteen of water, and be certain not to miss the natural spring that's available near the crest, just off to the right. After reaching the crest, the trail travels counterclockwise around the mountain, then drops into the Caribou Lakes Basin. Ignore your urge to stop at the first lake, because the best campsites, swimming, and views are from Caribou Lake, the last and largest lake you'll reach in this circuit. Because this is a popular destination, fishing is often poor. The lake is stocked, but these fish are very smart from the relatively large number of people making a cast over the course of a summer.

**User Groups:** Hikers and dogs. Horses are permitted but not recommended. No mountain bikes. No wheelchair facilities.

**Permits:** A wilderness permit is required for hikers planning to camp.

**Maps:** For a map, ask the U.S. Forest Service for Klamath National Forest or Trinity Alps Wilderness. For a topographic map, ask the USGS for Caribou Lakes.

**Directions:** From Weaverville, drive north on Highway 3 past Trinity Lake. At the Coffee Creek Ranger Station, turn west (left) on County Road 104 (Coffee Creek Road) and drive 17 miles to the trailhead at the end of the road, at Big Flat Campground.

**Contact:** Shasta-Trinity National Forest, Weaverville Ranger Station, P.O. Box 1190, 210 Main Street, Weaverville, CA 96093, 530/623-2121, website: www.fs.fed.us/r5 (click on Forest Offices); Klamath National Forest, Salmon River & Scott River Ranger Districts, 11263 North Highway 3, Fort Jones, CA 96032-9702, 530/468-5351, website: www.fs.fed.us/r5 (click on Forest Offices).

## 51 UNION LAKE TRAIL
**12.0 mi / 2.0 days**

in the Trinity Alps Wilderness northwest of
Trinity Lake

**Map 2.2, page 60**

Union Lake sits in a granite basin below Red
Rock Mountain. The hike in and out is a good
weekend affair, but most visitors are backpackers who are using the camp at the lake
as a first-day destination for a multiday trip.
Of the trailheads on Coffee Creek Road, this
one is often overlooked. The trail starts near
an old sawmill along Coffee Creek, heads
south (to the left), and in less than a mile
starts the climb adjacent to Union Creek (on
your right). Like most hikes that start at a
streambed, you pay for your pleasure, going
up, not down. After about two miles, the trail
crosses Union Creek and continues on for a
few miles, now with the stream on the left.
You'll pass a trail junction for Bullards Basin,
and about .5 mile later, turn right on the cutoff trail to Union Lake.

**User Groups:** Hikers, dogs, and horses. No
mountain bikes. No wheelchair facilities.

**Permits:** A wilderness permit is required for
hikers planning to camp.

**Maps:** For a map, ask the U.S. Forest Service
for Shasta-Trinity National Forest or Trinity
Alps Wilderness. For a topographic map, ask
the USGS for Caribou Lakes.

**Directions:** From Weaverville, drive north
on Highway 3 past Trinity Lake. At the Coffee Creek Ranger Station, turn west (left)
on County Road 104 (Coffee Creek Road)
and drive about 10 miles to the trailhead, on
the left.

**Contact:** Shasta-Trinity National Forest,
Weaverville Ranger Station, P.O. Box 1190,
210 Main Street, Weaverville, CA 96093,
530/623-2121, website: www.fs.fed.us/r5 (click
on Forest Offices).

## 52 BIG BEAR LAKE TRAIL
**8.0 mi / 2.0 days**

in the Trinity Alps Wilderness south
of Callahan

**Map 2.2, page 60**

The four-mile hike up to Big Bear Lake, a
large, beautiful lake by wilderness standards,
can make for a perfect weekend backpack
trip. If there's a negative to this trip, it's this:
The trail ends at the lake, so if the lakeside
campsites are already taken when you arrive,
you're out of luck for a quality place to camp.
The trailhead is easy to reach,—just off Highway 3 north of Trinity Lake. The route is simple but not easy. It follows Bear Creek for the
entire route, with one stream crossing, but
climbing all the way. Once you reach the lake,
a bonus is the side trip to Little Bear Lake,
which takes about a mile of scrambling cross-
country to reach. The trail is steep, popular,
and beautiful.

**User Groups:** Hikers and dogs. Horses are allowed but not recommended. No mountain
bikes. No wheelchair facilities.

**Permits:** A wilderness permit is required for
hikers planning to camp in the wilderness.

**Maps:** For a map, ask the U.S. Forest Service for Shasta-Trinity National Forest. For
a topographic map, ask the USGS for Tangle Blue Lake.

**Directions:** From I-5 at Yreka, take the Highway 3/Fort Jones exit and drive about 40 miles
to Callahan. Continue south on Highway 3 for
about 13 miles to Bear Creek Loop Road. Turn
right and drive a short distance (on an unpaved
road) to the signed trailhead (located near the
Bear Creek road crossing).

**Contact:** Shasta-Trinity National Forest,
Weaverville Ranger Station, P.O. Box 1190,
210 Main Street, Weaverville, CA 96093,
530/623-2121, website: www.fs.fed.us/r5 (click
on Forest Offices).

## 53 TAMARACK LAKE TRAILHEAD
### 5.0 mi / 4.0 hrs

in Shasta-Trinity National Forest southwest of Mount Shasta

**Map 2.2, page 60**

This is sacred country for some hikers, set high in the Trinity Divide at 5,900 feet. Tamarack is a beautiful alpine lake and a place of remarkable serenity. If you can pull yourself away from it, there's a rugged, cross-country route to the north that approaches the summit of Grey Rocks, a series of dark, craggy peaks. The route is steep and difficult, but the view of Castle Crags, Mount Shasta, the ridges of the Trinity Divide, and the Sacramento River Canyon will have you thanking a higher power for the privilege of breathing the air here.

**User Groups:** Hikers and dogs. Not suitable for horses or mountain bikes. No wheelchair facilities.

**Permits:** No permits are required.

**Maps:** For a map, ask the U.S. Forest Service for Shasta-Trinity National Forest. For a topographic map, ask the USGS for Chicken Hawk Hill.

**Directions:** From I-5 south of Dunsmuir, take the Castella/Castle Crags State Park exit and drive west on Castle Creek Road. Continue past the park (the road becomes Forest Road 25/Whalen Road) and continue 12.5 miles on to Forest Road 38N17 (Tamarack Road). Turn left on Forest Road 38N17 and drive about six miles to the trailhead. This road is extremely rough, with the last mile passable only to four-wheel-drive vehicles with large tires and high clearance. For other vehicles, before this bad section of road, there is a primitive parking area on the right side.

**Contact:** Shasta-Trinity National Forest, Mount Shasta Ranger District, 204 West Alma, Mount Shasta, CA 96067, 530/926-4511, website: www.fs.fed.us/r5 (click on Forest Offices).

## 54 ROOT CREEK TRAIL
### 2.3 mi / 1.75 hrs

in Castle Crags State Park south of Mount Shasta

**Map 2.2, page 60**

Castle Crags State Park features a series of huge granite spires that tower over the Sacramento River Canyon, the kind of sight that can take your breath away the first time you see it from I-5. That sight inspires a lot of people to take one of the hikes at the park, and while most don't have the time, energy, or body conditioning to complete Castle Crags Trail, Root Creek Trail is a good second choice.

As you drive up the access road, look for the signed trailhead to the left, just as you arrive at the parking area. The elevation is 2,500 feet at the trailhead. Start at this trailhead, which is signed for Castle Crags Trail, and walk .25 mile to a trail junction. Turn right on Root Creek Trail. From here, the trail is routed through a thick, cool forest, an easy walk that most visitors overlook. It continues to Root Creek, a pretty, babbling stream.

**User Groups:** Hikers only. No dogs, horses, or mountain bikes. No wheelchair facilities.

**Permits:** No permits are required. A state park entrance fee of $6 is charged for each vehicle.

**Maps:** A trail map can be obtained for a fee by contacting Castle Crags State Park at the address below. For a topographic map, ask the USGS for Dunsmuir.

**Directions:** From I-5 south of Dunsmuir, take the Castella/Castle Crags State Park exit. Turn west on Castle Creek Road and drive .25 mile to the park entrance, on the right. Turn right and drive to the kiosk. Just past the kiosk, bear right and drive two miles (past the campground) to the parking area for Vista Point. The signed trailhead is at the west edge of the parking area.

**Contact:** Castle Crags State Park, P.O. Box 80, Castella, CA 96017, 530/235-2684, website: www.parks.ca.gov (click on Find A Park).

## 55 CASTLE CRAGS TO MUMBO BASIN (PCT)

**25.0 mi one-way / 2.0 days**

**from Castle Crags State Park west into Shasta-Trinity National Forest**

**Map 2.2, page 60**

This is a key juncture for the PCT, where the trail climbs out of a river canyon and back to high ridgelines. It's in a classic region, the Trinity Divide, known for lakes sculpted in granite and sweeping views of Mount Shasta. The trail runs right beneath the spires of Castle Crags, a setting that can astonish newcomers. From the Sacramento River at Castle Crags, at an elevation of 2,000 feet, the trail laterals up the north side of Castle Creek Canyon, rising just below the base of the awesome crags. It finally hits the rim at the back side of Castle Ridge. Then it follows the rim in a half circle to the west, to the Seven Lakes Basin and beyond to the Mumbo Basin and the Gumboot Lake trailhead. The final five miles of this segment pass by a dozen pristine mountain lakes, but most are well off the trail.

To continue north on the PCT, see the Mumbo Basin to Scott Moutain (PCT) hike in this chapter. If you are walking this trail in reverse, see the Ash Camp to Castle Crags Wilderness (PCT) hike in this chapter to continue south.

**User Groups:** Hikers only. No dogs, horses, or mountain bikes. No wheelchair facilities.

**Permits:** No permits are required. A state park entrance fee of $6 is charged for each vehicle.

**Maps:** A trail map can be obtained for a fee by contacting Castle Crags State Park at the address below. For topographic maps, ask the USGS for Dunsmuir, Seven Lakes Basin, and Mumbo Basin.

**Directions:** From I-5 south of Dunsmuir, take the Castella/Castle Crags State Park exit. Turn west on Castle Creek Road and drive .25 mile to the park entrance, on the right. Turn right and drive to the kiosk. Just past the kiosk is a special parking area for PCT hikers. For day hikers, continue by bearing right, and then drive two miles to the end of the road, where there is a parking area for Vista Point. The sighned trailhead is back down the road about 50 yards.

**Contact:** Castle Crags State Park, P.O. Box 80, Castella, CA 96017, 530/235-2684, website: www.parks.ca.gov (click on Find A Park).

## 56 CRAGS TRAIL TO CASTLE DOME

**5.7 mi / 4.0 hrs**

**in Castle Crags State Park south of Mount Shasta**

**Map 2.2, page 60**

From Vista Point in Castle Crags State Park, hikers can gaze up at the wondrous crags and spot Castle Dome (at 4,966 feet), the leading spire on the crags' ridge. This is a high, rounded, missile-shaped piece of rock—and, yes, this is your destination on Castle Crags Trail. If you're out of shape, this climb is a butt-kicker, gaining elevation all the way.

As you drive up to the parking area, you will see the signed trailhead on your left just as you reach the parking area. The elevation is 2,500 feet. Start by taking Castle Crags Trail for .25 mile; when you reach a three-trail junction, continue on Castle Crags Trail. Here the trail launches off, rising through a thick forest. It climbs steeply at times before eventually turning to the right, emerging from the forest, and winding through the lower crags. Once above tree line, the views get better with each rising step. In spring, snow and ice fields are common this high. An excellent picnic spot is at Indian Springs (at 3,600 feet), and many hikers get no farther than this point. But the trail goes onward, always climbing, then getting quite steep before finally reaching a saddle at the foot of Castle Dome, where a few trees have somehow gained toeholds. When you set foot on this divine perch and gaze north at Mount Shasta, it will be a moment you'll prize forever.

It isn't quite pristine, unfortunately, because of highway noise emerging from the canyon, as well as the inevitable freight train. Regardless, the views and photographs are eye-popping, making it a must-do for those who rate their hikes based on the lookouts.

**User Groups:** Hikers only. No dogs, horses, or mountain bikes. No wheelchair facilities.

**Permits:** No permits are required. A state park entrance fee of $6 is charged for each vehicle.

**Maps:** A trail map can be obtained for a fee by contacting Castle Crags State Park at the address below. For a topographic map, ask the USGS for Dunsmuir.

**Directions:** From I-5 south of Dunsmuir, take the Castella/Castle Crags State Park exit. Turn west on Castle Creek Road and drive .25 mile to the park entrance, on the right. Turn right and drive to the kiosk. Just past the kiosk, bear right and drive two miles to its end, at the parking area for Vista Point. The signed trailhead is back down the road about 50 yards.

**Contact:** Castle Crags State Park, P.O. Box 80, Castella, CA 96017, 530/235-2684, website: www.parks.ca.gov (click on Find A Park).

## ⑤⑦ MIDDLE FALLS TRAIL
### 0.5–2.0 mi / 0.5–1.0 hr

**at Fowler's Camp in Shasta-Trinity National Forest east of McCloud**

**Map 2.2, page 60**

Middle Falls, on the McCloud River, is one of the prettiest waterfalls in Northern California. It is a wide and tall cascade of water that pours over a 50-foot cliff into a deep pool in a rock bowl. This easy hike is a 10- to 15-minute walk on a paved trail that starts at Lower Falls and skirts the left side of the McCloud River. You'll round a bend, probably hearing the waterfall before you see it, and then suddenly, there it is, this wide sheet of falling water. It's something like a miniature Niagara Falls. On summer weekends, teenagers climb to the rim above the falls, then plunge 50 feet into the pool like human missiles. It's a dangerous venture that we don't recommend.

From the base of the plunge pool, you can extend your walk by hiking up a series of switch-

backs that tops out at the volcanic rim encircling the pool. From here, you may continue to hike upstream to Upper Falls, a narrow, staircase-type waterfall. It is also possible to drive to a parking area near the brink of the falls, reducing the hike to about 50 yards. A restroom is available at this parking area.

The one frustrating element is that some visitors litter at this spot—or worse, they discard their cigarette butts on the trail. We try to reverse this offensive practice by packing out any trash that we see.

**User Groups:** Hikers and dogs. No horses or mountain bikes. The paved path from Lower Falls to Middle Falls is wheelchair accessible.

**Permits:** No permits are required. Parking and access are free.

**Maps:** For a map, ask the U.S. Forest Service for Shasta-Trinity National Forest. For a topographic map, ask the USGS for McCloud.

**Directions:** From I-5 in Redding, drive north for 47 miles to the Highway 89/McCloud-Reno exit. Bear right on Highway 89 and drive nine miles to McCloud. Continue southeast on Highway 89 for five miles to the sign for Fowler's Campground and Forest Road 39N28. Turn right and drive one mile to a fork. Bear left at the fork for Fowler's Campground, drive through the campground to the restroom, and park. The trailhead is across the road from the restroom.

**Contact:** Shasta-Trinity National Forest, McCloud Ranger District, P.O. Box 1620, 2019 Forest Road, McCloud, CA 96057, 530/964-2184, website: www.fs.fed.us/r5 (click on Forest Offices).

## ⑤⑧ ASH CAMP TO CASTLE CRAGS WILDERNESS (PCT)
### 30.0 mi one-way / 2.0 days

**from Ash Camp on the McCloud River west into Castle Crags State Park**

**Map 2.2, page 60**

Of the hundreds of rivers along the Pacific Crest Trail, it's the McCloud River that often seems most vibrant with life. This segment of the PCT starts right alongside the lush

McCloud River at Ash Camp, set at about 3,000 feet. The trail is then routed downstream above the McCloud for 2.5 miles, one of the most prized sections of trail in this region. At Ah-Di-Na Camp, the trail starts to rise, eventually turning up Squaw Valley Creek and climbing beyond to top Girard Ridge (at 4,500 feet), a long, tiring, and dry climb. But when you top the ridge, Mount Shasta, Black Butte, and Castle Crags suddenly pop into view. After traversing the ridge for a few miles, the trail suddenly drops and cascades down to the Sacramento River Canyon. Your toes will be jamming into your boots as you head downhill. At the river you might stop to soak your feet before picking up and heading west into Castle Crags State Park.

To continue north on the PCT, see the Castle Crags to Mumbo Basin (PCT) hike in this chapter. If you are walking this trail in reverse, see the McArthur-Burney Falls Memorial State Park to Ash Camp (PCT) hike, in the Lassen and Modoc chapter, to continue south.

**User Groups:** Hikers, dogs, and horses. No mountain bikes. No wheelchair facilities.

**Permits:** Wilderness permits are required only in Castle Crags Wilderness.

**Maps:** For topographic maps, ask the USGS for Shoeinhorse Mountain, Yellowjacket Mountain, and Dunsmuir.

**Directions:** From I-5 in Redding, drive north for 47 miles to the Highway 89/McCloud-Reno exit. Bear right on Highway 89 and drive nine miles to McCloud and Squaw Valley Road. Turn right on Squaw Valley Road, and drive about five miles. (Squaw Valley Road becomes Forest Road 11/Hawkins Creek Road.) Continue on Forest Road 11, keeping right past the McCloud boat ramp, and continue over the McCloud Dam. Turn right (it's still Forest Road 11) and drive down the canyon for one mile. At the turnoff for Ash Camp, bear right and drive a short distance to the parking area.

**Contact:** Shasta-Trinity National Forest, McCloud Ranger District, 2019 Forest Road, P.O.

Box 1620, McCloud, CA 96057, 530/964-2184, fax 530/964-2938, website: www.fs.fed.us/r5/ (click on Forest Offices).

## 59 McCLOUD NATURE TRAIL
**4.5 mi / 2.5 hrs**

**at Nature Conservancy on the McCloud River south of McCloud**

**Map 2.2, page 60**

Have you ever yearned for a place where old trees are left standing, deer and bobcat roam without fear, and a crystal-perfect river flows free in an untouched canyon? The McCloud River Preserve is such a place, and because it's managed by the Nature Conservancy, it will always remain that way. Although the lower McCloud River is best known for its fly-fishing for trout, there's an excellent hiking trail that runs alongside the river, spanning more than two miles from the parking area on downstream. It's an easy yet beautiful walk among woods and water, requiring a bit of boulder hopping in a few spots. It's well worth it to hike out to the end, where the river plunges into a series of deep holes and gorges. Note that an angler's trail also runs upstream from Ah-Di-Na Campground, but while pretty, this is not the feature walk here. The trailhead for this hike is another one-mile drive at road's end, at the Nature Conservancy section of land.

**User Groups:** Hikers only. No dogs, horses, or mountain bikes. No wheelchair facilities.

**Permits:** No permits are required. Parking and access are free.

**Maps:** For a map, ask the U.S. Forest Service for Shasta-Trinity National Forest. For a topographic map, ask the USGS for Lake McCloud.

**Directions:** From I-5 in Redding, drive north for 47 miles to the Highway 89/McCloud-Reno exit. Bear right on Highway 89 and drive nine miles to McCloud at Squaw Valley Road. Turn right on Squaw Valley Road and drive five miles (the road becomes Forest Road 11). At the McCloud boat ramp, bear right and drive on Forest Road 11 to the end of Battle Creek Cove and Forest Road 38N53/Ah-Di-Na Road (a dirt road) on the right. Turn right and drive four miles (past Ah-Di-Na Campground) to the road's end, at Fisher Creek. The Nature Conservancy boundary is .5 mile down the trail.

**Contact:** Shasta-Trinity National Forest, McCloud Ranger District, P.O. Box 1620, 2019 Forest Road, McCloud, CA 96057, 530/964-2184, website: www.fs.fed.us/r5 (click on Forest Offices).

## 60 NEW RIVER TRAILHEAD
### 18.0 mi / 2.0 days
**in the Trinity Alps Wilderness east of Willow Creek**

Map 2.3, page 61

Most backpackers in the Trinity Alps Wilderness like high mountain lakes, but here is a trail that features small streams and is set in the relative vicinity of the Megram burn area of 1999. The highlights are the headwaters of the New River (a tributary to the Trinity River), the history of the area, and Mary Blaine Meadow. Because this is a river trail, not a lake trail, and because of the Megram fire at the headwaters of the New River, it gets very little use.

The trail starts right along the New River and immediately begins by dropping to Barrow Creek. In about a mile, you'll reach the historic and largely eroded site of the Megram Cabin, the first landmark along the trail. After another mile, bear right at the fork in the trail and hike along Slide Creek. After two miles you'll arrive again at a fork, and you should again stay to the right. The trail passes Robbers Roost Mine, Emmons Cabin, and the Old Denny Cabin site, all on the way to Mary Blaine Meadow, a distance of about nine miles from the trailhead. The meadow is set below Mary Blaine Mountain, and to the north, Dees Peak. The whole region is cut with small streams in crevices and canyons. From the air, you can see how the fire burned a huge area but cut a mosaiclike swath, leaving patches of green amid blackened scars.

**User Groups:** Hikers, dogs, and horses. No mountain bikes. No wheelchair facilities.

**Permits:** A wilderness permit is required for hikers planning to camp.

**Maps:** For a map, ask the U.S. Forest Service for Shasta-Trinity National Forest or Trinity Alps Wilderness. For topographic maps, ask the USGS for Jim Jam Ridge, Dees Peak, and Trinity Mountain.

**Directions:** From Weaverville, take Highway 299 west about 45 miles. Turn north on County Road 402 (Denny Road) and drive about 21 miles. Turn left on Forest Road 7N15 and drive four miles north to the trailhead parking area.

**Contact:** Shasta-Trinity National Forest, Weaverville Ranger Station, P.O. Box 1190, 210 Main Street, Weaverville, CA 96093, 530/623-2121, website: www.fs.fed.us/r5 (click on Forest Offices).

## 61 EAST FORK LOOP
### 20.0 mi / 3.0 days
**in the Trinity Alps Wilderness east of Willow Creek**

Map 2.3, page 61

Where else can you hike 20 miles with a chance of not seeing anybody? The East Fork trailhead provides access to one of the more primitive, less-traveled regions of the Trinity Alps Wilderness. It's an area known for streams and forests in the lower reaches and bare limestone ridges in the higher reaches. The trip starts at East Fork trailhead, adjacent to the East Fork New River. It climbs along this watershed and, after two miles, turns before coming to Pony Creek. In the next six miles, which include sections that are quite steep, the trail climbs to Limestone Ridge, near little Rattlesnake Lake. At Limestone Ridge, turn right on New River Divide Trail and head south for six miles, passing Cabin Peak at 6,870 feet and arriving at White Creek Lake. To complete the loop, turn right on the trail at White Creek Lake and start the trip back, descending most of the way. The trail goes past Jakes Upper Camp and Jakes Lower Camp before linking up again with East Fork Trail for the jog back to the parking area. Note that some bypass this trip because of the fear of walking through burned areas from the Megram fire of 1999. The reality is the Megram fire was west of Slide Creek, and that East Fork is not in the fire area.

**User Groups:** Hikers, dogs, and horses. No mountain bikes. No wheelchair facilities.

**Permits:** A wilderness permit is required for hikers planning to camp.

**Maps:** For a map, ask the U.S. Forest Service for Shasta-Trinity National Forest or Trinity Alps Wilderness. For a topographic map, ask the USGS for Jim Jam Ridge.

**Directions:** From Weaverville, turn west on Highway 299 and drive about 32 miles. Turn north on County Road 402 (Denny Road) and drive 22 miles (the last four miles of the road become unpaved Forest Road 7N01) to the trailhead parking area.

**Contact:** Shasta-Trinity National Forest, Weaverville Ranger Station, P.O. Box 1190, 210 Main Street, Weaverville, CA 96093, 530/623-2121, website: www.fs.fed.us/r5 (click on Forest Offices).

## 62 CANYON CREEK LAKES TRAILHEAD

**16.0 mi / 2.0 days**

in the Trinity Alps Wilderness north of Weaverville

Map 2.3, page 61

This is the kind of place where wilderness lovers think they can find religion. But what they find, guaranteed, are tons of other people: Expect about 50 other hikers on weekdays and 200 to 300 on weekends. The destination is Canyon Creek Lakes, set high in a mountain canyon, framed by Sawtooth Mountain to the east and a series of high granite rims to the north. The route in is no mystery; it's a climb of 3,100 feet over the course of eight miles. The trail heads straight upstream along Bear Creek for about .25 mile, crossing Bear Creek before continuing along Canyon Creek. Four miles out, you'll reach the first of four waterfalls. The first is the smallest, then they get progressively taller, and all are gorgeous. After

the last waterfall, walk .5 mile to reach Lower Canyon Creek Lake, seven miles out from the trailhead. From this place, which is now largely above tree line, cross Stonehouse Gulch to reach the first of two lakes. The trail skirts the left side of the first of the Canyon Creek Lakes, then in .5 mile, it arrives at the head of the larger one. They are like jewels set in the bottom of a gray, stark, high mountain canyon, and once you've seen them, you'll have their picture branded permanently in your mind. This has become a special weekend favorite for hikers from Eureka and Redding.

**User Groups:** Hikers, dogs, and horses. No mountain bikes. No wheelchair facilities.

**Permits:** A wilderness permit is required for hikers planning to camp.

**Maps:** For a map, ask the U.S. Forest Service for Shasta-Trinity National Forest or Trinity Alps Wilderness. For a topographic map, ask the USGS for Dedrick.

**Directions:** From Weaverville, drive west on Highway 299 for eight miles to Junction City and Canyon Creek Road. Turn north on Canyon Creek Road and drive 13 miles to the trailhead, at the end of the road (.75 mile past Ripstein Campground).

**Contact:** Shasta-Trinity National Forest, Weaverville Ranger Station, P.O. Box 1190, 210 Main Street, Weaverville, CA 96093, 530/623-2121, website: www.fs.fed.us/r5 (click on Forest Offices).

## 63 NEW RIVER DIVIDE TRAIL

**30.0 mi / 3.0 days**

in the Trinity Alps Wilderness north of Trinity River's Big Bar

Map 2.3, page 61

The New River Divide Trail provides access to the Limestone Ridge of the Trinity Alps, taking a ridgeline route most of the way. This is an area known for having lookouts from mountain rims, the headwaters of many small feeder streams, and few people. The trip starts at the Green Mountain trailhead, at an elevation of 5,052 feet, and in the first three miles, the route skirts the southern flank of Brushy Mountain, past Panther Camp and Stove Camp, and along the eastern flank of Green Mountain. As the trail climbs toward the Limestone Ridge, you'll find yourself perched on a divide, where the streams on each side pour into different watersheds. Eventually the trail rises all the way to Cabin Peak (at 6,870 feet) and beyond to little Rattlesnake Lake, a one-way distance of about 15 miles. Note that the Megram fire of 1999 consumed a huge area of acreage at the headwaters of the New River, off to the northwest from this ridge route.

**User Groups:** Hikers, dogs, and horses. No mountain bikes. No wheelchair facilities.

**Permits:** A wilderness permit is required. Parking and access are free.

**Maps:** For a map, ask the U.S. Forest Service for Shasta-Trinity National Forest or Trinity Alps Wilderness. For a topographic map, ask the USGS for Del Loam.

**Directions:** From Weaverville, drive west on Highway 299 for 28 miles to French Creek Road (Forest Road 5913). Turn north (right) and drive seven miles (the road becomes Forest Road 5N04). Continue straight for four miles to the trailhead, at the Green Mountain parking area.

**Contact:** Shasta-Trinity National Forest, Big Bar Ranger Station, Star Route 1, Box 10, Big Bar, CA 96010, 530/623-6106, website: www.fs.fed.us/r5 (click on Forest Offices).

## 64 BURNT RANCH FALLS
### 1.25 mi / 1.0 hr

**in Shasta-Trinity National Forest on Highway 299 east of Willow Creek**

Map 2.3, page 61

Burnt Ranch Falls isn't a spectacular cascade of water like other, more famous waterfalls, but it is the center of a very pretty, easy-to-reach scene on the Trinity River. It's a relatively small but wide waterfall, comprised of about 10 feet of rock that creates a natural barrier for migrating salmon and steelhead during low-water conditions. Thus the highlight

comes when river flows rise a bit in the fall, so that you can watch the spectacular sight of salmon and steelhead jumping and sailing through the air to get over and past the falls.

The trail is a short but steep .75-mile jaunt down from the Burnt Ranch Campground. When you arrive at the river, walk out a short way on the rocky spot to watch the fish jump. The setting, in an area along Highway 299, has a magnificent natural landscape. From the river, the Trinity Canyon walls look like they ascend into the sky. Unlike most waterfalls, Burnt Ranch Falls is a far less compelling scene at high water. During high, turbid flows, it becomes much more difficult to see fish jumping past the falls.

**User Groups:** Hikers and dogs. No horses or mountain bikes. No wheelchair facilities.

**Permits:** No permits are required.

**Maps:** For a map, ask the U.S. Forest Service for Shasta-Trinity National Forest. For a topographic map, ask the USGS for Ironed Mountain.

**Directions:** From Weaverville, drive west on Highway 299 to Burnt Ranch. From Burnt Ranch, drive .5 mile west on Highway 299 to the trailhead at Burnt Ranch Campground, on the right.

**Contact:** Shasta-Trinity National Forest, Weaverville Ranger Station, P.O. Box 1190, 210 Main Street, Weaverville, CA 96093, 530/623-2121, website: www.fs.fed.us/r5 (click on Forest Offices).

## 65 SOUTH FORK NATIONAL RECREATION TRAIL
### 20.0 mi / 2.0 days

**in Shasta-Trinity National Forest east of Ruth Lake on Highway 36**

Map 2.3, page 61

This remote trail is best known for following along the South Fork Trinity River, heading south toward the Yolla Bolly Wilderness. This is also a great early-season trail, when so many others are still snowbound. And because of that, mountain bikers and equestrians often share the trail on warm spring weekends. There are no lakes anywhere near the trail, and for the most part, the trail just meanders along, with that stream nearby providing a constant point of reference. Even the trailhead, a short drive out of the Hell Gate Campground, is remote and obscure. Immediately, the trail picks up the stream, and in less than an hour, you might even feel as if you've discovered your own private little universe. The temperatures can really smoke out here in the summer, and the stream is your savior. How far might you go? For many, an hour in, an hour out is plenty. Hikers can keep going to St. Jacques Place, an abandoned camp about 10 miles farther one-way, or even another five miles to the trail's end at Double Cabin site, where you can leave a shuttle car and make this a one-way trip. Note that the trail crosses private property several times; stay on the trail, respect property rights, and help keep this trail open.

**User Groups:** Hikers and dogs. No horses or mountain bikes. No wheelchair facilities.

**Permits:** Campfire permits are required for overnight use. Parking and access are free.

**Maps:** For a map, ask the U.S. Forest Service for Shasta-Trinity National Forest. For a topographic map, ask the USGS for Forest Glen.

**Directions:** From Red Bluff, drive west on Highway 36 (very twisty) past Platina to the junction with Highway 3. Continue west on Highway 36 for 10 miles to the Hell Gate Campground, on the left. Turn left on Forest Road 1526 and drive to the trailhead.

**Contact:** Shasta-Trinity National Forest, Hayfork Ranger Station, P.O. Box 159, Hayfork, CA 96041, 530/628-5227 or 530/352-4211, website: www.fs.fed.us/r5 (click on Forest Offices).

## 66 BLACK ROCK LAKE TRAIL
**4.5 mi / 3.0 hrs**

**on the northern boundary of the Yolla Bolly Wilderness west of Red Bluff**

Map 2.3, page 61

The 2.25-mile hike from the Stuart Gap trailhead to Black Rock Lake is one of the best day hikes in the Yolla Bolly Wilderness. One of the highlights comes in mid- to late June, when the wildflower blooms are absolutely beautiful. From the trailhead at the northern tip of the wilderness, at 5,600 feet, hike about a mile on Pettyjohn Trail along the northwestern flank of North Yolla Bolly Mountain (7,863 feet) toward Pettyjohn Basin. Then turn right on Black Rock Lake Trail and tromp another 1.25 miles to the lake, with the trail contouring through open stands of pine and fir and some small meadows. Small Black Rock Lake is set just below Black Rock Mountain (7,755 feet), is ideal for swimming, and is stocked with trout by air every other year. There are many other excellent day hikes from this trailhead: Yolla Bolly Lake (stocked with trout every other year), Black Rock Mountain (great views), North Yolla Bolly Mountain (more sweeping vistas), and Cedar Basin (several creeks). Any of these make for classic days, remote and quiet. The trailhead can also be used as a jump-off spot for a hike straight south on Pettyjohn Trail into the wilderness interior. Note that this trail is usually impassable prior to Memorial Day.

**User Groups:** Hikers, dogs, and horses. No mountain bikes. No wheelchair facilities.

**Permits:** A campfire permit is required for hikers planning to camp.

**Maps:** For a map, ask the U.S. Forest Service for Shasta-Trinity National Forest or Yolla Bolly Wilderness. For a topographic map, ask the USGS for North Yolla Bolly.

**Directions:** From I-5 at Red Bluff, drive west on Highway 36 for 47 miles to Platina. Continue west on Highway 36 for 11 miles to Forest Road 30 (Wildwood–Mad River Road). Turn left (south) and drive nine miles to Forest Road 35. Turn left (east) on Forest Road 35 and drive 10 miles to the intersection of several roads. Take the signed fork for Stuart Gap trailhead and drive 1.8 miles (unpaved) to the trailhead parking area. Hike on Pettyjohn Trail for one mile to reach Black Rock Lake Trail.

**Contact:** Shasta-Trinity National Forest, Yolla

Bolly Ranger Station, HC01 Box 400, 2555 State Highway 36, Platina, CA 96076, 530/352-4211, website: www.fs.fed.us/r5 (click on Forest Offices).

## 67 SWIFT CREEK TRAIL TO GRANITE LAKE
**12.0 mi / 2.0 days**

**in the Trinity Alps Wilderness west of Trinity Center**

Map 2.4, page 62

When hikers scan wilderness maps, they often search for trails that are routed a short distance to a beautiful lake for a first night's camp. That's exactly what you get at Granite Lake, but although the trip in is only about six miles, it's anything but easy. From the trailhead, the hike starts simply enough, tracing the right side of Swift Creek. Don't be fooled. Just beyond the confluence of Swift and Granite Creeks, you must cross the stream to the left and then pick up Granite Lake Trail. This trail runs along the right side of Granite Creek for four miles and includes a very steep section in the final mile that will have you wondering why you ever thought this was going to be such a short, easy trip. (Two notes on the way in: 1. For the most part, the creek is not accessible as a water source, so monitor your canteen level. 2. There is a series of tumbling, churning waterfalls on Swift Creek—no great free falls, but lots of whitewater.) Finally you'll rise to Gibson Meadow and just beyond, Granite Lake, a gorgeous sight below Gibson Peak. For a natural mountain lake, it's a fair size, with good swimming during the day and trout fishing in the evening. This is a popular spot, so plan on company.

**User Groups:** Hikers, dogs, and horses. No mountain bikes. No wheelchair facilities.

**Permits:** A wilderness permit is required for hikers planning to camp.

**Maps:** For a map, ask the U.S. Forest Service for Shasta-Trinity National Forest or Trinity Alps Wilderness. For topographic maps, ask the USGS for Covington Mill and Trinity Center.

**Directions:** From Weaverville, drive north on Highway 3 for 28 miles to Trinity Center and Swift Creek Road. Turn left and drive 6.8 miles to the parking area, at the wilderness border.

**Contact:** Shasta-Trinity National Forest, Weaverville Ranger Station, P.O. Box 1190, 210 Main Street, Weaverville, CA 96093, 530/623-2121, website: www.fs.fed.us/r5 (click on Forest Offices).

## 68 LONG CANYON TRAILHEAD
**16.0 mi / 2.0 days**

**in the Trinity Alps Wilderness northwest of Trinity Lake**

Map 2.4, page 62

Your mission, should you choose to accept it, is the 6.5-mile largely uphill hike to the west side of Gibson Peak, where Deer Lake, Summit Lake, Luella Lake, Diamond Lake, and Siligo Peak can provide days of side-trip destinations. From the trailhead, the trip starts by tracing along the East Fork Stuart Fork, a feeder creek to Trinity Lake. After two miles you'll arrive at a fork in the trail. Take the right fork (the left fork is routed to Bowerman Meadows and little Lake Anna), which climbs farther along the stream and then traces the southern flank of Gibson Peak. At times the trail is steep in this area, but finally you'll pass Gibson Peak, and Siligo Peak will come into view. The trail also intersects a loop trail that circles Siligo Peak and provides access to four high mountain lakes. Summit Lake is the favorite.

**User Groups:** Hikers, dogs, and horses. No mountain bikes. No wheelchair facilities.

**Permits:** A wilderness permit is required for hikers planning to camp.

**Maps:** For a map, ask the U.S. Forest Service for Shasta-Trinity National Forest or Trinity Alps Wilderness. For a topographic map, ask the USGS for Covington Mill.

**Directions:** From Weaverville, drive north on Highway 3 to Covington Mill and Forest Road 115. Turn left and drive for 2.5 miles to the trailhead.

**Contact:** Shasta-Trinity National Forest, Weaverville Ranger Station, P.O. Box 1190,

210 Main Street, Weaverville, CA 96093, 530/623-2121, website: www.fs.fed.us/r5 (click on Forest Offices).

## 69 STUART FORK TRAILHEAD
**28.0 mi / 4.0 days**

**in the Trinity Alps Wilderness northwest of Trinity Lake**

Map 2.4, page 62

Don't say we didn't warn you: This trail doesn't have a difficulty rating of five for nothing. The hike requires an endless climb—very steep at times, particularly as you near the Sawtooth Ridge—spanning nearly 14 miles to Emerald Lake. The first nine miles are easy, and it will have you thinking that this hike is a piece of cake. But surprise: The last five miles from Morris Meadows are the killer. After arriving and resting up for a night, you'll find that ecstasy follows. Emerald Lake is one of three lakes set in line in a canyon below the Sawtooth Ridge; the others are Sapphire and Mirror. The surroundings are stark and prehistoric, and the lakes are gemlike, blue, and clear, with big rainbow trout and water that is perfect for refreshing swims. The trail continues a mile past Emerald Lake to Sapphire Lake, and from there, it's an off-trail scramble, often across big boulders, as you climb another mile to reach Mirror Lake. The entire scene is surreal.

Special note: On the way to Emerald Lake, you might notice a cutoff trail to the right. On your trail map, you'll notice that it crosses the Sawtooth Ridge and leads in to the acclaimed Caribou Lakes Basin. On the map it appears to be a short, easy trip, but in reality, it involves a terrible climb with more than 100 switchbacks.

**User Groups:** Hikers, dogs, and horses. No mountain bikes. No wheelchair facilities.

**Permits:** A wilderness permit is required for hikers planning to camp.

**Maps:** For a map, ask the U.S. Forest Service for Shasta-Trinity National Forest or Trinity Alps Wilderness. For a topographic map, ask the USGS for Covington Mill.

**Directions:** From Weaverville on Highway 299, turn north onto Highway 3 and drive 15 miles to Trinity Lake. Turn left on Trinity Alps Road and drive 2.5 miles to the trailhead at Bridge Camp.

**Contact:** Shasta-Trinity National Forest, Weaverville Ranger Station, P.O. Box 1190, 210 Main Street, Weaverville, CA 96093, 530/623-2121, website: www.fs.fed.us/r5 (click on Forest Offices).

## 70 HIRZ BAY TRAIL
**3.2 mi / 1.75 hrs**

**on the McCloud arm of Shasta Lake north of Redding**

Map 2.4, page 62

Most people discover this trail by accident, usually while camping at Hirz Bay Group Camp. That is because this trail, routed along the west side of the beautiful McCloud arm of Shasta Lake, is a natural hike from that camp. The trail traces the shoreline of the lake, in and out along small coves and creek inlets. Straight across the lake are pretty views of the deep coves at Campbell Creek and Dekkas Creek, of unique limestone outcrops, and of Minnesota Mountain (at 4,293 feet).

**User Groups:** Hikers and leashed dogs. No mountain bikes or horses. No wheelchair facilities.

**Permits:** No permits are required. A parking fee of $6 per vehicle is charged if parking at the Hirz Bay boat launch.

**Maps:** For a map, ask the U.S. Forest Service for Shasta-Trinity National Forest. For a topographic map, ask the USGS for O'Brien.

**Directions:** From I-5 north of Redding, take the Salt Creek/Gilman Road exit. Drive east on Gilman Road/County Road 7H009 for 10 miles to the access road for Hirz Bay boat launch and campground. Turn right and drive to the parking area.

**Contact:** Shasta-Trinity National Forest, Shasta Lake Ranger District, 14225 Holiday Road, Redding, CA 96003, 530/275-1587, website: www.fs.fed.us/r5 (click on Forest Offices); Shasta Lake Visitor Center, 530/275-1589.

## 71 GREENS CREEK BOAT-IN TRAIL

**1.0–12.0 mi / 0.5–7.0 hrs**

**on the McCloud arm of Shasta Lake north of Redding**

Map 2.4, page 62

Let's get a few things straight from the start: 1) almost no one hikes this entire trail, 2) almost no one hikes part of this trail, and 3) almost no one even knows about this trail. Why? Because even with two million people estimated to visit Shasta Lake every year, the only way to access this trail is from an obscure, boat-in campsite at Greens Creek, on the east side of the McCloud arm of the lake. At the back of the cove at Greens Creek, you'll find a small U.S. Forest Service billboard posted with recreation guide sheets, and behind it are the campground and trailhead. There are many fascinating side trips on the steep climb upward toward a saddle between Town Mountain, at 4,325 feet, and Horse Mountain, at 4,025 feet. The trail enters an oak and madrone forest that is interspersed with limestone formations. The latter are worth exploring, and if you spend enough time hiking and investigating, you may find some small caves, a highlight of the trip. Most people are inspired to hike just high enough to get a good clear view of the lake below, but not much farther.

**User Groups:** Hikers and leashed dogs. No horses or mountain bikes. No wheelchair facilities.

**Permits:** No permits are required. A parking fee of $6 per vehicle is charged.

**Maps:** For a map, ask the U.S. Forest Service for Shasta-Trinity National Forest. For a topographic map, ask the USGS for O'Brien.

**Directions:** This trail can be accessed only by boat. Boat ramps are located to the north at Hirz Bay Campground (see the directions in the previous hike for Hirz Bay Trail); to the south, at Lakeview Marina Resort (off Shasta Caverns Road); and at Bailey Cove. The trailhead is at Greens Creek Boat-In Camp, on the east side of the McCloud River arm.

**Contact:** Shasta-Trinity National Forest, Shasta Lake Ranger District, 14225 Holiday Road, Redding, CA 96003, 530/275-1587, website: www.fs.fed.us/r5 (click on Forest Offices); Shasta Lake Visitor Center, 530/275-1589.

## 72 BAILEY COVE LOOP TRAIL

**2.8 mi / 1.5 hrs**

**on the McCloud arm of Shasta Lake north of Redding**

Map 2.4, page 62

This hike is best done when the lake is full in May and June, or you'll be looking out at a lot of red dirt. A favorite part of Shasta Lake is the McCloud arm, where the mountain canyon features limestone formations and the lake's clear, emerald waters. This trail provides a great view of these phenomena, as well as a close-to-the-water loop hike on one of the lake's peninsulas. From the trailhead, start by hiking on the left fork, which travels out along Bailey Cove. As you continue, the loop trail heads in a clockwise direction, first along the McCloud arm of the lake, then back to the parking area along John's Creek Inlet. When you reach the mouth of Bailey Cove, stop and enjoy the view. Directly across the lake are the limestone formations, featuring North Gray Rocks (at 3,114 feet) and topped by Horse Mountain (at 4,025 feet). The famous Shasta Caverns are located just below North Gray Rocks. And hey, watch out for the poison oak; there's plenty off trail.

**User Groups:** Hikers and leashed dogs. No mountain bikes or horses. No wheelchair facilities.

**Permits:** No permits are required. A parking fee of $6 per vehicle is charged.

**Maps:** For a map, ask the U.S. Forest Service for Shasta-Trinity National Forest. For a topographic map, ask the USGS for O'Brien.

**Directions:** From I-5 north of Redding, take the O'Brien Road/Shasta Caverns exit. Turn east on Shasta Caverns Road and drive .1 mile to the sign for Bailey Cove Boat Ramp. Bear right at the sign and drive .5 mile to the day-use parking area.

**Contact:** Shasta-Trinity National Forest, Shasta Lake Ranger District, 14225 Holiday Road, Redding, CA 96003, 530/275-1587, website: www.fs.fed.us/r5 (click on Forest Offices); Shasta Lake Visitor Center, 530/275-1589.

## 73 WATERS GULCH OVERLOOK
### 3.8 mi / 2.0 hrs

at Packers Bay on Shasta Lake north of Redding

Map 2.4, page 62

Shasta Lake is so big—the biggest reservoir in California—that it can be difficult to know where to start in your mission to explore it. A good answer is right here on the Waters Gulch Loop. It connects to the Overlook Trail, a cutoff of .8 mile that climbs atop a small mountain and furnishes a view of the main lake. The trailhead is at Packers Bay, which is easily accessible off I-5. From the trailhead at the parking area, walk down the road and start hiking the trail from the Packer's Bay boat-ramp parking lots, and then finish back at the trailhead parking areas. This provides the best loop hike. Highlights of this trip include a route that extends onto one of the lake's peninsulas; Waters Gulch; a cove on the main Sacramento River arm of the lake; and several lookout points. Although there are many drive-to areas with lake views, you can get a little seclusion here as well.

**User Groups:** Hikers and leashed dogs. No horses or mountain bikes. No wheelchair facilities.

**Permits:** No permits are required. Parking and access are free.

**Maps:** For a map, ask the U.S. Forest Service for Shasta-Trinity National Forest. For a topographic map, ask the USGS for O'Brien.

**Directions:** From I-5 at Redding, drive north to Shasta Lake and take the Packers Bay exit. Drive southwest on Packers Bay Road for one mile to the trailhead, on the right (.25 mile before the boat ramp).

**Contact:** Shasta-Trinity National Forest, Shasta Lake Ranger District, 14225 Holiday Road,

Redding, CA 96003, 530/275-1587, website: www.fs.fed.us/r5 (click on Forest Offices); Shasta Lake Visitor Center, 530/275-1589.

## 74 DAVIS GULCH TRAIL
### 3.3 mi one-way / 3.5 hrs

at Whiskeytown Lake National Recreation Area west of Redding

Map 2.4, page 62

The Davis Gulch Trail is Whiskeytown Lake's best hike—an easy, meandering route along the southwest end of the lake. It starts out at 1,414 feet (at an information billboard along an access road) and winds its way down to the Brandy Creek Picnic Area, at 1,240 feet. It is a moderate descent on a wide, flat footpath surrounded mostly by oak and manzanita. Along the way, there are many good views of Whiskeytown Lake. The trail spans 3.3 miles and dead-ends. With two vehicles, it is possible to make it a one-way hike with a shuttle and then (better yet) hike the whole route downhill.

**User Groups:** Hikers and dogs. No horses or mountain bikes. No wheelchair facilities.

**Permits:** There's a parking fee of $5 per vehicle.

**Maps:** For a detailed trail map, contact Whiskeytown National Recreation Area at the address below. For a topographic map, ask the USGS for Igo.

**Directions:** From I-5 at Redding, turn west on Highway 299 and drive 10 miles to the Whiskeytown Visitors Center. Turn left at the visitors center and drive on J. F. Kennedy Memorial Drive for three miles to the Davis Gulch trailhead, on the right. To reach the Brandy Creek Picnic Area (and end of the trail), continue three more miles on J. F. Kennedy Memorial Drive.

**Contact:** Whiskeytown National Recreation Area, P.O. Box 188, 14412 J. F. Kennedy Memorial Drive, Whiskeytown, CA 96095, 530/246-1225, website: www.nps.gov/whis.

## 75 SYD CABIN RIDGE TRAIL
### 8.0 mi / 2.0 days

on the eastern boundary of the Yolla Bolly
Wilderness west of Red Bluff

Map 2.4, page 62

Not many people hike into the Yolla Bolly Wilderness, set up a camp, then hike back out the next day. But here is a chance to do exactly that. The trailhead is at the Tomhead Saddle, located just west of Tomhead Mountain, at an elevation of 6,757 feet. From here, hike past Tomhead Spring on Syd Cabin Ridge Trail, then drop down into Hawk Camp. Set just below the confluence of three feeder streams, Hawk Camp is an ideal spot to overnight. On the way back, expect a steady climb with no water between Tomhead Spring and Hawk Camp. If you plan on extending your trip for several days into the wilderness, a network of trails intersects just beyond Hawk Camp, but note that a stream crossing is required.

**User Groups:** Hikers, dogs, and horses. No mountain bikes. No wheelchair facilities.

**Permits:** A campfire permit is required for hikers planning to camp.

**Maps:** For a map, ask the U.S. Forest Service for Shasta-Trinity National Forest or Yolla Bolly Wilderness. For a topographic map, ask the USGS for North Yolla Bolly.

**Directions:** From I-5 at Red Bluff, drive west on Highway 36 about 13 miles. Turn left (south) on Cannon Road and go approximately five miles to Pettyjohn Road. Turn right (west) on Pettyjohn Road and drive to Forest Road 27N06. Turn left (south) on Forest Road 27N06 and continue three miles to the parking area at Tomhead Saddle Campground. This is a dirt road all the way in from Highway 36. A high-clearance vehicle is recommended. It can also be slippery when wet.

**Contact:** Shasta-Trinity National Forest, Yolla Bolly Ranger Station, HC01 Box 400, 2555 State Highway 36, Platina, CA 96076, 530/352-4211, website: www.fs.fed.us/r5 (click on Forest Offices).

## Chapter 3

© TOM STIENSTRA

# Lassen and Modoc

# Lassen and Modoc

**M**ount Lassen and its awesome volcanic past seem to cast a shadow everywhere you go in this region. At 10,457 feet, the mountain's domed summit is visible for more than 100 miles in all directions. It blew its top in 1914, with occasional releases after that through 1917. Although now dormant, the volcanic-based landscape dominates Lassen's vast sphere of influence.

The hike to the summit is one of the top day hikes in California—it's challenging enough to provide an aerobic reward, yet easy enough for ambitious children. Lassen Volcanic National Park is easily explored along the main route, the Lassen Park Highway. Along the way, you can pick a few trails for adventure. The best hikes are the Summit Climb (moderate to challenging), which is best done first thing in the morning, and Bumpass Hell (easy and great for kids), to see the sulfur vents and boiling mud pots. Another favorite for classic alpine beauty is Shadow Lake Trail. This area is often off the radarscope of mainstream vacationers, making it one of the few national parks where hikers can enjoy the wilderness in relative solitude.

Unique features of the region include its pumice boulders, volcanic rock, and spring-fed streams from the underground lava tubes. The highlights include the best still-water canoeing and fly-fishing at Fall River, Big Lake, and Ahjumawi State Park. Access to Ahjumawi is by canoe or powerboat only; it's a great boat-in campground with access to a matrix of clear, cold waters with giant trout, as well as trails you can have all to yourself.

Nearby is Burney Falls State Park, along with the Pit River and

Lake Britton, which together make up one of Northern California's best recreation destinations for families. This is also one of the best areas for fly-fishing, especially at Hat Creek, Pit River, Burney Creek, and Manzanita Lake. For more beautiful settings, you can visit Lake Almanor and Eagle Lake, both of which provide lakeside campgrounds and excellent fishing and boating recreation.

And there's more. In remote Modoc County, you'll find Lava Beds National Monument and the South Warner Wilderness. Lava Beds is a stark, pretty, and often lonely place. It's sprinkled with small lakes full of trout, it is home to large-antlered deer that migrate in after the first snow (and after the hunting season has closed), and it features a unique volcanic habitat with huge flows of obsidian (dark, smooth, natural glass formed by the cooling of molten lava) and dacite (gray, craggy volcanic flow). Lava Beds National Monument boasts 445 caves and lava tubes, including the 6,000-foot Catacomb Tunnel. Nearby is pretty Medicine Lake, formed in a caldera, which provides good trout fishing, hiking, and exploring.

This area includes the Hat Creek Rim section of the Pacific Crest Trail, where PCT through-hikers are challenged by 30 miles without a water stop. It is by far the worst section of the 2,650-mile PCT—even worse than stretches of the Mojave Desert. Yet when you hear people talk about having completed this hike, if you listen close, it's difficult to distinguish whether they are complaining or bragging.

It seems no matter where you go, there are so many great hikes in this area that you can always find a match for what you desire.

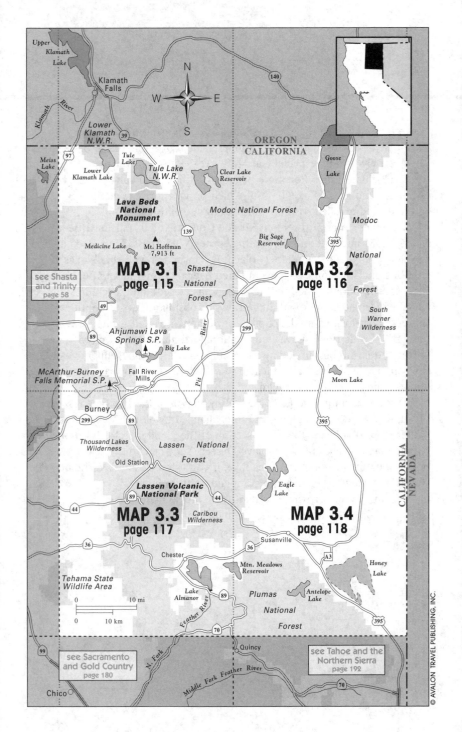

# Map 3.1

**Hikes 1–11**
**Pages 119–124**

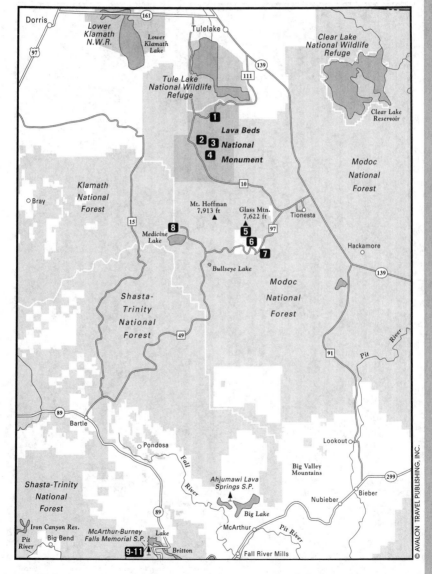

# Map 3.2

**Hikes 12–21**
**Pages 125–129**

© AVALON TRAVEL PUBLISHING, INC.

# Map 3.3

## Hikes 22–54
## Pages 130–149

© AVALON TRAVEL PUBLISHING, INC.

# Map 3.4

## Hike 55
## Page 149

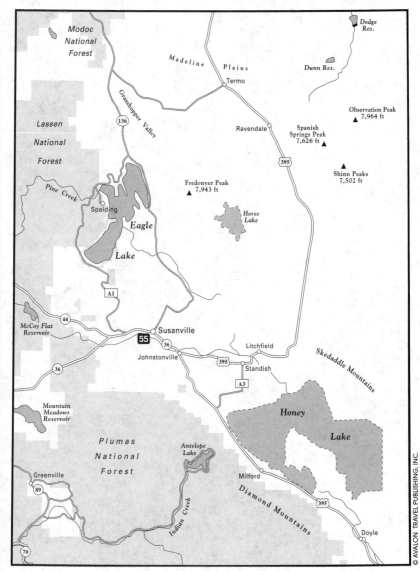

© AVALON TRAVEL PUBLISHING, INC.

# 1 CAPTAIN JACK'S STRONGHOLD

**1.7 mi / 1.5 hrs**

**in Lava Beds National Monument south of Klamath Wildlife Refuge**

Map 3.1, page 115

Captain Jack was a Modoc warrior who fought U.S. troops attempting to relocate Native Americans off their lands and onto a reservation. His hiding place was betrayed by his own troops, and in 1873, Captain Jack was finally captured and hanged, and this site was later named for him. Captain Jack's Stronghold provides a history lesson and an introduction to the Lava Beds National Monument. It's an easy walk on a clear trail amid a volcanic plateau, with a few trenches, dips, and rocks. From this trailhead, there are actually two loop trails available, including a shorter route that is just .5 mile long. The general terrain is level, with a trailhead elevation of 4,047 feet and a high point of 4,080 feet. Note that during the winter, this is an outstanding area to see mule deer. Many of the famous photographs of big bucks in California were taken in this area. The wildlife viewing is best at the onset of winter, after the first inch or two of snow has fallen. In addition, a good nearby side trip is Tule Lake, a favorite wintering area for waterfowl and bald eagles.

**User Groups:** Hikers only. No dogs, horses, or mountain bikes. No wheelchair access.

**Permits:** No permits are required. A park entrance fee of $10, good for seven days, is charged per vehicle.

**Maps:** A free brochure is available by contacting Lava Beds National Monument at the address below. For a topographic map, ask the USGS for Captain Jack's Stronghold.

**Directions:** From I-5 in Weed, take the Highway 97/Klamath Falls exit and drive through Central Weed to Highway 97. Turn north on Highway 97 and drive 54 miles to Highway 161. Turn right (east) on Highway 161 and drive 20 miles to Hill Road. Turn right (south), drive 18 miles to the visitors center, and look for the

main road of the Lava Beds National Monument (it's unnamed). Turn north and drive 13 miles on the main monument road to the Captain Jack's Stronghold access road. Turn right and drive to the trailhead.

**Contact:** Lava Beds National Monument, 1 Indian Well Headquarters, Tulelake, CA 96134, 530/667-2282, website: www.nps.gov/labe.

# 2 WHITNEY BUTTE TRAIL

**6.8 mi / 4.0 hrs**

**in Lava Beds National Monument south of Klamath Wildlife Refuge**

Map 3.1, page 115

The Whitney Butte Trail is one of three wilderness trails in Lava Beds National Monument, and for many, it's the best of the lot. From the trailhead at Merrill Cave, set at 4,880 feet, the trail goes west for 3.4 miles, skirting the northern flank of Whitney Butte (5,004 feet) and ending at the edge of the Callahan Lava Flow, on the park's southwest boundary. Be sure to climb Whitney Butte. This area bears a resemblance to the surface of the moon, and skilled photographers who know how to use sunlight to their advantage can take black-and-white pictures that can fool most people into thinking they are looking at a lunar surface. Most people arrive just to see the Merrill Ice Cave (which is actually a lava tube) at the beginning of the hike. If you plan to explore the cave, bring plenty of flashlight power, a hard hat, and knee pads.

**User Groups:** Hikers and horses. No dogs or mountain bikes. No wheelchair facilities.

**Permits:** No permits are required. A park entrance fee of $10, good for seven days, is charged per vehicle.

**Maps:** A free brochure is available by contacting Lava Beds National Monument at the address below. For a topographic map, ask the USGS for Schonchin Butte.

**Directions:** From I-5 in Weed, take the Highway 97/Klamath Falls exit and drive through Central Weed to Highway 97. Turn north on Highway 97 and drive 54 miles to Highway

161. Turn right (east) on Highway 161 and drive 20 miles to Hill Road. Turn right (south), drive 18 miles to the visitors center, and look for the main road of the Lava Beds National Monument (it's unnamed). Turn north and drive two miles north on the monument main road to the turnoff for Merrill Ice Cave. Turn left and drive .75 mile to parking lot and trailhead, at the end of the road.

**Contact:** Lava Beds National Monument, 1 Indian Well Headquarters, Tulelake, CA 96134, 530/667-2282, website: www.nps.gov/labe.

## 🖫 THOMAS WRIGHT TRAIL
**2.2 mi / 1.0 hr**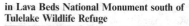

**in Lava Beds National Monument south of Tulelake Wildlife Refuge**

Map 3.1, page 115

After just .25 mile on this trail, hikers reach the awesome Black Crater, a spatter cone. It feels as if you are looking into the bowels of the earth. In time, as you continue on, you might even get the sense that ghosts are shadowing your footsteps. That is because some say this area is haunted by the ghosts of Modoc Indians, who fought troops in several violent battles for custody of the land. Though the Modoc warriors eventually lost that war, some say they actually won in the long run, since their spirits haunt modern-day visitors. At the end of the trail are interpretive signs that explain the Thomas Wright battlefield site. For an excellent side trip from here, continue off trail, clambering up to the Hardin Butte, a 130-foot climb, for a view. The butte sits on the western edge of the huge Schonchin Lava Flow.

**User Groups:** Hikers only. No dogs, horses, or mountain bikes. No wheelchair facilities.

**Permits:** No permits are required. A park entrance fee of $10, good for seven days, is charged per vehicle.

**Maps:** A free brochure is available by contacting Lava Beds National Monument at the address below. For a topographic map, ask the USGS for Captain Jack's Stronghold.

**Directions:** From I-5 in Weed, take the High-

way 97/Klamath Falls exit and drive through Central Weed to Highway 97. Turn north on Highway 97 and drive 54 miles to Highway 161. Turn right (east) on Highway 161 and drive 20 miles to Hill Road. Turn right (south) and drive five miles to the trailhead on the left (the visitors center is another five miles south).

**Contact:** Lava Beds National Monument, 1 Indian Well Headquarters, Tulelake, CA 96134, 530/667-2282, website: www.nps.gov/labe.

## 🛈 SCHONCHIN BUTTE TRAIL
**1.8 mi / 1.0 hr**

**in Lava Beds National Monument south of Tulelake Wildlife Refuge**

Map 3.1, page 115

This is a short hike, but for many, it's a butt-kicker. A portion of it is quite steep—enough to get most folks wheezing like old steam locomotives. The trail climbs 600 feet, from a trailhead elevation of 4,700 feet to the lookout at 5,300 feet. There are benches along the trail in case you need to catch your breath. Schonchin Butte has an old fire lookout, and the views are spectacular, of course, especially of the Schonchin Lava Flow to the northeast. Because of the proximity to the visitors center, as well as the short distance involved, many visitors make the tromp to the top. After completing this trip, always explore some of the caves in the matrix of underground lava tubes. You need a hard hat and flashlight to do it (available for a fee at the visitors center). For extensive caving, always wear knee pads. There are more than 500 caves in a five-mile radius, including 15 with signed entrances on the Cave Loop.

**User Groups:** Hikers only. No dogs, horses, or mountain bikes. No wheelchair facilities.

**Permits:** No permits are required. A park entrance fee of $10, good for seven days, is charged per vehicle.

**Maps:** A free brochure is available by contacting Lava Beds National Monument at the address below. For a topographic map, ask the USGS for Schonchin Butte.

**Directions:** From I-5 in Weed, take the Highway 97/Klamath Falls exit and drive through Central Weed to Highway 97. Turn north on Highway 97 and drive 54 miles to Highway 161. Turn right (east) on Highway 161 and drive 20 miles to Hill Road. Turn right (south), drive 18 miles to the visitors center, and look for the main road of the Lava Beds National Monument (it's unnamed). Turn north and drive 2.3 miles to the turnoff for Schonchin Butte. Turn right at the sign for Schonchin Butte and drive about one mile on a gravel road to the trailhead.

**Contact:** Lava Beds National Monument, 1 Indian Well Headquarters, Tulelake, CA 96134, 530/667-2282, website: www.nps.gov/labe.

## 5 MEDICINE LAKE LOOP
**4.5 mi / 2.5 hrs**

**in Modoc National Forest northeast of Mount Shasta**

Map 3.1, page 115

When you stand on the shore of Medicine Lake, it might be difficult to believe that this was once the center of a volcano. The old caldera is now filled with water and circled by conifers, and the lake is clear and crisp. Set at 6,700 feet, it's a unique and popular destination for camping, boating, and fishing. At some point in their stay, most campers will take a morning or afternoon to walk around the lake. Although there is no specific trail, the route is clear enough. There is a sense of timelessness here. Although its geology is comparable to Crater Lake in Oregon, Medicine Lake is neither as deep nor as blue. But a bonus here is the good shore fishing for large brook trout, often in the 12- to 14-inch class, buoyed by the largest stocks of trout of any lake in the region (30,000 per year). There are also many excellent nearby side trips—including ice caves (along the access road on the way in); a great mountaintop lookout from Little Mount Hoffman, just west of the lake; and nearby little Bullseye and Blanche Lakes.

**User Groups:** Hikers, dogs, horses, and mountain bikes. There are wheelchair facilities at the beach and the boat ramp.

**Permits:** No permits are required. Parking and access are free unless you're camping.

**Maps:** A free brochure on the Medicine Lake Highlands is available by contacting the Doublehead Ranger District at the address below. For a map, ask the U.S. Forest Service for Modoc National Forest. For a topographic map, ask the USGS for Medicine Lake.

**Directions:** From Redding, turn north on I-5 and drive 56 miles to Highway 89/McCloud exit. Bear right on Highway 89 and drive 28 miles east to Bartle. Just past Bartle, turn left (northeast) on Powder Hill Road (Forest Road 49), and drive 31 miles (it becomes Medicine Lake Road) to the campground and lake access road. Turn left and drive .25 mile to the lake.

**Contact:** Modoc National Forest, Doublehead Ranger District, P.O. Box 369, Tulelake, CA 96134, 530/667-2246, website: www.fs.fed.us/r5 (click on Forest Offices).

## 6 GLASS MOUNTAIN
**2.5 mi / 1.5 hrs**

**in Modoc National Forest east of Medicine Lake**

Map 3.1, page 115

Glass Mountain, a glass flow that covers 4,210 acres, is one of the most unusual settings in the Medicine Lake Highlands. It was created when glassy dacite and rhyolitic obsidian flowed from the same volcanic vent without mixing, creating a present-day phenomenon that exhibits no modification from weather, erosion, or vegetation. There are no designated trails on Glass Mountain, so visitors just wander about, inspecting the geologic curiosities as they go. Take care to stay clear of the obsidian, which is quite slippery and can have arrowhead-sharp edges. Don't walk on it, and don't handle it. Be sure to stay on the gray-colored dacite instead.

**User Groups:** Hikers and dogs. The terrain is not suitable for horses or mountain bikes. No wheelchair facilities.

**Permits:** No permits are required. Parking and access are free.

Maps: A free brochure on the Medicine Lake Highlands is available by contacting the Doublehead Ranger District at the address below. For a map, ask the U.S. Forest Service for Modoc National Forest. For a topographic map, ask the USGS for Medicine Lake.

Directions: From Redding, turn north on I-5 and drive 56 miles to the exit for Highway 89/McCloud. Bear right on Highway 89 and drive 28 miles to Bartle. Just past Bartle, turn left (northeast) on Powder Hill Road (Forest Road 49) and drive about 29 miles (it becomes Medicine Lake Road) to County Road 97. Turn right on County Road 97 and drive about six miles to Forest Road 43N99. Turn north on Forest Road 43N99 and drive to the southern border of Glass Mountain.

Contact: Modoc National Forest, Doublehead Ranger District, P.O. Box 369, Tulelake, CA 96134, 530/667-2246, website: www.fs.fed.us/r5 (click on Forest Offices).

## 7 BURNT LAVA FLOW
### 2.5 mi / 1.5 hrs

in Modoc National Forest south of Medicine Lake

Map 3.1, page 115

When you walk across the Burnt Lava Flow, a land of "rocks that float and mountains of glass," it may seem as if you're exploring some prehistoric area that resembles the moon. But get this: The lava formation is only about 200 years old, the youngest flow in the Medicine Lake Highlands. It's located south of Glass Mountain and covers some 8,760 acres, with little islands of forest amid the bare, jet-black lava flow. When we took an aerial survey of the area, the Burnt Lava Flow was one of the most fascinating portions of the entire region. On foot, it's even stranger. There is no trail, so pick any direction—most visitors go from tree island to tree island. There are a few weird spots where the ground can be like quicksand when dry and like wet concrete when wet. Just walk around those spots, staying on the hard, black lava flow.

User Groups: Hikers and dogs. The terrain is not suitable for mountain bikes or horses. No wheelchair facilities.

Permits: No permits are required. Parking and access are free.

Maps: For a map, ask the U.S. Forest Service for Modoc National Forest. For a topographic map, ask the USGS for Porcupine Butte.

Directions: From Redding, drive north on I-5 for 56 miles to Highway 89/McCloud. Bear right on Highway 89 and drive 28 miles to Bartle. Just past Bartle, turn left on Powder Hill Road (Forest Road 49) and drive 24 miles (the road becomes Medicine Lake Road) to Forest Road 42N25. Turn right and drive (the road becomes Forest Road 56) to the Burnt Lava Flow Geologic Area.

Contact: Modoc National Forest, Doublehead Ranger District, P.O. Box 369, Tulelake, CA 96134, 530/667-2246, website: www.fs.fed.us/r5 (click on Forest Offices).

## 8 MEDICINE LAKE LAVA FLOW
### 2.0 mi / 2.0 hrs

in Modoc National Forest north of Medicine Lake

Map 3.1, page 115

The Medicine Lake Lava Flow covers 570 acres but has no designated trails. You can explore in any direction you wish, investigating the ancient, stony-gray dacite, which runs 50 to 150 feet deep. This is part of the Medicine Lake Highlands, located just a mile north of Medicine Lake, where there are "rocks that float and mountains of glass" (a poetic description from Forest Service geologists). Before the first lunar landing, many originally believed this area to resemble the surface of the moon. That is why this area was selected by the Manned Spacecraft Center in 1965 for study by astronauts preparing for the first manned trip to the moon. Most people will just poke around for an hour or two, take a few pictures, and leave, saying they've never seen anything like it.

User Groups: Hikers and dogs. The terrain is

not suitable for mountain bikes or horses. No wheelchair facilities.

**Permits:** No permits are required. Parking and access are free.

**Maps:** A free brochure on the Medicine Lake Highlands is available by contacting the Doublehead Ranger District at the address below. For a map, ask the U.S. Forest Service for Modoc National Forest. For a topographic map, ask the USGS for Medicine Lake.

**Directions:** From Redding, turn north on I-5 and drive 56 miles to the exit for Highway 89/McCloud. Bear right on Highway 89 and drive 28 miles to Bartle. Just past Bartle, turn left (northeast) on Powder Hill Road (Forest Road 49) and drive 31 miles (it becomes Medicine Lake Road) to the Medicine Lake turnoff. Continue ahead (do not turn) for 2.5 miles, and look for the glass flow, on the left side of the road. Park and go for it.

**Contact:** Modoc National Forest, Doublehead Ranger District, P.O. Box 369, Tulelake, CA 96134, 530/667-2246, website: www.fs.fed.us/r5 (click on Forest Offices).

## 9 BURNEY FALLS LOOP TRAIL
### 1.2 mi / 0.5 hr

**in McArthur-Burney Falls Memorial State Park north of Burney**

Map 3.1, page 115

Visitors from across the West are attracted to this state park by the chance to see spectacular Burney Falls. At 129 feet high, the waterfall plunges over a cliff in two pieces, split at the rim by a small bluff, where two trees have managed toeholds (although the river flows over the top of them during high water from the spring snowmelt). Underground lava tubes also transport water to the site; water seems to ooze right from the surrounding moss. From the park entrance station, it's a 100-foot walk to the rocky Falls Overlook, a perfect place for photographs of the waterfall. This spot also marks the start of Burney Falls Loop Trail, an easy 1.2-mile loop around the waterfall and back. There is a 200-foot drop at the

start of the trail, where you skirt the plunge pool of the waterfall. Then the trail is routed downstream along Burney Creek and crosses a wood bridge. Turn right and hike upstream back to the waterfall for more fantastic views. The trail climbs up past the brink of the falls and continues upstream along Burney Creek. It then crosses another bridge and loops back to the Falls Overlook. It's a self-guided nature trail, but rather than having to carry a brochure with you, you can just read the small signs that explain the featured sites. To celebrate the expedition, the next destination is the park's snack bar, where visitors often go for an ice-cream cone. All in all, this is an easy, fun, beautiful, and memorable walk.

**User Groups:** Hikers only. No dogs, horses, or mountain bikes. There is paved wheelchair access at the falls overlook point, at the beginning of the trail.

**Permits:** No permits are required. A state park day-use fee of $6 is charged for each vehicle.

**Maps:** A trail guide is available for a fee at the state park at the address below. For a topographic map, ask the USGS for Burney Falls.

**Directions:** From I-5 at Redding, turn east on Highway 299 and drive 50 miles to Burney. Drive five miles east on Highway 299, turn north on Highway 89, and drive 5.8 miles to the state park entrance, on the left. Park at the main lot, and follow the signs to the trailhead.

**Contact:** McArthur-Burney Falls Memorial State Park, 24898 Highway 89, Burney, CA 96013, 530/335-2777, website: www.parks.ca.gov (click on Find A Park).

## 10 RIM TRAIL
### 3.0 mi / 1.75 hrs

**at Lake Britton in McArthur-Burney Falls Memorial State Park north of Burney**

Map 3.1, page 115

The Rim Trail provides an ideal hike for campers at Burney Falls State Park. The trail starts at the campground and is routed to the rim of Lake Britton, a distance of 1.5 miles. It's an easy walk, and pretty too, heading first through forest, then emerging with a good lookout of the lake. The total elevation gain and loss is less than 250 feet. An easy side trip takes you down to the beach. The lake, set in a gorge, seems to have special qualities, sometimes shimmering with effervescence. The fishing is good, too—especially for crappie, but bass, bluegill, and trout are plentiful as well.

**User Groups:** Hikers only. No dogs, horses, or mountain bikes. No wheelchair facilities.

**Permits:** No permits are required. A state park day-use fee of $6 is charged for each vehicle.

**Maps:** A trail guide is available for a fee at the state park at the address below. For a topographic map, ask the USGS for Burney Falls.

**Directions:** From I-5 at Redding, turn east on Highway 299 and drive 50 miles to Burney. Go five miles east on Highway 299 to Highway 89. Turn north on Highway 89 and drive 5.8 miles to the state park entrance, on the left. The trailhead is at the Falls Overlook.

**Contact:** McArthur-Burney Falls Memorial State Park, 24898 Highway 89, Burney, CA 96013, 530/335-2777, website: www.parks.ca.gov (click on Find A Park).

## 11 McARTHUR-BURNEY FALLS MEMORIAL STATE PARK TO ASH CAMP (PCT)

**52.0 mi one-way / 4.0 days**

**from McArthur-Burney Falls Memorial State Park west into Ash Camp in Shasta-Trinity National Forest**

Map 3.1, page 115

It may be difficult to leave the woods, waters, and aura of Burney Falls, but off you go, facing dry country and some of Northern California's least used portions of the Pacific Crest Trail. Typically the only hikers who complete this section are the ones hiking the entire route from Mexico to Canada; they're virtually forced to endure it, often at great hardship.

From Burney Falls, the PCT heads west, touching the Pit River arm of Lake Britton, and then continues forward into Lassen Volcanic National Park, crossing into Shasta-Trinity Na-

tional Forest and up to Grizzly Peak. Much of this route is across dry, hot, exposed slopes, where the trail has deteriorated in many spots due to the encroachment of brush and the zero trail maintenance by the U.S. Forest Service. Knowing you're smack between the lush beauty of Burney Falls (behind you) and the Mc-Cloud River (ahead of you) can make dealing with the present brush-infested landscape a frustrating encounter. Always fill your canteens with water wherever you find it, and don't hesitate to make a camp if, late in the day, you find even a small flat spot with water nearby. In extremely dry years it's possible to travel this entire stretch without finding any water.

After the hot, beastly climb near Grizzly Peak, most hikers will want to make a lightning-fast descent to the Eden of the McCloud River at Ash Camp. But hold your horses. As long as you've come this far, make the short side trip to Grizzly Peak, and while you're looking at the incredible view of Mount Shasta and the McCloud flats, congratulate yourself for completing such a terrible hike. Considering the PCT is the feature national recreation trail in America, this stretch is an embarrassment to the U.S. Forest Service and an abomination to hikers.

To continue north on the PCT, see the Ash Camp to Castle Crags Wilderness (PCT) hike in the Shasta and Trinity chapter. If you are walking this trail in reverse, see the Highway 44 to McArthur-Burney Falls Memorial State Park (PCT) hike in this chapter to continue south.

**User Groups:** Hikers, dogs (except in the state park boundaries), and horses. No mountain bikes. No wheelchair facilities.

**Permits:** A campfire permit (free) is required. A fee of $6 is charged per vehicle at the state park.

**Maps:** For USGS topographic maps, ask for Burney Falls, Skunk Ridge, and Grizzly Peak.

**Directions:** From I-5 at Redding, turn east on Highway 299 and drive 50 miles to Burney. Continue five miles east on Highway 299 to Highway 89. Turn north on Highway 89 and drive 5.8 miles to the state park entrance. Follow the signs to the trailhead.

**Contact:** McArthur-Burney Falls Memorial State Park, 24898 Highway 89, Burney, CA 96013, 530/335-2777, website: www.parks.ca.gov (click on Find A Park).

## 12 JANES RESERVOIR
**1.0 mi / 0.75 hr**

**in Modoc National Forest north of Alturas**

**Map 3.2, page 116**

A dirt road leads from the southwest corner of Janes Reservoir to Huffman Butte, about a two-mile drive. If your car can't handle the road, you can hike it. The best strategy is to park at the base of the butte and make the easy climb to the top of it. The reward is a nice view of the lake and the surrounding stark terrain.

This is sagebrush country, the high-plateau land of Modoc County. You're likely to see cattle, possibly wild mustangs, and—with the number of wetlands in the area—lots of waterfowl, particularly Canada geese. However, you're unlikely to see people. Even though it's very remote for a drive-to area, a bonus is that there are a number of side trips possible to other lakes. The best are the Alphabet Lakes (Reservoir C has the best trout fishing) and Big Sage Reservoir, on Crowder Flat Road.

**User Groups:** Hikers, dogs, horses, and mountain bikes. No wheelchair facilities.

**Permits:** No permits are required. Parking and access are free.

**Maps:** For a map, ask the U.S. Forest Service for Modoc National Forest. For a topographic map, ask the USGS for South Mountain.

**Directions:** From I-5 at Redding, turn east on Highway 299 and drive about 144 miles (17 miles past Canby). Turn left on Crowder Flat Road and continue approximately 30 miles to the reservoir.

**Contact:** Modoc National Forest, Devil's Garden Ranger District, 800 West 12th Street, Alturas, CA 96101, 530/233-5811, website: www.fs.fed.us/r5 (click on Forest Offices).

## 13 HI GRADE NATIONAL RECREATION TRAIL
**1.1 mi / 0.5 hr**

**in Modoc National Forest east of Goose Lake**

**Map 3.2, page 116**

The Hi Grade National Recreation Trail is actually 5.5 miles long, but only 1.1 miles are specifically designed for hiking. The remainder of this trail is designated for four-wheel-drive use, one of the only national four-wheel-drive trails in the state. Of course, you can still hike all of it, but it's better to use four-wheeling to get out there, then hike the final mile to get way out there. As you go, watch for signs of old, abandoned mining operations, because gold was discovered here. They never found enough to cause any outpouring of gold miners, though, and the result is a sparsely populated county, with this area being abandoned completely. The surrounding habitat is a mix of high desert and timber, although the trees tend to be small.

A good side trip from the nearby Buck Creek Ranger Station is to Fandango Pass, where there are nice views to the east of Surprise Valley and the Nevada Mountains. This is where a group of immigrants arrived, topped the ridge, looked west, saw Goose Lake, and shouted, "Aha! the Pacific Ocean! We have arrived!" So they started dancing the fandango; but, alas, as lore has it, they were massacred by marauding Indians. That's how the mountain pass got its name.

**User Groups:** Hikers, dogs, horses, and mountain bikes. No wheelchair facilities.

**Permits:** No permits are required. Parking and access are free.

**Maps:** For a map, ask the U.S. Forest Service for Modoc National Forest. For topographic maps, ask the USGS for Mount Bidwell and Willow Ranch.

**Directions:** From I-5 at Redding, turn east on Highway 299 and drive 146 miles to Alturas. Turn north on U.S. 395 and drive about 35 miles. Turn right on Forest Road 9 and drive

4.5 miles. At the Buck Creek Ranger Station, turn left on Forest Road 47N72 and drive about six miles to the trailhead. Four-wheel-drive vehicles are required.

**Contact:** Modoc National Forest, Warner Mountain Ranger District, P.O. Box 220, Cedarville, CA 96104, 530/279-6116, website: www.fs.fed.us/r5 (click on Forest Offices).

## 14 PEPPERDINE TRAILHEAD
### 12.0 mi / 2.0 days

on the northern boundary of the South Warner Wilderness east of Alturas

Map 3.2, page 116

The six-mile trip on Summit Trail to Patterson Lake is the most popular hike in the South Warner Wilderness. That still doesn't mean you'll run into other people or horses, because the Warners are a remote, lonely place rarely visited by hikers from the Bay Area, Sacramento, or Los Angeles. Patterson Lake is set in a rock basin at 9,000 feet, just below Warren Peak (9,718 feet), the highest lake in the wilderness and the highlight destination for most visitors. The Pepperdine trailhead (at 6,900 feet) is located just beyond Porter Reservoir, where a primitive campground and a horse corral are available. The hike is a sustained climb, gaining 2,100 feet, passing to the right of Squaw Peak (8,646 feet) and then tiny Cottonwood Lake. From Squaw Peak, looking east, you'll feel as if you're looking across hundreds of miles of a stark, uninhabited landscape.

**User Groups:** Hikers, dogs, and horses. No mountain bikes. No wheelchair facilities.

**Permits:** A campfire permit (free) is required. Parking and access are free.

**Maps:** For a map, ask the U.S. Forest Service for Modoc National Forest or South Warner Wilderness. For a topographic map, ask the USGS for Warren Peak.

**Directions:** From U.S. 395 at the south end of Alturas, turn east on County Road 56 and drive 13 miles to the Modoc National Forest boundary and Parker Creek Road. Turn left and drive six miles on Parker Creek Road, to the sign for Pepperdine Campground. Turn right and drive to the trailhead.

**Contact:** Modoc National Forest, Warner Mountain Ranger District, P.O. Box 220, Cedarville, CA 96104, 530/279-6116, website: www.fs.fed.us/r5 (click on Forest Offices).

## 15 PINE CREEK TRAILHEAD
### 4.0 mi / 3.0 hrs

on the northwestern boundary of the South Warner Wilderness east of Alturas

Map 3.2, page 116

Modoc County is the least populated and least known region of California, with only 10,000 residents sprinkled across a huge area. Yet there are many outstanding adventures available here, including one of the truly greatest short hikes anywhere. The Pine Creek Trail is a magnificent traipse into the beautiful South Warner Wilderness.

The trail starts along the south fork of Pine Creek, about 6,800 feet in elevation, then heads straight east into the wilderness, climbing the lush western slopes. In the course of two miles, the trail rises 1,000 feet to the Pine Creek Basin. Along the trail are several small lakes, the largest being the two set right along the trail as you enter the basin. Above you is a stark, volcanic-faced rim with few trees, where the headwaters of eight small creeks start from springs, pour down the mountain, join, and then flow into several small lakes. To lengthen the hike, go on to Patterson Lake, a gorgeous mountain lake surrounded by towering rock walls; the round-trip is 11 miles.

**User Groups:** Hikers, dogs, and horses. No mountain bikes. No wheelchair facilities.

**Permits:** No permits are required. Parking and access are free.

**Maps:** For a map, ask the U.S. Forest Service for Modoc National Forest or South Warner Wilderness. For a topographic map, ask the USGS for Eagle Peak.

**Directions:** On U.S. 395 at the south end of Alturas, turn east on County Road 56 and drive 13 miles to the Modoc National Forest boundary. Turn south on West Warner Road and go about 10 miles to the sign for the Pine Creek trailhead. Turn left (east) and head 1.75 miles to the parking area. The road is unpaved for the last 12 miles.

**Contact:** Modoc National Forest, Warner Mountain Ranger District, P.O. Box 220, Cedarville, CA 96104, 530/279-6116, website: www.fs.fed.us/r5 (click on Forest Offices).

## 16 SOUP SPRING TRAILHEAD
### 3.0 mi / 2.0 hrs

**on the western boundary of the South Warner Wilderness east of Alturas**

Map 3.2, page 116

Mill Creek is a small, pristine trout stream that brings the lonely Warner Mountains to life. It's a short hike to get here, up a hill and then down, heading into a valley. On this valley floor, you'll find Mill Creek, only a 1.5-mile walk out of the Soup Spring trailhead. Mill Creek is a great spot for a picnic lunch or a high-finesse fishing trip. The trout are extremely sensitive, so anything clumsy—like letting your shadow hit the water or clanking your boots on the shore—will spook them off the bite. The trout are small, dark, and chunky, unlike any seen elsewhere.

Some hikers use Slide Creek Trail as a way of climbing up near the Warner Rim and intersecting with Summit Trail, the feature hike in the South Warner Wilderness. That makes sense, as there is a primitive campground and corral at the trailhead; then it's a four-mile romp uphill to the Summit Trail junction. It includes a 1,000-foot climb on the way, with the trail routed up the Slide Creek Canyon over the last two miles.

**User Groups:** Hikers, dogs, and horses. No mountain bikes. No wheelchair facilities.

**Permits:** No permits are required. Parking and access are free.

**Maps:** For a map, ask the U.S. Forest Service for Modoc National Forest or South Warner Wilderness. For a topographic map, ask the USGS for Eagle Peak.

**Directions:** From Alturas, drive south on U.S. 395 for 18.5 miles to Likely and Jess Valley Road (County Road 64). Turn east on Jess Valley Road and drive nine miles to West Warner Road (Forest Road 5). Turn left on West Warner Road (Forest Road 5) and drive 4.5 miles to Soup Loop Road (Forest Road 40N24). Turn right and drive six miles (a gravel road) to the campground parking lot, on the right.

**Contact:** Modoc National Forest, Warner Mountain Ranger District, P.O. Box 220, Cedarville, CA 96104, 530/279-6116, website: www.fs.fed.us/r5 (click on Forest Offices).

## 17 MILL CREEK FALLS TRAILHEAD
### 0.5 mi / 0.5 hr

**on the southwestern boundary of the South Warner Wilderness east of Alturas**

Map 3.2, page 116

The short, easy walk from the Mill Creek Falls trailhead to Clear Lake leads to one of the prettiest spots in Modoc County. It's .5 mile to Mill Creek Falls and another .5 mile to Clear Lake. At the fork, bear left for the waterfalls, or bear right for the lake. Most hikers will take in both. The trail skirts along the perimeter of a pretty lake set at 6,000 feet. Of the lakes and streams in the Warners, it's Clear Lake that has the largest fish, with brown and rainbow trout ranging to more than 10 pounds. There just aren't many of them. Backpackers can head onward from Clear Lake on Poison Flat Trail, but expect a very steep howler of a climb before intersecting with Mill Creek Trail.

**User Groups:** Hikers, dogs, and horses. Some wheelchair-accessible facilities are available at the nearby campground, but there is no wheelchair access on this trail. No mountain bikes.

**Permits:** No permits are required. Parking and access are free.

**Maps:** For a map, ask the U.S. Forest Service for Modoc National Forest or South Warner Wilderness. For a topographic map, ask the USGS for Eagle Peak.

**Directions:** From Alturas, drive south on U.S. 395 about 18.5 miles to Likely and Jess Valley

Road (County Road 64). Turn east on Jess Valley Road and drive nine miles to a fork. At the fork, bear left on Forest Road 5 and drive 2.5 miles to Forest Road 40N46. Turn right and drive two miles to the trailhead.

**Contact:** Modoc National Forest, Warner Mountain Ranger District, P.O. Box 220, Cedarville, CA 96104, 530/279-6116, website: www.fs.fed.us/r5 (click on Forest Offices).

## 18 EMERSON TRAILHEAD
**7.0 mi / 2.0 days**

on the eastern boundary of the South Warner Wilderness east of Alturas

**Map 3.2, page 116**

Don't be yelpin' about the dreadful climb up to North Emerson Lake, because we're warning you right here, loud and clear, that it qualifies as a first-class butt-kicker. If you choose to go anyway, well, you asked for it. The trail climbs 2,000 feet in 3.5 miles, but much of that is in a hellish .5-mile stretch that'll have you howling for relief. Your reward is little North Emerson Lake at 7,800 feet, a wonderland in a rock bowl with a high sheer back wall.

The Emerson trailhead, the most remote of those providing access to the Warners, is located on the east side of the mountain rim, near stark, dry country. A primitive campground is available at the trailhead. Out of camp, take North Emerson Trail. And while you're at it, get yourself in the right frame of mind to cheerfully accept that you'll be getting your butt kicked. But rest assured that North Emerson Lake is worth every step.

**User Groups:** Hikers, dogs, and horses. No mountain bikes. No wheelchair facilities.

**Permits:** A campfire permit (free) is required. Parking and access are free.

**Maps:** For a map, ask the U.S. Forest Service for Modoc National Forest or South Warner Wilderness. For a topographic map, ask the USGS for Emerson Peak.

**Directions:** From Alturas, turn east on Highway 299 and drive 22 miles to Cedarville. Turn south on County Road 1 and go about 16 miles

to Eagleville. Drive another 1.5 miles south on County Road 1, turn right on Emerson Road, and head three miles to the trailhead. Emerson Road is very steep and can be slippery when wet.

**Contact:** Modoc National Forest, Warner Mountain Ranger District, P.O. Box 220, Cedarville, CA 96104, 530/279-6116, website: www.fs.fed.us/r5 (click on Forest Offices).

## 19 BLUE LAKE LOOP NATIONAL RECREATION TRAIL
**2.0 mi / 1.25 hrs**

at Blue Lake in Modoc National Forest southeast of Alturas

**Map 3.2, page 116**

Blue Lake, shaped like an egg and rimmed with trees, is one of the prettiest lakes you can reach by driving. That makes the easy two-mile loop hike around the lake on Blue Lake Loop National Recreation Trail very special. With a campground at the lake, this trail makes a good side trip for overnight visitors. In addition, a fishing pier and wheelchair-accessible restroom are available. A bonus is that there are some huge trout in this lake—brown trout in the 10-pound class—and they provide quite a treasure hunt amid good numbers of foot-long rainbow trout.

**User Groups:** Hikers and dogs. The fishing pier and restroom are wheelchair accessible. No horses or mountain bikes.

**Permits:** No permits are required. Parking and access are free.

**Maps:** For a map, ask the U.S. Forest Service for Modoc National Forest. For a topographic map, ask the USGS for Jess Valley.

**Directions:** From Alturas, drive south on U.S. 395 about 18.5 miles to Likely. Turn east on Jess Valley Road (County Road 64) and drive nine miles to a fork. When the road forks, bear right on Blue Lake Road (Forest Road 64) and drive seven miles to Forest Road 39N30 (signed for Blue Lake). Turn right and drive to the parking area.

**Contact:** Modoc National Forest, Warner Mountain Ranger District, P.O. Box 220, Cedarville, CA 96104, 530/279-6116, website: www.fs.fed.us/ r5 (click on Forest Offices).

## 20 EAST CREEK LOOP
### 15.0 mi / 2.0 days

**on the southern boundary of the South Warner Wilderness east of Alturas**

Map 3.2, page 116

The East Creek Loop is a favorite loop hike in the Warner Mountains. It can be completed in a weekend, not including driving time, and provides a capsule look at the amazing contrasts of the Warners. The hike includes small, seemingly untouched streams, as well as high, barren mountain rims. The East Creek Trail, elevation 7,100 feet, is routed 5.5 miles north into the wilderness. Just before the junction with Poison Flat Trail, a spring is located on the left side of the trail. Don't miss it—you'll need the water for the upcoming climb. Turn right at the junction with Poison Flat Trail to make the 800-foot climb above tree line, and turn right again on Summit Trail.

The loop is completed by taking Summit Trail back south, crossing high, stark country—most of it more than 8,000 feet in elevation. In the last two miles, the trail drops sharply, descending 1,000 feet on the way to Patterson Campground, which marks the end of the loop trail. Reaching the parking area at the East Creek trailhead requires a .5-mile walk on the forest road.

**User Groups:** Hikers, dogs, and horses. No mountain bikes. No wheelchair facilities.

**Permits:** A campfire permit (free) is required. Parking and access are free.

**Maps:** For a map, ask the U.S. Forest Service for Modoc National Forest or South Warner Wilderness. For a topographic map, ask the USGS for Emerson Peak.

**Directions:** From Alturas, drive south on U.S. 395 about 18.5 miles to Likely and Jess Valley Road (County Road 64). Turn east on Jess Valley Road and drive nine miles to South Warner Road (Forest Road 64). Turn right and drive

southeast (heading toward Patterson Campground) to the access road for East Creek Trail. Turn left and drive a short distance to the parking area.

**Contact:** Modoc National Forest, Warner Mountain Ranger District, P.O. Box 220, Cedarville, CA 96104, 530/279-6116, website: www.fs.fed.us/ r5 (click on Forest Offices).

## 21 SUMMIT LOOP
### 45.0 mi / 4.0 days

**on the southern boundary of the South Warner Wilderness east of Alturas**

Map 3.2, page 116

The Warner Mountains have a mystique about them, a charm cultivated by the thoughts of hikers who dream of an area where the landscape is remote and untouched, and the trails are empty. That is why the Summit Loop is the backpacking trek that most hikers yearn to take someday. However, only rarely do they get around to it. For most, the Warners are just too remote and too far away, and the trip requires too much time. If you are one of the lucky few to get here, you'll find this hike traverses both sides of the Warner ridge, providing an intimate look at a diverse place. The west side of the Warner Mountains is a habitat filled with small pine trees, meadows, and the headwaters of many small streams. The east side, however, is stark and rugged, with great long-distance lookouts to the east across high desert and miles of sagebrush and juniper.

Start the trip at the Patterson Camp trailhead (at 7,200 feet). From there the trail climbs quickly, rising to 8,200 feet in two miles, accessing high, barren country. Great views abound from here as hikers head north. To reach the north end of the wilderness, take the turn at Owl Creek Trail and hike to Linderman Lake—set at the foot of Devils Knob (8,776 feet)—and go beyond past Squaw Peak (8,646 feet). To return, make the hairpin left turn at Summit Trail and walk back on the mostly lush western slopes of the Warners. Highlights on the return loop include Patterson Lake (9,000 feet), the headwaters of Mill Creek and North Fork East Creek, and many beautiful and fragile meadows. The trail ends at the East Creek parking area, a .5-mile walk from the Patterson Camp trailhead. Savor every moment of this trip—it's one of the greatest little-known hikes anywhere in the United States.

**User Groups:** Hikers, dogs, and horses. No mountain bikes. No wheelchair facilities.

**Permits:** A campfire permit (free) is required. Parking and access are free.

**Maps:** For a map, ask the U.S. Forest Service for Modoc National Forest or South Warner Wilderness. For a topographic map, ask the USGS for Emerson Peak.

**Directions:** From Alturas, drive south on U.S. 395 for 18.5 miles to Likely and Jess Valley Road (County Road 64). Turn east on Jess Valley Road and drive nine miles to South Warner Road (Forest Road 64). Turn right and drive 16 miles to Patterson Campground. The trailhead is at the camp.

**Contact:** Modoc National Forest, Warner Mountain Ranger District, P.O. Box 220, Cedarville, CA 96104, 530/279-6116, website: www.fs.fed.us/r5 (click on Forest Offices).

## 22 BURNEY MOUNTAIN SUMMIT
0.25–8.0 mi / 0.25–3.0 hrs

**in Lassen National Forest south of Burney**

Map 3.3, page 117

The view is just so good from the top of Burney Mountain (elevation 7,863 feet) that the trip had to be included in this book. If you drive to the summit, the "hike" consists of just moseying around and gazing off in all directions. There is a fire lookout on top of the mountain. Occasionally, tours are available. Burney Mountain often gets lost in the shadow of its big brothers, Mount Lassen and Mount Shasta, but of the three, the view just might be best from Burney. That's because a view of Lassen or Shasta offers impressive panoramas that just can't be duplicated.

If you show up in the winter or after 6 P.M.,

when the access road is gated, or if you simply want the exercise, it's a four-mile hike up the road to the top of the mountain.

**User Groups:** Hikers, dogs, horses, and mountain bikes. No wheelchair facilities.

**Permits:** No permits are required. Parking and access are free.

**Maps:** For a map, ask the U.S. Forest Service for Lassen National Forest. For topographic maps, ask the USGS for Burney Mountain West and Burney Mountain East.

**Directions:** From I-5 at Redding, turn east on Highway 299 and drive 50 miles to Burney. Drive five more miles east to Highway 89. Turn south (right) on Highway 89 and drive 10.5 miles to Forest Road 26/Forest Road 34N19. Turn right on Forest Road 26 and drive 10 miles to Forest Road 34N23. Turn right and drive seven miles to the mountain summit. Note that the summit access road is blocked by a gate at 6 P.M. each day and throughout winter. You can park at the gate and hike to the top.

**Contact:** Lassen National Forest, Hat Creek Ranger District, 43225 East Highway 299, P.O. Box 220, Falls River Mills, CA 96028, 530/336-5521, website: www.fs.fed.us/r5 (click on Forest Offices).

## 23 CYPRESS TRAILHEAD
6.0 mi / 1.0 day

**on the north boundary of the Thousand Lakes Wilderness north of Lassen Volcanic National Park**

Map 3.3, page 117

You like lakes? You came to the right place. The Cypress trailhead at 5,400 feet is the number-one starting point for the Thousand Lakes Wilderness, with many small lakes sprinkled about in a radius of just two miles. The primary destination is Lake Eiler, a round-trip of six miles, though it is 9.9 miles if you also hike around the lake and return to the trailhead. It is the largest lake in this region, set just below Eiler Butte. But a network of trails here connects to other lakes, so an option is to keep on going for an overnighter. From the south side of Eiler Lake, the trail loops deeper into the wilderness in a clockwise arc. It passes near several other lakes, including Box and Barrett Lakes. Both of these provide good fishing for small trout.

**User Groups:** Hikers, dogs, and horses. No mountain bikes. No wheelchair facilities.

**Permits:** No permits are required. Parking and access are free.

**Maps:** For a map, ask the U.S. Forest Service for Lassen National Forest. A wilderness trail map is available for a fee from the Hat Creek Ranger District. For topographic maps, ask the USGS for Thousand Lakes Valley and Jacks Backbone.

**Directions:** From I-5 at Redding, turn east on Highway 299 and drive 50 miles to Burney. Continue east five more miles to Highway 89. Turn south on Highway 89 and drive 10.5 miles to Forest Road 26 (Forest Road 34N19). Turn west on Forest Road 26 (Forest Road 34N19) and drive 8.5 miles to Forest Road 34N60. Turn left and drive 2.5 miles to the parking area.

**Contact:** Lassen National Forest, Hat Creek Ranger District, 43225 East Highway 299, P.O. Box 220, Falls River Mills, CA 96028, 530/336-5521, website: www.fs.fed.us/r5 (click on Forest Offices).

## 24 TAMARACK TRAILHEAD
**6.0 mi / 3.5 hrs**

**on the east boundary of the Thousand Lakes Wilderness north of Lassen Volcanic National Park**

Map 3.3, page 117

From the Tamarack trailhead, your first destination is Lake Eiler, a three-mile hike. Tamarack is an alternative trailhead to Lake Eiler; the other is the previously listed Cypress trailhead. The difference is that this trailhead gets far less use, because the last 1.5 miles of the access road are very rough; a high-clearance, four-wheel-drive truck is required to make it in. Once in, it's on to Lake Eiler, where a variety of activities is available. Have a picnic,

swim, or fish, and then return; or if you have backpacking gear, head onward to several other wilderness lakes. The trailhead elevation is 5,200 feet, and from this point, the trail is routed into the northwestern interior of the Thousand Lakes Wilderness. After two miles, you'll reach a fork in the trail; turn left (south) to reach Barrett Lake in just another mile of hiking. Note that there is a complex trail network in this area with many junctions, creating a situation in which backpackers can invent their own multiday route. From Barrett Lake, other attractive destinations include Durbin Lake, .5 mile to the south, and Everett and Magee Lakes, another (very challenging) 2.7 miles away.

**User Groups:** Hikers, dogs, and horses. No mountain bikes. No wheelchair facilities.

**Permits:** No permits are required. Parking and access are free.

**Maps:** For a map, ask the U.S. Forest Service for Lassen National Forest. A wilderness trail map is available for a fee from the Hat Creek Ranger District. For topographic maps, ask the USGS for Thousand Lakes Valley and Jacks Backbone.

**Directions:** From I-5 at Redding, turn east on Highway 299 and drive 50 miles to Burney. Continue east on Highway 299 for five more miles to Highway 89. Turn south on Highway 89 and drive about 14 miles to Forest Road 33N25. Turn west on Forest Road 33N25 and drive five miles to Forest Road 33N23Y. Turn right and head to the parking area at the end of the road. The last 1.5 miles are very rough; four-wheel-drive, high-clearance trucks are recommended.

**Contact:** Lassen National Forest, Hat Creek Ranger District, 43225 East Highway 299, P.O. Box 220, Falls River Mills, CA 96028, 530/336-5521, website: www.fs.fed.us/r5 (click on Forest Offices).

## 25 BUNCHGRASS TRAILHEAD
8.0 mi / 2.0 days

on the south boundary of the Thousand Lakes Wilderness north of Lassen Volcanic National Park

**Map 3.3, page 117**

This trailhead is obscure and difficult to reach, and because of that, few visitors choose it as a jump-off spot for their treks. The destination is Durbin Lake, a four-mile hike one-way, making an easy weekend backpack trip. The trailhead elevation is 5,680 feet, and from there, it's a fair walk in, up, and down—and if you're not in shape, you'll know it well before you reach the lake. You'll come to Hall Butte (at 7,187 feet) and then Durbin Lake. A side-trip option is to climb Hall Butte. This is best done by breaking off the trail at three miles in, along the western side of Hall Butte. It is a .5-mile tromp to the top with no trail. This area does get frequent traffic in the fall from deer hunters.

**User Groups:** Hikers, dogs, and horses. No mountain bikes. No wheelchair facilities.

**Permits:** A campfire permit (free) is required. Parking and access are free.

**Maps:** For a map, ask the U.S. Forest Service for Lassen National Forest. A wilderness trail map is available for a fee from the Hat Creek Ranger District. For topographic maps, ask the USGS for Thousand Lakes Valley and Jacks Backbone.

**Directions:** From I-5 at Redding, turn east on Highway 299 and drive 50 miles to Burney. Continue east five more miles to Highway 89. Turn south on Highway 89 and drive 31 miles to Forest Road 16 (Forest Road 33N16). Turn right on Forest Road 16 and drive seven miles to Forest Road 32N45. Turn right on Forest Road 32N45 and drive two miles to Forest Road 32N42Y (which is very steep). Turn left and head to the parking area, at the end of the road.

**Contact:** Lassen National Forest, Hat Creek Ranger District, 43225 East Highway 299, P.O. Box 220, Falls River Mills, CA 96028, 530/336-5521, website: www.fs.fed.us/r5 (click on Forest Offices).

## 26 HIGHWAY 44 TO McARTHUR-BURNEY FALLS MEMORIAL STATE PARK (PCT)
40.0 mi one-way / 3.0 days

from the Highway 44 parking area north to McArthur-Burney Falls Memorial State Park

**Map 3.3, page 117**

The features of this segment of the Pacific Crest Trail are Hat Creek, Baum Lake, Crystal Lake, and spectacular Burney Falls. From the trailhead at Highway 44, the trail passes through the wooded watershed of Hat Creek to a long, shadeless section that will have you counting the drops of water in your canteen. This is the infamous Hat Creek Rim section of the PCT, the roughest section of the entire route from Mexico to Canada, with no water available for 27 miles of trail—a single drop of water will be valued more than a $10,000 bill. After departing from Hat Creek, the PCT heads past Baum and Crystal Lakes, the latter being 27 miles in from the trailhead. You cross Highway 299, and from there, it's an eight-mile romp to Burney Falls State Park and its breathtaking 129-foot waterfall. It is a portrait of serenity along with nearby Lake Britton.

To continue north on the PCT, see the McArthur-Burney Falls Memorial State Park to Ash Camp (PCT) hike in this chapter. If you are walking this trail in reverse, see the Lassen Volcanic National Park to Highway 44 (PCT) hike in this chapter to continue south.

**User Groups:** Hikers, dogs (except in the state park boundaries), and horses. No mountain bikes. No wheelchair facilities.

**Permits:** A campfire permit (free) is required. A state park entrance fee of $6 is charged per vehicle.

**Maps:** For topographic maps, ask the USGS for Cassel, Dana, Old Station, Murken Bench, Hogback Ridge, and Burney Falls.

**Directions:** From I-5 at Redding, turn east on Highway 44 and drive 60 miles to Highway 89/44. Turn left (north) on Highway 89/44 and drive 13 miles to Old Station. Just past Old Station, turn right (east) on Highway 44 and drive .25 mile beyond the Old Station Post Office to Forest Road 32N20. Turn right on Forest Road 32N20. The trail crosses the road about .5 mile from the junction of Highway 44 and Forest Road 32N20. If you have horses and need to park a horse trailer, use Mud Lake trailhead, located three miles from the junction of Highway 89 and Highway 44.

**Contact:** Lassen National Forest, Hat Creek Ranger District, 43225 East Highway 299, P.O. Box 220, Falls River Mills, CA 96028, 530/336-5521, website: www.fs.fed.us/r5 (click on Forest Offices).

## 27 NOBLES EMIGRANT TRAIL
### 2.0–10.0 mi / 1.0 hr–1.0 day

**from the Manzanita Lake Trailhead in Lassen Volcanic National Park east of Red Bluff**

Map 3.3, page 117

The most difficult part of this hike is the first two steps. Why? Because the trailhead is set near the northern park entrance amid a number of small roads and a maintenance area, and despite a trail sign, many visitors can't find it and give up. It's worth the search, because it's a great day hike for campers staying at Manzanita Lake. The trail, with its easy, moderate grade, passes first through an old forest with towering firs, cedars, and Jeffrey pines. About 2.5 miles in, however, you'll arrive at Lassen's strange Dwarf Forest. Not only are you surrounded by stunted trees, but you also get views of Chaos Crags, a jumble of pinkish rocks constituting what's left of an old broken-down volcano. Many visitors hike to this point, then turn around and return to the campground. The trail follows part of a historical route that was originally an east–west portion of California Trail, used by emigrants in the 1850s. There is no water available on the trail, so be sure to have at least one filled canteen per hiker. Because of the moderate slope, this trail is an ideal cross-country ski route in the winter months. Key note: No campfires are allowed in the park.

**User Groups:** Hikers and horses. No dogs or mountain bikes. No wheelchair facilities.

**Permits:** A wilderness permit (free) is required for hikers planning to camp in the backcountry. A park entrance fee of $10, good for seven days, is charged for each vehicle.

**Maps:** Trail maps are available for a fee from park visitors stations and at Lassen Loomis Museum Association. For a map, ask the U.S. Forest Service for Lassen National Forest. For a topographic map, ask the USGS for Manzanita Lake.

**Directions:** From I-5 at Redding, turn east on Highway 44 and drive 46 miles to the junction with Highway 89. Turn south on Highway 89 and drive one mile to the park entrance station. Continue on the main park road (Lassen Park Highway/Highway 89) for .5 mile to the turnoff for Manzanita Lake. The trailhead is across the road from Manzanita Lake, just past the Loomis Museum.

**Contact:** Lassen Volcanic National Park, P.O. Box 100, Mineral, CA 96063, 530/595-4444, website: www.nps.gov/lavo/home.htm; Lassen Loomis Museum Association, P.O. Box 220, Mineral, CA 96063, 530/595-3399, website: www.lassenloomis.info.

## 28 MANZANITA LAKE TRAIL
### 1.6 mi / 1.0 hr

**at the northern entrance to Lassen Volcanic National Park on Highway 44**

Map 3.3, page 117

There's no prettier lake that you can reach by car in Lassen Park than Manzanita Lake. That is why many consider the campground here a perfect destination. With 179 sites, it's the largest camp in the park, and it's easy to reach, located just beyond the entrance station at the western boundary of the park. The trail simply traces the shoreline of this pretty lake at a 5,950-foot elevation and is easily accessible from either the parking area just beyond the entrance station or from the campground. A good side trip is across the road to Reflection Lake, a small and also very pretty lake, which adds about .5 mile to the trip. Note that the fishing at Manzanita Lake is catch-and-release only with the use of artificials—do not use bait, and do pinch down your barbs.

**User Groups:** Hikers only. No dogs, horses, or mountain bikes. No wheelchair facilities.

**Permits:** No permits are required. A $10 park entrance fee, good for seven days, is charged for each vehicle.

**Maps:** Trail maps are available for a fee from park visitors stations and at Lassen Loomis Museum Association. For a map, ask the U.S. Forest Service for Lassen National Forest. For a topographic map, ask the USGS for Manzanita Lake.

**Directions:** From I-5 at Redding, turn east on Highway 44 and drive 46 miles to the junction with Highway 89. Turn south on Highway 89 and drive one mile to the park entrance station. Continue on the main park road (Lassen Park Highway/Highway 89) for .5 mile, to the turnoff for Manzanita Lake Campground. Turn right and drive .5 mile to the day-use parking area.

**Contact:** Lassen Volcanic National Park, P.O. Box 100, Mineral, CA 96063, 530/595-4444, website: www.nps.gov/lavo/home.htm; Lassen Loomis Museum Association, P.O. Box 220, Mineral, CA 96063, 530/595-3399, website: www.lassenloomis.info.

## 29 CINDER CONE TRAIL
**4.0 mi / 3.0 hrs**

**from Butte Lake Trailhead in Lassen Volcanic National Park**

Map 3.3, page 117

Huge chunks of Lassen Volcanic National Park are overlooked by visitors simply because access is not off the park's main roadway (Lassen Park Highway/Highway 89). Butte Lake and Cinder Cone Trail, set in the northeastern corner of the park, are such areas. When you arrive by car, you'll find large, attractive Butte Lake, quite a surprise for newcomers. The trailhead for Nobles Emigrant Trail/Cinder Cone Trail is set at an elevation of 6,100 feet, at the northwest corner of the lake. The trail starts

out easy, heading southwest through forest. But don't be fooled. After 1.5 miles, you'll reach the Cinder Cone cutoff, and there, everything suddenly changes. The last .5 mile rises to the top of the Cinder Cone, a short but very intense climb of 800 feet to the summit, at 6,907 feet. The views are unforgettable, especially south to the Painted Dunes and Fantastic Lava Beds, a classic volcanic landscape.

**User Groups:** Hikers only. No dogs, horses, or mountain bikes. No wheelchair facilities.

**Permits:** No permits are required. A park entrance fee of $10, good for seven days, is charged for each vehicle.

**Maps:** Trail maps are available for a fee from park visitors stations and at Lassen Loomis Museum Association. For a map, ask the U.S. Forest Service for Lassen National Forest. For a topographic map, ask the USGS for Prospect Peak.

**Directions:** From I-5 at Redding, turn east on Highway 44 and drive 60 miles to Highway 89/44. Bear left (north) on Highway 89/44 and drive 13 miles to Old Station. Just past Old Station, turn right (east) on Highway 44 and drive 10 miles to Butte Lake Road (Forest Road 32N21). Turn right (south) on Butte Lake Road (Forest Road 32N21) and drive six miles to Butte Lake. The trailhead is located near the boat ramp.

**Contact:** Lassen Volcanic National Park, P.O. Box 100, Mineral, CA 96063, 530/595-4444, website: www.nps.gov/lavo/home.htm; Lassen Loomis Museum Association, P.O. Box 220, Mineral, CA 96063, 530/595-3399, website: www.lassenloomis.info.

## 30 PROSPECT PEAK TRAIL
**6.6 mi / 4.5 hrs**

**at Butte Lake in Lassen Volcanic National Park**

Map 3.3, page 117

Hiking to the top of most mountains requires a long, grinding climb. Alas, gaining the summit of Prospect Peak is no different. Your reward is some of the best views in Lassen

Volcanic National Park and a trail that gets little use when compared to the others in the park. The trailhead (Nobles Emigrant Trail), at 6,100 feet, is adjacent to Butte Lake. After less than .5 mile, you'll turn right at the junction with Prospect Peak Trail. The trail immediately starts to climb—and get used to it, because there's no respite for several hours. It climbs more than 2,200 feet over the course of just 3.3 miles, finally topping the summit at 8,338 feet. From here, hikers can see most of the prominent peaks in the park—including Lassen Peak, Mount Hoffman, and Crater Butte—along with thousands and thousands of acres of national forest to the north. Since the snowmelt occurs earlier here than in the rest of the park, this trip makes a perfect hike in the early to mid-spring, when the air is still cool. If you wait until summer, you'll find this a dry, forsaken place.

**User Groups:** Hikers only. No dogs, horses, or mountain bikes. No wheelchair facilities.

**Permits:** No permits are required. A park entrance fee of $10, good for seven days, is charged for each vehicle.

**Maps:** Trail maps are available for a fee from park visitors stations and at Lassen Loomis Museum Association. For a map, ask the U.S. Forest Service for Lassen National Forest. For a topographic map, ask the USGS for Prospect Peak.

**Directions:** From I-5 at Redding, turn east on Highway 44 and drive 60 miles to Highway 89/44. Turn left (north) on Highway 89/44 and drive 13 miles to Old Station. Just past Old Station, turn right (east) on Highway 44 and drive 10 miles to Forest Road 32N21. Turn right (south) on Forest Road 32N21 and drive seven miles to Butte Lake and the parking area near the boat ramp. Look for Nobles Emigrant trailhead, and hike .5 mile to Prospect Peak Trail, on the right.

**Contact:** Lassen Volcanic National Park, P.O. Box 100, Mineral, CA 96063, 530/595-4444, website: www.nps.gov/lavo/home.htm; Lassen Loomis Museum Association, P.O. Box 220,

Mineral, CA 96063, 530/595-3399, website: www.lassenloomis.info.

## 31 CONE LAKE TRAILHEAD
### 4.0 mi / 2.5 hrs

on the northern boundary of the
**Caribou Wilderness east of Lassen Volcanic National Park**

Map 3.3, page 117

The prize destination on this excellent day hike is Triangle Lake, a pretty spot set in the northern Caribou Wilderness near Black Butte. The trailhead is located at tiny Cone Lake, just outside the wilderness. From here, you'll walk for nearly a mile before passing the wilderness boundary, which is clearly marked. At that point, you can sense the change in features, as the land becomes wild and untouched—in striking contrast to the start of the hike. Continue one mile south to Triangle Lake, which provides good fishing during the evening for pan-sized trout. If you want more, you can get more. Here the trail forks. The right fork is routed right into Lassen Volcanic National Park, a distance of only 1.5 miles, from which you can access Widow Lake (a free wilderness permit is required from Lassen Volcanic National Park for overnight use). The left fork, on the other hand, leads to Twin Lakes over the course of just .5 mile.

**User Groups:** Hikers, dogs, and horses. No mountain bikes. No wheelchair facilities.

**Permits:** No permits are required for day use. Campfire permits are required for overnight use. Parking and access are free.

**Maps:** A trail map is available for a fee from the Almanor Ranger District. For a map, ask the U.S. Forest Service for Lassen National Forest or Caribou Wilderness. For a topographic map, ask the USGS for Bogard Buttes.

**Directions:** From I-5 at Redding, turn east on Highway 44 and drive 60 miles to Highway 89/44. Bear left (north) on Highway 89/44 and drive 13 miles to Old Station. Just past Old Station, turn right (east) on Highway 44 and drive 30 miles to Bogard Work Station and nearby Forest Road 10. Turn right on Forest Road 10 and drive six miles to Forest Road 32N09. Then turn right on Forest Road 32N09 and drive three miles to the Cone Lake trailhead. Note that the roads are unpaved from Highway 44 to the trailhead.

**Contact:** Lassen National Forest, Almanor Ranger District, P.O. Box 767, Chester, CA 96020, 530/258-2141, website: www.fs.fed.us/r5 (click on Forest Offices).

## 32 CARIBOU LAKE TRAILHEAD
### 12.0 mi / 2.0 days

on the eastern boundary of the
**Caribou Wilderness east of Lassen Volcanic National Park**

Map 3.3, page 117

The Caribou Lake trailhead provides a hiking trip that is a parade past mountain lakes. Rarely are so many wilderness lakes this close to a trailhead. The trip starts at Caribou Lake, heading west, and in no time you pass all kinds of tiny lakes. The first one, Cowboy Lake, is only .25 mile down the trail. In another 15 minutes, you'll come to Jewel Lake. This procession of lakes never seems to stop—Eleanor Lake is next; then after turning left at the fork (two miles in), you pass Black Lake, North and South Divide Lakes, and, farther on, Long Lake. This lake, six miles from the trailhead, should be your destination, since it makes a great two-day backpack adventure. The Caribou Wilderness is quite small, just nine miles from top to bottom, and only five miles across, with elevations ranging from 5,000 to 7,000 feet. This trip will provide a visit to the best of it.

**User Groups:** Hikers, dogs, and horses (a horse corral is available at the trailhead). No mountain bikes. No wheelchair facilities.

**Permits:** A campfire permit (free) is required. Parking and access are free.

**Maps:** A trail map is available for a fee from the Almanor Ranger District. For a map, ask the U.S. Forest Service for Lassen National Forest or Caribou Wilderness. For a topographic map, ask the USGS for Red Cinder.

**Directions:** From I-5 at Red Bluff, turn east on Highway 36 and drive 83 miles to the town of Westwood (east of Lake Almanor) and County Road A21. Turn north on County Road A21 and go 14.1 miles to Silver Lake Road. Turn left on Silver Lake Road and drive five miles to a Y with Forest Road 10. Turn right on Forest Road 10 and drive .25 mile to a fork. Turn left and drive .25 mile to the trailhead.

**Contact:** Lassen National Forest, Almanor Ranger District, 900 East Highway 36, P.O. Box 767, Chester, CA 96020, 530/258-2141, website: www.fs.fed.us/r5 (click on Forest Offices).

## 33 ECHO AND TWIN LAKES
### 8.0 mi / 5.5 hrs

in Lassen Volcanic National Park east of **Red Bluff**

Map 3.3, page 117

You get it all on this hike to Lower Twin Lake: beautiful lakes, forest, meadows, and wildflowers—all a prime testimonial to the beauty of the Lassen Wilderness. It makes an outstanding day hike for campers staying at Summit Lake Campground or an easy overnighter for backpackers. The trailhead elevation is 7,000 feet. The trail starts on the north side of Summit Lake, rising 500 feet in the first mile. If you can endure this climb, the rest of the hike will be a breeze. You'll arrive at Echo Lake in just another mile and at Upper Twin and Lower Twin in the next two miles, dropping 500 feet on your way. It's all very pretty and is a great bonus for Summit Lake campers.

Special note: No campfires are permitted at any time in the wilderness at Lassen Volcanic National Park.

**User Groups:** Hikers and horses. No dogs or mountain bikes. No wheelchair facilities.

**Permits:** No permits are required. A park entrance fee of $10, good for seven days, is charged for each vehicle.

**Maps:** Trail maps are available for a fee at park visitors stations and at Lassen Loomis Museum Association. For a map, ask the U.S. Forest Service for Lassen National Forest.

For a topographic map, ask the USGS for Reading Peak.

**Directions:** From I-5 at Redding, turn east on Highway 44 and drive 46 miles to the junction with Highway 89. Turn south on Highway 89 and drive one mile to the park entrance station. Continue on the main park road (Lassen Park Highway/Highway 89) for 12 miles to the turnoff for Summit Lake North Campground. Turn left and park in the day-use area near the lake. Look for the boardwalk that leads to a trail sign, then turn left and start your hike.

**Contact:** Lassen Volcanic National Park, P.O. Box 100, Mineral, CA 96063, 530/595-4444, website: www.nps.gov/lavo/home.htm; Lassen Loomis Museum Association, P.O. Box 220, Mineral, CA 96063, 530/595-3399, website: www.lassenloomis.info.

## 34 SUMMIT LAKE LOOP
**0.5 mi / 0.5 hr**

**in Lassen Volcanic National Park east of Red Bluff**

Map 3.3, page 117

At 7,000 feet, Summit Lake is a beautiful spot where deer visit almost every summer evening. Nearby campgrounds on both sides of the lake (north and south) are set in conifers, with a pretty meadow just south of the lake along Kings Creek. This hike is a simple walk around Summit Lake, best taken at dusk, when the changing evening colors reflect a variety of tints across the lake surface. Though no lakes in Lassen Volcanic National Park are stocked with trout and the fishing is typically poor, you may still see a rising trout or two. The best place to see wildlife, especially deer, is in the meadow adjacent to Kings Creek, the lake's outlet stream.

**User Groups:** Hikers and horses. No dogs or mountain bikes. No wheelchair facilities.

**Permits:** No permits are required. A park entrance fee of $10, good for seven days, is charged for each vehicle.

**Maps:** Trail maps are available for a fee at park visitors stations and at Lassen Loomis Museum Association. For a map, ask the U.S. Forest Service for Lassen National Forest. For a topographic map, ask the USGS for Reading Peak.

**Directions:** From I-5 at Redding, turn east on Highway 44 and drive 46 miles to the junction with Highway 89. Turn south on Highway 89 and drive one mile to the park entrance station. Continue on the main park road (Lassen Park Highway/Highway 89) for 12 miles to the turnoff for Summit Lake North Campground. Turn left and park in the day-use area near the lake.

**Contact:** Lassen Volcanic National Park, P.O. Box 100, Mineral, CA 96063, 530/595-4444, website: www.nps.gov/lavo/home.htm; Lassen Loomis Museum Association, P.O. Box 220, Mineral, CA 96063, 530/595-3399, website: www.lassenloomis.info.

## 35 LASSEN PEAK TRAIL
**5.0 mi / 4.0 hrs**

**in Lassen Volcanic National Park east of Red Bluff**

Map 3.3, page 117

Lassen Peak crowns the horizon at 10,457 feet. It's a huge volcanic flume with hardened lava flows, craters, outcrops, and extraordinary views in all directions. Exploring Lassen Peak has become a popular hike—perhaps the best introduction to mountain climbing a hiker could desire. The climb to the top is a 2.5-mile zigzag on a hard, flat trail, ascending just over 2,000 feet in the process. The trailhead (at 8,500 feet) is adjacent to a large parking area, set at the base of the summit along the main park road (Lassen Park Highway/Highway 89), which means that many visitors can spontaneously decide to try the climb. But it's best to plan ahead, starting early, at least by 7:30 A.M. Bring a lunch and a canteen or two of water. In the morning, with the air still cool, it's about a two-hour walk to the top, with a 15 percent grade most of the way. The views are superb—Mount Shasta, 100 miles north, appears close enough to reach out and grab. To the east are hundreds of miles of forests and lakes, and to the west, the land drops off to several small volcanic cones and the northern Sacramento Valley. This is an exceptional first climb for youngsters, providing for plenty of encouragement and rest stops.

Special note: Winds are common at Lassen Summit, especially on summer afternoons. Hikers should stash a windbreaker in their day packs. It's always a mistake to suddenly climb the summit without planning the trip. Stay at lower elevations if there's any chance of lightning activity.

**User Groups:** Hikers only. No dogs, horses, or mountain bikes. No wheelchair facilities.

**Permits:** No permits are required. A park entrance fee of $10, good for seven days, is charged for each vehicle.

**Maps:** Trail maps are available for a fee at park visitors stations and at Lassen Loomis Museum Association. For a map, ask the U.S. Forest Service for Lassen National Forest. For a topographic map, ask the USGS for Lassen Peak.

**Directions:** From I-5 at Red Bluff, turn east on Highway 36 and drive 47 miles to the junction with Highway 89. Turn north (left) on Highway 89 and continue 4.5 miles to the park entrance. Continue seven miles on the main park road (Lassen Park Highway/Highway 89) to the parking area and trailhead, on the left.

**Contact:** Lassen Volcanic National Park, P.O. Box 100, Mineral, CA 96063, 530/595-4444, website: www.nps.gov/lavo/home.htm; Lassen Loomis Museum Association, P.O. Box 220, Mineral, CA 96063, 530/595-3399, website: www.lassenloomis.info.

## 36 SHADOW LAKE TRAIL
1.6 mi / 1.0 hr

**in Lassen Volcanic National Park east of Red Bluff**

Map 3.3, page 117

A hike of less than a mile on this trail will take you past little Terrace Lake (7,800 feet) and then shortly after to Shadow Lake (7,600 feet). It's rare to reach such a pretty lake surround-

ed by wildlands in such a short distance. The trail involves a short, steep climb to Terrace Lake, and then a .25-mile junket to skirt the southeast shoreline of Shadow Lake (which is at least three times the size of Terrace Lake). The lakes are set just north of Reading Peak, which reaches 8,701 feet. The trailhead is at 8,000 feet, and because of the altitude, some hikers may experience shortness of breath when making the climb to the lakes. But if you're still feeling good, then by all means continue .75 mile to Cliff Lake (7,250 feet), a beautiful spot that's well worth the extra hour.

**User Groups:** Hikers only. No dogs, horses, or mountain bikes. No wheelchair facilities.

**Permits:** No permits are required. A park entrance fee of $10, good for seven days, is charged for each vehicle.

**Maps:** Trail maps are available for a fee at park visitors stations and at Lassen Loomis Museum Association. For a map, ask the U.S. Forest Service for Lassen National Forest. For a topographic map, ask the USGS for Reading Peak.

**Directions:** From I-5 at Red Bluff, turn east on Highway 36 and drive 47 miles to the junction with Highway 89. Turn north (left) on Highway 89 and continue 4.5 miles to the park entrance. Continue nine miles on the main park road (Lassen Park Highway/Highway 89) to the parking area and trailhead, on the left (two miles past the parking area for Lassen Summit).

**Contact:** Lassen Volcanic National Park, P.O. Box 100, Mineral, CA 96063, 530/595-4444, website: www.nps.gov/lavo/home.htm; Lassen Loomis Museum Association, P.O. Box 220, Mineral, CA 96063, 530/595-3399, website: www.lassenloomis.info.

## 37 BUMPASS HELL TRAIL
3.0 mi / 2.0 hrs

**in Lassen Volcanic National Park east of Red Bluff**

Map 3.3, page 117

Bumpass Hell is like a walk into the land of perdition, complete with steam vents, boiling mud pots, and natural furnaces. It's all set amid volcanic rock and is prehistoric looking and a bit creepy, as if at any moment a dinosaur might come charging around the bend and start eating tourists. The trip to Bumpass Hell is the most popular hike in the park, and it makes sense, because it's not only the park's largest thermal area but also an excellent morning walk. The elevation at the trailhead is 8,200 feet.

The trail starts with a gradual 500-foot climb over the first mile, then descends 250 feet into the thermal area. It sits in a pocket just below Bumpass Mountain (8,753 feet). Exhibits explain the area. There are usually large numbers of tourists at Bumpass Hell, but you can get beyond them by extending your trip to Cold Boiling Lake, another 1.5 miles (one-way), which includes two steep portions of trail.

Special note: For obvious reasons, it's important to stay on the trail or boardwalk near hydrothermal areas.

**User Groups:** Hikers only. No dogs, horses, or mountain bikes. No wheelchair facilities.

**Permits:** No permits are required. A park entrance fee of $10, good for seven days, is charged for each vehicle.

**Maps:** Trail maps are available for a fee from park visitors stations and at Lassen Loomis Museum Association. For a topographic map, ask the USGS for Lassen Peak.

**Directions:** From I-5 at Red Bluff, turn east on Highway 36 and drive 47 miles to Highway 89. Turn north (left) on Highway 89 and drive 4.5 miles to the park entrance. Continue six miles on the main park road (Lassen Park Highway/Highway 89) to the trailhead, on the right.

**Contact:** Lassen Volcanic National Park, P.O. Box 100, Mineral, CA 96063, 530/595-4444, website: www.nps.gov/lavo/home.htm; Lassen Loomis Museum Association, P.O. Box 220, Mineral, CA 96063, 530/595-3399, website: www.lassenloomis.info.

## 38 DRAKE LAKE TRAIL

**4.5 mi / 2.75 hrs**

**at Drakesbad in Lassen Volcanic National Park**

**Map 3.3, page 117**

Drake is a somewhat swampy alpine lake that brightens a largely dry hillside, where deer are often more plentiful than people. Set in a remote forested pocket, it's very secluded and just difficult enough of a climb that many take a pass on the trip. From the trailhead at Drakesbad, at about 5,650 feet, it's about an 800-foot climb over the course of two miles to Drake Lake (6,482 feet). Midway up the grade, the hike becomes steep and stays that way for nearly 45 minutes.

The lake is the payoff—emerald green and circled by firs. After you catch your breath, you may feel like jumping in and cooling off, particularly if it's a hot summer day. Well, we've got news for you: In early summer, the water is still ice cold, and just when you realize that, a battalion of mosquitoes will show up and start feasting on all your bare, sumptuous flesh. Then what? Jump in and freeze your buns? Stand there and get devoured? Heck no, you'll have your clothes back on in record time.

**User Groups:** Hikers only. Horses are allowed on a portion of the trail. No dogs or mountain bikes. No wheelchair facilities.

**Permits:** No permits are required. A park entrance fee of $10, good for seven days, is charged for each vehicle.

**Maps:** Trail maps are available for a fee from park visitors stations and at Lassen Loomis Museum Association. For a topographic map, ask the USGS for Reading Peak.

**Directions:** From I-5 at Red Bluff, turn east on Highway 36 and drive 47 miles to Highway 89. Do not turn. Continue east on Highway 36 toward Lake Almanor and to Chester and Feather River Drive. Turn left on Feather River Drive and drive .75 mile. Bear left for Drakesbad and Warner Valley, and drive six miles to Warner Valley Road. Turn right and drive 11 miles to Warner Valley Campground. Continue for .5

mile to the trailhead, on the left. The last 3.5 miles is unpaved, and there is one steep hill that can be difficult for trailers or RVs.

**Contact:** Lassen Volcanic National Park, P.O. Box 100, Mineral, CA 96063, 530/595-4444, website: www.nps.gov/lavo/home.htm; Lassen Loomis Museum Association, P.O. Box 220, Mineral, CA 96063, 530/595-3399, website: www.lassenloomis.info.

## 39 DEVILS KITCHEN TRAIL
**4.4 mi / 2.5 hrs**
**at Drakesbad in Lassen Volcanic National Park**

Map 3.3, page 117

Drakesbad is the undiscovered Lassen—beautiful, wild, and remote. It gets missed by nearly everybody because access is obscure and circuitous on the way out of Chester en route to the Warner Valley Campground and nearby trailhead. In other words, there's no way to get here when entering from either of the main Lassen park entrances. But those who persevere will find a quiet paradise, along with this easy trip to Devils Kitchen, a unique geologic thermal area. The trail is an easy hike, heading west above Hot Springs Creek. The elevation at the trailhead is 5,650 feet, with a gradual climb of 300 feet. After two miles it ventures into this barren pocket of steaming vents, boiling mud pots, and fumaroles—you'll immediately see why it was tagged Devils Kitchen. It is dangerous to walk off trail in this area.

**User Groups:** Hikers only. Horses are allowed on a portion of the trail. No dogs or mountain bikes. No wheelchair facilities.

**Permits:** No permits are required. A park entrance fee of $10, good for seven days, is charged for each vehicle.

**Maps:** Trail maps are available for a fee from park visitors stations and at Lassen Loomis Museum Association. For a topographic map, ask the USGS for Reading Peak.

**Directions:** From I-5 at Red Bluff, turn east on Highway 36 and drive 47 miles to Highway 89. Do not turn. Continue east on Highway 36 toward Lake Almanor and to Chester and Feather River Drive. Turn left on Feather River Drive and drive .75 mile. Bear left for Drakesbad and Warner Valley, and drive six miles to Warner Valley Road. Turn right and drive 11 miles to Warner Valley Campground. Continue .5 mile to the trailhead, on the left. The last 3.5 miles is unpaved, and there is one steep hill that can be difficult for trailers or RVs.

**Contact:** Lassen Volcanic National Park, P.O. Box 100, Mineral, CA 96063, 530/595-4444, website: www.nps.gov/lavo/home.htm; Lassen Loomis Museum Association, P.O. Box 220, Mineral, CA 96063, 530/595-3399, website: www.lassenloomis.info.

## 40 LASSEN VOLCANIC NATIONAL PARK TO HIGHWAY 44 (PCT)
**32.0 mi one-way / 3.0 days**
**from Warner Valley Campground in Lassen Volcanic National Park to Highway 44**

Map 3.3, page 117

Every step is a pleasure in Lassen Volcanic National Park when starting from the wooded Warner Valley (at 5,680 feet), at Hot Springs Creek, and then heading north into the park's most remote terrain. The trail is routed across Grassy Swale, past Swan Lake, and on to Lower Twin Lake (seven miles in), a pretty body of water circled by conifers.

From here, the trail heads north through a strange but compelling volcanic area, skirting the western flank of Fairfield Peak (7,272 feet) and then going onward. It turns west past Soap Lake and Badger Flat, and continues out past the park's boundary. As you hike toward Highway 44, you'll be lateraling Badger Mountain (6,973 feet) to your right, with the Hat Creek drainage off to your immediate left. In this latter stretch of trail, you'll cross no major lakes or streams (plan your water well). You'll just forge on through the national forest, which is mostly second-growth, crossing a few roads along the way. In the spring, wildflowers are exceptional on the Hat Creek Rim. Several primitive

U.S. Forest Service campgrounds are located on the trail about 10 miles north of the border of Lassen Volcanic National Park. Note that no campfires are permitted at any time in the wilderness at Lassen Volcanic National Park.

To continue north on the PCT, see the Highway 44 to McArthur-Burney Falls Memorial State Park (PCT) hike in this chapter. If you are walking this trail in reverse, see the Domingo Springs to Lassen Volcanic National Park (PCT) hike in this chapter to continue south.

**User Groups:** Hikers and horses. No dogs or mountain bikes are allowed in the Lassen Volcanic National Park section of the hike. No wheelchair facilities.

**Permits:** A wilderness permit (free) is required for hikers planning to camp in the Lassen Volcanic National Park backcountry and for equestrians. You may not camp with horses in the national park's backcountry, but a horse corral is available by reservation for overnighters at Summit Lake and Juniper Lake, and a small corral is located near the park's northern boundary for exclusive use by those on the Pacific Crest Trail. A park entrance fee of $10, good for seven days, is charged for each vehicle.

**Maps:** For topographic maps, ask the USGS for Reading Peak, West Prospect Peak, and Old Station.

**Directions:** From I-5 at Red Bluff, turn east on Highway 36 and drive 70 miles to the town of Chester and Feather River Drive. Turn left (north) and drive .75 mile to Warner Valley Road (signed to Juniper Lake and Drakesbad). Turn left and drive six miles to Warner Valley Road. Turn right and drive 11 miles (on an improved dirt road) to the Warner Valley Campground and trailhead, on the right.

**Contact:** Lassen Volcanic National Park, P.O. Box 100, Mineral, CA 96063, 530/595-4444, website: www.nps.gov/lavo/home.htm; Lassen National Forest, Hat Creek Ranger District, 43225 East Highway 299, Falls River Mills, CA 96028, 530/336-5521, website: www.fs.fed.us/r5 (click on Forest Offices).

## 41 JUNIPER LAKE LOOP
**7.5 mi / 4.0 hrs**

**in Lassen Volcanic National Park north of Lake Almanor**

Map 3.3, page 117

The Juniper Lake Loop explores Lassen Volcanic National Park's least known yet most beautiful backcountry, with many lakes, many lookouts, and—because there are pretty trail camps along the route—the chance to turn the trip into an overnighter. The adventure starts at the trailhead adjacent to the Juniper Lake Ranger Station, which requires a long bumpy ride out of Chester just to reach it. If you arrive late, a campground is available at the lake, at an elevation of 6,792 feet. At the north end of Juniper Lake, the trail heads straight north, and though it has plenty of ups and downs, along with a fairly level stretch through Cameron Meadow, it's mostly down, descending 800 feet to Snag Lake, at an elevation of 6,076 feet. The best advice is to turn south at Snag Lake and take the trail along Grassy Creek to Horseshoe Lake. This section is the prettiest of the hike. If you want to extend your trip, options from Snag Lake include hiking out to into the backcountry to Rainbow Lake, a mile later to Lower Twin Lake (6,537 feet), and another mile farther to Swan Lake (6,628 feet). Any of these can make for a good trail camp. On the second day, you'll loop back, skirt the south flank of Crater Butte (7,267 feet), head past Horseshoe Lake, and then continue on to the starting point. Alas, this trip is not flawless. The fishing is poor, mosquitoes are rampant in the early summer, and nights are very cold in the fall.

Note: From the north end of Juniper Lake, the 400-foot climb to Inspiration Point provides a lookout for the park's backcountry, but trees partially block the view. No campfires are permitted at Lassen Volcanic National Park.

**User Groups:** Hikers and horses. No dogs or mountain bikes. No wheelchair facilities.

**Permits:** For overnight use, a wilderness permit (free) is required. A park entrance fee of $10, good for seven days, is charged for each vehicle.

**Maps:** Trail maps are available for a fee from park visitors stations and at Lassen Loomis Museum Association. For a topographic map, ask the USGS for Mount Harkness.

**Directions:** From I-5 at Red Bluff, turn east on Highway 36 and drive 47 miles to Highway 89. Do not turn. Continue east on Highway 36 toward Lake Almanor and to Chester and Feather River Drive. Turn left on Feather River Drive and drive .75 mile to a Y. Bear right at the Y to Juniper Lake Road and drive 13 miles to the Snag Lake trailhead, near the ranger station. The access road is rough. Trailers and RVs are not recommended.

**Contact:** Lassen Volcanic National Park, P.O. Box 100, Mineral, CA 96063, 530/595-4444, website: www.nps.gov/lavo/home.htm; Lassen Loomis Museum Association, P.O. Box 220, Mineral, CA 96063, 530/595-3399, website: www.lassenloomis.info.

## 42 HAY MEADOW TRAIL
### 6.0 mi / 2.0 days

**on the southern boundary of the Caribou Wilderness north of Lake Almanor**

Map 3.3, page 117

Hidden between South Caribou Peak and Black Cinder Rock is a little alpine pocket where dozens of small lakes are sprinkled about the southern Caribou Wilderness. It's a slice of paradise that some hikers call the Hidden Lakes. The trail out of Hay Meadow is a loop that crosses right through these lakes—Beauty, Long, Posey, and Evelyn—and the area's larger and most divine settings. Although the trip can be made in a day, you likely won't feel like leaving, and planning an easy overnight backpacking trip is recommended. Another bonus of an overnight trip is that you can take the side trip up to Hidden Lakes, a series of several small but pretty waters, set just below South Caribou Mountain.

After arriving at the trailhead at Hay Meadow, the trip starts easily enough, first crossing Hay Meadow. In another mile, you'll reach Beauty Lake, the first of four major lakes on this loop hike. They are all good for swimming, although a bit cold, and Beauty and Posey have the best trout fishing. Note that although the Caribou Wilderness abuts Lassen Volcanic National Park, it's often overlooked in the big park's shadow. That's to your benefit, as long as you know about this trail.

**User Groups:** Hikers, dogs, and horses (a horse corral is available at the trailhead). No mountain bikes. No wheelchair facilities.

**Permits:** A campfire permit (free) is required. Parking and access are free.

**Maps:** A trail map is available for a fee from the Almanor Ranger District. For a map, ask the U.S. Forest Service for Lassen National Forest or Caribou Wilderness. For a topographic map, ask the USGS for Red Cinder.

**Directions:** From Red Bluff, turn east on Highway 36 and drive to Chester. Continue east on Highway 36 for five miles to Forest Road 10. Turn north on Forest Road 10 and drive 9.5 miles to Forest Road 30N25. Turn left on Forest Road 30N25 and drive to the trailhead.

**Contact:** Lassen National Forest, Almanor Ranger District, P.O. Box 767, Chester, CA 96020, 530/258-2141, website: www.fs.fed.us/r5 (click on Forest Offices).

## 43 SPENCER MEADOW TRAIL
### 10.0 mi / 1.0 day

**in Lassen National Forest just south of Lassen Volcanic National Park**

Map 3.3, page 117

Spencer Meadow is a pretty mountain meadow on the southern flank of Mount Conrad. Here explorers can discover an effervescent spring pouring forth, one source of Mill Creek and the creation of the headwaters of a Sacramento River tributary. Hiking access is easy; the trailhead is located at a parking area just off Highway 36. From here, hike straight north toward Lassen on Spencer Meadow Trail. Over the course of five miles, the trail passes a small spring (about halfway in—look for the faint spur trail on the left), then tiny Patricia Lake (on the right, hidden), and finally Spencer Meadow and Mill Creek Spring. Note that fishing at Mill Creek is restricted to catch-and-release and the use of artificials with single barbless hooks.

Special note: There is a trailhead closer to Spencer Meadow on Forest Road 29N40, but reaching it involves a long, rough drive.

**User Groups:** Hikers, dogs, horses, and mountain bikes. No wheelchair facilities.

**Permits:** No permits are required for day use. Campfire permits are required for overnight use. Parking and access are free.

**Maps:** A trail map is available for a fee from the Almanor Ranger District. For a map, ask the U.S. Forest Service for Lassen National Forest. For a topographic map, ask the USGS for Childs Meadows.

**Directions:** From I-5 at Red Bluff, drive east on Highway 36 for 43 miles to Mineral. Continue east on Highway 36 for about seven miles to the trailhead parking area, on the left.

**Contact:** Lassen National Forest, Almanor Ranger District, P.O. Box 767, Chester, CA 96020, 530/258-2141, website: www.fs.fed.us/r5 (click on Forest Offices).

## 44 DOMINGO SPRINGS TO LASSEN VOLCANIC NATIONAL PARK (PCT)

11.0 mi one-way / 1.0 day

**at the Domingo Springs Trailhead in Lassen National Forest west of Lake Almanor**

Map 3.3, page 117

With each passing step, the scenery gets better and better. Hikers leave the dry, hot forest country and enter Lassen Volcanic National Park at Warner Valley. All the suffering seems over, and only paradise awaits. From Domingo Springs, the Pacific Crest Trail runs straight north through Lassen National Forest. The Little North Fork of the North Fork Feather River is located .25 mile to the west and is a good side trip, both for swimming and for fishing for large brown trout. As you enter Lassen

Volcanic National Park, you'll pass Little Willow Lake, and two miles later, you'll arrive at Boiling Springs Lake and the Warner Valley Campground. This is a good layover spot, and a side trip to Devils Kitchen is recommended.

To continue north on the PCT, see the Lassen Volcanic National Park to Highway 44 (PCT) hike in this chapter. If you are walking this trail in reverse, see the Feather River to Humboldt Summit (PCT) hike in this chapter to continue south.

**User Groups:** Hikers, dogs, and horses. No mountain bikes. No wheelchair facilities.

**Permits:** A campfire permit (free) is required. Parking and access are free.

**Maps:** For a map, ask the U.S. Forest Service for Lassen National Forest. For a topographic map, ask the USGS for Stover Mountain.

**Directions:** From Chico, drive north on Highway 32 to the junction with Highway 89/36. Turn right (east) and take Highway 36 toward Chester. In Chester, turn north on Warner Valley Road (County Road 312) and drive about six miles. Turn left on Old Red Bluff Road (County Road 311) and go three miles to the parking area at Domingo Springs.

**Contact:** Lassen National Forest, Almanor Ranger District, P.O. Box 767, Chester, CA 96020, 530/258-2141, website: www.fs.fed.us/r5 (click on Forest Offices).

## 45 McCLURE TRAIL

9.0 mi / 1.0 day

**in the Tehama Wildlife Area east of Red Bluff**

Map 3.3, page 117

At first glance, the Tehama Wildlife Area might appear to be nothing more than rolling oak woodlands. But this is a habitat managed expressly for wildlife, and it includes a beautiful stream, abundant vegetation, and plenty of animals. The area is huge, covering 44,862 acres, and is popular only in the fall, during hunting season for deer and wild pigs. This trail accesses the best of the wildlife area, heading down a steep canyon to Antelope Creek, buffered by riparian vegetation.

Deer are rampant in late fall (typically migrating in after the hunting season is over), and there are also lots of squirrels, hawks, and, alas, rattlesnakes. Wild pigs roam the canyons but are only occasionally seen from trails. In late winter and spring, the canyons and hillsides come alive in green, and all wildlife seems to prosper. They'd better when they have the chance, because the heat here can seem unbearable in summer. The stream is very pretty, and fishing is catch-and-release only with the use of artificials. You can count on lots of deer hunters in October and lots of turkey hunters from late March to May 1.

**User Groups:** Hikers and dogs. Mountain bikes and horses permitted but not recommended because of terrain. No wheelchair facilities.

**Permits:** A campfire permit (free) is required for overnight use. Parking and access are free.

**Maps:** For a free map, contact the Tehama Wildlife Area at the address below. For a map, ask the U.S. Forest Service for Lassen National Forest. For a topographic map, ask the USGS for Dewitt Peak.

**Directions:** From I-5 at Red Bluff, turn east on Highway 36 and drive 20 miles to the town of Paynes Creek. Turn south on Plum Creek Road and go to Ishi Conservation Camp. Drive about 2.5 miles south to High Trestle Road and follow it to Hogsback Road. Park across from the intersection of High Trestle and Hogsback Roads, and walk about .25 mile on the dirt road to the trailhead. Access to the Tehama Wildlife Area is closed to the public from February to the first Saturday in April. Access is also restricted for a short period during deer season in late September. There are no closures on U.S. Forest Service trails.

**Contact:** Lassen National Forest, Almanor Ranger District, 900 East Highway 36, P.O. Box 767, Chester, CA 96020, 530/258-2141, website: www.fs.fed.us/r5 (click on Forest Offices); Department of Fish and Game, Tehama Wildlife Area, P.O. Box 188, Paynes Creek, CA 96075, 530/597-2201; Department of Fish and Game, Region 1 Headquarters, 530/225-2300.

## 46 TABLE MOUNTAIN TRAIL
### 3.2 mi / 2.5 hrs

**in the Ishi Wilderness east of Red Bluff**

Map 3.3, page 117

This trail may be short, but it's anything but sweet. Except, that is, from the top of Table Mountain, at 2,380 feet, where you're supplied with a sweeping view of the Sacramento Valley and the surrounding land of Ishi. This is where Ishi, the last survivor of the Yahi Yana tribe, escaped from a band of white settlers who exterminated the rest of the Yahis. The Indians had lived here for 3,000 years before being killed off, another stellar moment in the history of the western frontier.

The trail starts from the northwest corner of the wilderness at the Table Mountain trailhead, and then goes 1.6 miles to the summit. It's very steep and challenging, and most hikers will be wheezing like worn-out donkeys before making the top. Because of the hot summers, it's absolutely critical either to start the trip very early in the morning or to time it so that it's done during cool weather. Bring plenty of water for your built-in radiator.

Special note: A wilderness trail map is strongly advised for those hiking in the Ishi Wilderness.

**User Groups:** Hikers, dogs, and horses. No mountain bikes. No wheelchair facilities.

**Permits:** A campfire permit is required for hikers planning to camp. Parking and access are free.

**Maps:** A trail map is available for a fee from Almanor Ranger District. For a map, ask the U.S. Forest Service for Lassen National Forest or Ishi Wilderness. For topographic maps, ask the USGS for Panther Spring and Butte Meadows.

**Directions:** From I-5 at Red Bluff, turn east on Highway 36, drive to the town of Paynes Creek, and continue to Little Giant Mill Road. Turn south on Little Giant Mill Road (Road 202) and drive about seven miles until you reach Ponderosa Way. Turn south at Ponderosa Way and drive about 10 miles to Forest Road

28N57. Turn right (west) on Forest Road 28N57 and follow Peligreen Jeep Trail for six miles to the trailhead. The last five miles of road are suitable only for four-wheel-drive vehicles.

**Contact:** Lassen National Forest, Almanor Ranger District, P.O. Box 767, Chester, CA 96020, 530/258-2141, website: www.fs.fed.us/r5 (click on Forest Offices).

## 47 RANCHERIA TRAIL
### 4.0 mi / 2.75 hrs

**in the Ishi Wilderness east of Red Bluff**

Map 3.3, page 117

On a map, the Rancheria trailhead looks like the closest and easiest trailhead to reach into the Ishi Wilderness from Red Bluff. And the trail also appears short as well. But when you go there, a completely different picture comes into focus. First off, the trailhead access road is quite rough, impassable for most cars, and that's just a prelude to what lies ahead. The trail starts by following an old jeep road, then leaves the road at a fence line off to the right. If it's hot, which is typical here most of the year, you'll already be reaching for your canteen. The trail then drops like a cannonball for 1,000 feet into the Mill Creek Canyon, a surprising and awesome habitat with some of the prettiest areas of the Ishi. The fishing is often good; rules mandate catch-and-release with the use of artificials. Too bad you can't enjoy it more, because shadowing your every move is the knowledge that you have to climb back out of that canyon—most likely during the hottest part of the day. By the time you reach the car, your butt will be thoroughly kicked.

Special note: A trail map is strongly advised for those hiking in the Ishi Wilderness.

**User Groups:** Hikers, dogs, and horses. No mountain bikes. No wheelchair facilities.

**Permits:** A campfire permit (free) is required for overnight use. Parking and access are free.

**Maps:** A trail map is available for a fee from Almanor Ranger District. For a map, ask the U.S. Forest Service for Lassen National Forest or

Ishi Wilderness. For topographic maps, ask the USGS for Panther Spring and Butte Meadows.

**Directions:** From I-5 at Red Bluff, turn east onto Highway 36, drive to the town of Paynes Creek, and continue to Little Giant Mill Road. Turn south on Little Giant Mill Road (Road 202) and drive seven miles to Ponderosa Way. Turn south and drive about 10 miles to Forest Road 28N57. Turn right (west) and follow the Peligreen Jeep Trail for two miles to the Rancheria trailhead. The last two miles of road are suitable only for four-wheel-drive vehicles.

**Contact:** Lassen National Forest, Almanor Ranger District, P.O. Box 767, Chester, CA 96020, 530/258-2141, website: www.fs.fed.us/r5 (click on Forest Offices).

## 48 LOWER MILL CREEK
### 13.0 mi / 1.0 day

**in the Ishi Wilderness east of Red Bluff**

Map 3.3, page 117

If you have time for only one trail in the Ishi Wilderness, Mill Creek Trail is the one to pick. That goes whether you want to invest just an hour or a full day, because any length of trip can be a joy here. The trail simply parallels the creek for 6.5 miles to its headwaters, at Papes Place, with magnificent scenery and many good fishing and swimming holes along the way. This is a dramatic canyon, and as you stand along the stream, the walls can seem to ascend into heaven. It's a land shaped by thousands of years of wind and water.

Directly across from the trailhead, on Ponderosa Way, is another trailhead, this one for a route that follows Upper Mill Creek into Lassen National Forest. Although not as spectacular as Lower Mill Creek, it provides a good option for hiking, fishing, and swimming. Note that fishing is restricted to catch-and-release and the use of artificials.

Special note: A trail map is strongly advised for those hiking in the Ishi Wilderness.

**User Groups:** Hikers, dogs, and horses. No mountain bikes. No wheelchair facilities.

**Permits:** A campfire permit (free) is required for overnight use. Parking and access are free.
**Maps:** A trail map is available for a fee from Almanor Ranger District. For a map, ask the U.S. Forest Service for Lassen National Forest or Ishi Wilderness. For topographic maps, ask the USGS for Panther Spring and Butte Meadows.
**Directions:** From I-5 at Red Bluff, turn east on Highway 36, drive to the town of Paynes Creek, and continue to Little Giant Mill Road. Turn south on Little Giant Mill Road (Road 202) and drive seven miles to Ponderosa Way. Turn south at Ponderosa Way and drive about 17 miles to the Mill Creek trailhead.
**Contact:** Lassen National Forest, Almanor Ranger District, P.O. Box 767, Chester, CA 96020, 530/258-2141, website: www.fs.fed.us/r5 (click on Forest Offices).

# 49 MOAK TRAIL
## 14.0 mi / 1.5 days

**in the Ishi Wilderness east of Red Bluff**

Map 3.3, page 117

Hit it right in the spring, and Moak Trail could be the best overnight hike in California's foothill country. Hit it wrong in the summer, and you'll wonder what you did to deserve such a terrible fate. In the spring, the foothill country is loaded with wildflowers and tall, fresh grass—and the views of the Sacramento Valley are spectacular. The trail includes a poke-and-probe section over a lava-rock boulder field, and there are good trail camps at Deep Hole (2,800 feet) and Drennan. It's an excellent weekend trip, including a loop route by linking Moak Trail with Buena Vista Trail, most of it easy walking. Alas, if you try this trip in the summer or fall, you'll need to have your gray matter examined at Red Bluff General. No wildflowers, no shade, 100-degree temperatures, and as for water, you're dreamin'.

Special note: A trail map is strongly advised for those hiking in the Ishi Wilderness.
**User Groups:** Hikers, dogs, and horses. No mountain bikes. No wheelchair facilities.

**Permits:** A campfire permit (free) is required for overnight use. Parking and access are free.
**Maps:** A trail map is available for a fee from Almanor Ranger District. For a map, ask the U.S. Forest Service for Lassen National Forest or Ishi Wilderness. For topographic maps, ask the USGS for Panther Spring and Butte Meadows.
**Directions:** From I-5 at Red Bluff, turn east on Highway 36, drive to the town of Paynes Creek, and continue to Little Giant Mill Road. Turn south on Little Giant Mill Road (Road 202) and drive seven miles to Ponderosa Way. Turn south at Ponderosa Way and drive about 24 miles to the Moak trailhead.
**Contact:** Lassen National Forest, Almanor Ranger District, P.O. Box 767, Chester, CA 96020, 530/258-2141, website: www.fs.fed.us/r5 (click on Forest Offices).

# 50 DEER CREEK TRAIL
## 14.0 mi / 1.5 days

**in the Ishi Wilderness east of Red Bluff**

Map 3.3, page 117

It's no accident that Deer Creek Trail is the most popular hike in the Ishi Wilderness. Not only are hikers rewarded with striking surroundings, but the hike is a pleasurable romp even if you cut the trip short to just an hour or two. That's because the trail runs midway up naked slopes, offering spectacular views of Deer Creek Canyon's basaltic cliffs and spires, and of the stream below. The trailhead is at the southeast border of the wilderness, and right from the start, it's routed along the north shore of Deer Creek. Iron Mountain (at 3,274 feet) is located to the immediate north. The trail continues along the stream into the wilderness interior, skirting past the northern edge of what is called the Graham Pinery—a dense island of ponderosa pine growing on a mountain terrace. A bonus is good bird-watching for hawks, eagles, and falcons at the rock cliffs, and looking for a large variety of wildlife—including rattlesnakes (here's your warning), wild pigs, and lots of squirrels and quail. Note that the stream is stocked with rainbow and brook trout near Potato Patch and Alder Creek Campgrounds. Below Potato Patch Campground, fishing is catch-and-release only with the use of artificials.

Special note: A trail map is strongly advised for those hiking in the Ishi Wilderness.

**User Groups:** Hikers, dogs, and horses. No mountain bikes. No wheelchair facilities.

**Permits:** A campfire permit (free) is required for overnight use. Parking and access are free.

**Maps:** A trail map is available for a fee from Almanor Ranger District. For a map, ask the U.S. Forest Service for Lassen National Forest or Ishi Wilderness. For topographic maps, ask the USGS for Panther Spring and Butte Meadows.

**Directions:** From I-5 at Red Bluff, turn east on Highway 36, drive to the town of Paynes Creek, and continue to Little Giant Mill Road. Turn south on Little Giant Mill Road (Road 202) and drive seven miles to Ponderosa Way. Turn south at Ponderosa Way and drive about 26 miles to the Deer Creek trailhead.

**Contact:** Lassen National Forest, Almanor Ranger District, P.O. Box 767, Chester, CA 96020, 530/258-2141, website: www.fs.fed.us/r5 (click on Forest Offices).

## 51 HUMBOLDT SUMMIT TO DOMINGO SPRINGS (PCT)

**28.0 mi one-way / 2.0 days**

at Humboldt Summit in Lassen National Forest southwest of Lake Almanor

Map 3.3, page 117

The idea of back-to-back 14-mile days to get through this chunk of trail may not appeal to many hikers, especially while carrying full-weight expedition packs. But that's standard for most hikers on this stretch of PCT, with little here to tarry for and with Lassen Volcanic National Park beckoning ahead. The trail starts just below Humboldt Peak, at 7,087 feet, and heads north along the ridge line—for the most part, past Butt Mountain (7,866 feet) and down to Soldier Meadows. A spring and stream

make this a delightful stop before crossing Highway 36, forging onward another three miles to the Stove Springs Campground. The trail then skirts around the western flank of North Stover Mountain and drops down to Domingo Springs, where another campground is available.

To continue north on the PCT, see Domingo Springs to Lassen Volcanic National Park (PCT) hike in this chapter. If you are walking this trail in reverse, see the Feather River to Humboldt Summit (PCT) hike in this chapter to continue south.

**User Groups:** Hikers, dogs, and horses. No mountain bikes. No wheelchair facilities.

**Permits:** A campfire permit (free) is required. Parking and access are free.

**Maps:** For a map, ask the U.S. Forest Service for Lassen National Forest. For topographic maps, ask the USGS for Humboldt Peak and Stover Mountain.

**Directions:** From Chico, drive north on Highway 32 to the junction with Highway 89/36. Turn right (east) and take Highway 36 toward Chester. Turn west on Highway 36 and drive two miles to the junction with Highway 89. Turn south on Highway 89 and proceed four miles; then turn right on County Road 308 (Humboldt Road) and drive 15 miles to the trailhead parking area.

**Contact:** Lassen National Forest, Almanor Ranger District, P.O. Box 767, Chester, CA 96020, 530/258-2141, website: www.fs.fed.us/r5 (click on Forest Offices).

## 52 DEER CREEK TRAIL

**1.0–8.0 mi / 1.0 day**

in Lassen National Forest along Highway 32 west of Lake Almanor

Map 3.3, page 117

The Deer Creek Trail has all the ingredients to make it ideal for a trout angler, an explorer, or somebody just looking for a dunk on a hot day. The gorgeous stream runs right alongside the trail, with good access throughout and fish (often plenty of them) in the summer months. From the parking area, the trail is routed downstream along the river for about 10 miles, but rarely does anybody ever walk all the way to the end. Instead they take their time, perhaps fishing or swimming along the way. In summer, Deer Creek is cold and clear, tumbling its way over rocks and into pools, with trout seemingly in every one. California Department of Fish and Game rules mandate catch-and-release fishing with artificials with a single barbless hook for most of the river. This trail has also become popular among mountain bikers; most are courteous to hikers, and on a single-track trail, that's important. An interesting note is that the canyon rim is made up of a series of volcanic crags and basalt spires.

**User Groups:** Hikers, dogs, and horses. Mountain bikes aren't advised. No wheelchair facilities.

**Permits:** No permits are required. Parking and access are free.

**Maps:** A trail map is available for a fee from Almanor Ranger District. For a map, ask the U.S. Forest Service for Lassen National Forest. For a topographic map, ask the USGS for Onion Butte.

**Directions:** Drive north from Chico on Highway 32 for 40 miles. Just after crossing a small, red, metal bridge (locals call it the Red Bridge) that crosses Deer Creek, park on the south side of the road, where there's a dirt pullout. The trailhead is just up from the bridge, on the north side of the road.

**Contact:** Lassen National Forest, Almanor Ranger District, P.O. Box 767, Chester, CA 96020, 530/258-2141, website: www.fs.fed.us/r5 (click on Forest Offices).

## 53 DEVILS DEN TRAIL
### 9.0 mi / 1.0 day

**in the Ishi Wilderness east of Red Bluff**

Map 3.3, page 117

The Devils Den trailhead is less than .5 mile from the Deer Creek trailhead, but there is

where the similarities between the two end. This trail includes a rough climb that's beastly in summer. Always bring a water filtration pump to fill your canteen at Deer Creek. The main attractions here are: 1) nobody else is usually around, and 2) the trail is routed through a series of habitat zones over the course of the first 3.5 miles, providing a number of striking contrasts. The trail starts easy, following along Deer Creek for the first mile. Enjoy yourself, because what follows is not exactly a picnic. Note that fishing here is restricted to catch-and-release and the use of artificials. The trail turns left, climbing up Little Pine Creek all the way to the ridge top, with the last mile on an old, hot, and chunky abandoned road. Along the way, the vegetation changes from riparian along the creek to woodland on the slopes, then chaparral on the ridge. In addition, an island of conifers, the Graham Pinery, is available for viewing with a .25-mile side trip.

Special note: A trail map is strongly advised for those hiking in the Ishi Wilderness.

**User Groups:** Hikers, dogs, and horses. No mountain bikes. No wheelchair facilities.

**Permits:** A campfire permit (free) is required for overnight use. Parking and access are free.

**Maps:** A trail map is available for a fee from Almanor Ranger District. For a map, ask the U.S. Forest Service for Lassen National Forest or Ishi Wilderness. For topographic maps, ask the USGS for Panther Spring and Butte Meadows.

**Directions:** From I-5 at Red Bluff, turn east on Highway 36, drive to the town of Paynes Creek, and continue to Little Giant Mill Road. Turn south on Little Giant Mill Road (Road 202) and drive seven miles to Ponderosa Way. Turn south at Ponderosa Way and drive 32.5 miles to the Devils Den trailhead (just south of the Deer Creek trailhead).

**Contact:** Lassen National Forest, Almanor Ranger District, P.O. Box 767, Chester, CA 96020, 530/258-2141, website: www.fs.fed.us/r5 (click on Forest Offices).

## 54 FEATHER RIVER TO HUMBOLDT SUMMIT (PCT)

**26.0 mi one-way / 2.0 days**

**at the Belden Trailhead on Highway 70 in Plumas National Forest**

Map 3.3, page 117

The trail is not only rough from Belden to Humboldt Summit, it's not particularly pretty either, especially compared to the nearby wilderness. The climb is a mighty dry slice of rattlesnake country. From the North Fork Feather River at Belden (elevation 2,310 feet), the PCT climbs 4,777 feet over the course of this two-day thumper to Humboldt Summit, at 7,087 feet. There are no lakes along this trail, only a few small water holes requiring short side trips. Instead, the prettiest sections are along streams, the first being Chips Creek, which runs adjacent to the trail for eight miles. Then later, there's a short crossing over the headwaters of Willow Creek. Some might prefer to take three days instead of two to hike this section, but with the stunning Lassen Volcanic National Park looming ahead, most hikers are willing to put in long days to get through this area.

To continue north on the PCT, see the Humboldt Summit to Domingo Springs to Lassen Volcanic National Park (PCT) hike in this chapter. If you are walking this trail in reverse, see the Bucks Summit to Feather River (PCT) hike, in the Sacramento and Gold Country chapter, to continue south.

**User Groups:** Hikers, dogs, and horses. No mountain bikes. No wheelchair facilities.

**Permits:** A campfire permit (free) is required. Parking and access are free.

**Maps:** For a map, ask the U.S. Forest Service for Plumas National Forest. For topographic maps, ask the USGS for Belden and Humboldt Peak.

**Directions:** From Quincy, drive west on Highway 70 about 26 miles to the trailhead, at the roadside rest area at Belden.

**Contact:** Plumas National Forest, Mount Hough Ranger District, 39696 State Highway 70, Quincy, CA 95971, 530/283-0555, fax

530/283-1821, website: www.fs.fed.us/r5/ (click on Forest Offices).

## 55 BIZZ JOHNSON

**1.0–25.0 mi one-way / 0.5 hour–3.0 days**

**west of Susanville**

Map 3.4, page 118

In the 1960s, when Shasta legend John Reginato heard that Southern Pacific was going to abandon a rail line between Westwood and Susanville, he urged that it be converted to a hiking trail. The idea struck home, and the Bureau of Land Management worked with the U.S. Forest Service to develop and refine it.

Today this trail is one of the true multiple-use routes in Northern California, with plenty of room for hikers, mountain bikers, and horseback riders. Fieldscout Stan Bales reports that it is ideal for day trips, with trailhead access spaced five to seven miles apart. People can hike or bike different portions of the trail; you don't have to complete the entire route, of course. The seven-mile stretch west of Susanville is the most popular stretch of the 25-mile route.

The trailhead is at 4,200 feet, and the high point of the route is at 5,600 feet, at Westwood Junction. The route traces the old Fernley and Lassen railroad line, a branch line of the South Pacific Railroad, following the Susan River Canyon along the Susan River for 15 miles. It is basically routed from the Susanville Railroad Depot to the Mason Station trailhead five miles north of Westwood. The surface is a mixture of compacted dirt and small gravel. It features beautiful views in many areas and passes through two old railroad tunnels and 11 old railroad bridges. You won't cross any developed areas.

One-way trips with shuttles are becoming popular, with a shuttle service available for a fee through Lassen Rural Bus or Mount Lassen Cab & Shuttle. The one negative: Like most rails-to-trails projects, it's way too wide for a premium hiking trail. In the winter, it makes a great trip on cross-country skis or on a snowmobile (snowmobiling is allowed on the western half of the trail, from Mason Station to just beyond Westwood Junction).

**User Groups:** Hikers, dogs (must be leashed near Susanville), horses, and mountain bikes. Wheelchair-accessible from Susanville and Hobo Camp trailhead.

**Permits:** No permits are required. Parking and access are free.

**Maps:** For a free brochure, contact the Bureau of Land Management at the address below. For a map, ask the U.S. Forest Service for Lassen National Forest. For topographic maps, ask the USGS for Westwood East, Fredonyer Pass, and Susanville.

**Directions:** In Susanville on Highway 36, turn south on Weatherlow Street and drive .5 mile (Weatherlow becomes Richmond Road) to the Susanville Depot Visitor Center (open May–early October) and the trailhead, on the right.

Alternate route: From Westwood on Highway 36, turn north on County Road A21 and drive three miles to the trailhead access road. Turn right (onto a dirt road) and drive .4 mile to the trailhead, on the left.

**Contact:** Lassen National Forest, Eagle Lake Ranger District, 477-050 Eagle Lake Road, Susanville, CA 96130, 530/257-4188, website: www.fs.fed.us/r5 (click on Forest Offices); Bureau of Land Management, Eagle Lake Field Office, 2950 Riverside Drive, Susanville, CA 96130, 530/257-0456, website: www.ca.blm.gov (click on Field Offices); Susanville Depot Visitor Center, 530/257-3252; Lassen Rural Bus, 530/257-7433; Mount Lassen Cab & Shuttle, 530/257-5187.

## Chapter 4

© ANN MARIE BROWN

# Mendocino and Wine Country

# Mendocino and Wine Country

For many people, this region offers the best possible combination around in terms of geography, weather, and outdoor activities.

The Mendocino coast is dramatic and remote, with several stellar state parks for hiking, while Sonoma Valley, in the heart of the wine country, produces some of the most popular wines in the world. Add in the self-indulgent options of mud baths and hot springs in Calistoga and a dash of mainstream recreation at Clear Lake, Lake Berryessa, or any other lake, and you have a capsule summary of why the Mendocino coast and the wine country have turned into getaway favorites.

The coast features excellent adventuring and hiking, including some of the best year-round day hikes in California. The Fort Bragg area alone has three state parks, all with outstanding recreation, including several easy hikes—many amid redwoods and along pretty streams. If you want a campsite at a state park on a summer weekend, make reservations far in advance. The weather is most agreeable in spring and fall, when your chances of blue skies and temperatures in the 60s are best. In summer, it is often foggy, with mist common at daybreak—so much of it that the forest canopy can be dripping with moisture by midmorning. In winter, it can be very wet; the streams and waterfalls are brought to life, ferns and forests are lush and fresh, and yet visitors are relatively few. On weekdays, it is common to have trails all to yourself.

The driving tour of Highway 1 along the coast is the fantasy of many, and it can live up to that fantasy if you don't mind the twists and turns of the road. Along the way, there are dozens of hidden beaches and untouched coastline, where you can stop, explore, and play tag with the waves. Some of the prize spots are MacKerricher State Park, Salt Point State Park, and Anchor Bay.

As you venture inland, the landscape changes in a dramatic fashion. The terrain consists of rolling foothills peppered with oaks and hot, dry weather in summer. Yet there are still pockets of redwoods hidden in canyons in a few surprise spots, including at Bothe-Napa Valley State Park, near Calistoga, and Hendy Woods, near Philo. This region is bordered to the east by the Yolla Bolly Mountains. This is where you will find the Yolla Bolla Wilderness, a landscape that features many small streams that eventually join to form the headwaters of the Eel River. Outside the wilderness boundary, the area has been heavily cut by loggers.

One of the best lookouts in Northern California is from the top of Mount St. Helena, a great all-day tromp. Bothe-Napa Valley State Park, near Calistoga, has a surprise redwood grove and a beautiful stream under forest canopy. Nearby Sugarloaf Ridge State Park is known for wide-open views from its ridges, yet it also hides a pretty waterfall in a wooded canyon that in winter transforms into a gorgeous easy hike and picnic setting.

Between the beautiful coastal state parks and the surprises in the inland foothills, you get the best of two worlds.

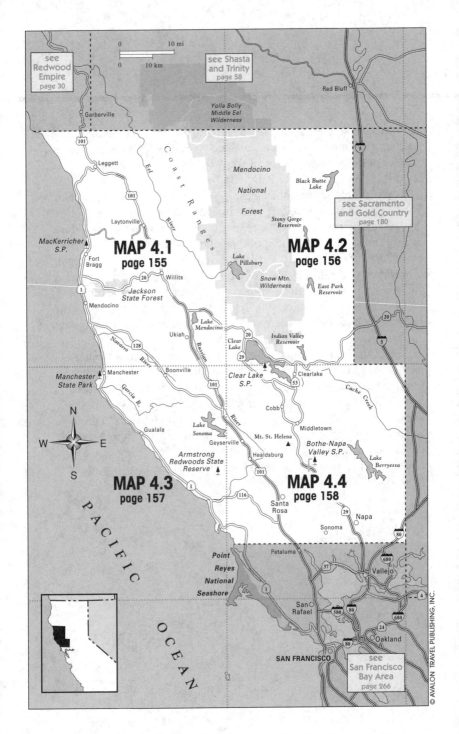

# Map 4.1

**Hikes 1–10**
**Pages 159–164**

# Map 4.2

**Hikes 11–16**
**Pages 164–167**

# Map 4.3

**Hikes 17–22**
**Pages 168–170**

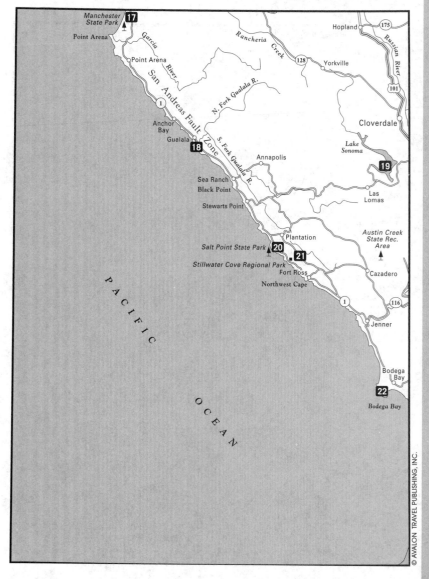

© AVALON TRAVEL PUBLISHING, INC.

# Map 4.4

## Hikes 23–31
## Pages 171–176

© AVALON TRAVEL PUBLISHING, INC.

# 1 LOST COAST TRAIL/SINKYONE TRAILHEAD

**16.7 mi one-way / 2.0 days**

in Sinkyone Wilderness State Park and on the Mendocino coast

Map 4.1, page 155

This remote and rugged wilderness of Northern California coastline, covering more than 7,000 acres, is now protected forever as Sinkyone Wilderness State Park. It was once one of the least traveled jewels of California. No more. It has become very popular, with thousands of hikers from early spring through summer—despite few directional signs along roads, no highways leading here, and virtually no park promotion. The primitive, steep, and unforgiving terrain provides a rare coastal wilderness experience. The best way to explore it is on Lost Coast Trail, which is best hiked north to south to keep the north winds out of your face. A shuttle service is available for a fee through Lost Coast Trail Transport Service.

Day 1: From the northern trailhead at Orchard Camp, Lost Coast Trail starts out flat and pleasant, arcing around Bear Harbor Cove. From here the trail climbs 800 feet and then back down, passing through a redwood grove and also breaking out for sweeping coastal views. Enjoy them, because the hike gets more difficult, including a steep climb up, over, and down a mountain. The trail finally descends into Little Jackass Creek Camp, which is set beside a small stream 10.5 miles from your start.

Day 2: The closeout of a two-day hike should always be as enjoyable as possible, and so it is here, with divine views in many spots along the 6.5-mile route. Alas, there's usually payment for views, and that comes in the form of several rugged climbs in the park's most remote sections. After climbing to nearly 1,000 feet, the trail ends with an 800-foot downgrade over the last mile, descending to the Usal Campground parking area.

Special note: At the northern boundary of the Sinkyone Wilderness, this trail continues north into the King Range National Conservation Area, where it's routed for another 30 miles to the mouth of the Mattole River.

**User Groups:** Hikers only. Horses allowed only on the section of trail between the trailhead at the park entrance and Wheeler Camp. No dogs or mountain bikes. No wheelchair facilities.

**Permits:** No permits are required. Parking and access are free unless you plan to camp.

**Maps:** A trail map and brochure is available for a fee from Sinkyone Wilderness State Park at the address below. For a topographic map, ask the USGS for Bear Harbor.

**Directions:** From U.S. 101 north of Garberville, take the Redway exit to Briceland Road. Turn west on Briceland Road and drive 17 miles to Whitethorn. From Whitethorn, continue six miles to the Four Corners Fork. Continue straight and drive six miles on a gravel road to the Needle Rock Ranger Station. Continue past the ranger station to the visitors center, and park at Orchard Camp. Be aware that the access road is unpaved, that it may close unexpectedly in the winter, and that four-wheel-drive vehicles are often required in wet weather. There are few signs pointing the way to the park. Trailers and RVs are not recommended.

**Contact:** Sinkyone Wilderness State Recreation Area, P.O. Box 245, Whitethorn, CA 95489, 707/986-7711; California State Parks, North Coast Redwoods District, Piercy Sector, 707/247-3319, website: www.parks.ca.gov (click on Find A Park); Lost Coast Trail Transport Service, 707/986-9909, website: www.lostcoasttrail.com.

# 2 SOLDIER RIDGE TRAIL

**11.2 mi / 2.0 days**

on the southern boundary of the Yolla Bolly Wilderness west of Red Bluff

Map 4.1, page 155

This wilderness trail features three linked segments, Soldier Ridge Trail, Minnie Lake Trail, and Kingsley Lake Trail, combining for a 5.6-mile walk to your destination, Kingsley Lake. The rugged climb on Soldier Ridge Trail to get there, along with the charm of this little lake, usually compels hikers to stay overnight.

Actually, it's a long drive in the middle of nowhere just to reach the trailhead, and then when you get there, you'll face a daunting 3.5-mile climb up the spine of Soldier Ridge toward the Yolla Bolly Crest. At the crest are three mountains lined in a row: Sugarloaf Mountain (elevation 7,367 feet), Solomon Peak (7,581 feet), and Hammerhorn Mountain (7,567 feet). The trail crosses a saddle between Sugarloaf Mountain and Solomon Peak, then drops down to little Kingsley Lake, which is created from the headwaters of Thomes Creek. All is quiet and peaceful here.

**User Groups:** Hikers, dogs, and horses. No mountain bikes. No wheelchair facilities.

**Permits:** A campfire permit is required for hikers planning to camp. Parking and access are free.

**Maps:** For a map, ask the U.S. Forest Service for Mendocino National Forest or Yolla Bolly Wilderness. For a topographic map, ask the USGS for South Yolla Bolly.

**Directions:** From Willits, drive north on U.S. 101 for 13 miles to Longvale and Highway 162. Turn east on Highway 162 and drive 30 miles to the turnoff for Highway 162 East. Turn right and drive nine miles to the Eel River Bridge and Forest Road M1 (Indian Dick Road). At the bridge, turn left (north) onto Forest Road M1 and drive 27 miles to the trailhead, at the end of the road.

**Contact:** Mendocino National Forest, Covelo Ranger District, 78150 Covelo Road, Covelo, CA 95428, 707/983-6118, website: www.fs.fed.us/r5 (click on Forest Offices).

# 🅱 WRIGHTS VALLEY TRAIL
## 8.0 mi / 4.5 hrs

**on the southern boundary of the Yolla Bolly Wilderness west of Red Bluff**

Map 4.1, page 155

The Rock Cabin Trail (also known as River Trail) extends north into the Yolla Bolly Wilderness and up, over, and down a short ridge before pouring into Wrights Valley. About halfway in, River Trail jumps to Wrights Valley Trail.

It's about a four-mile trip one way to your destination. Here you'll find the headwaters of the Middle Fork Eel River, one of the prettiest streams in the wilderness. The trail is well marked and includes two creek crossings. Whereas the Yolla Bollys provide few lakes, the Middle Fork awaits you. In order to protect endangered steelhead, no fishing is allowed.

Special note: Map-gazing hikers will likely notice small Henthorne Lake, complete with two wilderness cabins, set just 2.5 miles from the Rock Cabin trailhead. Resist the urge to visit. This is maintained as private property, a nature reserve for some lucky soul. Hikers are often tempted to hike in via a very faint cowboy trail (with a river crossing) and camp here illegally.

**User Groups:** Hikers, dogs, and horses. No mountain bikes. No wheelchair facilities.

**Permits:** A campfire permit is required for hikers planning to camp. Parking and access are free.

**Maps:** For a map, ask the U.S. Forest Service for Mendocino National Forest or Yolla Bolly Wilderness. For a topographic map, ask the USGS for South Yolla Bolly.

**Directions:** From Willits, drive north on U.S. 101 for 13 miles to Longvale and Highway 162. Turn east on Highway 162 and drive 30 miles to the turnoff for Highway 162 East. Turn right and drive nine miles to the Eel River Bridge and Forest Road M1 (Indian Dick Road). At the bridge, turn left (north) onto Forest Road M1 and drive 24 miles to Forest Road 25N15C. Turn left on Forest Road 25N15C and drive .75 mile to the turnoff for the Rock Cabin trailhead. Turn left and drive .25 mile to the trailhead, at the end of the road.

**Contact:** Mendocino National Forest, Covelo Ranger District, 78150 Covelo Road, Covelo, CA 95428, 707/983-6118, website: www.fs.fed.us/r5 (click on Forest Offices).

## 4 BRUHEL POINT TIDEPOOLS
1.2 mi / 1.0 hr

**on the Mendocino coast north of Fort Bragg**

Map 4.1, page 155

Some of the best tidepools on the Pacific Coast can be found in Mendocino, and one of the best of the best is here, located just south of Bruhel Point. When you first arrive, you'll find a CalTrans roadside vista point (no overnight parking), restrooms, and a beach access trail. This is your calling. The trail is routed north toward Bruhel Point, much of it along the edge of ocean bluffs. Freelancing a descent down the bluff is not recommended; rather, take only the cutoff trails, which lead to the best tidepool areas. Time your trip during a low tide— or better yet, a minus low tide. That is when the ocean pulls back, leaving a series of holes and cuts in a rock basin that remain filled with water, providing the perfect habitat and viewing areas for all kinds of tiny marine life.

**User Groups:** Hikers and dogs. Not suitable for mountain bikes or horses. No wheelchair facilities.

**Permits:** No permits are required. Parking and access are free.

**Maps:** For a topographic map, ask the USGS for Inglenook.

**Directions:** From Westport, drive south on Highway 1 about two miles to milepost marker 74.09. The tidepools are a short walk from the CalTrans Vista Point parking lot.

**Contact:** No managing agency for contact.

## 5 LAKE CLEONE TRAIL
1.2 mi / 0.5 hr

**in MacKerricher State Park on the Mendocino coast north of Fort Bragg**

Map 4.1, page 155

MacKerricher State Park is filled with enticing highlights, including free day-use access and the loop trail around Lake Cleone, which is not only easy but also definitely something special. Mrs. MacKerricher aptly named the trail Cleone, which means "gracious" or "beautiful" in Greek. The route includes several sections on raised wooden walkways, which provide routes through marshy areas. In the winter months, the southern part of the trail (without the boardwalk) can be flooded. Be sure to wear your high boots in the rainy season.

The trail burrows like a tunnel through a variety of trees and lush vegetation, providing many glimpses of pretty Lake Cleone. It loops all the way around the lake, which is almost always full. There is the beautiful Pacific Ocean just beyond to the west, a cypress grove to the south, and a marsh to the east. Historically the lake is stocked with trout by the Department of Fish and Game three times before Memorial Day weekend. The boardwalk is wheelchair accessible.

Special note: From the parking lot adjacent to the lake, you can walk under the built-up foundation of an old railroad line (now a bicycle trail called Old Haul Road) and connect to Headlands Trail. This is a must-do—it's an easy short walk (much of it on a raised walkway) that leads to a series of tidepools and the best seal- and whale-watching station on the coast.

**User Groups:** Hikers, leashed dogs, and wheelchairs (the trail is partially wheelchair accessible). No horses or mountain bikes. Horse trails and mountain bike routes are available elsewhere in the state park.

**Permits:** No permits are required. Parking and access are free.

**Maps:** A brochure and trail map is available for a fee at MacKerricher State Park at the address below. For a topographic map, ask the USGS for Inglenook.

**Directions:** From Fort Bragg drive north on Highway 1 for three miles to the park entrance. Turn left and drive to the parking area beside the lake. The trailhead is on the east side of the parking lot.

**Contact:** MacKerricher State Park, c/o California State Parks, Mendocino District, P.O. Box 440, Mendocino, CA 95460, 707/937-5804, website: www.parks.ca.gov (click on Find A Park).

## 6 CHAMBERLAIN CREEK WATERFALL TRAIL
### 0.5 mi / 0.5 hr

**in Jackson State Forest east of Fort Bragg**

Map 4.1, page 155

Hidden in Jackson State Forest is a 50-foot waterfall set in a canyon framed by redwoods—the kind of place where explorers can get religion. Set back off an old dirt logging road, the trail is short—yet steep, secluded, and beautiful. This access road (gravel/dirt), by the way, can get muddy in the winter and extremely dusty in the summer. After parking, you'll find the trail routed a short distance down the canyon to the stream, starting with a short series of steps. The trail simply heads down the canyon directly to the base of the waterfall. Despite the beauty of the area and the popularity of the Mendocino coast, Jackson State Forest is typically overlooked by most visitors, meaning you'll most likely have the place to yourself.

**User Groups:** Hikers and dogs. No horses or mountain bikes. No wheelchair facilities.

**Permits:** No permits are required. Parking and access are free.

**Maps:** For a free trail map, contact Jackson Demonstration State Forest at the address below. For a topographic map, ask the USGS for Northspur.

**Directions:** From Willits, drive west on Highway 20 for 17 miles to Forest Road 200, a dirt road just before the Chamberlain Creek bridge. Turn right and Drive one mile on Road 200 to a fork. Bear left and drive 3.5 miles. Look for the trailhead on the left. Park on the side of the road and follow the hand railing down a steep slope to access the trail. In the heaviest rainy season, note that State Forest Road 200 is sometimes closed due to weather; call ahead for the status.

**Contact:** Jackson Demonstration State Forest, 802 North Main Street, Fort Bragg, CA 95437, 707/964-5674, fax 707/964-0941.

## 7 FALLS LOOP TRAIL
### 7.0 mi / 4.0 hrs

**in Russian Gulch State Park on the Mendocino coast south of Fort Bragg**

Map 4.1, page 155

A 35-foot waterfall in deep forest makes this walk one of the prettiest on the Mendocino coast. Most of the year, this waterfall is a narrow silvery stream that pours atop and across a boulder. In winter it can build into a more powerful chute and land in the rock basin with surging splashes.

The route is simple. Take North Trail for 2.5 miles out to its junction with Falls Loop Trail. Turn left, and then you'll hike less than a mile to reach the falls. Even in the summer months, this is a pretty, if narrow, silver cascade, streaming 20 feet across a granite boulder and down into a pool. The entire trip has very little elevation gain—it's an easy walk out to Falls Loop Trail, then only a 200-foot gain to reach the waterfall. As you go, you'll delve deeper and deeper into dense forest, and although a lot of the old growth was taken a long time ago, much is still divine.

Special note: A paved bicycle trail runs parallel to North Trail and makes a great bike trip. But please note that bikes are not permitted on the dirt Falls Loop Trail. Bike racks are available at the intersection of these two trails, meaning bikers can make the trip to the falls with only a one-mile hike. In other words, ride to the Falls Loop Trail junction, park your bike, and walk one mile from there. This bike trail is also wheelchair accessible. A large number of people also walk the bike trail, a five-mile round-trip.

**User Groups:** Hikers only. No mountain bikes, dogs, or horses. However, a paved trail for bicycles and wheelchairs is routed 2.5 miles to the trailhead of Falls Loop Trail.

**Permits:** No permits are required. A state park entrance fee of $6 is charged for each vehicle.

**Maps:** A brochure and trail map is available for a fee at Russian Gulch State Park at the address below. For a topographic map, ask the USGS for Mendocino.

**Directions:** From Fort Bragg, drive south on Highway 1 for six miles to the Russian Gulch State Park entrance. Turn right and drive a very short distance to the state park entrance. After passing the kiosk, travel down the hill and to the bridge. Turn left and drive past the campsites to the trailhead.

**Contact:** Russian Gulch State Park, c/o California State Parks, Mendocino District, P.O. Box 440, Mendocino, CA 95460, 707/937-5804, website: www.parks.ca.gov (click on Find A Park).

# 8 FERN CANYON TRAIL
## 8.1 mi / 5.0 hrs

**in Van Damme State Park on the Mendocino coast south of Mendocino**

Map 4.1, page 155

This beautiful streamside walk amid coastal redwoods is one of the most popular trails on the Mendocino coast. The trail starts at the bottom of a canyon along the Little River and heads upstream, rising gently along the way, with a series of little bridges crisscrossing the water. The creek is pretty and often clear, the forest canopy is towering, and the understory of fern and sorrel is lush. Most people hike 2.3 miles (paved all the way) out to the junction of Loop Trail and then turn around and head back. Visitors can add on a three-mile loop, including a visit to the delightful Pygmy Forest, where an elevated wood walkway is routed amid this unusual setting. Note that heavy rains can flood out the trail and wash out the bridges. Also note that if you're a cheapskate, you can avoid paying the park entrance fee by parking in the beach parking lot next to the park entrance and walking in.

Special note: Do not get this Fern Canyon Trail confused with the Fern Canyon Loop Trail on the Humboldt County coast, which is listed in the Redwood Empire chapter.

**User Groups:** Hikers only. No dogs or horses. Wheelchairs and mountain bikes are allowed only on the first 2.3 miles of the trail.

**Permits:** No permits are required. A state park entrance fee of $6 is charged for each vehicle.

**Maps:** A brochure and trail map is available for a fee at Van Damme State Park at the address below. For a topographic map, ask the USGS for Mendocino.

**Directions:** From Mendocino, drive south on Highway 1 for 2.5 miles to the park entrance. Turn left and drive .75 mile (well signed) to the trailhead. For campers, start near campsite No. 26.

**Contact:** Van Damme State Park, c/o California State Parks, Mendocino District, P.O. Box 440, Mendocino, CA 95460, 707/937-5804, website: www.parks.ca.gov (click on Find A Park).

# 9 GLEN EDEN TRAIL
## 3.0–10.5 mi / 1.0–5.0 hrs

**in Cow Mountain Recreation Area east of Ukiah**

Map 4.1, page 155

This trail will have you sweating like Charles Manson's cellmate. The Glen Eden Trail is not only difficult to find (follow our directions precisely), but has several steep sections and is typically quite hot. The trail eventually crosses Mendo Rock Road (another trailhead possibility, see Directions) and continues up to a series of great overlooks of Clear Lake. To return, retrace your route. Few make the entire trip, but instead they just hike out to a good vista or two, then return. The chaparral-covered slopes are peppered with pine and oak, with many miles of trails and fire roads. But it's extremely rare to see other hikers, and no off-road vehicles are allowed (unlike the southern portion of the Cow Mountain Recreation Area). In addition, the views of Clear Lake and the Mayacmas Range are outstanding.

**User Groups:** Hikers, dogs, and horses. Mountain bikes are prohibited on the first 2.5 miles of trail, after which public property starts and bicycles are allowed. Bikers should access Glen Eden Trail from other trailheads on Bureau of Land Management (BLM) land.

**Permits:** No permits are required. Parking and access are free.

**Maps:** For a free trail map of the Cow Mountain Recreation Area, contact the Bureau of Land Management at the address below. For a topographic map, ask the USGS for Cow Mountain.

**Directions:** To Glen Eden trailhead from Ukiah on U.S. 101, drive north to Highway 20. Turn east on Highway 20 and drive to Scotts Valley Road (near Blue Lakes west of Upper Lake). Turn south on Scotts Valley Road and drive 2.5 miles to trailhead parking, on the left. The trailhead is directly across the road.

To Mendo Rock Road trailhead (midtrail) from Ukiah on U.S. 101, take the Talmage Road exit. Turn east and drive 1.5 miles to Eastside Road. Turn right and drive .3 mile to Mill Creek Road. Turn left and drive three miles to Mendo Rock Road. Turn left (sharp, signed North Cow Mountain), and drive 5.5 miles (steep, narrow) to a T intersection. Turn right and drive three miles to where Glen Eden Trail crosses the road.

**Contact:** Bureau of Land Management, Ukiah Field Office, 2550 North State Street, Ukiah, CA 95482, 707/468-4000, fax 707/468-4027, website: www.ca.blm.gov/ukiah/cowmtn.html.

## 10 BIG HENDY GROVE TRAIL
### 1.0 mi / 0.5 hr

**in Hendy Woods State Park in Mendocino National Forest**

Map 4.1, page 155

This easy and short walk through an ancient redwood forest can have visitors to Hendy Woods smiling for days. Hendy Woods is located in the redwood-filled canyon of the Navarro River, which flows to the sea on the Mendocino coast. Although the park covers 845 acres, the two old-growth redwood groves, Little Hendy (20 acres) and Big Hendy (80 acres), are most compelling.

When you first arrive, you'll be stunned at the sudden interface of the foothill grasslands with redwoods. At Big Hendy, start by taking the .5-mile Discovery Trail, which leaves the grasslands and enters the grove on a dirt path. Suddenly you'll be walking among towering redwoods, moss-covered stumps, and a sprinkling of giant fallen trees, all set amid ferns and sorrel. A great side trip is to walk uphill on the cutoff trail to the old hermit's hut in a hollowed-out tree stump, where one of the last of the real hermits lived for years. A newspaper clipping here details the old hermit's strange life—kind of like that of an outdoors writer.

**User Groups:** Hikers and wheelchairs. No dogs, horses, or mountain bikes.

**Permits:** No permits are required. A state park entrance fee of $6 is charged for each vehicle.

**Maps:** A brochure and trail map is available for a fee at Hendy Woods State Park at the address below. For a topographic map, ask the USGS for Philo.

**Directions:** From Mendocino, drive south on Highway 1 for about five miles to Highway 128. Turn east on Highway 128 and drive about 20 miles to Philo Greenwood Road. Turn south (right) and drive .5 mile to the entrance of Hendy Woods State Park, on the left. The trailhead begins just off the parking area.

**Contact:** Hendy Woods State Park, c/o California State Parks, Mendocino District, P.O. Box 440, Mendocino, CA 95460, 707/937-5804, website: www.parks.ca.gov (click on Find A Park).

## 11 IDES COVE NATIONAL RECREATION TRAIL
### 10.5 mi / 5.5 hrs

**on the southeastern boundary of the Yolla Bolly Wilderness west of Red Bluff**

Map 4.2, page 156

At 8,092 feet, South Yolla Bolly Mountain is the highest point in this wilderness. The Ides Cove National Recreation Trail skirts this mountain as part of one of the top one-day loop trails available in the Yolla Bollys. A bonus is that a shorter loop hike (3.5 miles) is also convenient here. Another bonus is that a free campground is available at the trailhead. Horse facilities are nearby, but not at the trailhead. Despite these things, the trail gets only light use. From the Ides Cove trailhead, the trail drops down to the headwaters of Slide Creek and heads out to the foot of Harvey Peak, at 7,361 feet, which is the halfway point and a good spot for lunch. The trail turns sharply and is routed back along the flank of the South Yolla Bolly Mountains. On the way, it passes both Long and Square Lakes, which are both tiny water holes stocked with brook trout.

**User Groups:** Hikers, dogs, and horses. No mountain bikes. No wheelchair facilities.

**Permits:** A campfire permit is required for hikers planning to camp.

**Maps:** For a map, ask the U.S. Forest Service for Mendocino National Forest or Yolla Bolly Wilderness. For a topographic map, ask the USGS for South Yolla Bolly.

**Directions:** From Corning on I-5, take the Corning Road/Paskenta Road exit and drive west about 20 miles to Paskenta. In the town of Paskenta, Corning/Paskenta Road will split, becoming Round Valley Road on the left and County Road M2/Toomes Creek Road straight ahead. Continue straight on County Road M2/Toomes Creek Road for 20 miles to Cold Springs Ranger Station. Turn right on County Road M22 and drive about 15 miles to the trailhead.

For an alternate route: From Red Bluff, drive west on County Road 356 (Forest Route 22) and drive about 41 miles to the signed access road for Ides Cove trailhead. Turn right and drive to the trailhead.

**Contact:** Mendocino National Forest, Stonyford Work Center, 5171 Stonyfork-Elk Creek Road, P.O. Box 160, Stonyford, CA 95979, 530/963-3128, website: www.fs.fed.us/r5 (click on Forest Offices).

## 12 BIG OAK TRAIL
**1.0 mi / 0.5 hr**

at the head of Black Butte Reservoir west of Orland

Map 4.2, page 156

The Big Oak Trail goes through a riparian area, and the habitat is constantly changing based on creek flows during the winter. The route, an easy jaunt, follows the Stony Creek drainage above the head of Black Butte Reservoir. The riparian habitat here is in a protected state, making it an excellent area to see wildlife in the sparse foothills of the Sacramento Valley. It has become part of California's Watchable Wildlife system. The best time for hiking is at dusk, when wildlife viewing is at its best. Alas, this hike is not without a few potential problems. First is the weather, which is close to intolerable in the summer—a real temperature tantrum—and very hot in spring and fall as well, and that's when most people have time to visit the area. Second, this was once an interpretive trail, but because a flood washed out all the signs, the Army Corps of Engineers simply decided not to replace them. Ranger Mary Ann Deeming said that in the future, the park hopes to provide visitors with a brochure featuring plant and animal information.

**User Groups:** Hikers, dogs, and mountain bikes. No horses. No wheelchair facilities.

**Permits:** No permits are required. Parking and access are free.

**Maps:** For a topographic map, ask the USGS for Julian Rocks.

**Directions:** From I-5 at Orland, take the Black Butte Lake exit. Drive 10 miles west on Newville Road (County Road 200) to County Road 206. Turn left on County Road 206 and drive to County Road 200A. Bear left on County Road 200A and drive to the trailhead.

**Contact:** U.S. Army Corps of Engineers, Black Butte Lake, 19225 Newville Road, Orland, CA 95963-8901, 530/865-4781, website: www.spk.usace.army.mil (click on Black Butte).

## 13 WATERFALL LOOP TRAIL
**13.0 mi / 1.0 day**

on the northwestern boundary of the Snow Mountain Wilderness in Mendocino National Forest

Map 4.2, page 156

Very few people know about the Snow Mountain Wilderness, and far fewer know about this excellent loop trail that traverses the region's most treasured areas. Double-peaked Snow Mountain itself is the big ridge located about midway between I-5 at Willows and U.S. 101 at Willits. This trail starts at the northern boundary of the wilderness at the West Crockett trailhead (just west of Crockett Peak). You hike two miles to get into Middle Fork Creek, and there it connects with the Waterfall Loop Trail. A waterfall is located on a spur trail off the loop (2.2 miles from the trailhead). The trail climbs much of the way, reaching a small loop set between East Snow Mountain (7,056 feet) and West Snow Mountain (7,038 feet). To return, take North Ridge Trail, which drops down from Snow Mountain and traces the Middle Fork of Stony Creek for a good portion of the route back to the parking area. Much of this area can be quite dry and hot in midsummer, especially on the North Ridge.

Two notes: Rattlesnakes are common, and hikers should always be certain to carry a lot of water here—twice as much as usual.

**User Groups:** Hikers, dogs, and horses. No mountain bikes. No wheelchair facilities.

**Permits:** A campfire permit is required for hikers planning to camp. Parking and access are free.

**Maps:** For a map, ask the U.S. Forest Service for Mendocino National Forest. For topographic maps, ask the USGS for Crockett Peak and St. John Mountain.

**Directions:** From Willows on I-5, drive west on Highway 162 for 21 miles to a T junction. Turn left and drive one mile through the town of Elk Creek to Ivory Mill Road. Turn right on Ivory Mill Road (Road 308) and drive 15 miles to Forest Road M3. Turn left on Forest Road M3 and drive 15.5 miles to the signed turnoff for West Crockett trailhead. Turn left and drive .5 mile to the trailhead.

**Contact:** Mendocino National Forest, Stonyford Work Center, 5171 Stonyfork-Elk Creek Road, P.O. Box 160, Stonyford, CA 95979, 530/963-3128, website: www.fs.fed.us/r5 (click on Forest Offices).

## 14 WINDY POINT TRAILHEAD
### 3.25 mi / 1.75 hrs

**on the northern boundary of the Snow Mountain Wilderness in Mendocino National Forest**

Map 4.2, page 156

Every wilderness has secret spots, and so it is here in the Snow Mountain Wilderness. On a hot summer day when every drop of water is counted as if it were liquid gold, you'll find a simple paradise on this short walk to the headwaters of a tiny fork of Bear Wallow Creek. The hike starts at Windy Point, the northernmost trailhead in the Snow Mountains. The trail heads straight east on Bear Wallow Trail for a little more than a mile across very dry country. About 1.5 miles in, start looking for a spur trail on the right side, and when you see it, take it. This spur drops a short distance down to the source of the north fork of Bear Wallow Creek, a truly secret little spot. If you think there are too many people in the world, just come here and look around.

**User Groups:** Hikers, dogs, and horses. No mountain bikes. No wheelchair facilities.

**Permits:** A campfire permit is required for hikers planning to camp. Parking and access are free.

**Maps:** For a map, ask the U.S. Forest Service for Mendocino National Forest. For topographic maps, ask the USGS for Crockett Peak and St. John Mountain.

**Directions:** From Willows on I-5, drive west on Highway 162 for 21 miles to a T junction. Turn left and drive one mile through the town of Elk Creek to Ivory Mill Road. Turn right on Ivory Mill Road (Road 308) and drive 15 miles to Forest Road M3. Turn left on Forest Road M3 and drive 13 miles to the trailhead.

**Contact:** Mendocino National Forest, Stonyford Work Center, 5171 Stonyfork-Elk Creek Road, P.O. Box 160, Stonyford, CA 95979, 530/963-3128, website: www.fs.fed.us/r5 (click on Forest Offices).

## 15 BEAR WALLOW TRAILHEAD
### 4.0 mi / 2.5 hrs

**on the eastern boundary of the Snow Mountain Wilderness in Mendocino National Forest**

Map 4.2, page 156

Whoa, it can get hot out here. In summer a very early start for a hike is mandatory, particularly on the east-facing slopes of the Snow Mountain Wilderness. Your destination is a pretty section of Bear Wallow Creek, a small feeder stream to the middle fork of Stony Creek. The hike starts at the Bear Wallow trailhead. From here the Bear Wallow Trail is routed north; after about two miles, start looking for a trail junction on the left side. Be sure not to miss it. Turn left and take the .25-mile traipse down to Bear Wallow Creek, a pretty spot and a decent destination for a day's walk. Typically you'll have the place all to yourself. But if you miss the turn, the Bear Wallow Trail continues all the way to Windy Point trailhead, and with no water available, you'll be chanting, "Beam me up, Scotty."

**User Groups:** Hikers, dogs, and horses. No mountain bikes. No wheelchair facilities.

**Permits:** A campfire permit is required for hikers planning to camp. Parking and access are free.

**Maps:** For a map, ask the U.S. Forest Service for Mendocino National Forest. For a topographic map, ask the USGS for Fouts Springs.

**Directions:** On I-5 in Maxwell, take the Maxwell exit west, to Maxwell-Sites Road. Turn west on Maxwell-Sites Road and drive to Sites and Sites-Lodoga Road. Turn left on Sites-Lodoga Road and drive to Lodoga and Lodoga-Stonyford Road. Turn left and loop around East Park Reservoir to reach Stonyford and Fouts Spring Road (Road M10). Turn west and drive eight miles to Forest Road 18N06. Turn right and drive nine miles (four-wheel drive is necessary) to the parking area for the trailhead, on the left.

**Contact:** Mendocino National Forest, Stonyford Work Center, 5171 Stonyfork-Elk Creek Road, P.O. Box 160, Stonyford, CA 95979, 530/963-3128, website: www.fs.fed.us/r5 (click on Forest Offices).

## 16 OVERLOOK LOOP
### 8.5 mi / 1.0 day

**on the southwestern boundary of the Snow Mountain Wilderness in Mendocino National Forest**

Map 4.2, page 156

This is not a trail for the indifferent. Do you yearn for the passion of the mountain experience? Do you crave the zest of life when you have a bad case of dry mouth and discover a mountain spring? Is the price of a climb worth it for the mountaintop payoff? Are you nuts? You need to answer yes, yes, yes, and yes to be ready for this loop hike. It includes two killer climbs, a wonderful little spring along the trail, and the ascent of West Snow Mountain, at 7,038 feet. Still interested? Then read on.

The trail starts at the Summit Spring trailhead, and in the first two miles, it includes a no-fun clamber up to High Rock. At the trail junction here, turn right on Box Spring Loop Trail and hike past the headwaters of Trout Creek to Box Spring, located just to the right of the trail, near another trail junction. In hot weather (typically all summer), this spot is paradise. Turn left and make the three-mile climb up West Snow Mountain, sweating it out every step of the way. Enjoy this victory for a while before dropping back down for the final three miles to the trailhead and parking area. This is an excellent loop hike, one that furnishes several rewards but makes you earn every one of them.

**User Groups:** Hikers, dogs, and horses. No mountain bikes. No wheelchair facilities.

**Permits:** A campfire permit is required for hikers planning to camp. Parking and access are free.

**Maps:** For a map, ask the U.S. Forest Service for Mendocino National Forest. For a topographic map, ask the USGS for Fouts Springs.

**Directions:** On I-5 in Maxwell, take the Maxwell

exit west and to Maxwell-Sites Road. Turn west on Maxwell-Sites Road and drive to Sites and Sites-Lodoga Road. Turn left on Sites-Lodoga Road and drive to Lodoga and Lodoga-Stonyford Road. Turn left and loop around East Park Reservoir to reach Stonyford and Fouts Spring Road (Road M10). Turn west and drive 25 miles to a signed access road for Summit Spring trailhead. Turn right and drive 1.5 miles to the parking area and trailhead, at the end of the road.

**Contact:** Mendocino National Forest, Stonyford Work Center, 5171 Stonyfork-Elk Creek Road, P.O. Box 160, Stonyford, CA 95979, 530/963-3128, website: www.fs.fed.us/r5 (click on Forest Offices).

## 🔢17 ALDER CREEK TRAIL
**4.0 mi / 1.75 hrs**

**in Manchester Beach State Park on the Mendocino coast north of Point Arena**
Map 4.3, page 157

Manchester State Beach has two moods—one sweet, one foul. In late winter and fall, radiant sunbeams set the Mendocino coast aglow, making for flawless beach walks. But in spring and early summer, with winds powering out of the north, it can feel as if your head would blow off if it weren't attached by the neck. The hike here starts by the park headquarters and is routed past Lake Davis to the beach, continuing north along the beach to the mouth of Alder Creek. This is an attractive coastal lagoon, known for many species of birds, including whistling swans. It's also the area where the San Andreas Fault heads off from land into the sea. Time it right here, and all can seem perfect.

**User Groups:** Hikers and horses. No dogs. The terrain isn't suitable for mountain bikes. No wheelchair facilities.

**Permits:** No permits are required. Parking and access are free.

**Maps:** A brochure and trail map is available for a fee at Manchester Beach State Park at the address below. For a topographic map, ask the USGS for Point Arena.

**Directions:** From Point Arena, drive north on Highway 1 for five miles to Kinney Lane. Turn left and drive one mile to the park entrance, on the right.

**Contact:** Manchester Beach State Park, c/o California State Parks, Mendocino District, P.O. Box 440, Mendocino, CA 95460, 707/937-5804, website: www.parks.ca.gov (click on Find A Park).

## 🔢18 HEADLANDS LOOP
**1.5 mi / 0.75 hr**

**in Gualala Point Regional Park on the Sonoma coast**
Map 4.3, page 157

The Headlands (to beach) Loop is an easy, short walk that furnishes coastal views (with a short cutoff on a spur trail) and a lookout over the Gualala River, not to mention a route amid giant coastal cypress trees. From the visitors center, the trail is routed along the Gualala River and then turns and loops to the left. Here you can take the short cutoff trail that leads to the beach. On the way back, the trail traces the ocean bluffs for a short spell (take the spur trail), and with it comes the coastal views. Then the trail turns inland and returns to the visitors center. Bonuses here include excellent whale-watching during the winter and good wildflower blooms on the grassy hillsides in spring. It is mostly level, with a trailhead elevation of 250 feet.

**User Groups:** Hikers and dogs. No horses.

**Permits:** No permits are required. There is a parking fee of $4 per vehicle.

**Maps:** For a topographic map, ask the USGS for Gualala.

**Directions:** From Gualala, drive south on Highway 1 for .25 mile (over the Gualala River) and turn west into the park entrance. Continue to the visitors center.

**Contact:** Gualala Point Regional Park, P.O. Box 95, Gualala, CA 95445, 707/785-2377; Sonoma County Regional Parks Department, 707/565-2041, website: www.sonoma-county.org/parks/.

## 19 SOUTHLAKE TRAIL
### 5.2 mi / 2.0 hrs

**at Lake Sonoma northwest of Healdsburg**

**Map 4.3, page 157**

Lake Sonoma is one of the best examples in California of where the government folks have done something right. They not only built this lake, they added a superb boat ramp, marina, and campgrounds (including many great boat-in sites) and started a good bass fishery. They also cut 43 miles of trail, enough to spend days traipsing around the hills. The South Lake trailhead is the best starting point, though the short trail at Vista Point (also called Overlook) has the best views (and the most wind in the spring and heat in the summer).

The Southlake Trail starts off of Stewart's Point Road below the Overlook. There are spectacular views of the lake the entire way. The trail is not very steep, but does have some changes in elevation. It features sun exposure, making it great for wildflowers in the spring but very hot on summer afternoons. The trail winds along the southwestern portion of Warm Springs Arm through gray pine and madrone woodlands. It traces alongside the lake, enters and exits a series of small groves, and extends along the lake's fingers. Most of the habitat is oak grasslands, and on rare occasion you may see wild pigs, deer, or rattlesnakes. At 2.7 miles, you'll reach Quicksilver Campground—it's the easiest hike to any lakeside campground at Lake Sonoma. A few trails bisect the route and extend into more-remote surrounding country, allowing ambitious hikers to create longer adventures. When you've had enough, just turn back.

**User Groups:** Hikers, dogs, and horses. No mountain bikes. No wheelchair facilities.

**Permits:** No permits are required. Parking and access are free.

**Maps:** For a free map, go to the visitors center or contact the U.S. Corps of Engineers at the address below. For a topographic map, ask the USGS for Warm Springs Dam.

**Directions:** From Santa Rosa, drive 12 miles north on U.S. 101 to the town of Healdsburg and Dry Creek Road. Make a left turn at the Dry Creek Road exit and drive about 11 miles, crossing Dry Creek (Dry Creek Road becomes Skaggs Springs Road) and continuing (passing the visitors center) to Skaggs Springs–Stewart Point Road. Turn left, drive .25 mile, and then turn right and drive to the trailhead, on the left.

**Contact:** U.S. Army Corps of Engineers, Lake Sonoma, 3333 Skaggs Springs Road, Geyserville, CA 95441, 707/433-9483, website: www.spn.usace.army.mil/lakesonoma.

## 20 SALT POINT BLUFF TRAIL
### 3.5 mi / 1.5 hrs

**in Salt Point State Park north of Jenner**

**Map 4.3, page 157**

The dramatic, rocky shoreline of Salt Point State Park is memorable to anyone who has seen it. This trail provides the best look at it, including some simply awesome views from a 100-foot-high ocean bluff. The trailhead is at the parking area set near the tip of Salt Point. From there, hike north over Warren Creek, a seasonal stream, and then across the bluffs. You can practically feel the crashing of ocean breakers below you, the spray rocketing skyward. The trail eventually winds around and down to Stump Beach Cove, a pretty, sandy beach where the calm waters are in sharp contrast to the nearby mauling ocean breakers. Salt Point State Park is known for excellent sport abalone diving in season, and also for providing one of the few marine reserves (Gerstle Cove) where no form of marine life may be taken or disturbed.

**User Groups:** Hikers only. Horses are allowed on designated trails only, and mountain bikes are allowed only on fire roads. One trail (Gerstle Cove) is paved for wheelchairs for 100 yards out to Salt Point. No dogs.

**Permits:** No permits are required. A state park day-use fee of $6 is charged per vehicle.

**Maps:** A trail map is available for a fee from Salt

Point State Park at the address below. For a topographic map, ask the USGS for Plantation.

**Directions:** From U.S. 101 north of Santa Rosa, drive to the River Road exit. Take that exit and drive west for 13 miles to Highway 116 and Guerneville. Turn west on Highway 116 and drive to Highway 1 at Jenner. Turn north on Highway 1 and drive 20 miles (nine miles past Fort Ross) to the park entrance. Turn left (west) and drive to the entrance kiosk. The trailhead is at the Salt Point parking area.

**Contact:** Salt Point State Park, 25050 Coast Highway 1, Jenner, CA 95450, 707/847-3221, website: www.parks.ca.gov (click on Find A Park).

## **21** STOCKOFF CREEK LOOP
### 1.25 mi / 0.75 hr

**in Stillwater Cove Regional Park north of Jenner**

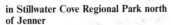

Highway 1 is one of the top tourist drives in the United States, which explains why the coastal state parks get such heavy use in the summer months. This little regional park, however, is sometimes overlooked by out-of-state traffic. The trailhead is located at the day-use parking lot, and after starting the walk, you'll almost immediately enter a surprising forest comprised of firs and redwoods. You then come to the Loop Trail junction, where you turn right (another good idea is to take Schoolhouse Trail, a spur trail that is routed a short distance to a historic schoolhouse, and then return). The trail is routed along the creek, crosses a few bridges, and eventually rises above the watershed and loops back through forest to the parking area. It's an easy, pretty, and secluded loop hike. The trailhead elevation is 100 feet; elevation changes on this hike amount to 140 feet. A bonus is visiting Stillwater Cove, which requires crossing Highway 1 and then dropping down to the beach, a dramatic rock-strewn shore.

**User Groups:** Hikers and dogs. No horses or mountain bikes. No wheelchair facilities.

**Permits:** No permits are required. A day-use fee of $6 is charged for each vehicle.

**Maps:** For a free brochure, contact Stillwater Cove Regional Park at the address below. For a topographic map, ask the USGS for Plantation.

**Directions:** Just north of Santa Rosa on U.S. 101, take the River Road exit. Turn left and follow River Road past Monte Rio. Go right on Highway 116 and drive to Highway 1. Turn right and head north, past the town of Jenner, for 16 miles to the park entrance, on the right at mile marker 37.01.

**Contact:** Stillwater Cove Regional Park, County of Sonoma, 2300 County Center Drive, Suite 120, Santa Rosa, CA 95403, 707/847-3245; Regional Parks Department, 707/565-2041, website: www.sonoma-county.org/parks/.

## **22** BODEGA HEAD LOOP
### 1.5 mi / 1.0 hr

**on the Sonoma coast west of Bodega Bay**

Map 4.3, page 157

The ocean seems to stretch to forever here. A short loop hike at Bodega Head will provide an introduction to one of California's great coastal areas for an easy hike and views that can set off feelings that you will never forget. The trail starts at the east parking lot, and in just 1.5 miles, it takes hikers into a wonderland—with views of cliffs and untouched beaches—and on southward to the sea and beyond. For a side trip, take a short tromp on a spur trail to the tip-top of Bodega Head for 360-degree views. Rarely does the ocean seem so vast as it does from here. In spring and early summer, the wind can really howl. In late summer, fall, or late winter, Bodega Bay gets its warmest—and often, most wind-free—weather. Bonuses: The whale-watching is great from January through April. And on clear, calm evenings, the parking lot provides a lookout for sunsets; they are so beautiful, they can break your heart.

**User Groups:** Hikers only. No horses, dogs, or mountain bikes. No wheelchair facilities.

**Permits:** No permits are required. Parking and access are free.

**Maps:** A trail map and brochure are available

for a fee from Sonoma Coast State Beach at the address below.

**Directions:** From U.S. 101 at Petaluma, take the East Washington exit. Turn west on East Washington Street and drive through Petaluma (it becomes Bodega Avenue) for about 10 miles to Valley Ford Road. Bear right and drive 7.5 miles to Highway 1. Turn north on Highway 1 and drive nine miles to Bodega Bay and continue to East Shore Road. Turn left on East Shore Road and drive less than .5 mile to a stop sign at Bay Flat Road. Turn right and drive five miles around Bodega Bay (the road turns into West Side Road). Continue past Spud Point Marina and drive to the Bodega Head parking area.

**Contact:** Sonoma Coast State Beach, 3095 Highway 1, Bodega Bay, CA 94923, 707/875-3483, website: www.parks.ca.gov (click on Find A Park).

## 23 BLUE RIDGE TRAIL
**1.0–17.0 mi / 1.0 day**

**north of Lake Berryessa**

Map 4.4, page 158

The Blue Ridge Trail provides a unique glimpse of the southern portion of the Cache Creek Natural Area and well beyond. Of course, there is a price. The Blue Ridge Trail includes a stretch with a 2,000-foot elevation gain in just over three miles, as well as many pieces of trail that are very steep, rocky, and dry. The trail follows the ridge for five miles (most folks don't last anywhere near that long) to a remote trailhead, and you'd better be as fit as a Sherpa to try it. But hey, in spring this can be a sensational hike, with wildflowers ablaze and bushes and trees in full bloom. You'll see songbirds, swallows, falcons, and eagles flitting, hovering, and soaring. There are also a good share of lizards and rattlesnakes. The views are exceptional in all directions, with the Sutter Buttes and Snow Mountain most prominent, but with even Shasta and Lassen in view on clear days. In fact, the area has just about everything—everything

that is, except water. You either bring at least two or three quarts per person, or you surrender, swearing never to hike here again.

**User Groups:** Hikers and dogs. Horses and mountain bikes, while allowed, aren't recommended because of the steep, rocky terrain. No wheelchair facilities.

**Permits:** No permits are required. Parking and access are free.

**Maps:** For a free primitive trail map, contact the Bureau of Land Management at the address below. For a topographic map, ask the USGS for Glascock.

**Directions:** From I-5 at Woodland, drive west on Highway 16 for about 45 miles to Lower Yolo County Park and the junction with County Road 40 (a gravel road). Turn left on County Road 40, drive .25 mile, and look for a concrete bridge (low water crossing). After crossing the bridge, drive 200 yards and look for the trailhead, on the left. Park in the unpaved area near Cache Creek. Walk down the dirt road through a meadow to the trailhead. In the winter, the dirt road is blocked by a locked gate; park instead at Lower Yolo County Park and walk down to the trailhead. Note that during the winter, the bridge is at times impassable due to high water.

**Contact:** Bureau of Land Management, Ukiah Field Office, 2550 North State Street, Ukiah, CA 95482, 707/468-4000, fax 707/468-4027, website: www.ca.blm.gov (click on Field Offices).

## 24 GILLIAM CREEK TRAIL
**8.9 mi / 1.0 day**

**in Austin Creek State Recreation Area north of Guerneville**

Map 4.4, page 158

The rolling hills, open forests, and streamside riparian habitat in Austin Creek State Recreation Area can seem a million miles away from the forests of Armstrong Redwoods. Yet the two parks together actually form 6,488 acres of contiguous parkland. While most tourists are walking around the redwoods at Armstrong, this trail offers a quieter, more ambitious alternative. From the trailhead (at 1,100 feet), you contour across the slope, then drop down to the headwaters of Schoolhouse Creek, at 400 feet. The trail then follows the stream, past the confluence with Gilliam Creek, extending 3.7 miles into the backcountry, all the way down to a 200-foot elevation. At the confluence of East Austin Creek, turn right and hike deeper into wild, hilly country along the stream, then return on the loop on East Austin Creek Trail, a fire road with a climb to boot. At this point, you may ask, "Are we having fun yet?" Visitors who love Armstrong Redwoods tend not to speak of the adjoining Austin Creek Recreation Area with any terms of endearment.

**User Groups:** Hikers and horses (no horses permitted during wet weather). Mountain bikes permitted on fire roads. No dogs. No wheelchair facilities.

**Permits:** No permits are required. A state park day-use fee of $6 is charged for each vehicle. A senior discount is available.

**Maps:** A trail map is available for $.50 from Armstrong Redwoods State Reserve at the address below. For a topographic map, ask the USGS for Guerneville.

**Directions:** From Santa Rosa, drive north on U.S. 101 to the River Road exit. Take that exit, turn west on River Road, and drive 13 miles to Guerneville. Continue to Armstrong Woods Road. Turn right (north) on Armstrong Woods Road and drive 2.5 miles to the Armstrong Redwoods State Reserve entrance. The trailhead is about four miles past the entrance. No trailers or vehicles more than 20 feet long are permitted in Austin Creek State Recreation Area.

**Contact:** Armstrong Redwoods State Reserve, 17000 Armstrong Redwoods Road, Guerneville, CA 95446, 707/869-2015 or 707/865-2391, website: www.parks.ca.gov (click on Find A Park).

## 25 EAST RIDGE TRAIL
**6.8 mi / 1.0 day**

**in Armstrong Redwoods State Reserve north of Guerneville**

Map 4.4, page 158

It's almost obligatory to hike either the Discovery Trail or Armstrong Nature Trail in Armstrong Redwoods—both are very short and beautiful strolls through the park's grove of huge redwoods. But after that taste, your appetite will likely be whetted for something more inspiring. The East Ridge Trail provides it, rising 1,400 feet over the course of 3.4 miles, at times offering lookouts below into a sea of redwood tops. The trailhead is at a 200-foot elevation, adjacent to Fife Creek. The route climbs gradually at first, then in the first .5 mile rises to cross the headwaters of Fife Creek, at an elevation of 600 feet. Your climb has only just begun, and if you're already running out of gas, you'd best head back. The trail continues climbing all the way, contouring its way up toward McCray Mountain (1,940 feet), topping out at a service road at 1,600 feet.

**User Groups:** Hikers and horses. No dogs or mountain bikes. No wheelchair facilities.

**Permits:** No permits are required. A state park day-use fee of $6 is charged for each vehicle. A senior discount is available. It is possible to park outside the entrance kiosk and walk in without paying a fee.

**Maps:** A trail map is available for $.50 from Armstrong Redwoods State Reserve at the address below. For a topographic map, ask the USGS for Guerneville.

**Directions:** From Santa Rosa, drive north on U.S. 101 to the River Road exit. Take that exit, turn west on River Road, and drive 13 miles to Guerneville. Continue to Armstrong Woods Road. Turn right (north) on Armstrong Woods Road and drive 2.5 miles to the Armstrong Redwoods State Reserve entrance. The trailhead is adjacent to the visitors center.

**Contact:** Armstrong Redwoods State Reserve, 17000 Armstrong Redwoods Road, Guerneville, CA 95446, 707/869-2015; Russian River District, 707/865-2391, website: www.parks.ca.gov (click on Find A Park).

## 26 MOUNT ST. HELENA TRAIL
**10.6 mi / 4.5 hrs**

**in Robert Louis Stevenson State Park north of Calistoga**

Map 4.4, page 158

Mount St. Helena is Sonoma County's highest mountain—the peak that strikes such a memorable silhouette when viewed from the Bay Area. This trail climbs to the summit (at 4,343 feet), requiring an ascent of 2,068 feet over the course of five miles. The route follows a moderate grade for the most part, then rises above the forest and includes two steep sections, one at the very end of your climb. In the summer, the hike can be pure hell: Much of the trail is actually a fire road with little shade, there's no water anywhere along the route, and the heat commonly blazes in the 90s and 100s out here. Most visitors make the trip when temperatures are more tolerable, of course, which makes the gradient feel pretty moderate. The mountain is most often visited in the winter, when passing storms often cause the summit to be flecked with snow (quite a treat for most folks in the area). In fact, when the snow level drops to 3,500 feet, the entire mountaintop can get a good pasting of a foot of snow. In spring, north winds clear the air, and visibility is best at this time, with remarkable views in all directions. Bill Grummer, a ranger pal, claims that on the best days, visitors can see Mount Shasta (192 miles away), but so far we haven't had that experience. But it is documented that in the late 19th century, surveyors sent signals back and forth between here and Mount Shasta, setting a record for longest signal distance. On other stellar days, you can see the Farallon Islands, 25 miles offshore from San Francisco, and a glimpse of the city itself (but not the Golden Gate Bridge). No matter when you hike, be certain to bring plenty of water, a day pack with high-energy food, a windbreaker, and a change of shirts (so you won't be making the return downhill trip with a cold, wet shirt).

**User Groups:** Hikers only on single-track trail. Mountain bikes allowed on a nearby fire road .25 mile north on Highway 29. No dogs or horses. No wheelchair facilities.

**Permits:** No permits are required. Parking and access are free.

**Maps:** A brochure/map is available for $1 at the park or for $1.60 by mail at the address below. For topographic maps, ask the USGS for Detert Reservoir and Mount St. Helena.

**Directions:** From Calistoga, drive about eight miles north on Highway 29 to the parking area at the highway summit, signed Robert Louis Stevenson State Park. The trailhead is next to the parking area. You can park on the east or west side of the road. The trail is located on the west side of the road (the trailhead is not signed from the road).

**Contact:** Robert Louis Stevenson State Park, c/o Bothe-Napa Valley State Park, 3801 St. Helena Highway North, Calistoga, CA 94515, 707/942-4575; Silverado District, 707/938-1519, website: www.parks.ca.gov (click on Find A Park).

## 27 PALISADES TRAIL
**4.0–9.5 mi one-way / 2.0–4.0 hr**

**near Calistoga**

Map 4.4, page 158

Calistoga is one of the best decompression chambers designed by mankind. But after a day or two of getting turned into Jell-O by soaks in steaming mineral water, massages, and mud baths, you can be brought back to life by the electrifying hike to the Palisades.

The Palisades? Aren't the Palisades a glacier-carved series of 14,000-foot peaks in the Sierra Nevada? Well, yep, but Napa County's Palisades are nearly as dramatic and accessible year-round: It's a stunning, mile-long volcanic wall set along a ridge that overlooks Calistoga and the Napa Valley. The Palisades is dramatic up close and personal, and provides gorgeous long-distances views. In addition, this trail is one of the best near Calistoga to see raptors (including a chance to spot peregrine falcons) and also for wildflowers, particularly bitteroot.

From Calistoga, it's a twisty, eight-mile drive up Highway 29 to the parking area and trailhead, the same staging area used for the Mount St. Helena Trail. It is signed Robert Louis Stevenson State Park. To climb Mount St. Helena (a 10-mile round-trip, a 2,000-foot climb), the trail is on the left (northwest) side of the road. To hike to Table Rock and the Palisades, the trailhead is on the right (southeast) side of the road.

This trip can be done three ways: A 4-mile round-trip to Table Rock and back, an 8-mile round-trip to the southern edge of the Palisades and back (recommended), or a wild 9.5-mile one-way trek (with a shuttle car) down to the valley. The best time for this getaway is from mid-March through mid-May, when the foothills are green, the skies are often crystal-clear, and the morning air is still cool.

From the southeast side of the parking area (elevation 2,250 feet), you start this hike on the Table Rock Trail. It's about two miles to Table Rock (2,465 feet), just enough of a climb to get you above the canyon woodlands. Some enjoy the views from atop Table Rock, have a picnic, and then head back to the car. But the trip gets better by continuing on the Palisades Trail. This drops down to Lasky Point (2,045 feet), and then climbs back up for about two miles along the base of the Palisades (2,930 feet). The trail is spectacular, set just beneath the sheer volcanic cliffs along the ridge. At 3.9 miles in, you will reach the junction of Historic Oat Hill Mine Road, a long abandoned rocky jeep road. Most people turn around and head back from here.

Oat Hill Mine Road is the route down to the valley for a one-way hike with a shuttle. But it plummets 2,000 feet over 4.5 miles, some of it rocky, and can be a thigh-burning, knee-wrenching, toe-jamming experience that's only for the deranged (like myself, for instance).

Note: There is no drinking water available anywhere on the trail. Rangers warn not to leave valuables in your car (covering them with a jacket or blanket isn't enough either).

**User Groups:** Hikers only. No dogs, horses, or mountain bikes. No wheelchair facilities.

**Permits:** Parking and access are free.

**Maps:** A brochure/map is available for a fee at the park or by mail at the address below. For topographic maps, ask the USGS for Detert Reservoir and Mount St. Helena.

**Directions:** From Calistoga, drive eight miles north on Highway 29 to the signed trailhead at the edge of the parking area, on the west side of the highway at Robert Louis Stevenson State Park.

**Contact:** Robert Louis Stevenson State Park, c/o Bothe-Napa Valley State Park, 3801 St. Helena Highway North, Calistoga, CA 94515, 707/942-4575; Silverado District, 707/938-1519, website: www.parks.ca.gov (click on Find A Park).

## 28 COYOTE PEAK/ REDWOOD TRAIL LOOP

4.4 mi / 3.0 hrs

**in Bothe-Napa Valley State Park south of Calistoga**

Map 4.4, page 158

Who ever heard of redwoods in the Napa Valley? Who ever heard of a mountain peak there, too? Only those who also know of Bothe-Napa Valley State Park, which is like an island of wildland in a sea of winery tourist traffic. Bothe-Napa has some of the most easterly stands of coastal redwoods, plus Douglas fir and an excellent lookout from Coyote Peak, all quite a surprise for newcomers. The best way to see it is on the Coyote Peak/Redwood Trail Loop, starting just past the Ritchey Creek Campground turnoff, near the picnic area. The first .5 mile is on the Ritchey Canyon Trail, a very pretty stretch of trail along beautiful Ritchey Creek. Then veer left onto the Redwood Trail, where you'll be surrounded by some of the park's highest stands of redwoods. The trail continues along Ritchey Creek for .25 mile, then connects to the Coyote Peak Trail. Take the Coyote Peak Trail, which rises quickly, skirting the northern flank of Coyote Peak. (A short spur trail will take you all the way to the top, elevation 1,170 feet.) Then the trail drops down the other side of the hill and intersects with South Fork Trail, which heads all the way back down to Ritchey Creek. Note that temperatures can be extremely hot in the summer—as high as 105 degrees in unshaded areas—but you'll find a cool paradise along Ritchey Creek. From the trailhead to the end of the hike, the elevation gain is roughly 800 feet, totaling the up-and-downs.

**User Groups:** Hikers only. Horses permitted on some designated trails. Mountain bikes allowed on fire roads and designated trails but not on most of this described loop. No dogs. No wheelchair facilities.

**Permits:** No permits are required. A state park fee of $6 is charged per vehicle.

**Maps:** A brochure and trail map are available for $1 at the park or $1.60 by mail at the address below. For a topographic map, ask the USGS for Calistoga.

**Directions:** From the town of St. Helena, drive north on Highway 128/29 for five miles (past Bale Grist Mill State Historic Park) to the park entrance, on the left side of the road. Turn left and drive past the entrance station to just past the Ritchey Creek Campground turnoff (near the picnic area), where there is trailhead parking.

**Contact:** Bothe-Napa Valley State Park, 3801 St. Helena Highway North, Calistoga, CA 94515, 707/942-4575; California State Parks, Silverado District, 707/938-1519, website: www.parks.ca.gov (click on Find A Park).

## 29 SPRING LAKE TRAIL
**2.0 mi / 1.0 hr**

**in Spring Lake Regional Park in eastern Santa Rosa**

Map 4.4, page 158

Spring Lake is Santa Rosa's backyard fishing hole, a popular place for trout fishing, an evening

picnic, or a short hike. For newcomers, we suggest you take the walk along the west shore of Spring Lake to the west dam, then turn left and head into adjoining Howarth Park and on to Lake Ralphine. It's an easy, enjoyable stroll. The lake is stocked with trout in winter and spring, and it provides a fair warm-water fishery in the summer. The lake is fun and quiet, with boats restricted to electric motors; no gas motors are allowed. The elevation is 300 feet, and the trail is mostly level.

**User Groups:** Hikers and dogs. Horses are allowed only on designated trails. The park has 2.3 miles of trail that are paved for wheelchair and bicycle use.

**Permits:** No permits are required. There is a parking fee of $5 per vehicle.

**Maps:** A free trail map is available from Spring Lake Regional Park at the address below. For a topographic map, ask the USGS for Santa Rosa.

**Directions:** From U.S. 101 in Santa Rosa, take the Highway 12 exit and drive east. Continue on Highway 12 (it becomes Hoen Avenue) to Newanga Avenue. Turn left on Newanga Avenue and drive .5 mile to the park entrance. The various trailheads are well marked and easily accessible from the parking area at the lake.

**Contact:** Spring Lake Regional Park, c/o Sonoma County Regional Parks, 2300 Country Center Drive, Santa Rosa, CA 95403, 707/539-8092; Sonoma County Regional Parks Department, 707/565-2041, website: www.sonoma-county .org/parks/.

## 30 BALD MOUNTAIN LOOP
**8.2 mi / 1.0 day**

**in Sugarloaf Ridge State Park north of Sonoma**

Map 4.4, page 158

Bald Mountain, elevation 2,729 feet, overlooks the Napa Valley, with Mount St. Helena to the north. On clear days from the summit, visitors can see portions of the San Francisco Bay Area and then be thankful they're here instead of there. The old mountain is the centerpiece of

Sugarloaf Ridge State Park, a 4,020-acre park featuring redwoods in the Sonoma Creek watershed, open meadows peppered with oaks on the hilltops, and some chaparral on ridges. The most ambitious hike in the park is the Bald Mountain Loop, an 8.2-mile trek that starts at the parking lot, then is routed in a loop by taking the Bald Mountain, Gray Pine, Brushy Peaks, and Meadow Trails. Many less-demanding hikes are available in the park, but this route will give hikers the greatest sense of the park's wildest lands. It's best hiked in the spring, when the air is still cool, the hills are green, and the wildflowers are in bloom. There's a bonus as well: When Sonoma Creek is really flowing, a 25-foot waterfall set in a wooded canyon tumbles downstream from the campground; a short trail is available from the park's entrance road, located at an unsigned turnout on the road's shoulder. A more formal route to the waterfall is on Canyon Trail.

**User Groups:** Hikers only. Horses are allowed on trails in summer and on fire roads in the park in winter. No dogs. No wheelchair facilities.

**Permits:** No permits are required. A state park day-use fee of $6 is charged for each vehicle.

**Maps:** A trail map and brochure are available for a fee from Sugarloaf Ridge State Park at the address below. For a topographic map, ask the USGS for Kenwood.

**Directions:** From U.S. 101 at Santa Rosa, take the Highway 12 exit east. Drive east on Highway 12 through Kenwood to Adobe Canyon Road. Turn left and drive 3.5 miles to the main park entrance, at the end of the road.

**Contact:** Sugarloaf Ridge State Park, 2605 Adobe Canyon Road, Kenwood, CA 95452, 707/833-5712; California State Parks, Silverado District, 707/938-1519, website: www.parks.ca.gov (click on Find A Park).

## 31 LAKE TRAIL
**2.0 mi / 0.75 hr**

**in Jack London State Historic Park**
**north of Sonoma**

Map 4.4, page 158

You'll likely feel the shadow of the ghost of Jack London as you walk in his steps on Lake Trail. It was here that London created his dreams as one of America's truly great writers and philosophers. It was also here that those dreams were shattered, first by a fire that devoured his ranch home, then by an illness at age 40 from which he never recovered. Most visitors start the trip by touring London's cottage, winery ruins, barns, and distillery. Yearning for more? The Lake Trail easily provides it. The short walk leads to a small pond, which served as a favorite recreation area for London and his guests. The trail circles it and then returns to the parking area.

**User Groups:** Hikers only. No dogs. Horses and mountain bikes are allowed on selected trails only. No wheelchair facilities.

**Permits:** No permits are required. A $6 state park day-use fee is charged for each vehicle.

**Maps:** For a trail map and brochure, send $1 to Jack London State Historic Park at the address below. For a topographic map, ask the USGS for Glen Ellen.

**Directions:** From U.S. 101 at Santa Rosa, take the Highway 12 exit east. Drive east to the Glen Ellen/Arnold Drive turnoff. Turn right on Arnold Drive and drive two miles to London Ranch Road. Turn right and drive one mile to the park entrance.

**Contact:** Jack London State Historic Park, 2400 London Ranch Road, Glen Ellen, CA 95442, 707/938-5216; California State Parks, Silverado District, 707/938-1519, website: www.parks.ca.gov (click on Find A Park).

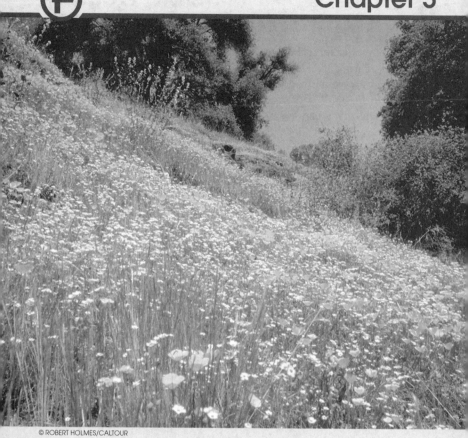
© ROBERT HOLMES/CALTOUR

## Chapter 5

# Sacramento and Gold Country

# Sacramento and Gold Country

**F**rom a distance, this section of the Sacramento Valley looks like flat farmland extending into infinity, with a sprinkling of cities and towns interrupting the view. But a closer look reveals a landscape filled with Northern California's most significant rivers—the Sacramento, Feather, Yuba, American, and Mokelumne. All of these provide water recreation (in both lakes and rivers), as well as serve as the lifeblood for a series of wildlife refuges.

This is an area for California-history buffs: Malakoff Diggins State Historic Park, Auburn State Recreation Area, and Spenceville Wildlife Area are all here, the center of the extraordinary gold rush era. This region also features Calaveras Big Trees in the foothills near Arnold along Highway 4, and, of course, the 32-mile American River Parkway, stretching from Sacramento on upstream along the American River to Rancho Cordova and Fair Oaks.

The highlight of the foothill country is a series of rivers and lakes that provide great hiking and water sports. Every canyon has a river, and every river has a trail. Some of these trails lead to fantastic waterfalls, such as Feather River Falls and Shingle Falls. The lakes include Camanche, Rollins, Oroville, Bucks, and many others, and several of these lakes provide trails along their shores.

In love and the great outdoors, timing is everything, and so it is in the Central Valley and the nearby foothills. Spring and fall are gorgeous here, along with many summer evenings. But there are always periods of 100-plus temperatures in the summer. But that's what gives the lakes and rivers such appeal, and in turn, it's why they are treasured. On a hot day, there is nothing quite like hiking deep into a remote canyon, then jumping into a cool river. It can make water seem more valuable than gold and a cold drink on ice worth more than silver.

# Map 5.1

## Hikes 1–6
## Pages 183–185

# Map 5.2

**Hikes 7–8**
**Page 186**

© AVALON TRAVEL PUBLISHING, INC.

## ■ BUCKS SUMMIT TO FEATHER RIVER (PCT)

**20.0 mi one-way / 2.0 days**

at Bucks Summit Trailhead at the southern boundary of the Bucks Lake Wilderness west of Quincy

Map 5.1, page 181

It's 20 miles from Bucks Summit to Belden, all of it on the Pacific Crest Trail through the Bucks Lake Wilderness. The trail passes across a granitic-based alpine area, where forest is interspersed with glacier-smoothed rock peaks. The trailhead is at Bucks Summit (elevation 5,531 feet), and from here, the route generally follows the ridgeline for many miles, climbing to the southern flank of Mount Pleasant, at 6,924 feet. Along the way, a short spur trail to little Rock Lake provides a good side trip. The trail heads past Three Lakes, where another spur trail provides another option, this one to Kellogg Lake. From here, the trail begins descending and then drops very sharply all the way down to 2,310 feet, to the North Fork Feather River at Belden. Your big toes will be sore for days from jamming into the front of your boots.

To continue north on the Pacific Crest Trail (PCT), see the Feather River to Humboldt Summit (PCT) hike, in the Lassen and Modoc chapter. If you are walking this trail in reverse, see the Fowler Peak to Bucks Summit (PCT) hike, in the Tahoe and the Northern Sierra chapter, to continue south.

**User Groups:** Hikers, dogs, and horses. No mountain bikes. No wheelchair access.

**Permits:** A wilderness permit (free) is required. Parking and access are free.

**Maps:** For a map, ask the U.S. Forest Service for Plumas National Forest. For a topographic map, ask the USGS for Bucks Lake.

**Directions:** From Quincy, turn west on Bucks Lake Road and drive about 11 miles to the trailhead, at Bucks Summit.

**Contact:** Plumas National Forest, Mount Hough Ranger District, 39696 State Highway 70, Quincy, CA 95971, 530/283-0555, website: www.fs .fed.us/r5 (click on Forest Offices).

## ■ HARTMAN BAR NATIONAL RECREATION TRAIL

**4.4 mi / 3.0 hrs**

in Plumas National Forest east of Lake Oroville

Map 5.1, page 181

Hikers often pay for their pleasure, and this hike involves two installments. The trail descends from the Hartman Ridge down the canyon to Hartman Bar Ridge, on the Middle Fork Feather River. Going down will have your toes jamming into your boots, and the trip back can have your heart firing off like cannon shots. But waiting is the Middle Fork Feather, one of the prettiest streams around, and with some of the best trout fishing as well. In fact, of the hundreds of trout streams in California, the Middle Fork Feather is clearly in the top five. If you don't like to fish but would rather explore further, a footbridge crosses the stream and climbs the other side of the canyon, meeting Catrell Creek at .5 mile. If you want to split the trip in two, the primitive Dan Beebe Camp is available along the river.

**User Groups:** Hikers, dogs, and horses. A horse corral is at the trailhead. Mountain bikes not recommended. No wheelchair facilities.

**Permits:** No permits are required. Parking and access are free.

**Maps:** For a map, ask the U.S. Forest Service for Plumas National Forest. For topographic maps, ask the USGS for Cascade and Haskins Valley.

**Directions:** From Oroville, drive east on Highway 162 for eight miles to Highway 174/Forbestown Road (and a junction signed Challenge/LaPorte). Turn right on Forbestown Road and drive east to Highway 120 (Quincy-LaPorte Road). Turn left and drive past LaPorte to Little Grass Valley Road. Turn left and drive a short distance to Black Rock Campground. Turn left on Forest Road 94 and drive 10 miles to Forest Road 22N42Y. Turn right and drive .25 mile to the parking area, at the end of the road.

**Contact:** Plumas National Forest, Feather River Ranger District, 875 Mitchell Avenue, Oroville,

CA 95965-4699, 530/534-6500, website: www.fs.fed.us/r5 (click on Forest Offices).

## 3 FEATHER FALLS NATIONAL RECREATION TRAIL
**9.5 mi / 4.0 hrs**

**in Plumas National Forest east of Lake Oroville**

Map 5.1, page 181

Ⓕ Feather Falls is heaven to look at—a 640-foot silver band of water free-falling into a granite canyon. It's the kind of sight that can leave you feeling refreshed for weeks. In the spring, it's wide and powerful, and in years when there is a big snowpack in the Sierra, it stays that way well into July. But it runs all year and is beautiful even in the fall. The prime viewing area is an awesome perch—a viewing deck set on a knife ridge directly adjacent to the waterfall and seemingly hanging in midair over the Feather River Canyon. The trail is a pretty easy loop route. It is best completed in a clockwise direction.

From the trailhead, this hike descends for a mile, crosses a stream and climbs out of the canyon, then is flat for the most part en route to the viewing area. Return on the loop, bearing left at the fork for a 4.5-mile cruise, mainly through forests and across small streams back to the parking area. Note that at the waterfall, some people crawl out on the brink of the falls on boulders; this is extremely dangerous. It is completely unnecessary to risk your life to get the exhilaration of this special and beautiful place.

**User Groups:** Hikers and dogs. Horses and mountain bikes permitted but not recommended. No wheelchair facilities.

**Permits:** No permits are required. Parking and access are free.

**Maps:** For a map, ask the U.S. Forest Service for Plumas National Forest. For a topographic map, ask the USGS for Brush Creek.

**Directions:** From Oroville, drive east on Highway 162 (Oroville Dam Boulevard) about eight miles to Forbestown Road. Turn right (east) on Forbestown Road east and drive six miles to Lumpkin Road. Turn left on Lumpkin Road and drive 10.5 miles to the sign for Feather Falls Trail. Turn left and drive 1.5 miles to the parking area, at the end of the road.

**Contact:** Plumas National Forest, Feather River Ranger District, 875 Mitchell Avenue, Oroville, CA 95965-4699, 530/534-6500, website: www.fs .fed.us/r5 (click on Forest Offices).

## 4 BULLARDS BAR TRAIL
**13.5 mi / 1.0 day**

**on Bullards Bar Reservoir in Tahoe National Forest**

Map 5.1, page 181

Don't be spooked by the seven-mile length of this trail (13.5 if you include the two loops). Most folks just saunter along for a few miles—maybe take a dunk in the water or cast out a fishing line and sit a spell—then turn back. From the trailhead at the Dark Day Picnic Area, the trail leads west and east along the shore of Bullards Bar Reservoir to Vista Point, overlooking the dam. The path is nearly flat, ranging between 2,243 and 2,250 feet in elevation. Along the way, there are many good fishing and swimming spots, as well as a sprinkling of huge ponderosa pines and Douglas firs. A bonus attraction is that the trail links up with a network of other trails that make up 23 miles of trails in this area. These include Rebel Ridge Trail, 7-Ball Trail, and 8-Ball Trail—all good. Because of the summer heat, this area is best hiked in spring; use then drops off in summer.

**User Groups:** Hikers, dogs, horses, and mountain bikes. No wheelchair facilities.

**Permits:** No permits are required. Parking and access are free.

**Maps:** For a map, ask the U.S. Forest Service for Tahoe National Forest. For topographic maps, ask the USGS for Camptonville and Challenge.

**Directions:** From Marysville, drive east on Highway 20 and drive 12 miles to Marysville Road. Turn left on Marysville Road (signed for Bullards Bar Reservoir) and drive 10 miles to Old Marysville Road. Turn right and drive 14 miles, over the dam, and continue four miles to Dark Day Road. Turn left and drive to the picnic area and trailhead.

**Contact:** Tahoe National Forest, Nevada City/Downieville Ranger Districts, North Yuba Ranger Station, 15924 Highway 49, Camptonville, CA 95922, 530/288-3231 or 530/478-6253, website: www.fs.fed.us/r5 (click on Forest Offices).

# 5 SOUTH YUBA INDEPENDENCE TRAIL
**1.0–9.0 mi / 0.5–3.0 hrs**

**near Nevada City**

Map 5.1, page 181

F This is a pleasant, virtually flat trail that is routed along Rush Creek Canyon with pretty views of the stream. A waterfall with a nearby water flume is a unique side attraction. From the trailhead, hike to the west (go right) to visit Rush Creek Falls and spectacular Flume 28, one mile from the trailhead. The entire trail is routed for 4.5 miles through beautiful forested terrain along the Yuba River Canyon, and it's equally loved by wheelchair users and hikers. The path was originally a canal route, built in 1859 to carry water from the Yuba to a hydraulic mining site in Smartville. This is considered the nation's first wheelchair-accessible wilderness trail; the wheelchair-accessible portion is a seven-mile round-trip. Guided nature walks for groups of six or more are offered by Sequoya Challenge, but reservations are required (see Contact, below). Note that this trailhead is set at midtrail along Highway 49, which gives you the option of hiking either direction.

**User Groups:** Hikers, dogs, and wheelchairs. No horses or mountain bikes.

**Permits:** No permits are necessary. Parking and access are free, but donations to Sequoya Challenge are accepted.

**Maps:** Trail maps/brochures are available at the trailhead or from the Bridgeport Ranger Station. For a topographic map, ask the USGS for Nevada City.

**Directions:** From Auburn, drive north on Highway 49 for 27 miles to Nevada City. Continue on Highway 49 for six miles past Nevada City to the trailhead parking area, along the highway. The parking area is a paved pullout located just before the South Yuba River bridge. If you reach the bridge, you have gone too far. Parking is limited.

**Contact:** South Yuba River State Park, Bridgeport Visitors Center and Ranger Station, 530/432-2546, website: www.parks.ca.gov (click on Find A Park); guided walks: Sequoya Challenge, P.O. Box 3166, Grass Valley, CA 95945, 530/477-4788.

# 6 SHINGLE FALLS
**5.0 mi / 2.5 hrs**

**in Spenceville Wildlife Area near Smartville**

Map 5.1, page 181

This is a pretty and surprise spot in the foothills of the Sacramento Valley. Many people call this place Dry Creek Falls. But the real name is Shingle Falls, named decades ago after a military officer from nearby Beale Air Force Base. Most of the trail here is on a gravel road set amid an oak-and-grassland country in the Sacramento Valley. The stream supports a surprising variety of creekside vegetation, including various oaks, willows, and alders. Your destination, of course, is Shingle Falls, which is easily reached by a five-mile round-trip hike. From the parking area and trailhead, walk across a worn-out bridge, and start hiking to your right on the fire road on the other side. After walking nearly a mile, you'll bear right and hike south on another dirt road. Keep alert, because wild turkeys are common here. At 2.5 miles from the trailhead, you'll come to the road's end, and in turn, to the creek, gorge, and waterfalls. The bigger one is about 60 feet, with steep cliffs walled off by a fence. If you follow use trails downstream along the creek, you'll find a smaller waterfall after about 100 yards. Both make fine spots for a springtime visit. Best time to hike the trail? December through April, preferably soon after a rain.

**User Groups:** Hikers and dogs. Horses and mountain bikes not allowed on this trail. Horses allowed on marked trails and service roads. Mountain bikes are allowed only on service roads. No wheelchair facilities.

**Permits:** No permits are necessary. Parking and access are free. Organized groups must obtain a free permit.

**Maps:** Free maps of Spenceville Wildlife Area are available at information signposts in the refuge. For a topographic map, ask the USGS for Camp Far West.

**Directions:** From Marysville, drive east on Highway 20 for 15 miles to Smartville and Smartville Road. Turn right (south) and drive 4.5 miles to Waldo Road (gravel). Turn left on Waldo Road and drive 2.1 miles to Spenceville Road. Turn left and drive two miles to the end of the road, at a closed bridge. Park, walk carefully across the bridge, and begin the hike.

**Contact:** Spenceville Wildlife Area, c/o Oroville Wildlife Area, Department of Fish and Game, 945 Oro Dam Boulevard West, Oroville, CA 95965, 530/538-2236.

## 7 CODFISH CREEK TRAIL
### 3.0 mi / 1.5 hrs

**in Auburn State Recreation Area**

Map 5.2, page 182

A little-known route along the North Fork American River, Codfish Creek Trail follows an old mining route downstream along its edge, then cuts up the canyon of Codfish Creek. The highlight here is Codfish Falls, but you should then hike up for canyon views. The lowlights are hot summer temperatures—too hot on summer afternoons for enjoyment.

The trail begins at the north side of the bridge, on Ponderosa Way, and heads downstream on sunny and exposed slopes. The path brings visitors to a series of cascades on Codfish Creek. If you can, plan your trip for March, April, or May, when you get the double bonus

of a full-flowing waterfall and lots of blooming wildflowers. At 1.2 miles, the trail turns right and leads upstream along Codfish Creek, heading away from the river.

**User Groups:** Hikers and dogs. No horses or mountain bikes. No wheelchair facilities.

**Permits:** No permits are necessary. Parking and access are free.

**Maps:** For a national forest map, which includes Auburn State Recreation Area lands, ask the U.S. Forest Service for Tahoe National Forest. For a topographic map, ask the USGS for Colfax.

**Directions:** Drive east from Sacramento on I-80 for 40 miles to Weimar and the Weimar Crossroad exit. Take that exit, turn south on Canyon Way (it becomes Ponderosa Way after a short distance), and drive 5.5 miles (the road turns to dirt) to a bridge at the American River. Park near the bridge and look for the trailhead, on the north side of the bridge, with the trail heading downstream past the beach area.

**Contact:** Auburn State Recreation Area, 501 El Dorado Street, Auburn, CA 95603, 916/885-4527, website: www.parks.ca.gov (click on Find A Park).

## 8 AMERICAN RIVER PARKWAY/JEDEDIAH SMITH MEMORIAL TRAIL
### 0.25–32.0 mi one-way / 0.5 hr–2.0 days

**along the American River from Sacramento to Folsom**

Map 5.2, page 182

The idea for the American River Parkway sounded good in concept, and it works even better in practice. The plan was to create a route along the American River that would link Sacramento all the way upstream past Rancho Cordova and Fair Oaks. The result was this multiuse trail that runs 32 miles from Discovery Park, in Sacramento, up to Folsom. There are actually two parallel trails, one paved for bicyclists and in-line skaters only, and a dirt trail for horses (note that there is no shoulder on the horse trail). Walkers and joggers should stay off the paved portion, and should instead use the dirt trail or the shoulder of the bike trail. The trail connects to Folsom Lake State Recreation Area, off Hazel Avenue (near Nimbus Dam), and continues for another nine miles one-way up to Beals Point, at Folsom Lake. Virtually no one hikes, bikes, or skates the entire length, of course; most people simply enjoy short sections, usually on evening walks, jogs, or rides.

Spring and fall are when the American River is prettiest. In spring, the trees and grass are green, the water is rolling fresh, and by May, schools of shad are swimming upstream. Come autumn, the leaves of the adjacent trees turn bright colors, lighting up the river. In the intervening summer months, 100-degree temperatures keep trail use low during the day, but when evening shade emerges, so do joggers and walkers.

Special Note: In-line skates or roller skates are allowed on the state park and county park portions of trail. The state park portion is two separate trails most of the route, but a .5 mile section is shared. All nine miles of state trail are paved, and wheelchairs are allowed. Elsewhere, wheelchairs are allowed on the actual trail, and wheelchair-accessible restrooms, fishing areas, and picnic grounds are available along the way.

**User Groups:** Hikers, dogs, mountain bikes, in-line skates, roller skates, and horses allowed, but horses are not advised. See the Special Note about restrictions for mountain bikes and hikers, above.

**Permits:** No permits are required. Folsom Lake State Recreation Area charges a fee of $7 per vehicle for developed parking and $3 per vehicle for undeveloped parking.

**Maps:** A trail map is available for a fee at the county parks department at the address below. For topographic maps, ask the USGS for Sacramento East, Carmichael, Citrus Heights, and Folsom.

**Directions:** The trail begins at Discovery Park, in Sacramento, on the north side of the American River. From I-5, take the Richards Boulevard exit and drive west to Jiboom Street. Turn right (north) and follow the road into the park.

Note: The trail's prettiest access point is Goethe Park, in Rancho Cordova. To get to Goethe Park, on the south side of the American River, drive east on U.S. 50 and take the Bradshaw North exit. Follow Bradshaw Road to Folsom Boulevard and turn right (east). Continue to Rod Beaudry Drive and turn left (north). Follow the road .5 mile into the park.

**Contact:** County of Sacramento, Parks and Recreation Division, Park Ranger Section, 4040 Bradshaw Road, Sacramento, CA 95827, 916/875-6672; Folsom Lake State Recreation Area, 916/988-0205, website: www.parks.ca.gov (click on Find A Park).

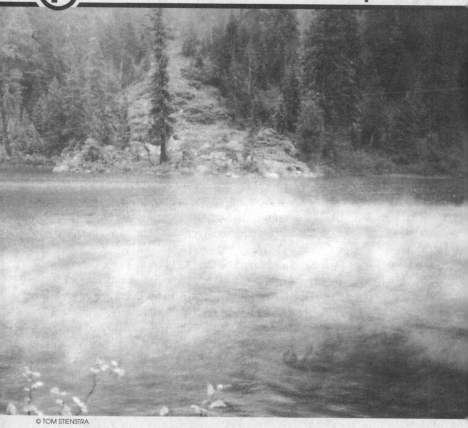

## Chapter 6

© TOM STIENSTRA

# Tahoe and the Northern Sierra

# Tahoe and the Northern Sierra

**M**ount Tallac affords a view across Lake Tahoe like no other: a cobalt blue expanse of water bordered by mountains that span miles of Sierra wildlands. The beauty is stunning. Lake Tahoe is one of the few places on earth where people feel an emotional response just by looking at it. Yosemite Valley, the giant sequoias, the Grand Canyon, a perfect sunset on the Pacific Ocean . . . these are a few other sights that occasionally evoke the same response. But Tahoe often seems to strike the deepest chord. It can resonate inside you for weeks, even after a short visit.

"What about all the people?" you ask. It's true that people come here in droves. But there are many spots that you'll share only with the chipmunks. You can enjoy these spots too—if you're willing to read our books, hunt a bit, and most importantly, time your trip to span Monday through Thursday.

Tahoe and the Northern Sierra feature hundreds of lakes, including dozens you can drive to. Many provide outstanding launch points for hikes. The best for scenic beauty are Tahoe, Echo Lakes, Donner, and Fallen Leaf in the immediate Tahoe region; Sardine, Gold Lake, and Salmon Lake in the Lakes Basin Recreation Area (also called the Gold Lakes Basin); Union Valley, Loon, and Wrights in the Crystal Basin; Carr, Feely, Lindsey, and Faucherie in the Bowman Lakes Recreation Area; and Caples, Woods, and Burnside near Carson Pass.

This list could go on and on. If you haven't figured it out by now, this is one of the most beautiful regions anywhere on earth.

The north end of the Sierra starts near Bucks Lake, a great lake for trout fishing, and extends to Bear River Canyon (and Caples Lake, Silver Lake, and Bear River Reservoir). In between are the Lakes Basin Recreation Area (containing Gold, Sardine, Packer, and other lakes), in southern Plumas County; the Crystal Basin (featuring Union Valley Reservoir and Loon Lake, among others), in the Sierra foothills west of Tahoe; Lake Davis (with the highest catch rates for trout), near Portola; and the Carson River Canyon and Hope Valley, south of Tahoe.

You could spend weeks exploring any of these places, having the time of your life, and still not get to Tahoe's magic. But it is Tahoe where the adventure starts for many, especially in the surrounding Tahoe National Forest, Desolation Wilderness, and Granite Chief Wilderness.

One of California's greatest day trips from Tahoe is to Echo Lakes, where you can take a hiker's shuttle boat across the two lakes to the Pacific Crest Trail, then hike a few miles into Desolation Wilderness and Aloha Lakes. Yet with so many wonderful ways to spend a day in this area, this day trip is hardly a blip on the radar scope.

With so many places and so little time, this region offers what can be the ultimate adventureland.

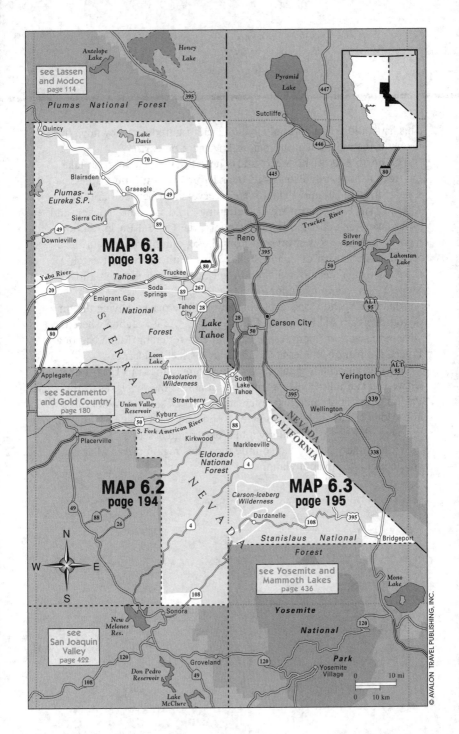

# Map 6.1

## Hikes 1–51
## Pages 196–224

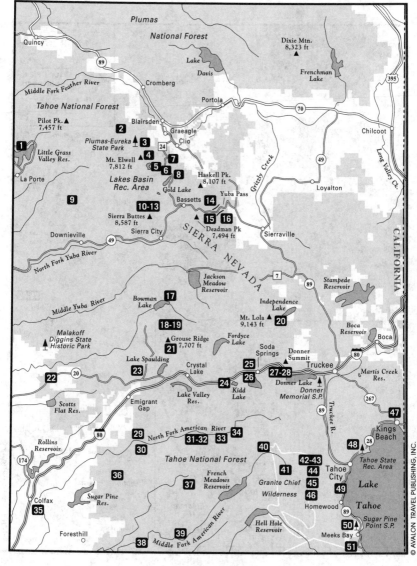

# Map 6.2

**Hikes 52–84**
**Pages 225–246**

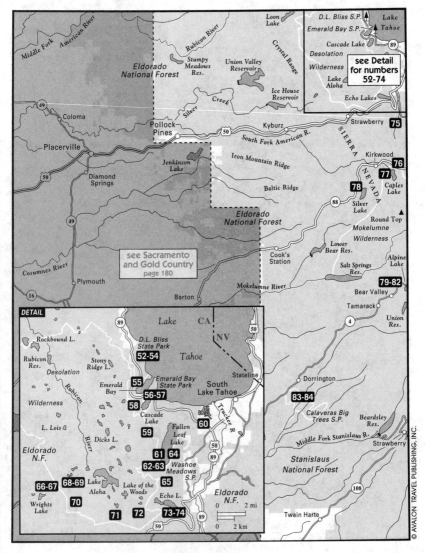

# Map 6.3

**Hikes 85–111**
**Pages 246–262**

# ◼ FOWLER PEAK TO BUCKS SUMMIT (PCT)

**26.0 mi one-way / 3.0 days**

**at Fowler Peak north of Little Grass Valley Reservoir in Plumas National Forest**

Map 6.1, page 193

Most Pacific Crest Trail (PCT) hikers will want to sprint through this section of trail. From Fowler Peak trailhead, it passes through Plumas National Forest country until reaching the southern border of the Bucks Lake Wilderness. It starts quite nicely, dropping down to the Middle Fork Feather River (3,180 feet), a great trout stream with an excellent footbridge to get you across a gorge. Enjoy it, because the rest of this route won't exactly have you writing postcards home. It climbs from the Middle Fork Feather to 6,955-foot Lookout Rock—a long, dry pull—then drops down to Bucks Creek. Most of this region is dry rattlesnake country, so watch your step, and time your water stops.

To continue north on the PCT, see the Bucks Summit to Feather River (PCT) hike in the Sacramento and Gold Country chapter. If you are walking this trail in reverse, see the Yuba River to Fowler Peak (PCT) hike in this chapter to continue south.

**User Groups:** Hikers, dogs, and horses. No mountain bikes. No wheelchair access.

**Permits:** A wilderness permit (free) is required. Parking and access are free.

**Maps:** For a map, ask the U.S. Forest Service for Tahoe and Plumas National Forests. For topographic maps, ask the USGS for Onion Valley, Dogwood Peak, and Bucks Lake.

**Directions:** From Oroville, drive east on Highway 162 for eight miles to Highway 174 (Forbestown Road and the junction signed Challenge/LaPorte). Turn right on Forbestown Road and drive east to Highway 120/Quincy-LaPorte Road. Turn left and drive past LaPorte to Little Grass Valley Road. Turn left on Little Grass Valley Road and drive to Black Rock Campground and Forest Road 94. Bear left on Forest Road 94 and drive three miles

to Forest Road 22N27. Turn right and drive four miles to the parking area.

**Contact:** Plumas National Forest, Feather River Ranger District, 875 Mitchell Avenue, Oroville, CA 95965-4699, 530/534-6500, website: www.fs.fed.us/r5 (click on Forest Offices).

# ◼ EUREKA PEAK LOOP

**3.0 mi / 2.0 hrs**

**in Plumas-Eureka State Park east of Quincy**

Map 6.1, page 193

The panoramic view of the Sierra Nevada from Eureka Peak (elevation 7,447 feet) includes all the peaks of the Gold Lakes Basin, with Mount Elwell (7,818 feet) most prominent to the south and Plumas National Forest to the north and west, crowned by Blue Nose Mountain (7,290 feet), Stafford Mountain (7,019 feet), and Beartrap Mountain (7,232 feet). It's the vista that compels people to make the climb—a serious three-mile loop, and the first half is a grunt to the top. The trailhead starts at Eureka Lake, (elevation 6,300 feet). It then climbs 1,150 feet—a good, hard pull to the top. Many people start this trail by accident after seeing the trailhead sign while visiting the lake. That's a mistake. The trip should be planned; bring plenty of water and snacks to enjoy from the summit.

**User Groups:** Hikers only. No dogs, horses, or mountain bikes. No wheelchair facilities.

**Permits:** No permits are required. A park entrance fee of $3 is charged for each vehicle.

**Maps:** A brochure and trail map is available for a fee from Plumas-Eureka State Park at the address below. For a topographic map, ask the USGS for Johnsville.

**Directions:** Take I-80 northeast to Truckee. Then take Highway 89 north and go past the town of Clio to County Road A14 (Graeagle-Johnsonville Road). Turn left (west) and drive six miles to the park entrance. Continue several miles to Eureka Lake (the road is rough, and high-clearance vehicles are recommended). The trailhead is located at the north end of Eureka Lake.

Contact: Plumas-Eureka State Park, 310 Johnsville Road, Blairsden, CA 96103, 530/836-2380, website: www.parks.ca.gov (click on Find A Park).

## ❸ UPPER JAMISON TRAIL
### 8.2 mi / 1.0–2.0 days

**in Plumas-Eureka State Park on the northern boundary of Gold Lakes Basin, east of Quincy**

**Map 6.1, page 193**

There's no reason to rush your way through this trail, which passes Grass, Jamison, and Rock Lakes. Rather, take your time at it, stopping to enjoy the lakes along the way—or even take this route and turn it into an overnight backpacking trip. The trail provides a glimpse of the beauty of the northern section of Lakes Basin Recreation Area, a country of alpine lakes and beveled granite mountains.

From the trailhead at the Jamison Mine building, start the trip by taking Grass Lake Trail. It follows along Little Jamison Creek; note that a 100-foot cutoff trail provides a route to Little Jamison Falls. Back on the trail, you will climb 1.75 miles (from the parking area) to Grass Lake, with the trail skirting the east side of the lake. For those on a day hike, this is far enough. However, we urge you to forge onward. It's another two miles to Jamison Lake, with the trail climbing more steeply, then crossing the creek twice before arriving at the outlet of Jamison Lake. Another .25 mile will route you over to Rock Lake, a pretty sight below Mount Elwell (elevation 7,818 feet). Several good trail campsites are available at Rock, Jamison, and Grass Lakes and are usually occupied on weekends. Note that the first half mile of trail is located in the state park, and the remainder is in Plumas National Forest.

**User Groups:** Hikers, dogs, horses, and mountain bikes. No wheelchair facilities.

**Permits:** No permits are required. A park entrance fee of $3 is charged for each vehicle.

**Maps:** A brochure and trail map is available for a fee from Plumas-Eureka State Park at

the address below. For a topographic map, ask the USGS for Johnsville.

**Directions:** From Truckee, take Highway 89 north and continue past the town of Clio to County Road A14 (Graeagle-Johnsonville Road); turn left (west) and drive 4.5 miles. Before reaching the Jamison Creek Bridge, look for a sign that reads Jamison Mine–Grass Lake Mine Complex. Turn left and drive on the dirt road for 1.5 miles to the Jamison Mine Complex. The trailhead starts at the far end of the parking lot.

**Contact:** Plumas-Eureka State Park, 310 Johnsville Road, Blairsden, CA 96103, 530/836-2380, website: www.parks.ca.gov (click on Find A Park).

## ❹ MOUNT ELWELL TRAIL
### 6.0 mi / 3.5 hrs

**at Smith Lake in Gold Lakes Basin south of Quincy**

**Map 6.1, page 193**

From atop Mount Elwell (7,818 feet), you're surrounded by the Gold Lakes Basin, a wildland filled with alpine lakes and granite mountains. You'll find yourself dreaming of the days when you might visit them. This trail is a good way to start. It begins at the Smith Lake trailhead and passes near Smith Lake (6,079 feet) on Smith Lake Trail, climbing all the way—2,018 feet over the course of three miles—to the top of Mount Elwell. It makes a great day trip for folks staying at the Gray Eagle Lodge. Though few go onward from Mount Elwell, the trip can be extended simply enough. The trail continues past Mount Elwell, descending .75 mile to the Long Lake Trail junction, then another mile to a four-wheel-drive route. From this junction, you can also make a loop back to the Smith Lake trailhead by descending to Long Lake and continuing north three miles on Long Lake Trail. This is one of the truly great hikes in the north Sierra.

**User Groups:** Hikers, dogs, mountain bikes, and horses. No wheelchair facilities.

**Permits:** No permits are required. Parking and access are free.

**Maps:** A trail map is available for a fee at the Beckwourth Ranger District. For a map, ask the U.S. Forest Service for Plumas National Forest. For a topographic map, ask the USGS for Gold Lake.

**Directions:** From Sacramento, drive northeast on I-80 to Truckee and take Highway 89 north to the town of Clio. Continue a short distance north on Highway 89 to Forest Road 24 (Gold Lake Highway). Turn left (west) on Gold Lake Highway and drive five miles to the sign for Gray Eagle Lodge. Turn right and drive .5 mile to the Smith Lake trailhead.

**Contact:** Plumas National Forest, Beckwourth Ranger District, P.O. Box 7, Mohawk Road, Blairsden, CA 96103, 530/836-2575, website: www.fs.fed.us/r5 (click on Forest Offices).

## 5 BEAR LAKES LOOP
### 5.6 mi / 3.0 hrs

**north of Sierra City**

Map 6.1, page 193

Long Lake is one of the celestial settings in the heavenly Gold Lakes Basin. It's the feature destination of this hike, a good tromp that includes some steep, rocky portions. The trailhead is just past the Lakes Basin Campground (elevation 6,300 feet). From here, the trail is clear and well maintained but requires a huff and a puff of a mile. Here you'll see the turnoff for .25-mile spur trail to Long Lake, one mile to little Silver Lake, .75 mile to Cub Lake, and another .5 mile to Little Bear and Big Bear Lakes, and then .75 mile back to the trailhead. Long Lake is always a surprise to newcomers, since it's much larger than most high-country lakes and is very pretty. The trail skirts along the southeast shoreline.

Special Note: Camping is permitted only at the Lakes Basin Campground. No camping is permitted at either Long or Silver Lakes.

**User Groups:** Hikers, dogs, mountain bikes, and horses. No wheelchair facilities.

**Permits:** No permits are required. Parking and access are free.

**Maps:** A trail map is available for a fee at the Beckwourth Ranger District at the address below. For a map, ask the U.S. Forest Service for Plumas National Forest. For a topographic map, ask the USGS for Gold Lake.

**Directions:** Take I-80 northeast from Sacramento to Truckee and then take Highway 89 north to the town of Clio. Continue a short distance north on Highway 89 to Forest Road 24 (Gold Lake Highway). Turn left on Gold Lake Highway and proceed about six miles until you see the sign for the Long Lake trailhead and Lakes Basin Campground, on the left (west) side of the road.

**Contact:** Plumas National Forest, Beckwourth Ranger District, P.O. Box 7, Mohawk Road, Blairsden, CA 96103, 530/836-2575, website: www.fs.fed.us/r5 (click on Forest Offices).

## 6 ROUND LAKE TRAILHEAD
### 1.4 mi / 1.0 hr

**on the southern boundary of Gold Lakes Basin north of Sierra City**

Map 6.1, page 193

The .7-mile hike to Big Bear Lake is an easy, popular, and pretty walk, most commonly taken by visitors staying at Gold Lake Lodge. The trailhead is located alongside the parking lot next to the road to the lodge, and the trail itself is actually a closed road to Round Lake. It becomes a trail within a few hundred yards when routed west to Big Bear Lake, the first in a series of beautiful alpine lakes in the Gold Lakes Basin. Although most day users return after a picnic at Big Bear Lake, the trip can easily be extended, either west to Round Lake or Silver Lake or north to Long Lake. Most of this country is in the 6,000- to 7,000-foot elevation range and is high granite filled with alpine lakes.

**User Groups:** Hikers, dogs, mountain bikes, and horses. No wheelchair facilities.

**Permits:** No permits are required. Parking and access are free.

**Maps:** A trail map is available for a fee from Beckwourth Ranger District at the address below. For a map, ask the U.S. Forest Service for Plumas National Forest. For a topographic map, ask the USGS for Gold Lake.

**Directions:** From Sacramento, drive northeast on I-80 to Truckee. Then take Highway 89 north to the town of Clio. Continue a short distance on Highway 89 north to Forest Road 24 (Gold Lake Highway). Turn left (west) on Forest Road 24 (Gold Lake Highway) and drive seven miles until you see the sign for Round Lake Trail. Turn right and continue to the parking area.

**Contact:** Plumas National Forest, Beckwourth Ranger District, P.O. Box 7, Mohawk Road, Blairsden, CA 96103, 530/836-2575, website: www.fs.fed.us/r5 (click on Forest Offices).

## ◪ FRAZIER FALLS TRAIL
### 1.0 mi / 1.0 hr

**north of Sierra City**

Map 6.1, page 193

Frazier Falls is a 178-foot, silver-tasseled waterfall that tumbles out of a chute into a rocky basin. It is like a miniature version of Feather Falls, near Lake Oroville. The trail is completely wheelchair-accessible and is a breeze, a .5-mile romp on a gentle route that leads to the scenic, fenced overlook of the falls. The best time to visit is early summer, when snowmelt from the high country is peaking, filling Frazier Falls like a huge fountain. In addition, wildflowers along the trail in early summer add a splash of color, with violet lupine the most abundant. The road to the trailhead is paved all the way, the hike is easy, the falls are beautiful, and as you might expect, thousands of people make the trip every summer.

**User Groups:** Hikers, wheelchairs, and dogs. No ATVs, mountain bikes, or horses. Wheelchair facilities are available.

**Permits:** No permits are required. Parking and access are free.

**Maps:** A trail map is available for a fee from Beckwourth Ranger District at the address below. For a map, ask the U.S. Forest Service for Plumas National Forest. For a topographic map, ask the USGS for Gold Lake.

**Directions:** From Sacramento, take I-80 northeast to Truckee. Then take Highway 89 north to the town of Clio. Continue a short distance on Highway 89 north to Forest Road 24 (Gold Lake Highway). Turn left (west) on Forest Road 24 (Gold Lake Highway) and drive until you see the sign for Frazier Falls. Turn left and drive four miles to the trailhead, on the left. Note: If you continue west on Gold Lake Highway for several miles, you will see another trailhead sign for Frazier Falls; it can also be reached on this route, but the road is rough and unpaved.

**Contact:** Plumas National Forest, Beckwourth Ranger District, P.O. Box 7, Mohawk Road, Blairsden, CA 96103, 530/836-2575, website: www.fs.fed.us/r5 (click on Forest Offices).

## ◪ HASKELL PEAK TRAIL
### 3.0 mi / 2.0 hrs

**north of Highway 49 in Tahoe National Forest**

Map 6.1, page 193

Haskell Peak is one of the great but unknown lookouts. On clear days, visitors can see many mountains both nearby and distant, including Mount Shasta and Mount Lassen, in Northern California; Mount Rose, in Nevada; and the closer Sierra Buttes. To get this view requires a 1,100-foot climb over the course of 1.5 miles, topping out at the 8,107-foot summit. The trail climbs at a decent, steady grade through heavy forest for the first mile. It then flattens and reaches an open area, where Haskell Peak comes into view. From here it's only a .25-mile (but very steep) climb to the top. You'll discover that Haskell Peak is the flume of an old volcano and has many unusual volcanic-rock formations. You'll also discover that just about nobody knows about this great hike. A fire lookout was once perched here, but it's gone now. Elevations range from 7,000 feet to 8,107 feet.

**User Groups:** Hikers, dogs, horses, and mountain bikes. No wheelchair facilities.

**Permits:** No permits are required. Parking and access are free.

**Maps:** For a map, ask the U.S. Forest Service for Tahoe National Forest. For a topographic map, ask the USGS for Clio.

**Directions:** From Truckee, turn north on Highway 89 and drive to Sierraville and Highway 49. Turn left on Highway 49 and drive 10 miles to Bassetts and the Gold Lake Highway. Turn right on Gold Lake Highway and drive 3.7 miles to Forest Road 9 (Haskell Peak Road). Turn right and drive 8.4 miles. The trailhead is on the left; parking is available on either side of the road.

**Contact:** Tahoe National Forest, Nevada City/Downieville Ranger Districts, 15924 Highway 49, Camptonville, CA 95922, 530/288-3231 or 530/478-6253, website: www.fs.fed.us/r5 (click on Forest Offices).

## 9 CHIMNEY ROCK TRAIL
**5.0 mi / 2.5 hrs**

**north of Downieville in Tahoe National Forest**

Map 6.1, page 193

Chimney Rock is a huge volcanic cone that's 12 feet in diameter at its base, and it rises nearly straight up for 25 feet. The great views from the top are well worth the trip. The elevations are roughly 6,400 to 6,800 feet. Yet brace yourself, because this little patch of land has undergone considerable change. First, the trail surface was hardened in 1999. In turn, off-highway-vehicle (OHV) users started showing up in force, especially with dirt bikes. Now nearly 50 percent of the trail users are OHV users, and 50 percent are mountain bikers— and between them, they have driven out the hikers. The Downieville area in general has been taken over by mountain bikes, and hikers looking for a natural, harmonious experience often encounter a pack of bikes. When that happens, it's "Adios, never to return." This trip was once a quiet spectacle, with side ventures around Needle Point and Rattlesnake Peak. Now you cringe when you hear the thunder of oncoming fast traffic; it's like all the problems of city driving have been transported to a mountain trail.

**User Groups:** Hikers, dogs, mountain bikes, horses, and OHVs (primarily motorcycles). No wheelchair facilities.

**Permits:** No permits are required. Parking and access are free.

**Maps:** A trail map is available for a fee at the Downieville Ranger District. For a map, ask the U.S. Forest Service for Tahoe National Forest. For a topographic map, ask the USGS for Mount Fillmore.

**Directions:** From Sacramento, drive east on I-80 to Auburn. Then take Highway 49 north to Nevada City and continue on Highway 49 (it jogs to the left in Nevada City, then narrows) for about 40 miles to an old cannon displayed on the right side of the road (.25 mile before reaching Downieville). Turn right at the cannon onto an unsigned road, make a U-turn back to Highway 49, and drive a short distance back to Saddleback Road. Turn right on Saddleback Road. (Note: When driving on Highway 49 toward Downieville, do not attempt to turn left across traffic to reach Saddleback Road. It is dangerous and illegal.) Continue north on Saddleback Road for eight miles to a five-way intersection. Drive straight through to Road 25-23-1 and continue for 2.6 miles to Road 25-23-1-2 (look for the Chimney Rock Trail sign). Bear right on Road 25-23-1-2 and drive .5 mile to an intersection and head straight through. Continue another mile to a turnout on the left side of the road. Park here and hike in .6 mile to the trailhead. The total mileage from Downieville is 13 miles.

Note: Sections of the road are quite rough.

**Contact:** Tahoe National Forest, Nevada City/Downieville Ranger Districts, 15924 Highway 49, Camptonville, CA 95922, 530/288-3231 or 530/478-6253, website: www.fs.fed.us/r5 (click on Forest Offices).

## 🔟 BUTCHER RANCH TRAIL
**8.0 mi / 5.0 hrs**

**west of Packer Lake in Tahoe National Forest**

**Map 6.1, page 193**

This used to be a great hike, a picture of harmony and beauty. It still is—for the few who are here at dawn and get it done before all the mountain bikes show up. The place is overrun now by mountain bikes and motorcycles; weekends are nearly intolerable. Hikers have virtually been driven out; hiker usage is down below 10 percent. This place was once a place of peace and harmony—a mountain canyon paradise where wildflowers were abundant, fishing was good, and a side trip would take hikers to a pristine stream with gorgeous deep pools. No more.

Elevations range from 6,200 to 4,320 feet. The trail follows the contour of Butcher Creek for 1.5 miles to the confluence of Pauley and Butcher Ranch Creeks. You then parallel Pauley Creek, with its deep and beautiful pools. On the way down, you'll drop nearly 2,000 feet over the course of four miles. Try not to laugh on your way down; what goes down must come up, and on the return, you'll be wondering why you ever talked yourself into this trip—especially if you run into a few motorcycles or a pack of mountain bikes heading downhill.

**User Groups:** Off-highway vehicles, mountain bikes, hikers, dogs, and horses. No wheelchair facilities.

**Permits:** No permits are required. Parking and access are free.

**Maps:** A trail map is available for a fee at the Downieville Ranger District. For a map, ask the U.S. Forest Service for Tahoe National Forest. For a topographic map, ask the USGS for Sierra City.

**Directions:** From Truckee, turn north on Highway 89 and drive to Sierraville and Highway 49. Turn left on Highway 49 and drive 10 miles to Bassetts and Gold Lake Highway. Turn right (north) on Gold Lake Highway and drive 1.4 miles to Sardine Lake Road. Turn left on Sardine Lake Road and drive a short distance. Cross the Salmon Creek Bridge and continue .3 mile to Packer Lake Road. Turn right on Packer Lake Road and drive 2.5 miles to a fork (near Packer Lake). Take the left fork (Packer Saddle Road/Forest Road 93), drive 2.1 miles, and look for the sign for Sierra Buttes Lookout. Turn left, drive .5 mile, and bear right; then continue .5 mile to a fork and sign for Butcher Ranch. Take the right fork (Forest Road 93-3) and drive .7 mile to a sign for the trailhead. Note: The road is quite steep and is only recommended for high-clearance or four-wheel-drive vehicles. Otherwise, park at the sign for the trailhead and hike .5 mile to the trailhead.

**Contact:** Tahoe National Forest, Nevada City/Downieville Ranger Districts, 15924 Highway 49, Camptonville, CA 95922, 530/288-3231 or 530/478-6253, website: www.fs.fed.us/r5 (click on Forest Offices).

## 1️⃣1️⃣ PAULEY CREEK TRAIL
**12.0 mi / 2.0 days**

**west of Packer Lake in Tahoe National Forest**

**Map 6.1, page 193**

The Pauley Creek Trail encompasses a land where there are streamside camps, spectacular wildflowers in early summer, and good trout fishing. Weekends are horrendous for dealing with high-speed mountain bikes and noisy motorcycles. Regardless, this is a beautiful stream, and this trail is the best way to see it. Wildlife is also abundant in this watershed. The trailhead is difficult to reach, and the return hike out of the canyon back to the trailhead involves a 1,800-foot climb. Elevations range from 6,200 to 4,400 feet.

**User Groups:** Hikers, dogs, horses, mountain bikes, and off-highway vehicles. No wheelchair facilities.

**Permits:** No permits are required. Parking and access are free.

**Maps:** A trail map is available for a fee at the Downieville Ranger District. For a map, ask the U.S. Forest Service for Tahoe National Forest. For topographic maps, ask the USGS for Downieville, Sierra City, and Gold Lake.

**Directions:** From Truckee, turn north on Highway 89 and drive to Sierraville and Highway 49. Turn left on Highway 49 and drive 10 miles to Bassetts and Gold Lake Highway. Turn right (north) on Gold Lake Highway and drive 1.4 miles to Sardine Lake Road. Turn left on Sardine Lake Road and drive a short distance. Cross the Salmon Creek Bridge and continue .3 mile to Packer Lake Road. Turn right on Packer Lake Road and drive 2.5 miles to a fork (near Packer Lake). Take the left fork (Packer Saddle Road/Forest Road 93), drive 2.1 miles, and look for the sign for Sierra Buttes Lookout. Turn left, drive .5 mile, bear right, and drive .5 mile to Forest Road 93-3. Bear right and drive 2.5 miles to a sign that says Gold Valley OHV Route. Turn left and drive 1.5 miles to an intersection. Bear left and cross Pauley Creek, then drive .25 mile to a Y intersection. Bear left and drive .25 mile to the trailhead, at the end of the road. Note: The access road is quite steep and is only recommended for high-clearance or four-wheel-drive vehicles. Otherwise, park at the sign for the trailhead and hike .5 mile to the trailhead.

**Contact:** Tahoe National Forest, Nevada City/Downieville Ranger Districts, 15924 Highway 49, Camptonville, CA 95922, 530/288-3231 or 530/478-6253, website: www.fs.fed.us/r5 (click on Forest Offices).

## 12 DEER LAKE TRAIL
**5.0 mi / 3.5 hrs**

**west of Packer Lake in Tahoe National Forest**

Map 6.1, page 193

Most lakes are green, but Deer Lake is the deepest azure blue you can imagine, and with the spectacular Sierra Buttes in the background, it's easy to understand why this trip is so popular—it gets some of the heaviest use of any trail in this section of Tahoe National Forest.

It's a 2.5-mile hike to the lake, climbing 1,000 feet and topping out at 7,110 feet. Elevations range from 6,080 to 7,110 feet.

From the trailhead, you'll climb through a basin and get a sweeping view of the massive Sierra Buttes and the surrounding forested slopes. As you head on, you'll cross a signed spur trail, a .25-mile route to Grass Lake. It's well worth the short detour, but approach quietly, because deer are common here. Then it's onward, over the ridge and down to Deer Lake. On warm evenings, the brook trout leave countless circles while feeding on surface insects. This hike has it all, and, alas, that's why it often includes so many other people. Good news for hikers: Mountain bikes are few, and off-highway-vehicle use is prohibited.

**User Groups:** Hikers, dogs, horses, and mountain bikes. No wheelchair facilities.

**Permits:** No permits are required. Parking and access are free.

**Maps:** A trail map is available for a fee at the Downieville Ranger District. For a map, ask the U.S. Forest Service for Tahoe National Forest. For a topographic map, ask the USGS for Sierra City.

**Directions:** From Truckee, turn north on Highway 89 and drive to Sierraville and Highway 49. Turn left onto Highway 49 and drive 10 miles to Bassetts and Gold Lake Highway. Turn right (north) on to Gold Lake Highway and drive 1.4 miles to Sardine Lake Road. Turn left on Sardine Lake Road and drive a short distance. Cross the Salmon Creek Bridge and continue .3 mile to Packer Lake Road. Turn right on Packer Lake Road and drive 2.5 miles to the trailhead. Parking is available in the Packsaddle camping area just opposite the trailhead.

**Contact:** Tahoe National Forest, Nevada City/Downieville Ranger Districts, 15924 Highway 49, Camptonville, CA 95922, 530/288-3231 or 530/478-6253, website: www.fs.fed.us/r5 (click on Forest Offices).

## 13 SIERRA BUTTES TRAIL
### 5.0 mi / 3.5 hrs

**near Packer Lake in Tahoe National Forest**

**Map 6.1, page 193**

The Sierra Buttes Lookout Station, sitting at 8,587 feet and with a railed stairway to its top, provides a destination for one of California's best day hikes and greatest viewpoints. Stand here one time, and you'll never forget it the rest of your life. The trip starts above Packer Lake, at 6,220 feet. The trail climbs through a series of shaded switchbacks to 6,700 feet, tracing the ridge that eventually leads to the summit, crowned by a series of jagged crags. On the way, you will rise to the rim of a mountain bowl that frames Sardine Lake, climbing 2,367 feet to reach the top. The trail traces this rim to the lookout and is capped by three stairways that seem to project into wide-open space. Climbing it is an astounding sensation—almost like climbing the cable at Half Dome. The lookout itself also juts out into space, and it can seem quite eerie as you scan miles and miles of Sierra mountain country, from Mount Lassen in the north all the way to the Tahoe Rim to the south, with a highlight being Union Valley Reservoir. Because the walkway around the lookout is grated, when you look straight down, you can see past your boots to a free fall. A bizarre sensation for many, this can even cause spatial disorientation.

**User Groups:** Hikers, dogs, and horses. No mountain bikes (except on jeep trail). No wheelchair access.

**Permits:** No permits are required. Parking and access are free.

**Maps:** A trail map is available for a fee from the Downieville Ranger District. For a map, ask the U.S. Forest Service for Tahoe National Forest. For a topographic map, ask the USGS for Sierra City.

**Directions:** From Truckee, turn north on Highway 89 and drive to Sierraville and Highway 49. Turn left on Highway 49 and drive 10 miles to Bassetts and the Gold Lake Highway. Turn right on Gold Lake Highway and drive 1.4 miles to Sardine Lake/Packer Lake Road. Turn left, cross a small bridge, and bear right on Packer Lake Road. Continue past Packer Lake and bear left at a fork, following the signs to a trailhead for the Pacific Crest Trail (do not bear right at a jeep road). Continue to a small parking area. The trail starts as a jeep trail next to the parking area (then becomes trail on the ridge).

**Contact:** Tahoe National Forest, Nevada City/Downieville Ranger Districts, 15924 Highway 49, Camptonville, CA 95922, 530/288-3231 or 530/478-6253, website: www.fs.fed.us/r5 (click on Forest Offices).

## 14 CHAPMAN CREEK TRAIL
### 3.0 mi / 2.0 hrs

**east of Sierra City in Tahoe National Forest**

**Map 6.1, page 193**

Chapman Creek is a babbling brook that you can walk alongside—or you can stop to picnic near it, fish a little in it, or do absolutely nothing. That's right, nothing. It's that kind of place. The trailhead, elevation 5,840 feet, is set at a campground, providing easy access. Outside of campers, few others know of it. The trail winds easily along the contours of Chapman Creek under the canopy of a dense forest, rising gently along the way. It climbs to 6,400 feet, 560 feet in a span of 1.5 miles. The river is the lifeblood for a variety of birds and wildlife, but few visitors make the trip for that reason. Rather they come to stroll and let their minds wander and be free.

**User Groups:** Hikers, dogs, horses, and mountain bikes. No wheelchair facilities.

**Permits:** No permits are required. Parking and access are free.

**Maps:** For a map, ask the U.S. Forest Service for Tahoe National Forest. For a topographic map, ask the USGS for Sierra City.

**Directions:** From Truckee, turn north on Highway 89 and drive to Sierraville and Highway 49. Turn left on Highway 49, drive over Yuba

Pass, and continue for four miles to the Chapman Creek Campground, on the right. The trailhead and a parking area are located at the north end of the campground.

**Contact:** Tahoe National Forest, Nevada City/Downieville Ranger Districts, 15924 Highway 49, Camptonville, CA 95922, 530/288-3231 or 530/478-6253, website: www.fs.fed.us/r5 (click on Forest Offices).

## 15 WILD PLUM LOOP/ HAYPRESS CREEK

**6.0 mi / 1.0 day**

**east of Sierra City in Tahoe National Forest**

Map 6.1, page 193

A canyon with a hidden stream and a waterfall that's surrounded by old-growth red fir make this a wonderful day hike for the properly inspired. Why properly inspired? Because the trail climbs from 4,400 feet up Haypress Creek to 5,840 feet, a 1,440-foot rise over just three miles. The trail starts out almost flat for the first .5 mile, and then it crosses over Haypress Creek on a footbridge. There's an excellent view of the Sierra Buttes in this area. Continue on Haypress Creek Trail, rising past a rocky area and into forest, and, alas, passing some logging activity where the trail turns to road for a short spell. Don't despair. The trail soon enters an old-growth forest, contouring along Haypress Canyon, and then passes by a lovely waterfall. This hike makes a great day trip with a picnic lunch, and trail use is typically quite light. Note that on the return trip, turn right on the Pacific Crest Trail to complete the loop. Walk .5 mile and turn left at the Wild Plum Loop sign to return.

**User Groups:** Hikers, dogs, and horses. No mountain bikes. No wheelchair facilities.

**Permits:** No permits are required. Parking and access are free.

**Maps:** For a map, ask the U.S. Forest Service for Tahoe National Forest. For a topographic map, ask the USGS for Haypress Valley.

**Directions:** From Truckee, drive north on Highway 89 to Sierraville and Highway 49. Turn left on Highway 49 and drive 12 miles (past Bassetts) to Wild Plum Road (near the eastern end of Sierra City) at the sign for Wild Plum Campground. Drive one mile on this road to the Wild Plum trailhead parking area. Walk through the campground to its upper loop, walk around a locked gate, and continue up the road .25 mile to the Wild Plum Loop Trail Sign. Walk .25 mile to the intersection with the Pacific Crest Trail, turn left, and cross a bridge over Haypress Creek. Continue for 200 yards to the trailhead, on the right.

**Contact:** Tahoe National Forest, Nevada City/Downieville Ranger Districts, 15924 Highway 49, Camptonville, CA 95922, 530/288-3231 or 530/478-6253, website: www.fs.fed.us/r5 (click on Forest Offices).

## 16 YUBA RIVER TO FOWLER PEAK (PCT)

**51.0 mi one-way / 4.0 days**

**in Tahoe National Forest, off Highway 49 east of Sierra City**

Map 6.1, page 193

Pristine alpine lakes and high mountain lookouts highlight this section of the Pacific Crest Trail. Although just as beautiful as the section of trail south near Tahoe, this stretch gets far less use. It starts at the Yuba River, and in the first two miles, it climbs an endless series of switchbacks up the back side of the Sierra Buttes—a terrible climb with a great reward. Note that the spur trail up to the Sierra Buttes Fire Lookout is an additional 1,400-foot climb, but it furnishes one of the top lookouts in California. The trail then heads north, skirting past the western border of the Gold Lakes Basin, where a dozen high alpine lakes make for easy side trips and camps. With some terrible switchbacks, the PCT passes Mount Gibraltar (7,343 feet), Stafford Mountain (7,019 feet), and Mount Etna (7,163 feet), and flanks below Pilot Peak (7,457 feet). It then heads along the western slope, eventually reaching the Fowler Peak trailhead.

To continue north on the PCT, see the Fowler Peak to Bucks Summit (PCT) hike in this chapter. If you are walking this trail in reverse, see the Donner Pass to the Yuba River (PCT) hike in this chapter.

**User Groups:** Hikers, dogs, and horses. No mountain bikes. No wheelchair access.

**Permits:** A wilderness permit (free) is required. Parking and access are free.

**Maps:** For a map, ask the U.S. Forest Service for Tahoe National Forest. For topographic maps, ask the USGS for Haypress Valley, Sierra City, Mount Fillmore, and Onion Valley.

**Directions:** From Truckee, turn north on Highway 89 and drive to Sierraville and Highway 49. Turn left on Highway 49 and drive 12 miles (passing Bassetts) to the eastern end of Sierra City. Look for the Pacific Crest Trail access sign and park on the right (north) side of the road.

**Contact:** Tahoe National Forest, Nevada City/Downieville Ranger Districts, 15924 Highway 49, Camptonville, CA 95922, 530/288-3231 or 530/478-6253, website: www.fs.fed.us/r5 (click on Forest Offices).

## 17 GROUSE RIDGE TRAIL (SAWMILL TO EAGLE LAKES)
### 6.0–16.5 mi / 1.0–2.0 days

in Tahoe National Forest north of Emigrant Gap

Map 6.1, page 193

This is a gorgeous hike. The Grouse Ridge Trail weaves up and down from a mountain crest, connecting Sawmill Lake to the north with the Eagle Lakes, for a one-way distance of 8.25 miles. The beauty of this hike is that along the way are a number of side trips you can take to make your choice of visits at a half dozen lakes. In fact, many people use Grouse Ridge Trail as a jump-off point to take short and spectacular day hikes. The elevation varies from 6,160 to 6,400 feet, with the ups and downs coming in short yet serious spurts. From Sawmill Lake, climb up a timbered slope to a ridge and a turnoff for Rock Lake, which is worth a visit itself. You then pass Shotgun Lake

(it's actually a wet meadow) and continue to Middle Lake, Crooked Lakes, and Milk Lake. The views are divine much of the way.

Special Note: At Sawmill Lake, the trail crosses the spillway of the dam, which may be impassable when high water spills into Canyon Creek.

**User Groups:** Hikers, dogs, horses, and mountain bikes. No wheelchair facilities.

**Permits:** A campfire permit (free) is required for overnight use. Parking and access are free.

**Maps:** For a map, ask the U.S. Forest Service for Tahoe National Forest. For topographic maps, ask the USGS for Cisco Grove and English Mountain.

**Directions:** From Auburn, drive east on I-80 for 45 miles to the Highway 20 exit. Take that exit, head west, and drive four miles to Bowman Lake Road (Forest Road 18). Turn right on Bowman Lake Road and drive 16 miles to Bowman Lake. Turn right and drive along Bowman Lake to Faucherie Lake Road. Turn right on Faucherie Lake Road and drive .5 mile to the north end of Sawmill Lake and the trailhead.

**Contact:** Tahoe National Forest, Nevada City/Downieville Ranger Districts, 15924 Highway 49, Camptonville, CA 95922, 530/288-3231 or 530/478-6253, website: www.fs.fed.us/r5 (click on Forest Offices); Big Bend Visitors Center, 530/426-3609.

## 18 LINDSEY LAKES TRAIL
### 7.0 mi / 3.0 hrs

in Tahoe National Forest north of Emigrant Gap

Map 6.1, page 193

The highlight of Lindsey Lakes Trail is that it intersects with other trails, including the beautiful Grouse Ridge Trail, and is set in a gorgeous landscape that features Sierra alpine beauty. But the trail itself from Lindsey Lakes to Rock Lake is a service road closed to public vehicle traffic, so you're hiking up a road. This 3.5-mile trail dead-ends after climbing past the three Lindsey Lakes, and it offers a great optional side trip. From the trailhead at Lower Lindsey Lake (elevation 6,160 feet), hike up to the other lakes on a short trail (it's quite steep in several places) before topping out at 6,400 feet. The route gets medium use and accesses good swimming holes with cold water, but the fishing is poor. The best fishing in this basin is at nearby Culbertson Lake, where you can make a wonderful side trip by hiking out to Rock Lake and up to Bullpen Lake. Note that Bullpen Lake was once one of the few lakes in California stocked with Arctic grayling, but that has not occurred for several years, and the unique fish has since disappeared here. Another side trip from Lindsey Lakes Trail is Crooked Lakes Trail.

**User Groups:** Hikers, dogs, and horses. Mountain bikes not advised. No wheelchair facilities.

**Permits:** No permits are required. Parking and access are free.

**Maps:** For a map, ask the U.S. Forest Service for Tahoe National Forest. For topographic maps, ask the USGS for English Mountain and Graniteville.

**Directions:** From Auburn, drive east on I-80 for 40 miles to Highway 20. Take the Highway 20 exit and head west, driving four miles to Bowman Lake Road (Forest Road 18). Turn right and drive 8.5 miles north until you see a sign that says Lindsey Lake, Feely Lake, Carr Lake. Turn right and follow the signs to the parking area for Lindsey Lake. The road can be rough for the last .5 mile; high-clearance vehicles are advised.

**Contact:** Tahoe National Forest, Nevada City/Downieville Ranger Districts, 15924 Highway 49, Camptonville, CA 95922, 530/288-3231 or 530/478-6253, website: www.fs.fed.us/r5 (click on Forest Offices); Big Bend Visitors Center, 530/426-3609.

## 19 PENNER LAKE
**4.5 mi / 3.0 hrs**

at Carr Lake in Tahoe National Forest north of Emigrant Gap

Map 6.1, page 193

The Round Lake Trail, which accesses a series of Sierra lakes (including Island Lake and Penner Lake), is extremely beautiful but also very popular; it's even crowded at the trailhead on weekends. From the trailhead at Feely Lake (elevation 6,720 feet), the route heads east, climbing first to Island Lake. This lake, named for the little rocky islands sprinkled about, has several good campsites. Turn left when you reach Island Lake and walk 1.5 miles on Crooked Lakes Trail through a fir forest to Penner Lake. The last half mile is uphill, but nothing serious. Penner Lake is one of the crown jewels of the Grouse Ridge area. Along with Island Lake, it has the most scenic beauty, is great for swimming, and is ideal for picnics or just gazing and taking in the mountain panorama. It is best experienced on an early weekday summer morning.

**User Groups:** Hikers, dogs, mountain bikes, and horses. No wheelchair facilities.

**Permits:** No permits are required. Parking and access are free.

**Maps:** For a map, ask the U.S. Forest Service for Tahoe National Forest. For topographic maps, ask the USGS for English Mountain and Graniteville.

**Directions:** From Auburn, drive east on I-80 to Highway 20 exit. Take that exit and head west, driving four miles to Bowman Lake Road (Forest Road 18). Turn right and drive 8.5 miles north until you see a sign that says Lindsey Lake, Feely Lake, Carr Lake. Turn right and follow the signs to the parking area at Carr Lake. Continue on foot to the trailhead at Feely Lake. Sections of the road can be rough; four-wheel-drive vehicles are advised.

**Contact:** Tahoe National Forest, Nevada City/Downieville Ranger Districts, 15924 Highway 49, Camptonville, CA 95922, 530/288-3231 or 530/478-6253, website: www.fs.fed.us/r5 (click on Forest Offices); Big Bend Visitors Center, 530/426-3609.

## 20 DONNER PASS TO THE YUBA RIVER (PCT)

**38.0 mi one-way / 3.0 days**

from Highway 80 to Highway 49 in Tahoe National Forest

**Map 6.1, page 193**

Though not one of the more glamorous sections of the Pacific Crest Trail, this stretch is hardly a stinker. For the most part, it follows a crest connecting a series of small mountaintops before dropping down to Jackson Meadow Reservoir and Highway 49. Some good views are to be had on the first leg of the trail—so many that some PCT hikers begin to take them for granted after awhile. Here the trail is routed past Castle Peak (elevation 9,103 feet), Basin Peak (9,015 feet), and Lacey Mountain (8,214 feet). Covering this much terrain makes for an ambitious first day, perhaps with stops at Paradise Lake or White Rock Lake. As the trail drops to Jackson Meadow Reservoir, the views end, but in time you'll catch sight of the lake; surrounded by firs, it is quite pretty. The PCT then skirts the east side of the reservoir, passes several drive-to campgrounds, heads through Bear Valley (not *the* Bear Valley), and drops steeply to Milton Creek and four miles beyond that to Loves Falls at Highway 49.

To continue north on the PCT, see the Yuba River to Fowler Peak (PCT) hike in this chapter. If you are walking this trail in reverse, see the Barker Pass to Donner Pass (PCT) hike in this chapter.

**User Groups:** Hikers, dogs, and horses. No mountain bikes. No wheelchair facilities.

**Permits:** A campfire permit (free) is required for overnight use. Parking and access are free.

**Maps:** For a map, ask the U.S. Forest Service for Tahoe National Forest. For topographic maps, ask the USGS for Norden, Soda Springs, Webber, Haypress Valley, Independence Lake, and English Mountain.

**Directions:** From Auburn, drive east on I-80 to Boreal/Donner Summit. Take the exit for the Pacific Crest trailhead parking area. There is no parking in the Donner Summit rest area.

**Contact:** Tahoe National Forest, Sierraville Ranger District, 317 South Lincoln Street, P.O. Box 95, Sierraville, CA 96126, 530/994-3401, website: www.fs.fed.us/r5 (click on Forest Offices).

## 21 GLACIER LAKE

**10.0 mi / 1.0 day**

in Tahoe National Forest north of Emigrant Gap

**Map 6.1, page 193**

In just a few hours you can be transported to heaven, though some call it Glacier Lake. It is a five-mile hike to get here, a pristine and peaceful high Sierra setting that can make you feel as if you're three days out on a backpacking expedition. The small lake is set in a rockbound bowl with the Black Buttes looming nearby. The tree cover is sparse, and the rock cover is abundant. To get there, start your hike by heading east on Round Lake Trail at Carr Lake, and hike almost three miles. You will pass a series of lakes, including Feely Lake, Island Lake, Round Lake, and Milk Lake. Then you'll drop down into forest and meadow landscape and reach a trail junction. Continue east on Glacier Lake Trail and continue through a meadow and some forest. Here you start a gradual climb, passing a small lake before entering a rocky area and then dropping down to the pretty lake. Several backpacking campsites are available.

Note that the map of Tahoe National Forest does not show the direct route to Glacier Lake, which rises up a beautiful canyon. Instead, take our suggested unmapped trail, which allows hikers to avoid the hot, exposed, mapped route on Sandy Ridge. Another note is that cows are often present in the lower meadow portions of the route, near the trail junction. A certain black-and-white cow is known to adopt female hikers, following for up to a mile, staring with lonely brown eyes as if saying, "Momma." Whatever you do, don't wear a cowbell around your neck.

Great side trips are also available. It is a

one-mile hike north to the Five Lakes Basin and a 1.5-mile hike south to Beyers Lake. The elevations here range from 5,500 to 7,000 feet.
**User Groups:** Hikers, dogs, and horses. Mountain bikes strongly discouraged. No wheelchair facilities.
**Permits:** No permits are required. Parking and access are free.
**Maps:** For a map, ask the U.S. Forest Service for Tahoe National Forest. For topographic maps, ask the USGS for Cisco Grove and English Mountain.
**Directions:** From Auburn, drive east on I-80 to the Highway 20 exit. Take that exit and head west, driving four miles to Bowman Lake Road (Forest Road 18). Turn right and drive 8.5 miles north until you see a sign that says Lindsey Lake, Feely Lake, Carr Lake. Turn right and follow the signs to the parking area at Carr Lake. Continue on foot to the trailhead at Feely Lake. Sections of the road can be rough; four-wheel-drive vehicles are advised.
**Contact:** Tahoe National Forest, Nevada City/Downieville Ranger Districts, 15924 Highway 49, Camptonville, CA 95922, 530/288-3231 or 530/478-6253, website: www.fs.fed.us/r5 (click on Forest Offices); Big Bend Visitors Center, 530/426-3609.

## 22 PIONEER TRAIL
1.0–24.0 mi /
0.5 hr–2.0 days

**east of Nevada City, off of Highway 20 in Tahoe National Forest**

Map 6.1, page 193

Hiking Pioneer Trail is like taking a history lesson as you trace the route of the first wagon road, opened by emigrants and gold seekers in 1850. Along the way are three campgrounds for backpackers, but the trail is better suited for mountain biking. From the trailhead at Five Mile House (elevation 3,500 feet), the trail heads east for 15 miles to Bear Valley, gaining 2,000 feet. You will pass Central House (once a stagecoach stop); White Cloud and Skillman Flat (former mill sites, one burned down); and the

Omega Overlook, which provides a view of a huge hydraulic gold mining operation. The Cal-Trans Omega rest area has parking, a restroom and a viewing platform perched over the South Yuba River Canyon. From the Omega Overlook, you will get dramatic views of the Yuba River and the surrounding granite cliffs. The traffic on this trail is increasing, particularly with all the mountain bikers making the one-way trip downhill from Omega rest area to Five Mile House. If you encounter others, demonstrate the utmost courtesy. Bikers should always dismount and walk when passing hikers.
**User Groups:** Hikers, dogs, mountain bikes, and horses. No wheelchair facilities.
**Permits:** A campfire permit (free) is required for overnight use. Parking and access are free.
**Maps:** For a map, ask the U.S. Forest Service for Tahoe National Forest. For a topographic map, ask the USGS for Washington.
**Directions:** From Nevada City, drive about seven miles east on Highway 20 to the trailhead, across from Lone Grave. If the parking lot there is full, additional parking and trail access are available at Skillman Flat, Upper Burlington Ridge, Harmony Ridge Market, the Omega rest area, and the Washington Overlook trailhead—all located to the east of Highway 20.
**Contact:** Tahoe National Forest, Nevada City/Downieville Ranger Districts, 15924 Highway 49, Camptonville, CA 95922, 530/288-3231 or 530/478-6253, website: www.fs.fed.us/r5 (click on Forest Offices); Big Bend Visitors Center, 530/426-3609.

## 23 SIERRA DISCOVERY TRAIL
1.0 mi / 0.5 hr

**off Highway 20 near Lake Spaulding**

Map 6.1, page 193

The waterfall at Bear River is your destination on this easy, short, and nearly flat trail that is accessible to wheelchair users (with a bit of assistance). This is not the wilderness—much of the trail is pavement, soil cement, and compressed gravel. It is designed as an interpretive loop walk, with information about ecosystems, wildlife, geology, and cultural history available as the trail winds through a forest of pines and incense cedars. This is an ideal mountain walk for seniors, youngsters, or the physically challenged. Bear River Falls is short but wide and is well framed by a forest canopy.

**User Groups:** Hikers, dogs, and wheelchairs (with assistance). No horses or mountain bikes. Dogs permitted, but rangers strongly discourage bringing them on this trail.

**Permits:** No permits are necessary. Parking and access are free.

**Maps:** For a topographic map, ask the USGS for Blue Canyon.

**Directions:** From Auburn, drive east on I-80 for 45 miles to the Highway 20 exit. Take that exit, head west, and drive four miles to Bowman Lake Road. Turn right and drive .6 mile to the Sierra Discovery Trail parking lot, on the left side of the road.

**Contact:** Pacific Gas & Electric, 916/386-5164 or 800/PGE-5000 (800/743-5000), website: www.pge.com.

## 24 LOCH LEVEN LAKES
**7.2 mi / 4.0 hrs**

**south of Cisco Grove in Tahoe National Forest**

Map 6.1, page 193

Most people would like to know what heaven is like but are not very willing to sign up for the trip. This trip to Loch Leven Lakes, however, won't be your final resting place, yet it provides a glimpse of what heaven might resemble. The 3.5-mile hike to Loch Leven Lakes provides sweeping vistas of ridges and valleys, gorgeous high alpine meadows, and glaciated mountain terrain with a series of perfect lakes. As hikers get deeper into the wildlands here, the lakes become progressively more beautiful and pristine. The lakes themselves are clear and blue, set in granite, and speckled with boulders—the perfect picnic site.

The trail starts at 5,680 feet then works its way upward on a moderate grade to the southwest. Granite outcrops are numerous, and huge boulders (deposited by receding glaciers) lie sprinkled among Jeffrey pine and lodgepole pine. The trail crosses a creek and railroad tracks, then climbs through a cool forest. Here the trail becomes steeper, climbing 800 feet in 1.25 miles. It then tops the summit and descends gently to Lower Loch Leven Lake (2.5 miles from the trailhead). Many people stop here, content to just take in the surroundings. But you can forge on for another mile, circling Middle Loch Leven Lake (2.8 miles from the trailhead) and heading east up to High Loch Leven Lake (3.6 miles from the trailhead), at 6,800 feet. At the south end of Lower Loch Leven Lake, turn left at the trail junction to see Middle and High Loch Leven Lakes (turning right at the junction will route you to Salmon Lake, a less-crowded alternative). Once you've come this far, beautiful High Loch Leven is an easy trip and a must-do.

But this hike is not without frustration: The first hour involves a continuous climb with the roar of I-80 traffic in the background. You do not escape the noise until you top the ridge. Elevations range from 5,680 feet to 6,850 feet at the ridge, a gain of 1,070 feet. With access so easy off I-80, the area can become inundated with people on summer weekends. With no trailhead quota, the numbers can affect the sense of wilderness.

Fishing is fair during the evening bite, and there are backcountry campgrounds at each lake. Restrooms are available at the trailhead (a plus). The trail is generally open for hiking from early June to November, weather permitting; it's not marked for winter use and can be difficult to find in snow conditions.

**User Groups:** Hikers, dogs, and horses. Mountain bikes not advised. No wheelchair facilities.

**Permits:** No permits are required. Parking and access are free.

**Maps:** For a map, ask the U.S. Forest Service

for Tahoe National Forest. For a topographic map, ask the USGS for Cisco Grove.

**Directions:** From Sacramento, take I-80 east into the Sierra Nevada and to the Big Bend exit. Take that exit and then turn left on Hampshire Rocks Road. Follow the signs to the Big Bend Visitors Center, located adjacent to the highway. The parking area and trailhead are about .2 mile east of the visitors center. The trailhead is on the opposite side of the road from the parking area.

From Reno, take I-80 west to the Cisco Grove exit. Take that exit and turn right on Hampshire Rocks Road. Continue as above.

**Contact:** Tahoe National Forest, Nevada City/Downieville Ranger Districts, 15924 Highway 49, Camptonville, CA 95922, 530/288-3231 or 530/478-6253, website: www.fs.fed.us/r5 (click on Forest Offices); Big Bend Visitors Center, 530/426-3609.

## 25 LOWER LOLA MONTEZ LAKE
**6.0 mi / 3.0 hrs**

**in Tahoe National Forest near Soda Springs**

Map 6.1, page 193

Partly because it's so easy, partly because it's right off the highway, and partly because the trail is favored by mountain bikers, the hike to Lower Lola Montez Lake is a bad choice for a July or August weekend afternoon. For hikers who enjoy peace and quiet, this is definitely an off-season trail, best left for the days of autumn, when the vacationers have abandoned Lake Tahoe. The path cuts through Toll Mountain Estates, a private community, and is a mix of wide dirt roads and single-track trails. The first .25 mile is on single track; then you reach a dirt road and turn right, cross Castle Creek, and continue until the road becomes single track again. And so it goes. Luckily, the route is marked all the way, and with all the people who visit here, it's unlikely you'll get lost and not be found. The good news is that the Lower Lola Montez Lake is popular for a reason; it's a beautiful alpine lake set at 7,200 feet but shal-

low enough to warm up for swimming. Fishing is half decent but is best early in the year.

**User Groups:** Hikers, dogs, horses, and mountain bikes. No wheelchair facilities.

**Permits:** No permits are required. Parking and access are free.

**Maps:** For a map, ask the U.S. Forest Service for Tahoe National Forest. For topographic maps, ask the USGS for Soda Springs and Norden.

**Directions:** Drive east from Auburn on I-80 for 55 miles to Soda Springs. Take the Soda Springs/Norden exit and cross over the overpass to the north side of the freeway. Follow the paved road east, past the fire station for .3 mile to the trailhead parking area.

**Contact:** Tahoe National Forest, Truckee Ranger District, 9646 Donner Pass Road, Truckee, CA 96161, 530/587-3558, website: www.fs.fed.us/r5 (click on Forest Offices).

## 26 PALISADE CREEK TRAIL TO HEATH FALLS
**10.0 mi / 6.0 hrs**

**in Tahoe National Forest near Soda Springs**

Map 6.1, page 193

The hike to Heath Falls is like going on vacation on your credit card. You can have all the fun you want, but when you return home, you have to pay up. That's because the trip to the Heath Falls Overlook is downhill nearly all the way, dropping 1,700 feet over five miles, through stunning alpine scenery that will have you smiling the whole time. The return trip is a long and steady five-mile climb back uphill, so be sure you have plenty of food, water, and energy left for it.

The trail begins at the dam between the two Cascade Lakes, the first of many lakes you'll see on this trip. The big hunk of imposing rock you have to walk around is 7,704-foot Devils Peak. Take the right fork signed for the North Fork American River, and get ready for a steady diet of granite, lakes, and vistas. At 2.2 miles, the trail leaves the rocks behind and enters the forest, switchbacking downhill for two miles to the Palisade Creek Bridge. Look for an unsigned junction 300 yards beyond it, where Heath Falls Overlook Trail heads east. Follow it for .5 mile to the trail's end, at a vista of the American River's Heath Falls. Camping is prohibited along this trail because much of it runs through private property, so after enjoying the falls overlook, you've got to make the long climb home. Hope you have at least one Power Bar left.

**User Groups:** Hikers, dogs, and horses. No mountain bikes. No wheelchair facilities.

**Permits:** No permits are required. Parking and access are free.

**Maps:** For a map, ask the U.S. Forest Service for Tahoe National Forest. For topographic maps, ask the USGS for Soda Springs and Norden.

**Directions:** From Auburn, drive east on I-80 for 55 miles to Soda Springs. Take the Soda Springs/Norden exit and follow Old Highway 40 east for .8 mile to Soda Springs Road. Turn south (right) and drive for another .8 mile to Pahatsi Road. Turn right. Pahatsi Road turns to dirt in .2 mile, and its name changes to Kidd Lakes Road. At 1.5 miles, you'll reach a fork. Continue straight for 2.3 more miles, passing Kidd Lake on your left and the Royal Gorge Devils Lookout Warming Hut on your right. Take the left fork after the warming hut and drive .5 mile farther. The trailhead, signed as Palisade Creek Trail, is on the north side of Cascade Lakes.

**Contact:** Tahoe National Forest, Truckee Ranger District, 9646 Donner Pass Road, Truckee, CA 96161, 530/587-3558, website: www.fs.fed.us/r5 (click on Forest Offices).

## 27 WARREN LAKE
### 14.0 mi / 2.0 days

**in Tahoe National Forest near Donner Summit**

Map 6.1, page 193

The first 1.6 miles of this trail follow the same route as Summit Lake Trail (see next listing), along the PCT access trail and underneath I-80. But Warren Lake hikers will take the left

fork where Summit Lake hikers go right. Whereas Summit Lake Trail is an easy stroll in the park, Warren Lake Trail climbs 1,500 feet and then drops 1,500 feet, which you must repeat on the return trip. The elevation change means you part company with most casual hikers. The route climbs through lodgepole pine and red fir forest to a saddle at three miles, where there are excellent views (you can see where you're going to be hiking next). Then the trail drops gently over the next 3.5 miles, into a wide valley basin that has a mix of volcanic and glaciated rocks. Wildflowers abound on the valley floor. After a brief climb to a ridge, the final mile is a steep descent, dropping 1,000 feet to Warren Lake, where you'll find many campsites on the lake's west and south sides. Note that just before you reach the top of the ridge, about 1.3 miles from Warren Lake, there is a left spur trail that leads to Devils Oven Lake. It's a good day hike for the following day.

**User Groups:** Hikers, dogs, horses, and mountain bikes. No wheelchair facilities.

**Permits:** No permits are required. Parking and access are free.

**Maps:** For a map, ask the U.S. Forest Service for Tahoe National Forest. For a topographic map, ask the USGS for Norden.

**Directions:** Drive east from Auburn on I-80 for 60 miles to the Castle Peak Area/Boreal Ridge Road exit just west of Donner Summit. Exit the freeway; turn right and then immediately left. Drive .4 mile to the trailhead for Donner Summit and the Pacific Crest Trail.

**Contact:** Tahoe National Forest, Truckee Ranger District, 9646 Donner Pass Road, Truckee, CA 96161, 530/587-3558, website: www.fs.fed.us/r5 (click on Forest Offices).

## 28 SUMMIT LAKE TRAIL
### 4.0 mi / 2.0 hrs

**in Tahoe National Forest near Donner Summit**

Map 6.1, page 193

It's hard to believe that this much fun is accessible right off I-80, but it's true. The Summit

Lake Trail is a quick and easy leg-stretcher and a great hike for families, leading two miles to a pretty alpine lake at 7,400 feet. Start hiking from the PCT trailhead, heading east and roughly paralleling the freeway. Watch carefully for an intersection .5 mile in; there, you must turn left and follow the PCT Access Trail north (signed for Castle Pass and Peter Grubb Hut), through a tunnel underneath I-80. (This is not the most scenic part of the trip, but it's not as bad as it sounds.) Once you're on the north side of the freeway, you'll reach a trail fork. Bear right for Summit Lake and Warren Lake, then start to climb a bit. The trail alternates through fir forest and occasional open ridges, with some excellent views to the south and east. At 1.6 miles, you'll see another trail fork—Warren Lake to the left, and Summit Lake to the right. Bear right, and finish out your walk to the lake's edge, where you can drop in a fishing line if you wish.

**User Groups:** Hikers, dogs, horses, and mountain bikes. No wheelchair facilities.

**Permits:** No permits are required. Parking and access are free.

**Maps:** For a map, ask the U.S. Forest Service for Tahoe National Forest. For a topographic map, ask the USGS for Norden.

**Directions:** From Auburn, drive 60 miles east on I-80 to the Castle Peak Area/Boreal Ridge Road exit just west of Donner Summit. Exit the freeway, turn right, and then immediately left. Drive .4 mile to the trailhead for Donner Summit and the Pacific Crest Trail.

**Contact:** Tahoe National Forest, Truckee Ranger District, 9646 Donner Pass Road, Truckee, CA 96161, 530/587-3558, website: www.fs.fed.us/r5 (click on Forest Offices).

## 29 EUCHRE BAR TRAIL
### 6.0 mi / 3.5 hrs

**on the North Fork American River near Baxter in Tahoe National Forest**

Map 6.1, page 193

A river runs through almost every Sierra gulch and canyon, and so it is with this portion of the North Fork American River. From the trailhead, the route winds steeply down to the river and Euchre Bar, where a suspension footbridge crosses the water. The trail then leads upriver for 2.4 miles, along an excellent stretch of water for fishing, camping, panning for gold, and swimming (it is cold). If you want a lesson in pain, continue hiking another five miles. You'll climb the old Dorer Ranch Road, passing mining ruins and abandoned equipment from the Gold Rush era, gaining 2,000 feet in elevation through this dry, dusty country.

**User Groups:** Hikers, dogs, and horses. Mountain bikes not advised. No wheelchair facilities.

**Permits:** Campfire permits are required for overnight use. Parking and access are free.

**Maps:** For a map, ask the U.S. Forest Service for Tahoe National Forest. For topographic maps, ask the USGS for Dutch Flat and Westville.

**Directions:** From I-80 east of Auburn, take the Alta exit. Turn right on Morton, then left on Casa Loma. Follow Casa Loma until you see the sign for the Rawhide Mine and then turn right. Follow the road .75 mile past the second railroad crossing to a parking area. The trailhead is .1 mile beyond the parking area.

**Contact:** Tahoe National Forest, Nevada City/Downieville Ranger Districts, 15924 Highway 49, Camptonville, CA 95922, 530/288-3231 or 530/478-6253, website: www.fs.fed.us/r5 (click on Forest Offices); Big Bend Visitors Center, 530/426-3609.

## 30 ITALIAN BAR TRAIL
### 4.5 mi / 3.5 hrs

**near the North Fork American River in Tahoe National Forest**

Map 6.1, page 193

Miners in the 1850s were like mountain goats, and they knew the most direct route between two points was a straight line. As a result, this route—which miners once used to reach the North Fork American River—is almost straight down going in and straight up coming out, gaining 3,000 feet in elevation over the course of 2.25 miles. It's about as fun as searching for a tiny gold nugget on the beach. As you head down from the trailhead at 5,400 feet, you get little help from switchbacks. The trail ends at the river, and from there, you must scramble and hop from rock to rock along the riverbanks. Eventually you end up at a secluded spot where all seems perfect—until you start the hike back. When you face the 3,000-foot climb out, you will wonder how you ever talked yourself into doing this hike.

**User Groups:** Hikers, dogs, and horses. Mountain bikes not advised. No wheelchair facilities.

**Permits:** No permits are required. Parking and access are free.

**Maps:** For a map, ask the U.S. Forest Service for Tahoe National Forest. For a topographic map, ask the USGS for Westville.

**Directions:** From I-80 at Auburn, turn east on Foresthill Road and drive 16 miles to the town of Foresthill. Continue another 13 miles northeast (the road becomes Foresthill Divide Road) to Humbug Ridge Road (Forest Road 66). Turn left and drive three miles north to the trailhead.

**Contact:** Tahoe National Forest, Nevada City/Downieville Ranger Districts, 15924 Highway 49, Camptonville, CA 95922, 530/288-3231 or 530/478-6253, website: www.fs.fed.us/r5 (click on Forest Offices); Big Bend Visitors Center, 530/426-3609.

## 31 MUMFORD BAR TRAIL
### 6.5 mi / 1.0 day

near the North Fork American River in Tahoe National Forest

Map 6.1, page 193

You'd have to be part mountain goat and part idiot to want to try this hike. Guess how we know? The trail leads almost straight down to the North Fork American River for more than 3.25 miles, and you know what that means. Right, it's almost straight up coming back.

From the trailhead at 5,360 feet, the first mile of trail follows an old four-wheel-drive route that deteriorates and then drops down to the river canyon at 2,640 feet. This stretch of river is designated as "wild and scenic" and

is quite pretty, with good canyon views and fishing spots. Consider extending your walk by taking American River Trail (see next listing) and staying overnight. Otherwise you will have to climb back out of the canyon on the same day, something even most mountain goats would choose not to do.

**User Groups:** Hikers, dogs, and horses. Mountain bikes are not advised. No wheelchair facilities.

**Permits:** No permits are required. Parking and access are free.

**Maps:** For a map, ask the U.S. Forest Service for Tahoe National Forest. For topographic maps, ask the USGS for Duncan Peak and Westville.

**Directions:** From I-80 at Auburn, turn east on Foresthill Road and drive 16 miles to the town of Foresthill. Continue another 17 miles northeast (the road becomes Foresthill Divide Road) to the Mumford trailhead, on the left side of the road.

**Contact:** Tahoe National Forest, Foresthill Ranger District, 22830 Foresthill Road, Foresthill, CA 95631, 530/367-2224, website: www.fs.fed.us/r5 (click on Forest Offices).

## 32 AMERICAN RIVER TRAIL
### 15.2 mi / 2.0 days

on the North Fork American River east of Foresthill in Tahoe National Forest

Map 6.1, page 193

A 90-minute hike from the Mumford Bar trailhead (see previous listing) gets you down into a steep canyon and alongside the beautiful and remote North Fork American River. There you turn right and start hiking upstream on American River Trail. This is what you came for, the chance to walk along a pristine stretch of river on a steady, easy grade. You will pass old mining sites and abandoned cabins, alternating between dense vegetation and pretty river views. This trail makes a great getaway, and hikers can enjoy exploring and trout fishing. Alas, nothing is perfect, and this hike does have some drawbacks: It crosses two creeks,

Tadpole and New York, which are difficult, even dangerous, to ford when running high during the snowmelt in spring and early summer. A mile upriver of Tadpole Creek and then again at New York Creek, the trail runs adjacent to private property—check your map and stay on the trail in these places. And the hike back out of the canyon to your car is a terrible grunt, going from 2,640 feet along the river up to 5,360 feet—a gain of 2,720 feet in just 3.25 miles.

Special Note: The Mumford trailhead is also accessible from Sailor Flat Trail (see listing in this chapter).

**User Groups:** Hikers, dogs, and horses. Mountain bikes not advised. No wheelchair facilities.

**Permits:** A campfire permit (free) is required for overnight use. Parking and access are free.

**Maps:** For a map, ask the U.S. Forest Service for Tahoe National Forest. For a topographic map, ask the USGS for Duncan Peak.

**Directions:** From I-80 at Auburn, turn east on Foresthill Road and drive 16 miles to the town of Foresthill. Continue another 17 miles northeast (the road becomes Foresthill Divide Road) to the Mumford trailhead, on the left side of the road.

**Contact:** Tahoe National Forest, Foresthill Ranger District, 22830 Foresthill Road, Foresthill, CA 95631, 530/367-2224, website: www.fs.fed.us/r5 (click on Forest Offices).

## 33 BEACROFT TRAIL
### 4.5 mi / 1.0 day

**near the North Fork American River in Tahoe National Forest**

Map 6.1, page 193

The Beacroft Trail is the "no-option" option to hiking down to the North Fork American River. The trailhead is located four miles beyond the Mumford trailhead, and after having reviewed the steep descent and climb required for that hike, you might want to look elsewhere for an easier route down. That's where Beacroft Trail comes in. Still, it isn't a much better option, requiring an even more

hellacious effort, as it drops 3,240 feet in only 2.25 miles. The trip back will have you howling. How can such a short trail be so steep? Ask the people who built the darn thing; those gold miners apparently had neither an abundance of useful gray matter between their ears nor much gold to carry on the return trip. When you reach the river, turn left on American River Trail, which traces some of the most beautiful, accessible portions of this stream. Alas, even here you face an obstacle. Within the first mile, you must cross New York Creek, a difficult (and sometimes dangerous) ford when full of snowmelt in early summer.

**User Groups:** Hikers, dogs, and horses. Mountain bikes are not advised. No wheelchair facilities.

**Permits:** No permits are required. Parking and access are free.

**Maps:** For a map, ask the U.S. Forest Service for Tahoe National Forest. For a topographic map, ask the USGS for Duncan Peak.

**Directions:** From I-80 at Auburn, turn east on Foresthill Road and drive 16 miles to the town of Foresthill. Continue another 19 miles northeast (the road becomes Foresthill Divide Road) to the trailhead, on the left side of the road (one mile past Secret House Campground).

**Contact:** Tahoe National Forest, Foresthill Ranger District, 22830 Foresthill Road, Foresthill, CA 95631, 530/367-2224, website: www.fs.fed.us/r5 (click on Forest Offices).

## 34 SAILOR FLAT TRAIL
### 6.5 mi / 1.0 day

**near the North Fork American River in Tahoe National Forest**

Map 6.1, page 193

There are several trailheads heading for Sailor Flat Trail on the Foresthill side of Foresthill Road that provide access to the North Fork American River. But this is the most distant, most remote, and, yes, most difficult—and in turn, the least traveled. The Sailor Flat trailhead lies at the end of the road, out in the middle of nowhere, at an elevation of 6,400 feet; yet the remains of a long-abandoned gold stamp mill still stand nearby. The hike starts out easily enough— the first 1.5 miles follow an old mining road on which hikers will confront nothing serious. Don't be fooled though. The trail becomes much steeper, with switchback after switchback leading down into the canyon. When you reach the river at 3,360 feet, you will have dropped 3,040 feet in only 3.25 miles. You can explore farther by turning left (west) on American River Trail, which traces the most beautiful sections of this river, heading downstream past meadows, canyon views, and good spots to fish and pan for gold.

Special Note: With a shuttle vehicle and a partner, you can create an excellent one-way hike covering 15.6 miles. From Sailor Flat trailhead, hike down to American River Trail, turn left, hike along the river to Mumford Bar, make a left turn, and hike out to Foresthill Road (see preceding hikes).

**User Groups:** Hikers, dogs, and horses. Mountain bikes not advised. No wheelchair facilities.

**Permits:** No permits are required. Parking and access are free.

**Maps:** For a map, ask the U.S. Forest Service for Tahoe National Forest. For topographic maps, ask the USGS for Royal Gorge and Duncan Peak.

**Directions:** From I-80 at Auburn, turn east on Foresthill Road and drive 16 miles to the town of Foresthill. Continue another 25 miles northeast (the road becomes Foresthill Divide Road) to Sailor Flat Road. Turn left and drive one mile north to the trailhead.

**Contact:** Tahoe National Forest, Foresthill Ranger District, 22830 Foresthill Road, Foresthill, CA 95631, 530/367-2224, website: www.fs.fed.us/r5 (click on Forest Offices).

## 35 STEVENS TRAIL
### 9.0 mi / 5.0 hrs

**near Colfax**

Map 6.1, page 193

The Stevens Trail is a surprisingly lush and peaceful trail that leaves noisy I-80 in Colfax

and drops down into the canyon of the North Fork American River. The feature here is a gentle terrain and long-distance canyon and stream views. You can also see the railroad line that was built by Chinese laborers dangling in rope-strung baskets from the cliffs above. In the spring, you will also pass blooming wildflowers and buckeye trees. The trail is well signed, except the section you take to see the waterfall. After parking, walk 1.3 miles, starting with a gentle climb, and keep a sharp eye off to the left, where a pretty waterfall is hidden just off the trail. From the ridge, continue on a gentle downhill path, descending 1,200 feet over the course of 4.5 miles if you choose to head all the way to the river. The return trip is up but is well graded and not too difficult for most hikers. The biggest problem here is timing. This is no fun on a summer afternoon, with 90-degree temperatures and an afternoon climb out of a canyon. Regardless, this is a great trip for many, especially for those cruising the interstate who desire a quick getaway into a pretty setting where the highway traffic seems like a million miles away. This trail became registered in 2002 as a National Historic Trail. It was originally part of a livery trail from the town of Iowa Hill to Colfax (the entire historic route is no longer connected).

**User Groups:** Hikers, dogs, horses, and mountain bikes. No wheelchair facilities.

**Permits:** No permits are necessary. Parking and access are free.

**Maps:** For a topographic map, ask the USGS for Colfax.

**Directions:** From Sacramento, drive east on I-80 for 45 miles to Colfax and the Colfax/Grass Valley exit. Take that exit and drive a short distance to a stop sign at North Canyon Way (a frontage road). Turn left at the stop sign and drive east .7 mile to the trailhead parking area.

**Contact:** Bureau of Land Management, Folsom Field Office, 63 Natoma Street, Folsom, CA 95630, 916/985-4474, website: www.ca.blm.gov (click on Field Offices).

## 36 GREEN VALLEY TRAIL
**4.5 mi / 1.0 day**

**on the North Fork American River near Sugar Pine Reservoir**

Map 6.1, page 193

It's amazing what people will go through to create a space that feels like their own. Hikers can do just that on Green Valley Trail by finding an idyllic spot along the North Fork American River and soaking up the serenity. But the price is steep, and the return trip will put you through more punishment than is typically handed out at Folsom Prison.

The trip starts at a little-known trailhead near Sugar Pine Reservoir (elevation 4,080 feet). From there, Green Valley Trail is steep and often rocky, dropping 2,240 feet in 2.25 miles before reaching the river. We do not advise extending your trip from here. It is possible to continue downriver a short way, or to cross the river (good luck) and hike upstream into Green Valley. However, these sections of the trail are in very poor condition, and the upstream route crosses private property owned by people who don't take kindly to visitors.

**User Groups:** Hikers, dogs, and horses. Mountain bikes are not advised. No wheelchair facilities.

**Permits:** No permits are required. Parking and access are free.

**Maps:** For a map, ask the U.S. Forest Service for Tahoe National Forest. For a topographic map, ask the USGS for Dutch Flat.

**Directions:** From I-80, drive to Auburn and Foresthill Road. Turn east onto Foresthill Road and drive 16 miles to the town of Foresthill. Continue northeast (it becomes Foresthill Divide Road) and drive seven miles to Forest Road 10. Turn left on Forest Road 10 (Sugar Pine Road) and drive five miles to Sugar Pine Dam. Continue one mile past the dam to Elliot Ranch Road (just past the entrance to Sugar Pine Campground, on the right). Turn north on Elliot Ranch Road and drive three miles to the trailhead.

**Contact:** Tahoe National Forest, Foresthill Ranger District, 22830 Foresthill Road, Foresthill, CA 95631, 530/367-2224, website: www.fs.fed.us/r5 (click on Forest Offices).

## 37 FOREST VIEW TRAIL
**1.5 mi / 0.75 hr**

**in Tahoe National Forest east of Foresthill**

Map 6.1, page 193

Giant sequoias, the world's largest trees, attract many visitors to this easy, well-maintained interpretive trail that leads through California's northernmost grove of sequoias. It is set at 5,200 feet on Mosquito Ridge Road, which provides generous views of the wild and superb landscape. The trail meanders through virgin old-growth forest, home to half a dozen truly monster-sized trees. Along the .5-mile Big Trees Interpretive Trail are 16 stops marked with numbers that coincide with numbered listings in a brochure that's available at the trailhead, allowing visitors to take an interesting and informative self-guided tour of the fascinating history of these massive trees. Linked with Forest View Trail, the entire loop extends 1.5 miles. Despite the long drive to the trailhead on Mosquito Ridge, the trail gets quite a bit of use.

**User Groups:** Hikers and dogs. No horses or mountain bikes. No wheelchair facilities.

**Permits:** No permits are required. Parking and access are free.

**Maps:** Free interpretive brochures are available at the trailhead. For a map, ask the U.S. Forest Service for Tahoe National Forest. For a topographic map, ask the USGS for Greek Store.

**Directions:** From I-80, drive to Auburn and Foresthill Road. Turn east onto Foresthill Road and drive 16 miles to the town of Foresthill and Mosquito Ridge Road. Turn right (east) on Mosquito Ridge Road and drive 23 miles to the trailhead.

**Contact:** Tahoe National Forest, Foresthill Ranger District, 22830 Foresthill Road, Foresthill, CA 95631, 530/367-2224, website: www.fs.fed.us/r5 (click on Forest Offices).

## 38 WESTERN STATES TRAIL/ MICHIGAN BLUFF TO DEADWOOD SEGMENT

4.0 mi / 2.5 hrs

**in Tahoe National Forest east of Foresthill**

Map 6.1, page 193

The attraction here is beautiful Eldorado Canyon, where you can fish for trout and camp along Eldorado Creek. From the trailhead at 3,520 feet, the trail quickly drops about two miles into the canyon, with switchbacks leading to a footbridge over Eldorado Creek. Extend the trip by crossing the bridge and hiking up the other side of the canyon to scenic views of the rugged topography.

Special Note: The Michigan Bluff Trail is a section of Western States Trail, which spans from Squaw Valley to Auburn.

**User Groups:** Hikers, dogs, horses, and mountain bikes. No wheelchair facilities.

**Permits:** No permits are required. Parking and access are free.

**Maps:** For a map, ask the U.S. Forest Service for Tahoe National Forest. For a topographic map, ask the USGS for Michigan Bluff.

**Directions:** From I-80, drive to Auburn and Foresthill Road. Turn east onto Foresthill Road and drive 16 miles to the town of Foresthill. Continue northeast (it becomes Foresthill Divide Road) and look for the signed turnoff to Michigan Bluff. Turn right on Michigan Bluff Road and drive five miles to the town of Michigan Bluff. The trailhead is located about .25 mile east of Michigan Bluff, at the end of the road.

**Contact:** Tahoe National Forest, Foresthill Ranger District, 22830 Foresthill Road, Foresthill, CA 95631, 530/367-2224, website: www.fs.fed.us/r5 (click on Forest Offices).

## 39 GROUSE FALLS

1.0 mi / 0.5 hr

**in Tahoe National Forest near Foresthill**

Map 6.1, page 193

Some waterfalls are simply mind-boggling in their beauty, and some provide the centerpiece of a beautiful setting. Grouse Falls is one of the latter. The hike is a 15-minute walk through old-growth forest to a viewing deck. From here you're looking out over a deep and wide canyon with absolutely no sign of human development. The waterfall is about .5 mile away across the canyon; it's several hundred feet long, and when it's running full, it can seem like a scene out of Yosemite. The overlook is a wooden platform with benches where you can sit and admire the beauty. You don't see or hear immense Grouse Falls until just before you come out to the overlook, and when you do, it can be a shock to your system.

**User Groups:** Hikers, dogs, horses, and mountain bikes. No wheelchair facilities.

**Permits:** No permits are necessary. Parking and access are free.

**Maps:** For a map, ask the U.S. Forest Service for Tahoe National Forest. For a topographic map, ask the USGS for Michigan Bluff.

**Directions:** From I-80, drive to Auburn and Foresthill Road. Turn east onto Foresthill Road and drive 16 miles to the town of Foresthill and Mosquito Ridge Road. Turn right (east) on Mosquito Ridge Road and drive 19 miles to Peavine Road (Road 33). Turn left on Peavine Road and drive 5.5 miles to the Grouse Falls turnoff, on the left. Turn left and drive .5 mile to the trailhead.

**Contact:** Tahoe National Forest, Foresthill Ranger District, 22830 Foresthill Road, Foresthill, CA 95631, 530/367-2224, website: www.fs.fed.us/r5 (click on Forest Offices).

## 40 WESTERN STATES TRAIL/ McGUIRE SEGMENT

7.8 mi / 4.0 hrs

at French Meadows Reservoir in Tahoe National Forest

**Map 6.1, page 193**

The McGuire Trail has become a favorite side trip for families visiting or camping at French Meadows Reservoir (elevation 5,290 feet). The trail traces the north shore of the lake, poking in and out of timber, then goes up an easy grade to the top of Red Star Ridge (5,600 feet), offering good views of the reservoir below. French Meadows is a beautiful and large lake, covering nearly 2,000 acres when full. It is stocked each year with more than 30,000 trout that join a healthy population of resident brown trout and holdovers from stocks of rainbow trout from prior years. Water drawdowns are a common problem in late summer, as they expose many stumps and boulders, creating a navigational hazard for boaters.

**User Groups:** Hikers, dogs, horses, and mountain bikes. No wheelchair facilities.

**Permits:** No permits are required. Parking and access are free.

**Maps:** For a map, ask the U.S. Forest Service for Tahoe National Forest. For a topographic map, ask the USGS for Bunker Hill.

**Directions:** From I-80, drive to Auburn and Foresthill Road. Turn east onto Foresthill Road and drive 16 miles to the town of Foresthill and Mosquito Ridge Road. Turn right (east) on Mosquito Ridge Road and drive 40 miles to the French Meadows Reservoir Dam. Cross the dam, turn left (still Mosquito Ridge Road), and drive 3.5 miles to the trailhead, near McGuire Boat Ramp.

**Contact:** Tahoe National Forest, Foresthill Ranger District, 22830 Foresthill Road, Foresthill, CA 95631, 530/367-2224, website: www.fs.fed.us/r5 (click on Forest Offices).

## 41 POWDERHORN TRAIL TO HELL HOLE

13.0 mi one-way / 2.0 days

in the Granite Chief Wilderness east of Hell Hole Reservoir in Tahoe National Forest

**Map 6.1, page 193**

Do you yearn for a challenging trek in a very remote high-mountain wilderness setting? This is it. The Hell Hole Trail requires hikers to have wilderness skills and, worst of all, to be prepared for a difficult stream crossing and traversing a landslide. Sound fun? Who said anything about fun?

Start at the remote Powderhorn trailhead, set at 6,400 feet on the boundary of the Granite Chief Wilderness. From there, you hike four miles down to Diamond Crossing (fording Powderhorn Creek), where you will meet Hell Hole Trail. Shortly after turning left, you will have to cross Five Lakes Creek, a difficult and sometimes dangerous endeavor, especially during snowmelt. After crossing, you will descend to Little Buckskin Creeks (two more fords, both a lot easier than the first one) and into Steamboat Canyon. Approximately .5 mile from Steamboat Canyon, hikers face a slippery landslide that demands caution. The trail then drops toward the Rubicon River and Hell Hole Reservoir.

Special Notes: The stream crossings required on this hike can be life threatening during periods of high snowmelt and runoff.

For a day hike or a weekend camping trip, start the trail at the Hell Hole Dam and walk three miles to a hike-in camp set at the head of the lake.

**User Groups:** Hikers, dogs, and horses. No mountain bikes. No wheelchair facilities.

**Permits:** A campfire permit (free) is required for overnight use. Parking and access are free.

**Maps:** For a map, ask the U.S. Forest Service for Tahoe National Forest. For a topographic map, ask the USGS for Wentworth Springs.

**Directions:** In Truckee, turn south on Highway 89 and drive to Tahoe City. Continue four miles south on Highway 89 to the Kaspian Picnic Area. Turn west (right) on Blackwood

Canyon Road and drive 2.3 miles. Cross the creek and continue for another 4.8 miles to Barker Pass.

**Contact:** Tahoe National Forest, Truckee Ranger District, 9646 Donner Pass Road, Truckee, CA 96161, 530/587-3558, website: www.fs.fed.us/r5 (click on Forest Offices).

## 42 GRANITE CHIEF TRAIL TO TINKER KNOB
### 14.0 mi / 8.0 hrs or 2.0 days

**in Tahoe National Forest near Squaw Valley**

**Map 6.1, page 193**

Tinker Knob is not an easy summit to attain, but those who reach it always remember it. From the Squaw Valley Fire Station, it's a demanding 3.5-mile hike to the intersection of the Granite Chief Trail and the Pacific Crest Trail. The total gain is 2,000 feet; most of the climb is forested, but there are occasional openings with views of Lake Tahoe and surrounding peaks. When at last you gain the PCT (at 8,200 feet), turn right (north) toward Tinker Knob. Now it's another 3.5 miles, most of it on an easier, winding grade along the top of a ridge, with only one surprising, cruel stretch in which you must drop downhill and then climb up again. The last section of trail is a series of switchbacks up to the Tinker Knob Saddle, then it's a brief .25-mile climb to the summit of Tinker Knob, at 8,950 feet. You like views? How about this one—a head-swiveling vista of Anderson Peak, Painted Rock, Silver Peak, the American River Canyon, Donner Lake, and Lake Tahoe. To cut some mileage off your trip, hike this trail as a shuttle trip, leaving one car at the Coldstream trailhead near Donner Memorial State Park. (It's at the horseshoe bend in the railroad tracks at the end of Coldstream Creek access road.) The Coldstream Trail meets the PCT just below the summit of Tinker Knob, so after gaining the summit via the route described above, follow Coldstream Trail four miles down to its trailhead. This makes an 11-mile one-way hike with a shuttle.

**User Groups:** Hikers, dogs, horses, and mountain bikes. No wheelchair facilities.

**Permits:** No permits are required. Parking and access are free.

**Maps:** For a map, ask the U.S. Forest Service for Tahoe National Forest. For topographic maps, ask the USGS for Tahoe City and Granite Chief.

**Directions:** Drive north from Tahoe City on Highway 89 for five miles and turn west on Squaw Valley Road. Drive 2.2 miles to the Squaw Valley Fire Station, where the trail begins on its east side. You must leave your car in the large parking lot by the ski lift buildings, not by the fire station. Walk back across the bridge to the trailhead.

**Contact:** Tahoe National Forest, Truckee Ranger District, 9646 Donner Pass Road, Truckee, CA 96161, 530/587-3558, website: www.fs.fed.us/r5 (click on Forest Offices).

## 43 GRANITE CHIEF TRAIL TO EMIGRANT PASS
### 12.0 mi / 7.0 hrs

**in Tahoe National Forest near Squaw Valley**

**Map 6.1, page 193**

The Granite Chief Trail begins at the Squaw Valley Fire Station (at 6,200 feet) and climbs, climbs, and climbs some more until it reaches the Pacific Crest Trail 3.5 miles later. This is why many hikers choose to ride the tram at Squaw Valley to reach the PCT, then start hiking around from there. But not you . . . you like a challenge, right? Well, in either case, see you at the top.

You'll climb 2,000 feet over those 3.5 miles, roughly paralleling Squaw Creek and mostly in the woods. When you reach the PCT, turn left (south) toward Twin Peaks. The view of Lake Tahoe and its cobalt blue waters is stunning. Still ascending, hike for one mile on the PCT to the eastern flank of Granite Chief Peak (elevation 9,086 feet). Finally you begin to descend, and in one more mile you reach an intersection with Western States Trail. Turn left and take a .5-mile walk to visit the Watson Monument, a stone marker at Emigrant Pass. You probably won't stay long if you arrive in the afternoon: Although the views are lovely, the wind is usually fierce by midday.

**User Groups:** Hikers, dogs, horses, and mountain bikes. No wheelchair facilities.

**Permits:** No permits are required. Parking and access are free.

**Maps:** For a map, ask the U.S. Forest Service for Tahoe National Forest. For topographic maps, ask the USGS for Tahoe City and Granite Chief.

**Directions:** From Tahoe City, drive north on Highway 89 for five miles and turn west on Squaw Valley Road. Drive 2.2 miles to the Squaw Valley Fire Station, where the trail begins on its east side. You must leave your car in the large parking lot by the ski lift buildings, not by the fire station. Walk back across the bridge to the trailhead.

**Contact:** Tahoe National Forest, Truckee Ranger District, 9646 Donner Pass Road, Truckee, CA 96161, 530/587-3558, website: www.fs .fed.us/r5 (click on Forest Offices).

## 44 FIVE LAKES
**4.2 mi / 2.0 hrs**

**in the Granite Chief Wilderness near Alpine Meadows**

Map 6.1, page 193

Some say that this trek into the Granite Chief Wilderness is too easy, and they may be right. Although the trail has a moderately steep grade, it's mercifully short, which makes it incredibly popular with hikers, especially on weekends. Make your trip in the off-season or during the week, and definitely make this a day trip instead of an overnight in order to minimize impact at the five granite-bound lakes.

The first .5 mile is the steepest grade, whereas the next .75 mile continues uphill more gradually to the top of a ridge. Switchbacks make it manageable, but there is almost no shade along the route as you climb 1,000 feet. At 1.8 miles, you reach the Granite Chief Wilderness

boundary and enter a land of red fir, white fir, and rocks. A signed junction .25 mile farther points you to the left toward the lakes, with your trail heading directly downhill to the largest of them. From there, you can follow numerous side trails to the four other lakes, all east of the big one. Most people don't go any farther than the first big lake, where the swimming is excellent—the shallow water is clear and warm. Remember: Minimize your impact in this heavily traveled area. The Five Lakes are set at 7,400 feet.

**User Groups:** Hikers, dogs, and horses. No mountain bikes. No wheelchair facilities.

**Permits:** No permits are required for day hiking. Parking and access are free.

**Maps:** For a map, ask the U.S. Forest Service for Tahoe National Forest. For topographic maps, ask the USGS for Tahoe City and Granite Chief.

**Directions:** From Tahoe City, drive north on Highway 89 for 3.5 miles to Alpine Meadows Road. Turn west on Alpine Meadows Road and drive two miles to the trailhead, on the right. Park alongside the road.

**Contact:** Tahoe National Forest, Truckee Ranger District, 9646 Donner Pass Road, Truckee, CA 96161, 530/587-3558, website: www.fs .fed.us/r5 (click on Forest Offices).

## 45 WARD CREEK TRAIL
**6.0 mi / 3.0 hrs**

**in Tahoe National Forest near Tahoe City**

Map 6.1, page 193

Compared to some of the more famous hikes at Lake Tahoe, Ward Creek Trail is rather tame: No stellar waterfall, no drop-dead gorgeous lake views, no towering granite monoliths. But then again, there are no crowds either. For many, the trade-off is a good one. The route passes through fields of mule's ears and forests of sugar pines, with enough open sections to provide wide-open views of the surrounding mountain ridges.

The trail begins as an old dirt road, paralleling Ward Creek for 1.5 miles to a washed-out bridge and a Road Closed sign. Cross the creek on logs and continue hiking, now on a single track. The trail climbs a little higher above Ward Creek, then enters a dense, lovely pine forest. You can go as far as you like (the trail continues to Twin Peaks, 5.3 miles from the trailhead), but for the mileage suggested above, turn around when you are about .5 mile into the trees and take an easy stroll home.

**User Groups:** Hikers, dogs, horses, and mountain bikes. No wheelchair facilities.

**Permits:** No permits are required. Parking and access are free.

**Maps:** For a map, ask the U.S. Forest Service for Lake Tahoe Basin Management Unit. For a topographic map, ask the USGS for Tahoe City.

**Directions:** From Tahoe City, drive two miles south on Highway 89 to Pineland Drive, just north of Kilner Park. Turn right on Pineland Drive and go .5 mile to Twin Peaks Drive. Turn left and drive 1.7 miles. (Twin Peaks Drive becomes Ward Creek Boulevard.) At 1.7 miles, park in the pullout on the left side of the highway and begin hiking at the gated dirt road, Forest Service Road 15N62. If the gate is open, you can drive inside and park along the dirt road.

**Contact:** Lake Tahoe Basin Management Unit, 35 College Drive, South Lake Tahoe, CA 96150, 530/543-2600, website: www.fs.fed.us/r5 (click on Forest Offices); Visitors Center (open only in summer), 530/543-2674.

# 46 ELLIS PEAK
**6.0 mi / 3.5 hrs**

**in Tahoe National Forest near Tahoe City**

Map 6.1, page 193

This short but steep trek leads to the top of Ellis Peak and to fabulous views of Lake Tahoe, Granite Chief and Desolation Wildernesses, and Hell Hole Reservoir. There is a total 1,300-foot elevation gain to the peak (at 8,740 feet), but the route is beautiful all the way, with close-up wildflowers rivaling the far-off views. The initial climb is a bit steep, but there is plenty of shade on this stretch. Then, for 1.5 miles, the route follows a sunny ridgeline with wide-open vistas, revealing Lake Tahoe to the east and Hell Hole Reservoir to the west. The perspective from this ridgeline alone is worth the trip. Plus, mule's ears and other wildflowers bloom in profusion all around your ankles.

After traversing the ridgeline, head downhill (surprise!) through the forest, dropping 400 feet in elevation. When you come to a wide dirt road, bear left to begin the trek to Ellis Peak. In .25 mile, you'll see a short left spur to tiny Ellis Lake, a worthy side trip of about 50 yards. If you ignore the spur and stay on the main trail for another 100 yards, you'll reach an old dirt road, where you turn east (left). In .25 mile, you come to Knee Ridge, from which the summit of Ellis Peak is plainly visible. Go for it. Note that the only downer along this route is that some of it is accessible to off-road-vehicle riders and mountain bikers, although we saw none of the former on our trip, and the latter were extremely courteous.

**User Groups:** Hikers, dogs, horses, and mountain bikes. No wheelchair facilities.

**Permits:** No permits are required. Parking and access are free.

**Maps:** For a map, ask the U.S. Forest Service for Lake Tahoe Basin Management Unit. For a topographic map, ask the USGS for Homewood.

**Directions:** Drive four miles south from Tahoe City on Highway 89 to Forest Service Road 03 (Barker Pass Road). Turn right (west) and drive seven miles to the summit of Barker Pass. The trailhead is on the left (south) side of the road.

**Contact:** Lake Tahoe Basin Management Unit, 35 College Drive, South Lake Tahoe, CA 96150, 530/543-2600, website: www.fs.fed.us/r5 (click on Forest Offices); Visitors Center (open only in summer), 530/543-2674.

## 47 STATELINE LOOKOUT
### 1.0 mi / 0.5 hr

off Highway 28 near Crystal Bay

Map 6.1, page 193

For years we avoided this trail because we thought it was just a tourist attraction, located at the lookout tower that straddles the Nevada and California state line. It turns out that *we* were the dumb tourists, because this little trail is great. You can learn all about the cultural history of Lake Tahoe's north shore—which includes stories of timber, railroads, casinos, and resorts—as well as a little about the natural history of the area as well. After you walk the short self-guided trail, be sure to check out the views of Lake Tahoe from the telescopes located at the lookout. Or, hey, forget the telescopes and just look with your own eyes. Either way, the view is unforgettable.

**User Groups:** Hikers, wheelchairs, and dogs. No horses or mountain bikes.

**Permits:** No permits are required. Parking and access are free.

**Maps:** For a map, ask the U.S. Forest Service for Lake Tahoe Basin Management Unit. For a topographic map, ask the USGS for Kings Beach.

**Directions:** From Tahoe City, drive east on Highway 28 for six miles to Reservoir Drive, just east of the old Tahoe Biltmore Casino. Turn left (north), drive to Lake View Avenue, and turn right. Continue through a residential area and then turn left on Forest Service Road 1601 at an unmarked iron gate. Park at the gate and walk .5 mile to the lookout. Parking is limited.

**Contact:** Lake Tahoe Basin Management Unit, 35 College Drive, South Lake Tahoe, CA 96150, 530/543-2600, website: www.fs.fed.us/r5 (click on Forest Offices); Visitors Center (open only in summer), 530/543-2674.

## 48 BURTON CREEK LOOP
### 5.0 mi / 2.5 hrs

off Highway 28 near Tahoe City

Map 6.1, page 193

At more than 2,000 acres, Burton Creek is Lake Tahoe's second-largest state park, so you might wonder why few people have ever heard of it. It's because the park has no visitors center, no campground, no entrance kiosk, and, unfortunately, no trail signs or official map. What really matters is that it has no crowds—a major bonus at Lake Tahoe. A five-mile loop trip is possible in the park, starting near North Tahoe High School and wandering through a mix of fir and pine forest, open meadows, and creekside riparian habitat. Although the trail is not signed at present, there are numbers painted at most intersections, which help you stay on track. The loop starts .25 mile from the trailhead; you can hike it in either direction. Just make sure you remember what the spur trail that leads from the loop back to the trailhead looks like; otherwise you may walk right past it on your return trip. Some advice: If you're visiting this park in summer, stop in at the campground at Tahoe State Recreation Area, across Highway 28 from the turnoff to Burton Creek State Park. Check with the kiosk to see if they have any updated trail information on Burton Creek.

**User Groups:** Hikers, leashed dogs, horses, and mountain bikes. No wheelchair facilities.

**Permits:** No permits are required. Parking and access are free.

**Maps:** For a topographic map, ask the USGS for Tahoe City.

**Directions:** From Tahoe City, drive northeast on Highway 28 for 2.3 miles to Old Mill Road. Turn left and drive .4 mile; then turn left on Polaris Road and drive .5 mile to North Tahoe High School and the dirt road by the school parking lot. Park alongside the dirt road, being careful not to block the gate.

**Contact:** Tahoe State Recreation Area, P.O. Box 266, Tahoma, CA 96142, 530/525-7232 or 530/583-3074, fax 530/525-0138.

## 49 BARKER PASS TO DONNER PASS (PCT)
**31.4 mi one-way / 3.0 days**

**from Barker Pass to Donner Pass**

**Map 6.1, page 193**

The trailhead at Barker Pass (7,650 feet), is one of the best anywhere, with direct access to the Granite Chief Wilderness to the north or the Desolation Wilderness to the south. Heading north on the PCT, the trip starts with a climb of 800 feet to enter Granite Chief, and once on the ridge, you're rewarded with 360-degree views of this high-mountain landscape, a mix of volcanic rock and granite ridges, much of it above tree line. Though hikers don't face the long, sustained climbs so common in the southern Sierra, it's enough of a roller-coaster ride to require hikers to be in excellent shape. The trail cuts the flank of Ward Peak, at 8,470 feet, then switchbacks steeply down to Five Lakes and Five Lakes Creek (where there's good camping). The trail then continues up and down canyons all the way to Donner Pass. You can expect to see lots of hikers, because along the way, you'll pass near two ski resorts (Alpine Meadows and Squaw Valley), where hikers can use the ski lifts in the summer to gain easy elevation to the ridgeline, rather than having to grind out long, all-day climbs. Before making the final push to Donner Pass, a descent of more than 1,000 feet, hikers can enjoy breathtaking views of Donner Lake and the miles of surrounding high country.

To continue north on the PCT, see the Donner Pass to the Yuba River (PCT) hike in this chapter. If you are walking this trail in reverse, see the Echo Lakes Resort to Barker Pass (PCT) hike in this chapter.

**User Groups:** Hikers, dogs, and horses. No mountain bikes. No wheelchair facilities.

**Permits:** A backcountry permit is required for traveling through various wilderness and special-use areas that the trail traverses. In addition, a campfire permit is required for the use of portable camp stoves or the building of campfires (where allowed). To make it simple, you can contact the national forest, Bureau of Land Management (BLM), or national park office at your point of entry for a combined permit that is good for traveling through multiple-permit areas during your dates of travel.

**Maps:** For topographic maps, ask the USGS for Emerald Bay, Rockbound Valley, Homewood, Tahoe City, Granite Chief, and Norden.

**Directions:** To reach the Barker Pass trailhead from Tahoe Pines on Highway 89, head north for .5 mile to the Kaspian Picnic Grounds, and then bear left (west) for seven miles on Forest Service Road 15N03. For the Donner Pass trailhead from Truckee, drive west on I-80 and exit at Castle Peak Area/Boreal Ridge, just west of the Donner Summit roadside rest area. The sign for the Pacific Crest trailhead is what you're looking for, and it's located on the south side of the highway.

**Contact:** Tahoe National Forest, Truckee Ranger District, 9646 Donner Pass Road, Truckee, CA 96161, 530/587-3558, website: www.fs .fed.us/r5 (click on Forest Offices); Lake Tahoe Basin Management Unit, 35 College Drive, South Lake Tahoe, CA 96150, 530/543-2600, website: www.fs.fed.us/r5 (click on Forest Offices) ; Visitors Center (open only in summer), 530/543-2674.

## 50 GENERAL CREEK TO LILY POND
**7.0 mi / 3.5 hrs**

**in Sugar Pine Point State Park near Lake Tahoe**

**Map 6.1, page 193**

This trail, in Sugar Pine Point State Park, follows a flat open stretch of General Creek and then leads gently uphill through the forest to marshy Lily Pond, a pretty, serene spot. Most of the trail is part of a popular cross-country skiing loop in the winter, which means it's on a dirt road. There are a couple key factors to enjoying this walk: If you're not staying in the General Creek Campground, the day-use parking area is more than .5 mile from campsite

No. 149, where the trail begins. To make this walk to the trailhead more pleasant, be sure to take the single-track trail from the parking lot instead of walking along the paved camp road. The trail is somewhat hidden from view, so if you don't see it, ask the attendant in the entrance kiosk where it is. Next, when you finally meet up with the loop, be sure to take the north side of it, which is prettier than the south side, with lots of big sugar pines interspersed with Jeffreys and lodgepoles. The south side is mostly open meadows. This was the site of the 1960 Olympics biathlon. At 2.5 miles from the campground, at the far end of the loop, you'll see the single-track turnoff signed for Lily Pond and Lost Lake. It's a one-mile hike through a rocky, dense forest to the pond, which is indeed covered with lilies. On your return, you can always take the south side of the loop for variety, then turn left on the bridge over General Creek to return to the start of the loop.

**User Groups:** Hikers and mountain bikes. No dogs or horses. No wheelchair facilities.

**Permits:** No permits are required. A day-use fee of $6 is charged per vehicle.

**Maps:** A map of Sugar Pine Point State Park is available for a fee at the entrance station. A Lake Tahoe map is available for a fee from Tom Harrison Maps. For a topographic map, ask the USGS for Homewood.

**Directions:** From Tahoe City, drive eight miles south on Highway 89 to the General Creek Campground entrance, on the right. Park in one of the day-use areas by the entrance kiosk, then walk into the campground to site No. 149 and the start of the trail. You can walk into the camp on the park road or take the single-track trail that leads from the parking lot.

**Contact:** Sugar Pine Point State Park, P.O. Box 266, Tahoma, CA 96142, 530/525-7982 or 530/525-7232, website: www.parks.ca.gov (click on Find A Park).

## 51 MEEKS CREEK TRAIL TO RUBICON LAKE

**15.0 mi / 1.0–2.0 days**

in the Desolation Wilderness

**Map 6.1, page 193**

If you don't mind sharing the trail with lots of other folks, this trek into the Desolation Wilderness is a moderate backpacking trip that's loaded with alpine lakes and classic Tahoe scenery. A closed dirt road (Road 14N42) leads from the Desolation Wilderness sign near Meeks Bay for 1.3 level miles to a trail sign for Phipps Pass and Tahoe-Yosemite Trail, a popular cross-country skiing route in winter. Bear right here and begin the gradual climb to a chain of alpine lakes, beginning with Lake Genevieve at 4.5 miles and culminating with Rubicon Lake at 7.5 miles. Hike parallel to Meeks Creek on a gently climbing trail, and pass the wilderness boundary at 2.5 miles. You're in forest most of the time, so don't expect a lot of panoramic views, but then again, don't expect any brutal, sunny, exposed ascents. Cross Meeks Creek and continue straight to Lake Genevieve, a shallow, swimmable body of water. The trail then climbs up to larger Crag Lake, then continues to climb farther to small, lily-covered Shadow Lake. (A right fork beyond Crag Lake leads to small Hidden Lake, less than .25 mile off the main trail; it's a good side trip.) From Shadow Lake, it's a mile farther to Stony Ridge Lake, the largest of this series of lakes, and then yet another mile to Rubicon Lake, 7.5 miles from the trailhead and with a total elevation gain of only 2,000 feet. The main steep stretch is right at the end, between Stony Ridge Lake and Rubicon Lake. Campsites can be found at most all of the lakes, but Rubicon Lake is the preferred site, since it's the most scenic of the group.

**User Groups:** Hikers, dogs, and horses. No mountain bikes. No wheelchair facilities.

**Permits:** Permits are required year-round for both day and overnight use. Day hikers may obtain a free permit from a ranger station or may self-issue at most major trailheads. Backpackers camping in Desolation Wilderness are subject to trailhead quotas. There is a $5 reservation fee, plus $5 per person for one night, $10 per person for two or more nights up to 14 days (nonrefundable). Children ages 12 and under are free. Golden Passes do not apply to personal-use permits. For groups, the cost of a single permit will not exceed $100.

**Maps:** For a map, ask the U.S. Forest Service for Desolation Wilderness or Lake Tahoe Basin Management Unit. A Lake Tahoe or Desolation Wilderness map is also available from Tom Harrison Maps. For topographic maps, ask the USGS for Homewood and Rockbound Valley.

**Directions:** From Tahoe City, drive south on Highway 89 for 10 miles to Meeks Bay Resort. Look for a small dirt parking lot across from the resort, on the west side of the highway, and park there. The trailhead is well marked.

**Contact:** Lake Tahoe Basin Management Unit, 35 College Drive, South Lake Tahoe, CA 96150, 530/543-2600, website: www.fs.fed.us/r5 (click on Forest Offices); Visitors Center (open only in summer), 530/543-2674.

## 52 RUBICON AND LIGHTHOUSE LOOP

**2.0 mi / 1.0 hr**

**in D. L. Bliss State Park on the west shore of Lake Tahoe**

Map 6.2, page 194

Not everybody is up for hiking the entire length of Rubicon Trail (see next listing). But if you're visiting Lake Tahoe, you should not leave the area without sampling at least a piece of this magnificent pathway, which edges along the steep cliffs on the west side of the lake. An excellent short trip on the Rubicon is this loop, which starts from Calawee Cove Beach, at D. L. Bliss State Park. Although the hike has very little elevation gain, it's not for those who are afraid of heights, because there are 100-foot drop-offs along the trail's edge, leading straight down to Lake Tahoe. Cables are in place in some sections to keep people from falling off

the trail. Hike .25 mile to a spur trail leading to the old lighthouse (don't bother with the spur; there's nothing to see), then continue beyond it for another .5 mile. The lake and mountain views are mind-boggling every step of the way. Bear right at the trail junction and walk to a parking lot, where you can pick up Lighthouse Trail and loop back to Calawee Cove Beach. On the other hand, if you want to see those lake vistas one more time, forget about the loop and just head back the way you came.

**User Groups:** Hikers only. No dogs, horses, or mountain bikes. No wheelchair facilities.

**Permits:** No permits are required. A day-use fee of $6 is charged per vehicle.

**Maps:** A map of D. L. Bliss State Park is available for a fee at the entrance station. A Lake Tahoe map is available for a fee from Tom Harrison Maps. For a topographic map, ask the USGS for Emerald Bay.

**Directions:** Drive south from Tahoe City on Highway 89 for 15 miles and turn left at the sign for D. L. Bliss State Park. Drive .5 mile to the entrance station and continue for .7 mile to a fork. Turn right and drive another .7 mile to Calawee Cove Beach and the parking lot. The Rubicon Trail begins on the far side of the lot. If this lot is full, you will have to use one of the other day-use parking lots in the park.

**Contact:** D. L. Bliss State Park, P.O. Box 266, Tahoma, CA 96142, 530/525-7277 or 530/525-7232, website: www.parks.ca.gov (click on Find A Park).

## 53 RUBICON TRAIL

**9.0 mi / 5.0 hrs**

**in D. L. Bliss State Park on the west shore of Lake Tahoe**

Map 6.2, page 194

The Rubicon Trail is the premier Lake Tahoe day hike; accept no substitutes. If you want the best scenery that Lake Tahoe offers, this is the trail to hike. The only problem? Right; it's you and about a zillion other hikers. If you possibly can, walk this trail in the off-season (late September is great), and do it on a weekday. Then get ready for eye-popping, film-burning scenery as you gaze out across the surface and deep into the depths of sparkling, clear, 12-mile-wide Lake Tahoe and the rim of mountains that surround it. The trail stays close to the lake edge and has very little elevation change, just some mild ups and downs, holding steady near 6,300 feet. Highlights include Rubicon Point, Emerald Point, Emerald Bay, Fannette Island, Vikingsholm Castle, and Eagle Point. If you prefer, you can start and end your Rubicon hike at Vikingsholm; just leave your car in the Emerald Bay Overlook parking lot. Finding room in the parking lot in summer is nearly impossible except for those arriving very early in the day. In addition, you'll add on nearly two miles round-trip getting from the parking lot to Vikingsholm, during which there is a 600-foot elevation change.

**User Groups:** Hikers only. No dogs, horses, or mountain bikes. No wheelchair facilities.

**Permits:** No permits are required. A day-use fee of $6 is charged per vehicle.

**Maps:** A map of D. L. Bliss State Park is available for a fee at the entrance station. A Lake Tahoe map is available for a fee from Tom Harrison Maps. For a topographic map, ask the USGS for Emerald Bay.

**Directions:** From Tahoe City, drive south on Highway 89 for 15 miles and turn left at the sign for D. L. Bliss State Park. Drive .5 mile to the entrance station, then continue for .7 mile to a fork. Turn right and drive another .7 mile to Calawee Cove Beach and the parking lot. The Rubicon Trail begins on the far side of the lot. If this lot is full, you will have to use one of the other day-use parking lots in the park.

**Contact:** D. L. Bliss State Park, P.O. Box 266, Tahoma, CA 96142, 530/525-7277 or 530/525-7232, website: www.parks.ca.gov (click on Find A Park).

## 54 BALANCING ROCK
**1.0 mi / 0.5 hr**

**in D. L. Bliss State Park on the west shore of Lake Tahoe**

Map 6.2, page 194

The Balancing Rock is a big hunk of granite that has been a curiosity at Lake Tahoe for eons. It's a 130-ton rock that sits balanced on a small rock pedestal, like a giant golf ball on an itty-bitty golf tee. The trail's interpretive brochure explains that eventually erosion will wear away the pedestal and cause the Balancing Rock to lose its balance, but Tahoe lovers have been awaiting this event forever, and it still hasn't happened. In addition to Balancing Rock, the trail shows off many of the plants and trees of the Tahoe area. It's a good learning experience for both kids and adults.

**User Groups:** Hikers only. No dogs, horses, or mountain bikes. No wheelchair facilities.

**Permits:** No permits are required. A day-use fee of $6 is charged per vehicle.

**Maps:** A map of D. L. Bliss State Park is available for a fee at the entrance station. A Lake Tahoe map is available for a fee from Tom Harrison Maps. For a topographic map, ask the USGS for Emerald Bay.

**Directions:** From Tahoe City, drive south on Highway 89 for 15 miles and turn left at the sign for D. L. Bliss State Park. Drive .5 mile to the entrance station, then continue for .7 mile to a fork. Turn left and drive .25 mile to the Balancing Rock parking lot, on the left.

**Contact:** D. L. Bliss State Park, P.O. Box 266, Tahoma, CA 96142, 530/525-7277 or 530/525-7232, website: www.parks.ca.gov (click on Find A Park).

## 55 VIKINGSHOLM
**2.0 mi / 1.0 hr**

**in Emerald Bay State Park on the west shore of Lake Tahoe**

Map 6.2, page 194

If you can take this walk very early in the morning, and preferably on a weekday, you'll experience the incredible beauty that has made

Lake Tahoe the revered vacation destination that it is. If you take this walk at almost any other time, be prepared for a lot of company. Although the destination of this one-mile trail (really a dirt road) is Vikingsholm, a Viking castle built by an heiress in 1929, the beauty lies in the scenery spread out before you as you hike downhill. You'll see spectacular Fannette Island and the deep blue waters of Emerald Bay, and you'll travel through an old-growth cedar and pine forest. You even gain access to some of Lake Tahoe's coveted sandy shoreline. Although visitors have to pay a buck to tour the inside of the castle, you can hike to it for free and add on a side trip to the base of 150-foot Eagle Falls, situated .25 mile from Vikingsholm. For many people, the surprise on this trail is that the return hike has a 500-foot elevation gain. What, you mean we have to breathe hard?

Special Note: Be sure to arrive early. By mid-morning on weekends, visitors are forced to park up to two miles away.

**User Groups:** Hikers only. No dogs, horses, or mountain bikes. No wheelchair facilities.

**Permits:** No permits are required. A fee of $3 is charged per vehicle. There is a fee to tour the inside of the castle.

**Maps:** A map of Emerald Bay and D. L. Bliss State Parks is available for a fee at the visitors center by Vikingsholm. A Lake Tahoe map is available for a fee from Tom Harrison Maps. For a topographic map, ask the USGS for Emerald Bay.

**Directions:** From South Lake Tahoe, drive northwest on Highway 89 for nine miles to the Emerald Bay Overlook parking lot on the east side of Highway 89. The trail begins from the lake side of the parking lot.

**Contact:** Emerald Bay State Park, P.O. Box 266, Tahoma, CA 96142, 530/525-7277 or 530/525-7232, website: www.parks.ca.gov (click on Find A Park).

## 56 UPPER EAGLE FALLS AND EAGLE LAKE
**2.0 mi / 1.0 hr**

**off Highway 89 near South Lake Tahoe**

Map 6.2, page 194

This is one of the most popular hikes in the entire Tahoe region, perhaps No. 2 only to the trail to Vikingsholm. A sign by the restroom at the Eagle Falls Picnic Area points hikers to Upper Eagle Falls Trail. Unfortunately this is something of a "designer" path, with natural granite cut into flagstonelike stairs and an elaborate wooden bridge that escorts visitors over the top of the falls. Still it's a beautiful walk, best taken early in the morning and during the week, when the masses aren't around. The waterfall pours right under the hikers' bridge. (If you want to see the "other" Eagle Falls, the one that drops right along Highway 89, see the previous listing). Immediately after the bridge, the designer aspect of the trail ends as you enter the Desolation Wilderness and climb 400 feet in less than a mile to reach rocky Eagle Lake, surrounded by granite cliffs. People fish and picnic here; some even try to swim in the icy water.

**User Groups:** Hikers and dogs. No horses or mountain bikes. No wheelchair facilities.

**Permits:** Day hikers must fill out a free permit at the wilderness trailhead. A $3 parking fee is charged per vehicle.

**Maps:** For a map, ask the U.S. Forest Service for Desolation Wilderness or Lake Tahoe Basin Management Unit. A Lake Tahoe map is available for a fee from Tom Harrison Maps. For a topographic map, ask the USGS for Emerald Bay.

**Directions:** From South Lake Tahoe, drive northwest on Highway 89 for 8.5 miles to the Eagle Falls Picnic Area and trailhead. Turn left into the parking area, or park in the roadside pullout just north of the picnic area on the west side of Highway 89.

**Contact:** Lake Tahoe Basin Management Unit, 35 College Drive, South Lake Tahoe, CA 96150,

530/543-2600, website: www.fs.fed.us/r5 (click on Forest Offices); Visitors Center (open only in summer), 530/543-2674.

## 57 VELMA LAKES
**10.0 mi / 5.0 hrs**

**in the Desolation Wilderness**

Map 6.2, page 194

Remember to bring your sunscreen, because the rocky trail to the Velma Lakes is exposed and open. The route follows the trail to Eagle Falls and Eagle Lake (see previous listing) for the first mile, then climbs through a rugged, glaciated landscape, with only occasional hardy lodgepole pines and twisted junipers providing meager shade. The lack of trees and the abundance of rock means wide-open views and plenty of granite drama: Welcome to the Sierra high country. At three miles, you intersect the trail heading southwest (left) to Dicks Lake, but you should head northwest (right) for Velma Lakes. Your trail heads directly to Middle Velma Lake (in one mile), the most popular of the lakes. It has several granite islands and is favored for swimming. You can take a left cutoff just before Middle Velma Lake and head south to Upper Velma Lake in .5 mile, or follow a use trail north along a creek to Lower Velma Lake (on your right, also .5 mile away). Note that hikers can also begin the Velma Lakes hike from the trailhead at Bayview Campground, but then they miss out on seeing Eagle Lake and a world-class view of Tahoe.

**User Groups:** Hikers and dogs. No horses or mountain bikes (the Bayview Trail provides access for horses; contact Tahoe Basin National Forest). No wheelchair facilities. To reach Velma Lakes, equestrians must access from another trailhead; Bayview trailhead is the best for this.

**Permits:** Permits are required year-round for both day and overnight use. Day hikers may obtain a free permit from a ranger station or may self-issue at most major trailheads. Backpackers camping in Desolation Wilderness are subject to trailhead quotas. There is a $5 reservation fee, plus $5 per person for one night, $10 per person for two or more nights up to 14 days (nonrefundable). Children ages 12 and under are free. Golden Passes do not apply to personal-use permits. For groups, the cost of a single permit will not exceed $100. A $3 parking fee is charged per vehicle.

**Maps:** For a map, ask the U.S. Forest Service for Desolation Wilderness or Lake Tahoe Basin Management Unit. A Lake Tahoe or Desolation Wilderness map is available from Tom Harrison Maps. For topographic maps, ask the USGS for Emerald Bay and Rockbound Valley.

**Directions:** From South Lake Tahoe, drive northwest on Highway 89 for 8.5 miles to the Eagle Falls Picnic Area and trailhead. Turn left into the parking area or park in the roadside pullout just north of the picnic area, on the west side of Highway 89.

**Contact:** Lake Tahoe Basin Management Unit, 35 College Drive, South Lake Tahoe, CA 96150, 530/543-2600, website: www.fs.fed.us/r5 (click on Forest Offices); Visitors Center (open only in summer), 530/543-2674.

## 58 CASCADE FALLS
**2.0 mi / 1.0 hr**

**off Highway 89 near South Lake Tahoe**

Map 6.2, page 194

This trail is far and away the best easy hike at Lake Tahoe. It's short and flat enough for almost anybody to make the trip, including young children, but it still feels like wilderness. The one-mile trail leads to a stunning 200-foot cascade that drops into the southwest end of Cascade Lake. Make sure you visit in spring or early summer, when the waterfall is flowing full and wide, because by August, it loses its drama. From the trailhead at Bayview Campground, take the left fork signed for Cascade Falls. In five minutes, you get tremendous views of Cascade Lake (elevation 6,464 feet); then you start to hear and see the falls. The trail disintegrates as it nears the waterfall's edge, and hikers with children shouldn't get too close.

But no matter; the best views are actually farther back on the trail. Upstream of the falls are some lovely pools surrounded by wide shelves of granite.

**User Groups:** Hikers and dogs. No horses or mountain bikes. No wheelchair facilities.

**Permits:** No permits are required. Parking and access are free.

**Maps:** For a map, ask the U.S. Forest Service for Lake Tahoe Basin Management Unit. A Lake Tahoe map is available for a fee from Tom Harrison Maps. For a topographic map, ask the USGS for Emerald Bay.

**Directions:** Drive northwest on Highway 89 from South Lake Tahoe for 7.5 miles to the Bayview Campground. Turn left and drive to the far end of the campground to the trailhead parking area. If it's full, park on the shoulder of Highway 89 by the campground entrance.

**Contact:** Lake Tahoe Basin Management Unit, 35 College Drive, South Lake Tahoe, CA 96150, 530/543-2600, website: www.fs.fed.us/r5 (click on Forest Offices); Visitors Center (open only in summer), 530/543-2674.

## 59 MOUNT TALLAC (TALLAC TRAILHEAD)
### 9.0 mi / 6.0 hrs

in the Desolation Wilderness near Fallen Leaf Lake

Map 6.2, page 194

Hikers short on time and long on energy hike to 9,735-foot Mount Tallac from this trailhead rather than from the Glen Alpine trailhead (see the Mount Tallac Loop listing in this chapter). The payment this trail extracts from you is a 2,600-foot climb over the final three miles (plus another 900 feet in the first 1.5 miles), but in exchange, you get a gorgeous route that passes by Floating Island and Cathedral Lakes on its way to Tallac's spectacular summit. It's 1.7 miles from the trailhead to Floating Island Lake, with excellent views of Fallen Leaf Lake and Lake Tahoe along the way. Then it's another .7 mile to a trail junction just before Cathedral Lake, where a trail from Fallen Leaf

Lake joins this trail. Cathedral Lake is a good rest stop before making the final ascent to the top of Mount Tallac, a 2.4-mile butt-kicker of a climb on a rocky trail. It's made easier by a continuous and ever-changing parade of vistas, including long looks at Gilmore Lake, Susie Lake, and Lake Aloha. The trail ends .25 mile below the summit, where it meets the other Mount Tallac trail coming from Gilmore Lake. Bear right, and boulder hop your way to the top. Not surprisingly, the views are wide reaching—of the Desolation Wilderness, Fallen Leaf Lake, Lake Tahoe, and even Mount Rose far off to the east. Is the vista spectacular? Yes, undeniably.

**User Groups:** Hikers and dogs. No horses or mountain bikes. No wheelchair facilities.

**Permits:** Permits are required year-round for both day and overnight use. Day hikers may obtain a free permit from a ranger station or may self-issue at most major trailheads. Backpackers camping in Desolation Wilderness are subject to trailhead quotas. There is a $5 reservation fee, plus $5 per person for one night, $10 per person for two or more nights up to 14 days (nonrefundable). Children ages 12 and under are free. Golden Passes do not apply to personal-use permits. For groups, the cost of a single permit will not exceed $100.

**Maps:** For a map, ask the U.S. Forest Service for Desolation Wilderness. A Lake Tahoe or Desolation Wilderness map is also available for a fee from Tom Harrison Maps. For a topographic map, ask the USGS for Emerald Bay.

**Directions:** From South Lake Tahoe, drive northwest on Highway 89 for 3.8 miles to the signed turnoff for Mount Tallac and Camp Concord (on the left, across the highway from the sign for Baldwin Beach). Drive .4 mile, turn left, and drive .6 mile to the trailhead.

**Contact:** Lake Tahoe Basin Management Unit, 35 College Drive, South Lake Tahoe, CA 96150, 530/543-2600, website: www.fs.fed.us/r5 (click on Forest Offices); Visitors Center (open only in summer), 530/543-2674.

## 60 RAINBOW AND LAKE OF THE SKY TRAILS

0.5 mi / 0.5 hr

in Tahoe National Forest near South Lake Tahoe

Map 6.2, page 194

Several short interpretive walks begin at the Lake Tahoe Visitors Center, the best of which are Rainbow Trail and Lake of the Sky Trail. You can hike them both from the same starting point at the visitors center and combine an interesting nature lesson with a walk along Lake Tahoe's shoreline for exceptional scenery and views. Start with Rainbow Trail, which leads from the visitors center's west side and takes you to Taylor Creek and its Stream Profile Chamber. The creek is where thousands of kokanee salmon come to spawn in the fall, and visitors can view them through the glass walls of the profile chamber. You can also see them the ordinary way, just by peering into the creek as you walk. Then loop back to the visitors center and pick up Lake of the Sky Trail. You'll pass by Taylor Creek Marsh on your way to Tallac Point and Tahoe's shoreline. In summer, people go swimming at this sandy stretch of beach.

**User Groups:** Hikers and wheelchair users. No dogs, horses, or mountain bikes.

**Permits:** No permits are required. Parking and access are free.

**Maps:** For a map, ask the U.S. Forest Service for Lake Tahoe Basin Management Unit. A free forest recreation newspaper is also available. A Lake Tahoe map is available for a fee from Tom Harrison Maps. For a topographic map, ask the USGS for Emerald Bay.

**Directions:** From South Lake Tahoe, drive northwest on Highway 89 for three miles to the Lake Tahoe Visitors Center turnoff, on the right. Turn right and drive to the visitors center parking lot, where the trails begin.

**Contact:** Lake Tahoe Basin Management Unit, 35 College Drive, South Lake Tahoe, CA 96150, 530/543-2600, website: www.fs.fed.us/r5 (click on Forest Offices); Visitors Center (open only in summer), 530/543-2674.

## 61 MOUNT TALLAC LOOP (GLEN ALPINE TRAILHEAD)

11.6 mi / 7.5 hrs

in the Desolation Wilderness near Fallen Leaf Lake

Map 6.2, page 194

You can hike to the top of 9,735-foot Mount Tallac from either of two trailheads. This trip from Glen Alpine is more gradual than the route from the Tallac trailhead (see Mount Tallac listing in this chapter). Start at the Glen Alpine trailhead, elevation 6,560 feet, and follow the main trail, which is lined with large, cobblestone-like rocks. It's a difficult walking surface for many, but fortunately, the surface flattens out shortly beyond the first mile. At the Grass Lake and Gilmore Lake junction, 1.5 miles in, bear right. Get ready for a well-graded series of switchbacks climbing out of Glen Alpine Canyon, with some shade (but not quite enough) to keep you somewhat refreshed. A good rest stop is at Gilmore Lake, 3.5 miles in, where you can stretch your hamstrings and munch a snack. From there, it's just under two miles to the top of Mount Tallac, climbing steeply up its smooth back side. This is the toughest part of the trail, and it slows down a lot of casual hikers. The official trail ends just below the summit; you must scramble over and around boulders for the last .25 mile to reach the top. The vista here is one of the finest in Northern California; you'll shoot plenty of photographs. Enjoy the eye-popping views of the Desolation Wilderness, Fallen Leaf Lake, Lake Tahoe, and Mount Rose.

To make this a loop hike, be prepared for a knee-jarring descent down the front face of Mount Tallac. (Hikers preferring a more gradual slope should retrace their steps back to the trailhead.) From the summit, head back down the Glen Alpine Trail and look for another trail heading east, toward Fallen Leaf Lake. Just past tiny Cathedral Lake, 2.3 miles from the summit, bear right at the fork (it's easy to miss) and continue downhill to Stanford Camp; walk through the camp, and pick up the road to Glen Alpine trailhead. A short stint on the road will deposit you back at your car.

**User Groups:** Hikers and dogs. No horses or mountain bikes. No wheelchair facilities.

**Permits:** Permits are required year-round for both day and overnight use. Day hikers may obtain a free permit from a ranger station or may self-issue at most major trailheads. Backpackers camping in Desolation Wilderness are subject to trailhead quotas. There is a $5 reservation fee, plus $5 per person for one night, $10 per person for two or more nights up to 14 days (nonrefundable). Children ages 12 and under are free. Golden Passes do not apply to personal-use permits. For groups, the cost of a single permit will not exceed $100.

**Maps:** For a map, ask the U.S. Forest Service for Desolation Wilderness. A Lake Tahoe or Desolation Wilderness map is also available for a fee from Tom Harrison Maps. For a topographic map, ask the USGS for Echo Lake.

**Directions:** From South Lake Tahoe, drive northwest on Highway 89 for 2.9 miles to Fallen Leaf Lake Road. Turn left and drive 4.8 miles on a narrow road past the Fallen Leaf Marina. Take the left fork on Road 1216, signed for Lily Lake and the Desolation Wilderness. Drive .7 mile to the trailhead, at the road's end.

**Contact:** Lake Tahoe Basin Management Unit, 35 College Drive, South Lake Tahoe, CA 96150, 530/543-2600, website: www.fs.fed.us/r5 (click on Forest Offices); Visitors Center (open only in summer), 530/543-2674.

## 62 GILMORE LAKE
**7.6 mi / 4.0 hrs**

**in the Desolation Wilderness near Fallen Leaf Lake**

> Map 6.2, page 194

If you only have time to day-hike to one destination near South Lake Tahoe, Gilmore Lake should be your choice. Everything about it is a classic Lake Tahoe and Desolation Wilderness trip—a roundup of the best the area has to offer. You get to visit a scenic alpine lake, and along the way, you are treated to fields of

wildflowers, mountain vistas, conifer forests, and more. Of course, we're not the only ones who like this trail, so all the usual disclaimers apply about timing your trip for the off-season or during the week.

With that said, take off from the Glen Alpine trailhead and hike down the road past the private cabins. The rocky road eventually becomes a rocky trail. This cobblestone-like stretch is by far the worst part of the hike; the rocks make it rough going for hikers' ankles and knees. Bear right at the junction with Grass Lake Trail, 1.5 miles in, where the trail surface improves dramatically. Get ready to do the majority of this trail's climbing, heading for more trail junctions at nearly three miles in, where paths lead off to the left, to Susie and Heather Lakes. Bear right instead for Gilmore Lake, the largest lake in this area between Fallen Leaf Lake and Lake Aloha. You'll reach it at 3.5 miles, with a total 1,700-foot elevation gain. Despite the fact that hundreds of people cruise by Gilmore Lake each day on their way to climb Mount Tallac, few take the time to hang out for long by the lake's sapphire blue waters. The lake, ringed by grassy, flower-filled meadows, manages to stay secluded and pristine.

**User Groups:** Hikers and dogs. No horses or mountain bikes. No wheelchair facilities.

**Permits:** Permits are required year-round for both day and overnight use. Day hikers may obtain a free permit from a ranger station or may self-issue at most major trailheads. Backpackers camping in Desolation Wilderness are subject to trailhead quotas. There is a $5 reservation fee, plus $5 per person for one night, $10 per person for two or more nights up to 14 days (nonrefundable). Children ages 12 and under are free. Golden Passes do not apply to personal-use permits. For groups, the cost of a single permit will not exceed $100.

**Maps:** For a map, ask the U.S. Forest Service for Desolation Wilderness. A Lake Tahoe or Desolation Wilderness map is also available for a fee from Tom Harrison Maps. For a topographic map, ask the USGS for Emerald Bay.

**Directions:** From South Lake Tahoe, drive northwest on Highway 89 for 2.9 miles to Fallen Leaf Lake Road. Turn left and drive 4.8 miles on an increasingly narrow road. Take the left fork on Road 1216, signed for Lily Lake and the Desolation Wilderness. Drive .7 mile to the trailhead.

**Contact:** Lake Tahoe Basin Management Unit, 35 College Drive, South Lake Tahoe, CA 96150, 530/543-2600, website: www.fs.fed.us/r5 (click on Forest Offices); Visitors Center (open only in summer), 530/543-2674.

## 63 SUSIE AND HEATHER LAKES
### 10.0 mi / 5.0 hrs

in the Desolation Wilderness near Fallen Leaf Lake

**Map 6.2, page 194**

Many people believe they must visit the beautiful Desolation Wilderness to see the rugged alpine beauty of the Tahoe wildlands. Not so. This trip, a day hike to Susie and Heather Lakes, is a perfect example.

The trail to Susie and Heather Lakes begins as a rocky road and passes some summer cabins and a waterfall on Glen Alpine Creek. At 1.2 miles, the road ends near an old resort and you'll see a sign for Gilmore, Susie, and Grass Lakes. Start to climb, and shortly, you'll enter the Desolation Wilderness boundary. You can take the short left cutoff to little Grass Lake (adding one mile each way to your trip) or continue straight, which is signed for Susie, Heather, and Aloha Lakes. At four miles, you'll reach the eastern shore of Susie Lake, then hike alongside it and around the lake's southern edge to continue another mile to Heather Lake. The granite-lined lake is deep and wide, and is set in a landscape of classic high Sierra scenery.

**User Groups:** Hikers, dogs, and horses. No mountain bikes. No wheelchair facilities.

**Permits:** Permits are required year-round for both day and overnight use. Day hikers may obtain a free permit from a ranger station or may self-issue at most major trailheads. Backpackers camping in Desolation Wilderness are subject to trailhead quotas. There is a $5 reservation fee, plus $5 per person for one night, $10 per person for two or more nights up to 14 days (nonrefundable). Children ages 12 and under are free. Golden Passes do not apply to personal-use permits. For groups, the cost of a single permit will not exceed $100.

**Maps:** For a map, ask the U.S. Forest Service for Desolation Wilderness. A Lake Tahoe or Desolation Wilderness map is also available for a fee from Tom Harrison Maps. For a topographic map, ask the USGS for Emerald Bay.

**Directions:** From South Lake Tahoe, drive northwest on Highway 89 for 2.9 miles to Fallen Leaf Lake Road. Turn left and drive 4.8 miles on a narrow road past the Fallen Leaf Lake Marina. Take the left fork on Road 1216, signed for Lily Lake and the Desolation Wilderness. Drive .7 mile to the trailhead, at the road's end.

**Contact:** Lake Tahoe Basin Management Unit, 35 College Drive, South Lake Tahoe, CA 96150, 530/543-2600, website: www.fs.fed.us/r5 (click on Forest Offices); Visitors Center (open only in summer), 530/543-2674.

## 64 FALLEN LEAF LAKE TRAIL
### 2.0 mi / 1.0 hr

near South Lake Tahoe

**Map 6.2, page 194**

Fallen Leaf Lake, at 6,400 feet in elevation, is the second-largest lake in the Tahoe Basin, and some say it's the prettiest. Too bad most of it is privately owned. But luckily, this path allows you access to the part that is public. The short, mostly flat trail leads from the trailhead to the lake and then along its northern edge to the dam, which you can walk across. Much of the trail hugs the lake's shoreline, so you can look out across the blue water and feel that sense of peace that comes from the sight of deep, sapphire waters. You also get excellent views of Glen Alpine Canyon and Mount Tallac. In the fall, the shoreline of Fallen Leaf Lake is one of the best spots near Tahoe to admire the quaking aspens turning gold. Campers staying at Fallen Leaf Lake Campground can access this trail from their tents.

**User Groups:** Hikers, dogs, horses, and mountain bikes. No wheelchair facilities.

**Permits:** No permits are required. Parking and access are free.

**Maps:** For a map, ask the U.S. Forest Service for Lake Tahoe Basin Management Unit. A Lake Tahoe map is available for a fee from Tom Harrison Maps. For a topographic map, ask the USGS for Emerald Bay.

**Directions:** From South Lake Tahoe, drive northwest on Highway 89 for 2.9 miles to Fallen Leaf Lake Road. Turn left and drive .8 mile to the Fallen Leaf Lake trailhead. The parking is not marked; look for a circular area that is not paved.

**Contact:** Lake Tahoe Basin Management Unit, 35 College Drive, South Lake Tahoe, CA 96150, 530/543-2600, website: www.fs.fed.us/r5 (click on Forest Offices); Visitors Center (open only in summer), 530/543-2674.

## 65 ANGORA LAKES TRAIL
### 1.0 mi / 0.5 hr

**at Angora Lake near South Lake Tahoe**

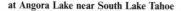
**Map 6.2, page 194**

First a warning: It's unwise to hike Angora Lakes Trail unless you are accompanied by a person under the age of seven. The Angora Lakes are extremely popular with children's day camps and groups, and all summer long, the little ones outnumber the old folks. Still it's a pretty hike, and the Upper Angora Lake is a sight to behold. Head uphill from the parking lot on the signed dirt road, and in 15 minutes, you'll be looking at Lower Angora Lake, which has a few cabins on its far side. Continue beyond its edge another .25 mile and, voilà, you reach the upper lake and Angora Lakes Resort, built in 1917. Although the resort cabins are always rented way in advance, day users can buy a lemonade and sit at a picnic table to watch the action at the small, picturesque lake. Action? What action?

Anglers fish from shore or rent rowboats for a few bucks per hour; toddlers wade around at the shallow beach area; and plenty of folks just plunk themselves down along the shoreline to stare at the bowl-shaped, glacial cirque lake. It has a high granite wall on its far side, where in early summer a waterfall of snowmelt flows down to the lake.

**User Groups:** Hikers, dogs, horses, and mountain bikes. No wheelchair facilities.

**Permits:** No permits are required. Parking and access are free.

**Maps:** For a map, ask the U.S. Forest Service for Lake Tahoe Basin Management Unit. A Lake Tahoe map is available for a fee from Tom Harrison Maps. For a topographic map, ask the USGS for Echo Lake.

**Directions:** From South Lake Tahoe, drive northwest on Highway 89 for 2.9 miles to Fallen Leaf Lake Road. Turn left and drive two miles to a fork. Turn left and drive .5 mile. Then bear right on Forest Service Road 12N14 and drive 2.3 miles, past the Angora Fire Lookout, to the road's end and the trailhead.

**Contact:** Lake Tahoe Basin Management Unit, 35 College Drive, South Lake Tahoe, CA 96150, 530/543-2600, website: www.fs.fed.us/r5 (click on Forest Offices); Visitors Center, (open only in summer), 530/543-2674.

## 66 ROCKBOUND PASS AND LAKE DORIS
### 12.0 mi / 6.0 hrs–2.0 days

**in the Desolation Wilderness**

**Map 6.2, page 194**

To make the epic trip to 8,650-foot Rockbound Pass, follow the trail notes for the route to Gertrude and Tyler Lakes (see next listing) for the first 1.9 miles. Bear left to stay on Rockbound Pass Trail and hike through mixed conifers to get your first glimpse of Rockbound Pass at 2.5 miles—a distant notch in the mountains to the north. To reach it, you must descend a bit and cross the Jones Fork of Silver Creek, then parallel the stream on its course from Maud Lake. You're traveling in very rocky terrain now; the trail is blasted out of granite in places. You'll reach the western shores of 7,700-foot Maud Lake at 4.5 miles. Many backpackers make camp here, while day hikers continue the ascent to the pass. It's not much farther; after a steady climb, you gain its wide summit at 5.9 miles. The views of Desolation Wilderness open wide, including views back at Maud Lake and ahead to Lake Doris, but the howling wind often prevents hikers from staying long. If that's the case, descend .5 mile to Lake Doris, just to the left of the trail, where you can make camp, or if you're day hiking, just hang out and rest. The total elevation gain on this trip is 1,700 feet, plus a short descent to Lake Doris.

**User Groups:** Hikers, dogs, and horses. No mountain bikes. No wheelchair facilities.

**Permits:** Permits are required year-round for both day and overnight use. Day hikers may obtain a free permit from a ranger station or may self-issue at most major trailheads. Backpackers camping in Desolation Wilderness are subject to trailhead quotas. There is a $5 reservation fee, plus $5 per person for one night, $10 per person for two or more nights up to 14 days (nonrefundable). Children ages 12 and under are free. Golden Passes do not apply to personal-use permits. For groups, the cost of a single permit will not exceed $100.

**Directions:** From Placerville, drive east on Highway 50 for 45 miles to the signed turnoff for Wrights Lake on the north side of the highway, about 15 miles west of South Lake Tahoe and five miles east of Kyburz. Drive north on Wrights Lake Road for eight miles to Wrights Lake Visitors Center. Continue straight past it for .5 mile to the Rockbound trailhead (on the way to Dark Lake).

**Contact:** Eldorado National Forest, Pacific Ranger District, 7887 Highway 50, Pollock Pines, CA 95726, 530/644-2349, website: www.fs.fed.us/r5 (click on Forest Offices).

# 67 GERTRUDE AND TYLER LAKES
## 9.0 mi / 5.0 hrs or 2.0 days 4 9

**in the Desolation Wilderness**

Map 6.2, page 194

There's a ton of hiking to be accomplished in the Wrights Lake area, and among all the possibilities, the trip to Gertrude and Tyler Lakes stands out, because it offers great scenery, a good workout, and a chance to practice your cross-country skills on the way to Tyler Lake. A clearly defined trail leads to pretty Gertrude Lake. But Tyler Lake, higher and lovelier, is found only by those who forge their own way. That makes for a fun little adventure if you desire. Begin on Rockbound Pass Trail, passing pastoral Beauty Lake .5 mile out and continuing on a remarkably easy path until you see a sign for Tyler Lake at 1.9 miles. There, bear right and prepare to work a lot harder for the rest of the hike. One memorable .5-mile stretch goes straight uphill and will cause you to question your sanity. Luckily the worst part doesn't last long, and the views of the spectacular peaks of the Crystal Range will distract you. At 3.5 miles you'll reach a hard-to-spot left spur trail (100 yards long) leading to the grave of William Tyler, a rancher who died here in a blizzard in the 1920s. A half mile beyond this cutoff is Gertrude Lake, at 8,000 feet. A nearly invisible right fork just past the grave cutoff is the start of an unmaintained trail to Tyler Lake, which lies 400 feet higher than Gertrude Lake. If you miss the use trail turnoff, watch for occasional rock cairns and keep an eye on your trail map. Tyler Lake lies .5 mile southeast of Gertrude Lake. Of the two lakes, Tyler is more beautiful, set in a granite basin with a few sparse pines on its shores. Because it's slightly difficult to locate, you have an excellent chance at solitude at Tyler Lake, even on summer weekends.

**User Groups:** Hikers, dogs, and horses. No mountain bikes. No wheelchair facilities.

**Permits:** Permits are required year-round for both day and overnight use. Day hikers may obtain a free permit from a ranger station or may self-issue at most major trailheads. Backpackers camping in Desolation Wilderness are subject to trailhead quotas. There is a $5 reservation fee, plus $5 per person for one night, $10 per person for two or more nights up to 14 days (nonrefundable). Children ages 12 and under are free. Golden Passes do not apply to personal-use permits. For groups, the cost of a single permit will not exceed $100.

**Maps:** For a map, ask the U.S. Forest Service for Desolation Wilderness or Eldorado National Forest. A Lake Tahoe or Desolation Wilderness map is also available from Tom Harrison Maps. For topographic maps, ask the USGS for Pyramid Peak and Rockbound Valley.

**Directions:** From Placerville, drive east on Highway 50 for 45 miles to the signed turnoff for Wrights Lake, on the north side of the highway, about 15 miles west of South Lake Tahoe and five miles east of Kyburz. Drive north on Wrights Lake Road for eight miles to Wrights Lake Visitors Center. Continue straight past the visitors center for .5 mile to the Rockbound trailhead (on the way to Dark Lake).

**Contact:** Eldorado National Forest, Pacific Ranger District, 7887 Highway 50, Pollock Pines, CA 95726, 530/644-2349, website: www.fs.fed.us/r5 (click on Forest Offices); Lake Tahoe Basin Management Unit, 35 College Drive, South Lake Tahoe, CA 96150, 530/543-2600, website: www.fs.fed.us/r5 (click on Forest Offices); Visitors Center (open only in summer), 530/543-2674.

## 68 TWIN AND ISLAND LAKES
### 6.4 mi / 4.0 hrs or 2.0 days

**in the Desolation Wilderness**

**Map 6.2, page 194**

The only downer on the trip to Twin and Island Lakes is the sheer number of people who make this journey every day during the summer months. Of course, when you see the lakes, you'll know why they are so darn popular. Of all the hiking possibilities in the Wrights Lake area, this trip is hands-down the most scenic, with the most striking views in the entire Desolation Wilderness and miles of solid granite under your feet as you walk. The trail is extremely well marked, and its moderate grade is suitable for all types of hikers. The first 1.2 miles from the Twin Lakes trailhead have only a gentle climb to the intersection with the trail to Grouse, Hemlock, and Smith Lakes. Bear left for Twin Lakes and climb up over granite until .75 mile later you crest a ridge and start to descend. The vistas of jagged Crystal Range peaks to the northeast make an awesome backdrop. At 2.5 miles, you'll reach the dam at Lower Twin Lake. Cross it and continue hiking along the lake's northwest shore to tiny Boomerang Lake, at three miles. The lake is shaped like its name and is shallow enough to provide warm water for swimming. Another .25 mile on the trail brings you to the south end of Island Lake, where the vistas of the Crystal Range are the best of the trip, and where most hikers burn a heck of a lot of film. If you ever wanted to sell somebody on the beauty of the Northern Sierra, this trail would be the place to do it.

**User Groups:** Hikers, dogs, and horses. No mountain bikes. No wheelchair facilities.

**Permits:** Permits are required year-round for both day and overnight use. Day hikers may obtain a free permit from a ranger station or may self-issue at most major trailheads. Backpackers camping in Desolation Wilderness are subject to trailhead quotas. There is a $5 reservation fee, plus $5 per person for one night, $10 per person for two or more nights up to 14 days (nonrefundable). Children ages 12 and under are free. Golden Passes do not apply to personal-use permits. For groups, the cost of a single permit will not exceed $100.

**Maps:** For a map, ask the U.S. Forest Service for Eldorado National Forest or Desolation Wilderness. A Lake Tahoe or Desolation Wilderness map is also available for a fee from Tom Harrison Maps. For a topographic map, ask the USGS for Pyramid Peak.

**Directions:** From Placerville, drive east on Highway 50 for 45 miles to the signed turnoff for Wrights Lake, on the north side of the highway, about 15 miles west of South Lake Tahoe and five miles east of Kyburz. Drive north on Wrights Lake Road for eight miles to Wrights Lake Visitors Center. Turn right and continue one mile beyond the campground to the end of the road and the Twin Lakes trailhead.

**Contact:** Eldorado National Forest, Pacific Ranger District, 7887 Highway 50, Pollock Pines, CA 95726, 530/644-2349, website: www.fs.fed.us/r5 (click on Forest Offices); Lake Tahoe Basin Management Unit, 35 College Drive, South Lake Tahoe, CA 96150, 530/543-2600, website: www.fs.fed.us/r5 (click on Forest Offices); Visitors Center (open only in summer), 530/543-2674.

## 69 GROUSE, HEMLOCK, AND SMITH LAKES
**6.0 mi / 3.0 hrs or 2.0 days**

**in the Desolation Wilderness**

> **Map 6.2, page 194**

The Crystal Basin area is a magical place on the western edge of Desolation Wilderness, where the nearly 10,000-foot peaks of the Crystal Range overlook the basin and its multitude of lakes. Several excellent day hikes and backpacking trips are possible in this area, most of which begin from popular Wrights Lake Campground. Of those, the trip to Grouse, Hemlock, and Smith Lakes is a favorite, despite the relentless climb required to reach all three lakes. From the parking area, Twin Lakes Trail winds past a meadow and then enters a pine and fir forest interspersed with stretches of hard granite. At a trail junction 1.2 miles out, head right for Grouse, Hemlock, and Smith Lakes. Small and pretty Grouse Lake is a one-mile, heart-pumping climb away, with many fine glances back at Wrights Lake and Icehouse Reservoir as you ascend. Many backpackers camp at Grouse Lake; look for wood posts that indicate designated campsites, and note that camp-

ing within 500 feet of Grouse Lake and its tributaries is prohibited. More hardy types and day hikers should head for Hemlock and Smith Lakes, farther uphill. The lakes get progressively prettier as you go, but the ascent gets steeper, too. Tiny Hemlock Lake is only .5 mile from Grouse Lake, and it boasts a spectacular rock slide on one shoreline and many scrawny hemlock trees on the other. Smith Lake lies another .5 mile beyond, way up high near tree line, at 8,700 feet, and it's a stunner. Don't forget your bathing suit.

**User Groups:** Hikers, dogs, and horses. No mountain bikes. No wheelchair facilities.

**Permits:** Permits are required year-round for both day and overnight use. Day hikers may obtain a free permit from a ranger station or may self-issue at most major trailheads. Backpackers camping in Desolation Wilderness are subject to trailhead quotas. There is a $5 reservation fee, plus $5 per person for one night, $10 per person for two or more nights up to 14 days (nonrefundable). Children ages 12 and under are free. Golden Passes do not apply to personal-use permits. For groups, the cost of a single permit will not exceed $100.

**Maps:** For a map, ask the U.S. Forest Service for Eldorado National Forest or Desolation Wilderness. A Lake Tahoe or Desolation Wilderness map is also available for a fee from Tom Harrison Maps. For a topographic map, ask the USGS for Pyramid Peak.

**Directions:** From Placerville, drive east on Highway 50 for 45 miles to the signed turnoff for Wrights Lake, on the north side of the highway, about 15 miles west of South Lake Tahoe and five miles east of Kyburz. Drive north on Wrights Lake Road for eight miles to Wrights Lake Visitors Center. Turn right and continue one mile beyond the campground to the end of the road and the Twin Lakes trailhead.

**Contact:** Eldorado National Forest, Pacific Ranger District, 7887 Highway 50, Pollock Pines, CA 95726, 530/644-2349, website: www.fs.fed.us/r5 (click on Forest Offices); Lake Tahoe Basin Management Unit, 35 College

Drive, South Lake Tahoe, CA 96150, 530/543-2600, website: www.fs.fed.us/r5 (click on Forest Offices); Visitors Center (open only in summer), 530/543-2674.

## ⁷⁰ LYONS CREEK TRAIL
**9.0 mi / 4.5 hrs or 2.0 days**

**in the Desolation Wilderness**

**Map 6.2, page 194**

This may be the easiest lake hike in the entire Wrights Lake area, with only a 1,700-foot elevation gain to visit two beautiful lakes. Because this trailhead is a few miles distant from popular Wrights Lake Campground, it gets fewer visitors than the trails that start right out of camp. The trip's total mileage is long, but the grade is mellow, except for the final .5 mile to Lyons Lake. If you're fond of walking along coursing waterways, following the gurgle and babble of a creek as you hike, you'll love this hike. Wildflowers proliferate in early summer, and views of Pyramid Peak (just shy of 10,000 feet in elevation) inspire you as you gently ascend. The trail keeps to the south side of Lyons Creek for four solid miles, passing through woods and meadows, then crosses the stream and reaches a junction .1 mile farther on. Lyons Lake is to the left and steeply uphill; Lake Sylvia is .5 mile to the right. Take your pick, or better yet, go see both. Lake Sylvia is shadowed by Pyramid Peak and has good campsites along its shoreline. Lyons Lake requires a nasty 450-foot climb in .5 mile, but its superior scenery makes it well worth the effort.

**User Groups:** Hikers, dogs, and horses. No mountain bikes. No wheelchair facilities.

**Permits:** Permits are required year-round for both day and overnight use. Day hikers may obtain a free permit from a ranger station or may self-issue at most major trailheads. Backpackers camping in Desolation Wilderness are subject to trailhead quotas. There is a $5 reservation fee, plus $5 per person for one night, $10 per person for two or more nights up to 14 days (nonrefundable). Children ages 12 and

under are free. Golden Passes do not apply to personal-use permits. For groups, the cost of a single permit will not exceed $100.

**Maps:** For a map, ask the U.S. Forest Service for Eldorado National Forest or Desolation Wilderness. A Lake Tahoe or Desolation Wilderness map is also available for a fee from Tom Harrison Maps. For a topographic map, ask the USGS for Pyramid Peak.

**Directions:** From Placerville, drive east on Highway 50 for 45 miles to the signed turnoff for Wrights Lake, on the north side of the highway. It's about 15 miles west of South Lake Tahoe and five miles east of Kyburz. Drive north on Wrights Lake Road for four miles and turn right at the sign for Lyons Creek Trail.

**Contact:** Eldorado National Forest, Pacific Ranger District, 7887 Highway 50, Pollock Pines, CA 95726, 530/644-2349, website: www.fs.fed.us/r5 (click on Forest Offices); Lake Tahoe Basin Management Unit, 35 College Drive, South Lake Tahoe, CA 96150, 530/543-2600, website: www.fs.fed.us/r5 (click on Forest Offices); Visitors Center (open only in summer), 530/543-2674.

## ⁷¹ HORSETAIL FALLS VISTA
**2.0 mi / 1.0 hr**

**in Eldorado National Forest near South Lake Tahoe**

**Map 6.2, page 194**

Horsetail Falls is the well-known waterfall that takes your breath away as you're driving west along U.S. 50. Approximately 15,000 people each summer glimpse the falls from their cars, then pull over at the giant parking lot by the trailhead and start hiking to get closer to it. The trail has been a source of controversy for many years, because the waterfall is located within the Desolation Wilderness boundary on a rough but serviceable route, but the first mile of trail is outside the wilderness boundary and is easily accessible from the highway. That first easy mile has encouraged many inexperienced visitors to try to hike to the falls, resulting in numerous accidents and even deaths in the wilderness area, where the trail dissipates and follows stream banks that are rough and slippery. The Forest Service has carried out the wilderness mandate by not making mechanical alterations to the trail, such as building bridges or blasting an obvious path into the granite. Instead, to decrease the frequent injuries, the 1.5-mile Pyramid Creek Loop Trail was built in 1999. Made specifically for day users who just want to see Horsetail Falls and spectacular, granite-lined Pyramid Creek, the Pyramid Creek Loop takes off from the main trail about a half mile in. Routed past a gorgeous stretch of Pyramid Creek called the Cascades, the trail stays outside of the wilderness boundary and provides a safe and easy alternative for casual visitors. Although the trail doesn't go all the way to the base of Horsetail Falls, it provides many excellent views of it, as well as of Pyramid Creek's glacier-carved canyon. This was a sensible solution to a difficult problem. The trail is a winner.

**User Groups:** Hikers and dogs. No horses or mountain bikes. No wheelchair facilities.

**Permits:** No permits are required if you stay out of the wilderness boundary. Parking is $3 per vehicle.

**Maps:** For a map, ask the U.S. Forest Service for Eldorado National Forest. A Lake Tahoe map is available for a fee from Tom Harrison Maps. For a topographic map, ask the USGS for Echo Lake.

**Directions:** From South Lake Tahoe, drive south on Highway 89 for five miles to Highway 50. Drive west on Highway 50 for about 15 miles to Twin Bridges, where there is a huge pullout on the north side of the highway, just before the bridge. The pullout is .5 mile west of the turnoff for Camp Sacramento. Park in the designated parking lot for the well-signed trailhead.

**Contact:** Eldorado National Forest, Pacific Ranger District, 7887 Highway 50, Pollock Pines, CA 95726, 530/644-2349, website: www.fs.fed.us/r5 (click on Forest Offices).

## 72 RALSTON PEAK
**8.0 mi / 5.0 hrs**

**in the Desolation Wilderness near South Lake Tahoe**

Map 6.2, page 194

The route to Ralston Peak has a little of everything—dense forest, open manzanita-covered slopes, meadows, and granite ridges. And a lot of one thing—elevation gain. From trailhead to summit, you ascend from 6,400 to 9,240 feet over the course of four miles. Begin by walking northward up the paved road from the east side of the parking area for 200 yards; look for the trail leading off on the left. Climb upward through nonstop trees (and nonstop switchbacks) for a mile; then enter a more open area as you pass the wilderness boundary sign at 1.5 miles. The views start to widen. Your lungs request a lunch break, but they don't get one until 2.5 miles up, when you finally gain the ridge. A half mile later, the break is over, and you climb again, this time to another ridge at 3.5 miles, covered in meadow grasses and wildflowers. Part ways with the main trail and look for a trail to your right leading to the top of Ralston Peak, .5 mile away. Scramble up over jumbled rock to gain the 9,235-foot summit, and take in the view of Lake Tahoe, Fallen Leaf Lake, Carson Pass, Echo Lakes—and below you (to the north), Ralston Lake. This is simply a spectacular lookout. To get it, you may also find that your butt gets kicked.

**User Groups:** Hikers and dogs. No horses or mountain bikes. No wheelchair facilities.

**Permits:** Permits are required year-round for both day and overnight use. Day hikers may obtain a free permit from a ranger station or may self-issue at most major trailheads. Backpackers camping in Desolation Wilderness are subject to trailhead quotas. There is a $5 reservation fee, plus $5 per person for one night, $10 per person for two or more nights up to 14 days (nonrefundable). Children ages 12 and under are free. Golden Passes do not apply to personal-use permits. For groups, the cost of a single permit will not exceed $100.

**Maps:** For a map, ask the U.S. Forest Service for Eldorado National Forest or Desolation Wilderness. A Lake Tahoe or Desolation Wilderness map is also available for a fee from Tom Harrison Maps. For a topographic map, ask the USGS for Echo Lake.

**Directions:** From South Lake Tahoe, drive south on Highway 89 for five miles to Highway 50. Drive west on U.S. 50 for about 14 miles to the turnoff for Camp Sacramento. (If you reach Twin Bridges, you've gone 1.5 miles too far west.) There is a parking area off the north side of U.S. 50 and a sign for Ralston Trail to Lake of the Woods.

**Contact:** Eldorado National Forest, Pacific Ranger District, 7887 Highway 50, Pollock Pines, CA 95726, 530/644-2349, website: www.fs.fed.us/r5 (click on Forest Offices); Lake Tahoe Basin Management Unit, 35 College Drive, South Lake Tahoe, CA 96150, 530/543-2600, website: www.fs.fed.us/r5 (click on Forest Offices); Visitors Center (open only in summer), 530/543-2674.

## 73 BOAT TAXI TO LAKE ALOHA
### 6.0–12.0 mi / 3.5–6.0 hrs    3    9

**in the Desolation Wilderness**

Map 6.2, page 194

Some people just like to take boat rides, and if you're one of them, you can have a great all-day adventure by taking the boat taxi from Echo Lakes Resort and then hiking to Lake Aloha and its neighboring lakes in Desolation Valley.

From the hiker's parking lot, walk .25 mile downhill to the resort and the boat launch area, at the edge of Echo Lake. The boat taxi leaves at frequent intervals (or whenever more than two people show up) from 8 A.M. to 6 P.M. daily all summer. The trip costs $7 and is well worth it to get you to the border of Desolation Wilderness. The boat carries hikers two miles to the far end of Upper and Lower Echo Lakes, passing many lovely lakeside cottages. From the boat taxi drop-off point, gain the main trail (Pacific Crest Trail) and head to your left. It

is a 3.5-mile hike to the eastern edge of Lake Aloha, a steady climb up to a ridge, then an easy saunter to a trail junction. You'll pass signed junctions with numerous trails along the way, all of which lead to various lakes in very short distances. Your best bet is to stay on the main path for Lake Aloha, then take some of the cutoffs to neighboring lakes on your way back. When you reach Lake Aloha's shore, hike along its beautiful north side for a distance, admiring the rocky coves and islands of the giant, shallow lake. At one time, Lake Aloha was several small lakes. They were dammed with a unique rock wall to create this huge body of water. The effect is a bit surreal, although beautiful. The lake's elevation is 8,116 feet.

On the trip back, take one or more of the signed trail junctions and visit Lake of the Woods, Lake Lucille, Lake Margery, Tamarack Lake, or Ralston Lake— all less than one mile off Lake Aloha Trail. Tamarack Lake is the best for scenery; Lake of the Woods is the best for fishing.

On the return trip, some bypass the boat taxi and continue on the Pacific Crest Trail back to the parking area. That will add 2.5 miles to your trip. The trail rises well above the lake, eventually passing a series of vacation homes.

**User Groups:** Hikers and dogs (not advised because sharp rocks can bruise their foot pads). No horses or mountain bikes. No wheelchair facilities.

**Permits:** Permits are required year-round for both day and overnight use. Day hikers may obtain a free permit from a ranger station or may self-issue at most major trailheads. Backpackers camping in Desolation Wilderness are subject to trailhead quotas. There is a $5 reservation fee, plus $5 per person for one night, $10 per person for two or more nights up to 14 days (nonrefundable). Children ages 12 and under are free. Golden Passes do not apply to personal-use permits. For groups, the cost of a single permit will not exceed $100.

**Maps:** For a map, ask the U.S. Forest Service for Desolation Wilderness. A Lake Tahoe or Desolation Wilderness map is also available for a fee from Tom Harrison Maps. For a topographic map, ask the USGS for Echo Lake.

**Directions:** From South Lake Tahoe, drive south on Highway 89 for five miles to U.S. 50. Drive west on U.S. 50 for 5.5 miles to the signed turnoff for Echo Lakes on the right. (It's one mile west of Echo Summit.) Turn right and drive .5 mile on Johnson Pass Road, then turn left on Echo Lakes Road. Drive one mile to a series of parking lots located .25 mile before the road ends at Echo Lakes Resort. Hikers not staying at the resort must park in one of the upper lots or alongside the road, not in the main lower lot by the resort.

**Contact:** Eldorado National Forest, Pacific Ranger District, 7887 Highway 50, Pollock Pines, CA 95726, 530/644-2349, website: www.fs.fed.us/r5 (click on Forest Offices); Lake Tahoe Basin Management Unit, 35 College Drive, South Lake Tahoe, CA 96150, 530/543-2600, website: www.fs.fed.us/r5 (click on Forest Offices); Visitors Center (open only in summer), 530/543-2674.

## 🗐 ECHO LAKES RESORT TO BARKER PASS (PCT)

**32.3 mi one-way / 3.0 days**

**from Echo Lake near U.S. 50 south of Lake Tahoe to Forest Road 3 near Barker Pass northwest of Emerald Bay**

Map 6.2, page 194

The Desolation Wilderness (and the neighboring Granite Chief Wilderness) are filled with sculpted granite domes and hundreds of gemlike lakes. All is pristine, yet access is also quite easy, making this the most heavily used section of the PCT all summer long. The trip starts at Echo Lake (elevation 7,400 feet), climbs through pines past Upper Echo Lake, and then continues up and north toward Triangle Lake, one of dozens of lakes you pass on your northward route. They come and go—Lake Margery, Lake Aloha, and then Heather, Susie, and

Gilmore Lakes, and finally Dicks Lake (at 9,380 feet). There are so many, in fact, that you can plan on a perfect campsite near a lake every night, providing you don't mind the company of other hikers drawn by classic beauty. The views are dramatic as well, across miles and miles of the glacial-carved granite, all of it marvelous high Sierra landscape. As you continue, you'll discover Upper and Middle Velma Lakes, both very pretty and with good fishing. The trail skirts the ridgeline, keeping the higher knobs to the east as it gradually descends toward Richardson Lake, just beyond the Desolation Wilderness boundary—ready now to enter the Granite Chief Wilderness.

To continue north on the PCT, see the Barker Pass to Donner Pass (PCT) hike in this chapter. If you are walking this trail in reverse, see the Carson Pass to Echo Lakes Resort (PCT) hike in this chapter.

**User Groups:** Hikers, dogs, and horses. No mountain bikes. No wheelchair facilities.

**Permits:** A backcountry permit is required for traveling through various wilderness and special-use areas the trail traverses. In addition, a campfire permit is required for the use of portable camp stoves or the building of campfires where allowed. To make it simple, you can contact the national forest, BLM, or national park office at your point of entry for a combined permit that is good for traveling through multiple-permit areas during your dates of travel.

**Maps:** For topographic maps, ask the USGS for Echo Lake, Emerald Bay, and Rockbound Valley.

**Directions:** For the Echo Lakes Resort trailhead, from South Lake Tahoe, drive south on Highway 89 for five miles to U.S. 50. Drive west on U.S. 50 for 5.5 miles to the signed turnoff for Echo Lakes, on the right. (It's one mile west of Echo Summit.) Turn right and drive .5 mile on Johnson Pass Road and then turn left on Echo Lakes Road. Drive one mile to a series of parking lots .25 mile before the road ends at Echo Lakes Resort. Park and walk downhill to the resort.

To reach the Barker Pass trailhead, from Tahoe Pines on Highway 89, head north for .5 mile to the Kaspian Picnic Grounds and then bear left (west) for seven miles on Forest Service Road 15N03.

**Contact:** Lake Tahoe Basin Management Unit, 35 College Drive, South Lake Tahoe, CA 96150, 530/543-2600, website: www.fs.fed.us/r5 (click on Forest Offices); Visitors Center (open only in summer), 530/543-2674.

## 75 DARDANELLES LAKE AND ROUND LAKE
7.6 mi / 4.5 hrs

**near Carson Pass**

Map 6.2, page 194

The route to Dardanelles Lake and Round Lake, along Tahoe Rim Trail, starts out steep but gets easier as it goes. It enters Meiss Country, that large and wonderful roadless area south of Lake Tahoe, where the forces that shaped the land were ice (glaciers) and fire (volcanic action). Both have made their presence clearly visible. The trail heads south from the parking lot, crosses Highway 89 in about 100 yards, then makes an initial climb through fir and pine forest to Big Meadow. The meadow makes lovely, level walking for .25 mile; then it's back into the trees. Follow the trail signs for Round Lake until you complete a steep, short descent at two miles out. At the bottom of the hill, turn sharply right on Meiss Meadow Trail toward Christmas Valley. Walk less than .25 mile, then turn left and cross a creek for the final 1.2 miles to Dardanelles Lake. The 7,740-foot lake is gorgeous, with a striking granite backdrop, and it's perfect for swimming, fishing, and picnicking. If you time your trip for autumn, you'll be treated to a marvelous color display from the aspens and alders that grow along this trail's many streams.

On your return, retrace your steps to the junction at the bottom of the hill, then hike .75 mile in the opposite direction to visit Round Lake. Although not quite as scenic as Dard-

anelles Lake, Round Lake provides a stark, fascinating contrast to its neighbor: It is surrounded by volcanic rock formations, not granite cliffs.

Note that this trail is open to mountain bikers. On weekdays you might not see a single bike, but on weekends it's another story.

**User Groups:** Hikers, dogs, horses, and mountain bikes. No wheelchair facilities.

**Permits:** No permits are required. Parking and access are free.

**Maps:** For a map, ask the U.S. Forest Service for Lake Tahoe Basin Management Unit. A Lake Tahoe map is available for a fee from Tom Harrison Maps. For a topographic map, ask the USGS for Echo Lake.

**Directions:** From South Lake Tahoe, drive south on Highway 89 for approximately 10 miles to the Big Meadow trailhead parking area, which is five miles south of the junction of U.S. 50 and Highway 89, on the northwest side of the road. Turn left off the highway, then bear left and park near the restrooms. The trail begins from the south side of the parking lot loop and crosses Highway 89 in about 100 yards.

**Contact:** Lake Tahoe Basin Management Unit, 35 College Drive, South Lake Tahoe, CA 96150, 530/543-2600, website: www.fs.fed.us/r5 (click on Forest Offices); Visitors Center (open only in summer), 530/543-2674.

## 76 LAKE MARGARET
4.6 mi / 3.0 hrs

**near Carson Pass and Kirkwood Lake**

Map 6.2, page 194

A hike to an alpine lake with only a 500-foot elevation gain? If it seems too good to be true, you need an easy-trail fix, and Lake Margaret should do the trick. The trail undulates gently, never gaining or losing more than a couple hundred feet. The first stretch is actually downhill; then the path climbs gently over a small ridge and then descends again over duck-marked granite slabs. You'll cross branches of Caples Creek twice in the first mile. At 1.5 miles, the trail passes by a couple of tiny ponds. At two miles out, after crossing another creek, you'll find yourself in a lovely grove of aspens and knee-high wildflowers. At 2.3 miles, after about an hour of walking and only a minor expenditure of energy, you'll reach the granite shoreline of Lake Margaret. Swimming is excellent. A few tiny islands and many shoreline boulders make fine sunbathing spots. Figure on staying a while. The lake's elevation is 7,500 feet.

Note that although most of the trails in the Carson Pass area are famous for wildflowers, the proximity of several small streams makes the bloom especially showy on this path. The peak wildflower season is from mid-June to mid-August.

**User Groups:** Hikers, leashed dogs, horses, and mountain bikes. No wheelchair facilities.

**Permits:** No permits are required. Parking and access are free.

**Maps:** For a map, ask the U.S. Forest Service for Eldorado National Forest or Mokelumne Wilderness. For a topographic map, ask the USGS for Caples Lake.

**Directions:** From Meyers at the junction of U.S. 50 and Highway 89, drive south on Highway 89 for 11 miles to Highway 88. Turn west on Highway 88 and drive 14.5 miles to the Lake Margaret sign, on the north side of the road. (It's 5.5 miles west of Carson Pass Summit, and 5.5 miles east of Silver Lake.) Turn north and park at the trailhead parking area.

**Contact:** Eldorado National Forest, Amador Ranger District, 26820 Silver Drive, Pioneer, CA 95666, 209/295-4251, website: www.fs .fed.us/r5 (click on Forest Offices).

## 77 EMIGRANT LAKE
### 8.0 mi / 4.0 hrs or 2.0 days

**in the Mokelumne Wilderness near Caples Lake**

Map 6.2, page 194

The trailhead at Caples Lake is often jam-packed with backpackers, so do yourself a favor—visit here midweek or in the off-season, or make your trip a day hike instead of an overnight. Why is this trail so popular? It's wonderfully scenic and surprisingly easy. The trail leads from the spillway at Caples Lake up and along the lake's south side, following an old emigrant route. The first two miles are right along the lake's edge, climbing gently above the shoreline, always in the shade of big conifers. If you enjoy hiking near water, you'll love this pathway. More climbing alongside Emigrant Creek leads hikers to a stream crossing at 3.5 miles, followed by another crossing. A few switchbacks carry you up to Emigrant Lake, a beautiful cirque lake set at 8,600 feet, with many fine sunbathing rocks. Covered Wagon Peak and Thimble Peak, at 9,500 feet, rise above the scene. The trail's total elevation gain is less than 1,000 feet, making this a surprisingly easy day hike, even with its eight-mile distance. But know before you go: Most of the trail's ascent is packed into the last 1.8 miles, which will leave you breathing hard. Note that no campfires are permitted above 8,000 feet.

**User Groups:** Hikers, leashed dogs, and horses. No mountain bikes. No wheelchair facilities.

**Permits:** No day hiking permits are required. A free wilderness permit is required for overnight stays; it is available from the Amador Ranger Station, the Carson Pass Information Station, or the Eldorado Information Center. Maximum group size for day use is 12. Maximum group size for overnight use is eight. No self-registration is available at the trailhead.

**Maps:** For a map, ask the U.S. Forest Service for Eldorado National Forest or Desolation Wilderness. For a topographic map, ask the USGS for Caples Lake.

**Directions:** From Meyers at the junction of U.S. 50 and Highway 89, drive south on Highway 89 for 11 miles to Highway 88. Turn west on Highway 88 and drive 14 miles to the west side of Caples Lake and the trailhead parking area, five miles west of Carson Pass Summit.

**Contact:** Eldorado National Forest, Amador Ranger District, 26820 Silver Drive, Pioneer, CA 95666, 209/295-4251, website: www.fs .fed.us/r5 (click on Forest Offices).

## 78 MINKALO TRAIL
7.0 mi / 3.5 hrs

**near Silver Lake**

Map 6.2, page 194

Since Silver Lake has a fair number of private homes on its shore, it appears less wild than nearby Caples Lake. Still, the big blue lake, at 7,300 feet in elevation, is beautiful, and if you want to hike near it, the Minkalo Trail is your best bet. The trail leads to Granite Lake in one mile and to Plasse's Resort, on the south side of the lake, in three miles. Why not hike to both, then buy a pizza or a Power Bar at Plasse's Resort Trading Post to fuel up for the hike back to the Minkalo trailhead? The trail starts out rocky and stays that way for the first .25 mile. Cross a bridge over Squaw Creek to a right fork that leads to Plasse's Resort. Take the left fork first, heading to Granite Lake, which you'll reach in about 20 minutes after a moderate climb. It's a pretty lake and good for swimming. After you've visited, return to the trail junction and hike southward, soon coming close to the edge of Silver Lake and staying in its proximity. You'll have many pretty lake views from here on out, including long looks at Treasure Island, Silver Lake's large island. It takes about an hour to reach the campground at Plasse's, an excellent place for horse lovers (and pizza lovers).

**User Groups:** Hikers, leashed dogs, horses, and mountain bikes. No wheelchair facilities.

**Permits:** No permits are required. Parking and access are free.

**Maps:** For a map, ask the U.S. Forest Service for Eldorado National Forest, or Desolation Wilderness. For a topographic map, ask the USGS for Caples Lake.

**Directions:** From Meyers at the junction of U.S. 50 and Highway 89, drive south on U.S. 89 for 11 miles to Highway 88. Turn west on Highway 88 and drive 15.5 miles to the Kit Carson Lodge turnoff, on the north side of the road. It's 10.8 miles west of Carson Pass Summit, at Silver Lake. Turn north and drive past Kit Carson Lodge, go left at the first fork, go right at the second fork, and wind up at the parking for Minkalo Trail. (It's a total 1.4 miles from Highway 88.) Walk back down the road for about 40 yards to find the start of the trail.

**Contact:** Eldorado National Forest, Amador Ranger District, 26820 Silver Drive, Pioneer, CA 95666, 209/295-4251, website: www.fs .fed.us/r5 (click on Forest Offices).

## 79 OSBORNE HILL
2.6 mi / 1.5 hrs

**on Highway 4 near Lake Alpine**

Map 6.2, page 194

We like the way Lake Alpine looks from close up on Lakeshore Trail, but then again, we like the way Lake Alpine looks from far up on Osborne Hill, also known as Osborne Point. A short, healthy climb brings you to the point, from which you can look down at the lake and beyond into the Carson-Iceberg Wilderness. The trail ends there but connects to Emigrant West Trail if you wish to hike farther. If you're itching for winter to be over so you can go hiking, you'll be happy to know that Highway 4 is always open as far east as Silvertip Campground, but not always farther. Thus if the snow is dwindling, you'll have access to this trailhead often long before you can access the others near Lake Alpine.

**User Groups:** Hikers, dogs, horses, and mountain bikes. No wheelchair facilities.

**Permits:** No permits are required. Parking and access are free.

**Maps:** For a map, ask the U.S. Forest Service for Stanislaus National Forest. For a topographic map, ask the USGS for Tamarack.

**Directions:** From Angels Camp at the intersection of Highways 4 and 49, drive east on Highway 4 for 40 miles to Bear Valley. Set your odometer at Bear Valley and drive three miles farther east on Highway 4 to the Osborne Ridge trailhead, just east of Silvertip Campground. Take the trail that leads from the south side of the road.

**Contact:** Stanislaus National Forest, Calaveras Ranger District, P.O. Box 500, Hathaway Pines, CA 95233, 209/795-1381, website: www.fs.fed.us/r5 (click on Forest Offices).

## 80 LAKESHORE TRAIL AND INSPIRATION POINT
**4.0 mi / 2.0 hrs**

**on Highway 4 near Lake Alpine**

Map 6.2, page 194

It's hard to say which trail is better, Lakeshore Trail or Inspiration Point Trail. To solve the dilemma, hike both of them together. The trip starts with a short walk down a dirt road; then turn right onto a single track. In a mere 10 minutes of hiking through a thick lodgepole pine forest littered with tiny pinecones, you're at the edge of Lake Alpine, elevation 7,350 feet. Follow the trail to your left, and in another 10 minutes, you reach a left fork for Inspiration Point (Lakeshore Trail continues straight). You'll want to head out and back on both trails; it makes no difference which one you take first.

The Lakeshore Trail is flat and stays within 100 feet of the water's edge, offering many pretty lake vistas. Eventually the trail meets up with Slick Rock, a four-wheel-drive road, but there's no need to go that far. Just walk a mile or so to the dam, and then turn around and head back. The Inspiration Point Trail is more of a workout: a steep one-mile climb to the summit at Inspiration Point, from which you can see for miles. Pick a clear day, and you'll be pointing out Lake Alpine, Elephant Rock, the Dardanelles, and Spicer Meadow Reservoir.
**User Groups:** Hikers, dogs, and horses. No mountain bikes. No wheelchair facilities.
**Permits:** No permits are required. Parking and access are free.
**Maps:** For a national forest map, ask for Stanislaus National Forest. For a topographic map, ask the USGS for Spicer Meadow Reservoir.
**Directions:** From Angels Camp at the intersection of Highways 4 and 49, drive east on Highway 4 for 40 miles to Bear Valley. Set your odometer at Bear Valley and drive 4.3 miles farther east on Highway 4 to the Lake Alpine East Shore trailhead turnoff, on the right. Turn right, drive .25 mile, and turn right again and drive .1 mile past Pine Marten Campground to the signed parking area and the trailhead.
**Contact:** Stanislaus National Forest, Calaveras Ranger District, P.O. Box 500, Hathaway Pines, CA 95233, 209/795-1381, website: www.fs.fed.us/r5 (click on Forest Offices).

## 81 DUCK LAKE
**3.0 mi / 1.5 hrs**

**in the Carson-Iceberg Wilderness off Highway 4 near Lake Alpine**

Map 6.2, page 194

The trailhead at Silver Valley Campground is the start of the route to Duck Lake, and it's also one of the busiest trailheads into the Carson-Iceberg Wilderness. The trip to Duck Lake is a perfect easy hike for families or people just in the mood for a stroll, and the more ambitious can continue past the lake on an eight-mile round-trip to Rock Lake. It's only one mile to reach Duck Lake, but once you're there, you'll want to walk the loop trail around its perimeter, adding another mile to your trip. The area is the site of a historic cow camp, where animals have grazed since the late 19th century. You can examine the remains of a couple of early-20th-century cowboy cabins.
**User Groups:** Hikers, dogs, and horses. No mountain bikes. No wheelchair facilities.
**Permits:** No day-use permits are required. Parking and access are free.
**Maps:** For a map, ask the U.S. Forest Service for Stanislaus National Forest or Carson-Iceberg Wilderness. For a topographic map, ask the USGS for Spicer Meadow Reservoir.
**Directions:** From Angels Camp at the intersection of Highways 4 and 49, drive east on Highway 4 for 40 miles to Bear Valley. Set your odometer at Bear Valley and drive 4.3 miles farther east on Highway 4 to the Lake Alpine East Shore trailhead turnoff, on the right. Turn

right and continue straight to Silver Valley Campground and the Silver Valley trailhead.

**Contact:** Stanislaus National Forest, Calaveras Ranger District, P.O. Box 500, Hathaway Pines, CA 95233, 209/795-1381, website: www.fs .fed.us/r5 (click on Forest Offices).

## 82 WOODCHUCK BASIN TO WHEELER LAKE

6.4 mi / 3.5 hrs

in the Mokelumne Wilderness off Highway 4 near Lake Alpine

**Map 6.2, page 194**

Located only a mile from the campgrounds at Lake Alpine, the Woodchuck Basin trailhead (elevation 7,800 feet) should have a parking lot full of cars, but it rarely does. The trail leads into the Mokelumne Wilderness, and after climbing uphill on it for 1.7 forested miles, you reach a junction where you can go left for Underwood Valley or right for tiny Wheeler Lake. Bear right, pass a Mokelumne Wilderness sign, and in moments, you are heading for a 1.5-mile steep descent to Wheeler Lake. Think it over before you go, because you'll need to regain those 1,000 feet on the way home. But if you're willing to take the plunge, you're treated to a picturesque, tree- and granite-lined lake, where you can pass the afternoon with little fear that you'll be bugged by a busload of other hikers. Dog owners should note that Tuolumne County has a leash law that is strictly enforced.

**User Groups:** Hikers, leashed dogs, and horses. No mountain bikes. No wheelchair facilities.

**Permits:** No permits are required. Parking and access are free.

**Maps:** For a map, ask the U.S. Forest Service for Stanislaus National Forest or Mokelumne Wilderness. For a topographic map, ask the USGS for Spicer Meadow Reservoir.

**Directions:** From Angels Camp at the intersection of Highways 4 and 49, drive east on Highway 4 for 40 miles to Bear Valley. Set your odometer at Bear Valley and drive 5.5 miles farther east on Highway 4 to the Woodchuck

Basin trailhead, on the left. Turn left and drive .25 mile to the parking area.

**Contact:** Stanislaus National Forest, Calaveras Ranger District, P.O. Box 500, Hathaway Pines, CA 95233, 209/795-1381, website: www.fs .fed.us/r5 (click on Forest Offices).

## 83 NORTH GROVE LOOP

1.0 mi / 0.5 hr

northeast of Arnold on Highway 4

**Map 6.2, page 194**

Even though there are 150 giant sequoias at Calaveras Big Trees State Park, the highlight is actually the one known as The Big Stump. Lore has it that the gent who first found this place wanted to prove how big the trees were, so naturally, he cut one down, leaving behind the giant stump. Makes perfect sense, right? Why don't you shoot Bigfoot while you're at it?

Well, the state park gets a lot of visitors, and this is the most popular walk here, so you can expect other people—lots of 'em—on weekends. The easy trail is routed among the giant sequoias, and the sweet fragrance of the massive trees fills the air. You will never forget that scent. These trees, of course, are known not for their height but for their tremendous diameter: It can take a few dozen people, linking hands, to encircle one.

**User Groups:** Hikers and wheelchairs. No dogs, horses, or mountain bikes.

**Permits:** No permits are required. A state park entrance fee of $6 is charged each vehicle.

**Maps:** A brochure and trail map is available for a fee at Calaveras Big Trees State Park at the address below. For a topographic map, ask the USGS for Dorrington.

**Directions:** From Angels Camp, drive east on Highway 4 for 23 miles to Arnold, and then continue east on Highway 4 for four miles to the park entrance. The trailhead is adjacent to the park entrance.

**Contact:** Calaveras Big Trees State Park, P.O. Box 120, Arnold, CA 95223, 209/795-2334;

Columbia State Park, 209/532-0150, website: www.parks.ca.gov (click on Find A Park).

## 84 SOUTH GROVE LOOP
### 5.0 mi / 3.0 hrs

**northeast of Arnold on Highway 4**

**Map 6.2, page 194**

The two largest sequoias in Calaveras Big Trees State Park are found on a spur trail of this hike, and that makes it a must-do for visitors. But so many tourists are content to just walk the little trail at the North Grove, look at the giant stump, and then hit the road. Why rush? As long as you're at the park, take the South Grove Loop. The loop itself is 3.5 miles long, but the highlight is a spur trail that branches off .75 mile to the Agassiz Tree and the Palace Hotel Tree, two monster-sized specimens. For a great photograph, have someone take a picture of you standing at the base of one of these trees; you will look like a Lilliputian from *Gulliver's Travels*.

**User Groups:** Hikers only. No dogs, horses, or mountain bikes. No wheelchair facilities.

**Permits:** No permits are required. A state park entrance fee of $6 is charged each vehicle.

**Maps:** A brochure and trail map is available for a fee at Calaveras Big Trees State Park at the address below. For a topographic map, ask the USGS for Boards Crossing.

**Directions:** From Angels Camp, drive east on Highway 4 for 23 miles to Arnold and then continue east on Highway 4 for four miles to the park entrance. From the park entrance, head down the parkway for nine miles to the trailhead, on the right. Note: The road is closed in winter.

**Contact:** Calaveras Big Trees State Park, P.O. Box 120, Arnold, CA 95223, 209/795-2334; Columbia State Park, 209/532-0150, website: www.parks.ca.gov (click on Find A Park).

## 85 CARSON PASS TO ECHO LAKES RESORT (PCT)
### 15.8 mi one-way / 1.0–2.0 days

**from Carson Pass at Highway 88 north to Echo Lake near U.S. 50, just south of Lake Tahoe**

**Map 6.3, page 195**

When you've hiked on the Pacific Crest Trail for weeks, the first glimpse of Lake Tahoe in the distance can seem like a privileged view into heaven. That view is just a few miles from Ebbetts Pass. You start by hiking over a short mountain rim (nice view to the west of Caples Lake) and then you drop into the headwaters of the Truckee River. As you look northward after making the rim, Lake Tahoe suddenly comes into view. It's like having a divine vision. And finally there is water available from several small creeks as you walk into the Truckee headwaters. At the same time, you will be greeted by a high meadow surrounded by a light forest. All seems right with the world again. With Echo Lakes Resort within one day's hiking time, you will be amazed at how inspired you can get on this section of trail. It's very pretty, weaving through lush canyons and along creeks, eventually reaching beautiful and tiny Showers Lake. Here the trail seems to drop off to never-never land, descending very quickly and steeply in the march toward Tahoe. Contentment reigns. When you reach Little Norway (it burned years ago, scheduled to reopen in 2003), however, reality sets in. Cars are everywhere. The trail suddenly grinds down amid cabins and vacation property. There's one last hill to climb, and then the PCT drops quickly to the parking lot for Echo Lake.

Almost nobody hiking the PCT immediately heads north into the Desolation Wilderness from here. Virtually everyone stops for at least a day to get cleaned up, resupplied, and fed by something other than a Power Bar. But after a day, the trail calls again. If you hear it, well, you just have to answer it.

To continue north on the PCT, see the Echo

Lakes Resort to Barker Pass (PCT) hike in this chapter. If you are walking this trail in reverse, see the Blue Lakes Road to Carson Pass (PCT) hike in this chapter.

**User Groups:** Hikers, dogs, and horses. No mountain bikes. No wheelchair facilities.

**Permits:** A backcountry permit is required for traveling through various wilderness and special-use areas that the trail traverses. In addition, a campfire permit is required for the use of portable camp stoves or the building of campfires where permitted. To make it simple, you can contact the national forest, BLM, or national park office at your point of entry for a combined permit that is good for traveling through multiple-permit areas during your dates of travel.

**Maps:** For national forest maps, ask for Lake Tahoe Basin Management Unit, Tahoe National Forest, Eldorado National Forest, and Stanislaus National Forest. For topographic maps, ask the USGS for Carson Pass, Caples Lake, and Echo Lake.

**Directions:** To reach the Carson Pass trailhead from the Highway 88/89 interchange at Hope Valley, head west on Highway 88 to Carson Pass.

For the Echo Lakes Resort trailhead, from South Lake Tahoe, drive south on Highway 89 for five miles to U.S. 50. Drive west on U.S. 50 for 5.5 miles to the signed turnoff for Echo Lakes on the right (one mile west of Echo Summit). Turn right and drive .5 mile on Johnson Pass Road and then turn left on Echo Lakes Road. Drive one mile to a series of parking lots .25 mile before the road ends, at Echo Lakes Resort. Park and walk downhill to the resort.

**Contact:** Eldorado National Forest, Amador Ranger District, 26820 Silver Drive, Pioneer, CA 95666, 209/295-4251, website: www.fs .fed.us/r5 (click on Forest Offices); Lake Tahoe Basin Management Unit, 35 College Drive, South Lake Tahoe, CA 96150, 530/543-2600, website: www.fs.fed.us/r5 (click on Forest Offices); Visitors Center (open only in summer), 530/543-2674.

## 86 SHOWERS LAKE
**10.0 mi / 6.0 hrs**

**near Caples Lake**

Map 6.3, page 195

Here's a day hike on the Pacific Crest Trail into the land of Meiss Country—the headwaters for the Upper Truckee River and the home of the endangered Lahontan cutthroat trout. Although Meiss Country is not designated wilderness, it might as well be, because there are no roads cutting into it, and all is peaceful and serene. The Pacific Crest Trail and a completed stretch of Tahoe Rim Trail are the main routes through Meiss Country.

For the trip to Showers Lake, head uphill from the trailhead on the PCT, climbing through Meiss Pass and then dropping into a huge valley basin. Views along the way include Mount Round Top, Elephant Back, and Red Lake Peak, expanding to include far-off Lake Tahoe, to the north. It's 2.9 miles to a fork with Tahoe Rim Trail (TRT), just beyond a crossing of Upper Truckee River, which is little more than a stream here. The right fork leads 2.2 miles to Round Lake, Meiss Country's—largest lake and a popular destination—but stay left on the PCT and TRT, and cross the river again on your way to Showers Lake, 2.1 miles farther. The last half mile of trail is a 350-foot descent to Showers Lake, with 9,590-foot Little Round Top poking up above it to the west. The trail leads along the east side of the lake, where campsites can be found. The lake is set at 8,790 feet and is the highest lake in the Upper Truckee River Basin.

This trip is popular with the horsy set. A separate trail leads to Showers Lake from Schneider Camp, a large horse camp, so weekends bring a fair amount of horse traffic. Also note that the trip begins in Eldorado National Forest, but two-thirds of the trail is within jurisdiction of the Lake Tahoe Basin Management Unit.

**User Groups:** Hikers, leashed dogs, and horses. No mountain bikes. No wheelchair facilities.

**Permits:** No permits are required. A $3 parking fee is charged per vehicle.

**Maps:** For a map, ask the U.S. Forest Service for Eldorado National Forest or Mokelumne Wilderness. For topographic maps, ask the USGS for Caples Lake and Carson Pass.

**Directions:** From Meyers at the junction of U.S. 50 and Highway 89, drive south on Highway 89 for 11 miles to Highway 88. Turn west on Highway 88 and drive 10 miles to Carson Pass Summit. The parking area and Meiss trailhead are on the right (north), across the highway from (and slightly west of) the Carson Pass Information Station.

**Contact:** Eldorado National Forest, Amador Ranger District, 26820 Silver Drive, Pioneer, CA 95666, 209/295-4251 website: www.fs .fed.us/r5 (click on Forest Offices).

## 87 WINNEMUCCA LAKE FROM WOODS LAKE

**3.0 mi / 1.5 hrs**

**in the Mokelumne Wilderness near Carson Pass**

Map 6.3, page 195

Woods Lake is a little magical spot where you can drive right up, walk a few feet to the water's edge, and plunk in your fishing line. It's also the trailhead for numerous great hikes into the Mokelumne Wilderness, including this easy trip to deep blue Winnemucca Lake, set at the base of fantastic-looking Mount Round Top (elevation 10,381 feet). The land here has been formed by volcanic action, so as you walk, you constantly have to remind yourself that you aren't at Mount Lassen or Mount Shasta—you're just south of Tahoe in Carson Pass. The beauty attracts a ton of people, often 200 to 300 on summer weekends.

After setting off down the trail, in a mile you will pass by the remains of an arrastra, a device used for crushing gold or silver ore—evidence of this area's mining past. Continue walking through big conifers until you come out to a glacial moraine, where your view of Mount Round Top—a huge old volcanic vent—

opens wide. Snowcapped almost all summer, imposing Round Top is a stunning sight. So are the early summer wildflowers that bloom in profusion on the open slopes surrounding the path. In 1.5 miles of gentle to moderate climbing, you reach the edge of Winnemucca Lake, right at the foot of Mount Round Top, a gorgeous circle of blue. Although there are several options for hiking farther from here (see next listing), for many people, this destination is perfect enough.

The peak season for wildflowers is mid-June to mid-August, at its very best in mid-to-late July. If you hiked this trail in years past, you may remember that it once started by crossing a footbridge. That is true no longer.

**User Groups:** Hikers, leashed dogs, and horses. No mountain bikes. No wheelchair facilities.

**Permits:** A free wilderness permit is required for overnight stays; it is available from the Amador Ranger Station, the Carson Pass Information Station, or the Eldorado Information Center. A parking fee of $3 is charged, good for overnight use.

**Maps:** For a map, ask the U.S. Forest Service for Mokelumne Wilderness or Eldorado National Forest. For topographic maps, ask the USGS for Caples Lake and Carson Pass.

**Directions:** From Meyers at the junction of U.S. 50 and Highway 89, drive south on Highway 89 for 11 miles to Highway 88. Turn west on Highway 88 and drive 12 miles to the Woods Lake Campground turnoff, on the south side of the road (1.5 miles west of Carson Pass Summit). Turn left and drive one mile to the trailhead parking area (.5 mile before reaching Woods Lake).

**Contact:** Eldorado National Forest, Amador Ranger District, 26820 Silver Drive, Pioneer, CA 95666, 209/295-4251, website: www.fs .fed.us/r5 (click on Forest Offices).

## 88 ROUND TOP SUMMIT AND WINNEMUCCA LAKE LOOP

**6.6 mi / 4.0 hrs**

in the Mokelumne Wilderness near
Carson Pass

Map 6.3, page 195

If you want all the scenic beauty of Winnemucca Lake Trail, but you also want a longer walk and a little more solitude, try this loop trip instead. Note that although the loop trail itself is a relatively easy hike, adding on a side trip to the summit of Mount Round Top gives this hike a difficulty rating of a resounding 4. There is no real trail to Round Top's summit, and the most obvious use trail goes straight uphill at a punishing grade.

The path is the same route as Winnemucca Lake Trail for the first 1.5 miles to Winnemucca's edge, but then you bear right and cross the stream on the west side of the lake. From there, it's one mile uphill to Round Top Lake—steep enough to get you puffing. The gorgeous volcanic scenery makes it all worthwhile. Round Top Lake is set below The Sisters, two peaks that are both over 10,000 feet high. You also have views of Mount Round Top and Fourth of July Peak. It's incredibly dramatic. From the eastern edge of Round Top Lake, you'll see an obvious path heading up the side of Mount Round Top. If you like a little challenge and you're surefooted, go for it. The grade is brutal, but when you reach the top after a final rocky scramble, you have a stunning view of The Dardanelles, Lake Tahoe, Caples Lake, Woods Lake, Round Top Lake, Winnemucca Lake, and Frog Lake. Perhaps most impressive is deep Summit City Canyon, 3,000 feet below the south side of Round Top. At 10,380 feet, Mount Round Top is the highest peak in the Carson Pass area and is the finest place for a bird's-eye view. The summit is more like a knife-thin, rocky ridge, so watch your footing. This is not a place for children or inexperienced hikers.

After your summit visit, return downhill to Round Top Lake to finish out your loop. Follow the lake's outlet creek on Lost Cabin Mine Trail for two miles back to Woods Lake Campground; then wind your way through the camp back to the Woods Lake Picnic Area, where you left your car.

**User Groups:** Hikers, leashed dogs, and horses. No mountain bikes. No wheelchair facilities.

**Permits:** A free wilderness permit is required for overnight stays; it is available from the Amador Ranger Station, the Carson Pass Information Station, or the Eldorado Information Center.

**Maps:** For a map, ask the U.S. Forest Service for Mokelumne Wilderness or Eldorado National Forest. For topographic maps, ask the USGS for Caples Lake and Carson Pass.

**Directions:** From Meyers at the junction of U.S. 50 and Highway 89, drive south on Highway 89 for 11 miles to Highway 88. Turn west on Highway 88 and drive 12 miles to the Woods Lake Campground turnoff, on the south side of the road. It's 1.5 miles west of Carson Pass Summit. Turn left and drive 1.5 miles to the trailhead parking area, by the picnic area at Woods Lake.

**Contact:** Eldorado National Forest, Amador Ranger District, 26820 Silver Drive, Pioneer, CA 95666, 209/295-4251, website: www.fs.fed.us/r5 (click on Forest Offices).

## 89 FOURTH OF JULY LAKE

**8.8 mi / 4.5 hrs or 2.0 days**

in the Mokelumne Wilderness near
Caples Lake

Map 6.3, page 195

The biggest problem in a trip to Fourth of July Lake is the high number of people. Carson Pass is a stellar trailhead, and with several lakes and Mount Round Top so close, there can be 200 to 300 hikers on summer weekends. So timing becomes key, along with deciding which way to go. There are so many ways from so many trailheads, including ones at Carson Pass and Upper Blue Lake. The shortest and most direct route is from Woods Lake trailhead, located .5 mile before the

Woods Lake Campground and picnic area. This includes a nice stopover at Round Top Lake, two miles in. You pass some old mining cabins before you enter the wilderness boundary. Pass the eastern flank of 9,000-foot Black Butte, an old volcanic vent that is similar in appearance to Mount Round Top a few miles to the east. In less than an hour, you arrive at Round Top Lake, a worthy destination in itself and a good spot for a snack break beneath the sturdy shoulders of the two peaks of The Sisters. It's only two miles more to Fourth of July Lake, but they are steep and downhill, which means you must climb back out on the way home. This is actually good news: It means you will leave the majority of the crowds behind. Most people give up at Fourth of July Saddle, a rocky overlook that sits 1,000 feet above the lake. In addition to the tough grade, the route is often dusty. At the lake, fishing is good for brook trout, and many campsites can be found near its edge. Late in the summer, a sandy beach gets exposed—perfect for swimmers.

**User Groups:** Hikers, leashed dogs, and horses. No mountain bikes. No wheelchair facilities.

**Permits:** A free wilderness permit is required for overnight stays; it is available from the Amador Ranger Station, the Carson Pass Information Station, or the Eldorado Information Center.

**Maps:** For a map, ask the U.S. Forest Service for Eldorado National Forest or Mokelumne Wilderness. For a topographic map, ask the USGS for Caples Lake.

**Directions:** From Meyers at the junction of U.S. 50 and Highway 89, drive south on Highway 89 for 11 miles to Highway 88. Turn west on Highway 88 and drive 12 miles to the Woods Lake Campground turnoff, on the south side of the road (located 1.5 miles west of Carson Pass Summit). Turn left and drive one mile to the trailhead (.5 mile before the campground and picnic area).

**Contact:** Eldorado National Forest, Amador Ranger District, 26820 Silver Drive, Pioneer,

CA 95666, 209/295-4251, website: www.fs .fed.us/r5 (click on Forest Offices).

## 90 FROG LAKE
### 1.8 mi / 1.0 hr

**in the Mokelumne Wilderness near Carson Pass**

Map 6.3, page 195

Any hiking trip from the Carson Pass trailhead is going to be packed with people. So it is here, with 200-plus people out on weekends. That known, this trail is educational and beautiful. At the visitors center, you can learn about Kit Carson, the great explorer for whom this pass was named, and you can learn about the geologic forces that shaped this region, which is called the Round Top Geologic Area. Evidence of both glacial and volcanic action can be seen with every step you take. The short walk to Frog Lake is suitable even for small children, and if you're more ambitious, you can continue another 1.5 miles to beautiful Winnemucca Lake. At Frog Lake, you are provided with a fascinating look at Elephant Back (elevation 9,585 feet), which looks exactly like its name. It's a lava dome—a round mass of solid lava. The lake is a beautiful turquoise color, perfect for picnicking, although because the area is rather open and exposed, the wind sometimes blows with ferocity.

Special Note: Plenty of people take this walk purely to see the wildflowers, especially lupine and Indian paintbrush, from mid-June to mid-August (best in late July). A huge patch of wild iris also blooms alongside Frog Lake. It's a sight to behold.

**User Groups:** Hikers, leashed dogs, and horses. No mountain bikes. No wheelchair facilities.

**Permits:** A free wilderness permit is required for overnight stays between April 1 and November 30; it is available from the Amador Ranger Station, the Carson Pass Information Station, or the Eldorado Information Center. A $3 parking fee is charged per vehicle.

**Maps:** For a map, ask the U.S. Forest Service for Eldorado National Forest or Mokelumne

Wilderness. For a topographic map, ask the USGS for Carson Pass.

**Directions:** From Meyers at the junction of U.S. 50 and Highway 89, drive south on Highway 89 for 11 miles to Highway 88. Turn west on Highway 88 and drive 10 miles to Carson Pass Summit. The parking area and trailhead are on the left, by the Carson Pass Information Station.

**Contact:** Eldorado National Forest, Amador Ranger District, 26820 Silver Drive, Pioneer, CA 95666, 209/295-4251, website: www.fs .fed.us/r5 (click on Forest Offices).

## 91 RAYMOND LAKE
### 11.0 mi / 1.0–2.0 days

**in the Mokelumne Wilderness near Blue Lakes**

Map 6.3, page 195

Considering how difficult it is, we're not sure why this trip in the Mokelumne Wilderness to Raymond Lake is so popular . . . unless you figure in the gorgeous alpine scenery. The 3,000-foot climb to the rocky alpine lake gets heavy use, despite the challenge it presents for some. The trail starts near Wet Meadows Reservoir and heads east from the access road on the Pacific Crest Trail. Keep following the PCT for 4.5 miles; then turn right on Raymond Lake Trail. (Most of those 4.5 miles are a moderate ascent.) The final stretch is only a mile but is a butt-kicker, mostly because you're already getting tired when you begin it. The lake is about 10 acres in size and is set at 9,000 feet. The best thing about the lake is that it is below 10,000-foot Raymond Peak, a ruggedly beautiful mountain.

**User Groups:** Hikers, dogs, and horses. No mountain bikes. No wheelchair facilities.

**Permits:** A free wilderness permit is required for overnight stays; it is available on the wilderness bulletin board at the trailhead, from the ranger station in Markleeville, the Carson Pass Information Station, or the Carson Ranger district in Carson City. Groups are limited to 12, and no campfires are permitted above 8,000 feet.

**Maps:** For a map, ask the U.S. Forest Service for Humboldt-Toiyabe National Forest, Carson District. For topographic maps, ask the USGS for Pacific Valley and Ebbetts Pass.

**Directions:** From Meyers, at the junction of U.S. 50 and Highway 89, drive south on Highway 89 for 11 miles to Highway 88. Turn west on Highway 88 and drive 2.5 miles to the Blue Lakes turnoff, on the south side of the road. Turn south and drive 11 miles to the left turnoff for Tamarack Lake and Wet Meadows. Bear left and drive three miles to the left turnoff for Lower Sunset Lake. Turn left and drive a short distance to the trailhead.

**Contact:** Humboldt-Toiyabe National Forest, Carson Ranger District, 1536 South Carson Street, Carson City, NV 89701, 775/882-2766, website: www.fs.fed.us/htnf.

## 92 GRANITE LAKE
### 4.0 mi / 2.0 hrs

**in the Mokelumne Wilderness near Blue Lakes**

Map 6.3, page 195

Campers at Middle Creek Campground can set out from their tents on this trail to Granite Lake, but everyone else must begin by the dam at Upper Blue Lake and follow a well-signed but meandering route to enter the Mokelumne Wilderness, one mile in. (Don't be concerned if there are lots of cars in the dam parking lot. Most of them belong to anglers, not hikers.) Only one mile beyond the wilderness boundary lies Granite Lake, requiring a total 550-foot climb over well-graded trail. You'll barely notice you're climbing; this is a very easy pathway. A quarter mile past the boundary sign, you'll see a large pond, but don't mistake that for Granite Lake, which is another 20 minutes farther on the trail. The granite basin it's set in and the granite that lines its shores are a dead giveaway that you've made it to the proper destination. Hope you brought your swimsuit for the deep, chilly waters. If you want to hike farther, Grouse Lake is another four miles beyond.

**User Groups:** Hikers, leashed dogs, and horses. No mountain bikes. No wheelchair facilities.

**Permits:** A free wilderness permit is required for overnight; it is available from the Amador Ranger Station, the Carson Pass Information Station, or the Eldorado Information Center.

**Maps:** For a map, ask the U.S. Forest Service for Eldorado National Forest. For a topographic map, ask the USGS for Pacific Valley.

**Directions:** From Meyers at the junction of U.S. 50 and Highway 89, drive south on Highway 89 for 11 miles to Highway 88. Turn west on Highway 88 and drive 2.5 miles to the Blue Lakes turnoff, on the south side of the road. Turn south and drive 12 miles to the fork at Lower Blue Lake. Turn right and drive 1.5 miles to the dam by Upper Blue Lake, shortly past Middle Creek Campground; turn left into the parking area. The Grouse Lake Trail leads to Granite Lake from the west side of the parking area.

**Contact:** Eldorado National Forest, Amador Ranger District, 26820 Silver Drive, Pioneer, CA 95666, 209/295-4251, website: www.fs.fed.us/r5 (click on Forest Offices).

## 93 HOT SPRINGS CREEK WATERFALL

**3.0 mi / 1.5 hrs**

in Grover Hot Springs State Park
near Markleeville

Map 6.3, page 195

Even without a waterfall, this would be a great trail to walk, because it leads through the giant Jeffrey pines of Hot Springs Valley, enclosed by rocky cliffs and 10,000-foot peaks. The route leaves from just beyond the campgrounds in Grover Hot Springs State Park and follows the Burnside Lake and Charity Valley Trails for .5 mile, then branches off on a left fork. The trail is well signed for the waterfall, so you'll have no chance of getting lost. There's one questionable part where the trail reaches a jumbled pile of boulders, but the correct answer is simply to go up and over them. Hot Springs Canyon gradually narrows on its way to the falls, and

when you near the creek's edge, you'll see many small trout swimming in its pools. The waterfall is about 50 feet high and is best seen from April to July. Technically it is outside of state parkland and in Toiyabe National Forest, so you'll see backpackers' campfire rings on the cliff above the falls. The trailhead elevation is 5,900 feet, and the waterfalls are set at 6,200 feet; hence, there's a 300 foot climb.

**User Groups:** Hikers and leashed dogs (not recommended). No horses or mountain bikes. No wheelchair facilities.

**Permits:** No permits are required. A day-use fee of $6 is charged per vehicle; there is a fee of $5 per person for use of the hot springs pool.

**Maps:** A map of Grover Hot Springs State Park is available for $.25 at the entrance station. For a topographic map, ask the USGS for Markleeville.

**Directions:** From Meyers at the junction of U.S. 50 and Highway 89, drive south on Highway 89 for 24 miles to Markleeville. At Markleeville turn right (west) on Hot Springs Road and drive 3.5 miles to the state park entrance. The signed trailhead is .25 mile beyond the entrance station and campground turnoffs, at a gated dirt road.

**Contact:** Grover Hot Springs State Park, P.O. Box 188, Markleeville, CA 96120, 530/694-2248 or 530/525-7232, website: www.parks.ca.gov (click on Find A Park).

## 94 BURNSIDE LAKE

**8.4 mi / 5.0 hrs**

in Humboldt-Toiyabe National Forest
near Markleeville

Map 6.3, page 195

The Burnside Lake Trail leaves Grover Hot Springs State Park at 5,900 feet in elevation and climbs west to Burnside Lake, at 8,160 feet—a gain of 2,260 feet. The climb is spaced out over four miles, so it's a steady workout to the lake. Along the way, you pass tall and majestic sugar pines and rocky outcrops, with 10,023-foot Hawkins Peak and 9,417-foot Markleeville Peak towering over the scene. The lake is about 10 surface acres and is popular for fishing. Although you can start hiking on the trail from Hot Springs Road shortly before the state park entrance, it's best to start from the park's trailhead. Not only does it shave one mile off your trip, but also when you return from your hike, you can take a dip in the 102- to 104-degree hot springs and soothe those aching muscles. Although you may encounter some mountain bikers on the trail at first, they will soon branch off on their way to Charity Valley.

**User Groups:** Hikers, dogs, horses, and mountain bikes. No wheelchair facilities.

**Permits:** No permits are required. A day-use fee of $6 is charged per vehicle at Grover Hot Springs State Park. Parking and access are free if you park and begin the trail outside the park entrance.

**Maps:** For a map, ask the U.S. Forest Service for Humboldt-Toiyabe National Forest, Carson District. A map of Grover Hot Springs State Park is available for $.25 at the entrance station. For a topographic map, ask the USGS for Markleeville.

**Directions:** From Meyers at the junction of Highway 50 and Highway 89, drive south on Highway 89 for 24 miles to Markleeville. At Markleeville turn right (west) on Hot Springs Road and drive 3.5 miles to the state park entrance. The signed trailhead is .25 mile beyond the entrance station and campground turnoffs, at a gated dirt road. Another trailhead is located outside the state park on Hot Springs Road, .75 mile before the state park entrance, and is signed for Charity Valley.

**Contact:** Grover Hot Springs State Park, P.O. Box 188, Markleeville, CA 96120, 530/694-2248 or 530/525-7232, website: www.parks.ca.gov (click on Find A Park); Humboldt-Toiyabe National Forest, Carson Ranger District, 1536 South Carson Street, Carson City, NV 89701, 775/882-2766, website: www.fs.fed.us/htnf.

## 95 BLUE LAKES ROAD TO CARSON PASS (PCT)

**12.0 mi one-way / 1.0 day**

**from Blue Lakes Road north to Carson Pass and Highway 88**

Map 6.3, page 195

Many hikers underestimate the climb over Elephant Back to reach Carson Pass. After all, on a map, it doesn't look like much, and from a distance, as you size it up, it looks easy enough. Wrong! It's a long, grueling pull. The trip out of Blue Lakes starts easily, with a dirt road often in view and adding a bit of early angst to the affair. As you go, you keep wondering when the climb will start. Well, eventually it does, and, alas, it takes a couple of hours—a long, steady march. After topping the Elephant Back, the route drops down to Carson Pass at a rest stop, where you'll likely meet humanity—but believe it or not, no water. Conserve yours if you plan to go onward, because it takes another hour of hiking before you'll reach the next trickle.

To continue north on the PCT, see the Carson Pass to Echo Lakes Resort (PCT) hike in this chapter. If you are walking this trail in reverse, see the Ebbetts Pass to Blue Lakes Road (PCT) hike in this chapter.

**User Groups:** Hikers, dogs, and horses. No mountain bikes. No wheelchair access.

**Permits:** A backcountry permit is required for traveling through various wilderness and special-use areas that the trail traverses. In addition, a campfire permit is required for the use of portable camp stoves or the building of campfires where allowed. To make it simple, you can contact the national forest, BLM, or national park office at your point of entry for a combined permit that is good for traveling through multiple-permit areas during your dates of travel.

**Maps:** For a map, ask the U.S. Forest Service for Lake Tahoe Basin Management Unit, Tahoe National Forest, Eldorado National Forest, and Stanislaus National Forest. For topographic maps, ask the USGS for Pacific Valley and Carson Pass.

**Directions:** To reach the Blue Lakes Road trailhead from the Highway 88/89 junction at Hope Valley, go west on Highway 88 to Blue Lakes Road and turn left. Stay on Blue Lakes Road for 11 miles to the trailhead parking, just before reaching Blue Lakes. For the Carson Pass trailhead from the Highway 88/89 junction at Hope Valley, go west on Highway 88 to Carson Pass.

**Contact:** Eldorado National Forest, Amador Ranger District, 26820 Silver Drive, Pioneer, CA 95666, 209/295-4251, website: www.fs .fed.us/r5 (click on Forest Offices).

## 96 KINNEY LAKES
**5.0 mi / 2.5 hrs**

**in Humboldt-Toiyabe National Forest near Ebbetts Pass**

Map 6.3, page 195

From the Ebbetts Pass trailhead, Kinney Lakes is an easy tromp north on the Pacific Crest Trail (as opposed to heading south from Ebbetts Pass to reach Noble Lake; see the Noble Lake listing in this chapter). You pass little Sherrold Lake on the way to large Upper Kinney Lake (which is actually a reservoir). You start hiking at 8,700 feet at the pass, so even though this trail has an easy to moderate grade, your lungs are getting a workout. The trail leads through a landscape of big conifers with little undergrowth—typical of the high country. When the trees thin out, your views open wide. Raymond Peak and Reynolds Peak rule the skyline. At 1.6 miles, you reach a signed junction for Upper and Lower Kinney Lakes, and you can take your pick as to which one to visit first. The Pacific Crest Trail leads directly to the upper lake, while the lower lake must be visited by following an eastward fork from the PCT. The upper lake, though smaller, is the prettier of the two.

**User Groups:** Hikers, dogs, and horses. No mountain bikes. No wheelchair facilities.

**Permits:** Wilderness permits are required for overnight use. No campfires are allowed above 8,000 feet. Parking and access are free.

**Maps:** For a map, ask the U.S. Forest Service for Humboldt-Toiyabe National Forest, Carson District. For a topographic map, ask the USGS for Ebbetts Pass.

**Directions:** From Angels Camp at the intersection of Highways 4 and 49, drive east on Highway 4 for about 40 miles to Bear Valley. Set your odometer at Bear Valley, and drive 15 miles farther east on Highway 4 to Ebbetts Pass and the trailhead parking area. The trail is on the north side of the road. If you are coming from Markleeville, drive south on Highway 89/Highway 4 for 15 miles to Ebbetts Pass.

**Contact:** Humboldt-Toiyabe National Forest, Carson Ranger District, 1536 South Carson Street, Carson City, NV 89701, 775/882-2766, website: www.fs.fed.us/htnf.

## 97 EBBETTS PASS TO BLUE LAKES ROAD (PCT)
**12.0 mi one-way / 1.0 day**

**from Highway 4 near Ebbetts Pass north to Blue Lakes Road just south of Carson Pass and Highway 88**

Map 6.3, page 195

As you leave Ebbetts Pass, you'll cross a series of fantastic volcanic formations in the Mokelumne Wilderness. The country here may look stark from a distance, but it is loaded with tiny wildflowers. The trail is quite good—a lot of hikers make great time in this area—but the lack of available water can become a concern. Tank up whenever you get the chance, such as at Eagle Creek below Reynold Peak (9,690 feet). The Mokelumne Wilderness is a relative breeze, and you'll find yourself approaching civilization at a series of small lakes in Tahoe National Forest. The trail rises up a stark, wind-blown, sandy ridge, with excellent views of the Blue Lakes—but again, there is no water for several miles until you drop down near Lost Lake. You'll actually cross several roads on this stretch of trail, and maybe even see a car—a moment of irony for long-distance PCT hikers. To continue north on the PCT, see the Blue Lakes Road to Carson Pass (PCT) hike in this chapter.

**User Groups:** Hikers, dogs, and horses. No mountain bikes. No wheelchair facilities.

**Permits:** A backcountry permit is required for traveling through various wilderness and special-use areas that the trail traverses. In addition, a campfire permit is required for the use of portable camp stoves or the building of campfires (where permitted). To make it simple, you can contact the national forest, BLM, or national park office at your point of entry for a combined permit good for traveling through multiple-permit areas during your dates of travel.

**Maps:** For a map, ask the U.S. Forest Service for Lake Tahoe Basin Management Unit, Tahoe National Forest, Eldorado National Forest, and Stanislaus National Forest. For topographic maps, ask the USGS for Ebbetts Pass, Pacific Valley, and Carson Pass.

**Directions:** To reach the Ebbetts Pass trailhead from Angels Camp, head east on Highway 4 to Ebbetts Pass. To reach the Blue Lakes Road trailhead from the Highway 88/89 interchange at Hope Valley, head west on Highway 88 to Blue Lakes Road and turn left. Stay on Blue Lakes Road to the trailhead parking area, just before reaching Blue Lakes.

**Contact:** Eldorado National Forest, Amador Ranger District, 26820 Silver Drive, Pioneer, CA 95666, 209/295-4251, website: www.fs .fed.us/r5 (click on Forest Offices).

## 98 NOBLE LAKE
**9.0 mi / 4.5 hrs**

**in Humboldt-Toiyabe National Forest near Ebbetts Pass**

Map 6.3, page 195

Noble Lake lies just outside of the Carson-Iceberg Wilderness and is reachable by a steady climb on Noble Canyon Trail out of Silver Creek Campground, or by a shorter, gentler route from Ebbetts Pass. The latter is the best choice. From Ebbetts Pass (elevation 8,700 feet), there's a 1,200-foot climb to the lake at 9,440 feet (which includes some descent as well). The lake is a fine spot for camping or

just spending an afternoon. The scenery is classic high Sierra—big conifers, snowcapped peaks, hard granite, and lush meadows. The hiking season is brief at this elevation, usually only from July to September, but that just makes being here seem all the more special.

The lake route follows an access trail to the Pacific Crest Trail from the trailhead parking area. After .25 mile of climbing, you will join the PCT proper and head south, first climbing and then making a long descent into Noble Canyon. The trail from Silver Creek Campground joins your trail here, and some switchbacks follow. At three miles, you will cross Noble Creek and then climb again to a high meadow. Soon you can see Noble Lake; the main lake is to the right of the trail, but a smaller, unnamed lake is to the left, about 650 feet off the trail. Both have decent campsites and many good rocks to sit on and relax. This lake is excellent for swimming but poor for fishing. For camping, group size is limited to 15 people, and a 100-foot setback from the lake is required. Dogs accompanying campers on this trip can have difficulty sleeping because of the high number of ground squirrels in the boulder field bordering the lake.

**User Groups:** Hikers, dogs, and horses. No mountain bikes. No wheelchair facilities.

**Permits:** No day-hiking permits are required. A free wilderness permit is available at the trailhead (self-issue). Parking and access are free.

**Maps:** For a map, ask the U.S. Forest Service for Humboldt-Toiyabe National Forest, Carson District. For a topographic map, ask the USGS for Ebbetts Pass.

**Directions:** From Angels Camp at the intersection of Highways 4 and 49, go east on Highway 4 for 40 miles to Bear Valley. Set your odometer at Bear Valley, and drive 15 miles farther east on Highway 4 to Ebbetts Pass and the trailhead parking area (located just east of Ebbetts Pass; do not park on Highway 4). The trailhead is on the south side of the road.

**Contact:** Humboldt-Toiyabe National Forest, Carson Ranger District, 1536 South Carson

Street, Carson City, NV 89701, 775/882-2766, website: www.fs.fed.us/htnf.

## 99 WOLF CREEK TRAIL
**9.6 mi / 5.0 hrs**

**in the Carson-Iceberg Wilderness
near Markleeville**

**Map 6.3, page 195**

When the temperature heats up around Markleeville, you've got two choices: Head for the mineral springs at Grover Hot Springs State Park (the cool pool, not the hot pool), or take a hike on Wolf Creek Trail in the Carson-Iceberg Wilderness—it's a tough choice. But if you pick the latter, you're in for a fine time on this easy trail along Wolf Creek, starting at 6,480 feet in elevation. The trail is an old jeep road and is almost entirely shaded, and it meanders upstream and slightly uphill for a total of nine miles one-way (most people do not hike the entire route, but rather our suggested trip to Wolf Creek Falls). A perfect day hike is just to stroll along the creek for an hour or two, find a good spot along the stream to hang out for a while, then turn around and stroll back. Energetic types can hike 4.3 miles out to a fork for the steep Bull Canyon Trail to Bull Lake, then bear left and continue a half mile beyond the fork to Wolf Creek Falls. The waterfall is found just off the trail to the left, about 50 yards beyond where the trail passes through a cattle fence. It's quite impressive early in the summer, as it thunders over a cliff of volcanic rock.

**User Groups:** Hikers, dogs, and horses. No mountain bikes. No wheelchair facilities.

**Permits:** A free wilderness permit is required for overnight stays; it is available at the trailhead. Parking and access are free.

**Maps:** For a map, ask the U.S. Forest Service for Humboldt-Toiyabe National Forest, Carson District, and Carson-Iceberg Wilderness. For a topographic map, ask the USGS for Wolf Creek.

**Directions:** From Meyers at the junction of U.S. 50 and Highway 89, drive south on Highway 89 for 24 miles to Markleeville. From Markleeville, continue south on Highway 89 for four miles to Monitor Pass Junction. Bear right (south) on Highway 4 and drive 2.5 miles to the signed turnoff for Wolf Creek, on the left. Turn left (south) and drive 4.9 miles to the trailhead, about 100 yards before the end of the road.

**Contact:** Humboldt-Toiyabe National Forest, Carson Ranger District, 1536 South Carson Street, Carson City, NV 89701, 775/882-2766, website: www.fs.fed.us/htnf.

## 100 EAST CARSON RIVER TRAIL
**4.0 mi / 2.0 hrs**

**in the Carson-Iceberg Wilderness
near Markleeville**

**Map 6.3, page 195**

If it's springtime, and you're itching to go hiking but there's still too much snow around Ebbetts Pass, the East Carson River Trail can be your salvation. Trailhead elevation is only 6,240 feet at the north side of Wolf Creek Meadows (private property), which means it's snow-free before other nearby areas. Bear left at the trail junction just uphill from the trailhead and the sign noting Carson-Iceberg Wilderness (the right fork is the High Trail northern terminus). An interesting journey is 1.5 miles to Wolf Creek Lake (sometimes dry) and Railroad Canyon, the site of 19th-century logging operations. Although this trail continues onward and eventually meets up with the southern terminus of High Trail (and ends at the junction with Golden Canyon Trail), it is nearly impossible to make a loop trip out of the two trails, especially in early season. The High Trail reaches an elevation of nearly 8,000 feet and is often covered in snow early in the season. So just hike as far as you like, then head back the way you came.

**User Groups:** Hikers, dogs, and horses. No mountain bikes. No wheelchair facilities.

**Permits:** A free wilderness permit is required for overnight stays; it is available at the trailhead. Parking and access are free.

Maps: For a map, ask the U.S. Forest Service for Humboldt-Toiyabe National Forest, Carson Distric, and Carson-Iceberg Wilderness. For a topographic map, ask the USGS for Wolf Creek.

Directions: From Meyers at the junction of U.S. 50 and Highway 89, drive south on Highway 89 for 24 miles to Markleeville. Continue south on Highway 89/Highway 4 for 7.5 miles to the signed turnoff for Wolf Creek on the left. Turn left (east) and drive 3.5 miles to the left turnoff signed for East Carson River Trail. Turn left and drive one mile to the road junction to Dixon Mine. Turn right and drive .25 mile to the trailhead.

Contact: Humboldt-Toiyabe National Forest, Carson Ranger District, 1536 South Carson Street, Carson City, NV 89701, 775/882-2766, website: www.fs.fed.us/htnf.

## 101 HEISER LAKE
### 4.8 mi / 2.5 hrs

in the Carson-Iceberg Wilderness near Ebbetts Pass

Map 6.3, page 195

You know you're in for a good trip when the trailhead is located at a spot as pretty as the Mosquito Lakes, set at an elevation of 8,000 feet on Highway 4. The tiny little lakes are popular with anglers from the nearby campgrounds, but this trail is popular with nature lovers, who set out on the short, moderate, day hike to Heiser Lake for a few hours of peace in the Carson-Iceberg Wilderness. The trail climbs and descends, then climbs and descends some more, mostly heading in a straight-line course due south to the lake. It's one of those trails where you've got to work equally hard traveling in both directions. At a junction with the trail from Bull Run Lake two miles in, bear left and finish out the last .5 mile to Heiser Lake, set at 8,300 feet. The lake is granite bound, with a couple of tiny islands sticking out of its shallow waters.

User Groups: Hikers, dogs, and horses. No mountain bikes. No wheelchair facilities.

Permits: No day hiking permits are required. Parking and access are free.

Maps: For a map, ask the U.S. Forest Service for Stanislaus National Forest and Carson-Iceberg Wilderness. For topographic maps, ask the USGS for Pacific Valley and Spicer Meadow Reservoir.

Directions: From Angels Camp at the intersection of Highways 4 and 49, drive east on Highway 4 for 40 miles to Bear Valley. Set your odometer at Bear Valley and drive 10 miles farther east on Highway 4 to the Mosquito Lakes trailhead and Heiser Lake Trail. Park on the right (south) side of the road, across from the campground; there is only enough space for a few cars.

Contact: Stanislaus National Forest, Calaveras Ranger District, P.O. Box 500, Hathaway Pines, CA 95233, 209/795-1381, website: www.fs.fed.us/r5 (click on Forest Offices).

## 102 BULL RUN LAKE
### 7.0 mi / 4.0 hrs

in the Carson-Iceberg Wilderness near Ebbetts Pass

Map 6.3, page 195

You might have to share the trail to Bull Run Lake with some horses. After all, their owners like the big parking lot at the trailhead, as it's large enough for horse trailers. Maybe you should pack along a few extra apples or carrots, eh? Although longer than the nearby trail to Heiser Lake, this trip to Bull Run Lake is actually easier, because the trail is well graded, and the only really steep section is in the last .5 mile. The trailhead is set at 7,800 feet. The first 1.3 miles are almost level, traveling slightly downhill through a grassy meadow that is filled with wildflowers in the early summer and turns golden by September. After that, you start to climb, mostly through pine forest and over duck-lined stretches of granite. Watch for a trail junction at 2.2 miles, where you should turn right for Bull Run Lake (straight ahead is Heiser Lake). After a brief flat stretch, prepare for a final mile of climbing, with the last part being the most challenging. The lake is set at 8,300 feet and is a fine reward for your effort, set in a steep-walled granite bowl, with many smooth rock slabs to lie on. Note that the ambitious can add on a trip to Heiser Lake, which is two miles away from the junction. But with a steep up and down, it's better saved for backpackers or day hikers with an early start.

**User Groups:** Hikers, dogs, and horses. No mountain bikes. No wheelchair facilities.

**Permits:** No day hiking permits are required. Parking and access are free.

**Maps:** For a map, ask the U.S. Forest Service for Stanislaus National Forest or Carson-Iceberg Wilderness. For topographic maps, ask the USGS for Pacific Valley and Spicer Meadow Reservoir.

**Directions:** From Angels Camp at the intersection of Highways 4 and 49, drive east on Highway 4 for 40 miles to Bear Valley. Set your odometer at Bear Valley and drive 8.5 miles farther east on Highway 4 to the Stanislaus Meadow turnoff, on the right (Road 8N13). Turn right and drive a short distance to the trailhead parking area.

**Contact:** Stanislaus National Forest, Calaveras Ranger District, P.O. Box 500, Hathaway Pines, CA 95233, 209/795-1381, website: www.fs.fed.us/r5 (click on Forest Offices).

## 103 CLARK FORK AND BOULDER LAKE
### 8.0 mi / 4.0 hrs

**in the Carson-Iceberg Wilderness on Clark Fork Stanislaus River**

Map 6.3, page 195

From this trailhead at Iceberg Meadow, you immediately enter the Carson-Iceberg Wilderness at the base of imposing Iceberg Peak. Hiking upstream on the northern edge of the Clark Fork Stanislaus River, you'll enjoy wildflowers and a lovely mixed forest of white firs and Jeffrey pines. At the water's edge, the trees are more leafy, including cottonwoods and aspens. The river pools are cold but useful for cooling off on a hot day. At 2.5 miles, you have a choice:

Bear right (really straight) and continue along the Clark Fork, or turn left and hike steeply uphill along Boulder Creek. We suggest the left fork, following Boulder Creek for 1.5 miles uphill to tiny Boulder Lake. It's a good workout to a pretty destination. But hey, if you get tired, just cut the trip short and turn around when you reach Boulder Creek. Plenty of fishing holes and picnic spots can be found along the Clark Fork.

**User Groups:** Hikers, dogs, and horses. No mountain bikes. No wheelchair facilities.

**Permits:** A free wilderness permit is required for overnight stays and is available from the Summit Ranger Station. Parking and access are free.

**Maps:** For a map, ask the U.S. Forest Service for Stanislaus National Forest or Carson-Iceberg Wilderness. For a topographic map, ask the USGS for Donnell Lake.

**Directions:** From Sonora, drive east on Highway 108 for 46 miles to the left turnoff for Clark Fork Road, approximately 17 miles east of Strawberry. Turn left and follow Clark Fork Road for about seven miles to its end, at the Clark Fork trailhead at Iceberg Meadow.

**Contact:** Stanislaus National Forest, Summit Ranger District, 1 Pinecrest Lake Road, Pinecrest, CA 95364, 209/965-3434, website: www.fs.fed.us/r5 (click on Forest Offices).

## 104 TRAIL OF THE GARGOYLES
### 3.0 mi / 1.5 hrs

**near Strawberry and Pinecrest Lake**

Map 6.3, page 195

 When you park your car at the nondescript trailhead, it's hard to guess what's in store on the Trail of the Gargoyles. Sure, the odd rock formations that line the trail are fascinating to look at, but what's more significant is that they (and you) are perched at the edge of a cliff at 7,400 feet in elevation. You walk just inches away from what appears to be the edge of the world, with only thin air between you and the densely forested basin several hundred feet below. It's an easy and nearly flat trail, but if you have kids with you, keep a handhold on them at all times. By the way, the rock formations don't look much like gargoyles except for the fact that they are hanging off the edge of this abrupt abyss. The trailhead is in the middle of the 1.5-mile trail, which means you'll want to walk out and back in both directions. The trail on the north rim is slightly steeper.

**User Groups:** Hikers and leashed dogs. No horses or mountain bikes. No wheelchair facilities.

**Permits:** No permits are required. Parking and access are free.

**Maps:** For a map, ask the U.S. Forest Service for Stanislaus National Forest. For a topographic map, ask the USGS for Pinecrest.

**Directions:** From Sonora, drive east on Highway 108 for 34 miles to Herring Creek Road (Road 4N12), 2.4 miles east of Strawberry. Turn right on Herring Creek Road and continue for 6.7 miles to an often-unsigned turnoff on the left. Turn left and drive .2 mile to the trailhead.

**Contact:** Stanislaus National Forest, Summit Ranger District, 1 Pinecrest Lake Road, Pinecrest, CA 95364, 209/965-3434, website: www.fs.fed.us/r5 (click on Forest Offices).

## 105 EAGLE MEADOW TO DARDANELLE
**4.0 mi one-way / 2.0 hrs**

**near Dardanelle**

Map 6.3, page 195

If you can convince someone to drop you off at Eagle Meadow and pick you up at Dardanelle Resort, or if you have two cars for a shuttle hike, you can take a scenic downhill stroll paralleling Eagle Creek. It's a trip for lovers of subalpine meadows, especially in the first mile. After it leaves the meadow, the trail enters a thick and lovely conifer forest, so you get a bit of shade along the path. The route gets a little steep in sections, so make sure your knees are in good enough shape for four miles of downhill before you make the trip.

**User Groups:** Hikers, leashed dogs, horses, and mountain bikes. No wheelchair facilities.

**Permits:** No permits are required. Parking and access are free.

**Maps:** For a map, ask the U.S. Forest Service for Stanislaus National Forest. For topographic maps, ask the USGS for Donnell Lake and Dardanelle.

**Directions:** From Sonora, drive east on Highway 108 for 41 miles to the turnoff for Niagara Creek Campground, on the right side of the highway, approximately 12 miles east of Strawberry. Turn right, then at .25 mile turn right again on Road 5N01. Follow Road 5N01 for seven miles to Eagle Meadow. This is the start of the one-way shuttle hike; the finish is at Dardanelle Resort on Highway 108, eight miles east of the Niagara Creek turnoff.

**Contact:** Stanislaus National Forest, Summit Ranger District, 1 Pinecrest Lake Road, Pinecrest, CA 95364, 209/965-3434, website: www.fs.fed.us/r5 (click on Forest Offices).

## 106 COLUMNS OF THE GIANTS
**0.5 mi / 0.5 hr**

**near Dardanelle**

Map 6.3, page 195

This is Highway 108's answer to Devils Postpile National Monument, and take it from us, it's no cheap imitation. The rock formations at the end of the Columns of the Giants geological trail were formed 150,000 years ago, when a series of volcanic eruptions occurred. The lava flow cooled rapidly, probably during cold weather, and cracked into narrow, hexagonal, basalt columns. Some of the remaining columns are 30 to 40 feet in height and three to four feet in diameter. Although many are still standing tall or at least at an angle, others have shattered into thousands of pieces, creating a giant pile of rubble. An interpretive trail sign explains that underneath this rock pile is evidence of the last small ice age in the Sierra—frozen remnants of ice fields that are replenished each year by winter snow and cold.

All this historical information gives you plenty to think about during your very short walk. Make sure you bring your camera—it's lots of fun taking pictures of your hiking partner standing right next to the jumbled heap of rocks.
**User Groups:** Hikers and leashed dogs. No horses or mountain bikes. No wheelchair facilities.
**Permits:** No permits are required. Parking and access are free.
**Maps:** For a map, ask the U.S. Forest Service for Stanislaus National Forest. For a topographic map, ask the USGS for Dardanelle.
**Directions:** From Sonora, drive east on Highway 108 for 50 miles to Pigeon Flat Campground, two miles east of Dardanelle and on the south side of the highway. If you're traveling west on Highway 108, the campground is 15 miles west of Sonora Pass. Park in the day-use parking lot just outside the camp.
**Contact:** Stanislaus National Forest, Summit Ranger District, 1 Pinecrest Lake Road, Pinecrest, CA 95364, 209/965-3434, website: www.fs.fed.us/r5 (click on Forest Offices).

## 107 KENNEDY LAKE
### 14.8 mi / 2.0 days

**in the Emigrant Wilderness near Dardanelle**

Map 6.3, page 195

If the number of cars in the Kennedy Meadows parking lot is scaring you, take heart. Many of them belong to people day hiking to fish at Relief Reservoir. If you have the time and inclination for a longer trip to Kennedy Lake, you will leave a lot of your fellow hikers behind. Even so, don't expect solitude. You'll likely share the lake with other backpackers, horse packers, and grazing cows. Follow the trail notes to Relief Reservoir (see next listing), but at 2.6 miles, take the left fork for Kennedy Lake. The trail climbs for another 1.6 miles, then goes flat for the final 3.2 miles to the lake. It's an easy two-day backpack trip, with low mileage and only a 1,200-foot elevation gain. Note that all the campsites are downstream of the lake rather than along its shoreline.

**User Groups:** Hikers, leashed dogs, and horses. No mountain bikes. No wheelchair facilities.
**Permits:** A free wilderness permit is required for overnight stays and is available from the Summit Ranger Station. Parking and access are free.
**Maps:** For a map, ask the U.S. Forest Service for Stanislaus National Forest or Emigrant Wilderness. For a topographic map, ask the USGS for Sonora Pass.
**Directions:** From Sonora, drive east on Highway 108 for 55 miles to the turnoff for Kennedy Meadows, six miles east of Dardanelle and on the south side of the highway. Turn right and follow the road for another mile to the large parking area. If you're traveling west on Highway 108, the Kennedy Meadows turnoff is 9.6 miles west of Sonora Pass.
**Contact:** Stanislaus National Forest, Summit Ranger District, 1 Pinecrest Lake Road, Pinecrest, CA 95364, 209/965-3434, website: www.fs.fed.us/r5 (click on Forest Offices).

## 108 RELIEF RESERVOIR
### 6.0 mi / 3.0 hrs

**on the edge of the Emigrant Wilderness near Dardanelle**

Map 6.3, page 195

From the mammoth trailhead and parking lot at Kennedy Meadows, you can hike to Relief Reservoir (elevation 7,200 feet), do a little fishing, then hike back out. The only downers are that pack animals have roughed up the trail, and the route is seriously overused. On weekends it seems you must constantly pull off the path to let horses and other hikers go by. The route, called the Huckleberry Trail, leads along the Stanislaus River, enters the Emigrant Wilderness at one mile, then skirts its edge. Quickly you understand why this trip is so popular— the river canyon gets more and more beautiful as you head deeper into it. The trail had to be blasted into the steep and rocky hillside. Pass the left turnoff for roaring Kennedy Creek and Kennedy Lake at 2.6 miles, and then proceed straight for another .5 mile to an overlook of the reservoir. It's a steep drop down to the water's edge in the last .25 mile, which must be regained on the return trip.

**User Groups:** Hikers, leashed dogs, and horses. No mountain bikes. No wheelchair facilities.
**Permits:** No day-use permits are required. Parking and access are free.
**Maps:** For a map, ask the U.S. Forest Service for Stanislaus National Forest or Emigrant Wilderness. For a topographic map, ask the USGS for Sonora Pass.
**Directions:** From Sonora, go east on Highway 108 for 55 miles to the Kennedy Meadows turnoff, on the south side of the highway, six miles east of Dardanelle. Turn right and follow the road a mile to the well-signed parking area. Day hikers can park .5 mile farther down the road, near Kennedy Meadows Resort. If you're traveling west on Highway 108, the Kennedy Meadows turnoff is 9.6 miles west of Sonora Pass.
**Contact:** Stanislaus National Forest, Summit Ranger District, 1 Pinecrest Lake Road, Pinecrest, CA 95364, 209/965-3434, website: www.fs.fed.us/r5 (click on Forest Offices).

## 109 SARDINE FALLS
**2.0 mi / 1.0 hr**

**near Sonora Pass**

Map 6.3, page 195

An easy hike through a high alpine meadow and culminating at a pretty waterfall is our idea of a fine way to spend an afternoon. The trip to Sardine Falls requires a little route-finding, because there is no formal trail, but since you can see the falls from the road and there are several overgrown jeep routes to follow, the going is easy. From where you've left your car, head across the northwest side of the meadow. Look for a route that is signed Route Closed to Motorized Vehicles; it's the most direct path. Cross Sardine Creek, which parallels Highway 108, and walk up the right side of larger McKay Creek. After climbing uphill over a rise, you'll hear and then see Sardine Falls, gracefully framed by a few sparse lodgepole pines.

**User Groups:** Hikers, leashed dogs, and horses. No mountain bikes. No wheelchair facilities.
**Permits:** No permits are required. Parking and access are free.
**Maps:** For a map, ask the U.S. Forest Service for Humboldt-Toiyabe National Forest, Bridgeport District. For a topographic map, ask the USGS for Pickel Meadow.
**Directions:** From the junction of U.S. 395 and Highway 108, drive 12.5 miles west on Highway 108. You will be 2.5 miles east of Sonora Pass Summit. Park along the road in the gravel pullouts near the overgrown jeep roads on the northwest side of the meadow.
**Contact:** Humboldt-Toiyabe National Forest, Bridgeport Ranger District, HCR1 Box 1000, Bridgeport, CA 93517, 760/932-7070, website: www.fs.fed.us/htnf.

## 110 SONORA PASS TO EBBETTS PASS (PCT)
**30.8 mi one-way / 3.0 days**
**from Highway 108 at Sonora Pass north to Highway 4 near Ebbetts Pass**

Map 6.3, page 195

While this section of the Pacific Crest Trail may not have the glamorous reputation of the stretch of trail in the southern Sierra, it's just as compelling for those who know it. From Sonora Pass, you're forced to climb out for a good hour or two. Then you'll rise over Wolf Creek Gap (10,300 feet) and make the easy drop down the Carson Canyon. This is the start of the Carson-Iceberg Wilderness, a giant swath of land that is a rare, unpeopled paradise. The Sierra riparian zones here are lined with flowers, seemingly all kinds and all colors, often in luxuriant beds of greenness. The PCT climbs out of Carson Canyon around Boulder Peak, then down and up two more canyons. All the while, you keep crossing creeks filled with natural gardens. You wind your way across and through these areas and eventually climb a ridge, then head down, steeply at times, to Ebbetts Pass. Alas, there's no water here. No problem. A short half-hour climb and you can be pumping water, and maybe setting up camp too, at little Sherrold Lake, not far from the edge of the Mokelumne Wilderness.

To continue north on the PCT, see the Ebbetts Pass to Blue Lakes Road (PCT) hike in this chapter.

**User Groups:** Hikers, dogs, and horses. No mountain bikes. No wheelchair facilities.

**Permits:** A wilderness permit is required for traveling through various wilderness and special-use areas the trail traverses. Contact the Stanislaus National Forest to obtain a permit that is good for the length of your trip.

**Maps:** For topographic maps, ask the USGS for Pickel Meadow, Disaster Peak, Dardanelles Cone, and Ebbetts Pass.

**Directions:** From Sonora, head east on Highway 108 to the trailhead and parking area at Sonora Pass.

**Contact:** Stanislaus National Forest, Summit Ranger District, 1 Pinecrest Lake Road, Pinecrest, CA 95364, 209/965-3434 or 209/532-3671 (for permits), website: www.fs.fed.us/r5 (click on Forest Offices).

## 111 SECRET AND POORE LAKES
### 6.5 mi / 3.5 hrs

**near Sonora Pass**

Map 6.3, page 195

This 6.5-mile loop trip begins at a footbridge over West Walker River at Leavitt Meadows Campground. After .25 mile, take the left fork for Secret Lake (you won't be alone, most likely). Climb for nearly two miles through sage and Jeffrey pines, then descend .5 mile to Secret Lake. Much larger Poore Lake is visible over your left shoulder. Take a break at Secret Lake, then continue around the right side of the lake, hiking through sparse junipers and pines for .5 mile to the left turnoff for Poore Lake. Take the rougher .75-mile route to the large lake. If it's quiet, you can swim or fish for a few hours, then retrace your steps to the junction. From there, loop back to the campground on a lower trail that follows closer to the West Walker River through Leavitt Meadow. If Poore Lake turns out to be less than perfect, you can always hike beyond the return loop junction to little Roosevelt Lake.

Special Notes: No mountain bikes are permitted beyond Poore Lake, so that means Roosevelt Lake is free of them. In addition, there is no bridge available for off-road vehicles, so though this area was once an off-roading spot, it is no longer. Finally, a nearby U.S. Marine training facility means it is possible you may see groups running along the road; they do not fire their weapons here and they almost never enter the forest.

**User Groups:** Hikers, dogs, horses, and mountain bikes. No wheelchair facilities.

**Permits:** No day-use permits are required. Campfire permits required for overnight use. Parking and access are free.

**Maps:** For a map, ask the U.S. Forest Service for Humboldt-Toiyabe National Forest, Bridgeport District. For a topographic map, ask the USGS for Pickel Meadow.

**Directions:** From the junction of U.S. 395 and Highway 108, drive seven miles west on Highway 108 to Leavitt Meadows Campground, on the south side of the road. If you are coming from the west, the camp is eight miles east of Sonora Pass. Day hikers may park inside the campground; backpackers must park .25 mile west of the camp on Highway 108.

**Contact:** Humboldt-Toiyabe National Forest, Bridgeport Ranger District, HCR1 Box 1000, Bridgeport, CA 93517, 760/932-7070, website: www.fs.fed.us/htnf.

## Chapter 7

© ANN MARIE BROWN

# San Francisco Bay Area

# San Francisco Bay Area

I t's ironic that many people who have chosen to live in the Bay Area are often the ones who complain the most about it. I've even heard some say, "Some day I'm going to get out of here and start having a good time."

Anyone who has ever had these thoughts should consider the view from an airplane encircling the Bay Area at 3,000 feet. What they'd see is that despite strips of roadways and pockets of cities where people are jammed together, most of the region is wild, unsettled, and beautiful. There is no metropolitan area in the world that offers better and more diverse recreation and open space so close to so many people.

The Bay Area has 150 significant parks (including 12 with redwoods), 7,500 miles of hiking and biking trails, 45 lakes, 25 waterfalls, 100 miles of coast, mountains with incredible lookouts, and bays with islands. And in all, there are 1.2 million acres of greenbelt, with hundreds of acres being added each year when land is bought by money earmarked from property taxes. The land has no limit. Enjoy it.

This chapter features 189 of the best hikes in the area, highlighted by Point Reyes National Seashore, Marin Headlands, California state parks, the East Bay Regional Park system, San Francisco Headlands, Midpeninsula Open Space District, Santa Clara and San Mateo county parks, and San Jose Department of Parks. These parks offer trails of all lengths—including long-distance hikes with campgrounds, such as Coast Trail (at Point Reyes), Ohlone Trail and East Bay National Skyline Trail (routed through several East Bay parks), and Skyline-to-the-Sea, in the Santa Cruz Mountains.

Note that proximity to a metropolitan area means one thing: The demand is higher. So plan ahead. Scheduling a hike on a Monday, Tuesday, Wednesday, or Thursday will decrease your chances of sharing the trail (and parking areas) with dozens of other people.

People from all over the world come here for good reason, so instead of going far away for a vacation, residents should consider this: Stay and discover the treasures in your own backyard.

see Sacramento and Gold Country page 180

see San Joaquin Valley page 422

San Joaquin River

Camanche Lake

Santa Nella

San Luis Reservoir

Manteca

Stockton

Rio Vista

Gilroy

**MAP 7.3 page 269**

Pittsburg

Concord

Danville

Livermore

Fremont

San Jose

Morgan Hill

**MAP 7.4 page 270**

Suisun City

Vallejo

Suisun Bay

Berkeley

Hayward

Santa Cruz

Richmond

Oakland

Redwood City

Petaluma

San Pablo Bay

San Francisco Bay

Woodside

San Rafael

San Francisco

Pacifica

Pescadero

**MAP 7.1 page 267**

**MAP 7.2 page 268**

Bolinas

Olema

10 mi

10 km

N
W — E
S

PACIFIC OCEAN

© AVALON TRAVEL PUBLISHING, INC.

# Map 7.1    Hikes 1–57    Pages 271–305

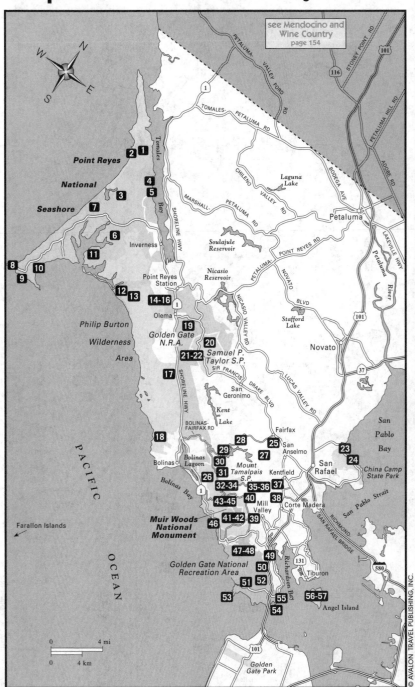

see Mendocino and
Wine Country
page 154

STONEY POINT RD

PETALUMA VALLEY FORD RD

PETALUMA HILL RD

ADOBE RD

101

116

TOMALES—PETALUMA RD

PETALUMA RD

Tomales Bay

**Point Reyes**

2  1

Tomales Bay

**National**

4
5

**Seashore**

3

7

CHILENO VALLEY RD

Laguna
Lake

MARSHALL—PETALUMA RD

BORGA AVE

Petaluma

6

Inverness

SHORELINE HWY

Soulajule
Reservoir

POINT REYES RD

PETALUMA NOVATO BLVD

LAKEVILLE HWY

Petaluma
River

11

8

10

9

Nicasio
Reservoir

Point Reyes
Station

BLVD

12  13

14–16    1

Olema

Stafford
Lake

101

**Philip Burton**

19

NICASIO VALLEY RD

Novato

37

**Wilderness**

**Golden Gate**
**N.R.A.**

20

21–22    Samuel P.
Taylor S.P.

**Area**

17

SIR FRANCIS DRAKE BLVD

LUCAS VALLEY RD

San
Geronimo

SHORELINE HWY

Kent
Lake

San
Pablo
Bay

BOLINAS—
FAIRFAX RD

Fairfax

18

28

25    San
Anselmo

23

24

China Camp
State Park

**Bolinas**

Bolinas
Lagoon

29

30

27

San
Rafael

P A C I F I C

26    31

Mount
Tamalpais
S.P.

Kentfield

32–34    35–36    37

San Pablo Strait

Bolinas Bay

1

43–45    40    38

Corte Madera

Mill
Valley

RICHMOND—SAN RAFAEL BRIDGE

41–42    39

**Muir Woods**
**National**
**Monument**

46

580

**Farallon Islands**

47–48    49

**Golden Gate National**
**Recreation Area**

50

131

Richardson Bay

Tiburon

51    52

O C E A N

53

55

56–57

54

Angel Island

0        4 mi

0        4 km

101

**Golden**
**Gate Park**

© AVALON TRAVEL PUBLISHING, INC.

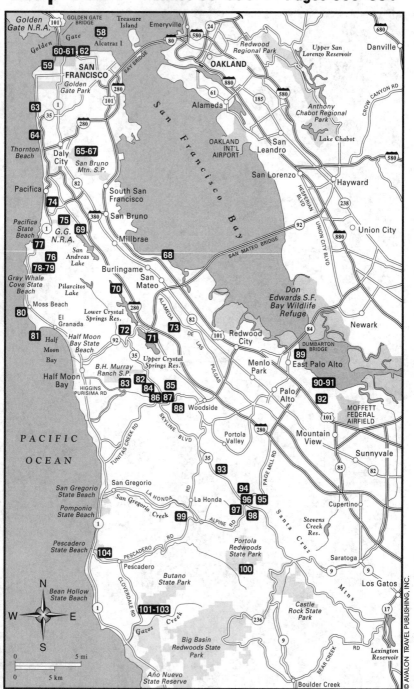

# Map 7.3   Hikes 105–150   Pages 335–364

# Map 7.4  Hikes 151–189  Pages 364–390

© AVALON TRAVEL PUBLISHING, INC.

## 1 TOMALES POINT TRAIL
### 6.0 mi / 3.5 hrs

**in Point Reyes National Seashore in northwest Marin County**

Map 7.1, page 267

Imagine meeting up with an elk that stands five feet at the shoulders and has antlers that practically poke holes in the clouds. That is likely to happen on this trail, the best hike in California for those who want to see wildlife. Elk often wander quite close to the parking area, and in the evening, the herd will usually congregate near a watering area set in a valley about three miles from the trailhead. The herd numbers over 500. We have seen as many as 75 elk on a single trip; on another, we counted 13 elk, six deer, three rabbits, and a fox—all within a two-hour span. Most people make this a five-mile round-trip, hiking north to the top of a grade, a great lookout of Dillon Beach and Bodega Bay. The reason most people turn around here is that the trail descends several hundred feet, so if they continue north, it means an additional climb on the way back.

The route has a flat walking surface and easy grades, and is flanked to the west by the Pacific Ocean and to the east by Tomales Bay—both beautiful sights. By following elk paths through the low brush, you can take numerous off-trail side trips, often discovering more beautiful views and elk—always a fun surprise. For a bonus, continue hiking the extra half mile past the elk watering area all the way to Tomales Point. The only negative to this trip is that wind and fog occasionally envelop the area in midsummer.

Special Note: It is a violation of federal law to herd, chase, or otherwise harass elk.

**User Groups:** Hikers and horses. Nearby Pierce Ranch (a former working ranch) is accessible to wheelchairs, but Tomales Point Trail is not. No dogs or mountain bikes.

**Permits:** No permits are required. Parking and access are free.

**Maps:** For a free map, write to Point Reyes National Seashore at the address below. For a topographic map, ask the USGS for Tomales.

**Directions:** From U.S. 101 in Marin, take the Sir Francis Drake Boulevard exit and drive about 20 miles west on Sir Francis Drake Boulevard to the town of Olema. Turn right on Highway 1 and drive a short distance to Bear Valley Road. Turn left on Bear Valley Road and drive two miles. Turn left on Sir Francis Drake Highway and drive 5.6 miles to Pierce Ranch Road. Bear right and drive nine miles to the Pierce Ranch parking area and the trailhead.

**Contact:** Superintendent, Point Reyes National Seashore, Point Reyes, CA 94956; Bear Valley Visitors Center, 415/464-5100, fax 415/663-8132, website: www.nps.gov/pore.

## 2 McCLURES BEACH TRAIL
### 1.0 mi / 0.5 hr

**in Point Reyes National Seashore in northwest Marin County**

Map 7.1, page 267

In the divine panorama of Point Reyes, McClures Beach is one easy-to-reach spot that is often overlooked. It sits in the shadow of nearby Pierce Ranch, with its 500-strong elk herd, and many visitors never drive to the road's end, except perhaps to use the restrooms and telephone there. But an easy .5-mile walk will lead you to McClures Beach, where you'll find tidepools to the south and beachfront to the north. The best time to visit is during minus low tides, so you can survey the tidepools and watch all manner of tiny marine creatures playing their war games. Beachcombing along McClures Beach and Driftwood Beach (to the immediate north) during these low tides also can unveil unusual finds. One other thing: The sunsets here can be spectacular, especially during fall and early winter, when the skies often look like a scene from *The Ten Commandments*.

Special Note: Tidepooling at this beach can be dangerous, as incoming tides can cut you off, leaving no way to escape. Consult a tide table, and never turn your back on the waves.

**User Groups:** Hikers only. No dogs, horses, or mountain bikes. No wheelchair facilities.

**Permits:** No permits are required. Parking and access are free.

**Maps:** For a free map, write to Point Reyes National Seashore at the address below. For a topographic map, ask the USGS for Tomales.

**Directions:** From U.S. 101 in Marin, take the Sir Francis Drake Boulevard exit and drive about 20 miles west on Sir Francis Drake Boulevard to the town of Olema. Turn right on Highway 1 and drive a short distance to Bear Valley Road. Turn left on Bear Valley Road and drive two miles. Turn left on Sir Francis Drake Highway and drive 5.6 miles to Pierce Ranch Road. Bear right and drive nine miles to the Pierce Ranch parking area, then turn left and drive .5 mile to the parking area and the trailhead.

**Contact:** Superintendent, Point Reyes National Seashore, Point Reyes, CA 94956; Bear Valley Visitors Center, 415/464-5100, fax 415/663-8132, website: www.nps.gov/pore.

## 3 ABBOTTS LAGOON TRAIL
### 3.2 mi / 1.5 hrs

**in Point Reyes National Seashore in northwest Marin County**

Map 7.1, page 267

What keeps this trail secluded is that a short ridge shields Abbotts Lagoon from the sight of park visitors driving on Pierce Point Road. It is an easy walk to an excellent destination. The trail is surfaced with what is known as "soil cement" and is wheelchair accessible about halfway to the ocean bluff. From the trailhead (look for the restrooms), the trail climbs the low ridge. When you pop over the top, just like that, below you lies Abbotts Lagoon, and beyond that, the Pacific Ocean. The lagoon is an ideal place for novice canoeists and kayakers, providing you don't mind the one-mile portage. Bird-watching is often good here, thanks to a rare mix of waterfowl that require freshwater and seabirds migrating along the coast. If you walk past the lagoon (a distance of 1.6 miles from the trailhead), you'll arrive at Point Reyes Beach, where miles and miles of

sand dunes and untouched waterfront stretch to the north and south.

**User Groups:** Hikers and mountain bikes (bikers on the first mile only; do not cross the bridge). The first portion of the trail is wheelchair accessible with assistance. No dogs or horses.

**Permits:** No permits are required. Parking and access are free.

**Maps:** For a free map, write to Point Reyes National Seashore at the address below. For a topographic map, ask the USGS for Drakes Bay.

**Directions:** From U.S. 101 in Marin, take the Sir Francis Drake Boulevard exit and drive about 20 miles west on Sir Francis Drake Boulevard to the town of Olema. Turn right on Highway 1 and drive a short distance to Bear Valley Road. Turn left on Bear Valley Road and drive two miles. Turn left on Sir Francis Drake Highway and drive 5.6 miles to Pierce Ranch Road. Bear right and drive 3.3 miles to a small parking area with restrooms. The trailhead is on the left side of the road.

**Contact:** Superintendent, Point Reyes National Seashore, Point Reyes, CA 94956; Bear Valley Visitors Center, 415/464-5100, fax 415/663-8132, website: www.nps.gov/pore.

## 4 MARSHALL BEACH TRAIL
### 2.4 mi / 1.25 hrs

**in Point Reyes National Seashore in northwest Marin County**

Map 7.1, page 267

What's the most secluded beach in Marin County? Marshall Beach might just qualify. This pretty spot is set on the demure waters of Tomales Bay, sheltered from north winds by Inverness Ridge. The trailhead tends to be overlooked, because there are no signs directing hikers to it until you reach the trailhead itself. In addition, the beach is overshadowed by Tomales Bay State Park, which you must drive past in order to get here—and many people don't continue driving. The hike is 1.2 miles one-way, taking an elliptical route down into a gulch to a protected cove that helps shelter the beach. It's the kind of place where you can just sit

and watch the water lap gently at the shore. Somehow, that is plenty.

**User Groups:** Hikers, horses, and mountain bikes. No dogs. No wheelchair facilities.

**Permits:** No permits are required. Parking and access are free.

**Maps:** For a free map, write to Point Reyes National Seashore at the address below. For a topographic map, ask the USGS for Tomales.

**Directions:** From U.S. 101 in Marin, take the Sir Francis Drake Boulevard exit and drive about 20 miles west on Sir Francis Drake Boulevard to the town of Olema. Turn right on Highway 1 and drive a short distance to Bear Valley Road. Turn left on Bear Valley Road and drive two miles. Turn left on Sir Francis Drake Highway and drive 5.6 miles to Pierce Ranch Road. Bear right and drive 1.3 miles (just past the entrance road to Tomales Bay State Park, on the right) to Duck Cove/Marshall Beach Road. Turn right and drive 2.6 miles (bear left at the fork) to the parking area for Marshall Beach Trail.

**Contact:** Superintendent, Point Reyes National Seashore, Point Reyes, CA 94956; Bear Valley Visitors Center, 415/464-5100, fax 415/663-8132, website: www.nps.gov/pore.

## 5 JOHNSTONE TRAIL
### 4.5 mi / 2.5 hrs

**in Tomales Bay State Park in northwest Marin County**

Map 7.1, page 267

The highlights of Tomales Bay State Park include Hearts Desire Beach, Indian Beach, Shell Beach, beautiful water views and the chance to hand-launch kayaks or canoes. The best hike for most is this 4.5-mile loop. Make sure you have a map. Some new to the park have missed the turn at the junction of the Johnstone Trail and the Jepson Trail on this recommended route.

From the parking area, start by taking the Johnstone Trail and hiking south along Tomales Bay. Bring a camera, because in the first mile, the picnic area provides a beautiful view of the bay, and the side trip to Pebble Beach is also a gorgeous setting. Continue on the Johnstone Trail, heading west with an easy climb, and then linking to the Jepson Trail. Your return on the Jepson Trail features dense forest and vegetation, with old-growth bishop pines with sprawling limbs. The trip ends with a water view. That's it. A stellar trip.

A must-do side trip is one of the best treasure hunts in the Bay Area, the short walk to Indian Beach. From the parking area, the trail meanders along the pretty shore of Tomales Bay. According to Carlos Porrata, head ranger at the park, this is where visitors have found perfectly crafted arrowheads, ancient bowls, and other Native American artifacts. He reminded that it is illegal, of course, to take any artifact or disturb any archeological site, and that any finds must be immediately reported.

If you have a car-top boat that can be launched by hand, such as a canoe or kayak, then don't leave it behind. Tomales Bay often provides the best flat-water paddling in the Bay Area. If you paddle north along the western shore, you can often spot many elk in shoreline ravines.

**User Groups:** Hikers only. The park headquarters is wheelchair accessible, but the trail is not. No dogs, horses, or mountain bikes.

**Permits:** A day-use fee of $6 is charged at the entrance station.

**Maps:** A small map/brochure is available for a fee at the entrance station to Tomales Bay State Park. For a topographic map, ask the USGS for Tomales.

**Directions:** From U.S. 101 in Marin, take the Sir Francis Drake Boulevard exit and drive about 20 miles west on Sir Francis Drake Boulevard to the town of Olema. Turn right on Highway 1 and drive a short distance to Bear Valley Road. Turn left on Bear Valley Road and drive two miles. Turn left on Sir Francis Drake Highway and drive 5.6 miles to Pierce Ranch Road. Bear right and drive 1.2 miles to the entrance road to Tomales Bay State Park, on the right. Turn right and drive 1.5 miles to the parking area and the trailhead, at Hearts Desire Beach.

**Contact:** Tomales Bay State Park, Star Route,

Inverness, CA 94937, 415/669-1140 or 415/898-4362, fax 415/669-1701, website: www.parks.ca.gov (click on Find A Park).

## 6 ESTERO TRAIL
**7.8 mi / 3.5 hrs**

**in Point Reyes National Seashore in northwest Marin County**

Map 7.1, page 267

The Estero Trail crosses a valley, parallels a bay, ascends a ridge, and leads down to the waterfront, where a perfect, quiet picnic spot awaits. It's an ideal hike for newcomers to Point Reyes National Seashore, providing glimpses of a variety of settings. After parking, Estero Trail starts by dropping down into a small valley, crossing a narrow inlet of Home Bay. The surroundings include pretty, low-lying coastal foothills set at the threshold of Drakes Estero, a drop-dead beautiful tidal lagoon. From here, the trail rises gently along the southeastern flank of the Estero. (If you own your own kayak or canoe, Drakes Estero is one of the prettiest settings in the Bay Area for an easy paddle trek; you can explore the four arms of the lagoon or paddle out to the mouth of the estuary and Limantour Spit.) At 2.4 miles in, you will reach a trail junction. Continue straight on Sunset Beach Trail, where it is an easy 1.5-miles down to Sunset Beach. This is a great picnic site for a trail lunch, set inside the mouth of the Estero, about a mile from the Pacific Ocean. This makes it a 7.8-mile round-trip. But there is a good option. When you reach the trail junction with Sunset Beach Trail (straight), an option is to instead turn left (south). A 15-minute climb will take you to a short ridge and the junction of Drakes Head Trail. Here you get a sweeping view of Drakes Bay, Estero de Limantour, and more foothills—well worth the effort. All of this is open to mountain bikes. Because it is set in foothill grasslands, visibility is good, so there are no surprises or uncomfortable encounters between hikers and bikers. Those on bikes have plenty of time to slow, stop, and give way to hikers, which is trail policy.

**User Groups:** Hikers, horses, and mountain bikes. The first two miles are wheelchair accessible, with assistance. No dogs.

**Permits:** No permits are required. Parking and access are free.

**Maps:** For a free map, write to Point Reyes National Seashore at the address below. For a topographic map, ask the USGS for Drakes Bay.

**Directions:** From U.S. 101 in Marin, take the Sir Francis Drake Boulevard exit and drive about 20 miles west on Sir Francis Drake Boulevard to the town of Olema. Turn right on Highway 1 and drive a short distance to Bear Valley Road. Turn left on Bear Valley Road and drive two miles. Turn left on Sir Francis Drake Highway and drive 7.5 miles to Estero Road, on the left. Turn left and drive one mile to the parking area.

**Contact:** Superintendent, Point Reyes National Seashore, Point Reyes, CA 94956; Bear Valley Visitors Center, 415/464-5100, fax 415/663-8132, website: www.nps.gov/pore.

## 7 SOUTH BEACH TRAIL
**0.1–20.0 mi / 0.25 hr–1 day**

**in Point Reyes National Seashore in northwest Marin County**

Map 7.1, page 267

If you desire miles of untouched beachfront, you've come to the right place. The Point Reyes beach extends for nearly 10 miles, all of it pristine with white, foaming surf that rolls on endlessly. An initial short trail leads from the parking area to South Beach, about three miles north of the Point Reyes Lighthouse. The beach makes a good picnic site and is one of the few places at Point Reyes where you can take a leashed dog. (Note that dogs may not be allowed if marine mammals are present.) For the best stroll, walk south for about a mile to an expanse of sand dunes. Or walk as far as you'd like and turn around. It is wise to call ahead for weather conditions, as low fog is common, especially during the summer. A word of warning: Do not swim or bodysurf here. This stretch of coast is known for its

treacherous undertow, the kind that can trap even the strongest swimmers, pulling people under and pushing them out to sea, despite their attempts to swim back to the beach.

**User Groups:** Hikers, dogs, and horses. No mountain bikes. No wheelchair facilities.

**Permits:** No permits are required. Parking and access are free.

**Maps:** For a free map, write to Point Reyes National Seashore at the address below. For a topographic map, ask the USGS for Drakes Bay.

**Directions:** From U.S. 101 in Marin, take the Sir Francis Drake Boulevard exit and drive about 20 miles west on Sir Francis Drake Boulevard to the town of Olema. Turn right on Highway 1 and drive a short distance to Bear Valley Road. Turn left on Bear Valley Road and drive two miles. Turn left on Sir Francis Drake Highway and drive 11.6 miles to the access turnoff for the South Beach parking lot, on the right. Turn right and drive to the parking lot for South Beach.

**Contact:** Superintendent, Point Reyes National Seashore, Point Reyes, CA 94956; Bear Valley Visitors Center, 415/464-5100, fax 415/663-8132, website: www.nps.gov/pore.

## 🔟 POINT REYES LIGHTHOUSE
**0.8 mi / 0.5 hr**

**in Point Reyes National Seashore in northwest Marin County**

**Map 7.1, page 267**

There may be no better place on land from which to watch migrating whales. From Point Reyes, you scan the ocean, searching for what looks like a little puff of smoke on the water's surface: a whale spout. When you find one, zoom in closer. If you are lucky, you might even get a tail salute. The chances are good, because 22,000 gray whales migrate past here every winter on what is called the Great Whale Highway, located just offshore of Point Reyes. The trail to the lookout is short and paved, and it includes a dramatic descent on a railed stairway. On the way back, of course, you face a modest climb. Those out of shape will even

find it steep, so three rest stops are available for some folks to stop to pant a bit. On clear weekends, particularly in winter, the place can be crowded. A fence on the edge of the cliff keeps visitors from falling overboard from one of the most dramatic coastal lookouts anywhere. Sunsets here are unforgettable.

**User Groups:** Hikers and mountain bikes (bikes are restricted from the stairs and not advised). No dogs or horses.

**Permits:** No permits are required. Parking and access are free. From January through April, a shuttle bus is required from Drakes Beach to Point Reyes Lighthouse or Chimney Rock Staging Areas ($6 per person, free for those under 16).

**Maps:** For a free map, write to Point Reyes National Seashore at the address below. For a topographic map, ask the USGS for Drakes Bay.

**Directions:** From U.S. 101 in Marin, take the Sir Francis Drake Boulevard exit and drive about 20 miles west on Sir Francis Drake Boulevard to the town of Olema. Turn right on Highway 1 and drive a short distance to Bear Valley Road. Turn left on Bear Valley Road and drive two miles. Turn left on Sir Francis Drake Highway and drive 17.6 miles. The road dead-ends at the parking area for the Point Reyes Lighthouse.

**Contact:** Superintendent, Point Reyes National Seashore, Point Reyes, CA 94956; Bear Valley Visitors Center, 415/464-5100, fax 415/663-8132, website: www.nps.gov/pore.

## 🔟 CHIMNEY ROCK TRAIL
**2.8 mi / 1.25 hrs**

**in Point Reyes National Seashore in northwest Marin County**

**Map 7.1, page 267**

A lot of visitors miss out on Chimney Rock because of its proximity to the Point Reyes Lighthouse, the feature destination of the national seashore. But the Chimney Rock lookout is easy to reach (about a half-hour hike), and the trail accesses a cutoff to a vista that is nearly the equal of that from the lighthouse. From the parking area, the trail is routed 1.4

miles to land's end. Chimney Rock, or at least what is supposed to be Chimney Rock, sits right offshore. Just beyond the halfway point to land's end, hikers can take a short cutoff trail that provides great views of the Pacific Ocean. During the winter, especially between late December and March, this is a great spot to watch for the spouts of migrating whales. Another bonus is that on the way back, you can complete the last .8 mile on a loop trail, so you don't have to walk the same route you followed on the way in. At the end of the trail, where a wooden guardrail keeps people from falling over the edge, look down at an assortment of coastal rocks and ask yourself, "So, which one of those suckers is Chimney Rock?"

**User Groups:** Hikers and mountain bikes. The first .25 mile of the trail is wheelchair accessible. No dogs or horses.

**Permits:** No permits are required. Parking and access are free.

**Maps:** For a free map, write to Point Reyes National Seashore at the address below. For a topographic map, ask the USGS for Drakes Bay.

**Directions:** From U.S. 101 in Marin, take the Sir Francis Drake Boulevard exit and drive about 20 miles west on Sir Francis Drake Boulevard to the town of Olema. Turn right on Highway 1 and drive a short distance to Bear Valley Road. Turn left on Bear Valley Road and drive two miles. Turn left on Sir Francis Drake Highway and drive 17.4 miles to Chimney Rock Road, on the left. Turn left and drive one mile to the parking area and trailhead.

**Contact:** Superintendent, Point Reyes National Seashore, Point Reyes, CA 94956; Bear Valley Visitors Center, 415/464-5100, fax 415/663-8132, website: www.nps.gov/pore.

## 10 SIR FRANCIS DRAKE TRAIL
### 1.9 mi / 1.0 hr

**in Point Reyes National Seashore in northwest Marin County**

Map 7.1, page 267

This spot is not exactly a secret. In fact, you might as well stand on the Golden Gate Bridge

with a megaphone and announce its existence to the world. At the trailhead, for instance, you will discover a large parking lot and visitors center, complete with exhibits, maps, and books (maybe even this one). The trail traces the back of the arcing beaches along Drakes Bay, providing scenic lookouts onto the bay's protected waters. The trail continues to the mouth of Drakes Estero, then returns via an inland loop that includes a short climb up, then down to a waterfront bluff. This is one of the more popular hikes at Point Reyes National Seashore, and why not? It is an easy walk, provides great scenic beauty, and traces three habitats: beach frontage, the mouth of a lagoon, and hillside bluffs.

**User Groups:** Hikers and mountain bikes. No dogs or horses. No wheelchair facilities.

**Permits:** No permits are required. Parking and access are free.

**Maps:** For a free map, write to Point Reyes National Seashore at the address below. For a topographic map, ask the USGS for Drakes Bay.

**Directions:** From U.S. 101 in Marin, take the Sir Francis Drake Boulevard exit and drive about 20 miles west on Sir Francis Drake Boulevard to the town of Olema. Turn right on Highway 1 and drive a short distance to Bear Valley Road. Turn left on Bear Valley Road and drive two miles. Turn left on Sir Francis Drake Highway, drive 11.1 miles, and look for the sign indicating a left turn to a visitors center. Turn left and drive 1.2 miles to the parking lot at the Kenneth Patrick Visitors Center and the trailhead.

**Contact:** Superintendent, Point Reyes National Seashore, Point Reyes, CA 94956; Bear Valley Visitors Center, 415/464-5100, fax 415/663-8132, website: www.nps.gov/pore.

## 11 MUDDY HOLLOW LOOP
### 7.1 mi / 3.25 hrs

**in Point Reyes National Seashore at Limantour Beach in northwest Marin County**

Map 7.1, page 267

This can be a wondrous coastal loop hike. The Muddy Hollow Loop is routed through various settings and terrain but starts and ends right on the beach. The most striking element of the hike is witnessing the regenerative powers of the land, as these coastal foothills—ravaged by wildfire in October 1995—are now revegetating and blooming. This is also the best place in the park to see the exotic fallow deer, which look like half moose and half elk, often pure white, with strange antlers. Elk have also been transplanted here and are forming a new herd. Finally, this is one of the best places in California to see wild iris bloom in April and early May. From the trailhead at Limantour Beach, hike north up Muddy Hollow, a shallow valley that drains rainfall into the Estero de Limantour. After 1.4 miles, turn left on Muddy Hollow "Road" and hike 2.1 miles. All of this area was devoured by the wildfire in October 1995. Here the trail crosses the coastal hills, climbing to about 300 feet, then dropping into another valley and crossing Glenbrook Creek. Seeing the remnants of fire damage being overcome by budding plant life here can leave a profound and lasting impact. Turn left at the Glenbrook/Estero Trail, which leads back to the parking area over the course of 3.9 miles. The latter sector traces the shore of the Estero, a serene setting on calm, blue-sky days. From the Limantour parking area, this is also an excellent jump-off spot for canoeing and kayaking. The Estero de Limantour is protected by the narrow Limantour sand spit.

**User Groups:** Hikers and horses. No dogs, mountain bikes, or wheelchair access.

**Permits:** No permits are required. Parking and access are free.

**Maps:** For a free map, write to Point Reyes National Seashore at the address below. For a topographic map, ask the USGS for Drakes Bay.

**Directions:** From U.S. 101 in Marin, take the Sir Francis Drake Boulevard exit and drive about 20 miles west on Sir Francis Drake Boulevard to the town of Olema. Turn right on Highway 1 and drive 100 yards. Turn left on Bear Valley Road and drive north for two miles (you pass the visitors center on your left) to Li-

mantour Road. Turn left and drive 7.6 miles to Limantour Beach and the trailhead.

**Contact:** Superintendent, Point Reyes National Seashore, Point Reyes, CA 94956; Bear Valley Visitors Center, 415/464-5100, fax 415/663-8132, website: www.nps.gov/pore.

## 12 COAST TRAIL
### 16.1 mi one-way / 2.0-plus days

in Point Reyes National Seashore in northwest Marin County

**Map 7.1, page 267**

Of the handful of overnight hiking trips available in the Bay Area, Coast Trail provides the most extended tour into a land of charm. Located north of Bolinas on the remote Marin coast, the trail offers camps at ocean bluffs, a beach with sculptured rocks and tidepools, bluff-top lookouts with a chance to see passing whales, a rare waterfall from an ocean bluff that pours like a fountain to a beach and then runs into the ocean, and coastal freshwater lakes. This continuous backcountry route is 16.1 miles long, enough to allow lingering hikers to spend a weekend at it, and short enough for the ambitious to tackle in a single day. There are only a few catches: You need a hiking partner who will double as a shuttle driver so you can leave a car at each end of the trail. You'll need to come prepared to cook your food using a small backpack stove, not a campfire. Tents are recommended, because the coastal weather is the most unpredictable in the Bay Area—clear, calm, and warm one day, then suddenly foggy, windy, moist, and clammy the next.

The best trailhead for Coast Trail is at the Point Reyes Hostel, from where you will hike north to south, keeping the wind at your back and out of your face. The first camp, Coast Camp, is an easy 2.8 miles, ideal for those heading out on a Friday evening after work. As you hike in, you'll have a panoramic view of the reborn coastal foothills that were burned in the wildfire of October 1995; the campground and trail were untouched. The sound of ocean waves will send you to sleep the first night—or in some sensitive cases, it might keep you awake.

The next day you will hike south, getting glimpses along the way of Sculptured Beach, with its magnificent rock stacks and tunnels. There are great cutoff trails along Coast Trail to Sculptured Beach, Kelham Beach, and Arch Rock. The Coast Trail continues south to Wildcat Camp, set on a bluff overlooking the ocean, making day two a hike of 7.8 miles.

On day three, figure on a 5.5-mile closeout with plenty of sideshows. You will hike past a series of coastal lakes—including nearby Wildcat Lake and little Ocean Lake—and you'll have the opportunity to see Alamere Falls, a drop-dead gorgeous waterfall that tumbles to the beach. After climbing to a short ridge, you will skirt above Pelican Lake and along the northern shore of Bass Lake. The trail then heads up a coastal hill, topping out at 563 feet, before lateraling down a canyon and back to ocean bluffs. Following the trail, you turn left and in a mile arrive at the Palomarin trailhead. You will be ready to reach your shuttle car and head for the barn. If you have a shuttle partner, this is one of the Bay Area's greatest hikes.

**User Groups:** Hikers and horses. Mountain bikes permitted only from the Laguna trailhead to the Coast Campground and are otherwise prohibited. Partially accessible to wheelchair users who have assistance. No dogs.

**Permits:** Parking and access are free, but camping requires a reservation, and there is a $12 fee per night per campsite for up to eight people.

**Maps:** For a free map, write to Point Reyes National Seashore at the address below. For topographic maps, ask the USGS for Inverness and Double Point.

**Directions:** To the northern trailhead from U.S. 101 in Marin, take the Sir Francis Drake Boulevard exit and drive about 20 miles west on Sir Francis Drake Boulevard to the town of Olema. Turn right on Highway 1 and drive about 100 yards. Turn left at Bear Valley Road and drive north for two miles (take the cutoff on the left to the Bear Valley Visitors Center to get your permits) to Limantour Road. Turn left and drive six miles. Turn left on the access road for the Point Reyes Hostel and continue to where it ends at the parking lot. After parking, hike back to the hostel and look for the trailhead on the left (west, across the road from the hostel).

To the southern trailhead from U.S. 101 in Marin, see the directions for Alamere Falls Trail (in this chapter).

**Contact:** Superintendent, Point Reyes National Seashore, Point Reyes, CA 94956; Bear Valley Visitors Center, 415/464-5100 or 415/663-8054 (camping reservations), fax 415/663-8132, website: www.nps.gov/pore.

# 13 LAGUNA LOOP TRAIL
## 5.5 mi / 2.5 hrs

**in Point Reyes National Seashore in northwest Marin County**

Map 7.1, page 267

The Laguna Loop Trail allows hikers to witness an amazing process known as "the genesis effect," in which land devoured by fire is reborn. The trailhead is just .2 mile down the road from the Point Reyes Hostel, adjacent to the park's Environmental Education Center. From there, the trail continues 1.8 miles up to Inverness Ridge, with great views of Drakes Bay along the way. At the ridge, turn right and hike .7 mile toward Mount Wittenberg, which at 1,407 feet is the highest point at Point Reyes National Seashore. On the north flank of Mount Wittenberg, hikers should turn right on the Fire Lane Trail, which loops back around for three miles to the Laguna trailhead. This excellent loop hike entails a bit of a climb and offers Pacific lookouts, yet it is short enough to complete in a few hours.

**User Groups:** Hikers and horses. Mountain bikes are permitted only from the Laguna trailhead to the Coast Campground and are otherwise prohibited. No dogs. No wheelchair facilities.

**Permits:** No permits are required. Parking and access are free.

**Maps:** For a free map, write to Point Reyes National Seashore at the address below. For a topographic map, ask the USGS for Inverness.
**Directions:** From U.S. 101 in Marin, take the Sir Francis Drake Boulevard exit and drive about 20 miles west on Sir Francis Drake Boulevard to the town of Olema. Turn right on Highway 1 and drive about 100 yards. Turn left at Bear Valley Road and drive north for two miles to Limantour Road. Turn left and drive six miles. Turn left on the access road for the Point Reyes Hostel and drive .2 mile past the hostel to the parking area and trailhead (on the right side of the road).
**Contact:** Superintendent, Point Reyes National Seashore, Point Reyes, CA 94956; Bear Valley Visitors Center, 415/464-5100, fax 415/663-8132, website: www.nps.gov/pore.

## 14 MOUNT WITTENBERG LOOP
**4.5 mi / 2.5 hrs**

**in Point Reyes National Seashore near Olema in northwest Marin County**

Map 7.1, page 267

This is one of the best short hikes in the entire Point Reyes National Seashore, providing a route through deep forest, a climb with a steady grade, and magnificent lookouts of Drakes Bay to the west and the Olema Valley to the east. The destination is Mount Wittenberg (at 1,407 feet, the highest point in the park), but the best views are from the ridge just west of the rounded summit. After parking at Bear Valley Visitors Center, where there's a huge parking lot, start the trip by taking Bear Valley Trail, located at the south end of the parking area. Hike on Bear Valley Trail for just .2 mile, and then bear right at the cutoff for Sky Trail. From here, it is a 1.4-mile hike with a climb of 1,200 feet at a steady grade, but it is easily handled by those in decent condition. You'll pass through old-growth forest and lush ravines, with occasional peephole-like lookouts to Olema Valley. It rises to the foot of Mount Wittenberg, and with another 100-foot climb, a cutoff trail takes hikers to the rounded summit. The views are

not the greatest from the top, but instead from just nearby. From here, return to Sky Trail and walk southwest .4 mile to Meadow Trail. In the process, there are dramatic views of Drakes Bay to the west and some hidden meadows to the east, where white deer can often be spotted. This is a must-do camera shot. You'll also have a panoramic shot of the coastal foothills, which are recovering from the wildfire of October 1995. From Meadow Trail, it is an easy downhill tromp of 1.5 miles back down to Bear Valley Trail. There you turn left, and the trail widens and flattens; then you'll walk out .8 mile to the parking lot. There you have it—to paradise and back in just a few hours.
**User Groups:** Hikers and horses. No dogs or mountain bikes. No wheelchair facilities.
**Permits:** No permits are required. Parking and access are free.
**Maps:** For a free map, write to Point Reyes National Seashore at the address below. For a topographic map, ask the USGS for Inverness.
**Directions:** From U.S. 101 in Marin, take the Sir Francis Drake Boulevard exit and drive about 20 miles west on Sir Francis Drake Boulevard to the town of Olema. Turn right on Highway 1 and drive about 100 yards. Turn left at Bear Valley Road and drive north .7 mile. Turn left at the Seashore Information sign and drive to the parking lot for the Bear Valley Visitors Center. The trailhead is at the south end of the parking lot.
**Contact:** Superintendent, Point Reyes National Seashore, Point Reyes, CA 94956; Bear Valley Visitors Center, 415/464-5100, fax 415/663-8132, website: www.nps.gov/pore.

## 15 BEAR VALLEY TRAIL
**8.2 mi / 4.0 hrs**

**in Point Reyes National Seashore near Olema in northwest Marin County**

Map 7.1, page 267

The Bear Valley Trail has all the ingredients needed to earn a 10 rating, but, alas, doesn't quite make it. Starting with a pretty route through forests, it leads past Divide Meadow to Bear

Valley, then down along Coast Creek to the beach, Arch Rock, and the Sea Tunnel, where the views are marvelous. So, you ask, why is it rated a 7? The answer is that the trail is actually a park service road made of compressed rock, and it gets a ton of traffic, including bicycles. This is the most heavily used trail in Point Reyes National Seashore. The best element is that it is wheelchair accessible and is, in fact, one of the prettiest wheelchair routes in California. Just put it in power drive, for there's a modest 215-foot climb from park headquarters to Divide Meadow. Wheelchairs and bikes are permitted to Glen Camp Trail, 3.2 miles from park headquarters. After that, you hike down the Coast Creek drainage on a .7-mile trek to the beach.

**User Groups:** Hikers, mountain bikes (first three miles only), and horses (weekdays only). The 1.5-mile trail to Divide Meadow is wheelchair accessible but requires a significant amount of assistance. No dogs.

**Permits:** No permits are required. Parking and access are free.

**Maps:** For a free map, write to Point Reyes National Seashore at the address below. For a topographic map, ask the USGS for Inverness.

**Directions:** From U.S. 101 in Marin, take the Sir Francis Drake Boulevard exit and drive about 20 miles west on Sir Francis Drake Boulevard to the town of Olema. Turn right on Highway 1 and drive about 100 yards. Turn left at Bear Valley Road and drive north .7 mile. Turn left at the Seashore Information sign and drive to the parking lot for the Bear Valley Visitors Center.

**Contact:** Superintendent, Point Reyes National Seashore, Point Reyes, CA 94956; Bear Valley Visitors Center, 415/464-5100, fax 415/663-8132, website: www.nps.gov/pore.

## 16 RIFT ZONE TRAIL
**5.2 mi one-way / 2.25 hrs**

in Point Reyes National Seashore near Olema in northwest Marin County

Map 7.1, page 267

Here's some advice to heed: Don't let school interfere with your education. Well, the Rift Zone Trail provides a lesson from the University of Nature, with one of the world's classic examples of an earthquake fault line: the San Andreas Fault. From park headquarters, it's a 5.2-mile one-way hike to the Five Brooks trailhead—best completed with a shuttle car. Along the way, the trail traces along Olema Creek, where horizontal movement of 21 feet was recorded during the 1906 earthquake. Much evidence of earthquake activity is visible on this trail, including parallel ridges, but the most obvious sign is the clear difference in vegetation types on each side of the fault. The trail gets heavy use, has no difficult grades, and requires only a few short ups and downs near its southern junction with the Five Brooks trailhead.

**User Groups:** Hikers and horses. No dogs or mountain bikes. No wheelchair facilities.

**Permits:** No permits are required. Parking and access are free.

**Maps:** For a free map, write to Point Reyes National Seashore at the address below. For a topographic map, ask the USGS for Inverness.

**Directions:** From U.S. 101 in Marin, take the Sir Francis Drake Boulevard exit and drive about 20 miles west on Sir Francis Drake Boulevard to the town of Olema. Turn right on Highway 1 and drive about 100 yards. Turn left at Bear Valley Road and drive north .7 mile. Turn left at the Seashore Information sign and drive to the parking lot for the Bear Valley Visitors Center.

**Contact:** Superintendent, Point Reyes National Seashore, Point Reyes, CA 94956; Bear Valley Visitors Center, 415/464-5100, fax 415/663-8132, website: www.nps.gov/pore.

## 17 OLEMA VALLEY
**5.3 mi one-way / 2.25 hrs**

in Point Reyes National Seashore south of Olema in northwest Marin County

Map 7.1, page 267

The phenomenon of two parallel creeks running in opposite directions is the featured attraction of the Olema Valley Trail, which starts at the Five Brooks trailhead (elevation 180 feet)

and runs adjacent to the San Andreas Fault rift zone. Two earth plates moving in opposite directions created the fault line and resulted in the strange marvel of Olema Creek and Pine Gulch Creek—the creeks are relatively parallel, but run in opposite directions. From the trailhead, it's 1.3 miles to the headwaters of Pine Gulch Creek. From there, hike southward for four miles along the pretty creek before the trail ends at Highway 1. Most hikers turn back long before that, but with a partner and a shuttle car, it makes a great one-way hike, 5.3 miles in all.

**User Groups:** Hikers, horses, and mountain bikes. No dogs. No wheelchair facilities.

**Permits:** No permits are required. Parking and access are free.

**Maps:** For a free map, write to Point Reyes National Seashore at the address below. For a topographic map, ask the USGS for Bolinas.

**Directions:** From U.S. 101 in Marin, take the Sir Francis Drake Boulevard exit and drive about 20 miles west on Sir Francis Drake Boulevard to the town of Olema. Turn left on Highway 1 and drive 3.6 miles to the Five Brooks trailhead, located on the west side of the road.

**Contact:** Superintendent, Point Reyes National Seashore, Point Reyes, CA 94956; Bear Valley Visitors Center, 415/464-5100, fax 415/663-8132, website: www.nps.gov/pore.

### 18 ALAMERE FALLS TRAIL
**8.4 mi / 4.0 hrs**

**in Point Reyes National Seashore northwest of Bolinas**

**Map 7.1, page 267**

The water from Alamere Falls tumbles down Alamere Creek and over an ocean bluff, cascading 40 feet to the beach below and into the Pacific Ocean. It is one of the few ocean-bluff waterfalls anywhere, and after winter rain, it is amazing how full, big, and beautiful it can become. A favorite thing to do is to lie prone on the rock right at the brink of the falls, peering over the cliffs, watching the water droplets

fall to the plunge p[...] course of the water thro[...] provides a fast-moving mos[...] ing point is the Palomarin t[...] which you'll hike the southern e[...] Trail. The trail is routed along the oc[...] about a mile, then heads up into the coa[...] hills to an elevation of about 500 feet and back down westward for two miles to the falls' access point. In the process, you will skirt the northern end of Bass Lake, and a mile later, you'll be along the ridge overlooking larger Pelican Lake. When you reach Alamere Creek, there is an unsigned cutoff route on the southern side of the creek. Although not maintained by the park, many people take this well-worn path down to Alamere Creek and the waterfall. Rangers urge visitors to hike instead to Wildcat Camp, drop down to the beach, and hike south on the beach to the base of Alamere Falls for the best views.

**User Groups:** Hikers and horses. No dogs or mountain bikes. No wheelchair facilities.

**Permits:** No permits are required. Parking and access are free.

**Maps:** For a free map, write to Point Reyes National Seashore at the address below. For topographic maps, ask the USGS for Bolinas and Double Point.

**Directions:** From U.S. 101 in Marin, take the Sir Francis Drake Boulevard exit and drive about 20 miles west on Sir Francis Drake Boulevard to the town of Olema and Highway 1. Turn left on Highway 1 and drive 9.3 miles to Olema-Bolinas Road on the right (if the sign is missing—a common event—note that a white ranch house is opposite the turn). Turn right on Olema-Bolinas Road and drive 2.1 miles to Mesa Road. Turn right and drive six miles (past an area known as The Towers because of all the antennas) to the parking area and Palomarin trailhead.

**Contact:** Superintendent, Point Reyes National Seashore, Point Reyes, CA 94956; Bear Valley Visitors Center, 415/464-5100, fax 415/663-8132, website: www.nps.gov/pore.

Park). The trailhead is on the left side of the road. Park along the road.

**Contact:** Golden Gate National Recreation Area, Fort Mason, Building 201, San Francisco, CA 94123, 415/561-4700, fax 415/331-1428, website: www.nps.gov/goga.

## 20 BARNABE PEAK LOOP
**6.0 mi / 3.5 hrs**

**in Samuel P. Taylor State Park west of San Rafael**

Map 7.1, page 267

Even well-known state parks can hide surprises and oft-missed, gemlike destinations. That's how it is at Samuel P. Taylor State Park, where a hidden waterfall and surprise mountaintop lookout—Barnabe Peak, at 1,466 feet—are the rewards for those willing to search out the extra mile (literally). Samuel P. Taylor is located along Sir Francis Drake Boulevard in western Marin, best known for its stand of redwoods and the lush undergrowth in the canyon along the headwaters of Lagunitas Creek. The park covers 2,700 acres and features excellent hiking, biking, and camping. But most people miss the best of it.

The trip starts by driving west on Sir Francis Drake, the pretty two-laner that leaves Marin's traffic for the redwood forests of the coastal foothills. Most turn left at the main entrance and parking area for the park's headquarters, and for access to campgrounds and a hike-in/bike-in site. For most, this is all they will ever know about this park.

Instead of parking at headquarters, drive one mile west from the park entrance on Sir Francis Drake and look for the dirt pullout parking area on the shoulder of the left side of the road. To find it, look for the small paved access road for the Devil's Gulch Horse Camp, on the right side. Park in the dirt pullout on the road's shoulder on the left, then walk across Sir Francis Drake and hike up Devil's Gulch Horse Camp access road for a short distance to a trailhead on your right, overlooking Devil's Gulch Creek. Thus starts a great adventure.

ing landscape once ... d slope and Kent Lake to the east, Olema Valley and Inverness Ridge to the west, and Bolinas Lagoon and the Pacific Ocean to the south. The trail crosses atop Bolinas Ridge, through some of the most remote land in the Golden Gate National Recreation Area. The trailhead near Olema starts with a 700-foot climb in the first 2.5 miles. Many hikers call it quits here, stopping to enjoy the view, then turning around and heading home. If you continue, though, you will discover that the trail keeps climbing to 1,329 feet in the first four miles. From that point on, the hike becomes much easier, with only moderate drops and ascents over the last 6.2 miles to the trail's end, on Bolinas-Fairfax Road. Mountain biking is permitted, but hikers need not fear: The trail is not only wide enough for everyone, but has very few hidden turns. Some people (especially bicyclists) prefer to complete this trail in the opposite direction in order to avoid the climb, but done in this direction, you need a rear-view mirror for the best views.

**User Groups:** Hikers, dogs, horses, and mountain bikes. No wheelchair facilities.

**Permits:** No permits are required. Parking and access are free.

**Maps:** For a free map, write to Point Reyes National Seashore at the address below. For topographic maps, ask the USGS for Inverness, San Geronimo, and Bolinas.

**Directions:** From U.S. 101 in Marin, take the Sir Francis Drake Boulevard exit. Turn west on this road and drive 18 miles (3.4 miles past the entrance station to Samuel P. Taylor State

From here, what awaits you is a six-mile loop hike with a 1,300-foot climb to Barnabe Peak (1,466 feet), with spectacular views on clear days of the Marin coast and western foothills. In the process, you will pass a cutoff trail that is routed for a half mile into a canyon to Stairstep Falls.

With a map in hand from park headquarters, the loop hike is easily traced. From the trailhead at Devil's Gulch, take the trail into the canyon and cross the creek on the small bridge. Take the signed left turn for Bill's Trail (also signed for Barnabe Peak). The hike starts off as a romp; it's an easy climb in forest for about a half hour to the cutoff trail for Stairstep Falls, on the left. After heavy rains, seeing this waterfall is a must-do trip for most. It goes dry in summer, but when fed by storm runoff, it creates a stepped cascade in a deep canyon that runs about 35 to 40 feet. At the base of the falls is wood debris that is slippery and dangerous, and hikers should stay clear.

If the weather is clear, most will be eager for the climb up to Barnabe Peak. Back at Bill's Trail, the hike gets steeper as you climb out of the canyon. Switchbacks help the grade, and eventually you will top the forest and reach a service road. Here you turn left and reach the lookout in about five minutes. An old lookout tower is positioned here, but there is no access. From the top, you get a sweeping lookout that spans from Mount Tamalpais to Point Reyes. Most will plan a picnic at the base of the old tower.

To return, most take the quickest route possible—after all, you got what you came for. Do that by taking the fire road, a fast two-mile drop back to the bottom.

**User Groups:** Hikers, dogs, and mountain bikes (bikes are not permitted on spur trails). No horses.

**Permits:** Free parking is available along the road. A state park day-use fee of $6 per vehicle is charged at the entrance station.

**Maps:** A small map/brochure is available for a fee at the entrance station to Samuel P. Tay-

lor State Park. For a topographic map, ask the USGS for San Geronimo.

**Directions:** To park headquarters: From U.S. 101 in Marin, take the Sir Francis Drake Boulevard exit. Turn west and drive 14.5 miles to the park entrance, on the left.

To Devil's Gulch trailhead: From park headquarters, drive west for one mile to the dirt pullout, on the left side of the road (across from the paved access road for Devil's Gulch Horse Camp). Park, cross the road, and walk up the access road to the trailhead, on the right.

**Contact:** Samuel P. Taylor State Park, P.O. Box 251, Lagunitas, CA 94938, 415/488-9897, fax 415/488-4315; Marin District Headquarters, 415/898-4362, website: www.parks.ca.gov (click on Find A Park).

## 21 PIONEER TREE TRAIL
### 2.0 mi / 1.0 hr

**in Samuel P. Taylor State Park west of San Rafael**

Map 7.1, page 267

If you like big trees and a simple, quiet walk, Pioneer Tree Trail in Samuel P. Taylor State Park will provide it. This loop circles through the park's prize grove of coastal redwoods, the species that produces the tallest trees in the world. The trailhead is at the south side of Lagunitas Creek, at the Redwood Grove Picnic Area, about .25 mile from park headquarters. From there, hike up Wildcat Canyon, then across to the Irving Creek drainage, and follow that creek down near its confluence with Lagunitas Creek. The last .5 mile traces the southern edge of the creek back to the picnic area. Surrounded by the scent of redwoods, it's a pleasant hike on a soft dirt trail and includes a 400-foot climb and drop. Bicycles are prohibited on this route from all but the .5-mile service road along Lagunitas Creek.

**User Groups:** Hikers only. No dogs, horses, or mountain bikes.

**Permits:** A state park day-use fee of $6 per vehicle is charged at the entrance station.

**Maps:** A small map/brochure is available for

a fee at the entrance station to Samuel P. Taylor State Park. For a topographic map, ask the USGS for San Geronimo.

**Directions:** From U.S. 101 in Marin, take the Sir Francis Drake Boulevard exit. Turn west on this road and drive 14.5 miles to the park entrance, on the left.

**Contact:** Samuel P. Taylor State Park, P.O. Box 251, Lagunitas, CA 94938, 415/488-9897, fax 415/488-4315; Marin District Headquarters, 415/898-4362, website: www.parks.ca.gov (click on Find A Park).

## 22 KENT DAM TRAIL
**1.8 mi / 1.0 hr**

**in northwest Marin County west of San Rafael**

Map 7.1, page 267

Most people are astounded the first time they see Kent Lake, for they have no idea such a huge lake is tucked away in a Marin canyon. But here it is, nearly four miles from north to south, with an additional large arm extending east into Big Carson Creek. One reason the lake remains little known to outsiders is that the parking at the trailhead is quite poor—just a few spaces along Sir Francis Drake Boulevard. From there, hike on a ranch road along Lagunitas Creek for about a mile, arriving at the east side of Peters Dam. By damming the canyon on Lagunitas Creek, the Marin Water District created this massive lake and at the same time annihilated the runs of steelhead and silver salmon by dewatering the stream and blocking the migratory path to spawning areas. No water contact is permitted, but quite a few people go swimming here anyway in the summer. Some get caught and cited when water district officials make the occasional patrol. Fishing is only fair for bass, and the Department of Fish and Game never makes stocks.

**User Groups:** Hikers, dogs, and mountain bikes. No horses. No wheelchair facilities.

**Permits:** No permits are required. Groups are limited to 19 people. Parking and access are free.

**Maps:** This trail is included on a free map of Point Reyes National Seashore (see address below). For topographic maps, ask the USGS for San Geronimo and Bolinas.

**Directions:** From U.S. 101 in Marin, take the Sir Francis Drake Boulevard exit. Turn west on this road and drive about 12 miles, just past Shafter Bridge, which spans Paper Mill Creek. Park here and look for the locked gate at the entrance to the trailhead, on the left.

**Contact:** Sky Oaks Ranger Station, 415/945-1181; Marin Municipal Water District, 220 Nellen Avenue, Corte Madera, CA 94925, 415/945-1195, website: www.marinwater.org; Superintendent, Point Reyes National Seashore, Point Reyes, CA 94956.

## 23 SHORELINE TRAIL
**5.0 mi / 2.5 hrs**

**in China Camp State Park east of San Rafael**

Map 7.1, page 267

The Shoreline Trail is the best introduction to China Camp State Park a hiker could ask for. From the well-signed trailhead at the parking area, the trail meanders along the shore of San Pablo Bay, bordered by undisturbed hills on one side and waterfront on the other. The first mile provides good lookouts across the bay; the last .5 mile crosses a meadow then runs adjacent to tidal areas, marshes, and wetlands—home to many species of waterfowl. The hike doesn't involve serious elevation gains or losses, so you won't face any surprise climbs. An option on the return trip is to take Miwok Fire Trail, which loops back to headquarters with a 300-foot climb and drop.

**User Groups:** Hikers, horses, and mountain bikes. No dogs. No wheelchair facilities.

**Permits:** No permits are required. A state park day-use fee of $5 per vehicle is charged at the entrance station.

**Maps:** A small map/brochure is available for a fee at park headquarters or by contacting the state parks district office at the address below. For a topographic map, ask the USGS for San Quentin.

**Directions:** From U.S. 101 in San Rafael, take the North San Pedro exit and drive east for four miles to the park entrance.

**Contact:** China Camp State Park, 415/456-0766; California State Parks, Marin District, 7665 Redwood Boulevard, Suite 150, Novato, CA 94945, 415/898-4362, fax 415/893-1583, website: www.parks.ca.gov (click on Find A Park).

## 24 McNEAR'S RIDGE/ PATRICK'S POINT

### 5.0 mi / 2.5 hrs

**in China Camp State Park east of San Rafael**

Map 7.1, page 267

The Bay View Trail is the most ambitious hike anywhere along the shore of San Pablo Bay. A stroke of genius by a state park ranger has created the Bay Area's greatest new lookout. In this case, the strokes of genius were made by a chainsaw. Ranger Patrick Robards, a fire science specialist, ordered a hilltop grove of eucalyptus taken out at China Camp State Park. The result at this spot is a jaw-dropping five-bridge view of the bay and the region's mountain peaks, as well as a Marin 360 that will have you wishing your head was mounted on a swivel. So, we named the spot Patrick's Point.

This trip starts with the drive on North San Pedro Road from San Rafael out to the Marin shoreline along San Pablo Bay. When you reach a fork to a ranger kiosk, instead stay left on the main road (turning right to the kiosk will take you to the park's campground entrance). Continue on the main road past the sensational picnic areas (on the left, at water's edge) to the turnoff on the right to the ranger station. This is your starting point.

From here, it is a 2.5-mile loop with a 500-foot climb to McNear's Ridge and Patrick's Point.

Near the ranger station, with the park map in hand, start at the Shoreline trailhead. Take the Shoreline Trail north (you'll have good views of the San Pablo Bay shore) to the Miwok Fire Trail. Here you climb steadily (passing the Oak Ridge Trail) to a junction with the

McNear's Fire Trail. Turn right and you pop out on top. Note that on the park map, the lookout is not marked.

What a view: On clear days, you can see the Bay Bridge, the Richmond–San Rafael Bridge, the Carquinez Bridge, the Benicia Bridge, and the tops of the Golden Gate Bridge. We've seen crystal clear days from this lookout where it seemed you could take a running start and then leap across the bay and land on Point Pinole.

**User Groups:** Hikers, horses, and mountain bikes. No dogs. No wheelchair facilities.

**Permits:** No permits are required. A fee of $5 per vehicle is charged at China Camp Village.

**Maps:** A small map/brochure is available for a fee at park headquarters or by contacting the state parks district office at the address below. For a topographic map, ask the USGS for San Quentin.

**Directions:** Take U.S. 101 to San Rafael and the exit for North San Pedro. Take that exit and drive east four miles to park. At the fork (with a kiosk and campground on right), stay left and drive one mile (past the picnic areas on the left) to the ranger station, on the right, and the trailheads.

**Contact:** China Camp State Park, 415/456-0766; California State Parks, Marin District, 7665 Redwood Boulevard, Suite 150, Novato, CA 94945, 415/898-4362, fax 415/893-1583, website: www.parks.ca.gov (click on Find A Park).

## 25 DEER PARK TRAIL

### 2.0 mi / 1.25 hrs

**on the northwest slopes of Mount Tamalpais near San Anselmo**

Map 7.1, page 267

The trailhead at Deer Park is quite popular, but by taking Deer Park Trail rather than one of the other options, you can find peace in addition to having quite a workout. You get both of these things because the trail climbs about 350 feet in less than a mile. This is one of those situations where you must pay for your pleasure. But pleasure you will get. As the trail rises up the slopes of Bald Hill, views open up around you, and not just of the surrounding countryside; it is common to see deer in this area, and wildflower blooms are quite good in the spring. If you want even more, you'll have an opportunity to link up with a spiderweb of other trails in the area.

**User Groups:** Hikers only. No dogs, horses, or mountain bikes. No wheelchair facilities.

**Permits:** No permits are required. Groups are limited to 19 people. Parking and access are free.

**Maps:** A hiking/biking map is available for a fee from the Marin Water District at the address below. A detailed hiking map of the area is available for a fee from Olmsted & Bros. Map Company. For a topographic map, ask the USGS for San Rafael.

**Directions:** From U.S. 101 in Marin, take the Sir Francis Drake Boulevard exit and drive six miles west to the town of Fairfax. Look for the Fairfax sign (in the center median), and turn left (the road is unsigned); turn right immediately onto Broadway Avenue (a frontage road). Drive one block to Bolinas Road. Turn left and drive west for .5 mile to Porteous Avenue. Turn left on Porteous Avenue and drive to Deer County Park.

**Contact:** Sky Oaks Ranger Station, 415/945-1181; Marin Municipal Water District, 220 Nellen Avenue, Corte Madera, CA 94925, 415/945-1195, website: www.marinwater.org.

## 26 AUDUBON CANYON RANCH TRAIL
### 0.4 mi / 0.25 hr

**on the Marin coast near Bolinas Lagoon**

Map 7.1, page 267

Here is a little slice of paradise, the premier place on the Pacific Coast to view herons and egrets—those large, graceful seabirds—as they court, mate, nest, and rear their young. From ranch headquarters, the hike is short but steep, requiring about 20 minutes to reach the canyon overlook. Benches are provided for rest stops. Scopes installed at the top can be used to peer across the valley and zero

in on the giant nests in the redwoods. Birdwatchers might want to repeat this great trip again and again, tracking the mating process of the great birds. May and June are usually the best times to come. In May the eggs start hatching, and by June, there can be as many as 200 hatchlings in the different nests. They eagerly await breakfast, lunch, and dinner, which are provided when their huge parents return from Bolinas Lagoon and vomit the goodies all over the nest. Hey, what's for dessert?

Special Note: It is important to remember that Audubon Canyon Ranch is open only on weekends and holidays, 10 A.M. to 4 P.M., mid-March to mid-July.

**User Groups:** Hikers only. No dogs, horses, or mountain bikes. No wheelchair facilities.

**Permits:** Entrance to the ranch is free, but donations are requested; a $10 donation from families is suggested.

**Maps:** A small trail map/brochure is available at ranch headquarters. For a topographic map, ask the USGS for Bolinas.

**Directions:** From U.S. 101 in Marin, take the Sir Francis Drake Boulevard exit and drive about 20 miles west on Sir Francis Drake Boulevard to the town of Olema. Turn left on Highway 1, drive south for 10.5 miles, and then turn left into Audubon Canyon Ranch.

**Contact:** Audubon Canyon Ranch, 4900 Highway 1, Stinson Beach, CA 94970, 415/868-9244, websites: www.egret.org, www.bayaudubon.org.

## 27 TWO LAKES TRAIL
### 5.0 mi / 2.5 hrs

**on the northwest slopes of Mount Tamalpais at Lagunitas Lake near San Anselmo**

Map 7.1, page 267

There is no officially designated Two Lakes Trail, so don't look for a sign. This trail gets its name from users who love the route, a loop hike that is made up of a series of trails that lead past pretty Bon Tempe and Lagunitas Lakes. A map is a must—you can get one at the entrance station. The trailhead lies at an elevation of 740 feet at the Lagunitas Picnic Area, adjacent to Lagunitas Lake, the smallest of Marin County's eight lakes. From here, the suggestion is to walk around Lagunitas Lake counterclockwise, eventually linking up with Pilot Knob Trail. Turn left, hike past the parking area, and connect with Bon Tempe Shadyside Trail. This circles the lake, eventually leading all the way back to the parking area.

**User Groups:** Hikers only. No dogs, horses, or mountain bikes. No wheelchair facilities.

**Permits:** A day-use fee of $7 is charged per vehicle. Groups are limited to 19 people.

**Maps:** A hiking/biking map is available for a fee from the Marin Water District at the address below. A detailed hiking map of the area is available for a fee from Olmsted & Bros. Map Company. For a topographic map, ask the USGS for Bolinas.

**Directions:** From U.S. 101 in Marin, take the Sir Francis Drake Boulevard exit and drive six miles west to the town of Fairfax. Look for the Fairfax sign (in the center median) and turn left (the road is unsigned); turn right immediately onto Broadway Avenue (a frontage road). Drive one block to Bolinas Road. Turn left and drive west for 1.5 miles to Sky Oaks Road, on the left. Bear left and drive .5 mile to the entrance kiosk. After paying the day-use fee, drive .25 mile to a fork. Bear left at the fork to the Lake Lagunitas parking area and the adjacent picnic area and trailhead.

**Contact:** Sky Oaks Ranger Station, 415/945-1181; Marin Municipal Water District, 220 Nellen Avenue, Corte Madera, CA 94925, 415/945-1195, website: www.marinwater.org.

## 28 PINE MOUNTAIN/ CARSON FALLS

**3.0 mi / 1.5 hrs**

**on the northwest slopes of Mount Tamalpais west of Fairfax**

Map 7.1, page 267

Your destination is Carson Falls, a set of small waterfalls that tumble into granite pools. The walk to this quiet, divine spot hidden on the north slopes of Mount Tamalpais is an easy stroll across hilly grassla[nd] nied by a hawk or two floati[ng] head), followed by a short jog do[wn] into the Carson Creek drainage.

The trailhead (at 1,078 feet) is adjacent one of the better parking areas provided on lands administered by the Marin Water District. After parking, cross Bolinas-Fairfax Road to reach the trailhead, Pine Mountain Road (a water district service road). The road climbs 400 feet over the course of a mile, reaching a junction with Oat Hill Road on the crest of a hill flanked on both sides by foothill grasslands. Turn left here, hike .3 mile, and turn right onto the hiking trail (look for the power lines; that's where the trail is). The trail is routed .2 mile down to Carson Creek and the series of waterfalls. The lowest of the falls is a stunning, high, silver stream that flows over a notch in a boulder and free-falls 30 feet into a beautiful pool. Of course, the cascades are best seen after a good rain, but there is usually at least a trickle of water into early summer. A trick: when nearing the waterfalls at the bottom of the valley, hop across the stream and then work your way down on the far side. From here looking up, you get a perfect view of four waterfalls, chutes, and cascades, each pouring into pools through a beautiful rock canyon. The final fall is a 35-foot free fall, silver and powerful. You can peer over its brink and look straight down, and in cool months, adjacent color is often added by nearby bright red toyon berries.

**User Groups:** Hikers, dogs, horses, and mountain bikes. No wheelchair facilities. Note that mountain bikes are allowed on Pine Mountain and Oat Hill Roads, but not on the hiking trail down to Carson Falls.

**Permits:** No permits are required. Groups are limited to 19 people. Parking and access are free.

**Maps:** A hiking/biking map is available for a fee from the Marin Water District at the address below. A detailed hiking map of the area is available for a fee from Olmsted & Bros. Map Company. For a topographic map, ask the USGS for Bolinas.

..., take the
...d drive six
...ook for the
...n) and turn
...ght immedi-
...ontage road).
...ad. Turn left
...(past the golf
course) to ... ...ing area on the
left. The trailhead for Pine Mountain Road
and an information billboard are across the
road from the parking area.

**Contact:** Sky Oaks Ranger Station, 415/945-
1181; Marin Municipal Water District, 220
Nellen Avenue, Corte Madera, CA 94925,
415/945-1195, website: www.marinwater.org.

## 29 ALPINE/KENT LAKE PUMP TRAIL

**1.0–8.6 mi / 1.0–4.5 hrs**

**on the northwest slopes of Mount Tamalpais
at Alpine Lake Dam**

Map 7.1, page 267

The Kent Lake Pump Trail can score a 100 on
the Blindfold Test. The Blindfold Test is where
you imagine that someone has blindfolded you
and taken you off on an adventure. At some
point deep into the trip, they suddenly stop,
remove the blindfold, and you answer true or
false to three statements:

1. If you really had been blindfolded, you
would have no idea of your exact surroundings.

2. It is more beautiful than you could have
imagined.

3. You can't believe you never heard about
this place or had never taken the time to make
the trip.

If the answers are true, true, and true, you
have not only achieved a perfect score on the
Blindfold Test, but you are on the way to a
great adventure. And you also have discovered
why the Kent Lake Pump Trail is treasured by
those who know about it.

This trip is located in the Marin foothills
along Lagunitas Creek, running from Alpine
Dam on through a streamside canyon to the
headwaters of Kent Lake. It passes through
beautiful riparian woodlands, eventually breaking out for views of well-hidden Kent Lake.

From the start, you get a view of the backside of Alpine Dam. In winter, when the lake
fills and overflows at the spillway, the dam
becomes a dramatic man-made waterfall.
From here you start your trip on a service
road, a downhill grade as the route enters
the canyon, with Lagunitas Creek on your
left. Stay alert for the second cutoff on your
left, which leads down to a beautiful, do-it-
yourself streamside picnic spot beneath a
canopy of Douglas fir and various hardwoods.
This is one of the prettiest picnic spots in the
Bay Area.

The Kent Lake Pump Trail continues over
the course of another four miles to the headwaters of Kent Lake, with small glimpses urg-
ing you forward for a more open look. The trail
gradient is generally good, involving a 250-foot
descent from Alpine Dam (648 feet) to Kent
Lake (403 feet). Few do the entire trip. Throughout this area, you can take a short departure
from the trail in the first mile to find an ideal
setting for a picnic along Lagunitas Creek.

**User Groups:** Hikers, dogs, horses, and mountain bikes. No wheelchair facilities.

**Permits:** No permits are required. Groups are
limited to 19 people. Parking and access are free.

**Maps:** A hiking/biking map is available for a
fee from the Marin Water District at the address below. A detailed hiking map of the area
is available for a fee from Olmsted & Bros.
Map Company. For a topographic map, ask
the USGS for Bolinas.

**Directions:** From U.S. 101 in Marin, take the
Sir Francis Drake Boulevard exit and drive six
miles west to the town of Fairfax. Look for the
Fairfax sign (in the center median, an unlighted
junction) and turn left (the road is unsigned);
turn right immediately onto Broadway Avenue
(a frontage road). Drive one block to Bolinas
Road. Turn left and drive west eight miles (continuing along Alpine Lake) to the Alpine Dam.
Park on the right side of the road (just before

the dam) and look for the gated service road/trailhead, on the right.

**Contact:** Sky Oaks Ranger Station, 415/945-1181; Marin Municipal Water District, 220 Nellen Avenue, Corte Madera, CA 94925, 415/945-1195, website: www.marinwater.org.

## 30 CATARACT FALLS
**2.5 mi / 1.5 hrs**

**on the northwest slopes of Mount Tamalpais at Alpine Lake Dam**

Map 7.1, page 267

Cataract Falls is not a single waterfall, but a series of cascades that rushes down a beautifully wooded canyon set in the northwest slopes of Mount Tamalpais. The hike requires a climb but is well worth every step. From the trailhead at the south end of Alpine Lake (elevation 644 feet), you face a 750-foot climb over the span of just a mile to reach the centerpiece falls at 1,400 feet. Some hikers take the easier route from the Laurel Dell trailhead, which has a 240-foot drop over .4 mile.

The trailhead is just over the west side of the dam at Alpine Lake. This is the best-known fall in the region, and parking along the road is extremely limited, often making for a frustrating encounter on weekends.

The trail starts by contouring along a cove of Alpine Lake. It then rises from the lake, climbing up into a lush canyon where there seems to be one small waterfall after another. These are not big free falls like in Yosemite, but rather small cascades, surrounded by luxuriant riparian beauty. Compared to almost anywhere in the Bay Area environs after such recent heavy rains, the collective beauty can seem nonpareil.

In late winter, especially when the skies have just cleared after heavy rains, the cascades in this canyon can look like something found in Hawaii. This is particularly true when rays of sunlight catch the droplets of water just right, and the refracted light makes them sparkle. From top to bottom, there's one cascade after another, ending with a silvery chute pouring into a plunge pool. After getting your fill of this sight, return the way you came.

**User Groups:** Hikers and dogs. No horses or mountain bikes. No wheelchair facilities.

**Permits:** No permits are required. Groups are limited to 19 people. Parking and access are free.

**Maps:** A hiking/biking map is available for a fee from the Marin Water District at the address below. For a topographic map, ask the USGS for Bolinas.

**Directions:** From U.S. 101 in Marin, take the Sir Francis Drake Boulevard exit and drive six miles west to the town of Fairfax. Look for the Fairfax sign (in the center median) and turn left (the road is unsigned); turn right immediately onto Broadway Avenue (a frontage road). Drive one block to Bolinas Road. Turn left and drive west for eight miles (continuing along Alpine Lake) to the Alpine Dam. Cross the dam and continue a short distance to the pullouts along the hairpin turn. Park here. The trailhead is on the south side of the road.

**Contact:** Sky Oaks Ranger Station, 415/945-1181; Marin Municipal Water District, 220 Nellen Avenue, Corte Madera, CA 94925, 415/945-1195, website: www.marinwater.org; Mount Tamalpais State Park, 801 Panoramic Highway, Mill Valley, CA 94941, 415/388-2070, fax 415/388-2968; California State Parks, Marin District, 415/898-4362, website: www.parks.ca.gov (click on Find A Park).

## 31 LAUREL DELL LOOP
**2.5 mi / 1.5 hrs**

**in Mount Tamalpais State Park**

Map 7.1, page 267

Cataract Falls is the most adored waterfall on Mount Tamalpais, and the Laura Dell trailhead provides the easiest route there. Instead of the gut-wrenching climb from Alpine Lake (see previous listing), here you start high and glide down to the falls, then return via a gentle loop. The trailhead is at 1,640 feet, and from there, hike .4 mile on the Laurel Dell Trail to the Laurel Dell Picnic Area. At the edge of the picnic area, get on the Cataract Falls Trail and continue to the waterfall, at 1,400 feet. When running at full strength, this cascade is a truly precious sight, especially when you realize it's so close to an urban setting. At the falls, turn right on the High Marsh Trail, hike onward, and turn right at any of the next three trail intersections to return to the Laurel Dell trailhead. Of the three choices, the second makes the best return loop, as the short cutoff will put you within a few hundred yards of the trailhead.

**User Groups:** Hikers and dogs. No horses or mountain bikes. No wheelchair facilities.

**Permits:** No permits are required. Parking and access are free.

**Maps:** A map/brochure of Mount Tamalpais State Park is available for a small fee at the visitors center or by writing to the address below. A detailed hiking map of the area is available for a fee from Olmsted & Bros. Map Company. For topographic maps, ask the USGS for Bolinas and San Rafael.

**Directions:** From U.S. 101 in Marin, take the Stinson Beach/Highway 1 exit. Drive west to the stoplight at the T intersection. Turn left and drive about 2.5 miles uphill to Panoramic Highway. Turn right on Panoramic Highway and continue up the hill for 5.5 miles (past the turnoff to Muir Woods). Turn right on Pantoll Road and drive about 1.5 miles to the T intersection. Turn left on Ridgecrest Road and drive 1.4 miles to the parking area for the Laura Dell trailhead.

**Contact:** Mount Tamalpais State Park, 801 Panoramic Highway, Mill Valley, CA 94941, 415/388-2070, fax 415/388-2968; California State Parks, Marin District, 415/898-4362, website: www.parks.ca.gov (click on Find A Park).

## 32 ROCK SPRINGS TRAIL
**0.6 mi / 0.5 hr**

**in Mount Tamalpais State Park**

Map 7.1, page 267

Five trails start at Rock Springs, but a favorite is the shorty to O'Rourke's Bench, where hik-

ers can have a picnic while enjoying an awesome view to the west. On one trip, the coast was socked in with low stratus clouds, appearing from this lookout like a sea of fog dotted with protruding mountaintops resembling islands. On another day, the sunset was simply extraordinary. O'Rourke's Bench is quite easy to reach. After parking at Rock Springs, cross Ridgecrest Boulevard and take O'Rourke's Bench Trail for .3 mile. After some 10 or 15 minutes, you will come upon a little bench set on a knoll at 2,071 feet. A plaque next to the bench reads: "Give me these hills and the friends I love. I ask no other heaven. To our dad O'Rourke, in joyous celebration of his 76th birthday, Feb. 25th, 1927. From the friends to whom he showed this heaven."

**User Groups:** Hikers only. No dogs, horses, or mountain bikes. No wheelchair facilities.

**Permits:** No permits are required. Parking and access are free.

**Maps:** A hiking/biking map is available for a fee from the Marin Water District at the address below. A detailed hiking map of the area is available for a fee from Olmsted & Bros. Map Company. For a topographic map, ask the USGS for San Rafael.

**Directions:** From U.S. 101 in Marin, take the Stinson Beach/Highway 1 exit. Drive west one mile to the stoplight at the T intersection at Highway 1/Shoreline Highway. Turn left and drive about 2.5 miles uphill to Panoramic Highway. Turn right on Panoramic Highway and continue up the hill for 5.5 miles (past the turnoff to Muir Woods). Turn right on Pantoll Road and drive 1.5 miles to a parking area across from a T intersection. This is the Rock Springs parking area and trailhead.

**Contact:** Mount Tamalpais State Park, 801 Panoramic Highway, Mill Valley, CA 94941, 415/388-2070, fax 415/388-2968; California State Parks, Marin District, 415/898-4362, website: www.parks.ca.gov (click on Find A Park).

## 33 BARTH'S RETREAT
2.0 mi / 1.0 hr

**in Marin Water District**

Map 7.1, page 267

Rarely can the features of the land change more quickly than on the hike to Barth's Retreat on Mount Tamalpais. In just a mile, you cross a serpentine swale, pass a small creek with riparian habitat, go through a forest, and then arrive at an open area called Barth's Retreat. Barth, by the way, was one Emil Barth, a prolific musician/hiker/trail-builder who constructed a camp here in the early 20th century. This hike provides a quick glimpse of the diversity Mount Tam offers. When you link it with the short hike to O'Rourke's Bench, which also starts from Rock Springs (see previous listing), you can feel as if you've seen the world in a two-hour time span.

**User Groups:** Hikers only. No dogs, horses, or mountain bikes. No wheelchair facilities.

**Permits:** No permits are required. Parking and access are free.

**Maps:** A hiking/biking map is available for a fee from the Marin Water District at the address below. A detailed hiking map of the area is available for a fee from Olmsted & Bros. Map Company. For a topographic map, ask the USGS for San Rafael.

**Directions:** From U.S. 101 in Marin, take the Stinson Beach/Highway 1 exit. Drive west one mile to the stoplight at the T intersection with Highway 1/Shoreline Highway. Turn left and drive about 2.5 miles uphill to Panoramic Highway. Turn right on Panoramic Highway and continue up the hill for 5.5 miles (past the turnoff to Muir Woods). Turn right on Pantoll Road and drive 1.5 miles to a parking area across from a T intersection. This is the Rock Springs trailhead; there is a sign noting Barth's Retreat.

**Contact:** Sky Oaks Ranger Station, 415/945-1181; Marin Municipal Water District, 220 Nellen Avenue, Corte Madera, CA 94925, 415/945-1195, website: www.marinwater.org; Mount Tamalpais State Park, 801 Panoramic Highway, Mill Valley, CA 94941, 415/388-2070, fax 415/388-2968; California State Parks, Marin District, 415/898-4362, website: www.parks.ca.gov (click on Find A Park).

## 34 MOUNTAIN THEATER
3.0 mi / 1.5 hrs

**in Marin Water District**

Map 7.1, page 267

The round-trip from the Mountain Theater to West Point Inn is a classic Mount Tamalpais walk—pretty, easy, and with a landmark on each end. Mount Tam's masterpiece outdoor amphitheater is actually a very short distance from the parking area; you cross right behind it on Rock Springs Trail en route to West Point Inn. The trail is quiet and tranquil—especially since it's off-limits to bikes—and it weaves in and out of a hardwood forest, descending easily for most of the way. Over the course of 1.5 miles, you drop 295 feet, from a trailhead elevation of 2,080 feet to the trail's end, at 1,785 feet. West Point Inn offers great views and a perfect spot for a picnic lunch, and lemonade is often available inside. Here's a secret: Small cabins without electricity can be rented for overnight stays.

**User Groups:** Hikers only. No dogs, horses, or mountain bikes. No wheelchair facilities.

**Permits:** No permits are required. Parking and access are free.

**Maps:** A hiking/biking map is available for a fee from the Marin Water District at the address below. A map/brochure of Mount Tamalpais State Park is available for a small fee at the visitors center or by writing to the address below. A detailed hiking map of the area is available for a fee from Olmsted & Bros. Map Company. For a topographic map, ask the USGS for San Rafael. Much of this trail is on Marin Water District land; contact that agency to obtain a detailed map for a fee.

**Directions:** From U.S. 101 in Marin, take the Stinson Beach/Highway 1 exit. Drive west one mile to the stoplight at the T intersection with

Highway 1/Shoreline Highway. Turn left and drive about 2.5 miles uphill to Panoramic Highway. Turn right on Panoramic Highway and continue up the hill for 5.5 miles (past the turnoff to Muir Woods). Turn right on Pantoll Road and drive 1.5 miles to the T intersection. Turn right, drive .25 mile to the parking area on the right side of the road, and walk the short distance to the Mountain Theater trailhead.

**Contact:** Sky Oaks Ranger Station, 415/945-1181; Marin Municipal Water District, 220 Nellen Avenue, Corte Madera, CA 94925, 415/945-1195, website: www.marinwater.org; Mount Tamalpais State Park, 801 Panoramic Highway, Mill Valley, CA 94941, 415/388-2070, fax 415/388-2968; California State Parks, Marin District, 415/898-4362, website: www.parks.ca.gov (click on Find A Park).

## 35 EAST PEAK MOUNT TAMALPAIS
**0.4 mi / 0.5–1 hr**

**in Mount Tamalpais State Park**

Map 7.1, page 267

There is simply no better place in the Bay Area to watch the sun set than atop Mount Tamalpais's East Peak, for the feelings this experience inspires will stay with you for many weeks. Mount Tam is one of those rare spots that projects a feeling of power, and while standing on its highest point, you can sense that power flowing right through you. The hike is very short (after all, a parking lot is set right at the foot of the summit trail) but is quite steep, rising about 330 feet to the top, at an elevation of 2,571 feet. An old lookout station is positioned at the summit, and hikers usually try to find a perch as close as possible to the top.

To the east, the bay resembles the Mediterranean Sea, an azure pool sprinkled with islands. And at night, the lights of the bridges and the surrounding cities can give the Bay Area an almost surreal look. But the true magic happens at sunset, particularly on foggy days.

The peak stands well above the fog line, and when the fiery sun dips into that low stratus to the west, orange light is refracted for hundreds of miles around. Witness this stunning sight even one time, and you will gain a new perspective about what might be possible in this world. Perhaps you'll even set some new horizons for yourself.

If you seek more hiking action, there are two great trailheads nearby. To visit lovely Cataract Falls, take the Laurel Dell Loop (see listing in this chapter). At the foot of the parking area, the Paradise Lookout Fire Road is another good trail on which to extend your hike.

**User Groups:** Hikers only. Dogs are permitted on the paved trail but not on the mountaintop overlook. No horses or mountain bikes. No wheelchair access on the trail, but good views are available from the wheelchair-accessible parking lot.

**Permits:** No permits are required. A parking fee of $6 per vehicle is charged.

**Maps:** A map/brochure of Mount Tamalpais State Park is available for a small fee at the visitors center, located adjacent to the parking area, or by writing to the address below. A detailed hiking map of the area is available for a fee from Olmsted & Bros. Map Company. For a topographic map, ask the USGS for San Rafael.

**Directions:** From U.S. 101 in Marin, take the Stinson Beach/Highway 1 exit. Drive west one mile to the stoplight at the T intersection with Highway 1/Shoreline Highway. Turn left and drive about 2.5 miles uphill to Panoramic Highway. Turn right on Panoramic Highway and continue up the hill 5.5 miles (past the turnoff to Muir Woods). Turn right on Pantoll Road and drive about 1.5 miles to the T intersection. Turn right on Ridgecrest Road and drive two miles to the East Peak. The road dead-ends at the parking area at the base of the summit.

**Contact:** Mount Tamalpais State Park, 801 Panoramic Highway, Mill Valley, CA 94941, 415/388-2070, fax 415/388-2968; California State Parks, Marin District, 415/898-4362, website: www.parks.ca.gov (click on Find A Park).

## 36 INSPIRATION POINT
**2.6 mi / 1.0 hr**

**in Mount Tamalpais State Park**

Map 7.1, page 267

Inspiration Point provides a nearby alternative to the East Peak, ideal if you want the same kind of magic found at that popular summit, yet without all the people. To get there, instead of heading up to the East Peak after parking, go the opposite direction and turn right on the fire road, Eldridge Grade. The trail wraps around the northern flank of the East Peak, then makes a hairpin turn to the left around North Knee, set at 2,000 feet. At this point, the bay comes into view to the east, and you start to understand the attraction. But keep on, because Inspiration Peak awaits just down the road. At the hairpin right turn, take the short but steep cutoff trail on the left, and you will quickly reach the top at 2,040 feet—your vantage point for miles and miles of charmed views. All can seem enchanted. Much of this trail is on Marin Water District land.

**User Groups:** Hikers, dogs, and mountain bikes. No horses. No wheelchair access on the trail, but good views are available from the wheelchair-accessible parking lot.

**Permits:** No permits are required. A parking fee of $6 per vehicle is charged.

**Maps:** A map/brochure of Mount Tamalpais State Park is available for a small fee at the visitors center, located adjacent to the parking area, or by writing to the address below. A detailed hiking map of the area is available for a fee from Olmsted & Bros. Map Company. For a topographic map, ask the USGS for San Rafael.

**Directions:** From U.S. 101 in Marin, take the Stinson Beach/Highway 1 exit. Drive west one mile to the stoplight at the T intersection with Highway 1/Shoreline Highway. Turn left and drive about 2.5 miles uphill to Panoramic Highway. Turn right on Panoramic Highway and continue up the hill 5.5 miles (past the turnoff to Muir Woods). Turn right on Pantoll Road and drive 1.5 miles to the T intersection. Turn right on Ridgecrest Road and drive two miles to the East Peak. The road dead-ends at the parking area at the base of the summit.

**Contact:** Mount Tamalpais State Park, 801 Panoramic Highway, Mill Valley, CA 94941, 415/388-2070, fax 415/388-2968; California State Parks, Marin District, 415/898-4362, website: www.parks.ca.gov (click on Find A Park).

## 37 PHOENIX LAKE TRAIL
**2.7 mi / 1.5 hrs**

**on the north slope of Mount Tamalpais near Ross**

Map 7.1, page 267

Of the eight lakes in Marin County, Phoenix is the least accessible. Not only is the parking situation terrible, but newcomers can have trouble finding the lake, an intolerable situation considering how beloved it is. The little 25-acre jewel set in a pocket just west of the town of Ross is indeed well loved. From Natalie Coffin Greene Park, it's an easy .2-mile walk to the lake. Stairs on one side of the small dam take visitors down to a trail at the water's edge. The distance around the entire lake is 2.3 miles. In the winter, the lake is stocked with trout twice a month, and in the spring, bass fishing can be decent. As at all Marin lakes, no one is permitted to make contact with the water.

**User Groups:** Hikers, leashed dogs, horses, and mountain bikes (restricted from the lake's southern shoreline). No wheelchair facilities.

**Permits:** No permits are required. Groups are limited to 19 people. Parking and access are free.

**Maps:** A hiking/biking map is available for a fee from the Marin Water District at the address below. A detailed hiking map of the area is available for a fee from Olmsted & Bros. Map Company. For a topographic map, ask the USGS for San Rafael.

**Directions:** From U.S. 101 in Marin, take the Sir Francis Drake Boulevard exit and head west for 2.5 miles to Lagunitas Road. Turn left on Lagunitas Road and drive 1.1 miles into Natalie Coffin Greene Park. The lake is .25 mile from the parking area. Parking is extremely limited.

**Contact:** Sky Oaks Ranger Station, 415/945-1181; Marin Municipal Water District, 220 Nellen Avenue, Corte Madera, CA 94925, 415/945-1195, website: www.marinwater.org.

## 38 DAWN FALLS
**1.8 mi / 1.0 hr**

**on the eastern slopes of Mount Tamalpais near Larkspur**

Map 7.1, page 267

The Bay Area has many hidden waterfalls, but this one is both easy to reach and a beautiful and energizing sight in winter and spring. Dawn Falls, a 25-foot fountain of water, is best seen in the early morning, when rays of sunlight penetrate the atmosphere. Note, however, that in summer and fall, day after day of dry weather reduces the cascade to a trickle, and in drought years, it can go completely dry.

At the trailhead, don't get confused and take Baltimore Canyon Fire Road; that route is far less intimate than Dawn Falls Trail, which probes a dense woodland with model riparian habitat on each side of Larkspur Creek near the falls. This walk starts out easy and stays that way, even with the moderate 300-foot rise to the waterfall. On the way in, many don't expect the waterfall to be much, especially if the creek appears as nothing but a tiny trickle. Surprise: In winter and early spring, it is very beautiful.

**User Groups:** Hikers, dogs, horses (on the adjacent fire road), and mountain bikes. No wheelchair facilities.

**Permits:** No permits are required. Groups are limited to 19 people. Parking and access are free.

**Maps:** A hiking/biking map is available for a fee from the Marin Water District at the address below. A detailed hiking map of the area is available for a fee from Olmsted & Bros. Map Company. For a topographic map, ask the USGS for San Rafael.

**Directions:** From U.S. 101 in Marin, take the Tamalpais Drive exit, and head west on Tamalpais Drive to Corte Madera Avenue. Turn right and drive about .5 mile to Madrone Avenue.

Turn left on Madrone Avenue and drive to Valley Way. The trailhead is at the road's end.
**Contact:** Marin County Parks, Marin Open Space, Civic Center Room 415, San Rafael, CA 94903, 415/499-6387; Ranger Field Office 415/507-2816, website: www.co.marin.ca.us.

## 39 DIPSEA TRAIL
**6.6 mi one-way / 3.5 hrs**

**on Mount Tamalpais from Mill Valley to Stinson Beach**

Map 7.1, page 267

For Marin hikers, completing the Dipsea Trail is a rite of passage, an experience that offers a glimpse into both heaven and hell in a single morning. The annual Dipsea Race has turned the trail into something of a legend, and many people have developed a classic love/hate relationship with the hike. They love it because it's the perfect east-to-west crossing of Mount Tamalpais, from Mill Valley to Stinson Beach, passing through Muir Woods in the process and making a beautiful descent to the coast. Yet they hate it because it starts at an infamous set of seemingly unending staircase steps, crosses paved roads, and, just when hikers start to get tired, throws in a killer climb up Cardiac Hill. And, this is a one-way-only hike; a shuttle partner is required.

The trail starts in Mill Valley on Cascade Way at those hated steps: 671 in all. According to park rangers, the steps spawned the legend that Marin hikers never die, they just reach the 672nd step. When the trail tops the stairs and reaches pavement, look for the arrows painted on the street to mark the way (at times, the arrows can be faint). They will route you along Sequoia Road, Walsh Drive, then Bay View, where you cross Panoramic Highway and finally get off the pavement and start descending into Muir Woods. From there, the trail is well signed. Noted spots include Cardiac Hill, where you are handed a 480-foot climb in .4 mile. In return, you are also presented with phenomenal views of the Pacific Ocean and San Francisco, as well as the knowledge that most of the rest of the trail is downhill. Over the final 2.3 miles, you descend across the Marin hills, dip into lush Steep Ravine Canyon, and push across coastal bluffs to the parking area at Stinson Beach. Like we said, it's a rite of passage.

**User Groups:** Hikers only. No dogs, horses, or mountain bikes. No wheelchair facilities.

**Permits:** No permits required. Parking and access is free at the primary trailhead, but the trail can be accessed from Muir Woods and Mt. Tamalpais State Park, where there are fees. In Muir Woods, the fee is $3 per person (free for hikers under 16). If you start at Mount Tamalpais State Park, a $6 fee is charged per vehicle.

**Maps:** The Dipsea Trail crosses several jurisdictions. A map/brochure of Mount Tamalpais State Park is available for a small fee at the visitors center or by contacting Mount Tamalpais State Park at the address below. A detailed hiking map of the area is available for a fee from Olmsted & Bros. Map Company. For topographic maps, ask the USGS for San Rafael and Bolinas.

**Directions:** From U.S. 101 in Marin, take the East Blithedale/Tiburon Boulevard exit. Head west on East Blithedale (it becomes Throckmorton Street) into Mill Valley, and follow Throckmorton to Old Mill Park. The trailhead is at Old Mill Creek and the bridge, which leads to the staircase.

**Contact:** Mount Tamalpais State Park, 801 Panoramic Highway, Mill Valley, CA 94941, 415/388-2070, fax 415/388-2968; California State Parks, Marin District, 415/898-4362, website: www.parks.ca.gov (click on Find A Park); Muir Woods Visitors Center, 415/388-7368; Muir Woods National Monument, Mill Valley, CA 94941, 415/388-2596, website: www.nps.gov/muwo/.

## 40 MOUNTAIN HOME TRAIL
### 2.4 mi / 1.0 hr

**in Mount Tamalpais State Park**

Map 7.1, page 267

Want unique? You got unique: a 1.2-mile hike at Mount Tamalpais that ends at a great little inn called the Tourist Club, where you can "slake your thirst," as they say here, with your favorite elixir. This walk is short and has only one small steep portion. To reach the Tourist Club, park at the lot at Mountain Home along Panoramic Highway. From there, take Panoramic Trail .4 mile (it parallels Panoramic Highway) to its junction with Redwood Trail, which you then follow for .75 mile. The route laterals across the mountain slope before dropping into a pocket where the Tourist Club is perched on a slope. On weekends at this wood-framed building, not only can you get liquid refreshments, you can often drink while listening to German music. There is no other hiking destination like it in California. The Tourist Club is open on Saturdays and Sundays year-round from noon to sunset. It's closed Mondays, and otherwise during the week, it's hit-and-miss, according to the availability of the caretaker.

**User Groups:** Hikers only. No dogs, horses, or mountain bikes. No wheelchair facilities.

**Permits:** No permits are required. Parking and access are free.

**Maps:** A map/brochure of Mount Tamalpais State Park is available for a small fee at the visitors center or by writing to the address below. A detailed hiking map of the area is available for a fee from Olmsted & Bros. Map Company. For a topographic map, ask the USGS for San Rafael.

**Directions:** From U.S. 101 in Marin, take the Stinson Beach/Highway 1 exit. Drive west one mile to the stoplight at the T intersection. Turn left and drive about 2.5 miles uphill to Panoramic Highway. Turn right on Panoramic Highway and continue up the hill 5.5 miles (past the turnoff to Muir Woods). Turn right on Pantoll Road and continue to the Mountain Home Inn parking area. The trailhead (Panoramic Trail) is on the west side of the road.

**Contact:** Tourist Club, 415/388-9987; Mount Tamalpais State Park, 801 Panoramic Highway, Mill Valley, CA 94941, 415/388-2070, fax 415/388-2968; California State Parks, Marin District, 415/898-4362, website: www.parks.ca.gov (click on Find A Park).

## 41 MAIN TRAIL
**2.0–3.0 mi / 1.0–1.5 hr**

**in Muir Woods National Monument near Mill Valley**

**Map 7.1, page 267**

This just might be the most heavily used trail in the Bay Area, yet not necessarily by Bay Area residents. You see, tourists from all over the world visiting San Francisco tend to follow the same routine: After taking the obligatory picture of the Golden Gate Bridge from Vista Point, they drive to Muir Woods to see a real redwood tree. Soon enough they find themselves on Main Trail, a paved route set along Redwood Creek and completely encompassed by the giant trees. The trail is both very pretty and easy to walk, but more often than not, it resembles a parade route. After about a mile, the trail starts to climb to the left, and just like that, most of the tourists head back to the parking lot. An option is to turn this into a loop hike by taking Hillside Trail up the west side of the canyon and looping back to the Muir Woods headquarters. The loop trail is three miles long and includes a pleasant climb.

**User Groups:** Hikers only. No dogs (except for seeing-eye dogs), horses, or mountain bikes. The first section of the trail is wheelchair accessible.

**Permits:** An entry fee is charged for visitors age 17 and over. No permits are required.

**Maps:** A map/brochure is available for a fee at the visitors center or by contacting Muir Woods National Monument at the address below. For a topographic map, ask the USGS for San Rafael.

**Directions:** From U.S. 101 in Marin, take the Stinson Beach/Highway 1 exit. Drive west to the stoplight at the T intersection with Highway 1/Shoreline Highway. Turn left and drive 2.5 miles uphill to Panoramic Highway. Turn right and drive .7 mile to the Muir Woods junction. Turn left and drive .8 mile to the Muir Woods parking area.

**Contact:** Muir Woods Visitors Center, 415/388-7368; Muir Woods National Monument, Mill Valley, CA 94941, 415/388-2596, website: www.nps.gov/muwo/.

## 42 OCEAN VIEW TRAIL (PANORAMIC HIGHWAY TRAIL)
**3.0 mi / 1.75 hrs**

**in Muir Woods National Monument near Mill Valley**

**Map 7.1, page 267**

When you arrive at Muir Woods and see tour buses shooting out people like popcorn from a popping machine, you'll be glad you read this, because Ocean View Trail provides the best chance of getting away from the crowds. After passing the information stand and starting down the paved path on the valley floor, turn right on Ocean View Trail. In under a minute you will enter a different world, a world of solitude, beautiful redwoods, and, alas, a steep ascent.

From the valley floor, the trail heads up the east side of the canyon on a steady grade, steep enough to get you puffing. It climbs 570 feet in 1.2 miles, rising above the valley to where you can look down into a sea of redwoods. To complete the loop, turn left on Lost Trail, elevation 750 feet, which descends quite steeply over just .4 mile back to the valley floor, at 300 feet. There you turn left and return to headquarters on Fern Creek Trail. It's a great escape.

**Special Note:** While this trail is listed as Ocean View Trail, most people call it Panoramic Highway Trail. It is listed both ways on various maps and signs. Ironically, there is no ocean view.

**User Groups:** Hikers only. No dogs (except for seeing-eye dogs), horses, or mountain bikes. The first section of the trail is wheelchair accessible.

**Permits:** An entry fee is charged for visitors age 17 and over. No permits are required.

**Maps:** A map/brochure is available for a fee at the visitors center or by contacting Muir Woods National Monument at the address below. For a topographic map, ask the USGS for San Rafael.

**Directions:** From U.S. 101 in Marin, take the Stinson Beach/Highway 1 exit. Drive west to the stoplight at the T intersection with Highway 1/Shoreline Highway. Turn left and drive 2.5 miles uphill to Panoramic Highway. Turn right and drive .7 mile to the Muir Woods junction. Turn left and drive .8 mile to the Muir Woods parking area.

**Contact:** Muir Woods Visitors Center, 415/388-7368; Muir Woods National Monument, Mill Valley, CA 94941, 415/388-2596, website: www.nps.gov/muwo/.

## 43 BOOTJACK LOOP
**6.2 mi / 3.0 hrs**

**in Mount Tamalpais State Park**

Map 7.1, page 267

Few hikes provide glimpses of such a dynamic, diverse, and delightful habitat as the Bootjack Loop. The trail crosses a meadow, oak woodlands, and some hilly grasslands, then submerges deep into a redwood forest and climbs back out, all in the space of 6.2 miles. It entails a steady downgrade, so you face a huff-puffer climb on the return trip, but the redwoods make it worth the grunt.

Starting at the Pantoll Ranger Station and trailhead (elevation 1,500 feet) in Mount Tamalpais State Park, hike north .4 mile on the Alpine Trail to Van Wyck Meadow, descending 450 feet in the process. From there, turn right on the Bootjack Trail, heading downhill along a small stream. This leg leads 1.3 miles into Muir Woods National Monument, where you turn right on Ben Johnson Trail and begin the steep return trip. Over the next mile, the trail climbs 500 feet, flanked the entire way by one of the Bay Area's richest redwood groves, home to many gigantic trees. To complete the loop, continue up, up, and up on Ben Johnson Trail (to the Stapelveldt Trail) for the final .9 mile to the Pantoll trailhead, a total elevation gain of 1,080 feet.

**User Groups:** Hikers only. No dogs, horses, or mountain bikes. No wheelchair facilities.

**Permits:** No permits are required. A parking fee of $6 per vehicle is charged.

**Maps:** A map/brochure of Mount Tamalpais State Park is available for a small fee at the visitors center or by writing to the address below. A detailed hiking map of the area is available for a fee from Olmsted & Bros. Map Company. For a topographic map, ask the USGS for San Rafael.

**Directions:** From U.S. 101 in Marin, take the Stinson Beach/Highway 1 exit. Drive west one mile to the stoplight at the T intersection with Highway 1/Shoreline Highway. Turn left and drive about 2.5 miles uphill to Panoramic Highway. Turn right on Panoramic Highway and continue up the hill for 5.5 miles (past the turnoff to Muir Woods) to Pantoll Road. Turn left at Pantoll parking area.

**Contact:** Mount Tamalpais State Park, 801 Panoramic Highway, Mill Valley, CA 94941, 415/388-2070, fax 415/388-2968; California State Parks, Marin District, 415/898-4362, website: www.parks.ca.gov (click on Find A Park).

## 44 MATT DAVIS/COASTAL TRAIL
**1.0–3.2 mi one-way / 0.5–1.5 hrs**

**on the western slopes of Mount Tamalpais**

Map 7.1, page 267

The 3.2-mile section of Matt Davis Trail from the Pantoll trailhead down to Stinson Beach offers dramatic views of the Pacific Ocean. There are many places where you can stop, spread your arms wide, and feel as if the entire world were within your grasp. It is a great one-way hike—just make sure you go with a partner, and have a shuttle car waiting at the trail's end, at the Stinson Beach Firehouse. After parking at Pantoll, elevation 1,500 feet, cross the road and look for the sign marking Matt Davis/Coastal Trail. Soon enough, you will start descending toward the beach, but not before first entering a lush grove of fir trees. Here the trail is level for nearly a mile. When you emerge, the trail begins its steep descent across open grasslands down to Stinson Beach. Only thick fog can ruin the day. Note that the entire Matt Davis Trail is technically nearly double this suggested route, with the trailhead at Mountain Home. Also note that many people just enjoy a mile or two of the expansive sea views, then return.

**User Groups:** Hikers only. No dogs, horses, or mountain bikes. No wheelchair facilities.

**Permits:** No permits are required. A parking fee of $6 per vehicle is charged.

**Maps:** A map/brochure of Mount Tamalpais State Park is available for a small fee at the visitors center or by writing to the address below. A detailed hiking map of the area is available for a fee from Olmsted & Bros. Map Company. For a topographic map, ask the USGS for San Rafael.

**Directions:** From U.S. 101 in Marin, take the Stinson Beach/Highway 1 exit. Drive west one mile to the stoplight at the T intersection. Turn left and drive about 2.5 miles uphill to Panoramic Highway. Turn right on Panoramic Highway and drive up the hill 5.5 miles (past the turnoff to Muir Woods) to Pantoll Road. Turn left at the Pantoll parking area.

**Contact:** Mount Tamalpais State Park, 801 Panoramic Highway, Mill Valley, CA 94941, 415/388-2070, fax 415/388-2968; California State Parks, Marin District, 415/898-4362, website: www.parks.ca.gov (click on Find A Park).

## 45 STEEP RAVINE TRAIL
### 4.0 mi / 1.5 hrs

**on the western slopes of Mount Tamalpais**

**Map 7.1, page 267**

Hiking Steep Ravine Trail is like being baptized by the divine spirit of nature, and those who set foot on it will find a place where they can get their own brand of religion. The trail passes through remarkably beautiful terrain, including cathedral-like redwoods, lush undergrowth, and a pretty stream. Believe it or not, this is one of the few hikes that is best

done during a rainstorm. In the canyon, the forest canopy protects you from a direct assault by the raindrops. Everything becomes vibrant with life as it drips with water. From the trailhead at Pantoll, the route descends 1,100 feet over the course of two miles, ending at Highway 1 near Rocky Point. After departing and heading downhill, it doesn't take long before the redwoods surround you. The trail follows Webb Creek, crossing the stream eight times in all. At one point, you have to climb down a ladder adjacent to a small waterfall. The junction with Dipsea Trail is a trail landmark; from this point, it's .5 mile to the end.

**User Groups:** Hikers only. No dogs, horses, or mountain bikes. No wheelchair facilities.

**Permits:** No permits are required. A parking fee of $6 per vehicle is charged.

**Maps:** A map/brochure of Mount Tamalpais State Park is available for a small fee at the visitors center or by writing to the address below. A detailed hiking map of the area is available for a fee from Olmsted & Bros. Map Company. For a topographic map, ask the USGS for San Rafael.

**Directions:** From U.S. 101 in Marin, take the Stinson Beach/Highway 1 exit. Drive west to the stoplight at the T intersection. Turn left on Shoreline Highway/Highway 1, drive about 2.5 miles uphill to Panoramic Highway, and turn right on Panoramic Highway. Continue up the hill 5.5 miles (past the turnoff to Muir Woods) to Pantoll Road. Turn left at the Pantoll parking area.

**Contact:** Mount Tamalpais State Park, 801 Panoramic Highway, Mill Valley, CA 94941, 415/388-2070, fax 415/388-2968; California State Parks, Marin District, 415/898-4362, website: www.parks.ca.gov (click on Find A Park).

## 46 OWL TRAIL
### 3.5 mi / 1.5 hrs

**on the Marin coast south of Stinson Beach**

**Map 7.1, page 267**

This is a delightful walk on a sunny day. This trail laterals down the coastal hillside to a secluded, rocky beach, with several sideshows along the way. The trailhead is near the Muir Beach Overlook, which alone is worth the trip for the great views of the southern Marin coast. Don't stop there like so many visitors do, but instead hike northward on Owl Trail. From the unsigned trailhead on the north side of the parking area, the trail is routed through low-lying brush, which makes wearing shorts a sticky proposition. Starting at 440 feet, the trail descends 240 feet in .9 mile on its northward course to Slide Ranch. Slide Ranch consists of a hamlet of wood huts and a small farm with goats, sheep, chickens, and even some duck—all favorites of youngsters. Two-foot-tall great horned owls sometimes roost in the giant cypress trees at Slide Ranch, but they can be difficult to see in their natural camouflage. From here, the trip down to the beach adds another 15 minutes to your walk; the descent is slippery, and a rope has been affixed to aid hikers through the worst spot. Once down, you can explore numerous secret spots amid rocks of all sizes, stacks, and tidepools. On one visit, hundreds of tiny rock crabs were sparring in the shallows.

**User Groups:** Hikers only. No dogs, horses, or mountain bikes. The Muir Beach Overlook is wheelchair accessible, but Owl Trail is not.

**Permits:** No permits are required. Parking and access are free.

**Maps:** A map/brochure is available at the Marin Headlands Visitors Center or by contacting the Golden Gate National Recreation Area, Marin Headlands, at the address below. A detailed hiking map of the area is available for a fee from Olmsted & Bros. Map Company. For a topographic map, ask the USGS for Point Bonita.

**Directions:** From U.S. 101 in Marin, take the Stinson Beach/Highway 1 exit and drive to the coast. Turn left at the Muir Beach Overlook and drive a short distance to the parking area. The trailhead may at first seem hidden. It is located at the north side of the parking area.

**Contact:** Muir Woods Visitors Center, 415/388-

7368
Valle
www.r

**47** M
**3.5 mi**

in the Ma

Map 7.1,

The Miwok ⸺⸺⸺ ⸺⸺ ⸺ hike that traverses the ⸺⸺ ⸺⸺⸺⸺ands of the Marin Headlands, connecting a number of trails to provide a decent physical workout. Good views are found throughout, including those from a great 880-foot lookout to the west, at the junction of Ridge Road and Fox Trail. The hike starts at the Miwok Stables (elevation 200 feet), where you head north on Miwok Trail, rising into higher country. The trail turns left, then heads west .6 mile, still climbing to the junction of Miwok Trail and Coyote Ridge Road. At this point, to make the loop hike, turn left on Ridge Road, where the trail tops out at 1,000 feet. The next mile offers spectacular views of the ocean, and every step can be special. To return to the Miwok Stables, turn left at the Fox Trail, and hike 1.1 miles; go left again on the paved Tennessee Valley Trail, and hike out the last .4 mile to the stables. Trail use is typically high on weekends, and that includes mountain bike traffic on Coyote Ridge Road.

**User Groups:** Hikers, dogs, horses, and mountain bikes (partial access). No wheelchair facilities.

**Permits:** No permits are required. Parking and access are free.

**Maps:** A map/brochure is available at the Marin Headlands Visitors Center or by contacting the Golden Gate National Recreation Area at the address below. A detailed hiking map of the the area is available for a fee from Olmsted & Bros. Map Company. For a topographic map, ask the USGS for Point Bonita.

**Directions:** From U.S. 101 in Marin, take the Stinson Beach/Highway 1 exit. Drive .6 mile and turn left on Tennessee Valley Road. Drive two miles until the road dead-ends at the trailhead.

**Contact:** Golden Gate National Recreation Area, Marin Headlands, Fort ing 948, 415/331-154

National Recreation
...ds Visitors Center, Build-
...arry, Sausalito, CA 94965,
..., website: www.nps.gov/goga.

## TENNESSEE VALLEY
4.2 mi / 2.0 hrs

**in the Marin Headlands near Sausalito**

Map 7.1, page 267

This is a very popular and scenic trail in the Marin Headlands that traces Tennessee Valley out to Tennessee Cove and the Pacific Ocean. Although the area is not wooded, the views of the Pacific Ocean can be gorgeous and the sunsets memorable. The best trailhead is at the Miwok Stables, elevation 200 feet. From there, the first .8 mile is paved and attracts many mountain bikers. The route turns to gravel for the final 1.1 miles, tracing along a pretty lagoon before dropping the final .2 mile to Tennessee Cove. This trail has become a favorite for family hiking or biking trips.

**User Groups:** Hikers, horses, and mountain bikes. (Horses and mountain bikes must take the forked fire road.) No dogs. No wheelchair facilities.

**Permits:** No permits are required. Parking and access are free.

**Maps:** A map/brochure is available at the Marin Headlands Visitors Center or by contacting the Golden Gate National Recreation Area at the address below. A detailed hiking map of the area is available for a fee from Olmsted & Bros. Map Company. For a topographic map, ask the USGS for Point Bonita.

**Directions:** From U.S. 101 in Marin, take the Stinson Beach/Highway 1 exit. Drive .6 mile and turn left on Tennessee Valley Road. Drive two miles until the road dead-ends at the trailhead.

**Contact:** Golden Gate National Recreation Area, Marin Headlands Visitors Center, Building 948, Fort Barry, Sausalito, CA 94965, 415/331-1540, website: www.nps.gov/goga.

## 49 BICENTENNIAL BIKE PATH
4.5 mi / 2.0 hrs

**on the San Francisco Bay shoreline from Sausalito to Corte Madera**

Map 7.1, page 267

Can folks out for an easy stroll mix well with joggers and bikers? The Bicentennial Bike Path proves this is possible, primarily because it was designed just for that purpose. This paved byway starts in Sausalito and heads north, tracing the shoreline of Richardson Bay into Corte Madera. It is a great nature walk—easy and pleasant. From Sausalito, the route passes beneath the U.S. 101 overpass, then pushes toward Bothin Marsh along the edge of Richardson Bay, crossing two exceptional little bridges that provide passage over tidelands. At low tide, hundreds of tiny sandpipers frequently poke around in the mud; in the nearby sloughs bordered by pickleweed, you can often spot egrets, night herons, and maybe even a pelican. Drop into the Richardson Bay Audubon Center for a good side trip. Bikers can continue all the way to Ross but will have to make a few connections on city streets (on an exceptionally well-designed bike trail) to do so.

**User Groups:** Hikers, dogs, mountain bikes, and wheelchairs. No horses.

**Permits:** No permits are required. Parking and access are free.

**Maps:** A detailed hiking map of the area is available for a fee from Olmsted & Bros. Map Company. For a topographic map, ask the USGS for San Francisco North.

**Directions:** From San Francisco, drive north on U.S. 101 over the Golden Gate Bridge. In Marin, take the Sausalito exit. Follow 2nd Street/Bridgeway through Sausalito to Harbor Drive, then park. The trail starts there.

**Contact:** Richardson Bay Audubon Center, 376 Greenwood Road, Tiburon, CA 94920, 415/388-2524, fax 415/388-0717, websites: www.bayaudubon.org, www.egret.org.

## 50 MORNING SUN TRAIL
**0.2–5.2 mi / 0.5–3.0 hr**

**in the Marin Headlands near Sausalito**

Map 7.1, page 267

This trail didn't get its name by accident. After the short but steep climb to the junction with Alta Trail, you will discover this is a magnificent location to watch the sun come up, casting varying hues of yellow and orange across San Francisco Bay. In fact, it is one of the best places in the Bay Area to catch a sunrise. There is a good parking area at the trailhead, and from there you climb about 400 feet, peaking out at 800 feet at the Alta Trail junction. From Alta, you can easily extend your trip in either direction, or you can create a pretty 5.2-mile loop by linking Rodeo Valley Trail and Bobcat Trail.

**User Groups:** Hikers only. No dogs, horses, or mountain bikes. No wheelchair facilities.

**Permits:** No permits are required. Parking and access are free.

**Maps:** A map/brochure is available at the Marin Headlands Visitors Center or by contacting the Golden Gate National Recreation Area at the address below. A detailed hiking map of the area is available for a fee from Olmsted & Bros. Map Company. For a topographic map, ask the USGS for San Francisco North.

**Directions:** From San Francisco, drive north on U.S. 101 through the Waldo Tunnel. Take the Spencer Avenue exit, but keep straight on the frontage road on the east side of the freeway. (Do not turn right onto Spencer Avenue.) Drive about .5 mile, turn left, and drive under the freeway to the commuter parking area at the trailhead.

**Contact:** Golden Gate National Recreation Area, Marin Headlands Visitors Center, Building 948, Fort Barry, Sausalito, CA 94965, 415/331-1540, website: www.nps.gov/goga.

## 51 COASTAL TRAIL/ FORT CRONKHITE
**5.2 mi / 2.5 hrs**

**in the Marin Headlands at the mouth of San Francisco Bay**

Map 7.1, page 267

Fort Cronkhite, perched on an ocean bluff above Rodeo Beach, was the "support community" for the Marin Headlands military fortifications in the 1930s and 1940s. From here, a paved pathway extends north up to Wolf Ridge, climbing to a 960-foot summit at what is known as Hill 88. The land consists primarily of coastal grasslands, so from the summit, you get outstanding views of the Pacific Ocean. The entire route is paved, and you may encounter bikers who careen downhill hell-bent for leather, sending hikers scattering for the bushes. Enforcement of the speed limit has helped, as has peer pressure from more ethical riders. Although the round-trip distance is 5.2 miles, you'll surely make the 2.6-mile return hike at least twice as fast as the journey up.

**User Groups:** Hikers, dogs, horses, and mountain bikes. Fort Cronkhite and the picnic area are partially wheelchair accessible.

**Permits:** No permits are required. Parking and access are free.

**Maps:** A map/brochure is available at the Marin Headlands Visitors Center or by contacting the Golden Gate National Recreation Area, Marin Headlands, at the address below. A detailed hiking map of the area is available for a fee from Olmsted & Bros. Map Company. For a topographic map, ask the USGS for Point Bonita.

**Directions:** From San Francisco, drive north on U.S. 101 over the Golden Gate Bridge. In Marin, take the Alexander Avenue exit and turn left underneath the highway. Take the wide paved road to the right (Conzelman Road, but there is no sign), and look for the Marin Headlands sign. Drive one mile, make a right on McCullough Road (the downhill fork), and soon after, turn left on Bunker Road. Drive about 2.5 miles to where the road dead-ends, at the Fort Cronkhite/Rodeo Beach parking lot.

**Contact:** Golden Gate National Recreation Area, Marin Headlands Visitors Center, Building 948, Fort Barry, Sausalito, CA 94965, 415/331-1540, website: www.nps.gov/goga.

## 52 COASTAL TRAIL/FORT BARRY
1.4 mi / 0.75 hr 🥾 ⏱9

**in the Marin Headlands near Rodeo Lagoon**

Map 7.1, page 267

Fort Barry was a nerve center for military operations in an era long past. Today it's a place that can calm the nerves of frazzled hikers. After parking and exploring at Fort Barry a bit, take the unpaved road/trail that heads west from the fort. Covering just .7 mile, the trail is routed along the south side of Rodeo Lagoon and out to the bluffs overlooking the ocean. This is a great walk, and easy, with good views all around on clear days. The fort, set at the foot of Rodeo Valley, offers a living history lesson.

**User Groups:** Hikers, dogs, and horses. No mountain bikes. No wheelchair facilities.

**Permits:** No permits are required. Parking and access are free.

**Maps:** A map/brochure is available at the Marin Headlands Visitors Center or by contacting the Golden Gate National Recreation Area, Marin Headlands, at the address below. A detailed hiking map of the area is available for a fee from Olmsted & Bros. Map Company. For a topographic map, ask the USGS for Point Bonita.

**Directions:** From San Francisco, drive north on U.S. 101 over the Golden Gate Bridge. In Marin, take the Alexander Avenue exit and turn left underneath the highway. Take the wide paved road to the right (Conzelman, but there is no sign), and look for the Marin Headlands sign. Drive one mile, make a right on McCullough Road (the downhill fork), and soon after, turn left on Bunker Road. Proceed a short distance to Fort Barry. After parking,

walk from the visitors center across the street and up the hill to the trailhead.

**Contact:** Golden Gate National Recreation Area, Marin Headlands Visitors Center, Building 948, Fort Barry, Sausalito, CA 94965, 415/331-1540, website: www.nps.gov/goga.

## 53 POINT BONITA LIGHTHOUSE
1.0 mi / 1.0 hr 🥾 ⏱10

**in the Marin Headlands at the mouth of San Francisco Bay**

Map 7.1, page 267

The walk to the Point Bonita Lighthouse is the most sensational easy hike in the Bay Area. In addition to the sweeping boat-level views, what makes it special is that you cross through a tunnel and then over a one-of-a-kind suspension bridge to reach the lighthouse and its perch, on a rock at the mouth of the bay. The hike starts with an easy traipse downhill; within .25 mile, you enter a 50-foot tunnel. You emerge seeing what looks like a miniature suspension bridge; some people say it looks like the Golden Gate Bridge in miniature. Cross the mini-suspension bridge (most often, just two people at a time cross, but five is the maximum it can hold), and arrive at the lighthouse. It's a fantastic lookout point, looking east at the Golden Gate Bridge, as well as across the entrance to the bay. Sound good? Is good. The only catch is that this trail is open only on weekends and Mondays, 12:30 to 3:30 P.M., but there are guided walks available on those days at 12:30 P.M. Also note this trail is sometimes closed during wet or windy weather.

**User Groups:** Hikers only. No dogs, horses, or mountain bikes are permitted.

**Permits:** No permits are required. Parking and access are free.

**Maps:** A map/brochure is available at the Marin Headlands Visitors Center or by contacting the Golden Gate National Recreation Area at the address below. For a topographic map, ask the USGS for Point Bonita.

**Directions:** From San Francisco, drive north on U.S. 101 over the Golden Gate Bridge. In

Marin, take the Alexander Avenue exit and turn left underneath the highway. Take the wide paved road to the right (Conzelman Road, but there is no sign), and look for the Marin Headlands sign. Continue on Conzelman to its end, at the Point Bonita Lighthouse parking lot.

**Contact:** Golden Gate National Recreation Area, Marin Headlands Visitors Center, Building 948, Fort Barry, Sausalito, CA 94965, 415/331-1540, website: www.nps.gov/goga.

## 54 VISTA POINT/ EAST FORT BAKER

**2.5 mi / 1.5 hrs**

**in the Marin Headlands at the northern foot of the Golden Gate Bridge**

Map 7.1, page 267

Vista Point, the famous lookout at the northern end of the Golden Gate Bridge, is like a miniature United Nations, as travelers from around the world stop there to take photos. Little do they know that with a short walk, they can get even better views. A paved trail from the parking area loops under the north foot of the bridge, then works its way back and forth, descending to East Fort Baker. There you will find a bay cove; as you look up from the shoreline, the Golden Gate Bridge is even more inspiring. You can stroll along the shore and out to a fishing pier or check out the Bay Area Discovery Museum, which is ideal for families. A nearby large grassy area makes an excellent picnic site, and picnic tables are available near Lime Point, set below the north end of the bridge. You can also extend the trip out to Yellow Bluff for more spectacular views and picnic sites.

**User Groups:** Hikers, dogs, and mountain bikes. Vista Point is wheelchair accessible, but the trail is not. No horses.

**Permits:** No permits are required. Parking and access are free.

**Maps:** A map/brochure is available at the East Fort Baker Visitors Center or by contacting the Golden Gate National Recreation Area at the address below. A detailed hiking map of

the area is available for a fee from Olmsted & Bros. Map Company. For a topographic map, ask the USGS for San Francisco North.

**Directions:** From San Francisco, drive north on U.S. 101 over the Golden Gate Bridge, get in the right lane, and take the Vista Point exit.

**Contact:** Golden Gate National Recreation Area, Marin Headlands Visitors Center, Building 948, Fort Barry, Sausalito, CA 94965, 415/331-1540, website: www.nps.gov/goga.

## 55 YELLOW BLUFF TRAIL

**1.5 mi / 1.0 hr**

**in the Marin Headlands at the northern foot of the Golden Gate Bridge**

Map 7.1, page 267

This is a little piece of heaven. From your vantage point on Yellow Bluff, San Francisco looks like the land of Oz. The first major land point along the Marin shore east of the Golden Gate, Yellow Bluff provides a stunning lookout across San Francisco Bay and the surrounding landmarks. The trail is flat, short, and (best of all) unpublicized, and there are a few picnic tables nearby. From East Fort Baker, walk on the trail that heads east near the shoreline of the bay. You can turn the trip into a triangular loop hike by continuing along the shore, heading toward Sausalito, turning left at the trail junction, and hiking back to Fort Baker. One of the great features of this area is that it is often sunny, even when the Marin Headlands to the west lie buried in fog.

**User Groups:** Hikers, dogs, and mountain bikes. Fort Baker is wheelchair accessible, but the trail is not. No horses.

**Permits:** No permits are required. Parking and access are free.

**Maps:** A map/brochure is available at the East Fort Baker Visitors Center or by contacting the Golden Gate National Recreation Area, Marin Headlands, at the address below. A detailed hiking map of the area is available for a fee from Olmsted & Bros. Map Company. For a topographic map, ask the USGS for San Francisco North.

**Directions:** From San Francisco, drive north on U.S. 101 over the Golden Gate Bridge. In Marin, take the Alexander Avenue exit and stay to the right at the split. Drive a very short distance, turn left, and drive a few hundred yards to a stop sign. Turn right and drive .5 mile to the parking area for Fort Baker.

**Contact:** Golden Gate National Recreation Area, Marin Headlands Visitors Center, Building 948, Fort Barry, Sausalito, CA 94965, 415/331-1540, website: www.nps.gov/goga.

## 56 PERIMETER ROAD
**5.0 mi / 2.5 hrs**

**in Angel Island State Park in San Francisco Bay**

Map 7.1, page 267

A hike around Angel Island on Perimeter Trail provides great views of the bay and a historical tour amid remnants of the island's military past. And it's long enough to provide a decent workout to boot. The trail winds past old barracks and abandoned military buildings, climbs through lush eucalyptus forests and across high bluffs, and looks out over San Francisco Bay and its world-class landmarks. Heavy logging of nonnative eucalyptus has dramatically changed the character of this island and the trail.

When linked with Perimeter/Summit Trail, this is the most scenic hike in the entire Bay Area. The only downer is that the trail is actually a road, but somehow it still manages to inspire. From each lookout, you see San Francisco Bay from a completely new angle.

**User Groups:** Hikers and mountain bikes (helmets are required for bikers 17 years and under). The Perimeter Road is accessible to wheelchairs, but many portions are too steep for use. No dogs (except for seeing-eye dogs) or horses.

**Permits:** No permits are required. Ferry ticket fees, which include day-use fees, vary according to departure point and season; a fee is charged per bicycle.

**Maps:** You can purchase a topographic map/brochure for a fee at the park or by mail from the Angel Island Association. For a topographic map, ask the USGS for San Francisco North.

**Directions:** Ferry service to Angel Island is available from Tiburon, San Francisco, Vallejo, and Oakland/Alameda.

To the Tiburon ferry: Take U.S. 101 in Marin to the exit for Tiburon Boulevard. Head east on Tiburon Boulevard (curving along the bay's shoreline). Park at one of the pay lots in Tiburon, then walk a short distance to the Tiburon Ferry (well signed).

To the San Francisco ferry: Take U.S. 101 to the exit for Marina Boulevard exit (near the southern foot of the Golden Gate Bridge). Take that exit and drive east on Marina Boulevard toward Fisherman's Wharf. Park at a parking garage or pay lot. The ferry departs from Pier 41.

To the Vallejo ferry: Take I-80 to U.S. 780. Take U.S. 780 and drive to Curtola Parkway. Take Curtola Parkway (which becomes Mare Island Way) and continue to 495 Mare Island Way, where free parking is available. The docking area is directly across from the parking lot.

To the Oakland/Alameda ferry: In Oakland drive south on Highway 980 to the exit for Webster. Take that exit and drive west to the ferry dock at Jack London Square.

**Contact:** Angel Island State Park, 415/435-1915 or 415/435-5390 (ranger's office); California State Parks, Marin District, 415/898-4362, website: www.parks.ca.gov (click on Find A Park); kayak rentals: Sea Trek Ocean Kayaking 415/488-1000, website: www.seatrekkayak.com; bike rentals: The Picnic People, 925/426-3071; tram tours: 415/897-0715, website: www.angelisland.com; picnic reservations: 800/444-7275; ferry information: San Francisco and Oakland/Alameda 415/773-1188, Tiburon 415/435-2131, websites: www.angelislandferry.com, www.blueandgoldfleet.com; maps: Angel Island Assocation, Box 866, Tiburon, CA 94920.

## 57 PERIMETER/SUMMIT TRAIL
### 6.0 mi / 3.0 hrs

**in Angel Island State Park in San Francisco Bay**

Map 7.1, page 267

When standing atop Mount Livermore, you will be surrounded by dramatic scenery in every direction. That is because at 781 feet, this is the highest point on Angel Island, the virtual center of San Francisco Bay. The views are superb even at night, when the lights of the Golden Gate Bridge and the city glow with charm. The trail is steep, with a 550-foot climb in just .5 mile, which will have even the best-conditioned hikers puffing like locomotives by the time they reach the top. The Summit Trail is actually a cutoff from Perimeter Trail; for the ambitious, it's the highlight of a six-mile loop hike on Angel Island.

**User Groups:** Hikers only. No dogs (except for seeing-eye dogs), horses, or mountain bikes (they may not even be walked on this trail). No wheelchair facilities.

**Permits:** No permits are required. Ferryboat ticket fees, which include day-use fees, vary according to departure point and season; a fee is charged per bicycle.

**Maps:** You can purchase a topographic map/brochure for a fee at the park or by mail from the Angel Island Association. For a topographic map, ask the USGS for San Francisco North.

**Directions:** Ferry service to Angel Island is available from Tiburon, San Francisco, Vallejo, and Oakland/Alameda.

To the Tiburon ferry: Take U.S. 101 in Marin to the exit for Tiburon Boulevard. Head east on Tiburon Boulevard (curving along the bay's shoreline). Park at one of the pay lots in Tiburon, then walk a short distance to the Tiburon Ferry (well signed).

To the San Francisco ferry: Take U.S. 101 to the exit for Marina Boulevard exit (near the southern foot of the Golden Gate Bridge). Take that exit and drive east on Marina Boulevard toward Fisherman's Wharf. Park at a parking garage or pay lot. The ferry departs from Pier 41.

To the Vallejo ferry: Take I-80 to U.S. 780. Take U.S. 780 and drive to Curtola Parkway. Take Curtola Parkway (which becomes Mare Island Way) and continue to 495 Mare Island Way, where free parking is available. The docking area is directly across from the parking lot.

To the Oakland/Alameda ferry: In Oakland drive south on Highway 980 to the exit for Webster. Take that exit and drive west to the ferry dock at Jack London Square.

**Contact:** Angel Island State Park, 415/435-1915 or 415/435-5390 (ranger's office); California State Parks, Marin District, 415/898-4362, website: www.parks.ca.gov (click on Find A Park); kayak rentals: Sea Trek Ocean Kayaking 415/488-1000, website: www.seatrekkayak.com; bike rentals: The Picnic People, 925/426-3071; tram tours: 415/897-0715, website: www.angel-island.com; picnic reservations: 800/444-7275; ferry information: San Francisco and Oakland/Alameda 415/773-1188, Tiburon 415/435-2131, websites: www.angelislandferry.com, www.blueandgoldfleet.com; topographic map/brochure: Angel Island Association, Box 866, Tiburon, CA 94920.

## 58 AGAVE TRAIL
### 1.5 mi / 1.5 hrs

**on Alcatraz Island**

Map 7.2, page 268

The Agave Trail at Alcatraz Island has made accessible one-third of the island that was previously closed to visitors. The catch is you must come in winter, when the trail is open from late September to February; the trail is closed from late winter on into spring and summer to protect nesting birds. The trail also provides some of the most breathtaking views found on any of the 15,000 miles of Bay Area hiking trails. The trail—named after the agave plant, which is common here—starts at the ferry landing on the east side of Alcatraz and traces the island rim to its southern tip. It is quite wide, with a few benches and cement picnic tables situated for sweeping views of both the East Bay and San Francisco.

From its southern end, the trail is routed back to the historic parade ground atop the island, where you find some sculptural masterpieces, which include 110 stone steps. The parade ground is a haven for nesting birds, and this area is closed to the public in the spring each year so the birds will not be disturbed. If you visit during a low tide, you can discover some relatively little-known tidepools at the island's southwest corner. This part of the island also has abundant bird life, including a population of night herons; in terms of pure cuteness, they're right up there with chipmunks and baby ducks. The old cell block is located at the center of the island, with other buildings sprinkled along the eastern shore and on the northern tip. Ranger-led park tours are available, and visitors can rent audiotapes for a self-guided cell-house tour. The ghost of Al Capone is said to roam here, trying to figure out a way to pay his taxes.

**User Groups:** Hikers only. No dogs, horses, or mountain bikes. No wheelchair facilities.

**Permits:** No permits are required. Entry tickets include the ferryboat trip to the island ($11.50 for adults, discounts for seniors and children) and are available from Blue & Gold Fleet. A cassette tape audio tour may be purchased for an additional $4.50. Ferries depart from Pier 41 in San Francisco.

**Maps:** A map is available at the ferry landing for a fee. For a topographic map, ask the USGS for San Francisco North.

**Directions:** Take I-80 into San Francisco to the exit for Embarcadero/Harrison Street. Take that exit and drive to Harrison Street. Turn right on Harrison Street and drive five blocks to Embarcadero Street. Turn left on Embarcadero and drive (past the piers) to Bay Street. Continue on Embarcadero Street for two blocks to the Pier 39 garage, on the left. Walk to Pier 41 at Fisherman's Wharf and look for the prominent sign for Blue & Gold Fleet.

**Contact:** Alcatraz Island, website: www.nps.gov/alcatraz; Blue & Gold Fleet, 415/705-5555, websites: www.blueandgoldfleet.com; San Francisco Convention & Visitor Bureau, 415/391-2000; California Welcome Center, 415/956-3493; Golden Gate National Recreation Area, Fort Mason, Building 201, San Francisco, CA 94123, 415/561-4700 or 415/705-8214 (group reservations), fax 415/561-4710.

## 59 LANDS END TRAIL

2.5 mi / 1.0 hr

**on the San Francisco headlands at the entrance to San Francisco Bay**

Map 7.2, page 268

One glance from Lands End can take in the mouth of San Francisco Bay and the crashing breakers, with the Golden Gate Bridge and Marin Headlands in the foreground and the Pacific Ocean, Farallon Islands, and Point Reyes in the background. By now you've probably figured out that this is one of San Francisco's greatest lookouts. From the trailhead by the Cliff House Restaurant, you meander eastward on a dirt trail set near bluffs topped with cypress trees. You can also tromp down past the ruins of Sutro Baths, then head toward the Golden Gate Bridge atop bluffs, occasionally sighting the masts of a few sunken ships along shore, and taking in a series of beautiful views. The path is nearly flat and traces Coastal Trail between Lands End and China Beach on a 2.5-mile round-trip course from the parking area. It is a great destination on Sunday mornings, when hikers take a brisk walk, enjoying the sea breeze on their faces, and then brunch at one of two nearby restaurants, the Cliff House or Louis'. The entire route was once a railroad track out to Sutro Baths. If you time it during a low tide, the alert can spot the top of ships' masts (from old shipwrecks in the rocks) below poking through the sea surface.

**User Groups:** Hikers, wheelchairs, dogs, and mountain bikes (mountain bikes must be walked through narrow sections of the trail). No horses.

**Permits:** No permits are required. Parking and access are free.

**Maps:** For a free map, contact the Golden Gate National Recreation Area at the address below. For a topographic map, ask the USGS for San Francisco North.

**Directions:** From the Peninsula: Take I-280 to Highway 1 in San Bruno. Turn west and drive one mile to Highway 35/Skyline Boulevard. Turn right on Highway 35 and drive past Lake Merced in San Francisco, jogging left at the lake, and continue to the Cliff House and Louis' Restaurants. Continue just past Louis' to the parking areas.

From San Francisco: Take Geary Boulevard west until it reaches the ocean and Louis' and Cliff House Restaurants. Just before Louis', look for the parking area, on the right.

**Contact:** Fort Funston Ranger Station, 415/239-2366; Golden Gate National Recreation Area, Fort Mason, Building 201, San Francisco, CA 94123, 415/561-4700, websites: www.nps.gov/goga, www.californiacoastaltrail.org/san_francisco.html.

# 60 COASTAL TRAIL
## 2.5 mi / 1.0 hr

**in the Presidio on the
San Francisco headlands**

Map 7.2, page 268

While Vista Point at the north end of the Golden Gate Bridge may be the most popular place from which to take snapshots of the bridge, a lookout on Coastal Trail provides an even more scenic view. This spot is just north of Baker Beach, where San Francisco Bay, the bridge, and the Marin coast form a postcardlike scene that fits easily into a 35mm frame.

After parking, hike southwest on Coastal Trail, passing the Fort Scott Overlook, Battery Crosby, and Battery Chamberlin en route to the south end of Baker Beach. The best strategy for photographers is to make the 30-minute walk in, scanning for photo opportunities along the way, and then capture any ideas on film on the return trip. The soft dirt pathway is set

in cypress, but don't forget that this is the big, bad city: Hikers should travel in pairs or go very early in the morning to avoid encounters with homeless campers. For more postcard views of the bridge, take a side trip down to mile-long Baker Beach.

**User Groups:** Hikers and wheelchairs. Dogs are not advised. No horses or mountain bikes.

**Permits:** No permits are required. Parking and access are free.

**Maps:** For a free map, contact the Golden Gate National Recreation Area at the address below. For a topographic map, ask the USGS for San Francisco North.

**Directions:** From U.S. 101 at the southern end of the Golden Gate Bridge, take the toll plaza parking area exit. Limited parking is available directly east of the toll plaza in a paved area (after parking, you must walk through a short tunnel to reach the trailhead). There is additional unpaved parking 50 yards west of the toll plaza, near the trailhead.

**Contact:** Contact: Presidio Visitors Center, 415/561-4323; Golden Gate National Recreation Area, Fort Mason, Building 201, San Francisco, CA 94123, 415/561-4700, website: www.nps.gov/prsf/index.htm.

# 61 GOLDEN GATE BRIDGE
## 3.0 mi / 1.25 hrs

**from San Francisco to Marin**

Map 7.2, page 268

Relatively few Bay Area residents ever get around to taking the No. 1 tourist walk in the world: the Golden Gate Bridge. From the center of the bridge, the view is incomparable. Looking eastward, you can see Alcatraz, Angel Island, and the bay framed by the San Francisco waterfront and the East Bay hills. Parking is available at the north end of the bridge (at Vista Point) and at the south end, on each side of the toll station. If you park on the west side, walk through a short tunnel that runs under U.S. 101 and loops up to the pathway entrance. The path on the east side of the bridge is reserved for pedestrians, while the west side is for bicyclists only on weekends and evenings. From one end to the other, the bridge is 1.2 miles long (and 220 feet above the water), but most folks walk only halfway out, then return to their cars, for a round-trip of 1.5 miles.

**User Groups:** Hikers, wheelchairs, dogs, and mountain bikes (on the west side of the bridge only). No horses.

**Permits:** No permits are required. Parking and access are free.

**Maps:** For a free map, contact the Golden Gate National Recreation Area at the address below. For a topographic map, ask the USGS for San Francisco North.

**Directions:** From U.S. 101 at the southern end of the Golden Gate Bridge, take the toll plaza parking area exit. Limited parking is available directly east of the toll plaza. There is additional unpaved parking 50 yards west of the toll plaza; from there you must walk through a short tunnel to reach the foot of the bridge.

**Contact:** Golden Gate National Recreation Area, Fort Mason, Building 201, San Francisco, CA 94123, 415/561-4700, website: www.nps.gov/goga/.

## 62 GOLDEN GATE PROMENADE
**3.0 mi / 1.25 hrs**

**on the shore of San Francisco Bay in San Francisco**

Map 7.2, page 268

This paved trail leads along the shoreline of San Francisco Bay from Marina Green to Fort Point. It is virtually flat and the views are magnificent, with a scenic backdrop of the Golden Gate Bridge, Alcatraz, Tiburon, Sausalito, and the bay itself. From the parking area at Marina Green, simply follow the paved pathway through Crissy Field along the way out to Fort Point, and then to the southern foot of the Golden Gate Bridge. The entire trail is popular with joggers and walkers, especially in the morning. In the afternoon it can get quite windy. People looking for a workout can find one of the Bay Area's most popular par

courses at Marina Green. Side trips include the old Muni Pier, the Presidio (which borders much of the route), Fort Point Pier, and Fort Point itself, with its cannons at the foot of the Golden Gate Bridge. The recent reclamation of Crissy Field as wetlands, dunes, and picnic area is another highlight.

**User Groups:** Hikers, wheelchairs, dogs, and mountain bikes. No horses.

**Permits:** No permits are required. Parking and access are free.

**Maps:** For a free map, contact the Golden Gate National Recreation Area at the address below. For a topographic map, ask the USGS for San Francisco North.

**Directions:** From U.S. 101 at the southern end of the Golden Gate Bridge in San Francisco, take the Marina Boulevard exit. Head southeast toward Fisherman's Wharf. Parking lots are available off Marina Boulevard at Fort Mason, Marina Green, Crissy Field, and near the St. Francis Yacht Club.

**Contact:** Presidio Visitors Center, 415/561-4323; Golden Gate National Recreation Area, Fort Mason, Building 201, San Francisco, CA 94123, 415/561-4700, website: www.nps.gov/prsf/index.htm.

## 63 OCEAN BEACH ESPLANADE
**6.0 mi / 2.25 hrs**

**on the San Francisco coast**

Map 7.2, page 268

At Ocean Beach, located along San Francisco's coastal Great Highway, you discover a long expanse of sand, a paved jogging trail, and small parks at Fort Funston and Thornton Beach. The nature of both the trail and the adjacent beach allows visitors to create trips of any length. The beach spans four miles, from Seal Rock (near the Cliff House) south to Fort Funston, from which you can continue to explore south all the way past Center Hole to Mussel Rock, at the north end of Pacifica. The huge swath of sand at Ocean Beach is popular with joggers, especially during low tides, when the hard-packed sand is uncovered. A paved jogging trail is located just east of the Great Highway. Warning: Do not swim here. There have been several drownings in this area due to rip tides.

**User Groups:** Hikers, dogs, and horses. Partially wheelchair accessible. No mountain bikes.

**Permits:** No permits are required. Parking and access are free.

**Maps:** For a free map, contact the Golden Gate National Recreation Area at the address below. For a topographic map, ask the USGS for San Francisco South.

**Directions:** From the Peninsula: Take I-280 to Highway 1 in San Bruno. Turn west and drive one mile to Highway 35/Skyline Boulevard. Turn right on Highway 35 and drive five miles, bearing left to pass Lake Merced. Park on the left along the beach.

From San Francisco: Take Geary Boulevard west until it dead-ends, at the ocean and the Cliff House Restaurant. Turn left on the Great Highway and drive one mile to the parking area, on the right.

**Contact:** Fort Funston Ranger Station, 415/239-2366; Golden Gate National Recreation Area, Fort Mason, Building 201, San Francisco, CA 94123, 415/561-4700, website: www.nps.gov/goga/fofu/index.htm.

## 64 FORT FUNSTON SUNSET TRAIL
### 1.5 mi / 0.5 hr

**on the San Francisco coast**

Map 7.2, page 268

Fort Funston is perched on San Francisco's coastal bluffs, with the ocean on one side and Lake Merced on the other. The park is one of the most popular places around to take dogs. It is also the top hang gliding spot in the Bay Area, and watching those daredevils soar is the main attraction. A viewing deck is provided adjacent to the parking area, where Sunset Trail begins. From here, the trail is routed north through coastal bluffs and above sand dunes for .75 mile to the park's border. In the

fall and winter, the fog clears, and each evening the kinds of sunsets that can make your spine tingle put on quite a show. Those hang gliders are worth gawking at, too, especially in the spring, when the north winds come up every afternoon.

A few highlights: Petrified saber-toothed tiger teeth have been discovered in the veins of volcanic ore on the cliff faces. The replanting of native flowers and plants, as well as the protection of the bluffs, has inspired a return of burrowing owls and bank swallows. A ton of sand dollars seem to turn up on the beach walk that leads south from Fort Funston less than a mile to Thornton Beach (collecting them is a violation of park rules).

**User Groups:** Hikers, dogs, and horses. Partially wheelchair accessible (on the paved jogging route). No mountain bikes.

**Permits:** No permits are required. Parking and access are free.

**Maps:** For a free map, contact the Golden Gate National Recreation Area at the address below. For a topographic map, ask the USGS for San Francisco South.

**Directions:** From the Peninsula: Take I-280 to Highway 1 in San Bruno. Turn west and drive one mile to Highway 35/Skyline Boulevard. Turn right (north) on to Highway 35 and drive five miles to the park entrance, on the left. Turn left and drive to the parking areas or park office.

From San Francisco: Take Geary Boulevard west until it dead-ends, at the ocean and the Cliff House Restaurant. Turn left on to the Great Highway and drive four miles to the park entrance, on the right. Turn right and drive to the parking areas or park office.

**Contact:** Fort Funston Ranger Station, 415/239-2366; Golden Gate National Recreation Area, Fort Mason, Building 201, San Francisco, CA 94123, 415/561-4700, website: www.nps.gov/goga/fofu/index.htm.

## 65 SUMMIT LOOP TRAIL
3.1 mi / 1.5 hrs

**in San Bruno Mountain State and County Park near South San Francisco**

Map 7.2, page 268

An island of peace and stunning views are bypassed each week by millions of drivers who need a heck of a lot of both. From a perch high on San Bruno Mountain, you can look down on U.S. 101 in South San Francisco and easily imagine the temporary insanity that grips some drivers in their mission to reach San Francisco International Airport. In fact, a secret to keeping your cool while on U.S. 101's rat maze of a road is to take a moment, gaze up at the old mountain, and then imagine you are up there at the lookout bench, enjoying the sweeping view and surrounding tranquility. Or better yet, take the Cow Palace exit and get it first hand.

San Bruno Mountain State Park is located on the north Peninsula, cresting at 1,314 feet above the Cow Palace. Millions have seen the old mountain from a distance. Yet those who know the place more intimately treasure its natural riches and rate it as a paradise island amid a sea of urban and industrial development.

The trailhead for the Summit Loop is well marked and is located at the parking lot on the south side of Guadalupe Canyon Parkway. This hike starts with a short spur that leads to the three-way junction for the Summit Loop. For the fastest payoff, turn left. A short climb rises over the course of a mile, and with it come the first views of San Francisco and the South Bay. Just after passing a junction (on the left) to the Dairy Ravine Trail, look for another fork on the left. Take this. This turn leads a short distance to a bench with one of the most dramatic lookouts of Bay Area parks.

When you are ready, return to the Summit Loop. The trail meanders in a clockwise circle, climbing near the mountain top (splintered by antennas), and more long-distance views abound. After swiveling your head to see it all, you may need a trip to the chiropractor. The trail eventually descends into Guadalupe Canyon. You cross radio road, reconnect with the short spur, then turn left and walk the final 100 yards to the parking lot. The complete loop is 3.1 miles and takes about 90 minutes.

The views from the Summit Loop Trail provide the payoff. From the lookout bench, you can swivel your head from north to south and take in hundreds of well-known landmarks: San Francisco's Twin Peaks, the downtown high-risers, the Bay Bridge, Oakland Hills, Mount Diablo on the horizon—and then to the south, San Francisco International Airport, Coyote Point, the San Mateo Bridge, and South San Francisco Bay. Other views from the Summit Loop Trail include the wilderness flank of Montara Mountain (about 10 miles to the west), and a sighting of Mount Tamalpais to the north.

Note: In summer of 2004, this park was closed on a temporary basis on Tuesdays, Wednesdays, and Thursdays because of park budget issues in San Mateo County. Call park headquarters at 650/363-4020 before planning a trip on those days.

**User Groups:** Hikers and horses. No dogs or mountain bikes. No wheelchair facilities.

**Permits:** No permits are required. An entrance fee of $5 per vehicle is charged.

**Maps:** For a free trail map, contact San Bruno Mountain State and County Park at the address below. For a topographic map, ask the USGS for San Francisco South.

**Directions:** Take U.S. 101 to the exit for the Brisbane/Cow Palace. Take that exit and drive two miles to Guadalupe Canyon Parkway. Turn west and drive 2.3 miles to the park entrance. Turn right to the entrance kiosk. Continue to the parking lot, at the south side of Guadalupe Canyon Parkway.

**Contact:** San Bruno Mountain State and County Park, 555 Guadalupe Canyon Parkway, Brisbane, CA 94005, 650/992-6770 or 650/573-2592 (park administered by Coyote Point); County Parks, 455 County Center, 4th Floor, Redwood City, CA 94063-1646, 650/363-4020, fax 650/599-1721, website: www.parks.ca.gov (click on Find A Park).

## 66 SADDLE TRAIL
**2.5 mi / 1.25 hrs**

**in San Bruno Mountain State and County Park**

Map 7.2, page 268

Guadalupe Canyon Parkway splits San Bruno Mountain State and County Park in two, leaving hikers to decide which section to visit on a given day. The north half provides a pair of good loop hikes: Saddle Trail (the featured hike from the parking area/trailhead on the north side) and Bog Trail. Both are easier than Summit Loop/Ridge Trail, in the park's southern half. From the north parking area, start walking on Old Guadalupe Trail, which junctions with Saddle Trail after about 20 minutes. From here, you'll take Saddle Trail and loop around the northern boundaries of the park, climbing about 150 feet in the process. The wind can absolutely howl through this area at times, so pick your hiking days with care. Most of the surrounding terrain is open hillside grasslands, so the views of the South Bay are unblocked and on clear days are just spectacular.

Note: In the summer of 2004, this park was closed on a temporary basis on Tuesdays, Wednesdays, and Thursdays because of park budget issues in San Mateo County. Call park headquarters at 650/363-4020 before planning a trip on those days.

**User Groups:** Hikers and horses. No dogs or mountain bikes. No wheelchair facilities.

**Permits:** No permits are required. An entrance fee of $5 per vehicle is charged.

**Maps:** For a free trail map, contact San Bruno Mountain State and County Park at the address below. For a topographic map, ask the USGS for San Francisco South.

**Directions:** From U.S. 101 north of South San Francisco, take the Brisbane/Cow Palace exit and drive two miles to Guadalupe Canyon Parkway. Turn left and follow Guadalupe Canyon Parkway for about two miles to the park entrance, on the right. After passing the entrance kiosk, drive to the parking area, on the north side of the road.

**Contact:** San Bruno Mountain State and County Park, 555 Guadalupe Canyon Parkway, Brisbane, CA 94005, 650/992-6770; County Parks, 455 County Center, 4th Floor, Redwood City, CA 94063-1646, 650/363-4020, fax 650/599-1721, website: www.parks.ca.gov (click on Find A Park).

## 67 BOG TRAIL
**0.8 mi / 0.5 hr**

**in San Bruno Mountain State and County Park**

Map 7.2, page 268

The Bog Trail provides a good introduction to San Bruno Mountain State and County Park, although you need to hike other trails here if you desire a more passionate experience. The trail starts at the trailhead on Guadalupe Canyon Parkway's north side and is routed along the north flank of the mountain, changing only 30 feet in elevation. By turning right at the junction with Old Guadalupe Trail, you can make this a short loop hike. Open hillsides surround the trail and are quite pretty on clear days in the spring, when the grasslands turn green and are sprinkled with an explosion of wildflowers. Hikers who make this easy trip quickly get a sense of the importance of the open-space buffer the park provides for the congested north Peninsula.

Note: In summer of 2004, this park was closed on a temporary basis on Tuesdays, Wednesdays, and Thursdays because of park budget issues in San Mateo County. Call park headquarters at 650/363-4020 before planning a trip on those days.

**User Groups:** Hikers only. The upper part of the trail is wheelchair accessible. No dogs, horses, or mountain bikes.

**Permits:** No permits are required. An entrance fee of $5 per vehicle is charged.

**Maps:** For a free trail map, contact San Bruno Mountain State and County Park at the address below. For a topographic map, ask the USGS for San Francisco South.

**Directions:** From U.S. 101 north of South San

Francisco, take the Brisbane/Cow Palace exit and drive two miles to Guadalupe Canyon Parkway. Turn left and follow Guadalupe Canyon Parkway for about two miles to the park entrance, on the right. After passing the entrance kiosk, drive to the parking area, on the north side of the road.

**Contact:** San Bruno Mountain State and County Park, 555 Guadalupe Canyon Parkway, Brisbane, CA 94005, 650/992-6770; County Parks, 455 County Center, 4th Floor, Redwood City, CA 94063-1646, 650/363-4020, fax 650/599-1721, website: www.parks.ca.gov (click on Find A Park).

## 68 BAY TRAIL/COYOTE POINT
### 1.0–10.0 mi / 0.5–3.0 hrs

**in Coyote Point County Park in San Mateo**

Map 7.2, page 268

The Bay Trail extends from Coyote Point on north for five miles along the shoreline of the South Bay to what is called Hotel Row, in Burlingame. The first thing you will notice is the dramatic expanse of the South Bay; up close, it is much bigger that most envision, particularly at high tide. There seems to be the highest variety of marine birds during low tides, when mud flats are exposed for miles. Egrets, coots, and sandpipers are residents of wetlands habitat here, and other the avocets that arrive every March are among the migrants that make regular appearances.

This trip makes a great family bike ride, because the route is flat, and it extends far enough to the north to provide a decent round-trip (10 miles). When the wind is blowing out of the north, the jets will make their approach from the south. That provides a sideshow from the Bay Trail.

A shorter trip is the .25-mile walk from the boat ramp out to land's end. The point provides a great lookout of the South Bay, where you can watch boats heading out, as well as good shore-fishing access for rays, sharks, and jacksmelt. From the lookout over the pretty

South Bay on a clear day, it looks as if you could get a running start, jump, and glide across the water to the land's edge.

**User Groups:** Hikers, wheelchairs, and mountain bikes. No dogs or horses.

**Permits:** No permits are required. An entrance fee of $5 per vehicle is charged.

**Maps:** For a free trail map, contact Coyote Point County Park at the address below. For a topographic map, ask the USGS for San Mateo.

**Directions:** From the north: Take U.S. 101 to San Mateo and the exit for Poplar. Take that exit and drive to Humboldt (at the first stoplight). Turn right on Humboldt and go to Peninsula. Turn right and continue over the highway to a frontage road (Bayshore Boulevard). Turn left on the frontage road and drive a short distance to the signed turn and entrance to the park.

From the south: Take U.S. 101 to San Mateo and the exit for Dore. Take that exit and make an immediate left turn on the frontage road (Bayshore Boulevard). Continue a short distance to the signed turn and entrance to the park.

**Contact:** Coyote Point County Park, 1701 Coyote Point Drive, San Mateo, CA 94401, 650/573-2592; San Mateo County Parks, 650/363-4020, website: www.eparks.net (click on Parks).

## 69 SAN ANDREAS TRAIL
### 6.0 mi / 2.5 hrs

**in the San Mateo County foothills southwest of San Bruno**

Map 7.2, page 268

The San Andreas Trail overlooks Upper San Andreas Lake, winding most of its way through wooded foothills. The only downer is that much of the route runs adjacent to Highway 35/Skyline Boulevard. Regardless, it is worth the trip, because to the west you can see the untouched slopes of Montara Mountain, a game preserve, and that sparkling lake—all off-limits to the public. The trail starts near the northern end of the lake; a signed trailhead marker is posted on Skyline Boulevard. It goes about three miles until the next access point, at Hillcrest Boulevard, and from there, it connects to Sawyer Camp Trail. The view of Montara Mountain to the west is particularly enchanting during the summer, when rolling fog banks crest the ridgeline: a spectacle.

**User Groups:** Hikers, horses, and mountain bikes. Note that the northern section is paved, but the southern section is not. There are some wheelchair-accessible facilities. No dogs.

**Permits:** No permits are required. Parking and access are free.

**Maps:** For a free trail map, contact San Mateo County Parks at the address below. For a topographic map, ask the USGS for Montara Mountain.

**Directions:** To access the north gate: From I-280 in San Bruno, take the Westborough exit and drive west up the hill to the intersection with Highway 35/Skyline Boulevard. Turn left on Highway 35 and drive about 2.5 miles to the trailhead entrance on the right side of the road.

To access the south gate: On I-280 drive to the Millbrae Avenue exit. Take that exit and drive north on Skyline Boulevard, a frontage road on the west side of Highway 280, and continue to the parking area on the left.

**Contact:** San Mateo County Parks and Recreation, 455 County Center, 4th Floor, Redwood City, CA 94063-1646, 650/363-4020, website: www.eparks.net (click on Parks).

## 70 SAWYER CAMP TRAIL
### 12.0 mi / 5.0 hrs

**in the San Mateo County foothills south of San Bruno**

Map 7.2, page 268

By taking Sawyer Camp Trail, hikers get everything that there is on the connecting link to the north (the San Andreas Trail) and more. Alas, not all of the "more" is good. On a positive note, the trail is set away from the road, so you get more peace (at least, that seems the intent). It is routed along a pretty lake and through a forest, so you get more nature. But since this route is paved and hardly a secret,

you also get more people. In fact, ever since the biking speed limit was raised to 15 miles per hour, there's been a real problem with hikers being used as flags in a slalom course. The result is that many hikers would rather stay away from this area than be put into fight-or-run showdowns with warp-speed bikers. Although the listed one-way distance is six miles, at any point, you can just turn around and go back, cutting the trip as short as you wish. Or better yet, bring two vehicles, leave one at each of the two trailheads along Highway 35/Skyline Boulevard, and make it a one-way walk. From north to south, the hike includes a drop of 400 feet, so if you plan on a return trip, there will be a little huff-and-puff on the way back. Park benches are provided at viewpoints along the lake, where you can often see trout rising and feeding on summer evenings.

**User Groups:** Hikers, horses, and mountain bikes. There are some wheelchair-accessible facilities at the south end. No dogs.

**Permits:** No permits are required. Parking and access are free.

**Maps:** For a free trail map, contact San Mateo County Parks at the address below. For a topographic map, ask the USGS for Montara Mountain.

**Directions:** From I-280 in San Bruno, take the Westborough exit and drive west up the hill to the intersection with Highway 35/Skyline Boulevard. Turn left on Highway 35 and drive about six miles to the trailhead entrance, on the right.

**Contact:** San Mateo County Parks and Recreation, 455 County Center, 4th Floor, Redwood City, CA 94063-1646, 650/363-4020, website: www.eparks.net (click on Parks).

## 71 CRYSTAL SPRINGS TRAIL
### 6.4 mi / 3.0 hrs

**along Crystal Springs Reservoir in the Woodside foothills**

Map 7.2, page 268

From the parking area, the trail runs along the border of San Francisco watershed land, adjacent to Cañada Road. Beautiful Crystal

Springs Reservoir is off to the west, occasionally disappearing from view behind a hill as you walk south. Deer are commonly seen in this area (a nice bonus). Your destination is 3.2 miles away, the Pulgas Water Temple (closed to the public), where waters from Hetch Hetchy in Yosemite arrive via canal and thunder into this giant, bathtublike structure surrounded by Roman pillars and a canopy. At the Pulgas Water Temple, you have the option of continuing for another 4.2 miles to Huddart Park. With a shuttle car, that makes a great one-way hike. This general route is a sensational family bike trip on Cañada Road, which is closed to all vehicles on Bicycle Sundays.

**User Groups:** Hikers and mountain bikes. No dogs or horses. No wheelchair facilities.

**Permits:** No permits are required. Parking and access are free.

**Maps:** For a free trail map, contact San Mateo County Parks at the address below. For a topographic map, ask the USGS for San Mateo.

**Directions:** From I-280 in San Mateo, take the Highway 92 exit and drive west to Cañada Road/Highway 95. Turn south on Cañada Road and drive .2 mile to the parking area, on the right.

**Contact:** San Mateo County Parks and Recreation, 455 County Center, 4th Floor, Redwood City, CA 94063-1646, 650/363-4020, website: www.eparks.net (click on Parks).

## 72 BAY RIDGE TRAIL/ CRYSTAL SPRINGS

**6.4 mi / 3.0 hrs**

**along Cahill/Fifield ridges in the Woodside foothills**

Map 7.2, page 268

The fight that took 70 years to win was resolved with one turn of a key. A locked gate at the Crystal Springs Watershed on the Peninsula was finally cracked open to the public. Access to the 23,000-acre watershed—which we once nicknamed the Forbidden Paradise—is finally possible, though by reservations only, where you join a group. Still, this is something special.

If you can get a trailhead reservation for the Skylawn access near the Highway 92 summit, then you have the chance for a sensational 12-mile romp, one-way with a shuttle. From the trailhead adjacent to Skylawn Memorial Gardens, the Bay Ridge Trail is routed north through the heart of the watershed, past Pilarcitos Lake, to Sweeney Ridge, and beyond to the trailhead at the end of Sneath Lane in San Bruno—where you should place an awaiting car.

The trips starts along Cahill Ridge. This section is a gentle downhill route set on the east side of the ridge, occasionally burrowing through beautiful forests of cypress, Douglas fir and redwood. If you hit it right in late afternoon, refracted sunlight through the branches can send dancing streaks of light and shadows across the road. After passing a turnoff on the right (Quarry Road, nice views to the east), you continue three miles to a five-way road junction called Five Points.

From Five Points, you get a glimpse of awesome Pilarcitos Lake to your left, one of the only protected fish reserves in America. But you are not allowed to get any closer and take in the full beauty of this double-canyoned jewel. Guess why? Because someone in the water department lives at the lake in a private cabin with a picnic area set in redwoods, along with boat dock and boat? Yep.

You continue north at Five Points and gain Fifield Ridge. Here you emerge from forest and climb atop and amid high foothills peppered thickly with chaparral. The long-distance views are eye-popping: the wilderness east flank of Montara Mountain, the outstanding wildflower blooms in spring, San Andreas Lake, and the South Bay.

The views get even better in the next mile. To the east, there's gemlike San Andreas Lake below, and beyond are the South Bay and the East Bay's prominent peaks: Mount Diablo, Mission Peak, and Mount Hamilton. To the west are the hidden wildlands of the eastern slopes of Montara Mountain, the boundary for the San Francisco Fish and Game Refuge, and 25 miles out to sea, you can see the Farallon Islands.

As good as this is, it could get far better. For instance, another service road junctions with Fifield Ridge, providing a route up the little-seen eastern flank of Montara Mountain all the way to the 1,898-foot summit. Then the route goes over the top to McNee State Park and San Pedro Valley County Park. Opening that route would provide a sensational one-way hike, starting from the Sneath Lake access. You would climb to Sweeney Ridge, then into the watershed and to the summit of Montara Mountain, and then down the north side to McNee Ranch State Park in Montara.

**User Groups:** Hikers, mountain bikes, horses. No dogs. Limited wheelchair access from Skylawn trailhead.

**Permits:** A permit and reservation are required at 650/652-3203 or at www.sfwater.org (click on the butterfly, then on Reservations). Public access is restricted to groups under the supervision of a trained leader on Wednesdays, Saturdays, and Sundays.

**Maps:** For a free trail map, contact San Francisco Public Utilities Commission. For a topographic map, ask the USGS for San Mateo.

**Directions:** From the Peninsula, take Highway 280 to Highway 92. Turn west on Highway 92, drive over Crystal Springs and continue to the summit, at Skylawn Memorial Gardens. Just before Skylawn, look for the access road for parking. Group leaders usually arrive early at trailhead.

**Contact:** San Francisco Public Utilities Commission, 650/652-3203, website: www.sfwater.org.

# 73 WATERDOG LAKE TRAIL
### 4.0 mi / 1.75 hrs

**in the Belmont foothills**

Map 7.2, page 268

The lack of public access to a half dozen lakes on the Peninsula makes little Waterdog Lake all the more special. Out of the way and often forgotten, the lake was created by damming Belmont Creek in Diablo Canyon. Although not exactly a jewel, it still makes for a unique recreation site; it gets overlooked because the parking access is so obscure. It takes only 15 minutes to reach the lake, and the trail skirts the northern edge of the shore. Many people stop here, but if you forge on, you will be well compensated. The trail, which is more of a dirt road, rises above the lake and enters John Brooks Memorial Open Space. At the crest of the hill, which is reached after a climb of about 300 feet, there are pretty views of Crystal Springs Reservoir. An option is to extend your trip on Sheep Camp Trail, a dirt road that is linked to a gravel road set adjacent to the San Francisco Fish and Game Refuge.

**User Groups:** Hikers and mountain bikes. No dogs or horses. No wheelchair facilities.

**Permits:** No permits are required. Parking and access are free.

**Maps:** For a trail map, contact the City of Belmont at the address below. For a topographic map, ask the USGS for San Mateo.

**Directions:** From Highway 92 in San Mateo, take the Ralston Avenue exit and turn south on Lyall Way. Drive to the corner of Lyall Way and Lake Road to find the parking entrance. Parking is available along the street.

**Contact:** City of Belmont, Parks, 1225 Ralston Avenue, Belmont, CA 94002, 650/595-7441, website: www.belmont.gov (click on Parks and Recreation).

# 74 MILAGRA RIDGE
### 2.0 mi / 0.75 hr

**in Pacifica near Skyline College**

Map 7.2, page 268

A mile-long paved road/trail is routed to the top of Milagra Ridge, one of the best places imaginable to fly a kite. Those coastal breezes can almost put a strong kite into orbit; some people even use saltwater fishing rods and reels filled with line, playing the kite as if it were a big fish. Kite flying is allowed only inside the gate on the hill to the left. Hikers must stay on the trail to protect the endangered mission blue butterfly.

The parking area that hikers use to gain access to Milagra Ridge is small and obscure—nobody winds up here by accident. Once you park your car, the hike up to the ridge top is an easy mile and is suitable for wheelchair users who have some assistance. The summit was flattened in the 1950s to accommodate a missile site, which has been abandoned long since. Looking westward, visitors are surprised at the sheer drop-off from the ridge down into Pacifica. Alas, in the summer months, this can be one of the foggiest places in the world.

**User Groups:** Hikers and mountain bikes (bikes allowed on only one mile of paved trail). Wheelchair accessible with assistance. No dogs or horses.

**Permits:** No permits are required. Parking and access are free.

**Maps:** For a free map, contact the Golden Gate National Recreation Area at the address below. For a topographic map, ask the USGS for San Francisco South.

**Directions:** From I-280 in San Bruno, take the Westborough exit and then drive west up the hill and across Highway 35/Skyline Boulevard. Drive to College Avenue and turn right (north). Continue a very short distance to the end of the road and the trailhead. Limited parking is available.

**Contact:** Golden Gate National Recreation Area, Fort Mason, Building 201, San Francisco, CA 94123, 415/561-4700, website: www.nps.gov/goga.

## 75 SWEENEY RIDGE
**4.2 mi / 3.0 hrs**

**on the Peninsula ridgeline in San Bruno**

Map 7.2, page 268

No matter how long you've lived in the Bay Area, there's always a chance to make it new again. You can do this by literally going the extra mile, and it works at even the region's most famous landmarks.

Try it at Sweeney Ridge, set on the ridge between San Bruno and Pacifica, less than 10 miles south of San Francisco. Just about everybody's heard about Sweeney Ridge and Bay Discovery Site, and many have visited it to relive a bit of Bay Area history. But get this: Just an extra 10 minutes of walking can provide an overlook of one of the most pristine meadows on public land in the whole Bay Area—where deer, rabbits, quail, and hawks are common on quiet evenings, and where the ocean views can knock your heart out.

Plan on three hours to enjoy the trip. You'll want to stop often for the views and enjoy a picnic at the meadow overlook, although the trip can easily be done in less time. It's a 4.2-mile round-trip (1.8 miles to Bay Discovery Site), including an easy 550-foot climb on the way in from the Sneath Lane access.

There are four access points and trailheads, but the best is at the end of Sneath Lane in San Bruno, where the road dead-ends at a hiker's access gate. As you start the climb (on a service road), you will immediately notice that the views are gorgeous off to your left—especially the views of San Andreas Lake and beyond to the South Bay. As you rise, Crystal Springs also comes into the view. The route heads up to the ridge, where you turn left and then arrive at the Discovery Site. The views from here are stunning, not only of the Bay Area to the east, but of the fantastic wildlands that extend across 100,000 acres, topped by Montara Mountain, San Pedro Mountain, Mori Ridge, and the Crystal Springs Watershed. On clear days, there are also views across the bay to Mount Diablo and the Mount Hamilton range.

For many, this is the end of the trip. After all, how can it get any better? Just walk a little more, that's how. Continue south on the ridge for about eight minutes and look for a cutoff trail on the right (it is unsigned and not on maps). Turn right, and in just five minutes, this small cutoff provides an overlook to what is known as South Meadow—an outstanding wildlife habitat with a stunning view of the ocean.

**User Groups:** Hikers, dogs, horses, and mountain bikes. No wheelchair facilities.

**Permits:** No permits are required. Parking and access are free.

**Maps:** For a free map, contact the Golden Gate National Recreation Area at the address below. For a topographic map, ask the USGS for San Francisco South.

**Directions:** From San Francisco, drive south on Highway 280 to San Bruno and Sneath Lane. Take that exit and drive west on Sneath Lane (crossing Skyline Boulevard) until it deadends at the trail access.

**Contact:** Sweeney Ridge, c/o Fort Funston, 415/239-2366; Golden Gate National Recreation Area, Fort Mason, Building 201, San Francisco, CA 94123, 415/561-4700, websites: www.nps.gov/goga/sites.htm (click on Sweeney Ridge), www.nps.gov/goga/clho/swri/index.htm, www.ci.pacifica.ca.us.

## 76 MONTARA MOUNTAIN/ BROOKS CREEK TRAIL
**7.0 mi / 2.5 hrs**

**in San Pedro Valley County Park in Pacifica**

Map 7.2, page 268

Just 20 minutes south of San Francisco is this secluded trail in San Pedro Valley County Park, where visitors are few, the coastal beauty is divine, and hikers can carve out their own personal slice of heaven. The Montara Mountain/ Brooks Creek Trail is the prize of the park, featuring the best viewing area for Brooks Falls (read on) and great lookouts to the Pacific Coast. After parking, walk about 50 yards along Montara Mountain/Brooks Creek Trail. The trail then splits, with Brooks Creek Trail on the left and Montara Mountain Trail on the right. The two merge again about one mile up Brooks Creek and continue as a common route to the peak. Turn right on the well-signed Montara Mountain Trail. From here, the next mile

climbs several hund[...] Brooks Falls appears in [...] down a canyon.

The fall is connected in three [...] tasseled tiers, falling 175 feet in all. A[...] there never seems to be enough water [...] waterfall, it still is a very pretty gorge amid[...] chaparral-covered mountain slope. One reason Brooks Falls is so little known is that it doesn't flow year-round. As a tributary to San Pedro Creek, Brooks Creek runs only in late winter and spring (best of course after several days of rain). Note that a great coastal lookout is available another 10 minutes up the trail on a dramatic rock outcrop. The hike continues all the way to the North Peak of Montara Mountain (at 1,898 feet), a trip of 3.5 miles one-way, including a final 1.1-mile push on a fire road to reach the summit. On a clear spring day, the views are absolutely stunning in all directions—highlighted by the Pacific Ocean, the Farallon Islands, and miles of the adjacent off-limits Crystal Springs Watershed.

This route is the first link in one of the few great one-way hikes (using a shuttle) in the Bay Area. From the top of Montara Mountain, you enter McNee Ranch State Park and hike 3.8 miles to Montara State Beach, descending all the way, with glorious views for the entire route. So with cars parked at each end of the trail, you can hike 7.3 miles one-way from San Pedro Valley County Park, up Montara Mountain, and down to Montara State Beach.

Note: In the summer of 2004, this park was closed on a temporary basis on Tuesdays, Wednesdays, and Thursdays because of park budget issues in San Mateo County. Call park headquarters at 650/363-4020 before planning a trip on those days.

**User Groups:** Hikers and horses (on designated trails only). Some trails and facilities are wheelchair accessible. No dogs or mountain bikes.

**Permits:** No permits are required. An entrance fee of $5 per vehicle is charged.

**Maps:** For a free trail map, contact San Pedro Valley County Park at the address below. For losophizing about life while looking down into the mouth of a beer bottle rather than taking this walk and experiencing the full fabric of the place.

**User Groups:** Hikers and dogs. No horses or mountain bikes. No wheelchair facilities.

**Permits:** No permits are required. Parking and access are free.

**Maps:** For a topographic map, ask the USGS for Montara Mountain.

**Directions:** From San Francisco, head south on I-280 to Daly City. Turn south on Highway 1 and drive about five miles into Pacifica. Drive to the southern end of Pacifica and turn right at the parking lot for Pacifica State Beach/Linda Mar. The trail starts at the north end of the beach.

**Contact:** City of Pacifica, Parks Department, 170 Santa Maria Avenue, Pacifica, CA 94044, 650/738-7300, websites: www.ci.pacifica.ca.us/recreation/rec.html, www.eparks.net/parks.

on-
igh-
inda
:nds,
ive to
ds on
st side

**Contact:** ... k, 600 Oddstad Boulevard, Pacifica, CA 94044, 650/355-8289, website: www.eparks.net (click on Parks); City of Pacifica, Parks Department, 170 Santa Maria Avenue, Pacifica, CA 94044, 650/738-7300, website: www.ci.pacifica.ca.us/recreation/rec.html.

## 77 LINDA MAR/ ROCKAWAY POINT TRAIL
### 2.5 mi / 1.5 hrs

**on the Pacifica shoreline near Pacifica State Beach/Linda Mar**

Map 7.2, page 268

Sure, you could probably hike this route to the end and back in a flash. But sometimes, as you will discover here, taking the time to go slowly sure beats rushing through as quickly as possible. You just plain won't want to miss anything after you park at the Pacifica State Beach parking lot at Linda Mar and start hiking north on the beach. The northern end of this sand stretch is a great place to throw sticks to a dog (but be aware that the sand dune area provides habitat for the endangered snowy plover) and to fish for striped bass in the summer.

At the end of the beach, climb up on the dirt trail that traces around Rockaway Point. Here you'll find beautiful views of San Pedro Point, Montara Mountain, and of course, the Pacific Ocean. Just meander along, listen to the waves, and let the beauty flow through you. Then when you feel like it, turn around and follow the same route back to your car. When you first drive up, don't get spooked if the parking lot seems crowded. Why? Because many people often prefer to spend time phi-

## 78 SAN PEDRO MOUNTAIN
### 6.0 mi / 2.5 hrs

**in McNee Ranch State Park in Montara**

Map 7.2, page 268

For people who like dramatic coastal views, this is an ideal trail. It traces the top of coastal bluffs and provides many flawless vistas. To reach them, take note at the entrance gate and look for the trail that is routed off to the left and up through the hilly grasslands. With those first few steps, it doesn't look like much of a trail. But as you continue, rising atop the first crest, you see how it tracks up the spine of the coastal ridgeline, eventually providing a lookout above Gray Whale Cove. From this viewpoint, you may feel an odd sense of irony: Below is Highway 1, typically filled with a stream of slow-moving cars driven by people who want to get somewhere else; meanwhile, you are in a place of peace and serenity, happy right where you are.

The hike includes a few short climbs across grasslands and can be converted to a loop hike by turning right at the junction with Montara Mountain Trail.

**User Groups:** Hikers and dogs. No horses or mountain bikes. No wheelchair facilities.

**Permits:** No permits are required. Parking and access are free.

**Maps:** For a topographic map, ask the USGS for Montara Mountain.

**Directions:** From San Francisco, drive about 17 miles south on Highway 1. Continue through Pacifica, then through Devils Slide, and down to the base of the hill. Look for a small pullout area on the left. The access point is at a yellow gate with a state park property sign. There is room for just a few cars. Do not block the gate. If the pullout area is full, drive south on Highway 1 a short distance and park at the lot on the west side of the highway, at Montara State Beach.

**Contact:** Half Moon Bay State Parks, 650/726-8820; Half Moon Bay State Ranger, 650/726-8819, website: www.parks.ca.gov (click on Find A Park).

## 79 MONTARA MOUNTAIN/ McNEE RANCH
**7.6 mi / 3.75 hrs**

**in McNee Ranch State Park in Montara**

Map 7.2, page 268

On a clear day from the top of Montara Mountain, the Farallon Islands to the northwest appear so close you may think you could reach out and pluck them from the ocean. To the east, it looks as if you could take a giant leap across the bay and land atop Mount Diablo.

Some 10 miles to the north and south, there's nothing but mountain wilderness connecting Sweeney Ridge to an off-limits state game preserve. By now you should be properly motivated for the climb, which for many is a genuine butt-kicker. From the main access gate to the top, it's 3.8 miles, a rise of nearly 2,000 feet that includes three killer "ups." Follow the ranch road up the San Pedro Mountain ridgeline to the Montara Coastal Range; at the fork, stay to the right on the dirt road as it climbs and

turns. After a 20-minute wheezer of an ascent, look for a garbage can at a flat spot on the left side of the trail. This garbage can serves as a landmark to a 30-yard cutoff trail to a perch for a dazzling view of Pacifica and northward along the Pacific Coast. After catching your breath, continue on, heading up, up, and up, eventually topping out at the summit. Only the radio transmitter here mars an otherwise pristine setting. All you need for this hike is a clear day, some water, and plenty of inspiration.

**User Groups:** Hikers, dogs, and mountain bikes. No horses. No wheelchair facilities.

**Permits:** No permits are required. Parking and access are free.

**Maps:** For a topographic map, ask the USGS for Montara Mountain.

**Directions:** From San Francisco, drive about 17 miles south on Highway 1. Continue through Pacifica, then through Devils Slide, and down to the base of the hill. Look for a small pullout area on the left. The access point is at a yellow gate with a state park property sign. There is room for just a few cars. Do not block the gate. If the pullout area is full, drive south on Highway 1 a short distance and park at the lot on the west side of the highway, at Montara State Beach.

**Contact:** Half Moon Bay State Parks, 650/726-8820; Half Moon Bay State Ranger, 650/726-8819, website: www.parks.ca.gov (click on Find A Park).

## 80 FITZGERALD MARINE RESERVE
**1.0 mi / 1.0 hr**

**in Moss Beach**

Map 7.2, page 268

The closer you look, the better it gets. When you go tidepool hopping, there is nothing more fascinating than discovering a variety of tiny sea creatures. That's what's so attractive about the Fitzgerald Marine Reserve—a shallow, 30-acre reef that exposes hundreds and hundreds of tidal pockets every time a minus low tide rolls back to the ocean. After parking, it's a short walk down to the tidepools; from here, you walk on exposed rock, watching the wonders of the tidal waters. Be sure to wear boots that grip well, and take care not to crush any fragile sea plants as you walk. In the tidepools, you may see hermit crabs, rock crabs, sea anemones, sculpins, starfish, sea snails, and many other animals and plants in various colors. An option during low tides is to continue walking south on the beach to a beautiful cove at the foot of the Moss Beach Distillery, a popular watering hole. Note: No dogs, no beachcombing, no shell gathering. In other words, OK looky, but no touchy. After all, this is a preserve.

**User Groups:** Hikers only. No dogs, horses, or mountain bikes. No wheelchair facilities.

**Permits:** No permits are required. Parking and access are free.

**Maps:** For a topographic map, ask the USGS for Montara Mountain.

**Directions:** From San Francisco: Take I-280 to Highway 1 in Daly City and drive through Pacifica, over Devils Slide, and into Moss Beach. Turn right (west) at the signed turnoff at California Street and continue one mile to the parking area.

From the Peninsula: Take Highway 92 into Half Moon Bay and then head north on Highway 1 for seven miles to Moss Beach. Turn left (west) at the signed turnoff at California Street and drive one mile to the parking area.

**Contact:** Fitzgerald Marine Reserve, P.O. Box 451, Moss Beach, CA 94022, 650/728-3584; San Mateo County Parks and Recreation, 455 County Center, 4th Floor, Redwood City, CA 94063-1646, 650/363-4020 or 650/340-7598 (group tour reservations), website: www.eparks .net (click on Parks).

## 81 PILLAR POINT
**2.5 mi / 1.5 hrs**

### in Princeton at Half Moon Bay

**Map 7.2, page 268**

When things are right, this easy walk has the prospects of being one of the truly great coastal walks. It includes a secluded beach with in-shore kelp beds and sea lions playing peeka-boo, and during low tide, you can walk around the corner at Pillar Point and boulder hop in wondrous seclusion. But watch your tide book, because the Pillar Point tidal area is under-water most of the time. Also keep an eye out for weather reports, because Pillar Point can be buried in fog for what seems weeks on end in the summer.

To start the trip, park at the small lot set just below the radar station, on the western side of Princeton Harbor. Then walk out along the west side of the harbor. The trail here is on hard-packed dirt above two quiet beaches where grebes, cormorants, and pelicans often cavort. During the evening, the harbor lights are quite pretty here. When you reach the Princeton jetty, turn right and walk along the beach toward Pillar Point; this is where the sea lions frequently play "now-you-see-me, now-you-don't." At low tides, continue around Pillar Point and enjoy the rugged beauty, solitude, and ocean views, taking your time as you hop along from rock to rock. Some people wonder if you can hop your way all the way around the Pillar Point Head and to the beach at the south end of Fitzgerald Marine Reserve. Nope.

**User Groups:** Hikers, dogs, and horses (not advised). No mountain bikes. No wheelchair facilities.

**Permits:** No permits are required. Parking and access are free.

**Maps:** For a topographic map, ask the USGS for Half Moon Bay.

**Directions:** From the Peninsula, take I-280 to San Mateo and Highway 92. Turn west on Highway 92 and drive to Half Moon Bay. Turn right on Highway 1 and drive five miles to Princeton. Turn left at the traffic signal, drive about .5 mile through Princeton Village, and turn left again, going one mile toward a radar station. There is limited parking at a small lot on the left side of the road. Follow the trail on the west side of the harbor.

**Contact:** There is no managing agency. For

weather and general information: Capt. John's, 650/726-2913; Huck Finn Sportfishing (closed November through December 26), 650/726-7133; website: www.smharbor.com/pillarpoint.

## 82 WHITTEMORE GULCH FROM SKYLINE
### 4.3 mi / 3.0 hrs

**in Purisima Creek Redwoods Open Space Preserve on Skyline Ridge near San Mateo**

Map 7.2, page 268

Purisima Creek Redwoods is a magnificent 2,633-acre redwood preserve set on the western slopes of the Santa Cruz Mountains, from Skyline Boulevard down to Half Moon Bay. One of the best ways to explore the area is on Harkins Ridge Trail. You can make it a one-way trip by having a shuttle car waiting at the trail's end at the Higgins Purisima parking access.

The trail starts at the Skyline Access on Skyline Boulevard, elevation 2,000 feet, located at a parking area just south of a small store. From here, you descend for .75 mile across open hills for beautiful views (best to the north of Half Moon Bay and Pillar Point) on your way to the rim of Whittemore Gulch.

At the canyon rim, the two ends of the trail are connected by a series of switchbacks, that is, the trail on top is linked with that on the bottom through the redwood canyon. This section of trail covers a 1,000-foot elevation change. It is well graded (about 10 percent), and with a rhythmic huff and a puff, it makes for a steady climb on the way back up.

The round-trip, from top to bottom and back, is 4.3 miles with an one-way elevation change of 1,600 feet, a great trip.

Then there is the timing. On weekday mornings, this place can be paradise—Purisima can feel like a vast uninhabited wilderness, complete with the long-distance coastal views and a hidden redwood canyon. On Sunday afternoons, however, it's often a zoo, especially on the adjacent Harkins Fire Trail, where hikers can find themselves jumping out of the way of mountain bikers ripping downhill.

For those who want a pristine experience, a good option is to take Soda Gulch Trail: About a mile down Harkins Ridge Trail, turn left at the junction. No mountain bikes are allowed on this portion of the trail, which heads past giant trees, redwood sorrel, and fern-lined creek banks.

**User Groups:** Hikers only. Mountain bikes permitted on adjacent Harkins Fire Trail. Horses and mountain bikes are sometimes restricted due to wet weather, so check with a ranger beforehand. No dogs. No wheelchair facilities.

**Permits:** No permits are required. Parking and access are free.

**Maps:** For a free map, contact the Midpeninsula Regional Open Space District at the address below or pick one up at the trailhead. For a topographic map, ask the USGS for Woodside.

**Directions:** From San Francisco, drive south on I-280 for about 15 miles to the Highway 92 cutoff. Turn west on Highway 92 and drive to Highway 35/Skyline Boulevard. Turn south (left) on Highway 35 and drive 4.5 miles to the Purisima Creek Redwoods parking area, on the right (west side of the road, just past a small store).

**Contact:** Midpeninsula Regional Open Space District, 330 Distel Circle, Los Altos, CA 94022, 650/691-1200, website: www.openspace.org (click on Preserve Locator). During nonbusiness hours, a touch-tone phone menu is available for trail news, conditions, and events.

## 83 WHITTEMORE GULCH FROM HALF MOON BAY
### 4.3 mi / 3.0 hrs

**in Purisima Creek Redwoods Open Space Preserve near Half Moon Bay**

Map 7.2, page 268

Most folks come to this popular trailhead, located just south of Half Moon Bay, to take a short stroll along Purisima Creek and then turn back. The Whittemore Gulch Trail, however, offers more of a challenge, especially near the end. It also forms the return route for a loop hike starting at Skyline Boulevard.

The trail begins innocently enough from the Higgins Purisima parking area, set in the beautiful foothills southeast of Half Moon Bay. The trail is routed right up Whittemore Gulch for a gentle climb over the first mile. This stretch is even suitable for wheelchairs and strollers. All seems well with the world as you pass through a grove of shaded redwoods and by a small stream. Cross the stream and continue up the canyon amid a beautiful redwood forest, complete with enclosed canopy and this beautiful little creek. At the head of the canyon, you then begin to climb. In a series of switchbacks, the trail climbs 600 feet in just over .25 mile. After the switchbacks, the trail climbs another 400 feet in a more gracious fashion to reach the Whittemore Gulch parking access on Skyline Boulevard, which, at 2,000 feet, features a great lookout of Half Moon Bay and Pillar Point Harbor. The trailhead elevation is 400 feet, so that means it's a 1,600-foot climb to Skyline Boulevard. Of course, it also means that this trip can also be started from Skyline, but then your return trip will be up rather than down.

**User Groups:** Hikers only. Mountain bikes permitted on adjacent Harkins Fire Trail. Horses and mountain bikes are sometimes restricted due to wet weather, so check with a ranger beforehand. No dogs. No wheelchair facilities.

**Permits:** No permits are required. Parking and access are free.

**Maps:** For a free map, contact the Midpeninsula Regional Open Space District at the address below or pick one up at the trailhead. For a topographic map, ask the USGS for Woodside.

**Directions:** From San Francisco, drive south on I-280 for about 15 miles to the Highway 92 cutoff. Turn west on Highway 92 and drive to Half Moon Bay. At the stoplight, turn left on Main Street and drive south through town to Higgins Purisima Road. Turn left and drive on the winding road for four miles to the trailhead parking area, on the left.

**Contact:** Midpeninsula Regional Open Space District, 330 Distel Circle, Los Altos, CA 94022, 650/691-1200, website: www.openspace.org (click on Preserve Locator). During nonbusiness hours, a touch-tone phone menu is available for trail news, conditions, and events.

## 84 REDWOOD TRAIL

**0.5 mi / 0.5 hr**

**in Purisima Creek Redwoods Open Space Preserve on Skyline Ridge near Woodside**

Map 7.2, page 268

The .25-mile-long Redwood Trail allows just about anybody to experience the grandeur of a redwood forest. Anybody? People with baby strollers, wheelchairs, or walkers, as well as those recovering from poor health, will be able to do this trail. It starts at 2,000 feet on Skyline Boulevard and is routed north under a canopy of giant redwoods. At the end, there are picnic tables and restrooms. And the return trip is just as easy. Most people don't really hike the trail, they just kind of mosey along, seeing how it feels to wander freely among ancient trees.

**User Groups:** Hikers and wheelchairs. No dogs, horses, or mountain bikes.

**Permits:** No permits are required. Parking and access are free.

**Maps:** For a free map, contact the Midpeninsula Regional Open Space District at the address below or pick one up at the trailhead. For a topographic map, ask the USGS for Woodside.

**Directions:** From San Francisco, drive south on I-280 for approximately 15 miles to the Highway 92 cutoff. Turn west on Highway 92 and continue driving to Highway 35/Skyline Boulevard. Turn west on Highway 35 and drive to the Purisima Creek parking area, located at mile marker 16.65.

**Contact:** Midpeninsula Regional Open Space District, 330 Distel Circle, Los Altos, CA 94022, 650/691-1200, website: www.openspace.org (click on Preserve Locator). During nonbusiness hours, a touch-tone phone menu is available for trail news, conditions, and events.

## 85 HUDDART PARK LOOP
**5.0 mi / 3.25 hrs**

**in the Woodside foothills**

> **Map 7.2, page 268**

Huddart Park is a Peninsula treasure, covering 1,000 acres from the foothills near Woodside on up to Skyline Boulevard. Redwoods grow on much of the land, a creek runs right through the park, and when you hike high on the east slope, there are occasional views of the South Bay. Although several short loop trips are available here, including the .5-mile Redwood Trail, this loop hike that circles the park has a little bit of everything. Some of the shorter trips here do not provide the kind of payoff in natural beauty that many are looking for.

At the Werder Picnic Area, start on the Dean Trail. To make a complete loop and return to the trailhead, connect to Richard Road's Trail, Summit Springs Trail, and Archery Fire Trail. In the process, you will get a good overview of the entire area.

Be sure to grab a trail map first, though. There are dozens of loop options at virtually every trail junction. Add variety to your hike, or make it shorter or longer, by carrying a map. A unique option is taking Skyline Ridge Trail, which connects Huddart Park with Wunderlich Park.

**User Groups:** Hikers and horses. Mountain bikes are permitted on paved roads only. The Chickadee Trail at Huddart Park is wheelchair accessible. No dogs.

**Permits:** No permits are required. An entrance fee of $5 per vehicle is charged.

**Maps:** For a trail map, contact Huddart Park at the address below. For a topographic map, ask the USGS for Woodside.

**Directions:** From I-280 in Woodside, take the Woodside Road/Highway 84 exit and drive about nine miles west to King's Mountain Road. Turn right and drive 2.2 miles to the park entrance.

**Contact:** Huddart Park, 1100 Kings Mountain Road, Woodside, CA 94062, 650/851-1210 or 650/363-4021 (group reservations); San Mateo County Parks and Recreation, 455 County Center, 4th Floor, Redwood City, CA 94063-1646, 650/363-4020, website: www.eparks.net (click on Parks).

## 86 TAFONI MONOLITH
**3.0 mi / 1.5 hrs**

**El Corte de Madera Open Space Preserve**

> **Map 7.2, page 268**

The Tafoni Monolith is the surprise show-stopper at El Corte de Madera Open Space Preserve, set on the San Francisco Peninsula. Most just call it The Tafoni. You emerge from a forest trail to suddenly arrive at a series of 50-foot high Goliaths. These huge sandstone formations are filled with natural carved-out hollows, holes, cuts, and what rangers call "fretwork" and "tree trunks." All of it is the product of erosion over hundreds of years, as wind and rain slowly engraved the soft sandstone into this etched monolith—and it's a stunner.

At El Corte de Madera Open Space Preserve, the trailhead to visit the Tafoni Monolith is located near the CalTrans' Skeggs Vista Point, set on the Peninsula's Skyline Ridge above Woodside. Most park at the vista point and then walk or bike about 50 yards north on the road's shoulder to reach the trailhead, a gated service road.

From here, the Tafoni Trail is routed through a dense second-growth forest (primarily Douglas fir) for 1.2 miles to a junction. Turn right, and in .25 mile, look for the signed fork on the right, a hiking path signed Tafoni (bikes are prohibited here; bikers should bring a lock and hike out the last piece). This is it: A short descent will lead you to the monolith, and a route circling it provides access to all the strange honeycombs, "petrified tree trunks," and fretwork seemingly etched into rock. It is strange and unforgettable.

In the Bay Area, sandstone formations were originally undersea deposits where sand grains were cemented together. The Tafoni is the softest of the Bay Area sandstone formations and crumbles easily. That is why rangers request visitors to keep their hands off.

Visiting the Tafoni usually whets the appetite for more adventure, whether riding or hiking. This park can certainly provide it. It is a big preserve, covering 2,821 acres and with 36 miles of trails for biking, hiking, and horseback riding. The trails are linked at many junctions, providing a fantastic network to self-style your trip.

In addition to the Tafoni, a must-see is the view from vista point off the Manzanita Trail. It's a breathtaking lookout across foothills, canyons, coast, and ocean.

Special Note: The Resolution Trail is the site of a 1953 DC-6 plane crash. The knoll off Fir Trail served as the rescue base. Taking artifacts is illegal. Those breaking this law are subject to a ghost curse.

**User Groups:** Hiking, mountain bikes, horses. No dogs. No bikes or horses on short spur to Tafoni Monolith. No wheelchairs.

**Permits:** Parking and access free.

**Maps:** Obtain a free map at the trailhead or from the Midpeninsula Regional Open Space District at the address below. For a topographic map, ask the USGS for Woodside.

**Directions:** From the Peninsula: Take Highway 280 to Woodside and Highway 84. Turn east on Highway 84 and go to Skylonda and Highway 35 (Skyline Boulevard). Turn right (north) and go 3.9 miles to CalTrans Skeggs Vista Point, on the right. Park and then walk 50 yards north on road's shoulder to the trailhead, on the west side of road.

From the East Bay: Take Highway 92 west to the junction of Highway 280, and continue straight for three miles to Highway 35/Skyline Boulevard. Turn left (south) and go 8.5 miles to Vista Point, on the left (you must continue straight, then make U-turn and return to Vista Point). Park and continue as above.

**Contact:** Midpeninsula Regional Open Space District, 330 Distel Circle, Los Altos, CA 94022, 650/691-1200, website: www.openspace.org

(click on Preserve Locator). During nonbusiness hours, a touch-tone phone menu is available for trail news, conditions, and events.

## 87 ALAMBIQUE TRAIL/ SKYLINE TRAILHEAD
**4.5 mi / 2.5 hrs**

### in Wunderlich Park

Map 7.2, page 268

Comes a time when you don't want to be bugged by anything. Not by traffic, work pressures, or the latest nightmare on the front page. That is when you search out places so quiet that to speak above a whisper seems irreverent. Sure, most everybody loves the excitement of an adventure with sizzle, but sometimes, only harmony will do.

An overlooked trailhead on Skyline Boulevard provides the jump-off point for such a place. It is the Skyline trailhead at Wunderlich Park, a short drive north of Sky Londa. On some Sundays, it's possible that you could not see another soul—despite the thousands of people out biking, hiking, and horseback riding at the half dozen parks and scenic roads in the surrounding foothills.

This trailhead features a 4.5-mile loop hike that drops into a remote redwood canyon with a creek, then rises back up, looping back through forest to the starting point.

The trip starts on the east side of Skyline Boulevard, where a large blue sign for the Bay Ridge Trail marks the trailhead. From Skyline, start the trip on the Alambique Trail (signed). Here you work your way down a canyon for two miles amid a second-growth redwood forest. On foggy mornings, moisture can be so heavy that it can drip from the branches of redwoods and Douglas fir like a sparse rain. Everything smells wet, dense, and old. Our personal preference is a fogbound morning, when the heavy air smothers distant sounds, creating perfect quiet.

It takes only about 40 minutes to reach a canyon bottom, where you cross a feeder stream to Alambique Creek. This watershed is home to many banana slugs and newts, and when the forest is dripping with moisture, they are often on the trail—so be careful not to accidentally squish the little fellers. Though the canyon is cool and moist, it is the kind of place you can sit for a while and enjoy a trail lunch in complete peace. For the moment, you can let the rest of the world worry about their latest problems. There's always something, right?

Shortly after a creek crossing, you will reach a four-way junction with the Skyline Trail. To return to the starting point, take the sharpest right on the Skyline Trail and climb back out (with a few short drops) for 2.4 miles to a staging area.

If you want to extend your trip at the junction, instead turn left on the Alambique Trail. This is routed further down into the park to an additional network of trails. The best offshoots are to The Meadows or to Alambique Flat. Amid the second-growth forest along the lower portion of the Alambique Trail, there is a single awesome redwood giant, called The Methuselah Tree, that still remains. Its trunk is roughly 45 feet around, with massive burls and a burned-out gap.

**User Groups:** Hikers and horses. No dogs or mountain bikes. No wheelchair facilities.

**Permits:** No permits are required. Parking and access are free.

**Maps:** For a trail map, contact Huddart Park at the address below. For a topographic map, ask the USGS for Woodside.

**Directions:** From the Peninsula: Take Highway 280 to Woodside and Highway 84. Turn east on Highway 84 and go to Sky Londa and Highway 35/Skyline Boulevard. Turn right (north) and go 2.5 miles to the trailhead, on the right (signed Bay Ridge Trail). Limited parking is available on the road's shoulder.

From the East Bay: Take Highway 92 west to the junction of Highway 280 and continue three miles to Highway 35/Skyline Boulevard. Turn left (south) and go 10 miles to the trailhead, on the left.

**Contact:** Wunderlich Park, c/o Huddart Park, 1100 Kings Mountain Road, Woodside, CA 94062, 650/851-1210 or 650/851-0326, fax 650/851-9558; San Mateo County Parks and Recreation, 455 County Center, 4th Floor, Redwood City, CA 94063-1646, 650/363-4020, fax 650/599-1721, website: www.eparks.net (click on Parks).

## 88 MEADOWS LOOP TRAIL
**5.5 mi / 3.0 hrs**

**in Wunderlich Park in the Woodside foothills**

Map 7.2, page 268

Wunderlich Park is one of the better spots on the Peninsula for clearing out the brain cobwebs. The network of trails here provides a variety of adventures, from short strolls to all-day treks. Take your pick. The Meadows Loop is the preferred route; it circles much of the park, crossing first through oak woodlands, then rising to open grasslands, and finally passing a redwood forest on the way back. Make sure you have a trail map, then take this route: Near the park office, look for the signed trailhead for Alambique Trail, and hike .5 mile. At the junction with Meadows Trail, turn right, hike a short distance, and then turn left on to Meadows Trail and climb up to The Meadows. This is a perfect picnic site, with rolling hills, grasslands, and great views. To complete the loop, forge onward, then turn right at Bear Gulch Trail and take it all the way back, including switchbacks, to the park entrance. This hike includes an elevation gain of nearly 1,000 feet, so come prepared for a workout.

**User Groups:** Hikers and horses. No dogs or mountain bikes. No wheelchair facilities.

**Permits:** No permits are required. A $5 fee is charged per vehicle.

**Maps:** For a free map, contact San Mateo County Parks at the address below. For a topographic map, ask the USGS for Woodside.

**Directions:** From I-280 on the Peninsula in Woodside, take the Woodside/Highway 84 exit. Drive west for 2.5 miles to the park on the right.

**Contact:** Wunderlich Park, c/o Huddart Park, 1100 Kings Mountain Road, Woodside, CA 94062, 650/851-1210 or 650/851-0326, fax 650/851-9558; San Mateo County Parks and Recreation, 455 County Center, 4th Floor, Redwood City, CA 94063-1646, 650/363-4020, fax 650/599-1721, website: www.eparks.net (click on Parks).

## 89 RAVENSWOOD OPEN SPACE PRESERVE

**2.0 mi / 0.75 hr**

**on the shore of South San Francisco Bay at Ravenswood**

Map 7.2, page 268

This 370-acre parcel of land is rich in marshland habitat and is home to many types of birds. The highlights are two excellent observation decks. From the parking area at the end of Bay Road, backtrack by walking across a bridged slough to the trailhead, on the north side of the road. You will immediately come to a fork in the road. You can turn right and walk 200 feet to an observation deck with great views of the South Bay. If you go left instead, you will find a hard-surface path that heads north and hooks out toward the bay to another wood observation deck. This is the primary destination for most visitors.

**User Groups:** Hikers, wheelchairs, and mountain bikes. No dogs or horses.

**Permits:** No permits are required. Parking and access are free.

**Maps:** For a free map, contact the Midpeninsula Regional Open Space District at the address below. For a topographic map, ask the USGS for Mountain View.

**Directions:** From U.S. 101 in Palo Alto, take the University Avenue exit and drive east to Bay Road. Turn right on Bay Road and drive to the end of the road. The preserve entrance is adjacent to Cooley Landing.

**Contact:** Midpeninsula Regional Open Space District, 330 Distel Circle, Los Altos, CA 94022, 650/691-1200, website: www.openspace.org (click on Preserve Locator). During nonbusi-ness hours, a touch-tone phone menu is available for trail news, conditions, and events.

## 90 BAYLANDS TRAIL

**4.0 mi / 1.5 hrs**

**on the shore of South San Francisco Bay in Palo Alto**

Map 7.2, page 268

The farther you go on this trail, the better it gets. The Baylands Trail starts without much fanfare: a simple hard-gravel road with an ugly slough on the left and the Palo Alto Golf Course on the right. If you keep looking ahead, you will often see ground squirrels scurrying about, as well as an occasional jackrabbit. The trail then reaches a fork. Bikers should turn left, taking the outstanding Baylands Bike Trail; it extends all the way to the Dumbarton Bridge, which has a bike lane, and across the bay to San Francisco Bay Wildlife Refuge, Coyote Hills, and Alameda Creek Trail. Hikers are better off turning right. Here the trail softens, and the slough melds into the tidal waters of San Francisquito Creek. The pathway continues along past the golf course, then crosses near the departure runway for the Palo Alto Airport and leads out to Land's End, where the creek pours into the bay. This is a classic salt marsh habitat, with lots of birds and wildlife. The views are pretty, the walk is as flat as it gets, and hikers are always sighting squirrels, rabbits, egrets, coots, and ducks.

**User Groups:** Hikers, wheelchairs, and mountain bikes. No dogs or horses.

**Permits:** No permits are required. Parking and access are free.

**Maps:** For a topographic map, ask the USGS for Mountain View.

**Directions:** From U.S. 101 in Palo Alto, take the Embarcadero East exit. At the second light, across from Ming's Restaurant, turn left on Geng Street and drive to the end of the road. The trailhead is right behind the Baylands Baseball Park grandstand.

**Contact:** Palo Alto Baylands Nature Center, 650/329-2506; Parks, Recreation, & Open

Spaces Division, 650/463-4900, website: www.city.paloalto.ca.us/ross/naturepreserve/baylands.html.

## 91 BAYLANDS CATWALK
**0.25 mi / 0.5 hr**

**on the shore of South San Francisco Bay in Palo Alto**

Map 7.2, page 268

What the heck is the Baylands Catwalk, you ask? As you will discover here, it is an old wooden walkway placed across tidal marshland and routed under giant electrical towers and out to the shoreline of South San Francisco Bay. In recent years, the catwalk has been improved, with a new observation deck set on the edge of the bay waters. You start at the Baylands Interpretive Center, which houses exhibits explaining the marshland habitat. From there you can make the short walk straight east out to the observation deck, about a 10-minute trip. The marsh supports an abundant population of bird life, especially egrets, coots, and ducks. Migrants can surprise, such as avocets by the dozen in early summer. Occasional dawn and sunset walks are led by naturalists; call the Baylands Interpretive Center for information.

Special Note: The catwalk extends north and south across the marsh for a mile. This was once a great easy walk, but access is now forbidden in order to protect an endangered mouse, and a barbed-wire-edged gate blocks passage.

**User Groups:** Hikers only. No dogs, horses, or mountain bikes. No wheelchair facilities.

**Permits:** No permits are required. Parking and access are free.

**Maps:** For a topographic map, ask the USGS for Mountain View.

**Directions:** From U.S. 101 in Palo Alto, take the Embarcadero East exit. Drive toward the bay, bearing left past the airport to a stop sign. Turn left and drive past the yacht harbor until you reach a sharp right turn. Park at the lot on the right (south). The nature preserve is on the left (north). Note: A gate is closed on the access route each evening just after sunset and is opened each day at 8 A.M. year-round; access is still possible by foot or bike.

**Contact:** Palo Alto Baylands Nature Center, 650/329-2506; Parks, Recreation, & Open Spaces Division, 650/463-4900, website: www.city.palo-alto.ca.us/ross/naturepreserve/baylands.html.

## 92 CHARLESTON SLOUGH
**4.0 mi / 1.5 hrs**

**in a South Bay marshland in Palo Alto**

Map 7.2, page 268

This trail is actually an old levee road that borders Charleston Slough, providing access to an expanse of wetlands and marsh habitat. It connects to a similar levee road that in turn connects to Shoreline Regional Park, in Mountain View—a great bike route and also good for hikes. From this trailhead, the best option is to head straight out the levee along the slough. Within 10 or 15 minutes, with each step you will gain access to marshland that has been preserved in its natural state. From afar, the surroundings may appear to be nothing more than pickleweed and mud, but look closer, and you will begin to see the huge diversity of birds and wildlife that thrive in this very rich ecosystem. Egrets seem particularly plentiful. Way back in the 1950s, striped bass used to enter the mouth of Charleston Slough here, providing some excellent fishing. Although the stripers are long gone, the serene atmosphere and the variety of birds remain, making this a favorite destination for many people. The trail/road extends out near the shore of the South Bay, near the mouth of San Francisquito Creek. This is an excellent route for a family bike trip.

**User Groups:** Hikers and mountain bikes. No dogs or horses. No wheelchair facilities.

**Permits:** No permits are required. Parking and access are free.

**Maps:** For a topographic map, ask the USGS for Mountain View.

**Directions:** From U.S. 101 in south Palo Alto, take the San Antonio exit and turn east toward the bay. After a short distance, turn left on Bayshore Frontage Road and drive about a mile (curving) to Charleston Slough. The parking area is on the right side of the road.

**Contact:** Palo Alto Baylands Nature Center, 650/329-2506; Parks, Recreation, & Open Spaces Division, 650/463-4900, website: www.city.palo-alto.ca.us/ross/naturepreserve/baylands.html.

## 93 WINDY HILL LOOP
**8.2 mi / 4.0 hrs**

in the Windy Hill Open Space Preserve in the Portola Valley foothills

**Map 7.2, page 268**

Windy Hill may be known for the north winds that blow through on spring afternoons, but it is even better known among hikers for offering remarkable views on clear days in any season. From the 1,900-foot summit, a grass-covered hilltop west of Portola Valley, hikers can see San Francisco Bay on one side and the Pacific Ocean on the other. If views are all you want, the .7-mile Anniversary Trail, which is routed from the parking area to the summit, provides them. If you want more, you can get more by taking an excellent loop hike that drops down into forests and climbs back out to grasslands. To do this, take Hamms Gulch Trail, dropping 1,000 feet in elevation through a remote, pristine, wooded environment. Loop back on Razorback Ridge Trail, hiking an extended series of switchbacks to make the return climb. The trail emerges from the woodlands and turns right on Lost Trail. The last 2.1 miles to the parking area offer great views and a refreshing end to the hike.

**User Groups:** Hikers, horses, and dogs (allowed on Hamms Gulch Trail, Eagle Trail, and Anniversary Trail; prohibited on others). No mountain bikes (except on the preserve's Spring Ridge Trail). There are wheelchair facilities in the picnic area adjacent to the parking area.

**Permits:** No permits are required. Parking and access are free.

**Maps:** For a free trail map and brochure, contact the Midpeninsula Regional Open Space

District at the address below. For a topographic map, ask the USGS for Mindego Hill.

**Directions:** From I-280 or U.S. 101 on the Peninsula, take Highway 84 west to Highway 35/Skyline Boulevard. Turn left on Highway 35 and drive 2.3 miles to the parking area, on the left.

**Contact:** Midpeninsula Regional Open Space District, 330 Distel Circle, Los Altos, CA 94022, 650/691-1200, website: www.openspace.org (click on Preserve Locator). During nonbusiness hours, a touch-tone phone menu is available for trail news, conditions, and events.

## 94 SAN ANDREAS FAULT TRAIL
**0.6 mi / 0.5 hr**

in Los Trancos Open Space Preserve in the Palo Alto foothills

**Map 7.2, page 268**

The air at Los Trancos Open Space Preserve always seems to have a special scent to it, freshened by leaves and damp woods. There are only seven miles of trails at the preserve, but one of the Peninsula's more unique hikes is found here: the San Andreas Fault Trail. This is a self-guided tour of an earthquake trail, and it includes several examples of fault movement. The 13 numbered signposts along the way correspond with numbered explanations in the park brochure. If you don't want a geology lesson, you may be content with the good views of the Peninsula from the 2,000-foot ridgeline. Most hikers connect San Andreas Fault Trail to Lost Creek Loop Trail, a pleasant and easy bonus leg that is routed into secluded spots along a pretty creek. With the Monte Bello Open Space Preserve located on the other side of Page Mill Road, there are nearly 3,000 contiguous acres of public open space here.

**User Groups:** Hikers only. The trail is not wheelchair accessible, but the parking lot is and offers a nice view. No dogs, horses, or mountain bikes.

**Permits:** No permits are required. Parking and access are free.

**Maps:** For a free trail map, contact the Midpeninsula Regional Open Space District at the address below. A map and trail guide are also available at the parking area. For a topographic map, ask the USGS for Mindego Hill.

**Directions:** From I-280 in Palo Alto, turn west on Page Mill Road and drive seven twisty miles to the signed parking area, on the right. The Monte Bello Open Space Preserve is directly across the street, on the left (south).

**Contact:** Midpeninsula Regional Open Space District, 330 Distel Circle, Los Altos, CA 94022, 650/691-1200, website: www.openspace.org (click on Preserve Locator). During nonbusiness hours, a touch-tone phone menu is available for trail news, conditions, and events.

## 95 BLACK MOUNTAIN
**3.5 mi / 2.0 hrs**

**in the Monte Bello Open Space Preserve in the Palo Alto foothills**

Map 7.2, page 268

The Monte Bello Open Space Preserve encompasses more than 2,700 acres of the most natural and scenic lands on the Peninsula. It includes 2,800-foot Black Mountain, the headwaters of Stevens Creek, and this pretty trail, which is crowned by great views and offers the opportunity to camp at a little-known backpack site.

Though the route to the camp and nearby Black Mountain is short, a map/brochure is a must. From the parking area, start the trip by taking the Stevens Creek Nature Trail for a few minutes (ignore the fork) to Canyon Trail. Turn right on Canyon Trail, and go .25 mile to the Bella Vista Trail. Turn left and climb a mile to the ridge and the Old Ranch Trail. Turn right, and you will arrive at the Black Mountain Backpack Camp in about a half mile.

In the process, you will pass the headwaters of Stevens Creek as well as the San Andreas Fault. You'll also get long-distance views of the valley and the ridge above San Jose, and opportunities to see squirrels, hawks, rabbits, and deer. It's about a 500-foot climb from the parking area to the campsites.

From camp, it's a five-minute walk on Monte Bello Road to the summit of Black Mountain

(some transmitters mar the perfection). On clear spring days, the views are eye-popping. For campers, bring flashlights with fresh batteries, and be sure to make the walk here in darkness for stargazing, or to time the trip for a meteor shower.

From the summit, another bonus is available by continuing on Monte Bello Road for a short distance to a picnic site on the right. It is set adjacent to a sprinkling of rock crags that look like a movie set simulating another planet (great for kids). There are more stellar views of the canyon and foothills below to the east.

**User Groups:** Hikers, horses, and mountain bikes (restricted from some trails). This trail is not open to wheelchairs, but the parking lot and a short side trail are wheelchair accessible and offer a good view. No dogs.

**Permits:** No permits are required for day-use. Campers must have reservation and permit for the backpack camp.

**Maps:** For a free trail map, contact the Midpeninsula Regional Open Space District at the address below. A map and trail guide are also available at the trailhead. For a topographic map, ask the USGS for Mindego Hill.

**Directions:** From I-280 in Palo Alto, turn west on Page Mill Road and drive seven twisty miles to the signed parking area for Monte Bello Open Space Preserve on the left (south). Los Trancos Open Space Preserve is directly across the street to the right (north).

**Contact:** Midpeninsula Regional Open Space District, 330 Distel Circle, Los Altos, CA 94022, 650/691-1200, website: www.openspace.org (click on Preserve Locator). During nonbusiness hours, a touch-tone phone menu is available for trail news, conditions, and events.

## 96 COAL CREEK OPEN SPACE
**4.0 mi / 2.0 hrs**

**in the Coal Creek Open Space Preserve on the Peninsula's Skyline Ridge**

Map 7.2, page 268

Most residents of the Peninsula have never heard of the Coal Creek Open Space Preserve.

That makes sense, as this is one of the lesser-developed parklands in the Bay Area. Yet it is worth making a trip to the 490-acre parcel of land set just east of Skyline Ridge, with its rolling meadows, open grasslands, and the forested headwaters of two creeks. The park's trails—actually old ranch roads—cover only four miles as they traverse the grasslands past a classic-looking barn and down along a small creek. Plan on enjoying nothing more than a short walk and a picnic. A bonus is that the parking area is adjacent to the CalTrans Vista Point, one of the best lookouts on the Peninsula.

**User Groups:** Hikers, dogs, horses, and mountain bikes. No wheelchair facilities.

**Permits:** No permits are required. Parking and access are free.

**Maps:** For a free trail map, contact the Midpeninsula Regional Open Space District at the address below. For a topographic map, ask the USGS for Mindego Hill.

**Directions:** From Highway 280 in Palo Alto, take the Page Mill Road exit and drive west on a winding two-lane road up the mountain to Skyline Boulevard. Turn right on Skyline Boulevard and drive one mile to the parking area, located on the right at the CalTrans Vista Point.

**Contact:** Midpeninsula Regional Open Space District, 330 Distel Circle, Los Altos, CA 94022, 650/691-1200, website: www.openspace.org (click on Preserve Locator). During nonbusiness hours, a touch-tone phone menu is available for trail news, conditions, and events.

## 97 BOREL HILL TRAIL
1.4 mi / 1.0 hr

**in the Russian Ridge Open Space Preserve on the Peninsula's Skyline Ridge**

Map 7.2, page 268

Borel Hill is one of the great lookouts on the San Francisco Peninsula, topping out at 2,572 feet and surrounded by grasslands so hikers get unobstructed, 360-degree views. Yet the hill is not well known and remains a favorite destination of only a few hikers who visit the Russian Ridge Open Space Preserve. Russian Ridge is that big

grassy ridge near the intersection of Alpine Road and Skyline Boulevard above Palo Alto. From the parking area, hike southeast on Ridge Trail, climbing about 250 feet over the course of .7 mile to Borel Hill. You'll see it just southwest of the trail: The hill is the highest spot around, bordered by grasslands and no trees. From the summit, with just a turn of the head, you can see Monterey Bay one moment, Mount Diablo and the South Bay the next. There are several other trails at the preserve, the best being the 2.6-mile (one-way) hike out to Mindego Ridge Trail, which is routed through an oak woodland forest.

**User Groups:** Hikers, horses, and mountain bikes. A wheelchair-accessible trail starting at the parking area leads to Alpine Pond in the Skyline Ridge Open Space Preserve. No dogs.

**Permits:** No permits are required. Parking and access are free.

**Maps:** For a free trail map, contact the Midpeninsula Regional Open Space District at the address below. Maps are usually available at the trailhead. For a topographic map, ask the USGS for Mindego Hill.

**Directions:** From I-280 in Palo Alto, take the Page Mill Road exit and drive west on a winding two-lane road up the mountain to Skyline Boulevard. Cross Skyline Boulevard, drive a short distance, and then turn right into the parking lot, at the northwest corner of the intersection.

**Contact:** Midpeninsula Regional Open Space District, 330 Distel Circle, Los Altos, CA 94022, 650/691-1200, website: www.openspace.org (click on Preserve Locator). During nonbusiness hours, a touch-tone phone menu is available for trail news, conditions, and events.

## 98 SKYLINE RIDGE TRAIL
3.0 mi / 1.5 hrs

**in the Skyline Ridge Open Space Preserve on the Peninsula's Skyline Ridge**

Map 7.2, page 268

Most people discover this park by accident in December, when they come up Skyline Boulevard (Highway 35) to the adjacent choose-and-cut Christmas tree farm. They see the parking area and a trailhead, and become a little curious. At some point many return to satisfy their curiosity with a hike, and most leave feeling good for taking the time. From the parking area on the west side of Skyline Boulevard, Skyline Ridge Trail is routed around Horseshoe Lake, a pretty little farm pond (incredibly, no fishing is permitted). From there, the trail pushes into the interior of the parkland, skirting the flank of the highest mountain in park boundaries (2,493 feet), and then looping back to Skyline Boulevard. You play peekaboo here, heading in and out of woodlands and gaining occasional views of plunging canyons to the west. You can create a loop hike, but that requires going back on a fire road; most people return to the parking area via the same route they walked in on the way in.

**User Groups:** Hikers, horses, and mountain bikes. A wheelchair-accessible trail leads to Horseshoe Lake. No dogs.

**Permits:** No permits are required. Parking and access are free.

**Maps:** For a free trail map, contact the Midpeninsula Regional Open Space District at the address below. For a topographic map, ask the USGS for Mindego Hill.

**Directions:** From Highway 280 in Palo Alto, take the Page Mill Road exit and drive west on a winding two-lane road up the mountain to Skyline Boulevard. Turn left on Skyline Boulevard and drive .8 mile to the main entrance and parking area, on the right.

**Contact:** Midpeninsula Regional Open Space District, 330 Distel Circle, Los Altos, CA 94022, 650/691-1200, website: www.openspace.org (click on Preserve Locator). During nonbusiness hours, a touch-tone phone menu is available for trail news, conditions, and events.

## 99 RIDGE TRAIL LOOP
**4.3 mi / 2.0 hrs**

**in Sam McDonald County Park near La Honda**

Map 7.2, page 268

This loop trail provides a stellar introduction to the area and makes an excellent hike year-round. It features about a 700-foot climb, a route through deep redwood canyons, and then ridge-top views across coastal foothills.

After a quick orientation with the park map (they're self-serve at the ranger station), choose the posted four-mile Ridge Trail Loop. The hike starts on a narrow dirt path that is carved in the side of a steep redwood canyon, heading north. Even on hot Bay Area days, this forest is cool and refreshing, with occasional banana slugs on the trail. The trail contours up and down, then eventually rises into hardwood forest (mainly oaks, bays, and madrones) to a sub-ridge with a partial lookout to the north across miles of pretty foothills.

Here the trail to curves left (west) and climbs toward Towne Ridge. You emerge at a crossing of Pescadero Road (now heading south). Here the trail turns from single track to a service road, and you are rewarded with sweeping views of the coastal foothills, into the Pescadero Creek Canyon, and across to Butano Rim. In March, April, and early May, there are also many blooming wildflowers, highlighted by occasional rafts of sprawling forget-me-nots. The trail continues to contour up and down, generally climbing until you reach a horse camp and the Towne Trail, which are set atop foothill grasslands. Turn left on the Towne Trail and you descend into another deep redwood canyon. At a massive water tank, turn right on the Big Tree Loop, which is highlighted by a massive redwood. The Big Tree Loop is routed to a crossing of Pescadero Road and the parking lot.

For a longer trip, this hike can be extended on the Towne Creek Loop. For a short side trip, visit the adjacent Heritage Grove, which is accessible on Alpine Road.

**User Groups:** Hikers only. No dogs, horses, or mountain bikes. No wheelchair facilities.

**Permits:** No permits are required. A parking fee of $5 is charged per vehicle.

**Maps:** A trail map is available for $1 at the ranger station. For a topographic map, ask the USGS for La Honda.

**Directions:** From I-280 on the Peninsula, take

the Woodside/Highway 84 exit. Drive up the hill past Skyline Boulevard and continue another 10 miles to La Honda. Turn left on La Honda/Pescadero Road and drive two miles to a Y. Bear right at the Y and drive a short distance to Sam McDonald County Park, on the right.

**Contact:** Sam McDonald County Park, Memorial Park Visitors Center, 650/879-0212; San Mateo County Parks and Recreation Department, 455 County Center, 4th Floor, Redwood City, CA 94063-1646, 650/363-4020, fax 650/599-1721, website: www.eparks.net (click on Parks).

## 100 SEQUOIA TRAIL
### 1.0 mi / 0.5 hr

**in Portola Redwoods State Park in the Santa Cruz Mountains**

Map 7.2, page 268

The Shell Tree is one of the most unusual forest specimens on the Peninsula. This giant redwood is a strange-looking creature that has been ravaged by fire yet still lives and measures some 17 feet in diameter. The Sequoia Trail, a short, easy loop, is a good way to see this tree. Even on such a short hike, the surrounding forest (much of it redwood and Douglas fir) can provide a sense of remoteness. If you want more of a workout, Sequoia Trail is linked to Summit Trail (across from the group camping area), which ventures into remote lands on the eastern border of the park. Portola Redwoods State Park covers about 1,000 acres, primarily second-growth redwoods, though a few ancient monsters remain. The park has only 14 miles of trails, but Iverson Trail connects to Memorial County Park and an additional trail network.

**User Groups:** Hikers only. No dogs, horses, or mountain bikes. No wheelchair facilities.

**Permits:** No permits are required. A state park entrance fee of $6 is charged per vehicle; pay at the visitors center.

**Maps:** A trail map is available for $1 at the visitors center. For a topographic map, ask the USGS for Mindego Hill.

**Directions:** From I-280 in Palo Alto, take the Page Mill Road exit. Turn west and drive nine miles to Highway 35 (Skyline Boulevard). Cross Highway 35 and continue on Alpine Road for three miles to Portola State Park Road. Turn left at Portola State Park Road and drive three miles to the park. The trailhead is just south of park headquarters.

**Contact:** Portola Redwoods State Park, 9000 Portola State Park Road, La Honda, CA 94020, 650/948-9098, website: www.parks.ca/gov (click on Find A Park).

## 101 MILL OX LOOP
### 5.0 mi / 2.75 hrs

**in Butano State Park near Pescadero**

Map 7.2, page 268

If you love redwoods and ferns but are also partial to sun and warm afternoons, the Mill Ox Loop at Butano State Park may be the ideal hike for you. Why? Because you get all these things in good doses. The trail starts by crossing a small creek in a dense redwood forest, then it heads up a very steep grade on switchbacks, emerging at the top of the canyon on Butano Fire Road. Many are surprised by how steep this section is, but it is short, and the worst of the climb is over quickly. Here you turn right and climb more gradually as you head toward the park's interior. The fire road gets plenty of sun, and plenty of shirts come off en route to 1,138 feet. If you turn and look back to the west, you have views of the Pacific Ocean. When you reach a junction with Jackson Flats Trail, turn right; the trail descends quite steeply over a bare rock facing for .25 mile, then drops into Butano Canyon and the surrounding redwood forest. The rest of the hike is beautiful and pleasant, a meandering walk past ferns, trillium, redwoods, and plenty of wild iris. This is one of our favorites.

**User Groups:** Hikers only. No dogs, horses, or mountain bikes. No wheelchair facilities.

**Permits:** No permits are required. A state park entrance fee of $6 is charged per vehicle.

**Maps:** For a free trail map, contact Butano State Park at the address below. For a topographic map, ask the USGS for Franklin Point.

**Directions:** In Half Moon Bay, at the junction of Highway 1 and Highway 92, drive south on Highway 1 for 17 miles to the Pescadero Road exit. Turn left on Pescadero Road and drive past the town of Pescadero (for three miles) to Cloverdale Road. Turn right and drive 5.5 miles to the park entrance, on the left. After paying the entrance fee, continue into the park and look for the Mill Ox trailhead, on your left. A small dirt parking area is on the shoulder of the road.

**Contact:** Butano State Park, 650/879-2040; Half Moon Bay State Parks, 650/726-8820, website: www.parks.ca/gov (click on Find A Park).

## 102 BUTANO RIM LOOP
### 11.0 mi / 2.0 days

**in Butano State Park near Pescadero**

**Map 7.2, page 268**

A trail camp makes this one of the few loop hikes in the Bay Area that can be turned into an overnight backpack trip. Note that water for drinking and cooking is usually not available at the camp, so campers must pack in their own. In addition, most of the route is on fire roads, and with the popularity of mountain bike use, most people make this trip on bikes, not on foot. Regardless, hikers can still arrange it so that almost half of the trip follows trails instead of roads, and they can enjoy a mix of redwood-filled canyons and sunny lookouts from ridgelines. By following this route, the first day of the hike will be spent primarily in the sun; you'll walk through redwoods for most of the second day.

Start at the Mill Ox trailhead, at an elevation of 200 feet; then hike up the steep grade, turning right on Butano Fire Road (700 feet). From here, trace the rim of Butano Canyon, and enjoy views of the redwood-filled valley (below) and the Pacific Ocean (behind you, off to the west). The trail climbs steadily be-

fore reaching 1,713 feet. Then it crosses an old, abandoned airstrip on the ridgeline, and then drops down to Butano Trail Camp (at 1,550 feet) for a first-day total of 5.5 miles. Reservations are required, and since this is an environmental camp, only lightweight camp stoves are permitted for cooking.

On day two, return by turning right on Olmo Fire Trail; then take the Doe Ridge/Goat Hill Trails back to the starting point. Much of this route (on a soft dirt trail amid redwoods) laterals and descends into the south side of Butano Canyon. During the winter, when the Sierra Nevada is entombed in snow and ice, this loop provides an answer for those looking for an overnight backpack trip.

**User Groups:** Hikers only. No dogs, horses, or mountain bikes. No wheelchair facilities.

**Permits:** A state park entrance fee of $6 is charged per vehicle. For overnight use, camping reservations are required, and a small camping fee is charged.

**Maps:** For a free trail map, contact Butano State Park at the address below. For a topographic map, ask the USGS for Franklin Point.

**Directions:** In Half Moon Bay, at the junction of Highway 1 and Highway 92, drive south on Highway 1 for 17 miles to the Pescadero Road exit. Turn left on Pescadero Road and drive past the town of Pescadero (for three miles) to Cloverdale Road. Turn right and drive 5.5 miles to the park entrance, on the left. After paying the entrance fee, continue into the park and look for the Mill Ox trailhead, on your left. A small dirt parking area is on the shoulder of the road.

**Contact:** Butano State Park, 650/879-2040; Half Moon Bay State Parks, 650/726-8820, website: www.parks.ca/gov (click on Find A Park).

## 103 AÑO NUEVO LOOKOUT
### 2.75 mi / 1.5 hrs

**in Butano State Park near Pescadero**

**Map 7.2, page 268**

The destination here is a little bench that once provided a picture-perfect view of Año Nuevo, to the south. The view even seemed to be framed on all four sides by conifers. Well, trees grow, and the view is gone. What remains is a loop trip with a steep ascent followed by a beautiful downhill tromp through redwoods. It still is a decent hike, but not the best at Butano (pronounced BEWT-uh-no, not Bew-TAH-no). Park at the entrance station and start at the trailhead directly to the right (south). The trail to the lookout climbs 730 feet in less than a mile. Some figure the bench is positioned here for you to have a sit and catch your breath. From here, it's best to continue on Año Nuevo Trai, then return on Goat Hill Trail, to complete the loop. Although short, this hike provides a good climb and a chance to walk through redwoods on the return descent. Pileated woodpeckers are occasionally seen on this loop.

**User Groups:** Hikers only. No dogs, horses, or mountain bikes. No wheelchair facilities.

**Permits:** No permits are required. A day-use fee of $6 is charged per vehicle.

**Maps:** For a free trail map, contact Butano State Park at the address below. For a topographic map, ask the USGS for Franklin Point.

**Directions:** In Half Moon Bay, at the junction of Highway 1 and Highway 92, drive south on Highway 1 for 17 miles to the Pescadero Road exit. Turn left on Pescadero Road and drive past the town of Pescadero (for three miles) to Cloverdale Road. Turn right and drive 5.5 miles to the park entrance, on the left.

**Contact:** Butano State Park, 650/879-2040; Half Moon Bay State Parks, 650/726-8820, website: www.parks.ca/gov (click on Find A Park).

## 104 PESCADERO MARSH
3.0 mi / 1.5 hrs

**in Pescadero Marsh south of Pescadero**

Map 7.2, page 268

The centerpiece of a vast wetland lagoon and coastal estuary is Pescadero Marsh Natural Preserve, located just east of Highway 1 along Pescadero Creek, 15 miles south of Half Moon Bay. This is a 600-acre wetlands and lagoon that provides a year-round haven for blue heron, egrets, and owls, as well as a refuge for more than 200 species of shorebirds, waterfowl, and raptors on their migrant routes. The most spectacular is the blue heron, which often grows nearly four feet tall and can have a wingspan of seven feet. A classic experience at any wetlands is watching these huge birds lift off with labored wing beats.

A great way to start the trip is with a three-mile loop walk through the marsh; it's an easy hike that gives you a chance to see the most, and at the same time, you can lose yourself in the surrounding wetlands habitat. To make it work, start by taking the North Pond Trail to Audubon Marsh. Then return on the Sequoia Trail, which traces the edge of the marsh and then is routed along Pescadero Creek. This trail is a dirt path that ventures through the heart of the wetlands, providing a good chance to see many birds, as well as occasional deer. We've been coming here for years and have also seen a fox, a skunk, and a badger.

Just across the highway from Pescadero Marsh is the parking lot and access point for Pescadero State Beach. This features an extended beach edged by cliffs, cuts in the bluffs, and sandy coves. It acts as a natural collection point for washed-up driftwood, bottles with notes, and other occasional goodies.

**User Groups:** Hikers only. No dogs, horses, or mountain bikes. No wheelchair facilities.

**Permits:** No permits are required. Parking and access are free.

**Maps:** A map is available from Half Moon Bay State Parks. For a topographic map, ask the USGS for San Gregorio.

**Directions:** From the Peninsula in San Mateo, take Highway 92 west to Half Moon Bay. Turn south on Highway 1 and drive 17 miles to Pescadero Road. Turn left and drive less than 0.25 mile to an unsigned turn at a small dirt road. Turn left and drive a short distance to an information board and small parking area.

**Contact:** Pescadero State Beach, 650/879-2170; Half Moon Bay State Parks, 650/726-8820, website: www.parks.ca/gov (click on Find A Park).

## 105 BAY VIEW LOOP
### 3.0 mi / 1.5 hrs

### in Point Pinole Regional Shoreline

Map 7.3, page 269

On the Bay View Loop, you can walk several miles along the shore of San Pablo Bay and see nothing but water, passing ships, and birds. That's because visitors to Point Pinole must park at the entrance station and catch a shuttle bus to the shoreline. There you will find a long, pretty, cobbled beach and beautiful views of San Pablo Bay, Marin, and Mount Tamalpais. An excellent fishing pier is also here. The park covers 2,147 acres, and this loop trail is a great way to explore it. From the parking area, it is routed along the shore to Point Pinole, then it swings back on Woods Trail, which runs through a large grove of eucalyptus.

You could drive I-80 a thousand times without realizing what's right next door in Pinole: the former site of the nation's largest dynamite factory; the best cobbled stone beach in the bay; a fishing pier where you might catch sturgeon and striped bass; hiking access with a shuttle bus; and great, easy bike trails with sensational views of San Pablo Bay, passing ships, and Mount Tamalpais.

In the World War II era, this was the site of the Giant Powder Company—that is, dynamite manufacturers. This was their fourth site in the Bay Area after factories blew up in San Francisco, South San Francisco, and Albany. So no one wanted to be anywhere near the place. The dynamite company built all the present trails and roads, planted eucalyptus, and is responsible for the basic layout of the park.

After parking, the trip starts with a shuttle ride (or with a bike ride) for 1.5 miles to a staging area adjacent to the 1,250-foot fishing pier. This is the launch point for adventuring in this park, whether you're hiking, biking, or fishing.

The best trip is on the Bay View Trail. This walk extends along the shore of San Pablo Bay, offering pretty views of the water, occasional passing tankers, fishing boats, and marine birds.

The long-distance views across the bay—of the Marin shoreline backed by Mount Tamalpais—are exceptional. The highlight of Point Pinole Regional Shoreline is a long, undisturbed stretch of shoreline on a cobbled beach along San Pablo Bay. The stone beach is unparalleled; it's as if this is the final resting place of every stone ever cast in the bay. It is a quiet place, where you can watch passing ships, go for an easy hike, take a dog for a walk, or fish from the pier. Yet the defining feature of the park is the Hayward Fault—marked by the cliffs and Point Pinole itself as it goes out to sea.

To turn this into a three-mile loop, turn back (left) on the Woods Trail. This trail is routed through a small eucalyptus forest, and eventually goes back to the staging area.

**User Groups:** Hikers, dogs, horses, and mountain bikes. The trail is partially wheelchair accessible.

**Permits:** No permits are required. A $4 dayuse fee is charged on weekends when the kiosk is attended. The shuttle costs $1 round-trip for people ages 12 through 61; it's free for seniors, and $.25 for youngsters 6 through 11. There is a $1 pet fee on weekends.

**Maps:** For a free trail map, contact the East Bay Regional Parks District at the address below and ask for the Point Pinole Regional Shoreline brochure. For a topographic map, ask the USGS for Richmond.

**Directions:** Take I-80 to San Pablo and the exit for Hilltop. Take that exit and drive west on Hilltop to the intersection with San Pablo Avenue. Turn right on San Pablo Avenue and drive north for a short distance to Richmond Parkway. Turn left on Richmond Parkway and drive a few miles to Giant Highway. Turn right and drive a short distance to the park entrance (it's well-signed), on the left. Take the shuttle to the bay.

**Contact:** Point Pinole Regional Park, 510/237-6896; East Bay Regional Parks District, 2950 Peralta Oaks Court, P.O. Box 5381, Oakland, CA 94605-0381, 510/562-7275, website: www.ebparks.org (click on Regional Parks and Trails).

## 106 FRANKLIN RIDGE LOOP TRAIL

2.8 mi / 1.75 hrs

**at Carquinez Strait Regional Shoreline near Martinez**

Map 7.3, page 269

What you get at Franklin Ridge is a great, easy romp with a number of little side trails to different hilltop lookouts of Carquinez Strait. In just two hour's time, this is an experience that can realign your brain—and there is no better place to salvage the day and make a break from a bad case of I-80 tunnel vision. Franklin Ridge is the centerpiece of the Carquinez Straight Regional Shoreline. From I-80, it's about a 10-minute drive to the trailhead, and by then, your personal transformation has already started.

Here's a summary of the adventure: The round-trip hike is 2.8 miles, including a 420-foot climb, with the opportunity to extend the trip on several little cutoffs to additional viewpoints. The trailhead for this adventure is at a parking area called the Carquinez Strait East Staging Area, located on Carquinez Scenic Drive between Hercules and Martinez. The trail is accessible for hikers, dogs, joggers, mountain bikes, and equestrians, and it has parking for trailers.

After parking, you start the trip by heading off on the signed trailhead for the California Riding and Hiking Trail. After just 10 minutes (less than a half mile), you will reach a junction with the Franklin Ridge Loop, a park service road. Here you turn right on the loop trail, generally climbing up Franklin Ridge. By taking the loop counterclockwise, it makes the climb a bit more benign. This loop covers two miles, rising an estimated 620 feet to the highest point on the trip. Although this is mighty short as far as hills go, it still is plenty high enough to provide great views of Carquinez Strait.

Sunsets can be absolutely spectacular here in winter, often with sunlight refracted through distant stratus and a dark silhouette of Mount Tamalpais. Even after sunset, it remains pretty as the lights of the Benicia Bridge and nearby towns take hold.

The loop reconnects with the California Hiking and Riding Trail, from which you make the 10-minute tromp back to the parking area. Some people can rip this loop off in little over an hour, but the views are so good that most spend well over two hours. Late in the day, this water scene features a changing of light and color, almost minute by minute. The boats and bridges add a timeless perspective.

The park covers 2,795 acres, most of it foothill country, with oaks, short ridges, and ravines. It is wild enough to provide habitat for wildlife; redtail hawks and deer are the most common. At dusk, it's possible to see great horned owls, kestrels, and occasionally even golden eagles.

**User Groups:** Hikers, dogs, horses, and mountain bikes. No wheelchair facilities.

**Permits:** No permits are required. Parking and access are free.

**Maps:** For a free trail map, contact the East Bay Regional Parks District at the address below and ask for the Carquinez Strait Regional Shoreline brochure. For a topographic map, ask the USGS for Benicia.

**Directions:** From Berkeley, drive east on I-80 to Hercules and Highway 4. Take Highway 4 east to Martinez and the Alhambra Avenue exit. Take that exit to Alhambra Avenue, turn left, and go two miles to Escobar. Turn left for three blocks to Talbart Street, then turn right and go .5 mile (Talbart Street becomes Carquinez Scenic Drive) to the parking area, on the left side of the road.

**Contact:** Carquinez Strait Regional Shoreline, 925/228-0112; East Bay Regional Parks District, 2950 Peralta Oaks Court, P.O. Box 5381, Oakland, CA 94605-0381, 510/562-7275, website: www.ebparks.org (click on Regional Parks and Trails).

## 107 MARTINEZ SHORELINE
**2.2 mi / 1.0 hr**

**at Martinez Regional Shoreline near Martinez**

Map 7.3, page 269

The Shoreline Trail is the most attractive walk at Martinez Waterfront Park, a 343-acre parcel that includes marshlands and bay frontage. Start hiking from the parking area (at the foot of the Martinez Fishing Pier) and walk back on North Court Street to the trailhead at Sand Beach. The hike skirts a pond, crosses Arch Bridge over Alhambra Creek, and runs along the waterfront, past an old schooner hull, to the park's western boundary. The trail is easy and flat, with the bay on one side, marshlands on the other. It is popular for bicycling, jogging, and bird-watching. An option is to walk a short distance from the parking lot to the Martinez Pier, one of the few piers in the Bay Area where striped bass, sturgeon, and steelhead are occasionally caught in the winter.

**User Groups:** Hikers, dogs, horses, and mountain bikes. The restrooms are wheelchair accessible, but the trail is not.

**Permits:** No permits are required. Parking and access are free.

**Maps:** For a free trail map, contact the East Bay Regional Parks District at the address below and ask for the Martinez Regional Shoreline brochure. For a topographic map, ask the USGS for Benicia.

**Directions:** From Highway 4 in Martinez, take the Alhambra Avenue exit. Drive north on Alhambra Avenue for two miles and turn right on Escobar Street. Continue for three blocks to Ferry Street and turn left. Drive across the railroad tracks and bear right onto Joe DiMaggio Drive. Turn left on North Court Street and drive to the parking area, next to the fishing pier.

**Contact:** Martinez Regional Shoreline, 925/228-0112; East Bay Regional Parks District, 2950 Peralta Oaks Court, P.O. Box 5381, Oakland, CA 94605-0381, 510/562-7275, website: www.ebparks.org (click on Regional Parks and Trails).

## 108 FALSE GUN
**1.0 mi / 0.75 hr**

**in Miller-Knox Regional Shore** Richmond on the shore of San F.

Map 7.3, page 269

A little-known lookout over San Francis is the highlight of Miller-Knox Regional Si. line, and getting to it requires only a short hik and climb. This parkland covers 260 acres of hill and shoreline property at Point Richmond, where strong afternoon winds in the summer create excellent conditions for kite flying. Whereas most people juts make the short stroll along Keller Beach, this hike is preferred for the view. From the parking area, it leads about .5 mile up Old Country Road and Marine View Trail, making a right turn on Crest Trail to reach the False Gun Vista Point. In the process, the trail climbs 300 feet to the lookout, at 322 feet. On clear days, you get picture-perfect views of San Francisco Bay and its many surrounding landmarks.

**User Groups:** Hikers and dogs. No horses or mountain bikes. No wheelchair facilities.

**Permits:** No permits are required. Parking and access are free.

**Maps:** For a free trail map, contact the East Bay Regional Parks District at the address below and ask for the Miller-Knox Regional Shoreline brochure. For a topographic map, ask the USGS for San Quentin.

**Directions:** From Berkeley: Drive north on I-80 to I-580 west. Take I-580 west to Canal Boulevard/Garrard Boulevard. Turn right on Canal Boulevard and drive .25 mile to Garrard Boulevard. Turn left and drive through the tunnel (the road becomes Dornan Drive). Continue on Dornan Drive for .5 mile to the parking area, on the right.

From Richmond: Drive south on I-80, exit west at Cutting Boulevard, and drive to Garrard Boulevard. Turn left and drive through the tunnel. The road becomes Dornan Drive; follow Dornan Drive .5 mile to the parking area, on the right.

**Contact:** Miller-Knox Regional Shoreline,

nal Parks Dis-
...rt, P.O. Box 5381,
..., 510/562-7275, web-
510/235-163
trict, 2950 (click on Regional Parks
Oaklar
site:

## PABLO RIDGE LOOP
### 3.0 hrs

**Wildcat Canyon Regional Park in the
Richmond foothills**

Map 7.3, page 269

Newcomers to Wildcat Canyon Regional Park may find it hard to believe how quickly they can get to a remote land with great views. But it is true. Just east of Richmond, San Pablo Ridge rises about 1,000 feet. It takes a short grunt of a hike to get to the top, but you'll find it well worth the grunting. That's because you get great views of San Pablo Reservoir and Briones Reservoir off one side of the ridge, and of San Francisco Bay on the other. Of all the views of San Francisco, this is certainly one of the best. Start at the parking area and hike up Belgum Trail, turning right at San Pablo Ridge and climbing about 700 feet over the course of 2.5 miles. Once on top, slow down and enjoy the cruise. To loop around, turn right on Mezue Trail, then right again on Wildcat Creek Trail, and walk back to the parking area.

**User Groups:** Hikers, dogs, horses, and mountain bikes. No wheelchair facilities.

**Permits:** No permits are required. Parking and access are free.

**Maps:** For a free trail map, contact the East Bay Regional Parks District at the address below and ask for the Wildcat Canyon Regional Park brochure. For a topographic map, ask the USGS for Richmond.

**Directions:** In Richmond, head north on I-80 to the Amador/Solano exit. Take that exit, turn left on Amador, and drive three blocks to McBryde Avenue. Turn right on McBryde Avenue and head east. After passing Arlington Boulevard, drive straight (the road becomes Park Avenue) and bear left through a piped gate to the parking area.

**Contact:** Wildcat Canyon Park Office, 510/236-1262; Tilden Nature Area, 510/525-2233; East Bay Regional Parks District, 2950 Peralta Oaks Court, P.O. Box 5381, Oakland, CA 94605-0381, 510/562-7275, website: www.ebparks.org (click on Regional Parks and Trails).

## 110 LAUREL LOOP TRAIL
### 0.7 mi / 0.5 hr

**in the Kennedy Grove Regional Recreation Area near the San Pablo Reservoir in El Sobrante**

Map 7.3, page 269

Kennedy Grove is set at the base of San Pablo Dam, where visitors will discover a rich grove of eucalyptus adjacent to a large lawn/meadow. This loop hike takes hikers through the eucalyptus and then back, skirting the lawn areas. It is best hiked in a clockwise direction, departing from the trailhead at the gate in the northeast corner of the parking area. This is the kind of park where people toss Frisbees, pass footballs, or play low-key games of softball.

A must-do: A hiking and equestrian trail is located off Laurel Loop Trail; it can extend your adventure and provide sensational views. From the other side of the grove, take the one-mile Seafoam Trail. It ascends a hill through a woodland of bay and oak trees and provides spectacular views of San Pablo Ridge, Wildcat Canyon, San Pablo Reservoir, and San Pablo Bay.

**User Groups:** Hikers, dogs, horses, and mountain bikes. No wheelchair facilities.

**Permits:** No permits are required. An entrance fee of $4 per vehicle is charged when the kiosk is attended.

**Maps:** For a free trail map, contact the East Bay Regional Parks District at the address below and ask for the Kennedy Grove Regional Recreation Area brochure. For a topographic map, ask the USGS for Richmond.

**Directions:** From Richmond on I-80, take the San Pablo Dam Road exit. Turn east and drive through El Sobrante for 3.5 miles to the park entrance, on the left. Follow the pavement to the northwestern parking lot.

Alternatively, from Orinda on Highway 24, turn north on Camino Pablo and drive north along San Pablo Reservoir to the park entrance, on the right.

**Contact:** Kennedy Grove Regional Park, 510/223-7840; East Bay Regional Parks District, 2950 Peralta Oaks Court, P.O. Box 5381, Oakland, CA 94605-0381, 510/562-7275, website: www.ebparks.org (click on Regional Parks and Trails).

## 111 SOBRANTE RIDGE TRAIL
**1.6 mi / 1.0 hr**

**in the Sobrante Ridge Regional Preserve near El Sobrante**

Map 7.3, page 269

Sobrante Ridge Park was the missing link in an East Bay corridor of open space until it was finally acquired in the mid-1980s. The wild and scenic land is now protected and should remain that way forever. The park covers 277 acres of rolling hills, open ridgeline, and wooded ravines, and this hike accesses the best of it. From the trailhead at Coach Drive, take Sobrante Ridge Trail, which rises in an elliptical half loop to the left. After .7 mile, you will come to the junction with Broken Oaks Trail. Turn left here and make the short loop (less than .25 mile long), and then retrace your steps on Sobrante Ridge Trail. This walk provides an easy yet intimate look at one of the Bay Area's newest parklands.

**User Groups:** Hikers, dogs, horses, and mountain bikes. No wheelchair facilities.

**Permits:** No permits are required. Parking and access are free.

**Maps:** For a free trail map, contact the East Bay Regional Parks District at the address below and ask for the Sobrante Ridge Regional Preserve brochure. For a topographic map, ask the USGS for Briones Valley.

**Directions:** From I-80 in Richmond, take the San Pablo Dam Road exit. Drive east for three miles and turn left on Castro Ranch Road.

## ⌐REST LOOP
**5.6 mi / 3.25 hrs**

**in Briones Regional Park north of Lafayette**

Map 7.3, page 269

Briones Regional Park is a 5,700-acre sanctuary of peace set amid several fast-growing communities. With its intricate network of trails, it is one of the best parks for hiking in the East Bay, and this is the best of the lot. There are many trail junctions on the loop, and a map will help you from making a wrong turn. From the trailhead, take Alhambra Creek Trail and Spengler Trail (turn right) to Briones Crest Trail, and turn left. This stretch rises to Briones Peak (at 1,483 feet) in just 2.5 miles. It is the highest point in the park and grants a panoramic view of the East Bay's rolling hillsides, quiet and tranquil. The view includes Mount Diablo, the west delta, Suisun Bay, and the Mothball Fleet. To complete the loop, turn left on the Spengler Trail, then right on Diablo View Trail. The latter closes out the hike in 1.1 miles, offering great views of the slopes of Mount Diablo.

**User Groups:** Hikers, dogs, and horses. Mountain bikes are allowed on all but the last mile of the loop. No wheelchair facilities.

**Permits:** No permits are required. An entrance fee of $4 per vehicle is charged when the kiosk is attended (there are five entrances at Briones, and only two have kiosks).

**Maps:** For a free trail map, contact the East Bay Regional Parks District at the address below and ask for the Briones Regional Park

map, ask the

[...] orth of Pleasant Hill, [...] for three miles to the Al- [...] exit. Turn south on Alhambra [...] for .5 mile, and bear right onto [...] a Valley Road. Drive another mile to [...] z Valley Road. Turn left and follow Re- [...] ez Valley Road .5 mile to the park entrance. Turn right and drive .5 mile to the parking area. Look for the trailhead indicating Alhambra Creek Trail.

**Contact:** Briones Regional Park, 925/370-3020; East Bay Regional Parks District, 2950 Peralta Oaks Court, P.O. Box 5381, Oakland, CA 94605-0381, 510/562-7275, website: www.ebparks.org (click on Regional Parks and Trails).

## 113 POINT ISABEL SHORELINE
### 1.0 mi / 0.75 hr

**at Point Isabel Regional Shoreline**
**near Berkeley**

Map 7.3, page 269

Beautiful bayfront views of San Francisco and the Golden Gate—plus the fact that it's a popular place to walk dogs—attract visitors to the Point Isabel Regional Shoreline. The point extends into San Francisco Bay just north of Golden Gate Fields Racetrack, and the 21-acre park provides an easy shoreline walk, rich bird-watching opportunities, and those great views. From the parking area, the trail extends northward along the shore of the bay, then east along Hoffman Channel, and ends with a short loop trail around the edge of Hoffman Marsh. The best time to see birds here is in the fall, when year-round residents are joined by migratory species.

**User Groups:** Hikers and dogs. No horses or mountain bikes. The restrooms are wheelchair accessible, but the trail is not.

**Permits:** No permits are required. Parking and access are free.

**Maps:** For a free trail map, contact the East Bay Regional Parks District at the address below and ask for the Point Isabel Regional

Shoreline brochure. For a topographic map, ask the USGS for Richmond.

**Directions:** From I-80 in south Richmond, take the Central Avenue exit and drive west to Isabel Street. Turn right and drive to the parking area, at the end of the road.

**Contact:** Point Isabel Regional Shoreline, 510/235-1631; East Bay Regional Parks District, 2950 Peralta Oaks Court, P.O. Box 5381, Oakland, CA 94605-0381, 510/562-7275, website: www.ebparks.org (click on Regional Parks and Trails).

## 114 NIMITZ WAY
### 4.0–10.0 mi / 1.5–4.0 hrs

**in Tilden Regional Park at Inspiration Point**
**in the Berkeley hills**

Map 7.3, page 269

When you start down this trail, you might wonder why it is rated so high. But the farther you go, the better it gets, and then everything explains itself. The views? Sure, the sweeping vistas of the East Bay foothills are great, but hey, the paved trail seems more appropriate for bikes, wheelchairs, and joggers than hikers. And so it is for the first four miles, until suddenly you enter a different universe. After passing a gate, the trail turns to dirt, and just like that, there's no one else around as you climb San Pablo Ridge. The views are stunning in all directions from a series of hilltops along the ridge, with the best views of Briones and San Pablo Reservoirs to the east, and San Francisco Bay and the city's skyline to the west. If you are not ready to commit to the full 10 miles, your goal should be at least two miles out to Wildcat Peak (elevation 1,250 feet; just off the trail) before turning around and heading for home. This is one of the best sections of the 31-mile East Bay Skyline National Trail.

**User Groups:** Hikers, dogs, horses, and mountain bikes. The trail is partially wheelchair accessible.

**Permits:** No permits are required. Parking and access are free.

**Maps:** For a free trail map, contact the East

Bay Regional Parks District at the address below and ask for the Tilden Regional Park brochure. For a topographic map, ask the USGS for Briones Valley.

**Directions:** From Highway 24 in the East Bay, drive to just east of the Caldecott Tunnel and take the Fish Ranch Road exit northwest to Grizzly Peak Boulevard. Turn right, drive up the hill, and turn right again on South Park Drive. Drive one mile to Wildcat Canyon Road, bear right, and drive to the parking area at Inspiration Point, on the left.

Note that South Park Drive is closed each year from November through March to protect migrating newts. To avoid South Park Drive, from Highway 24 drive through the Caldecott Tunnel and exit at Orinda. Turn left on Camino Pablo. Drive north for about two miles, turn left on Wildcat Canyon Road, and continue to Inspiration Point, on the right.

**Contact:** Tilden Nature Area, Environmental Education Center, 510/525-2233; East Bay Regional Parks District, 2950 Peralta Oaks Court, P.O. Box 5381, Oakland, CA 94605-0381, 510/562-7275, website: www.ebparks.org (click on Regional Parks and Trails).

## 115 BERKELEY PIER
**1.2 mi / 0.75 hr**

**near Berkeley on the shore of San Francisco Bay**

Map 7.3, page 269

This historic structure extends 3,000 feet into San Francisco Bay amid landmarks that people come from around the world to see. The walk is easy—straight and flat—and while most people can get to the end of the pier in 20 minutes, there is no reason to hurry. The Golden Gate Bridge is a classic sight from the end of the pier, especially during sunsets, when you will discover how the Golden Gate earned its name. Things look different here, especially if you bring a loaf of French bread to nibble on and maybe your favorite elixir to wash it down. Fishing success varies; the best time is early summer, when halibut school on the Berkeley flats.

**User Groups:** Hikers and wheelchairs. No dogs, horses, or mountain bikes.

**Permits:** No permits are required. Parking and access are free.

**Maps:** For a topographic map, ask the USGS for Oakland West.

**Directions:** From I-80 in Berkeley, take the University Avenue exit and follow the signs to the Berkeley marina. The pier is at the foot of University Avenue, on the west side of I-80, just past the bait shop and marina on the shore of San Francisco Bay.

**Contact:** Berkeley City Parks, 510/644-6376; Berkeley Marina Bait & Tackle, 510/849-2727, website: www.ci.berkeley.ca.us/parks.

## 116 ROUND TOP LOOP TRAIL
**1.7 mi / 1.0 hr**

**in the Robert Sibley Volcanic Regional Preserve in the Berkeley hills**

Map 7.3, page 269

The remains of the Bay Area's long-extinct volcano, Mount Round Top, can be explored at the Sibley preserve. As you walk along the exposed volcanic rock, you can take a self-guided tour using a pamphlet you get at the trailhead. After the volcano blasted out its lava contents about nine million years ago, the interior of the mountain collapsed into the void left by the outburst, and blocks of volcanic stone lie scattered everywhere around the flanks of the mountain. A gated road leads to the top (elevation 1,763 feet), but the best way to see the mountain is on Round Top Loop Trail. Hike in a clockwise direction so the numbered posts (one through nine) on the self-guided tour correspond in order with the most interesting volcanic outcrops.

**User Groups:** Hikers and dogs. Partially accessible to wheelchairs, horses, and mountain bikes.

**Permits:** No permits are required. Parking and access are free.

**Maps:** For a free trail map, contact the East Bay Regional Parks District at the address below and ask for the Sibley Volcanic Regional

Preserve brochure. For a topographic map, ask the USGS for Briones Valley.

**Directions:** From Highway 24 in the East Bay, drive to just east of the Caldecott Tunnel and take the Fish Ranch Road exit northwest to Grizzly Peak Boulevard. Turn left and drive to Skyline Boulevard. Then drive straight ahead for another .25 mile to the park entrance and parking area, on the left.

From Montclair Village, east of Highway 13 in Oakland, take Snake Road uphill to Skyline Boulevard. Turn left on Skyline Boulevard and drive .5 mile to the park entrance, on the right.

**Contact:** Robert Sibley Volcanic Regional Preserve, 510/644-0436; East Bay Regional Parks District, 2950 Peralta Oaks Court, P.O. Box 5381, Oakland, CA 94605-0381, 510/562-7275, website: www.ebparks.org (click on Regional Parks and Trails).

## 117 LAFAYETTE-MORAGA TRAIL
**7.75 mi one-way / 4.0 hrs**

**north of the San Leandro Reservoir**

**Map 7.3, page 269**

The Lafayette-Moraga Trail is a 7.75-mile linear park. In other words, the trail is a park that forms a line from Lafayette to Moraga. Much of it is paved, while the rest is either dirt or compacted soil, making most of the route more popular with bikers and joggers than hikers. On warming weekend mornings, this trail is a real hit with the locals. The hike starts at the Olympic Staging Area in Lafayette and curls to the left for the first 3.5 miles, eventually heading south along Las Trampas Creek to Bollinger Canyon. It then passes through downtown Moraga to the Valle Vista Staging Area on Canyon Road. For most, this is the end of the trip, as bicycles, dogs, and horses are not allowed to continue. Hikers, however, may keep walking west on land managed by the East Bay Municipal Utility District (EBMUD).

**User Groups:** Hikers, wheelchairs, dogs, horses, and mountain bikes.

**Permits:** No permits are required except on EBMUD lands. Parking and access are free.

**Maps:** For a free trail map, contact the East Bay Regional Parks District at the address below and ask for the Lafayette-Moraga Regional Trail brochure. For topographic maps, ask the USGS for Walnut Creek and Las Trampas Ridge.

**Directions:** From Highway 24 near Lafayette, take the Pleasant Hill Road exit south. Drive one mile to Olympic Boulevard. Turn right and drive .25 mile to the Olympic Staging Area.

**Contact:** Lafayette-Moraga Linear Park, 925/687-3419; East Bay Regional Parks District, 2950 Peralta Oaks Court, P.O. Box 5381, Oakland, CA 94605-0381, 510/562-7275, website: www .ebparks.org (click on Regional Parks and Trails); East Bay Municipal Utility District (EBMUD), 510/287-0459 (permits).

## 118 IRON HORSE REGIONAL TRAIL
**15.0 mi one-way / 1.0 day**

**in the San Ramon Valley from San Ramon to Walnut Creek**

**Map 7.3, page 269**

The Iron Horse Regional Trail is a focal point of the national Rails to Trails program, which converts abandoned rail lines into hiking trails. When complete, Iron Horse Trail will span northward from Shadow Cliffs Lake (in Pleasanton) all the way to Suisun Bay (near Martinez). The rail route that it follows was established in 1890 and was abandoned officially in 1976. It took only two years to remove all the tracks, but the trail conversion is requiring quite a bit more time.

The completed portion starts at Amador Valley Boulevard, in Dublin, and heads about 17 miles north to Walnut Creek. It is often hot and dry out here, with little shade (the trail is 75 feet wide in places) and no drinking water, but the trail deserves mention anyway. When shade trees are planted, drinking water is made available, and the route is lengthened, Iron Horse will become a prominent long-distance trail for jogging, biking, and walking.

**User Groups:** Hikers, wheelchairs, dogs, horses, and mountain bikes.

**Permits:** No permits are required. Parking and access are free.

**Maps:** For a free trail map, contact the East Bay Regional Parks District at the address below and ask for the Iron Horse Regional Trail brochure. For a topographic map, ask the USGS for Las Trampas Ridge.

**Directions:** From I-680 in Walnut Creek, take the Rudgear Road exit. Turn east and park at either the park-and-ride lot (on the east side of the freeway) or the staging area (south side).

**Contact:** Iron Horse Regional Trail, 925/687-3419; East Bay Regional Parks District, 2950 Peralta Oaks Court, P.O. Box 5381, Oakland, CA 94605-0381, 510/562-7275, website: www.ebparks.org (click on Regional Parks and Trails).

## 119 HUCKLEBERRY LOOP PATH
**1.7 mi / 1.25 hrs**

**in the Huckleberry Botanic Regional Preserve in the Oakland hills**

Map 7.3, page 269

If you know what you're looking for, this is a trip into an ecological wonderland. If you don't, well, it's still a rewarding, tranquil venture. The only reason people come to Huckleberry is to hike—not to play games or fish. That is because the Huckleberry Loop is routed through a remarkable variety of rare and beautiful plants. From the parking area, follow the path to the left fork, where you then descend steeply through a mature bay forest for a mile. The trail returns by turning right and climbing .7 mile out of the canyon. This last section is particularly rich in diverse plant life.

**User Groups:** Hikers only. No dogs, horses, or mountain bikes. No wheelchair facilities.

**Permits:** No permits are required. Parking and access are free.

**Maps:** For a free trail map, contact the East Bay Regional Parks District at the address below and ask for the Huckleberry Botanic Regional Preserve brochure. For a topographic map, ask the USGS for Oakland East.

**Directions:** From Highway 24 in the East Bay, drive to just east of the Caldecott Tunnel and take the Fish Ranch Road exit northwest to Grizzly Peak Boulevard. Drive two miles and bear left onto Skyline Boulevard (the roads merge). Drive a short distance past Robert Sibley Volcanic Regional Preserve to the park entrance and parking lot, on the left.

**Contact:** Huckleberry Botanic Regional Preserve, 510/644-0436; East Bay Regional Parks District, 2950 Peralta Oaks Court, P.O. Box 5381, Oakland, CA 94605-0381, 510/562-7275, website: www.ebparks.org (click on Regional Parks and Trails).

## 120 GRAHAM TRAIL LOOP
**0.75 mi / 0.5 hr**

**in the Roberts Regional Recreation Area in the Oakland hills**

Map 7.3, page 269

Because the entrance to Roberts Regional Recreation Area lies amid redwood trees, it has proven to be a popular stop for visitors who want to see *Sequoia sempervirens* with a minimum effort. If you want to enter a redwood forest in the East Bay without having to walk far, this is the best bet. From the entrance of the parking area, near the swimming pool, take the short trail that is linked to Graham Trail. Turn right, and you will be routed in a short circle past a restroom to Diablo Vista; then turn right and head back to the parking area. The walk is short and sweet—just right for those who do not wish for a more challenging encounter.

**User Groups:** Hikers and dogs. No horses or mountain bikes. The restroom is wheelchair accessible, but the trail is not.

**Permits:** No permits are required. An entrance fee of $4 per vehicle is charged on weekends and holidays; a fee is charged for access to the swimming pool (wheelchair accessible).

**Maps:** For a free trail map, contact the East Bay Regional Parks District at the address below and ask for the Roberts Regional Recreation Area and Redwood Regional Park brochures. For a topographic map, ask the USGS for Oakland East.

**Directions:** From Highway 24 in the East Bay, drive to Highway 13 in Oakland. Turn south on Highway 13 (follow the signs carefully) and drive three miles to Joaquin Miller Road. Turn left (east) on Joaquin Miller Road and drive one mile to Skyline Boulevard. Turn left on Skyline Boulevard and drive about one mile to the park entrance, on the right.

**Contact:** Roberts Regional Recreation Area, 510/482-6028; East Bay Regional Parks District, 2950 Peralta Oaks Court, P.O. Box 5381, Oakland, CA 94605-0381, 510/562-7275, website: www.ebparks.org (click on Regional Parks and Trails).

## 121 ROCKY RIDGE LOOP
**4.4 mi / 2.5 hrs**

**in Las Trampas Regional Wilderness south of Moraga**

Map 7.3, page 269

The primary destination at Las Trampas Regional Wilderness is Rocky Ridge and its 2,024-foot summit. Though the surrounding landscape consists of rolling hills edged by canyons with small creeks, Rocky Ridge is a spectacular sandstone wall with diagonal striations on its west face.

On top, you get spectacular views to the east of Mount Diablo and the Livermore Valley, and to the west of Crow Canyon plunging at your feet and beyond to the South Bay.

The adventure is best started at the trailhead at the end of Bollinger Road. Newcomers should always pick up a map/brochure from the self-serve box at the trailhead. From the parking area, it is a 2.2-mile trip on a service road to Rocky Ridge, with a climb of 800 feet in a stretch of 1.5 miles. At the ridge, there are several options. To complete a 4.4-mile loop trail, turn left (south) on the Upper Trail and then left again on the Elderberry Trail.

Another option is the side trip to what is called the Wind Caves. These are actually more like sandstone hollows. To get there from the

Upper Trail (with map in hand), turn right on the Sycamore Trail and tromp a little more than a quarter-mile down to the caves. This is a fairly steep descent, though short.

The land can also be trekked following game trails, exploring the edge of canyons and watersheds, and free climbing and scrambling atop the ridge itself.

Perched atop the ridge, you might be lucky to watch the hawks and falcons at eye-level, floating on the thermals and gliding with scarcely a wingbeat. The cliffs here provide nesting areas for many raptors, including red-tailed hawks, prairie falcons, and the fastest creature on earth—the peregrine falcon (this is where we saw our first peregrine). Golden eagles are also commonly sighted in the region in the winter months. An abundant population of ground squirrels provides a reliable food source, and in turn, the eagles migrate long distances to use the area as a wintering ground.

At 3,800 acres, Las Trampas represents a sprawling wilderness island amid civilization. With other contiguous regional parklands and watershed lands, it is ringed generally by Castro Valley to the south, Upper San Leandro Reservoir and Crow Canyon to the west, and Danville to the northeast.

**User Groups:** Hikers, dogs, and horses. No mountain bikes (but permitted on the park's service roads). No wheelchair facilities.

**Permits:** No permits are required. Parking and access are free. A permit is required to access and hike on adjoining EBMUD lands.

**Maps:** For a free trail map, contact the East Bay Regional Parks District at the address below and ask for the Las Trampas Regional Wilderness brochure. For a topographic map, ask the USGS for Las Trampas Ridge.

**Directions:** Take I-680 to San Ramon. Take the exit for Crow Canyon Road and drive west to Bollinger Canyon Road. Turn north on Bollinger Canyon Road and drive five miles to parking area and trailhead.

**Contact:** Las Trampas Regional Wilderness, 925/837-3250; East Bay Regional Parks District, 2950 Peralta Oaks Court, P.O. Box 5381, Oakland, CA 94605-0381, 510/562-7275, website: www.ebparks.org (click on Regional Parks and Trails); East Bay Municipal Utility District (EBMUD), 510/287-0459 (permits).

## 122 SHORELINE TRAIL
**5.0 mi / 2.25 hrs**

at Crown Memorial State Beach on the shore of San Francisco Bay in Alameda

Map 7.3, page 269

The tide book is your bible at Crown Memorial State Beach, which is set along the shore of San Francisco Bay just south of Crab Cove. High tide is the best time to observe seabirds such as loons, grebes, and ducks. Low tide, however, is the best time to watch shorebirds such as sandpipers poking around the exposed mudflats. The trail is a paved bicycle path that follows the bay's shoreline, running 2.5 miles south to an overlook of the Elsie Roemer Bird Sanctuary. The bay views are also quite good. When the wind is down, this is one of the best swimming areas in the bay; when the wind is up, it's excellent for windsurfing.

**User Groups:** Hikers, wheelchairs, dogs (on the paved trail only, not the beach), and mountain bikes. No horses.

**Permits:** No permits are required. An entrance fee of $4 per vehicle is charged February through October; there is also a fee for dogs.

**Maps:** For a free trail map, contact the East Bay Regional Parks District at the address below and ask for the Crown Memorial State Beach brochure. For a topographic map, ask the USGS for Oakland West.

**Directions:** From I-580, take I-980 west into Oakland. Take the 12th Street/Alameda exit. Follow the road under I-880 and turn left onto 5th Street. Drive to the Oakland/Alameda Tube. At the end of the tube, you will be on Webster Street, which dead-ends at Central. Turn left on Central and drive two blocks to 8th Street. Turn right on 8th Street and drive .25 mile to the Crown Beach entrance, on the right.

**Contact:** Crown Memorial State Beach, Crab

Cove Visitors Center, 510/521-6887; East Bay Regional Parks District, 2950 Peralta Oaks Court, P.O. Box 5381, Oakland, CA 94605-0381, 510/562-7275, website: www.ebparks.org (click on Regional Parks and Trails).

## 123 ARROWHEAD MARSH
**2.0 mi / 1.0 hr**

at Martin Luther King Regional Shoreline on San Leandro Bay near Oakland

Map 7.3, page 269

Arrowhead Marsh is one of the best bird-watching areas in the East Bay, with 30 species that are commonly sighted—including several pairs of blue-winged teal. At high tide, this is also a top spot to see rails, which are typically elusive birds that are more often heard than seen. The paved trail skirts the edge of the marsh, which is set along San Leandro Bay. From the parking area, the trail is routed one mile out along the Airport Channel, with the marsh on your left. If you want, extend your walk across a bridge at San Leandro Creek and continue along the shore to Garretson Point, adding 1.4 miles round-trip. This parkland covers 1,220 acres, including some of the bay's most valuable wetlands habitat.

**User Groups:** Hikers, wheelchairs, and mountain bikes. No dogs or horses.

**Permits:** No permits are required. Parking and access are free.

**Maps:** For a free trail map, contact the East Bay Regional Parks District at the address below and ask for the Martin Luther King Regional Shoreline brochure. For a topographic map, ask the USGS for San Leandro.

**Directions:** From I-880 in Oakland, take the Hegenberger Road exit and follow it toward the airport and Doolittle Drive. Turn right on Doolittle Drive and proceed to Swan Way. Turn right again and drive a short distance to the park entrance. Turn left and drive to the parking area at the end of the road.

Alternate route: From I-880 in Oakland, take the Hegenberger Road exit and drive .5 mile to Pardee Drive. Turn right and drive a few blocks to Swan Way. Turn left and drive one block to Gravel Access Road. Turn right on Gravel Access Road and drive .5 mile to the marsh area.

**Contact:** Martin Luther King Regional Shoreline, 510/562-1373; East Bay Regional Parks District, 2950 Peralta Oaks Court, P.O. Box 5381, Oakland, CA 94605-0381, 510/562-7275, website: www.ebparks.org (click on Regional Parks and Trails).

## 124 STREAM TRAIL LOOP
### 3.5 mi / 2.0 hrs

**in Redwood Regional Park in the Oakland hills**

Map 7.3, page 269

Newcomers to Redwood Regional Park are often amazed at the beauty of this trail. After all, whoever heard of redwood forests and trout streams in Oakland? But visitors to this park get both of these things here. For the best loop route, hike up Stream Trail for .25 mile, then turn left on French Trail. Climb along the western slopes of the redwood canyon, rising to 1,000 feet. With the puffing part behind you (always hike up when you're fresh), turn right on Fern Trail, and you'll soon meet a junction with Stream Trail. The rest of the route back to the park entrance is easy and downhill, tracing along pretty Redwood Creek through the center of the redwood forest. In late winter and spring, trout swim upstream from San Leandro Reservoir to spawn in these waters (fishing is not permitted).

**User Groups:** Hikers, wheelchairs, dogs, and horses. No mountain bikes.

**Permits:** No permits are required. An entrance fee of $4 per vehicle is charged when the kiosk is attended; there's a dog fee year-round.

**Maps:** For a free trail map, contact the East Bay Regional Parks District at the address below and ask for the Redwood Regional Park brochure. For a topographic map, ask the USGS for Oakland East.

**Directions:** From Highway 24 in Oakland, turn south on Highway 13 and drive to Redwood

Road. Turn left on Redwood Road and drive two miles past Skyline Boulevard to the park entrance, on the left. Turn left and park at the Canyon Meadow Staging Area, at the end of the road.

Alternate route: From the Bay Bridge, take I-580 to the 35th Avenue exit. Drive east on 35th Avenue, which becomes Redwood Road, and continue past Skyline Boulevard for about two miles to the park entrance, on the left.

**Contact:** Redwood Regional Park, 510/482-6024; East Bay Regional Parks District, 2950 Peralta Oaks Court, P.O. Box 5381, Oakland, CA 94605-0381, 510/562-7275, website: www.ebparks.org (click on Regional Parks and Trails).

## 125 EAST RIDGE LOOP
### 4.0 mi / 2.5 hrs

**in Redwood Regional Park in the Oakland hills**

Map 7.3, page 269

From atop the East Ridge, at 1,100 feet, you can look down into a canyon that appears to be a sea of redwoods. The view is quite a treat after climbing nearly 900 feet from the trailhead. The payback comes when you turn left and loop down into that canyon, where Redwood Creek awaits under the cool canopy of a lush forest. This trip is an option to the Stream Trail Loop (see previous listing) for ambitious hikers and mountain bikers; unlike on that trail, bikes are allowed on the East Ridge. From the parking area, turn right on Canyon Trail, climbing up to the East Ridge in .5 mile. Turn left and make the loop by hiking out on the ridge, climbing much of the way, turning left again on Prince Road, and returning on Stream Trail.

**User Groups:** Hikers, dogs, and horses. Mountain bikes and wheelchairs permitted on the paved part of the trail.

**Permits:** No permits are required. An entrance fee of $4 per vehicle is charged when the kiosk is attended.

**Maps:** For a free trail map, contact the East Bay Regional Parks District at the address below and ask for the Redwood Regional Park brochure. For a topographic map, ask the USGS for Oakland East.

**Directions:** From Highway 24 in Oakland, turn south on Highway 13 and drive to Redwood Road. Turn left on Redwood Road and drive two miles past Skyline Boulevard to the park entrance, on the left. Turn left and park at the Canyon Meadow Staging Area, at the end of the road.

Alternate route: From the Oakland side of the Bay Bridge, take I-580 to the 35th Avenue exit. Drive east on 35th Avenue, which becomes Redwood Road, and continue past Skyline Boulevard for about two miles to the park entrance, on the left.

**Contact:** Redwood Regional Park, 510/482-6024; East Bay Regional Parks District, 2950 Peralta Oaks Court, P.O. Box 5381, Oakland, CA 94605-0381, 510/562-7275, website: www .ebparks.org (click on Regional Parks and Trails).

## 126 GRASS VALLEY LOOP
**2.8 mi / 1.5 hrs**

**in Anthony Chabot Regional Park in the Oakland hills**

Map 7.3, page 269

Grass Valley lies hidden in the East Bay hills, providing a simple paradise. This meadow lines more than a mile of a valley floor that is framed on each side by the rims of miniature mountains. In the spring, the land glows with the various hues of green from wild grasses, along with wild radish, blue-eyed grass, and golden poppies. The scene is quiet and beautiful, and Grass Valley Loop is one of the quickest routes into tranquillity. Starting at the Bort Meadow Staging Area, at a trailhead for the East Bay Skyline National Trail, hike downhill to the Bort Meadow Picnic Area. Turn left and head south through Grass Valley, continuing on to Stonebridge, for a distance of 1.5 miles. To get back from Stonebridge, walk north on Brandon Trail, which is routed along the west side of Grass Valley. To crown a perfect day, end the hike with lunch at Bort Meadow.

**User Groups:** Hikers, dogs, horses, and mountain bikes. No wheelchair facilities.

**Permits:** No permits are required. Parking and access are free.

**Maps:** For a free trail map, contact the East Bay Regional Parks District at the address below and ask for the Anthony Chabot Regional Park brochure. For a topographic map, ask the USGS for Las Trampas Ridge.

**Directions:** From I-580 in Oakland, take the 35th Avenue exit and drive east (35th Avenue becomes Redwood Road). Follow Redwood Road past Skyline Boulevard and continue three more miles to the Bort Meadow Staging Area, on the right.

**Contact:** Anthony Chabot Regional Park, 510/639-4751; East Bay Regional Parks District, 2950 Peralta Oaks Court, P.O. Box 5381, Oakland, CA 94605-0381, 510/562-7275, website: www.ebparks.org (click on Regional Parks and Trails).

## 127 BORT MEADOW
**5.4 mi / 3.25 hrs**

**in Anthony Chabot Regional Park north of Castro Valley**

Map 7.3, page 269

This trail has good views of a beautiful valley, and in the spring, there is a diverse array of pretty wildflowers. Start at the Bort Meadow Staging Area, a trailhead for the East Bay Skyline National Trail. Head out north (to the right), where the trail meanders along an old ranch road, climbing only slightly above Bort Meadow and Grass Valley. At the ridge, turn and look south for a great view of Grass Valley—a divine sight in the springtime. From the ridge, the trail/road proceeds north, with valley and hilltop views along the way; watch closely for the hidden bench on the right side of the trail; here, you can sit and look out over the remote foothill country. After enjoying the views, return the way you came. The trail eventually drops steeply and connects to Redwood Regional Park, but most people turn around and return when they reach the drop in the trail.

**User Groups:** Hikers, dogs, horses, and mountain bikes. No wheelchair facilities.

**Permits:** No permits are required. Parking and access are free.

**Maps:** For a free trail map, contact the East Bay Regional Parks District at the address below and ask for the Anthony Chabot Regional Park brochure. For a topographic map, ask the USGS for Las Trampas Ridge.

**Directions:** From I-580 in Oakland, take the 35th Avenue exit and drive east (35th Avenue becomes Redwood Road). Follow Redwood Road past Skyline Boulevard and drive three more miles to the Bort Meadow Staging Area, on the right.

**Contact:** Anthony Chabot Regional Park, 510/639-4751; East Bay Regional Parks District, 2950 Peralta Oaks Court, P.O. Box 5381, Oakland, CA 94605-0381, 510/562-7275, website: www.ebparks.org (click on Regional Parks and Trails).

## 128 EAST BAY SKYLINE NATIONAL TRAIL

**31.0 mi one-way / 2.0–4.0 days**

in the East Bay Regional Parks District, from Chabot Regional Park near Castro Valley to Wildcat Canyon Regional Park in the Richmond hills

> **Map 7.3, page 269**

A 31-mile trail along the East Bay's skyline offers a unique opportunity for a long-distance hike that can be chopped into many short segments over the course of days or even weeks. The trail spans from the Castro Valley foothills northward to the ridgeline behind Richmond, crossing six regional parks for a view into the area's prettiest and wildest lands. Called the East Bay Skyline National Trail, it is the Bay Area's longest single continuous trail. The trail can be hiked from south to north in two days, but it can also be divided into seven sections from the different access points at the parking areas. Bicycles and horses are permitted on 65 percent of the trail, where it is wide enough to accommodate them.

It is a great trip, whether you do it all in one weekend or cover a bit at a time over several weeks. No permits are needed, leashed dogs are allowed, and access is free. There are no campgrounds along the way, which makes backpacking and overnights impossible, but you can use a shuttle car and come back to do a different section each day. The absence of piped drinking water is another drawback. Water is available at only four points over the 31 miles, at Lomas Cantadas, Sibley Preserve, Skyline Gate, and Bort Meadow. So come prepared with a full canteen or two of water per person, along with a hat and sunscreen. Following is a detailed description of the trail from south to north.

**User Groups:** Hikers, dogs, horses, and mountain bikes. Horses and mountain bikes are restricted in some sections. Also see individual trailhead listings, below.

**Permits:** No permits are required. A parking fee may be charged at some trailheads.

**Maps:** For a brochure and map of the East Bay Skyline National Trail or individual maps on each regional park, contact the East Bay Regional Parks District at the address below.

**Directions:** See individual trailhead listings below for specific directions.

**Contact:** East Bay Regional Parks District, 2950 Peralta Oaks Court, P.O. Box 5381, Oakland, CA 94605-0381, 510/562-7275, website: www .ebparks.org (click on Regional Parks and Trails).

• **Proctor Gate to Bort Meadow, Chabot Regional Park:** The trail starts adjacent to a golf course and is routed up a ridge. It then meanders on a ranch road in Chabot Regional Park. At Stonebridge (don't turn left at the trail junction!), the trail leads into Grass Valley and on to Bort Meadow. Distance: 6.5 miles; climbs 600 feet, then drops 320 feet.

**Directions:** From I-580 in Oakland, take the 35th Avenue exit and drive east (35th Avenue becomes Redwood Road). Drive on Redwood Road to the Proctor Gate Staging Area, located on the east border of the park, next to a golf course.

• **Bort Meadow to MacDonald Gate, Chabot Regional Park:** If you are hiking the entire East Bay National Skyline Trail, the trail climbs steeply out of Bort Meadow. If you are starting at the parking area, however, no such climb is needed. The trail becomes a service road, from which you can turn and look south for the great view of Grass Valley. Hikers are completely exposed on the ascent; it's hot and dry in the afternoon, so it's best to go early in the morning. Once on top, it's an easy hike, with many wildflowers in spring. It then descends into a canyon, crosses Redwood Road, and puts you at the entrance to Redwood Regional Park. Distance: 2.7 miles; climbs 300 feet, then drops 500 feet.

**Directions:** From I-580 in Oakland, take the 35th Avenue exit and drive east (35th Avenue becomes Redwood Road). Drive on Redwood Road three miles past Skyline Boulevard to the Bort Meadow Staging Area, on the right.

• **MacDonald Gate to Skyline Gate, Redwood Regional Park:** Hikers have two options here, and the suggested route is to split off at French Trail to hike up the canyon bottom on Stream Trail, enveloped by redwoods. Note that bikes are banned from this section. The alternative, a must-do for bikers, is to take West Ridge Trail for a steep climb to the canyon rim, then drop to the junction at Skyline Gate. Distance: five miles; French Trail drops 200 feet, then climbs 400 feet; West Ridge Trail climbs 900 feet, then drops 200 feet.

**Directions:** From I-580 to the west or I-680 to the east, drive to Highway 24, then to Highway 13 and go south. Drive to Redwood Road and turn left. Drive to the park entrance, turn south, and park at the MacDonald Gate Staging Area.

• **Skyline Gate through Huckleberry Preserve to Sibley Preserve:** This section of trail is a choice hike for nature lovers, who will see an abundance of birdlife and other animals, especially in the early morning and late evening. The trail passes through a deciduous woodland habitat, with a short but quite steep climb after entering Huckleberry Preserve. Distance: three miles; drops 200 feet, then climbs 480 feet.

**Directions:** From Highway 24 in Oakland, drive east to Highway 13. Go south and drive to Joaquin Miller Road, then head east until you hit Skyline Boulevard. Turn left on Skyline Boulevard and drive to the Skyline Gate Staging Area.

• **Sibley Preserve to Lomas Cantadas, Tilden Regional Park:** A unique section of trail, this part crosses over the Caldecott Tunnel in a relatively unpeopled area. Many hawks are seen here, a nice bonus. Sibley is best known for its volcanic past, and hikers can take a side trip to Mount Round Top (see listing in this chapter), a one-time volcano that blew its top off. No bicycles are permitted. Distance: 3.4 miles; drops 300 feet, then climbs 600 feet.

**Directions:** From I-580 to the west or I-680 to the east, drive to Highway 24. Continue to just east of the Caldecott Tunnel and take the Fish Ranch Road exit northwest to Grizzly Peak Boulevard. Turn left and drive to Skyline Boulevard. The park entrance and parking area are on the left.

• **Lomas Cantadas to Inspiration Point, Tilden Regional Park:** This section of trail starts at a major access area off Grizzly Peak Boulevard. Also possible is an adjacent side trip to Vollmer Peak, the highest point on East Bay Skyline National Trail. The trail is then routed north to Inspiration Point at Wildcat Canyon Road, another well-known access point, losing elevation most of the way. Many sweeping views of the East Bay's untouched foothills are found on this hike. Distance: three miles; drops 860 feet.

**Directions:** From I-580 to the west or I-680 to the east, drive to Highway 24. Continue to just east of the Caldecott Tunnel and take the Fish Ranch Road exit to Grizzly Peak Boulevard. At the stop sign, turn right and drive on Grizzly Peak Boulevard to Lomas Cantadas Road. Turn right, then immediately turn left, following the signs for the Steam Train to the parking area.

• **Inspiration Point (Tilden Regional Park) to Wildcat Canyon Regional Park:** The last stretch starts at the most heavily used section of the entire route, then crosses its most dramatic and unpeopled terrain. From Inspiration Point, the trail is actually paved for four miles—ideal for bicycles and wheelchairs. Beyond that, the trail turns to dirt and traces San Pablo Ridge, with inspiring views in all directions before dropping steeply into Wildcat Canyon Regional Park in the Richmond foothills. Distance: 7.2 miles; drops 800 feet.

**Directions:** From I-580 to the west or I-680 to the east, drive to Highway 24. Continue to just east of the Caldecott Tunnel and take the Fish Ranch Road exit northwest to Grizzly Peak Boulevard. Turn right, drive up the hill, and turn right on South Park Drive. Drive one mile to Wildcat Canyon Road, bear right, and drive to the parking area at Inspiration Point, on the left.

Alternate Route: To avoid South Park Drive, which is sometimes closed in the winter due to newt migrations, from Highway 24 go through the Caldecott Tunnel and exit at Orinda. Turn left on Camino Pablo. Drive north for about two miles, then turn left on Wildcat Canyon Road. Follow the road to Inspiration Point on the right.

# 129 SHORELINE LOOP TRAIL
## 1.75 mi / 1.0 hr

**in the Cull Canyon Regional Recreation Area in the Castro Valley foothills**

Map 7.3, page 269

Little Cull Canyon Reservoir, covering just 18 acres, is the backdrop for a picnic lunch in a canyon, and this short hike along the lake is popular with park visitors. From the parking area, walk over to the picnic areas, and turn left along Shoreline Trail. It skirts the western bank of the narrow lake then loops back along a lagoon. This is a pleasant walk most of the year. However, just plain forget it on summer afternoons, when the hot sun brands everything in sight. That is why this park is most fa-mous for its swimming complex—complete with bathhouse and snack bar—not for the hiking and, heaven knows, not for the fishing.

**User Groups:** Hikers and dogs. No horses or mountain bikes. No wheelchair facilities.

**Permits:** No permits are required. There is no entrance fee. A fee for swimming is charged.

**Maps:** For a free trail map, contact the East Bay Regional Parks District at the address below and ask for the Cull Canyon Regional Recreation Area brochure. For a topographic map, ask the USGS for Hayward.

**Directions:** From eastbound I-580 in Castro Valley, take the Center Street exit and drive north to Heyer Avenue. Turn right on Heyer and proceed to Cull Canyon Road. Turn left and drive to the park entrance.

From westbound I-580, take the Castro Valley exit and turn left onto Castro Valley Boulevard. Drive to Crow Canyon Road, turn right, and drive .5 mile. Turn left on Cull Canyon Road and drive to the park entrance.

**Contact:** Cull Canyon Regional Recreation Area, 510/537-2240; East Bay Regional Parks District, 2950 Peralta Oaks Court, P.O. Box 5381, Oakland, CA 94605-0381, 510/562-7275, website: www.ebparks.org (click on Regional Parks and Trails).

# 130 DON CASTRO LAKE LOOP
## 1.7 mi / 1.0 hr

**in the Don Castro Regional Recreation Area in the Castro Valley foothills**

Map 7.3, page 269

Don Castro is a small (23 acres) but pretty lake that attracts swimmers to its lagoon and its clear, warm, blue waters. Hiking is typically an afterthought for visitors, who come primarily to picnic or fish. The trail (actually, it's a road) is routed completely around the lake for an easy walk or jog in a nice setting. From the parking area, walk a short distance along the West Lawn to the dam, and start your hike there, circling the water in a clockwise direction. In the first .25 mile, you will pass a fishing pier, with the lake on your right and the swimming lagoon on your left. The route continues to the headwaters of the lake at San Lorenzo Creek, crosses the creek, and then hems the southern shoreline all the way to the lake's spillway. After climbing a short staircase, you will be on top and can hike over the dam and back to the parking area. It's an easy circle.

**User Groups:** Hikers and dogs. Portions of the trail are paved for bicycle and wheelchair use. No horses.

**Permits:** No permits are required. An entrance fee of $4 per vehicle is charged when the kiosk is attended; there is also a dog fee. A swimming fee is extra.

**Maps:** For a free trail map, contact the East Bay Regional Parks District at the address below and ask for the Don Castro Regional Recreation Area brochure. For a topographic map, ask the USGS for Hayward.

**Directions:** From eastbound I-580 in Castro Valley, take the Center Street exit and turn right. Drive to Kelly Street. Turn left and drive .5 mile to Woodroe. Turn left on Woodroe and drive to the park entrance.

From westbound I-580, take the Castro Valley exit and drive west on East Castro Valley Boulevard to Grove Way. Turn left and drive to Center Street. Drive .5 mile, turn left, and drive to Kelly Street. Make another left onto Kelly Street and drive to Woodroe. Turn left and drive to the park entrance.

**Contact:** Don Castro Regional Recreation Area, 510/538-1148; East Bay Regional Parks District, 2950 Peralta Oaks Court, P.O. Box 5381, Oakland, CA 94605-0381, 510/562-7275, website: www.ebparks.org (click on Regional Parks and Trails).

## 131 COGSWELL MARSH LOOP
**2.8 mi / 1.5 hrs**

at Hayward Regional Shoreline on South San Francisco Bay in Hayward

Map 7.3, page 269

Cogswell Marsh is the heart of an 800-acre marshy wetlands, a great place to take short nature hikes and try to identify many rare

birds. It's always a good choice for viewing shorebirds; as a bonus, peregrine falcons are typically seen either hovering over the marsh or perched on power pylons. As many as 200 white pelicans have been seen here, along with the occasional merlin. From the parking area, the trail starts with a .37-mile hike across landfill; then it enters the marshlands, where a loop trail circles the most vital habitat. To keep your feet from getting wet, two short sections are bridged. The loop is best hiked clockwise, so you face the Bay Bridge and the San Francisco skyline (an outstanding view) as you walk along the water's edge of the South Bay. Guided weekend nature walks are available.

**User Groups:** Hikers and mountain bikes. No dogs (south of flood control channel) or horses. No wheelchair facilities.

**Permits:** No permits are required. Parking and access are free.

**Maps:** For a free trail map, contact the East Bay Regional Parks District at the address below and ask for the Hayward Regional Shoreline brochure. For a topographic map, ask the USGS for San Leandro.

**Directions:** From I-880 in Hayward, take the West Winton Avenue exit and follow the road west toward the bay to the entrance and parking area.

**Contact:** Hayward Regional Shoreline, 510/783-1066; East Bay Regional Parks District, 2950 Peralta Oaks Court, P.O. Box 5381, Oakland, CA 94605-0381, 510/562-7275, website: www.ebparks.org (click on Regional Parks and Trails).

## 132 BAYVIEW TRAIL
**3.0 mi / 1.5 hrs**

in Coyote Hills Regional Park on the shore of the South Bay near Fremont

Map 7.3, page 269

Evidence of Coyote Hills Regional Park's rich history is visible throughout its 966 acres: four Indian shell middens (heaps of discarded shells from ancient tribes, who ate a lot of shellfish) can be seen. The Bayview Trail is the favorite hike in the park, offering excellent views of the South Bay. This walk circles the park, including a 1.5-mile stretch that borders the bay and a shorter piece that runs adjacent to a marsh. The park is a wildlife sanctuary, with grassy hills and marshes that provide significant habitat for numerous migrating waterfowl. The best way to hike this loop is in a counterclockwise direction from the main parking area. For a short but enjoyable side trip from the main parking area, take the wooden boardwalk out through the north marsh.

**User Groups:** Hikers, dogs, horses, and mountain bikes. The trail is paved and is technically wheelchair accessible but is quite steep in some sections.

**Permits:** No permits are required. An entrance fee of $4 per vehicle is charged when the kiosk is attended, and a dog fee is charged year-round.

**Maps:** For a free trail map, contact the East Bay Regional Parks District at the address below and ask for the Coyote Hills Regional Park brochure. For a topographic map, ask the USGS for Newark.

**Directions:** From Fremont, drive west on Highway 84 to the Paseo Padre Parkway exit. Turn right on Paseo Padre Parkway and drive to Patterson Ranch Road. Turn left and drive to the parking area.

From I-880 in Fremont, take the Highway 84/Decoto Road exit and drive on Highway 84 to Paseo Padre Parkway. Proceed as above.

From the Peninsula, turn east on Highway 84, cross the Dumbarton Bridge, and take the Thornton Avenue exit. Turn left (the road becomes Paseo Padre Parkway) and drive north to Patterson Ranch Road. Turn left on Patterson Ranch Road and drive to the parking area.

**Contact:** Coyote Hills Regional Park, Visitors Center, 8000 Patterson Ranch Road, Fremont, CA 94555, 510/795-9385; East Bay Regional Parks District, 2950 Peralta Oaks Court, P.O. Box 5381, Oakland, CA 94605-0381, 510/562-7275, website: www.ebparks.org (click on Regional Parks and Trails).

## 133 DUMBARTON BRIDGE
**4.5 mi / 2.5 hrs**

**on the Dumbarton Bridge from Fremont to East Palo Alto**

Map 7.3, page 269

Let this be a lesson for future bridge designers. When the Dumbarton Bridge was constructed, a biking and hiking path was added along the south side of the roadway, separated from traffic by a cement cordon. That means you can safely hike to the top of the center span for a unique view of the South Bay. This hike is best started from the Fremont side of the bridge, because it is unsafe to leave cars unattended at the western foot of the bridge, in East Palo Alto.

Special Note: The bridge is a link in an outstanding bicycle trip. Start at Alameda Creek Regional Trail in Niles, head over the Dumbarton Bridge, turn left on the Baylands Trail, and ride through Palo Alto; then go farther south at Charleston Slough on Baylands Trail to Mountain View Baylands.

**User Groups:** Hikers, wheelchairs, and mountain bikes. No dogs or horses.

**Permits:** No permits are required. Parking and access are free.

**Maps:** For a topographic map, ask the USGS for Newark.

**Directions:** From Redwood City, head east on Highway 84 and cross the Dumbarton Bridge. Take the first exit after the toll plaza, Thornton Avenue. Turn right and drive .25 mile to Marshland Road. Turn right and drive four miles to the parking area at the fishing pier.

**Contact:** Don Edwards San Francisco Bay National Wildlife Refuge, P.O. Box 524, Newark, CA 94560, 510/792-4275 or 510/792-0222, website: http://desfbay.fws.gov.

## 134 TIDELANDS TRAIL
**2.5 mi / 1.5 hrs**

in the San Francisco Bay National
Wildlife Refuge at the eastern foot of the
Dumbarton Bridge

Map 7.3, page 269

Bird-watchers won't soon forget the diversity
of birdlife at the San Francisco Bay National
Wildlife Refuge, with more than 250 species
in a given year using this habitat for food, resting space, and nesting sites. It is not unusual
to see a half dozen species of ducks, an egret,
a sandpiper, a willet, and herons in just 15 or
20 minutes. The refuge is big, covering 23,000
acres in all, and Tidelands Trail pours right
through it. This is actually a wide dirt pathway on a levee routed amid salt marsh and
bay tidewaters. Group nature tours on this
trail are offered regularly on weekends. The
views of the South Bay and (on clear days)
the surrounding foothills are a panoramic
urban backdrop. Don't forget to stop by refuge
headquarters before your hike to see the exhibits and pamphlets, which will make your
walk more enjoyable.

**User Groups:** Hikers, dogs, and mountain
bikes. There are no wheelchair facilities, but
the trail can be navigated by most wheelchair
users. No horses.

**Permits:** No permits are required. Parking and
access are free.

**Maps:** For a free brochure, contact the refuge
at the address below. For a topographic map,
ask the USGS for Newark.

**Directions:** From San Francisco, drive south
on U.S. 101 to the Willow Road–Dumbarton
exit. Drive east across the Dumbarton Bridge
and take the first exit (Thornton Avenue) after
the toll plaza. Turn right and drive .25 mile to
Marshland Road. Turn right and drive a short
distance to the visitors center.

**Contact:** Don Edwards San Francisco Bay National Wildlife Refuge, P.O. Box 524, Newark,
CA 94560, 510/792-4275 or 510/792-0222: website: http://desfbay.fws.gov.

## 135 DUMBARTON PIER
**1.0 mi / 1.0 hr**

in South San Francisco Bay in the
San Francisco Bay National Wildlife Refuge
in Fremont

Map 7.3, page 269

Here is an example of how the government
did something right. This pier was once the
old Dumbarton Bridge, but when the new
high-rise span was built in the 1980s, the roadway extending from Fremont was converted
to a fishing pier and was made part of the
San Francisco Bay National Wildlife Refuge.
The pier reaches all the way to the channel
of the South Bay, a natural migratory pathway for sharks (in the summer), bat rays (winter), sturgeon (winter), perch (late fall), and
jacksmelt (spring). Many seabirds and waterfowl live in this area year-round. The easy
walk out to the end of the pier also renders
pretty sea views of the South Bay's shoreline;
looking north on a clear day, you can see the
city of San Francisco as well as the San Mateo
and Bay Bridges.

**User Groups:** Hikers, wheelchairs, and mountain bikes. No dogs or horses.

**Permits:** No permits are required. Parking and
access are free.

**Maps:** For a free brochure, contact the refuge
at the address below. For a topographic map,
ask the USGS for Newark.

**Directions:** From San Francisco, drive south
on U.S. 101 to the Willow Road–Dumbarton
exit. Drive east across the Dumbarton Bridge
and take the first exit (Thornton Avenue) after
the toll plaza. Turn right and drive to Marshlands Road. Turn right again and drive past
the San Francisco Bay National Wildlife Refuge
entrance and visitors center for about three
miles, following the signs to Dumbarton Pier
(and the entrance to a leg of the San Francisco Bay bicycle trail).

**Contact:** Don Edwards San Francisco Bay National Wildlife Refuge, P.O. Box 524, Newark,
CA, 510/792-4275 or 510/792-0222, website: http://desfbay.fws.gov.

## 136 CONTRA LOMA LOOP
1.6 mi / 1.0 hr

**in Contra Loma Regional Park near Antioch**

Map 7.3, page 269

Most people go to Contra Loma Regional Park to fish, swim, sunbathe, or picnic at Contra Loma Lake. This short loop trail provides an alternative to those activities, tracing along the northwest shore of the lake, then climbing up and over a short hill and looping back to the starting point. From the parking area, head out on the trail to the Cattail Cove Picnic Area. Just after that, the trail turns right, and you'll follow the shore of the lake, pass a fishing pier, and then start a 10-minute climb up a small hill. To close out the loop, glide down the hill. The trail turns left and a mile later returns to the Cattail Cove Picnic Area.

**User Groups:** Hikers, wheelchairs, dogs, horses, and mountain bikes.

**Permits:** No permits are required. A parking fee of $4 per vehicle is charged; there is a dog fee year-round. An additional fee is charged for access to the swim lagoon.

**Maps:** For a free trail map, contact the East Bay Regional Parks District at the address below and ask for the Contra Loma Regional Park brochure. For a topographic map, ask the USGS for Antioch South.

**Directions:** From Highway 4 at Antioch, take the Lone Tree Way exit and drive south to Golf Course Road. Turn right, drive to Frederickson Lane, bear right, and drive to the gate. Turn right, pass the kiosk, and bear left. Drive to the parking lot by the beach.

**Contact:** Contra Loma Regional Park, 925/757-0404; East Bay Regional Parks District, 2950 Peralta Oaks Court, P.O. Box 5381, Oakland, CA 94605-0381, 510/562-7275, website: www.ebparks.org (click on Regional Parks and Trails).

## 137 PROSPECT TUNNEL LOOP
4.5 mi / 2.5 hrs

**in the Black Diamond Mines Regional Preserve in the Mount Diablo foothills near Antioch**

Map 7.3, page 269

Bring a flashlight with fresh batteries so you can explore 200 feet of mountain tunnel—the featured attraction of Black Diamond Mines Regional Preserve. The Prospect Tunnel, driven in the 1860s by miners in search of coal, probes 400 feet into the side of Mount Diablo, and half of that length is now accessible to the public. To reach the tunnel, it's about a 1.5-mile hike from the trailhead, taking Stewartville Trail (which is well signed) off Frederickson Lane. It is a paved road at the beginning but then turns to dirt. Most of the surrounding area is grasslands and foothill country. After exploring the Prospect Tunnel, you can tack a loop onto your hike. Turn left on Star Mine Trail, which loops for 1.6 miles and passes by a barred tunnel, one of the last active coal mines in the area. The Prospect Tunnel and the Star Mine are two of the most unusual spots in the preserve's 3,700 acres.

**User Groups:** Hikers, dogs, horses, and mountain bikes. A short portion of the trail is accessible to hikers only. No wheelchair facilities.

**Permits:** No permits are required. A parking fee of $4 per vehicle is charged when the kiosk is attended. Guided tours of the underground mining museum cost $3 per person; an underground visitors center is free.

**Maps:** For a free trail map, contact the East Bay Regional Parks District at the address below and ask for the Black Diamond Mines Regional Preserve brochure. For a topographic map, ask the USGS for Antioch South.

**Directions:** From Highway 4 at Antioch, take the Lone Tree Way exit and drive south to Golf Course Road. Turn right, drive to Frederickson Lane, bear right, and drive about one mile to the gate. There is limited parking on the left (at the corner of a right turn). Note: The signs along the way say Contra Loma Regional Park—

not Black Diamond Mines. Once past the gate, you will be in Black Diamond Mines Regional Preserve.

**Contact:** Black Diamond Mines Regional Preserve, 925/757-2620; East Bay Regional Parks District, 2950 Peralta Oaks Court, P.O. Box 5381, Oakland, CA 94605-0381, 510/562-7275, website: www.ebparks.org (click on Regional Parks and Trails).

## 138 DONNER FALLS
**6.5 mi / 2.5 hr**

**in Mount Diablo State Park near Danville**

Map 7.3, page 269

At Mount Diablo, the Bay Area's grand old mountain rising above the East Bay hills, there is a series of hidden waterfalls that can be as pretty as anything after a heavy rain. Reaching them requires a 6.5-mile hike, a good climb, and something of a fortune hunt. In return, you get an experience that shows why the Bay Area is one of the most special places on earth.

The trailhead for Donner Creek Falls is at the end of Regency Drive, which is located off Clayton Road (and becomes Marsh Creek Road) out of Clayton. From here, turn left on an old ranch road and walk alongside a pretty creek set amid rolling hills peppered with oaks. At Cardinet Junction, turn left, and after a short time, cross the creek. Then it's a 600-foot climb in five switchbacks before you reach the signed turnoff for the falls trail. Rewards feature views to the north of Clayton, Suisun Bay, and the Mothball Fleet, as well as a good chance of seeing rabbits, deer, and hawks.

From here, the trail turns to single track and laterals the left side of a canyon. One by one, the falls start to come in view. The first is a 20-foot cascade across the other side of the canyon. Then, moments later, another one, straight ahead, and more of a chute. Moving along, two more come into view, including one short but pretty free fall. Continuing straight, the trail will guide you right across two streams, the source of the falls. The trail loops back to

Cardinet Junction, and from there it's an easy (but often muddy in winter) traipse downhill back to the trailhead. It's hard to imagine Diablo any prettier than on this hike.

**User Groups:** Hikers and horses. No dogs. Mountain bikes permitted on the service road, but not the single-track trail that provides access to the waterfalls. The first half of the trail is designed for wheelchair use.

**Permits:** No permits are required. Parking and access are free.

**Maps:** A state park brochure/map or and trail map are available for a fee at Mount Diablo Interpretive Association, P.O. Box 346, Walnut Creek, CA 94597, 925/927-7222. Ask the USGS for a topographic map of Diablo.

**Directions:** From I-680 in Walnut Creek, take the Ygnacio Valley Road exit. Drive east on Ygnacio Valley Road for 7.5 miles to Clayton Road. Turn right on Clayton Road and drive three miles (the road becomes Marsh Creek Road) to Regency Drive. Turn right on Regency Drive and drive .5 mile, to the end of the road and the trailhead.

**Contact:** Mount Diablo State Park, 96 Mitchell Canyon Road, Clayton, CA 94517, 925/837-2525 (recording), 925/837-0904 (ranger), or 925/838-9225 (weather conditions at summit); Mount Diablo Interpretive Association, 925/927-7222, website: www.mdia.org.

## 139 LITTLE GIANT LOOP
**8.1 mi / 4.0 hrs**

**in Mount Diablo State Park near Danville**

Map 7.3, page 269

High on the north flank of Mount Diablo, the world seems simple and clean, with a view that never ends. From Deer Flat and Meridian Ridge, you can peer down Mitchell Canyon, across the Carquinez Strait and lower delta, and across miles of greenbelt to the silhouette of Mount St. Helena, north of Calistoga. At Mount Diablo, the best way to commemorate the annual coronation of spring is from the Mitchell Canyon trailhead.

Our favorite trip here is an 8.1-mile loop, named the Little Giant Loop, and it takes most hikers about four hours to complete. It features an elevation gain of about 1,600 feet, a great picnic site with sensational views, and the option to fork off and create more ambitious trips.

The trip starts at the Mitchell Canyon trailhead (elevation 600 feet), located just outside of Clayton. This provides access to Mount Diablo's prettiest regions in spring.

In the first two miles, the climb is steady, and you can establish a good rhythm as you open the day and gain entry to Mitchell Canyon. You will pass amid grasslands, chaparral and the first wildflowers of the year. In late March and April, this area features rafts of a purple bloom on a long stalk (linathus), along with dozens of other species. In April and early May, there can also be hummingbirds, butterflies, and ladybugs galore (don't laugh—on one trip we saw maybe 50,000 ladybugs in a 100-yard radius).

Then it gets steep, climbing about 1,000 feet in a mile, but it's graded with switchbacks, making for a strong aerobic rhythm for hikers—but it's at butt-kicker level for bikers. You will top out at Deer Flat and reach a fork in the trail. Everybody stops here, turns, and takes in the long distance views, often enjoying a drink and maybe a trail snack at the picnic table. Deer Flat is primarily grasslands and chaparral, sprinkled with some small pines. The lookout points here tower over Mitchell Canyon and beyond to the valley flatlands to the north.

To complete the loop, turn left at Deer Flat to the Meridian Ridge Fire Road (more great views) and continue to Murchio Gap at a major junction. The best route is to continue straight for a short distance to the Back Trail, turn left and enjoy the saunter downhill into a canyon setting. At the Coulter Pine Trail (single track, no bikes), turn left, which is routed back to the Mitchell Canyon trailhead and parking area.

Mount Diablo is rarely so beautiful as here and now. Sometimes we wish the experience could be captured in a bottle, and then taken in little doses when needed for the rest of the year.

**User Groups:** Hikers and horses. Mountain bikes are allowed on a portion of this route. No dogs. No wheelchair facilities.

**Permits:** No permits are required. A state park entrance fee of $4 is charged for each vehicle.

**Maps:** A trail map is available for a fee from Mount Diablo Interpretive Association, P.O. Box 346, Walnut Creek, CA 94597. For a topographic map, ask the USGS for Diablo.

**Directions:** From I-680 in Walnut Creek, take the Ygnacio Valley Road exit and drive 7.5 miles on Ygnacio Valley Road into Clayton. Turn right on Clayton Road and drive one mile to Mitchell Canyon Road. Turn right and drive to the trailhead at the end of the road.

**Contact:** Mount Diablo State Park, 96 Mitchell Canyon Road, Clayton, CA 94517, 925/837-2525 (recorded info) or 925/837-0904 (ranger at kiosk); weather conditions at summit, 925/838-9225; Mount Diablo Interpretive Association, 925/927-7222, website: www.mdia.org.

## 140 MOUNT DIABLO DOUBLE SUMMIT

**4.0 mi / 2.0 hrs**

### in Mount Diablo State Park near Danville

Map 7.3, page 269

Mount Diablo and its nearby sphere of influence was considered the sacred birthplace of the world by the Ohlone in ancient days. Its Native American name was "Tuyshtak."

The trip up Mount Diablo starts with a winding drive on country two-laners that heads up to the summit parking lot. The visitors center is roosted right on the summit, with the tiptop of the mountain actually rising through the floor of the building, ringed by a small enclosure, and set at 3,849 feet. The distant scenic points feature the Golden Gate Bridge (66 miles) and Mount Lassen (165 miles). On perfect days, the rangers say you can see the Farallon Islands (91 miles) to the west and a piece of Half Dome (135 miles) to the east. The view from the top of Mount Diablo is said to be second only to that of Mount Kilimanjaro in terms of the amount of visible earth surface. After this mandatory summit tour, you are ready for adventure.

Start at the Devil's Elbow trailhead, located .25 mile below the main parking area at a pullout on the east side of the road. The trail begins with an easy downhill saunter to Prospector's Gap, a junction set at a mountain saddle between Diablo Summit and North Peak. Bear right at the junction, heading to North Peak—you'll see it plain enough. This is where the 500-foot climb starts, and it's steep enough to get you into an aerobic rhythm. From North Peak, at 3,557 feet, the views can be breathtaking, highlighted by a tremendous drop below toward Brentwood. At times starting in October, the fog below to the east can look like a sea across the valley floor. There can also be a phenomenon on cool days where fog or mist seems to rise and fall in the surrounding canyons as if alive. There is also a good view of Los Vaqueros Reservoir.

**User Groups:** Hikers and horses. No dogs or mountain bikes. The first half of the trail is designed for wheelchair use.

**Permits:** No permits are required. A state park entrance fee of $6 is charged for each vehicle.

**Maps:** Send $1.50 for a state park brochure/map or $5.50 for a trail map to Mount Diablo Interpretive Association, P.O. Box 346, Walnut Creek, CA 94597, fax 877/349-5016. For a topographic map, ask the USGS for Diablo.

**Directions:** From San Francisco, take the Bay Bridge east to I-580 and continue to Highway 24. Take Highway 24 east to the I-680 interchange and look for the Ygnacio Valley Road exit on the right. Take that exit and drive four miles to Oak Grove Road. Turn right and drive three miles to North Gate Road. Turn left on North Gate Road and continue to the state park entrance kiosk. Continue 10 miles to the summit. The trailhead is just above the lower

parking area just before the road becomes a one-way road.

From Danville on I-680, take the Diablo Road exit and drive east (after .75 mile, bear right to stay on Diablo Road) for three miles to Mount Diablo Scenic Boulevard. Turn left and drive 3.7 miles (the road becomes South Gate Road) to the park entrance station. Continue for 7.3 miles to the summit. The trailhead is just above the lower parking area just before the road becomes a one-way road.

**Contact:** Mount Diablo State Park, 96 Mitchell Canyon Road, Clayton, CA 94517, 925/837-2525 (recorded info) or 925/837-0904 (ranger at kiosk); weather conditions at summit, 925/838-9225; Mount Diablo Interpretive Association, 925/927-7222, website: www.mdia.org.

## 141 CHINA WALL LOOP
**3.3 mi / 2.0 hrs**

**in Diablo Foothills Regional Park on the northwest slopes of Mount Diablo near Danville**

Map 7.3, page 269

First of all, there is no sign for the China Wall Loop at the trailhead. But after taking this hike, some call this loop hike by that name anyway, hence the unofficial recognition. So at the trailhead, look instead for Borges Ranch trailhead and Briones-to-Mount Diablo Trail although China Wall is your destination. The China Wall rock formation sits on the slopes of Mount Diablo. What you see on this hike is a line of rocks that looks like the Great Wall of China in miniature (well, kind of)—they are prehistoric-looking sandstone formations. In addition, on the hike out, you will get glimpses to the east of Castle Rocks and other prominent sandstone outcrops located just outside the park's boundary. Look closer and you might also see golden eagles, hawks, and falcons, all of which nest here. Reaching China Wall requires only a 1.5-mile hike from the Borges Ranch trailhead, heading off on Briones-to-Mount Diablo Trail. Turn right at the junction with Alamo Trail, which runs .5 mile along the base of China Wall. To complete the loop, turn right again on Hanging Valley Trail and hike back to the trailhead.

**User Groups:** Hikers, dogs, horses, and mountain bikes. No wheelchair facilities.

**Permits:** No permits are required. Parking and access are free.

**Maps:** For a free trail map, contact the East Bay Regional Parks District at the address below and ask for the Diablo Foothills Regional Park brochure. For a topographic map, ask the USGS for Diablo.

**Directions:** Northbound on I-680 in Walnut Creek, take the Ygnacio Valley Road exit. Turn right, drive several miles to Walnut Avenue, and turn right. Drive to Oak Grove Road, turn right, then turn right again on Castle Rock Road, and drive to Borges Ranch Road. Turn right and drive to the parking area at the end of Borges Ranch Road.

Alternate route: Southbound on I-680, drive south to the North Main Street exit. Drive south on North Main Street to Ygnacio Valley Road. Turn left and proceed as above.

**Contact:** Diablo Foothills Regional Park, 925/837-3250 (Las Trampas); East Bay Regional Parks District, 2950 Peralta Oaks Court, P.O. Box 5381, Oakland, CA 94605-0381, 510/562-7275, website: www.ebparks.org (click on Regional Parks and Trails).

## 142 VOLVON LOOP TRAIL/ BOB WALKER RIDGE

**5.7 mi / 3.0 hrs**

**in the Morgan Territory Regional Preserve north of Livermore**

Map 7.3, page 269

Morgan Territory Regional Preserve is located within the traditional homeland of the Volvon, one of five historical Indian nations in the Mount Diablo area. This trail, named after the first people to live here, is the preserve's featured hike. You can create an easy 5.7-mile loop, tracing along a ridge as it rises along sandstone hills to a ridgeline with terrific views.

From the trailhead at about 2,000 feet, take

Volvon Trail for two miles (for this trip, ignore several side trails). Here the trail is routed northward on a ranch road to a rounded mountain peak. There are beautiful views of Los Vaqueros Reservoir, as well as below to Round Valley. The trail loops (take the right fork at Volvon Loop) around a prominent lookout at Bob Walker Ridge (1,977 feet). Rather than return the way you hiked in, a better choice is to turn this adventure into a loop hike. This is done by continuing on Volvon Trail and walking a short distance to Corral Trail (a ranch road). Turn right on Corral Trail and hike .7 mile to Coyote Trail (single-track). Turn left and hike 1.5 mile back to the starting and parking area.

This parkland is most beautiful in the spring, and not just because the hills are greened up; one of the best wildflower displays in the Bay Area occurs here at that time. Views of Mount Diablo are also excellent. The one downer: too many cows. But here's a secret: There are Native American grinding bowls carved out of bedrock mortars to be discovered by those who search out these bedrock depressions.

Finally, although the name Volvon Loop Trail is still used, many are calling this hike "Bob Walker Ridge," as in, "Hey, let's do the Bob Walker Ridge Trail out at Morgan Territory." The ridge was named in the 1990s for Bob Walker, a landscape photographer and open-space advocate who helped ensure that Morgan Territory was added to the East Bay Regional Parks District.

**User Groups:** The first half of the loop is accessible to hikers, dogs, horses, and mountain bikes. The second half is for hikers and dogs only. No wheelchair facilities.

**Permits:** No permits are required. Parking and access are free.

**Maps:** For a free trail map, contact the East Bay Regional Parks District at the address below and ask for the Morgan Territory Regional Preserve brochure. For a topographic map, ask the USGS for Tassajara.

**Directions:** From I-580 in Livermore, take the N. Livermore Avenue exit and turn north.

Drive to the junction of Morgan Territory Road and turn right. Drive 10.7 miles to the staging area on the right side of the road.

From I-680 in Concord, take the Clayton Road exit and head east. Clayton Road becomes Marsh Creek Road, and continue to Morgan Territory Road. Turn right and drive 9.4 miles to the staging area on the left side of the road.

**Contact:** Morgan Territory Regional Preserve, 925/757-2620 (Black Diamond); East Bay Regional Parks District, 2950 Peralta Oaks Court, P.O. Box 5381, Oakland, CA 94605-0381, 510/562-7275, website: www.ebparks.org (click on Regional Parks and Trails).

## 143 NORTH ARROYO TRAIL
**1.3 mi / 0.75 hr**

**in the Shadow Cliffs Regional Recreation Area in Pleasanton**

Map 7.3, page 269

Though you can't walk all the way around Shadow Cliffs Lake, you can explore a series of smaller ponds in the Arroyo area. There's no place else like it in the East Bay. From the back of the first parking area, you take a trail over the top of a levee and down to the shore of the first pond. Then just follow North Arroyo Trail along the shores of several ponds for about .5 mile. For a view of the ponds, make the short climb up the adjacent levee. These ponds are water holes left over from a gravel quarry. Shadow Cliffs Lake, the biggest pond covering some 80 acres, has been stocked with trout and is one of the better fishing spots in the East Bay. It is also a good place to swim, as the water is often quite clear.

**User Groups:** Hikers and dogs. Portions of the trail are accessible to horses and mountain bikes. No wheelchair facilities.

**Permits:** No permits are required. A fee of $6 per vehicle is charged for parking; there is also a fee for dogs.

**Maps:** For a free trail map, contact the East Bay Regional Parks District at the address below and ask for the Shadow Cliffs Region-

al Recreation Area brochure. For a topographic map, ask the USGS for Livermore.

**Directions:** From I-580 in Pleasanton, take Santa Rita Road south. Drive two miles, turn left on Valley Avenue, and drive to Stanley Boulevard. Turn left and drive to the park entrance.

**Contact:** Shadow Cliffs Regional Recreation Area, 925/846-3000; East Bay Regional Parks District, 2950 Peralta Oaks Court, P.O. Box 5381, Oakland, CA 94605-0381, 510/562-7275, website: www.ebparks.org (click on Regional Parks and Trails).

## 144 RIDGELINE TRAIL
**7.0 mi / 4.0 hrs**

**in Pleasanton Ridge Regional Park west of Pleasanton**

Map 7.3, page 269

People often overlook Pleasanton Ridge Regional Park, not knowing it offers a quiet, natural setting with excellent views from Ridgeline Trail. Development in and around the park has purposely been limited so the surroundings could retain as natural a feel as possible. The plan has succeeded, and the best way to experience it is on this hike. The Ridgeline Trail climbs to elevations of 1,600 feet, with the northern sections giving way to sweeping views featuring miles of rolling foothills and valleys at the threshold of Mount Diablo. From the parking area, elevation 300 feet, start hiking on Oak Tree Trail, which is routed 1.4 miles up to Ridgeline Trail, climbing 750 feet. Turn right and hike two miles along the ridge. You can return on a loop route by turning left on Thermalito Trail, which is recommended.

**User Groups:** Hikers, dogs, horses, and mountain bikes. No wheelchair facilities.

**Permits:** No permits are required. Parking and access are free.

**Maps:** For a free trail map, contact the East Bay Regional Parks District at the address below and ask for the Pleasanton Ridge Regional Park brochure. For a topographic map, ask the USGS for Dublin.

**Directions:** From I-680 in Pleasanton, take the

Bernal Road exit west and drive to Foothill Road. Turn left and drive three miles to the parking area and information center on the right.

**Contact:** Pleasanton Ridge Regional Park, 925/862-2963; East Bay Regional Parks District, 2950 Peralta Oaks Court, P.O. Box 5381, Oakland, CA 94605-0381, 510/562-7275, website: www.ebparks.org (click on Regional Parks and Trails).

## 145 HIGH RIDGE LOOP
**3.3 mi / 2.0 hrs**

**in Garin Regional Park in the Hayward foothills**

Map 7.3, page 269

The hilltops in Garin Regional Park render sweeping views of the East Bay foothills westward to South San Francisco Bay, the number-one attraction at this 3,000-acre parkland. The hills span for miles, and in the fall there are times late in the day when sunbeams will pour through openings between cumulus clouds, creating a divine scene. Of the 20 miles of trails in the park, Ridge Loop Trail is the best way to see the surrounding wildlands, primarily oak grasslands amid rolling foothills. From the parking area (at 380 feet), walk .25 mile past the picnic areas to Arroyo Flats and turn left on High Ridge Trail. In another .25 mile, it links up with the Vista Peak Loop, best hiked in a clockwise direction. You will start climbing, rising 550 feet in a mile, topping out at Vista Peak (934 feet) and shortly after, Garin Peak (948 feet). Take your time and enjoy the views.

**User Groups:** Hikers, dogs, horses, and mountain bikes. No wheelchair facilities.

**Permits:** No permits are required. An entrance fee of $4 per vehicle is charged when the kiosk is attended; there is also a dog fee.

**Maps:** For a free trail map, contact the East Bay Regional Parks District at the address below and ask for the Garin and Dry Creek Pioneer Regional Parks brochure. For a topographic map, ask the USGS for Hayward.

**Directions:** From Fremont, take Highway 238 (Mission Boulevard) north through Union City

to Garin Avenue. Turn right onto Garin Avenue and drive one mile to the park entrance.

**Contact:** Garin Regional Park, 510/582-2206; East Bay Regional Parks District, 2950 Peralta Oaks Court, P.O. Box 5381, Oakland, CA 94605-0381, 510/562-7275, website: www.ebparks.org (click on Regional Parks and Trails).

## 146 ALAMEDA CREEK REGIONAL TRAIL
**11.0 mi one-way / 4.5 hrs**

**on Alameda Creek from Niles to the South Bay**

Map 7.3, page 269

An unusual solution to the biker-versus-hiker conflict has been implemented here with the construction of a double trail. Two trails, one on each side of Alameda Creek, are routed from Niles Community Park to the shoreline of the South Bay. The trail on the north bank is designed for horseback riders and hikers. The one on the south bank is paved, perfect for bicyclists and joggers. Markers set at .25-mile intervals help joggers keep track of their exact distances. From Niles, the trail goes past Shinn Pond, Alameda Creek Quarries, and Coyote Hills Regional Park. For access to Coyote Hills Regional Park and the San Francisco Bay National Wildlife Refuge, take the trail on the south side of the creek; there is no direct access to either of those areas on the northside trail.

**User Groups:** South Trail: Hikers, dogs, and mountain bikes. North Trail: Hikers, dogs, and horses. No wheelchair facilities.

**Permits:** No permits are required. Parking and access are free.

**Maps:** For a free trail map, contact the East Bay Regional Parks District at the address below and ask for the Alameda Creek Regional Trail brochure. For a topographic map, ask the USGS for Niles.

**Directions:** From I-680 in Fremont, take the Mission Boulevard exit and drive west to Highway 84/Niles Canyon Road. Turn right and make another immediate right on Old Canyon Road. The staging area is on the left.

Contact: Alameda Creek Regional Trail, 510/790-2612 (Quarry Lakes); East Bay Regional Parks District, 2950 Peralta Oaks Court, P.O. Box 5381, Oakland, CA 94605-0381, 510/562-7275, website: www.ebparks.org (click on Regional Parks and Trails).

## 147 MISSION PEAK TRAIL
**7.0 mi / 4.0 hrs**

**in the Mission Peak Regional Preserve near Fremont**

Map 7.3, page 269

Breathtaking views of the South Bay, wildflowers galore and a memorable perspective of the Bay Area are the rewards for those who take on the climb to the top of Mission Peak. Among the mainstream public, this is one of the Bay Area's lesser-known peaks. At 2,517 feet, it looms over the Ohlone College campus in Fremont and the South Bay. Yet Mount Hamilton, Mount Diablo and Mount Umunhum dwarf Mission Peak in size and stature, and for that reason, some overlook it; that equals your gain, others' loss. Hot days don't work here because this tromp to the top features a climb of 2,000 feet in a span of about 3.5 miles (a round-trip of just under 7 miles).

While there are multiple trailheads for this trip, the best is at the end of Stanford Ave., a short drive from either I-880 or I-680, where you will find a parking area and gated trailhead with a box that contains a free brochure/map from the East Bay Regional Park District. From the parking area, you get a good view to the east of the awaiting landscape: rolling grassland foothills cut by a few tree-filled ravines and a barren ridge that promises a great lookout.

Start the trip by taking the Ohlone Wilderness Trail/Hidden Valley Trail, the left fork at the trailhead, well-signed and mapped. The trail is a dirt road, crumbling in spots. As you rise up, the views start quickly of the South Bay, and then beyond across the Santa Clara Valley. Although there is a network of routes that eventually can be linked to the top, the best route is to stay on the Ohlone Wilderness

Trail up to the foot of the last summit rise. Here you will reach the Peak Trail. Turn right and climb the last half mile to the summit (ignore the left fork you will pass). The summit is marked by a post. Everybody, and we mean everybody, touches the darn thing. It's like part ceremony, part official procedure.

The views provide a stunning new outlook on a familiar homeland. On clear days, all the prominent peaks in the Bay Area come into view, Tamalpais, Diablo, Hamilton and Umunhum, and to the distant east, you can see the snow-crested Sierra. There must be 100 points of sunlit charm in a 50-mile radius that stand out as landmarks. Other highlights are high numbers of hawks out hovering in rising thermals, and on some weekends, a number of hang gliders joining them. A herd of feral goats is supposed to roam wild in this area, but in several visits, we've never seen them.

**User Groups:** Hikers, dogs, and horses. No mountain bikes. No wheelchair facilities.

**Permits:** No permits are required. Parking is free.

**Maps:** For a free trail map, contact the East Bay Regional Parks District at the address below and ask for the Mission Peak Regional Preserve brochure. For a topographic map, ask the USGS for Niles.

**Directions:** From I-880: Take I-880 to Fremont and the exit for Mission Boulevard. Take that exit to Mission Boulevard, turn east and go 1.5 miles to Stanford Ave. Turn right and go a half mile to parking.

From I-680: Take I-680 to Fremont and exit for Durham Road. Take that exit east and go 1 mile to Mission Boulevard. Turn right and go 0.75 mile to Stanford Ave. Turn left and go half mile to parking.

**Contact:** Mission Peak Regional Preserve, 925/862-2244 (Sunol kiosk); East Bay Regional Parks District, 2950 Peralta Oaks Court, P.O. Box 5381, Oakland, CA 94605-0381, 510/562-7275, website: www.ebparks.org (click on Regional Parks and Trails).

## 148 OHLONE WILDERNESS TRAIL
**28.0 mi one-way / 3.0 days** 🥾 🎒

**in the Sunol-Ohlone Regional Wilderness from Del Valle Regional Park south of Livermore to Mission Peak in Fremont**

Map 7.3, page 269

Hikers can traverse the East Bay's most unspoiled backcountry via the spectacular 28-mile Ohlone Wilderness Trail, which lies entirely on wildlands. Starting south of Livermore at Del Valle Regional Park and cutting west to Fremont, the trail rises through fields of wildflowers, grasslands, and oaks. It also climbs three major summits: Rocky Ridge, Rose Peak (elevation 3,817 feet), and Mission Peak (2,517 feet). It makes an ideal three-day backpacking venture, as hikers can set up trail camps at designated wilderness sites. Backpackers will cover about 12 miles the first day, followed by two days at about eight miles each. Some people close out the final 16 miles in one day. And it's not unusual for cross-country runners to run the entire route in a single day; an organized race is held here every year.

Hiking the trail east to west is the only way to fly. That way you'll face the steepest ascent right at the beginning, when you are still fresh, and end with sweeping views of the South Bay. The trip starts at Del Valle Regional Park, and the route first tackles Rocky Ridge for an elevation gain of 1,600 feet in just 1.5 miles (a side trip from here, by the way, is to Murietta Falls; see next hike).

It is absolutely essential to have your itinerary and water supply timed for the trail camps. This isn't difficult, but those who don't do this may have to be carried out by a camel. The route in the interior of the wilderness is an undulating up-and-down as you make your way past and around a series of foothill ridges. You might even encounter a moment of irony as you begin to feel a strange sense of solitude, yet know that just over the final ridge to the west is a pit with 6.8 million people.

As you crest the final ridge, Mission Peak, you'll face a moment of truth: You can actually see your car waiting at the parking lot—even though it's so far away. This last stretch drops 2,100 feet in 3.5 miles, a terrible toe-jammer that will have your knees and thighs screaming for mercy. Weeks later, though, when you replay this adventure in your memory banks, the hike will suddenly seem like "fun."

**User Groups:** Hikers, dogs (daytime only, not permitted on overnight trips), and horses. No mountain bikes. No wheelchair facilities.

**Permits:** A trail permit/map for the Ohlone Wilderness Trail is required. You can obtain one for $2 at the park office or for $2.50 by mail from the East Bay Regional Parks District at the address below. A fee of $6 per vehicle is charged at the trailhead at Del Valle Regional Park. There is also a fee for dogs.

**Maps:** You will receive a trail map when you purchase your permit. For a topographic map, ask the USGS for Mendenhall Springs.

**Directions:** To the east trailhead from I-580 East at Livermore, take the North Livermore Avenue exit and turn right. Drive south for 3.5 miles (the road becomes Tesla Road) to Mines Road. Turn right on Mines Road and drive 3.5 miles to Del Valle Road. Continue on Del Valle Road for three miles to the Del Valle Regional Park entrance. Drive less than a mile to the dam at Del Valle Reservoir, cross it, then turn right and drive a half mile to the Lichen Bark Picnic Area and the trailhead for the Ohlone Trail.

To the west trailhead from I-680 near Fremont, take the Highway 238 (Mission Boulevard) exit. Turn east on Stanford Avenue and drive to the parking lot and trailhead at the end of the road.

**Contact:** Del Valle Regional Park, 925/373-0332; Sunol-Ohlone Regional Wilderness, 925/862-2244; East Bay Regional Parks District, 2950 Peralta Oaks Court, P.O. Box 5381, Oakland, CA 94605-0381, 510/562-7275, website: www.ebparks.org (click on Regional Parks and Trails).

## 149 MURIETTA FALLS TRAIL

**12 mi / 1.0 day**

**in the Sunol-Ohlone Regional Wilderness, from Del Valle Regional Park south of Livermore to Mission Peak in Fremont**

Map 7.3, page 269

If you want to unplug from the world for a day, one of the best places to do it in winter and spring is at Murietta Falls in the Ohlone Wilderness. Yet this can be a star-crossed adventure. It is the most demanding one-day hike in the Bay Area, a butt-kicker on the way in, a knee-jammer one the way out. And meanwhile, the reward at the end of the rainbow can be dubious.

When the foothills are saturated and the Murietta Canyon has been recharged by a big storm with a heavy spring rain, this is one of the region's most stunning destinations. Best seen standing below the waterfall, looking up, this waterfall is a 100-foot cataract that tumbles down a rocky gorge, a beautiful mix of short freefalls, horsetails, cascades and chutes. The sharp contrast of white, churning water against the surrounding oak grasslands/foothills is enough to make you forget all the problems of the world, and maybe even a few of your own. Except it isn't always churning. In fact, it doesn't churn but a few times a year. If you don't time it after a spring rain, the flows can be reduced to a wisp of a trickle. Typically, the window of hope closes by early May.

The trailhead for Murietta Falls is the Ohlone Wilderness Trail out of the southern end of Del Valle Regional Park, located south of Livermore. The trip is a round-trip hike of 12 miles with a cumulative elevation gain of 4,000 feet, and virtually no shade. Right. This is the mother of all Bay Area butt-kickers. It must have been configured by a roller-coaster designer.

You'll know within the first hour if you made a mistake. The hike starts with a 1,700-foot gain to Rocky Ridge (2.4 miles), with a pretty view to the north of Del Valle Reservoir and beyond, and then drops 500 feet in a half mile to the bottom of a canyon. This is just the start.

You then climb out of the canyon, gutting it out up 1,200 feet as you rise toward Wauhab Ridge (pretty long-distance foothill views). You will pass a series of impressive rock outcrops and then reach a little watering hole for cows (mapped as Johnny's Pond). From the pond, continue a short distance to the junction with the Springboard Trail, signed Murietta Falls, signpost 35.

Turn on this trail and walk about a quarter mile (to a sharp turn in the trail)—then be sharp-eyed for the footpath on your left, along a small creek. Take this path to the brink of the falls. Alas, the view is lousy. No problem. From here, there is a well-worn route that everybody takes that leads down to the plunge pool of the falls. Here you get a picture-perfect view of the gorge and enjoy a long picnic.

Some choose to extend the trip to two days by camping at a trail site called Stewart's Camp, located about a half mile from the base of the falls. Although this splits the hiking distance into two days, it also means you must carry all your backpacking gear in and out, a heavy price.

Murietta Falls is named after Joaquin Murietta, of course, the legendary outlaw of the 1800s. If you hit it right, when the waterfall is gushing, you might wonder why such a beautiful place was named after a notorious killer. If you hit it wrong, however, you will understand. It is his final curse.

**User Groups:** Hikers, dogs (daytime only, not permitted on overnight trips), and horses. No mountain bikes. No wheelchair facilities.

**Permits:** A trail permit/map for the Ohlone Wilderness Trail is required. You can obtain one for $2 at the park office or for $2.50 by mail from the East Bay Regional Parks District at the address below. A fee of $6 per vehicle is charged at the trailhead at Del Valle Regional Park. There is also a fee for dogs.

**Maps:** You will receive a trail map when you purchase your permit. For a topographic map, ask the USGS for Mendenhall Springs.

**Directions:** From I-580 east at Livermore, take the North Livermore Avenue exit and turn right. Drive south for 3.5 miles (the road becomes Tesla Road) to Mines Road. Turn right on Mines Road and drive 3.5 miles to Del Valle Road. Continue on Del Valle Road for three miles to the Del Valle Regional Park entrance. Drive less than a mile to the dam at Del Valle Reservoir, cross it, and then turn right and drive .5 mile to the Lichen Bark Picnic Area and the trailhead for Ohlone Trail.

**Contact:** Del Valle Regional Park, 925/373-0332; Sunol-Ohlone Regional Wilderness, 925/862-2244; East Bay Regional Parks District, 2950 Peralta Oaks Court, P.O. Box 5381, Oakland, CA 94605-0381, 510/562-7275, website: www.ebparks.org (click on Regional Parks and Trails).

# **150** SUNOL LOOP
## 4.75 mi / 3.5 hrs

**in the Sunol Regional Wilderness near Sunol**

Map 7.3, page 269

There are hidden places around the Bay Area that make you feel as if only you know about them. This is one such place. Sunol Regional Wilderness is a 6,400-acre wilderness. This loop trail leads past many of its most striking spots. They include Little Yosemite, a miniature canyon with a pretty stream (Alameda Creek) with little pool-and-drop waterfalls at high flow in late winter; Cerro Este, at 1,720 feet, one of the higher points in the park; Cave Rocks, a series of natural, gouged-out rock forms; and Indian Joe Creek, a little brook that runs along the start of the trail. This park is a habitat center for the largest number of nesting golden eagles in the world. And in recent years, peregrine falcons have been found nesting on the edges of cliffs.

From the parking area, begin the loop hike by heading north on Indian Joe Creek Trail, then climb one mile to Cave Rocks. Turn right onto Rocks Road/Cerro Este Trail and climb up over the summit and down the other side all the way to Canyon View Trail. Turn right and return to the parking area.

This trip has many options. In winter, a must-do on the Canyon View Trail is to take the short gated cutoff trail that drops down to the floor of Little Yosemite. In the winter, the creek at the bottom of the valley has many tiny pool-and-drop waterfalls.

Another great trip in late winter and early spring is the tromp up the Flag Hill Trail to a prominent rock outcropping that overlooks the valley floor. It's only a 1.5-mile hike, but it can be a real butt-kicker for some, with an 800-foot climb to make it to the top. But the views are gorgeous. Directly below is the Alameda Creek watershed and valley, where you are often at eye-level at hawks gliding in the rising thermals.

**User Groups:** Hikers, dogs, horses, and mountain bikes. The Indian Joe Creek section of the loop is limited to hikers. No wheelchair facilities.

**Permits:** No permits are required for day use. A fee of $4 per vehicle is charged; there is also a fee for dogs. A wilderness permit and a camping reservation are required for overnight backpackers.

**Maps:** For a free trail map, contact the East Bay Regional Parks District at the address below and ask for the Sunol-Ohlone Regional Wilderness brochure. For a topographic map, ask the USGS for La Costa Valley.

**Directions:** From I-680 in the East Bay, take the Calaveras Road exit in Sunol. Turn south on Calaveras Road to Geary Road. Turn left on Geary Road and continue into the park.

**Contact:** Sunol-Ohlone Regional Wilderness, 925/862-2244; East Bay Regional Parks District, 2950 Peralta Oaks Court, P.O. Box 5381, Oakland, CA 94605-0381, 510/562-7275, website: www.ebparks.org (click on Regional Parks and Trails).

# **151** SHORELINE REGIONAL PARK
## 2.0 mi / 1.0 hr

**along South San Francisco Bay in Mountain View**

Map 7.4, page 270

An ideal family destination, Shoreline Regional Park offers a wide variety of activities, including pleasant walks and bike rides on wide, crushed-gravel byways. There is also a small lake that makes an excellent spot for windsurfing, and many good kite-flying areas on tiny hills. The best trail at the park is routed along the east side of the lake and then northward on a levee through marshlands. It is quite popular with bird-watchers, who can spot everything from egrets to LBJs (Little Brown Jobs). A concession stand near the lake gets a lot of use from the corn-dog-and-Coke crowd, which kind of puts everything in perspective.

**User Groups:** Hikers, wheelchairs, and mountain bikes. No dogs or horses.

**Permits:** No permits are required. Parking and access are free (there is a kiosk that will provide a map if requested).

**Maps:** For a topographic map, ask the USGS for Mountain View.

**Directions:** From U.S. 101 in Mountain View, take Shoreline Boulevard east and drive past the Shoreline Amphitheater to the park entrance station.

**Contact:** Shoreline Regional Park, City of Mountain View, 3070 N. Shoreline Boulevard, Mountain View, CA 94043, 650/903-6392, website: www.ci.mtnview.ca.us/citydepts/cs/sd/trails_wildlife.htm.

## 152 LONG RIDGE LOOP
**4.6 mi / 2.0 hrs**

**in the Long Ridge Open Space Preserve on Skyline Ridge**

Map 7.4, page 270

Long Ridge provides a great escape hatch for a quick launch into the wild outdoors. In just two hours on the trail here, this place has the ability to recharge your senses. Long Ridge is located on Skyline Boulevard, just south of the junction of Page Mill Road. Trails are routed through a variety of beautiful landscapes, included sheltered canyons, creeks, meadows and oak woodlands, past a beautiful hidden pond, and up on Long Ridge itself for great open views to the west of the Butano Rim and Pacific Ocean. And you can get this with one

4.6-mile loop trip, including only about a 400-foot climb.

After parking, get the brochure/trail map from the box near the trailhead to orient yourself. This adventure starts by heading west (past the intersection with the Bay Ridge Trail at 0.4 mile) and reaching the junction with the Long Ridge Trail and Peters Creek Trail (at 0.5 mile). Here you turn right and make a climb through oak woodlands, including one short, steep spot, where the trail horseshoes its way eventually to the south up to Long Ridge Road (at 1.2 miles; a dirt service road). This is a great coastal lookout, one of the best on the Peninsula.

From here, the going is easy to Four Corners, heading south on Long Ridge, with a slight elevation gain, rewarded by gorgeous views off to the west. On clear days, you get long-distance views of the ocean, and as you continue south, across miles of foothills and forested valleys. The highest point in San Mateo County, 2,600 feet, is just off the trail here.

At Four Corners (2.5 miles), you turn left, encounter a series of switchbacks as you descend into a heavily wooded canyon, extremely lush in late winter and spring. The surprise of the trip is just ahead: You will pass a surprise and secret pond (3.0 miles), ringed by tules and quite pretty. To complete the loop hike, continue on the Peters Creek Trail, a rich riparian zone, back to the junction with Long Ridge Trail (4.1 miles). Turn right and hike back to the parking area (4.6 miles).

There is also a good chance of spotting wild turkey, rabbits, deer, raptors and songbirds.

**User Groups:** Hikers, horses, and mountain bikes (restricted from some trails, signed). No dogs. No wheelchair facilities.

**Permits:** No permits are required. Parking and access are free.

**Maps:** For a free trail map, contact the Midpeninsula Regional Open Space District at the address below. Maps are usually available at the trailhead. For a topographic map, ask the USGS for Mindego Hill.

**Directions:** From Highway 280 in Palo Alto,

take the Page Mill Road exit and drive west to Skyline Boulevard. Turn left (south) and drive three miles (just past Portola Heights Road) to a dirt parking area on the right (west) side of the road (note that a larger parking area is also on the east side of the road). The trailhead is on the west side of the road.

**Contact:** Midpeninsula Regional Open Space District, 330 Distel Circle, Los Altos, CA 94022, 650/691-1200, fax 650/691-0485, website: www.openspace.org (click on Preserve Locator). During nonbusiness hours, a touch-tone phone menu is available for trail news, conditions, and events.

## 153 SARATOGA GAP LOOP
**9.0 mi / 5.0 hrs**

**in the Saratoga Gap Open Space Preserve on Skyline Ridge in the Santa Cruz Mountains**

Map 7.4, page 270

Saratoga Gap serves as a trailhead center for hikers exploring the Peninsula's Skyline Ridge. Trails from here lead to five other parklands, making it possible for hikers to create trips of any length. The best is the nine-mile Saratoga Gap Loop. The trail starts off northward, adjacent to Highway 35 on the Skyline Ridge. After one mile, turn right on Charcoal Road, which is routed down the slope (bikes are permitted here) and into Upper Stevens Creek County Park. The trail descends to the headwaters of Stevens Creek, a quiet, wooded spot. Cross the creek and soon you will reach a trail junction, where you turn left (west) on Canyon Trail; after crossing a small creek, turn left on Grizzly Flat Trail. This trail climbs back to Skyline Boulevard, where you cross the road, enter the Long Ridge Open Space Preserve, and hike south to where the trail crosses Skyline Boulevard once again. Return on Saratoga Gap Trail to the parking area. The hills here are grassy knobs sprinkled with oaks and madrones, while the canyons are heavily wooded, most prominently with Douglas firs.

**User Groups:** Hikers, horses, and mountain bikes. No dogs. No wheelchair facilities.

**Permits:** No permits are required. Parking and access are free.

**Maps:** For a free trail map, contact the Midpeninsula Regional Open Space District at the address below. Maps are usually available at the trailhead. For topographic maps, ask the USGS for Mindego Hill and Cupertino.

**Directions:** From I-280 near Santa Clara, turn west on Saratoga Avenue and drive to Highway 9. Take Highway 9 up to the ridge to the junction of Highway 9 and Highway 35. At the junction, look for the CalTrans parking area on the left (southeast) corner. Park there. The preserve is on the northeast corner of this junction, across the road from the parking lot.

**Contact:** Midpeninsula Regional Open Space District, 330 Distel Circle, Los Altos, CA 94022, 650/691-1200, fax 650/691-0485, website: www.openspace.org (click on Preserve Locator). During nonbusiness hours, a touch-tone phone menu is available for trail news, conditions, and events.

## 154 SUMMIT ROCK LOOP
**2.0 mi / 1.0 hr**

**in Sanborn-Skyline County Park on Skyline Ridge in the Santa Cruz Mountains**

Map 7.4, page 270

The Santa Clara Valley never looks prettier than it does from Summit Rock, set just east of the Skyline Ridge. This is the ideal perch for a lookout to the valley below, and getting there is not difficult when you take the featured hike at Sanborn-Skyline County Park. The park is so named because it connects Sanborn Creek with the Skyline Ridge, covering some 2,850 acres of mountain terrain in between. From the trailhead across Highway 35 from Castle Rock State Park, hikers start on the Skyline Trail and head north, adjacent to the road. The Skyline Trail leads right into the Summit Rock Loop, providing easy access to this great lookout. For people who like their views to come even easier, a popular option at the Skyline trailhead is the .25-mile hike that leads to Indian Rock. Note that park headquarters are not located at this trailhead, but rather off Sanborn Road, where full facilities and other trails are available.

**User Groups:** Hikers and horses. No dogs or mountain bikes. No wheelchair facilities.

**Permits:** No permits are required. A day-use fee of $5 is charged per vehicle.

**Maps:** For a free trail map, contact Sanborn-Skyline County Park at the address below. For a topographic map, ask the USGS for Castle Rock Ridge.

**Directions:** From I-280 near Santa Clara, turn west on Saratoga Avenue and drive to Highway 9. Drive west on Highway 9 to the junction with Highway 35 (Skyline Boulevard). Turn south and drive 2.5 miles to Sanborn-Skyline County Park on the left. The trailhead is located roughly across from Castle Rock State Park on Skyline Boulevard.

**Contact:** Sanborn-Skyline County Park, 16055 Sanborn Road, Saratoga, CA 95070, 408/867-9959; Upper Stevens Creek, 408/741-5375; Santa Clara County Parks and Recreation, 408/355-2200; guided walks, 408/867-9959. Website: www.parkhere.org (click on Find A Park).

## 155 TRAIL CAMP LOOP
### 5.3 mi / 2.5 hrs

**in Castle Rock State Park on Skyline Ridge in the Santa Cruz Mountains**

Map 7.4, page 270

Here you can discover a great and easy 5.3-mile walk that takes about 2.5 hours. It is highlighted by a surprise waterfall with a viewing deck, honeycombed sandstone formations, sweeping views of the Santa Cruz Mountains and Monterey Bay to the west, and then a top-of-the-world perch atop Goat Rock.

Begin on Saratoga Gap Trail. In the first few minutes, the trail descends into a lush riparian canyon. Within a half mile, you arrive at a viewing deck to your left. This puts you at the brink of a canyon and adjacent to the waterfall, which is at its fullest after recent rainfall. From here, the trail breaks out into the open along a rock facing. On stellar days, those with sharp vision can see the white foam of the breakers on the beaches to the west. As you head on, you will pass a series of sandstone formations to your right, where material has eroded over time to create a series of holes and cavities. The most dramatic of these is at Goat Rock, where the trail runs right past its base. At this spot there is a permanent climbing cable, and on weekends, climbers practice technical skills here.

The trail continues to a junction with Ridge Trail, a distance of 2.6 miles from the parking lot. At this junction, turn right and start the loop back to the parking area. The return loop features a gentle climb, primarily amid chaparral and woodlands. Be certain to watch for a cutoff trail on the right to Goat Rock Lookout—don't miss this side trip; walk a short distance to a sweeping, long-distance view across a sea of conifers and beyond to the ocean. Goat Rock is also an excellent picnic site for those with trail snacks.

There are 32 miles of hiking trails in 3,600 acres of semiwilderness at this park, so extending your adventure can be done quite easily.

**User Groups:** Hikers and horses. No dogs or mountain bikes. No wheelchair facilities.

**Permits:** No permits are required, but you must self-register at the park entrance. A day-use fee of $6 per vehicle is charged.

**Maps:** A trail map of Castle Rock State Park is available for $1.75, including postage, from Mountain Parks Foundation, 525 North Big Trees Road, Felton, CA 95018, 831/335-3174. For a free brochure, contact Castle Rock State Park at the address below. For a topographic map, ask the USGS for Castle Rock Ridge.

**Directions:** From I-280 near Santa Clara, turn west on Saratoga Avenue and drive to Highway 9. Drive west on Highway 9 to the junction with Highway 35 (Skyline Boulevard). Turn south and drive 2.5 miles to the entrance to Castle Rock State Park on the right.

**Contact:** Castle Rock State Park, 15000 Skyline

Boulevard, Los Gatos, CA 95020, 408/867-2952; California State Parks, Santa Cruz District, 831/429-2850; trail camp reservations, 831/338-8861; websites: www.parks.ca/gov (click on Find A Park), www.mountainparks.org.

## 156 SKYLINE-TO-THE-SEA TRAIL
### 34.0 mi one-way / 2.5 days 🥾 ◁10

**from Castle Rock State Park via Big Basin to Waddell Creek on the Pacific coast**
Map 7.4, page 270

This is one of the most worshipped trails in the Bay Area. The workings of this trail started with a vision to create a route that connected Castle Rock State Park on Skyline Ridge to Big Basin and then to Waddell Creek on the coast. The result, much of it built by volunteers, is this 34-mile backpack route, complete with primitive trail camps. It is ideal in many ways, including the fact that the hike is generally downhill, starting at 3,000 feet at Castle Rock and dropping all the way down to sea level. Fantastic views, redwood forests, waterfalls, and backpack camps are among the rewards. Only in extremely rare conditions will you come across a discarded cigarette butt or a piece of litter; after all, most people won't trash a piece of heaven. Most hike the trail in three days, camping at Waterman Gap and at Big Basin, with a shuttle car waiting at the end of the trail at Waddell Creek on Highway 1.

From the trailhead at Castle Rock State Park, head out to the Waterman Gap trail camp (water is available) for a first-day hike of 9.6 miles. This portion includes crossing an open rock facing with fantastic views of Big Basin and the Pacific Coast to the west, which will help you envision the upcoming route. Other highlights include the headwaters of the San Lorenzo River, an old homestead, and mixed forest.

The logical plan for the second day is to hike 9.5 miles to Jay Camp at Big Basin headquarters. Once you cross Highway 9, enter the state park; for a few miles the route roughly parallels the park's access road. Then it breaks off, passes an open sandstone face with great westerly views, traces a narrow ridge, and drops down into a lush redwood canyon with a stream. Eventually it emerges at the bottom of Big Basin, and you camp relatively near park headquarters. Although this camp is not a backcountry experience, the convenience of restrooms, coin showers, drinking water, and a small store are usually well received.

On the last day, you face hiking 12.5 miles out, up, and over the Big Basin rim, then down a wooded canyon, passing beautiful 70-foot Berry Creek Falls, crossing Waddell Creek, and finishing up at the coast. It is a fantastic trip, highlighted by the gigantic old-growth redwoods and a series of spectacular waterfalls. At Berry Creek Falls, be sure to hike up the stairs to the brink of the waterfall, then head up the canyon to see Silver Falls (a gorgeous free fall, perfect for photographs), and then above that, Golden Falls, where clear water cascades over golden sandstone like a gigantic water slide. From Berry Creek Falls to the coast is a breeze, crossing over the stream with a make-shift bridge, then making the sea-level walk to Rancho del Oso and the parking area. It's a shortcut to hike out on the service road and bike path, but in the spring, take the longer, official route that loops around the valley hills (to the north) and down to the parking area to see 20 or 30 species of wildflowers, including occasional rafts of forget-me-nots.

**User Groups:** Hikers and horses. No dogs or mountain bikes. No wheelchair facilities.

**Permits:** Trail camp reservations are required with a reservation fee, plus a camping fee per night, plus a fee per extra vehicle at the trailheads. Call 831/338-8861.

**Maps:** Detailed trail maps of Castle Rock State Park and Big Basin Redwoods State Park are available for a fee from Mountain Parks Foundation, 525 North Big Trees Road, Felton, CA 95018, 831/335-3174. A free information sheet and a mileage chart between trail camps are available by phoning 831/338-8861, or writing Big Basin Redwoods State Park at the address below. For topographic maps, ask the USGS for Castle Rock Ridge and Big Basin.

**Directions:** To Castle Rock State Park from I-280 near Santa Clara, turn west on Saratoga Avenue and drive to Highway 9. Drive west on Highway 9 to the junction with Highway 35 (Skyline Boulevard). Turn south and drive 2.5 miles to the entrance to Castle Rock State Park on the right. Your vehicle must be registered in advance with park rangers.

To Waddell Creek/Rancho del Oso from I-280 in San Mateo, turn west on Highway 92 and drive to Half Moon Bay. Turn left (south) on Highway 1 and drive about 35 miles, (two miles past Año Nuevo State Reserve) and look for the signs indicating Big Basin Redwoods State Park/Rancho del Oso, just past the Santa Cruz County line. Turn and park at Rancho del Oso. Your vehicle must be registered in advance with park rangers.

**Contact:** Big Basin Redwoods State Park, 21600 Big Basin Way, Boulder Creek, CA 95006, 831/338-8860, trail camp reservations 831/338-8861; Castle Rock State Park, 15000 Skyline Boulevard, Los Gatos, CA 95020, 408/867-2952, district headquarters 831/429-2850, trail camp reservations 831/338-8861, websites: www.parks.ca/gov (click on Find A Park), www.mountainparks.org.

## 157 REDWOOD LOOP
**0.6 mi / 0.5 hr**

**in Big Basin Redwoods State Park in the Santa Cruz Mountains near Boulder Creek**

Map 7.4, page 270

Most people come to Big Basin Redwoods State Park to see giant redwoods, and the Redwood Loop is a short, easy path that meanders around many of these giants. This trail gets a lot of use, which is why the rating has been knocked down a few notches. By using the numbered posts along the way and a trail brochure, you can take a self-guided nature walk. The sights include pretty Opal Creek, the Chimney Tree (which has survived many fires), and several other ancient redwoods. The Santa Clara Tree, located across Opal Creek at signpost three, is 17 feet in diameter; the Fa-

ther-of-the-Forest is about 2,000 years old and stands at signpost eight; and the Mother-of-the-Forest, the tallest tree in the park at 329 feet, is at signpost nine. Many people take as much as an hour to complete the loop. There is no reason to rush.

**User Groups:** Hikers only. Partially wheelchair accessible. No dogs, horses, or mountain bikes.

**Permits:** No permits are required. A state park entrance fee of $6 per vehicle is charged. For backpack campsites, reservations are required at 831/338-8861.

**Maps:** Detailed trail maps of Big Basin Redwoods State Park are available for a fee from Mountain Parks Foundation, 525 N. Big Trees Road, Felton, CA 95018, 831/335-3174. For topographic maps, ask the USGS for Castle Rock Ridge and Big Basin.

**Directions:** From the San Francisco Peninsula, take I-280 to Sunnyvale/Saratoga Road. Turn south and drive five miles to Saratoga and Highway 9. Turn right at Highway 9 and drive up the hill for about seven miles to Skyline Ridge. Continue over the other side of Highway 9 about seven more miles to Highway 236. Turn right and drive about 10 miles to Big Basin Redwoods State Park. Note: Highway 236 is extremely twisty and not recommended for RVs or trailers.

Alternatively, from San Francisco, take Highway 1 south to Santa Cruz and Highway 9. Turn left on Highway 9 and drive about 12 miles to Boulder Creek and the traffic light for Highway 236. Turn left on Highway 236 and drive 10 miles to park headquarters.

**Contact:** Big Basin Redwoods State Park, 21600 Big Basin Way, Boulder Creek, CA 95006, 831/338-8860; district headquarters, 831/429-2851, fax 831/429-2876.

## 158 BERRY CREEK FALLS
**12.0 mi / 5.5 hrs**

**in Big Basin Redwoods State Park in the Santa Cruz Mountains near Boulder Creek**

Map 7.4, page 270

The prettiest sight in the Bay Area just might be Berry Creek Falls, a 70-foot waterfall framed by a canyon and complete with ferns, redwoods, and the sound of rushing water. Yet many believe that just upstream the views of Silver Falls, a beautiful free fall enclosed by a bowl of redwoods, or Golden Falls, a gorgeous cascade over gold sandstone, are even more beautiful. These three waterfalls, along with the redwood forest, make this the No. 1 hike in the Bay Area. It is worth repeating many times.

Getting an early start helps to ensure a carefree trip with no pressure to complete the loop by a certain time. Start at park headquarters and take Skyline-to-the-Sea Trail amid the giant redwoods up to the Big Basin rim; then head down the other side, hiking west toward the coast. After topping the rim at 1,200 feet, the hike descends 600 feet over the course of about four miles to Berry Creek Falls (4.7 miles from the trailhead). You round a bend and suddenly, there it is, a divine waterfall. A small bench is perfectly situated for viewing the scene while eating a picnic lunch.

To return, it's best to go the long way: up the staircase and past the Cascade Falls—both Silver Falls and Golden Falls—and return on Sunset Trail. At Silver Falls, it is possible to dunk your head into the streaming water without getting the rest of your body wet—a real thrill. Golden Falls is a beautiful cascade of water over golden sandstone, like a giant water slide. Once you pass Golden Falls, the trail climbs out to a service road near Sunset Camp. Do not miss the right turn off the service road to Sunset Trail. From here, Sunset Trail meanders through the most remote sections of the park, in and out of chaparral and forest, then loops back into redwoods, and leads back to park headquarters. However, you can trim the hiking time down to about 4.5 hours if you double back on the same trail you came in on. But in such a beautiful place, why cut the experience short?

**User Groups:** Hikers only. No dogs, horses, or mountain bikes. No wheelchair facilities.

**Permits:** No permits are required. A state park entrance fee of $6 per vehicle is charged. For backpack campsites, reservations are required at 831/338-8861.

**Maps:** Detailed trail maps of Big Basin Redwoods State Park are available for a fee from Mountain Parks Foundation, 525 N. Big Trees Road, Felton, CA 95018, 831/335-3174. For topographic maps, ask the USGS for Castle Rock Ridge and Big Basin.

**Directions:** From the San Francisco Peninsula, take I-280 to Sunnyvale/Saratoga Road. Turn south and drive five miles to Saratoga and Highway 9. Turn right at Highway 9 and drive up the hill for about seven miles to Skyline Ridge. Continue over the other side of Highway 9 about seven more miles to Highway 236. Turn right and drive about 10 miles to Big Basin Redwoods State Park. Note: Highway 236 is extremely twisty and not recommended for RVs or trailers.

From San Francisco, take Highway 1 south to Santa Cruz and Highway 9. Turn left on Highway 9 and drive about 12 miles to Boulder Creek and the traffic light for Highway 236. Turn left on Highway 236 and drive 10 miles to park headquarters.

**Contact:** Big Basin Redwoods State Park, 21600 Big Basin Way, Boulder Creek, CA 95006, 831/338-8860, websites: www.bigbasin.org, www.parks.ca.gov (click on Find A Park); Santa Cruz District, 831/429-2850; camping reservations 800/444-7275; backpack camping reservations 831/338-8861; tent cabin reservations 800/874-8368.

## 159 METEOR TRAIL
**5.2 mi / 2.5 hrs**

**in Big Basin Redwoods State Park in the Santa Cruz Mountains near Boulder Creek**

Map 7.4, page 270

Under the heavy redwood canopy of Big Basin, most hikers don't worry about whether or not it's foggy on the coast. But on this hike there's a unique reason to worry, as the park's best coastal lookout is at trail's end. The Meteor Trail starts at park headquarters on Skyline-to-the-Sea Trail and heads northeast. (If you see a sign for Berry Creek Falls, you're going in the wrong direction.)

For much of the route, you hike along Opal Creek, a pretty stream in the spring, surrounded by redwoods. Two miles out, you will arrive at the intersection with Meteor Trail, where you turn left and climb 400 feet over the space of a mile to the Middle Ridge Fire Road. The Ocean View Summit (1,600 feet) is only a couple hundred yards off, featuring a glimpse to the west of the Waddell Creek watershed and the Pacific Coast—though the view is largely eclipsed now by trees. Return by doubling back the way you came. If you visit Big Basin and don't have time for the Berry Creek Falls hike, this is the next best option.

**User Groups:** Hikers only. No dogs, horses, or mountain bikes. No wheelchair facilities.

**Permits:** No permits are required. A state park entrance fee of $6 per vehicle is charged.

**Maps:** Detailed trail maps of Big Basin Redwoods State Park are available for a fee from Mountain Parks Foundation, 525 N. Big Trees Road, Felton, CA 95018, 831/335-3174. For topographic maps, ask the USGS for Castle Rock Ridge and Big Basin.

**Directions:** From the San Francisco Peninsula, take I-280 to Sunnyvale/Saratoga Road. Turn south and drive five miles to Saratoga and Highway 9. Turn right at Highway 9 and drive up the hill for about seven miles to Skyline Ridge. Continue over the other side of Highway 9 about seven more miles to Highway 236. Turn right and drive about 10 miles to Big Basin Redwoods State Park. Note: Highway 236 is extremely twisty and not recommended for RVs or trailers.

From San Francisco, take Highway 1 south to Santa Cruz and Highway 9. Turn left on Highway 9 and drive about 12 miles to Boulder Creek and the traffic light for Highway 236. Turn left on Highway 236 and drive 10 miles to park headquarters.

**Contact:** Big Basin Redwoods State Park, 21600 Big Basin Way, Boulder Creek, CA 95006, 831/338-8860, websites: www.bigbasin.org,

www.parks.ca.gov (click on Find A Park); Santa Cruz District, 831/429-2850, camping reservations 800/444-7275, backpack camping reservations 831/338-8861, tent cabin reservations 800/874-8368.

## 160 AÑO NUEVO TRAIL
**3.0 mi / 2.0 hrs**

in Año Nuevo State Reserve on the San Mateo County coast south of Pescadero

**Map 7.4, page 270**

One of the more curious adventures in the Bay Area has become one of the most popular: touring Año Nuevo State Reserve to see the elephant seals. Yep, this is the place where these giant creatures arrive every winter to fight, mate, give birth, sunbathe, and make funny noises. So many people want to watch them that you must make reservations and join a tour group, from December 15 through March 31. The rest of the year you are free to hike on your own.

Elephant seals look like giant slugs, often weighing 2,000 to 3,000 pounds—even the newborns weigh 75 pounds. The old boars reach nearly 20 feet in length and weigh as much as 5,000 pounds. As part of a tour group, you'll walk along roped-off trails, winding your way amid the animals. With a 200 mm camera lens, you can get excellent pictures. The best times to visit are in mid-December, when the males battle for harems, and in late January, when hundreds of pups are born. The rest of the year this is a nice place to enjoy a quiet beach walk.

**User Groups:** Hikers only. No dogs, horses, or mountain bikes. No wheelchair facilities.

**Permits:** A year-round parking fee of $6 is charged per vehicle. From mid-December through March, access to the park is available only by accompanying a ranger on a scheduled walk, $5 per person. To make a reservation, call 800/444-7275.

**Maps:** A map is available at the entrance station for a fee. For a topographic map, ask the USGS for Año Nuevo.

**Directions:** From I-280 in San Mateo, turn

west on Highway 92 and drive to Half Moon Bay and Highway 1. Turn left (south) on Highway 1 and drive about 27 miles to the park entrance on the right (well signed).

**Contact:** Año Nuevo State Reserve, New Year's Creek Road, Pescadero, CA 94060, 650/879-2025, website: www.anonuevo.org; Half Moon Bay state parks, 650/726-8820.

## 161 SKYLINE-TO-THE-SEA (FROM RANCH DEL OSO)/ McRARY RIDGE LOOP
### 13.6 mi / 7.0 hrs

**at Rancho del Oso on the Santa Cruz County coast south of Año Nuevo**

Map 7.4, page 270

The wide dirt road that leads from Rancho del Oso into the Waddell Creek canyon is very popular with mountain bikers who use this out-and-back route to access Berry Creek Falls, 5.8 miles in. Because of the number of bikes on the dirt road, it doesn't always make the best hiking trip, especially on weekends. A better choice is to use it as part of a longer loop, on which you'll spend much of your time on lovely single-track trail (no bikes).

Follow the wide road/trail inland from Highway 1. Where the road is gated near a restroom at .2 mile, cut off to the left on the hikers-only alternate trail. Follow this path to Alder Trail Camp, then rejoin the wide dirt road for 1.5 miles to Camp Herbert. Here is the start of your loop. Note the McCrary Ridge Trail cutting off to the right; this is your return route. For now, stay on the wide dirt road all the way to Berry Creek Falls (the last .7 mile is a narrow trail for hikers only). Enjoy the refreshing sight and sound of the gorgeous 70-foot falls, then retrace your steps for .25 mile to Howard King Trail. This redwood-lined path leads 1.8 miles to Hihn Hammond Road; cross it and pick up McCrary Ridge Trail. Follow it 2.6 miles back to the wide Skyline-to-the-Sea Trail, then cruise through the last three easy miles back to your car.

In the spring, this is a great wildflower walk, with 15 to 20 species commonly sighted, including a few pockets of virtual rafts of Forget-Me-Nots.

**User Groups:** Hikers, horses (not permitted past Henry Trail), and mountain bikes (not permitted past Waddell Creek Bridge). No dogs. No wheelchair facilities.

**Permits:** No permits are required. A fee of $6 is charged per vehicle.

**Maps:** A trail map is available on weekends at the ranger station for a fee. It can be obtained by mail by calling Mountain Parks Foundation, 831/335-3174, credit cards accepted. For a topographic map, ask the USGS for Franklin Point.

**Directions:** From I-280 in San Mateo, turn west on to Highway 92 and drive to Half Moon Bay. Turn left (south) onto Highway 1 and drive about 35 miles (two miles past Año Nuevo State Reserve) and look for the signs indicating Big Basin Redwoods State Park/Rancho del Oso on the east side of the highway, just past the Santa Cruz County line. Turn and park at Rancho del Oso.

**Contact:** Rancho del Oso, 831/425-1218; Rancho del Oso Nature Center, 831/427-2288; trail camp reservations, 831/338-8861; equestrian camping, 831/425-1218; Big Basin Redwoods State Park, 21600 Big Basin Way, Boulder Creek, CA 95006, 831/338-8860; California State Parks, Santa Cruz District, 831/429-2850, websites: www.parks.ca.gov (click on Find A Park), www.mountainparks.org.

## 162 MONUMENT PEAK TRAIL
### 7.5 mi / 4.0 hrs

**in Ed R. Levin County Park in the Milpitas foothills**

Map 7.4, page 270

At 2,594 feet, Monument Peak offers views that nearly rival those on Mount Hamilton, with far-ranging vistas over the Santa Clara Valley. Yet the peak gets bypassed by many people, including regular visitors to Ed R. Levin County Park. Of the 13 trails in the park, the summit hike is clearly the longest, steepest, and most difficult. And most park visitors do not come for a challenge, but to play golf at Spring Valley, go fishing at Sandy Wool Lake, or just enjoy a picnic. Those who do want a challenge will find one on this climb. There are two routes to the top: The Monument Peak Trail is actually a road, and you may run head-on into mountain bikers ripping downhill on it; instead, take Tularcitos/Agua Caliente Trail for a more gentle climb without having to contend with bikes. It junctions with the Monument Peak Road near the top, where you turn left for the final push to the summit. With the trailhead at 300 feet at Sandy Wool Lake, figure on a 2,300-foot climb over the course of about 3.75 miles.

**User Groups:** Hikers and horses. Leashed dogs permitted only on Calera Creek Trail and Agua Caliente Trail, a service road. No mountain bikes. No wheelchair facilities.

**Permits:** No permits are required. A day-use fee of $5 per vehicle is charged. Hikers are encouraged to wait two days after a rain before hiking in order to prevent trail damage.

**Maps:** For a free trail map, contact Ed R. Levin County Park at the address below. For topographic maps, ask the USGS for Milpitas and Calaveras Reservoir.

**Directions:** Take I-680 to Milpitas and the exit for Calaveras Road East. Take that exit and drive east for 3.5 miles to Downing Street. Turn left on Downing Street and drive .5 mile to the park entrance (straight ahead). Proceed to the parking area near Sandy Wool Lake.

**Contact:** Ed R. Levin County Park, 3100 Calaveras Road, Milpitas, CA 95035, 408/262-4527 or 408/262-6980, websites: www.parkhere.org (click on Find A Park).

## 163 SUNNYVALE BAYLANDS
### 2.0 mi / 1.0 hr

**on South San Francisco Bay in Sunnyvale**

Map 7.4, page 270

Sunnyvale Baylands County Park really isn't much of a park at all, but rather a wildlife preserve surrounded by a levee that makes a trail

for hiking and jogging. It covers 177 acres of South Bay marshland, home to blue herons, great egrets, avocets, black-necked stilts, mallards, pintails, and burrowing owls. On nearly every trip, you will also see a jackrabbit or two. In fact, these rabbits have a way of scaring the bejesus out of hikers. They hide in the weeds until you get close, then suddenly pop up and take off at warp speed, shocking you every time.

From the parking area adjacent to Highway 237, hike along the levee, turning left as it parallels Calabazas Creek. To your left is a seasonal wetlands preserve. The trail continues along the creek, then turns left again and runs alongside Guadalupe Slough. An open-water bird preserve lies to the left. The adjacent proximity of the highway is a downer.

**User Groups:** Hikers only. No dogs, horses, or mountain bikes. No wheelchair facilities.

**Permits:** No permits are required. An entrance fee of $4 per vehicle is charged from May to October (season pass available), with no parking fee from November to April. No fees for walk-in or bike-in traffic.

**Maps:** For a free map, write to Sunnyvale Baylands County Park at the address below. For a topographic map, ask the USGS for Mountain View.

**Directions:** From Highway 237 in Sunnyvale, take the Caribbean exit. The park is immediately on your right hand side at 999 East Caribbean (well signed, located next to Twin Creeks baseball facility).

**Contact:** Sunnyvale Baylands County Park, P.O. Box 3707, Sunnyvale, CA 94088, 408/730-7709, websites: www.ci.sunnyvale.ca.us/baylands, www.parkhere.org (click on Find A Park).

## 164 SOUTH BAY NATURE TRAIL
### 2.0 mi / 1.0 hr

**in San Francisco Bay National Wildlife Refuge near Alviso**

Map 7.4, page 270

Everybody knows about South Bay Nature Trail at the San Francisco Bay National Wildlife

Refuge, right? That's the big nature center located at the eastern foot of the Dumbarton Bridge, right? Very popular, right? Wrong, wrong, and wrong. A little-known portion of the wildlife refuge is set deep in the South Bay marsh near Alviso, where it receives scant attention compared to its big brother to the north at the Dumbarton Bridge. Headquarters are at the Environmental Education Center; from there, you walk on a dirt path along a wild tidal marshland. As you stroll northward, you will delve into wilder and wilder habitat, and in the process have a chance at seeing a dozen species of birds in a matter of minutes. The endangered harvest salt mouse lives in this habitat. Guided nature walks are held regularly on weekend mornings, and they are well worth attending. The sloughs and quiet waters here also make for a unique opportunity for saltwater canoeing and kayaking.

**User Groups:** Hikers and mountain bikes. No dogs or horses. No wheelchair facilities.

**Permits:** No permits are required. Parking and access are free.

**Maps:** For a topographic map, ask the USGS for Mountain View.

**Directions:** From U.S. 101 near Sunnyvale, take Highway 237. Drive east on Highway 237 to Zanker Street. Turn left on Zanker Street and drive to the parking area at the Environmental Education Center.

**Contact:** Environmental Education Center, 408/262-5513; Don Edwards San Francisco Bay National Wildlife Refuge, P.O. Box 524, Newark, CA 94560, 510/792-4275 or 510/792-0222; website: http://desfbay.fws.gov/.

## 165 EAGLE ROCK LOOP
### 2.2 mi / 1.0 hr

**in Alum Rock City Park in the San Jose foothills**

Map 7.4, page 270

Eagle Rock is pretty short as far as mountains go, only 795 feet. But at Alum Rock City Park, it's the best perch in the vicinity for a picnic site and a view of the Santa Clara Valley. In the winter, after rain has cleared the air, it becomes a choice spot. For this hike, park at the lot at the road's end at the eastern end of the park, where you'll find a major trailhead for several routes. Take the one on the left, North Rim Trail, to reach Eagle Rock. The hike climbs 300 feet to a canyon rim overlooking the valley cut by Penitencia Creek, before a short, signed cutoff trail takes you to Eagle Rock. To complete the loop, return to North Rim Trail and continue on, working your way back down the valley floor. Turn left on Creek Trail (more like a road), which is routed along Penitencia Creek to the parking area. Thirteen miles of trails provide access to the park's 700 acres, but this hike is our favorite.

**User Groups:** Hikers, horses, and mountain bikes. No dogs. No wheelchair facilities.

**Permits:** No permits are required. An entrance fee of $6 per vehicle is charged daily from Memorial Day through Labor Day; at other times, it is charged only on weekends.

**Maps:** For a free trail map, contact Alum Rock City Park at the address below. For a topographic map, ask the USGS for Calaveras Reservoir.

**Directions:** From I-680 in San Jose, take the Alum Rock Avenue exit. Turn east on Alum Rock Avenue and drive 3.5 miles to the park entrance.

**Contact:** Alum Rock City Park, 16240 Alum Rock Avenue, San Jose, CA 95127, 408/277-4539; group picnic reservations, 408/277-5561; Youth Science Institute, 408/258-4322. Website: www.ci.san-jose.ca.us/cae/parks/arp/.

## 166 PENITENCIA CREEK
### 4.0 mi / 1.75 hrs

**in Penitencia Creek County Park in east San Jose**

Map 7.4, page 270

This isn't much of a hiking trail, but rather more of a bike path. But with the stream running alongside, it makes a pleasant route for a leisurely stroll, jog, or bicycle ride. Two more bonuses make it worth a trip: The park's eastern boundary abuts Alum Rock City Park, providing access to an additional 13 miles of trails. And near

Piedmont Road, behind the fire station, you'll find an additional 40 acres called Creek Park, which is linked to this trail, providing an optional loop hike. The Penitencia Creek Trail traces the stream for four miles, adjacent to Penitencia Creek Road, so joggers making the round-trip can have an easy eight-miler. Most hikers do about half that or extend their walks into Creek Park or Alum Rock City Park.

**User Groups:** Hikers and mountain bikes. No dogs or horses. No wheelchair facilities.

**Permits:** No permits are required. Parking and access are free.

**Maps:** For a free trail map, contact Penitencia Creek County Park at the address below. For a topographic map, ask the USGS for Calaveras Reservoir.

**Directions:** From I-680 in San Jose, take the Berryessa Road exit. Drive east on Berryessa Road to Capitol Avenue. Turn right on Capitol Avenue and drive to Penitencia Creek Road. Turn left and drive to the parking area on the left.

**Contact:** Penitencia Creek County Park (Levin County Park), 408/262-6980; Santa Clara County Parks and Recreation, 408/355-2200. Website: www.parkhere.org (click on Find A Park).

## 167 HALLS VALLEY LOOP
**5.5 mi / 3.0 hrs**

in Joseph D. Grant County Park in the Mount Hamilton foothills east of San Jose

Map 7.4, page 270

Grant County Park is the Bay Area's great undiscovered playland. The wild area covers 9,000 acres in the foothills of Mount Hamilton and can be the perfect setting for hiking and mountain biking. There is plenty of room for both endeavors, with nearly 40 miles of hiking trails (horses permitted) and 20 miles of old ranch roads for both mountain biking and hiking. The Halls Valley Loop provides the best introduction to what many call Grant Ranch. From the parking area along Mount Hamilton Road, take the main trail/road out past Grant Lake and bear left at the junction on Halls Valley Trail. This route skirts Halls Valley to the left, an open landscape of foothills and grasslands sprinkled with oaks, a quiet and pretty scene. The trail heads out 2.5 miles, climbing east toward Mount Hamilton until it meets Cañada de Pala Trail. Turn right, hike up .4 mile, and turn right again on Los Huecos Trail to complete the loop. From here, it's a 1.8-mile trip back to the parking area, descending steeply most of the way.

Special note: There are many great side trips on this route. After a rain, one of the best is searching out the little creek at the bottom of Halls Valley, then following it upstream to discover a procession of little waterfalls. For the ambitious, another is climbing 2.2 miles and 500 feet up the ridge on Pala Seca Trail above Halls Valley to the park's highest point; from Antler Point at 2,995 feet, you can look out over the Santa Clara Valley.

**User Groups:** Hikers, horses, and mountain bikes. No dogs. No wheelchair facilities.

**Permits:** No permits are required. An entrance fee of $5 per vehicle is charged.

**Maps:** For a free trail map, contact Joseph D. Grant County Park at the address below. For a topographic map, ask the USGS for Lick Observatory.

**Directions:** From I-680 in San Jose, take the Alum Rock Avenue East exit and drive to Mount Hamilton Road. Turn right on Mount Hamilton Road and drive eight miles east to the parking area on the left.

**Contact:** Joseph D. Grant County Park, 18405 Mount Hamilton Road, San Jose, CA 95140, 408/274-6121; Santa Clara County Parks and Recreation, 408/355-2200, website: www.parkhere.org/prkpages/grant.htm.

## 168 HOTEL TRAIL
**7.0 mi / 3.25 hrs**

in Joseph D. Grant County Park in the Mount Hamilton foothills east of San Jose

Map 7.4, page 270

The remote landscape around Eagle Lake in Grant County Park provides visitors with precious tranquillity as well as good chances of seeing wildlife. Eagle Lake, set in the southernmost reaches of the park's 9,000 acres, is the prime destination of Hotel Trail. After parking at the lot along Mount Hamilton Road, cross the road and look for the trailhead on the south side. Start hiking southeast on the ranch road (Hotel Trail), scanning your surroundings for the wild turkeys that are commonly seen in this area. As you head deeper into the interior, you will be hiking through foothill country; bovines are the most frequently encountered animal (keep your distance from the bulls, of course), but you might see a herd of wild pigs, too. These pigs tend to sprint off when they see or hear people, so don't worry about playing out the fearless-hiker-meets-ferocious-boar scene. The route to Eagle Lake is a direct shot of 3.5 miles, climbing a couple of hundred feet in the process. There are several options for side trips along the way: the best is to turn right on Cañada de Pala Trail and drop down about .5 mile to San Felipe Creek, the prettiest stream in the park.

**User Groups:** Hikers, horses, and mountain bikes. No dogs. No wheelchair facilities.

**Permits:** No permits are required. An entrance fee of $5 per vehicle is charged.

**Maps:** For a free trail map, contact Joseph D. Grant County Park at the address below. For a topographic map, ask the USGS for Lick Observatory.

**Directions:** From I-680 in San Jose, take the Alum Rock Avenue East exit and drive to Mount Hamilton Road. Turn right on Mount Hamilton Road and drive eight miles east to the parking area on the left. The Hotel Trail starts on the south side of the road, opposite the parking area.

**Contact:** Joseph D. Grant County Park, 18405 Mount Hamilton Road, San Jose, CA 95140, 408/274-6121; Santa Clara County Parks and Recreation, 408/355-2200, website: www.parkhere.org/prkpages/grant.htm.

## 169 COYOTE PEAK LOOP
### 3.4 mi / 2.0 hrs

**in Santa Teresa County Park south of San Jose**

Map 7.4, page 270

Golfers know Santa Teresa County Park best, but hikers are discovering that the park has something for them as well. Most notable is the walk up to Coyote Peak, the feature destination of a good loop hike that provides a surprise lookout to the southern Santa Clara Valley. This park covers 1,688 acres, but the main attractions are the golf course, driving range, bar, and restaurant. You can quickly leave development behind, however, by hiking south from the Hidden Springs trailhead off Bernal Road. After one mile, the trail junctions with Coyote Peak Trail, which climbs up Coyote Peak, with a short loop cutoff getting you to the summit. To complete the loop, continue on Coyote Peak Trail, then take Ohlone Trail one mile back to the parking area. In contrast to the manicured greens of the golf course, this trail provides an insight into the park's most primitive and rugged areas and gives you a good view for your efforts.

**User Groups:** Hikers, leashed dogs, and horses. No mountain bikes, except on Ohlone Trail. No wheelchair facilities.

**Permits:** No permits are required. A $5-per-vehicle park entrance fee is charged.

**Maps:** For a free trail map, contact Santa Teresa County Park at the address below. For a topographic map, ask the USGS for Santa Teresa Hills.

**Directions:** From San Jose on U.S. 101, drive south to Bernal Road (north of Morgan Hill). Take that exit and turn west on Bernal Road and drive .75 mile to the park. Park in the main day-use lot.

**Contact:** Santa Teresa County Park, 408/225-0225 (Hellyer); Santa Clara County Parks, 408/355-2200, websites: www.parkhere (click on Find A Park).

## 170 RIDGE TRAIL
**6.0 mi / 2.75 hrs**

**in El Sereno Open Space Preserve in the Saratoga foothills**

Map 7.4, page 270

El Sereno Open Space is one of the lesser-used parklands in the Bay Area. Why? Not only is it remote, but there's room at the trailhead for only two vehicles to park. The preserve covers 1,112 acres and is named for Mount El Sereno, a prominent peak on the adjacent ridge. From the trailhead at the pullout on Montevina Road, hike on the jeep trail, which traces a ridgeline. Though the trail bobs and weaves, you will generally head east, topping out on a rim and then descending toward Los Gatos for a distance of three miles to the end of the trail. This is where you'll find panoramic views of Lyndon Canyon, Lexington Reservoir, and the South Bay. After taking time to enjoy the vistas, return via the same route.

**User Groups:** Hikers, horses, and mountain bikes. No dogs. No wheelchair facilities.

**Permits:** No permits are required. Parking and access are free.

**Maps:** For a free trail map, contact the Midpeninsula Regional Open Space District at the address below. For a topographic map, ask the USGS for Castle Rock Ridge.

**Directions:** From the intersection of I-280 and Highway 17 in San Jose, turn south on Highway 17 and drive about eight miles to Los Gatos. Continue south for about three miles to Montevina Road. Turn right and park at the roadside turnout at the end of the road. There is space for only a few cars.

**Contact:** Midpeninsula Regional Open Space District, 330 Distel Circle, Los Altos, CA 94022, 650/691-1200, website: www.openspace.org (click on Preserve Locator). During nonbusiness hours, a touch-tone phone menu is available for trail news, conditions, and events.

## 171 ST. JOSEPH'S HILL TRAIL
**2.7 mi / 1.75 hrs**

**in the St. Joseph's Hill Open Space Preserve near Lexington Reservoir**

Map 7.4, page 270

For most people to be willing to hike up, there had better be considerable compensation waiting at the trail's end. And so there is on this hike, which climbs 600 feet in the space of about 1.5 miles to a perch on top of St. Joseph's Hill, with views of Lexington Reservoir, the Santa Clara Valley, and the adjacent Sierra Azul Range. From the parking area just east of the dam at elevation 645 feet, you hike north adjacent to Los Gatos Creek for about .5 mile. At the trail junction, turn right and begin the climb up St. Joseph's Hill; a loop route is available near the top. Lexington Reservoir never looked so good.

**User Groups:** Hikers, dogs, and mountain bikes. No horses. No wheelchair facilities.

**Permits:** No permits are required. A fee of $5 per vehicle is charged at Lexington Reservoir County Park.

**Maps:** For a free trail map, contact the Midpeninsula Regional Open Space District at the address below. For a topographic map, ask the USGS for Los Gatos.

**Directions:** From San Jose: Take Highway 17 (to about four miles east of Los Gatos) to the exit for Bear Creek Road. Take that exit, bear right, cross over the freeway, and re-enter Highway 17 and drive a short distance to the exit for Alma Bridge Road. Take that exit and drive east for 1.5 miles (across the Lexington Dam). Parking is available just east of the dam in Lexington Reservoir County Park. The trail starts opposite the boat launching area beyond the dam.

From Santa Cruz: Take Highway 17 (to about four miles east of Los Gatos) to the exit for Alma Bridge Road. Take that exit and drive east for 1.5 miles (across the Lexington Dam). Parking is available just east of the dam in Lexington Reservoir County Park. The trail starts opposite the boat launching area beyond the dam.

**Contact:** Lexington Reservoir County Park, c/o Vasona Lake County Park, 298 Garden Hill Drive, Los Gatos, CA 95030, 408/356-2729; Santa Clara County Parks and Recreation, 408/355-2200, website: www.parkhere.org (click on Find A Park); Midpeninsula Regional Open Space District, 330 Distel Circle, Los Altos, CA 94022, 650/691-1200, website: www.openspace.org (click on Preserve Locator). During nonbusiness hours, a touch-tone phone menu is available for trail news, conditions, and events.

## 172 LEXINGTON DAM TRAIL
**1.0 mi / 0.5 hr**

**in Lexington Reservoir County Park in the Saratoga foothills**

Map 7.4, page 270

Lexington Reservoir can be one of the prettiest places in Santa Clara County, as well as one of the ugliest. The lake might be full of water one year, then drained down to nothing the next. And after a hot summer it can resemble a dust bowl. But when it is full, some people show up in the spring just to stare at all the water. Well, you can take it literally the extra mile for a nice bonus. Park at the lot just east of the dam, then walk across the dam and turn right on the "Pedway." That's as far as many people get, as most come for the view of the lake from the dam. Keep walking, though, and you will be surprised, as the trail drops down along Los Gatos Creek. After 1.5 miles, it links up with Los Gatos Creek Trail, which you can follow all the way into town; it's a popular bike route. Note: Alma Bridge Road circles the reservoir, and for more ambitious walks, there are several parklands nearby.

**User Groups:** Hikers and mountain bikes. No dogs or horses. No wheelchair facilities.

**Permits:** No permits are required. A day-use fee of $5 per vehicle is charged.

**Maps:** For a free trail map, contact Lexington Reservoir County Park at the address below. For a topographic map, ask the USGS for Los Gatos.

**Directions:** From San Jose: Take Highway 17 (to about four miles east of Los Gatos) to the exit for Bear Creek Road. Take that exit, bear right, cross over the freeway, and re-enter Highway 17 and drive a short distance to the exit for Alma Bridge Road. Take that exit and drive east for 1.5 miles (across the Lexington Dam). Parking is available just east of the dam in Lexington Reservoir County Park.

From Santa Cruz: Take Highway 17 (to about four miles east of Los Gatos) to the exit for Alma Bridge Road. Take that exit and drive east for 1.5 miles (across the Lexington Dam). Parking is available just east of the dam in Lexington Reservoir County Park.

**Contact:** Lexington Reservoir (c/o Vasona), 408/356-2729, website: www.valleywater.org (click on Reservoirs); Santa Clara County Parks and Recreation, 408/355-2200, website: www.parkhere.org (click on Find A Park); City of San Jose Parks and Recreation, 408/277-5561.

## 173 PRIEST ROCK TRAIL
**6.1 mi / 4.5 hrs**

**in the Sierra Azul Open Space Preserve near Lexington Reservoir**

Map 7.4, page 270

Many people find it difficult to believe these wildlands could exist so close to so many homes. But they do, and you can explore them on the Sierra Azul Loop, a strenuous hike that climbs, climbs, and climbs as it probes the Sierra Azul Range.

At the entrance to the Sierra Azul Open Space Preserve, the trail rises in the first mile to 1,762 feet at Priest Rock. There it nearly levels out for about a mile, until you reach the loop junction. Bear to the left; the trail starts climbing again and climbs another thousand feet or so in the next 1.5 miles to reach the ridgeline at 2,628 feet. Turn right at the ridge and enjoy finally being on top, cruising over the 1.6-mile stretch on the mountain rim. Turn right at the next ridge junction and take the trail back (three miles to the loop junction), relaxing on the downhill cruise.

**User Groups:** Hikers, horses, and mountain bikes. No dogs. No wheelchair facilities.

**Permits:** No permits are required. No fee.

**Maps:** For a free trail map, contact the Midpeninsula Regional Open Space District at the address below. For a topographic map, ask the USGS for Santa Teresa Hills.

**Directions:** From Los Gatos, drive south on Highway 17 for about four miles to the Alma Bridge Road exit at Lexington Reservoir. Turn east and drive 1.5 miles across the dam. When you reach the parking area for county parks (a fee is charged), continue on Alma Bridge Road to another parking area (free) on the right.

**Contact:** Midpeninsula Regional Open Space District, 330 Distel Circle, Los Altos, CA 94022, 650/691-1200, fax 650/691-0485, website: www.openspace.org (click on Preserve Locator). During nonbusiness hours, a touch-tone phone menu is available for trail news, conditions, and events.

## 174 BALD MOUNTAIN TRAIL
### 1.0 mi / 1.0 hr

**in the Sierra Azul Range south of Los Gatos**

Map 7.4, page 270

It's hard to beat standing atop a mountain, especially when you're near Mount Umunhum. At 3,486 feet, it's the highest point in the Sierra Azul Range. From anywhere in the Santa Clara Valley, Mount Umunhum is the most prominent landmark on the western horizon—it's that mountain with the big abandoned radar station on top. Alas, the public is not permitted to hike to the summit of Umunhum due to toxic contaminates and restrictions related to private property. But the trip to adjacent Bald Mountain is the next best thing. The trail here is a .5-mile route on Mount Umunhum Road to Bald Mountain, a hilltop knoll with views of the Almaden Valley and across San Jose to Mount Hamilton, then south to San Benito County. As we said, public access to Mount Umunhum is prohibited, and the Midpeninsula Regional Open Space District requests that

you call prior to visiting Bald Mountain. By the way, guess what "Umunhum" means in the Ohlone Indian language: 1. Eagle? 2. Bear? 3. Hummingbird? The answer: hummingbird.

**User Groups:** Hikers, horses, and mountain bikes. No dogs. No wheelchair facilities.

**Permits:** No permits required. Parking and access are free.

**Maps:** For a free trail map, contact the Midpeninsula Regional Open Space District at the address below. For a topographic map, ask the USGS for Santa Teresa Hills.

**Directions:** In San Jose, take Almaden Expressway south to Camden Avenue. Turn west on Camden Avenue and drive to the intersection with Hicks Road. Turn south on Hicks Road and drive to Mount Umunhum Road. Turn west and drive a small parking area at district pipe gate SA-7. There is limited roadside parking only with space for two vehicles.

**Contact:** Midpeninsula Regional Open Space District, 330 Distel Circle, Los Altos, CA 94022, 650/691-1200, fax 650/691-0485, website: www.openspace.org (click on Preserve Locator). During nonbusiness hours, a touch-tone phone menu is available for trail news, conditions, and events.

## 175 MINE HILL TRAIL
### 2.0–14.5 mi / 1.0–7.0 hrs

**in Almaden Quicksilver County Park in the San Jose foothills**

Map 7.4, page 270

Of the dozen trails at Almaden Quicksilver County Park, this is the most unusual. Although Almaden covers 3,600 acres and has two lakes (Almaden and Guadalupe), it is the evidence of historical mining operations that makes it fascinating. With a network of trails here, many routes and long trips are possible, but most people cut it short, enjoying a portion.

The Mine Hill Trail starts just inside the park entrance off of New Almaden Road (Hacienda entrance). From here, Mine Hill Trail is routed north to a junction. Turn left (staying on Mine Hill Trail) and you will pass the Dan Tunnel and

San Cristobel Tunnel, remnants of the mining days. At that point, most people just return. Some will take the .75-mile April Trail Loop, a short cutoff loop off Mine Hill Trail.

Note that some areas adjacent to Mine Hill Trail are closed to public access because of hazardous residual materials from the mercury mines. Almaden was the site of the first quicksilver mine in North America. Mining began in 1845 and continued until 1975. There are still burnt ore dumps along the trail. A bonus is that wildflower blooms are good in this park in the spring.

**User Groups:** Hikers and horses. Leashed dogs and mountain bikes are permitted on some trails; mountain bikes must enter from the Hacienda entrance. No wheelchair trail access.

**Permits:** No permits are required. Park entrance is free.

**Maps:** A trail map is also available at the trailhead. For a topographic map, ask the USGS for Santa Teresa Hills.

**Directions:** Take Highway 85 to the exit for Almaden Expressway. Take that exit and drive south on Almaden Expressway to Almaden Road. Turn right on Almaden Road and drive through New Almaden to the Hacienda park entrance on the right. (note that there are three major access points to the park).

**Contact:** Almaden Quicksilver County Park office, (Calero Reservoir County Park), 23205 McKean Road, San Jose, CA 95120, 408/268-3883; San Jose Regional Park, 408/277-5562; Almaden Lake Park (City of San Jose), 408/277-5130; nature walks 408/268-3883, websites: www.parkhere.org (click on Find A Park), www.valleywater.org (click on Reservoirs).

## 176 JUAN CRESPI LOOP
### 4.8 mi / 2.0 hrs

**in Calero Reservoir County Park southeast of San Jose**

Map 7.4, page 270

You'd better know the difference between horse droppings and Shinola if you plan to do this hike. Why? Because this is a very popular horseback trail, and if you don't watch where you're going, well, you won't be stepping in shoe polish. And many people have trouble watching their steps because of the nice views of Calero Reservoir to the north. Start near the entrance gate and follow Juan Crespi Trail, turning right toward Calero Reservoir. The trail runs along the southern shoreline of the lake for more than a mile before making a nearly 180-degree looping left turn. There it becomes Los Cerritos Trail and climbs the ridgeline bordering the southern end of the lake. When it tops the ridge, it connects to Peña Trail. To complete the loop, turn left on Peña Trail, making a descent. A great way to go is to descend Peña Trail, turn right on Vallecitos Trail and then left on Figueroa Trail. It adds two miles to the trip but is well worth it.

**User Groups:** Hikers and horses. No dogs or mountain bikes. No wheelchair facilities.

**Permits:** No permits are required. Park entrance is free (at this access point for hiking).

**Maps:** For a free map, contact Calero Reservoir County Park at the number below. For a topographic map, ask the USGS for Santa Teresa Hills.

**Directions:** From San Jose, drive south on U.S. 101 for five miles to Coyote and Bernal Road. Take the Bernal Road exit west and drive a short distance to the Monterey Highway exit. Turn south on Monterey and drive a short way to Bailey Avenue. Turn right and drive to McKean Road. Turn left on McKean Road and drive one-half mile to the park/reservoir entrance. Drive to the sign for the horse stables. Park adjacent to the ranger office.

**Contact:** Calero Reservoir County Park, 408/268-3883, websites: www.parkhere.org (click on Find A Park), www.valleywater.org (click on Reservoirs); Santa Clara County Parks, 408/355-2200, boat launching reservations 408/355-2201, group picnic reservations 408/355-2201; Coyote Discount Bait & Tackle, 408/463-0711, website: www.coyotebait.com; Calero Ranch Horse rentals, 408/268-2567, website: www.caleroranchstables.com.

## 177 DEL COYOTE NATURE TRAIL
1.2 mi / 0.5 hr

in Coyote-Hellyer County Park downstream
of Anderson Dam south of San Jose

**Map 7.4, page 270**

Thousands and thousands of people roar up
and down U.S. 101 south of San Jose with nary
a clue about the peaceful little park that sits
so nearby. Yet just east of the highway is Coyote-Hellyer County Park with its small, shaded stream that is stocked with rainbow trout
in the late spring and early summer. The hike
starts at a picnic area, meandering along the
stream from there. The flowing waters come
from nearby Anderson Dam, and steady releases are made well into summer. That is what
makes this park so attractive to local residents,
who know this is a nice spot for a respite.

**User Groups:** Hikers only. No dogs, horses, or
mountain bikes. No wheelchair facilities.

**Permits:** No permits are required. A day-use
fee of $5 is charged per vehicle.

**Maps:** For a free map, contact Coyote-Hellyer
County Park at the address below. For a topographic map, ask the USGS for Morgan Hill.

**Directions:** To Nature Trail/fishing access: From
San Jose, drive south on U.S. 101 for six miles
to the town of Coyote and the Cochran Road
exit. Take the Cochran Road exit and drive
east (toward the base of Anderson Dam) to
the parking area on the left (Coyote Creek runs
downstream of the dam).

To Coyote Creek Parkway (for mountain bikers): From San Jose, drive south on U.S. 101
for six miles to the town of Coyote and the
Cochran Road exit. Take the Cochran Road
exit west and drive a very short distance to Monterey Road. Turn right at Monterey and drive
one mile to Burnett Avenue and the trailhead.

**Contact:** Coyote-Hellyer County Park, 985
Hellyer Avenue, San Jose, CA 95111, 408/225-
0025; Santa Clara County Parks, 408/355-2200,
website: www.parkhere.org (click on Find A
Park); Coyote Discount Bait & Tackle, 408/463-
0711; DFG Trout Plant hot line, 707/944-5581
(updated late Friday).

## 178 FROG POND LOOP
4.7 mi / 3.0 hrs

in Henry W. Coe State Park in the Hamilton
Range east of Morgan Hill

**Map 7.4, page 270**

A good pair of hiking boots, a horse, or a mountain bike—and an honest reality check—are your
tickets to the Bay Area's backyard wilderness:
Henry Coe State Park. This wildland covers is
located south of Mount Hamilton and covers
86,000 acres, 134 square miles (larger than the
land mass of San Francisco), with access provided by 100 miles of ranch roads and 250 miles
of trails. The Frog Pond Loop is a short day
hike from headquarters that provides a glimpse
of the park's primitive charms, along with a
sampling of a few of the ups and downs. Think
of it as a test case: If you like this, then pack a
lunch and two canteens and launch off on one
of the butt-kickers.

Start this trip from park headquarters at
Monument Trail (.1 mile from the visitors center), elevation 2,500 feet. The trip starts by hiking .5 mile to Hobbs Road, climbing to nearly
3,000 feet. At Hobbs Road, turn left and tromp
down for .8 mile into Little Fork Coyote Creek
(2,400 feet). This stream is very pretty in the
spring, and though you must then walk out of
the canyon, it is a tranquil and memorable setting. Then make the short .25-mile rise from
the creek up to Frog Pond. This first leg is
about 1.6 miles, and most visitors will stop
along the creek for a reality check and to re-
assess what awaits in the wilderness. Frog Pond
is a pretty little spot, complete with fishing line
hanging from tree limbs (this lake is fished
often and the catch rates are low). Many people then simply return the way they came. A
preferred option is to turn the trip into a loop.
This is done by returning to Little Fork Coyote Creek and then turning left onto Flat Frog
Trail at a junction on the east side of the road.
The route laterals around the ridge that provided the up-and-down huff-and-puff on the
way in, extending 2.3 miles with more gradual
climbs. It eventually reaches Manzanita Point

Road. Cross the road and pick up Corral Trail, which provides a .6-mile finish to the trip. This hike gives you just enough to whet your appetite for more challenging routes into the park's interior.

**User Groups:** Hikers, horses, and mountain bikes. No dogs. No wheelchair facilities. After .5 inch of rain or more, bikes are prohibited from single-track trails for 48 hours.

**Permits:** A state park day-use fee of $5 per vehicle is charged. No permits are required unless you plan to camp in the backcountry.

**Maps:** A map/brochure is available at park headquarters. For a detailed topographic map, contactto Pine Ridge Association, P.O. Box 846, Morgan Hill, CA 95038. For a topographic map, ask the USGS for Mount Sizer.

**Directions:** From U.S. 101 in Morgan Hill, take the East Dunne Avenue exit and drive east (over Lake Anderson) for 13 miles (slow and twisty) to the park headquarters and visitors center.

**Contact:** Henry W. Coe State Park, P.O. Box 846, Morgan Hill, CA 95038, 408/779-2728 or 408/848-4006, website: www.coepark.org; California State Parks, Four Rivers District, 209/826-1197, website: www.parks.ca.gov (click on Find A Park).

## 179 MISSISSIPPI LAKE TRAIL
### 27.0 mi / 3.0 days

**in Henry W. Coe State Park in the Hamilton Range east of Morgan Hill**

Map 7.4, page 270

Mississippi Lake is set in the virtual center of Henry W. Coe State Park, borders the 23,000-acre Orestimba Wilderness to the east, and is the largest lake and the preeminent destination for many who venture into these vast wildlands. Fishing for bass, swimming in cool waters in early summer, and viewing wildflower blooms in spring are exceptional. If you catch it just right, the color of the lake seems almost tourmaline, a beautiful sight in this foothill wildland. Improvements in this trail grade at China Hole, once a nightmare climb, has made this one of the best mountain bike trips in the Bay

Area, as well as an exceptional overnight backpack trip for hikers.

This is a grueling hike from headquarters, and many unprepared hikers have suffered from dehydration and had to be rescued by park staff. Some hikers will try to short-cut the trip by bringing a mountain bike, but find themselves pushing the bike uphill, then speeding fast on downhill portions. Many can accomplish the hike in two days, but after the workout, you'll most likely want to relax on day two and head back to your car on day three.

An early start is paramount. From park headquarters, start this ambitious expedition by hiking out on Corral Trail for 1.9 miles to its junction with Manzanita Point Road. Turn right and hike 1.5 miles, past the group campgrounds, to China Hole Trail on the left. This can seem like a launch point off the edge of the earth—China Hole Trail drops from 2,320 feet elevation to 1,150 feet in the course of 2.6 miles. Though as field scout Lee Dittman points out, switchbacks have improved the trail gradient to about 10 percent.

At China Hole, you'll reach the East Fork of Coyote Creek, a beautiful trout stream, cool and fresh and full of water in late winter and early spring. Then you'll hike through The Narrows en route to Los Cruzeros, a junction of canyons and streams, in the process adding 1.1 miles to the day. A trail camp is available at Los Cruzeros, one of the park's prettiest spots. Make sure you pump two canteens full of water before leaving Los Cruzeros.

From here, you start to climb, hiking out on Willow Ridge Trail for 1.6 miles with an elevation gain of 1,350 feet to Willow Ridge Road. Turn left on Willow Ridge Road for a series of foothill-like climbs and drops as the trip extends 3.8 miles to the southern edge (and earth dam) at Mississippi Lake. The nearest trail camp, Mississippi Creek Horse Camp, is one mile south of the lake. That makes the trip a one-way excursion of 13.5 miles—a long and challenging day, especially if temperatures are hot.

All of this could be short-cutted if the California Department of Parks could negotiate a permanent easement at Bell Station from Highway 152/Pacheco Pass Highway for access to this remote section. We have made the trip to Mississippi from this alternate access and it cuts the hiking time down by 75 percent. Each year, Coe arranges a special weekend when hikers can enter from the Bell Station trailhead, with the lucky few picked by a drawing.

Even though Henry W. Coe State Park has been open to the public only since 1981, a few legends have already developed, and the most mysterious involves Mississippi Lake. The lake once had a one-of-a-kind ability to create huge trout. Scientists documented 26-inch wild trout that were only 18 months old. The trout are gone now, as low water in the feeder creek prevented spawning during the 1988 to 1992 drought; any trout you catch should be released immediately. Still, the legendary huge trout of Mississippi Lake have inspired many to make the trip out, often out of curiosity, to see such a unique habitat. (Bass were planted in 1991 and have taken over the lake, providing good fishing.)

**User Groups:** Hikers, horses, and mountain bikes. No dogs. No wheelchair facilities. After .5 inch of rain, bikes are prohibited from single-track trails for 48 hours.

**Permits:** A trail map and camp permit are required. A state park day-use fee of $5 per vehicle is charged.

**Maps:** A map/brochure is available at park headquarters. For a detailed topographic map, contactto Pine Ridge Association, P.O. Box 846, Morgan Hill, CA 95038. For topographic maps, ask the USGS for Mount Sizer and Mississippi Creek.

**Directions:** From U.S. 101 in Morgan Hill, take the East Dunne Avenue exit and drive east over Lake Anderson for 13 miles (a twisty road) to the park headquarters and visitors center.

**Contact:** Henry W. Coe State Park, P.O. Box 846, Morgan Hill, CA 95038, 408/779-2728 or 408/848-4006, website: www.coepark.org; California State Parks, Four Rivers District, 209/826-1197, website: www.parks.ca.gov (click on Find A Park).

# 180 COIT LAKE
**11.6 mi / 2.0 days**

**in Henry W. Coe State Park in the Hamilton Range east of Morgan Hill**

Map 7.4, page 270

The canyons and ridges at Henry W. Coe State Park seem to stretch to infinity. Exploring the wild foothill country, combined with the likely chance of seeing wild pigs, is the primary attraction for visitors. It is a good trip for ambitious naturalists, with 400 species of wildflowers documented, as well as deer, coyote, bobcat, fox, wild turkey, hawks, owls, eagles, and of course, tons of pigs. This park also attracts fishermen—there are 140 ponds with small Bass—with Coit one of the best. Finally, it provides backcountry camping for a small fee.

Heading off to Coit Lake (and stopping at Kelly Cabin Lake on the way in) is the best introduction to this wild land. But come prepared: The reality for many turns into an endurance test. You go up one canyon, then down the next, over and over. Some people get so worn down, hot, and exhausted that they are practically reduced to nothing more than a little pile of hair lying in the dirt.

From the Coyote Creek gate (there is limited parking at the gate—see note at end of listing for alternate parking at Hunting Hollow), walk a short distance (about .1 mile) and look for Grizzly Gulch Trail off to the right. Take Grizzly Gulch Trail. After just five minutes (.2 mile) you will reach a fork. Take the left fork to stay on Grizzly Gulch Trail, where you will start a climb through oak woodlands, ridges, and canyons. This extends for 1.2 miles to another fork, with the elevation nearly 1,900 feet. Bear right, staying on Grizzly Gulch Trail, and head out for one mile on the road to a fork with Dexter Trail (2,000 feet). Bear to the left on Dexter Trail, and continue the climb for another .6 mile (topping out at 2,400 feet)

before finally reaching Wasano Ridge and Wasano Ridge Road. Turn left and hike .2 mile on the road to Kelly Lake Trail. Turn right and enjoy the one-mile descent to Kelly Lake. So far you have invested 4.3 miles with a 1,500-foot climb and 300-foot descent.

After enjoying pretty Kelly Cabin Lake, you are ready to top off the trip by heading 1.5 miles to Coit Lake and the campground that is available there. Most of this is a climb. From below the earth dam at Kelly Cabin Lake, take the right fork on Coit Road and climb out .8 mile to the junction with Willow Road (2,386 feet). Simply continue straight for .3 mile and you will reach the inlet to Coit Lake. A well-worn trail circles the lake. From the Coyote Creek Gate trailhead to Coit Lake with this route will make for a 5.8-mile hike for the day, one-way.

At one time at Coit Lake, you could catch nearly a bass per cast just by flipping out a one-inch floating Rapala lure. That is no longer true, but it does offer a rare chance for pond-style fishing in the greater Bay Area. For the best fishing, longer trips are often required (see next listing) to more remote lakes that are only occasionally fished. Unfortunately, the vision of great fishing inspires many excited people to start hiking off to the lake without first taking a litmus test of the quest they are about to undertake. Venturing here requires long hikes with difficult climbs both ways, particularly if the weather is hot and dry, as is common out here. Many get busted by the heat before reaching the lake and return frustrated, sometimes extremely angry (at me for inspiring the adventure; you should see the letters) without making a cast. So get the difficulty of this trip in focus before heading out.

Note that overnight users are required to obtain a camping/wilderness permit. Hikers who choose to enter by the Coyote Creek access point must have a trail map. And if the limited parking along the road's shoulder at the Coyote Creek Gate is full, you must instead park at the Hunting Hollow parking area

(along Gilroy Springs Road, the access road you drove in on), which will add two miles to this route.

**User Groups:** Hikers, horses, and mountain bikes. No dogs. No wheelchair facilities.

**Permits:** A trail map and camp permit are required. A self-registration area is available at the Hunting Hollow parking area, located just off the trailhead access road. A state park day-use fee of $5 per vehicle is charged. After .5 inch of rain or more, bikes are prohibited from single-track trails for 48 hours.

**Maps:** A map/brochure is available at park headquarters. For a detailed topographic map for a fee, contact Pine Ridge Association, P.O. Box 846, Morgan Hill, CA 95038. For topographic maps, ask the USGS for Gilroy Hot Springs and Mississippi Creek.

**Directions:** From U.S. 101 in Gilroy, drive east on Leavesley Road to New Avenue. Turn left on New Avenue and drive to Roop Road. Turn right on Roop Road and drive up into the hills to the Coyote Lake County Park turnoff. Continue past that turnoff, across the cattle guard, to Gilroy Hot Springs Road/Coyote Creek Road and continue five miles to the end of the road. If parking along the road's shoulder is taken, return two miles to the Hunting Hollow parking area. Route is well-signed.

**Contact:** Henry W. Coe State Park, P.O. Box 846, Morgan Hill, CA 95038, 408/779-2728 or 408/848-4006, website: www.coepark.org; California State Parks, Four Rivers District, 209/826-1197, website: www.parks.ca.gov (click on Find A Park).

## 181 ROOSTER COMB LOOP
**70.0 mi / 6.0 days**

in Henry W. Coe State Park in the Mount Hamilton Range southeast of San Jose

Map 7.4, page 270

You have to be something of a deranged soul to try this hike, and that's why we signed up! Not only is it just plain long, but it includes seven climbs that'll have you cussing, and yet explores the park's most remote and arid wildlands where anything over 10 inches of rain a year is considered a flood. So why do it? Because no trail on public land in the Bay Area leads to more isolated spots. A series of short cutoff trips can take you to the park's best fishing spots and little-seen gems: Mississippi Lake, Mustang Pond, Jackrabbit Lake, Paradise Lake, and all the way out to Orestimba Creek—and climb the Rooster Comb, a rock formation that looks something like a miniature stegosaurus-back rim.

You could search across California and not find a more remote wildland—and yet here it is within range of the Bay Area and 6.5 million people. But you have to pay dearly for your pleasures—either that or border insanity. Paradise Lake will seem like a mirage after you've walked 33 miles.

While many routes are available, the best suggestion is to take the most direct way out to the Orestimba Wilderness Zone. The best suggested starting point is not park headquarters, but rather the Coyote Creek entrance gate, or the nearby (two miles) Hunting Hollow parking area. From the gate, it's an 11.6-mile trip to Coit Lake (see prior listing).

From Coit Lake, take Coit Road out 4.2 miles to Pacheco Junction, then continue on Coit Road another 1.8 miles to a major fork. This fork marks the beginning and the end of the Rooster Comb Loop. At this point, you have traveled 15.8 miles.

Turn left at this fork, taking County Line Road, to start the Rooster Comb Loop and a route through the Orestimba Wilderness Zone in a clockwise manner. From the fork, it is 2.7 miles to the short cutoff to Mississippi Lake. Stop, rest up, tank up, fuel up, and get your thoughts straight before heading out. Because from Mississippi Lake, the trip heads off into a land that seems to have no end. It is 7.8 miles north to Red Creek Road. Turn right, and it is another 6.1 miles to Robinson Creek Trail. Turn left and hike along Robinson Creek, a remote canyon with a sliver of water, for 5.6 miles to Orestimba Creek Road. This is so far

away from anything that it is unbelievable, and it is also typically dry and hot most of the year.

Turn right on Orestimba Creek Road and you start your return from the depths of the wilderness (though it won't seem like it). The route heads 3.2 miles to a cutoff trail on the right for Rooster Comb Summit Trail. This is a must-do, if you've come this far, a 1.4-mile hike (2.8 round-trip) up the north flank of the Rooster Comb, topping out at 1,836 feet, a 600-foot climb.

From here you head back, heading south on Orestimba Creek Road, passing short cutoff trails for Paradise Lake, Mustang Pond, and Kingbird Pond, a distance of 8.7 miles back to the fork with Coit Road. When you reach the junction with Coit Road, you have completed the loop, a distance of 36.9 miles (including the Rooster Comb Summit trail).

Turn left and return the final 11.6 miles back to the Coyote Creek entrance station. With this route, in all you have completed a loop trip of 60.1 miles, not including side-trip cutoff trails to several lakes, which can typically add another 10 miles to the trip.

So there you have it: 70 miles, best done in five or six days, exploring a land that few have seen, and fewer yet have experienced.

Several trail camps are situated along the way, and camping is permitted throughout the wilderness area. If the weather turns hot, physically unprepared hikers can find themselves in real danger. Let me say that again before you head off full of excitement and a limited amount of logic: unprepared hikers can find themselves in real danger. OK? Got it?

To best explore the park, the perfect approach would be to come in on horseback or with a burro carrying your gear and water, then take a day and set up a base camp in Pacheco Canyon; note that no bikes are permitted in the designated Orestimba Wilderness, and in addition, all single-track trails are closed to bikes for 48 hours after a half inch of rain.

**User Groups:** Hikers, horses, and mountain

bikes. No dogs. No wheelchair facilities. After .5 inch of rain, bikes are prohibited from single-track trails for 48 hours.

**Permits:** A trail map and camp permit are required. A self-registration area is available at the Hunting Hollow parking area, located just off the trailhead access road. A state park day-use fee of $5 per vehicle is charged.

**Maps:** A map/brochure is available at park headquarters. For a detailed topographic map for a fee, contact Pine Ridge Association, P.O. Box 846, Morgan Hill, CA 95038. For topographic maps, ask the USGS for Gilroy Hot Springs and Mississippi Creek.

**Directions:** From U.S. 101 in Gilroy, drive east on Leavesley Road to New Avenue. Turn left on New Avenue and drive to Roop Road. Turn right on Roop Road and drive up into the hills to the Coyote Lake County Park turnoff. Continue past that turnoff, across the cattle guard to Gilroy Hot Springs Road/Coyote Creek Road and continue five miles to the end of the road. If parking along the road's shoulder is taken, return two miles to the Hunting Hollow parking area.

**Contact:** Henry W. Coe State Park, P.O. Box 846, Morgan Hill, CA 95038, 408/779-2728 or 408/848-4006, website: www.coepark.org; California State Parks, Four Rivers District, 209/826-1197, website: www.parks.ca.gov (click on Find A Park).

## 182 UVAS PARK WATERFALL LOOP
**1.0–4.5 mi / 0.5–2.0 hrs**

**in Uvas Canyon County Park near Morgan Hill**

Map 7.4, page 270

Uvas Canyon County Park is a little slice of waterfall heaven on the east side of the Santa Cruz Mountains. Although the park has only short hiking trails, it's living proof that good things come in small packages. What's the one key element to a perfect trip? Visit during the rainy season, preferably just after a good downpour. Although the park's creeks flow year-round, only immediately following a good rain can you witness the full watery spectacle. The one-mile Waterfall Loop Trail parades around Swanson Creek's canyon, crossing wooden footbridges and passing 30-foot Black Rock Falls and several smaller falls. Be sure to walk .1 mile past the far end of the loop to see Basin Falls and Upper Falls, both pretty cascades 15 to 25 feet high. The entire canyon comes alive with the sound of rushing water, and a myriad of ferns and foliage grow on every inch of ground. It's a happy place where you can hike around in your rain gear and be smiling the whole time.

This trip can also be extended to 4.5 miles for the full show, including a surprise lookout over the south Santa Clara Valley. For the longer version, bear left on the Alec Canyon Trail and climb to the canyon rim for a sweeping view of the South Santa Clara Valley (well worth the short climb). Triple Falls can be reached from a short cutoff trail located just past the lookout, another must-see. To return down into the canyon, take the Contour Trail. It is routed back down to Swanson Creek, where it links up with the Waterfall Loop, and your return to the picnic area. Always remember this place. It can save a wet winter day—or salvage a long drive to the southland.

**User Groups:** Hikers and dogs. No horses or mountain bikes. No wheelchair facilities.

**Permits:** No permits are required. A day-use fee of $5 is charged per vehicle.

**Maps:** A free map of Uvas Canyon County Park is available at the visitors center. For a topographic map, ask the USGS for Loma Prieta.

**Directions:** From San Jose, take U.S. 101 south and exit at Bernal Road. At the stoplight, turn right, then right again to reach Monterey Highway. Turn left (south) on Monterey Highway. Turn right on Bailey Avenue and drive 2.8 miles to McKean Road. Turn left on McKean Road and drive six miles. McKean Road becomes Uvas Road. Turn right on Croy Road and drive 4.5 miles to the park. Continue past Svaedal, a private camp and resort. Park near the park visitors center or farther up the hill in one of the picnic area parking lots. The railhead is the gated dirt road at Black Oak Picnic Area.

**Contact:** Uvas Canyon County Park, 8515 Croy Road, Morgan Hill, CA 95037, 408/779-9232, Santa Clara County Parks and Recreation, 408/355-2200, website: www.parkhere.org.

## 183 ALEC CANYON AND CONTOUR LOOP

**4.5 mi / 2.5 hrs**

**in Uvas Canyon County Park near Morgan Hill**

Map 7.4, page 270

For hikers looking for more of a workout than the Waterfall Loop in Uvas Park provides, this hike up Alec Canyon Trail will get your heart pumping. It's a good trip for a clear winter day when the views from the trail's overlook at Manzanita Point are at their best. Start hiking on the gated road at Black Oak Picnic Area and then bear left, heading up and away from the canyon and Waterfall Loop Trail. You'll get to hike that trail on your way back down. A steep climb up the wide road brings you to Manzanita Point, where you can see far off to the north and east—a dramatic valley view. Continue .25 mile beyond the point and take the right cutoff to cascading Triple Falls, the most secluded of all the waterfalls in Uvas Park. Then retrace your steps on Alec Canyon Trail, this time bearing left on Contour Trail less than .5 mile past Manzanita Point. Contour Trail is pure fun, winding like a snake along the hillsides, with minimal elevation change but many curves and twists. Finally it drops back down to Swanson Creek, where you can walk back to the trailhead via the Waterfall Loop.

**User Groups:** Hikers and dogs. No horses or mountain bikes. No wheelchair facilities.

**Permits:** No permits are required. A day-use fee of $5 is charged per vehicle.

**Maps:** A free map of Uvas Canyon County Park is available at the visitors center. For a topographic map, ask the USGS for Loma Prieta.

**Directions:** From San Jose take U.S. 101 south and exit at Bernal Road. At the stoplight turn right and then right again to reach Monterey Highway. Turn left (south) on Monterey Highway. Turn right on Bailey Avenue and drive 2.8 miles to McKean Road. Turn left on McKean Road and drive six miles (McKean Road becomes Uvas Road) to Croy Road. Turn right on Croy Road and drive 4.5 miles to the park. Continue past Svaedal, a private camp and resort. Park near the park visitors center or farther up the hill in one of the picnic area parking lots. The trailhead is the gated dirt road at Black Oak Picnic Area.

**Contact:** Uvas Canyon County Park, 8515 Croy Road, Morgan Hill, CA 95037, 408/779-9232, Santa Clara County Parks and Recreation, 408/355-2200, website: www.parkhere.org.

## 184 LOCH LOMOND LOOP

**5.0 mi / 3.25 hrs**

**in Loch Lomond Recreation Area in the Santa Cruz Mountains near Ben Lomond**

Map 7.4, page 270

There is no prettier lake in the greater Bay Area than Loch Lomond Reservoir, a jewel set in the Santa Cruz Mountains, complete with an island and circled by conifers. Newcomers are always surprised by its beauty and by the nearby hiking opportunities as well. Of the 12 miles of trails here, the best hike is the Loch Lomond Loop. You start on Loch Trail, a level path that extends northward along the lakeshore for 1.5 miles out to Deer Flat. There you turn uphill on Highland Trail, climbing and looping to the east up the ridge on a moderate ascent. It peaks out at a remote weather station where you get a sweeping view of the lake below and the surrounding forested mountains. Bring your camera.

To complete the loop, continue southward along the ridgecrest down to the Glen Corrie Picnic Area, or you can take the paved road back to the starting point. A bonus at Loch Lomond is good trout fishing, especially from April through June, and good bass and bluegill fishing in the summer. Great lake, great views, great hike.

Note that the park is closed from mid-September through February, and swimming is not permitted—this is a drinking-water supply lake.
**User Groups:** Hikers and dogs. No horses or mountain bikes. No wheelchair facilities.
**Permits:** No permits are required. A day-use fee of $4 per vehicle is charged; there is also a fee for dogs. The Loch Lomond Recreation Area is open only from March 1 through September 15. Rangers are on duty during the winter and will cite trespassers.
**Maps:** For a free trail map, contact Loch Lomond Recreation Area at the address below. For a topographic map, ask the USGS for Felton.
**Directions:** From Santa Cruz: Take Highway 1 to Highway 9. Turn north on Highway 9 and drive to Felton and Graham Hill Road. Turn right and drive two stoplights to East Zayante Road. Turn left and drive 2.5 miles to Lompico Road. Turn left, and drive 1.5 miles to West Drive. Turn left and go 0.75 mile to Sequoia Drive. Turn right, continue to park entrance. Well-signed.

From San Jose: Take Highway 17 south to Scotts Valley and the Mount Hermon Road exit. Take that exit and drive west 3.5 miles to Graham Hill Road. Turn left and continue as above.

The trailhead is located adjacent to the boat ramp.
**Contact:** Loch Lomond Recreation Area, 100 Loch Lomond Way, Felton, CA 95018, 831/420-5320 or 831/335-7424, website: www.ci.santa-cruz.ca.us/wt (click on Loch Lomond Recreation Area).

## 185 BIG TREES NATURE TRAIL
**1.0 mi / 0.5 hr**

**in Loch Lomond Recreation Area in the Santa Cruz Mountains near Ben Lomond**
Map 7.4, page 270

This short but steep trail starts at the Glen Corrie Picnic Area and provides an excellent reminder of the power and the glory of Mother Nature. As the trail ascends, its numbered signs explore many natural features and plants of the redwood forest (pick up a free trail guide at the park store before you go). Near the ridgecrest are the only remaining old-growth redwoods in this watershed. These massive, 500- to 1,000-year-old trees offer a glimpse into the area's prelogging magnificence. Just around the bend from the giant trees is a highly disturbed area that suffered major storm damage during the 1970s and 1980s from high winds, snowfall, and heavy rainfall. The biggest hit came from a January 1982 storm in which 15 inches of rain fell in a 24-hour period, causing major debris flows (mud slides). As the trail descends through this now-recovering area, you'll notice many trees that had their tops knocked off. The debris flows clogged existing drainage channels and created several massive log jams. Remnants of early 20th-century logging activities can also be seen along this short, fascinating trail.

Note that the park is closed from mid-September through February, and swimming is not permitted—this is a drinking-water supply lake.
**User Groups:** Hikers and dogs. No horses or mountain bikes. No wheelchair facilities.
**Permits:** No permits are required. A day-use fee of $4 per vehicle is charged; there is also a fee for dogs. The Loch Lomond Recreation Area is open only from March 1 through September 15. Rangers are on duty during the winter and will cite trespassers.
**Maps:** For a free trail map, contact Loch Lomond Recreation Area at the address below. For a topographic map, ask the USGS for Felton.
**Directions:** From Santa Cruz: Take Highway 1 to Highway 9. Turn north on Highway 9 and drive to Felton and Graham Hill Road. Turn right and drive two stoplights to East Zayante Road. Turn left and drive 2.5 miles to Lompico Road. Turn left, and drive 1.5 miles to West Drive. Turn left and go 0.75 mile to Sequoia Drive. Turn right, continue to park entrance. Well-signed.

# Newsweek

## SUBSCRIBER SAVINGS VOUCHER

**Just use this card to get Newsweek for 84% off the cover price. That's only 79¢ an issue. (Order two years for just 69¢ per issue and save even more!)**

| Newsweek's Cover Price | Your Cost* | You Save |
|---|---|---|
| $133.65 | $21.33 | $112.32 |

**Check one:**
*I'LL TAKE THE BEST DEAL*

☐ 24 months (106 issues) just 69¢ per issue.

☐ 12 months (53 issues) just 79¢ per issue.

☐ 6 months (27 issues) just 79¢ per issue.

**Check one:**
○ Payment enclosed.
○ Bill me later.
○ Renewal (attach label).

Mr./Mrs./Ms.(circle one) _____
please print

Street _____ Apt No. _____

City _____ State _____ Zip _____

*27 issues. Residents of DC and GA add applicable sales tax. Offer good in U.S. only and subject to change. Newsweek publishes weekly, except when combined issues are published that count as two issues, and when an additional special issue may be published.

JO723DC

NO POSTAGE
NECESSARY
IF MAILED
IN THE
UNITED STATES

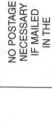

# BUSINESS REPLY MAIL

FIRST-CLASS MAIL     PERMIT NO. 309     HARLAN IA

POSTAGE WILL BE PAID BY ADDRESSEE

## Newsweek

PO BOX 5551
HARLAN IA 51593-3051

From San Jose: Take Highway 17 south to Scotts Valley and the Mount Hermon Road exit. Take that exit and drive west 3.5 miles to Graham Hill Road. Turn left and continue as above.

The trailhead is located near the restrooms at the Glen Corrie Picnic Area.

**Contact:** Loch Lomond Recreation Area, 100 Loch Lomond Way, Felton, CA 95018, 831/ 420-5320 or 831/335-7424, website: www.ci .santa-cruz.ca.us/wt (click on Loch Lomond Recreation Area).

## 186 FALL CREEK LOOP
**8.0 mi / 4.0 hrs**

**in Henry Cowell Redwoods State Park near Santa Cruz**

Map 7.4, page 270

Where in the Santa Cruz area can you find a fast-running, full-flowing stream even in the driest months of summer and fall? Almost nowhere except here, at the Fall Creek Unit of Henry Cowell Redwoods State Park. Located a few miles distant from the main area of Henry Cowell, which is well known for its campground and steam trains, the Fall Creek Unit is a less developed area that is perfectly suited for hikers. Crystal-clear Fall Creek tumbles and cascades through the park year-round. Many visitors just hike a short stretch along the stream, but your best bet is to make a big loop around the park. In addition to its perennial stream and second- and third-growth redwood forest, the park features three 1870s lime kilns, an old railroad grade, and other evidence of this area's history as an important lime producer. The lime was used to make mortar to build the brick buildings of San Francisco and San Jose.

From the parking lot, take Bennett Creek Trail gently downhill for .2 mile, then turn left on Fall Creek Trail. Meander along this fern-laden, creekside path to South Fork Trail spur to the lime kilns. This is the start of the loop. After marveling at the kilns, follow Cape Horn Trail to Lost Empire Trail. The next two miles are a sustained climb with a short level stretch

in the middle near Barrel Mill Creek. The high point of the loop is reached at Big Ben Tree, a large virgin redwood situated at a junction of trails. You'll finish out the loop by heading downhill on Big Ben Trail, then turning right on Fall Creek Trail, and finally heading back up Bennett Creek Trail to your car.

**User Groups:** Hikers and horses. No dogs or mountain bikes. No wheelchair facilities.

**Permits:** No permits are required. A fee of $6 is charged per vehicle.

**Maps:** Park maps are available at the visitors center at the main unit of Henry Cowell State Park on Highway 9. For a topographic map, ask the USGS for Felton.

**Directions:** From San Jose, drive south on Highway 17 for 24 miles to Scotts Valley. Take the Mount Hermon Road exit and drive west toward Felton for 3.7 miles. Turn right on Graham Hill Road and drive .1 mile to Highway 9. Go straight across Highway 9 onto Felton Empire Road and drive .6 mile to the Fall Creek trailhead on the right.

**Contact:** Henry Cowell Redwoods State Park, Fall Creek Unit, 101 N. Big Trees Road, Felton, CA 95018, 831/335-4598, 831/335-7077 (Nature Center), or 831/429-2851, websites: www.parks.ca.gov (click on Find A Park), www.mountainparks.org.

## 187 EAGLE CREEK TRAIL
**3.0 mi / 1.5 hrs**

**in Henry Cowell Redwoods State Park near Santa Cruz**

Map 7.4, page 270

There are two places you don't want to miss on a visit to Henry Cowell Redwoods State Park. The first one is Eagle Creek Trail, the most direct hiking route to River Trail and the San Lorenzo River. The other is the park's observation deck, offering first-class views on clear days.

The Eagle Creek Trail starts between campsites 82 and 84, crosses Eagle Creek, and continues adjacent to the stream as it heads out toward the San Lorenzo River. As you hike this portion of the trail, you are surrounded by redwoods. The trail then crosses Pipeline Road and junctions with River Trail. Many people turn around and head back at this point. However, a great way to extend your hike is to head north on River Trail alongside the river, adding an extra three miles to the trip. Another bonus is the observation deck, the highest point in the park. Trees obscure views of Santa Cruz and Monterey Bay. It's only a .3-mile hike from the campground via Pine Trail, which starts near campsite 49. Right alongside the observation deck are a few ponderosa pine trees, growing far from their normal range in the Sierra Nevada. You'll recognize them by their distinctive jigsaw-puzzle bark.

**User Groups:** Hikers and horses. No dogs or mountain bikes. No wheelchair facilities.

**Permits:** No permits are required. A day-use fee of $6 is charged per vehicle.

**Maps:** Park maps are available at the campground entrance station or at the park visitors center off Highway 9. For a topographic map, ask the USGS for Felton.

**Directions:** From San Jose, drive south on Highway 17 for 24 miles to Scotts Valley. Take the Mount Hermon Road exit and drive west toward Felton for about one mile. Turn left on Lockewood Lane and drive one mile. Turn left on Graham Hill Road and drive .5 mile to the campground entrance on the right.

**Contact:** Henry Cowell Redwoods State Park, 101 N. Big Trees Road, Felton, CA 95018, 831/335-4598, 831/335-7077 (Nature Center), or 831/429-2851, websites: www.parks.ca.gov (click on Find A Park), www.mountainparks.org.

## 188 SPRIG LAKE LOOP
### 4.2 mi / 2.5 hrs

**in Mount Madonna County Park in the Santa Cruz Mountains west of Gilroy**

Map 7.4, page 270

This loop hike from the Sprig Lake parking area at Mount Madonna County Park provides a close-up look at beautiful Blackhawk Creek canyon, a shady sanctuary filled with redwoods, giant ferns, and a carpet of sorrel. Plan this trip for a cool day, though, because the first mile has an 800-foot climb. After that, the rest of the hike is much easier. From the parking area, follow the dirt road to Blackhawk Trail, where you turn left. Huff and puff your way uphill until the trail enters the redwoods; soon thereafter the grade lessens. The loop tops out at a junction of several trails near Pole Line Road. From that junction, take Sprig Lake Trail (signed for the campgrounds) and start heading downhill. After another stint in the redwoods, you drop into a drier forest of manzanita, pines, and madrones. Outcrops of sandstone make an appearance here and there. Finally you move back into a shady mixed forest and wind your way back to the west side of Sprig Lake. By the way, Sprig Lake isn't really a lake; it's a fishing pond that is popular with the youngsters.

**User Groups:** Hikers, horses, and dogs. No mountain bikes. No wheelchair facilities.

**Permits:** No permits are required. A day-use fee of $5 is charged per vehicle.

**Maps:** A free trail map is available at the entrance station. For a topographic map, ask the USGS for Mount Madonna.

**Directions:** From San Jose, take U.S. 101 south to Gilroy. Turn west on Highway 152 and drive about five miles. Turn north off Highway 152 at the Sprig Lake entrance to the park (five miles east of the main entrance at Pole Line Road).

**Contact:** Mount Madonna County Park, 7850 Poleline Road, Watsonville, CA 95076, 408/842-2341, website: www.parkhere.org.

## 189 BAYVIEW LOOP
### 2.5 mi / 1.75 hrs

**in Mount Madonna County Park in the Santa Cruz Mountains west of Gilroy**

Map 7.4, page 270

Mount Madonna County Park provides great scenic beauty, good hiking, camping, and horseback riding. The park is set around the highest peak in the southern range of the Santa

Cruz Mountains, and with 18 miles of hiking trails, the best routes are combinations of different trails. So it is with this triangular loop, starting at the park entrance station at Hecker Pass, elevation 1,270 feet. Take Bayview Trail and hike north for 1.1 miles, scanning west to Monterey Bay along the way. Turn right on Redwood Trail (it will cross Poleline Road) and head into the forest. To complete the loop, take Redwood, Rock Springs, Blackhawk, and Bayview Trails as they join in sequence. Confused? This park is filled with a spiderweb of short hikes. By linking them, you can customize your adventure. This suggested loop provides a look at some of the park's prettiest settings.

**User Groups:** Hikers, horses, and dogs. No mountain bikes. No wheelchair facilities.

**Permits:** No permits are required. A day-use fee of $5 is charged per vehicle.

**Maps:** A free trail map is available at the park entrance station. For a topographic map, ask the USGS for Mount Madonna.

**Directions:** From San Jose, take U.S. 101 south to Gilroy. Turn west on Highway 152 and drive 10 miles, turn right on Poleline Road, and drive to the entrance station. The trailhead is on the left.

**Contact:** Mount Madonna County Park, 7850 Poleline Road, Watsonville, CA 95076, 408/842-2341, website: www.parkhere.org.

## Chapter 8

© ANN MARIE BROWN

# Monterey and Big Sur

# Monterey and Big Sur

I t wouldn't be easy to choose the most spectacular stretch of California coastline, but if pressed, most beach connoisseurs would agree there is no place as visually stunning as the 130 miles of cliffs, rocks, and waves that run from Davenport to San Simeon.

There's nothing not to like here, from the mild climate to the wild landscape. Much of this area is isolated, undeveloped, and difficult to access, with high cliffs and few roads. Hiking in this land means wandering along gravel beaches, pausing to watch sunsets over glimmering seas, and walking in the shadows of giant redwoods.

South of Carmel, services are clustered in a few small towns: Big Sur, Lucia, and Gorda. In between is a string of coastal state parks that provide a bounty of hiking trails. The long list of options includes the rock-lined coves of Point Lobos State Reserve; the flower-covered hills of Garrapata State Park; the windswept beaches of Andrew Molera State Park; and the redwood-lined canyons of Julia Pfeiffer Burns State Park, Pfeiffer Big Sur State Park, and Limekiln State Park.

Whereas towns are few and traffic is light on the shore, a different story takes place out at sea. Every winter and spring, like clockwork, thousands of gray whales pass by on their long migrations. Traveling from their summer home in Alaska's Bering Sea to their winter breeding grounds in Baja, then back again a few months later, the whales display occasional flashes of fins or tails and leave hundreds of frothy spouts as their calling cards. Whale-watching is at its best from December to May, on days when the sea is flat and deep blue, with no wind or whitecaps. Hikers have a chance to witness this great natural spectacle from coastside trails at several Santa Cruz, Monterey, and Big Sur parks, and also while driving scenic Highway 1.

Neighboring this region's coastal splendor is a mountainous area of deeply carved canyons and steep escarpments, where the Santa Cruz Mountains in the north give way to the Santa Lucia Mountains in the south. Here, dense redwood forests thin out, and the forest gradually transitions to drier groves of oaks and pines. Hikers can explore these mountains on the paths of the spectacular Ventana Wilderness and its neighbor, Silver Peak Wilderness. Trails are easily accessed on the west side of Ventana (off Highway 1) or the east side (off U.S. 101). Although some wilderness destinations, such as Sykes Hot Springs, are notorious for crowds, a hiking trip in the off-season (autumn or winter) can provide solitude on even the most popular trails.

Last but not least, the Monterey and Big Sur region also contains one of California's most unusual national parks, Pinnacles National Monument. Its jagged cliffs, crags, and peaks are not part of any nearby mountain range; instead they are the remains of an ancient volcano that erupted 200 miles to the southeast. Whereas rock climbers flock to the vertical surfaces of the high crags, hikers can choose from a variety of well-built trails that tunnel through caves and ascend over and around the pinnacles. Springtime brings a spectacular display of wildflowers in the park's grasslands.

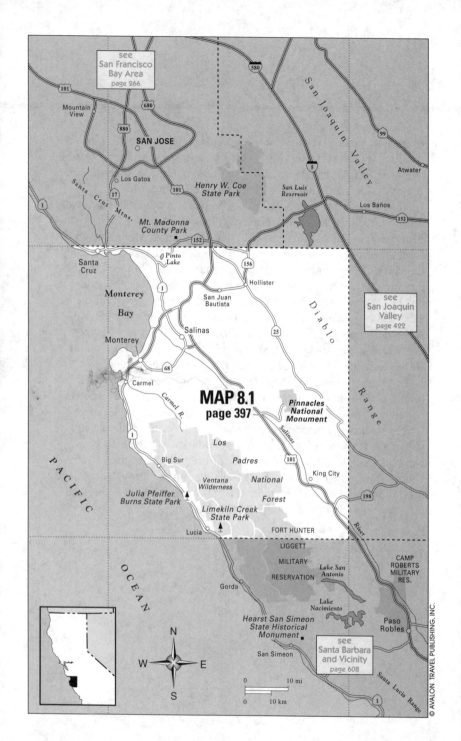

# Map 8.1

## Hikes 1–34
## Pages 398–417

# 1 OLD LANDING COVE TRAIL
## 2.5 mi / 1.5 hrs

**in Wilder Ranch State Park north of Santa Cruz**

Map 8.1, page 397

When you visit Wilder Ranch, you may notice that on some maps and park signs this trail is called Old Cove Landing, while on others it's called Old Landing Cove. Take your pick. The Old Landing Cove Trail is a gem of a coastal hike that offers a look at a seal rookery, some spectacular pocket beaches, and a hidden fern cave. Although the trail is open to both hikers and mountain bikers, everybody seems to mind their manners and get along fine.

The trail leads past brussels sprouts fields to the coast. An odd but interesting fact is that 12 percent of our nation's brussels sprouts production happens right here in this park. The trail leads from the main parking lot toward the ocean, then traces along the coastal blufftops, with farm fields on your right and the dramatic coastline on your left. In short order you reach the trail's namesake, Old Landing Cove, where small schooners loaded lumber in the late 19th century. A little more walking brings you to the bluffs above the seal rookery, where you look down on huge flat rocks covered with wall-to-wall seals. Finally, near post No. 8, a spur trail leads down to a small beach cove. Follow the spur and you will find on the inland side of the cove a shallow cave filled with ferns from floor to ceiling. A quarter mile past the fern-cave beach is another excellent pocket beach, perfect for picnicking or lying around. Although this is a fine destination for most visitors, you can keep hiking along the bluffs beyond this beach to several more beaches in the next few miles. (The trail's name changes from Old Landing Cove Trail to Ohlone Bluff Trail.) If you decide to keep going, be forewarned that you might get an anatomy lesson along the way: Both Three-Mile and Four-Mile beaches often attract nude sunbathers.

**User Groups:** Hikers and mountain bikes. No horses or dogs. No wheelchair facilities.

**Permits:** No permits are required. A $6 day-use fee is charged per vehicle.

**Maps:** A free map of Wilder Ranch State Park is available at the entrance station. For a topographic map, ask the USGS for Santa Cruz.

**Directions:** From Santa Cruz, drive north on Highway 1 for four miles. Turn left into the entrance for Wilder Ranch State Park and follow the park road to its end, at the main parking area. Take the signed trail from the southwest side of the parking lot.

**Contact:** Wilder Ranch State Park, 1401 Old Coast Road, Santa Cruz, CA 95060, 831/423-9703 or 831/426-0505, website: www.parks.ca.gov.

# 2 WILDER RIDGE AND ZANE GREY TRAILS
## 6.0 mi / 3.0 hrs

**in Wilder Ranch State Park north of Santa Cruz**

Map 8.1, page 397

Once you find your way to the hiker/biker tunnel underneath Highway 1 near the farm buildings at Wilder Ranch, you're on your way to a great six-mile hike with just enough of a climb to give you a workout and a spectacular vista of Monterey Bay. Keep in mind that this side of the park is the domain of mountain bikers—hundreds of them on weekends—but the trails are wide, and there's plenty of room for everybody. The Wilder Ridge Trail features a 500-foot climb to a coastal overlook. You reach it by exiting the tunnel and heading straight and then uphill on Wilder Ridge, then bearing right on the Wilder Ridge Loop. At about 2.5 miles out, shortly after Twin Oaks Trail forks right, you come to an obvious grassy overlook at the top of the ridge—about 40 feet off the main trail. Enjoy the wide vista, then continue hiking along the ridgetop on Wilder Ridge Loop. For an interesting loop, take the Zane Grey cutoff on the left (it's single track) and then go left again on the other side of the Wilder Ridge Loop.

**User Groups:** Hikers, horses, and mountain bikes. No dogs. No wheelchair facilities.

**Permits:** No permits are required. A $6 day-use fee is charged per vehicle.

**Maps:** A free map of Wilder Ranch State Park is available at the entrance station. For a topographic map, ask the USGS for Santa Cruz.

**Directions:** From Santa Cruz, drive north on Highway 1 for four miles. Turn left into the entrance for Wilder Ranch State Park and follow the park road to its end, at the main parking area. Take the trail signed Nature Trail from the southwest side of the parking lot. Walk down the park road to the Wilder Ranch and Cultural Preserve, then through the cultural preserve to the picnic area and chicken coops, to reach the tunnel that leads underneath Highway 1.

**Contact:** Wilder Ranch State Park, 1401 Old Coast Road, Santa Cruz, CA 95060, 831/423-9703 or 831/426-0505, website: www.parks.ca.gov.

## 3 MAPLE FALLS
**7.0–9.0 mi / 4.5 hrs**

**in Forest of Nisene Marks State Park
near Aptos**

**Map 8.1, page 397**

It's either a seven- or nine-mile round-trip hike to Maple Falls, and it all depends on whether the park road is gated at Porter Picnic Area, the main trailhead. In winter and spring, the road is usually closed, which means you need to walk an extra mile in each direction in order to see the falls. Winter and spring are the best seasons to go, of course, because that's when Maple Falls is flowing at its fullest. The trip starts out with an easy walk on Aptos Creek Fire Road, which you'll share with mountain bikers. Follow it .25 mile past Porter Picnic Area, where you turn left on Loma Prieta Grade Trail. The second-growth redwood and Douglas fir forest just keeps getting thicker, greener, and prettier, and the trail turns to sweet single track. Where Loma Prieta Grade splits, stay to the right, heading toward Bridge Creek Historic Site, for the shortest route to the falls. You can take the other side of the Loma Prieta Grade loop on your way back if

you still have the energy. When you reach Bridge Creek Historic Site, the site of a former logging camp, the maintained trail ends, and you begin a fun .5-mile stream scramble to Maple Falls, following the course of Bridge Creek. The canyon narrows as you travel through a dense green world of ferns, moss, foliage, and water, and at last you reach the back of the canyon, where 50-foot Maple Falls spills over the wall.

**User Groups:** Hikers only. No dogs or horses. Mountain bikes allowed only on fire roads. No wheelchair facilities.

**Permits:** No permits are required. A $6 day-use fee is charged per vehicle.

**Maps:** A free map of The Forest of Nisene Marks State Park is available at the entrance kiosk. For topographic maps, ask the USGS for Laurel, Soquel, and Loma Prieta.

**Directions:** From Santa Cruz, drive south on Highway 1 for six miles to the Aptos exit. Bear left at the exit, turn right on Soquel Drive, and drive .5 mile. Turn left on Aptos Creek Road. Stop at the entrance kiosk, then continue up the park road and park at Porter Picnic Area. In the winter months, you must park at George's Picnic Area, a mile before Porter Picnic Area, because the park road is gated off at that point.

**Contact:** Forest of Nisene Marks State Park, c/o Sunset State Beach, 201 Sunset Beach Road, Watsonville, CA 95076, 831/763-7063 or 831/429-2850, website: www.parks.ca.gov.

## 4 LOMA PRIETA EPICENTER AND FIVE FINGER FALLS
**4.0–12.0 mi /
2.0 hrs or 1.0 day**

**in Forest of Nisene Marks State Park
near Aptos**

**Map 8.1, page 397**

The destination on this trail is the epicenter of the 1989 Loma Prieta earthquake, but the pleasure of the trip has little to do with its interesting geological history. Instead, the joy is in the scenery, a lush second-growth redwood forest that regenerated after a clear-cut operation at the end of the 19th century. The hike follows Aptos Creek Fire Road, which leads gently uphill (expect plenty of mountain bikers and joggers on the weekends). At 1.5 miles from the Porter Picnic Area, cross a footbridge and descend a bit on the trail until you come to the spot where a large sign once proclaimed the proximity of the earthquake epicenter (the sign was stolen). There's a small bike rack there. Cross the creek and continue up the single-track Aptos Creek Trail for .5 mile to the actual epicenter, where you will see surprisingly little evidence of anything earthshaking, but rather a lovely and peaceful redwood forest. Turn around here for a four-mile round-trip (or six miles if you had to start from George's Picnic Area instead of Porter Picnic Area). If you want to hike more, keep following Aptos Creek Trail from the epicenter as far as you wish.

If you are an intrepid hiker and get an early start, you can follow Aptos Creek Trail a full five miles to Five Finger Falls, one of the least visited waterfalls in the Santa Cruz Mountains. This will make a long, 14-mile day, and it can only be accomplished when the flow is low enough in Aptos Creek to allow for numerous stream crossings. It's a challenging adventure, so it changes the difficulty rating of this hike from a 2 to a 4.

**User Groups:** Hikers and mountain bikes. No dogs or horses. No wheelchair facilities.

**Permits:** No permits are required. A $6 day-use fee is charged per vehicle.

**Maps:** A free map of the Forest of Nisene Marks State Park is available at the entrance kiosk. For topographic maps, ask the USGS for Laurel, Soquel, and Loma Prieta.

**Directions:** From Santa Cruz, drive south on Highway 1 for six miles to the Aptos exit. Bear left at the exit, turn right on Soquel Drive, and drive .5 mile. Turn left on Aptos Creek Road. Stop at the entrance kiosk, continue up the park road, and park at Porter Picnic Area. In the winter months, you must park at George's Picnic Area, a mile before Porter Picnic Area, because the park road is closed at that point.

**Contact:** Forest of Nisene Marks State Park, c/o Sunset State Beach, 201 Sunset Beach Road, Watsonville, CA 95076, 831/763-7063 or 831/429-2850, website: www.parks.ca.gov.

## 5 WEST RIDGE AND APTOS CREEK LOOP

**12.5 mi / 7.0 hrs or 2.0 days**

**in Forest of Nisene Marks State Park near Aptos**

Map 8.1, page 397

The West Ridge and Aptos Creek Loop is the grand tour of the Forest of Nisene Marks State Park, suitable only for hikers in good condition and with a lot of time on their hands. An option is to get reservations for West Ridge Trail Camp and turn this into an overnight trip; the camp is situated conveniently near Sand Point Overlook—a great spot for sunsets. (Backpacking stoves are necessary; no campfires are allowed.) From George's Picnic Area, walk up Aptos Creek Road for .25 mile to the left cutoff for West Ridge Trail, and start climbing uphill along the west ridge of Aptos Canyon. (You can also take Loma Prieta Grade Trail if you prefer. Follow the left side of its loop, then take the connector trail to West Ridge Trail.) Finally you ascend all the way to Hinckley Ridge (at 1,300 feet) and meet up with the fire road that leads to West Ridge Trail Camp and Sand Point Overlook. From the overlook at 1,500 feet, you can see down into the densely forested Bridge Creek drainage and far off across sky-blue Monterey Bay. Finish out the loop with a long downhill walk on Aptos Creek Fire Road, a wide path through dense redwoods and Douglas firs.

**User Groups:** Hikers and mountain bikes. No dogs or horses. No wheelchair facilities.

**Permits:** No permits are required. A $6 day-use fee is charged per vehicle. An advance reservation is necessary to stay overnight at West Ridge Trail Camp; call the park for reservations.

**Maps:** A free map of Forest of Nisene Marks State Park is available at the entrance kiosk.

For topographic maps, ask the USGS for Laurel, Soquel, and Loma Prieta.

**Directions:** From Santa Cruz, drive south on Highway 1 for six miles to the Aptos exit. Bear left at the exit, turn right on Soquel Drive, and drive .5 mile. Turn left on Aptos Creek Road. Stop at the entrance kiosk, continue up the park road, and park at George's Picnic Area.

**Contact:** Forest of Nisene Marks State Park, c/o Sunset State Beach, 201 Sunset Beach Road, Watsonville, CA 95076, 831/763-7063 or 831/429-2850, website: www.parks.ca.gov.

## 6 ELKHORN SLOUGH SOUTH MARSH LOOP
**2.8 mi / 1.5 hrs**

**near Moss Landing**

Map 8.1, page 397

Elkhorn Slough is 2,500 acres of marsh and tidal flats, the precious borderline between sea and land that is home to thousands of species of birds, fish, and invertebrates. It's the second-largest salt marsh in California, and in the peak of the migration season, over 20,000 birds per day congregate here. Hikers with binoculars (and sometimes with just their own eyes) frequently spot golden eagles and peregrine falcons. Endangered clapper rails and least terns are also among the sanctuary's inhabitants. The South Marsh Loop Trail is a three-mile tour of this salty, marshy, bird-filled land, crossing footbridges over the slough and staying close to mudflats and the water's edge. Make sure you take all the short spurs off the loop. A highlight in the spring is walking through the heron rookery, where you may be able to spot tiny great blue heron babies. If you want to walk more, two other loop trails are available.

Special Note: The reserve is open Wednesday through Sunday only. Guided tours are available on Saturday and Sunday.

**User Groups:** Hikers only. No dogs, horses, or mountain bikes. Several boardwalks and overlook areas are wheelchair accessible.

**Permits:** No permits are required. A $2.50 entrance fee is charged per person. Children under 16 and anyone in possession of a California fishing or hunting license can enter free.

**Maps:** A map of Elkhorn Slough is available at the visitors center. For a topographic map, ask the USGS for Moss Landing.

**Directions:** From Highway 1 at Moss Landing, turn east on Dolan Road by the PG&E power station. Drive three miles to Elkhorn Road, turn left (north), and drive two miles to the reserve entrance. The trail begins by the visitors center.

**Contact:** Elkhorn Slough National Estuarine Reserve, 1700 Elkhorn Road, Watsonville, CA 95076, 831/728-2822, website: www.elkhornslough.org.

## 7 FREMONT PEAK TRAIL
**0.6 mi / 0.5 hr**

**in Fremont Peak State Park near San Juan Bautista**

Map 8.1, page 397

Fremont Peak State Park is a small park with a big view. There isn't much of a choice of hiking trails here—just a short, .6-mile trail to the summit of Fremont Peak (elevation 3,169 feet). But that one little trip packs one heck of a punch. Pick a clear day in winter or spring (summer gets brutally hot, and the visibility worsens), make the narrow and winding drive from San Juan Bautista, and prepare for a panorama of Monterey Bay, Santa Cruz, Salinas, Watsonville, Hollister, and the Santa Lucia Mountains. (They say that on the clearest of days you can see the Sierra, but we've never seen it.) From the southwest parking area, walk up the gated, paved service road for a few hundred yards, and then cut off to the right on the signed Peak Trail, which winds its way up the mountain. The last .1 mile is very rocky, and the final summit climb is a bit of a scramble. Ignore the close-by transmitters, and check out the far-off views.

Another popular activity at the park is stargazing. Fremont Peak Observatory is open to the public on some weekends, and rangers hold astronomy programs here.

**User Groups:** Hikers only. No dogs, horses, or mountain bikes. No wheelchair facilities.

**Permits:** No permits are required. A $4 day-use fee is charged per vehicle.

**Maps:** A map of Fremont Peak State Park is available at the information kiosk. For a topographic map, ask the USGS for San Juan Bautista.

**Directions:** From Gilroy, drive south on U.S. 101 for 10 miles to the Highway 156 East/San Juan Bautista exit. Turn east on Highway 156 and drive three miles to San Juan Bautista. Then turn right (south) on the Alameda and then right on San Juan Canyon Road. (It's signed for the state park.) Follow it 11 miles to its end, in Fremont Peak State Park. Park in the southwest parking area.

**Contact:** Fremont Peak State Park, P.O. Box 787, San Juan Bautista, CA 95045, 831/623-4255; Fremont Peak Observatory, website: www.fpoa.net.

## 8 ASILOMAR COAST TRAIL
### 2.4 mi / 1.5 hrs

**in Pacific Grove**

Map 8.1, page 397

Even if you aren't lucky enough to attend a conference at the historic Asilomar Conference Center, you can still walk its adjoining Asilomar Coast Trail, a spectacular 1.2-mile trail along coastal bluffs above rugged, windswept Asilomar Beach. There's plenty to look at and many side trails to explore. You'll see waves crashing against jagged rocks, plentiful tidepools, tiny pocket beaches, wide sandy stretches with big white dunes, and much sea life. Be sure to take the separate boardwalk trail (on the west side of the conference center) that leads across the dunes. Kite flying is also popular along some stretches of Asilomar Beach.

**User Groups:** Hikers and dogs. No horses or mountain bikes. Portions of the trail are wheelchair accessible.

**Permits:** No permits are required. Parking and access are free.

**Maps:** For a topographic map, ask the USGS for Monterey.

**Directions:** From Salinas on U.S. 101, take the Highway 68/Monterey exit and continue into Monterey and then Pacific Grove, where Highway 68 becomes Sunset Drive. Continue to Asilomar State Beach. Park alongside Sunset Drive; the trail begins opposite the conference center.

**Contact:** Asilomar State Beach, 804 Crocker Avenue, Pacific Grove, CA 93950, 831/372-4076, website: www.parks.ca.gov.

## 9 SKYLINE NATURE AND JACKS PEAK TRAILS
### 1.2 mi / 0.5 hr

**in Jacks Peak County Park near Monterey**

Map 8.1, page 397

At 1,068 feet, Jacks Peak is the highest point on the Monterey Peninsula. Hey, it's not the Sierra, but it's high and pretty. The peak and its surrounding park are named after David Jacks, the guy who got his name on Monterey Jack cheese. The Skyline Nature Trail is an easy loop walk around the summit of Jacks Peak, set amid Monterey pines. The Jacks Peak Trail is a smaller loop inside Skyline Nature Trail loop, and you can easily branch off the latter to join the former for a half-hour walk that provides unparalleled views of Carmel Valley, the Monterey Peninsula, Point Lobos, the Santa Lucia Mountains, and the Pacific Ocean. Even though the view is about the same on both trail loops, make sure you walk a leg of Jacks Peak Trail to the top of Jacks Peak, where you can sit on a bench and pull out a picnic of Jack cheese sandwiches. Don't plan on watching the sun set from here, though; unfortunately the park closes before then.

**User Groups:** Hikers and dogs. No horses or mountain bikes. No wheelchair facilities.

**Permits:** No permits are required. A $3 entrance fee is charged per vehicle on weekdays; $4 on weekends and holidays.

**Maps:** A free map of Jacks Peak County Park

is available at the entrance station. For a topographic map, ask the USGS for Seaside.

**Directions:** From Monterey, take Highway 68 east from Highway 1 for 1.7 miles to Olmsted Road. Turn right on Olmsted Road and drive 1.5 miles to Jacks Peak Drive, then follow Jacks Peak Drive to the park entrance. After passing through the entrance kiosk, turn right and drive to the parking area for Jacks Peak.

**Contact:** Jacks Peak County Park, 25020 Jacks Peak Road, Monterey, CA 93940, 831/372-8551, website: www.co.monterey.ca.us/parks.

## 10 OLLASON PEAK
### 7.5 mi / 3.5 hrs

in Toro County Park near Monterey

Map 8.1, page 397

Pick a cool day in spring to take this inspiring jaunt to the top of Ollason Peak (elevation 1,800 feet), far from the madding crowds of popular Toro County Park. Even with a cool breeze, Ollason Trail can be a butt-kicker, with many steep sections over a less-than-smooth route. It leads from the Quail Meadow Group Picnic Area and climbs through wide grasslands and occasional oak groves, most of the time on wide double-track trail. Increasingly wide views and an excellent variety of grassland wildflowers are your reward for the work. After a long stint heading southwest, the trail suddenly veers east, then resumes its southern course for the final climb to Ollason Peak, four miles from the trailhead. You get lovely views toward Monterey Bay and the Central Valley from the summit, plus a set of rugged-looking peaks to the east. Retrace your steps from there or continue a little farther to Coyote Spring Trail, bearing left for a 7.5-mile loop. If you're making the loop, be sure to watch for the left turnoff on Cougar Ridge from Coyote Spring, which returns you to a connector trail back to Quail Meadow.

**User Groups:** Hikers and dogs. Mountain bikes and horses allowed on only a portion of the trail. No wheelchair facilities.

**Permits:** No permits are required. A $4 entrance fee is charged per vehicle on weekdays; $6 on weekends and holidays.

**Maps:** A free map of Toro County Park is available at the entrance station. For a topographic map, ask the USGS for Spreckels.

**Directions:** From Monterey, take Highway 68 east from Highway 1 for 13 miles to the Portola Drive exit. Turn right into the Toro County Park entrance road. Drive .5 mile past the entrance kiosk to the parking area by Quail Meadow Group Picnic Area.

**Contact:** Toro County Park, 501 Monterey Highway, Salinas, CA 93908, 831/484-1108, website: www.co.monterey.ca.us/parks.

## 11 SEA LION POINT TRAIL
### 0.6 mi / 0.5 hr

in Point Lobos State Reserve near Carmel

Map 8.1, page 397

On summer weekends, the cars are parked in a long line along the road outside Point Lobos State Reserve, one of the crown jewels of the state park system. Even on weekdays, the parking lots are surprisingly full here, but the park's stunning coastal beauty and plentiful wildlife explain why. One of the biggest attractions at the park is Sea Lion Point Trail, a round-trip loop of just over .5 mile, part of which is suitable for wheelchairs. Along the way you can look for cute little sea otters floating on their backs in the kelp and chubby harbor seals hauling out on the rocks. When the trail reaches a rocky staircase, wheelchair users will have to turn back, but other visitors can continue down to a lower trail. Rocks jut out of the breakers just offshore; these are named Sea Lion Rocks for obvious reasons. Test your hiking partner's literary knowledge with this fact: Robert Louis Stevenson used Point Lobos as the inspiration for his novel *Treasure Island.*

**User Groups:** Hikers and wheelchairs. No dogs, horses, or mountain bikes. Part of the trail is wheelchair accessible.

**Permits:** No permits are required. An $8 day-use fee is charged per vehicle.

**Maps:** A map of Point Lobos State Reserve is available for $1 at the entrance station. For a topographic map, ask the USGS for Monterey.

**Directions:** From Carmel at Rio Road, drive south on Highway 1 for three miles to the entrance to Point Lobos State Reserve, on the right. Turn right and drive through the entrance kiosk, and continue straight to the information station and Sea Lion Point parking area.

**Contact:** Point Lobos State Reserve, Route 1, Box 62, Carmel, CA 93923, 831/624-4909, website: www.pointlobos.org.

## 12 WHALER'S KNOLL AND CYPRESS GROVE
4.0 mi / 2.0 hrs

**in Point Lobos State Reserve near Carmel**

Map 8.1, page 397

Two excellent trails lead from the north side of the Sea Lion Point parking area near the information station at Point Lobos, and you can connect them to make a stellar four-mile round-trip. Start by hiking on Cypress Grove Trail, which shows off the park's Monterey cypress trees, one of only two remaining native Monterey cypress groves on earth. In addition to getting a look at the marvelous windswept trees, you walk through coastal scrub to rocky cliffs with picture-perfect ocean views. The trail loops around and heads back toward the parking area, but just before you reach it, you can turn left on North Shore Trail and climb a bit to the right turnoff for Whaler's Knoll Trail. Whaler's Knoll Trail makes loose switchbacks uphill to the top of Whaler's Knoll, where you get the best view in the whole park. Luckily there's a bench there, so you can sit down, catch your breath, and enjoy it. The knoll was where early-20th-century whalers would watch for whales, then hang a signal flag when they spotted them. You can continue hiking from there, heading downhill and making a loop along the coast on North Shore Trail.

**User Groups:** Hikers only. No dogs, horses, or mountain bikes. No wheelchair facilities.

**Permits:** No permits are required. An $8 day-use fee is charged per vehicle.

**Maps:** A map of Point Lobos State Reserve is available for $1 at the entrance station. For a topographic map, ask the USGS for Monterey.

**Directions:** From Carmel at Rio Road, drive south on Highway 1 for three miles to the entrance to Point Lobos State Reserve on the right. Turn right and drive through the entrance kiosk and continue straight to the information station and Sea Lion Point parking area.

**Contact:** Point Lobos State Reserve, Route 1, Box 62, Carmel, CA 93923, 831/624-4909, website: www.pointlobos.org.

## 13 POINT LOBOS PERIMETER
6.0 mi / 3.0 hrs

**in Point Lobos State Reserve near Carmel**

Map 8.1, page 397

 The perimeter hike at Point Lobos connects a number of trails to view the best highlights of the park. Make sure you get a park map at the entrance station before hiking so you can scope out the many side-trip options that are possible (and the many shortcuts if you're getting tired). Starting from the Sea Lion Point parking area, make your first destination Sea Lion Point. Then bear left on Sand Hill Trail and connect to South Shore Trail. The latter leads along the quieter, south part of the park, past numerous spectacular beaches and coves, to Bird Island Trail. Make sure you take the short side path to Bird Island Overlook, then maybe walk the stairs down to the sandy beaches at China Cove and Gibson Beach. (China Cove is one of the most beautiful spots on earth, in our opinion.) From Bird Island Trail, connect with South Plateau Trail, follow it northward, cross the park road to follow Carmelo Meadow Trail, and bear right for a side trip to Granite Point. Don't miss this; it's a rocky outcrop on a short loop trail with great views toward Carmel to the north. Then retrace your steps along Granite Point Trail and finish out your loop by hiking along the park's northern shoreline, following Granite Point Trail to Cabin Trail to North Shore Trail. Possible side trips are to Whaler's Cabin Museum, to a lookout of Guillemot Island and its millions of birds (from a spur trail), or to Whaler's Knoll and Cypress Grove. If you take all of the possible side trips along the route, this hike will take you almost all day—and what a fine day it will be.

**User Groups:** Hikers only. No dogs, horses, or mountain bikes. No wheelchair facilities.

**Permits:** No permits are required. An $8 day-use fee is charged per vehicle.

**Maps:** A map of Point Lobos State Reserve is available for $1 at the entrance station. For a topographic map, ask the USGS for Monterey.

**Directions:** From Carmel at Rio Road, drive south on Highway 1 for three miles to the entrance to Point Lobos State Reserve on the right. Turn right and drive through the entrance kiosk; continue straight to the information station and Sea Lion Point parking area.

**Contact:** Point Lobos State Reserve, Route 1, Box 62, Carmel, CA 93923, 831/624-4909, website: www.pointlobos.org.

## 14 ROCKY RIDGE AND SOBERANES CANYON LOOP
6.0 mi / 3.0 hrs

**in Garrapata State Park south of Carmel**

Map 8.1, page 397

Garrapata State Park is situated on both sides of Highway 1, with some trails leading to the ocean and others leading up inland canyons and hillsides. Hikers looking for a long, leg-stretching walk will enjoy this loop trip on the inland side of the park, which travels through a remarkable variety of terrain.

Begin hiking on Soberanes Canyon Trail. What starts out as a ranch road through cactus- and chaparral-covered hillsides quickly becomes single-track trail through an increasingly narrow and wet canyon. The big surprise is a gorgeous stand of redwoods along Soberanes Creek, an extreme contrast to the chaparral

and cacti at the start of the trail. The grove is a good turnaround spot for those looking for a shorter trip. If you continue on, the trail makes a substantial climb with few switchbacks and heads north to a right-hand spur to Peak Trail (also signed as North Ridge Trail) and an intersection with Rocky Ridge Trail. Forget the spur and finish out your loop on Rocky Ridge Trail, where on a clear day you can look out over the ocean for miles. The trail then winds back down the hillsides and deposits you back at your car on Highway 1. Note that the ideal time to hike this trail is in spring; the profusion of wildflowers in the high grassy hills will dazzle you.

**User Groups:** Hikers only. No dogs, horses, or mountain bikes. No wheelchair facilities.

**Permits:** No permits are required. Parking and access are free.

**Maps:** For a topographic map, ask the USGS for Soberanes Point.

**Directions:** From Carmel at Rio Road, drive south on Highway 1 for seven miles to marker 13 and the dirt pullouts along the highway at Garrapata State Park. It's four miles south of Point Lobos State Park and easy to miss; go slowly and watch for cars parked alongside the road. The Soberanes Canyon Trail begins on the east side of the road.

**Contact:** Garrapata State Park, c/o Big Sur Station, Highway 1, Big Sur, CA 93920, 831/667-2315 or 831/649-2836, website: www.parks.ca.gov.

## 15 SOBERANES POINT TRAIL
2.0 mi / 1.0 hr

**in Garrapata State Park south of Carmel**

Map 8.1, page 397

You can access Soberanes Point Trail from three different gates along Highway 1, so if you miss marker 13, you can always stop at markers 15 or 16. Wherever you begin, you'll end up on a spectacular and easy set of trails that joins in a series of loops around Soberanes Point, all basically around Whale Peak. If you time your trip at low tide, you'll have access to some excellent tidepools, and even if not, you have views of rocky shoreline bluffs and plenty of birdlife and other animals. Many anglers try their luck rock fishing here at the point, and it's also a popular spot for whale-watching from November to January. Note that if you start from marker 13, you can hike a short loop to your right and then a much larger loop to your left. If you start from marker 15, you're at the middle of the larger loop, so you can start hiking either right or left. Just wander as you please; the coastline and the perimeter of the point make it impossible to get lost.

**User Groups:** Hikers only. No dogs, horses, or mountain bikes. No wheelchair facilities.

**Permits:** No permits are required. Parking and access are free.

**Maps:** For a topographic map, ask the USGS for Soberanes Point.

**Directions:** From Carmel at Rio Road, drive south on Highway 1 for seven miles to marker 13 and the dirt pullouts along the highway at Garrapata State Park. It's four miles south of Point Lobos State Park and easy to miss; go slowly and watch for cars parked alongside the road. The Soberanes Point Trail begins on the east side of the road.

**Contact:** Garrapata State Park, c/o Big Sur Station, Highway 1, Big Sur, CA 93920, 831/667-2315 or 831/649-2836, website: www.parks.ca.gov.

### 16 LUPINE, WATERFALL, AND MESA LOOP
3.0 mi / 1.5 hrs

in Garland Ranch Regional Park
near Carmel

Map 8.1, page 397

Garland Ranch's excellent visitors center is the perfect place to begin your trip to the park. Take a look inside, get a trail map, and learn a few things about the area's animals, trees, and wildflowers. The center is also the trailhead for this combined loop on Lupine, Waterfall, and Mesa Trails. Although the park's waterfall only flows during the rainy season,

the trails are good to walk year-round, and they're well maintained and well signed to boot. Begin by heading to the left (northwest) from the visitors center on Lupine Loop, which travels along the open, flat floodplains of the Carmel River. In .5 mile, leave the loop and continue straight on the Waterfall Trail, then climb through a more shady area to the rocky cliff where the waterfall sometimes falls. Beyond it, you'll ascend more seriously, following a few switchbacks to the mesa, a large high meadow with views of Carmel Valley and beyond. Follow Mesa Trail back downhill to the other side of the Lupine Loop and take the Lupine Loop back to the visitors center. Expect an excellent wildflower show in the grasslands in springtime.

**User Groups:** Hikers, dogs, and horses. No mountain bikes. No wheelchair facilities.

**Permits:** No permits are required. Parking and access are free.

**Maps:** A free map of Garland Ranch Regional Park is available at the visitors center. For topographic maps, ask the USGS for Mount Carmel and Carmel Valley.

**Directions:** From Highway 1 at Carmel, turn east on Carmel Valley Road. Drive 8.6 miles on Carmel Valley Road to the Garland Ranch parking area, on the right side of the road. Walk across the river bridge to get to the visitors center and trailheads.

**Contact:** Garland Ranch Regional Park, P.O. Box 935, Carmel Valley, CA 93924, 831/659-6065 or 831/372-3196, website: www.mprpd.org.

### 17 SNIVLEY'S RIDGE TRAIL
5.6 mi / 3.0 hrs

in Garland Ranch Regional Park
near Carmel

Map 8.1, page 397

If it's winter or spring, a trip to the top of Snivley's Ridge could be just what you need to keep your hiking legs in shape. It's a healthy, 1,600-foot climb up to the ridge, plus a 250-foot climb to get to the ridge's highest point, so be prepared to pant a little. Much of the walk is exposed; be sure to bring water, and pick a cool day to hike the trail. From the visitors center, set out on either side of Lupine Loop (heading left is a little shorter), and continue uphill on Mesa Trail to its junction with Fern Trail. This stretch is moist and shady, so enjoy it while you're in it. Follow Fern Trail, turn left and quickly right on Sky Trail, and begin the serious portion of the climb. Well-graded switchbacks make it easier. Many people stop where Sky Trail meets Snivley's Ridge Trail, at a bench with a panoramic view of Carmel Valley, the forested Santa Lucia Mountains, and the ocean. But those determined to go as high as possible should turn right on Snivley's Ridge, walk another .5 mile, and turn left on a spur trail that leads to the park's highest point, at 2,038 feet.

**User Groups:** Hikers, dogs, and horses. No mountain bikes. No wheelchair facilities.

**Permits:** No permits are required. Parking and access are free.

**Maps:** A free map of Garland Ranch Regional Park is available at the visitors center. For topographic maps, ask the USGS for Mount Carmel and Carmel Valley.

**Directions:** From Highway 1 at Carmel, turn east on Carmel Valley Road. Drive 8.6 miles on Carmel Valley Road to the Garland Ranch parking area, on the right side of the road. Walk across the river bridge to get to the visitors center and trailheads.

**Contact:** Garland Ranch Regional Park, P.O. Box 935, Carmel Valley, CA 93924, 831/659-6065 or 831/372-3196, website: www.mprpd.org.

# 🔳 CONDOR GULCH AND HIGH PEAKS LOOP

**5.0 mi / 2.5 hrs**

**in Pinnacles National Monument near Soledad**

Map 8.1, page 397

The Condor Gulch Trail begins across the road from the Bear Gulch Visitors Center, and it's a good 30-minute climb up the hill on a smooth, switchback trail to an overlook of High Peaks. The scent of wild sage and rosemary is entic-

ingly aromatic along the route, and your eyes are continually drawn to the colorful lichen growing on equally colorful rocks. The overlook is just a piped railing on a ledge above a huge boulder, but it's a good spot to get your bearings and look out over the trail you just climbed. It's also a good turnaround spot if you don't want to go farther. If you do, continue uphill to a junction with High Peaks Trail (at 1.7 miles) and turn left. In just over a half mile, you'll reach a junction with the Tunnel Trail. (People afraid of heights should consider taking the Tunnel Trail downhill. They can then turn left on the Juniper Canyon Trail to meet up with their fellow hikers at a bench and an overlook area at the junction of Juniper Canyon Trail and High Peaks Trail.) Those willing for the adventure should continue on High Peaks Trail through narrow passageways and over and under steep rock formations. In many places, the trail has been blasted into the rock, and the steep drop-offs can be dizzying. Use the handholds and guard rails. After .7 mile, you'll reach the intersection with Juniper Canyon Trail, where there is a bench, a fine view to the west, and a restroom. Take advantage of any or all of these, then turn left to stay on High Peaks Trail and head back to Bear Gulch. You'll have to walk down Moses Spring Trail a short distance to get back to your car.

**User Groups:** Hikers only. No dogs, horses, or mountain bikes. No wheelchair facilities.

**Permits:** No permits are required. There is a $5 per vehicle entrance fee, good for seven days, at Pinnacles National Monument.

**Maps:** A free map of Pinnacles National Monument is available at the visitors center. For topographic maps, ask the USGS for Bickmore Canyon and North Chalone Peak.

**Directions:** From King City on U.S. 101, take the First Street exit and head east. First Street turns into Highway G13/Bitterwater Road. Follow it for 15 miles to Highway 25, where you turn left (north). Follow Highway 25 for 14 miles to Highway 146. Turn left on Highway 146 and drive 4.8 miles to the park visitors center. The trailhead for the Condor Gulch Trail is across the road from the visitors center.

Alternatively, from Gilroy, drive south on U.S. 101 for two miles and take the Highway 25 exit. Drive south on Highway 25 for 43 miles to Highway 146. Turn right on Highway 146 and drive 4.8 miles to the park visitors center. **Contact:** Pinnacles National Monument, 5000 Highway 146, Paicines, CA 95043, 831/389-4485, website: www.nps.gov/pinn.

## 19 NORTH CHALONE PEAK
### 8.4 mi / 4.0 hrs

**in Pinnacles National Monument near Soledad**

Map 8.1, page 397

Sure, the High Peaks at Pinnacles National Monument are high—about 2,700 feet. But if you want to go higher and get a better look around, take this hike to North Chalone Peak. It's in the southern area of the park at 3,304 feet in elevation, and it has a closed fire lookout tower on its summit. It's a great place to take in the view and enjoy some peace and quiet—this trail is much less traveled than the popular High Peaks Loop.

Take Moses Spring Trail from the visitors center parking lot, and then climb the stairsteps up to Bear Gulch Reservoir. Turn left on the signed trail for North Chalone Peak, skirting the edge of the reservoir and admiring the ubiquitous rock climbers who are busy doing their thing on the cliff faces. Once you're past the reservoir, you're only one mile from the visitors center, but you've left the vast majority of people behind. Enjoy the fascinating volcanic rock formations and spring wildflowers on the next stretch of trail. At 3.5 miles, you'll reach a gate; go through it, follow the trail uphill, then pass through a second gate and join the fire road to the summit. The final .75 mile is the steepest stretch of the whole trip, but the reward at the top is a fine view of the Salinas River curving through its valley, the Santa Lucia Mountains, and all of Pinnacles. On very rare, crystal-clear days, you can see all the way to the Pacific Ocean.

**User Groups:** Hikers only. No dogs, horses, or mountain bikes. No wheelchair facilities.
**Permits:** No permits are required. There is a $5 per vehicle entrance fee at Pinnacles National Monument, good for seven days.
**Maps:** A free map of Pinnacles National Monument is available at the visitors center. For topographic maps, ask the USGS for Bickmore Canyon and North Chalone Peak.
**Directions:** From King City on U.S. 101, take the First Street exit and head east. First Street turns into Highway G13/Bitterwater Road. Follow it for 15 miles to Highway 25, where you turn left (north). Follow Highway 25 for 14 miles to Highway 146. Go left on Highway 146 and drive 4.8 miles to the park visitors center; continue beyond it to the parking lot at the end of the road. If this lot is full, park by the visitors center and walk down the road to the trailhead.

Alternatively, from Gilroy, drive south on U.S. 101 for two miles and take the Highway 25 exit. Drive south on Highway 25 for 43 miles to Highway 146. Turn right on Highway 146 and drive 4.8 miles to the park visitors center. **Contact:** Pinnacles National Monument, 5000 Highway 146, Paicines, CA 95043, 831/389-4485, website: www.nps.gov/pinn.

## 20 BALCONIES CAVES
### 2.4 mi / 1.5 hrs

**in Pinnacles National Monument near Soledad**

Map 8.1, page 397

Pinnacles National Monument has two famous sets of caves: the Bear Gulch Caves, on the east side of the park; and the Balconies Caves, on the west. Access to the Bear Gulch Caves is often totally or partially restricted in order to protect the resident nesting bats, but the Balconies Caves are always open to visitors and are tons of fun. Got your flashlight? Okay; then set off on the Balconies Trail, following the often dry west fork of Chalone Creek. A mere .6 mile brings you to some huge, colorful, lichen-covered volcanic rocks—a preview of the caves to come. The sounds of the wind in the gray pines and the scurrying of squirrels keep you company. At the fork with the Balconies Cliffs Trail, turn right to enter the caves. Turn on your flashlight for some good clean fun and adventure—squeezing through clefts in the rock, ducking under ledges, and climbing down rocky staircases. When you exit the caves, you can turn left and loop back to the parking area on the Balconies Cliffs Trail, gaining many lovely views of the park's rocky landscape as you climb over the top of the caves.

**User Groups:** Hikers only. No dogs, horses, or mountain bikes. No wheelchair facilities.

**Permits:** No permits are required. There is a $5 per vehicle entrance fee at Pinnacles National Monument, good for seven days.

**Maps:** A free map of Pinnacles National Monument is available at the ranger station. For topographic maps, ask the USGS for Bickmore Canyon and North Chalone Peak.

**Directions:** From Salinas, drive south on U.S. 101 for 22 miles to Soledad, and take the Soledad/Highway 146 exit. Drive east on Highway 146 for 12 miles. (The road is signed for West Pinnacles.) Highway 146 dead-ends at the Chaparral Ranger Station and trailhead parking lot.

**Contact:** Pinnacles National Monument, 5000 Highway 146, Paicines, CA 95043, 831/389-4485, website: www.nps.gov/pinn.

## 21 JUNIPER CANYON AND HIGH PEAKS LOOP

**8.4 mi / 5.0 hrs**

in **Pinnacles National Monument** near **Soledad**

Map 8.1, page 397

Pinnacles National Monument is a hiker's park. The first clue you get is that no road connects the east and west sides of the park, so the only way to get from one side to the other is to walk. And that's just fine, especially since the park's first-rate trail system makes it possible to string together a loop tour around the park on the Juniper Canyon Trail, High Peaks Trail, Old

Pinnacles Trail, and Balconies Trail. If you follow the trails in this order, you get almost all your climbing done in the first half of the trip and then have a fairly easy and flat homestretch.

Begin hiking from the right side of the large parking lot near the Chaparral Ranger Station, following Juniper Canyon Trail from grasslands into the rocky hills. The trail gets steeper as you go, but it's well built and has many switchbacks. Ignore the Tunnel Trail turnoff at 1.2 miles, and keep climbing to the junction with High Peaks Trail, at 1.8 miles. Here, at a saddle, are fine views to the west and east, as well as a bench and restroom. The High Peaks Trail goes both north and southeast. Turn north (left) and prepare yourself for the most exciting part of the trip: a narrow and exciting stretch of trail with many handholds and footholds carved into the rock. Continue on the High Peaks Trail for 3.3 miles all the way to the Chalone Creek Picnic Area. There you can fill up your water bottles, take a rest, and then head north on the Old Pinnacles Trail, a pleasant route that meanders along the west fork of Chalone Creek. In winter, the creek even has water in it, and spring wildflowers are tremendous. In 2.3 miles, you'll reach a fork for the Balconies Trail, and if you've never been to Balconies Caves, take the left fork, which leads you through them. (The right fork climbs above the caves, and offers some excellent views.) After ducking your head and bending your knees a lot as you wander through the caves, you'll come out to an easy and flat section of the Balconies Trail, which brings you right back to the Chaparral Ranger Station and trailhead parking lot. If you pick a cool day and carry plenty of water, this is a stellar long-day hike in Pinnacles.

**User Groups:** Hikers only. No dogs, horses, or mountain bikes. No wheelchair facilities.

**Permits:** No permits are required. There is a $5 per vehicle entrance fee at Pinnacles National Monument, good for seven days.

**Maps:** A free map of Pinnacles National Monument is available at the ranger station. For topographic maps, ask the USGS for Bickmore Canyon and North Chalone Peak.

**Directions:** From Salinas, drive south on U.S. 101 for 22 miles to Soledad and take the Soledad/Highway 146 exit. Drive east on Highway 146 for 12 miles. The road is signed for West Pinnacles. Highway 146 dead-ends at the Chaparral Ranger Station and trailhead parking lot.

**Contact:** Pinnacles National Monument, 5000 Highway 146, Paicines, CA 95043, 831/389-4485, website: www.nps.gov/pinn.

## 22 SKINNER RIDGE TRAIL TO DEVILS PEAK
### 7.6 mi / 3.5 hrs or 2.0 days  🥾 ◢8

**in the Ventana Wilderness near Carmel Valley**

Map 8.1, page 397

What's the best thing about this trip? The far-off ocean views in the first mile of the climb? The white marble of giant Pico Blanco to the southwest? The colors of the oak leaves in autumn? The huge old madrone trees that pepper Skinner Ridge? It's hard to decide; you'd better go see for yourself. Pick a cool and clear day to make the trip, preferably in autumn, or arm yourself with a ton of sunscreen and water in summer. The trailhead is at 2,000 feet, and the initial climb is through chaparral, with many open views. Then the trail enters the trees (madrones and oaks) and twists its way to a short, steep ascent to the top of Skinner Ridge, at 3,450 feet and 2.1 miles out. A wide bulldozer line runs up the ridge, left from the huge Marble Cone fire of the 1970s. From the ridge, backpackers usually continue down the other side for .75 mile to a trail junction for Turner Creek. Apple Tree Camp is a left turn and one mile away—a good place for an overnight. Day hikers should proceed straight ahead at that junction for the climb to Devils Peak, elevation 4,158 feet, and one mile farther. That final mile will get you huffing and puffing for sure, but hey, exercise is good for you, right?

**User Groups:** Hikers, dogs, and horses. No mountain bikes. No wheelchair facilities.

**Permits:** No day hiking permits are required. A national forest recreation pass is required for each vehicle; fees are $5 for one day, or $30 for a year. If you don't have a recreation pass, you can pay $5 at the trailhead parking lot.

**Maps:** For a map, ask the U.S. Forest Service for Los Padres National Forest or Ventana Wilderness. For topographic maps, ask the USGS for Mount Carmel and Big Sur.

**Directions:** From Carmel, drive south on Highway 1 for 12 miles, past Garrapata State Park, to the left (east) turnoff for Palo Colorado Road, south of Rocky Point Restaurant. Turn left and drive eight miles to Bottcher's Gap Campground. The Skinner Ridge Trail begins at the edge of the parking lot.

**Contact:** Big Sur Station, Highway 1, Big Sur, CA 93920, 831/667-2315 or 831/649-2836; Los Padres National Forest, Monterey Ranger District, 406 South Mildred Avenue, King City, CA 93930, 831/385-5434, website: www.fs.fed.us/r5/lospadres.

## 23 MOLERA POINT TRAIL
### 2.5 mi / 1.5 hrs  🥾 ◢9

**in Andrew Molera State Park north of Big Sur**

Map 8.1, page 397

Andrew Molera is a low-key state park without all the development and fanfare that often come with state park status. But the park has plenty to offer for hikers and coast lovers. An easy trail leads from the park's main parking lot to Molera Point, where you can look down on spectacular Molera Beach and count the sea lions lying on the rocks. To reach the point, take the trail from the right side of the main parking lot, signed for the campground (not the main trail to the beach, which starts with a bridge crossing). Molera Point Trail stays on the north side of the Big Sur River and winds past the park's walk-in camp, set in a wide meadow, and historic Cooper Cabin, which was built in 1861 and is the oldest structure on the Big Sur coast. At the river's mouth, the trail forks to the right, heading out to Molera Point. Check out the view from this often windswept promontory; then if the tide is low, go play on the beach at the river's edge before heading back.

**User Groups:** Hikers, dogs, and horses. No mountain bikes. No wheelchair facilities.

**Permits:** No permits are required. An $8 day-use fee is charged per vehicle.

**Maps:** A map of Andrew Molera State Park is available at the entrance station. For a topographic map, ask the USGS for Big Sur.

**Directions:** From Carmel, drive 22 miles south on Highway 1 to Andrew Molera State Park's main entrance, on the west side of the highway. Trails begin at the parking lot. The park is two miles north of Big Sur.

**Contact:** Andrew Molera State Park, c/o Big Sur Station, Highway 1, Big Sur, CA 93920, 831/667-2315 or 831/649-2836, website: www.parks.ca.gov.

## 24 MOLERA STATE PARK LOOP
**8.0 mi / 4.0 hrs**

in Andrew Molera State Park north of Big Sur

Map 8.1, page 397

This big loop around the western side of Andrew Molera State Park is easiest in summer, when the footbridge is in place over the Big Sur River. If the bridge isn't there, you must take off your shoes and socks and suffer through a very cold ford over smooth, rounded rocks. But this trail is worth the effort. It offers several miles of lovely ocean vistas, plus a visit to a remote beach. Start by taking the path from the west side of the parking lot and immediately crossing the river. In a few minutes of walking, you'll leave the crowds behind as you turn left (south) on River Trail, then in less than a mile, turn right on single-track Hidden Trail. Enjoy a heart-pumping climb through forest and meadows up to Ridge Trail, where you turn left and hike southward, paralleling the ocean. Ridge Trail is a wide fire road and rolls gently, still heading generally uphill. In addition to the ocean vistas to the west, you also have fine views inland of Big Sur's rugged peaks,

and you pass through a small, surprising grove of redwood trees.

At 3.5 miles, Ridge Trail meets Panorama Trail at a bench and overlook point. Turn right and start to switchback steeply downhill toward the ocean, enjoying more wide views all the way. Spring wildflowers are lovely along the open hillsides. As you near the coast, you'll reach a junction with Spring Trail. Turn left for a few hundred feet to a lovely, driftwood-laden beach. This makes a perfect lunch stop, provided the wind isn't howling. A fascinating log jam at the beach's entrance makes great photographs. For your return, follow Bluffs Trail 2.5 miles back to Molera Beach. This is the most lovely stretch of the entire loop, offering long and beautiful looks at Molera Point and beach and Point Sur Light Station. Finally, take the trail from Molera Beach back to the parking lot. Wow, what a perfect Big Sur day.

**User Groups:** Hikers, dogs, and horses. Mountain bikes are allowed on Ridge Trail and part of Bluffs Trail only. No wheelchair facilities.

**Permits:** No permits are required. An $8 day-use fee is charged per vehicle.

**Maps:** A map of Andrew Molera State Park is available at the entrance station. For a topographic map, ask the USGS for Big Sur.

**Directions:** From Carmel, drive 22 miles south on Highway 1 to Andrew Molera State Park's main entrance, on the west side of the highway. Trails begin at the parking lot. (The park is two miles north of Big Sur.)

**Contact:** Andrew Molera State Park, c/o Big Sur Station, Highway 1, Big Sur, CA 93920, 831/667-2315 or 831/649-2836, website: www.parks.ca.gov.

## 25 PFEIFFER FALLS AND VALLEY VIEW LOOP
**1.6 mi / 1.0 hr**

in Pfeiffer Big Sur State Park near Big Sur

Map 8.1, page 397

A loop hike to a 60-foot waterfall and an overlook of the Big Sur Valley? Sounds great; let's go. And don't forget, there's a gorgeous red-wood forest along the way. You get all of this when you set out on the Pfeiffer Falls Trail from the nature center at Pfeiffer Big Sur State Park and return on the Valley View Trail. After a slightly uphill walk on the Pfeiffer Falls Trail along Pfeiffer Redwood Creek (ignore all the trail junctions and stay along the creek, crossing it a couple of times on bridges), you'll wind up at the foot of tall and narrow Pfeiffer Falls, which stream down a vertical, dark rock face. You can sit for a while at the waterfall's viewing platform, then backtrack along the trail .1 mile to its junction with the Valley View Trail. Follow Valley View Trail as it climbs up and out of the canyon. You'll leave the redwoods almost immediately and hike in an oak forest for .5 mile. Look for the brilliant blooms of Douglas iris in the spring. The trail reaches an overlook of the Big Sur Valley and Point Sur. Unfortunately, the sight of Highway 1 somewhat diminishes the beauty of the view. Head back down Valley View Trail and take the right fork (.25 mile from the overlook) to finish out your loop. This last downhill stretch is on the steep side, so wear a good pair of boots.

**User Groups:** Hikers only. No dogs, horses, or mountain bikes. No wheelchair facilities.

**Permits:** No permits are required. An $8 day-use fee is charged per vehicle.

**Maps:** A map of Pfeiffer Big Sur State Park is available at the entrance station. For a topographic map, ask the USGS for Big Sur.

**Directions:** From Carmel, drive 26 miles south on Highway 1 to Pfeiffer Big Sur State Park, on the east side of the highway. It's two miles south of Big Sur. Drive through the entrance kiosk, turn left at the lodge, and then turn right, following the signs to Pfeiffer Falls trailhead and the nature center. Park just beyond the nature center. The trail is on the left side of the lot, signed as Oak Grove Trail, Valley View Trail, and Pfeiffer Falls Trail. If the small parking lot is full, you may have to park by the lodge and walk to the trailhead.

**Contact:** Big Sur Station, Highway 1, Big Sur,

CA 93920, 831/667-2315 or 831/649-2836; Los Padres National Forest, Monterey Ranger District, 406 South Mildred Avenue, King City, CA 93930, 831/385-5434, website: www.fs.fed.us/r5/lospadres.

## 26 MOUNT MANUEL
**9.0 mi / 5.0 hrs**

**on the southern edge of the Ventana Wilderness near Big Sur**

Map 8.1, page 397

This trail leads to one of the best vantage points in the Ventana Wilderness—the summit of Manuel Peak, where all of Big Sur, the Santa Lucia Mountains, and the Pacific Ocean are spread out before you—but it starts out by the softball field at Pfeiffer Big Sur State Park. You might say this is a good example of the expression "from one extreme to the other." Over its 4.5-mile length, the route climbs 3,100 feet to Mount Manuel's summit, at 3,379 feet in elevation, so make sure you have fresh soles on your boots and plenty of water. Pick a cool day to make the climb, because although the trail starts in the trees, the vast majority of the route is shadeless. Winter or spring are usually ideal.

Negotiate your way through a half-mile series of signed state park trails to access the official start of the Mount Manuel Trail. You'll enter Los Padres National Forest and head in to a long series of switchbacks over chaparral-covered slopes. These quickly provide views of the Big Sur River canyon and the coast. About three miles from the start, the trail enters a forest of tan oaks, madrones, and redwoods, then exits it again, returning to the chaparral. Finally you near the summit—rather, a series of summits. Head for the highest point, where the view is no disappointment. Time to pull out your sandwich and contemplate the vastness of the Pacific Ocean and the wonders of the Ventana Wilderness.

**User Groups:** Hikers only. No dogs, horses, or mountain bikes. No wheelchair facilities.

**Permits:** No day hiking permits are required. An $8 day-use fee is charged per vehicle.

**Maps:** For a map, ask the U.S. Forest Service for Los Padres National Forest or Ventana Wilderness. For topographic maps, ask the USGS for Pfeiffer Point and Big Sur.

**Directions:** From Carmel, drive 26 miles south on Highway 1 to Pfeiffer Big Sur State Park, on the east side of the highway. It's two miles south of Big Sur. Drive through the entrance kiosk and continue straight past the campfire center to the parking lot near the picnic areas and softball field. The trailhead is signed for Oak Grove Trail and Mount Manuel.

**Contact:** Big Sur Station, Highway 1, Big Sur, CA 93920, 831/667-2315 or 831/649-2836, website: www.parks.ca.gov.

## 27 BUZZARDS ROOST OVERLOOK
### 4.0 mi / 2.0 hrs

**in Pfeiffer Big Sur State Park near Big Sur**

Map 8.1, page 397

Hikers looking for a bit of a challenge in Pfeiffer Big Sur State Park will want to try out this trail to the Buzzards Roost Overlook. Compared to the Pfeiffer Falls Trail, this trail gets surprisingly little traffic, unless there are large groups camping at the nearby group campground. The trail leads along the Big Sur River through a forest of many splendid redwoods, switches back uphill onto slopes filled with oaks and bays, and finally climbs into chaparral country. You get to walk in every kind of Big Sur terrain. High up on Pfeiffer Ridge, there's a 360-degree view of the Pacific Ocean, the Big Sur River gorge, and the Santa Lucia Mountains, providing a fine reward for your effort in climbing here. The trailhead is at 200 feet in elevation, and the overlook is at nearly 1,000 feet.

**User Groups:** Hikers only. No dogs, horses, or mountain bikes. No wheelchair facilities.

**Permits:** No permits are required. An $8 day-use fee is charged per vehicle.

**Maps:** A map of Pfeiffer Big Sur State Park

is available at the entrance station. For topographic maps, ask the USGS for Big Sur and Pfeiffer Point.

**Directions:** From Carmel, drive 26 miles south on Highway 1 to Pfeiffer Big Sur State Park, on the east side of the highway. It's two miles south of Big Sur. Drive through the entrance kiosk, go past the lodge, and turn right to cross the bridge over the Big Sur River. A parking area is on the left side of the road. The Buzzards Roost trailhead is signed.

**Contact:** Pfeiffer Big Sur State Park, c/o Big Sur Station, Highway 1, Big Sur, CA 93920, 831/667-2315 or 831/649-2836, website: www.parks.ca.gov.

## 28 SYKES HOT SPRINGS
### 20.0 mi / 2.0 days

**in the Ventana Wilderness near Big Sur**

Map 8.1, page 397

The trip to Sykes Hot Springs is one that just about every California backpacker takes at one time or another. This is a quintessential Big Sur/Ventana Wilderness trip, with deep swimming holes, three hot springs pools, and plenty of coastal mountain scenery. And yes, it's incredibly popular, so plan your trip for the off-season if possible. Fall or winter are beautiful times to visit, and if you go on a weekday, you might just get the hot springs all to yourself. The first four miles of trail will have you huffing and puffing through shadeless switchbacks, with only occasional breaks as the path travels through small redwood groves. Hang on, because the route eventually levels and gets much easier. At a junction just past the four-mile mark, the left trail leads to Ventana Camp, one mile farther. This camp, with nearby swimming holes on Ventana Creek, makes a great overnight for people who have gotten a late start. If it's still early, continue straight. At 5.4 miles, you pass Terrace Creek Camp, another option for spending the night. At seven miles, you reach the Big Sur River for the first time, and another camp at Barlow Flat. You'll cross the river at 9.7 miles and head for Sykes Camp and the hot springs. Note that after a period of rain, this can be a difficult or even impossible ford, so if you plan to hike in the wet season, check on conditions before setting out. The hot springs are less than a quarter mile from the camp. Depending on current conditions, two or three pools are terraced along the Big Sur River. The largest of the group is 10 feet long and gracefully sheltered by a large boulder. It averages 100 degrees, although the other pools are slightly cooler.

**User Groups:** Hikers, dogs, and horses. No mountain bikes. No wheelchair facilities.

**Permits:** A free wilderness permit is required for overnight stays and is available from Big Sur Station. Parking and access are free.

**Maps:** For a map, ask the U.S. Forest Service for Los Padres National Forest or Ventana Wilderness. For topographic maps, ask the USGS for Pfeiffer Point, Partington Ridge, and Ventana Cones.

**Directions:** From Carmel, drive 30 miles south on Highway 1 to Big Sur Station, on the east side of the highway. It's three miles south of Big Sur. The Pine Ridge Trail begins behind the ranger station at the backpacking parking lot.

**Contact:** Big Sur Station, Highway 1, Big Sur, CA 93920, 831/667-2315 or 831/649-2836; Los Padres National Forest, Monterey Ranger District, 406 South Mildred Avenue, King City, CA 93930, 831/385-5434, website: www.fs.fed.us/r5/lospadres.

## 29 PARTINGTON POINT AND TAN BARK TRAILS

4.0 mi / 2.0 hrs

in Julia Pfeiffer Burns State Park south of Big Sur

Map 8.1, page 397

If you want to hike at Julia Pfeiffer Burns State Park without the crowds, a combined out-and-back trip on Partington Point and Tan Bark Trails could be just your cup of tea. The two trails are about as different as any trails could be, except that they both start from the same point along Highway 1. The Partington Point Trail is a dirt road that leads westward and downhill to the rocky cove at Partington Point. A short, fun section goes through a tunnel in the rock. The point is home to the park's underwater playground of caves and natural bridges, but unless you're a scuba diver, you won't be able to see them. Instead, you can have a seat on a rock and look for sea otters, sea lions, and pelicans. Also keep your eyes peeled for spouting whales. Another short fork in this trail leads to the other side of the point, where there is a small sand-and-rock beach.

When you've seen enough, hike back uphill and cross the highway to the start of Tan Bark Trail, a thickly forested route that leads along Partington Creek, heading inland. You can hike a short .5-mile loop on the trail (a bridge carries you across Partington Creek and then back down the other side), or you can continue farther on the route, climbing steeply uphill for a mile or so until you gain some lovely views out to the coast.

**User Groups:** Hikers only. No dogs, horses, or mountain bikes. No wheelchair facilities.

**Permits:** No permits are required. Parking and access are free.

**Maps:** A map of Julia Pfeiffer Burns State Park is available at the entrance kiosk (2.2 miles south of this trailhead). For a topographic map, ask the USGS for Partington Ridge.

**Directions:** From Carmel, drive 34 miles south on Highway 1 to a dirt pullout along the highway and the trailheads for the Partington Point and Tan Bark Trails. The trailheads are 10.5 miles south of Big Sur and 2.2 miles north of the main entrance to Julia Pfeiffer Burns State Park. Partington Point Trail is on the west side of the highway; Tan Bark Trail is on the east side.

**Contact:** Julia Pfeiffer Burns State Park, c/o Big Sur Station, Highway 1, Big Sur, CA 93920, 831/667-2315 or 831/649-2836, website: www.parks.ca.gov.

## 30 McWAY FALLS OVERLOOK
### 0.5 mi / 0.5 hr

in Julia Pfeiffer Burns State Park south of Big Sur

Map 8.1, page 397

After Yosemite Falls and Bridalveil Fall, McWay Falls is probably the waterfall that appears most often on family snapshots of California vacations. Although few know its name, its image is unforgettable: an 80-foot waterfall leaping off a rugged ocean bluff and pouring gracefully into the Pacific. The walk to the waterfall's overlook is on a paved trail that leads through a tunnel underneath Highway 1 and comes out to a spectacular overlook of McWay Cove. A bench is placed along the trail, and you can sit there and admire the action—and maybe even catch sight of a passing gray whale. You can continue a few hundred feet beyond the bench, where the trail ends at the ruins of Waterfall House, the home of Lathrop and Helen Hooper Brown in the 1940s. There's not much left of it now, but at one time, it was obviously quite a place.

**User Groups:** Hikers only. No dogs, horses, or mountain bikes. The McWay Falls Overlook Trail is wheelchair accessible via a special bridge that bypasses the stairs from the parking lot.

**Permits:** No permits are required. Parking and access are free.

**Maps:** A map of Julia Pfeiffer Burns State Park is available at the entrance kiosk. For a topographic map, ask the USGS for Partington Ridge.

**Directions:** From Carmel, drive 37 miles south on Highway 1 to Julia Pfeiffer Burns State Park, located on the east side of the highway, 13 miles south of Big Sur. Drive through the entrance kiosk and park near the restrooms. The Overlook Trail starts on a series of wooden stairs across the pavement from the restrooms.

**Contact:** Julia Pfeiffer Burns State Park, c/o Big Sur Station, Highway 1, Big Sur, CA 93920, 831/667-2315 or 831/649-2836, website: www.parks.ca.gov.

## 31 EWOLDSEN LOOP TRAIL
### 4.3 mi / 2.0 hrs

in Julia Pfeiffer Burns State Park south of Big Sur

Map 8.1, page 397

Some say that Ewoldsen Trail is the best hiking trail in all of Big Sur, and they get no argument from us. The trail begins with an easy saunter along McWay Creek and its spectacular redwood forest; then the trail splits, with Canyon Trail to the left and Ewoldsen Trail switchbacking uphill. Take the short Canyon Trail spur to its end, .25 mile away, and visit McWay Canyon's sweet little waterfall. It's not the big one (McWay Falls) that cascades into the ocean, but it's pretty to look at. Then retrace your steps to the junction and head uphill on Ewoldsen Trail, which climbs steadily above the tops of the tall redwood trees below. The next fork, about 1.5 miles in, is the beginning of the loop. Hike the right side first. You'll alternate between dense redwood forest and more sparse oak woodland until at 2.5 miles you'll see a spur trail signed as Overlook. Take it and climb very steeply uphill for .25 mile until you come out to a wide, grassy ridgetop with stunning views over McWay Canyon and out to the ocean. After all your time in the forest, this bald, open viewpoint comes as quite a surprise. Pull out your lunch and your camera. After a rest, retrace your steps to the junction, bear right, and take the downhill side of the loop. You're treated to more fine views of the ocean before dropping back into redwood forest. The total elevation gain along the trail is 1,600 feet.

**User Groups:** Hikers only. No dogs, horses, or mountain bikes. No wheelchair facilities.

**Permits:** No permits are required. Parking and access are free.

**Maps:** A map of Julia Pfeiffer Burns State Park is available at the entrance kiosk. For a topographic map, ask the USGS for Partington Ridge.

**Directions:** From Carmel, drive 37 miles south on Highway 1 to Julia Pfeiffer Burns State

Park, on the east side of the highway. It's 13 miles south of Big Sur. Drive through the entrance kiosk, and park near the restrooms. The Ewoldsen Trail starts near the picnic areas on the inland side of the parking area.

**Contact:** Julia Pfeiffer Burns State Park, c/o Big Sur Station, Highway 1, Big Sur, CA 93920, 831/667-2315 or 831/649-2836, website: www .parks.ca.gov.

## 32 PINE VALLEY
### 10.6–13.0 mi / 6.0 hrs or 2.0 days

**in the Ventana Wilderness near Carmel Valley**

Map 8.1, page 397

The Pine Valley hike is a great one-night backpacking trip or long day hike into the Ventana Wilderness and can easily be extended into a 13-mile loop. The hike begins on the northern end of Pine Ridge Trail at China Campground, following an up-and-down course that soon becomes more down than up. At 3.5 miles, you turn right on Carmel River Trail and descend some more to the headwaters of the Carmel River and the beginning of a fir and ponderosa pine forest. Pine Valley Camp is 5.3 miles from the trailhead, set in lush Pine Valley, a spacious high meadow lined with ferns, ponderosa pines, and rocky sandstone formations. A short side trip to Pine Falls is possible from the camp; follow a well-worn route downstream along the river for .5 mile to the waterfall. From there, you can retrace your steps to the trailhead for a 10.6-mile round-trip, or make camp at Pine Valley, or take the trail from the upper end of camp, which meets up with Pine Ridge Trail. Turn left on Pine Ridge Trail and hike back to the trailhead to complete a 13-mile loop.

**User Groups:** Hikers, dogs, and horses. No mountain bikes. No wheelchair facilities.

**Permits:** A free campfire permit is required for overnight stays from May through December and is available from the Monterey Ranger District or the Big Sur Station. A national forest

recreation pass is required for each vehicle; fees are $5 for one day or $30 for a year.

**Maps:** For a map, ask the U.S. Forest Service for Los Padres National Forest or Ventana Wilderness. For a topographic map, ask the USGS for Chews Ridge.

**Directions:** From Greenfield on U.S. 101, take the G-16/Monterey County Road exit and drive west for 29 miles. Turn south on Tassajara Road and drive 1.3 miles to Cachagua Road. Turn left and drive nine miles to the trailhead, located just past the turnoff for China Campground. High-clearance vehicles are recommended. The county sometimes closes the road during bad weather; call the Monterey Ranger District before traveling.

**Contact:** Los Padres National Forest, Monterey Ranger District, 406 South Mildred Avenue, King City, CA 93930, 831/385-5434, website: www.fs.fed.us/r5/lospadres.

## 33 LIMEKILN TRAIL
### 1.8 mi / 1.0 hr

**in Limekiln State Park south of Big Sur**

Map 8.1, page 397

What's Big Sur's best-kept secret? That's easy—the hiking trail at Limekiln State Park. The state park is so new and so small that it hasn't been inundated by visitors, as have Pfeiffer Big Sur and Julia Pfeiffer Burns State Parks. The Limekiln Trail leads from the inland campground into a gorgeous redwood forest. It follows Limekiln Creek for a half mile to the park's namesake limekilns, which were used to make limestone bricks and cement in the 1880s. The four kilns look like giant smokestacks with mossy, brick bottoms; they're interesting to see and photograph, but they're not the highlight of this trail. What is? A spur trail off the main route leads to Limekiln Falls, a spectacular 100-foot waterfall that drops over a limestone face. The spur is not marked, but it comes up immediately after you cross the second bridge on your way to the limekilns. (The first bridge is right by the campground.)

Getting to the waterfall requires some boulder hopping, and in spring, you may end up with wet feet, but it's good fun.

**User Groups:** Hikers only. No dogs, horses, or mountain bikes. No wheelchair facilities.

**Permits:** No permits are required. A $6 day-use fee is charged per vehicle.

**Maps:** A map of Limekiln State Park is available at the entrance kiosk. For a topographic map, ask the USGS for Lopez Point.

**Directions:** From Carmel, drive 52 miles south on Highway 1 to Limekiln State Park, on the east side of the highway. It's 2.5 miles south of Lucia and 14.8 miles south of Julia Pfeiffer Burns State Park. The trailhead is at the far side of the inland campground.

**Contact:** Limekiln State Park, c/o Big Sur Station, Highway 1, Big Sur, CA 93920, 831/667-2315 or 831/667-2403, website: www.parks.ca.gov.

## 34 CONE PEAK LOOKOUT TRAIL
### 4.8 mi / 2.5 hrs

in the Ventana Wilderness north of Lucia

Map 8.1, page 397

The 2.4-mile climb to Cone Peak is a classic Ventana Wilderness adventure, and the fun begins with the drive to the trailhead. After leaving Highway 1, first you get wide coastal views and then views of the inland mountain ranges as your car chugs its way uphill. But those are nothing compared to the views you get at the fire lookout on Cone Peak, at 5,155 feet above sea level. The hike is a relentless climb, and the last mile sometimes seems to go straight up, but the total elevation gain is surprisingly only 1,400 feet. Make sure you have plenty of water with you.

After switchbacking upward through a mix of low brush, hardwoods, and then conifers (mostly Coulter pines), you reach a trail junction at 1.9 miles. Go east (right) and walk the final half mile to the fire lookout, where in the summer months the lookout person will usually be happy to see you. How's the view? Excellent. From the historic lookout tower, built on tinker toy-style stilts in 1923, you can see as far as 100 miles on clear days. Perched at the lofty elevation of 5,155 feet, the tower looks down the west side of Cone Peak for almost a vertical mile to the ocean. Be sure to pack along a good map, so you can name all the peaks and valleys in the 360-degree panorama that surrounds you.

**User Groups:** Hikers, dogs, and horses. No mountain bikes. No wheelchair facilities.

**Permits:** No permits are required. A national forest recreation pass is required for each vehicle; fees are $5 for one day or $30 for a year.

**Maps:** For a map, ask the U.S. Forest Service for Los Padres National Forest or Ventana Wilderness. For a topographic map, ask the USGS for Cone Peak.

**Directions:** From Big Sur, drive 27 miles south on Highway 1 to Kirk Creek Campground, on the west side of the highway, and the left turnoff for Nacimiento-Fergusson Road, on the east side of the highway. Turn left and drive seven miles, then turn left on Cone Peak Road (dirt) and drive 5.5 miles to the trailhead, on the left (do not follow the road to its end). Park off the road.

**Contact:** Los Padres National Forest, Monterey Ranger District, 406 South Mildred Avenue, King City, CA 93930, 831/385-5434, website: www.fs.fed.us/r5/lospadres.

## Chapter 9

© ANN MARIE BROWN

# San Joaquin Valley

# San Joaquin Valley

**S**tretching from Stockton, in the north, to Bakersfield, in the south, the San Joaquin Valley is best known for its agricultural bounty. This "fruit basket of the nation" is part of the larger Central Valley, a giant basin which reaches all the way north to Chico. Snowmelt from the western Sierra Nevada mountains irrigates this immense valley via the Sacramento and San Joaquin Rivers, which join in the delta before flowing to San Francisco Bay and the Pacific Ocean.

The San Joaquin region is bisected by two major freeways—I-5 and Highway 99. While traveling these corridors, drivers cruise past endless acres of cotton, orchards, cattle grazing lands, and stick-straight concrete aqueducts that transport water. Most regard this flat, nondescript landscape as nothing more than an irritation—an obstacle that must be passed on the way to someplace better. But this land was once much different from what you see today. Before the Europeans settled here in the 19th century, the San Joaquin Valley was a vast wetland. Its millions of acres of marshes, vernal pools, and riparian streams and creeks were the homeland of immense populations of waterfowl and elk. Native Americans lived bountifully year-round in this wildlife-rich area.

Enterprising European settlers saw that the San Joaquin Valley could be useful for growing their nonnative vegetables, and for farming livestock. They diked and dammed the land to create vast dry patches suitable for ranching and farming, then built irrigation systems to water the crops. In relatively short order, populations of native wildlife soon dwindled, having lost their natural habitat. Larger animals, like the tule elk, completely disappeared (but were later brought back by wildlife managers).

Today, we recognize that this dramatic transformation of the land was not beneficial to either people or wildlife. Through ongoing conservation efforts, large stretches of the San Joaquin Valley's agricultural fields are now purposefully flooded in winter to provide a haven for migrating ducks and geese. Farming and irrigation strategies are being rethought and redesigned. In protected habitat areas, such as wildlife refuges and at Tule Elk State Reserve, tule elk are being reintroduced to their native habitat.

What all this means for hikers is that the few natural areas found in this region should be appreciated for their very existence, and also for their unique look into California's past. The state's largest remaining wetland ecosystem—160,000 acres of grassland wetlands—is preserved at Los Banos Wildlife Area and the San Luis National Wildlife Refuge complex. Within these protected boundaries, winter visitors can see lakes and ponds that are completely covered by hundreds of thousands of geese and ducks. Smaller regional, county, and privately operated parks provide access to special places like the riparian forest and valley oak woodland at Kaweah Oaks Preserve—a rare, remnant example of what this vast landscape once looked like.

Perhaps the most impressive preservation of "old California" is at Carrizo Plain, which was declared a national monument in 2000. The plains are considered to be California's largest nature preserve, stretching for 50 miles north to south along the San Andreas Fault. Here, hikers have the chance to see the largest remaining example of San Joaquin Valley grassland habitat. Amid the waving grasses live reintroduced pronghorn antelope and tule elk, plus thousands of visiting sandhill cranes in the winter months.

Next time you're driving 70 miles per hour down I-5 or Highway 99, pull off the road, tie up your boot laces, and take a closer look at the landscape of the San Joaquin Valley. You might be surprised at the rare and precious beauty that awaits you.

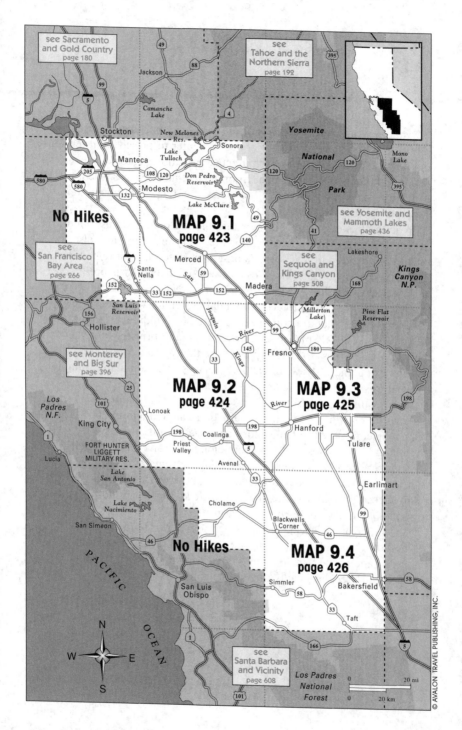

# Map 9.1

Hikes 1–2
Page 427

© AVALON TRAVEL PUBLISHING, INC.

# Map 9.2

**Hikes 3–4**
**Page 428**

# Map 9.3

## Hikes 5–6
## Page 429

# Map 9.4

## Hikes 7–8
## Pages 430–431

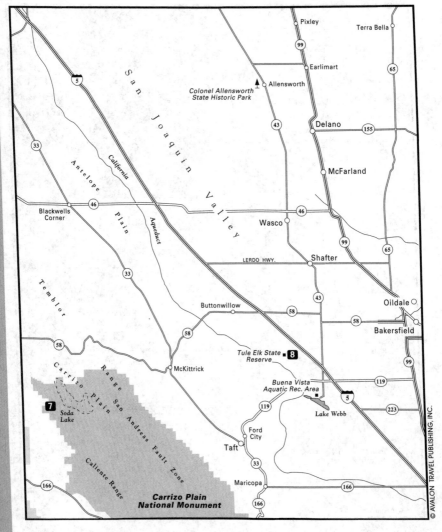

# 1 CHESTER, SOUSA, AND WINTON MARSH TRAILS
## 4.0 mi / 2.0 hrs

in the San Luis National Wildlife Refuge north of Los Banos

Map 9.1, page 423

The San Luis National Wildlife Refuge offers two main driving tours: the Tule Elk Auto Tour Loop and the Waterfowl Auto Tour Loop, and both are great opportunities for visitors to see wildlife. But if you want to get out of your car and on to your feet for a while, check out the three short hiking trails located off the 9.7-mile Waterfowl Auto Tour Loop. Walk all three, and you can easily chalk up about four miles of exercise. The trails lead to three different marsh areas, each with its own character.

As you drive the auto route, the first trailhead you reach is for the Chester Marsh Trail. It's open for hiking only from February to September; from October to January, it is part of the refuge's hunting area. It's a one-mile loop, and you can pick up an interpretive brochure at the trailhead. After your walk, get back in your car and continue driving along the Waterfowl Auto Tour Route until you reach the trailhead for the Sousa Marsh. This area consists of an inner and outer loop trail through a canopy of riparian trees. The longest trail (1.2 miles) goes to the Sousa observation platform, with its telescope and benches. The .7-mile Winton Marsh Trail, located just beyond the Sousa Marsh parking lot, also leads to an observation platform and several benches situated slightly above the marsh, so you can pull out your binoculars and peer at the feathered fowl below. What will you see? The usual cabal: ducks, geese, moorhens, coots, pheasants, snipe, hawks, owls, egrets, herons, and even some rare types, like the endangered tricolored blackbird. In case you haven't gotten the idea yet, this place is crawling with wildlife. Even while just driving around, we saw a coyote and about a zillion bunnies, in addition to numerous Swainson's hawks.

User Groups: Hikers and dogs. No horses or mountain bikes. No wheelchair facilities.

Permits: No permits are required. Parking and access are free.

Maps: A free map is available by contacting the refuge headquarters at the address below. For a topographic map, ask the USGS for Los Banos.

Directions: From Los Banos on Highway 152/33, drive north on Highway 165 (Mercey Springs Road) for 6.4 miles to Wolfsen Road. Bear right and follow Wolfsen Road for 2.5 miles into the National Wildlife Refuge. Follow the signs for the Waterfowl Auto Tour Loop.

Contact: San Luis National Wildlife Refuge, P.O. Box 2176, Los Banos, CA 93635, 209/826-3508, website: http://sanluis.fws.gov.

# 2 MEADOWLARK TRAIL
## 0.25 mi / 0.25 hr

in the Merced National Wildlife Refuge southwest of Merced

Map 9.1, page 423

It doesn't seem like a .25-mile loop trail could offer much in the way of a payoff, but you may be surprised by the rewards on the diminutive Meadowlark Trail. First off, it's one of only two places in the Merced National Wildlife Refuge where you're allowed to get out of your car and walk. Walking is prohibited in most of the preserve in order to reduce the disturbance to the thousands of geese and cranes that winter here. Driving your car along the Auto Tour Route is okay, though; it turns out that birds aren't bothered much by cars. The Meadowlark Trail gives you a chance to stretch your legs within the wildlife refuge, which serves as a precious island of wildlife habitat in the midst of Merced's vast agricultural fields. A thicket of tules, cattails, and willows in the refuge provides heavy cover for birds—particularly raptors, wintering shorebirds, and waterfowl. Because morning fog is common here in the winter months, bird-watching is often better at midday, when you may see concentrations of snow geese and Ross' geese. Magnificent sandhill cranes also make an appearance in winter.

The rest of the year, you're more likely to see a variety of raptors. Barn owls are particularly common—one visitor saw 14 of them while walking this short loop. Great horned owls and a variety of hawks are also frequently sighted.

**User Groups:** Hikers and dogs. No horses or mountain bikes. No wheelchair facilities.

**Permits:** No permits are required. Parking and access are free.

**Maps:** A free map is available by contacting the refuge headquarters at the address below. For a topographic map, ask the USGS for Los Banos.

**Directions:** From Merced, take Highway 59 south for eight miles. Turn west on Sandy Mush Road and drive eight miles to the refuge entrance.

**Contact:** San Luis National Wildlife Refuge, P.O. Box 2176, Los Banos, CA 93635, 209/826-3508, website: http://sanluis.fws.gov.

## 🛇 PATH OF THE PADRES
### 5.0 mi / 3.0 hrs

**on Los Banos Creek, south of San Luis Reservoir**

Map 9.2, page 424

You have to plan way in advance to take this unusual hike at Los Banos Creek Reservoir. That's because the only way to go is by boat and with a guide, and guided trips are offered only on weekends in March and April. The trip has become so popular that it usually sells out as soon as reservations are available, which is the first week of February each year, so don't procrastinate on making your call for reservations. If you've reserved a spot, your trip begins with a boat ride down the long and narrow reservoir, which is set in a steep-walled canyon and is popular for windsurfing and canoeing. At the reservoir's far end, everyone gets off the boat and starts hiking up the narrow canyon of Los Banos Creek, where old-growth sycamore groves and a cornucopia of spring wildflowers can be seen. The guide will teach you how to spot and identify various animal tracks along the canyon floor, and bird-watchers may thrill to see a peregrine falcon or other

cliff-dwelling species. The hike ends with a climb to the top of a knoll that offers wide views of the Los Banos valley. So why is this trail called the Path of the Padres? Because the fathers at Mission San Juan Bautista came here in the early 19th century to recruit the Yokut Indians to work for them. On the trip, you'll see bedrock mortars and other evidence of the Native Americans who once lived in this canyon.

**User Groups:** Hikers only. No dogs, horses, or mountain bikes. No wheelchair facilities.

**Permits:** Reservations are required; call to reserve a space during the first week of February. A $5 fee is charged per person for the reservation and guided tour. An additional $6 day-use fee is charged per vehicle.

**Maps:** For a topographic map, ask the USGS for Los Banos Valley.

**Directions:** From I-5 at the junction with Highway 152 (south of Santa Nella), turn east on Highway 152 and drive 2.5 miles. Turn right (south) on Volta Road and drive one mile. Turn left (east) on Pioneer Road and drive .8 mile, then right on Canyon Road. Drive south on Canyon Road for five miles to Los Banos Creek Reservoir. (You will cross back to the west side of I-5.) Park near the boat ramp.

**Contact:** San Luis Reservoir State Recreation Area, Four Rivers District, 31426 Gonzaga Road, Gustine, CA 95322, 209/826-4714 or 209/826-1196, website: www.parks.ca.gov.

## 🛇 COALINGA MINERAL SPRINGS NATIONAL RECREATION TRAIL
### 4.8 mi / 2.5 hrs

**northwest of Coalinga**

Map 9.2, page 424

Most people don't realize that there's a National Recreation Trail out here near Coalinga, the town that was made famous by an earthquake, but it's true. In winter and spring, this is a first-class hike to the summit of Kreyenhagen Peak (elevation 3,558 feet), climbing through chaparral-covered hillsides. The trail begins at the far end of the picnic area and crosses a dry streambed, then begins to ascend. It's well graded all the way, with the second mile slightly steeper than the first. Plenty of switchbacks ease you through it. Views are good all the way up this 2.4-mile trail, but the impressive vista from the summit ridge includes the Diablo Range, the San Joaquin Valley, and miles of surrounding Bureau of Land Management (BLM) land. That's a pretty wide scope, considering how little effort is required to get here. Have a seat on one of the rock outcrops, pull out your picnic lunch, and enjoy the show.

**User Groups:** Hikers, dogs, horses, and mountain bikes. No wheelchair facilities.

**Permits:** No permits are required. A $3 day-use fee is charged per vehicle.

**Maps:** Free trail maps are available at the trailhead. For a topographic map, ask the USGS for Curry Mountain.

**Directions:** From Coalinga, drive 20 miles west on Highway 198 to the Coalinga Mineral Springs County Park exit. Turn right (north) and drive four miles to Coalinga Mineral Springs County Park. Park in the main lot and walk to the far end of the park. The trail begins across the creek bed.

**Contact:** Bureau of Land Management, Hollister Field Office, 20 Hamilton Court, Hollister, CA 95023, 831/630-5000, website: www.ca.blm.gov/hollister.

## 5 LEWIS S. EATON TRAIL
### 1.0–10.0 mi / .5–5.0 hrs

**on the San Joaquin River near Fresno**

**Map 9.3, page 425**

Woodward Park is the kind of city park that has a par course, children's playgrounds, and barbecue areas. But it's also a convenient access point for the San Joaquin River Parkway, also called the Lewis S. Eaton Trail. When completed, the multiuse parkway will cover a 22-mile distance between Highway 99 and Friant Dam in Millerton Lake State Park. Currently five miles are finished, which means you

can walk, jog, rollerblade, bike, or cruise in a wheelchair up to 10 miles round-trip on a paved trail that parallels the river and Friant Road for its entire distance. The good folks at the San Joaquin River Parkway and Conservation Trust are working hard to add to the current trail system; various loops and extensions from the paved trail are in the works. If you want to explore some of them, start with the River Access Trail, which branches off the Lewis S. Eaton Trail on the north side of Woodward Park. The trail meanders down to the riverbanks at the Jensen River Ranch, a small park that is under restoration by the conservancy.

**User Groups:** Hikers, dogs, horses, mountain bikes, and wheelchairs.

**Permits:** No permits are required. A $3 fee is charged per vehicle.

**Maps:** A park map is available at the entrance kiosk. For a topographic map, ask the USGS for Fresno North.

**Directions:** From Highway 41 heading north in Fresno, take the Friant Road exit. Turn left on Audubon Avenue and then turn right into Woodward Park.

**Contact:** Woodward Regional Park, 7775 Friant Road, Fresno, CA 93710, 559/621-2900; San Joaquin River Parkway and Conservation Trust, 1550 East Shaw Avenue, Suite 114, Fresno, CA 93710, 559/248-8480, website: www.riverparkway.org.

## 6 KAWEAH OAKS PRESERVE
### 2.0 mi / 1.0 hr

**east of Visalia**

**Map 9.3, page 425**

The Kaweah Oaks Preserve is Tulare County's premier private nature preserve, the slim remains of what was once a vast valley oak forest. Some marvelous big oaks still stand, as well as wild grapes growing as high as 30 feet. Four easy hiking trails feature a riparian forest, valley oak woodlands, alkali meadow, and a small swamp. From the parking area, enter through the fence opening to the right of the cattle gate. Head west down the old ranch road to the picnic area on the right (less than a quarter mile). Follow the ranch road west or north to hike the self-guided interpretive trails. Because this is a grazing area, leave all cattle gates the way you found them—open or closed. As you stroll, listen for sounds of birdlife, and look for herons, hawks, and owls, as well as the preserve's five species of woodpeckers. In addition to the diverse birdlife, you'll enjoy abundant native flora, including California sycamores, cottonwoods, and willows growing near the streams. This is a good walk for late winter, spring, or fall. In the heat of summer, confine your visits to the early morning or evening, when the valley is at its coolest.

**User Groups:** Hikers only. No dogs, horses, or mountain bikes. No wheelchair facilities.

**Permits:** No permits are required. Parking and access are free.

**Maps:** For a topographic map, ask the USGS for Visalia.

**Directions:** From Tulare on Highway 99, drive north for 10 miles and turn east on Highway 198. Drive 13 miles on Highway 198, passing Visalia, to the left turnoff for Road 182. Turn left on Road 182 and drive .4 mile to the trailhead parking area, on the left.

**Contact:** Kaweah Oaks Preserve, Sierra Los Tulares Land Trust, 711 North Court Street, Visalia, CA 93291, 559/738-0211, website:kaweah oaks.com.

## �７ CARRIZO PLAIN AND PAINTED ROCK
**1.5 mi / 1.0 hr**

in eastern San Luis Obispo County, south of California Valley

Map 9.4, page 426

Ⓕ Carrizo Plain is one of California's newest national monuments (as of 2000) and is also considered to be California's largest nature preserve. Its biggest draw is the massive number of sandhill cranes, who hang around from late November to February. Although thousands of migrating and resident birds can be seen in this area, it's the cranes that bring the hordes of bird lovers and photographers to alkali Soda Lake and the surrounding plains. Since the birds don't stay in one place, most people spot them while driving around Carrizo Plain, or while stopping at the overlook platform near Soda Lake. The birds are unmistakable—drab gray in color but with seven-foot wing spans and three-foot-long legs. After checking out the big birds, head for the Painted Rock Interpretive Trail, where you can walk the flat dirt road that leads to 55-foot-tall Painted Rock. The interior of the rounded sandstone amphitheater has some of the best Native American pictographs in the country, although some have been eroded by time and weather. Spring wildflowers are beautiful all across the plains.

Special note: The area is closed from March 1 to July 15 to protect nesting falcons, but you can still sign up for a guided hike to Painted Rock on Saturdays from March through May. The rest of the year, you are free to hike on your own.

**User Groups:** Hikers, dogs, horses, and mountain bikes. No wheelchair facilities.

**Permits:** No permits are required. Parking and access are free.

**Maps:** A brochure on Carrizo Plain National Monument is available from the BLM at the address below. For a topographic map, ask the USGS for Painted Rock.

**Directions:** From San Luis Obispo on U.S. 101, drive north for 10 miles and take the Santa Margarita/Highway 58 exit. Drive east on Highway 58 for 50 miles to the Soda Lake Road turnoff, on the right. Turn right (south) and drive 13.5 miles to the Painted Rock Trail and visitors center turnoff, on the right. Turn right and drive to the visitors center, then turn left and drive two miles to the Painted Rock trailhead.

**Contact:** Bureau of Land Management, Bakersfield Field Office, 3801 Pegasus Drive, Bakersfield, CA 93308, 661/391-6000; Goodwin Education Center at Carrizo Plain (open Thursday through Sunday from December through May), 805/475-2131, website: www.ca.blm .gov/bakersfield.

# 8 TULE ELK STATE RESERVE
## 0.25 mi / 0.25 hr

**off I-5 west of Bakersfield**

Map 9.4, page 426

Most people just don't know that there's a herd of magnificent tule elk wandering around a few miles from I-5. If you didn't know, better pull off the highway and get yourself to the Tule Elk State Reserve near Tupman. There aren't a lot of trails to choose from, and you won't do much that resembles true hiking here, but if you've been driving on I-5 long enough, just getting out of the car and stretching your legs is a big deal. The animals are most active in the late summer, when their rutting season begins. Bring binoculars for your best chance at a good view, or take a stroll to the walk-up platform, where you can look through a spotting scope at the elk. Make sure you stop in at the visitors center and check out the interesting displays on the elk and the history of the Central Valley.

**User Groups:** Hikers and dogs. No horses or mountain bikes. Some facilities are wheelchair accessible.

**Permits:** No permits are required. A $3 day-use fee is charged per vehicle.

**Maps:** For a topographic map, ask the USGS for Tupman.

**Directions:** From the junction of I-5 and Highway 99 north of the Grapevine, drive north on I-5 for 33 miles to the Stockdale Highway exit. Drive west for 1.2 miles and turn left (south) on Morris Road. Drive 1.6 miles on Morris Road and turn left into the Tule Elk State Reserve. The route is well signed.

**Contact:** Tule Elk State Reserve, 8653 Station Road, Buttonwillow, CA 93206, 661/764-6881, website: www.parks.ca.gov.

## Chapter 10

© ANN MARIE BROWN

# Yosemite and Mammoth Lakes

# Yosemite and Mammoth Lakes

Plunging waterfalls, stark granite, alpine lakes, pristine meadows, giant sequoias, and raging rivers—you'll find them all in the Yosemite and Mammoth Lakes region, which encompasses not only world-famous Yosemite National Park but also the popular recreation areas of Mammoth Lakes and the Eastern Sierra.

The centerpiece of this region, of course, is Yosemite National Park, a must-see on every hiker's itinerary. From Yosemite Valley's famous waterfalls—three of which are among the tallest in the world—to the towering granite domes and glistening meadows of Tioga Pass, Yosemite is a place that can only be described in superlatives. Hikers can choose from short-and-easy jaunts to world-class destinations (like Taft Point and Vernal Falls) or exhaustive treks to the summits of Half Dome or Clouds Rest—but there's also a wealth of moderate trails in between the two extremes. One thing is certain: Every trail in Yosemite leads to a destination that is completely worth the effort to reach it.

As scenic as the national park itself are the resort areas just to the east, particularly Mammoth Lakes and June Lake, on the U.S. 395 corridor, as well as the surrounding wilderness areas—Hoover, Ansel Adams, and John Muir. Best known for skiing and snowboarding in winter, the resort towns of the Eastern Sierra are ideal base camps for hiking trips in the warmer seasons.

The alpine lakes of this region are a major draw for day hikers and backpackers alike, but equally as compelling are the Eastern Sierra's alpine meadows, fir and pine forests, and sagebrush-covered plains. This is a region known for its unusual diversity—including volcanic craters, hot springs, lava flows, and the strange beauty of Mono Lake, an ancient and majestic body of water covering 60 square miles. An easy, popular hiking trail provides access to its lakeshore.

More uncommon geologic features are found nearby at Devils Postpile National Monument. This 800-acre national park preserves the Devils Postpile—a "pile" of 60-foot-high basalt columns that are remnants of an ancient lava flow—plus breathtaking 101-foot Rainbow Falls. Hikers can spend a day walking to these and other destinations within the monument, or they can hike beyond park borders into the glacially carved backcountry of the Ansel Adams Wilderness.

Key to enjoying your experience in the Yosemite and Mammoth Lakes region is planning your visit for the least crowded months of the year. Summer weekends are the busiest time and are best avoided, especially in the national park. After school starts in September, the crowds lessen substantially. Autumn is a fine time for hiking in and around Yosemite, even though most of the valley's famous waterfalls (except for dependable Bridalveil) have run dry by midsummer. This lack of falling water is more than made up for by the show of fall colors on the valley floor and the chance for solitude in this too well-loved park. (Another option, especially for waterfall aficionados, is to show up before school lets out in June. Although the high country is snowed in and inaccessible at this time, Yosemite Valley is in its full splendor in April and May.)

Likewise, if there is a perfect time to visit the Eastern Sierra, it's in the transition between summer and winter. Autumn transforms the scenic canyons and pristine lakeshores into a wave of blazing color. Aspens, willows, and cottonwoods turn showy hues of orange, yellow, and red. The trees generally begin their color change early in September; peak viewing time is usually late September and early October.

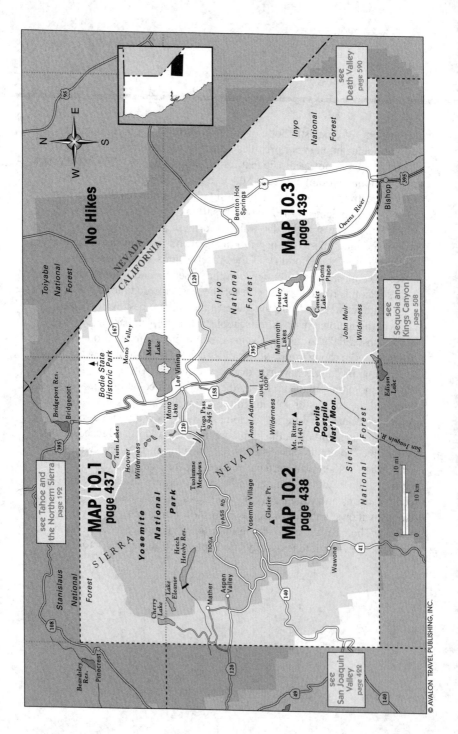

MAP 10.1
page 437

MAP 10.2
page 438

MAP 10.3
page 439

No Hikes

see Tahoe and
the Northern Sierra
page 192

see San Joaquin
Valley page 492

see Death Valley
page 590

see Sequoia and
Kings Canyon
page 508

NEVADA
CALIFORNIA

Toiyabe
National
Forest

Inyo
National
Forest

Inyo
National
Forest

Bodie State
Historic Park

Mono Valley

Mono Lake

Mono Lake

Lee Vining

Benton Hot
Springs

Owens River

Bishop

Crowley
Lake

Convict
Lake

Toms
Place

Mammoth
Lakes

John Muir
Wilderness

Edison
Lake

Bridgeport Res.

Bridgeport

Twin Lakes

Hoover
Wilderness

Yosemite
National
Park

Tuolumne
Meadows

Tioga Pass
9,945 ft

Ansel Adams
Wilderness

JUNE LAKE
LOOP

Mt. Ritter
13,140 ft

Devils
Postpile
Nat'l Mon.

Sierra
National
Forest

San Joaquin R.

Stanislaus
National
Forest

SIERRA

Cherry
Lake

Lake
Eleanor

Hetch
Hetchy Res.

Mather

Aspen
Valley

Yosemite Village

Glacier Pt.

NEVADA

Wawona

Beardsley
Res.

Pinecrest

TIOGA    PASS   RD.

10 mi

10 km

© AVALON TRAVEL PUBLISHING, INC.

# Map 10.1

**Hikes 1–10**
**Pages 440–445**

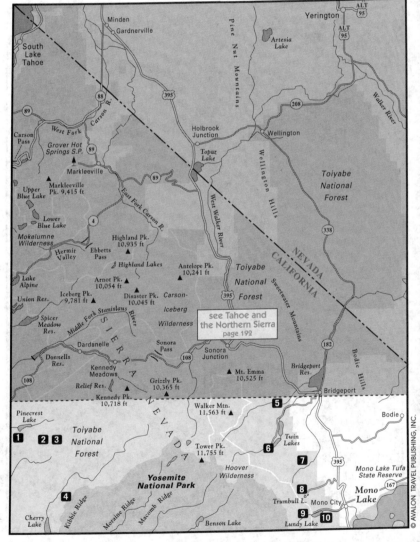

# Map 10.2

**Hikes 11–88**
**Pages 446–498**

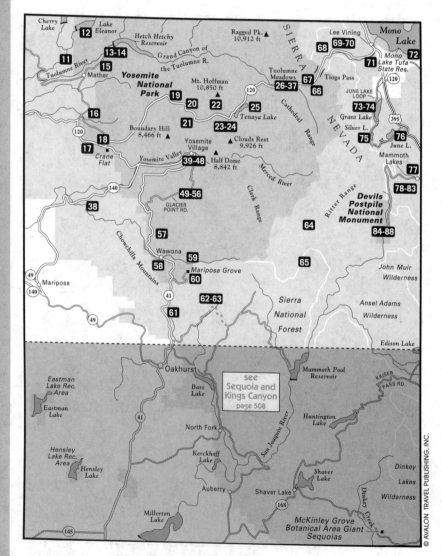

© AVALON TRAVEL PUBLISHING, INC.

# Map 10.3

**Hikes 89–96**
**Pages 499–503**

# 1 PINECREST LAKE NATIONAL RECREATION TRAIL
## 4.0 mi / 2.0 hrs

**on Pinecrest Lake near Strawberry**

Map 10.1, page 437

Pinecrest Lake is a tremendously popular family vacation resort just off Highway 108, the kind of place that people go year after year for a week of boating, camping, and fishing. The trail that circles its shoreline is a lot like the lake itself—it's pretty, it's popular, and it's no place to go if you like solitude. However, the four-mile loop makes a good early morning walk or run if you're up and at it before the crowds get out of bed. In the afternoons, you can hike to the east side of the lake and follow a spur trail along the South Fork Stanislaus River to some excellent swimming holes, called Cleo's Bath.

The main downer: The south side of the loop is littered with vacation homes, which detract from your nature experience. The weird part: Pay telephones are located alongside the trail.
**User Groups:** Hikers and dogs. No horses or mountain bikes. No wheelchair facilities except at the fishing ramp and day-use area.
**Permits:** No permits are required. Parking and access are free.
**Maps:** For a map, ask the U.S. Forest Service for Stanislaus National Forest. For a topographic map, ask the USGS for Pinecrest.
**Directions:** From Sonora, drive east on Highway 108 for 31 miles to the Pinecrest turnoff. Turn right on Pinecrest Lake Road and continue for another mile to the day-use parking area, on the south side of the lake. Park as close to the end of the road as possible.
**Contact:** Stanislaus National Forest, Summit Ranger District, 1 Pinecrest Lake Road, Pinecrest, CA 95364, 209/965-3434, website: www.fs.fed.us/r5/stanislaus.

# 2 CAMP AND BEAR LAKES
## 8.0 mi / 4.0 hrs

**in the Emigrant Wilderness near Pinecrest Lake**

Map 10.1, page 437

The Crabtree trailhead, at elevation 7,180 feet, is the trailhead of choice for most casual hikers and backpackers entering the Emigrant Wilderness. It's easy to reach and allows access to many excellent destinations with a relatively short walk. From Crabtree, it's a moderate 2.5-mile hike to Camp Lake, which is just inside the Emigrant Wilderness boundary. Ironically, camping is not allowed at Camp Lake, so while day-users may choose to linger along its shores, backpackers must continue another 1.5 miles to Bear Lake, accessible via a one-mile left spur trail. Both lakes offer stellar granite-country scenery, good (but icy) swimming, decent rainbow trout fishing, and the chance of seeing plenty of wildflowers along the route in summer. You, too, can be wowed by the wandering daisies and blue lupine. You'll face only one sustained hill climb along the route; most of the trail gently undulates. You'll also note some beaver evidence at Bear Lake.
**User Groups:** Hikers, dogs, and horses. No mountain bikes. No wheelchair facilities.
**Permits:** A free wilderness permit is required for overnight stays and is available from the Summit Ranger Station. Parking and access are free.
**Maps:** For a map, ask the U.S. Forest Service for Stanislaus National Forest or Emigrant Wilderness. For a topographic map, ask the USGS for Pinecrest.
**Directions:** From Sonora, drive east on Highway 108 for 31 miles to the Pinecrest turnoff. Turn right on Pinecrest Lake Road and continue .5 mile to the right fork for Dodge Ridge Ski Area. Bear right and drive 2.9 miles, then turn right at the sign for Aspen Meadow and Gianelli trailhead. Drive .5 mile, turn left, and drive four miles to the turnoff for Crabtree trailhead (follow the signs). Turn right and drive .25 mile.

**Contact:** Stanislaus National Forest, Summit Ranger District, 1 Pinecrest Lake Road, Pinecrest, CA 95364, 209/965-3434, website: www.fs.fed.us/r5/stanislaus.

## ⓷ BURST ROCK/POWELL LAKE
**4.0 mi / 2.5 hrs**

**in the Emigrant Wilderness near Pinecrest Lake**

Map 10.1, page 437

Both Burst Rock and Powell Lake are supreme day-hike destinations, but they present a problem for first-time visitors: Neither one is located right along the trail and neither one is signed. This results in a lot of people wandering around asking, "So which rock is Burst Rock?"

The short answer is it doesn't matter all that much. After hiking gently but steadily uphill for one mile, you'll reach an interpretive sign that details the difficulties of pioneers who tried to use this route, called the West Walker–Sonora Emigrant Trail, to cross the Sierra in the 1850s. From the wilderness boundary sign, cut off to your left for about 50 yards, and you'll witness an incredible vista and drop-off to the valley below—and who knows, you might even be standing on Burst Rock. After feeling suitably humbled, retrace your steps and continue another mile until you reach an unsigned fork. Go left for less than .25 mile to Powell Lake, a favorite spot of young anglers. If you miss the fork, shortly you'll catch sight of the lake, off to your left, and you'll know to go back and find it. The peninsula of rocks that juts out into the water is the perfect place to launch into a swan dive.

**User Groups:** Hikers, dogs, and horses. No mountain bikes. No wheelchair facilities.

**Permits:** A free wilderness permit is required for overnight stays and is available from the Summit Ranger Station. Parking and access are free.

**Maps:** For a map, ask the U.S. Forest Service for Stanislaus National Forest or Emigrant Wilderness. For a topographic map, ask the USGS for Pinecrest.

**Directions:** From Sonora, drive east on Highway 108 for 31 miles to the Pinecrest turnoff. Turn right on Pinecrest Lake Road and continue for .5 mile to the right fork for Dodge Ridge Ski Area. Bear right, drive 2.9 miles, and turn right at the sign for Aspen Meadow and Gianelli trailhead. Drive .5 mile, turn left, and drive 8.3 miles to the trailhead parking area. The route is well signed.

**Contact:** Stanislaus National Forest, Summit Ranger District, 1 Pinecrest Lake Road, Pinecrest, CA 95364, 209/965-3434, website: www.fs.fed.us/r5/stanislaus.

## ⓸ KIBBIE LAKE
**8.4 mi / 1.0–2.0 days**

**in northwest Yosemite National Park**

Map 10.1, page 437

This day hike or easy backpacking trip starts in Stanislaus National Forest and heads into the Hetch Hetchy region of Yosemite. The trip is easy enough that it makes a rewarding weekend trip for beginning backpackers, who can easily carry a pack over the 4.2-mile distance. From the trailhead, you hike the Kibbie Ridge Trail 1.2 miles to the Kibbie Lake Trail, then go right and head for the lake in another 3.0 miles. The route leads through lodgepole pine forest to the southern tip of the granite-bound lake, at elevation 6,800 feet. Long and narrow Kibbie Lake is fairly shallow and supports a good population of rainbow trout, although it gets fished heavily.

Special Note: Check your calendar before you go. The gate at Cherry Lake is closed every year one week before deer season, which is usually sometime in September, and doesn't reopen until spring. Most years, the road is open from May 1 to September 15.

**User Groups:** Hikers and horses. No dogs or mountain bikes. No wheelchair facilities.

**Permits:** There is a $20 per vehicle entrance fee at Yosemite National Park, good for seven days. Free wilderness permits are required for overnight stays. They are available on a first-come, first-served basis up to one day in advance at the Yosemite Wilderness kiosk near your chosen trailhead, or farther in advance by mail, phone, or email using the contact information below.

**Maps:** A Yosemite map is available from Tom Harrison Maps. For topographic maps, ask the USGS for Kibbie Lake and Hetch Hetchy Reservoir.

**Directions:** From Groveland, drive east on Highway 120 for 13 miles toward Yosemite National Park. Turn left on Cherry Lake Road and drive 24 miles to Cherry Lake's dam, then cross it. Turn left on Road 1N45Y and follow it about five miles to its end.

**Contact:** Yosemite National Park Public Information Office, P.O. Box 577, Yosemite National Park, CA 95389, 209/372-0200, website: www.nps.gov/yose.

## 5 BUCKEYE CREEK TRAIL
### 5.0 mi / 2.5 hrs

**in Humboldt-Toiyabe National Forest west of Bridgeport and Highway 395**

Map 10.1, page 437

You can hike up to eight miles one-way along Buckeye Creek to the Hoover Wilderness boundary at the Buckeye Roughs. But most hikers do less than that; they just take off from Buckeye Campground (7,000 feet), maybe pack along their fishing rods, and walk a couple of miles each way up and down the stream. Brook trout are planted close to the campground all summer. It's rare to hike far in the Eastern Sierra without having to climb, but that's what you get here at the base of Buckeye Canyon. If you don't like to fish, there's plenty of other stuff to do, like admire the wildflowers in the meadows or gape at the impressive walls of glacial summits and ridges that surround you. A popular hot spring is found in Buckeye Creek less than a mile from the campground, but be forewarned: You might get an anatomy lesson there. Occasional Buckeye Creek bathers have been spotted wearing only birthday suits.

**User Groups:** Hikers, dogs, and horses. No mountain bikes. No wheelchair facilities.

**Permits:** No permits are required. Parking and access are free.

**Maps:** Humboldt-Toiyabe National Forest (Bridgeport). For a topographic map, ask the USGS for Twin Lakes.

**Directions:** From Bridgeport on U.S. 395, drive west on Twin Lakes Road for seven miles to the Buckeye Road turnoff. Turn right on Buckeye Road and drive 3.5 miles to the Buckeye Campground and trailhead. (Buckeye Road turns to dirt at Doc and Al's Resort.)

**Contact:** Humboldt-Toiyabe National Forest, Bridgeport Ranger District, HCR1 Box 1000, Bridgeport, CA 93517, 760/932-7070, website: www.fs.fed.us/htnf.

## 6 ROBINSON CREEK TRAIL
### 7.8 mi / 5.0 hrs

**in the Hoover Wilderness west of Bridgeport**

Map 10.1, page 437

Some call it Barney Lake Trail and others call it Robinson Creek Trail. Whatever you call it, you should know that this is the busiest trail into the Hoover Wilderness. Why? It gains only 1,000 feet along its four-mile length. The remedy for the crowds? Start hiking very early in the day, before the hundreds of campers in the Twin Lakes area have risen from their sleeping bags. You must park outside Mono Village Campground and then walk straight through it to reach the trailhead, which is signed for Barney Lake. The trail parallels Robinson Creek with off-and-on views of the mammoth, jagged Sawtooth Ridge. It enters the Hoover Wilderness at 2.6 miles, then climbs a bit more steeply and reaches the lake at 3.9 miles. If you get there before everyone else, you are one lucky hiker. Backpackers can continue another 3.5 miles to larger Peeler Lake.

**User Groups:** Hikers, dogs, and horses. No mountain bikes. No wheelchair facilities.

**Permits:** A wilderness permit is required for overnight stays and is available from the

Bridgeport Ranger Station. Quotas are in effect from the last Saturday in June to September 18; permits are available in advance by mail for this period for a $3 per person fee. See the website www.sierranevadawild.gov for a permit application.

**Maps:** Humboldt-Toiyabe National Forest (Bridgeport) or Hoover Wilderness. For a topographic map, ask the USGS for Twin Lakes.

**Directions:** From Bridgeport on U.S. 395, drive west on Twin Lakes Road for 13.2 miles to the signed parking area, on the west end of the lakes, near Mono Village Campground.

**Contact:** Humboldt-Toiyabe National Forest, Bridgeport Ranger District, HCR1 Box 1000, Bridgeport, CA 93517, 760/932-7070, website: www.fs.fed.us/htnf.

## 7 GREEN, EAST, AND WEST LAKES
### 8.6–11.6 mi / 5.0 hrs

**in the Hoover Wilderness west of Bridgeport**

Map 10.1, page 437

Three beautiful lakes—Green, East, and West—are situated right around 9,000 feet in elevation. They offer fair trout fishing and are accessible via Green Creek Trail (sometimes called Green Lake Trail). It's only 4.6 miles round-trip to Green Lake, but you can go two miles farther for an 8.6-mile round-trip that includes East Lake as well. Or, you can take a 1.5-mile spur off the main trail for a jaunt to West Lake. Some people make a short backpacking trip out of it and see all three lakes. If you do, note that Green Lake is the only one of the three that is just below 9,000 feet in elevation, which means it is the only one where campfires are permitted. (You must use the established campfire rings.) At the other, higher lakes, only backpacking stoves are allowed. The fishing is generally better at East and West Lakes than at Green Lake, although it's nothing to write home about. The high mountain scenery, on the other hand, will knock your socks off.

The Green Creek Trail climbs, of course—but not so much that you'll be worn out when you reach Green Lake; just enough to provide you with expansive valley views most of the way. The path closely parallels the tumbling cascades of the west fork of Green Creek, and the July wildflower show is outstanding here. (The autumn aspen show is also noteworthy.) The turnoff for West Lake is on the right at 2.2 miles and makes a steep 1,000-foot ascent over 1.5 miles. The main trail reaches Green Lake at 2.3 miles. East Lake can be reached by heading left off the main trail and gaining another 500 feet in elevation over two miles. All three lakes are sparkling, rock-bound gems. West Lake is the toughest to reach.

**User Groups:** Hikers, dogs, and horses. No mountain bikes. No wheelchair facilities.

**Permits:** A wilderness permit is required for overnight stays and is available from the Bridgeport Ranger Station. Quotas are in effect from the last Saturday in June to September 18; permits are available in advance by mail for this period for a $3 per person fee. See the website www.sierranevadawild.gov for a permit application.

**Maps:** Humboldt-Toiyabe National Forest (Bridgeport) or Hoover Wilderness. For a topographic map, ask the USGS for Twin Lakes.

**Directions:** From Bridgeport, drive south on U.S. 395 for 4.5 miles to Green Creek Road (dirt). Turn west and drive 8.2 miles to the signed trailhead parking area, shortly before Green Creek Campground.

**Contact:** Humboldt-Toiyabe National Forest, Bridgeport Ranger District, HCR1 Box 1000, Bridgeport, CA 93517, 760/932-7070, website: www.fs.fed.us/htnf.

## 8 VIRGINIA LAKES TRAIL
### 6.2–10.2 mi / 3.0 hrs–2.0 days

**in the Hoover Wilderness south of Bridgeport**

Map 10.1, page 437

Virginia Lakes form the gateway to a beautiful high-mountain basin that contains eight small alpine lakes within a two-mile radius. The trailhead is at the Big Virginia Lake day-use area, set at 9,500 feet between mountain peaks that jut 12,000 feet into the sky. From here, you hike west past Blue Lake to Cooney Lake and on to Frog Lakes (a very easy 1.4 miles), then start climbing seriously, continuing 1.8 more miles to 11,100-foot Summit Pass. The landscape here is windswept, barren, and beautiful—a mix of rock, occasional whitebark pines, and high alpine wildflowers. Many hikers take a look at the scene from the pass, then retreat to one of the aforementioned lakes to spend the afternoon, making a 6.2-mile day. If you continue beyond the pass, you curve downhill through dozens of switchbacks for 1.4 miles, then climb gently .5 mile west to Summit Lake (at 10,203 feet), on the northeast boundary of Yosemite National Park. Summit Lake is set between Camiaca Peak (11,739 feet) to the north and Excelsior Mountain (12,446 feet) to the south. This is the logical place for backpackers to make camp, and for day-trippers to turn around for a 10.2-mile day. If you want to take a longer trip into even wilder country, you can do so from this point. The trail skirts Summit Lake's north side, then enters Yosemite National Park in Virginia Canyon, one of the least visited areas of the park. Another option is to take the fork right before Summit Lake that leads east (right) to the double Hoover Lakes, connecting with the Green Creek Trail. Some backpackers and day hikers make a one-way hike of about 11 miles out of this trip by arranging to have a shuttle car waiting for them at the Green Creek trailhead (see the previous hike).

**User Groups:** Hikers, dogs, and horses. No dogs on trail in the Yosemite National Park portion. No mountain bikes. No wheelchair facilities.

**Permits:** A wilderness permit is required for overnight stays and is available from the Bridgeport Ranger Station. Quotas are in effect from the last Saturday in June to September 18; permits are available in advance by mail for this period for a $3 per person fee. See the website www.sierranevadawild.gov for a permit application.

**Maps:** Humboldt-Toiyabe National Forest (Bridgeport) or Hoover Wilderness. For a topographic map, ask the USGS for Dunderberg Peak.

**Directions:** From Bridgeport, drive 13.5 miles south on U.S. 395 (or from Lee Vining, drive 12 miles north on U.S. 395) to Conway Summit. Turn west on Virginia Lakes Road and drive 6.5 miles to the trailhead, at the Big Virginia Lake day-use area.

**Contact:** Humboldt-Toiyabe National Forest, Bridgeport Ranger District, HCR 1, Box 1000, Bridgeport, CA 93517, 760/932-7070, website: www.fs.fed.us/htnf.

## 9 LUNDY CANYON TRAIL
### 4.4–10.0 mi /
### 2.0 hrs–2.0 days

**south of Bridgeport in the Hoover Wilderness**

**Map 10.1, page 437**

The Lundy Canyon Trail is the back door into the 20 Lakes Basin, a well-traveled area of the Hoover Wilderness that is most commonly accessed from Saddlebag Lake off Highway 120. This is your passport into the sculpted-granite high country, complete with half a dozen gemlike lakes. The trailhead lies about two miles past Lundy Lake, a long, narrow pool set at 7,800 feet. From here, the trail rises along Mill Creek, passing several beaver ponds, a dilapidated miner's cabin, and two small but boisterous waterfalls (Lower and Upper Lundy Falls) as it heads into the Hoover Wilderness. Most visitors hike to the first or second falls, enjoying the gorgeous Eastern Sierra scenery with a relatively mellow walk, then hike back out. Those who continue find that the trail, which climbed gently but steadily for the first 2.2 miles, suddenly reaches what appears to be the back of the canyon. But look straight up the canyon wall to your left—that's where the path continues, although it isn't much of a path. An unmaintained, marginally switchbacked route leads .8 mile upward through a frighteningly steep wall of shale, and the difficulty rating for this trail changes abruptly from a 3 to a 4 (and maybe a 5 on the way back downhill). Use great caution here; one slip and you could take a nasty fall. You don't want to be carrying a pack that is too heavy or unbalanced on this stretch. When you finally make it to the top of the canyon wall, you come out to a beautiful high mountain meadow and a junction near the austere shores of Lake Helen, elevation 10,100 feet (3.3 miles from your start). By going right, you can take a lesser-traveled trail to Shamrock and Steelhead Lakes. Shamrock is .3 mile farther and dotted with many islands; Steelhead is another .5 mile beyond and is framed by 12,242-foot North Peak, towering above.

The main trail goes left to Odell Lake (3.6 miles from your start). From Odell Lake, you could continue on to Hummingbird Lake, then to the north shore of Saddlebag Lake. If you can arrange a car shuttle at Saddlebag Lake, you can extend your trip into a one-way hike of seven miles, and that would save you the harrowing trip back down that shale-covered slope.

Note that one of the best times to visit here is in October, when Lundy Canyon's stands of quaking aspen turn bright gold and seem to dance in the breeze. This is one of the best places to admire fall colors in the Eastern Sierra. July is another first-rate time to visit; the canyon's wildflower displays are remarkable.

**User Groups:** Hikers and dogs. Note that the high country region bordering the trail is closed to dogs for the protection of endangered Sierra bighorn sheep. No horses or mountain bikes. No wheelchair facilities.

**Permits:** A wilderness permit is required for overnight stays and is available from the Mono Basin Scenic Area Visitors Center. There are no quotas on this trail, so advance reservations are not required.

**Maps:** For a map, ask the U.S. Forest Service for Inyo National Forest or Hoover Wilderness. For topographic maps, ask the USGS for Lundy and Dunderberg Peak.

**Directions:** From Lee Vining, drive north on U.S. 395 for seven miles to Lundy Lake Road. Turn west on Lundy Lake Road and drive five miles to Lundy Lake. Continue two miles farther (on an unpaved road) to the trailhead, at the end of the road.

**Contact:** Inyo National Forest, Mono Basin Scenic Area Visitors Center, P.O. Box 429, Lee Vining, CA 93541, 760/647-3044, website: www.fs.fed.us/r5/inyo.

## 🔟 LAKE CANYON AND MAY LUNDY MINE
**7.0 mi / 3.5 hrs or 2.0 days**

**south of Bridgeport in the Hoover Wilderness**

**Map 10.1, page 437**

The Lundy Lake area is blessed with two first-rate day hiking trails that lead into two separate and distinct canyons: Lundy Canyon (see previous listing) and Lake Canyon. Both paths offer so many rewards that when you drive up to Lundy Lake, it's hard to decide which one to take. History buffs and scenery lovers would do well to take this trip from Lundy's dam into Lake Canyon, where they can see the remains of the May Lundy Mine. The mine was worked continuously for two decades starting in 1878, producing a total of about $2 million in gold. As a result, the surrounding community of Lundy grew to support 500 people, despite severe winters and deadly avalanches. The hike to the May Lundy Mine is a fairly steep 3.5 miles one-way, climbing above Lundy Lake on the old mine road that was built in 1881. The road/trail passes Blue Lake and Crystal Lake, where old mining relics can be found. (Crystal Lake is .3 mile off the trail via a left fork.) Continue on the main trail, and you'll see the mine remains—old railcar tracks, tailings, and a closed-off mine shaft. Just beyond is Oneida Lake, whose waters were used to run the stamp mill for the mine. Even without the fascinating traces of history, this is an extraordinarily beautiful place. You'll want to linger a while at sparkling Oneida Lake.

**User Groups:** Hikers and dogs (note that the high-country region bordering the trail is closed to dogs for the protection of endangered Sierra bighorn sheep). No horses or mountain bikes. No wheelchair facilities.

**Permits:** A wilderness permit is required for overnight stays and is available from the Mono Basin Scenic Area Visitors Center. There are no quotas on this trail, so advance reservations are not required.

**Maps:** For a map, ask the U.S. Forest Service for Inyo National Forest or Hoover Wilderness. For topographic maps, ask the USGS for Lundy.

**Directions:** From Lee Vining, drive north on U.S. 395 for seven miles to Lundy Lake Road. Turn west on Lundy Lake Road and drive five miles to Lundy Lake's dam. Turn left and drive .25 mile to a locked gate and trailhead.

**Contact:** Inyo National Forest, Mono Basin Scenic Area Visitors Center, P.O. Box 429, Lee Vining, CA 93541, 760/647-3044, website: www.fs.fed.us/r5/inyo.

## **11** PRESTON FLAT TRAIL
### 8.4 mi / 4.0 hrs or 2.0 days

**in Stanislaus National Forest**

Map 10.2, page 438

If you want access to the free-flowing stretch of the Tuolumne River west of Hetch Hetchy Reservoir—whether it is to fish, swim, or just take a nice mellow hike—there aren't many places where you can find it without taking a long hike downhill, followed by a long hike uphill. The solution is the Preston Flat Trail, which on a winter or spring day is an ideal path for day hiking. If you want to stay overnight, you can do that, too. Several good campsites are found along the trail, which sticks closely to the river for most of its 4.2-mile length. The trail ends at an overlook of Preston Falls, a 15-foot waterfall that lies just .5 mile downstream of the boundary line for Yosemite National Park. Shortly before the trail's end are the remains of an old cabin that was built here by a homesteader named Preston. The trail's grade is very mellow—level or nearly so all the way—and spring wildflowers can be abundant.

**User Groups:** Hikers, horses, dogs and mountain bikes. No wheelchair facilities.

**Permits:** A free campfire permit is required for overnight stays. Parking and access are free.

**Maps:** For a map, ask the U.S. Forest Service for Stanislaus National Forest. For a topographic map, ask the USGS for Cherry Lake South.

**Directions:** From Groveland, drive east on Highway 120 for 14 miles toward Yosemite National Park. Turn left on Cherry Lake Road, drive 8.5 miles to Early Intake, and cross the bridge across the Tuolumne River. Turn right and drive .8 mile to the trailhead parking area at the end of the road, just beyond Kirkwood Powerhouse.

**Contact:** Stanislaus National Forest, Groveland Ranger District, 24545 Highway 120, Groveland, CA 95321, 209/962-7825, website: www.fs.fed.us/r5/stanislaus.

## **12** LAKE ELEANOR
### 3.0 mi / 1.5 hrs

**in northwest Yosemite National Park**

Map 10.2, page 438

Up here in the Hetch Hetchy region of Yosemite, elevations are low, and temperatures can heat up. Whereas that may not be good news in July and August, it's great news early in the year, when the Yosemite high country is still buried in snow. Lake Eleanor (elevation 4,657 feet) is a favorite of anglers and hikers who head for the easy trail that skirts the three-mile-long lake's edge. Swimming and canoeing are also popular in summer. Originally a naturally shallow glacial lake, Lake Eleanor was "improved" by the city of San Francisco by damming Eleanor Creek in 1928, five years before the dam at Hetch Hetchy was completed. Today, Lake Eleanor is the second-largest lake in Yosemite National Park (after Hetch Hetchy). The access road to Lake Eleanor ends .25 mile before the lake, so you start your hike there, then take a mellow walk along the lake's south shore. Much of the lake's western side is dotted with picturesque islands.

Special Note: Check your calendar before you go. The gate at Cherry Lake is closed every year one week before deer season, which is usually sometime in September, and doesn't reopen until spring. Most years the road is open from May 1 to September 15.

**User Groups:** Hikers and horses. No dogs or mountain bikes. No wheelchair facilities.

**Permits:** No permits are required. Parking and access are free (the trailhead is outside Yosemite National Park).

**Maps:** Free park maps are available at park entrance stations or by contacting Yosemite National Park at the address below. A Yosemite map is available from Tom Harrison Maps. For a topographic map, ask the USGS for Lake Eleanor.

**Directions:** From Groveland, drive east on Highway 120 for 13 miles toward Yosemite National Park. Turn left on Cherry Lake Road and drive 24 miles to Cherry Lake's dam, then cross it and turn right on Road 1N14, a dirt road that is signed for Lake Eleanor. Follow this road four miles to its end, at the gated Yosemite National Park boundary, .25 mile south of the lake.

**Contact:** Yosemite National Park Public Information Office, P.O. Box 577, Yosemite National Park, CA 95389, 209/372-0200, website: www.nps.gov/yose.

## 13 HETCH HETCHY RESERVOIR
**13.0 mi / 1.0 or 2.0 days**

**in northwest Yosemite National Park**

Map 10.2, page 438

It's spring and you're hungering for a Yosemite backpacking trip, but Tuolumne Meadows is knee-deep in melting snow. Then you'll want to hike the northern edge of Hetch Hetchy Reservoir (elevation 3,796 feet), admiring three stunning waterfalls along the way: Tueeulala, Wapama, and Rancheria. It's a long round-trip day hike or an easy overnight backpacking trip to the eastern edge of the reservoir and Rancheria Falls, where the bears are some of the boldest in all of Yosemite. (Bear canisters are required for backpackers.)

Whereas Rancheria Falls is a series of cascades, Wapama Falls, on Falls Creek, is a Bridalveil-like plume of whitewater, plunging daringly into the reservoir. In spring, Wapama Falls sometimes flows so furiously that the park service closes the trail. In contrast, Tueeulala Falls is a delicate wisp of a fall that dries up by early summer. Many day hikers simply walk the 2.4 miles to see Tueeulala Falls and Wapama Falls and then turn back, having had a very satisfying day. Those who continue onward find that the trail is generally level, with a total elevation gain of only 1,300 feet. It is manageable even for beginning backpackers. Fishing in the reservoir is fair in spring and fall, but remember: Swimming is not allowed. The trail starts by crossing the giant O'Shaughnessy Dam, giving you pause to curse the San Francisco politicians who in 1908 believed that flooding Hetch Hetchy's valley, a near twin to stunning Yosemite Valley, was a good idea. It just goes to show you—the good old days were not always so good.

**User Groups:** Hikers and horses. No dogs or mountain bikes. No wheelchair facilities.

**Permits:** There is a $20 per vehicle entrance fee at Yosemite National Park, good for seven days. Free wilderness permits are required for overnight stays. They are available on a first-come, first-served basis up to one day in advance at the Yosemite Wilderness kiosk near your chosen trailhead, or farther in advance by mail, phone, or email for a $5 per person reservation fee.

**Maps:** Free park maps are available at park entrance stations or by contacting Yosemite National Park at the address below. A Yosemite map is available from Tom Harrison Maps. For topographic maps, ask the USGS for Lake Eleanor and Hetch Hetchy Reservoir.

**Directions:** From Groveland, drive east on Highway 120 for 22.5 miles to the Evergreen Road turnoff signed for Hetch Hetchy Reservoir on the left, a mile west of the Big Oak Flat entrance to Yosemite. Drive north on Evergreen Road for 7.4 miles and turn right on Hetch Hetchy Road. Drive 16 miles to the dam and trailhead.

**Contact:** Yosemite National Park Public Information Office, P.O. Box 577, Yosemite National Park, CA 95389, 209/372-0200 or 209/372-0740 (permit reservations), websites: www.nps.gov/yose or www.nps.gov/yose/wilderness (permit reservations).

## 14 LAUREL LAKE
### 14.6 mi / 1.0 or 2.0 days

**in northwest Yosemite National Park**

Map 10.2, page 438

The Hetch Hetchy region of Yosemite is ideal for late-spring backpacking trips, with far less crowds than Yosemite Valley and far less snow than Tuolumne Meadows. And Laurel Lake is an ideal weekend destination in the region—just far enough to make you feel like you've gotten away, but close enough for a two-day trip (or even a one-day trip, if you're an ambitious day hiker). The trip begins at Hetch Hetchy Reservoir, and after an initial one-mile stretch along the lakeshore, you turn left and head up, up, and up on the Beehive Trail. The trail follows an old road through a series of switchbacks, climbing 1,200 feet over 1.8 miles to the canyon rim and a junction. Turn right, and your trail departs from the road and meanders on a much easier grade through pine and incense cedar forest. In another 2.4 miles, turn right and stroll for a mile to Beehive Meadow, then take either of two trails to the lake (most people opt for the shorter trail; both are signed). Beautiful Laurel Lake is surrounded by aspen groves, firs, and lodgepole pines, and its waters are a fair bet for rainbow trout fishing. Those who want to add on another night to this trip can set out for even more scenic Lake Vernon the next day (four miles away).

**User Groups:** Hikers and horses. No dogs or mountain bikes. No wheelchair facilities.

**Permits:** There is a $20 per vehicle entrance fee at Yosemite National Park, good for seven days. Free wilderness permits are required for overnight stays. They are available on a first-come, first-served basis up to one day in advance at the Yosemite Wilderness kiosk near your chosen trailhead, or farther in advance by mail, phone, or email for a $5 per person reservation fee.

**Maps:** Free park maps are available at park entrance stations or by contacting Yosemite National Park at the address below. A Yosemite map is available from Tom Harrison Maps. For topographic maps, ask the USGS for Lake Eleanor and Hetch Hetchy Reservoir.

**Directions:** From Groveland, drive east on Highway 120 for 22.5 miles to the Evergreen Road turnoff signed for Hetch Hetchy Reservoir (on the left), a mile west of the Big Oak Flat entrance to Yosemite. Drive north on Evergreen Road for 7.4 miles and turn right on Hetch Hetchy Road. Drive 16 miles to the dam and trailhead.

**Contact:** Yosemite National Park Public Information Office, P.O. Box 577, Yosemite National Park, CA 95389, 209/372-0200 or 209/372-0740 (permit reservations), websites: www.nps.gov/yose or www.nps.gov/yose/wilderness (permit reservations).

## 15 LOOKOUT POINT
### 2.6 mi / 1.2 hrs

**in northwest Yosemite National Park**

Map 10.2, page 438

Check your calendar. Is it springtime? Are most of the high-country trails in Yosemite National Park still snowed in? Then it's time to take the easy jaunt to Lookout Point, where you can admire Hetch Hetchy Reservoir and its waterfalls from an unusual perspective, and count the plentiful wildflowers along the trail as you walk. The Lookout Point Trail begins by the Mather Ranger Station, on Hetch Hetchy Road. Begin hiking at the trail sign for Cottonwood and Smith Meadows and Hetch Hetchy (it's not signed for Lookout Point). Turn left at the first junction, then follow the trail as it roughly parallels Hetch Hetchy Road for .5 mile. You turn away from the road with a brief uphill stretch, then you enter a level, forested area that was severely burned in the wildfires of 1996. This is where the flowers bloom profusely in springtime. Look for a trail junction at one mile out, and bear left for Lookout Point, .3 mile away. The path gets rather faint in places, but rock cairns mark the way. Just head for the highest point you see atop a granite knob dotted with a few Jeffrey pines. You'll know you're at Lookout Point when you can see the west end of Hetch Hetchy Reservoir (including its immense dam) and two of Hetch Hetchy's beautiful waterfalls: Wapama and Tueeulala. If you visit much later than May or June, you may see only Wapama, the most robust of Hetch Hetchy's waterfalls. (Tueeulala dries up early in the year.) Although the vista is not perfect from Lookout Point—it would be better if it were 500 feet higher or perhaps farther away from the fast-growing ponderosa pines—this is still a fine spot to spread out a picnic.

**User Groups:** Hikers and horses. No dogs or mountain bikes. No wheelchair facilities.

**Permits:** No permits are required. There is a $20 per vehicle entrance fee at Yosemite National Park, good for seven days.

**Maps:** Free park maps are available at park entrance stations or by contacting Yosemite National Park at the address below. A Yosemite map is available from Tom Harrison Maps. For a topographic map, ask the USGS for Lake Eleanor.

**Directions:** From Groveland, drive east on Highway 120 for 22.5 miles to the Evergreen Road turnoff (on the left), signed for Hetch Hetchy Reservoir (it's a mile west of the Big Oak Flat entrance to Yosemite). Drive north on Evergreen Road for 7.4 miles, then turn right on Hetch Hetchy Road. Drive 1.7 miles to the entrance kiosk by the Mather Ranger Station; the trail begins 100 yards past the entrance kiosk, just beyond the ranger station, on the right.

**Contact:** Yosemite National Park Public Information Office, P.O. Box 577, Yosemite National Park, CA 95389, 209/372-0200, website: www.nps.gov/yose.

# 16 CARLON FALLS
**3.8 mi / 2.5 hrs**

on the border of Stanislaus National Forest and northwest Yosemite National Park

**Map 10.2, page 438**

Carlon Falls is a pretty cascade on the South Fork Tuolumne River in the far western region of Yosemite. It is so far west that the trailhead is actually in Stanislaus National Forest, outside the park border. You hike about 100 feet and then you enter Yosemite National Park. This means there is no $20 entrance fee, no waiting in line at the entrance kiosk, and no crowds. The trailhead is across from Carlon Day-Use Area, a popular picnicking and fishing spot on the Tuolumne River. Follow the trail along the northern bank of the river to reach the falls, in just under two miles. The path is completely shaded, mostly level (except for one short climb that skirts a landslide area), and fairly easy to follow—although it does require clambering over a lot of fallen trees. The waterfall drops in two tiers over wide granite ledges, and the riverbanks surrounding it are covered with big conifers and dense foliage. A bonus is that unlike most Yosemite waterfalls, Carlon Falls runs year-round. It's great to visit in the autumn, when the deciduous dogwoods and oaks show their brilliant colors.

**User Groups:** Hikers only. No dogs, horses, or mountain bikes. No wheelchair facilities.

**Permits:** No permits are required. Parking and access are free.

**Maps:** For a map, ask the U.S. Forest Service for Stanislaus National Forest. For a topographic map, ask the USGS for Ackerson Mountain.

**Directions:** From Groveland, drive east on Highway 120 for 22.5 miles to the Evergreen Road turnoff, signed for Hetch Hetchy Reservoir, one mile west of the Big Oak Flat entrance to Yosemite. Follow Evergreen Road north for one mile to the far side of the bridge just past Carlon Day-Use Area. Park on the right, at the closed-off dirt road on the north side of the bridge. There is room for about five cars. Begin hiking on the closed road, heading upstream. The road turns to single track after about 100 yards.

**Contact:** Stanislaus National Forest, Groveland Ranger District, 24545 Highway 120, Groveland, CA 95321, 209/962-7825, website: www.fs.fed.us/r5/stanislaus.

## 17 MERCED GROVE
**3.0 mi / 1.5 hrs**

**in western Yosemite National Park**

> **Map 10.2, page 438**

There are three giant sequoia groves in Yosemite National Park—Merced, Tuolumne, and Mariposa. Because the Merced Grove is the smallest of the three groves, it is usually the least visited, which makes it the best in our opinion. Generally it only gets traffic from people who enter Yosemite at the Big Oak Flat entrance (in the north) and drive by it on their way to Yosemite Valley. The hiking is on a closed-off dirt road that is ideal for snowshoeing in winter. The trail is level and straight for the first .5 mile; bear left at the only junction, and head downhill through a lovely mixed forest of white firs, incense cedars, ponderosa pines, and sugar pines. You reach the small sequoia grove at 1.5 miles; the first group of six trees will take your breath away. Continue another 100 yards past these beauties; the two largest sequoias of the Merced Grove are directly across from a handsome old log cabin. It was originally built as a retreat for the park superintendent but is no longer used. Retrace your steps from the cabin, hiking uphill for your return.

**User Groups:** Hikers only. No dogs, horses, or mountain bikes. No wheelchair facilities.

**Permits:** No permits are required. There is a $20 per vehicle entrance fee at Yosemite National Park, good for seven days.

**Maps:** Free park maps are available at park entrance stations or by contacting Yosemite National Park at the address below. A Yosemite map is available from Tom Harrison Maps. For a topographic map, ask the USGS for Ackerson Mountain.

**Directions:** From Merced, drive 70 miles northeast on Highway 140 to Yosemite National Park. Follow the signs toward Yosemite Valley, entering through the Arch Rock entrance station. Continue 4.5 miles to the left turnoff for Tioga Road/Highway 120, looping back out of the valley on Big Oak Flat Road. Continue straight on Big Oak Flat Road for 13.5 miles (past the Tioga Road turnoff) to the Merced Grove parking area, on the left. If you enter Yosemite at the Big Oak Flat entrance station on Highway 120, drive 4.3 miles southeast to reach the trailhead, on your right.

**Contact:** Yosemite National Park Public Information Office, P.O. Box 577, Yosemite National Park, CA 95389, 209/372-0200, website: www.nps.gov/yose.

## 18 TUOLUMNE GROVE
**2.5 mi / 1.5 hrs**

**in western Yosemite National Park**

> **Map 10.2, page 438**

What's nice about the Tuolumne Grove of giant sequoias in Yosemite National Park is that you have to walk a mile to access it, unlike the old days, before 1993, when motorists were allowed to drive right in. The grove is located on the old Big Oak Flat Road, which is a six-mile historic road/trail that is open to bikes and hikers (although bikes are a rarity here). Leave your car at the parking lot near Crane Flat and hike downhill into the big trees. It is one mile to the first sequoias; a .5-mile loop trail continues from here through more of the grove. Don't forget about the uphill return trip; save some energy for the moderate grade, which climbs about 500 feet. The Tuolumne Grove's big claim to fame is that it has one of the two remaining walk-through trees in Yosemite; this one is called the Dead Giant. It's a stump that was tunneled in 1878. Go ahead, walk through it–everybody does. The grove is especially beautiful in winter or early spring, when you can take a snowshoe walk through the sequoias. Of all the sights in Yosemite, there's nothing quite like the vision of these gentle giants crowned with snow.

**User Groups:** Hikers and mountain bikes. No dogs or horses. No wheelchair facilities.

**Permits:** No permits are required. There is a $20 per vehicle entrance fee at Yosemite National Park, good for seven days.

**Maps:** Free park maps are available at park entrance stations or by contacting Yosemite National Park at the address below. A Yosemite map is available from Tom Harrison Maps. For a topographic map, ask the USGS for Ackerson Mountain.

**Directions:** From Merced, drive 70 miles northeast on Highway 140 to Yosemite National Park. Follow the signs toward Yosemite Valley, entering through the Arch Rock entrance station. Continue 4.5 miles to the left turnoff for Tioga Road/Highway 120, looping back out of the valley on Big Oak Flat Road. In 9.3 miles, turn right on Tioga Road, then drive .5 mile to the Tuolumne Grove parking lot, on the left, near Crane Flat. If you enter Yosemite at the Big Oak Flat entrance station on Highway 120, drive 7.7 miles southeast to the Crane Flat/Highway 120 East turnoff. Turn left and drive .5 mile to the Tuolumne Grove trailhead.

**Contact:** Yosemite National Park Public Information Office, P.O. Box 577, Yosemite National Park, CA 95389, 209/372-0200, website: www.nps.gov/yose.

## 19 LUKENS LAKE
### 1.5–4.6 mi / 1.0–2.0 hr

**off Tioga Road in Yosemite National Park**

Map 10.2, page 438

The Lukens Lake Trail is the perfect introductory lake hike for families in Yosemite National Park. A six-year-old could make the trip easily. A bonus is that the trailhead is on the western end of Tioga Road, so it is quickly reached from points in Yosemite Valley. The trail is .75 mile long, leading from Tioga Road up to a saddle, then dropping down to the lake. It winds through a dense red fir forest, filled with mammoth trees, then cuts across a corn lily-filled meadow to the edge of the shallow lake. Swimming is highly recommended; by midsummer, this is one of the warmest lakes in the park. Note that if you want to take a longer hike to Lukens Lake, you can start from the trailhead at White Wolf, and make a 4.6-mile round-trip.

**User Groups:** Hikers only. No dogs, horses, or mountain bikes. No wheelchair facilities.

**Permits:** No permits are required. There is a $20 per vehicle entrance fee at Yosemite National Park, good for seven days.

**Maps:** Free park maps are available at park entrance stations or by contacting Yosemite National Park at the address below. A Yosemite map is available from Tom Harrison Maps. For a topographic map, ask the USGS for Tamarack Flat.

**Directions:** From Merced, drive 70 miles northeast on Highway 140 to Yosemite National Park. Follow the signs to Yosemite Valley, entering through the Arch Rock entrance station. Continue 4.5 miles to the left turnoff for Tioga Road/Highway 120, looping back out of the valley on Big Oak Flat Road. In 9.3 miles, turn right on Tioga Road and drive 16.2 miles to the Lukens Lake trailhead parking area, on the south side of the road. The trail begins across the road.

**Contact:** Yosemite National Park Public Information Office, P.O. Box 577, Yosemite National Park, CA 95389, 209/372-0200, website: www.nps.gov/yose.

## 20 TEN LAKES/GRANT LAKES
### 12.8 mi / 1.0 or 2.0 days

**off Tioga Road in Yosemite National Park**

Map 10.2, page 438

The Ten Lakes area is incredibly popular with backpackers, so get your wilderness permit early. Or get an early-morning start and make this trip as a day hike; just be prepared for some serious climbing and long miles. From the Ten Lakes trailhead at Tioga Road (elevation 7,500 feet), the path climbs steadily for the first four miles. There's only one brutally steep stretch, which comes between miles four and five, after a pretty stroll around Half Moon Meadow. A series of tight switchbacks pulls you through a nasty 800-foot elevation gain to the top of a ridge and the Ten Lakes/Grant Lakes junction. From there, you make a choice. Turn right to reach Grant Lakes and head mostly downhill for a mile; or, to reach Ten Lakes, continue straight, soon heading steeply downhill for 1.4 miles. The Grant Lakes offer a little more solitude (good for day hikers), while the two larger of the Ten Lakes have the best campsites, with many trees along their shorelines offering protection from the wind. All of the lakes are sparkling, rockbound beauties. Whether you go to Ten Lakes or Grant Lakes, don't miss taking a side trip to the rocky overlook above the Ten Lakes Basin. It's only .5 mile from the Ten Lakes/Grant Lakes junction (continue straight for Ten Lakes, then take the unsigned trail to the left of the main trail and head for the highest point). Four of the Ten Lakes are visible from this promontory, as well as a section of the Grand Canyon of the Tuolumne. Wow!

**User Groups:** Hikers only. No dogs, horses, or mountain bikes. No wheelchair facilities.

**Permits:** There is a $20 per vehicle entrance fee at Yosemite National Park, good for seven days. Free wilderness permits are required for overnight stays. They are available on a first-come, first-served basis up to one day in advance at the Yosemite Wilderness kiosk near your chosen trailhead or farther in advance by mail, phone, or email for a $5 per person reservation fee.

**Maps:** Free park maps are available at park entrance stations or by contacting Yosemite National Park at the address below. A Yosemite map is available from Tom Harrison Maps.

For topographic maps, ask the USGS for Yosemite Falls and Ten Lakes.

**Directions:** From Merced, drive 70 miles northeast on Highway 140 to Yosemite National Park. Follow the signs toward Yosemite Valley, entering through the Arch Rock entrance station. Continue 4.5 miles to the left turnoff for Tioga Road/Highway 120, looping back out of the valley on Big Oak Flat Road. In 9.3 miles, turn right on Tioga Road and drive 19.4 miles to the Yosemite Creek and Ten Lakes trailhead parking area which is on the south side of the road. The trail begins on the north side of the road.

**Contact:** Yosemite National Park Public Information Office, P.O. Box 577, Yosemite National Park, CA 95389, 209/372-0200 or 209/372-0740 (permit reservations), websites: www.nps.gov/yose or www.nps.gov/yose/wilderness (permit reservations).

## 21 NORTH DOME
### 9.0 mi / 5.0 hrs

**off Tioga Road in Yosemite National Park**

> Map 10.2, page 438

There are those who say that climbing Half Dome is a bit of a disappointment, and not just because of the crowds. When you reach the top and check out the commanding view, the panorama of granite is not quite as awesome as you might expect, and that's because you can't see Half Dome—you're standing on it.

That's a dilemma that's easy to fix. If Half Dome is an absolute necessity in your view of Yosemite, climb North Dome instead, which offers a heart-stopping view of that big piece of granite. The route is not for the faint of heart, but when you are way up high looking down at Tenaya Canyon and across at Half Dome and Clouds Rest—well, you'll know why you came. You could hike to North Dome from Yosemite Valley, but it's a long, butt-kicking trip. A much preferred route begins at the Porcupine Creek trailhead on Tioga Road. The dirt access road shortly brings you to a proper trail, signed as Porcupine Creek. Continue straight at two possible junctions near the 2.5-mile mark, heading due south for North Dome. After the third mile, your views begin to open up, providing fine vistas of North Dome and Half Dome and increasing your anticipation. At the trail junction at 4.5 miles, take the left spur for the final hike to North Dome's summit. Surprise—it's a downhill grade to reach it. Hope you brought plenty of film with you; the view from the top is sublime. Half Dome, just across the canyon, appears close enough to touch. Clouds Rest is a dramatic sight to the northeast. To the southwest, you can see cars crawling along the Yosemite Valley floor. On your return trip, consider taking the unsigned spur trail two miles from North Dome, at an obvious saddle. The spur leads a steep .25 mile to Indian Rock, the only natural arch on land in Yosemite. It's great fun to climb around on.

**User Groups:** Hikers only. No dogs, horses, or mountain bikes. No wheelchair facilities.

**Permits:** There is a $20 per vehicle entrance fee at Yosemite National Park, good for seven days. Free wilderness permits are required for overnight stays. They are available on a first-come, first-served basis up to one day in advance at the Yosemite Wilderness kiosk near your chosen trailhead or farther in advance by mail, phone, or email for a $5 per person reservation fee.

**Maps:** Free park maps are available at park entrance stations or by contacting Yosemite National Park at the address below. A Yosemite map is available from Tom Harrison Maps. For a topographic map, ask the USGS for Yosemite Falls.

**Directions:** From Merced, drive 70 miles northeast on Highway 140 to Yosemite National Park. Follow the signs toward Yosemite Valley, entering through the Arch Rock entrance station. Continue 4.5 miles to the left turnoff for Tioga Road/Highway 120, looping back out of the valley on Big Oak Flat Road. In 9.3 miles, turn right on Tioga Road and drive 24.5 miles to the Porcupine Creek trailhead parking area, on the right, a mile past Porcupine Flat Campground.

**Contact:** Yosemite National Park Public Information Office, P.O. Box 577, Yosemite National Park, CA 95389, 209/372-0200 or 209/372-0740 (permit reservations), websites: www.nps.gov/yose or www.nps.gov/yose/wilderness (permit reservations).

## 22 MAY LAKE AND MOUNT HOFFMAN
**2.4–6.0 mi / 2.0–4.0 hrs**

**off Tioga Road in Yosemite National Park**

Map 10.2, page 438

Here's a hike that you can take the kids on—well, the first part, anyway. It's an easy 1.2 miles to May Lake, tucked in below 10,850-foot Mount Hoffman. The trail to the lake has a total elevation gain of only 400 feet, and better yet, it's downhill all the way home. Attaining the summit of Mount Hoffman, on the other hand, requires a challenging ascent, and is best left to more seasoned hikers. (Leave the kids at home if you are going to continue this hike from the shores of May Lake to the top of Mount Hoffman.) The trail to both destinations begins at the Snow Flat trailhead (two miles off Tioga Road), passes through a lodgepole pine forest, climbs up a granite-lined slope, then drops down to May Lake's southern shore. A High Sierra Camp is located here. Unfortunately, swimming is not allowed in May Lake, because it is the water source for the camp. Nonetheless, wandering along the scenic, granite-ringed shoreline is a pleasant way to spend the afternoon.

To turn this easy walk into a butt-kicker, follow the obvious use trail to the west, which leads around to the north side of May Lake. From the northwest shore, a fairly distinct use trail leads to Hoffman's summit. This is not an official park trail, and it requires scrambling skills and sure footing, especially as you near the top. It also requires good lungs and legs: you have to gain another 1,500 feet in about two miles. So why do it? The view from Mount Hoffman's ridgeline is first-class, with Half Dome, Clouds Rest, Tenaya Lake, and May Lake all in sight. Mount Hoffman is the exact geographical center of Yosemite National Park. The peak has two main summits; the one with the weather station on top is the highest. Explore the entire ridgeline, and visit both summits if you have the time; the view is surprisingly different.

**User Groups:** Hikers and horses. No dogs or mountain bikes. No wheelchair facilities.

**Permits:** No permits are required. There is a $20 per vehicle entrance fee at Yosemite National Park, good for seven days.

**Maps:** Free park maps are available at park entrance stations or by contacting Yosemite National Park at the address below. A Yosemite map is available from Tom Harrison Maps. For a topographic map, ask the USGS for Tenaya Lake.

**Directions:** From Merced, drive 70 miles northeast on Highway 140 to Yosemite National Park. Follow the signs toward Yosemite Valley, entering through the Arch Rock entrance station. Continue 4.5 miles to the left turnoff for Tioga Road/Highway 120, looping back out of the valley on Big Oak Flat Road. In 9.3 miles, turn right on Tioga Road and drive 26.6 miles to the May Lake Road turnoff, on the left (near road marker T-21). Drive two miles to the trailhead parking lot.

**Contact:** Yosemite National Park Public Information Office, P.O. Box 577, Yosemite National Park, CA 95389, 209/372-0200, website: www.nps.gov/yose.

## 23 CLOUDS REST
**14.0 mi / 8.0 hrs**

**off Tioga Road in Yosemite National Park**

Map 10.2, page 438

Hiking to Clouds Rest is a trip that's as epic as climbing Half Dome, but with far less people elbowing you along the way. With a 2,300-foot climb and 14 miles to cover, it's not for those who are out of shape. The trail ascends steadily for the first four miles, descends steeply for .5 mile, then climbs again more moderately. Keep the faith—the first 2.5 miles from the trailhead are the toughest. The final summit ascent is a little dicey because of the terrifying dropoffs, but as with other Yosemite peaks, watch your footing on the granite slabs, and you'll be fine. Overall, the route is much safer than climbing Half Dome, because the final ascent is far more gradual, and there are no cables to maneuver. The view from the top of Clouds Rest—of Tenaya Canyon, Half Dome, Yosemite Valley, Tenaya Lake, the Clark Range, and various peaks and ridges—will knock your socks off (hope you brought along an extra pair). Note that if this long hike has made you hot and sweaty, you can stop at the Sunrise Lakes for a swim on the way back—the first lake is only .25 mile from the Clouds Rest/Sunrise Trail junction.

**User Groups:** Hikers only. No dogs, horses, or mountain bikes. No wheelchair facilities.

**Permits:** No permits are required. There is a $20 per vehicle entrance fee at Yosemite National Park, good for seven days.

**Maps:** Free park maps are available at park entrance stations or by contacting Yosemite National Park at the address below. A Yosemite map is available from Tom Harrison Maps. For a topographic map, ask the USGS for Tenaya Lake.

**Directions:** From Merced, drive 70 miles northeast on Highway 140 to Yosemite National Park. Follow the signs toward Yosemite Valley, entering through the Arch Rock entrance station. Continue 4.5 miles to the left turnoff for Tioga Road/Highway 120, looping back out of the valley on Big Oak Flat Road. In 9.3 miles, turn right on Tioga Road and drive 30.3 miles to the Sunrise Lakes trailhead, on the south side of Tioga Road just west of Tenaya Lake.

**Contact:** Yosemite National Park Public Information Office, P.O. Box 577, Yosemite National Park, CA 95389, 209/372-0200, website: www.nps.gov/yose.

## 24 SUNRISE LAKES
**7.5 mi / 4.5 hrs or 2.0 days**

**off Tioga Road in Yosemite National Park**

**Map 10.2, page 438**

With all the people hiking to Clouds Rest, combined with all the people hiking to the Sunrise Lakes, the Sunrise trailhead can look like a mall parking lot on a Saturday. But don't be scared off; the hike to Sunrise Lakes is a great day hike or easy backpacking trip, especially during the week or off-season, with only a 1,000-foot elevation gain and a ton of stellar scenery, including great views of Clouds Rest at your back as you hike the final stretch to the lakes. You follow the trail as it climbs steeply above the edge of Tenaya Canyon. At 2.5 miles, turn left at the sign for the Sunrise High Sierra Camp. In about 10 minutes of easy walking, Lower Sunrise Lake shows up on the right, and the other lakes are shortly after it, on the left. The upper lake is the largest and by far the most popular; lots of folks like to swim and picnic there on warm summer days. Backpackers can pick a site here or continue onward for two more miles to the backpackers' camp or the High Sierra Camp, depending on where they've made their plans.

**User Groups:** Hikers only. No dogs, horses, or mountain bikes. No wheelchair facilities.

**Permits:** There is a $20 per vehicle entrance fee at Yosemite National Park, good for seven days. Free wilderness permits are required for overnight stays. They are available on a first-come, first-served basis up to one day in advance at the Yosemite Wilderness kiosk near your chosen trailhead or farther in advance by mail, phone, or email for a $5 per person reservation fee.

**Maps:** Free park maps are available at park entrance stations or by contacting Yosemite National Park at the address below. A Yosemite map is available from Tom Harrison Maps. For a topographic map, ask the USGS for Tenaya Lake.

**Directions:** From Merced, drive 70 miles northeast on Highway 140 to Yosemite National Park. Follow the signs toward Yosemite Valley, entering through the Arch Rock entrance station. Continue 4.5 miles to the left turnoff for Tioga Road/Highway 120, looping back out of the valley on Big Oak Flat Road. In 9.3 miles, turn right on Tioga Road and drive 30.3 miles to the Sunrise Lakes trailhead, on the south side of Tioga Road just west of Tenaya Lake.

**Contact:** Yosemite National Park Public Information Office, P.O. Box 577, Yosemite National Park, CA 95389, 209/372-0200 or 209/372-0740 (permit reservations), websites: www.nps.gov/yose or www.nps.gov/yose/wilderness (permit reservations).

## 25 TENAYA LAKE
**2.0 mi / 1.0 hr**

**off Tioga Road in Yosemite National Park**

**Map 10.2, page 438**

Lots of people drive east down Tioga Road in a big rush to get to Tuolumne Meadows, but when they see giant Tenaya Lake right along the road, they stop short in their tire tracks. Luckily the 150-acre, sapphire-blue lake has a parking lot and picnic area at its east end, where you can leave your car and take a stroll down to the lake's edge. Although most people stop at the white-sand beach and picnic tables to watch the rock climbers on nearby Polly Dome, you can leave the crowds behind and stroll to the south side of the beach. Pick up the trail there; it leads along the back side of Tenaya Lake, far from the road on the north side. When you get to the lake's west end, where the trail continues but the water views end, just turn around and walk back. It's a perfect, easy hike alongside one of the most beautiful lakes in Yosemite.

**User Groups:** Hikers only. No dogs, horses, or mountain bikes. No wheelchair facilities.

**Permits:** No permits are required. There is a $20 per vehicle entrance fee at Yosemite National Park, good for seven days.

**Maps:** Free park maps are available at park

entrance stations or by contacting Yosemite National Park at the address below. A Yosemite map is available from Tom Harrison Maps. For a topographic map, ask the USGS for Tenaya Lake.

**Directions:** From Merced, drive 70 miles northeast on Highway 140 to Yosemite National Park. Follow the signs toward Yosemite Valley, entering through the Arch Rock entrance station. Continue 4.5 miles to the left turnoff for Tioga Road/Highway 120, looping back out of the valley on Big Oak Flat Road. In 9.3 miles, turn right on Tioga Road and drive 31.7 miles to the eastern Tenaya Lake Picnic Area (another Tenaya Lake picnic area lies .5 mile west). The trail leads from the parking lot.

**Contact:** Yosemite National Park Public Information Office, P.O. Box 577, Yosemite National Park, CA 95389, 209/372-0200, website: www.nps.gov/yose.

## 26 CATHEDRAL LAKES
**7.4 mi / 4.0 hrs or 2.0 days**

**near Tuolumne Meadows in Yosemite National Park**

**Map 10.2, page 438**

The Cathedral Lakes are a tremendously popular easy backpacking destination in Yosemite, but it's such a short hike to reach them that they also make a great day trip. Located on a .5-mile spur off John Muir Trail, the lakes are within a classic glacial cirque, tucked in below 10,840-foot Cathedral Peak. It's as scenic a spot as you'll find anywhere in Yosemite. Campsites are found close to the lakes, but you will need to secure your wilderness permit way in advance in order to spend the night. From the trail's start at Tioga Road, you hike 3.2 miles on John Muir Trail, with a 1,000-foot elevation gain. Much of the trail is shaded by lodgepole pines, but when the path breaks out of the trees, views of surrounding peaks (especially distinctive Cathedral Peak, which looks remarkably different from every angle) keep you oohing and

ahhing the whole way. At 3.2 miles, turn right on the Cathedral Lake spur to reach the lower, larger lake in .5 mile. You'll follow the lake's inlet stream through a gorgeous meadow to the water's edge—then start snapping photographs like crazy. To reach the upper lake, retrace your steps to John Muir Trail and continue another .5 mile. Fishing is often better in the upper lake, and the scenery is equally sublime.

**User Groups:** Hikers and horses. No dogs or mountain bikes. No wheelchair facilities.

**Permits:** There is a $20 per vehicle entrance fee at Yosemite National Park, good for seven days. Free wilderness permits are required for overnight stays. They are available on a first-come, first-served basis up to one day in advance at the Yosemite Wilderness kiosk near your chosen trailhead or farther in advance by mail, phone, or email for a $5 per person reservation fee.

**Maps:** Free park maps are available at park entrance stations or by contacting Yosemite National Park at the address below. A Yosemite map is available from Tom Harrison Maps. For a topographic map, ask the USGS for Tenaya Lake.

**Directions:** From Merced, drive 70 miles northeast on Highway 140 to Yosemite National Park. Follow the signs toward Yosemite Valley, entering through the Arch Rock entrance station. Continue 4.5 miles to the left turnoff for Tioga Road/Highway 120, looping back out of the valley on Big Oak Flat Road. In 9.3 miles, turn right on Tioga Road and drive 37.4 miles to the Cathedral Lakes trailhead, on the right, by Tuolumne Meadows. Park your car in the pullouts on either side of Tioga Road near the trailhead; there is no formal parking lot.

**Contact:** Yosemite National Park Public Information Office, P.O. Box 577, Yosemite National Park, CA 95389, 209/372-0200 or 209/372-0740 (permit reservations), websites: www.nps.gov/yose or www.nps.gov/yose/wilderness (permit reservations).

## 27 VOGELSANG LOOP
### 19.0 mi / 3.0 or 4.0 days

**near Tuolumne Meadows in Yosemite National Park**

**Map 10.2, page 438**

Although this loop is popular with hikers staying at the Vogelsang High Sierra Camp, backpackers who plan early can get a wilderness permit for their own self-designed trip. The traditional route is to head out on the western side of the loop along Rafferty Creek, then take a short spur and spend the night at Vogelsang Lake, which is without question the most visually dramatic spot seen on this trip. It's flanked by Fletcher Peak, a steep and rugged wall of glacier-carved granite. Few trees can grow in this sparse, high-alpine environment. The next day, you rejoin the loop and continue eastward to Evelyn Lake, another favorite camping spot. When it's time to return, you hike down to Lyell Fork, a 2,000-foot descent that takes a few hours, then meet up with John Muir Trail and follow it north through lush green and gorgeous Lyell Canyon, back to the trailhead at Tuolumne Meadows. The trailhead is at 8,600 feet—plenty high to start—and for the most part, the trail undulates along, never gaining or losing more than 2,000 feet.

**User Groups:** Hikers and horses. No dogs or mountain bikes. No wheelchair facilities.

**Permits:** There is a $20 per vehicle entrance fee at Yosemite National Park, good for seven days. Free wilderness permits are required for overnight stays. They are available on a first-come, first-served basis up to one day in advance at the Yosemite Wilderness kiosk near your chosen trailhead or farther in advance by mail, phone, or email for a $5 per person reservation fee.

**Maps:** Free park maps are available at park entrance stations or by contacting Yosemite National Park at the address below. A Yosemite map is available from Tom Harrison Maps. For a topographic map, ask the USGS for Vogelsang Peak.

**Directions:** From Merced, drive 70 miles north-east on Highway 140 to Yosemite National Park. Follow the signs toward Yosemite Valley, entering through the Arch Rock entrance station. Continue 4.5 miles to the left turnoff for Tioga Road/Highway 120, looping back out of the valley on Big Oak Flat Road. In 9.3 miles, turn right on Tioga Road and drive 39.5 miles to the Tuolumne Lodge and Wilderness Permits turnoff, on the right. Turn right and drive .4 mile toward Tuolumne Lodge. Park in the lot on the left signed for Dog Lake and John Muir Trail. The trail begins across the road from the parking lot. Additional parking is available in the Wilderness Permit parking lot, at the turnoff from Tioga Road.

**Contact:** Yosemite National Park Public Information Office, P.O. Box 577, Yosemite National Park, CA 95389, 209/372-0200 or 209/372-0740 (permit reservations), websites: www.nps.gov/yose or www.nps.gov/yose/wilderness (permit reservations).

## 28 LOWER GAYLOR LAKE
### 8.0 mi / 4.0 hrs

**near Tioga Pass in Yosemite National Park**

**Map 10.2, page 438**

This mellow, pretty hike starts on John Muir Trail near Tuolumne Lodge, then heads east along the south side of the Dana Fork Tuolumne River. After two miles, the trail crosses the river and Tioga Road, and heads uphill to Lower Gaylor Lake (elevation 10,049 feet). Note that if you want to get to the Middle and Upper Gaylor Lakes from the lower lake, you have to go cross-country. An easier way is to drive to the Tioga Pass trailhead and follow the trail notes in this chapter for the Middle and Upper Gaylor Lakes hike. Elevation at this trailhead is 9,250 feet; the total gain is about 800 feet to Lower Gaylor Lake, a gentle climb the whole way. The lake is a deep turquoise color and is hemmed in by granite. From its edge, you gain wide vistas of the peaks in the Tuolumne Meadows area. This is classic high-country beauty at its finest.

**User Groups:** Hikers only. No dogs, horses, or mountain bikes. No wheelchair facilities.

**Permits:** No permits are required. There is a $20 per vehicle entrance fee at Yosemite National Park, good for seven days.

**Maps:** Free park maps are available at park entrance stations or by contacting Yosemite National Park at the address below. A Yosemite map is available from Tom Harrison Maps. For topographic maps, ask the USGS for Vogelsang Peak and Tioga Pass.

**Directions:** From Merced, drive 70 miles northeast on Highway 140 to Yosemite National Park. Follow the signs toward Yosemite Valley, entering through the Arch Rock entrance station. Continue 4.5 miles to the left turnoff for Tioga Road/Highway 120, looping back out of the valley on Big Oak Flat Road. In 9.3 miles, turn right on Tioga Road and drive 39.5 miles to the Tuolumne Lodge and Wilderness Permits turnoff, on the right. Turn right and drive .4 mile toward Tuolumne Lodge, then park in the lot on the left signed for Dog Lake and John Muir Trail. The trail begins across the road from the parking lot. Additional parking is available in the Wilderness Permit parking lot, at the turnoff from Tioga Road.

**Contact:** Yosemite National Park Public Information Office, P.O. Box 577, Yosemite National Park, CA 95389, 209/372-0200, website: www.nps.gov/yose.

## 29 ELIZABETH LAKE
### 4.5 mi / 2.5 hrs

**near Tuolumne Meadows in Yosemite National Park**

Map 10.2, page 438

Starting at the trailhead elevation of 8,600 feet, you have a mere 900-foot elevation gain over 2.25 miles to get to pretty Elizabeth Lake, a day hike that is attainable for almost everybody. The only problem is that the trailhead is tricky to find—it's tucked into the back of Tuolumne Meadows Campground, across from the group camp restrooms. Once you locate it, be prepared to climb steeply for the first mile, then

the trail levels out, and you can breathe easier. Luckily the route is mostly shaded by lodgepole pines. Your reward is a gorgeous little lake at the base of Unicorn Peak that is suitable for swimming or fishing. Some folks try to climb Unicorn Peak (10,900 feet) from here, but most are happy to sit at the lake's edge and admire the views of the sculpted peak and its neighbors in the Cathedral Range.

**User Groups:** Hikers only. No dogs, horses, or mountain bikes. No wheelchair facilities.

**Permits:** No permits are required. There is a $20 per vehicle entrance fee at Yosemite National Park, good for seven days.

**Maps:** Free park maps are available at park entrance stations or by contacting Yosemite National Park at the address below. A Yosemite map is available from Tom Harrison Maps. For a topographic map, ask the USGS for Vogelsang Peak.

**Directions:** From Merced, drive 70 miles northeast on Highway 140 to Yosemite National Park. Follow the signs toward Yosemite Valley, entering through the Arch Rock entrance station. Continue 4.5 miles to the left turnoff for Tioga Road/Highway 120, looping back out of the valley on Big Oak Flat Road. In 9.3 miles, turn right on Tioga Road and drive 39 miles to the Tuolumne Meadows Campground. Turn right and follow the signs through the main camp to the group camp. The trail begins across from the group camp restrooms, near group site No. .B49.

**Contact:** Yosemite National Park Public Information Office, P.O. Box 577, Yosemite National Park, CA 95389, 209/372-0200, website: www.nps.gov/yose.

## 30 LYELL CANYON
### 6.0 mi / 3.0 hrs

**near Tuolumne Meadows in Yosemite National Park**

Map 10.2, page 438

This hike is one of the easiest in the Yosemite high country, and since it starts out beautiful and stays that way, you can hike it as long or as short as you like. The total trail length is eight miles one-way, paralleling the Lyell Fork of the Tuolumne River on the Pacific Crest Trail/John Muir Trail. But most people just head out for two or three miles, carrying their fishing rods, and turn back. To reach the Lyell Fork, you must first cross the Dana Fork on a footbridge less than .5 mile from the parking lot. Then after .5 mile, you cross the Lyell Fork on a second footbridge, and head left along the river's south side. A third bridge takes you across Rafferty Creek and into Lyell Canyon. If you like looking at gorgeous meadows and a meandering river, this is your hike. Small trout are plentiful. A bonus is that backpacking sites are located three to four miles out on the trail, so if you get a wilderness permit, you can linger for a few days in paradise.

**User Groups:** Hikers and horses. No dogs or mountain bikes. No wheelchair facilities.

**Permits:** No permits are required. There is a $20 per vehicle entrance fee at Yosemite National Park, good for seven days.

**Maps:** Free park maps are available at park entrance stations or by contacting Yosemite National Park at the address below. A Yosemite map is available from Tom Harrison Maps. For a topographic map, ask the USGS for Vogelsang Peak.

**Directions:** From Merced, drive 70 miles northeast on Highway 140 to Yosemite National Park. Follow the signs toward Yosemite Valley, entering through the Arch Rock entrance station. Continue 4.5 miles to the left turnoff for Tioga Road/Highway 120, looping back out of the valley on Big Oak Flat Road. In 9.3 miles, turn right on Tioga Road and drive 39.5 miles to the Tuolumne Lodge and Wilderness Permits turnoff, on the right. Turn right and drive .4 mile toward Tuolumne Lodge; park in the lot on the left signed for Dog Lake and John Muir Trail. The John Muir Trail begins across the road from the parking lot. Additional parking is available in the Wilderness Permit parking lot, at the turnoff from Tioga Road.

**Contact:** Yosemite National Park Public Information Office, P.O. Box 577, Yosemite National Park, CA 95389, 209/372-0200, website: www.nps.gov/yose.

## 31 YOUNG LAKES LOOP
### 12.5 mi / 1.0 or 2.0 days

near Tuolumne Meadows in Yosemite National Park

Map 10.2, page 438

Starting from the Lembert Dome parking lot, the Young Lakes Loop is a classic Yosemite trip that works equally well as a short backpacking trip or a long day hike. The destination is a series of lakes set in a deep and wide glacial cirque—the kind of awesome scenery that sticks in your mind months later, when you're sitting at a desk somewhere staring at your computer screen. The trip starts with a walk down the wide dirt road that leads to Soda Spring. Pick up the trail near Parson's Lodge that leads to Glen Aulin, and follow it through lodgepole pines for 1.8 miles until you see the right turnoff for Young Lakes. Follow Young Lakes Trail for three more miles, climbing steadily. At five miles out, you'll see the return leg of your loop leading off to the right (signed for Dog Lake). You'll continue straight for another 1.5 miles to Lower Young Lake and a stunning view of Ragged Peak, Mount Conness, and White Mountain. Two more lakes are accessible within a mile to the east. If you have the energy, don't miss the third, upper lake, the most visually stunning of them all. When you're ready to head home, retrace your steps to the junction, and take the eastern (left) fork, returning via Dog Lake and Lembert Dome. Be forewarned: If you loop back this way, it won't be an all-downhill cruise, but the scenery makes the additional climbing worthwhile. If you're exhausted from your trip to the lakes, skip the loop and return the way you came—it's downhill all the way.

**User Groups:** Hikers and horses. No dogs or mountain bikes. No wheelchair facilities.

**Permits:** There is a $20 per vehicle entrance

fee at Yosemite National Park, good for seven days. Free wilderness permits are required for overnight stays. They are available on a first-come, first-served basis up to one day in advance at the Yosemite Wilderness kiosk near your chosen trailhead or farther in advance by mail, phone, or email for a $5 per person reservation fee.

**Maps:** Free park maps are available at park entrance stations or by contacting Yosemite National Park at the address below. A Yosemite map is available from Tom Harrison Maps. For topographic maps, ask the USGS for Tioga Pass and Falls Ridge.

**Directions:** From Merced, drive 70 miles northeast on Highway 140 to Yosemite National Park. Follow the signs toward Yosemite Valley, entering through the Arch Rock entrance station. Continue 4.5 miles to the left turnoff for Tioga Road/Highway 120, looping back out of the valley on Big Oak Flat Road. In 9.3 miles, turn right on Tioga Road and drive 39 miles to the Lembert Dome/Soda Spring/Dog Lake/Glen Aulin trailhead parking, on the left. Begin hiking on the western edge of the parking lot, where there is a gated dirt road signed for Soda Spring.

**Contact:** Yosemite National Park Public Information Office, P.O. Box 577, Yosemite National Park, CA 95389, 209/372-0200 or 209/372-0740 (permit reservations), websites: www.nps.gov/yose or www.nps.gov/yose/wilderness (permit reservations).

## 32 WATERWHEEL FALLS
**16.0 mi / 1.0 or 2.0 days**

**near Tuolumne Meadows in Yosemite National Park**

**Map 10.2, page 438**

Ⓕ This hike could be called the Epic Waterfall Trip. If you hike the entire route, you'll see so many waterfalls and so much water along the way that you'll have enough memories to get you through a 10-year drought. Arrange for a wilderness permit in advance, or reserve a stay at the Glen Aulin High Sier-

ra Camp, so that you can divide the 16 miles over two or more days. If you're in good enough shape, you can do the trip in one day, because the trail is nearly level for the first four miles (a 400-foot elevation loss), then descends more steeply over the next four miles (a 1,500-foot elevation loss). Unfortunately, all the climbing must be done on the way home, so you must reserve your energy and have plenty of food and water (or at least a purifying device so you can filter water from the river).

Follow the trail notes for Glen Aulin and Tuolumne Falls (see next listing) for the first four miles of trail; then continue downstream past Glen Aulin Camp, alternating between stretches of stunning flower- and aspen-lined meadows and stark granite slabs. Waterwheel Falls is only three miles from the camp, and two other major cascades, California and LeConte, are along the way. To see all three falls, make sure you take each spur trail you see that leads to the river; none of the waterfalls is apparent from the main trail. Other hikers will stop you on the trail to ask if you know where the waterfalls are. Whereas all three falls are long whitewater cascades, Waterwheel is considered Yosemite's most unusual-looking waterfall because it has sections of churning water that dip into deep holes in the granite, then shoot out with such velocity that they double back on themselves. When the river level is high, they actually appear to circle around like waterwheels.

**User Groups:** Hikers and horses. No dogs or mountain bikes. No wheelchair facilities.

**Permits:** There is a $20 per vehicle entrance fee at Yosemite National Park, good for seven days. Free wilderness permits are required for overnight stays. They are available on a first-come, first-served basis up to one day in advance at the Yosemite Wilderness kiosk near your chosen trailhead or farther in advance by mail, phone, or email for a $5 per person reservation fee.

**Maps:** Free park maps are available at park entrance stations or by contacting Yosemite National Park at the address below. A Yosemite map is available from Tom Harrison Maps. For topographic maps, ask the USGS for Tioga Pass and Falls Ridge.

**Directions:** From Merced, drive 70 miles northeast on Highway 140 to Yosemite National Park. Follow the signs toward Yosemite Valley, entering through the Arch Rock entrance station. Continue 4.5 miles to the left turnoff for Tioga Road/Highway 120, looping back out of the valley on Big Oak Flat Road. In 9.3 miles, turn right on Tioga Road and drive 39 miles to the Lembert Dome/Soda Spring/Dog Lake/Glen Aulin trailhead parking, on the left. Begin hiking on the western edge of the parking lot, where there is a gated dirt road signed for Soda Spring.

**Contact:** Yosemite National Park Public Information Office, P.O. Box 577, Yosemite National Park, CA 95389, 209/372-0200 or 209/372-0740 (permit reservations), websites: www.nps.gov/yose or www.nps.gov/yose/wilderness (permit reservations).

## 33 GLEN AULIN AND TUOLUMNE FALLS
**9.0 mi / 5.0 hrs**

**near Tuolumne Meadows in Yosemite National Park**

Map 10.2, page 438

Ⓕ Those who aren't up for the Epic Waterfall Trip to Waterwheel Falls (see previous listing) can take this trip instead and maybe even sneak in a good meal at the Glen Aulin High Sierra Camp. To stay in the camp, you must reserve a spot far in advance, but you can often purchase a hot meal just by showing up. Tuolumne Falls drop right by the High Sierra Camp, and reaching the waterfall requires only a 4.5-mile walk with a 400-foot elevation loss. The return climb is easy, with most of the ascent being in the first mile as you head up and over the various cascades of Tuolumne Falls on granite stairs. Follow the dirt road from the Lembert Dome parking lot toward Soda Spring. When you near Parson's Lodge, veer right

on the signed trail to Glen Aulin. You'll walk through lodgepole pine forest, then move closer to the Tuolumne River and get incredible views of Cathedral and Unicorn Peaks, as well as Fairview Dome. After three miles, you'll cross the Tuolumne on a footbridge, and in another .25 mile, you'll reach the first stunning drop of Tuolumne Falls, a 100-foot, churning free fall. Keep descending past more cascades to the base of the falls, where another footbridge leads back across the river and to Glen Aulin. Pick a spot downstream beside a river pool or near the bridge at the base of the waterfall, have a seat, and ponder the exquisite beauty of this place.

**User Groups:** Hikers and horses. No dogs or mountain bikes. No wheelchair facilities.

**Permits:** No permits are required. There is a $20 per vehicle entrance fee at Yosemite National Park, good for seven days.

**Maps:** Free park maps are available at park entrance stations or by contacting Yosemite National Park at the address below. A Yosemite map is available from Tom Harrison Maps. For topographic maps, ask the USGS for Tioga Pass and Falls Ridge.

**Directions:** From Merced, drive 70 miles northeast on Highway 140 to Yosemite National Park. Follow the signs toward Yosemite Valley, entering through the Arch Rock entrance station. Continue 4.5 miles to the left turnoff for Tioga Road/Highway 120, looping back out of the valley on Big Oak Flat Road. In 9.3 miles, turn right on Tioga Road and drive 39 miles to the Lembert Dome/Soda Spring/Dog Lake/Glen Aulin trailhead parking, on the left. Begin hiking on the western edge of the parking lot, where there is a gated dirt road signed for Soda Spring.

**Contact:** Yosemite National Park Public Information Office, P.O. Box 577, Yosemite National Park, CA 95389, 209/372-0200, website: www.nps.gov/yose.

## 34 LEMBERT DOME
**2.8 mi / 1.5 hrs**

**near Tuolumne Meadows in Yosemite National Park**

Map 10.2, page 438

Lembert Dome is a *roche moutonnée* (a French geologic term that means it looks something like a sheep). We never see the resemblance, but we did feel like a couple of mountain goats when we climbed Lembert Dome, elevation 9,450 feet. From the parking area at Lembert Dome's base, you can see rock climbers practicing their stuff on the steep side of the dome, but luckily the hiker's trail heads around to the more-sloped back side. You can walk right up the granite—no ropes necessary. The Dog Lake and Lembert Dome Trail winds its way steeply around to the dome's north side (see next listing); from there, pick any route along the granite that looks manageable. When you reach the top of the dome, you know that you've accomplished something. The view from its highest point—of Tuolumne Meadows and surrounding peaks and domes—is more than worth the effort.

**User Groups:** Hikers only. No dogs, horses, or mountain bikes. No wheelchair facilities.

**Permits:** No permits are required. There is a $20 per vehicle entrance fee at Yosemite National Park, good for seven days.

**Maps:** Free park maps are available at park entrance stations or by contacting Yosemite National Park at the address below. A Yosemite map is available from Tom Harrison Maps. For a topographic map, ask the USGS for Tioga Pass.

**Directions:** From Merced, drive 70 miles northeast on Highway 140 to Yosemite National Park. Follow the signs toward Yosemite Valley, entering through the Arch Rock entrance station. Continue 4.5 miles to the left turnoff for Tioga Road/Highway 120, looping back out of the valley on Big Oak Flat Road. In 9.3 miles, turn right on Tioga Road and drive 39 miles to the Lembert Dome/Soda Spring/Dog Lake/ Glen Aulin trailhead park-ing, on the left. Begin hiking on the trail near the restrooms.

**Contact:** Yosemite National Park Public Information Office, P.O. Box 577, Yosemite National Park, CA 95389, 209/372-0200, website: www.nps.gov/yose.

## 35 DOG LAKE
**3.4 mi / 2.0 hrs**

**near Tuolumne Meadows in Yosemite National Park**

Map 10.2, page 438

Dog Lake is an easy-to-reach destination from Tuolumne Meadows, a perfect place for a family to spend an afternoon in the high country. The hike begins near the base of Lembert Dome, then heads through a gorgeous meadow that offers views of snowy Cathedral and Unicorn Peaks. The trail traverses a granite slab, then splits off from the path to Lembert Dome and starts to climb quite steeply through a lodgepole pine and fir forest. When you reach an intersection with Young Lakes Trail, you're only .25 mile from Dog Lake. The lake is a delight, although with its grassy shoreline, it is often plagued with mosquitos (don't forget the bug spray). Set at 9,170 feet in elevation, it is wide, shallow, and deep blue. The colorful peaks to the east are Mount Dana and Mount Gibbs. You can hike around Dog Lake's perimeter if you please, take a swim in late summer, or just sit by the peaceful shoreline and relax.

**User Groups:** Hikers and horses. No dogs or mountain bikes. No wheelchair facilities.

**Permits:** No permits are required. There is a $20 per vehicle entrance fee at Yosemite National Park, good for seven days.

**Maps:** Free park maps are available at park entrance stations or by contacting Yosemite National Park at the address below. A Yosemite map is available from Tom Harrison Maps. For a topographic map, ask the USGS for Tioga Pass.

**Directions:** From Merced, drive 70 miles northeast on Highway 140 to Yosemite National Park. Follow the signs toward Yosemite Valley, entering through the Arch Rock entrance station. Continue 4.5 miles to the left turnoff for Tioga Road/Highway 120, looping back out of the valley on Big Oak Flat Road. In 9.3 miles, turn right on Tioga Road and drive 39 miles to the Lembert Dome/Soda Spring/Dog Lake/Glen Aulin trailhead parking, on the left. Begin hiking on the trail near the restrooms.

**Contact:** Yosemite National Park Public Information Office, P.O. Box 577, Yosemite National Park, CA 95389, 209/372-0200, website: www.nps.gov/yose.

## 36 TUOLUMNE MEADOWS TO SONORA PASS (PCT)

**77.0 mi one-way / 8.0 days**

from Tuolumne Meadows on Highway 120 north to Sonora Pass on Highway 108

Map 10.2, page 438

This is a spectacular week-plus backpack trip that follows a section of the Pacific Crest Trail (PCT). The beauty of this region's deep canyons, glacial-cut peaks, verdant meadows, and abundant wildlife make it a hiker's paradise.

From Tuolumne Meadows, the trail starts out deceptively easily as it follows the Tuolumne River toward the Grand Canyon of the Tuolumne River. It heads gently downhill to Glen Aulin, where you get a great view of Tuolumne Falls. When you cross the bridge at the base of the falls and head up-canyon, you'll leave the day hikers behind. In the next three days, you'll go up one canyon and down the next, one after another, with breathtaking views and long, demanding climbs. Highlights include Matterhorn Canyon (many deer, trout, and views), Benson Lake (the largest white-sand beach in the Sierra Nevada), Dorothy Lake (panoramic views to the north), and many pristine, high-country meadows. The incredible clouds of mosquitoes at the Wilmer Lake area during early summer can be a major annoyance.

When you leave Yosemite and enter Humboldt-Toiyabe National Forest, the landscape changes quickly from glacial-cut granite to volcanic rock. The trail drops past several pretty lakes and into a river drainage, and at points can be difficult to follow. In a few areas, you may be surprised to meet up with grazing cows, especially from midsummer onward. You'll make a long, slow, climb up toward Leavitt Pass, set just below 10,800-foot Leavitt Peak. This landscape is entirely above tree line, in gray, stark country. At Leavitt Pass, the wind whistles by at high speed almost year-round. The final drop down to Sonora Pass is a one-hour descent that seems to wind all over the mountain. When you reach Highway 108, cross the road and walk about 100 yards west to a large day-use parking area. That's where your car shuttle should be waiting for you.

**User Groups:** Hikers and horses. No dogs or mountain bikes. No wheelchair facilities.

**Permits:** A wilderness permit is required for traveling through various wilderness and special-use areas the trail traverses. Contact either the Wilderness Office of the National Park Service or the Stanislaus National Forest for a permit that is good for the length of your trip.

**Maps:** For maps, ask the U.S. Forest Service for Yosemite National Park, Stanislaus National Forest, and Humboldt-Toiyabe National Forest. For topographic maps, ask the USGS for Pickel Meadow, Tower Peak, Piute Mountain, Matterhorn Peak, Dunderberg Peak, Vogelsang Peak, Tioga Pass, Falls Ridge, Buckeye Ridge, and Sonora Pass.

**Directions:** From Merced, drive 70 miles northeast on Highway 140 to Yosemite National Park. Follow the signs toward Yosemite Valley, entering through the Arch Rock entrance station. Continue 4.5 miles to the left turnoff for Tioga Road/Highway 120, looping back out of the valley on Big Oak Flat Road. In 9.3 miles, turn right on Tioga Road and drive 39 miles to the Lembert Dome/Soda Spring/Dog Lake/Glen Aulin trailhead parking, on the left. Begin hiking on the western edge of the parking lot, where there is a gated dirt road signed for Soda Spring.

**Contact:** Yosemite National Park Public Information Office, P.O. Box 577, Yosemite

National Park, CA 95389, 209/372-0200, website: www.nps.gov/yose; Stanislaus National Forest, Calaveras Ranger Station, P.O. Box 500, Hathaway Pines, CA 95233, 209/795-1381, website: www.fs.fed.us/r5/stanislaus.

## 37 TUOLUMNE MEADOWS TO YOSEMITE VALLEY (JMT)

**22.0 mi one-way / 2.0 days**

from Tuolumne Meadows Campground in Yosemite

**Map 10.2, page 438**

The first glimpses of Yosemite Valley will seem like a privileged view into heaven after having hiked the entire John Muir Trail (JMT) from Mount Whitney. For hikers making only this 22-mile section, the rewards can seem just as profound. The trip starts at Tuolumne Meadows, where backpackers can buy a good cheap breakfast, obtain wilderness permits, and camp in a special area set aside for JMT hikers. When you take your first steps away from Tuolumne Meadows, resist the urge to rush to the finish line in order to close out a historic expedition. Instead, relax and enjoy the downhill glide, always remembering that you are in sacred land. Compared to the rest of the JMT, this leg will come with far less strain, starting with a 3.1-mile tromp past Cathedral Lakes and requiring a .5-mile walk on a signed cutoff trail. If you can time it right, this area can make a great layover camp, with deep, emerald-green water and Cathedral Peak in the background. Beyond Cathedral Lakes, the trail makes a relatively short 500-foot climb over Cathedral Pass, skirts Tresidder Peak, and then descends through pristine Long Meadow. After passing Sunrise Trail Camp, a decent layover, the trail picks up little Sunrise Creek and follows it all the way down to Little Yosemite Valley, a popular trail camp. From Cathedral Lakes, it's 14.5 miles to the junction of Half Dome Trail, and another 2.2 miles to Little Yosemite.

For JMT hikers, making the climb to the top of Half Dome is a must, even though it often means putting up with a parade of people and even delays waiting for the line to move at the climbing cable. The Half Dome climb starts with a steep hike for the first mile, followed by steep switchbacks across granite on good trail to the foot of Half Dome's back wall. Here you'll find climbing cables to aid your final 300-foot ascent, and as you go, you'll discover breathtaking views of Tenaya Canyon. This is considered one of the world's glamour hikes, and while it turns hiking into an act of faith, we have seen eight-year-olds and 70-year-olds make the cable climb. By the way, if you take on Half Dome, be certain to have two canteens of water per person. Adding the Half Dome side trip to the rest of the JMT leg will add a round-trip of 5.2 miles to your hike. Because of its proximity to Half Dome, the Little Yosemite Valley Trail Camp is often crowded. From here, though, it's an easy five-mile hike downhill to Yosemite Valley. Again, try not to speed through to the end, even though it's an easy tromp downhill all the way. The magic is in the moment.

From Little Yosemite, the JMT is routed along the Merced River. In a mile, you'll reach Liberty Cap, and shortly later, Nevada Fall. Then down, down you go, with the trail often turning to giant granite steps, down past Emerald Pool and then to Vernal Fall, another spectacular waterfall. Since Vernal Fall is just 1.7 miles from the end of the trail, you'll start meeting lots of day hikers coming from the other direction, many gasping for breath as they make the uphill climb out of Yosemite Valley. Many will ask how far you've hiked; some may even want to take your photograph. It may feel a bit inane, but, hey, enjoy it. After all, you just finished John Muir Trail, the greatest hiking trail in the world.

**User Groups:** Hikers and horses. No dogs or mountain bikes. No wheelchair facilities.

**Permits:** A wilderness permit is required for traveling through various wilderness and special-use areas that the trail traverses. Contact the Wilderness Office of the National Park Service for a permit that is good for the length of your trip.

**Maps:** Free park maps are available at park

entrance stations or by contacting Yosemite National Park at the address below. A more detailed map is available for a fee from Tom Harrison Maps. For topographic maps, ask the USGS for Vogelsang Peak, Half Dome, Yosemite Falls, and Tenaya Peak.

**Directions:** From Groveland in the Central Valley foothills, drive east on Highway 120 into Yosemite National Park and continue toward Yosemite Valley. At Crane Flat, turn left on Highway 120/Tioga Pass Road and continue for about an hour, driving past Tenaya Lake to the Tuolumne Meadows Campground. There is a signed parking area for John Muir Trail just beyond the campground.

**Contact:** Yosemite National Park, P.O. Box 577, Yosemite National Park, CA 95389, 209/372-0200, website: www.nps.gov/yose; Wilderness Office of the National Park Service, 209/372-0200 (permits).

## 38 HITES COVE TRAIL
### 9.0 mi / 5.0 hrs

**on the South Fork Merced River**

Map 10.2, page 438

 The best part of the 22-mile South Fork Merced River Trail is the Hites Cove portion, which begins at Savage's Trading Post on Highway 140. It runs 4.5 miles one-way to Hites Cove on a four-wheel-drive road. Considered by many to be the premier Sierra spring wildflower trail, Hites Cove Trail offers hikers a look at 60 flower varieties, including goldfields, lupine, poppies, brodaiea, monkeyflower, shooting stars, fiesta flowers, fairy lanterns, baby blue eyes, and Indian pinks. To see them, visit from March to May, before the show is over. Conveniently, this is usually the only time of the year when the trail is open, because the first .75 mile of trail is on private property, and access is restricted during fire season.

You start hiking on a paved driveway, but the asphalt only lasts for a few yards, then the trail transitions to a narrow single track that hugs the side of the steep canyon wall, high above the South Fork Merced River. Even if you aren't terribly interested in wildflowers, the river and canyon views are tremendous. About one mile out is an obvious rock outcrop, a few feet off the trail, where you can sit and enjoy the rushing river below. Another .5 mile farther, the trail drops down right alongside the river, and where the current mellows out, there are many tempting swimming holes. Hikers wishing to turn this hike into an overnight trip can camp at Hites Cove (the site of the 1879 Hites Cove Hotel), then continue hiking to Devils Gulch, 2.5 miles farther. To do so, however, requires crossing the South Fork Merced River at Hites Cove, a difficult feat early in the year.

Special Note: Call the Bass Lake Ranger Station to make sure this trail is open before planning your trip. Access to the trail is restricted during fire season.

**User Groups:** Hikers, dogs, and horses. No mountain bikes. No wheelchair facilities.

**Permits:** No permits are required. Parking and access are free.

**Maps:** For a map, ask the U.S. Forest Service for Sierra National Forest. For a topographic map, ask the USGS for El Portal.

**Directions:** From Mariposa, drive 22 miles east on Highway 140 to Savage's Trading Post. The parking area is on the north side of the road, but the trail begins on the south side, near Savage's Trading Post.

**Contact:** Sierra National Forest, Bass Lake Ranger Station, 57003 Road 225, North Fork, CA 93643, 559/877-2218, website: www.fs.fed.us/r5/sierra.

## 39 UPPER YOSEMITE FALL
### 7.2 mi / 6.0 hrs

**in Yosemite Valley**

Map 10.2, page 438

 If you tucker out on this demanding climb to Upper Yosemite Fall, just remember that you always have a fallback position: You can hike only 1.2 miles one-way to the Columbia Point viewpoint (also called Columbia Rock) for a total gain of 1,200 feet in elevation, and then call it a day. The view of Yosemite Valley from Columbia Point is a stunner, and plenty of people who planned on hiking to Upper Yosemite Fall turn around here and still leave satisfied. Nonetheless, it's worth pushing on for at least another .5 mile, where after a level section of trail and then a surprising descent, hikers obtain their first full-impact view of the horsetail-shaped Upper Yosemite Fall. Those who push on are further rewarded: The trail switchbacks up and up, leaving the waterfall views behind and entering a canyon to the west of the fall, which allows passage to the top of the north rim of Yosemite Valley. At this point, you've gained 2,700 feet and hiked 3.5 miles; it's only another .2 mile to the brink of Upper Yosemite Fall. (Make sure you take the spur trail signed as Overlook.) From the metal fence above the fall's lip, you gain an incredible perspective on the waterfall's drop and the valley floor far below. It's a great feeling to stand here and realize that you're on top of the tallest waterfall in North America. After visiting the overlook, return to the main trail and hike a short distance farther to the wide bridge over Yosemite Creek. Still haven't had enough? You can continue another .75 mile beyond the bridge to Yosemite Point (6,936 feet), where you get a stunning view of the south rim of the canyon, Half Dome, and North Dome, as well as a look at the top of Lost Arrow Spire, a single shaft of granite jutting into the sky. Believe it or not, this is a popular rock-climbing route.

**User Groups:** Hikers only. No dogs, horses, or mountain bikes. No wheelchair facilities.

**Permits:** No permits are required. There is a $20 per vehicle entrance fee at Yosemite National Park, good for seven days.

**Maps:** Free park maps are available at park entrance stations or by contacting Yosemite National Park at the address below. A Yosemite map is available from Tom Harrison Maps.

For a topographic map, ask the USGS for Yosemite Falls.

**Directions:** From Merced, drive 70 miles northeast on Highway 140 to Yosemite National Park. Follow the signs toward Yosemite Valley, entering through the Arch Rock entrance station. Continue on Highway 140/El Portal Road, which becomes Southside Drive, for 10.5 miles. Just beyond the Yosemite Chapel, bear left at the fork and head toward the village and visitors center, then turn left and drive west on Northside Drive .75 mile to the Yosemite Lodge parking lot. Turn left and park in the lot; then walk to the Upper Fall trailhead, which is across the road and .25 mile to the west, between the parking lot for Camp 4 and the camp itself. You may not park in the campground lot unless you are camping there. If you are riding the free Yosemite Valley shuttle bus, get off on stop No. 8 and walk to the trailhead.

**Contact:** Yosemite National Park Public Information Office, P.O. Box 577, Yosemite National Park, CA 95389, 209/372-0200, website: www.nps.gov/yose.

## 40 EAGLE PEAK
**13.5 mi / 1.0 or 2.0 days**

**in Yosemite Valley**

Map 10.2, page 438

If you seek more of a challenge than the day hike to Upper Yosemite Fall, the trail to Eagle Peak delivers the stunning destinations of the shorter trip (Columbia Point and Upper Yosemite Fall) plus an additional three miles one-way to a lookout atop of the highest rock of the Three Brothers formation. Here, the vista is sublime. All of Yosemite comes into view from the top of Eagle Peak. Just make sure you pick a clear day.

Follow the trail notes for the hike to Upper Yosemite Fall (see previous listing), then after taking the spur trail to the fall's brink, backtrack .25 mile to the trail junction for Eagle Peak Trail. Follow Eagle Peak Trail northwest for 1.5 miles, then hike south for one mile through

Eagle Peak Meadows. At a trail junction with El Capitan Trail, bear left for a .5-mile ascent to your final destination—the summit of Eagle Peak, elevation 7,779 feet. After completing this trip, you'll never view the Three Brothers from the valley floor the same way again.

**User Groups:** Hikers only. No dogs, horses, or mountain bikes. No wheelchair facilities.

**Permits:** There is a $20 per vehicle entrance fee at Yosemite National Park, good for seven days. Free wilderness permits are required for overnight stays. They are available on a first-come, first-served basis up to one day in advance at the Yosemite Wilderness kiosk near your chosen trailhead or farther in advance by mail, phone, or email for a $5 per person reservation fee.

**Maps:** Free park maps are available at park entrance stations or by contacting Yosemite National Park at the address below. A Yosemite map is available from Tom Harrison Maps. For a topographic map, ask the USGS for Yosemite Falls.

**Directions:** From Merced, drive 70 miles northeast on Highway 140 to Yosemite National Park. Follow the signs toward Yosemite Valley and enter through the Arch Rock entrance station. Continue on Highway 140/El Portal Road, which becomes Southside Drive, for 10.5 miles. Just beyond the Yosemite Chapel, bear left at the fork and head toward the village and visitors center; then turn left and drive west on Northside Drive .75 mile to the Yosemite Lodge parking lot. Turn left and park in the lot; then walk to the Upper Yosemite Fall trailhead, which is across the road and .25 mile to the west, between the parking lot for Camp 4 and the camp itself. You may not park in the campground lot unless you are camping there. If you are riding the free Yosemite Valley shuttle bus, take stop No. 8 and walk to the trailhead.

**Contact:** Yosemite National Park Public Information Office, P.O. Box 577, Yosemite National Park, CA 95389, 209/372-0200 or 209/372-0740 (permit reservations), websites: www.nps.gov/yose or www.nps.gov/yose/wilderness (permit reservations).

## 41 LOWER YOSEMITE FALL
**0.5 mi / 0.5 hr**

**in Yosemite Valley**

**Map 10.2, page 438**

The trail to Lower Yosemite Fall is undoubtedly one of the most famous and popular pathways in all of the Western United States, and as this book goes to press, it is getting a much-needed facelift. In the long term, this is great news for the millions of people who visit Yosemite Valley each year. In the short term, it's a pain in the neck for those same visitors. That's because the ongoing construction mess has created difficulties for visitors trying to park near, or even just access on foot, the falls trailhead. At present, your best bet is to park in one of the large day-use lots near Yosemite Village, then walk or ride the shuttle bus to the Yosemite Lodge area. The waterfall is found across Northside Drive from Yosemite Lodge—just look for the obvious construction site.

Despite the current confusion, the trail to Lower Yosemite Fall remains an absolute must for valley visitors, especially in the spring months. When the falls are roaring with snowmelt, they never fail to thrill even the most jaded hiker. At present, you still follow the main paved trail out-and-back from the old trailhead parking area to the footbridge below the falls. When the construction is finally completed, the pavement will be torn out, and the out-and-back trail will be replaced by a loop trail. One feature will remain the same as it ever was: In the spring months, you will still get soaking wet from the incredible mist and spray. Another fact that will not change is that by late summer, Yosemite Falls will still go dry, or nearly so. If you like to see substantial water in your waterfalls, plan your trip for sometime between April and June. And if you can time it right, check out the spectacle that occurs on full moon nights in the spring, when you can sometimes see "moonbows" in the lower fall.

**User Groups:** Hikers and wheelchairs. No dogs, horses, or mountain bikes.

**Permits:** No permits are required. There is a $20 per vehicle entrance fee at Yosemite National Park, good for seven days.

**Maps:** Free park maps are available at park entrance stations or by contacting Yosemite National Park at the address below. A Yosemite map is available from Tom Harrison Maps. For a topographic map, ask the USGS for Half Dome.

**Directions:** From Merced, drive 70 miles northeast on Highway 140 to Yosemite National Park. Follow the signs to Yosemite Valley, entering through the Arch Rock entrance station. Continue on Highway 140/El Portal Road, which becomes Southside Drive, for 10.5 miles. Just beyond the Yosemite Chapel, bear left at the fork and head toward the village and visitors center. Park in one of the day-use lots in Yosemite Village and walk or ride the free Yosemite Valley shuttle bus to the Yosemite Lodge area (stop No. 7). The old parking lot for the Lower Yosemite Fall Trail no longer exists; visitors must park elsewhere and walk or ride the bus to access the trail.

**Contact:** Yosemite National Park Public Information Office, P.O. Box 577, Yosemite National Park, CA 95389, 209/372-0200, website: www.nps.gov/yose.

## 42 MIST TRAIL TO TOP OF VERNAL FALL
**3.0 mi / 2.0 hrs**

**in Yosemite Valley**

**Map 10.2, page 438**

To hike to the top of Vernal Fall, you must take the free Yosemite shuttle bus to the trailhead at Happy Isles, or add on an extra mile each way by hiking from the day-use parking area in Curry Village to Happy Isles. But once that's accomplished, prepare yourself for a stellar, world-class walk to one of the most photographed waterfalls in the world. The only minus is the hordes of people, so make your trip more enjoyable by starting early in the morning, before they're out in full force. Although many people

hike only to the Vernal Fall footbridge (.8 mile from Happy Isles), it's definitely worth the extra effort to push on another .5 mile to reach the top of Vernal Fall. To do so means ascending the Mist Trail's famous granite stairway that curves around the side of Vernal Fall, so close to it that you feel as if you are practically a part of the waterfall. Often you are—hikers are frequently drenched in spray and mist, particularly in springtime. Be sure to bring a rain poncho if you don't like getting wet. The route is a fairly easy climb to the Vernal Falls bridge; then it's a steep tromp up the seemingly endless stairs to the top of the falls. Total elevation gain is 1,050 feet. When you first look over the metal railing perched above the waterfall's brink, you'll understand why this is a trip that everyone should do at least once in their life. If it's your first trip, make sure you go in the spring months so you get the full effect.

**User Groups:** Hikers only. No dogs, horses, or mountain bikes. No wheelchair facilities.

**Permits:** No permits are required. There is a $20 per vehicle entrance fee at Yosemite National Park, good for seven days.

**Maps:** Free park maps are available at park entrance stations or by contacting Yosemite National Park at the address below. A Yosemite map is available from Tom Harrison Maps. For a topographic map, ask the USGS for Half Dome.

**Directions:** From Merced, drive 70 miles northeast on Highway 140 to Yosemite National Park. Follow the signs toward Yosemite Valley, entering through the Arch Rock entrance station. Continue on Highway 140/El Portal Road, which becomes Southside Drive, for 11.6 miles to the day-use parking lot at Curry Village. Then ride the free Yosemite Valley shuttle bus to Happy Isles, stop No. 16. In winter, when the shuttle does not run, you must hike from the day-use parking lot in Curry Village, adding two miles to your round-trip. Trails may be closed in winter; call to check on weather conditions.

**Contact:** Yosemite National Park Public Information Office, P.O. Box 577, Yosemite National Park, CA 95389, 209/372-0200, website: www.nps.gov/yose.

## 43 MIST AND JOHN MUIR LOOP TO NEVADA FALL
**6.5 mi / 4.0 hrs**

**in Yosemite Valley**

**Map 10.2, page 438**

You can hike either John Muir Trail or Mist Trail to reach Yosemite's classic Nevada Fall, but the best choice is to make a loop out of it by hiking up on Mist Trail, then down partway or all the way on John Muir Trail. Both trails join above and below Nevada Fall, so you have some options. By hiking uphill rather than downhill on the Mist Trail's treacherous granite staircase, you can look around at the gorgeous scenery every time you stop to catch your breath. The John Muir Trail is somewhat less scenic, especially in its lower reaches, so save it for the way back downhill.

Start at Happy Isles and follow the signed trail to the footbridge over the Merced River, below Vernal Fall. After crossing the bridge, stay close along the river's edge on Mist Trail for 1.2 miles to the top of Vernal Fall. If it's early spring, make sure you bring your rain gear for this stretch. After a brief rest at the waterfall overlook, continue along the river's edge, passing a gorgeous stretch of stream known as the Emerald Pool, still following Mist Trail. In .5 mile, the path crosses the river again, then climbs another mile to the brink of Nevada Fall. Total elevation gain to the top of the 594-foot falls is 2,600 feet, a healthy ascent. But when you get to walk this close to two world-class waterfalls, who's complaining? For your return trip, cross the footbridge above Nevada Fall and follow John Muir Trail to loop back. As you descend, check out the great view of Nevada Fall with Liberty Cap in the background. This is one of the most famous scenes in Yosemite Valley.

Note that you can cut back over to Mist Trail at Clark Point, just above Vernal Fall, if you so desire. That way, you get a second chance to

see Vernal Fall and hike the Mist Trail's granite staircase. In our humble opinion, this beats taking John Muir Trail all the way back by a long shot. But let your knees decide—plenty of hikers don't want to face those stairsteps a second time, especially in the downhill direction.

**User Groups:** Hikers only. No dogs or mountain bikes. Horses are allowed only on John Muir Trail. No wheelchair facilities.

**Permits:** No permits are required. There is a $20 per vehicle entrance fee at Yosemite National Park, good for seven days.

**Maps:** Free park maps are available at park entrance stations or by contacting Yosemite National Park at the address below. A Yosemite map is available from Tom Harrison Maps. For a topographic map, ask the USGS for Half Dome.

**Directions:** From Merced, drive 70 miles northeast on Highway 140 to Yosemite National Park. Follow the signs toward Yosemite Valley, entering through the Arch Rock entrance station. Continue on Highway 140/El Portal Road, which becomes Southside Drive, for 11.6 miles to the day-use parking lot at Curry Village. Then ride the free Yosemite Valley shuttle bus to Happy Isles, stop No. 16. In winter, when the shuttle does not run, you must hike from the day-use parking lot in Curry Village, adding two miles to your round-trip. Trails may be closed in winter; call to check on weather conditions.

**Contact:** Yosemite National Park Public Information Office, P.O. Box 577, Yosemite National Park, CA 95389, 209/372-0200, website: www.nps.gov/yose.

## 44 MIRROR LAKE LOOP
**4.5 mi / 2.0 hrs**

**in Yosemite Valley**

**Map 10.2, page 438**

You can add 1.5 miles round-trip to this trail by walking to Mirror Lake Junction, or you can ride the free shuttle from Curry Village parking lot. Either way, you're heading for an easy, mostly level loop trip around Mirror Lake. From the bus stop, walk .5 mile on pavement to Mirror Lake, follow the foot trail beyond it up Tenaya Creek for 1.5 miles, and circle back. You can add 1.5 miles round-trip to this trail by walking to Mirror Lake Junction, or you can ride the free shuttle from Curry Village Parking lot. Either way, you're heading for an easy, mostly level loop trip around Mirror Lake. From the bus stop, walk .5 mile on pavement to Mirror Lake, follow the foot trail beyond it up Tenaya Creek for 1.5 miles. Check out the great views of Half Dome and Basket Dome as you hike. If you want to see Mirror Lake looking more like a lake and less like a meadow, make this trip in springtime. The lake is slowly undergoing the process of sedimentation (it's filling with sand and gravel from Tenaya Creek), and even in spring, it is quite shallow. The loop trail is nearly level the whole way, and once you get past Mirror Lake and into the lower Tenaya Creek Canyon, you may even find a little privacy.

**User Groups:** Hikers only. No dogs, horses, or mountain bikes. No wheelchair facilities.

**Permits:** No permits are required. There is a $20 per vehicle entrance fee at Yosemite National Park, good for seven days.

**Maps:** Free park maps are available at park entrance stations or by contacting Yosemite National Park at the address below. A Yosemite map is available from Tom Harrison Maps. For a topographic map, ask the USGS for Half Dome.

**Directions:** From Merced, drive 70 miles northeast on Highway 140 to Yosemite National Park. Follow the signs toward Yosemite Valley, entering through the Arch Rock entrance station. Continue on Highway 140/El Portal Road, which becomes Southside Drive, for 11.6 miles to the day-use parking lot at Curry Village. Then ride the free Yosemite Valley shuttle bus to Mirror Lake Junction.

**Contact:** Yosemite National Park Public Information Office, P.O. Box 577, Yosemite National Park, CA 95389, 209/372-0200, website: www.nps.gov/yose.

## 45 HALF DOME
### 17.0 mi / 1.0 or 2.0 days

**in Yosemite Valley**

Map 10.2, page 438

No argument about it, Half Dome is one of those once-in-your-life-you-gotta-do-it hikes. Just be sure you know what you're in for before you set out on this epic trail: You're looking at 17 miles round-trip, a 4,800-foot elevation gain, and an unbelievable amount of company. During the summer, about 500 people a day make this trip. Plenty of them do it as a day hike, and if you do so, make sure to bring a load of water and food with you. You'll be handing it out to others who are not so well prepared, as well as gulping it down yourself. Follow either John Muir Trail or Mist Trail from Happy Isles to the top of Nevada Fall, then go left and enter Little Yosemite Valley. At 6.2 miles, John Muir Trail splits off from Half Dome Trail, and you head left for Half Dome. Everything usually goes smoothly until you reach the steel cables that run 250 yards up the back of the dome, at which point you'll start praying a lot and wishing there weren't so many other hikers on the cables with you. Do some soul-searching before you begin the cable ascent—turning around is not an option once you are halfway up. When you reach the top, the views are so incredible that you forget all about your tired arms and feet. To make the trip easier, camp at Little Yosemite Valley, 4.7 miles in (wilderness permit required), and save the final ascent for the next day. Don't plan on sleeping much, though. Little Yosemite Valley is one zoo of a backpacking camp.

**User Groups:** Hikers only. No dogs, horses, or mountain bikes. No wheelchair facilities.

**Permits:** There is a $20 per vehicle entrance fee at Yosemite National Park, good for seven days. Free wilderness permits are required for overnight stays. They are available on a first-come, first-served basis up to one day in advance at the Yosemite Wilderness kiosk near your chosen trailhead or farther in advance by mail, phone, or email for a $5 per person reservation fee.

**Maps:** Free park maps are available at park entrance stations or by contacting Yosemite National Park at the address below. A Yosemite map is available from Tom Harrison Maps. For a topographic map, ask the USGS for Half Dome.

**Directions:** From Merced, drive 70 miles northeast on Highway 140 to Yosemite National Park. Follow the signs toward Yosemite Valley, entering through the Arch Rock entrance station. Continue on Highway 140/El Portal Road, which becomes Southside Drive, for 11.6 miles to the day-use parking lot at Curry Village. Then ride the free Yosemite Valley shuttle bus to Happy Isles, stop No. 16.

**Contact:** Yosemite National Park Public Information Office, P.O. Box 577, Yosemite National Park, CA 95389, 209/372-0200 or 209/372-0740 (permit reservations), websites: www.nps.gov/yose or www.nps.gov/yose/wilderness (permit reservations).

## 46 INSPIRATION AND STANFORD POINTS
7.6 mi / 4.0 hrs

**in Yosemite Valley near the Wawona Tunnel**

Map 10.2, page 438

You need a little inspiration? You came to the right place. The view from the Wawona Tunnel trailhead should be enough to inspire you (check out the panorama of Yosemite Valley, El Capitan, Half Dome, and Bridalveil Fall), but if it's not, just do a little climbing on Pohono Trail to Inspiration Point and Stanford Point. The trail is uphill but well graded and just long enough to give you a good workout. The first mile of trail has numerous switchbacks, with great views every time you face eastward. The trail climbs 1,000 feet over this stretch. At 1.3 miles, the route reaches Inspiration Point, where the view is largely obscured by trees, but keep heading upward for another 1,000-foot

climb. Eventually you'll cross Meadow Brook and reach the left cutoff trail for Stanford Point. You're 3.8 miles from the trailhead, and you've climbed 2,200 feet, but your reward is an eagle's-eye view of the valley floor (3,000 feet below), and a vista to the east of Half Dome and all its granite neighbors.

**User Groups:** Hikers only. No dogs, horses, or mountain bikes. No wheelchair facilities.

**Permits:** No permits are required. There is a $20 per vehicle entrance fee at Yosemite National Park, good for seven days.

**Maps:** Free park maps are available at park entrance stations or by contacting Yosemite National Park at the address below. A Yosemite map is available from Tom Harrison Maps. For a topographic map, ask the USGS for El Capitan.

**Directions:** From Merced, drive 70 miles northeast on Highway 140 to Yosemite National Park. Follow the signs to Yosemite Valley, entering through the Arch Rock entrance station. Continue 6.3 miles on Highway 140/El Portal Road, which becomes Southside Drive, and turn right at the fork for Highway 41/Wawona/Fresno. Continue 1.5 miles to the parking lots on either side of the road just before you enter the Wawona Tunnel. The trailhead is at the parking lot on the left (south) side of the road.

**Contact:** Yosemite National Park Public Information Office, P.O. Box 577, Yosemite National Park, CA 95389, 209/372-0200, website: www.nps.gov/yose.

## 47 BRIDALVEIL FALL
0.5 mi / 0.5 hr

**in Yosemite Valley**

Map 10.2, page 438

Bridalveil Fall is right up there with Lower Yosemite Fall as a must-do walk for visitors (including nonhikers) to Yosemite Valley. Like that other famous waterfall walk, the path to Bridalveil Fall is paved with people. But the best thing about this waterfall is that unlike other falls in Yosemite Valley, Bridalveil runs year-round; it never dries up and disappoints visitors. The walk to its overlook is short and nearly level, and the trail delivers you to a small viewing area about 70 yards from the fall. You can look straight up and see Bridalveil Creek plunging 620 feet off the edge of the south canyon wall. In high wind, the fall billows and sways; if you are lucky, you might see rainbows dancing in its mist. Another bonus is that your position at the Bridalveil overlook is such that if you make an about-face, you have an excellent view of Ribbon Fall flowing off the northern Yosemite Valley rim. Ribbon Fall is the highest single drop in the park (1,612 feet), but it only flows in the earliest months of spring.

**User Groups:** Hikers and wheelchairs. No dogs, horses, or mountain bikes.

**Permits:** No permits are required. There is a $20 per vehicle entrance fee at Yosemite National Park, good for seven days.

**Maps:** Free park maps are available at park entrance stations or by contacting Yosemite National Park at the address below. A Yosemite map is available from Tom Harrison Maps. For a topographic map, ask the USGS for El Capitan.

**Directions:** From Merced, drive 70 miles northeast on Highway 140 to Yosemite National Park. Follow the signs toward Yosemite Valley, entering through the Arch Rock entrance station. Continue for 6.3 miles on Highway 140/El Portal Road, which becomes Southside Drive, and turn right at the fork for Highway 41/Wawona/Fresno. Turn left almost immediately into the Bridalveil Fall parking lot. The trail begins at the end of the parking lot. If you are driving into the park from the southern entrance near Wawona, watch for the Bridalveil Fall turnoff on your right as you drive into the valley on Highway 41.

**Contact:** Yosemite National Park Public Information Office, P.O. Box 577, Yosemite National Park, CA 95389, 209/372-0200, website: www.nps.gov/yose.

## 48 FOUR-MILE TRAIL
### 9.6 mi / 6.0 hrs

**in Yosemite Valley**

**Map 10.2, page 438**

Many years ago, we hiked this trail on our first-ever visit to Yosemite and were shocked when we got to the top and found a giant parking lot and refreshment stand located there. What, you mean we could have driven to the high point on this trail? It's true, but your arrival at dramatic Glacier Point is somehow made all the more meaningful if you get there the hard way, which means hiking Four-Mile Trail all the way up from the valley floor, gaining 3,220 feet in 4.8 miles (not 4.0 miles, as the name implies). The trail is partially shaded and makes for a terrific day hike with an early morning start. Then you can have a leisurely brunch or lunch from your bird's-eye perch on Glacier Point. Don't like what you brought in your daypack? No problem. A snack shop sells hot dogs and the like all summer. From Glacier Point, you have unobstructed views of just about every major landmark in Yosemite Valley—most notably Half Dome, Basket Dome, Yosemite Falls, Vernal and Nevada Falls, and the valley floor far, far below you.

**User Groups:** Hikers only. No dogs, horses, or mountain bikes. No wheelchair facilities.

**Permits:** No permits are required. There is a $20 per vehicle entrance fee at Yosemite National Park, good for seven days.

**Maps:** Free park maps are available at park entrance stations or by contacting Yosemite National Park at the address below. A Yosemite map is available from Tom Harrison Maps. For a topographic map, ask the USGS for Half Dome.

**Directions:** From Merced, drive 70 miles northeast on Highway 140 to Yosemite National Park. Follow the signs to Yosemite Valley, entering through the Arch Rock entrance station. Continue on Highway 140/El Portal Road, which becomes Southside Drive, for 9.5 miles. The trailhead is located next to mile marker

V18 on the right side of Southside Drive. Park in the pullouts along the road.

**Contact:** Yosemite National Park Public Information Office, P.O. Box 577, Yosemite National Park, CA 95389, 209/372-0200, website: www.nps.gov/yose.

## 49 McGURK MEADOW & DEWEY POINT
### 2.0–7.0 mi / 1.0–4.0 hrs

**off Glacier Road in Yosemite National Park**

Map 10.2, page 438

Some hikes make you feel joyful to be alive, and McGurk Meadow Trail is one of those. The trailhead is the first one you reach as you wind along Glacier Point Road to spectacular Glacier Point, and it's definitely worth stopping to take the short walk through a fir and pine forest to pristine McGurk Meadow. A quarter mile before you reach the meadow, you pass an old pioneer cabin on your left, still standing in half-decent repair. Next, you come out to the mile-long meadow, and a footbridge carries you across a tiny stream that makes lazy S-turns through the grasses. You can follow the trail along the north edge of McGurk Meadow as far as you please. The route connects to Pohono Trail, which traverses Yosemite's south rim, so many hikers continue from McGurk Meadow to Dewey Point, a spectacular promontory just off Pohono Trail. That option turns this into a seven-mile round-trip.

**User Groups:** Hikers only. No dogs, horses, or mountain bikes. No wheelchair facilities.

**Permits:** No permits are required. There is a $20 per vehicle entrance fee at Yosemite National Park, good for seven days.

**Maps:** Free park maps are available at park entrance stations or by contacting Yosemite National Park at the address below. A Yosemite map is available from Tom Harrison Maps. For a topographic map, ask the USGS for El Capitan.

**Directions:** From Merced, drive 70 miles northeast on Highway 140 to Yosemite National Park. Follow the signs toward Yosemite Valley, entering through the Arch Rock entrance station. Continue 6.3 miles on Highway 140/El Portal Road, which becomes Southside Drive, and turn right at the fork for Highway 41/Wawona/Fresno. Continue for 9.2 miles, turn left on Glacier Point Road, and drive 7.5 miles to the McGurk Meadow trailhead, on the left. Park in the pullout about 75 yards farther up the road.

**Contact:** Yosemite National Park Public Information Office, P.O. Box 577, Yosemite National Park, CA 95389, 209/372-0200, website: www.nps.gov/yose.

## 50 BRIDALVEIL CREEK
### 3.2 mi / 1.5 hrs

**off Glacier Point Road in Yosemite National Park**

Map 10.2, page 438

Maybe the best time to hike to Bridalveil Creek is immediately after visiting Bridalveil Fall. After a short walk from Glacier Point Road through a regenerated forest fire area, you wind up at the edge of Bridalveil Creek, a babbling brook that seems far too tame to produce the giant waterfall downstream. It's a great lesson for children, as is the abundance of new growth in the burned areas of the forest. To make the trip, follow Ostrander Lake Trail from Glacier Point Road for 1.4 miles. This stretch is almost completely level and is framed by colorful bunches of lupine in midsummer. When the trail splits, take the right fork toward Bridalveil Creek. The stream is so tame here that there is no bridge to cross—it's an easy rock hop by midsummer, although it can be a dangerous crossing in late spring. Pick a spot along its banks, and spend some time counting the wildflowers or the small, darting trout.

**User Groups:** Hikers only. No dogs, horses, or mountain bikes. No wheelchair facilities.

**Permits:** No permits are required. There is a $20 per vehicle entrance fee at Yosemite National Park, good for seven days.

**Maps:** Free park maps are available at park

entrance stations or by contacting Yosemite National Park at the address below. A Yosemite map is available from Tom Harrison Maps. For a topographic map, ask the USGS for Half Dome.

**Directions:** From Merced, drive 70 miles northeast on Highway 140 to Yosemite National Park. Follow the signs toward Yosemite Valley, entering through the Arch Rock entrance station. Continue for 6.3 miles on Highway 140/El Portal Road, which becomes Southside Drive, and turn right at the fork for Highway 41/Wawona/Fresno. Continue for 9.2 miles, turn left on Glacier Point Road, and drive another 8.9 miles to the Ostrander Lake trailhead, on the right.

**Contact:** Yosemite National Park Public Information Office, P.O. Box 577, Yosemite National Park, CA 95389, 209/372-0200, website: www.nps.gov/yose.

## 51 OSTRANDER LAKE
**12.5 mi / 1.0 or 2.0 days**

**off Glacier Point Road in Yosemite National Park**

Map 10.2, page 438

While many people take short day hikes from Glacier Point Road, a longer 12.5-mile trip to Ostrander Lake may better suit your desires. The trail is surprisingly easy, considering the long miles, and the first half is quite level. You can hike out and back in a day, or get a wilderness permit and camp near the lake's shores. The wide blue lake, set at 8,580 feet, is a popular destination for cross-country skiers in the winter, as is evidenced by the stone Ostrander Ski Hut and the yellow ski markers high up on trees along the route. Although the trail (really an old road) begins in a regenerated forest fire area, it traverses a typical high-country landscape of firs, pines, and, as you ascend, granite. You have to gain 1,600 feet along the way, most of it in the final three miles to the lake. The culmination of the climb occurs at nearly six miles out, as you reach the trail's highest point, a sad-

dle on top of 8,700-foot Horizon Ridge. You are rewarded with excellent views of Half Dome, North Dome, Basket Dome, and Liberty Cap. This is a fine place to catch your breath. From here, the lake is less than .5 mile farther. On summer days, bring your swimsuit and a book, and plan to spend a few hours on Ostrander's sand- and boulder-lined shoreline.

**User Groups:** Hikers only. No dogs, horses, or mountain bikes. No wheelchair facilities.

**Permits:** There is a $20 per vehicle entrance fee at Yosemite National Park, good for seven days. Free wilderness permits are required for overnight stays. They are available on a first-come, first-served basis up to one day in advance at the Yosemite Wilderness kiosk near your chosen trailhead or farther in advance by mail, phone, or email for a $5 per person reservation fee.

**Maps:** Free park maps are available at park entrance stations or by contacting Yosemite National Park at the address below. A Yosemite map is available from Tom Harrison Maps. For topographic maps, ask the USGS for Half Dome and Mariposa Grove.

**Directions:** From Merced, drive 70 miles northeast on Highway 140 to Yosemite National Park. Follow the signs toward Yosemite Valley, entering through the Arch Rock entrance station. Continue for 6.3 miles on Highway 140/El Portal Road, which becomes Southside Drive, and turn right at the fork for Highway 41/Wawona/Fresno. Continue for 9.2 miles, turn left on Glacier Point Road, and drive 8.9 miles to the Ostrander Lake trailhead, on the right.

**Contact:** Yosemite National Park Public Information Office, P.O. Box 577, Yosemite National Park, CA 95389, 209/372-0200 or 209/372-0740 (permit reservations), websites: www.nps.gov/yose or www.nps.gov/yose/wilderness (permit reservations).

## 52 SENTINEL DOME
2.0 mi / 1.0 hr

**off Glacier Point Road in Yosemite National Park**

Map 10.2, page 438

 It's hard to believe you can get so much for so little, but on Sentinel Dome Trail, you can. The granite dome is located about a mile before Glacier Point on Glacier Point Road, and its elevation is 1,000 feet higher than the point's, which means stellar views are yours for the asking. A nearly flat one-mile walk leads you to the base of the dome, and a 50-yard scramble up its smooth granite back side brings you to its summit. There, you are greeted by stunning vistas in all directions, including an unusual perspective on Upper and Lower Yosemite Falls. This is one of the best places in Yosemite to watch the sun set. To make a longer excursion, you can easily combine this hike with the hike to Taft Point and the Fissures (see next listing), which starts from the same trailhead but heads in the opposite direction.

**User Groups:** Hikers only. No dogs, horses, or mountain bikes. No wheelchair facilities.

**Permits:** No permits are required. There is a $20 per vehicle entrance fee at Yosemite National Park, good for seven days.

**Maps:** Free park maps are available at park entrance stations or by contacting Yosemite National Park at the address below. A Yosemite map is available from Tom Harrison Maps. For a topographic map, ask the USGS for Half Dome.

**Directions:** From Merced, drive 70 miles northeast on Highway 140 to Yosemite National Park. Follow the signs to Yosemite Valley, entering through the Arch Rock entrance station. Continue 6.3 miles on Highway 140/El Portal Road, which becomes Southside Drive, and turn right at the fork for Highway 41/Wawona/Fresno. Continue for 9.2 miles, turn left on Glacier Point Road, and drive 13.2 miles to the Taft Point/Sentinel Dome trailhead parking lot, on the left side of the road.

**Contact:** Yosemite National Park Public Information Office, P.O. Box 577, Yosemite National Park, CA 95389, 209/372-0200, website: www.nps.gov/yose.

## 53 TAFT POINT AND THE FISSURES
2.0 mi / 1.0 hr

**off Glacier Point Road in Yosemite National Park**

Map 10.2, page 438

It's not so much the sweeping vista from Taft Point that you remember (although certainly you could say that the views of Yosemite's north rim and the valley floor are stunning). What you remember is the incredible sense of awe that you feel, perhaps mixed with a little fear and a lot of respect, as you peer down into the fissures in Taft Point's granite—huge cracks in the rock that plunge hundreds of feet down toward the valley. One of the fissures has a couple of large boulders captured in its jaws; they're stuck there, waiting for the next big earthquake or ice age to set them free. Be sure to walk to the metal railing along the edge of Taft Point's cliff, where you can hold on tight and peer down at the valley far, far below. If you have kids with you or anyone who is afraid of heights, be sure to keep a tight handhold on them.

**User Groups:** Hikers only. No dogs, horses, or mountain bikes. No wheelchair facilities.

**Permits:** No permits are required. There is a $20 per vehicle entrance fee at Yosemite National Park, good for seven days.

**Maps:** Free park maps are available at park entrance stations or by contacting Yosemite National Park at the address below. A Yosemite map is available from Tom Harrison Maps. For a topographic map, ask the USGS for Half Dome.

**Directions:** From Merced, drive 70 miles northeast on Highway 140 to Yosemite National Park. Follow the signs to Yosemite Valley, entering through the Arch Rock entrance station. Continue for 6.3 miles on Highway 140/El Portal Road, which becomes Southside Drive, and turn right at the fork for Highway 41/Wawona/Fresno. Continue for 9.2 miles, turn left on Glacier Point Road, and drive 13.2 miles to the Taft Point/Sentinel Dome trailhead parking lot, on the left side of the road.

**Contact:** Yosemite National Park Public Information Office, P.O. Box 577, Yosemite National Park, CA 95389, 209/372-0200, website: www.nps.gov/yose.

## 54 POHONO TRAIL
### 13.0 mi one-way / 7.0 hrs

**off Glacier Point Road in Yosemite National Park**

Map 10.2, page 438

If you can arrange a shuttle trip, Pohono Trail from Glacier Point downhill to its end (at Wawona Tunnel) is worth every step of its 13 miles. The two ends of the trail have the best drive-to viewpoints in all of Yosemite, and in between, you are treated to dozens of other scenic spots (including Sentinel Dome, at 1.5 miles, and Taft Point, at 3.8 miles), as well as four bird's-eye lookouts over the valley floor: Inspiration, Stanford, Dewey, and Crocker Points. Starting at Glacier Point and ending at Wawona Tunnel, you'll cover a 2,800-foot descent, but there are some "ups" along the way, too—like at the very beginning (from Glacier Point to Sentinel Dome), and between Bridalveil Creek and Dewey Point. The trail stays on or near Yosemite Valley's southern rim the entire way except for one major detour into the woods to access the bridge crossing of Bridalveil Creek. Remember to bring along a good map, because many of the trail's best offerings are just off the main path. If you don't take the short spur routes to reach them, you'll miss out on some spectacular scenery.

The view of Yosemite Falls from Pohono Trail in front of Sentinel Dome is the best in all of Yosemite. For the best overall vista along the trail, it's a toss-up between Glacier Point, Taft Point, and Dewey Point.

**User Groups:** Hikers only. No dogs, horses, or mountain bikes. No wheelchair facilities.

**Permits:** There is a $20 per vehicle entrance fee at Yosemite National Park, good for seven days. Free wilderness permits are required for overnight stays. They are available on a first-come, first-served basis up to one day in advance at the Yosemite Wilderness kiosk near your chosen trailhead, or farther in advance by mail, phone, or email for a $5 per person reservation fee.

**Maps:** Free park maps are available at park entrance stations or by contacting Yosemite National Park at the address below. A Yosemite map is available from Tom Harrison Maps. For topographic maps, ask the USGS for Half Dome and El Capitan.

**Directions:** From Merced, drive 70 miles northeast on Highway 140 to Yosemite National Park. Follow the signs to Yosemite Valley, entering through the Arch Rock entrance station. Continue for 6.3 miles on Highway 140/El Portal Road, which becomes Southside Drive, and turn right at the fork for Highway 41/Wawona/Fresno. Continue for 9.2 miles, turn left on Glacier Point Road, and drive 15.7 miles to Glacier Point. Park and walk toward the main viewing area across from the café and gift shop. Look for the Pohono Trail sign about 150 feet southeast of the café building, on your right.

**Contact:** Yosemite National Park Public Information Office, P.O. Box 577, Yosemite National Park, CA 95389, 209/372-0200 or 209/372-0740 (permit reservations), websites: www.nps.gov/yose or www.nps.gov/yose/wilderness (permit reservations).

## 55 PANORAMA TRAIL
### 8.5 mi one-way / 5.0 hrs

**off Glacier Point Road in Yosemite National Park**

Map 10.2, page 438

The Panorama Trail is an incredibly spectacular route from Glacier Point to Yosemite Valley, heading downhill most of the way, but you must have a shuttle car waiting at the end, or it's a heck of a long climb back up. A great option is to take the Yosemite Lodge tour bus for one leg of the trip.

The aptly named Panorama Trail begins at Glacier Point (elevation 7,214 feet), the trailhead with what is probably the grandest view in the West. You switchback down from the point accompanied by ever-changing perspectives on Half Dome, Basket Dome, North Dome, Liberty Cap, and far-off Vernal and Nevada Falls. You will gape a lot. After passing Illilouette Fall and ascending a bit for the first time on the trip, continue eastward to Panorama Trail's end, near the top of Nevada Fall. Turn right to reach the top of the fall, and have a snack at the overlook, then continue downhill on Mist Trail, on the north side of the river. After a view-filled descent along the north side of Nevada Fall, you'll cross the river in 1.4 miles and walk alongside lovely Emerald Pool on your way to the top of Vernal Fall. Enjoy the show here, then tromp down the granite staircase on the busy trail back to Happy Isles. There you can take the free valley shuttle bus to your shuttle car, parked somewhere in the valley. Note that the entire route has a 3,200-foot elevation loss over its course, but there is also a 760-foot climb after you cross Illilouette Creek. Also be forewarned that while the starting miles of the trip are very peaceful, the final two miles by Vernal Fall can be a parade of people.

**User Groups:** Hikers only. No dogs, horses, or mountain bikes. No wheelchair facilities.

**Permits:** No permits are required. There is a $20 per vehicle entrance fee at Yosemite National Park, good for seven days.

**Maps:** Free park maps are available at park entrance stations or by contacting Yosemite National Park at the address below. A Yosemite map is available from Tom Harrison Maps. For a topographic map, ask the USGS for Half Dome.

**Directions:** From Merced, drive 70 miles northeast on Highway 140 to Yosemite National Park. Follow the signs to Yosemite Valley, entering through the Arch Rock entrance station. Continue for 6.3 miles on Highway 140/El Portal Road, which becomes Southside Drive, and turn right at the fork for Highway 41/Wawona/Fresno. Continue for 9.2 miles, turn left on Glacier Point Road, and drive 15.7 miles to Glacier Point. Park and walk toward the main viewing area, across from the café and gift shop. Look for the Panorama Trail sign about 150 feet southeast of the café building, on your right.

**Contact:** Yosemite National Park Public Information Office, P.O. Box 577, Yosemite National Park, CA 95389, 209/372-0200, website: www.nps.gov/yose; Yosemite Lodge Tour Buses, 209/372-1240.

## 56 ILLILOUETTE FALL
**4.0 mi / 2.5 hrs**

**off Glacier Point Road in Yosemite National Park**

Map 10.2, page 438

Those who can't afford the time or make the car shuttle arrangements necessary to hike the entire Panorama Trail should at least take this incredible out-and-back trip on the top portion of the route. Glacier Point is your starting point, and the bridge above Illilouette Fall becomes your destination, but what happens in between is sheer magic. Some say that hiking Panorama Trail is like staring at a life-size Yosemite postcard, but we say it's more like being in the postcard. As you walk, you feel as if you've become one with the magnificent panorama of Half Dome, Basket Dome, North Dome, Liberty Cap, and far-off Vernal and Nevada Falls. The trail is downhill all the way to Illilouette Fall in two miles, which means you have a 1,200-foot elevation gain on the return trip. The path is extremely well graded though, so even children can make the climb. After viewing the waterfall from a trailside overlook, walk another .25 mile and stand on the bridge that is perched just above the 370-foot drop. For obvious reasons, don't think about swimming here.

**User Groups:** Hikers only. No dogs, horses, or mountain bikes. No wheelchair facilities.

**Permits:** No permits are required. There is a $20 per vehicle entrance fee at Yosemite National Park, good for seven days.

**Maps:** Free park maps are available at park entrance stations or by contacting Yosemite National Park at the address below. A Yosemite map is available from Tom Harrison Maps. For a topographic map, ask the USGS for Half Dome.

**Directions:** From Merced, drive 70 miles northeast on Highway 140 to Yosemite National Park. Follow the signs to Yosemite Valley, entering through the Arch Rock entrance station. Continue for 6.3 miles on Highway 140/El Portal Road, which becomes Southside Drive, and turn right at the fork for Highway 41/Wawona/Fresno. Continue for 9.2 miles, turn left on Glacier Point Road, and drive 15.7 miles to Glacier Point. Park and walk toward the main viewing area, across from the café and gift shop. Look for the Panorama Trail sign on your right, about 150 feet southeast of the café building.

**Contact:** Yosemite National Park Public Information Office, P.O. Box 577, Yosemite National Park, CA 95389, 209/372-0200, website: www.nps.gov/yose.

## 57 ALDER CREEK FALLS
**8.2 mi / 5.0 hrs**

**off Highway 41 near Wawona in Yosemite National Park**

Map 10.2, page 438

Maybe the best thing about Alder Creek Falls is that with all the world-famous waterfalls in Yosemite, this one just plain gets overlooked. Or maybe the best thing is the fun hike to reach it, starting with the challenge of locating the hidden trailhead along Highway 41. After you accomplish this feat, you begin with a one-mile beeline hike straight uphill through the forest, which will surely get your heart pumping. At the top of the ridge and a trail junction, turn left and hike through the trees for two more miles, still heading uphill but now more gently. Three miles from the trailhead, the route

suddenly goes level as it joins an old railroad grade, and then it's a one-mile easy stroll to the spot where Alder Creek takes the plunge off a granite lip. The waterfall is about 250 feet tall, and the best view of it is from the trail, about 100 yards from it. If you choose to keep hiking beyond the falls, you'll find many picnic spots among meadows and wildflowers.

**User Groups:** Hikers and horses. No dogs or mountain bikes. No wheelchair facilities.

**Permits:** There is a $20 per vehicle entrance fee at Yosemite National Park, good for seven days. Free wilderness permits are required for overnight stays. They are available on a first-come, first-served basis up to one day in advance at the Yosemite Wilderness kiosk near your chosen trailhead, or farther in advance by mail, phone, or email for a $5 per person reservation fee.

**Maps:** Free park maps are available at park entrance stations or by contacting Yosemite National Park at the address below. A Yosemite map is available from Tom Harrison Maps. For a topographic map, ask the USGS for Wawona.

**Directions:** From Merced, drive 55 miles northeast on Highway 140 to Yosemite National Park. Follow the signs to Yosemite Valley, entering through the Arch Rock entrance station. Continue for 6.3 miles on Highway 140/El Portal Road, which becomes Southside Drive, and turn right at the fork for Highway 41/Wawona/Fresno. Drive south on Highway 41 for 21 miles to a hairpin turn in the road (if you are coming from the south, it is exactly 4.2 miles north of Chilnualna Falls Road in Wawona). Park in the large dirt pullout on the west side of the road; the trailhead is on the east side of Highway 41. There is no marker except for a Yosemite Wilderness sign.

**Contact:** Yosemite National Park Public Information Office, P.O. Box 577, Yosemite National Park, CA 95389, 209/372-0200 or 209/372-0740 (permit reservations), websites: www.nps.gov/yose or www.nps.gov/yose/wilderness (permit reservations).

## 58 WAWONA MEADOW LOOP
3.2 mi / 1.25 hrs

**off Highway 41 near Wawona in Yosemite National Park**

Map 10.2, page 438

Hey, sometimes you just want to take a stroll in the park, and the Wawona Meadow Loop is just that. On many trips to Yosemite, we ignored this trail because of its proximity to the Wawona Golf Course, the presence of which insulted our national-park sensibilities. But then one day, we gave the Wawona Meadow Loop a try and wound up liking it. On the easy, level trail, you see and smell terrific wildflowers in late spring and summer, enjoy the good company of butterflies, and take a soothing lazy stroll around a pretty meadow. From the signed trailhead across the road from the Wawona Hotel, hike to your left on the dirt road, following the split rail fence, and then loop around the meadow. You can even bring your dog or ride your bike on this trail—a rarity in Yosemite. If you're staying at the Wawona Hotel, you can hike from there, crossing Highway 41 on your way out and back.

**User Groups:** Hikers, dogs, and mountain bikes. No horses. No wheelchair facilities.

**Permits:** No permits are required. There is a $20 per vehicle entrance fee at Yosemite National Park, good for seven days.

**Maps:** Free park maps are available at park entrance stations or by contacting Yosemite National Park at the address below. A Yosemite map is available from Tom Harrison Maps. For a topographic map, ask the USGS for Wawona.

**Directions:** From Merced, drive 70 miles northeast on Highway 140 to Yosemite National Park. Follow the signs toward Yosemite Valley, entering through the Arch Rock entrance station. Continue for 6.3 miles on Highway 140/El Portal Road, which becomes Southside Drive, and turn right at the fork for Highway 41/Wawona/Fresno. Drive 27 miles to the trailhead, which is just south of the golf course and across the road from the Wawona Hotel.

**Contact:** Yosemite National Park Public Information Office, P.O. Box 577, Yosemite National Park, CA 95389, 209/372-0200, website: www.nps.gov/yose.

## 59 CHILNUALNA FALL
8.2 mi / 5.0 hrs

**off Highway 41 near Wawona in Yosemite National Park**

Map 10.2, page 438

Are you ready to climb? Pick a nice, cool day—because this trail is in the lower-elevation part of Yosemite—and prepare for a steady four-mile uphill, gaining 2,400 feet to reach the top of Chilnualna Fall. Your nose will be continually assaulted with the intoxicating smell of bear clover, which together with manzanita and oaks makes up the majority of the vegetation along the route. Halfway up, you get a great view of Wawona Dome (elevation 6,897 feet) from a granite overlook. This is a great place to take a break and stretch your hamstrings. Shortly thereafter, you glimpse a section of Chilnualna Fall high up on a cliff wall, still far ahead of you. When you get closer, you see that the lower drop of the waterfall is a plunging free fall. The trail leads above the brink of the free fall (unfortunately not in front of it, so you never get to see it head-on) to a series of higher cascades. Keep walking until you reach the top cascade (consisting of five pool-and-drop tiers), which is just 100 yards to the right of the granite-lined trail. It's a great spot for a picnic before you begin the long descent back downhill.

**User Groups:** Hikers and horses. No dogs or mountain bikes. No wheelchair facilities.

**Permits:** There is a $20 per vehicle entrance fee at Yosemite National Park, good for seven days. Free wilderness permits are required for overnight stays. They are available on a first-come, first-served basis up to one day in advance at the Yosemite Wilderness kiosk near your chosen trailhead, or farther in advance by mail, phone, or email for a $5 per person reservation fee.

**Maps:** Free park maps are available at park entrance stations or by contacting Yosemite National Park at the address below. A Yosemite map is available from Tom Harrison Maps. For topographic maps, ask the USGS for Wawona and Mariposa Grove.

**Directions:** From Merced, drive 55 miles northeast on Highway 140 to Yosemite National Park. Follow the signs to Yosemite Valley, entering through the Arch Rock entrance station. Continue for 6.3 miles on Highway 140/El Portal Road, which becomes Southside Drive, and turn right at the fork for Highway 41/Wawona/Fresno. Drive south on Highway 41 for 25 miles to Wawona, and turn left on Chilnualna Falls Road. Drive 1.7 miles east and park in the lot on the right side of the road. Walk back to Chilnualna Falls Road and pick up the single-track trail across the pavement.

**Contact:** Yosemite National Park Public Information Office, P.O. Box 577, Yosemite National Park, CA 95389, 209/372-0200 or 209/372-0740 (permit reservations), websites: www.nps.gov/yose or www.nps.gov/yose/wilderness (permit reservations).

## 60 MARIPOSA GROVE
**2.0–6.5 mi / 1.0–3.0 hrs**

**off Highway 41 near Wawona in Yosemite National Park**

Map 10.2, page 438

The Mariposa Grove is the largest of the three groves of giant sequoias in Yosemite National Park. That's why on summer weekends the parking lot fills up and people wait in line in their cars to see the 250 or so big trees here. To save yourself the parking struggle, ride the free shuttle bus from the Wawona Store in the summer months. We hate to spill the beans, but the truth is that there are far bigger and more peaceful groves of sequoias just a few miles south, in Sierra National Forest. Still, the Mariposa Grove is worth seeing, especially if you can time your trip for when the crowds are somewhere else. (Early in the morning or just before sunset are usually the most peaceful times

to visit.) The star tree in the Mariposa Grove is the Grizzly Giant, with a circumference of more than 100 feet. At approximately 2,700 years old, it's one of the oldest known giant sequoias. If you want to see only the most famous trees in the grove—the Grizzly Giant, California Tunnel Tree, the Bachelor, and Three Graces—take the well-signed two-mile hike through the lower grove and turn around when you see the signs pointing to the upper grove. If you hike the entire lower and upper grove, you will cover about 6.5 miles. One surprise to first-time visitors is that motorized shuttles run through the grove. Some people ride the shuttle to the top of the upper grove, then walk back downhill, making an easy hike of about 3.2 miles with no climbing.

**User Groups:** Hikers only. No dogs, horses, or mountain bikes. No wheelchair facilities.

**Permits:** No permits are required. There is a $20 per vehicle entrance fee at Yosemite National Park, good for seven days.

**Maps:** A trail map/brochure is available at the trailhead. Free park maps are available at park entrance stations or by contacting Yosemite National Park at the address below. A Yosemite map is available from Tom Harrison Maps. For a topographic map, ask the USGS for Mariposa Grove.

**Directions:** From Merced, drive 70 miles northeast on Highway 140 to Yosemite National Park. Follow the signs toward Yosemite Valley, entering through the Arch Rock entrance station. Continue for 6.3 miles on Highway 140/El Portal Road, which becomes Southside Drive, and turn right at the fork for Highway 41/Wawona/Fresno. Drive 32 miles to the well-signed Mariposa Grove access road by Yosemite's south entrance. Turn east and drive two miles to the parking lot. During the busy summer months, you should park your car at the Wawona Store and ride the free shuttle bus into the Mariposa Grove. During the winter, this two-mile-long road into the grove is often closed due to snow, but you can still walk or snowshoe in.

If you enter the park on Highway 41 from the south, the Mariposa Grove is on the right, just after you drive through the park entrance station.

**Contact:** Yosemite National Park Public Information Office, P.O. Box 577, Yosemite National Park, CA 95389, 209/372-0200, website: www.nps.gov/yose.

## 61 LEWIS CREEK TRAIL
**4.0 mi / 2.0 hrs**

**off Highway 41 north of Oakhurst**

**Map 10.2, page 438**

Three separate trailheads access Lewis Creek Trail, but unless you want to hike its entire 3.5-mile one-way distance, the best place to start is at the trail's midpoint, just off Highway 41. From this roadside trailhead, you can take a 10-minute walk south to Corlieu Falls and/or walk 1.8 miles north to see Red Rock Falls. Neither waterfall is a showstopper, although both are pretty. Instead, the highlight of the trip is the hike itself, a gorgeous walk along flower-lined Lewis Creek, following the route of the historic Madera Sugar Pine lumber flume. You'll pass many anglers along the way; Lewis Creek is stocked with catchable trout. In addition, the white western azaleas along the stream bloom in profusion in early summer, shaded by a thick canopy of oaks, ponderosa pines, and incense cedars.

**User Groups:** Hikers and dogs. No horses or mountain bikes. No wheelchair facilities.

**Permits:** No permits are required. Parking and access are free.

**Maps:** For a map, ask the U.S. Forest Service for Sierra National Forest. For a topographic map, ask the USGS for Ahwahnee.

**Directions:** From Oakhurst, drive north on Highway 41 for eight miles to the signed trailhead for Lewis Creek Trail, on the east side of the highway. The trailhead is four miles south of Westfall Picnic Area.

**Contact:** Sierra National Forest, Bass Lake Ranger Station, 57003 Road 225, North Fork,

CA 93643, 559/877-2218, website: www.fs.fed.us/r5/sierra.

## 62 SHADOW OF THE GIANTS
**1.2 mi / 0.5 hr**

**off Highway 41 south of Yosemite National Park and north of Oakhurst**

**Map 10.2, page 438**

Shadow of the Giants is a National Recreation Trail that is located within the Nelder Grove of giant sequoias. For the sheer numbers of sequoias and the blissful peace and quiet, it beats the heck out of the sequoia groves a few miles north, in Yosemite National Park. On a Saturday afternoon in June, it's not impossible to walk the one-mile interpretive trail all by yourself. The self-guided signs along the trail are interesting and informative, and the babble of Nelder Creek is a perfect accompaniment to the huge, majestic trees. In addition to the sequoias, the forest is filled with western azaleas, dogwoods, incense cedars, wild rose, sugar pines, and white firs. What's the best thing we learned on the trail? The bark of mature sequoias is so soft that squirrels use it to line their nests. The trail makes an easy loop and is set at 5,000 feet in elevation. The best sequoias are at the far end of the loop, so make sure you walk all the way.

**User Groups:** Hikers and dogs. No horses or mountain bikes. No wheelchair facilities.

**Permits:** No permits are required. Parking and access are free.

**Maps:** For a map, ask the U.S. Forest Service for Sierra National Forest. For a topographic map, ask the USGS for Bass Lake.

**Directions:** From Oakhurst, drive north on Highway 41 for five miles to Sky Ranch Road/Road 632. Turn east on Sky Ranch Road and drive six miles to the turnoff for Nelder Grove. Turn left, drive 1.5 miles, and take the left fork, signed for Shadow of the Giants. Drive .5 mile to the trailhead.

**Contact:** Sierra National Forest, Bass Lake Ranger Station, 57003 Road 225, North Fork, CA 93643, 559/877-2218, website: www.fs.fed.us/r5/sierra.

## 63 FRESNO DOME

**2.0 mi / 1.0 hr**

off Highway 41 south of Yosemite National
Park and north of Oakhurst

Map 10.2, page 438

It's best to plan one hour of time for this
trip, but you might want to leave room
for more, because once you reach the top of
Fresno Dome, you won't want to leave. The
trailhead elevation is 8,000 feet, and the trail
is beautiful right from the start. It traverses
a verdant meadow filled with corn lilies, quaking aspens, and lavender shooting stars. The
first .5 mile is completely flat; in the second
.5 mile, you climb up the sloped back side of
Fresno Dome. After a moderate ascent (manageable by almost anybody), you're rewarded
with 360-degree views, mostly of conifer-filled
valleys. You can just make out a corner of
Bass Lake, the town of Oakhurst, and the far-
off snowy peaks of the John Muir Wilderness. From up on top of Fresno Dome, it all
looks like heaven.

**User Groups:** Hikers and dogs. No horses or
mountain bikes. No wheelchair facilities.

**Permits:** No permits are required. Parking and
access are free.

**Maps:** For a map, ask the U.S. Forest Service
for Sierra National Forest. For a topographic
map, ask the USGS for Bass Lake.

**Directions:** From Oakhurst, drive north on
Highway 41 for five miles to Sky Ranch
Road/Road 632. Turn east on Sky Ranch
Road, drive approximately 12 miles, and bear
left at the sign for Fresno Dome Campground.
Drive 4.8 miles to the trailhead (two miles
past the camp).

**Contact:** Sierra National Forest, Bass Lake
Ranger Station, 57003 Road 225, North Fork,
CA 93643, 559/877-2218, website: www.fs.fed
.us/r5/sierra.

## 64 THE NICHE AND CORA LAKES

**8.6 mi / 4.0 hrs–2.0 days**

in the Ansel Adams Wilderness southeast of
Yosemite National Park

Map 10.2, page 438

Reaching the trailhead for The Niche and Cora
Lakes requires a long drive on the Sierra Vista
National Scenic Byway, the showpiece road of
the North Fork area. If you have the time for
it, it's a great trip. The best approach is to drive
out and spend the night at Granite Creek Campground or nearby Clover Meadow Campground,
then start hiking the next day. The trip starts
with a 3.1-mile gentle ascent through red firs
and lodgepole pines to The Niche (at 8,000
feet), where you enter the Ansel Adams Wilderness boundary. Bear left and follow the signs
to Cora Lakes, at 4.3 miles. Only one of the
Cora Lakes is of substantial size; that's the
lower lake, the first one you come to, on the
left. The lake is partly forested and has dependable trout fishing. Because the total ascent
to Cora Lakes is only 1,200 feet, you may have
some energy left to burn. Backpackers should
consider adding on a jaunt to Joe Crane Lake,
another four miles to the north. The lake has
a long and lovely sandy beach, good fishing,
and even better swimming than at Cora Lakes.

**User Groups:** Hikers, dogs, and horses. No
mountain bikes. No wheelchair facilities.

**Permits:** A free wilderness permit is required
for overnight stays and is available from the
Bass Lake Ranger Station. Quotas are in effect from May 1 to November 1; for this period, permits are available in advance online or
by phone, fax, or mail for a $5 per person fee.

**Maps:** For a map, ask the U.S. Forest Service
for Sierra National Forest or Ansel Adams
Wilderness. For a topographic map, ask the
USGS for Timber Knob.

**Directions:** From the town of North Fork south
of Bass Lake, drive southeast on Road 225 to
Minarets Road. Turn left (north) on Minarets
Road/Road 81 and follow it for approximate-
ly 50 winding miles to the Clover Meadow
Ranger Station/Granite Creek turnoff, on the

right. Drive 4.5 miles to the Isberg trailhead, just beyond Granite Creek Campground.

**Contact:** Sierra National Forest, Bass Lake Ranger Station, 57003 Road 225, North Fork, CA 93643, 559/877-2218, website: www.fs.fed .us/r5/sierra.

## 65 JACKASS LAKES
### 7.2 mi / 4.0 hrs or 2.0 days

**in the Ansel Adams Wilderness southeast of Yosemite National Park**

**Map 10.2, page 438**

Campers in the Clover Meadow and Upper Chiquito campground areas have this pleasant day hike to look forward to. The trailhead is an easy reach (right off of Beasore Road), and in about two hours of hiking, you can be cooling your toes in the crystal-blue waters of Lower Jackass Lake. The trail climbs immediately from the road, then enters the Ansel Adams Wilderness boundary in one mile. This first mile can be hot and steep, but it's over with quickly. At the boundary, the grade mellows out, and you reach a junction just before the lakes, at 3.4 miles. The right fork goes to Lower Jackass Lake (the largest of three choices) in .2 mile, and the left fork goes to the tiny upper lake. A third lake lies in the basin above the upper lake. Many people just bear right at the junction and visit Lower Jackass Lake, which at 8,600 feet is backed by granite cliffs and offers good swimming and fishing prospects. No, this isn't the most beautiful lake in the Sierra, but if you just want to visit a pretty spot without a whole lot of effort, this trip fits the bill.

**User Groups:** Hikers, dogs, and horses. No mountain bikes. No wheelchair facilities.

**Permits:** A free wilderness permit is required for overnight stays and is available from the Bass Lake Ranger Station. Quotas are in effect from May 1 to November 1; for this period, permits are available in advance online or by phone, fax, or mail for a $5 per person fee.

**Maps:** For a map, ask the U.S. Forest Service for Sierra National Forest or Ansel Adams Wilderness. For a topographic map, ask the USGS for Timber Knob.

**Directions:** From Oakhurst, drive north on Highway 41 for four miles, then turn right on Road 222 toward Bass Lake. In four miles, bear left on Road 274. Drive two miles and turn left on Beasore Road (gravel). Drive 29 miles to a turnoff for the Norris Trailhead. Bear left and drive two miles to the trailhead parking area.

**Contact:** Sierra National Forest, Bass Lake Ranger Station, 57003 Road 225, North Fork, CA 93643, 559/877-2218, website: www.fs.fed .us/r5/sierra.

## 66 MONO PASS
### 8.4 mi / 4.5 hrs

**near Tioga Pass in Yosemite National Park**

**Map 10.2, page 438**

With an elevation gain of only 900 feet spread out over four miles, you'll hardly even notice you're climbing on the route to Mono Pass. (That's if you're acclimated, of course, because you're starting out at 9,700 feet, where the air is mighty thin.) The trail passes through lodgepole pine forests and meadows, and crosses the Dana fork of the Tuolumne River (an easy boulder hop by midsummer). Besides Mono Pass itself, the big attractions on the trail are some 19th-century mining cabins, which have been beautifully restored. Take the right spur at the Mono Pass sign (3.8 miles from the trailhead) to see the group of four side-by-side cabins. Take a photo of your hiking partner posing as a miner in one of their doorways. The hike to the pass offers great views of Mount Gibbs, Mount Dana, and the Kuna Crest. But don't turn around at the Mono Pass sign; continue past it for another .5 mile for the best views, looking down at Mono Lake and the surrounding desert.

**User Groups:** Hikers and horses. No dogs or mountain bikes. No wheelchair facilities.

**Permits:** No permits are required. There is a $20 per vehicle entrance fee at Yosemite National Park, good for seven days.

**Maps:** Free park maps are available at park entrance stations or by contacting Yosemite National Park at the address below. A Yosemite map is available from Tom Harrison Maps. For a topographic map, ask the USGS for Tioga Pass.

**Directions:** From Merced, drive 70 miles northeast on Highway 140 to Yosemite National Park. Follow the signs toward Yosemite Valley, entering through the Arch Rock entrance station. Continue 4.5 miles to the left turnoff for Tioga Road/Highway 120, looping back out of the valley on Big Oak Flat Road. In 9.3 miles, turn right on Tioga Road and drive 44.5 miles to the Mono Pass trailhead, parking on the south side of the road near road marker T-37, 1.5 miles west of Tioga Pass.

**Contact:** Yosemite National Park Public Information Office, P.O. Box 577, Yosemite National Park, CA 95389, 209/372-0200, website: www.nps.gov/yose.

## 67 MIDDLE AND UPPER GAYLOR LAKES
**4.0 mi / 2.5 hrs**

**near Tioga Pass in Yosemite National Park**

Map 10.2, page 438

The trail to Middle and Upper Gaylor Lakes is incredibly popular, which is another way of saying that it offers world-class scenery that completely wows visitors. Starting near Tioga Pass (at nearly 10,000 feet), the trail climbs a steep ridge and then drops down to Middle Gaylor Lake. Though it's only one mile of ascent, it's a high-elevation butt-kicker that makes many beg for mercy. From the middle lake, you can follow the creek gently uphill to the east to reach smaller Upper Gaylor Lake in another mile. Take the trail around its north side and uphill for a few hundred yards to the site of the Great Sierra Mine and the remains of an old stone cabin. The Great Sierra Mine turned out to be not so great—no silver ore was ever refined, and the mine was eventually abandoned. The haunt-ingly beautiful glacial scenery is what remains. The total elevation gain on the hike to Upper Gaylor Lake is about 1,000 feet, and it's worth every step.

**User Groups:** Hikers only. No dogs, horses, or mountain bikes. No wheelchair facilities.

**Permits:** No permits are required. There is a $20 per vehicle entrance fee at Yosemite National Park, good for seven days.

**Maps:** Free park maps are available at park entrance stations or by contacting Yosemite National Park at the address below. A Yosemite map is available from Tom Harrison Maps. For a topographic map, ask the USGS for Tioga Pass.

**Directions:** From Merced, drive miles northeast on Highway 140 to Yosemite National Park. Follow the signs toward Yosemite Valley, entering through the Arch Rock entrance station. Continue 4.5 miles to the left turnoff for Tioga Road/Highway 120, looping back out of the valley on Big Oak Flat Road. In 9.3 miles, turn right on Tioga Road and drive 46 miles to the parking lot just west of the Tioga Pass entrance station, on the north side of Tioga Road.

**Contact:** Yosemite National Park Public Information Office, P.O. Box 577, Yosemite National Park, CA 95389, 209/372-0200, website: www.nps.gov/yose.

## 68 BENNETTVILLE
**2.0 mi / 2.0 hrs**

**in Inyo National Forest just east of Tioga Pass**

Map 10.2, page 438

This trail is sure to spark your imagination. The remote high-country region of Bennettville was the site of a 19th-century silver mining community. Although the town thrived only from 1882 to 1884, it was the primary reason for the construction of the Tioga Pass Road from the west. The original road was built by the Great Sierra Consolidated Silver Company in anticipation of the riches they would make from the mines at Bennettville and nearby. Ultimately, no valuable minerals were ever extracted, and the company went broke in record time. A mostly level trail leads to the two buildings that remain from Bennettville's heyday: the assay office and barn/bunkhouse. An open mine tunnel lined with railcar tracks can also be seen, as well as some rusting mining equipment. Other than the mining town's remains, this area has plenty to offer in the way of high-country beauty. The elevation is well over 10,000 feet, and the forest is filled with graceful whitebark pines and chattering Clark's nutcrackers. Many hikers become enchanted with the scenery here, and if you want to see more, you can extend this hike by following the trail .5 mile uphill from the old buildings to small Shell Lake, or proceed onward past another small pothole lake to Fantail Lake and another mine site, .5 mile beyond.

**User Groups:** Hikers only. No dogs, horses or mountain bikes. No wheelchair facilities.

**Permits:** No permits are required. Parking and access are free.

**Maps:** For a map, ask the U.S. Forest Service for Inyo National Forest. For a topographic map, ask the USGS for Tioga Pass.

**Directions:** From Merced, drive 70 miles northeast on Highway 140 to Yosemite National Park. Follow the signs toward Yosemite Valley, entering through the Arch Rock entrance station. Continue 4.5 miles to the left turnoff for Tioga Road/Highway 120, looping back out of the valley on Big Oak Flat Road. In 9.3 miles, turn right on Tioga Road and drive 48 miles (you'll exit the park) to the Saddlebag Lake turnoff, on the left, two miles east of Tioga Pass. Turn left, and then left again immediately, to enter Junction Campground. The trail begins at the campground entrance.

**Contact:** Inyo National Forest, Mono Basin Scenic Area Visitors Center, P.O. Box 429, Lee Vining, CA 93541, 760/647-3044, website: www.fs.fed.us/r5/inyo.

## 69 GARDISKY LAKE
### 2.0 mi / 2.0 hrs

**in Inyo National Forest just east of Tioga Pass**

**Map 10.2, page 438**

How can a two-mile round-trip hike be rated a 3 for difficulty? It can because it goes straight up, gaining 800 feet in just one mile, with not nearly enough switchbacks. Although the trail distance is short, the trailhead is set at 10,000 feet, which means you need to be well acclimated to pant your way through that steep of a grade. The trip offers many rewards, though—such as much fewer people than at nearby Saddlebag Lake and a stellar high-alpine setting. Once you gain the ridgetop, you have a nearly level .25-mile stroll through a fragile alpine meadow to reach the lake, a shallow body of water. It's not the lake itself that is the highlight of this trail; it's the beauty and delicacy of the total landscape at this high elevation. That 11,500-foot mountain you see as you climb (ahead and to your right) is Tioga Peak; some hikers choose to ascend to its summit from Gardisky Lake. White Mountain and Mount Conness are also prominent, both over 12,000 feet.

**User Groups:** Hikers and dogs. No horses or mountain bikes. No wheelchair facilities.

**Permits:** No permits are required. Parking and access are free.

**Maps:** For a map, ask the U.S. Forest Service for Inyo National Forest. For a topographic map, ask the USGS for Tioga Pass.

**Directions:** From Merced, drive 70 miles northeast on Highway 140 to Yosemite National Park. Follow the signs toward Yosemite Valley, entering through the Arch Rock entrance station. Continue 4.5 miles to the left turnoff for Tioga Road/Highway 120, looping back out of the valley on Big Oak Flat Road. In 9.3 miles, turn right on Tioga Road and drive 48 miles (you'll exit the park) to the Saddlebag Lake turnoff, on the left, two miles east of Tioga Pass. Turn left and go 1.3 miles to the trailhead parking area, on the west side of the road before you reach Saddlebag Lake. The trail begins across the road.

**Contact:** Inyo National Forest, Mono Basin Scenic Area Visitors Center, P.O. Box 429, Lee Vining, CA 93541, 760/647-3044, website: www.fs.fed.us/r5/inyo.

## 70 SADDLEBAG LAKE LOOP
**3.6–8.4 mi / 2.0–4.0 hrs**

**in Inyo National Forest just east of Tioga Pass**

Map 10.2, page 438

Located just east of Tioga Pass and in the heart of the 20 Lakes Basin, Saddlebag Lake (at 10,087 feet) is a slice of paradise that's just outside the border of Yosemite National Park. The high-alpine setting is as good as anything in the park, and unfortunately, on summer weekends, the crowds are just as apparent. A fun aspect of hiking here is that you can make a shuttle trip by hiking one-way along the length of Saddlebag Lake, then taking the boat taxi back for a fee. It cuts 1.5 miles off your total mileage, and it increases the number of places you can access if you wish to go farther than this loop around the lake. You can also take the shuttle both ways and cut three miles off your trip. The only downer to the boat taxi is that it sometimes attracts yahoos who bring coolers of food and drink with them and leave their litter behind. That's one reason our favorite time to hike here is after Labor Day, when the summer crowds have dispersed.

To hike alongside Saddlebag Lake instead of riding in the boat taxi, you can follow either of two trails—the one on the lake's east side, or the one on the west side. The east-side trail is more scenic; the west-side trail is shorter. Take your pick. If you just want a short 3.6-mile loop, hike out on one and back on the other, but be sure to take the .2-mile spur to Greenstone Lake, which is backed by photogenic North Peak. If you want to hike farther, you can continue past Greenstone Lake to Wasco Lake and then on to deep, stark Steelhead Lake (three miles out if you start on the

west-side trail). Several more lakes lie beyond, including Shamrock and Helen. Bring a map with you; if you hike the entire loop and visit all six lakes that lie immediately beyond Saddlebag, you'll have an 8.4-mile day (or a 5.4-mile day, if you take the boat taxi round-trip). No matter how far you go, you'll be awed by the incredible high-country scenery—a blend of blue sky, granite, water, and hardy whitebark pines.

**User Groups:** Hikers and dogs. No horses or mountain bikes. No wheelchair facilities.

**Permits:** No permits are required. Parking and access are free.

**Maps:** For a map, ask the U.S. Forest Service for Inyo National Forest or Hoover Wilderness. For a topographic map, ask the USGS for Tioga Pass.

**Directions:** From Merced, drive 70 miles northeast on Highway 140 to Yosemite National Park. Follow the signs toward Yosemite Valley, entering through the Arch Rock entrance station. Continue 4.5 miles to the left turnoff for Tioga Road/Highway 120, looping back out of the valley on Big Oak Flat Road. In 9.3 miles, turn right on Tioga Road and drive 48 miles (you'll exit the park) to the Saddlebag Lake turnoff, on the left, two miles east of Tioga Pass. Turn left and drive another 2.5 miles to the trailhead parking area.

**Contact:** Inyo National Forest, Mono Basin Scenic Area Visitors Center, P.O. Box 429, Lee Vining, CA 93541, 760/647-3044, website: www.fs.fed.us/r5/inyo.

## 71 GIBBS LAKE TRAIL
**5.4 mi / 2.5 hrs or 2.0 days**

**west of Lee Vining on the northern boundary of the Ansel Adams Wilderness**

Map 10.2, page 438

The 2.7-mile hike from Upper Horse Meadow to Gibbs Lake is a great day hike that sees surprisingly few people. Since the trailhead isn't located at a lake or some other attractive setting, nobody gets here by accident. The trail starts at Upper Horse Meadow (elevation 8,000 feet), and climbs up Gibbs Canyon to Gibbs Lake, at 9,530 feet. That's about a 1,500-foot climb, but unfortunately the first stretch goes straight uphill on an old dirt road with nary a switchback. Once you get through that grunt of an ascent, the rest of the route is on a much mellower grade as it travels alongside Gibbs Creek. The trail ends at Gibbs Lake, a lovely glacial cirque that is backed by bare granite and fronted by conifers. Are you feeling ambitious? If you study the lake's back wall for a few minutes, it will soon become obvious that there is another, higher lake in this drainage. If you are sure-footed and have plenty of energy, you can pick out your route and go take a look at that lake. Although Gibbs Lake is pretty, the higher Kidney Lake (10,388 feet) is a stunner. It will take you about 40 minutes of challenging cross-country scrambling to get from Gibbs to Kidney; you'll gain almost 900 feet in less than a mile. Just pick your route carefully and go slow. Kidney Lake is indeed kidney-shaped, and it is flanked by Mount Dana (13,057 feet) on one side and Mount Gibbs (12,773 feet) on the other.

Special Note: Forest Road 1N16 requires a vehicle with high clearance.

**User Groups:** Hikers, horses, and mountain bikes (up to the wilderness border). No dogs permitted in order to protect endangered Sierra bighorn sheep. No wheelchair facilities.

**Permits:** A free wilderness permit is required for overnight stays and is available from the Mono Basin Scenic Area Visitors Center. Quotas are in effect from May 1 to November 1; for this period, permits are available in advance online or by phone, fax, or mail for a $5 per person fee.

**Maps:** For a map, ask the U.S. Forest Service for Inyo National Forest or Ansel Adams Wilderness. A map of the Mammoth High Country is available from Tom Harrison Maps. For a topographic map, ask the USGS for Lee Vining.

**Directions:** From Lee Vining, drive about two miles south on U.S. 395 and turn west on Forest Road 1N16 (look for the sign indicating Horse Meadow). Drive 3.4 miles to the trailhead at the end of the road. Forest Road 1N16 requires a vehicle with high clearance.

**Contact:** Inyo National Forest, Mono Basin Scenic Area Visitors Center, P.O. Box 429, Lee Vining, CA 93541, 760/647-3044, website: www.fs.fed.us/r5/inyo.

## 72 MONO LAKE SOUTH TUFA TRAIL
1.0 mi / 0.5 hr

**at the southern end of Mono Lake**

**Map 10.2, page 438**

The strange and remarkable tufa towers at Mono Lake create one of the most extraordinary landscapes in California. The terrain resembles a moonscape, but a strangely beautiful one. The area is extremely popular with photographers, especially at sunset. This short loop trail is the best way to get a good look at the tufa formations, which are formed when calcium-rich underwater springs are released from the lake bottom and then combine with Mono Lake's saline water, forming calcium carbonate. The trail leads through sagebrush plains to the southern shore of the lake, where the tufas rest like old, untouched earth castles. Some of them poke out of the lake surface; others are high and dry on land. Mono Lake itself is vast (covering 60 square miles) and is estimated to be more than 700,000 years old, making it one of the oldest lakes in North America. The lake's basin has become one of the world's most prolific stopover points for gulls, grebes, plovers, and phalaropes during their annual southbound flights. That's because the alkaline properties of the water create prime habitat for brine shrimp (an ideal food for these birds), and the lake's two large islands provide isolation from predators. Eighty-five percent of the California gull population was born at Mono Lake.

**User Groups:** Hikers and wheelchairs. No dogs, horses, or mountain bikes.

**Permits:** No permits are required. A $3 entrance fee is charged per adult. Youth ages 17 and under are free.

**Maps:** Trail maps are available at the Mono Basin Scenic Area Visitors Center. For topographic maps, ask the USGS for Lee Vining and Mono Mills.

**Directions:** From Lee Vining, drive five miles south on U.S. 395 and turn east on Highway 120 (signed for Mono Lake South Tufa). Drive 4.7 miles, then turn left and drive one mile on a dirt road to the parking area.

**Contact:** Mono Lake Tufa State Reserve, 760/647-6331, website: www.ceres.ca.gov/sierradsp/mono.html; Inyo National Forest, Mono Basin Scenic Area Visitors Center, P.O. Box 429, Lee Vining, CA 93541, 760/647-3044, website: www.fs.fed.us/r5/inyo.

## 73 BLOODY CANYON TRAIL
**8.2 mi / 5.0 hrs**

**southwest of Lee Vining at the northeastern boundary of the Ansel Adams Wilderness**

**Map 10.2, page 438**

Lower Sardine Lake is a jewel cradled in a high glacial bowl at 9,888 feet, the kind of lake that made the Ansel Adams Wilderness one of the most treasured places in the world. The hike in is tough and steep, with only one short, level section to provide much of a break. The trail is a historic Native American trading route, used by the Indians of the Mono Basin to visit the Indians of the Yosemite high country. The first mile to Walker Lake gains 600 feet and is very steep. From there, you head up Bloody Canyon, climbing nearly 2,000 feet in less than three miles. The hike parallels Walker Creek, requiring two stream crossings on the way up to Lower Sardine Lake. For anyone who is either out of shape or not acclimated to the altitude, the climb can be rough going. As you near Sardine Lake, a beautiful waterfall (the lake's outlet stream) will help to spur you on. When you reach the high-elevation lake, you'll find it is surrounded by rocky cliffs on one side and that it offers great views of the Mono Basin

to the east. Backpackers can continue hiking up and over Mono Pass and into Yosemite National Park's remote backcountry.

**User Groups:** Hikers, horses, and mountain bikes (up to the wilderness border). No dogs are permitted in order to protect endangered Sierra bighorn sheep. No wheelchair facilities.

**Permits:** A free wilderness permit is required for overnight stays and is available from the Mono Basin Scenic Area Visitors Center. Quotas are in effect from May 1 to November 1; for this period, permits are available in advance online or by phone, fax, or mail for a $5 per person fee.

**Maps:** For a map, ask the U.S. Forest Service for Inyo National Forest or Ansel Adams Wilderness. A map of the Mammoth High Country is available from Tom Harrison Maps. For topographic maps, ask the USGS for Mount Dana and Koip Peak.

**Directions:** From Lee Vining, drive five miles south on U.S. 395 to the north end of the June Lake Loop (Highway 158). Turn right and drive 1.3 miles on Highway 158, then turn right on a dirt road signed for Parker and Walker Lakes. Drive .5 mile to a junction, turn right, then drive another .5 mile and turn right again. Drive 2.9 miles to the trailhead.

**Contact:** Inyo National Forest, Mono Basin Scenic Area Visitors Center, P.O. Box 429, Lee Vining, CA 93541, 760/647-3044, website: www.fs.fed.us/r5/inyo.

## 74 PARKER LAKE TRAIL
**3.8 mi / 2.0 hrs**

**in the Ansel Adams Wilderness west of Grant Lake**

**Map 10.2, page 438**

This short trail has a whole lot going for it. The beauty of Parker Lake and towering Parker Peak just might knock your boots off—or at least your socks. Although the nearby June Lake Loop gets a lot of vacation traffic, this trailhead is obscure enough that most visitors pass it by. And get this: the 1.9-mile-long trail has an elevation gain of only a little more than 300 feet. Beginning at an elevation of 8,000 feet above Parker Creek, the trail follows the creek upstream on a fairly mellow grade before arriving at Parker Lake, at 8,318 feet. As you ascend, the landscape transitions from sagebrush plains into a mixed forest alongside Parker Creek, complete with quaking aspens and mammoth-sized Jeffrey pines. Look behind you once in a while, and you'll catch great views of Mono Lake. In short order, you will suddenly emerge from the forest onto the lake's shore. The lake is surrounded by granite walls that are impassable, so just pick a spot along the shoreline and pull out a snack. The only downer on this trip is that many of the largest aspen trees have had their trunks carved with initials by idiots. Let's hope they didn't know any better. Please teach your children never, ever to carve into trees.

**User Groups:** Hikers, dogs, and horses. No mountain bikes. No wheelchair facilities.

**Permits:** A free wilderness permit is required for overnight stays and is available from the Mono Basin Scenic Area Visitors Center. Quotas are in effect from May 1 to November 1; for this period, permits are available in advance online or by phone, fax, or mail for a $5 per person fee.

**Maps:** For a map, ask the U.S. Forest Service for Inyo National Forest or Ansel Adams Wilderness. A map of the Mammoth High Country is available from Tom Harrison Maps. For topographic maps, ask the USGS for Mount Dana and Koip Peak.

**Directions:** From Lee Vining, drive five miles south on U.S. 395 to the north end of the June Lake Loop (Highway 158). Turn right and drive 1.3 miles on Highway 158, then turn right on a dirt road signed for Parker and Walker Lakes. Drive 2.4 miles to the Parker Lake trailhead, at the end of the road.

**Contact:** Inyo National Forest, Mono Basin Scenic Area Visitors Center, P.O. Box 429, Lee Vining, CA 93541, 760/647-3044, website: www.fs.fed.us/r5/inyo.

## 75 RUSH CREEK TRAIL
**19.2 mi / 3.0 days**

on the eastern boundary of the Ansel Adams Wilderness west of June Lake

Map 10.2, page 438

Some places will never change, and people are drawn to them because they provide a sense of permanence that can't be found anywhere else. That is how it is at the Rush Creek headwaters. Created from drops of melting snow near the Sierra crest (at 10,500 feet), this stream runs downhill for miles, rolling into the forest like a swirling, emerald green fountain. Even a short visit requires a long drive to the trailhead, followed by a demanding backpacking trek. In the process, hikers contend with a 10-mile climb out, ice-cold stream crossings, and the possibility of afternoon thunderstorms, in which lightning bolts and thunderclaps rattle off the canyon rims.

The trailhead lies at Silver Lake (elevation 7,200 feet). After departing Silver Lake, follow the trail adjacent to Lower Rush Creek upstream toward the Ansel Adams Wilderness. Just before Agnew Lake, you reach a trail junction, 2.2 miles from your start. Turn right, and in one more mile, you arrive at beautiful Gem Lake (8,058 feet) and then Waugh Lake (9,442 feet), at the seven-mile point. Many visitors never venture farther than these lakes, simply stopping to camp, swim, or fish. But upstream of Waugh Lake is where you find the Rush Creek headwaters, along with the flawless symmetry of the untouched high country. Getting there requires a total climb of 3,300 feet over the course of 9.6 miles, but it is one of the prettiest streams anywhere and is well worth the effort.

**User Groups:** Hikers, dogs, and horses. No mountain bikes. No wheelchair facilities.

**Permits:** A free wilderness permit is required for overnight stays and is available from the Mono Basin Scenic Area Visitors Center. Quotas are in effect from May 1 to November 1; for this period, permits are available in advance online or by phone, fax, or mail for a $5 per person fee.

**Maps:** For a map, ask the U.S. Forest Service for Inyo National Forest or Ansel Adams Wilderness. A map of the Mammoth High Country is available from Tom Harrison Maps. For topographic maps, ask the USGS for June Lake and Koip Peak.

**Directions:** From Lee Vining, drive about 11 miles south on U.S. 395 to June Lake Junction. Turn right on Highway 158/June Lake Road and drive seven miles to the Rush Creek trailhead, across the road from Silver Lake Campground.

**Contact:** Inyo National Forest, Mono Basin Scenic Area Visitors Center, P.O. Box 429, Lee Vining, CA 93541, 760/647-3044, website: www.fs.fed.us/r5/inyo.

## 76 YOST LAKE
### 4.8–9.4 mi / 2.5 hr–1.0 day

**in Inyo National Forest near June Lake**

Map 10.2, page 438

Yost Lake is a small glacial lake hidden at 9,000 feet on the June Mountain slopes. Many people visit the June Lake area for years without even knowing Yost exists. But it is up here, tucked away and accessible only to those willing to hike. From the trailhead (7,800 feet) at June Lake, Yost Meadows Trail rises very steeply in the first mile, climbing 800 feet—a real butt-kicker for many. That discourages many from going farther—after all, it is 4.7 miles to the lake. But after that first grunt of a climb, the trail gets much easier, contouring across the mountain slopes. It rises gradually to the headwaters of Yost Creek and then drops into the small basin that guards the lake.

A shorter option is to begin at the Yost Creek/Fern Lake trailhead, making it a much shorter, 4.8-mile round-trip. It is just as pretty, but it has a more difficult grade and can be slippery for those not wearing heavy, firm-gripping hiking boots. The trailhead is located three miles west of the town of June Lake, on the west (left) side of June Lake Road, past the ski resort.

**User Groups:** Hikers, dogs, and horses. No mountain bikes. No wheelchair facilities.

**Permits:** No permits are required. Parking and access are free.

**Maps:** For a map, ask the U.S. Forest Service for Inyo National Forest. A map of the Mammoth High Country is available from Tom Harrison Maps. For topographic maps, ask the USGS for June Lake and Mammoth Mountain.

**Directions:** From Lee Vining, drive about 11 miles south on U.S. 395 to June Lake Junction. Go right on Highway 158/June Lake Road and drive two miles to the town of June Lake. The trailhead is on the west (left), across the road from the fire station.

**Contact:** Inyo National Forest, Mono Basin Scenic Area Visitors Center, P.O. Box 429, Lee Vining, CA 93541, 760/647-3044, website: www.fs.fed.us/r5/inyo.

## 77 INYO CRATERS
### 0.5 mi / 0.5 hr

**in Inyo National Forest north of Mammoth Lakes**

Map 10.2, page 438

A geologic phenomenon, the Inyo Craters make a great destination for an easy day hike in the Mammoth Lakes area. They are part of a chain of craters and other volcanic formations that reaches from Mammoth Lake to Mono Lake. The craters—evidence of Mammoth's fiery past—are the remains of a volcanic explosion of steam that occurred a mere 600 years ago. At that time, the mountain was a smoldering volcano. Melted snow found its way inside, and when the cold water hit hot magma—kaboom! The hike is a short, gentle uphill, but the elevation sucks the air out of many visitors who have just arrived in Mammoth. The trail leads through a lovely open forest of red fir and Jeffrey pine. In each of the two Inyo Craters lies a tiny pond that fills with melted snow each spring, then dries up during summer.

**User Groups:** Hikers, horses, and dogs. No mountain bikes. No wheelchair facilities.

**Permits:** No permits are required. Parking and access are free.

**Maps:** For a map, ask the U.S. Forest Service for Inyo National Forest. For a topographic map, ask the USGS for Mammoth Mountain.

**Directions:** From Lee Vining, drive about 20 miles south on U.S. 395 to the Mammoth Lakes Scenic Loop/Forest Road 3S23. Turn right and drive 3.2 miles to Forest Road 3S30. Turn right and drive .3 mile to Forest Road 3S29. Turn right and drive to the parking area for the Inyo Craters Picnic Area. The last 1.3 miles is unpaved.

**Contact:** Inyo National Forest, Mammoth Ranger Station, P.O. Box 148, Mammoth Lakes, CA 93546, 760/924-5500, website: www.fs.fed .us/r5/inyo.

## 78 BARRETT AND TJ LAKES
### 1.0 mi / 0.5 hr

**at Lake George in Mammoth Lakes**

Map 10.2, page 438

Campers at Lake George, and Mammoth visitors who just want a short and easy day hike, will be pleased to find that this no-sweat trail provides access to hidden Barrett and TJ Lakes. The trail starts on the northeast shore of Lake George (which in itself is a gorgeous spot), follows the lakeshore for about 100 yards, then climbs alongside a small stream to little Barrett Lake. The tiny lake is framed by Red Mountain in the background. Hey, this was so easy, you might as well continue another .25 mile to TJ Lake, the more scenic of the two lakes. The distinctive granite fin of Crystal Crag (10,377 feet) towers above TJ Lake's basin, adding drama to the scene. In addition to the pretty but popular lakes, this trail shows off some lovely mountain meadows, gilded with colorful penstamen, shooting stars, and paintbrush in midsummer.

**User Groups:** Hikers, horses, and dogs. Mountain bikes are not advised. No wheelchair facilities.

**Permits:** No permits are required. Parking and access are free.

**Maps:** For a map, ask the U.S. Forest Service for Inyo National Forest. A map of the Mammoth High Country is available from Tom Harrison Maps. For a topographic map, ask the USGS for Crystal Crag.

**Directions:** From the Mammoth Lakes junction on U.S. 395, turn west on Highway 203 and drive four miles through the town of Mammoth Lakes to the junction of Minaret Road/Highway 203 and Lake Mary Road. Continue straight on Lake Mary Road and drive four miles to a juction for Lake George. Turn left here, drive .3 mile, then turn right and drive another .3 mile to Lake George. The trailhead is located near the campground.

**Contact:** Inyo National Forest, Mammoth Ranger Station, P.O. Box 148, Mammoth Lakes, CA 93546, 760/924-5500, website: www.fs.fed .us/r5/inyo.

## 79 CRYSTAL LAKE
### 3.8 mi / 2.0 hrs

**at Lake George in Mammoth Lakes**

Map 10.2, page 438

If you think Lake George is gorgeous, wait until you see Crystal Lake, located southwest of Lake George in a bowl scoured by glaciers and tucked into a hollow below 10,377-foot Crystal Crag. The trail to reach it has a 700-foot elevation gain and is pleasantly shaded by a hearty hemlock, pine, and fir forest. The path begins near the cabins at Woods Lodge but rises quickly above them. Many hikers huff and puff as they climb this ridge. But the view of the Mammoth Lakes Basin makes it all worthwhile. This high ridge gives you a bird's-eye look at the basin's four major lakes: George, Mary, Mamie, and Twin. At a junction at one mile, go left and descend to Crystal Lake. The lake is a true jewel, highlighted by permanent snowfields that line its granite backdrop. You aren't likely to find much solitude here, since the lake is so easy to reach, but the scenery more than makes up for it.

If you want to turn this into a longer hike,

you can take the other trail at the fork and head for Mammoth Crest, at 10,400 feet, two miles farther. The trail gains another 700 feet as it leaves the forest and enters a stark, volcanic landscape peppered with whitebark pines. The expansive view from the high point on the crest includes the Mammoth Lakes Basin, the San Joaquin River, the Minaret Range, and Mammoth Mountain. If this hike hasn't taken your breath away, the vista will.

**User Groups:** Hikers, horses, and dogs. Mountain bikes are not advised. No wheelchair facilities.

**Permits:** No permits are required. Parking and access are free.

**Maps:** For a map, ask the U.S. Forest Service for Inyo National Forest. A map of the Mammoth High Country is available from Tom Harrison Maps. For a topographic map, ask the USGS for Crystal Crag.

**Directions:** From the Mammoth Lakes junction on U.S. 395, turn west on Highway 203 and drive four miles through the town of Mammoth Lakes to the junction of Minaret Road/Highway 203 and Lake Mary Road. Continue straight on Lake Mary Road and drive four miles to a junction for Lake George. Turn left, drive .3 mile, then turn right and drive another .3 mile to Lake George. The trailhead is on the right, near some cabins.

**Contact:** Inyo National Forest, Mammoth Ranger Station, P.O. Box 148, Mammoth Lakes, CA 93546, 760/924-5500, website: www.fs.fed .us/r5/inyo.

## 80 EMERALD LAKE AND SKY MEADOWS
**4.0 mi / 2.0 hrs**

**at Lake Mary in Mammoth Lakes**

Map 10.2, page 438

This is one of the Eastern Sierra's premier wildflower trails, and it's easy enough for children to hike. The trail starts just south of Lake Mary, at the end of the Coldwater Campground road. The hike is short and direct, climbing straight

to Emerald Lake on an easy grade. Picnickers are often found seated among the rocks by the water's edge, although by midsummer, the tiny lake dwindles to something that more closely resembles a pond. No matter, the lake is not the star of the show here—the flowers are. The trail skirts the east shore of Emerald Lake and continues along its inlet stream. Three brief climbs lead you past Gentian Meadow to the southeast edge of Sky Meadows, which is filled with wildflowers throughout the summer. Beyond the meadows, permanent snow fields decorate the granite cliffs of Mammoth Crest. Among the wide variety of flower species to be seen and admired, one standout is the tall orange tiger lilies, a flower that is showy enough to be in a florist's shop. Please be careful not to trample any of the blooms here, and by all means, refrain from picking samples. They say that for every wildflower that is picked, 100 will not grow next summer.

**User Groups:** Hikers, dogs, and horses. No mountain bikes allowed past the wilderness boundary. No wheelchair facilities.

**Permits:** No day permits are required. Parking and access are free.

**Maps:** For a map, ask the U.S. Forest Service for Inyo National Forest. A map of the Mammoth High Country is available from Tom Harrison Maps. For a topographic map, ask the USGS for Crystal Crag.

**Directions:** From the Mammoth Lakes junction on U.S. 395, turn west on Highway 203 and drive four miles through the town of Mammoth Lakes to the junction of Minaret Road/Highway 203 and Lake Mary Road. Continue straight on Lake Mary Road and drive 3.5 miles to a fork just before Lake Mary; turn left and drive .6 mile to the Coldwater Campground turnoff, on the left. Turn left and drive .5 mile through the camp to the trailhead, at the first parking lot.

**Contact:** Inyo National Forest, Mammoth Ranger Station, P.O. Box 148, Mammoth Lakes, CA 93546, 760/924-5500, website: www.fs.fed .us/r5/inyo.

## 81 DUCK LAKE
### 10.0 mi / 6.0 hrs or 2.0 days

**in the John Muir Wilderness near Mammoth Lakes**

Map 10.2, page 438

How far you hike on Duck Pass Trail is up to you, but if it were up to us, we'd hike at least as far as five miles to Duck Lake, elevation 10,450 feet. Sure, lots of people stop at the other lakes this trail passes along the way—Arrowhead Lake at 1.3 miles out, Skelton Lake at two miles, or Barney Lake at three miles—and these make fine destinations. But you might as well see them all and then keep climbing through Duck Pass to much larger Duck Lake, at five miles. The pass is a 1,600-foot climb from the trailhead at Coldwater Campground. Just beyond the pass, the trail drops 300 feet to reach Duck Lake, one of the largest natural lakes in the Eastern Sierra. (It's bigger than Convict Lake, for example, which you can drive to.) Most of the climbing is in the stretch from Barney Lake to the pass, as the trail switchbacks up a talus-covered slope. Day hikers can make their way from Duck Lake on a side trail to Pika Lake, which is visible in the distance. Backpackers can continue on to Purple Lake (at 7.5 miles) and Lake Virginia (at nine miles). The only downer on this trail is the presence of horses and pack mules, which can make the trail quite dusty by late summer. There are tons of people on the trail, too, but with this kind of scenery, everybody is in a good mood.

**User Groups:** Hikers, dogs, and horses. No mountain bikes allowed past the wilderness boundary. No wheelchair facilities.

**Permits:** A free wilderness permit is required for overnight stays and is available from the Mammoth Ranger Station. Quotas are in effect from May 1 to November 1; for this period, permits are available in advance online or by phone, fax, or mail for a $5 per person fee.

**Maps:** For a map, ask the U.S. Forest Service for Inyo National Forest. A map of the Mammoth High Country is available from Tom Harrison Maps. For a topographic map, ask the USGS for Crystal Crag.

**Directions:** From the Mammoth Lakes junction on U.S. 395, turn west on Highway 203 and drive four miles, through the town of Mammoth Lakes, to the junction of Minaret Road/Highway 203 and Lake Mary Road. Continue straight on Lake Mary Road and drive 3.5 miles to a fork just before Lake Mary; turn left and drive .6 mile to the Coldwater Campground turnoff, on the left. Turn left and drive .5 mile through the camp to the trailhead at the farthest parking lot.

**Contact:** Inyo National Forest, Mammoth Ranger Station, P.O. Box 148, Mammoth Lakes, CA 93546, 760/924-5500, website: www.fs.fed .us/r5/inyo.

## 82 VALENTINE LAKE TRAIL
### 11.2 mi / 6.0 hrs or 2.0 days

**in the John Muir Wilderness south of Mammoth Lakes**

Map 10.2, page 438

The Mammoth Lakes area is one of the Eastern Sierra's star attractions, yet nearby Valentine Lake is perhaps overlooked because the trailhead (at 7,600 feet) is not found at one of the lakes in the Mammoth Lakes Basin. Or perhaps it's because the climb required to get there is so steep. Regardless of the reason, a morning's hike—rising some 1,900 feet over 5.6 miles, but with most of the climb compressed into two miles—gets you to the lake, which sits at 9,698 feet.

Some say the lake is shaped like a teardrop, but we think it looks more like a drop of sweat. The hike starts out with a very steep climb (including .5 mile of sandy switchbacks in a dry pine forest) and doesn't level out for the first two miles. You'll pass a side trail to the Sherwin Lakes at 2.9 miles (a fine destination for those who have had enough, or those who just want to catch fish). Continue uphill, much more gently now, finally meeting up with Valentine Lake's outlet stream. Valentine Lake has rocky cliffs ringing its edges, making it difficult to explore its shoreline. Pick a spot and toss in a line; the lake has plentiful brook trout.

**User Groups:** Hikers, dogs, and horses. No

mountain bikes allowed past the wilderness boundary. No wheelchair facilities.

**Permits:** A free wilderness permit is required for overnight stays and is available from the Mammoth Ranger Station. Quotas are in effect from May 1 to November 1; for this period, permits are available in advance online or by phone, fax, or mail for a $5 per person fee.

**Maps:** For a map, ask the U.S. Forest Service for Inyo National Forest or John Muir Wilderness. A map of the Mammoth High Country is available from Tom Harrison Maps. For a topographic map, ask the USGS for Crystal Crag.

**Directions:** From the Mammoth Lakes junction on U.S. 395, turn west on Highway 203 and drive 2.6 miles to Old Mammoth Road. Turn left and drive .8 mile to Sherwin Creek Road. Turn left and drive 2.7 miles to the signed trailhead for Valentine Lake (past the Sherwin Creek Campground.)

**Contact:** Inyo National Forest, Mammoth Ranger Station, P.O. Box 148, Mammoth Lakes, CA 93546, 760/924-5500, website: www.fs.fed .us/r5/inyo.

## 83 RED CONES LOOP
**6.7 mi / 4.0 hrs**

**at Horseshoe Lake in Mammoth Lakes**

**Map 10.2, page 438**

Horseshoe Lake, elevation 8,900 feet, lies at the end of the Mammoth Lakes road and has an excellent trailhead that makes for a great day hike. Don't be put off by the dead trees and the barren look of the place. A relatively small area by the lake has been affected by carbon-dioxide gas venting up through the soil—the result of seismic activity. You get away from this strange-looking forest quickly. Set out from the northwest side of the lake, ascend the slope, and take the left fork for McLeod Lake. In just under two miles, you'll reach the start of the loop. Go right to reach Crater Meadow, a beautiful little spot set just

below Red Cones, and then circle around to Upper Crater Meadow. Either meadow is a fine destination for a picnic lunch in peace. The contrast is striking: Just a short distance below, there are typically many people at Twin Lakes, Lake Mary, Lake Mamie, and Lake George, yet you are separated from them by Mammoth Pass. You will be surprised at how relatively few people take this loop hike, and glad that you made the choice to do so.

**User Groups:** Hikers, dogs, and horses. No mountain bikes are allowed past the wilderness border. No wheelchair facilities.

**Permits:** No permits are required. Parking and access are free.

**Maps:** For a map, ask the U.S. Forest Service for Inyo National Forest. A map of the Mammoth High Country is available from Tom Harrison Maps. For a topographic map, ask the USGS for Crystal Crag.

**Directions:** From the Mammoth Lakes junction on U.S. 395, turn west on Highway 203 and drive four miles through the town of Mammoth Lakes to the junction of Minaret Road/Highway 203 and Lake Mary Road. Continue straight on Lake Mary Road and drive 4.8 miles to the road's end, at Horseshoe Lake. The trailhead is on the northwest side of the lake, signed for Mammath Pass.

**Contact:** Inyo National Forest, Mammoth Ranger Station, P.O. Box 148, Mammoth Lakes, CA 93546, 760/924-5500, website: www.fs.fed .us/r5/inyo.

## 84 DEVILS POSTPILE AND RAINBOW FALLS
**2.0–5.0 mi / 1.0–2.0 hrs**

**in Devils Postpile National Monument west of Mammoth Lakes**

**Map 10.2, page 438**

The first time you lay eyes on 101-foot Rainbow Falls, the tall, wide, and forceful waterfall comes as an awesome surprise. Most first-time visitors see it before or after a trip to the Devils Postpile, a fascinating collection of volcanic rock columns and rubble left from a lava flow nearly 100,000 years ago. It's like nothing you've seen anywhere else. You can hike to Rainbow Falls two ways, either from the ranger station at Devils Postpile National Monument or from the Rainbow Falls trailhead, near Reds Meadow Resort. Either way, this is one of the best short hikes in California.

Your best bet is to start at the ranger station, then pass by the Devils Postpile lava columns in only .5 mile. Stop and gape at this geologic wonder, and perhaps take the short but steep side trip to the top of the columns, then continue downhill to Rainbow Falls, at 2.5 miles. (If you start at the trailhead by Reds Meadow, your trip to Rainbow Falls is only one mile, but you'll miss out on the postpile.)

In order to see the rainbow that gives the waterfall its name, you must show up in late morning or at midday. The rainbow is the result of a prism effect from sun's rays refracting through the falling water. Two overlook areas across from the waterfall's brink give you an excellent view, but you can hike down a series of stairsteps to the falls' base for an even better vantage point. If you're inspired, you can travel another .5 mile on the trail to find a smaller waterfall on the San Joaquin River, called Lower Falls.

**User Groups:** Hikers and horses. No mountain bikes. Dogs must be leashed in national monument. No wheelchair facilities.

**Permits:** Each person entering the Devils Postpile/Reds Meadow area must purchase an access pass. (See Access Note, below.) The fee is $7 per adult and $4 for children ages 3 to 12. Children ages two and under are free. Passes may be purchased at the Mammoth Mountain shuttle bus terminal or at Minaret Station.

**Maps:** For a map, ask the U.S. Forest Service for Inyo National Forest. A map of the Mammoth High Country is available from Tom Harrison Maps. For a topographic map, ask the USGS for Mammoth Mountain.

**Directions:** From the Mammoth Lakes junction on U.S. 395, turn west on Highway 203 and drive four miles through the town of Mammoth Lakes to Minaret Road (still Highway 203). Turn right and drive 4.5 miles to the shuttle bus terminal (adjacent to the Mammoth Mountain Ski Area). Purchase an access pass and board a shuttle bus here. Disembark at the Devils Postpile Ranger Station or Rainbow Falls trailhead, which is just before Reds Meadow Resort.

Access Note: Visitors arriving between 7 A.M. and 7 P.M. are required to ride a shuttle bus (free with purchase of an access pass) from Mammoth Mountain Ski Area. If you are camping in the Devils Postpile area, you are permitted to drive your own car instead of taking the shuttle, but each passenger in the car must purchase an access pass.

**Contact:** Inyo National Forest, Mammoth Ranger Station, P.O. Box 148, Mammoth Lakes, CA 93546, 760/924-5500, website: www.fs.fed.us/r5/inyo; Devils Postpile National Monument, 760/934-2289 (summer only).

## 85 MINARET LAKE
**16.0 mi / 2.0 days**

**in the Ansel Adams Wilderness west of Mammoth Lakes**

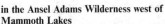
Map 10.2, page 438

Minaret Lake is a real prize, set just below the awesome glacial-carved Ritter Range, at 9,793 feet. Reaching it requires an eight-mile hike with a 1,800-foot elevation gain, and every step is completely worth it. From the trailhead at Devils Postpile Ranger Station, you hike south to access a bridge across the San Joaquin River, then head northward two miles on John Muir Trail. (You can also start from Upper Soda Spring Campground and hike south on the Pacific Crest Trail, then turn north on the John Muir Trail. The distance is about the same.) After passing tiny Johnston Lake, you reach the junction with Minaret Lake Trail. Turn left and follow Minaret Creek. The trail rises with the creek and in the last mile climbs steeply above tree line before skirting the Minaret Lake outlet and tracing the line of the north shore. The granite peaks that form the lake's backdrop are Clyde and Ken Minaret. Good campsites are found near Minaret Lake's rocky shore. If you want to do some exploring, Cecile Lake (at 10,239 feet) can be reached via a cross-country route to the northwest of the lake.

**User Groups:** Hikers, dogs, and horses. Dogs must be leashed in national monument. No mountain bikes. No wheelchair facilities.

**Permits:** Each person entering the Devils Postpile/Reds Meadow area must purchase an access pass. (See Access Note, below.) The fee is $7 per adult and $4 for children ages 3 to 12. Children ages two and under are free. Passes may be purchased at the Mammoth Mountain shuttle bus terminal or at Minaret Station.

A free wilderness permit is required for overnight stays and is available from the Mammoth Ranger Station. Quotas are in effect from May 1 to November 1; for this period, permits are available in advance online or by phone, fax, or mail for a $5 per person fee.

**Maps:** For a map, ask the U.S. Forest Service for Inyo National Forest or Ansel Adams Wilderness. A map of the Mammoth High Country is available from Tom Harrison Maps. For topographic maps, ask the USGS for Mammoth Mountain and Mount Ritter.

**Directions:** From the Mammoth Lakes junction on U.S. 395, turn west on Highway 203 and drive four miles through the town of Mammoth Lakes to Minaret Road (still Highway 203). Turn right and drive 4.5 miles to the shuttle bus terminal (adjacent to the Mammoth Mountain Ski Area). Purchase an access pass and board a shuttle bus here. Disembark at the Devils Postpile Ranger Station.

Access Note: Visitors arriving between 7 A.M. and 7 P.M. are required to ride a shuttle bus (free with purchase of an access pass) from Mammoth Mountain Ski Area. If you are camping in the Devils Postpile area, you are permitted to drive your own car instead of taking the shuttle, but each passenger in the car must purchase an access pass.

**Contact:** Inyo National Forest, Mammoth Ranger Station, P.O. Box 148, Mammoth Lakes, CA 93546, 760/924-5500, website: www.fs.fed .us/r5/inyo.

## 86 FERN LAKE LOOP
**10.0–16.0 mi / 1.0–2.0 days** 🥾 🏕

**in the Ansel Adams Wilderness west of Mammoth Lakes**

Map 10.2, page 438

Fern Lake can be the destination on an ambitious day hike from Devils Postpile, or the start of a great 15-mile backpacking loop. Either way, this is an excellent hike that has become very popular. Starting from the ranger station at Devils Postpile, you head south to access the bridge across the San Joaquin River, then follow Fern Lake Trail. About two miles in, you face a crossing of King Creek that can be tricky early in the summer. Exercise some caution. Then climb through the pine forest to reach a junction, at 4.9 miles. Follow the spur to Fern Lake, elevation 8,800 feet, where many good campsites are found. The lake is set in a small rock bowl at tree line, below Iron Mountain, in the Minarets. Day hikers will often while away a few hours here and then retrace their steps for a 10-mile round-trip.

Those continuing onward will find the trail pokes in and out of sparse forest for the next two miles to Becks Cabin. From here, a one-mile side trip leads to Superior Lake (7.5 miles from your start, and at 9,400 feet), another excellent spot for an overnight. A faint path leads .7 mile from Superior Lake to the two Beck Lakes (at 9,800 feet), which are surrounded by high granite ridges. A visit to Beck Lakes—set in a glacial-formed pocket below the Minarets and amid celestial mountain scenery—is highly recommended. When you return to the loop at Becks Cabin, you have a 4.8-mile descent to reach John Muir Trail, where you turn right and head back to the bridge and the ranger station.

**User Groups:** Hikers, dogs, and horses. Dogs must be leashed in national monument. No mountain bikes. No wheelchair facilities.

**Permits:** Each person entering the Devils Postpile/Reds Meadow area must purchase an access pass. (See Access Note, below.) The fee is $7 per adult and $4 for children ages 3 to 12. Children ages two and under are free. Passes may be purchased at the Mammoth Mountain shuttle bus terminal or at Minaret Station.

A free wilderness permit is required for overnight stays and is available from the Mammoth Ranger Station. Quotas are in effect from May 1 to November 1; for this period, permits are available in advance online or by phone, fax, or mail for a $5 per person fee.

**Maps:** For a map, ask the U.S. Forest Service for Inyo National Forest or Ansel Adams Wilderness. A map of the Mammoth High Country is available from Tom Harrison Maps. For topographic maps, ask the USGS for Mammoth Mountain and Mount Ritter.

**Directions:** From the Mammoth Lakes junction on U.S. 395, turn west on Highway 203 and drive four miles through the town of Mammoth Lakes to Minaret Road (still Highway 203). Turn right and drive 4.5 miles to the shuttle bus terminal (adjacent to the Mammoth Mountain Ski Area). Purchase an access pass and board a shuttle bus here. Disembark at the Devils Postpile Ranger Station.

Access Note: Visitors arriving between 7 A.M. and 7 P.M. are required to ride a shuttle bus (free with purchase of an access pass) from Mammoth Mountain Ski Area. If you are camping in the Devils Postpile area, you are permitted to drive your own car instead of taking the shuttle, but each passenger in the car must purchase an access pass.

**Contact:** Inyo National Forest, Mammoth Ranger Station, P.O. Box 148, Mammoth Lakes, CA 93546, 760/924-5500, website: www.fs.fed.us/r5/inyo.

## 87 SHADOW LAKE
**7.6 mi / 4.0 hrs or 2.0 days**

**in the Ansel Adams Wilderness west of Mammoth Lakes**

Map 10.2, page 438

Shadow Lake is one of the most popular destinations in the Devils Postpile region simply because of its sheer beauty. The only unpleasant part of this hike is making your way through the busy trailhead parking lots at Agnew Meadows. Once that's accomplished and you're on the trail, all is bliss, as long as you're in good condition and ready for a sustained climb. (Campers at Agnew Meadows can cut a half mile off this trip each way by starting from the trail at camp, not from the trailhead parking lot.) The route starts out quite mellow as it wanders through the wildflowers at Agnew Meadows. It then follows the River Trail along the middle fork of the San Joaquin River. Just beyond shallow Olaine Lake (at two miles) lies a junction, where you go left for Shadow Lake. Cross a bridge and prepare to climb. A long series of steep, shadeless switchbacks ensues as you climb alongside a narrow creek gorge. Fortunately the view looking down the San Joaquin River Canyon becomes ever more grand as you rise upward. At last you reach the waterfall on Shadow Lake's outlet stream and then climb the final stretch to the lake. Its backdrop is like something you've seen on a million Sierra postcards, with the Minarets and Mounts Ritter and Banner towering above the lake. Day hikers have the best deal here; they can just pick a spot along the 8,737-foot lakeshore and drink in the view. Camping is not permitted at Shadow Lake, so backpackers must continue on to smaller Rosalie Lake (much more climbing over the next two miles). Ediza Lake is also a popular overnight option, 2.5 miles from Shadow Lake.

**User Groups:** Hikers, dogs, and horses. No mountain bikes. No wheelchair facilities.

**Permits:** Each person entering the Devils Postpile/Reds Meadow area must purchase an access pass. (See Access Note, below.) The fee is $7 per adult and $4 for children ages 3 to 12. Children ages two and under are free. Passes may be purchased at the Mammoth Mountain shuttle bus terminal or at Minaret Station.

A free wilderness permit is required for overnight stays and is available from the Mammoth Ranger Station. Quotas are in effect from May 1 to November 1; for this period, permits are available in advance online or by phone, fax, or mail for a $5 per person fee.

**Maps:** For a map, ask the U.S. Forest Service for Inyo National Forest or Ansel Adams Wilderness. A map of the Mammoth High Country is available from Tom Harrison Maps. For topographic maps, ask the USGS for Crystal Crag and Cattle Mountain.

**Directions:** From the Mammoth Lakes junction on U.S. 395, turn west on Highway 203 and drive four miles through the town of Mammoth Lakes to Minaret Road (still Highway 203). Turn right and drive 4.5 miles to the shuttle bus terminal (adjacent to the Mammoth Mountain Ski Area). Purchase an access pass and board a shuttle bus here. Disembark at the Agnew Meadows Campground. Walk through the trailhead parking lots to the Shadow Lake trailhead.

Access Note: Visitors arriving between 7 A.M. and 7 P.M. are required to ride a shuttle bus (free with purchase of an access pass) from Mammoth Mountain Ski Area. If you are camping in the Devils Postpile area, you are permitted to drive your own car instead of taking the shuttle, but each passenger in the car must purchase an access pass.

**Contact:** Inyo National Forest, Mammoth Ranger Station, P.O. Box 148, Mammoth Lakes, CA 93546, 760/924-5500, website: www.fs.fed.us/r5/inyo.

## 88 AGNEW MEADOWS TO TUOLUMNE MEADOWS (JMT/PCT)

**28.0 mi one-way / 3.0 days**

from the Agnew Meadows trailhead north to the trailhead parking area at Tuolumne Meadows on Highway 120

**Map 10.2, page 438**

This section of the JMT/PCT features breathtaking views of the Minarets, many glacial-cut lakes, and the wondrous descent into Yosemite. The PCT starts here by leaving Reds Meadows, an excellent place to arrange a food drop and a chance to eat your first cheeseburger in weeks. The trail heads out into the most beautiful section of Inyo National Forest and the Ansel Adams Wilderness. All in a row, the PCT passes Rosalie, Shadow, Garnet, and Thousand Island Lakes. If they look like Ansel Adams' pictures in real life, it's because they are. The background setting of Banner and Ritter Peaks is among the most spectacular anywhere. From Thousand Island Lake, the PCT makes a fair climb over Island Pass (10,200 feet), then drops down into the headwaters of Rush Creek, where emerald green flows swirl over boulders, pouring like a wilderness fountain. From here, it's a decent, steady ascent back above tree line to Donohue Pass (11,056 feet), the southern wilderness border of Yosemite National Park. It was here, while munching a trail lunch, that we saw a huge landslide on the westward canyon wall. A massive amount of rock material fell in just a few seconds—an unforgettable show of natural forces. The trail becomes quite blocky at Donohue Pass, and you rock hop your way down to the headwaters of Lyell Fork, a pretzel-like stream that meanders through the meadows. It pours all the way to Tuolumne Meadows, and following it, the trail is nearly flat for more than four miles. At Tuolumne Meadows you can resupply—and get another cheeseburger.

To continue north on the JMT, see the Tuolumne Meadows to Yosemite Valley (JMT) hike in this chapter. If you are walking this trail in reverse, see the Lake Thomas Edison to Agnew Meadows (JMT/PCT) hike in the Sequoia and Kings Canyon chapter.

**User Groups:** Hikers and horses. No dogs or mountain bikes. No wheelchair facilities.

**Permits:** A wilderness permit is required for traveling through various wilderness and special-use areas the trail traverses. Contact either the Inyo National Forest or Yosemite National Park for a permit that is good for the length of your trip.

**Maps:** For a map, ask the U.S. Forest Service for Inyo National Forest and Sierra National Forest. For topographic maps, ask the USGS for Vogelsang Peak, Mount Ritter, Koip Peak, and Mammoth Mountain.

**Directions:** From Lee Vining, drive 26 miles south on Highway 395 to Mammoth Junction. Turn west on Highway 203/Minaret Summit Road to the town of Mammoth Lakes and drive 14 miles to the Agnew Meadows Campground and the trailhead parking area.

**Contact:** Yosemite National Park, P.O. Box 577, Yosemite National Park, CA 95389, 209/372-0200, website: www.nps.gov/yose; Inyo National Forest, Mono Basin Scenic Area Visitors Center, P.O. Box 429, Lee Vining, CA 93541, 760/647-3044, website: www.fs.fed.us/r5/inyo.

## 89 CONVICT CANYON TO LAKE DOROTHY

**15.0 mi / 2.0 days**

in the John Muir Wilderness south of Mammoth Lakes

Map 10.3, page 439

Framed by a back wall of bare granite peaks, Convict Lake is a mountain shrine, and the trail that leads from here into the backcountry wilderness makes hikers feel as if they're ascending into heaven. But this is no easy trip. Not only is there a 2,700-foot climb, but a tricky and sometimes dangerous stream crossing is involved. The trail starts near Convict Lake (at 7,621 feet), skirts along the lake's north shore, and then leads up through a canyon alongside Convict Creek. At

2.8 miles, you have to ford the creek, which usually requires getting wet and can be dangerous in the early summer because of high snowmelt. The trail meets the creek in the middle of a small waterfall. Many attempts to bridge this crossing have failed, as the bridge always gets washed out by high flows in early summer.

If you can get past that crossing, you follow the trail up to a series of large, untouched lakes: Mildred Lake at 4.9 miles, Lake Dorothy at 6.2 miles (10,275 feet), Lake Genevieve at 7.2 miles (10,000 feet), and beyond them, Bighorn, Edith, and Cloverleaf Lakes. Take your pick. Lake Dorothy is by far the largest of the lot. You can spend days exploring this high-mountain paradise.

Special Note: The crossing of Convict Creek is considered to be one of the most treacherous in the Sierra Nevada. This trail should only be hiked late in the season, when the stream flow has dropped. Check with the Mammoth Ranger Station for current conditions before planning a trip.

**User Groups:** Hikers, dogs, and horses. No mountain bikes. No wheelchair facilities.

**Permits:** A free wilderness permit is required for overnight stays and is available from the Mammoth Ranger Station. Quotas are in effect from May 1 to November 1; for this period, permits are available in advance online or by phone, fax, or mail for a $5 per person fee.

**Maps:** For a map, ask the U.S. Forest Service for Inyo National Forest or John Muir Wilderness. A map of the Mammoth High Country is available from Tom Harrison Maps. For a topographic map, ask the USGS for Bloody Mountain.

**Directions:** From U.S. 395 at the Mammoth Lakes junction, drive south for six miles to Convict Lake Road. Turn west and drive 1.8 miles to a spur road on the right as you near the lake. Turn right and drive .25 mile to the parking area for the trailhead.

**Contact:** Inyo National Forest, Mammoth Ranger Station, P.O. Box 148, Mammoth Lakes, CA 93546, 760/924-5500, website: www.fs.fed.us/r5/inyo.

## 90 McGEE CREEK TO STEELHEAD LAKE

**11.4 mi / 6.0 hrs or 2.0 days**

**in the John Muir Wilderness**

Map 10.3, page 439

Unlike many trails leading into the John Muir Wilderness, the McGee Creek Trail has the benefit of starting out with a mostly level stretch. It follows the remains of an old mining road, giving your legs and lungs the opportunity to warm up before you start to climb. In the first two miles, you pass plains of sage and rabbit brush, heading toward a colorful and dramatic mountain backdrop: Mount Baldwin on the right, Mount Crocker on the left, and Red and White Mountain straight ahead—all at over 12,000 feet in elevation. To your left, along McGee Creek, grows a lush garden of aspens and cottonwoods. Pass Horsetail Falls on the right at two miles out. Soon the trail enters a lodgepole pine forest and the climb steepens, and at 4.5 miles, you reach a junction with Steelhead Lake Trail heading left (east). Switchbacks carry you to a short spur to tiny Grass Lake, then to much larger Steelhead Lake (10,350 feet). The total climb is 2,300 feet over 5.7 miles, but most of the work is in the last 1.2 miles.

**User Groups:** Hikers, dogs, and horses. No mountain bikes. No wheelchair facilities.

**Permits:** A free wilderness permit is required for overnight stays and is available from the Bishop/White Mountain Ranger Station. Quotas are in effect from May 1 to November 1; for this period, permits are available in advance online or by phone, fax, or mail for a $5 per person fee.

**Maps:** For a map, ask the U.S. Forest Service for Inyo National Forest or John Muir Wilderness. A map of the Mammoth High Country is available from Tom Harrison Maps. For a topographic map, ask the USGS for Convict Lake.

**Directions:** From U.S. 395 at the Mammoth Lakes junction, drive south eight miles to the McGee Creek Road turnoff on the right (30 miles north of Bishop). Drive three miles southwest on McGee Creek Road (past the pack station) to the trailhead.

**Contact:** Inyo National Forest, White Mountain Ranger District, 798 North Main Street, Bishop, CA 93514, 760/873-2500, website: www.fs.fed.us/r5/inyo.

## 91 MONO PASS

**7.4 mi / 4.0 hrs**

**in the John Muir Wilderness**

Map 10.3, page 439

Since wilderness permits are hard to come by for this trail, your best bet is a day hike up to scenic, austere Mono Pass, where William Brewer and his party crossed the Sierra in 1864. Trailhead elevation is 10,300 feet, and the pass is at 12,600 feet, so get ready to climb in thin air (gasp). Also, expect it to be cold and windy at the pass, no matter how warm it is at the trailhead. Start your trip by following the trail alongside Rock Creek, with a wall of mammoth mountain peaks surrounding you. A half mile in, leave most of the crowds behind as you bear right for Mono Pass, switchbacking uphill. As you climb, you gain a view of Little Lakes Valley below, as well as continual eyefuls of classic Sierra scenery—clear blue sky, jagged mountain backdrops, and plenty of rock. Pass the side trail to Ruby Lake at two miles out (save this .25-mile spur for your return trip). Continue on the rocky, treeless trail until at last you reach the summit, where you get a full panoramic view, which is probably hardly different from when Brewer saw it more than a century ago. That peak just to the east of you is Mount Starr, elevation 12,835 feet. To the south, the 13,000-foot-plus peaks reign: Mount Abbot and Mount Mills. Mono Rock and the Mono Recesses lie to the west, and the blue lakes of the Pioneer Basin are to the north.

**User Groups:** Hikers, dogs, and horses. No mountain bikes. No wheelchair facilities.

**Permits:** No permits are required. Parking and access are free.

**Maps:** For a map, ask the U.S. Forest Service for Inyo National Forest or John Muir Wilderness. A map of the Mono Divide High Country is available from Tom Harrison Maps. For topographic maps, ask the USGS for Mount Morgan and Mount Abbot.

**Directions:** From U.S. 395 at the Mammoth Lakes junction, drive south 15 miles to Tom's Place and the Rock Creek Road turnoff, on the right (24 miles north of Bishop). Follow Rock Creek Road southwest for 10.5 miles to its end, at the Mosquito Flat parking area.

**Contact:** Inyo National Forest, White Mountain Ranger District, 798 North Main Street, Bishop, CA 93514, 760/873-2500, website: www.fs.fed.us/r5/inyo.

## 92 LITTLE LAKES VALLEY
### 3.0–9.0 mi / 2.0–5.0 hrs

**in the John Muir Wilderness**

Map 10.3, page 439

If the mileage shown above reflects some indecision, that's because the Little Lakes Valley makes it hard to decide which lake to visit or how far to hike. It's best to decide as you go, depending on how busy the trail is and how your energy is holding up. The Little Lakes Valley is a spectacularly beautiful, glacially carved area that is littered with lakes both large and small, and is surrounded by 13,000-foot peaks. What makes it even more special is that its trailhead is at 10,300 feet, so your car does most of the climbing, instead of your feet. For this reason, the trail is extremely popular, especially with beginning backpackers, day hikers, and dog walkers.

The trail leads past Mack Lake and shallow Marsh Lake to Heart Lake, 1.5 miles in. Box Lake is .25 mile farther, and then another .25 mile farther is the still larger Long Lake, both popular destinations right along the trail. Those with more stamina can continue to Chickenfoot Lake, at three miles out, or the Gem Lakes,

at 3.5 miles. Most people consider the Gem Lakes to be the most gorgeous of the lot, but frankly, it's pretty hard to choose. Those who are willing and able continue upward through 11,100-foot Morgan Pass and descend a couple hundred feet to Upper and Lower Morgan Lakes, at 4 and 4.5 miles out, respectively. There are enough hiking options along this one trail to keep most lake-lovers busy for a week.

**User Groups:** Hikers, dogs, and horses. No mountain bikes. No wheelchair facilities.

**Permits:** A free wilderness permit is required for overnight stays and is available from the Bishop/White Mountain Ranger Station. Quotas are in effect from May 1 to November 1; for this period, permits are available in advance online or by phone, fax, or mail for a $5 per person fee.

**Maps:** For a map, ask the U.S. Forest Service for Inyo National Forest or John Muir Wilderness. A map of the Mono Divide High Country is available from Tom Harrison Maps. For topographic maps, ask the USGS for Mount Morgan and Mount Abbot.

**Directions:** From U.S. 395 at the Mammoth Lakes junction, drive south 15 miles to Tom's Place and the Rock Creek Road turnoff, on the right (24 miles north of Bishop). Follow Rock Creek Road southwest for 10.5 miles to its end, at the Mosquito Flat parking area.

**Contact:** Inyo National Forest, White Mountain Ranger District, 798 North Main Street, Bishop, CA 93514, 760/873-2500, website: www.fs.fed.us/r5/inyo.

## 93 TAMARACK LAKES
### 9.4 mi / 6.0 hrs or 2.0 days

**in the John Muir Wilderness**

Map 10.3, page 439

This fantastic Eastern Sierra hike offers a great deal of variety in terrain, a couple of gorgeous lakes with good fishing prospects, and the chance of seeing bighorn sheep. Perhaps best of all, this trail sees a lot less foot traffic than the other pathways in the popular Rock Creek area. The trailhead elevation at Rock Creek Lake is 9,700 feet, so the first stretch of this trail can be a bit breathtaking as you climb steadily for a mile on a brushy slope. Soon the trail levels out and follows an old dirt road for a while, which connects to a mountain biking route in Sand Canyon. The terrain you are walking through is dry and sandy, with only a few pines to create some sparse shade, and it gives little indication of the dramatic high-country scenery that lies ahead. You'll pass a turnoff for Francis Lake on the right (.7 mile distant), and shortly thereafter, Kenneth Lake on the left (.1 mile distant). Kenneth Lake is really just a muddy pond, but its surrounding meadow is filled with blooming gentian in late summer. Stay on the path to Tamarack Lakes, and you'll find that the climbing you will face will result in a dramatic change of landscape. The trail ascends over a series of glacial moraines, and you soon find yourself in a high-alpine area, where bighorn sheep are sometimes seen grazing on the fragile grasses. You'll pass the left turnoff for Dorothy Lake (there are good fishing prospects for brook trout here, as well as good camping spots), but stay right, and in another mile, you will begin to follow the outlet stream from the Tamarack Lakes. Now the real work begins, as you must gain 800 more feet to climb into the high basin where the Tamarack Lakes lie. The trail ends at a small tarn just before the largest Tamarack Lake. Just beyond the big Tamarack Lake is Buck Lake, which most people assume is just another of the Tamarack Lakes. The lakes are set in a steeply sloped rocky bowl and have that barren, austere look that is common to lakes above 11,000 feet. You won't find much in the way of flat, soft spots to put your tent, but the scenery more than makes up for it. The largest Tamarack Lake has good fishing for golden trout. The total elevation gain on this hike is 2,000 feet, and it is worth every bit of it.

**User Groups:** Hikers, dogs, and horses. No mountain bikes. No wheelchair facilities.

**Permits:** A free wilderness permit is required for overnight stays and is available from the Bishop/White Mountain Ranger Station. Quotas are in effect from May 1 to November 1; for this period, permits are available in advance online or by phone, fax, or mail for a $5 per person fee.

**Maps:** For a map, ask the U.S. Forest Service for Inyo National Forest or John Muir Wilderness. A map of the Mono Divide High Country is available from Tom Harrison Maps. For a topographic map, ask the USGS for Mount Morgan.

**Directions:** From U.S. 395 at the Mammoth Lakes junction, drive south 15 miles to Tom's Place and the Rock Creek Road turnoff, on the right (24 miles north of Bishop). Follow Rock Creek Road southwest for 8.5 miles to the east shore of Rock Creek Lake and the trailhead parking for Tamarack Lakes, on the left.

**Contact:** Inyo National Forest, White Mountain Ranger District, 798 North Main Street, Bishop, CA 93514, 760/873-2500, website: www.fs.fed.us/r5/inyo.

## 94 RUBY LAKE
**4.5 mi / 2.5 hrs**

**in the John Muir Wilderness**

Map 10.3, page 439

For both day hikers and backpackers, the Little Lakes Valley is the premier destination from the Rock Creek Canyon trailhead. The only problem is the crowds, especially on the weekends, which can turn a supposedly peaceful wilderness experience into a large group encounter. A visit to Ruby Lake is a possible solution, because it's off the main trail that leads into the Little Lakes Valley, situated instead on the right fork that leads to Mono Pass. Since most trail users on this fork are backpackers heading to Mono Pass and the Pioneer Basin beyond, few take the time to stop at Ruby Lake, .25 mile off the main trail. From the trailhead, hike .5 mile, and bear right at the junction for Mono Pass. Grunt it out through the switchbacks as you enjoy a series of stunning vistas of the Little Lakes Valley. You'll reach the Ruby Lake spur trail at two miles out, on the left. A .25-mile walk brings you to cliffbound Ruby Lake, which is much larger than you'd expect and perfectly ringed by granite. The fishing is not great, but the picnicking is highly recommended. The lake's elevation is 11,121 feet.

**User Groups:** Hikers, dogs, and horses. No mountain bikes. No wheelchair facilities.

**Permits:** No permits are required. Parking and access are free.

**Maps:** For a map, ask the U.S. Forest Service for Inyo National Forest or John Muir Wilderness. A map of the Mono Divide High Country is available from Tom Harrison Maps. For topographic maps, ask the USGS for Mount Abbot and Mount Morgan.

**Directions:** From U.S. 395 at the Mammoth Lakes junction, drive south 15 miles to Tom's Place and the Rock Creek Road turnoff, on the right (24 miles north of Bishop). Follow Rock Creek Road southwest for 10.5 miles to its end, at the Mosquito Flat parking area.

**Contact:** Inyo National Forest, White Mountain Ranger District, 798 North Main Street, Bishop, CA 93514, 760/873-2500, website: www.fs.fed.us/r5/inyo.

## 95 WHITE MOUNTAIN PEAK TRAIL
### 14.4 mi / 8.0 hrs   

**in Inyo National Forest northeast of Bishop**

Map 10.3, page 439

 White Mountain Peak is the third-tallest peak in California, only 249 feet lower than the highest, Mount Whitney (Mount Williamson is second in line), yet it is little known to hikers outside of the area. In contrast to Whitney, this 14,246-foot summit is not reached by a narrow foot trail, but instead via an old Navy-built road that climbs 2,600 feet in 7.2 miles. The trail starts at a locked gate at 11,630 feet in elevation and then leads past Mount Barcroft (13,040 feet) on a long grind. The road/trail is completely above tree line, so it's exposed and often windswept. Sunscreen alone won't do it here—wear a hat to give yourself a break from the sun. If you aren't

acclimated, the high altitude will make the trip very difficult. The summit constitutes an impressive granite massif with grand views. To the east, you can see 200 miles into Nevada; to the west, the Owens Valley and Volcanic Tableland, plus a wide panorama of the Sierra Nevada. Some hikers choose to pack along their headlamps and do all or part of the trip by moonlight. The road/trail is simple to navigate, so this is easily accomplished. Forget turning this into a backpack trip: The area is so exposed that you won't find a suitable place to camp. Also, if you are planning an early summer visit, call the White Mountain Ranger Station to be sure the dirt road to the trailhead is open.

**User Groups:** Hikers only. Dogs, horses, and mountain bikes permitted, but not advised due to extremely high altitudes. No wheelchair facilities.

**Permits:** No permits are required. Parking and access are free.

**Maps:** For a map, ask the U.S. Forest Service for Inyo National Forest. For a topographic map, ask the USGS for White Mountain Peak.

**Directions:** From U.S. 395 at Big Pine, take Highway 168 east for 13 miles to White Mountain Road. Turn left on White Mountain Road and drive north for 10.5 miles to Schulman Grove. Continue on White Mountain Road (it becomes unpaved just past the Schulman Grove turnoff) for 16 miles to the locked gate and trailhead, at the road's end.

**Contact:** Inyo National Forest, White Mountain Ranger Station, 798 North Main Street, Bishop, CA 93514, 760/873-2500, website: www.fs.fed.us/r5/inyo.

## 96 METHUSELAH TRAIL
### 4.2 mi / 2.5 hrs   

**in Inyo National Forest northeast of Bishop**

Map 10.3, page 439

 The Methuselah Tree is the prize of the Ancient Bristlecone Pine Forest. Here for more than 4,000 years, it's the oldest documented living tree in the world. But forest rangers won't tell you which one it is, out of fear that some dimwit will cut it down. So you have to be satisfied just knowing you have walked among the ancients, rather than actually seeing the grandfather of all trees. No matter—each one of the thousands of trees here will impress you with its beautifully sculpted form. Amateur photographers have a field day along this trail. The path starts at the patio of the Schulman Grove Visitors Center (elevation 10,100 feet) and follows a meandering route through a forest of ancient and younger bristlecone pines, plus a few limber pines (the only other trees that grow up here). The first half of the loop drops 800 feet, which of course must be regained on your return, but the climb is nicely spread out. Still, if you're not acclimated, the high elevation will leave you huffing and puffing. Plan on bringing a picnic with you (you're a long way from the nearest convenience store), and make sure you spend some time at the excellent visitors center, which is open daily. If you want to hike a bit more, try the one-mile Discovery Trail loop (more bristlecone pines) or the one-mile Bristlecone Cabin Trail, which leads to an old Mexican mine site.

**User Groups:** Hikers and leashed dogs. No horses or mountain bikes. No wheelchair facilities.

**Permits:** No permits are required. There is a $2 fee per person, with a maximum of $5 per group.

**Maps:** For a map, ask the U.S. Forest Service for Inyo National Forest. For a topographic map, ask the USGS for Westgard Pass. Trail maps/brochures are available at the trailhead.

**Directions:** From U.S. 395 at Big Pine, take Highway 168 east for 13 miles to White Mountain Road. Turn left on White Mountain Road and drive north for 10.5 miles to Schulman Grove, on the right.

**Contact:** Inyo National Forest, White Mountain Ranger Station, 798 North Main Street, Bishop, CA 93514, 760/873-2500, website: www.fs.fed.us/r5/inyo.

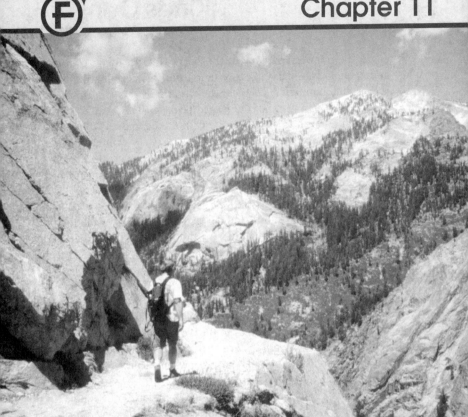

## Chapter 11

© ANN MARIE BROWN

# Sequoia and
# Kings Canyon

# Sequoia and Kings Canyon

Located on the western slope of the Sierra Nevada, Kings Canyon and Sequoia National Parks are famous for their giant sequoia groves, tall mountains, deep canyons, roaring rivers, and spectacular hiking trails with views of the jagged peaks of the Great Western Divide. Often referred to as "Yosemite without the masses," these two side-by-side national parks offer classic Sierra scenery without the infamous overcrowding that plagues that great park to the north. Kings Canyon and Sequoia have been managed jointly by the National Park Service since 1943.

The parks abound with superlatives. The highest peak in the contiguous United States—Mount Whitney, at 14,494 feet—is located in Sequoia National Park, although most people hike to it from the east side, in Inyo National Forest. Several other park summits top out at more than 14,000 feet. The largest living tree in the world, the Sherman Tree, is found in Sequoia National Park. At 275 feet tall and with a 103-foot circumference at the ground, the massive tree is still growing; every year it adds enough wood to make another 60-foot-tall tree. The second- and third-largest trees in the world, named Washington and General Grant, respectively, are also found in Sequoia and Kings Canyon. No nature experience is quite as awe-inspiring or as humbling as hiking through a grove of these giant trees.

Three powerful rivers course through the boundaries of Sequoia and Kings Canyon: the Kings, Kern, and Kaweah. The canyon of the Kings River is carved to a depth of 8,000 feet below the summit of neighboring Spanish Mountain, making Kings Canyon deeper than the Grand Canyon or any other canyon in North America. Hikers who make the long drive on Highway 180 alongside this dramatic river eventually find themselves at Roads End, where civilization ends and the wilderness begins. To continue through the Sierra from here, your only choice is to walk. Trail options range from easy strolls along the riverbanks to long, steep treks into the Monarch Wilderness.

A less-visited area of the parks, but a mecca for hikers, is the Mineral King region. A glacier-carved bowl surrounded by massive peaks, Mineral King Valley is crowned by the distinct, pointed pinnacle known as Sawtooth Peak. Reaching the 7,800-foot valley requires a circuitous 25-mile drive from the foothills of Three Rivers. Once that's accomplished, hikers can choose from a wide variety of day hiking and backpacking trails, many of which lead to 10,000-foot-plus alpine lakes.

Since December 2000, a new park joins the borders of Sequoia and Kings Canyon: Giant Sequoia National Monument. Administered by the U.S. Forest Service, not the National Park Service, the national monument contains two noncontiguous land areas, both designated to increase protection for the last remaining giant sequoia groves in the world. Hiking opportunities are already plentiful in the monument; more trails are in the planning stages.

The recreation options don't stop at the national park and monument borders. Hikers can walk through much-less-visited giant sequoia groves in national forest and state forest lands near Dinkey Creek (McKinley Grove), Oakhurst (Nelder Grove), and Springville (Mountain Home State Forest). Visitors seeking the polished granite landscape of the national parks without the accompanying crowds can find it along the trails of the Kaiser Pass area, near Huntington Lake. And far across the Sierra Nevada, on the U.S. 395 corridor in the Eastern Sierra, hikers can access one trailhead after another at the end of almost every road leading west off the highway. From Bishop to Big Pine to Independence to Lone Pine, each mountainbound road is a gateway to a world of hiking opportunities.

# Map 11.1

**Hikes 1–12
Pages 513–518**

11.2

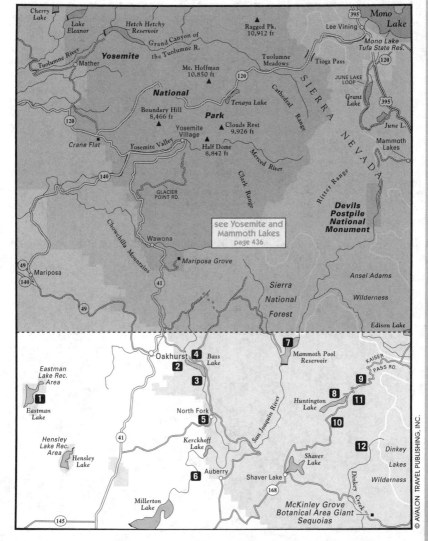

see Yosemite and Mammoth Lakes page 436

© AVALON TRAVEL PUBLISHING, INC.

# Map 11.2

**Hikes 13–22**
**Pages 519–525**

see Yosemite and Mammoth Lakes page 436

© AVALON TRAVEL PUBLISHING, INC.

# Map 11.3

**Hikes 23–107**
**Pages 525–577**

# Map 11.4

**Hikes 108–121**
**Pages 577–584**

## 1 LAKEVIEW TRAIL
**4.2 mi one-way / 2.0 hrs**

**on the southeast shore of Eastman Lake east of Chowchilla**

Map 11.1, page 509

Let's get one thing straight: You don't want to hike here at midday in July. Got it? Good. But if it's March and the wildflowers are in bloom, you'd be wise to head out here to Eastman Lake, then hike the Lakeview Trail that leads along its south and east sides. Sure, a reservoir is a reservoir, but when the water level is high, the grasslands are green, and the flowers are blooming, this reservoir can seem like a little slice of paradise in the Central Valley. The Lakeview Trail leads a total of 4.2 miles one-way from the trailhead at the group campgrounds to Raymond Bridge. Hike as little or as much of it as you please, watching for birds and identifying the wildflowers as you go. The trail is usually quite uncrowded; after all, most people come to Eastman Lake to fish, not hike. In addition to its trophy bass fishery, the lake also boasts populations of crappie, bluegill, and catfish. They even stock rainbow trout here in the winter when the temperature cools down.

**User Groups:** Hikers, dogs, horses, and mountain bikes. No wheelchair facilities.

**Permits:** No permits are required. A $4 day-use fee is charged.

**Maps:** A free map of Eastman Lake is available at the visitors center. For a topographic map, ask the USGS for Raymond.

**Directions:** From Merced, drive south on Highway 99 for 20 miles to Chowchilla. Take the Avenue 26 exit and head east for 17 miles. Turn north on County Road 29 and drive eight miles to the lake entrance. Turn right and drive to the parking area by Cordorniz Group Campground.

**Contact:** U.S. Army Corps of Engineers, Eastman Lake, P.O. Box 67, Raymond, CA 93653, 559/689-3255, website: www.spk.usace.army.mil/ organizations/cespk-co/lakes/eastman.html.

## 2 WAY OF THE MONO
**0.5 mi / 0.5 hr**

**on the northwest end of Bass Lake near Oakhurst**

Map 11.1, page 509

Pick up an interpretive brochure at the trailhead or the Bass Lake Recreation Office before you set off on this .5-mile loop trail. The Way of the Mono is an educational trail that teaches about the Western Mono Indians, who once inhabited the Bass Lake area. You visit a grain-grinding place and learn about how the Monos survived through the area's seasonal changes. In addition to a cultural history lesson, the trail also offers beautiful vistas of Bass Lake and its surroundings. Check out the view from the large granite outcrop.

**User Groups:** Hikers and dogs. No horses or mountain bikes. No wheelchair facilities.

**Permits:** No permits are required. Parking and access are free.

**Maps:** For a map, ask the U.S. Forest Service for Sierra National Forest. For a topographic map, ask the USGS for Bass Lake.

**Directions:** From Oakhurst, drive north on Highway 41 for four miles and then turn right on Road 222. Drive four miles and bear right to stay on Road 222. The signed trailhead parking area is across from Little Denver Church Picnic Area, between the Forks Resort and the California Land Management Office.

**Contact:** Sierra National Forest, Bass Lake Ranger Station, 57003 Road 225, North Fork, CA 93643, 559/877-2218, website: www.fs.fed .us/r5/sierra.

## 3 GOAT MOUNTAIN FIRE LOOKOUT
**8.4 mi / 5.0 hrs**

**on the south end of Bass Lake near Oakhurst**

Map 11.1, page 509

The 4.2-mile route to Goat Mountain Fire Lookout can be hiked from trailheads at either Forks Campground or Spring Cove Campground. Both are equally good and of similar length, so take your pick. Both trails climb two miles on a well-built, moderate grade, then join and form one path for another .5 mile before meeting up with a dirt road leading the lookout. As you climb up the trail, you have nearly nonstop views of Bass Lake and the forested valleys surrounding it. You'll also be breathing hard. Heading south on the fire road, you'll reach the fire lookout (4,675 feet) in 1.7 miles. Stop in and say hello to the lookout person. If you can talk someone into driving a second car to the other trailhead and campground, you can turn this into a pleasant semiloop trip by hiking up one trail and down the other. Note that this trail has become increasingly popular with mountain bikers in the last few years. If you don't like sharing the trail with them, plan your hike for a weekday, when you're more likely to be out here by yourself.

**User Groups:** Hikers, dogs, horses, and mountain bikes. No wheelchair facilities.

**Permits:** No permits are required. Parking and access are free.

**Maps:** For a map, ask the U.S. Forest Service for Sierra National Forest. For a topographic map, ask the USGS for Bass Lake.

**Directions:** From Oakhurst, drive north on Highway 41 for four miles and turn right on Road 222. Drive four miles and bear right to stay on Road 222. Continue along the western shore of Bass Lake for about five miles to Spring Cove Campground. The Spring Cove Trail begins on the left side of the campground entrance. If there is no parking there, you can park at Rocky Point Picnic Area. You can also hike to Goat Mountain Fire Lookout from Forks Campground, three miles north on Road 222.

**Contact:** Sierra National Forest, Bass Lake Ranger Station, 57003 Road 225, North Fork, CA 93643, 559/877-2218, website: www.fs.fed.us/r5/sierra.

# 4 WILLOW CREEK
## 4.8 mi / 2.5 hrs

**on the northeast end of Bass Lake near Oakhurst**

Map 11.1, page 509

Most people hike Willow Creek Trail with one of two things in mind: fishing or swimming. You can't blame them, since the trail runs alongside Willow Creek and offers myriad quiet pools and fast, granite-lined cascades. The forest service requests that visitors don't swim upstream of Angel Falls—a wide cascade that looks like angel wings—because the creek is used as a domestic water supply. Downstream swimming is allowed, but be wary of the slippery granite. At 2.4 miles from the trailhead, be sure to take the left spur for Devils Slide, at a junction where the main trail continues to its end at McLeod Flat Road. Devils Slide is a remarkable granite water slide, with large rounded indentations in the rock. A chain-link fence keeps hikers off the dangerously slick granite. From Devils Slide, head back to the main trail and retrace your steps downhill. Expect to see some great views of bright blue Bass Lake on the return trip.

**User Groups:** Hikers and dogs. No horses or mountain bikes. No wheelchair facilities.

**Permits:** No permits are required. Parking and access are free.

**Maps:** For a map, ask the U.S. Forest Service for Sierra National Forest. For a topographic map, ask the USGS for Bass Lake.

**Directions:** From Oakhurst, drive north on Highway 41 for four miles and turn right on Road 222. Drive four miles and bear left on Road 274. Drive one mile to the trailhead parking area, on the left side of the road, on the west side of the highway bridge over Willow Creek. Alternatively, you can park near Falls Beach Picnic Area on Road 222 by Bass Lake's dam and access the trail via a connector route alongside Willow Creek.

**Contact:** Sierra National Forest, Bass Lake Ranger Station, 57003 Road 225, North Fork, CA 93643, 559/877-2218, website: www.fs.fed.us/r5/sierra.

## 5 CEDARS INTERPRETIVE WALK
0.5 mi / 0.5 hr

**in North Fork**

Map 11.1, page 509

When people stop in at the North Fork Ranger Station to figure out how to spend their time in these parts, they'd be wise to take the .5-mile Cedars Interpretive Walk that begins next to the station. That way they can learn about the local flora and fauna of the area and about the people who lived on these lands long before us—the Mono Indians. A bonus is that the trail is surfaced, so wheelchair users can make the trip. Trailhead elevation is 2,600 feet.

**User Groups:** Hikers, wheelchairs, and dogs. No horses or mountain bikes.

**Permits:** No permits are required. Parking and access are free.

**Maps:** For a map, ask the U.S. Forest Service for Sierra National Forest. For a topographic map, ask the USGS for North Fork.

**Directions:** From Oakhurst, drive north on Highway 41 for four miles and turn right on Road 222. Drive four miles and bear left on Road 274, following it approximately 10 miles to its end, in North Fork. At the four-way intersection, turn right and drive .25 mile to the Bass Lake Ranger Station.

**Contact:** Sierra National Forest, Bass Lake Ranger Station, 57003 Road 225, North Fork, CA 93643, 559/877-2218, website: www.fs.fed.us/r5/sierra.

## 6 SQUAW LEAP LOOP
7.8 mi / 4.0 hrs

**near Millerton Lake**

Map 11.1, page 509

The Squaw Leap area, managed by the Bureau of Land Management, straddles the San Joaquin River upstream of Millerton Lake State Park. This pretty foothill country is best visited in winter or spring, primarily due to the cooler temperatures but also for a chance to see wildflowers. The well-built Six-Mile Loop Trail, which is actually 7.8 miles as described here, rolls through chaparral country. Ceanothus and manzanita line the hillsides; gray pines and blue oaks dot the landscape. The trail begins with a one-mile stretch that leads you down to the river and the start of the loop. A surprisingly well-built footbridge takes you across the river canyon, where you have fine views of whitewater cascades, both upstream and down. On the far side of the bridge, go left on River Trail for .7 mile, then bear right on Ridge Trail. At mileage marker No. 3, you have a fine view of the river canyon; this is the best place to stop for a snack. Ridge Trail brings you right back downhill to the bridge you crossed earlier; cross it again and head back to your car to finish out the trip.

**User Groups:** Hikers, dogs, horses, and mountain bikes. No wheelchair facilities.

**Permits:** No permits are required. Parking and access are free.

**Maps:** For a topographic map, ask the USGS for Millerton Lake East.

**Directions:** From Fresno, drive 37 miles east on Highway 168 and turn left on Auberry Road. Drive through Auberry and turn left on Powerhouse Road. Drive 1.9 miles and turn left on Smalley Road at the sign for Squaw Leap Management Area. Park by the campground and signed trailhead.

**Contact:** Bureau of Land Management (BLM), Bakersfield Field Office, 3801 Pegasus Drive, Bakersfield, CA 93308, 661/391-6000, website: www.ca.blm.gov/bakersfield.

## 7 FRENCH TRAIL AT MAMMOTH POOL
4.0 mi / 2.0 hrs

**at the Mammoth Pool Reservoir on the North Fork San Joaquin River**

Map 11.1, page 509

The French Trail is a 75-mile trail that follows the route of the San Joaquin River from Redinger Lake, near North Fork, to south of Devils Postpile National Monument. It was surveyed in 1880 and was intended to become a wagon road, although there was never enough money or interest to make it happen. One section of French Trail runs along the west side of Mammoth Pool Reservoir. Along this stretch, you hike through a pine and cedar forest and open chaparral hillsides, with constant views of the big lake, which is a long, narrow reservoir with steep, high walls. Just remember this: If it's summertime, confine your activities at Mammoth Pool to swimming, boating, and fishing. It's too hot to hike at this 3,300-foot elevation except in spring and fall. Spring is best, because that's when the lake is full and pretty.

**User Groups:** Hikers, dogs, horses, and mountain bikes. No mountain bikes allowed on portion of French Trail that enters the Ansel Adams Wilderness. No wheelchair facilities.

**Permits:** No permits are required. Parking and access are free.

**Maps:** For a map, ask the U.S. Forest Service for Sierra National Forest. For a topographic map, ask the USGS for Mammoth Pool Dam.

**Directions:** From the town of North Fork, south of Bass Lake, drive southeast on Road 225 to Minarets Road. Turn left (north) on Minarets Road/Road 81 and follow it for approximately 35 winding miles to the Mammoth Pool Road/Road 25 turnoff, on the right. Turn right and drive past Wagner's Resort to the trailhead at Logan Meadow.

**Contact:** Sierra National Forest, Bass Lake Ranger Station, 57003 Road 225, North Fork, CA 93643, 559/877-2218, website: www.fs.fed.us/r5/sierra.

## 8 KAISER PEAK
### 10.6 mi / 6.0 hrs or 2.0 days

**in the Kaiser Wilderness north of Huntington Lake near Lakeshore**

Map 11.1, page 509

While many visitors to Huntington Lake take the short strolls to Rancheria Falls or the Indian Pools on Big Creek, far fewer attempt the ascent of Kaiser Peak. Why? Because it's a butt-kicking, 5.3-mile climb to the top, gaining 3,000 feet of elevation on the way to the 10,320-

foot peak. Luckily, you get many excellent views of Huntington Lake on the way up, and at the halfway point, you can scramble up for a view and a rest on huge College Rock. Then it's up, up, and up some more, for what seems like an eternity. Finally, you gain the rocky summit, and at last you know why you came. You're wowed by incredible 360-degree views, which take in Mammoth Pool Reservoir, Huntington Lake, Shaver Lake, Mount Ritter, and Mount Goddard. Wow. Backpackers looking for more mileage can turn the hike into a 14-mile loop trip.

**User Groups:** Hikers, dogs, and horses. No mountain bikes. No wheelchair facilities.

**Permits:** A free wilderness permit is required for overnight stays and is available from the High Sierra/Prather Ranger Station. Quotas are in effect from May 1 to September 15; permits are available in advance by mail for this period for a $5 per person reservation fee.

**Maps:** For a map, ask the U.S. Forest Service for Sierra National Forest or Kaiser Wilderness. For a topographic map, ask the USGS for Kaiser Peak.

**Directions:** From Fresno, drive northeast on Highway 168 through Clovis for 70 miles to Huntington Lake, turn left on Huntington Lake Road, and drive one mile. Look for the large sign for the horse stables and pack station, and turn right. Follow the pack station road (Deer Creek Road) for .5 mile to the hikers' parking area. The trailhead is signed Kaiser Loop Trail.

**Contact:** Sierra National Forest, High Sierra Ranger District, P.O. Box 559, Prather, CA 93651, 559/855-5360, website: www.fs.fed.us/r5/sierra.

## 9 TWIN LAKES AND GEORGE LAKE
### 8.0–9.8 mi / 6.0–7.0 hrs or 2.0 days

**in the Kaiser Wilderness north of Huntington Lake near Lakeshore**

Map 11.1, page 509

Trails into the Kaiser Wilderness always seem to come with a climb, and the route to Twin

Lakes and George Lake is no exception. But if you're willing to work your heart and lungs, your reward is a spectacular day hike or backpacking trip to three scenic alpine lakes. Along the way, you must ascend to Kaiser Ridge and cross over it through Potter Pass. You're witness to wildflower-filled meadows, dense conifer forests, and a classic Sierra view from the pass—you can easily make out the jagged outline of the Minarets. It's a great spot to stop and catch your breath. Then it's downhill from the pass to the granite-lined Twin Lakes, at three miles out. Many people make this their destination, then turn around for a six-mile round-trip. If you do, make sure you visit the second Twin Lake, which is much prettier than the first. For those continuing onward, it's uphill again to George Lake, 1.3 miles from Upper Twin Lake. The final push is definitely worth it. Trailhead elevation is 8,200 feet, Twin Lakes are at 8,800 feet, and George Lake is at 9,300 feet. Another good route to these lakes is from the trailhead near Sample Meadow Campground, farther north on Kaiser Pass Road. If you're willing to drive farther, this trail has less of a climb.

**User Groups:** Hikers, dogs, and horses. No mountain bikes. No wheelchair facilities.

**Permits:** A free wilderness permit is required for overnight stays and is available from the High Sierra/Prather Ranger Station. Quotas are in effect from May 1 to September 15; permits are available in advance by mail for this period for a $5 per person reservation fee.

**Maps:** For a map, ask the U.S. Forest Service for Sierra National Forest or Kaiser Wilderness. For a topographic map, ask the USGS for Kaiser Peak.

**Directions:** From Fresno, drive northeast on Highway 168 through Clovis for 70 miles to Huntington Lake; turn right on Kaiser Pass Road and drive 4.8 miles to a large parking area on the south side of the road. The trail begins across the road from the parking area. Look for a trail sign for Trail 24E03, Twin Lakes and Potter Pass. Park on the south side of the road; the trail begins on the north side of the road.

**Contact:** Sierra National Forest, High Sierra Ranger District, P.O. Box 559, Prather, CA 93651, 559/855-5360, website: www.fs.fed .us/r5/sierra.

## 10 INDIAN POOLS
### 1.5 mi / 1.0 hr

**off Highway 168 near Huntington Lake**

Map 11.1, page 509

When campers at Huntington Lake's many campgrounds are looking for a place to cool off in the afternoon, Indian Pools is where they go. The hike is really a walk, suitable for all ages and abilities. You can stop almost anywhere you like along Big Creek, pick a pool, and wade in. The trailhead is a bit tricky to find—it's all the way at the far end of the Sierra Summit Ski Area parking lot, near some mobile homes and trailers. Ignore the wide dirt road and instead look for the single-track trail signed for Indian Pools. It's a smooth, dirt path that quickly meets up with Big Creek. Flowers bloom in profusion along the stream and the rocky areas of the trail. The official path ends .7 mile east of the trailhead, at a huge, clear pool that is big enough to jump into and swim across. A use trail continues farther upstream, marked by trail cairns. If you follow it, you can reach quieter, more private pools.

**User Groups:** Hikers and dogs. No horses or mountain bikes. No wheelchair facilities.

**Permits:** No permits are required. Parking and access are free.

**Maps:** For a map, ask the U.S. Forest Service for Sierra National Forest. For a topographic map, ask the USGS for Huntington Lake.

**Directions:** From Fresno, drive northeast on Highway 168 through Clovis for 70 miles, past Shaver Lake. One mile before reaching Huntington Lake, turn right at the signed Sierra Summit Ski Area. Drive .5 mile to the far end of the ski area parking lot and look for the signed trailhead for Indian Pools. Occasionally the Sierra Summit parking lot is closed, and you must park on Highway 168 and walk the short distance into the ski area.

**Contact:** Sierra National Forest, High Sierra Ranger District, P.O. Box 559, Prather, CA 93651, 559/855-5360, website: www.fs.fed .us/r5/sierra.

## 11 RANCHERIA FALLS
**2.0 mi / 1.0 hr**

**off Highway 168 near Huntington Lake**

Map 11.1, page 509

At 7,760 feet in elevation in Sierra National Forest, the air is clean and fresh, butterflies flutter amid the wildflowers, and a 150-foot waterfall sparkles in the sunlight. Wanna go? It's an easy trip, with the trailhead located close to popular Huntington Lake. The hike to Rancheria Falls is a well-graded one mile on a National Recreation Trail, suitable for hikers of all levels. The route leads through a fir forest with an understory of wildflowers and gooseberry, and it delivers you at Rancheria Falls' base, where you watch the creek tumble over a 50-foot-wide rock ledge. On weekends the destination can be a little crowded, but you can pick a boulder downstream from the falls and call it your own. Then have a seat and watch the watery spectacle unfold.

**User Groups:** Hikers, dogs, horses, and mountain bikes. No wheelchair facilities.

**Permits:** No permits are required. Parking and access are free.

**Maps:** For a map, ask the U.S. Forest Service for Sierra National Forest. For a topographic map, ask the USGS for Huntington Lake.

**Directions:** From Fresno, drive northeast on Highway 168 through Clovis for 70 miles, past Shaver Lake. A half mile before reaching Huntington Lake, take the right turnoff signed for Rancheria Falls (Road 8S31). Follow the dirt road for 1.3 miles to the signed trailhead, at a sharp curve in the road. Park off the road.

**Contact:** Sierra National Forest, High Sierra Ranger District, P.O. Box 559, Prather, CA 93651, 559/855-5360, website: www.fs.fed .us/r5/sierra.

## 12 DINKEY LAKES
**7.0 mi / 4.0 hrs or 2.0 days**

**in Dinkey Lakes Wilderness off Highway 168 near Shaver Lake**

Map 11.1, page 509

We've never met anybody who doesn't love the Dinkey Lakes. What's not to love? The small wilderness area has dozens of lakes, and most are so easily accessible that you can see them in a day hike rather than packing along all your gear for an overnight stay. The trip begins with a stream crossing over Dinkey Creek, where you are immediately awed by the incredible array of colors in the rock streambed. Walk on level trail through a flower-filled forest, re-cross the creek, and start to climb. At 1.3 miles, you reach the junction for the start of the loop. Go right and meet Mystery Lake at 1.6 miles, Swede Lake at 2.3 miles, South Lake at 3.2 miles, and finally First Dinkey Lake at 3.8 miles. First Dinkey Lake is the most beautiful of them all. After taking in the scenery, continue on the loop, now heading westward back to the parking lot. One caveat: Don't expect much solitude. The easy hiking here makes this area extremely popular. Note that the loop described here works as either a day hike or back-packing trip, but if you choose to backpack, you can explore much farther, taking the spurs off the end of the main loop, between South Lake and First Dinkey Lake, to Second Dinkey Lake, Island Lake, Rock Lake, and so on.

**User Groups:** Hikers, dogs, and horses. No mountain bikes. No wheelchair facilities.

**Permits:** A wilderness permit is required for overnight stays and is available from the High Sierra/Prather Ranger Station. Quotas are in effect from May 1 to November 1; permits are available in advance by phone, fax, or mail for this period for a $5 per person reservation fee.

**Maps:** For a map, ask the U.S. Forest Service for Sierra National Forest or Dinkey Lakes Wilderness. A Mono Divide High Country map is available from Tom Harrison Maps. For topographic maps, ask the USGS for Huntington Lake and Dogtooth Peak.

**Directions:** From Fresno, drive northeast on Highway 168 through Clovis for 50 miles to the town of Shaver Lake. Turn right on Dinkey Creek Road and drive nine miles. Turn left on Rock Creek Road/9S09, drive six miles, turn right on 9S10, and drive 4.7 miles. Turn right at the sign for Dinkey Lakes, on Road 9S62, and drive 2.2 miles to the trailhead. These last two miles are very rough road. Stay left at the fork to bypass the four-wheel-drive area and go straight to the trailhead.

**Contact:** Sierra National Forest, High Sierra Ranger District, P.O. Box 559, Prather, CA 93651, 559/855-5360, website: www.fs.fed.us/r5/sierra.

## 13 LAKE THOMAS EDISON TO AGNEW MEADOWS (JMT/PCT)

**38.0 mi one-way / 3.0 days**

**from Lake Thomas Edison north to Agnew Meadows**

Map 11.2, page 510

The world is not perfect, but the scene from Silver Pass comes close. At 10,900 feet, you scan a bare, high-granite landscape sprinkled with alpine lakes. Just north of the pass are five small lakes: Chief, Papoose, Warrior, Squaw, and Lake of the Lone Indian. This is the highlight on this 38-mile section of the Pacific Crest Trail. The trip starts at Mono Creek, with a good resupply point at Edison Lake (7,650 feet), just two miles away. From the Mono Creek junction, you head north toward Silver Pass, climbing along Silver Pass Creek much of the way. Before you get to Silver Pass, there's a stream crossing that can be dangerous in high-runoff conditions. Top Silver Pass at 10,900 feet, and enjoy a five-mile descent and then a quick ascent to Tully Hole (9,250 feet). Climbing north, you pass Deer Creek, Purple Lake, and Lake Virginia. You head up to Red Cones and then make a steady descent toward Devils Postpile National Monument. A good resupply point is at nearby Reds Meadows Pack Station.

To continue north on the John Muir Trail/Pacific Crest Trail (JMT/PCT), see the Agnew Meadows to Tuolumne Meadows (JMT/PCT) hike in the Yosemite and Mammoth Lakes chapter. If you are walking this trail in reverse, see the Whitney Portal to Lake Thomas Edison (JMT/PCT) hike in this chapter.

Special Note: For food drop information, call the Vermillion Valley Resort. It is open only in summer and fall.

**User Groups:** Hikers, dogs, and horses. No mountain bikes. No wheelchair facilities.

**Permits:** A wilderness permit is required for traveling through various wilderness and special-use areas the trail traverses. Contact the Inyo National Forest.

**Maps:** For a map, ask the U.S. Forest Service for Inyo National Forest. For topographic maps, ask the USGS for Mammoth Mountain, Crystal Crag, Bloody Mountain, Graveyard Peak, Mount Ritter, and Coip Peak.

**Directions:** From Fresno, drive northeast on Highway 168 for about 68 miles to the Lakeshore Resort Area, at Huntington Lake. Turn northeast onto Kaiser Pass Road/Forest Service 4S01. Kaiser Pass Road becomes Edison Lake Road at Mono Hot Springs. Drive another five miles north, past the Vermillion Resort and Campground, and beyond to the parking area for backcountry hikers. The trail begins near the west end of the lake.

**Contact:** Inyo National Forest, Mammoth Ranger Station, P.O. Box 148, Mammoth Lakes, CA 93546, 760/924-5500 or 760/873-2400 (permits), website: www.fs.fed.us/r5/inyo; Sierra National Forest, High Sierra Ranger District, P.O. Box 559, Prather, CA 93651, 559/855-5360, website: www.fs.fed.us/r5/sierra; Vermillion Valley Resort, 559/855-6558 (food drop).

## 14 HONEYMOON LAKE

**12.0 mi / 1.0–2.0 days**

**in the John Muir Wilderness**

Map 11.2, page 510

Since the trailhead elevation in Pine Creek Canyon is only 7,400 feet, the best destinations must be gained with a climb. That includes Honeymoon Lake, six miles and a 3,000-foot ascent away. Luckily, you pass Upper and Lower Pine Lake along the route, and there's enough spectacular scenery to keep you motivated as you huff and puff. The route begins by the pack station in the trees along Pine Creek, then joins a mining road that leads to the Brownstone Mine. (Don't be put off by the mining activity at this trailhead. You soon leave it behind as you enter the John Muir Wilderness.) As you switchback up and out of the trees, you gain views of the Owens River Valley and the desertlike White Mountains. Above the mine, the road becomes a trail and also becomes extremely rocky as it ascends more switchbacks to meet first Lower and then Upper Pine Lake, at 4.7 and 5.7 miles. The upper lake is at 10,400 feet and is reached by following the trail along the lower lake's northwest shore. A quarter mile beyond the upper lake, you reach a trail junction and take the right fork toward Italy Pass, heading west to Honeymoon Lake (in .1 mile). Many campsites are found near the granite-bound lake, set at 10,400 feet.

**User Groups:** Hikers, dogs, and horses. No mountain bikes. No wheelchair facilities.

**Permits:** A free wilderness permit is required for overnight stays and is available from the Bishop/White Mountain Ranger Station. Quotas are in effect from May 1 to November 1; permits are available in advance by phone, fax, or mail for this period for a $5 per person reservation fee.

**Maps:** For a map, ask the U.S. Forest Service for Inyo National Forest or John Muir Wilderness. A map of the Mono Divide High County is available from Tom Harrison Maps. For topographic maps, ask the USGS for Bishop and Tungsten Hills.

**Directions:** From Bishop, drive north on U.S. 395 for seven miles and turn left (west) on Pine Creek Road. Drive 9.5 miles to the trailhead parking area, near the pack station, on the left side of the road.

**Contact:** Inyo National Forest, White Mountain Ranger Station, 798 North Main Street, Bishop, CA 93514, 760/873-2500, website: www.fs.fed.us/r5/inyo.

## 15 BLUE LAKE
### 6.0 mi / 3.0 hrs or 2.0 days  3

**in the John Muir Wilderness**

Map 11.2, page 510

The Sabrina Basin Trail leads to a series of gorgeous alpine lakes set below lofty, 13,000-foot granite peaks. Of these, one of the easiest to reach is scenic Blue Lake, a popular spot for photographers, trout anglers, and cold-water swimmers. If you catch the light just right, you can take pictures of Blue Lake with towering Mount Thompson and the Thompson Ridge mirrored on its surface. It's a 1,250-foot climb to the lake (at 10,400 feet), but it is spread out gradually over three miles. Nonetheless, be prepared for the thin air here, which can make the climb seem pretty strenuous if you're not acclimated. Start by hiking along the shore of Lake Sabrina, then switchback your way uphill to Blue Lake. The trail is very rocky in places; wear good boots. If you get inspired to see more of this high-alpine scenery, you can bear left from Blue Lake to Donkey Lake and the Baboon Lakes (1.5 miles farther), or bear right and hike eastward to the Emerald Lakes and Dingleberry Lake (1.8 miles farther). Any of these are likely to have fewer visitors than Blue Lake.

**User Groups:** Hikers, dogs, and horses. No mountain bikes. No wheelchair facilities.

**Permits:** A free wilderness permit is required for overnight stays and is available from the Bishop/White Mountain Ranger Station. Quotas are in effect from May 1 to November 1; permits are available in advance by phone, fax, or mail for this period for a $5 per person reservation fee.

**Maps:** For a map, ask the U.S. Forest Service for Inyo National Forest or John Muir Wilderness. A Bishop Pass map is available from Tom Harrison Maps. For topographic maps, ask the USGS for Mount Thompson and Mount Darwin.

**Directions:** From Bishop on U.S. 395, turn west on Line Street/Highway 168 and drive 18.5 miles to Lake Sabrina. Day-use parking is located near the end of the road, just before the boat launch area. Backpackers' parking is located at a turnout near the road to North Lake, .5 mile before the end of the road.

**Contact:** Inyo National Forest, White Mountain Ranger Station, 798 North Main Street, Bishop, CA 93514, 760/873-2500, website: www.fs.fed.us/r5/inyo.

## 16 LAMARCK LAKES
### 6.0 mi / 3.0 hrs or 2.0 days

**in the John Muir Wilderness**

Map 11.2, page 510

The only downer on the Lamarck Lakes Trail is that from the trailhead parking area, you have to walk .5 mile down the road to get to the actual trailhead, which is located in North Lake Campground. No problem, though; the scenery is so lovely around here you won't mind the extra walk. Once you access the trailhead, the path heads through the aspens and crosses Bishop Creek on a footbridge. You'll climb gently for one mile through a lodgepole pine forest, gaining only 600 feet to the left fork for Grass Lake, a small and shallow lake in a wide meadow. Grass Lake is worth a brief glance, but it doesn't hold a candle to the Lamarck Lakes. Back on the main trail, the climb begins in earnest, but it's less than a mile more to the short right spur to Lower Lamarck Lake. The lower lake is quite scenic, set in a rock-lined granite basin. Look for Mount Emerson, Mount Lamarck, and the red-colored Piute Crags in the background. Many people make this their destination for the day, but if you want to see more, cross the lake's outlet creek and continue .5 mile farther to the Upper Lamarck Lake, which is nearly double in size. There isn't much in the way of a formal trail

to Upper Lamarck; you just make your way by following the course of the outlet creek. Those looking for an adventure can make their way from the Lower Lamarck Lake to the Wonder Lakes, set in the basin northwest of Lower Lamarck. Trailhead elevation for this hike is 9,300 feet, the lower lake is at 10,662 feet, and the upper lake is at 10,918 feet.

**User Groups:** Hikers, dogs, and horses. No mountain bikes. No wheelchair facilities.

**Permits:** A free wilderness permit is required for overnight stays and is available from the Bishop/White Mountain Ranger Station. Quotas are in effect from May 1 to November 1; permits are available in advance by phone, fax, or mail for this period for a $5 per person reservation fee.

**Maps:** For a map, ask the U.S. Forest Service for Inyo National Forest or John Muir Wilderness. A Bishop Pass map is available from Tom Harrison Maps. For topographic maps, ask the USGS for Mount Thompson and Mount Darwin.

**Directions:** From Bishop on U.S. 395, turn west on Line Street/Highway 168 and drive 18 miles toward Lake Sabrina. Just before reaching the lake, turn right at the turnoff for North Lake. Drive 1.5 miles and turn right to park in the hiker parking lot by North Lake, near the pack station. Then walk .5 mile down the road to the trailhead, at the edge of North Lake Campground.

**Contact:** Inyo National Forest, White Mountain Ranger Station, 798 North Main Street, Bishop, CA 93514, 760/873-2500, website: www.fs.fed.us/r5/inyo.

## 17 LOCH LEVEN LAKE
### 5.0 mi / 3.0 hrs

**in the John Muir Wilderness**

Map 11.2, page 510

If you're in the mood for a shorter hike in the Bishop Creek and North Lake area, Loch Leven Lake could fit the bill. After walking .5 mile from the trailhead parking area to North Lake

Campground's trailhead, take the trail marked for Piute Pass. A steep climb in the first mile will leave you panting. Luckily, the route is shaded by lodgepole pines. After you leave the forest, the grade lessens. You traverse a series of switchbacks that take you to the top of a high ridge, where Loch Leven Lake is nestled at 10,740 feet. As you curve your way up the ridge, be sure to stop occasionally and look back at the incredible valley below and the reddish-colored Piute Crags towering above. You'll say "wow" a bunch of times.

Loch Leven Lake is set right alongside the trail in a rocky glacial bowl. It is very long and narrow, with little accessible shoreline. A steep talus slope, usually snow covered, frames its back side. There are a few campsites on the far side of the lake in the whitebark pines. Ambitious hikers can continue another 1.2 miles to Piute Lake, with little additional elevation gain. A bonus on this trip: In autumn, the quaking aspens along the lower reaches of the route can take your breath away. Total elevation gain to Loch Leven Lake is 1,400 feet.

**User Groups:** Hikers, dogs, and horses. No mountain bikes. No wheelchair facilities.

**Permits:** No permits are required. Parking and access are free.

**Maps:** For a map, ask the U.S. Forest Service for Inyo National Forest or John Muir Wilderness. A Bishop Pass map is available from Tom Harrison Maps. For topographic maps, ask the USGS for Mount Thompson and Mount Darwin.

**Directions:** From Bishop on U.S. 395, turn west on Line Street/Highway 168 and drive 18 miles toward Lake Sabrina. Just before reaching the lake, turn right at the turnoff for North Lake. Drive 1.5 miles and turn right to park in the hiker parking lot by North Lake, near the pack station. Walk .5 mile down the road to the trailhead, at the edge of North Lake Campground.

**Contact:** Inyo National Forest, White Mountain Ranger Station, 798 North Main Street, Bishop, CA 93514, 760/873-2500, website: www.fs.fed.us/r5/inyo.

## 18 TYEE LAKES
### 7.0 mi / 4.0 hrs or 2.0 days

**in the John Muir Wilderness**

Map 11.2, page 510

There's so much excellent hiking in the South Fork Bishop Creek Canyon, it's hard to choose where to go. Since so many backpackers opt for Bishop Pass Trail and its many lakes, which are described in the next listing, day hikers might do well to choose this trail to the Tyee Lakes instead. Just make sure that you are in the mood for hiking up, because you'll do plenty of that, with a total 2,000-foot elevation gain to the highest lakes. From the bridge over Bishop Creek, your climb begins immediately as you tromp up a hillside covered with sagebrush and aspens, gradually making your way through a few dozen switchbacks. You get great views of the Bishop Creek Canyon as you climb—an especially beautiful sight when the aspens are putting on their autumn color show. Finally you enter a lodgepole pine forest, and after two miles of climbing, the grade eases up. You reach one of the smaller, lower Tyee Lakes at 2.3 miles. Another .5 mile of climbing brings you to the next small lake (called Tyee Lake number two). These first two lakes are small and pondlike, edged with grass, and not worth much more than a second glance. But keep pushing onward, and in another .5 mile, you reach one of the larger Tyee Lakes (number three). The fourth and fifth lakes are only .25 mile further and are separated by a small boulder field. The fifth lake is very small, but the fourth lake (elevation 11,015 feet) is large and beautiful. Backpackers usually set up their tent at the third lake and then day hike to the fourth and fifth lakes. Named for a brand of salmon eggs, the Tyee Lakes offer dependably good trout fishing and the chance to enjoy plenty of classic high Sierra scenery. Backpackers looking to make a semiloop can arrange to have a car waiting at Lake Sabrina in Bishop Creek Canyon, then continue from the Tyee Lakes to George Lake and then Lake Sabrina.

**User Groups:** Hikers, dogs, and horses. No mountain bikes. No wheelchair facilities.

**Permits:** A free wilderness permit is required for overnight stays and is available from the Bishop/White Mountain Ranger Station. Quotas are in effect from May 1 to November 1; permits are available in advance by phone, fax, or mail for this period for a $5 per person reservation fee.

**Maps:** For a map, ask the U.S. Forest Service for Inyo National Forest or John Muir Wilderness. A Bishop Pass map is available from Tom Harrison Maps. For a topographic map, ask the USGS for Mount Thompson.

**Directions:** From Bishop on U.S. 395, turn west on Line Street/Highway 168 and drive 14 miles to the junction for South Lake. Go left and drive 4.5 miles on South Lake Road to the footbridge that crosses Bishop Creek. It is on the right, just before Willow Campground, and it is signed as Tyee Lakes and George Lake trailhead. Park alongside the road.

**Contact:** Inyo National Forest, White Mountain Ranger Station, 798 North Main Street, Bishop, CA 93514, 760/873-2500, website: www.fs.fed.us/r5/inyo.

## 19 GREEN AND BROWN LAKES
### 6.6 mi / 3.0 hrs

**in the John Muir Wilderness**

**Map 11.2, page 510**

Brown Lake and Green Lake are two excellent day hiking destinations from the South Lake trailhead in Bishop Creek's South Fork Canyon. With only a 1,500-foot climb, you can visit both lakes, maybe do a little fishing for rainbow trout, and be home in time for supper. Access the trail from the pack station trailhead, and follow a stock trail as it climbs along Bishop Creek through a conifer forest and joins the main Green Lake Trail at one mile. Bear left and level out to an alpine meadow at two miles, where you have a spectacular view of Mount Tom behind you. Soon you'll meet Brown Lake's outlet stream and the little lake itself (really a

pond), at 2.5 miles and 10,750 feet. Pay a brief visit, then continue another .5 mile to much larger and prettier Green Lake, at 11,050 feet, surrounded by wildflowers and ancient-looking whitebark pines. Both lakes host an abundance of rainbow trout, who might just invite themselves to dinner.

**User Groups:** Hikers, dogs, and horses. No mountain bikes. No wheelchair facilities.

**Permits:** No permits are required. Parking and access are free.

**Maps:** For a map, ask the U.S. Forest Service for Inyo National Forest or John Muir Wilderness. A Bishop Pass map is available from Tom Harrison Maps. For a topographic map, ask the USGS for Mount Thompson.

**Directions:** From Bishop on U.S. 395, turn west on Line Street/Highway 168 and drive 14 miles to the junction for South Lake. Go left and drive six miles on South Lake Road to Parchers Resort and pack station, on the left side of the road, just beyond Willow Campground.

**Contact:** Inyo National Forest, White Mountain Ranger Station, 798 North Main Street, Bishop, CA 93514, 760/873-2500, website: www.fs.fed.us/r5/inyo.

## 20 RUWAU AND CHOCOLATE LAKES LOOP
### 6.6 mi / 3.5 hrs or 2.0 days

**in the John Muir Wilderness**

**Map 11.2, page 510**

Lakes, lakes, lakes everywhere. That's how it is on Bishop Pass Trail, where in the space of only five miles you can access Long Lake, Spearhead Lake, Saddlerock Lake, Bishop Lake, and so on. But if you prefer a loop trip to an out-and-back hike, Bishop Pass Trail provides another lake-filled option: a two-mile hike to Long Lake, then a circular route to Ruwau Lake, the Chocolate Lakes, and Bull Lake. It's the kind of trip that fills your mind with precious memories of blue-sky Sierra scenery and gemlike, rock-lined lakes. Still, the trip is not for everyone; some of the trail is an indistinct route with steep, rocky sections that are not an official trail. Bring a good map with you.

The trail begins on the south side of the parking lot, and you head uphill along the eastern shore of South Lake. The views begin almost immediately, particularly of South Lake, Mount Thompson, and Mount Goode. Take the left fork at .75 mile, heading for Long Lake and Bishop Pass. Continue straight, ignoring all turnoffs as you hike up around the spectacular western shore of Long Lake, popular with anglers and backpackers. At 2.5 miles (before you reach the lake's far end), instead of continuing straight to Saddlerock Lake and Bishop Pass, take the left fork for Ruwau Lake, a steep but short .5 mile away. Skirt the edge of Ruwau Lake for about 75 yards, then look for a use trail leading uphill to your left. Make a steep uphill climb for .5 mile to the ridgetop, where you'll look down and see the Chocolate Lakes, set below Chocolate Peak. Make the steep descent to the lakes, picking your way along the rocky slope. Once you're there, the hard part is over. You'll find an easy-to-follow trail at the Chocolate Lakes, and then you'll walk downhill for .5 mile to Bull Lake, which is big, round, and beautiful. From Bull Lake, you keep on hiking, and in less than .25 mile, you rejoin Bishop Pass Trail. Turn right and walk just under two miles back to the parking lot. Wow, what a day.

**User Groups:** Hikers, dogs, and horses. No mountain bikes. No wheelchair facilities.

**Permits:** A free wilderness permit is required for overnight stays and is available from the Bishop/White Mountain Ranger Station. Quotas are in effect from May 1 to November 1; permits are available in advance by phone, fax, or mail for this period for a $5 per person reservation fee.

**Maps:** For a map, ask the U.S. Forest Service for Inyo National Forest or John Muir Wilderness. A Bishop Pass map is available from Tom Harrison Maps. For a topographic map, ask the USGS for Mount Thompson.

**Directions:** From Bishop on U.S. 395, turn west on Line Street/Highway 168 and drive 14 miles to the junction for South Lake. Go left and drive 7.5 miles on South Lake Road to the end of the road and the trailhead parking area. This parking is for day-use only. If you are backpacking, you must park 1.5 miles from the trailhead, east of Parchers Resort.

**Contact:** Inyo National Forest, White Mountain Ranger Station, 798 North Main Street, Bishop, CA 93514, 760/873-2500, website: www.fs.fed.us/r5/inyo.

## 21 FIRST AND SECOND FALLS
### 3.0 mi / 1.5 hrs

**in the John Muir Wilderness**

Map 11.2, page 510

If you're camping or fishing in Big Pine Canyon, or maybe just wandering around exploring the area, there's a great walk to take starting from the end of the road near Glacier Lodge. Since it's just a day hike, you can park in the parking area right by the lodge and save yourself the long walk from the backpackers' parking lot.

Head west from the trailhead on the wide road, passing some private cabins, and in seconds you cross a bridge over First Falls, a noisy, 200-foot-long whitewater cascade. Bear right onto a narrower trail and start switchbacking uphill, paralleling the cascade. As you climb, you get awesome views into Big Pine Canyon's South Fork. At the top of the falls, cross another bridge over the creek and take a hard left onto a dirt road, staying along the creek. Now it's a flat stroll into the north fork of Big Pine Canyon. Your goal is Second Falls, a larger, more impressive cascade than First Falls; it's less than a mile away and clearly visible from the trail. Since the route is set along the canyon bottom, you get many interesting vistas along the way, from the tall surrounding canyon walls to occasional lodgepole pines and many mountain wildflowers. When the trail starts to climb out of the canyon, take the left spur cutoff to head closer to the waterfall, or just pick a big rock to sit on and admire the scenery.

**User Groups:** Hikers, dogs, and horses. No mountain bikes. No wheelchair facilities.

**Permits:** No permits are required. Parking and access are free.

**Maps:** For a map, ask the U.S. Forest Service for Inyo National Forest or John Muir Wilderness. For a topographic map, ask the USGS for Coyote Flat.

**Directions:** From Bishop, drive 15 miles south on U.S. 395 to Big Pine. Turn right (west) on Crocker Street, which becomes Glacier Lodge Road, and drive 10.5 miles to Glacier Lodge and the Big Pine Canyon trailhead, at the end of the road. Day hikers may park in the day-use area near the lodge, but backpackers must park .5 mile east, on Glacier Lodge Road, in the backpackers' parking lot.

**Contact:** Inyo National Forest, White Mountain Ranger Station, 798 North Main Street, Bishop, CA 93514, 760/873-2500, website: www.fs.fed.us/r5/inyo.

## 22 FIRST AND SECOND LAKES
### 9.6 mi / 6.0 hrs or 2.0 days

**in the John Muir Wilderness**

Map 11.2, page 510

The trail to First and Second Lakes in Big Pine Canyon follows the same route as the trail to First and Second Falls, above, but then continues onward, climbing up and over Second Falls on the well-graded trail to Cienaga Mirth, at three miles out. Here you'll see a stone cabin (now a back-country ranger residence) built by movie star Lon Chaney. Wildflowers are excellent at the swampy, spring-fed mirth. You reach First Lake at 4.5 miles, and Second Lake is just a few hundred yards further. By Second Lake, you've climbed to over 10,000 feet, and the lake water is a stunning glacial blue-green. Those who wish to see more lakes can continue on a loop past Second Lake to Third, Fourth, Fifth, and Black Lakes, making a long, 14-mile day. Fifth Lake, just off the loop by .25 mile, is the most scenic. You'll see hardy mountaineer-types with climbing equipment turning left beyond Third Lake. They're hiking a full nine miles one-way to the edge of Palisade Glacier, the southernmost glacier in the

Sierra. With a 5,000-foot elevation gain, the route to the glacier is not for everybody.

**User Groups:** Hikers, dogs, and horses. No mountain bikes. No wheelchair facilities.

**Permits:** A free wilderness permit is required for overnight stays and is available from the Bishop/White Mountain Ranger Station. Quotas are in effect from May 1 to November 1; permits are available in advance by phone, fax, or mail for this period for a $5 per person reservation fee.

**Maps:** For a map, ask the U.S. Forest Service for Inyo National Forest or John Muir Wilderness. For topographic maps, ask the USGS for Coyote Flat and Split Mountain.

**Directions:** From Bishop, drive 15 miles south on U.S. 395 to Big Pine. Turn right (west) on Crocker Street, which becomes Glacier Lodge Road, and drive 10.5 miles to Glacier Lodge and the Big Pine Canyon trailhead, at the end of the road. Day hikers may park in the day-use area near the lodge, but backpackers must park .5 mile east, on Glacier Lodge Road, in the backpackers' parking lot.

**Contact:** Inyo National Forest, White Mountain Ranger Station, 798 North Main Street, Bishop, CA 93514, 760/873-2500, website: www.fs.fed.us/r5/inyo.

## 23 BIG STUMP TRAIL
### 1.0 mi / 0.5 hr

**in the Grant Grove area of Kings Canyon National Park**

Map 11.3, page 511

Normally it would be hard for us to get excited about a trail called the Big Stump Trail. In fact, this sort of thing could be quite depressing. But Big Stump Trail, at the entrance to Kings Canyon National Park, is a pleasant nature walk and provides an excellent history lesson as well. The size of the mammoth trees—oops, make that stumps—just blows you away. Most of the big trees were cut for timber in the 1880s, and you'll see the remains of logging activities. Be sure to pick up a trail brochure at the Grant Grove Visitors Center or at the trailhead. It's a fun read, cleverly written in the voice of a late 19th-century logger. The trail is a short loop that circles a meadow. A few sequoias still thrive along the route, including one in the first 50 feet from the parking lot. The path's highlights include the Burnt Monarch, a shell of a giant sequoia that has been ravaged by fire but still stands, and the Mark Twain Stump. The latter belonged to a 26-foot-wide tree that took two men 13 days to cut down.

**User Groups:** Hikers only. No dogs, horses, or mountain bikes. No wheelchair facilities.

**Permits:** No permits are required. There is a $10 per vehicle entrance fee at Sequoia and Kings Canyon National Parks, good for seven days.

**Maps:** Free park maps are available at park entrance stations or by contacting Sequoia and Kings Canyon National Parks at the address below. A more detailed map is available from Tom Harrison Maps. For a topographic map, ask the USGS for Hume.

**Directions:** From Fresno, drive east on Highway 180 for 55 miles to the Big Stump entrance station at Kings Canyon National Park. The trail begins .5 mile past the entrance station, at the Big Stump Picnic Area.

**Contact:** Sequoia and Kings Canyon National Parks, 47050 General Highway, Three Rivers, CA 93271-9651, 559/565-3341 or 559/335-2856, website: www.nps.gov/seki.

## 24 SUNSET TRAIL
### 5.0 mi / 2.5 hrs

**in the Grant Grove area of Kings Canyon National Park**

Map 11.3, page 511

The Sunset Trail leaves Sunset Campground (elevation 6,590 feet) and heads gently downhill for 2.25 miles to Ella Falls, a pretty 40-foot cascade on Sequoia Creek. At 1.5 miles down the trail, you reach a junction with South Boundary Trail and can take a short side trip to the left to Viola Falls, which isn't much of a waterfall but is a memorably scenic spot on granite-sculpted Sequoia Creek. Most people just mosey down the trail, enjoying the big pines and firs and the flow-

ering western azaleas, and maybe stealing a kiss on one of the wooden footbridges. If you like, you can follow the trail for its entire 2.5-mile length to Sequoia Lake. Although the lake is privately owned, hikers are allowed to walk along its edge as long as they stay out of the camp area. While you're having fun, don't forget that the return trip is all uphill, with a 1,300-foot elevation gain, so save some water and energy.

**User Groups:** Hikers only. No dogs, horses, or mountain bikes. No wheelchair facilities.

**Permits:** No permits are required. There is a $10 per vehicle entrance fee at Sequoia and Kings Canyon National Parks, good for seven days.

**Maps:** Free park maps are available at park entrance stations or by contacting Sequoia and Kings Canyon National Parks at the address below. A more detailed map is available from Tom Harrison Maps. For topographic maps, ask the USGS for Hume and General Grant Grove.

**Directions:** From Fresno, drive east on Highway 180 for 55 miles to the Big Stump entrance station at Kings Canyon National Park. Continue 1.5 miles and turn left for Grant Grove. Drive 1.5 miles to Grant Grove Village, and park in the large parking lot near the visitors center. Cross the road and walk on the paved trail toward Sunset Campground's amphitheater. Continue heading left through the camp to site No. 179, where the trail begins.

**Contact:** Sequoia and Kings Canyon National Parks, 47050 General Highway, Three Rivers, CA 93271-9651, 559/565-3341 or 559/335-2856, website: www.nps.gov/seki.

## 25 MANZANITA AND AZALEA LOOP
### 3.3 mi / 2.0 hrs

**in the Grant Grove area of Kings Canyon National Park**

Map 11.3, page 511

This hike is a good exercise route for vacationers staying in Grant Grove Village or in the nearby campgrounds. It climbs 800 feet, which gives your heart and lungs a workout, and it's pretty every step of the way. From the edge of the dirt service road, Manzanita Trail climbs a dry slope uphill to Park Ridge. Near the top, you'll parallel the dirt road that leads to the Park Ridge Fire Lookout. Then Manzanita Trail meets up with Azalea Trail, and you'll descend on a much shadier, moister slope. The azaleas bloom bright white, with prolific, showy blossoms, in June and July. To complete the loop, the trail skirts the boundary of Wilsonia, a private community within the national park, then crosses both the Wilsonia Road and the park road and ends across from the visitors center.

**User Groups:** Hikers only. No dogs, horses, or mountain bikes. No wheelchair facilities.

**Permits:** No permits are required. There is a $10 per vehicle entrance fee at Sequoia and Kings Canyon National Parks, good for seven days.

**Maps:** Free park maps are available at park entrance stations or by contacting Sequoia and Kings Canyon National Parks at the address below. A more detailed map is available from Tom Harrison Maps. For a topographic map, ask the USGS for Hume.

**Directions:** From Fresno, drive east on Highway 180 for 55 miles to the Big Stump entrance station at Kings Canyon National Park. Continue 1.5 miles and turn left for Grant Grove. Drive 1.5 miles to Grant Grove Village and park in the large parking lot near the visitors center. Walk on the service road behind the village buildings and near the tent cabins to reach the start of Manzanita Trail.

**Contact:** Sequoia and Kings Canyon National Parks, 47050 General Highway, Three Rivers, CA 93271-9651, 559/565-3341 or 559/335-2856, website: www.nps.gov/seki.

## 26 PANORAMIC POINT AND PARK RIDGE LOOKOUT

**4.7 mi / 3.0 hrs**

**in the Grant Grove area of Kings Canyon National Park**

Map 11.3, page 511

Start your trip by taking the 300-yard paved walk from the parking area to Panoramic Point, which delivers what its name implies. An in-

terpretive display names the many peaks and valleys you can see, including the big pointy one—Mount Goddard, at 13,560 feet. From Panoramic Point, take the dirt Park Ridge Trail that leads to the right along the ridge. Your views continue as you contour along the ridgeline, climbing gently uphill. The trail intersects a dirt road, which you follow for about 50 yards; then bear left onto trail again. You'll intersect this dirt road once more about 100 yards before the Park Ridge Fire Lookout. Follow the road to the lookout tower, and check out the nifty outdoor shower at its base. If someone is stationed in the tower and gives you permission to come up, do so and sign the visitors register. (The lookout person rarely gets visitors on cloudy days, but he or she gets a good number of them when it's sunny, and you can see for miles around.) The lookout is only operated during the fire season, which is usually May to October. For your return trip, you can walk down the trail back to Panoramic Point or take the shorter fire road, which also leads back to the parking lot. Views are far better along the trail than on the fire road.

**User Groups:** Hikers only. No dogs, horses, or mountain bikes. No wheelchair facilities.

**Permits:** No permits are required. There is a $10 per vehicle entrance fee at Sequoia and Kings Canyon National Parks, good for seven days.

**Maps:** Free park maps are available at park entrance stations or by contacting Sequoia and Kings Canyon National Parks at the address below. A more detailed map is available from Tom Harrison Maps. For a topographic map, ask the USGS for Hume.

**Directions:** From Fresno, drive east on Highway 180 for 55 miles to the Big Stump entrance station at Kings Canyon National Park. Continue 1.5 miles and turn left for Grant Grove. Drive 1.5 miles to Grant Grove Village and turn right by the visitors center and store. Follow the road past the cabins and take the right fork for Panoramic Point. It's 2.3 miles from the visitors center to Panoramic Point.

Contact: Sequoia and Kings Canyon National Parks, 47050 General Highway, Three Rivers, CA 93271-9651, 559/565-3341 or 559/335-2856, website: www.nps.gov/seki.

## 27 GENERAL GRANT TREE TRAIL
0.6 mi / 0.5 hr

in the Grant Grove area of Kings Canyon National Park

Map 11.3, page 511

This paved loop through a giant sequoia grove allows both wheelchair users and hikers to have a look at the General Grant Tree. Estimated to be 1,800 to 2,000 years old, the General Grant is 267 feet tall and 107 feet in circumference at its base, making it the third-largest tree in the world. Every year since 1926, the park has held a Christmas celebration around its base, and so the tree is dubbed "the nation's Christmas tree." Its neighbors include the Fallen Monarch, a hollow downed tree that is so wide, it was once used as a park employee camp. Also nearby is a group of big sequoias named after various U.S. states. It may seem a little campy, but there are many excellent photo opportunities in the grove.

**User Groups:** Hikers and wheelchairs. No dogs, horses, or mountain bikes.

**Permits:** No permits are required. There is a $10 per vehicle entrance fee at Sequoia and Kings Canyon National Parks, good for seven days.

**Maps:** Free park maps are available at park entrance stations or by contacting Sequoia and Kings Canyon National Parks at the address below. A more detailed map is available from Tom Harrison Maps. For topographic maps, ask the USGS for Hume and General Grant Grove.

**Directions:** From Fresno, drive east on Highway 180 for 55 miles to the Big Stump entrance station at Kings Canyon National Park. Continue 1.5 miles and turn left for Grant Grove. Drive two miles, passing Grant Grove Village, to the left turnoff for General Grant Tree. Turn left and follow the access road for one mile to the parking lot.

Contact: Sequoia and Kings Canyon National Parks, 47050 General Highway, Three Rivers, CA 93271-9651, 559/565-3341 or 559/335-2856, website: www.nps.gov/seki.

## 28 NORTH GROVE AND DEAD GIANT LOOP
3.0 mi / 1.5 hrs

in the Grant Grove area of Kings Canyon National Park

Map 11.3, page 511

For people who want a little more hiking than what the General Grant Tree Trail (see previous listing) provides, the combined North Grove and Dead Giant Loop Trails are the answer. The walk begins on an old dirt road that leads downhill through a mixed forest of sequoia, sugar pine, white fir, and dogwood. Don't expect to see dense groves of sequoias here; the big trees are few and far between. However, the forest is pleasant, quiet, and shady.

Stay to the right at the first junction to follow the North Grove Loop. At the bottom of the hill, you'll pass an obscure junction with an old wagon road that was used to take logged sequoias to the mill. Continue to a more obvious junction at one mile out. Turn right and walk .25 mile downhill to Lion Meadow. Turn right on a single-track trail and circle around the meadow, heading for the Dead Giant. This sequoia, like some others in the park, is a nearly hollow, dead tree that somehow keeps standing. From the Dead Giant, it's a short tromp to the Sequoia Lake Overlook, a tranquil high point where you can have a snack and enjoy the view of the large, private lake in Sequoia National Forest. From the overlook, backtrack a few yards and turn right to finish out the loop, returning uphill on the wide dirt road. There is a 400-foot gain on the return.

**User Groups:** Hikers only. No dogs, horses, or mountain bikes. No wheelchair facilities.

**Permits:** No permits are required. There is a $10 per vehicle entrance fee at Sequoia and Kings Canyon National Parks, good for seven days.

**Maps:** Free park maps are available at park entrance stations or by contacting Sequoia and Kings Canyon National Parks at the address below. A more detailed map is available from Tom Harrison Maps. For topographic maps, ask the USGS for Hume and General Grant Grove.

**Directions:** From Fresno, drive east on Highway 180 for 55 miles to the Big Stump entrance station at Kings Canyon National Park. Continue 1.5 miles and turn left for Grant Grove. Drive two miles, passing Grant Grove Village, to the left turnoff for General Grant Tree. Turn left and follow the access road for one mile to the parking lot. The North Grove Loop starts from the far end of the lower parking lot.

**Contact:** Sequoia and Kings Canyon National Parks, 47050 General Highway, Three Rivers, CA 93271-9651, 559/565-3341 or 559/335-2856, website: www.nps.gov/seki.

## 29 CHICAGO STUMP TRAIL
**0.5 mi / 0.5 hr**

**in Giant Sequoia National Monument north of the Grant Grove area of Kings Canyon National Park**

Map 11.3, page 511

The Converse Basin once sheltered one of the largest and finest groves of giant sequoias in the world—before the loggers had their way. Where the giants once stood, second-growth sequoias have now taken hold. This short and easy stroll takes you through a regenerated mixed forest to the Chicago Stump, a massive stump that belonged to one of the largest trees in the world. The tree was cut down in 1883, and the lower portion of the tree was reassembled and exhibited at the Chicago World's Fair. The stump that remains is at least 10 feet high and remarkably wide. In addition to its historical interest, this easy trail provides a pleasant, peaceful change from the hustle and bustle of the neighboring national parks.

**User Groups:** Hikers, horses, and dogs. No mountain bikes. No wheelchair facilities.

**Permits:** No permits are required. There is

a $10 per vehicle entrance fee at Sequoia and Kings Canyon National Parks, good for seven days.

**Maps:** For a map, ask the U.S. Forest Service for Sequoia National Forest. A map of Sequoia and Kings Canyon is available from Tom Harrison Maps. For a topographic map, ask the USGS for Hume.

**Directions:** From Fresno, drive east on Highway 180 for 55 miles to the Big Stump entrance station at Kings Canyon National Park. Continue 1.5 miles and turn left for Grant Grove. Drive approximately 4.5 miles, passing Grant Grove Village, and turn left at the sign for Forest Service Road 13S03. Drive two miles, turn right on Road 13S65, and continue .1 mile to the Chicago Stump trailhead.

**Contact:** Giant Sequoia National Monument/Sequoia National Forest, Hume Lake Ranger District, 35860 East Kings Canyon Road, Dunlap, CA 93621, 559/338-2251, website: www.fs.fed.us/r5/sequoia.

## 30 BOOLE TREE LOOP
**2.5 mi / 1.0 hr**

**in Giant Sequoia National Monument north of the Grant Grove area of Kings Canyon National Park**

Map 11.3, page 511

The drive in to the Boole Tree trailhead is worth the trip by itself—you pass through a beautiful, ghostly meadow filled with giant sequoia stumps. The sight of them is so otherworldly that it will stay engrained in your memory for a long time. The Boole Tree hike is a loop, and it's a good idea to take the right side of the loop first, making the ascent more gradual. You climb 500 feet to the top of a ridge, then descend the other side, reaching the Boole Tree in one mile. (It's just off the main loop, accessible via a short, obvious spur.) At 269 feet tall and with a diameter of 35 feet, the Boole Tree is the largest tree in any of the national forests, and it's one of the largest trees in the world. Unfortunately, it is one of a very few giant sequoias left standing in the Converse

Basin grove, as the rest were clear-cut at the turn of the century. Although some people go see the Boole Tree and then turn around, it's better to finish out the loop. You'll be rewarded with a stellar view of Spanish Mountain and the Kings Canyon area.

**User Groups:** Hikers, horses, and dogs. No mountain bikes. No wheelchair facilities.

**Permits:** No permits are required. There is a $10 per vehicle entrance fee at Sequoia and Kings Canyon National Parks, good for seven days.

**Maps:** For a map, ask the U.S. Forest Service for Sequoia National Forest. A map of Sequoia and Kings Canyon is available from Tom Harrison Maps. For a topographic map, ask the USGS for Hume.

**Directions:** From Fresno, drive east on Highway 180 for 55 miles to the Big Stump entrance station at Kings Canyon National Park. Continue 1.5 miles and turn left for Grant Grove. Drive approximately six miles, passing Grant Grove Village. Turn left at the sign for Forest Service Road 13S55, Boole Tree, Converse Basin, and Stump Meadow. Drive 2.6 miles, and park in the wide parking pullout.

**Contact:** Giant Sequoia National Monument/Sequoia National Forest, Hume Lake Ranger District, 35860 Kings Canyon Road, Dunlap, CA 93621, 559/338-2251, website: www.fs.fed.us/r5/sequoia.

## 31 YUCCA POINT
### 4.0 mi / 2.25 hrs

in Giant Sequoia National Monument west of the Cedar Grove area of Kings Canyon National Park

Map 11.3, page 511

The Yucca Point Trail is an upside-down hike—the kind where you go down on the way in (so easy) and up on the way back (not so easy). The path descends from Highway 180 to the Kings River, dropping 1,200 feet along the way. As long as you don't climb uphill at high noon, the hike back is not as bad as it looks from the top. The trail is well graded; the only

hardship is that the terrain is all chaparral, so there's almost no shade, just the occasional tall yucca plant. The path is mostly used by anglers heading down to the wild trout section of the Kings River, but hikers like the excellent views it provides and the access to the river's cool, emerald green pools.

**User Groups:** Hikers only. No dogs, horses, or mountain bikes. No wheelchair facilities.

**Permits:** No permits are required. There is a $10 per vehicle entrance fee for access to this section of Sequoia National Forest, payable at any of the entrance stations to Kings Canyon and Sequoia National Parks. The fee is good for seven days in both the national forest and the national parks.

**Maps:** For a map, ask the U.S. Forest Service for Sequoia National Forest. A map of Sequoia and Kings Canyon is available from Tom Harrison Maps. For a topographic map, ask the USGS for Wren Peak.

**Directions:** From Fresno, drive east on Highway 180 for 55 miles to the Big Stump entrance station at Kings Canyon National Park. Continue 1.5 miles and turn left for Grant Grove and Cedar Grove. Continue 16 miles on Highway 180, past Kings Canyon Lodge, to the Yucca Point trailhead, on the left. Park in the pullouts alongside Highway 180.

**Contact:** Giant Sequoia National Monument/Sequoia National Forest, Hume Lake Ranger District, 35860 Kings Canyon Road, Dunlap, CA 93621, 559/338-2251, website: www.fs.fed.us/r5/sequoia.

## 32 WINDY CLIFFS
### 3.0 mi / 1.5 hrs

in Giant Sequoia National Monument west of the Cedar Grove area of Kings Canyon National Park

Map 11.3, page 511

The forest service concessionaire charges a fee for tours of Boyden Cave, one of many limestone caverns in the vicinity of Kings Canyon and Sequoia National Parks, and the parking lot is always busy with carloads and busloads of people waiting to take the tour. The cave is fascinating and worth a visit, but if you're low on cash, you can take this stellar hike instead and get million-dollar views of Kings Canyon for free. From the cave gift shop, walk up the paved path and take the left fork near the entrance to the cave. The trail is signed as unmaintained, but never fear, it's fairly well used. It does have some steep drop-offs, however. In no time, you'll climb a little higher and see a sweeping panorama of Highway 180 and the fast-flowing Kings River below. In one mile, Boulder Creek cascades down the hillside. The path ends when it reaches creekside at 1.5 miles, and you turn around and head back. Note that poison oak is prolific along this trail, so it might be a good idea to wear long pants and long sleeves.

**User Groups:** Hikers only. No dogs, horses, or mountain bikes. No wheelchair facilities.

**Permits:** No permits are required. There is a $10 per vehicle entrance fee for access to this section of Sequoia National Forest, payable at any of the entrance stations to Kings Canyon and Sequoia National Parks. The fee is good for seven days in both the national forest and the national parks.

**Maps:** For a map, ask the U.S. Forest Service for Sequoia National Forest. A map of Sequoia and Kings Canyon is available from Tom Harrison Maps. For a topographic map, ask the USGS for Wren Peak.

**Directions:** From Fresno, drive east on Highway 180 for 55 miles to the Big Stump entrance station at Kings Canyon National Park. Continue 1.5 miles and turn left for Grant Grove and Cedar Grove. Continue 22 miles on Highway 180 to the parking area for Boyden Cave, on the right side of the road.

**Contact:** Giant Sequoia National Monument/Sequoia National Forest, Hume Lake Ranger District, 35860 Kings Canyon Road, Dunlap, CA 93621, 559/338-2251, website: www.fs.fed.us/r5/sequoia.

## 33 LEWIS CREEK TRAIL

**11.6 mi / 6.0 hrs or 2.0 days**

off Highway 180 in the Cedar Grove area of Kings Canyon National Park

**Map 11.3, page 511**

Up, up, and up. If you're willing to climb 3,200 feet over the course of 5.5 miles, your reward is pristine Frypan Meadow, at 7,800 feet in elevation. In early summer, the meadow is green and littered with wildflowers—a glorious sight after the hot, sunny climb. But there's no way to see it without first putting in some effort on Lewis Creek Trail. The good news is that if the first mile or so proves to be too demanding, or too hot if you don't start first thing in the morning, you can always take the right fork at 1.6 miles and head back downhill on Hotel Creek Trail, making a seven-mile loop out of the trip. If you push onward on Lewis Creek Trail, you cross lovely Comb Creek (at 3.2 miles), then Lewis Creek one mile farther. Many day hikers make the Lewis Creek crossing their destination; its pools make fine swimming holes. Backpackers continue another 1.5 miles to Frypan Meadow. If you've got your wilderness permit, campsites are available there.

**User Groups:** Hikers and horses. No dogs or mountain bikes. No wheelchair facilities.

**Permits:** There is a $10 per vehicle entrance fee at Sequoia and Kings Canyon National Parks, good for seven days. Wilderness permits are required for overnight stays. They are available on a first-come, first-served basis at the wilderness kiosk at Roads End, or in advance by mail or fax for a $15 reservation fee. For more information, call 559/565-3708.

**Maps:** Free park maps are available at park entrance stations or by contacting Sequoia and Kings Canyon National Parks at the address below. A more detailed map is available from Tom Harrison Maps. For a topographic map, ask the USGS for Cedar Grove.

**Directions:** From Fresno, drive east on Highway 180 for 55 miles to the Big Stump entrance station at Kings Canyon National Park. Continue 1.5 miles and turn left for Grant Grove and Cedar Grove. Drive 31 miles on Highway 180 to the Lewis Creek Trail parking area, on the north side of the road, before you reach Cedar Grove Village.

**Contact:** Sequoia and Kings Canyon National Parks, 47050 General Highway, Three Rivers, CA 93271-9651, 559/565-3341 or 559/335-2856, website: www.nps.gov/seki.

## 34 KINGS CANYON OVERLOOK
**5.0 mi / 2.5 hrs**

off Highway 180 in the Cedar Grove area of Kings Canyon National Park

Map 11.3, page 511

The destination on this trip is a stunning overlook of Kings Canyon—the deepest canyon in the continental United States, with a plunge of 8,200 feet at its deepest point. In truth, the canyon vistas are continual for most of the hike, so if you don't make it to the overlook, you'll still get an eyeful. The Hotel Creek Trail consists of dozens of switchbacks over open, sunny slopes, climbing 1,200 feet over two miles to a trail junction with Overlook Trail. Turn left to head to the overlook, which peers down on Cedar Grove and the length of Kings Canyon. Some of the best views are of Monarch Divide's high peaks to the north. Hope you came with picnic supplies. For a five-mile round-trip, retrace your steps back to Cedar Grove. If you want to walk farther, you can continue from the overlook junction for another 1.5 miles and turn left, hiking downhill on Lewis Creek Trail and making a seven-mile loop out of the trip. This stretch of Lewis Creek Trail is lined with sweet-smelling ceanothus. The final 1.2 miles of the loop are a dull stretch paralleling a park road, but the rest of the hike is so good that you won't complain.

**User Groups:** Hikers and horses. No dogs or mountain bikes. No wheelchair facilities.

**Permits:** No permits are required. There is a $10 per vehicle entrance fee at Sequoia and Kings Canyon National Parks, good for seven days.

**Maps:** Free park maps are available at park entrance stations or by contacting Sequoia and

Kings Canyon National Parks at the address below. A more detailed map is available from Tom Harrison Maps. For a topographic map, ask the USGS for Cedar Grove.

**Directions:** From Fresno, drive east on Highway 180 for 55 miles to the Big Stump entrance station at Kings Canyon National Park. Continue 1.5 miles and turn left for Grant Grove and Cedar Grove. Drive 31.5 miles on Highway 180 to Cedar Grove Village. Turn left at the sign for the visitors center and Cedar Grove Lodge. Continue on the main road past the lodge for .25 mile and turn right. The Hotel Creek trailhead is on the left after a few hundred feet.

**Contact:** Sequoia and Kings Canyon National Parks, 47050 General Highway, Three Rivers, CA 93271-9651, 559/565-3341 or 559/335-2856, website: www.nps.gov/seki.

## 35 LOOKOUT PEAK
**12.0 mi / 7.0 hrs**

off Highway 180 in the Cedar Grove area of Kings Canyon National Park

Map 11.3, page 511

Lookout Peak, at 8,531 feet in elevation, is a summit worth ascending, even though it's an all-day trip with a 3,900-foot elevation gain. From the top, you get an unforgettable Sierra view, with Cedar Grove far below you and peaks and ridges all around. In addition, just a few hundred yards from the summit is Summit Meadow, filled with summer wildflowers. The key is to carry plenty of water and plan on an early-morning start to beat the heat. You can filter water from Sheep Creek, one mile in. Luckily, there's a decent amount of shade in the first few miles. Even though this trailhead is located right by the Cedar Grove campgrounds, few people hike all the way to the peak, so you have a chance at peace and quiet along the trail. The only downer on this hike is that when you near the summit, you see that other people have driven their cars on an alternate route to Lookout Peak (from the Big Meadows area of Giant Sequoia

National Monument), and they are gaining the summit after only a .25-mile hike. Hey, at least you earned it.

**User Groups:** Hikers and horses. No dogs or mountain bikes. No wheelchair facilities.

**Permits:** No permits are required. There is a $10 per vehicle entrance fee at Sequoia and Kings Canyon National Parks, good for seven days.

**Maps:** Free park maps are available at park entrance stations or by contacting Sequoia and Kings Canyon National Parks at the address below. A more detailed map is available from Tom Harrison Maps. For a topographic map, ask the USGS for Cedar Grove.

**Directions:** From Fresno, drive east on Highway 180 for 55 miles to the Big Stump entrance station at Kings Canyon National Park. Continue 1.5 miles and turn left for Grant Grove and Cedar Grove. Drive 31.5 miles on Highway 180 and take the right fork for Cedar Grove. The Don Cecil trailhead is on the right side of the road, just beyond the turnoff for Cedar Grove Village and the visitors center. If you reach Canyon View and Moraine Campgrounds, you've gone too far.

**Contact:** Sequoia and Kings Canyon National Parks, 47050 General Highway, Three Rivers, CA 93271-9651, 559/565-3341 or 559/335-2856, website: www.nps.gov/seki.

## 36 ROARING RIVER FALLS
0.4 mi / 0.25 hr

off Highway 180 in the Cedar Grove area of Kings Canyon National Park
Map 11.3, page 511

It's an easy stroll to Roaring River Falls, a pretty waterfall that drops through a narrow gorge into the South Fork Kings River. It's the only waterfall in Sequoia and Kings Canyon National Parks that is accessible via wheelchair. If hikers want a longer walk, they can continue downstream on the River Trail to Zumwalt Meadow in 1.6 miles or Road's End in 2.7 miles. What's extraordinary about the waterfall is not the cascade itself, but the

giant rocky pool into which it falls; it's at least 50 feet wide. From where the paved trail ends, at the edge of the pool, the waterfall is perfectly framed by two big conifers. About a zillion photos have been snapped here.

**User Groups:** Hikers and wheelchairs. No dogs, horses, or mountain bikes.

**Permits:** No permits are required. There is a $10 per vehicle entrance fee at Sequoia and Kings Canyon National Parks, good for seven days.

**Maps:** Free park maps are available at park entrance stations or by contacting Sequoia and Kings Canyon National Parks at the address below. A more detailed map is available from Tom Harrison Maps. For a topographic map, ask the USGS for Sphinx.

**Directions:** From Fresno, drive east on Highway 180 for 55 miles to the Big Stump entrance station at Kings Canyon National Park. Continue 1.5 miles and turn left for Grant Grove and Cedar Grove. Continue 35 miles on Highway 180 to the sign for Roaring River Falls and the River Trail, three miles past Cedar Grove Village. The trailhead is on the right side of the road.

**Contact:** Sequoia and Kings Canyon National Parks, 47050 General Highway, Three Rivers, CA 93271-9651, 559/565-3341 or 559/335-2856, website: www.nps.gov/seki.

## 37 ZUMWALT MEADOW LOOP
1.5 mi / 1.0 hr

off Highway 180 in the Cedar Grove area of Kings Canyon National Park
Map 11.3, page 511

What's the prettiest easy hike in Kings Canyon National Park? The Zumwalt Meadow Loop Trail wins hands down. A scenic 1.5-mile walk along the South Fork Kings River, the Zumwalt Meadow Loop is a delight for hikers of all abilities. Many people bring their fishing rods along to try their luck in the river, but for most, the hiking is better than the fishing. From the parking area, walk downstream along the river to an old suspension footbridge, cross it, and walk back upstream. The loop begins at an obvious fork, and you can hike it in either direction. The south side traverses a boulder field of jumbled rocks that have tumbled down from the Grand Sentinel (elevation 8,504 feet). The north side cuts through a thick, waist-high fern forest and follows a wooden walkway over a marsh. Views of 8,717-foot North Dome are awe inspiring. Trees, meadow, rock, stream, river, canyon walls—Zumwalt Meadow Trail has it all.

**User Groups:** Hikers only. No dogs, horses, or mountain bikes. No wheelchair facilities.

**Permits:** No permits are required. There is a $10 per vehicle entrance fee at Sequoia and Kings Canyon National Parks, good for seven days.

**Maps:** Free park maps are available at park entrance stations or by contacting Sequoia and Kings Canyon National Parks at the address below. A more detailed map is available from Tom Harrison Maps. For a topographic map, ask the USGS for Cedar Grove.

**Directions:** From Fresno, drive east on Highway 180 for 55 miles to the Big Stump entrance station at Kings Canyon National Park. Continue 1.5 miles and turn left for Grant Grove and Cedar Grove. Continue 36 miles on Highway 180 to the parking area for Zumwalt Meadow, on the right side of the road.

**Contact:** Sequoia and Kings Canyon National Parks, 47050 General Highway, Three Rivers, CA 93271-9651, 559/565-3341 or 559/335-2856, website: www.nps.gov/seki.

## 38 MIST FALLS
**8.8 mi / 5.0 hrs**

off Highway 180 in the Cedar Grove area of Kings Canyon National Park
Map 11.3, page 511

The Mist Falls Trail is probably the most well-used pathway in Kings Canyon National Park, with good reason. It's a stellar 4.4-mile walk to an impressive cascade on the South Fork Kings River, with only a 650-foot gain in elevation along the way. Many backpackers use this trail to access Paradise Valley and points

beyond, while most day hikers turn around at Mist Falls. The first two miles are a flat walk up the Kings River Valley, with canyon walls towering above you on both sides. You spend a lot of time craning your neck, looking up at the high canyon rims, from which springtime waterfalls cascade down. You're in a dry, open forest much of the time.

At two miles, you'll reach a trail junction. Bear left, then start to climb over granite. The farther you go, the more expansive the views become; make sure you keep turning around so you can take in the whole panorama. A highlight is the huge stone face of the Sphinx—you'll know it when you see it. At four miles, the river starts to look more waterfall-like, with crashing pools and rocky granite slides becoming increasingly vertical. A quarter mile later you reach Mist Falls, which fans out over a 45-foot wide granite ledge and crashes into a boulder-lined pool. It creates a tremendous spray and mist in early summer, and mellows out as the season goes on. Take a look at the falls, then walk back down the trail .2 mile to the obvious, immense slab of flat granite you just passed. This is a favorite spot to have lunch, with its wide-open view of the Sphinx and 10,007-foot Avalanche Peak.

There are two ways to beat the crowds on this path, so listen carefully. First, start early in the morning. Second, hike part of the route on an alternate trail on the south side of the river, which runs from the Road's End parking lot to the Bailey Bridge at the trail intersection mentioned above. If you get an early start, save this alternate route for the return trip. By then, the day hikers will be out in full force.

**User Groups:** Hikers and horses. No dogs or mountain bikes. No wheelchair facilities.

**Permits:** No permits are required. There is a $10 per vehicle entrance fee at Sequoia and Kings Canyon National Parks, good for seven days.

**Maps:** Free park maps are available at park entrance stations or by contacting Sequoia and Kings Canyon National Parks at the address below. A more detailed map is available from

Tom Harrison Maps. For a topographic map, ask the USGS for Sphinx.

**Directions:** From Fresno, drive east on Highway 180 for 55 miles to the Big Stump entrance station at Kings Canyon National Park. Continue 1.5 miles and turn left for Grant Grove and Cedar Grove. Continue 38 miles on Highway 180 to Road's End, six miles past Cedar Grove Village. The trailhead is at the east end of the parking lot, near the wilderness ranger station.

**Contact:** Sequoia and Kings Canyon National Parks, 47050 General Highway, Three Rivers, CA 93271-9651, 559/565-3341 or 559/335-2856, website: www.nps.gov/seki.

## 39 COPPER CREEK TRAIL
### 21.0 mi / 3.0–4.0 days

**off Highway 180 in the Cedar Grove area of Kings Canyon National Park**

Map 11.3, page 511

The Copper Creek trailhead is at 5,000 feet, and Granite Lake is at 9,972 feet, so it's not hard to do the math. If you're up for a backpacking trip with a 5,000-foot elevation gain over 10 miles, the Granite Lake Basin is your ticket to happiness. But keep in mind that the route can be hot and dry as it switchbacks up manzanita-covered slopes; this trail is considered one of the most strenuous in the Cedar Grove area. Your first night's camp is at Lower Tent Meadow, four miles in and at 7,800 feet. After that, things start to get really good. With Mount Hutchings looming over your left shoulder, the second day's six miles will go easier, bringing you to rocky, jewel-like Granite Lake in only a few hours. You must have a backpacking stove for camping by the lake or anywhere above 10,000 feet.

**User Groups:** Hikers and horses. No dogs or mountain bikes. No wheelchair facilities.

**Permits:** There is a $10 per vehicle entrance fee at Sequoia and Kings Canyon National Parks, good for seven days. Wilderness permits are required for overnight stays. They are available on a first-come, first-served basis at

the wilderness kiosk at Roads End, or in advance by mail or fax for a $15 reservation fee. For more information, call 559/565-3708.

**Maps:** Free park maps are available at park entrance stations or by contacting Sequoia and Kings Canyon National Parks at the address below. A more detailed map is available from Tom Harrison Maps. For a topographic map, ask the USGS for Sphinx.

**Directions:** From Fresno, drive east on Highway 180 for 55 miles to the Big Stump entrance station at Kings Canyon National Park. Continue 1.5 miles and turn left for Grant Grove and Cedar Grove. Continue 38 miles on Highway 180 to Road's End, six miles past Cedar Grove Village. The trail begins at the long-term parking area.

**Contact:** Sequoia and Kings Canyon National Parks, 47050 General Highway, Three Rivers, CA 93271-9651, 559/565-3341 or 559/335-2856, website: www.nps.gov/seki.

## 40 REDWOOD CANYON
### 4.0 mi / 2.0 hrs

**southeast of the Grant Grove area of Kings Canyon National Park**

Map 11.3, page 511

Several loop trips are possible in the Redwood Mountain area of Kings Canyon National Park, but one of the prettiest and simplest trips is just an out-and-back walk on Redwood Canyon Trail, paralleling Redwood Creek. The beauty begins before you even start walking; on the last mile of the drive to the trailhead, the road winds through giant sequoias that are so close, you can reach out your car window and touch them. The trail leads downhill from the parking area, and in just over .3 mile, you reach a junction and follow Redwood Creek Trail to the right. You'll find that this sequoia grove is far denser than many. Because they are situated by Redwood Creek, the sequoias grow amid a thriving background of dogwoods, firs, ceanothus, and mountain misery. Though the standing sequoias are impressive, some of the fallen ones are really amazing, because you get a close-up look at their immense size. Make sure you hike the full two miles to the stream crossing of Redwood Creek—some of the best tree specimens are down there, near the junction with Sugar Bowl Loop Trail. The return trip is all uphill but easier than you'd expect.

**User Groups:** Hikers only. No dogs, horses, or mountain bikes. No wheelchair facilities.

**Permits:** No permits are required. There is a $10 per vehicle entrance fee at Sequoia and Kings Canyon National Parks, good for seven days.

**Maps:** Free park maps are available at park entrance stations or by contacting Sequoia and Kings Canyon National Parks at the address below. A more detailed map is available from Tom Harrison Maps. For a topographic map, ask the USGS for General Grant Grove.

**Directions:** From Fresno, drive east on Highway 180 for 55 miles to the Big Stump entrance station at Kings Canyon National Park. Continue 1.5 miles and turn right on the Generals Highway, heading for Sequoia National Park. Drive approximately three miles on the Generals Highway to Quail Flat, signed for Hume Lake to the left, and turn right on the dirt road to Redwood Saddle. Drive 1.5 miles and park in the parking lot. Take the trail signed for the Hart Tree and Redwood Canyon.

**Contact:** Sequoia and Kings Canyon National Parks, 47050 General Highway, Three Rivers, CA 93271-9651, 559/565-3341 or 559/335-2856, website: www.nps.gov/seki.

## 41 REDWOOD MOUNTAIN LOOP

**10.0 mi / 5.0 hrs**

**southeast of the Grant Grove area of Kings Canyon National Park**

Map 11.3, page 511

If you have most of a day to hike in the Redwood Mountain area of Kings Canyon National Park, you're in luck. This is one of the best day hikes in all of Kings Canyon. The Redwood Mountain Loop combines the best highlights of the area into one long trail, on which you'll wander in near solitude among the giant sequoias. If the paved, crowded trails to the General Grant Tree and the General Sherman Tree turn you off, this trail will turn you on. Start by hiking on the signed Burnt Grove/Sugar Bowl Loop Trail, which leads uphill from the parking lot. It's one mile to Burnt Grove and 2.5 miles to Sugar Bowl Grove; both are very dense stands of sequoias. Beyond the groves you descend for two miles to intersect with Redwood Canyon Trail. Head downhill and cross Redwood Creek, then proceed to the Fallen Goliath, a mammoth downed tree. One mile farther, you reach the Hart Tree, the largest tree in this area and a real show-stopper. In the final three miles, you get to walk through the Tunnel Log, a hollowed sequoia, and pass by pretty Hart Meadow. Note that if you tire out halfway through this loop, you can always follow the Redwood Canyon Trail uphill back to the start, cutting three miles off your round-trip.

**User Groups:** Hikers only. No dogs, horses, or mountain bikes. No wheelchair facilities.

**Permits:** No permits are required. There is a $10 per vehicle entrance fee at Sequoia and Kings Canyon National Parks, good for seven days.

**Maps:** Free park maps are available at park entrance stations or by contacting Sequoia and Kings Canyon National Parks at the address below. A more detailed map is available from Tom Harrison Maps. For a topographic map, ask the USGS for General Grant Grove.

**Directions:** From Fresno, drive east on Highway 180 for 55 miles to the Big Stump entrance station at Kings Canyon National Park. Continue 1.5 miles and turn right on the Generals Highway, heading for Sequoia National Park. Drive approximately three miles on the Generals Highway to Quail Flat, signed for Hume Lake to the left, and turn right on the dirt road to Redwood Saddle. Drive 1.5 miles and park in the parking lot. Take the trail signed as Burnt Grove/Sugar Bowl Loop.

**Contact:** Sequoia and Kings Canyon National Parks, 47050 General Highway, Three Rivers,

CA 93271-9651, 559/565-3341 or 559/335-2856, website: www.nps.gov/seki.

## 42 BUENA VISTA PEAK
**2.0 mi / 1.0 hr**

**southeast of the Grant Grove area of Kings Canyon National Park**

Map 11.3, page 511

Forget driving to the Kings Canyon Overlook, because just across the road is a trailhead with an easy walk and even better views, plus a chance at a private picnic spot. Buena Vista Peak is really a rocky dome, peaking at 7,603 feet, and is one of the highest points west of Generals Highway. It offers 360-degree views—you can see a million conifers at your feet and the hazy foothills to the southwest, but the best vistas are to the east, looking out at the snow-capped peaks of the John Muir and Monarch Wildernesses. It's an easy half-hour walk up the back side of the dome, passing through pine and fir forest, manzanita, and sage, and walking by some interesting rock formations—check out the giant boulder sculptures in the trail's first .25 mile. At the top of Buena Vista Peak, you can wander all around the spacious granite summit, enjoying different perspectives on the vista, before heading back to the parking lot. It's downhill all the way.

**User Groups:** Hikers only. No dogs, horses, or mountain bikes. No wheelchair facilities.

**Permits:** No permits are required. There is a $10 per vehicle entrance fee at Sequoia and Kings Canyon National Parks, good for seven days.

**Maps:** Free park maps are available at park entrance stations or by contacting Sequoia and Kings Canyon National Parks at the address below. A more detailed map is available from Tom Harrison Maps. For a topographic map, ask the USGS for General Grant Grove.

**Directions:** From Fresno, drive east on Highway 180 for 55 miles to the Big Stump entrance station at Kings Canyon National Park. Continue 1.5 miles and turn right on the Generals Highway, heading for Sequoia National Park. Drive approximately five miles on the Gener-als Highway to the Buena Vista trailhead on the right, just across the road and slightly beyond the large pullout for the Kings Canyon Overlook, on the left.

**Contact:** Sequoia and Kings Canyon National Parks, 47050 General Highway, Three Rivers, CA 93271-9651, 559/565-3341 or 559/335-2856, website: www.nps.gov/seki.

## 43 WEAVER LAKE
**4.2 mi / 2.0 hrs or 2.0 days**

**in the Jennie Lakes Wilderness**

Map 11.3, page 511

Tucked into a corner just outside the border of Kings Canyon and Sequoia National Parks, the Jennie Lakes Wilderness is a 10,500-acre wilderness area that is often overlooked by park visitors. It offers much of the same scenery as the parks—beautiful lakes, meadows, forests, and streams—but without all the fanfare. Weaver Lake is the easiest-to-reach destination in the wilderness, and it makes a perfect family backpacking trip or an equally nice day hike. The trail is well signed and passes through a mix of fir forest and meadows. At .7 mile, take the left fork for Weaver Lake, climbing uphill to the lake's basin. You'll spy the shelflike slabs of Shell Mountain peeking out above the trees. At just over two miles, shallow but pretty Weaver Lake is set at 8,700 feet, positioned at the base of Shell Mountain's high, rounded ridge. You can try your luck fishing, or just find a lakeside seat and gaze at the view. On warm days, the brave go swimming.

Note that the road to Big Meadows and Fox Meadows is usually the last road to open in the area after snowmelt. If you're planning an early season trip, call to check on road and trail conditions.

**User Groups:** Hikers, dogs, and horses. No mountain bikes. No wheelchair facilities.

**Permits:** A free campfire permit is required for overnight stays and is available from the Hume Lake Ranger Station. There is a $10 per vehicle entrance fee at Sequoia and Kings Canyon

National Parks, good for seven days in both the national forest and the national parks.
**Maps:** For a map, ask the U.S. Forest Service for Sequoia National Forest or Monarch/Jennie Lakes Wilderness. A map of Sequoia and Kings Canyon is available from Tom Harrison Maps. For a topographic map, ask the USGS for Muir Grove.
**Directions:** From Fresno, drive east on Highway 180 for 55 miles to the Big Stump entrance station at Kings Canyon National Park. Continue 1.5 miles and turn right on the Generals Highway, heading for Sequoia National Park. Drive seven miles and turn left on Forest Service Road 14S11, at the sign for Big Meadows and Horse Corral. Drive four miles, passing Big Meadows trailhead and Big Meadows Campground, and turn right on the dirt road .5 mile beyond the camp (it's just past the bridge over Big Meadows Creek). Drive .5 mile to the fork, turn left, and turn right immediately afterward. Drive one more mile, and park at the road's end at the Fox Meadow trailhead. Total mileage from Big Meadows Road is 1.5 miles.
**Contact:** Giant Sequoia National Monument/Sequoia National Forest, Hume Lake Ranger District, 35860 Kings Canyon Road, Dunlap, CA 93621, 559/338-2251, website: www.fs.fed.us/r5/sequoia.

## 44 JENNIE LAKE
**10.0 mi / 6.0 hrs or 2.0 days**

**in the Jennie Lakes Wilderness**

**Map 11.3, page 511**

This trail into the Jennie Lakes Wilderness offers more of a challenge than the route to Weaver Lake, climbing 1,500 feet over five miles with some short, steep pitches. The rewards are also greater, because Jennie Lake is a beauty and receives fewer visitors than Weaver Lake. The trail is the same as the Weaver Lake Trail for .7 mile, but at the fork, you bear right for Jennie Lake. The trail climbs and dips through fir, pine, and manzanita forest, then crosses Poop Out Pass at 3.7 miles, the high-

est point on this trip. At five miles, you reach the outlet stream for Jennie Lake. Follow the short spur trail to the lake, set at 9,000 feet. With a white granite backdrop and some sparse trees, the shoreline looks austere and barren, but beautiful just the same. Campsites are found around the lake, and catching fish for dinner is a fair possibility. If you only came for the day, find a comfortable spot to sit and admire the scenery before you head back.
**User Groups:** Hikers, dogs, and horses. No mountain bikes. No wheelchair facilities.
**Permits:** A free campfire permit is required for overnight stays and is available from the Hume Lake Ranger Station. There is a $10 per vehicle entrance fee at Sequoia and Kings Canyon National Parks, good for seven days in both the national forest and the national parks.
**Maps:** For a map, ask the U.S. Forest Service for Sequoia National Forest or Monarch/Jennie Lakes Wilderness. A map of Sequoia and Kings Canyon is available from Tom Harrison Maps. For a topographic map, ask the USGS for Muir Grove.
**Directions:** From Fresno, drive east on Highway 180 for 55 miles to the Big Stump entrance station at Kings Canyon National Park. Continue 1.5 miles and turn right on the Generals Highway, heading for Sequoia National Park. Drive seven miles and turn left on Forest Service Road 14S11, at the sign for Big Meadows and Horse Corral. Drive four miles, passing Big Meadows trailhead and Big Meadows Campground, and turn right on the dirt road .5 mile beyond the camp (it's just past the bridge over Big Meadows Creek). Drive .5 mile to the fork, turn left, and turn right immediately afterward. Drive one more mile and park at the road's end at the Fox Meadow trailhead. Total mileage from Big Meadows Road is 1.5 miles.
**Contact:** Giant Sequoia National Monument/Sequoia National Forest, Hume Lake Ranger District, 35860 Kings Canyon Road, Dunlap, CA 93621, 559/338-2251, website: www.fs.fed.us/r5/sequoia.

## 45 MITCHELL PEAK
### 5.2 mi / 3.0 hrs

**in the Jennie Lakes Wilderness**

Map 11.3, page 511

If you have the legs for a 2,000-foot climb over 2.6 miles, you can stand atop the summit of Mitchell Peak, the highest point in the Jennie Lakes Wilderness, at 10,365 feet in elevation. The peak used to have a fire lookout tower on top of it, but the forest service stopped using it and burned it down. What remains is the fabulous view, one of the best in this area. It's a one-mile climb from the trailhead to Marvin Pass and the boundary of the Jennie Lakes Wilderness. Bear left (east) and climb some more. At 1.6 miles, you reach the next junction, signed for Mitchell Peak. Head left (north), and in one more mile, you'll make the brief climb to Mitchell's summit, which straddles the border of Kings Canyon National Park. From your rocky perch, you can look out on the Great Western Divide and the Silliman Crest. It's an exemplary spot to catch your breath.

**User Groups:** Hikers, dogs, and horses. No mountain bikes. No wheelchair facilities.

**Permits:** A free campfire permit is required for overnight stays and is available from the Hume Lake Ranger Station. There is a $10 per vehicle entrance fee at Sequoia and Kings Canyon National Parks, good for seven days in both the national forest and the national parks.

**Maps:** For a map, ask the U.S. Forest Service for Sequoia National Forest or Monarch/Jennie Lakes Wilderness. A map of Sequoia and Kings Canyon is available from Tom Harrison Maps. For a topographic map, ask the USGS for Muir Grove.

**Directions:** From Fresno, drive east on Highway 180 for 55 miles to the Big Stump entrance station at Kings Canyon National Park. Continue 1.5 miles and turn right on the Generals Highway, heading for Sequoia National Park. Drive seven miles and turn left on Forest Service Road 14S11, at the sign for Big Meadow and Horse Corral. Drive four miles to the Big

Meadow Campground and continue six more miles to Horse Corral Meadow. Turn right on Forest Service Road 13S12 and drive 2.8 miles to the Marvin Pass trailhead.

**Contact:** Giant Sequoia National Monument/Sequoia National Forest, Hume Lake Ranger District, 35860 Kings Canyon Road, Dunlap, CA 93621, 559/338-2251, website: www.fs.fed.us/r5/sequoia.

## 46 BIG BALDY
### 4.6 mi / 2.5 hrs

**southeast of the Grant Grove area of Kings Canyon National Park**

Map 11.3, page 511

The trip to Big Baldy comes with a million views and a little workout besides. Views? We're talking Redwood Canyon, Redwood Mountain, Buena Vista Peak, Little Baldy, Buck Rock, and the Great Western Divide. A little workout? You've got to climb 1,000 feet, but it's nicely spread out over two miles. The trail alternates between thick forest cover and open granite areas as it winds along the rim of Redwood Canyon. In the forested stretches, we were amazed at how many birds were singing in the tall firs and cedars. The trail's initial vistas are to the west, but they keep changing and getting more interesting all the way to Big Baldy's 8,209-foot summit, where your view opens up to 360 degrees. Here you get your first wide-open views of the high Sierra peaks and the Great Western Divide to the east. This trail is so fun and rewarding, with so little suffering involved, that you may feel like you're getting away with something. A bonus: Because the first mile of trail faces to the west, this is a great area for watching the sunset. Big Baldy Trail is also ideal for snowshoeing in the winter.

**User Groups:** Hikers only. No dogs, horses, or mountain bikes. No wheelchair facilities.

**Permits:** No permits are required. There is a $10 per vehicle entrance fee at Sequoia and Kings Canyon National Parks, good for seven days.

**Maps:** Free park maps are available at park entrance stations or by contacting Sequoia and

Kings Canyon National Parks at the address below. A more detailed map is available from Tom Harrison Maps. For a topographic map, ask the USGS for Muir Grove.

**Directions:** From Fresno, drive east on Highway 180 for 55 miles to the Big Stump entrance station at Kings Canyon National Park. Continue 1.5 miles and turn right on the Generals Highway, heading for Sequoia National Park. Drive approximately 6.5 miles on the Generals Highway to the Big Baldy trailhead, on the right, shortly before the turnoff for Big Meadows, on the left.

**Contact:** Sequoia and Kings Canyon National Parks, 47050 General Highway, Three Rivers, CA 93271-9651, 559/565-3341 or 559/335-2856, website: www.nps.gov/seki.

## 47 MUIR GROVE
### 4.0 mi / 2.0 hrs

northwest of the Lodgepole area of Sequoia National Park

**Map 11.3, page 511**

Few people hike this trail unless they are staying at Dorst Campground, so you have a lot better chance of seeing giant sequoias in solitude in the Muir Grove than at many places in the park. After crossing a wooden footbridge, the trail enters a mixed forest of red fir, white fir, sugar pines, and incense cedars. In early summer, you can count the many varieties of wildflowers along the trail, especially where you cross tiny streams. The trail heads west and curves around a deeply carved canyon at one mile out. Just off the trail to your right is a bare granite slab with an inspiring westward view. The trail undulates, never climbing or dropping much, making this an easy and pleasant stroll. At 1.9 miles, you reach the Muir Grove, a small, pristine grove of huge sequoias—the first one you come to on your left is a doozy. The grove is made even more enchanting by the thick undergrowth of blue and purple lupine blooming amid the trees in early summer.

**User Groups:** Hikers only. No dogs, horses, or mountain bikes. No wheelchair facilities.

**Permits:** No permits are required. There is a $10 per vehicle entrance fee at Sequoia and Kings Canyon National Parks, good for seven days.

**Maps:** Free park maps are available at park entrance stations or by contacting Sequoia and Kings Canyon National Parks at the address below. A more detailed map is available from Tom Harrison Maps. For a topographic map, ask the USGS for Muir Grove.

**Directions:** From Fresno, drive east on Highway 180 for 55 miles to the Big Stump entrance station at Kings Canyon National Park. Continue 1.5 miles and turn right on the Generals Highway, heading for Sequoia National Park. Drive approximately 17 miles on the Generals Highway to the right turnoff for Dorst Campground. Turn right and drive through the campground to the amphitheater parking lot. Park there; the trail begins at a footbridge between the amphitheater parking lot and the group campground.

**Contact:** Sequoia and Kings Canyon National Parks, 47050 General Highway, Three Rivers, CA 93271-9651, 559/565-3341 or 559/335-2856, website: www.nps.gov/seki.

## 48 LITTLE BALDY
### 3.5 mi / 2.0 hrs

northwest of the Lodgepole area of Sequoia National Park

**Map 11.3, page 511**

Little Baldy, Big Baldy, Buena Vista Peak—along this stretch of the Generals Highway, there are so many peak trails that offer far-reaching views, it's hard to choose where to start. Start here, on the Little Baldy Trail. It's a little more challenging than the Buena Vista Peak Trail, but it's shorter than Big Baldy Trail, and it offers eye-popping drama for remarkably little effort. Some claim that Little Baldy's view of the Silliman Crest, the Great Western Divide, Castle Rocks, Moro Rock, the Kaweah River Canyon, and the San Joaquin foothills is the best panorama in the park.

To see for yourself, set out from the trailhead, climbing through long, tree-shaded switchbacks, heading first north, then south. Check out the unusual view of Big Baldy off to your left (far across the highway) as you climb. After 1.2 miles, the trail leaves the forest and its many wildflowers, and your views start to open up. Hike along Little Baldy's ridgeline and make the final steep summit ascent. The trail gets a little hard to discern as you near Little Baldy's wide, bare summit, but just wander around until you find the highest spot with the best view. Take a seat—you'll want to stay a while.

Special Note: Be sure to pick a clear day for this hike. In summer, your best bet is to hike the trail early in the morning, before the Central Valley haze rises to the mountains.

**User Groups:** Hikers only. No dogs, horses, or mountain bikes. No wheelchair facilities.

**Permits:** No permits are required. There is a $10 per vehicle entrance fee at Sequoia and Kings Canyon National Parks, good for seven days.

**Maps:** Free park maps are available at park entrance stations or by contacting Sequoia and Kings Canyon National Parks at the address below. A more detailed map is available from Tom Harrison Maps. For topographic maps, ask the USGS for Muir Grove and Giant Forest.

**Directions:** From Fresno, drive east on Highway 180 for 55 miles to the Big Stump entrance station at Kings Canyon National Park. Continue 1.5 miles and turn right on the Generals Highway, heading for Sequoia National Park. Drive approximately 18 miles on the Generals Highway to the Little Baldy trailhead, on the left, a mile beyond the turnoff for Dorst Campground.

**Contact:** Sequoia and Kings Canyon National Parks, 47050 General Highway, Three Rivers, CA 93271-9651, 559/565-3341 or 559/335-2856, website: www.nps.gov/seki.

## 49 THE LAKES TRAIL
### 13.0 mi / 2.0–3.0 days

**off the Generals Highway in the Wolverton area of Sequoia National Park**

Map 11.3, page 511

The Wolverton trailhead is at 7,200 feet, which gives you a boost at the start for this trip into the high country. The Lakes Trail is the most popular backpacking trip in Sequoia National Park, and it's easy to see why. Wide-open views and dramatic granite walls are standard fare as you hike. Part of the route is on a loop, with one side of the loop traveling to the Watchtower—a 1,600-foot-tall granite cliff that offers incredible vistas of Tokopah Valley and beyond. The trailside scenery begins in red fir forest, then enters polished granite country, and culminates in a rocky basin with three gemlike lakes—Heather, Emerald, and Pear—as well as many sparkling creeks. The total climb to Pear Lake is a mere 2,300 feet, spread out over 6.5 miles. Backpackers take note: You may camp only at Emerald and Pear Lakes, and no campfires are allowed.

Special Note: The Watchtower Trail usually isn't open until midsummer. When it is closed, you must take the alternate Hump Trail, which is not as scenic. If you're planning a trip for early in the year, check with the park to be sure Watchtower Trail is open.

**User Groups:** Hikers only. No dogs, horses, or mountain bikes. No wheelchair facilities.

**Permits:** There is a $10 per vehicle entrance fee at Sequoia and Kings Canyon National Parks, good for seven days. Wilderness permits are required for overnight stays. They are available on a first-come, first-served basis at the Lodgepole Visitors Center or in advance by mail or fax for a $15 reservation fee. For more information, call 559/565-3708.

**Maps:** Free park maps are available at park entrance stations or by contacting Sequoia and Kings Canyon National Parks at the address below. A more detailed map is available from Tom Harrison Maps. For a topographic map, ask the USGS for Lodgepole.

**Directions:** From Fresno, drive east on Highway 180 for 55 miles to the Big Stump entrance station at Kings Canyon National Park. Continue 1.5 miles and turn right on the Generals Highway, heading for Sequoia National Park. Drive approximately 27 miles on the Generals Highway, past the Lodgepole Village turnoff, to the Wolverton turnoff, on the left (east) side of the road. Turn left and drive to the parking area and trailhead.

**Contact:** Sequoia and Kings Canyon National Parks, 47050 General Highway, Three Rivers, CA 93271-9651, 559/565-3341 or 559/335-2856, website: www.nps.gov/seki.

## 50 HEATHER LAKE AND THE WATCHTOWER

**9.0 mi / 5.0 hrs**

**off the Generals Highway in the Wolverton area of Sequoia National Park**

Map 11.3, page 511

There's no reason that day hikers should be denied the incredible joys of hiking Lakes Trail from the Wolverton area of Sequoia National Park. You don't have to carry a backpack, get a wilderness permit, or have two or more free days to hike the first part of Lakes Trail, which ascends to the top of the 1,600-foot Watchtower (a big chunk of granite) and then continues to rocky Heather Lake. If you're hiking in spring or early summer, call the park first to make sure Watchtower Trail is open. Otherwise you'll have to take the alternate Hump Trail, which is steeper and nowhere near as scenic. The route to the Watchtower is a ledge trail, blasted into hard granite, which creeps along the high rim of Tokopah Valley. Your view is 1,500 feet straight down. You can even see tiny people walking on the path to Tokopah Falls. It's incredible, although perhaps not a good idea for people who are afraid of heights. Walking up to the Watchtower is plenty exciting, but it's even more so when you reach the other side, where you can look back and see what you were walking on. Just .75 mile farther and you're at Heather Lake, which is designated for day use only, so it has no campsites. It has a steep granite backdrop and a few rocky ledges to sit on. Too many people here when you arrive? No big deal. It's only another .5 mile to even prettier Emerald Lake, and the trail is nearly level. After a rest, you get to head back and hike the Watchtower route all over again.

**User Groups:** Hikers only. No dogs, horses, or mountain bikes. No wheelchair facilities.

**Permits:** No permits are required. There is a $10 per vehicle entrance fee at Sequoia and Kings Canyon National Parks, good for seven days.

**Maps:** Free park maps are available at park entrance stations or by contacting Sequoia and Kings Canyon National Parks at the address below. A more detailed map is available from Tom Harrison Maps. For a topographic map, ask the USGS for Lodgepole.

**Directions:** From Fresno, drive east on Highway 180 for 55 miles to the Big Stump entrance station at Kings Canyon National Park. Continue 1.5 miles and turn right on the Generals Highway, heading for Sequoia National Park. Drive approximately 27 miles on the Generals Highway, past the Lodgepole Village turnoff, to the Wolverton turnoff on the left (east) side of the road. Turn left and drive to the parking area and trailhead.

**Contact:** Sequoia and Kings Canyon National Parks, 47050 General Highway, Three Rivers, CA 93271-9651, 559/565-3341 or 559/335-2856, website: www.nps.gov/seki.

## 51 ALTA PEAK

**13.0 mi / 1.0–2.0 days**

**off the Generals Highway in the Wolverton area of Sequoia National Park**

Map 11.3, page 511

You say you like heights? You like vistas? Here's your trail, a 4,000-foot climb to the top of Alta Peak, an 11,204-foot summit in the Alta Country. Alta Peak and Mount Whitney are the only major summits in Sequoia National Park that have established trails, but both of them are still butt-kickers to reach. The trail to Alta Peak and Alta Meadow starts out the same as Lakes Trail (from the Wolverton parking area), then it heads south (right) to Panther Gap, at 1.8 miles. After climbing through the forest to Panther Gap (at 8,450 feet), you get your first set of eye-popping views—of the Middle Fork Kaweah River and the Great Western Divide.

Continue on Alta Trail to Mehrten Meadow (at 3.9 miles), a popular camping spot, then reach a junction where you can go left for Alta Peak or right to Alta Meadow. You'll want to take both spurs if you have the time and energy. If you're exhausted, just walk to Alta Meadow, with its flower-filled grasses and exquisite mountain views a flat one mile away. Alta Peak is two miles away via the left fork, with a 2,000-foot climb. These two miles are considered one of the toughest stretches of trail in Sequoia National Park due to the brutal grade and the 10,000-plus foot elevation here above tree line. The summit is at 11,204 feet, and, of course, it offers a complete panorama. Even Mount Whitney and the Coast Range are visible on a clear day.

**User Groups:** Hikers only. No dogs, horses, or mountain bikes. No wheelchair facilities.

**Permits:** There is a $10 per vehicle entrance fee at Sequoia and Kings Canyon National Parks, good for seven days. Wilderness permits are required for overnight stays. They are available on a first-come, first-served basis at the Lodgepole Visitors Center or in advance by mail or fax for a $15 reservation fee. For more information, call 559/565-3708.

**Maps:** Free park maps are available at park entrance stations or by contacting Sequoia and Kings Canyon National Parks at the address below. A more detailed map is available from Tom Harrison Maps. For a topographic map, ask the USGS for Lodgepole.

**Directions:** From Fresno, drive east on Highway 180 for 55 miles to the Big Stump entrance station at Kings Canyon National Park. Continue 1.5 miles and turn right on the Generals Highway, heading for Sequoia National Park. Drive approximately 27 miles on the Generals Highway, past the Lodgepole Village turnoff, to the Wolverton turnoff, on the left (east) side of the road. Turn left and drive to the parking area and trailhead.

**Contact:** Sequoia and Kings Canyon National Parks, 47050 General Highway, Three Rivers, CA 93271-9651, 559/565-3341 or 559/335-2856, website: www.nps.gov/seki.

# 52 PANTHER GAP LOOP
**6.0 mi / 3.5 hrs**

off the Generals Highway in the Wolverton area of Sequoia National Park

Map 11.3, page 511

If you're not up for the marathon trip to Alta Peak, you can still get a taste of the high country on this loop from the Wolverton trailhead. Start hiking on the Lakes Trail from the east end of the Wolverton parking lot, and at 1.8 miles, bear right on Alta Trail to parallel Wolverton Creek, following it to Panther Gap. Here, at 8,450 feet, you get an inspiring vista of the Middle Fork Kaweah River and the Great Western Divide. Check out 9,081-foot Castle Rocks, an obvious landmark. From the gap, turn right (west) and follow the Alta Trail to Panther Peak and Panther Meadow, then on to Red Fir Meadow. Finally, at 4.6 miles, bear right and complete the loop by descending to Long Meadow and then edging along its east side to return to the parking lot. By the way, don't get any smart ideas about hiking this loop in the opposite direction—it's a much steeper climb.

**User Groups:** Hikers and horses. No dogs or mountain bikes. No wheelchair facilities.

**Permits:** No permits are required. There is a $10 per vehicle entrance fee at Sequoia and Kings Canyon National Parks, good for seven days.

**Maps:** Free park maps are available at park entrance stations or by contacting Sequoia and Kings Canyon National Parks at the address below. A more detailed map is available from Tom Harrison Maps. For a topographic map, ask the USGS for Lodgepole.

**Directions:** From Fresno, drive east on Highway 180 for 55 miles to the Big Stump entrance station at Kings Canyon National Park. Continue 1.5 miles and turn right on the Generals Highway, heading for Sequoia National Park. Drive approximately 27 miles on the Generals Highway, past the Lodgepole Village turnoff, to the Wolverton turnoff, on the left (east) side of the road. Turn left and drive to the parking area and trailhead.

**Contact:** Sequoia and Kings Canyon National Parks, 47050 General Highway, Three Rivers, CA 93271-9651, 559/565-3341 or 559/335-2856, website: www.nps.gov/seki.

## 53 TOKOPAH FALLS
### 3.6 mi / 2.0 hrs

off the Generals Highway in the Lodgepole area of Sequoia National Park

Map 11.3, page 511

This is unquestionably the best waterfall day hike in Sequoia and Kings Canyon National Parks, leading to 1,200-foot-high Tokopah Falls. It's also a perfect family hike, easy on the feet and even easier on the eyes. The scenery is spectacular the whole way, from the up-close looks at wildflowers and granite boulders to the more distant views of the Watchtower, a 1,600-foot glacially carved cliff on the south side of Tokopah Valley. Then there's the valley itself, with Tokopah Falls pouring down the smooth back curve of its U shape. Because the trail begins by the three huge Lodgepole Campgrounds, it sees a lot of foot traffic. Your best bet is to start early in the morning. Another unusual feature of the trail? Hikers see more yellow-bellied marmots on the Tokopah Falls route than anywhere else in the two parks. We saw at least 40 of the cute little blond guys sunning themselves on rocks. If you're lucky, one of them will whistle at you as you walk by.

**User Groups:** Hikers and horses. No dogs or mountain bikes. No wheelchair facilities.

**Permits:** No permits are required. There is a $10 per vehicle entrance fee at Sequoia and Kings Canyon National Parks, good for seven days.

**Maps:** Free park maps are available at park entrance stations or by contacting Sequoia and Kings Canyon National Parks at the address below. A more detailed map is available from Tom Harrison Maps. For a topographic map, ask the USGS for Lodgepole.

**Directions:** From Fresno, drive east on Highway 180 for 55 miles to the Big Stump entrance station at Kings Canyon National Park. Continue 1.5 miles and turn right on the Generals

Highway, heading for Sequoia National Park. Drive approximately 25 miles on the Generals Highway to the Lodgepole Campground turnoff, then drive .75 mile to the Log Bridge area of Lodgepole Camp. Park in the large lot just before the bridge over the Marble Fork Kaweah River, and walk 150 yards to the trailhead, which is just after you cross the bridge.

**Contact:** Sequoia and Kings Canyon National Parks, 47050 General Highway, Three Rivers, CA 93271-9651, 559/565-3341 or 559/335-2856, website: www.nps.gov/seki.

## 54 TWIN LAKES
### 13.6 mi / 1.0–2.0 days

off the Generals Highway in the Lodgepole area of Sequoia National Park

Map 11.3, page 511

From the Lodgepole Campground trailhead (at 6,740 feet), the Twin Lakes are a 2,800-foot elevation gain and 6.8 miles away, making this a moderate backpacking trip or a long, strenuous day hike. It's a classic Sequoia National Park trip; one that is heavily traveled each summer. The terrain is an interesting mix of dense conifer forests, glacial moraine, and open meadows. From the trailhead, you climb past Wolverton's Rock to Cahoon Meadow at three miles, .5 mile beyond a crossing of Silliman Creek. You then continue to Cahoon Gap at 4.2 miles, cross over Clover Creek at five miles (campsites are found along the creek), bear right at the J. O. Pass Trail junction at 5.5 miles, and reach the Twin Lakes at 6.8 miles. The trail leads you directly to the larger Twin Lake; the smaller one is reached by following a spur. Both are shallow and have forested banks; some hikers try their luck fishing in the larger lake. Backpackers spending the night at Twin Lakes can hike farther the next day—over rocky Silliman Pass (at 10,100 feet) to the less-visited Ranger Lakes, three miles farther. Note that campfires are not allowed at Twin Lakes.

**User Groups:** Hikers and horses. No dogs or mountain bikes. No wheelchair facilities.

**Permits:** There is a $10 per vehicle entrance

fee at Sequoia and Kings Canyon National Parks, good for seven days. Wilderness permits are required for overnight stays. They are available on a first-come, first-served basis at the Lodgepole Visitors Center or in advance by mail or fax for a $15 reservation fee. For more information, call 559/565-3708.

**Maps:** Free park maps are available at park entrance stations or by contacting Sequoia and Kings Canyon National Parks at the address below. A more detailed map is available from Tom Harrison Maps. For a topographic map, ask the USGS for Lodgepole.

**Directions:** From Fresno, drive east on Highway 180 for 55 miles to the Big Stump entrance station at Kings Canyon National Park. Continue 1.5 miles and turn right on the Generals Highway, heading for Sequoia National Park. Drive approximately 25 miles on the Generals Highway to the Lodgepole Campground turnoff, and then drive .75 mile to the Log Bridge area of Lodgepole Camp. The Twin Lakes trailhead is just beyond the Tokopah Falls trailhead and the bridge over the Marble Fork Kaweah River.

**Contact:** Sequoia and Kings Canyon National Parks, 47050 General Highway, Three Rivers, CA 93271-9651, 559/565-3341 or 559/335-2856, website: www.nps.gov/seki.

## 55 CONGRESS TRAIL LOOP
**2.1 mi / 1.0 hr**

off the Generals Highway in the Giant Forest area of Sequoia National Park

Map 11.3, page 511

The Congress Trail, a two-mile loop that starts (and ends) at the General Sherman Tree, is a much-traveled route through the Giant Forest's prize grove of sequoias. The General Sherman gets the most visitors, of course, because it is recognized as the largest living thing in the world (not by height, but by volume). After you leave its side, the crowds lessen substantially. You'll pass by many huge trees with very patriotic names, like the House and Senate clusters, the McKinley Tree, the Lincoln Tree, and—you get the idea.

Every single giant tree is worth stopping to gape at. We rate the Congress Trail as the best level, easy trail for sequoia viewing in the park. Plus, the farther you walk, the more solitude you get. Make sure you pick up an interpretive brochure at the trailhead or at the Lodgepole Visitors Center, and get away from the crowds at the Sherman Tree as fast as you can.

**User Groups:** Hikers only. No dogs, horses, or mountain bikes. Wheelchair users can access this trail; in some areas they may need assistance.

**Permits:** No permits are required. There is a $10 per vehicle entrance fee at Sequoia and Kings Canyon National Parks, good for seven days.

**Maps:** Free park maps are available at park entrance stations or by contacting Sequoia and Kings Canyon National Parks at the address below. A more detailed map is available from Tom Harrison Maps. For a topographic map, ask the USGS for Giant Forest.

**Directions:** From Fresno, drive east on Highway 180 for 55 miles to the Big Stump entrance station at Kings Canyon National Park. Continue 1.5 miles and turn right on the Generals Highway, heading for Sequoia National Park. Drive approximately 28 miles on the Generals Highway, past Lodgepole and Wolverton, to the signed turnoff (on the left) for the General Sherman Tree.

**Contact:** Sequoia and Kings Canyon National Parks, 47050 General Highway, Three Rivers, CA 93271-9651, 559/565-3341 or 559/335-2856, website: www.nps.gov/seki.

## 56 HAZELWOOD AND HUCKLEBERRY LOOP
**4.5 mi / 2.0 hrs**

off the Generals Highway in the Giant Forest area of Sequoia National Park

Map 11.3, page 511

This hike combines two loop trails in the Giant Forest area for an easy but excellent day hike, passing by many giant sequoias and peaceful grassy meadows. A bonus: These trails are generally less crowded than the other day hikes in the Giant Forest area.

From the Generals Highway, pick up the Hazelwood Nature Trail and take the right side of the loop to join Alta Trail and Huckleberry Meadow Trail Loop. Take Alta Trail for .25 mile and bear right on Huckleberry Meadow Trail, climbing a bit for one mile to the site of Squatter's Cabin, one of the oldest structures in Sequoia National Park, dating back to the 1880s. To stay on the loop, turn left by the cabin (don't take the trail signed for The Dead Giant). The trail skirts the edge of Huckleberry Meadow and heads north to Circle Meadow, where giant sequoias line the meadow's edges. There are several junctions, but stay on Huckleberry Meadow Trail. A half mile farther is a short spur trail on the left heading to the Washington Tree. Follow the spur to see the second-largest tree in the world (after General Sherman)—it's 30 feet in diameter and 246.1 feet tall. The trip finishes out on Alta Trail, where you return to Hazelwood Nature Trail and walk the opposite side of its short loop back to the Generals Highway.

**User Groups:** Hikers only. No dogs, horses, or mountain bikes. No wheelchair facilities.

**Permits:** No permits are required. There is a $10 per vehicle entrance fee at Sequoia and Kings Canyon National Parks, good for seven days.

**Maps:** Free park maps are available at park entrance stations or by contacting Sequoia and Kings Canyon National Parks at the address below. A more detailed map is available from Tom Harrison Maps. For topographic maps, ask the USGS for Giant Forest and Lodgepole.

**Directions:** From Fresno, drive east on Highway 180 for 55 miles to the Big Stump entrance station at Kings Canyon National Park. Continue 1.5 miles and turn right on the Generals Highway, heading for Sequoia National Park. Drive approximately 30 miles on the Generals Highway, past Lodgepole and Wolverton, to the Giant Forest area of Sequoia National Park. The Hazelwood trailhead is on the south side of the highway, .25 mile before you reach the Giant Forest Museum.

**Contact:** Sequoia and Kings Canyon National Parks, 47050 General Highway, Three Rivers, CA 93271-9651, 559/565-3341 or 559/335-2856, website: www.nps.gov/seki.

## 57 HIGH SIERRA TRAIL TO HAMILTON LAKE

**30.0 mi / 3.0 days**

**off the Generals Highway in the Giant Forest area of Sequoia National Park**

**Map 11.3, page 511**

This is a classic, easy-to-moderate, three-day backpacking trip in the High Sierra, with a two-night stay at Bearpaw Meadow Camp, a shady campground that clings to the edge of a granite gorge. The route follows High Sierra Trail from Crescent Meadow to Eagle View, then continues for 10 nearly level miles along the north rim of the Middle Fork Kaweah River Canyon. It's views, views, views all the way.

After a good night's sleep at Bearpaw Meadow, elevation 7,700 feet (reservations for a wilderness permit are definitely necessary in the summer months), you start out on an eight-mile round-trip day hike to Upper and Lower Hamilton Lake (at 8,300 feet), set in a glacially carved basin at the base of the peaks of the Great Western Divide. On the final day, you hike 11 miles back to Crescent Meadow, once again witnessing 180-degree views from the sunny High Sierra Trail. By the time it's all over and you're back home, your mind is completely blown by all the high-country beauty, and you've shot about a million pictures, none of which can compare to the experience of actually being there.

**User Groups:** Hikers only. No dogs, horses, or mountain bikes. No wheelchair facilities.

**Permits:** There is a $10 per vehicle entrance fee at Sequoia and Kings Canyon National Parks, good for seven days. Wilderness permits are required for overnight stays. They are available on a first-come, first-served basis at the Lodgepole Visitors Center or in advance by mail or fax for a $15 reservation fee. For more information, call 559/565-3708.

Maps: Free park maps are available at park entrance stations or by contacting Sequoia and Kings Canyon National Parks at the address below. A more detailed map is available from Tom Harrison Maps. For topographic maps, ask the USGS for Giant Forest and Lodgepole.

Directions: From Fresno, drive east on Highway 180 for 55 miles to the Big Stump entrance station at Kings Canyon National Park. Continue 1.5 miles and turn right on the Generals Highway, heading for Sequoia National Park. Drive approximately 30 miles on the Generals Highway, past Lodgepole and Wolverton, to the Giant Forest area of Sequoia National Park. Just beyond the museum, turn left on Crescent Meadow Road and drive 3.5 miles to the Crescent Meadow parking area.

Contact: Sequoia and Kings Canyon National Parks, 47050 General Highway, Three Rivers, CA 93271-9651, 559/565-3341 or 559/335-2856, website: www.nps.gov/seki.

## 58 HIGH SIERRA TRAIL AND EAGLE VIEW
1.5 mi / 1.0 hr

**off the Generals Highway in the Giant Forest area of Sequoia National Park**

Map 11.3, page 511

Are you ready to be wowed? From the lower parking lot at Crescent Meadow, follow the trail that leads to the southern edge of Crescent Meadow, and at .1 mile, take the right fork that leads up the ridge on High Sierra Trail toward Eagle View. The High Sierra Trail is a popular trans-Sierra route that eventually leads to Mount Whitney, the highest peak in the contiguous United States. On this trip you won't go quite that far, but you will get a taste of the visual delights of this extraordinary trail. In less than .5 mile, you'll gain the ridge and start getting wondrous, edge-of-the-world views. Numerous wildflowers line the path, which hugs the edge of this high ridge. At .7 mile, you'll reach Eagle View, an unsigned but obvious lookout from which you get a fascinating look at Moro

Rock to your right, Castle Rocks straight ahead, and dozens of peaks and ridges of the Western Divide far across the canyon. The vistas are so fine and the trail is so good that you might just want to keep walking all the way to Mount Whitney.

User Groups: Hikers only. No dogs, horses, or mountain bikes. No wheelchair facilities.

Permits: No permits are required. There is a $10 per vehicle entrance fee at Sequoia and Kings Canyon National Parks, good for seven days.

Maps: Free park maps are available at park entrance stations or by contacting Sequoia and Kings Canyon National Parks at the address below. A more detailed map is available from Tom Harrison Maps. For topographic maps, ask the USGS for Giant Forest and Lodgepole.

Directions: From Fresno, drive east on Highway 180 for 55 miles to the Big Stump entrance station at Kings Canyon National Park. Continue 1.5 miles and turn right on the Generals Highway, heading for Sequoia National Park. Drive approximately 30 miles on the Generals Highway, past Lodgepole and Wolverton, to the Giant Forest area of Sequoia National Park. Just beyond the museum, turn left on Crescent Meadow Road and drive 3.5 miles to the Crescent Meadow parking area.

Contact: Sequoia and Kings Canyon National Parks, 47050 General Highway, Three Rivers, CA 93271-9651, 559/565-3341 or 559/335-2856, website: www.nps.gov/seki.

## 59 CRESCENT MEADOW AND THARP'S LOG
1.6 mi / 1.0 hr

**off the Generals Highway in the Giant Forest area of Sequoia National Park**

Map 11.3, page 511

Crescent Meadow is more than 1.5 miles long and is surrounded by giant sequoias. John Muir called it "the gem of the Sierras." We don't know how Muir would feel about the pavement that lines the trail around this precious meadow, but we hope he'd like this loop hike anyhow. Follow the pavement for 200 yards from the eastern side of the parking lot, and just like that, you're at the southern edge of beautiful Crescent Meadow. Take the right fork and head for Log Meadow and Tharp's Log. Log Meadow is as large and beautiful as Crescent Meadow, and Tharp's Log was the homestead of Hale Tharp, the first white man to enter this forest. He grazed cattle and horses here, and built a modest home inside a fallen, fire-hollowed sequoia. You can look inside Tharp's Log and see his bed, fireplace, dining room table, and the door and windows he fashioned into the log. (Children find this incredibly thrilling.) From Tharp's Log, continue your loop back to Crescent Meadow and around its west side, where you return to the north edge of the parking lot.

**User Groups:** Hikers and wheelchairs (with assistance). No dogs, horses, or mountain bikes.

**Permits:** No permits are required. There is a $10 per vehicle entrance fee at Sequoia and Kings Canyon National Parks, good for seven days.

**Maps:** Free park maps are available at park entrance stations or by contacting Sequoia and Kings Canyon National Parks at the address below. A more detailed map is available from Tom Harrison Maps. For topographic maps, ask the USGS for Giant Forest and Lodgepole.

**Directions:** From Fresno, drive east on Highway 180 for 55 miles to the Big Stump entrance station at Kings Canyon National Park. Continue 1.5 miles and turn right on the Generals Highway, heading for Sequoia National Park. Drive approximately 30 miles on the Generals Highway, past Lodgepole and Wolverton, to the Giant Forest area of Sequoia National Park. Just beyond the museum, turn left on Crescent Meadow Road and drive 3.5 miles to the Crescent Meadow parking area.

**Contact:** Sequoia and Kings Canyon National Parks, 47050 General Highway, Three Rivers, CA 93271-9651, 559/565-3341 or 559/335-2856, website: www.nps.gov/seki.

# 60 MORO ROCK
## 0.6 mi / 0.5 hr

off the Generals Highway in the Giant Forest area of Sequoia National Park

**Map 11.3, page 511**

Just about everybody has heard of Moro Rock, the prominent, pointy granite dome with the top-of-the-world sunset vistas, and if you're visiting the Giant Forest area of Sequoia National Park, well, you just have to hike to the top of it. When you climb those 380 stairs to the dome's summit and check out the view, you realize that unlike many famous attractions, Moro Rock is not overrated. It's as great as everybody says, and maybe even better. If you start your trip from the Moro Rock parking area, it's only .3 mile to the top, climbing switchbacks, ramps, and granite stairs the whole way. Railings line the rock-blasted trail to keep you from dropping off the 6,725-foot granite dome. What's the view like? Well, on a clear day, you can see all the way to the Coast Range, 100 miles away. In closer focus is the Middle Fork Kaweah River, the Great Western Divide, Castle Rocks (at 9,180 feet), Triple Divide Peak (at 12,634 feet), Mount Stewart (at 12,205 feet) . . . and on and on. In a word, it's awesome. And even better, you don't get this view just from the top of Moro Rock—you get it all the way up, at every turn in the trail.

If you want the absolute best visibility, show up early in the morning, before the afternoon haze from the Central Valley obscures the view. On the other hand, that same haze creates amazingly colorful sunsets, so early evening is another fine time to be on top of Moro Rock.

**User Groups:** Hikers only. No dogs, horses, or mountain bikes. No wheelchair facilities.

**Permits:** No permits are required. There is a $10 per vehicle entrance fee at Sequoia and Kings Canyon National Parks, good for seven days.

**Maps:** Free park maps are available at park entrance stations or by contacting Sequoia and Kings Canyon National Parks at the address below. A more detailed map is available from

Tom Harrison Maps. For a topographic map, ask the USGS for Giant Forest.

**Directions:** From Fresno, drive east on Highway 180 for 55 miles to the Big Stump entrance station at Kings Canyon National Park. Continue 1.5 miles and turn right on the Generals Highway, heading for Sequoia National Park. Drive approximately 30 miles on the Generals Highway, past Lodgepole and Wolverton, to the Giant Forest area of Sequoia National Park. Just beyond the museum, turn left on Crescent Meadow Road, drive 1.5 miles, and take the right fork to the Moro Rock parking area.

**Contact:** Sequoia and Kings Canyon National Parks, 47050 General Highway, Three Rivers, CA 93271-9651, 559/565-3341 or 559/335-2856, website: www.nps.gov/seki.

## 61 SUNSET ROCK
**2.0 mi / 1.0 hr**

**off the Generals Highway in the Giant Forest area of Sequoia National Park**

Map 11.3, page 511

The trail to Sunset Rock is a first-rate easy hike, perfect at sunset or any time. It gets much less traffic than you might expect, considering its proximity to Giant Forest. Leave your car in the vicinity of the new Giant Forest museum (make sure you stop in before or after your trip), then cross the road and pick up the signed trail. The level path leads through a mixed forest (with a handful of giant sequoias) and crosses Little Deer Creek on its way to Sunset Rock. The rock is a gargantuan, flat piece of granite—about the size of a football field—set at 6,412 feet in elevation. Standing on it, you get a terrific overlook of Little Baldy to your right and a sea of conifers below, in the Marble Fork Kaweah River Canyon.

**User Groups:** Hikers only. No dogs, horses, or mountain bikes. No wheelchair facilities.

**Permits:** No permits are required. There is a $10 per vehicle entrance fee at Sequoia and Kings Canyon National Parks, good for seven days.

**Maps:** Free park maps are available at park entrance stations or by contacting Sequoia and

Kings Canyon National Parks at the address below. A more detailed map is available from Tom Harrison Maps. For a topographic map, ask the USGS for Giant Forest.

**Directions:** From Fresno, drive east on Highway 180 for 55 miles to the Big Stump entrance station at Kings Canyon National Park. Continue 1.5 miles and turn right on the Generals Highway, heading for Sequoia National Park. Drive approximately 30 miles on the Generals Highway, past Lodgepole and Wolverton, to the Giant Forest area of Sequoia National Park. Park near the Giant Forest museum.

**Contact:** Sequoia and Kings Canyon National Parks, 47050 General Highway, Three Rivers, CA 93271-9651, 559/565-3341 or 559/335-2856, website: www.nps.gov/seki.

## 62 PARADISE CREEK TRAIL
**1.2 mi / 0.75 hr**

**off Highway 198 in the Foothills region of Sequoia National Park**

Map 11.3, page 511

From Buckeye Flat Campground, Paradise Creek Trail meanders through oaks and buckeyes, and crosses a long, picturesque footbridge over the Middle Fork Kaweah River. An inviting, Olympic-sized pool is on the right side of the bridge, where campers often go swimming on summer afternoons. Save the pool for after your hike; for now, take the signed Paradise Creek Trail, at the far side of the bridge. You'll briefly visit the creek and then leave it, climbing into oak and grassland terrain. There are some high views of Moro Rock and Hanging Rock, but most of the beauty is right at your feet, in the springtime flowers that grow in the grasses and in the leafy blue oaks that shade them. The maintained trail ends when it reaches Paradise Creek again, although a faint route continues along its banks.

**User Groups:** Hikers only. No dogs, horses, or mountain bikes. No wheelchair facilities.

**Permits:** No permits are required. There is a $10 per vehicle entrance fee at Sequoia and Kings Canyon National Parks, good for seven days.

**Maps:** Free park maps are available at park entrance stations or by contacting Sequoia and Kings Canyon National Parks at the address below. A more detailed map is available from Tom Harrison Maps. For a topographic map, ask the USGS for Giant Forest.

**Directions:** From Visalia, drive east on Highway 198 for 47 miles to the turnoff, on the right, for Buckeye Flat Campground, across from Hospital Rock. Turn right and drive .6 mile to the campground. Park in any of the dirt pullouts outside of the camp entrance; no day-use parking is allowed in the camp. You can also park at Hospital Rock and walk to the campground. The trailhead is near campsite 28.

**Contact:** Sequoia and Kings Canyon National Parks, 47050 General Highway, Three Rivers, CA 93271-9651, 559/565-3341 or 559/565-3135, website: www.nps.gov/seki.

## 63 MIDDLE FORK TRAIL TO PANTHER CREEK

**6.0 mi / 3.0 hrs**

**off Highway 198 in the Foothills region of Sequoia National Park**

Map 11.3, page 511

You want to be alone? You don't want to see anybody else on the trail? Just sign up for this trip any time between June and September, when the foothills have warmed up to their summer extremes. Don't be fooled by this path's name: The Middle Fork Trail is no streamside meander. Rather, it's a shadeless, exposed trail that leads high along the canyon of the Middle Fork Kaweah River—always at least 250 feet above it. In summer, it's hot as Hades, but this trail is perfect in winter and spring. Whereas most other trails in Sequoia and Kings Canyon are still snowed under, you can take an early-season day hike or backpacking trip along Middle Fork Trail. The main destination is Panther Creek (at three miles), where the trail leads across the brink of Panther Creek's

100-foot dive into the Kaweah River. But you can hike farther if you wish. Although Middle Fork Trail is set in grasslands and chaparral, it offers some stunning views of the area's geology, including Moro Rock, Castle Rocks, and the Great Western Divide. We hiked this trail in August, and despite the fact that we were wilting from the heat, the expansive views kept our spirits up.

**User Groups:** Hikers only. No dogs, horses, or mountain bikes. No wheelchair facilities.

**Permits:** No permits are required. There is a $10 per vehicle entrance fee at Sequoia and Kings Canyon National Parks, good for seven days.

**Maps:** Free park maps are available at park entrance stations or by contacting Sequoia and Kings Canyon National Parks at the address below. A more detailed map is available from Tom Harrison Maps. For a topographic map, ask the USGS for Giant Forest.

**Directions:** From Visalia, drive east on Highway 198 for 47 miles to the turnoff, on the right, for Buckeye Flat Campground, across from Hospital Rock. Turn right and drive .5 mile to a left fork just before the campground. Bear left on the dirt road and drive 1.3 miles to the trailhead and parking area. In the winter, you must park at Hospital Rock and walk in to the trailhead, adding 3.6 miles to your round-trip.

**Contact:** Sequoia and Kings Canyon National Parks, 47050 General Highway, Three Rivers, CA 93271-9651, 559/565-3341 or 559/565-3135, website: www.nps.gov/seki.

## 64 POTWISHA TO HOSPITAL ROCK

**5.0 mi / 2.5 hrs**

**off Highway 198 in the Foothills region of Sequoia National Park**

Map 11.3, page 511

First, some advice: Don't hike this trail on a hot day. If it's summertime and you want to the see the Monache Indian historical sites at Potwisha and Hospital Rock, drive to each of them and see them separately. In winter or spring, however, it's far more fun to take this five-mile hike through chaparral and oak woodlands, especially in March, when the wildflowers bloom. In the first 100 yards from the trailhead, you'll see Native American grinding holes and pictographs that look roughly like people and animals. You'll also pass many tempting pools in the Middle Fork Kaweah, which are frequented by swimmers and bathers in the summer. The trail climbs a gradual 2.5 miles from Potwisha to Hospital Rock, crossing the highway after the first mile. When you reach Hospital Rock, which is just a few feet off the road to Buckeye Flat Campground, you see a huge display of pictographs on its side. Across the campground road are more grinding holes in the boulders, and near them, a short paved path leads to deep pools and sandy beaches on the middle fork. Another path leads from the camp road to the underside of Hospital Rock, where there's a large, cavelike shelter. This is where a Native American medicine man healed the sick and injured, resulting in a white man naming this place Hospital Rock.

**User Groups:** Hikers only. No dogs, horses, or mountain bikes. No wheelchair facilities.

**Permits:** No permits are required. There is a $10 per vehicle entrance fee at Sequoia and Kings Canyon National Parks, good for seven days.

**Maps:** Free park maps are available at park entrance stations or by contacting Sequoia and Kings Canyon National Parks at the address below. A more detailed map is available from Tom Harrison Maps. For a topographic map, ask the USGS for Giant Forest.

**Directions:** From Visalia, drive east on Highway 198 for 44 miles to the turnoff, on the left, for Potwisha Campground, 3.8 miles east of the Ash Mountain entrance station to Sequoia National Park. Don't turn left into Potwisha campground; instead, turn right on the paved road opposite the campground. Drive past the RV dumping station to the signed trailhead and parking area.

**Contact:** Sequoia and Kings Canyon National Parks, 47050 General Highway, Three Rivers, CA 93271-9651, 559/565-3341 or 559/565-3135, website: www.nps.gov/seki.

## 65 MARBLE FALLS
### 7.0 mi / 4.0 hrs

off Highway 198 in the Foothills region of Sequoia National Park

Map 11.3, page 511

This is the waterfall to see in Sequoia National Park in late winter and spring. March and April are particularly good months to visit because of high flows in the Marble Fork Kaweah River and blooming wildflowers in the grasslands and chaparral that line the trail. From its rather banal start as a dirt road, this trail just keeps getting better as it follows the Marble Fork Kaweah River. There are no trail junctions to worry about; at 3.5 miles, the path simply dead-ends near the lower cascades of Marble Falls. Although much of the falls are hidden in the narrow, rocky river gorge, tucked out of sight, what is visible is an impressive billowing cascade of whitewater. Be very careful on the slippery granite near the river's edges; the current and the cold water are even more dangerous than they look. Aside from the waterfalls and the wildflowers, the other highlights on this trail are the colorful outcroppings of marble, particularly in the last mile as you near the falls. Remember, though, that in summer this area of the park can bake like an oven. If you make the trip to the falls from late May to September, get an early morning start.

**User Groups:** Hikers only. No dogs, horses, or mountain bikes. No wheelchair facilities.

**Permits:** No permits are required. There is a $10 per vehicle entrance fee at Sequoia and Kings Canyon National Parks, good for seven days.

**Maps:** Free park maps are available at park entrance stations or by contacting Sequoia and Kings Canyon National Parks at the address below. A more detailed map is available from Tom Harrison Maps. For a topographic map, ask the USGS for Giant Forest.

**Directions:** From Visalia, drive east on Highway 198 for 44 miles to the turnoff, on the left, for Potwisha Campground, 3.8 miles east of the Ash Mountain entrance station to Sequoia

National Park. The trail begins next to campsite No. 16 in Potwisha Campground; park in the day-use parking area in the camp.

**Contact:** Sequoia and Kings Canyon National Parks, 47050 General Highway, Three Rivers, CA 93271-9651, 559/565-3341 or 559/565-3135, website: www.nps.gov/seki.

## 66 PARADISE RIDGE
**3.2 mi / 1.5 hrs**

**off Highway 198 in the Mineral King region of Sequoia National Park**

Map 11.3, page 511

OK, you've just driven the 20 twisting miles into Mineral King from Three Rivers. You're tired, dusty, and itching to get out of the car and move your legs. What's the first trail you can reach in Mineral King? The Paradise Ridge Trail, and it climbs right away, getting you huffing and puffing and clearing out the road dust from your lungs. After the initial steepness of the trail, the grade becomes easier as it moves into switchbacks ascending the hill. The path is loaded with giant sequoia trees, some in clusters as large as 10 or more. At your feet are tons of ferns. As you climb, the views just keep improving—you see the East Fork Kaweah River Canyon below you, and far off, the Great Western Divide. You can hike all the way to the top of the ridge at three miles, but the views aren't any better there than they are on the way up. Most people just cruise uphill a way, and turn around when they've had enough. Besides the big trees and the big views, our favorite thing about this trail was that we saw more bears than people.

**User Groups:** Hikers and horses. No dogs or mountain bikes. No wheelchair facilities.

**Permits:** No permits are required. There is a $10 per vehicle entrance fee at Sequoia and Kings Canyon National Parks, good for seven days.

**Maps:** Free park maps are available at park entrance stations or by contacting Sequoia and Kings Canyon National Parks at the address below. A more detailed map is available from Tom Harrison Maps. For a topographic map, ask the USGS for Silver City.

**Directions:** From Visalia, drive east on Highway 198 for 38 miles to Mineral King Road, 2.5 miles east of Three Rivers. If you reach the Ash Mountain entrance station, you've gone too far. Turn right on Mineral King Road and drive 20 miles to the Hockett Trail parking area, on the right, .25 mile past Atwell Mill Camp. Park there and walk back west on Mineral King Road about .3 mile to the trailhead for Paradise Ridge, on the north side of the road.

**Contact:** Sequoia and Kings Canyon National Parks, 47050 General Highway, Three Rivers, CA 93271-9651, 559/565-3341 or 559/565-3135, website: www.nps.gov/seki.

## 67 HOCKETT TRAIL TO EAST FORK BRIDGE
**4.0 mi / 2.0 hrs**

**off Highway 198 in the Mineral King region of Sequoia National Park**

Map 11.3, page 511

The Hockett Trail makes a fine day hiking path in Mineral King. It's suitable for all kinds of hikers. Families with small children can just walk a mile downhill to the footbridge over the East Fork Kaweah River, where there is a small waterfall and many sculptured granite pools, and then turn around and head back. People looking for a longer trip can continue another mile to the East Fork Grove of sequoias and Deer Creek. Both groups get to hike through a beautiful forest of big conifers—pines, cedars, and firs—and fields of mountain misery. The trail starts in an area of sequoia stumps, near where the Atwell Mill cut lumber in the 1880s. Live sequoias still flourish farther down the path, near the river's edge; apparently they were spared because of their distance from the mill. The trail is well graded, and even the uphill return is only a moderate climb.

**User Groups:** Hikers and horses. No dogs or mountain bikes. No wheelchair facilities.

**Permits:** No permits are required. There is a $10 per vehicle entrance fee at Sequoia and Kings Canyon National Parks, good for seven days.

Maps: Free park maps are available at park entrance stations or by contacting Sequoia and Kings Canyon National Parks at the address below. A more detailed map is available from Tom Harrison Maps. For a topographic map, ask the USGS for Mineral King.

Directions: From Visalia, drive east on Highway 198 for 38 miles to Mineral King Road, 2.5 miles east of Three Rivers. If you reach the Ash Mountain entrance station, you've gone too far. Turn right on Mineral King Road and drive 20 miles to the Hockett Trail parking area, on the right, .25 mile past Atwell Mill Camp. Park there and walk into the campground to campsite No. 16, where the trail begins.

Contact: Sequoia and Kings Canyon National Parks, 47050 General Highway, Three Rivers, CA 93271-9651, 559/565-3341 or 559/565-3135, website: www.nps.gov/seki.

## 68 COLD SPRINGS NATURE TRAIL

2.0 mi / 1.0 hr

**off Highway 198 in the Mineral King region of Sequoia National Park**

Map 11.3, page 511

You may not expect much from a campground nature trail, but Cold Springs Nature Trail is guaranteed to exceed your expectations. Not only is it lined with wildflowers along the East Fork Kaweah River and informative signposts that teach you to identify junipers, red and white firs, cottonwoods, and aspens, but the views of the Sawtooth Ridge are glorious. The loop is less than .5 mile, but from the far end of it, the trail continues along the East Fork Kaweah River, heading another mile into Mineral King Valley. Walk to the loop's far end, and then continue at least another .25 mile along the trail. It just gets prettier as it goes. You're in for a real treat if you take this walk right before sunset, when the valley's surrounding mountain peaks turn every imaginable shade of pink, orange, and coral, reflecting the sun setting in the west. The vistas are so beautiful that they can practically make you weep.

User Groups: Hikers and horses. No dogs or mountain bikes. No wheelchair facilities.

Permits: No permits are required. There is a $10 per vehicle entrance fee at Sequoia and Kings Canyon National Parks, good for seven days.

Maps: Free park maps are available at park entrance stations or by contacting Sequoia and Kings Canyon National Parks at the address below. A more detailed map is available from Tom Harrison Maps. For a topographic map, ask the USGS for Mineral King.

Directions: From Visalia, drive east on Highway 198 for 38 miles to Mineral King Road, 2.5 miles east of Three Rivers. If you reach the Ash Mountain entrance station, you've gone too far. Turn right on Mineral King Road and drive 23.5 miles to Cold Springs Campground on the right. The trail begins near site six. If you aren't staying in the camp, you can park by the Mineral King Ranger Station and walk into the campground.

Contact: Sequoia and Kings Canyon National Parks, 47050 General Highway, Three Rivers, CA 93271-9651, 559/565-3341 or 559/565-3135, website: www.nps.gov/seki.

## 69 FAREWELL GAP TRAIL TO ASPEN FLAT

2.0 mi / 1.0 hr

**off Highway 198 in the Mineral King region of Sequoia National Park**

Map 11.3, page 511

If ever there was a perfect family hike, this would have to be it. Actually, if ever there was a perfect hike for every two-legged person on the planet, this would have to be it. The glacial-cut Mineral King Valley—a peaceful paradise of meadows, streams, and 100-year-old cabins—has to be one of the most scenic places in the West, and possibly in the world. An easy stroll along the canyon floor leads you past waterfalls and along the headwaters of the East Fork Kaweah River, in the awesome shelter of thousand-foot cliffs. After walking to the trailhead near the pack station, you follow Farewell Gap Trail (an old dirt road)

for a mile, then cross Crystal Creek and take the right fork off the main trail. This brings you closer to the river, where you follow a narrow use trail to Aspen Flat (a lovely grove of trees), or to Soda Springs, situated right along the river's edge. There you can see mineral springs bubbling up from the ground, turning the earth around them a bright orange color. Bring a fishing rod on this trail if you like, but be absolutely certain to bring your camera.

**User Groups:** Hikers and horses. No dogs or mountain bikes. No wheelchair facilities.

**Permits:** No permits are required. There is a $10 per vehicle entrance fee at Sequoia and Kings Canyon National Parks, good for seven days.

**Maps:** Free park maps are available at park entrance stations or by contacting Sequoia and Kings Canyon National Parks at the address below. A more detailed map is available from Tom Harrison Maps. For a topographic map, ask the USGS for Mineral King.

**Directions:** From Visalia, drive east on Highway 198 for 38 miles to Mineral King Road, 2.5 miles east of Three Rivers. If you reach the Ash Mountain entrance station, you've gone too far. Turn right on Mineral King Road and drive 25 miles to the end of the road and the Eagle/Mosquito trailhead. Take the right fork at the end of the road to reach the parking area. Walk back out of the parking lot and follow the road to the pack station; the Farewell Gap Trail begins just beyond it.

**Contact:** Sequoia and Kings Canyon National Parks, 47050 General Highway, Three Rivers, CA 93271-9651, 559/565-3341 or 559/565-3135, website: www.nps.gov/seki.

## 70 MOSQUITO LAKES
**8.0 mi / 4.0 hrs or 2.0 days**

**off Highway 198 in the Mineral King region of Sequoia National Park**

Map 11.3, page 511

Ah, paradise. You know you're in it as soon as you park your car at the end of Mineral King Road. The Eagle/Mosquito trailhead is at 7,830 feet, and you set out from the parking lot near one of Mineral King's adorable cabins, left from the early 20th century and privately owned. Feel jealous? Keep walking; you'll get over it. In minutes you cross a footbridge over Spring Creek's cascade, called Tufa Falls because of the calcium carbonate in Spring Creek's water. Don't expect to see much of a waterfall—most of it is hidden by brush. At one mile, you reach the junction for Eagle Lake, the Mosquito Lakes, and White Chief Trails. Take the right fork, climbing steadily. At two miles, you reach the Mosquito Lakes junction and go right, leaving Eagle Lake Trail for another day. Climb up and then down the other side of Miner's Ridge, at 9,300 feet. The final descent covers .5 mile; you reach Mosquito Lake number one at 9,040 feet and 3.6 miles. It's considered to be the easiest lake to reach in Mineral King, with a mostly shaded trail and only a 1,500-foot gain on the way in, plus a 250-foot gain on the way out. Still, if you've visited any of the other spectacular Mineral King lakes, this lake will look a little disappointing. It's small, shallow, and greenish. But fear not: This is the first of several Mosquito Lakes, all of which are linked by Mosquito Creek. Hikers with excess energy can follow the stream uphill to four more lakes. There is no maintained trail to the upper lakes, but if you follow the use trail near the stream, the going is easier. The use trail begins on the west side of the stream at the first lake, navigates around the rocky slope behind the lake, and then crosses the stream above it. The climb from lake number one to lake number two is steep, with a 600-foot elevation gain in .5 mile, but it's worth it. Lake number two is the usual destination for day hikers; it's a blue, deep, granite-bound beauty and makes for an eight-mile round-trip. Backpackers will find the first campsites at Mosquito Lake number two (no camping is allowed at the first lake). Mosquito Lake number five is five miles from the Eagle/Mosquito trailhead.

**User Groups:** Hikers and horses. No dogs or mountain bikes. No wheelchair facilities.

**Permits:** There is a $10 per vehicle entrance fee at Sequoia and Kings Canyon National Parks, good for seven days. Wilderness permits are required for overnight stays. They are available on a first-come, first-served basis at the Mineral King Ranger Station, or in advance by mail or fax for a $15 reservation fee. For more information, call 559/565-3708.

**Maps:** Free park maps are available at park entrance stations or by contacting Sequoia and Kings Canyon National Parks at the address below. A more detailed map is available from Tom Harrison Maps. For a topographic map, ask the USGS for Mineral King.

**Directions:** From Visalia, drive east on Highway 198 for 38 miles to Mineral King Road, 2.5 miles east of Three Rivers. If you reach the Ash Mountain entrance station, you've gone too far. Turn right on Mineral King Road and drive 25 miles to the end of the road and the Eagle/Mosquito trailhead. Take the right fork at the end of the road to reach the parking area. The trail begins at the far end of the parking lot.

**Contact:** Sequoia and Kings Canyon National Parks, 47050 General Highway, Three Rivers, CA 93271-9651, 559/565-3341 or 559/565-3135, website: www.nps.gov/seki.

## 71 EAGLE LAKE TRAIL
**6.8 mi / 4.0 hrs**

off Highway 198 in the Mineral King region of Sequoia National Park

Map 11.3, page 511

Eagle Lake has always been the glamour destination in Mineral King; the trail to hike if you can hike only one trail in the area. Why? The blue-green lake is drop-dead gorgeous, that's why, and the trail to reach it is challenging but manageable for most day hikers, with a 2,200-foot elevation gain spread out over 3.4 miles. Nonetheless, hikers who made the trek to Eagle Lake in the summer of 2003 were heartily disappointed when they arrived. The lake's historic dam had sprung a leak, and the water had dropped to a sadly diminished level.

However, the park service got to work on fixing the dam, and as of the summer of 2004, Eagle Lake has been restored to its formerly gorgeous self. The Eagle Lake Trail follows the same route as the Mosquito Lakes Trail (see previous listing) until the two-mile point, near the Eagle Sink Holes. These geological oddities are small craters in the ground where Eagle Creek suddenly disappears underground. At the trail junction by the sinkholes, go left for Eagle Lake. Enjoy the brief flat stretch here, because shortly, you'll gain another 1,000 feet over 1.4 miles. Much of the climb is in an exposed, rocky area—a large boulder field that gets baked by the sun on warm days. Well-graded switchbacks and beautiful scenery make it easier. Soon you arrive at Eagle Lake's dam, at 10,000 feet. The big lake is surrounded by glacially carved rock and has a few rocky islands. Brook trout swim in its clear waters. The trail continues along the lake's west side to many good picnicking spots and photo opportunities. Campsites are found near the lake; no camping is allowed between the trail and the lake.

**User Groups:** Hikers and horses. No dogs or mountain bikes. No wheelchair facilities.

**Permits:** There is a $10 per vehicle entrance fee at Sequoia and Kings Canyon National Parks, good for seven days. Wilderness permits are required for overnight stays. They are available on a first-come, first-served basis at the Mineral King Ranger Station, or in advance by mail or fax for a $15 reservation fee. For more information, call 559/565-3708.

**Maps:** Free park maps are available at park entrance stations or by contacting Sequoia and Kings Canyon National Parks at the address below. A more detailed map is available from Tom Harrison Maps. For a topographic map, ask the USGS for Mineral King.

**Directions:** From Visalia, drive east on Highway 198 for 38 miles to Mineral King Road, 2.5 miles east of Three Rivers. If you reach the Ash Mountain entrance station, you've gone too far. Turn right on Mineral King Road and drive 25 miles to the end of the road and the Eagle/Mosquito trailhead. Take the right fork at the end of the road to reach the parking area. The trail begins at the far end of the parking lot.

**Contact:** Sequoia and Kings Canyon National Parks, 47050 General Highway, Three Rivers, CA 93271-9651, 559/565-3341 or 559/565-3135, website: www.nps.gov/seki.

## 7.2 FRANKLIN LAKES
**10.8 mi / 6.0 hrs or 2.0 days**

**off Highway 198 in the Mineral King region of Sequoia National Park**

Map 11.3, page 511

Maybe the best thing about hiking to Franklin Lakes is the waterfalls you get to pass along the way—especially our favorite cascades, on Franklin Creek. Or maybe it's the prolific wildflowers along the trail, or the spectacular views over Mineral King Valley that you gain as you climb. Maybe it's the big lake itself, set below Tulare Peak, or the fact that the trail to reach it is so well graded, with a 2,500-foot elevation gain spread out over 5.4 miles. What the heck—this trail is about as close to hiking perfection as you get.

The first two miles are nearly flat; the route winds along the bottom of Mineral King's canyon, following Farewell Gap Trail alongside the East Fork Kaweah River. You'll pass Tufa Falls, across the canyon, at .25 mile and Crystal Creek's cascades, on your side of the canyon, at one mile. The trail leaves the valley floor and starts to climb moderately, reaching the bottom of Franklin Creek's cascades at 1.7 miles. After crossing Franklin Creek, you continue south along Farewell Canyon, negotiating some switchbacks as you gain elevation. The views get better and better. One mile farther, Franklin Lakes Trail forks left off Farewell Gap Trail and starts climbing in earnest up the Franklin Creek Valley. At nearly 10,000 feet, the trail crosses Franklin Creek again, then parallels the creek for another mile to the largest Franklin Lake. Note that when you see the lake's dam straight ahead and an obvious campsite about 150 yards below it to the right of the trail, you

should cut off the main trail. Walk to the camp and follow its use trail to the dam and the lake. The main trail switchbacks up and above the lake but doesn't go directly to its shoreline. Franklin Lake is a dramatic sight, surrounded by steep, snow-covered slopes and a few pines and junipers. Rainbow Mountain is on its northeast side; Tulare Peak is to the southwest.

**User Groups:** Hikers and horses. No dogs or mountain bikes. No wheelchair facilities.

**Permits:** There is a $10 per vehicle entrance fee at Sequoia and Kings Canyon National Parks, good for seven days. Wilderness permits are required for overnight stays. They are available on a first-come, first-served basis at the Mineral King Ranger Station, or in advance by mail or fax for a $15 reservation fee. For more information, call 559/565-3708.

**Maps:** Free park maps are available at park entrance stations or by contacting Sequoia and Kings Canyon National Parks at the address below. A more detailed map is available from Tom Harrison Maps. For a topographic map, ask the USGS for Mineral King.

**Directions:** From Visalia, drive east on Highway 198 for 38 miles to Mineral King Road, 2.5 miles east of Three Rivers. If you reach the Ash Mountain entrance station, you've gone too far. Turn right on Mineral King Road and drive 25 miles to the end of the road and the Eagle/Mosquito trailhead. Take the right fork at the end of the road to reach the parking area. Walk back out of the parking lot, and follow the road to the pack station; Farewell Gap Trail begins just beyond it.

**Contact:** Sequoia and Kings Canyon National Parks, 47050 General Highway, Three Rivers, CA 93271-9651, 559/565-3341 or 559/565-3135, website: www.nps.gov/seki.

## 7.3 WHITE CHIEF MINE TRAIL
**5.8 mi / 3.0 hrs**

**off Highway 198 in the Mineral King region of Sequoia National Park**

Map 11.3, page 511

If you're one of those liberated hikers who

doesn't need to have an alpine lake in your itinerary to be happy, the trail to White Chief Bowl is a scenic route with much to offer, including an exploration of the White Chief Mine tunnel. Until the park service purchased it in 1998, the mine was private property within the national park and off-limits to hikers.

The first mile of the trail is the same as the route to Eagle and Mosquito Lakes, but you'll leave most everyone behind when you continue straight at the one-mile junction, while they bear right for Eagle Lake and the Mosquito Lakes. The White Chief Trail continues with a hefty grade—this second mile is the toughest part of the whole trip—until it tops out at the edge of a gorgeous meadow. Just after you cross a seasonal stream (often a dry ravine by late summer), look for the ruins of Crabtree Cabin, to the right of the trail. The cabin ruins are what is left of the oldest remaining structure in Mineral King. It was built by the discoverer of the White Chief Mine in the 1870s. Next comes White Chief Meadows, surrounded by high granite walls and filled with summer wildflowers in the wet areas around White Chief Creek. The meadow is also filled with dozens of downed trees, evidence of harsh winter avalanches.

Beyond the meadow, the trail ascends slightly until it nears a waterfall on White Chief Creek. Shortly before the falls, the trail crosses the creek and heads uphill. Look for the opening to White Chief Mine in a layer of white rock just above the trail. Scramble off the trail a few yards to reach it. The mine tunnel is tall enough to walk into and dead-ends in about 150 feet. It's a fascinating piece of history in a gorgeous, high-country location.

**User Groups:** Hikers and horses. No dogs or mountain bikes. No wheelchair facilities.

**Permits:** No permits are required. There is a $10 per vehicle entrance fee at Sequoia and Kings Canyon National Parks, good for seven days.

**Maps:** Free park maps are available at park entrance stations or by contacting Sequoia and Kings Canyon National Parks at the address

below. A more detailed map is available from Tom Harrison Maps. For a topographic map, ask the USGS for Mineral King.

**Directions:** From Visalia, drive east on Highway 198 for 38 miles to Mineral King Road, 2.5 miles east of Three Rivers. If you reach the Ash Mountain entrance station, you've gone too far. Turn right on Mineral King Road and drive 25 miles to the end of the road and the Eagle/Mosquito trailhead. Take the right fork at the end of the road to reach the parking area. The trail begins from the far end of the parking lot.

**Contact:** Sequoia and Kings Canyon National Parks, 47050 General Highway, Three Rivers, CA 93271-9651, 559/565-3341 or 559/565-3135, website: www.nps.gov/seki.

## 7.4 TIMBER GAP TRAIL
### 4.0 mi / 2.0 hrs
**off Highway 198 in the Mineral King region of Sequoia National Park**

Map 11.3, page 511

On this short but steep trail, you'll stand witness to the mining history of Mineral King. The trail climbs abruptly from the Sawtooth trailhead on an old mining path along Monarch Creek, and forks in .25 mile. Take the left fork for Timber Gap, which climbs through a dense fir forest and then opens out to switchbacks in a wide and treeless slope—the result of continual winter avalanches. The exposed slope is home to many mountain wildflowers. The climb ends in two miles at Timber Gap, elevation 9,450 feet, a forested pass. The stumps you see among the red firs remain from early miners who cut down the trees to fuel their fires and support their mining tunnels. A faint path heads east from the pass and leads to the remains of the Empire Mine in just over one mile.

**User Groups:** Hikers and horses. No dogs or mountain bikes. No wheelchair facilities.

**Permits:** No permits are required. There is a $10 per vehicle entrance fee at Sequoia and Kings Canyon National Parks, good for seven days.

**Maps:** Free park maps are available at park entrance stations or by contacting Sequoia and Kings Canyon National Parks at the address below. A more detailed map is available from Tom Harrison Maps. For a topographic map, ask the USGS for Mineral King.

**Directions:** From Visalia, drive east on Highway 198 for 38 miles to Mineral King Road, 2.5 miles east of Three Rivers. If you reach the Ash Mountain entrance station, you've gone too far. Turn right on Mineral King Road and drive 24.5 miles to the Sawtooth parking area, .5 mile before the end of the road.

**Contact:** Sequoia and Kings Canyon National Parks, 47050 General Highway, Three Rivers, CA 93271-9651, 559/565-3341 or 559/565-3135, website: www.nps.gov/seki.

## 75 MONARCH LAKES
**8.4 mi / 5.0 hrs or 2.0 days**

**off Highway 198 in the Mineral King region of Sequoia National Park**

Map 11.3, page 511

The Monarch Lakes Trail leads from the Sawtooth trailhead at 8,000 feet in elevation and climbs 2,500 feet to the rocky, gemlike Monarch Lakes. The first lake is good, but the second lake is simply awesome, and the scenery along the trail is unforgettable. Walk .25 mile from the trailhead and take the right fork for Monarch and Crystal Lakes. After one steep mile, you'll reach Groundhog Meadow, named for the adorable yellow-bellied marmots that inhabit the area. (We like their blond coats and shrill whistles.) Beyond the meadow, the trail starts seriously switchbacking in and out of red fir forest, making a gut-thumping climb to the Crystal Lake trail junction. The trail forks sharply right for Crystal Lake, but you head left for one more mile—a relatively smooth mile, with the easiest grade of the whole route—to Lower Monarch Lake. (This section crosses an incredible talus slope.) Snow can often be found near the lake even in late summer, and the vista is dramatic, with Sawtooth Peak dom-

inating the skyline. If you have a wilderness permit and a backpacking stove, you can find a campsite near the lake.

While the main trail continues north to Sawtooth Pass, a use trail leads southeast from the lower lake for .5 mile to Upper Monarch Lake. Basically you head directly up the cliff that forms the back wall of the lower lake. It's worth the climb. The upper lake is wide, deep blue, and dramatic, set at the base of barren, pointy Monarch Peak. The view from the upper lake's basin, looking back down at the lower lake and various Mineral King peaks, is breathtaking. A big surprise is that the upper lake has been dammed, like many of the high lakes in Mineral King, and is operated by Southern California Edison. Note: If you're backpacking and want to take a first-rate side trip, the trail to Sawtooth Pass is a 1.3-mile, 1,200-foot climb that's not easy, but Sawtooth Pass offers one of the best views in the Southern Sierra.

**User Groups:** Hikers and horses. No dogs or mountain bikes. No wheelchair facilities.

**Permits:** There is a $10 per vehicle entrance fee at Sequoia and Kings Canyon National Parks, good for seven days. Wilderness permits are required for overnight stays. They are available on a first-come, first-served basis at the Mineral King Ranger Station, or in advance by mail or fax for a $15 reservation fee. For more information, call 559/565-3708.

**Maps:** Free park maps are available at park entrance stations or by contacting Sequoia and Kings Canyon National Parks at the address below. A more detailed map is available from Tom Harrison Maps. For a topographic map, ask the USGS for Mineral King.

**Directions:** From Visalia, drive east on Highway 198 for 38 miles to Mineral King Road, 2.5 miles east of Three Rivers. If you reach the Ash Mountain entrance station, you've gone too far. Turn right on Mineral King Road and drive 24.5 miles to the Sawtooth parking area, .5 mile before the end of the road.

**Contact:** Sequoia and Kings Canyon National Parks, 47050 General Highway, Three Rivers, CA 93271-9651, 559/565-3341 or 559/565-3135, website: www.nps.gov/seki.

## 76 CRYSTAL LAKE TRAIL
**9.8 mi / 6.0 hrs or 2.0 days**

**off Highway 198 in the Mineral King region of Sequoia National Park**

Map 11.3, page 511

The long and arduous path to Crystal Lake follows the same route as the trail to Monarch Lakes (see previous listing) for the first 3.2 miles. In Chihuahua Bowl, a sharp right-hand turn puts you on the trail to Crystal Lake. In .5 mile, the trail leads past the ruins of the Chihuahua Mine (on the right), one of Mineral King's last hopes for silver riches. Like the other mines in the area, it never produced ore to equal the miners' dreams. The trail climbs abruptly over a rocky slope to a ridge of reddish foxtail pines, where your vista opens wide. Far off you can see the Farewell Gap peaks, and down below you see the Cobalt Lakes and Crystal Creek, pouring down to the Mineral King Valley and the East Fork Kaweah River. The trail continues, following more switchbacks, to upper Crystal Creek and Crystal Lake, which has been dammed. Off to the left (north), Mineral Peak stands out at 11,500 feet, and to the right (south), Rainbow Mountain shows off its colorful rock. Views are spectacular in every direction. If you scramble .25 mile off-trail toward Mineral Peak, you will reach Little Crystal Lake, where you have a near guarantee of solitude and a vista you won't forget.

**User Groups:** Hikers and horses. No dogs or mountain bikes. No wheelchair facilities.

**Permits:** There is a $10 per vehicle entrance fee at Sequoia and Kings Canyon National Parks, good for seven days. Wilderness permits are required for overnight stays. They are available on a first-come, first-served basis at the Mineral King Ranger Station, or in advance by mail or fax for a $15 reservation fee. For more information, call 559/565-3708.

**Maps:** Free park maps are available at park entrance stations or by contacting Sequoia and Kings Canyon National Parks at the address below. A more detailed map is available from Tom Harrison Maps. For a topographic map, ask the USGS for Mineral King.

**Directions:** From Visalia, drive east on Highway 198 for 38 miles to Mineral King Road, 2.5 miles east of Three Rivers. If you reach the Ash Mountain entrance station, you've gone too far. Turn right on Mineral King Road and drive 24.5 miles to the Sawtooth parking area, .5 mile before the end of the road.

**Contact:** Sequoia and Kings Canyon National Parks, 47050 General Highway, Three Rivers, CA 93271-9651, 559/565-3341 or 559/565-3135, website: www.nps.gov/seki.

## 77 BLACK WOLF FALLS
**0.5 mi / 0.5 hr**

**off Highway 198 in the Mineral King region of Sequoia National Park**

Map 11.3, page 511

This hike is really just a stroll, and the destination is readily apparent from the Sawtooth trailhead: Black Wolf Falls, tumbling down the canyon wall in Mineral King Valley. But aside from the chance to get close to a pretty waterfall, the hike is interesting because of its historical significance. Black Wolf's name is actually an alteration of its original moniker, which was Black Wall Falls, named for the Black Wall copper mine that was located at the waterfall's base. Back in the 1870s, when miners believed that Mineral King was rich in more than just scenery, they mined the base of Monarch Creek with a modicum of success. Today you can walk right up to the falls and see the mine tunnel on its right side (it looks like a cave, but don't go inside; it's unstable). In summer, rangers lead group hikes to the waterfall and talk about Mineral King's mining history. Although the route to Black Wolf Falls isn't an official trail, the path is well used and clearly visible. If you can find its beginning across the road from the No

Parking Any Time sign, the rest of the hike is easy.

**User Groups:** Hikers only. No dogs, horses, or mountain bikes. No wheelchair facilities.

**Permits:** No permits are required. There is a $10 per vehicle entrance fee at Sequoia and Kings Canyon National Parks, good for seven days.

**Maps:** Free park maps are available at park entrance stations or by contacting Sequoia and Kings Canyon National Parks at the address below. A more detailed map is available from Tom Harrison Maps. For a topographic map, ask the USGS for Mineral King.

**Directions:** From Visalia, drive east on Highway 198 for 38 miles to Mineral King Road, 2.5 miles east of Three Rivers. If you reach the Ash Mountain entrance station, you've gone too far. Turn right on Mineral King Road and drive 24.5 miles to the Sawtooth parking area, .5 mile before the end of the road. Walk up the road toward Black Wolf Falls, then look for a use trail across the road from the No Parking Any Time sign, just beyond where Monarch Creek flows under the road.

**Contact:** Sequoia and Kings Canyon National Parks, 47050 General Highway, Three Rivers, CA 93271-9651, 559/565-3341 or 559/565-3135, website: www.nps.gov/seki.

## 78 LADYBUG TRAIL
### 3.8 mi / 2.0 hrs
off Highway 198 in the South Fork region of Sequoia National Park

Map 11.3, page 511

The South Fork area is the forgotten region of Sequoia National Park. Accessible only by a 13-mile dead-end road out of Three Rivers, South Fork is the place to go when you just want to get away from it all. Solitude in a national park? You can find it here. The elevation is low (only 3,600 feet), so the area is accessible year-round, and there may be no finer winter walk than a hike on Ladybug Trail out of South Fork. The trail leaves the far end of South Fork Campground and heads through an oak and bay forest along the South Fork Kaweah River. At 1.7 miles, you reach Ladybug Camp, a primitive camping area along the river's edge, in the shade of pines and firs. A short scramble downstream of the camp gives you a look at Ladybug Falls, a 25-foot waterfall set in a rocky grotto. If you continue upstream, the trail leads another few hundred yards and then switchbacks uphill, heading for Whiskey Log Camp. A use trail leaves the main trail and continues a short distance upriver, where there are many beautiful rocky pools. And in case you haven't guessed, the trail, camp, and falls are named for the millions of ladybugs that winter near the river, then take flight in the spring to head back to the Central Valley to feed.

**User Groups:** Hikers and horses. No dogs or mountain bikes. No wheelchair facilities.

**Permits:** No permits are required. There is a $10 per vehicle entrance fee at Sequoia and Kings Canyon National Parks, good for seven days.

**Maps:** Free park maps are available at park entrance stations or by contacting Sequoia and Kings Canyon National Parks at the address below. A more detailed map is available from Tom Harrison Maps. For a topographic map, ask the USGS for Dennison Peak.

**Directions:** From Visalia, drive east on Highway 198 for 35 miles to one mile west of Three Rivers. Turn right on South Fork Drive and drive 12.8 miles to South Fork Campground. (At nine miles, the road turns to dirt.) Day-use parking is available just inside the camp entrance. The trailhead is at the far end of the campground loop.

**Contact:** Sequoia and Kings Canyon National Parks, 47050 General Highway, Three Rivers, CA 93271-9651, 559/565-3341 or 559/565-3135, website: www.nps.gov/seki.

## 79 GARFIELD-HOCKETT TRAIL
### 5.8 mi / 3.0 hrs
off Highway 198 in the South Fork region of Sequoia National Park

Map 11.3, page 511

The trip to the magnificent Garfield Grove is only 2.9 miles from South Fork Campground, and if you don't mind a steep climb and possibly sharing the trail with horse packers, you should be sure to take this hike. The trail climbs immediately and keeps climbing, but fortunately, it is shaded by oaks most of the way. The ascent rewards you with a continual view of distant Homer's Nose, a granite landmark that, although prominent, looks little like anybody's nose. In just under three miles of nonstop climbing, you reach the first of many sequoias in the Garfield Grove, reported to be one of the largest groves in the national parks. By the time you reach it, you've gained 2,000 feet in elevation, so pick a big tree to lean against, pull out a snack, and take a breather.

**User Groups:** Hikers and horses. No dogs or mountain bikes. No wheelchair facilities.

**Permits:** No permits are required. There is a $10 per vehicle entrance fee at Sequoia and Kings Canyon National Parks, good for seven days.

**Maps:** Free park maps are available at park entrance stations or by contacting Sequoia and Kings Canyon National Parks at the address below. A more detailed map is available from Tom Harrison Maps. For topographic maps, ask the USGS for Dennison Peak.

**Directions:** From Visalia, drive east on Highway 198 for 35 miles to one mile west of Three Rivers. Turn right on South Fork Drive and drive 12.8 miles to South Fork Campground. (At nine miles, the road turns to dirt.) Day-use parking is available just inside the camp entrance. The trailhead is on the right side of the campground.

**Contact:** Sequoia and Kings Canyon National Parks, 47050 General Highway, Three Rivers, CA 93271-9651, 559/565-3341 or 559/565-3135, website: www.nps.gov/seki.

## 80 BALCH PARK NATURE TRAIL
**1.0 mi / 0.5 hr**

in Mountain Home Demonstration State Forest off Highway 190 near Springville
Map 11.3, page 511

Balch Park is the small county-run park within the borders of Mountain Home Demonstration State Forest, and its easy, one-mile nature trail is a great place to take your kids for the afternoon. The trail begins next to the main entrance to Balch Park Camp, across from the museum, and your first stop is a visit to the Hollow Log, which was used as a dwelling by various pioneers, Indians, and prospectors. You also get to see the Lady Alice Tree, which was incorrectly billed in the early 20th century as the largest tree in the world. Nonetheless, it's no slacker in the size department. Continuing along the route, you'll see and learn all about dogwoods, bracken ferns, manzanita, and gooseberry. When you're finished hiking the nature trail, you can cross the road and throw a line into one of Balch Park's two small fishing ponds, which are stocked weekly.

**User Groups:** Hikers, dogs, and horses. No mountain bikes. No wheelchair facilities.

**Permits:** No permits are required. Parking and access are free.

**Maps:** A free map/brochure of Mountain Home Demonstration State Forest, which includes Balch Park, is available from park headquarters. For a topographic map, ask the USGS for Camp Wishon.

**Directions:** From Porterville, drive east on Highway 190 for 18 miles to Springville. At Springville, turn left (north) on Balch Park Road/Road 239, drive 3.5 miles, and turn right on Bear Creek Road/Road 220. Drive 14 miles to Mountain Home Demonstration State Forest Headquarters, pick up a free park map, and then continue 1.5 miles farther to the entrance to Balch Park and the nature trail.

**Contact:** Balch Park, 559/539-3896; Mountain Home Demonstration State Forest, P.O. Box 517, Springville, CA 93265, 559/539-2321 (summer) or 559/539-2855 (winter).

## 81 ADAM AND EVE LOOP TRAIL
**2.0 mi / 1.0 hr**

in Mountain Home Demonstration State Forest off Highway 190 near Springville
Map 11.3, page 511

On Adam and Eve Loop Trail you can see the Adam Tree standing tall and proud, but its companion, the Eve Tree, is no longer thriving. It (she?) was axed during the infamous sequoia logging years, and it's strangely touching to see the gaping slash in her side. Begin your trip by taking the left side of the loop, heading uphill to the Adam Tree, the second-largest tree in this state forest, at 240 feet tall and 27 feet in diameter. The Eve Tree is shortly after. The big draw on the trail is visiting the "Indian bathtubs" at Tub Flat, halfway around the loop; these are basins, formed in solid granite, that were probably used by Native Americans. No one is sure whether they are man-made. The basins are much larger than the traditional Indian grinding holes that are found elsewhere in the Sierra; they are truly large enough to take a bath in.

**User Groups:** Hikers, dogs, and horses. No mountain bikes. No wheelchair facilities.

**Permits:** No permits are required. Parking and access are free.

**Maps:** A free map/brochure of Mountain Home Demonstration State Forest is available from park headquarters. For a topographic map, ask the USGS for Camp Wishon.

**Directions:** From Porterville, drive east on Highway 190 for 18 miles to Springville. At Springville, turn left (north) on Balch Park Road/Road 239 and drive 3.5 miles; then turn right on Bear Creek Road/Road 220. Drive 14 miles to Mountain Home Demonstration State Forest Headquarters, pick up a free park map, and then continue one mile farther, turing right at the sign for Hidden Falls Recreation Area. Drive three miles to just past the pack station and before Shake Camp Campground, to the trailhead for Adam and Eve Loop Trail, on the left.

**Contact:** Mountain Home Demonstration State Forest, P.O. Box 517, Springville, CA 93265, 559/539-2321 (summer) or 559/539-2855 (winter).

## 82 REDWOOD CROSSING
**4.0 mi / 2.0 hrs**

**in Mountain Home Demonstration State Forest off Highway 190 near Springville**

Map 11.3, page 511

An excellent easy hike for campers and day visitors at Mountain Home Demonstration State Forest is on Long Meadow Trail, from Shake Camp Campground to Redwood Crossing, on the Tule River. The trail starts by the public corral (elevation 6,800 feet) and leads through logged sequoia stumps to a thick mixed forest on the slopes high above the Wishon Fork Tule River. When the trail reaches clearings in the trees, the views of the Great Western Divide are excellent. At two miles out, you reach Redwood Crossing, a boulder-lined stretch of the river. Those willing to ford can cross to the other side and head into the Golden Trout Wilderness, but day hikers should pull out a picnic at the river's edge and make an afternoon of it. Backpackers heading for the wilderness need to secure a wilderness permit from the Tule River Ranger District office at the address below.

**User Groups:** Hikers, dogs, and horses. No mountain bikes. No wheelchair facilities.

**Permits:** No permits are required. Parking and access are free.

**Maps:** A free map/brochure of Mountain Home Demonstration State Forest is available from park headquarters. For a topographic map, ask the USGS for Camp Wishon.

**Directions:** From Porterville, drive east on Highway 190 for 18 miles to Springville. At Springville, turn left (north) on Balch Park Road/Road 239, drive 3.5 miles, and turn right on Bear Creek Road/Road 220. Drive 14 miles to Mountain Home Demonstration State Forest Headquarters, pick up a free park map, and then continue one mile farther. Turn right at the sign for Hidden Falls Recreation Area. Drive 3.5 miles to Shake Camp Campground. The Long Meadow trailhead is located by the public corral.

**Contact:** Mountain Home Demonstration State

Forest, P.O. Box 517, Springville, CA 93265, 559/539-2321 (summer) or 559/539-2855 (winter); Tule River Ranger District, 32588 Highway 190, Springville, CA 93265, 559/539-2607, website: www.fs.fed.us/r5/sequoia.

## 83 MOSES GULCH TRAIL
**4.0 mi / 2.0 hrs**

**in Mountain Home Demonstration State Forest off Highway 190 near Springville**

Map 11.3, page 511

For a less-crowded alternate to the popular Redwood Crossing (see previous listing), you can take the other trail from the public corral at Shake Flat Campground and wind your way through stands of beautiful virgin sequoias to the Wishon Fork Tule River at Moses Gulch Campground. The Moses Gulch Trail crosses park roads twice—the only downer—but it's an easy walk for families, and it's peaceful besides. Once you reach the river (at two miles), you have the option of hiking alongside it to the north or south, adding some distance to your trip. The northern stretch leads to Hidden Falls Campground (the home of many small falls and pools), and the southern stretch crosses pretty Galena and Silver Creeks, leading past a mining cabin and an old copper mine.

**User Groups:** Hikers, dogs, and horses. No mountain bikes. No wheelchair facilities.

**Permits:** No permits are required. Parking and access are free.

**Maps:** A free map/brochure of Mountain Home Demonstration State Forest is available from park headquarters. For a topographic map, ask the USGS for Camp Wishon.

**Directions:** From Porterville, drive east on Highway 190 for 18 miles to Springville. At Springville, turn left (north) on Balch Park Road/Road 239, drive 3.5 miles, and then turn right on Bear Creek Road/Road 220. Drive 14 miles to Mountain Home Demonstration State Forest Headquarters and pick up a free park map, then continue one mile farther and turn right at the sign for Hidden Falls Recreation Area. Drive 3.5 miles to Shake Camp Campground. The Moses Gulch trailhead is by the public corral.

**Contact:** Mountain Home Demonstration State Forest, P.O. Box 517, Springville, CA 93265, 559/539-2321 (summer) or 559/539-2855 (winter).

## 84 DOYLE TRAIL
**6.0 mi / 3.0 hrs**

**in Giant Sequoia National Monument near Springville**

Map 11.3, page 511

The Doyle Trail is a great alternative to the heat of the Springville and Porterville Valleys. It's in the transition zone between foothills and conifers, with plenty of shade from tall manzanita, oaks, madrones, and pines. Squirrels and lizards are your primary companions on the trail, which laterals along the slopes above the Wishon fork of the Tule River. From the gated trailhead, hike up the paved road and bear left to bypass Doyle Springs, a community of private cabins. Follow the trail that is signed Trail to Upstream Fishing. The route climbs gently through the forest for 2.5 miles and then suddenly descends to the same level as the river, where there are some primitive campsites available. Then the trail rises again, climbing for another .5 mile to a clearing on the right, where there is an outcrop of jagged green rock alongside the river. Leave the trail and cross over the rock, where you'll find a few picture-perfect swimming holes and small waterfalls.

**User Groups:** Hikers, dogs, horses, and mountain bikes. No wheelchair facilities.

**Permits:** No permits are required. Parking and access are free.

**Maps:** For a map, ask the U.S. Forest Service for Sequoia National Forest. For a topographic map, ask the USGS for Camp Wishon.

**Directions:** From Porterville, drive east on Highway 190 for 18 miles to Springville. From Springville, continue east on Highway 190 for 7.5 miles to Wishon Drive/Road 208, a left fork. Turn left and drive four miles on Wishon Drive, then take the left fork, which is signed for day-use parking (above the campground). Drive .25 mile and park off the road, near the gate.

**Contact:** Giant Sequoia National Monument/Sequoia National Forest, Tule River Ranger District, 32588 Highway 190, Springville, CA 93265, 559/539-2607, website: www.fs.fed.us/r5/sequoia.

## 85 JORDAN PEAK LOOKOUT
### 1.8 mi / 1.0 hr

in Giant Sequoia National Monument near Quaking Aspen

Map 11.3, page 511

You'll see some logging activity out here by Jordan Peak, but if you can put up with it, you can climb a mere 600 feet over less than a mile to reach the summit of this 9,100-foot mountain. Few summits are so easily attained (it's a well-graded and well-maintained trail), and this one is not lacking in dramatic vistas. You can see the Wishon Fork Canyon of the Tule River, Camp Nelson, the Sequoia Crest, Slate Mountain, Maggie Mountain, and Moses Mountain close up, and the Tehachapis and the Coast Range far, far away. The peak is covered with microwave equipment, but it doesn't mar the stupendous view. Head west from the trailhead on Jordan Lookout Trail, switchbacking up until you reach the catwalked stairs to the lookout, which was built in 1934.

**User Groups:** Hikers, dogs, horses, and mountain bikes. No wheelchair facilities.

**Permits:** No permits are required. Parking and access are free.

**Maps:** For a map, ask the U.S. Forest Service for Sequoia National Forest. For a topographic map, ask the USGS for Sentinel Peak.

**Directions:** From Porterville, drive 45 miles east on Highway 190 to Forest Service Road 21S50, near Quaking Aspen Campground. Turn left on Road 21S50 and drive five miles. Bear left and continue on Road 21S50 for 2.8 miles, bearing left on Road 20S71, signed for Jordan Peak Lookout, and following it one mile to its end, at the trailhead.

**Contact:** Giant Sequoia National Monument/Sequoia National Forest, Tule River Ranger District, 32588 Highway 190, Springville, CA 93265, 559/539-2607, website: www.fs.fed.us/r5/sequoia.

## 86 CLICKS CREEK TRAIL
### 14.0 mi / 2.0 days

in the Golden Trout Wilderness near Quaking Aspen

Map 11.3, page 511

If you like peace and quiet on your backpacking trips, Clicks Creek Trail, in the Golden Trout Wilderness, may suit you just fine. The trail leads northeast from Log Cabin Meadow (elevation 7,800 feet), heading steadily downhill along Clicks Creek to the Little Kern River. The route crosses the creek several times. Shade lovers will thrill at the conifer forests that line the route, interspersed by large and grassy meadows, and anglers can bring along their gear to try their luck with the golden trout in the river. There are many possible campsites along the Little Kern, where the elevation is 6,200 feet.

**User Groups:** Hikers, dogs, and horses. No mountain bikes. No wheelchair facilities.

**Permits:** A free wilderness permit is required for overnight stays and is available from the Springville or Kernville Ranger Stations at the addresses below. Parking and access are free.

**Maps:** For a map, ask the U.S. Forest Service for Sequoia National Forest or Golden Trout Wilderness. For a topographic map, ask the USGS for Sentinel Peak.

**Directions:** From Porterville, drive 45 miles east on Highway 190 to Forest Service Road 21S50 near Quaking Aspen Campground. Turn left on Road 21S50 and drive five miles; bear left and continue on Road 21S50 for 1.5 miles to the Clicks Creek trailhead, at Log Cabin Meadow.

**Contact:** Sequoia National Forest, Tule River Ranger District, 32588 Highway 190, Springville, CA 93265, 559/539-2607, website: www.fs.fed.us/r5/sequoia; Cannell Meadow Ranger District, P.O. Box 9, Kernville, CA 93238, 760/376-3781, website: www.fs.fed.us/r5/sequoia.

## 87 JOHN JORDAN/HOSSACK MEADOW TRAIL
### 5.0–6.0 mi / 2.5–3.0 hrs

**in Giant Sequoia National Monument near Quaking Aspen**

Map 11.3, page 511

Your route on John Jordan Trail begins with a crossing of McIntyre Creek, then traverses a level mile to an old fence, gate, and McIntyre Rock—a huge pile of granite boulders with an excellent view. Climb on top of the rock's well-graded, cracking-granite back side and peer over its startlingly steep front side. Surprise! It's straight down, about 600 feet. The trail heads downhill through a red fir forest to Nelson Creek, the site of some logging work. Although you can walk another .5 mile to the trail's end (at Hossack Meadow), most people turn around at the sight of logged trees, making for a five-mile round-trip with a 1,000-foot elevation gain on the return. So who was John Jordan, anyway? He was a trailblazer in the 1870s who unfortunately was most famous for drowning in the Kern River on his way back to the Central Valley to tell everybody he had completed this trail, a proposed toll road.

**User Groups:** Hikers, dogs, horses, and mountain bikes. No wheelchair facilities.

**Permits:** No permits are required. Parking and access are free.

**Maps:** For a map, ask the U.S. Forest Service for Sequoia National Forest. For a topographic map, ask the USGS for Sentinel Peak.

**Directions:** From Porterville, drive 45 miles east on Highway 190 to Forest Service Road 21S50, near Quaking Aspen Campground. Turn left on Road 21S50 and drive 6.6 miles, then bear left on Road 20S81. Follow Road 20S81 for 1.4 miles to the signed trailhead.

**Contact:** Giant Sequoia National Monument/Sequoia National Forest, Tule River Ranger District, 32588 Highway 190, Springville, CA 93265, 559/539-2607, website: www.fs.fed.us/r5/sequoia.

## 88 FREEMAN CREEK TRAIL
### 4.0 mi / 2.0 hrs

**in Giant Sequoia National Monument near Quaking Aspen**

Map 11.3, page 511

The easternmost grove of sequoias in the world is your destination on Freeman Creek Trail. Compared to most sequoia groves in the Sierra, the trees of the 1,700-acre Freeman Creek Grove are mere adolescents—probably not more than 1,000 years old. Among them is a tree named for former President George Bush Sr., who visited the grove in 1992. The trail is a pleasant downhill stroll along Freeman Creek, reaching the first sequoias in about one mile, after crossing the creek. In between the big trees are large meadow areas (many of which bloom with spring and summer wildflowers) and forests of red firs. Many campsites are found along the creek. The path finally ends at Lloyd Meadows, three miles from the trailhead, but most people don't travel that far, since it requires too much climbing on the way back. Two miles out and back is just about perfect.

**User Groups:** Hikers, dogs, horses, and mountain bikes. No wheelchair facilities.

**Permits:** No permits are required. Parking and access are free.

**Maps:** For a map, ask the U.S. Forest Service for Sequoia National Forest. For topographic maps, ask the USGS for Sentinel Peak.

**Directions:** From Porterville, drive 45 miles east on Highway 190 to Forest Service Road 21S50, near Quaking Aspen Campground. Turn left on Road 21S50 and drive .5 mile, then turn right at the sign for the Freeman Creek Grove.

**Contact:** Giant Sequoia National Monument/Sequoia National Forest, Tule River Ranger District, 32588 Highway 190, Springville, CA 93265, 559/539-2607, website: www.fs.fed.us/r5/sequoia.

## 89 SUMMIT TRAIL TO SLATE MOUNTAIN

**8.0 mi / 4.0 hrs**

in Giant Sequoia National Monument near Quaking Aspen

Map 11.3, page 511

If you're staying at Quaking Aspen Campground, you can set out on Summit National Recreation Trail from outside your tent door, but if you're not, drive to the trailhead just south of the camp off Road 21S78. Few people hike all 12 miles of the trail, but many take this four-mile jaunt to the summit of 9,302-foot Slate Mountain, the highest peak in the area. The first two miles of trail are easy, climbing gently through meadows and forest (some logging activity can be seen); then the route climbs more steeply, ascending first the east side and then the north side of Slate Mountain. Views of the granite spires of The Needles and Olancha Peak can be seen. At 3.8 miles you reach a junction with Bear Creek Trail, and from there, it's a short scramble to your left to the top of Slate Mountain, which is a big pile of rocks with a tremendous 360-degree view. There's no trail, but a couple well-worn routes are visible.

**User Groups:** Hikers, dogs, horses, and mountain bikes. No wheelchair facilities.

**Permits:** No permits are required. Parking and access are free.

**Maps:** For a map, ask the U.S. Forest Service for Sequoia National Forest. For a topographic map, ask the USGS for Sentinel Peak.

**Directions:** From Porterville, drive 46 miles east on Highway 190 to Forest Service Road 21S78, which is .5 mile south of Quaking Aspen Campground. Turn right on Road 21S78 and drive .5 mile to the Summit trailhead.

**Contact:** Giant Sequoia National Monument/Sequoia National Forest, Tule River Ranger District, 32588 Highway 190, Springville, CA 93265, 559/539-2607, website: www.fs.fed .us/r5/sequoia.

## 90 NEEDLES LOOKOUT

**5.0 mi / 2.5 hrs**

in Giant Sequoia National Monument near Quaking Aspen

Map 11.3, page 511

Here it is, the perfect easy day hike in Giant Sequoia National Monument. It's just long enough and undulating enough for beginning and intermediate hikers, without being too demanding, and it's full of visual rewards. The trail starts with a placard bearing a great old black-and-white photo that shows what the fire lookout on top of The Needles looked like early in the 20th century. Five minutes down the trail, you leave the forest and come out to two wooden benches, good places to stare out at the magnificent view of the Kern River Basin before you. If you look ahead, you get a glimpse of the fire lookout, perched in what looks like a precarious fashion on top of The Needles' tall granite spires. As you continue along the trail, you lose your view of the lookout. The trail goes up, then down, then up again, through firs, ponderosa, sugar pines, granite, and sand. The only steep section is the final set of switchbacks up The Needles; the lead to a series of stairs and catwalks that ascend to the lookout tower. When you reach the first catwalk, the rest is a cakewalk. A sign tells you if the tower is open and you may come up and visit. If it's closed, just climb up on any boulder to admire the view— it's just as fine from the base of the tower as it is from above. You look out over Lloyd Meadow and the western half of the Golden Trout Wilderness. This is a perfect place to take someone who needs to get inspired.

**User Groups:** Hikers, dogs, horses, and mountain bikes. No wheelchair facilities.

**Permits:** No permits are required. Parking and access are free.

**Maps:** For a map, ask the U.S. Forest Service for Sequoia National Forest. For topographic maps, ask the USGS for Sentinel Peak and Durrwood Creek.

**Directions:** From Porterville, drive 46 miles east on Highway 190 to Forest Service Road

21S05, which is .5 mile south of Quaking Aspen Campground. Turn left (east) on Road 21S05 and drive 2.8 miles to the trailhead.

**Contact:** Giant Sequoia National Monument/Sequoia National Forest, Tule River Ranger District, 32588 Highway 190, Springville, CA 93265, 559/539-2607, website: www.fs.fed.us/r5/sequoia.

## 91 TRAIL OF 100 GIANTS
**0.5 mi / 0.5 hr**

in Giant Sequoia National Monument
near Johnsondale

Map 11.3, page 511

The Trail of 100 Giants is as good as many of the giant sequoia trails in Sequoia and Kings Canyon National Parks. Trailhead elevation is 6,400 feet, and the trail is an easy and nearly flat loop that is paved and suitable for wheelchairs and baby strollers. Located within the Long Meadow Giant Sequoia Grove, the second-most southern grove where sequoias are found, the big trees on the Trail of 100 Giants are situated amid a mixed forest of cedars and pines. A dozen interpretive signs along the path unlock the secrets of this forest. As you walk in from the parking lot across the road, the first sequoia tree on your right is a doozy—probably the best one on the loop. Of all the sequoia groves we've seen and admired, the Trail of 100 Giants grove stands out because it has an unusual amount of twins—two sequoias growing tightly side by side in order to share resources. In fact, this grove even has one twin that rangers call a "sequedar," a sequoia and a cedar that have grown together. If you're staying at Redwood Meadow Campground, you have your own entrance to this loop, so you don't have to drive down the road to the main trailhead and parking lot.

**User Groups:** Hikers, wheelchairs, dogs, and horses. No mountain bikes.

**Permits:** No permits are required. A $3 parking fee is charged per vehicle.

**Maps:** For a map, ask the U.S. Forest Service for Sequoia National Forest. For a topographic map, ask the USGS for Johnsondale.

**Directions:** From Kernville on the north end of Isabella Lake, drive north on Sierra Way/Road 99 for 27 miles to Johnsondale R-Ranch. Continue west (the road becomes Road 50) for 5.5 miles, turn right on the Western Divide Highway, and drive 2.4 miles to the trailhead parking area, on the right, just before Redwood Meadow Campground. Cross the road to begin the trail.

**Contact:** Giant Sequoia National Monument/Sequoia National Forest, Tule River Ranger District, 32588 Highway 190, Springville, CA 93265, 559/539-2607, website: www.fs.fed.us/r5/sequoia.

## 92 MULE PEAK LOOKOUT
**1.2 mi / 1.0 hr**

in Giant Sequoia National Monument
near Johnsondale

Map 11.3, page 511

While rock climbers come to Mule Peak to do their daring work, hikers can take a not-so-daring walk up the back side of Mule Peak; it's attainable for all ages and levels of hikers. The area around the peak has been logged, unfortunately, but growth is coming back with moderate success. The trail follows a series of easy switchbacks up the hillside, gaining 600 feet to the summit of Mule Peak (elevation 8,142 feet). A lookout tower is positioned there, still in operation by Sequoia National Forest, and views are excellent of Onion Meadow Peak, Table Mountain, and the Tule River Valley.

**User Groups:** Hikers, dogs, horses, and mountain bikes. No wheelchair facilities.

**Permits:** No permits are required. Parking and access are free.

**Maps:** For a map, ask the U.S. Forest Service for Sequoia National Forest. For a topographic map, ask the USGS for Sentinel Peak.

**Directions:** From Kernville on the north end of Isabella Lake, drive north on Sierra Way/Road 99 for 27 miles to Johnsondale R-Ranch. Continue west (the road becomes Road 50), then in 5.5 miles, turn right on the Western Divide Highway. Drive five miles to the left turnoff signed for Mule Peak/Road 22S03. Turn left and follow Road 22S03 for five miles to the Mule Peak trailhead.

**Contact:** Giant Sequoia National Monument/Sequoia National Forest, Tule River Ranger District, 32588 Highway 190, Springville, CA 93265, 559/539-2607, website: www.fs.fed.us/r5/sequoia.

## 93 DOME ROCK
### 0.25 mi / 0.5 hr

**in Giant Sequoia National Monument near Quaking Aspen**

Map 11.3, page 511

Dome Rock wins the prize for "Granite Dome with the Most Pedestrian Name." But never mind. It also wins the prize for "Shortest Walk to an Incredible View." Trailhead elevation is 7,200 feet, and the trail is really just a route leading from the left side of the parking lot. Signs at the parking lot warn you not to drop or throw anything off the top of the dome, because there are rock climbers down below on the dome's steep side. It's a mere five-minute walk to the top of Dome Rock—a huge cap of bare granite—where the views are incredible of Slate Mountain, Isabella Lake, and The Needles. If you look very carefully, you can just make out the fire lookout tower on top of The Needles. You'll want to hang around here for a while to ooh-and-aah. If your scrambling skills are good, consider checking out another stunning destination just a few miles from here. Jump back in your car and drive back to the Western Divide Highway, then head south for four miles to an unmarked pullout on the east side of the road, .25 mile south of the Crawford Road turnoff. Start hiking on the dirt road that begins at the turnout; bear right where it forks. The path draws near to Nobe Young Creek, and soon you will hear a noisy waterfall. Take one of several spur trails on your left leading down to the base of the 125-foot fall, which drops over three granite ledges. The entire hike is only one mile round-trip, but because there is no formal trail, it's

not for novices. Wear good boots and use caution on the steep and slippery slope.

**User Groups:** Hikers, dogs, horses, and mountain bikes. No wheelchair facilities.

**Permits:** No permits are required. Parking and access are free.

**Maps:** For a map, ask the U.S. Forest Service for Sequoia National Forest. For a topographic map ask the USGS for Sentinel Peak.

**Directions:** From Kernville on the north end of Isabella Lake, drive north on Sierra Way/Road 99 for 27 miles to Johnsondale R-Ranch. Continue west (the road becomes Road 50) for 5.5 miles, and turn right on the Western Divide Highway. Drive 12 miles to the Dome Rock/Road 21S69 turnoff, on the right, across from Peppermint Work Center. Turn right and follow the dirt road for a few hundred yards; where it forks, bear left and continue to the trailhead, .5 mile from the Western Divide Highway. If you're traveling from the north, the turnoff is two miles south of Ponderosa Lodge.

**Contact:** Giant Sequoia National Monument/Sequoia National Forest, Tule River Ranger District, 32588 Highway 190, Springville, CA 93265, 559/539-2607, website: www.fs.fed.us/r5/sequoia.

## 94 ALDER CREEK TRAIL
### 1.8 mi / 1.0 hr

**in Giant Sequoia National Monument near Johnsondale**

Map 11.3, page 511

The granite slabs and pools on Alder Creek have gotten so popular with hikers, swimmers, and picnickers that the forest service has installed No Parking Any Time signs all over the road near the trailhead. But as long as you park where you're supposed to (off the road, in the day-use parking area), you can still pay a visit to the tons-of-fun pools and slides along Alder Creek. To reach them, walk up the gated dirt road (Road 22S83) and turn right on the single-track trail. The path descends to the confluence of Alder Creek and

Dry Meadow Creek, where there is a long length of swimming holes and rocky slides that pour into them. Make sure you wear denim or some other heavy material on your backside so you can while away many happy hours pretending you are a river otter. It's exhilarating, but please use caution as you slip and slide. Slick granite can be very unforgiving.

**User Groups:** Hikers and dogs. No horses or mountain bikes. No wheelchair facilities.

**Permits:** No permits are required. Parking and access are free.

**Maps:** For a map, ask the U.S. Forest Service for Sequoia National Forest. For a topographic map, ask the USGS for Sentinel Peak.

**Directions:** From Kernville on the north end of Lake Isabella, drive north on Sierra Way/Road 99 for 27 miles to .5 mile north of Johnsondale R-Ranch. Turn right on Road 22S82 and drive 5.7 miles to the day-use parking area, on the right side of the road. Walk across Road 22S82 to the gated dirt road and the trailhead.

**Contact:** Giant Sequoia National Monument/Sequoia National Forest, Tule River Ranger District, 32588 Highway 190, Springville, CA 93265, 559/539-2607, website: www.fs.fed.us/r5/sequoia.

## 95 KEARSAGE PASS
**10.0 mi / 6.0 hrs or 2.0 days**

**in the John Muir Wilderness in Inyo National Forest**

Map 11.3, page 511

The trailhead elevation for Kearsage Pass Trail is 9,200 feet, and the elevation at Kearsage Pass is 11,823 feet. Five miles and a good amount of climbing lie in between, but the route is well graded, and the scenery is spectacular. The trail, which was once an Indian trading route, leads to the backcountry of Kings Canyon National Park, but most day hikers just make the trip to the pass. Along the way, you are witness to several sparkling lakes and whitewater cascades, and a wealth of high-country wildflowers. Not surprisingly, this is a very popular trail. Remember to bring sunglasses, sunscreen, and a jacket for the summit, which is windy and exposed.

The trail climbs gradually from the trailhead, often nearing Independence Creek then veering away again as it winds through a multitude of switchbacks. You pass Little Pothole Lake at 1.5 miles, Gilbert Lake at 2.2 miles, and Flower Lake at 2.6 miles. Continue climbing high above tree line to Kearsage Pass. You'll get a long-distance view of Heart Lake and pass the left spur trail leading to Big Pothole Lake along the way. Finally, just when you think you can climb no farther, you reach the pass, at five miles. A sign announces your arrival in Kings Canyon Park, and extraordinary Sierra views surround you. You'll gaze at Bullfrog and Kearsage Lakes, University Peak, and Mount Gould.

Note that if you decide to turn this into an overnight trip and continue into the backcountry of Kings Canyon National Park, food storage regulations are in effect. The bears have smartened up to the old hang-the-food-in-the-tree routine, so bear-resistant canisters are required for all backpackers. Also, you must have a backpacking stove, because campfires are not permitted. Good camping and fishing is located 3.5 miles beyond the pass, at Charlotte Lake, but a one-night stay limit is in effect.

**User Groups:** Hikers, dogs, and horses. Dogs are allowed to Kearsage Pass, but not beyond it. No mountain bikes. No wheelchair facilities.

**Permits:** A free wilderness permit is required for overnight stays and is available from the Lone Pine/Mount Whitney Ranger Station. Quotas are in effect from May 1 to November 1; during this time, permits are also available in advance by phone, fax, or mail for a $5 per person reservation fee.

**Maps:** For a map, ask the U.S. Forest Service for Inyo National Forest or John Muir Wilderness. For a topographic map, ask the USGS for Kearsage Peak.

**Directions:** From Lone Pine, drive 15 miles north on U.S. 395 to Independence. Turn west on Market Street, which becomes Onion Valley Road. Drive 14 miles to the end of the road and the trailhead parking area.

**Contact:** Inyo National Forest, Mount Whitney Ranger Station, P.O. Box 8, Lone Pine, CA 93545, 760/876-6200, website: www.fs.fed.us/r5/inyo.

## 96 FLOWER AND MATLOCK LAKES
**6.4 mi / 3.5 hrs**

in the John Muir Wilderness in Inyo National Forest

Map 11.3, page 511

If you don't have the time or the energy for Kearsage Pass (see previous listing), the route to Flower Lake and Matlock Lake is a good second choice. Although it doesn't offer the astounding views that the pass has, it is still a stellar trip into dramatic granite country. Both lakes are deep blue waterways that draw in all the color of the Sierra sky. The trail climbs gradually from the trailhead, switchbacking along Independence Creek. You pass Little Pothole Lake at 1.5 miles and Gilbert Lake at 2.2 miles, reaching a junction for Matlock Lake at 2.5 miles. Continue straight for .1 mile to Flower Lake, then retrace your steps to the junction and head south for .7 mile to larger Matlock Lake. Pull out your camera and a picnic, and while away some time before returning to the trailhead.

**User Groups:** Hikers, dogs, and horses. No mountain bikes. No wheelchair facilities.

**Permits:** No permits are required. Parking and access are free.

**Maps:** For a map, ask the U.S. Forest Service for Inyo National Forest or John Muir Wilderness. For a topographic map, ask the USGS for Kearsage Peak.

**Directions:** From Lone Pine, drive 15 miles north on U.S. 395 to Independence. Turn west on Market Street, which becomes Onion Valley Road. Drive 14 miles to the end of the road and the trailhead parking area.

**Contact:** Inyo National Forest, Mount Whit-

ney Ranger Station, P.O. Box 8, Lone Pine, CA 93545, 760/876-6200, website: www.fs.fed.us/r5/inyo.

## 97 ROBINSON LAKE
**3.0 mi / 2.0 hrs**

in the John Muir Wilderness in Inyo National Forest

Map 11.3, page 511

The Robinson Lake Trail is best described as relentlessly steep but mercifully short. The hike is challenging in places due to the grade, loose surface, and relative obscurity of the trail, but the destination is superlative. In addition to beautiful Robinson Lake (at 10,500 feet), you get a close and personal view of 11,744-foot Independence Peak and an excellent wildflower display along Robinson Creek. Start at the trailhead by campsite No. 7 in Onion Valley Campground. Watch out for the overgrown vegetation that can sometimes hide the trail. Just climb, catch your breath, and climb some more. After a fairly punishing ascent, you'll reach the small, shallow lake in less than an hour. Campsites and picnicking sites are found in the sand on the lake's east side, or in the pine forest on the northwest side. Equally as pretty as the lake are the views from its shores of the valley below. Plan your trip for July to September; the trail is usually free of snow by midsummer. But whenever you go, watch your footing carefully. This trail is not maintained very often.

**User Groups:** Hikers, dogs, and horses. No mountain bikes. No wheelchair facilities.

**Permits:** No permits are required. Parking and access are free.

**Maps:** For a map, ask the U.S. Forest Service for Inyo National Forest or John Muir Wilderness. For a topographic map, ask the USGS for Kearsage Peak.

**Directions:** From Lone Pine, drive 15 miles north on U.S. 395 to Independence. Turn west on Market Street, which becomes Onion Valley Road. Drive 14 miles to the end of the road and the hikers parking area. Walk into Onion Valley Campground to find the trailhead, by site No. 7.

**Contact:** Inyo National Forest, Mount Whitney Ranger Station, P.O. Box 8, Lone Pine, CA 93545, 760/876-6200, website: www.fs.fed.us/r5/inyo.

## 98 MOUNT WHITNEY TRAIL
### 22.0 mi /
### 15.0 hrs or 2.0–3.0 days

**in the John Muir Wilderness**

**Map 11.3, page 511**

Mount Whitney, at 14,494 feet in elevation, is the highest peak in the contiguous United States and is also probably the most frequently climbed. It has become so well traveled that not only are quotas enforced for backpackers, but even day hikers must obtain a wilderness permit to hike the trail. And, yes, many people do hike the entire 22-mile trail in one day, ascending and descending more than a vertical mile along the way (6,131 feet in all), but it means a pre-dawn start and a grueling march. Many people who try this suffer from altitude sickness and never make it to the top; others make it but realize they would have had a lot more fun if they had divided the trip into two or even three days. So here's the smart way to hike Mount Whitney: Get your wilderness permit way in advance (see the permit information below), and plan your trip for a weekday, not a weekend. If possible, wait to make the climb until September or early October, when the crowds have thinned considerably. (August sees the highest trail usage.) Spend a couple days at high elevation before you set out on Mount Whitney Trail, and come prepared with sunglasses, sunscreen, good boots, and warm clothes for the summit. And here's our Good Samaritan tip: Bring extra food and water so you can give it out to less-fortunate hikers you meet along the trail. For more information on Mount Whitney Trail, see the trail notes for the Whitney Portal to Lake Thomas Edison (JMT/PCT) hike in this chapter.

**User Groups:** Hikers only. No dogs, horses, or mountain bikes. (Dogs are allowed on the first 6.2 miles of trail, but not beyond.) No wheelchair facilities.

**Permits:** A wilderness permit is required for both day hikers and backpackers. Quotas are in effect from May 1 to November 1 for both day hikers and backpackers; during this period, permits are available in advance by mail or fax. Permit applications are accepted from February 1 to February 28 for all dates during the quota period. The lottery begins on February 15. There is a $15 per person reservation fee. Any unreserved or cancelled permits for the quota period become available on a first-come, first-served basis. Contact the Mount Whitney Ranger Station for more information.

**Maps:** For a map, ask the U.S. Forest Service for Inyo National Forest or John Muir Wilderness. A Mount Whitney Zone map is available from Tom Harrison Maps. For topographic maps, ask the USGS for Mount Whitney and Mount Langley.

**Directions:** From Lone Pine on U.S. 395, drive west on Whitney Portal Road for 13 miles to the end of the road and the trailhead.

**Contact:** Inyo National Forest, Mount Whitney Ranger Station, P.O. Box 8, Lone Pine, CA 93545, 760/876-6200, website: www.fs.fed.us/r5/inyo.

## 99 WHITNEY PORTAL NATIONAL RECREATION TRAIL
### 4.0 mi one-way / 2.0 hrs

**in Inyo National Forest near Whitney Portal**

**Map 11.3, page 511**

Don't confuse this trail with Mount Whitney Trail, because except for their nearby trailheads, they have zero in common. Although if you try to hike Whitney Portal National Recreation Trail in both directions, instead of as a one-way downhill hike, you may find it feels darn nearly as demanding as Mount Whitney Trail, which climbs nearly 6,000 feet to the top of Mount Whitney. (Okay, maybe not quite that demanding.) The recreation trail begins at Whitney Portal (elevation 8,360 feet) and heads downhill through conifers and granite to Lone Pine Campground (elevation 5,640). The best thing about the route is that no matter how crowded it is at Whitney Portal, this trail gets surprisingly few hikers, especially after the first .5 mile, which skirts Whitney Portal Campground. You get to leave the multitudes behind as you walk downhill along Lone Pine Creek, among the good company of granite formations and big pines. Vistas are excellent along the way, including Mount Whitney to the west and the Alabama Hills and White Mountains to the east.

**User Groups:** Hikers, dogs, and horses. No mountain bikes. No wheelchair facilities.

**Permits:** No permits are required. Parking and access are free.

**Maps:** For a map, ask the U.S. Forest Service for Inyo National Forest. A Mount Whitney High Country map is available from Tom Harrison Maps. For a topographic map, ask the USGS for Mount Langley.

**Directions:** From Lone Pine on U.S. 395, drive west on Whitney Portal Road for 13 miles to the end of the road and the trailhead, located across from the fishing pond. You will need to leave a shuttle car or arrange a pickup at Lone Pine Campground, four miles downhill on Whitney Portal Road.

**Contact:** Inyo National Forest, Mount Whitney Ranger Station, P.O. Box 8, Lone Pine, CA 93545, 760/876-6200, website: www.fs.fed .us/r5/inyo.

## 100 MEYSAN LAKE
### 11.0 mi / 6.0 hrs or 2.0 days 🥾

**in the John Muir Wilderness near Mount Whitney**

Map 11.3, page 511

The Meysan Lake Trail is less popular than the neighboring trail to the top of Mount Whitney, but still, you should get your wilderness permit in advance or plan on day hiking. Better yet, plan your trip for late September and during the week. The trail to Meysan Lake is long, steep, hot, and dry—let's just say it's gru-

eling—but it leads to a beautiful alpine lake basin and provides spectacular views of granite walls. It also gives climbers access to climbing routes on Mount Mallory and Lone Pine Peak. The trail is parallel to Meysan Creek and is not well maintained, which makes it even more demanding. You reach a left fork for Grass Lake at 4.5 miles, where the first water is available. The right fork continues to Camp Lake and its beautiful meadow (at five miles). Elevation here is 11,200 feet. The trail from Camp Lake to Meysan Lake is rather sketchy. Head to the right of Camp Lake, cross the inlet stream, and watch for rock cairns marking the way up the steep, rocky slope. Meysan Lake is often still frozen as late as June, even though the trail can be as hot as an oven. Trailhead elevation is 7,900 feet; Meysan Lake is at 11,460 feet. No fires are allowed at Meysan Lake, so make sure your stove is packed.

**User Groups:** Hikers and dogs. No horses or mountain bikes. No wheelchair facilities.

**Permits:** A free wilderness permit is required for overnight stays and is available from the Lone Pine/Mount Whitney Ranger Station. Quotas are in effect from May 1 to November 1; during this time, permits are also available in advance by phone, fax, or mail for a $5 per person reservation fee.

**Maps:** For a map, ask the U.S. Forest Service for Inyo National Forest or John Muir Wilderness. A Mount Whitney Zone map is available from Tom Harrison Maps. For topographic maps, ask the USGS for Mount Whitney and Mount Langley.

**Directions:** From Lone Pine on U.S. 395, drive west on Whitney Portal Road for 12 miles to Whitney Portal Campground and the Meysan Lake trailhead. Park on the side of Whitney Portal Road by the camp and walk through the camp to reach the trailhead.

**Contact:** Inyo National Forest, Mount Whitney Ranger Station, P.O. Box 8, Lone Pine, CA 93545, 760/876-6200, website: www.fs.fed .us/r5/inyo.

## 101 LONE PINE LAKE

**5.8 mi / 3.0 hrs**

**in the John Muir Wilderness near Whitney Portal**

Map 11.3, page 511

The route to the top of Mount Whitney is so popular and so overcrowded that it has permits and quotas and regulations up the wazoo, but guess what? Sweet little Lone Pine Lake is just outside of the regulated Mount Whitney Zone, so you can hike to it anytime without dealing with any bureaucracy. It's a fun trip for people who have always dreamed of climbing Mount Whitney, because it follows the first three miles of the summit trail. While other people are trudging along carrying heavy backpacks, you're stepping lightly, with only a sandwich and a bottle of water in your day pack. The trail leads through Jeffrey pines and manzanita to the John Muir Wilderness border at one mile, then switchbacks uphill and opens up to views of the Alabama Hills far below. You'll cross Lone Pine Creek at 2.8 miles, then bear left at a junction to leave the main Mount Whitney Trail and head a few hundred yards to Lone Pine Lake. It's a sweet spot, and although privacy is rare, you have a greater chance of it after Labor Day and on a weekday. Who knows, you might just get so inspired that next time you'll come back and hike all the way to the summit.

**User Groups:** Hikers and dogs. No horses or mountain bikes. No wheelchair facilities.

**Permits:** No permits are required. Parking and access are free.

**Maps:** For a map, ask the U.S. Forest Service for Inyo National Forest or John Muir Wilderness. A Mount Whitney Zone map is available from Tom Harrison Maps. For topographic maps, ask the USGS for Mount Whitney and Mount Langley.

**Directions:** From Lone Pine on U.S. 395, drive west on Whitney Portal Road for 13 miles to the end of the road and the Mount Whitney trailhead.

**Contact:** Inyo National Forest, Mount Whit-

ney Ranger Station, P.O. Box 8, Lone Pine, CA 93545, 760/876-6200, website: www.fs.fed.us/r5/inyo.

## 102 WHITNEY PORTAL TO LAKE THOMAS EDISON (JMT/PCT)

**112.0 mi one-way / 11.0 days**

**from the trailhead parking area at Whitney Portal north to the trailhead parking area at Lake Thomas Edison**

Map 11.3, page 511

You can have a foothold in the sky with every step on John Muir Trail. This part of the trail is shared with the PCT and starts at practically the tip-top of North America—Mount Whitney—and takes you northward across a land of 12,000-foot passes and Ansel Adams-style panoramas.

From the trailhead at Whitney Portal, the hike climbs more than 6,100 feet over the course of 10 miles to reach the Whitney Summit, at 14,494 feet. That includes an ascent over 100 switchbacks (often snow covered) to top Wotan's Throne and reach Trail Crest (13,560 feet). Here you turn right and take Summit Trail. In the final stretch to the top, the ridge is cut by huge notch windows in the rock; you look through, and the bottom drops out more than 10,000 feet to the town of Lone Pine below, at an elevation of 3,800 feet. Finally you make it to the top and notice how the surrounding giant blocks of rock look as if they were sculpted with a giant hammer and chisel. From here, the entire Western Divide is visible, and to the north, rows of mountain peaks are lined up for miles to the horizon. Be sure to sign your name in the register, kept in a lightning-proof metal box. You may feel a bit dizzy from the altitude, but you'll know you're someplace very special.

The journey farther north is just as captivating. The route drops into Sequoia National Park, then climbs above timberline for almost a day's worth of hiking as it nears Forester Pass, 13,180 feet. It's not only the highest point on the PCT; it's the most dangerous section of trail on the entire route as well. The trail is narrow and steep, cut into a high vertical slab of rock, and is typically icy, with an iced-over snowfield near the top that's particularly treacherous. An ice ax is an absolute must—slip here, and you could fall thousands of feet.

Once through Forester, the trail heads onward into the John Muir Wilderness along Bubbs Creek, with great wildflowers at nearby Vidette Meadow. Then it's up and over Kearsage Pass (10,710 feet), and after a short drop, you're back climbing again, this time over Glen Pass (11,978 feet)—a spectacular, boulder-strewn ridge with great views to the north looking into Kings Canyon National Park. Just two miles from Glen Pass is Rae Lakes, a fantasy spot for camping (one-night limit), with pristine meadows, shoreline campsites, and lots of eager brook trout.

The JMT then heads through Kings Canyon National Park by following sparkling streams much of the way, finally climbing up and over Pinchot Pass (12,130 feet), then back down along the upper Kings River for a long, steady ascent over Mather Pass (12,100 feet). The wonders continue as you hike along Palisade Lakes, then down into LeConte Canyon, followed by an endless climb up to Muir Pass (11,965 feet). In early summer, snowfields are common here, and this can be difficult and trying, especially if your boots keep postholing through the snow. The country near Muir Pass is extremely stark—nothing but sculpted granite, ice, and a few small turquoise lakes—crowned by the stone Muir Hut at the pass, where hikers can duck in and hide for safety from sudden afternoon thunderstorms and lightning bolts.

The views astound many visitors as the trail drops into Evolution Valley. It's like a trip back to the beginning of time, where all is pure and primary, yet incredibly lush and beautiful. You finally leave Kings Canyon National Park, following the headwaters of the San Joaquin River into Sierra National Forest. After bottoming out at 7,890 feet, the trail rises steeply in switchback after switchback as it enters the John Muir Wilderness. Finally you top Selden Pass (10,900 feet), take in an incredible view (where the rows of surrounding mountaintops look like the Great Pyramids), then make the easy one-mile descent to Marie Lakes, a pretty campsite with excellent trout fishing near the lake's outlet.

The final push on this section of the JMT is climbing up Bear Mountain, then down a terrible, toe-jamming stretch to Mono Creek. Here you make a left turn and continue for two more miles until you come to Edison Lake, an excellent place to have a food stash waiting. (To continue north on the JMT/PCT, see the Lake Thomas Edison to Agnew Meadows hike in this chapter.)

Special Note: Crossing Mono Creek at the north fork can be dangerous during high-runoff conditions.

**User Groups:** Hikers and horses. No dogs or mountain bikes. No wheelchair facilities.

**Permits:** A wilderness permit is required for traveling through various wilderness and special-use areas the trail traverses. Contact the Inyo National Forest Supervisor's Office.

**Maps:** For a map, ask the U.S. Forest Service for Sierra National Forest, Inyo National Forest, and Sequoia National Forest. For topographic maps, ask the USGS for Mount Whitney, Mount Williamson, Kearsarge Peak, Mount Clarence King, Mount Pinchot, North Palisade, Mount Goddard, Mount Darwin, Mount Henry, Ward Mountain, Florence Lake, and Graveyard Peak.

**Directions:** To reach the Mount Whitney trailhead from Lone Pine and U.S. 395, head west on Whitney Portal Road for approximately 13 miles to Whitney Portal and the trailhead for the Mount Whitney Trail. To reach the Lake Thomas Edison trailhead from the town of Shaver Lake, drive north on Highway 168 for approximately 21 miles to the town of Lakeshore. Turn northeast onto Kaiser Pass Road/Forest Service 4S01. Kaiser Pass Road becomes Edison Lake Road at Mono Hot Springs. Drive another five miles north past town to the Vermillion Campground and parking area for backcountry hikers. The PCT begins near the east end of the lake.

**Contact:** Inyo National Forest, Mount Whitney Ranger Station, P.O. Box 8, Lone Pine, CA 93545, 760/876-6200 or 760/873-2400 (permits), website: www.fs.fed.us/r5/inyo; Sierra National Forest, High Sierra Ranger District, P.O. Box 559, Prather, CA 93651, 559/855-5360, website: www.fs.fed.us/r5/sierra; Sequoia National Forest, Cannell Meadow Ranger District, P.O. Box 9, Kernville, CA 93238, 760/376-3781, website: www.fs.fed.us/r5/sequoia.

## 103 COTTONWOOD LAKES
### 10.0–12.5 mi /
### 6.0 hrs or 2.0 days

**in the John Muir Wilderness south of Mount Whitney**

Map 11.3, page 511

Trailhead elevation is just over 10,000 feet here at Horseshoe Meadow, which makes this a wildly popular trailhead for climbing deeper into the backcountry. With the trailhead situated so high, you get a jump on the ascent; your four wheels do the work, instead of your two feet. An unusual feature of this hike is that it passes through two wilderness areas—first a small portion of the Golden Trout Wilderness and then the John Muir Wilderness. Cottonwood Creek accompanies you for much of the trip. The trail starts out in a sandy pine forest with a mellow grade. At 3.7 miles you reach a junction. Most hikers go left; the trail forms a loop around Cottonwood Lakes numbers one, two, and three. If you just want to see the closest lake and head back without making a loop, Cottonwood Lake number one is to the left, 1.5 miles from the junction. Your round-trip will be an even 10 miles. If you complete the whole loop, passing all three lakes, you'll travel 11.5 miles. But the most beautiful lakes by far are numbers four and five, worth an extra .5 mile of hiking beyond the far end of the loop. Total elevation gain is only 1,000 feet. Once at the lakes, remember a few points: 1) Because the Cotton-

wood Lakes are home to golden trout, special fishing regulations are in effect, so get updated on the latest rules. 2) No wood fires are allowed, so bring your backpacking stove. 3) The wildflowers are spectacular, but the mosquitoes can be voracious; come prepared.

**User Groups:** Hikers, dogs, and horses. No mountain bikes. No wheelchair facilities.

**Permits:** A free wilderness permit is required for overnight stays and is available from the Mount Whitney Ranger Station. Quotas are in effect from May 1 to November 1; during this time, permits are also available in advance by phone, fax, or mail for a $5 per person reservation fee.

**Maps:** For a map, ask the U.S. Forest Service for Inyo National Forest or John Muir Wilderness. For a topographic map, ask the USGS for Cirque Peak.

**Directions:** From Lone Pine on U.S. 395, drive west on Whitney Portal Road for 3.3 miles and turn left (south) on Horseshoe Meadow Road. Continue 19.5 miles and bear right for the Cottonwood Lakes trailhead parking area, near the end of Horseshoe Meadow Road.

**Contact:** Inyo National Forest, Mount Whitney Ranger Station, P.O. Box 8, Lone Pine, CA 93545, 760/876-6200, website: www.fs.fed.us/r5/inyo.

## 104 COTTONWOOD PASS
### 8.0 mi / 5.0 hrs or 2.0 days

**in the Golden Trout Wilderness**

Map 11.3, page 511

The Cottonwood Pass Trail provides access to the Pacific Crest Trail and the Kern Plateau, a land of stark, subalpine meadows. You're entering the Golden Trout Wilderness, home of California's state fish and located at the very south end of the Sierra Nevada. This is where the steep, nearly perpendicular mountains start to mellow out into more gentle terrain—mostly in the form of rolling high-country hills and meadows. Start from wide Horseshoe Meadow and climb gently through forest for the first two miles of trail. Shortly, the switchbacks begin and the ascent becomes serious. After an 1,100-foot climb, you reach the pass (at four miles), where you can gaze out at the Great Western Divide, Big Whitney Meadows, and the Inyo Mountains. Bring a jacket with you for the windy, 11,250-foot summit. Ambitious hikers can continue beyond the pass and take the right fork for Chicken Spring Lake, one mile away on the Pacific Crest Trail (no campfires allowed).

**User Groups:** Hikers, dogs, and horses. No mountain bikes. No wheelchair facilities.

**Permits:** A free wilderness permit is required for overnight stays and is available from the Mount Whitney Ranger Station. Quotas are in effect from May 1 to November 1; during this time, permits are also available in advance by phone, fax, or mail for a $5 per person reservation fee.

**Maps:** For a map, ask the U.S. Forest Service for Inyo National Forest or Golden Trout Wilderness. For a topographic map, ask the USGS for Cirque Peak.

**Directions:** From Lone Pine on U.S. 395, drive west on Whitney Portal Road for 3.3 miles and turn left (south) on Horseshoe Meadow Road. Continue 19.5 miles to the Horseshoe Meadow trailhead, on the left, at the end of Horseshoe Meadow Road.

**Contact:** Inyo National Forest, Mount Whitney Ranger Station, P.O. Box 8, Lone Pine, CA 93545, 760/876-6200, website: www.fs.fed.us/r5/inyo.

## 105 TRAIL PASS
5.0 mi / 3.0 hrs

in the Golden Trout Wilderness

Map 11.3, page 511

Trail Pass may not be as spectacular as the other trails at Horseshoe Meadow, but it has two things going for it—far fewer people and an easier grade. It's only five miles round-trip from the trailhead to the pass, with a mere 500-foot elevation gain, unheard of in these parts. The main folks using the trail are back-packers accessing the Pacific Crest Trail and Golden Trout Wilderness, so a lot of the time, you can have this gently rolling, high-country terrain all to yourself. Follow the trail from the parking area to a junction .25 mile in, and bear left. In another .5 mile, the trail forks, and you bear right for Trail Pass. Pass by Horseshoe Meadow and Round Valley, where you'll have the company of many packhorses. Views are good of Mount Langley and Cirque Peak. The pass is situated at 10,500 feet, just below Trail Peak (at 11,600 feet).

**User Groups:** Hikers, dogs, and horses. No mountain bikes. No wheelchair facilities.

**Permits:** No permits are required. Parking and access are free.

**Maps:** For a map, ask the U.S. Forest Service for Inyo National Forest or Golden Trout Wilderness. For a topographic map, ask the USGS for Cirque Peak.

**Directions:** From Lone Pine on U.S. 395, drive west on Whitney Portal Road for 3.3 miles and turn left (south) on Horseshoe Meadow Road. Continue 19.5 miles to the Horseshoe Meadow trailhead, on the right, at the end of Horseshoe Meadow Road.

**Contact:** Inyo National Forest, Mount Whitney Ranger Station, P.O. Box 8, Lone Pine, CA 93545, 760/876-6200, website: www.fs.fed.us/r5/inyo.

## 106 CASA VIEJA MEADOW
4.0 mi / 2.0 hrs

in the Golden Trout Wilderness

Map 11.3, page 511

The Blackrock Mountain trailhead, at 8,800 feet, is the jump-off point for a variety of backpacking trips into the Golden Trout Wilderness. But day hikers can also sample the delights of this large, waterway-filled land, the home of California's state fish, the golden trout. From the end of Blackrock Road, walk for less than .25 mile to the wilderness boundary, then head gently downhill through a red fir forest to the western edge of Casa

Vieja Meadow. There you'll find a snow survey cabin and a wide expanse of grass and wildflowers. Hope your day pack is full of picnic supplies. At the far end of the meadow, you must ford Ninemile Creek to continue hiking farther, so make this your turnaround point. Some people try their luck fishing here. You'll have a gradual 800-foot elevation gain on your return trip.

**User Groups:** Hikers, dogs, and horses. No mountain bikes. No wheelchair facilities.

**Permits:** No permits are required. Parking and access are free.

**Maps:** Sequoia National Forest, Inyo National Forest, or Golden Trout Wilderness. For a topographic map, ask the USGS for Casa Vieja Meadows.

**Directions:** From Kernville on the north end of Isabella Lake, drive north on Sierra Way/Road 99 for 22 miles to the turnoff for Sherman Pass Road/22S05. Turn right and drive approximately 35 miles on Sherman Pass Road to the Blackrock Information Station; continue straight on Road 21S03/Blackrock Road. Follow Road 21S03 north for eight miles to the end of the road and the Blackrock Mountain trailhead.

**Contact:** Sequoia National Forest, Cannell Meadow Ranger District, P.O. Box 9, Kernville, CA 93238, 760/376-3781, website: www.fs.fed.us/r5/sequoia; Inyo National Forest, Mount Whitney Ranger Station, P.O. Box 8, Lone Pine, CA 93545, 760/876-6200, website: www.fs.fed.us/r5/inyo.

## 107 JORDAN HOT SPRINGS
**12.0 mi / 7.0 hrs or 2.0 days** 🥾 ⬅9

**in the Golden Trout Wilderness**

Map 11.3, page 511

You can do it in a day if you're ambitious, or you can take a more leisurely two-day trip to Jordan Hot Springs. But however you do it, it's critical to remember that almost all the work is on the way home. The trail is a descent (sometimes knee-jarring) to the grounds of an old hot springs resort, which was closed when this area became part of the Golden Trout Wilderness. The original buildings still stand, and the hot springs are still hot, which is the reason that this is one of the most popular trips in the wilderness. From the trailhead, take Blackrock Trail for two miles to Casa Vieja Meadow (see previous listing), then cross Ninemile Creek and turn left (west) on Jordan Hot Springs Trail. Hike another three miles downhill along Ninemile Creek, crossing it a few more times. Once you reach the old resort, have a good soak and pull your energy together, because you've got a 2,600-foot gain on the return trip.

**User Groups:** Hikers, dogs, and horses. No mountain bikes. No wheelchair facilities.

**Permits:** A free wilderness permit is required for overnight stays and is available from the Cannell Meadow Ranger Station. Parking and access are free.

**Maps:** Sequoia National Forest, Inyo National Forest, or Golden Trout Wilderness. For a topographic map, ask the USGS for Casa Vieja Meadows.

**Directions:** From Kernville on the north end of Isabella Lake, drive north on Sierra Way/Road 99 for 22 miles to the right turnoff for Sherman Pass Road/22S05. Turn right and drive approximately 35 miles on Sherman Pass Road to the Blackrock Information Station; continue straight on Road 21S03/Blackrock Road. Follow Road 21S03 north for eight miles to the end of the road and the Blackrock Mountain trailhead.

**Contact:** Sequoia National Forest, Cannell Meadow Ranger District, P.O. Box 9, Kernville, CA 93238, 760/376-3781, website: www.fs.fed.us/r5/sequoia.

## 108 NORTH FORK KERN RIVER TRAIL
**10.4 mi / 5.0 hrs or 2.0 days** 🥾 ⬅8

**in Sequoia National Forest north of Kernville**

Map 11.4, page 512

Sometimes you just want to walk alongside a beautiful river, and if that's what you're in the mood for, the Wild and Scenic North Fork Kern is a first-rate choice. From the giant parking lot, walk across the hikers' bridge (separate from but next to the highway bridge) to reach the far side of the river, and then descend on stairs to reach the trail. The North Fork Kern River Trail winds along gently, heading deep into the dramatic Kern Canyon—sometimes under the shade of digger pines, live oaks, and incense cedars, and sometimes out in the bright sunshine. Spring wildflowers are stunning, especially in March and April. Spring river rafters are also entertaining to watch. Most people who walk this trail bring a fishing rod with them, and if you do, make sure you're up-to-date on the special fishing regulations. They're in effect for the first four miles of river, which is a wild trout area. Backpackers will find many campsites along the trail, including some that are under the cavelike canopy of big boulders. This easy, mellow trail offers something for everyone. Note that if you venture out here at the height of spring runoff, parts of the trail may be submerged.

**User Groups:** Hikers, dogs, and mountain bikes. No horses. No wheelchair facilities.

**Permits:** A free campfire permit is required for overnight stays and is available from the Springville or Kernville Ranger Stations at the addresses below. Parking and access are free.

**Maps:** For a map, ask the U.S. Forest Service for Sequoia National Forest. For a topographic map, ask the USGS for Fairview.

**Directions:** From Kernville on the north end of Lake Isabella, drive north on Sierra Way/Road 99 for 22 miles to the Johnsondale highway bridge over the Kern River. Turn right and park in the large paved parking lot by the signboard at the bridge.

**Contact:** Sequoia National Forest, Cannell Meadow Ranger District, P.O. Box 9, Kernville, CA 93238, 760/376-3781, website: www.fs.fed .us/r5/sequoia; Tule River Ranger District, 32588 Highway 190, Springville, CA 93265, 559/539-2607, website: www.fs.fed.us/r5/sequoia.

## 109 SHERMAN PEAK TRAIL
### 4.0 mi / 2.0 hrs

**in Sequoia National Forest near Sherman Pass**

Map 11.4, page 512

From the Sherman Pass Vista along the highway, you can look to the north to Mount Whitney and the Great Western Divide. After crossing the highway and hiking Sherman Peak Trail to the top of Sherman Peak (at 9,909 feet), you can pivot around and have a panoramic look at an even bigger chunk of the world. The trail is mostly forested with red firs and pines, and is gradual enough for children to climb. If you read the interpretive display at the vista, you'll be able to identify the myriad mountains you're looking at from the peak, including Split Rock and Dome Rock. It's only a 700-foot climb to the summit, mostly through a series of easy switchbacks.

**User Groups:** Hikers, dogs, horses, and mountain bikes. No wheelchair facilities.

**Permits:** No permits are required. Parking and access are free.

**Maps:** For a map, ask the U.S. Forest Service for Sequoia National Forest. For topographic maps, ask the USGS for Durrwood Creek and Sirretta Peak.

**Directions:** From Kernville on the north end of Lake Isabella, drive north on Sierra Way/Road 99 for 22 miles to the right turnoff for Sherman Pass Road/22S05. Turn right and drive approximately 15 miles on Sherman Pass Road to the Sherman Pass Vista. The trailhead is across the road.

**Contact:** Sequoia National Forest, Cannell Meadow Ranger District, P.O. Box 9, Kernville, CA 93238, 760/376-3781, website: www.fs.fed .us/r5/sequoia.

## 110 BALD MOUNTAIN LOOKOUT
### 0.25 mi / 0.25 hr

**in Sequoia National Forest on the north edge of the Dome Land Wilderness**

Map 11.4, page 512

This short hike to the summit of 9,382-foot Bald Mountain is the easiest possible introduction to the Dome Land Wilderness. It's a brief stroll to the lookout, which is perched on the very northern edge of the wilderness. This region is famous for its many granite domes and monolithic rocks—the happy hunting ground of rock climbers from all over Southern California. Of the many big hunks of rock, Church Dome is perhaps the most outstanding, and it can be seen from here directly to the south. White Dome and Black Mountain are also visible (east of Church Dome), as well as a sweeping vista of the Kern Plateau, the Whitney Range, and the Great Western Divide.

**User Groups:** Hikers, dogs, horses, and mountain bikes. No wheelchair facilities.

**Permits:** No permits are required. Parking and access are free.

**Maps:** For a map, ask the U.S. Forest Service for Sequoia National Forest or Dome Land Wilderness. For a topographic map, ask the USGS for Crag Peak.

**Directions:** From Kernville on the north end of Lake Isabella, drive north on Sierra Way/Road 99 for 22 miles to the right turnoff for Sherman Pass Road/22S05. Turn right and drive approximately 25 miles on Sherman Pass Road to Forest Service Road 22S77, signed for Bald Mountain Lookout. Turn east (right) on Road 22S77 and follow it for one mile to its end.

**Contact:** Sequoia National Forest, Cannell Meadow Ranger District, P.O. Box 9, Kernville, CA 93238, 760/376-3781, website: www.fs.fed .us/r5/sequoia.

## 111 JACKASS CREEK NATIONAL RECREATION TRAIL

**5.0 mi / 2.5 hrs**

in Sequoia National Forest near the South Sierra Wilderness

Map 11.4, page 512

The Jackass Creek Trail is way out there on the Kern Plateau, at a trailhead elevation of 8,000 feet. The trail climbs 5.5 miles to Jackass Peak (elevation 9,245 feet) on the border of the South Sierra Wilderness. Most people don't bother traveling that far; instead, they follow the trail along Jackass Creek for a couple of miles through red fir forest to the western edge of Jackass Meadow. In addition to the beautiful meadow, the trail offers a look at many handsome old-growth aspens. The trail is an old dirt road, wide enough for holding hands with your hiking partner. Unfortunately, it's also wide enough for motorcycles, which are allowed here. Our recommendation? Hike this trail in late September or early October for the best show of autumn colors, and for the best chance at having the trail to yourself. If you drive all the way out here and see a parking lot full of motorcycle trailers, try hiking the nearby Hooker Meadow Trail instead (the trailhead is at the end of Road 21S29, just east of Fish Creek Campground). The machines aren't allowed there, and this trail also leads to an outstanding grove of quaking aspens.

**User Groups:** Hikers, dogs, horses, and mountain bikes. No wheelchair facilities.

**Permits:** No permits are required. Parking and access are free.

**Maps:** For a map, ask the U.S. Forest Service for Sequoia National Forest. For a topographic map, ask the USGS for Crag Peak.

**Directions:** From Kernville on the north end of Lake Isabella, drive north on Sierra Way/Road 99 for 22 miles to the right turnoff for Sherman Pass Road/22S05. Turn right and drive approximately 35 miles on Sherman Pass Road to the four-way intersection with Road 21S03, near Blackrock Information Station. Turn right to continue on Road 22S05, and drive five miles to Fish Creek Campground and Road 21S01, where the trail begins.

**Contact:** Sequoia National Forest, Cannell Meadow Ranger District, P.O. Box 9, Kernville, CA 93238, 760/376-3781, website: www.fs.fed .us/r5/sequoia.

## 112 WHISKEY FLAT TRAIL
### 5.0 mi / 2.5 hrs

**in Sequoia National Forest near Fairview**

**Map 11.4, page 512**

The Whiskey Flat Trail is a 14.5-mile trail that parallels the Kern River from Fairview Lodge all the way south to Burlando Road in Kernville. Primarily used by anglers working the Kern River, it's also a good springtime stroll for river lovers. If you walk out and back for a few miles on the northern end of the trail by Fairview, you can end the day with a meal at Fairview Lodge's restaurant, where you can brag about the fish you did or didn't catch, like everybody else there. The Whiskey Flat Trail can be somewhat difficult to follow, especially in springtime, when the numerous creeks you must cross are running full. Early in the year, the creeks can sometimes be impassable. The path begins on a suspension bridge, which is reminiscent of Huck Finn and his friends. You can hike as far as you please; a good distance is 2.5 miles out, or about an hour's walk each way. The terrain is grasslands and chaparral, with occasional digger pines, which means no shade but plenty of spring wildflowers. Although the route is basically level, there are numerous steep stretches where you climb in and out of stream drainages running into the Kern. The trailhead elevation is 2,800 feet.

**User Groups:** Hikers, dogs, horses, and mountain bikes. No wheelchair facilities.

**Permits:** No permits are required. Parking and access are free.

**Maps:** For a map, ask the U.S. Forest Service for Sequoia National Forest. For a topographic map, ask the USGS for Fairview.

**Directions:** From Kernville on the north end of Lake Isabella, drive north on Sierra Way/Road 99 for 17 miles to Fairview and the Fairview Lodge, on the left side of the road. To the right of the lodge is a large parking area and a trailhead for the Whiskey Flat Trail.

**Contact:** Sequoia National Forest, Cannell Meadow Ranger District, P.O. Box 9, Kernville, CA 93238, 760/376-3781, website: www.fs.fed .us/r5/sequoia.

## 113 PACKSADDLE CAVE TRAIL
### 4.6 mi / 2.3 hrs

**in Sequoia National Forest near Fairview**

**Map 11.4, page 512**

Everybody enjoys the trip to Packsaddle Cave, even though the cave was long ago vandalized of its jewel-like stalactites and stalagmites. Nonetheless, the appeal of visiting the limestone cave keeps this trail well used and fairly well maintained. From the parking lot on Sierra Way, cross the highway and hike uphill on the path, huffing and puffing through some steep pitches. This is not a trail for summertime, because there is little shade among the manzanita, sagebrush, and deer brush, and the total climb is about 1,200 feet. At 1.8 miles, you cross Packsaddle Creek and see several campsites near it. Continue a short distance farther; the cave is off to the left, .25 mile before this trail's junction with Rincon Trail. Don't forget your flashlight so you can take a peek inside.

**User Groups:** Hikers, dogs, horses, and mountain bikes. No wheelchair facilities.

**Permits:** No permits are required. Parking and access are free.

**Maps:** For a map, ask the U.S. Forest Service for Sequoia National Forest. For a topographic map, ask the USGS for Fairview.

**Directions:** From Kernville on the north end of Lake Isabella, drive north on Sierra Way/Road 99 for 18 miles to the Packsaddle Cave trailhead, on the right, .25 mile beyond Fairview Campground. The parking area is across the road.

**Contact:** Sequoia National Forest, Cannell Meadow Ranger District, P.O. Box 9, Kernville, CA 93238, 760/376-3781, website: www.fs.fed .us/r5/sequoia.

## 114 RINCON TRAIL
### 4.0 mi / 2.0 hrs

**in Sequoia National Forest near Fairview**

Map 11.4, page 512

Let's say right away that this Rincon has absolutely nothing in common with the other Rincon, the classic surfing break on the Ventura coast. For one, there's no water here, and two, there's no cool ocean breeze. That means you should plan your hike for winter or spring, before the Kern Valley heats up. The trail leads first east and then steadily north along the Rincon Fault, heading for Forks of the Kern. It undulates, following the drainages of Salmon and other creeks. The destination on this trail is the long-distance view of Salmon Creek Falls, about two miles in, and the good fishing and camping prospects on the way along Salmon Creek. The trail crosses Salmon Creek on a bridge 1.7 miles in, but the waterfall view is about .25 mile farther. You might want to bring your binoculars to get a good look. If you wish to hike farther on Rincon Trail, it intersects the route to Packsaddle Cave in another two miles, then crosses Sherman Pass Road in another 2.5 miles, and keeps going straight north all the way to Forks of the Kern. The total one-way trail length is a whopping 19.5 miles. Be forewarned that Rincon Trail is popular with motorcycle enthusiasts, so your peaceful nature experience may be shattered by their noise.

**User Groups:** Hikers, dogs, and mountain bikes. No horses. No wheelchair facilities.

**Permits:** No permits are required. Parking and access are free.

**Maps:** For a map, ask the U.S. Forest Service for Sequoia National Forest. For a topographic map, ask the USGS for Kernville.

**Directions:** From Kernville on the north end of Isabella Lake, drive north on Sierra Way/Road 99 for 13 miles to the Rincon trailhead, on the right, across from the Ant Canyon dispersed camping area.

**Contact:** Sequoia National Forest, Cannell Meadow Ranger District, P.O. Box 9, Kernville, CA 93238, 760/376-3781, website: www.fs.fed.us/r5/sequoia.

## 115 SUNDAY PEAK TRAIL
### 3.4 mi / 2.0 hrs

**in Sequoia National Forest near Wofford Heights**

Map 11.4, page 512

From the Sunday Peak trailhead, at 7,200 feet in the Greenhorn Mountains, it's a 1,000-foot climb to the top of Sunday Peak, an excellent day hike for families. The grade is moderate and shaded by big conifers, and the destination is perfect on a day when the heat is sweltering down near Isabella Lake. From the top, you can look down at the Kern River Valley and feel sorry for all those people sweating it out down there. Although the peak's fire lookout tower was abandoned and then destroyed by the forest service in the 1950s, the wide-angle views remain—of the Kern Valley, Kern Plateau, and far-off high Sierra peaks. There are many good picnicking spots on the summit.

**User Groups:** Hikers, dogs, horses, and mountain bikes. No wheelchair facilities.

**Permits:** No permits are required. Parking and access are free.

**Maps:** For a map, ask the U.S. Forest Service for Sequoia National Forest. For a topographic map, ask the USGS for Posey.

**Directions:** From Wofford Heights on the west side of Isabella Lake, turn west on Highway 155 and drive eight miles to Greenhorn Summit. Turn right on Road 24S15/Forest Highway 90, signed for Portuguese Pass, and drive 6.5 miles north to the parking area for Sunday Peak Trail, near the Girl Scout Camp.

**Contact:** Sequoia National Forest, Greenhorn Ranger District, c/o Isabella Lake Visitors Center, P.O. Box 3810, Lake Isabella, CA 93240, 760/379-5646, website: www.fs.fed.us/r5/sequoia.

## 116 UNAL TRAIL
3.0 mi / 1.5 hrs

in Sequoia National Forest near
Wofford Heights

Map 11.4, page 512

This is a first-rate trail for families or for anybody who wants a good leg-stretching walk or run around a beautiful mountain. The Unal Trail is a three-mile loop that climbs gently for two miles to Unal Peak, and then descends in one mile of switchbacks back to the trailhead. (After the first 100 yards, where the trail forks, be sure you take the left fork and hike the trail clockwise.) The trail passes a Native American cultural site on the return of the loop, the homestead of the Tubatulabal Indians. With only a 700-foot climb and an excellent grade, even mountain bikers can manage this trail, although few bother with it. You'll likely see some deer on the hillsides, and the view from the top of Unal Peak makes the whole world seem peaceful and serene. Although most of the trail is lined with conifers, the top of the loop is a little exposed and catches a strong breeze.

**User Groups:** Hikers, dogs, horses, and mountain bikes. No wheelchair facilities.

**Permits:** No permits are required. Parking and access are free.

**Maps:** For a map, ask the U.S. Forest Service for Sequoia National Forest. For a topographic map, ask the USGS for Posey.

**Directions:** From Wofford Heights on the west side of Lake Isabella, turn west on Highway 155 and drive eight miles to Greenhorn Summit. Turn left at the sign for Shirley Ski Meadows and drive 100 yards to the Greenhorn Fire Station and Unal trailhead, on the right side of the road.

**Contact:** Sequoia National Forest, Greenhorn Ranger District, c/o Isabella Lake Visitors Center, P.O. Box 3810, Lake Isabella, CA 93240, 760/379-5646, website: www.fs.fed.us/r5/sequoia.

## 117 CANNELL MEADOW NATIONAL RECREATION TRAIL
24.0 mi / 3.0 days

in Sequoia National Forest north of Kernville

Map 11.4, page 512

The Cannell Meadow National Recreation Trail is the first trailhead you reach out of Kernville, and if it's summertime, you should start at the other end of this 12-mile trail. That's because the Kernville end is at 2,800 feet, set in rocky chaparral and digger pine country, and, baby, it's hot out here. Still, if you can time your trip for late winter or spring, hiking this end of Cannell Trail is a great adventure, watching the terrain and environment change as the elevation rises. The shadeless trail climbs right away, through sage and occasional live oaks, affording views of the Kern River Valley. The trail gets more and more steep as you near conifer country at Pine Flat, but then you also get some blessed shade. It crosses Cannell Creek twice and reaches the Cannell Meadow Forest Service Cabin, a log cabin that was built in 1904. Cannell Meadow is a beautiful spot on the western edge of the Kern Plateau, edged by Jeffrey and lodgepole pines. Elevation is 7,500 feet, which means a total climb of 4,700 feet. Spread it out over a few days.

**User Groups:** Hikers, dogs, horses, and mountain bikes. No wheelchair facilities.

**Permits:** A free campfire permit is required for overnight stays and is available from the Kernville Ranger Station. Parking and access are free.

**Maps:** For a map, ask the U.S. Forest Service for Sequoia National Forest. For a topographic map, ask the USGS for Kernville.

**Directions:** From Kernville on the north end of Isabella Lake, drive north on Sierra Way/Road 99 for 1.4 miles to the Cannell Meadow trailhead, on the right. Parking is available near the horse corrals.

**Contact:** Sequoia National Forest, Cannell Meadow Ranger District, P.O. Box 9, Kernville, CA 93238, 760/376-3781, website: www.fs.fed.us/r5/sequoia.

## 118 SALMON CREEK FALLS
### 8.0 mi / 4.0 hrs or 2.0 days

**in Sequoia National Forest near Big Meadow**

**Map 11.4, page 512**

The eight-mile round-trip to the brink of Salmon Creek Falls is a stellar walk through lodgepole pines and white fir, with a chance for fishing, skinny-dipping, and admiring a lot of beautiful scenery at 7,600 feet in elevation. Since there are campsites located along the trail, it's easy enough to turn the trip into an overnight excursion, but the trail also makes a good long day hike. The trail is downhill all the way, dropping 600 feet over .5 mile, and follows granite-lined Salmon Creek. After skirting the edge of Horse Meadow, you simply follow the creek's meander. Trails run on both sides of the stream for the first two miles, so you can walk either side, but then they join as one. The path comes to an end above Salmon Creek Falls, where you can swim, fish, and camp, but don't expect to gaze out at the big waterfall—there's no way to get a good look at it from here, since you're perched on top of it.

**User Groups:** Hikers, dogs, horses, and mountain bikes. No wheelchair facilities.

**Permits:** A free campfire permit is required for overnight stays and is available from the Springville or Kernville Ranger Stations at the addresses below. Parking and access are free.

**Maps:** For a map, ask the U.S. Forest Service for Sequoia National Forest. For topographic maps, ask the USGS for Sirretta Peak and Fairview.

**Directions:** From Kernville on the north end of Isabella Lake, drive north on Sierra Way/Road 99 for 22 miles to the right turnoff for Sherman Pass Road/22S05. Turn right and drive 6.1 miles on Sherman Pass Road, then turn right on Road 22S12, signed for Horse Meadow Campground. Drive 6.3 miles on Road 22S12 until you reach a fork. Stay straight. At eight miles, bear left. At 9.3 miles, turn right at the Horse Meadow Campground sign (Road 23S10). You'll reach the camp at 10.7

miles, but take the right turnoff just before the camp to reach the trailhead.

**Contact:** Sequoia National Forest, Cannell Meadow Ranger District, P.O. Box 9, Kernville, CA 93238, 760/376-3781, website: www.fs.fed .us/r5/sequoia; Tule River Ranger District, 32588 Highway 190, Springville, CA 93265, 559/539-2607, website: www.fs.fed.us/r5/sequoia.

## 119 SIRRETTA PEAK
### 8.0 mi / 5.0 hrs

**near the Dome Land Wilderness**

**Map 11.4, page 512**

Hey, what's that big meadow down there? It's Big Meadow, of course—that huge expanse of green you see from the top of Sirretta Peak. From Sirretta's summit, you get an eyeful of it, as well as long, lingering glances at the many granite domes of the Dome Land Wilderness Area, Sirretta and Deadwood Meadows, and the peaks of the High Sierra. The route to the peak starts at Big Meadow's northern edge, then travels north on Cannell Trail for .5 mile. Bear right (northeast) at the fork with Sirretta Peak Trail and climb 2.5 miles to a spur trail that leads to the summit. There are many switchbacks and plenty of fine views along the way. Take the left spur (it's obvious) for .5 mile to the rocky summit, and congratulate yourself on your fine mountaineering skills. The trail has an elevation gain of 1,200 feet, and if you decide to make the final summit climb, you'll add on another 700 feet. Sirretta Peak is just shy of 10,000 feet in elevation.

**User Groups:** Hikers and dogs. No horses or mountain bikes. No wheelchair facilities.

**Permits:** No permits are required for day hiking. Parking and access are free.

**Maps:** For a map, ask the U.S. Forest Service for Sequoia National Forest. For a topographic map, ask the USGS for Sirretta Peak.

**Directions:** From Kernville on the north end of Isabella Lake, drive north on Sierra Way/Road 99 for 22 miles to the right turnoff for Sherman Pass Road/22S05. Turn right and drive 6.1 miles on Sherman Pass Road. Turn right on Road 22S12, signed for Horse Meadow Campground, and drive 6.3 miles on Road 22S12 until you reach a fork. Stay straight. At eight miles, bear left, staying on Road 22S12. Continue four more miles, passing the Horse Meadow Campground turnoff, to Road 23S07, at the northern edge of Big Meadow. Turn left on Road 23S07 and drive .5 mile to the Cannell trailhead.

**Contact:** Sequoia National Forest, Cannell Meadow Ranger District, P.O. Box 9, Kernville, CA 93238, 760/376-3781, website: www.fs.fed .us/r5/sequoia.

## 120 MANTER MEADOW LOOP
### 10.0 mi / 6.0 hrs

**in the Dome Land Wilderness**

Map 11.4, page 512

For people who love meadows, granite, and solitude, this loop trip is just about perfect. From the South Manter trailhead at 7,800 feet, the trail goes uphill for four miles to Manter Meadow, so bring your wildflower identification book and a map to identify surrounding peaks and domes. Along the way, several side trails branch off the main trail, leading to some of the granite domes of the Dome Land Wilderness, including spectacular Taylor Dome and Church Dome. A two-mile loop trail encircles the entire perimeter of the meadow, which you can add on to your trip if you wish. At the meadow's western edge, South Manter Trail meets North Manter Trail, and you follow the latter back to Forest Service Road 23S07 (the road you drove in on). Then it's a 1.5-mile walk on the dirt road back to your car. If you want to avoid the road, hike South Manter Trail both ways, and take the loop walk around the meadow. The mileage is about equal to the other trip.

**User Groups:** Hikers, dogs, and horses. No mountain bikes. No wheelchair facilities.

**Permits:** No permits are required. Parking and access are free.

**Maps:** For a map, ask the U.S. Forest Service for Sequoia National Forest or Dome Land Wilderness. For a topographic map, ask the USGS for Sirretta Peak.

**Directions:** From Kernville on the north end of Isabella Lake, drive north on Sierra Way/Road 99 for 22 miles to the right turnoff for Sherman Pass Road/22S05. Turn right and drive 6.1 miles on Sherman Pass Road. Turn right on Road 22S12, signed for Horse Meadow Campground, and drive 6.3 miles on Road 22S12 until you reach a fork. Stay straight. At eight miles, bear left, staying on Road 22S12. Continue four more miles, passing the Horse Meadow Campground turnoff, to Road 23S07 at the northern edge of Big Meadow. Turn left on Road 23S07 and drive three miles to the southeast edge of Big Meadow and the South Manter trailhead.

**Contact:** Sequoia National Forest, Cannell Meadow Ranger District, P.O. Box 9, Kernville, CA 93238, 760/376-3781, website: www.fs.fed .us/r5/sequoia.

## 121 ROCKHOUSE BASIN
### 4.0 mi / 2.0 hrs

**on the eastern side of the Dome Land Wilderness**

Map 11.4, page 512

You're driving along in no-man's-land on Highway 178 between U.S. 395 and Lake Isabella, staring at thousands of those odd-looking piñon pines. This is the transition zone between the Mojave Desert to the east and the Sierra Nevada to the west, and it doesn't look quite like either one of them. Want to see this strange land up close? This easy hike to Rockhouse Basin can take you there, and since it requires a long drive on dirt roads to reach the trailhead, you're likely to be free of the Eastern Sierra's hiking masses. A half mile from the trailhead, turn right and head north to Rockhouse Basin, where the noise of cicadas serenades you almost as loudly as the river. Explore the rocks, cool off in the river, and admire those piñon pines. It can be as hot as Hades out here, so plan your trip for early in the year, when you can hike along the Kern River in relative comfort.

**User Groups:** Hikers, dogs, and horses. No mountain bikes. No wheelchair facilities.

**Permits:** No permits are required. Parking and access are free.

**Maps:** For a map, ask the U.S. Forest Service for Sequoia National Forest or Dome Land Wilderness. For a topographic map, ask the USGS for Rockhouse Basin.

**Directions:** From the junction of Highway 14 and Highway 178 north of Mojave, drive west on Highway 178 for 18 miles to the right turnoff for Chimney Peak National Backcountry Byway, or Canebrake Road. Turn right and drive approximately nine miles.

Turn left (west) on Long Valley Loop Road and drive 14 miles to the gate at the start of Rockhouse Basin Trail. You can also reach the trailhead by taking Ninemile Canyon Road west for 11 miles from the Bureau of Land Management (BLM) administration site. Go past the BLM office, take the second dirt road on the left, and drive eight miles to the trailhead. (This road is much rougher.)

**Contact:** Bureau of Land Management, Ridgecrest Field Office, 300 South Richmond Road, Ridgecrest, CA 93555, 760/384-5400, website: www.ca.blm.gov/ridgecrest; Sequoia National Forest, Cannell Meadow Ranger District, P.O. Box 9, Kernville, CA 93238, 760/376-3781, website: www.fs.fed.us/r5/sequoia.

## Chapter 12

© ANN MARIE BROWN

# Death Valley

# Death Valley

The Death Valley region includes our largest national park outside of Alaska. The landscape in this part of California is dramatically different from anywhere else in the United States—and in fact, from most of the world.

Although its name is foreboding, Death Valley National Park comprises a vast region of desert beauty, from soaring sand dunes and mountain ranges to below-sea-level salt flats. In summer, the park is the hottest place in North America—over 120 degrees Fahrenheit is common—but in winter, temperatures are cool and mild.

Death Valley is home to the lowest point in elevation in the Western hemisphere: Badwater, at 282 feet below sea level. In stark contrast, it's also home to Telescope Peak, elevation 11,048 feet, which is snow-covered six months of the year. With a little effort, hikers can set foot in both places in the same day. In between these extremes are a wide range of ecological communities, from desert scrub to piñon and juniper woodlands. More than 900 plant species and 50 mammal species live in Death Valley. Hikers can choose from an amazing diversity of trails that lead to destinations such as 700-foot-high sand dunes, colorful badlands, towering rock walls, volcanic craters, old mining ruins, and even a waterfall in the desert.

Plan ahead before making a trip to the park. Because of its immense size, hikers need at least a few days to best experience it. The driving distance from one trailhead to another can take up half a day. Accommodations, services, and towns are few and far between. Only three lodgings are available within the massive park's borders, and only a few more are found within a wide surrounding area. Reservations are strongly advised.

MAP 12.1
page 591

MAP 12.2
page 592

MAP 12.3
page 593

Tonopah

N
W    E
S

Scotty's Junction

Eureka
Dunes

Scotty's
Castle

*Death*

Beatty

0        15 mi
0        15 km

*Valley*

Lone
Pine

Stovepipe
Wells

Furnace
Creek

*National*

Olancha

Death Valley
Junction

*Panamint Valley*

Telescope Pk.
11,049 ft

★ Badwater
-282 ft

NV
CA

*Park*

Shoshone

see
Sequoia and
Kings Canyon
page 508

Tecopa

Trona

Inyokern

Ridgecrest

see
The Southern
Deserts
page 724

Baker

*Mojave*

*National*

Mojave

*Preserve*

Four
Corners

© AVALON TRAVEL PUBLISHING, INC.

# Map 12.1

**Hikes 1–2**
**Page 594**

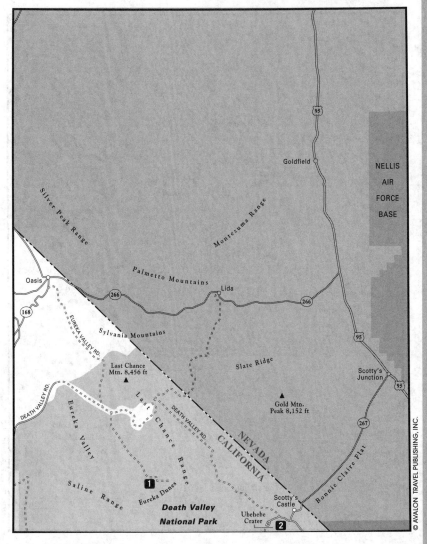

12.2

NELLIS

AIR

FORCE

BASE

Silver Peak Range

Goldfield

95

Montezuma Range

Palmetto Mountains

Oasis

266

Lida

266

168

EUREKA VALLEY RD

Sylvania Mountains

95

Slate Ridge

Scotty's
Junction

Last Chance
Mtn. 8,456 ft
▲

Gold Mtn.
Peak 8,152 ft
▲

95

DEATH VALLEY RD

DEATH VALLEY RD

Eureka
Valley

Last Chance Range

267

NEVADA

CALIFORNIA

Bonnie Claire Flat

Saline Range

Eureka Dunes

**1**

**Death Valley
National Park**

Scotty's
Castle

Ubehebe
Crater

**2**

© AVALON TRAVEL PUBLISHING, INC.

# Map 12.2

## Hikes 3–9
## Pages 595–599

# Map 12.3

**Hikes 10–16**
**Pages 599–602**

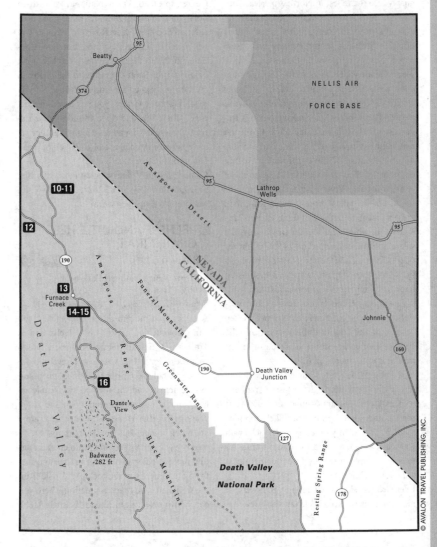

# ❶ EUREKA DUNES
## 2.0 mi / 1.0 hr

**in Death Valley National Park north of Scotty's Castle**

Map 12.1, page 591

It takes a heck of a lot of time and patience to drive to Eureka Dunes, but as soon as you see those giant icons of the desert, you'll know why you came. Eureka Dunes are the tallest sand dunes in California and are arguably also the tallest in North America. They rise nearly 700 feet from their base, creating a sandy, miniature mountain range that is home to several rare and endangered desert plants. Simply put, Eureka Dunes are a must-see in Death Valley. Hike to the top and snap a few pictures, and you'll go home with many weird and wonderful photographs of wind patterns on sand or your hiking partner traversing swirling dune ridge tops. From the trailhead, simply head for the clearly visible dunes. Because of the continually shifting desert sand, there is no marked trail, so make your own path. Your best bet is to climb to the top of the tallest dune you can find, then trace a ridgeline path from dune to dune. It's a strange, wonderful feeling to walk on the silky-soft sand crystals. And as you might expect, climbing the dunes is a slow proposition—take two steps forward, slide one step back, then repeat the process. Just take your time and enjoy the uniqueness of the experience. Also, be extremely careful not to step on any of the fragile dune vegetation—the Eureka Dunes are home to three different rare and endangered plants.

A few tips: Prepare yourself mentally and physically for the long drive to the trailhead (especially the bumpy 44-mile section on dirt roads), and you'll be far more likely to enjoy the trip. Take plenty of water and snacks with you for a long day. And most important: Attempt this adventure only when temperatures are cool in Death Valley.

**User Groups:** Hikers only. No dogs, horses, or mountain bikes. No wheelchair facilities.

**Permits:** No permits are required. There is a $10 entrance fee at Death Valley National Park, good for seven days.

**Maps:** Free park maps are available at park entrance stations or by contacting Death Valley National Park at the address below. A more detailed map is available from Tom Harrison Maps. For a topographic map, ask the USGS for Last Chance Range Southwest.

**Directions:** From the Furnace Creek Visitors Center, in Death Valley National Park, drive north on Highway 190 for 17 miles, then bear right on Scotty's Castle Road. In 32 miles you will pass the Grapevine entrance station. Continue northwest for three miles (keep left; don't bear right for Scotty's Castle) to the dirt road on the right signed for Eureka Dunes. (If you reach Ubehebe Crater, you've passed the dirt road.) Turn right and drive 44 miles to the Eureka Dunes parking area. A high-clearance vehicle is recommended; call to check on road conditions before heading out.

**Contact:** Death Valley National Park, P.O. Box 579, Death Valley, CA 92328, 760/786-3200, website: www.nps.gov/deva.

# ❷ UBEHEBE AND LITTLE HEBE CRATER TRAIL
## 1.0 mi / 0.5 hr

**in Death Valley National Park near Scotty's Castle**

Map 12.1, page 591

A walk along the rim of a not-so-ancient volcano is what you get on Little Hebe Crater Trail. The trail leads along Ubehebe Crater's southwest rim to Little Hebe and several older craters. Ubehebe Crater is 500 feet deep and .5 mile across, and was formed by volcanic activity that occurred between 1,000 and 2,000 years ago. Little Hebe and the other craters are much smaller but similar in appearance—mostly black and ash colored, with eroded walls that reveal a colorful blend of orange and rust from the minerals in the rock. At .5 mile from the trailhead, you reach a junction where you can continue straight ahead to Little Hebe

Crater or just loop all the way around Ube-hebe's rim. Take your pick—from the high rim of Ubehebe, it's easy to see where you're going, as well as down into the valley below, and far off to the Last Chance Range. Note that the trail surface is a mix of loose gravel and cin-ders, so it's a good idea to bring hiking boots or high-top shoes. A side note: Most visitors to Ubehebe Crater don't even bother with this trail. Instead, they just get out of their cars, make a beeline run for the bottom of the huge crater, and then moan and groan when they realize they have to make the steep climb back up. Go figure.

**User Groups:** Hikers only. No dogs, horses, or mountain bikes. No wheelchair facilities.

**Permits:** No permits are required. There is a $10 entrance fee at Death Valley National Park, good for seven days.

**Maps:** Free park maps are available at park entrance stations or by contacting Death Valley National Park at the address below. A more detailed map is available from Tom Harrison Maps. For a topographic map, ask the USGS for Ubehebe Crater.

**Directions:** From the Furnace Creek Visitors Center, in Death Valley National Park, drive north on Highway 190 for 17 miles, then bear right on Scotty's Castle Road. In 32 miles you will pass the Grapevine entrance station. Con-tinue northwest for five miles to the left turnoff to Ubehebe Crater.

**Contact:** Death Valley National Park, P.O. Box 579, Death Valley, CA 92328, 760/786-3200, website: www.nps.gov/deva.

## 🖪 FALL CANYON
### 5.6 mi / 3.0 hrs

**in Death Valley National Park near Scotty's Castle**

Map 12.2, page 592

Most park visitors take the one-way drive through Titus Canyon to see a desert canyon with giant alluvial fans and towering rock walls. But if you want to witness a similarly imposing desert scene on foot, take a hike in Titus Canyon's next-door neighbor, Fall Canyon. There is no formal trail, but the canyon walls keep you funneled in the right direction. From the parking area, hike to your left (north) on the unsigned trail. In .5 mile, you'll reach a wash, but its walls quickly nar-row, then later widen again, then repeat the process. A gravel surface makes the walking a bit strenuous. Scan the walls' colorful sur-faces as you walk, and you'll notice tiny arch formations and miniature caves and alcoves. At 2.8 miles, you are faced with a 20-foot dry fall, and this is where most hikers turn back. If you are experienced at rock scrambling, however, you can locate and follow a use trail on the canyon's south side to bypass the fall. After doing so, you'll enter a .5-mile-long, pol-ished narrows area, which many consider to be as beautiful as the narrows in Death Val-ley's Mosaic Canyon.

**User Groups:** Hikers only. No dogs, horses, or mountain bikes. No wheelchair facilities.

**Permits:** No permits are required. There is a $10 entrance fee at Death Valley National Park, good for seven days.

**Maps:** Free park maps are available at park entrance stations or by contacting Death Val-ley National Park at the address below. A more detailed map is available from Tom Harrison Maps. For a topographic map, ask the USGS for Ubehebe Crater.

**Directions:** From the Furnace Creek Visitors Center, in Death Valley National Park, drive north on Highway 190 for 17 miles, then bear right on Scotty's Castle Road. In 14 miles, turn right at the sign for Titus Canyon. Drive 2.7 miles to the parking area, just before Titus Canyon Road becomes a one-way road. Begin hiking to the left of Titus Canyon on a narrow, unsigned trail heading north.

**Contact:** Death Valley National Park, P.O. Box 579, Death Valley, CA 92328, 760/786-3200, website: www.nps.gov/deva.

## 4 UBEHEBE PEAK
### 6.0 mi / 3.0 hrs

**in Death Valley National Park**

Map 12.2, page 592

Are you prepared for a long drive and then a difficult hike? If you are, the rewards on this trip are great. The climb to Ubehebe Peak would be strenuous enough if you just accounted for the steep grade, but add in the fact that this is Death Valley, and the hike becomes a butt-kicker. The peak offers tremendous views of both the snowy Sierra Nevada and the desertlike Last Chance Range, as well as Racetrack and Saline Valleys. The trail is a narrow miners' route that switchbacks up and up and up, and you can be darn sure that you won't come across any shade on the way. There is no trail for the final .5 mile to the summit; most hikers content themselves with the view from the saddle below. (If you stop there, you won't miss out. The view is incredible, especially of the Grandstand rock formation far below, and the salt flats of the Saline Valley to the west.) Experienced climbers can make the final summit scramble. Total elevation gain is 1,900 feet; the summit is at 5,678 feet in elevation. Note: Before or after your trip, be sure to explore around the Racetrack area, where you can see the tracks of rocks that have slid along the surface of the mudflats, pushed by strong winds. To see them, drive about two miles south of this trailhead to the pullout and interpretive sign for the sliding rocks, then walk about a half mile out on the playa. Many a fine photograph has been shot of these fascinating rock tracks.

**User Groups:** Hikers only. No dogs, horses, or mountain bikes. No wheelchair facilities.

**Permits:** No permits are required. There is a $10 entrance fee at Death Valley National Park, good for seven days.

**Maps:** Free park maps are available at park entrance stations or by contacting Death Valley National Park at the address below. A more detailed map is available from Tom Harrison Maps. For a topographic map, ask the USGS for Ubehebe Peak.

**Directions:** From the Furnace Creek Visitors Center, in Death Valley National Park, drive north on Highway 190 for 17 miles, then bear right on Scotty's Castle Road. In 32 miles, you will pass the Grapevine entrance station, then continue northwest for 5.8 miles (keep left; don't bear right for Scotty's Castle). Turn right on the dirt road signed for Racetrack. Drive 20 miles on Racetrack Road. Bear right at Teakettle Junction and drive 5.9 miles to a pullout on the right side of the road, across from the large rock formation called the Grandstand. High-clearance vehicles are necessary on Racetrack Road.

**Contact:** Death Valley National Park, P.O. Box 579, Death Valley, CA 92328, 760/786-3200, website: www.nps.gov/deva.

## 5 MESQUITE FLAT SAND DUNES
### 3.0 mi / 1.0 hr

**in Death Valley National Park near Stovepipe Wells**

Map 12.2, page 592

Nothing makes a better introduction to Death Valley than a visit to the 80-foot-high Mesquite Flat sand dunes, near Stovepipe Wells. No, these aren't the giant sand dunes that Death Valley is famous for; those are the Eureka Dunes. But if you've just driven into the park, this hike will convince your senses that you're really in Death Valley, a place like no place else. There is no marked trail because of the continually shifting desert sands, so you just make a beeline from the roadside parking area to the dunes. How far you wander is completely up to you. Early in the morning or right about sunset are the best times to visit because of the incredible show of color and light in the ghostlike dunes. Full-moon nights are also popular, and it's easy to imagine why. They'll have you dreaming of Arabian nights. Note that there used to be another trailhead for these dunes off Scotty's Castle Road, but the access road has been closed. Now everybody heads to the dunes directly from Highway 190.

**User Groups:** Hikers only. No dogs, horses, or mountain bikes. No wheelchair facilities.

**Permits:** No permits are required. There is a $10 entrance fee at Death Valley National Park, good for seven days.

**Maps:** Free park maps are available at park entrance stations or by contacting Death Valley National Park at the address below. A more detailed map is available from Tom Harrison Maps. For a topographic map, ask the USGS for Stovepipe Wells.

**Directions:** From Lone Pine on U.S. 395, drive east on Highway 136 for 18 miles. Continue east on Highway 190 for approximately 62 miles, past Stovepipe Wells Village, to the pull-outs alongside the road near the sand dunes (exactly 2.2 miles east of Stovepipe Wells). Park alongside the road.

**Contact:** Death Valley National Park, P.O. Box 579, Death Valley, CA 92328, 760/786-3200, website: www.nps.gov/deva.

# **6** MOSAIC CANYON
## 1.0 mi / 0.5 hr

**in Death Valley National Park near Stovepipe Wells**

Map 12.2, page 592

The Mosaic Canyon hike is one of the scenic highlights of Death Valley, and it's accessible to all levels of hikers. The trail shows off plenty of colorful slickrock and polished marble as it winds its way up a narrow, high-walled canyon, which was formed by a fault zone. A rock formation called mosaic breccia—multicolored rock fragments that appear to be cemented together—is embedded in the canyon walls. The best mosaics are visible in the first .25 mile, making this trip rewarding even for those who don't like to hike more than a short distance.

From the trailhead, the route enters the canyon almost immediately, and the smooth marble walls close in around you. At various points, the fissure you're walking through opens wider into "rooms" bordered by marble walls, then narrows again. After .3 mile, the canyon

walls open out to a wide alluvial fan that is not quite as interesting as the narrows area. Many people turn around here, but if you like, you can continue walking another 1.5 miles. The path ends at a dry waterfall that is too high to be scaled.

**User Groups:** Hikers only. No dogs, horses, or mountain bikes. No wheelchair facilities.

**Permits:** No permits are required. There is a $10 entrance fee at Death Valley National Park, good for seven days.

**Maps:** Free park maps are available at park entrance stations or by contacting Death Valley National Park at the address below. A more detailed map is available from Tom Harrison Maps. For a topographic map, ask the USGS for Stovepipe Wells.

**Directions:** From Lone Pine on U.S. 395, drive east on Highway 136 for 18 miles. Continue east on Highway 190 for approximately 60 miles to .25 mile west of Stovepipe Wells Village. Look for the Mosaic Canyon turnoff, on the right. If you reach Stovepipe Wells Village, you missed the turnoff. Turn right and drive 2.2 miles to the trailhead parking lot. The last two miles are rough dirt road but are usually passable by passenger cars.

**Contact:** Death Valley National Park, P.O. Box 579, Death Valley, CA 92328, 760/786-3200, website: www.nps.gov/deva.

# **7** DARWIN FALLS
## 2.2 mi / 1.0 hr

**in Death Valley National Park near Panamint Springs**

Map 12.2, page 592

Darwin Falls is a must-do desert hike. A waterfall in the desert is a rare and precious thing, a miracle of life in a harsh world. The trip is easy enough for young children, and although the temperatures in this area can be extreme in the summer, an early-morning start makes the short hike manageable almost year-round. Of course, be sure to carry water with you. Follow the trail into the canyon, and you'll soon see a trickle of water on the ground that grows wider and more substantial the farther you walk. You simply follow the stream, crossing it a few times, for about a mile. The canyon walls narrow, and the vegetation becomes much more lush. Just beyond a small stream-gauging station, you come to the waterfall—a 30-foot cascade tucked into a box canyon. A large cottonwood tree grows at its lip. In the spring, more than 80 species of resident and migrating birds have been sighted in this canyon.

**User Groups:** Hikers only. No dogs, horses, or mountain bikes. No wheelchair facilities.

**Permits:** No permits are required. Parking and access are free.

**Maps:** Free park maps are available at park entrance stations or by contacting Death Valley National Park at the address below. A more detailed map is available from Tom Harrison Maps. For a topographic map, ask the USGS for Panamint Springs.

**Directions:** From Lone Pine on U.S. 395, drive east on Highway 136 for 18 miles, and then continue straight on Highway 190 for 30 miles. The right (south) turnoff for Darwin Falls is exactly one mile before you reach the Panamint Springs Resort. Look for a small Darwin Falls sign and a dirt road. Turn right and drive 2.5 miles on the dirt road to a fork in the road; bear right and park at the signed trailhead. Alternatively, you can exit U.S. 395 at Olancha and Highway 190 and drive east on Highway 190 for 44 miles.

**Contact:** Death Valley National Park, P.O. Box 579, Death Valley, CA 92328, 760/786-3200, website: www.nps.gov/deva.

## 8 WILDROSE PEAK TRAIL
**8.4 mi / 5.0 hrs**

**in Death Valley National Park**

**Map 12.2, page 592**

If it's boiling in Death Valley, you can always make the long drive out to Wildrose Canyon and begin your hike at a trailhead elevation of 6,800 feet. Get this: You'll even find trees here. Whew, what a relief—at least until

you start climbing in earnest, heading for 9,064-foot Wildrose Peak. The hike begins at the 10 charcoal kilns (they look strangely like beehives) that were built in the 1870s to make charcoal for the local mines. Walk to the north end of the kilns to find the signed trail, then start climbing through scattered piñon pines and junipers. You can see far off to the Sierra, even Mount Whitney, and then as you climb higher, you can look down at Death Valley and Panamint Valley. Well-graded switchbacks make the 2,200-foot climb manageable, and the panoramic views make the energy expenditure completely worth it. If you tire out, at least try to hike the first 2.5 miles of trail, where you'll get a good dose of vistas from a saddle below the summit. The last mile to the summit is the steepest.

Special Note: This trail can be snowed in any time between November and May. Check with the park before making the long drive.

**User Groups:** Hikers and horses. No dogs or mountain bikes. No wheelchair facilities.

**Permits:** No permits are required. There is a $10 entrance fee at Death Valley National Park, good for seven days.

**Maps:** Free park maps are available at park entrance stations or by contacting Death Valley National Park at the address below. A more detailed map is available from Tom Harrison Maps. For a topographic map, ask the USGS for Wildrose Peak.

**Directions:** From Stovepipe Wells, drive west on Highway 190 for eight miles to Emigrant Canyon Road, then turn left (south). Drive 21 miles to a junction with Wildrose Canyon Road. Turn left (east) and drive seven miles to the parking area on the right, across from the Charcoal Kilns.

**Contact:** Death Valley National Park, P.O. Box 579, Death Valley, CA 92328, 760/786-3200, website: www.nps.gov/deva.

## 9 TELESCOPE PEAK TRAIL
**14.0 mi / 9.0 hrs**

**in Death Valley National Park**

Map 12.2, page 592

The chief highlight of the long hike to the summit of Telescope Peak is this: When you get there, you can pivot around and in one long, sweeping glance take in Mount Whitney to the west and Badwater to the east. For the uninitiated, that means you're seeing the highest point in the contiguous United States and the lowest point in the Western Hemisphere from the same spot (one is ahead of you, one to your back). The other big deal about the hike is that the trailhead is at 8,000 feet, so you don't have to worry about passing out from the valley's heat. The peak (at 11,049 feet) is the highest in Death Valley National Park, and the trail to reach it is well graded and well maintained. Nonetheless, the 3,000-foot climb and the long mileage take their toll, so don't try this hike unless you're in good shape. In addition to passing piñon pines and junipers, you'll also see some ancient bristlecone pine trees once you climb above 10,000 feet. To supplement the vistas of Mount Whitney and Badwater, you are also witness to Death Valley and Panamint Valley, as well as the White Mountains to the north. It's beyond spectacular. But the climb is one heck of a workout, so be prepared.

Special Note: This trail can be snowed in any time between November and May. Check with the park before making the long drive.

**User Groups:** Hikers only. No dogs, horses, or mountain bikes. No wheelchair facilities.

**Permits:** No permits are required. There is a $10 entrance fee at Death Valley National Park, good for seven days.

**Maps:** Free park maps are available at park entrance stations or by contacting Death Valley National Park at the address below. A more detailed map is available from Tom Harrison Maps. For a topographic map, ask the USGS for Telescope Peak.

**Directions:** From Stovepipe Wells, drive west on Highway 190 for eight miles to Emigrant Canyon Road, then turn left (south). Drive 21 miles to a junction with Wildrose Canyon Road. Turn left (east) and drive nine miles to the end of Wildrose Canyon Road at Mahogany Flat Campground. The road gets very rough and steep for the last two miles after the charcoal kilns. High-clearance vehicles are recommended.

**Contact:** Death Valley National Park, P.O. Box 579, Death Valley, CA 92328, 760/786-3200, website: www.nps.gov/deva.

## 10 KEANE WONDER MINE TRAIL
**3.2 mi / 2.0 hrs**

**in Death Valley National Park**

Map 12.3, page 593

You wouldn't think a three-mile round-trip trail could be this hard. But then again, most people don't usually climb 1,600 feet in 1.5 miles, and especially not this close to sea level, in the desert. The million-dollar vistas on Keane Wonder Mine Trail are worth the trek, though, and they're sure to pay off at least as well as the Wonder gold and silver mine did in the early 20th century. The mine had such promise, in fact, that ambitious miners built an aerial tramway to carry loads of rock down the mountainside to the mill. The vein of ore ran dry in 1915, but the mine's mill and tramway ruins still exist, and you'll see them on this steep trek into the Funeral Mountains. After only .5 mile of climbing, the views of Death Valley open wide; meanwhile, the path steepens and continues straight upward. When you pass mine shafts along the trail, remember to stay out of them; their list of hazards is long. The vistas, on the other hand, are perfectly safe and yours for the taking.

**User Groups:** Hikers only. No dogs, horses, or mountain bikes. No wheelchair facilities.

**Permits:** No permits are required. There is a $10 entrance fee at Death Valley National Park, good for seven days.

**Maps:** Free park maps are available at park entrance stations or by contacting Death Valley National Park at the address below. A more detailed map is available from Tom Harrison Maps. For a topographic map, ask the USGS for Chloride City.

**Directions:** From the Furnace Creek Visitors Center, in Death Valley National Park, drive 10 miles north on Highway 190 to the Beatty Cutoff Road. Bear right (north) on Beatty Cutoff Road and drive 5.7 miles to the right turnoff for Keane Wonder Mine. Turn right and drive 2.8 miles on a rough dirt road to the parking area.

**Contact:** Death Valley National Park, P.O. Box 579, Death Valley, CA 92328, 760/786-3200, website: www.nps.gov/deva.

## 11 KEANE WONDER SPRING
### 2.0 mi / 1.0 hr

**in Death Valley National Park**

Map 12.3, page 593

If you aren't up for the steep climb to the top of the tramway at Keane Wonder Mine (see previous listing), this easy and flat trail to Keane Wonder Spring provides a pleasant alternative. The mineral spring once provided water for the mining operation; now it provides a gathering place for birds and wildlife. Walk from the trailhead toward the large metal water tank to find the trail (on its left side). Follow an old pipeline northward along the base of the mountains, cross a wash, and pass mounds of travertine (a marblelike rock formed by the sulfur-rich springwater). The spring is just slightly off the trail .75 mile from the trailhead and not really worth the scramble required to access it. (It's a hole in the ground that reeks of hydrogen sulfide.) Instead, continue another .25 mile beyond the spring to the remains of an old stamp mill and cabin.

**User Groups:** Hikers only. No dogs, horses, or mountain bikes. No wheelchair facilities.

**Permits:** No permits are required. There is a $10 entrance fee at Death Valley National Park, good for seven days.

**Maps:** Free park maps are available at park entrance stations or by contacting Death Valley National Park at the address below. A more

detailed map is available from Tom Harrison Maps. For a topographic map, ask the USGS for Chloride City.

**Directions:** From the Furnace Creek Visitors Center, in Death Valley National Park, drive 10 miles north on Highway 190 to the Beatty Cutoff Road. Bear right (north) on Beatty Cutoff Road and drive 5.7 miles to the turnoff for Keane Wonder Mine. Turn right and drive 2.8 miles on a rough dirt road to the parking area.

**Contact:** Death Valley National Park, P.O. Box 579, Death Valley, CA 92328, 760/786-3200, website: www.nps.gov/deva.

## 12 SALT CREEK INTERPRETIVE TRAIL
### 1.0 mi / 0.5 hr

**in Death Valley National Park**

Map 12.3, page 593

Salt Creek is exactly what its name implies—a stream of saline water—and it's home to the Salt Creek pupfish, a species that lives nowhere else. The fish underwent an incredible evolutionary change in order to live in this saline creek, which was once a part of a much larger freshwater lake. The biological alteration would be roughly the same as if humans decided to drink gasoline instead of water. In late winter and spring, you can look down into Salt Creek and spot the minnow-sized pupfish swimming about. The plants along the stream are typical of California coastal wetlands—salt grass and pickleweed. Birds congregate by the stream, including great blue herons. Because the trail is on a wooden boardwalk, it is accessible to all hikers, including wheelchair users.

**User Groups:** Hikers and wheelchairs. No dogs, horses, or mountain bikes.

**Permits:** No permits are required. There is a $10 entrance fee at Death Valley National Park, good for seven days.

**Maps:** Interpretive trail brochures are available at park visitors centers or at the trailhead. Free park maps are available at park entrance stations or by contacting Death Valley National Park at the address below. A more detailed map is available from Tom Harrison Maps. For a topographic map, ask the USGS for Beatty Junction.

**Directions:** From the Furnace Creek Visitors Center, in Death Valley National Park, drive 12 miles north on Highway 190 to the turnoff for Salt Creek. Turn left and drive one mile to the Salt Creek parking area.

**Contact:** Death Valley National Park, P.O. Box 579, Death Valley, CA 92328, 760/786-3200, website: www.nps.gov/deva.

## 13 HARMONY BORAX WORKS AND BORAX FLATS
1.0 mi / .5 hr

**in Death Valley National Park**

Map 12.3, page 593

A stroll on Harmony Borax Works Interpretive Trail, combined with a longer excursion on neighboring Borax Flats. makes an easy and interesting walk through Death Valley's history. Borax was first discovered in Death Valley in 1881, but transporting it proved difficult, because the nearest railroad was 165 miles away, in Mojave, over fierce, rugged terrain. Enterprising miners figured out the solution: build specially designed wagons that could carry huge, extra-heavy loads pulled by teams of 20 mules. The rest, as they say, is history. The paved loop leads past examples of the 20-mule team wagons, as well as equipment used for refining borax. At the west end of the loop, you can leave the pavement and walk out to the site where Chinese laborers gathered the stuff from the salt flats. The flats are easy to walk on, with a crusty, hard surface. Eventually the trail dissipates in the mud, so when you curiosity is satisfied, just turn around and head back.

**User Groups:** Hikers only. No dogs, horses, or mountain bikes. No wheelchair facilities.

**Permits:** No permits are required. There is a $10 entrance fee at Death Valley National Park, good for seven days.

**Maps:** Free park maps are available at park entrance stations or by contacting Death Valley National Park at the address below. A more detailed map is available from Tom Harrison Maps. For a topographic map, ask the USGS for Furnace Creek.

**Directions:** From the Furnace Creek Visitors Center, in Death Valley National Park, drive north on Highway 190 for 1.3 miles to the left turnoff for Harmony Borax Works and Mustard Canyon. Turn left, then stay to the left to reach the trailhead parking area.

**Contact:** Death Valley National Park, P.O. Box 579, Death Valley, CA 92328, 760/786-3200, website: www.nps.gov/deva.

## 14 GOLDEN CANYON INTERPRETIVE TRAIL
2.0 mi / 1.0 hr

**in Death Valley National Park**

Map 12.3, page 593

The Golden Canyon Interpretive Trail is a perfect path for first-timers in Death Valley National Park. Because the trail is so short, most people continue beyond the end of the self-guided stretch, heading deeper into Golden Canyon to Red Cathedral, .3 mile from the last numbered trail marker. The interpretive trail follows the path of an old road through a flat alluvial fan exhibiting a colorful array of volcanic rocks, sand, and gravel. Imagine every shade of gold you can think of—from yellow to orange to apricot. That's what you'll see here in the cliffs, which are composed of the layered remains of ancient lake beds. They're especially gorgeous near sunrise and sunset. At the final interpretive post, you can turn around and head back, or take the left fork of the trail and continue to Red Cathedral, the huge red cliff that looms in the background. Its lovely hue is caused by the weathering of rocks containing a large quantity of iron. A surprise is that by the time you reach Red Cathedral, you've gained some 300 feet in elevation—enough to provide some wide views looking back the way you came.

**User Groups:** Hikers only. No dogs, horses, or mountain bikes. No wheelchair facilities.

**Permits:** No permits are required. There is a $10 entrance fee at Death Valley National Park, good for seven days.

**Maps:** Interpretive trail brochures are available at park visitors centers or at the trailhead. Free park maps are available at park entrance stations or by contacting Death Valley National Park at the address below. A more detailed map is available from Tom Harrison Maps. For a topographic map, ask the USGS for Furnace Creek.

**Directions:** From the Furnace Creek Visitors Center, in Death Valley National Park, drive southeast on Highway 190 for 1.2 miles to the right turnoff for Badwater. Bear right and drive south for two miles to the Golden Canyon parking area, on the east side of the road.

**Contact:** Death Valley National Park, P.O. Box 579, Death Valley, CA 92328, 760/786-3200, website: www.nps.gov/deva.

## 15 GOWER GULCH LOOP
### 5.5 mi / 3.0 hrs

**in Death Valley National Park**

Map 12.3, page 593

This hike is an extension of Golden Canyon Interpretive Trail (see previous listing) for slightly more experienced hikers. When you reach the last interpretive trail marker on Golden Canyon Trail, take the right fork for Gower Gulch Loop. The path is signed with small hiker symbols; watch for them as you continue your trek into the colorful badlands—deeply creased, eroded, and barren hillsides. Hike across the shoulder of Manly Beacon, a yellow sandstone hill with lovely views. At the base of Manly Beacon's south slope, you reach a junction. Turn right to loop back through Gower Gulch (the left fork leads to Zabriskie Point, a popular drive-to overlook). On your return, remember to stay in the wide main wash and keep heading downhill; this will keep you from making a wrong turn in the canyons

of Gower Gulch. You'll notice white outcroppings in the rock, the raison d'être for the old borax mines still found in the area. Also look for mine shafts; several are bored into the canyon walls. Eventually the canyon narrows, and the trail leads around the side of a 40-foot dry fall. The final mile of the loop parallels the highway, heading back to the mouth of Golden Canyon and its parking area.

One thing to keep in mind: Be sure to carry enough water for the few hours you'll be out on the trail. The total elevation gain is only 800 feet, but it's pretty darn hot out here.

**User Groups:** Hikers only. No dogs, horses, or mountain bikes. No wheelchair facilities.

**Permits:** No permits are required. There is a $10 entrance fee at Death Valley National Park, good for seven days.

**Maps:** Free park maps are available at park entrance stations or by contacting Death Valley National Park at the address below. A more detailed map is available from Tom Harrison Maps. For a topographic map, ask the USGS for Furnace Creek.

**Directions:** From the Furnace Creek Visitors Center, in Death Valley National Park, drive southeast on Highway 190 for 1.2 miles to the turnoff for Badwater. Turn right and drive south for two miles to the Golden Canyon parking area, on the east side of the road.

**Contact:** Death Valley National Park, P.O. Box 579, Death Valley, CA 92328, 760/786-3200, website: www.nps.gov/deva.

## 16 NATURAL BRIDGE CANYON
### 1.2 mi / 1.0 hr

**in Death Valley National Park**

Map 12.3, page 593

Natural Bridge Canyon is a good spot to take a short walk and get a good taste of what Death Valley is all about. Because the canyon has an abrupt slope, the hike is not as easy as you might expect. The loose gravel surface of its floor makes walking a workout. Still, you should at least go as far as the natural bridge the canyon is named for, which is only .3 mile in, or about 15 minutes from your car. The "bridge" is an imposing overhang about 40 feet high and 25 feet wide. It was formed by repeated flash flooding over thousands of years. Take a walk underneath it, then head up the canyon a little farther and watch other visitors walk underneath it. All the while, you can't help but ponder the amazing geologic action that has created Death Valley. If you want to head farther back into the canyon, you'll find more interesting features, such as dry waterfalls and "wax drippings," which are formed when water drips down the canyon walls and forms a type of mud. The canyon walls come together at a 15-foot dry fall .6 miles in, so that's your turn-around point.

**User Groups:** Hikers only. No dogs, horses, or mountain bikes. No wheelchair facilities.

**Permits:** No permits are required. There is a $10 entrance fee at Death Valley National Park, good for seven days.

**Maps:** Free park maps are available at park entrance stations or by contacting Death Valley National Park at the address below. A more detailed map is available from Tom Harrison Maps. For a topographic map, ask the USGS for Furnace Creek.

**Directions:** From the Furnace Creek Visitors Center, in Death Valley National Park, drive southeast on Highway 190 for 1.2 miles to the right turnoff for Badwater. Bear right and drive south for 13.2 miles to the left turnoff for Natural Bridge Canyon. Turn left and drive 1.7 miles to the trailhead.

**Contact:** Death Valley National Park, P.O. Box 579, Death Valley, CA 92328, 760/786-3200, website: www.nps.gov/deva.

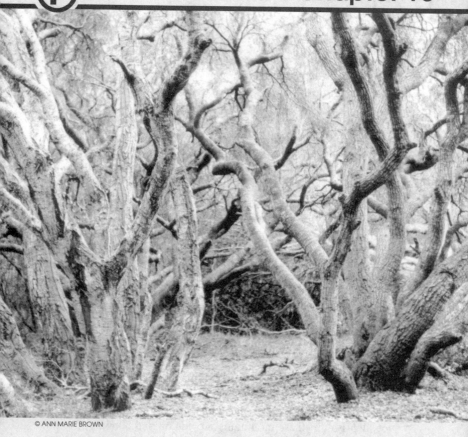

## Chapter 13

© ANN MARIE BROWN

# Santa Barbara
# and Vicinity

# Santa Barbara and Vicinity

The Santa Barbara region, which extends 200 miles from the artsy town of Cambria and terraced vineyards of Paso Robles to the white sands of Ventura, encompasses what many consider to be Southern California's finest stretch of coast. The Santa Barbara County shoreline, curving upcoast from Carpinteria to Point Conception, has a southern, not western, exposure, which results in exceptionally mild weather. To the south, Ventura County's coast offers 40 miles of fine sandy beaches.

Hikers can explore this meeting of land and sea on a wealth of trails in state-protected lands: San Simeon State Beach, Morro Bay State Park, Montaña de Oro State Park, Gaviota State Park, McGrath State Beach, and Point Mugu State Park. Trails wind along the tops of oceanside bluffs, across coastal grasslands gilded with wildflowers in the spring, and on top of boardwalks spanning coastal dunes and wetlands.

Lest you think the Santa Barbara region is all sun and sand, note that it also contains more than a million acres of national forest land in the Santa Barbara and Ojai backcountry—the southern section of Los Padres National Forest. This landscape is a conglomeration of pine-clad high mountain peaks, river-cut canyons, and chaparral-covered hillsides. The Santa Ynez Mountains, a centerpiece of southern Los Padres National Forest, are part of the unique Transverse Range, a system of mountains that defies the rules of California geography: They run from east to west, rather than north to south.

Not surprisingly, these mountains provide myriad hiking opportunities, although most trails are little known except by Santa Barbara locals. Hikers wishing to explore the remote backcountry can choose from five wilderness areas: San Rafael, Dick Smith, Matilija, Chumash, and Sespe. Those seeking easily accessible day-use areas will find Los Padres National Forest trails just beyond the town limits in Santa Barbara, Montecito, and Ojai. Paths lead to waterfalls, high overlooks of mountains and ocean, and sculpted sandstone formations, and many destinations can be visited with only a small investment of mileage and time.

Perhaps the most remarkable stretch of land in the Santa Barbara region is a parcel surrounded entirely by water—the five rugged and remote islands of Channel Islands National Park. The islands are often referred to as "the Galapagos of California" because of the amount and diversity of endemic animals and plant life. More than 100 species of plants and animals are found on the Channel Islands and nowhere else.

Although reaching the islands requires more effort than simply driving your car (boat concessionaires are located in Santa Barbara and Ventura), hikers who make the trip are rewarded with a chance to see coastal California in a nearly primitive state. Wildlife—particularly seals, sea lions, and seabirds—are remarkably plentiful. Depending on which island you visit, you can take an easy stroll past 10-foot-tall blooming coreopsis or a demanding trek to see a ghost forest of caliche formations—calcium-carbonate sand castings of dead plants. Catch a glimpse of the endemic island scrub jay or the island gray fox. Visit a stand of Torrey pines—the only existing grove outside of Torrey Pines State Reserve, in San Diego. One trip to the Channel Islands, and you'll be convinced: This place is California like you've never seen it before.

# Map 13.1

**Hikes 1–3**
**Pages 614–615**

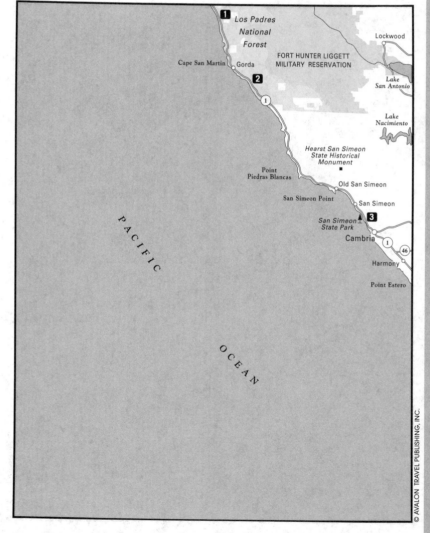

Los Padres National Forest

Lockwood

FORT HUNTER LIGGETT MILITARY RESERVATION

Cape San Martin  Gorda

Lake San Antonio

Lake Nacimiento

Hearst San Simeon State Historical Monument

Point Piedras Blancas

Old San Simeon

San Simeon Point  San Simeon

San Simeon State Park

Cambria

Harmony

Point Estero

PACIFIC OCEAN

© AVALON TRAVEL PUBLISHING, INC.

# Map 13.2

**Hikes 4–14**
**Pages 615–622**

13.1

13.3

1 2
3 4

see
San Joaquin
Valley
page 422

33

41

Salinas R.

101

Lake San
Antonio

Cholame Hills

San Andreas

CAMP
ROBERTS
MILITARY
RES.

San Miguel

Cholame

Antelope Valley

46

Lake
Nacimiento

46

Shandon

Fault

Zone

Paso Robles

41

Temblor Range

46

41

Santa

Templeton

Lucia

Atascadero

229

58

1

Cayucos

41

Range

101

La Panza Range

Morro Strand
State Beach

4-5

Estero

Morro Bay

6 Morro Bay S.P.

Santa
Margarita

Santa
Margarita
Lake

Morro
Bay

Baywood Park

Bay

7-8

Los
Osos

9

1

San Luis
Obispo

Garcia Mountain

Point
Buchon

Montaña de Oro S.P.

10-11

Los Padres

Irish Hills

227

12-13

Lopez
Lake

Rancho Arroyo
Grande

National Forest

Avila Beach

Pismo State
Beach

Point San
Luis

San Luis
Obispo Bay

Pismo
Beach

Arroyo Grande

Oceano

101

Oceano Dunes
State Vehicular
Rec. Area

14

1

Nipomo

Twitchell
Reservoir

166

© AVALON TRAVEL PUBLISHING, INC.

# Map 13.3

**Hikes 15–19**
**Pages 622–624**

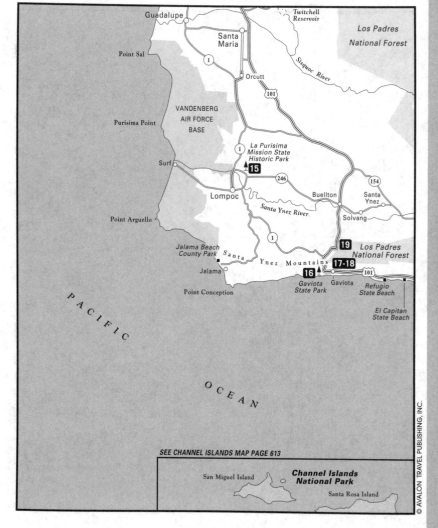

SEE CHANNEL ISLANDS MAP PAGE 613

© AVALON TRAVEL PUBLISHING, INC.

# Map 13.4

**Hikes 20–45**
**Pages 625–639**

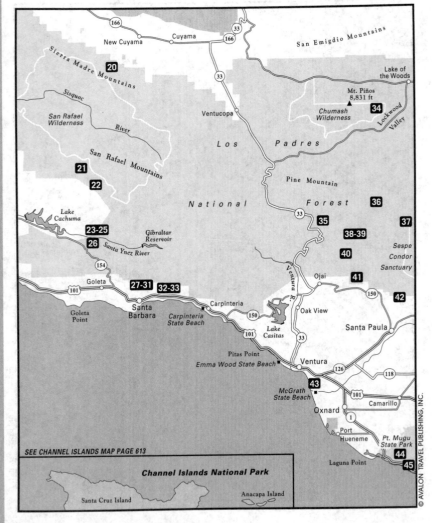

SEE CHANNEL ISLANDS MAP PAGE 613

© AVALON TRAVEL PUBLISHING, INC.

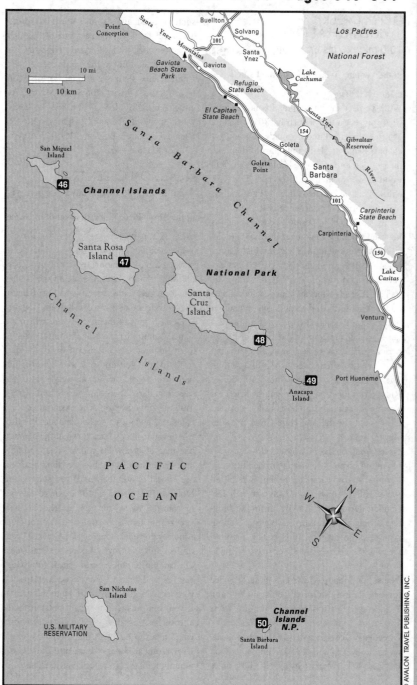

Point Conception
Buellton
Solvang
101
Los Padres
National Forest
Santa Ynez
Mountains
Santa Ynez
Gaviota Beach State Park
Gaviota
Santa Ynez
Lake Cachuma
Refugio State Beach
El Capitan State Beach
154
Goleta
Gibraltar Reservoir
Santa Ynez River
San Miguel Island
46
Channel Islands
Goleta Point
Santa Barbara
101
Carpinteria State Beach
Carpinteria
Santa Rosa Island
47
National Park
Santa Cruz Island
150
Lake Casitas
Channel
Islands
48
49
Anacapa Island
Port Hueneme
Ventura

PACIFIC

OCEAN

N
W   E
S

San Nicholas Island

U.S. MILITARY RESERVATION

Channel Islands N.P.
50
Santa Barbara Island

© AVALON TRAVEL PUBLISHING, INC.

0   10 mi
0   10 km

## 1 KIRK CREEK/ VICENTE FLAT TRAIL

**10.0 mi / 6.0 hrs or 2.0 days**

**in the Ventana Wilderness south of Lucia**

Map 13.1, page 609

What you see at the trailhead is not exactly what you get on this popular backpacking trail. You see chaparral and no shade, but you get chaparral and no shade only part of the time; the rest of the time, you're hiking in shady redwood groves or along lush ravines. The Kirk Creek Trail (also called Vicente Flat Trail) is full of surprises. The absence of trees in some sections is actually a positive, because it allows for wide-reaching views over the big, blue Pacific. Your destination is Vicente Flat Camp, reached after five miles, with a 1,700-foot elevation gain, mostly on a well-graded trail. The trail leads steadily northeast, passing occasional odd-looking rocks and meandering in and out of the trees. Pass small Espinoza Camp at 3.2 miles, which is seldom used because of the superiority of Vicente Flat Camp, a larger camp with a nearby stream and a beautiful setting. The final .5 mile of trail is a descent to Stone Ridge Trail junction, where you bear left for Vicente Flat Camp. You have a choice of sites in the shade or the sun; Hare Creek provides a water source.

**User Groups:** Hikers, dogs, and horses. No mountain bikes. No wheelchair facilities.

**Permits:** A free campfire permit is required for overnight stays from May through December; permits are available from the Monterey Ranger District or the Big Sur Station. A national forest recreation pass is required for each vehicle; fees are $5 for one day or $30 for a year.

**Maps:** For a map, ask the U.S. Forest Service for Los Padres National Forest or Ventana Wilderness. For topographic maps, ask the USGS for Lopez Point and Cone Peak.

**Directions:** Drive 55 miles south from Carmel on Highway 1 to Kirk Creek Campground, on the west side of the highway. (It's four miles

south of Lucia and six miles north of Gorda.) The trailhead is on the east side of the highway; you must park alongside Highway 1 in the pullout and not in the campground.

**Contact:** Los Padres National Forest, Monterey Ranger District, 406 South Mildred Avenue, King City, CA 93930, 831/385-5434, website: www.fs.fed.us/r5/lospadres; Big Sur Station, Highway 1, Big Sur, CA 93920, 831/667-2315 or 831/649-2836.

## 2 SALMON CREEK TRAIL

**4.2 mi / 2.0 hrs or 2.0 days**

**in the Silver Peak Wilderness south of Gorda**

Map 13.1, page 609

While heading for a day hike or short backpacking trip on Salmon Creek Trail, many people walk right by and miss seeing spectacular Salmon Creek Falls, which is just off Salmon Creek Trail and a .25-mile walk from Highway 1. Don't be one of them; start your trip at the signed Salmon Creek Trail, but after walking a few hundred feet, cut off on any of the spur trails to your left and pay a visit to the impressive 100-foot waterfall, surrounded by cabin-sized boulders. Then return to Salmon Creek Trail, say good-bye to the creekside shade and dampness, and start a healthy climb to the ridge, where you can look back down at the highway and marvel at how far you've gone, and how fast. From there, it's still more climbing, gaining a total of 800 feet, until you start to see Douglas firs, a sure sign that you're nearing misnamed Spruce Camp, at 1,325 feet. At Spruce Creek Trail fork, stay straight (left). The final .1 mile is downhill along Spruce Creek, a beautiful stream with myriad pools and cascades. The camp here is in gorgeous shade from Douglas firs, and there are many good spots to stick your feet (or other body parts) into the stream. If you want to spend the night but somebody already has this spot, you can continue another 1.5 miles to Estrella Camp.

**User Groups:** Hikers, dogs, and horses. No mountain bikes. No wheelchair facilities.

**Permits:** A free campfire permit is required for overnight stays from May through December; permits are available from the Monterey Ranger District or the Big Sur Station. A national forest recreation pass is required for each vehicle; fees are $5 for one day or $30 for a year.

**Maps:** For a map, ask the U.S. Forest Service for Los Padres National Forest. For a topographic map, ask the USGS for Villa Creek.

**Directions:** From Big Sur, drive 33 miles south on Highway 1 to Gorda; continue 7.6 miles south of Gorda to the trailhead for Salmon Creek Trail, on the east side of the highway at a hairpin turn. Park in the large parking pullout along the road. The Salmon Creek Trail leads from the south end of the guardrail.

**Contact:** Los Padres National Forest, Monterey Ranger District, 406 South Mildred Avenue, King City, CA 93930, 831/385-5434, website: www.fs.fed.us/r5/lospadres; Big Sur Station, Highway 1, Big Sur, CA 93920, 831/667-2315 or 831/649-2836.

## ❸ LEFFINGWELL LANDING AND MOONSTONE BEACH
**4.0 mi / 2.0 hrs**　　

**near Cambria**

> **Map 13.1, page 609**

What's the best time to make the trip to Cambria? That's easy—in the spring, when the rolling hills along Highway 46 on the drive to the coast are lush and green. Of course, any time of year is a good time to walk the trail that leads from Leffingwell Landing along the bluffs above Moonstone Beach. Although Moonstone Beach Drive parallels the trail all the way, the road isn't much of a bother, because the vistas out to sea hold all of your attention. The parking lot at Leffingwell Landing is in the middle of this trail, which means you can walk out and back in both directions. To the south you may have a wet creek crossing at Leffingwell Creek, but you can go around it via the golf course. The bluff trail's southern terminus is at the in-

tersection of Moonstone Beach Drive and Weymouth Street, but you can descend to the beach there and keep walking. If you head in the other direction, about .25 mile north of Leffingwell Landing the trail again descends on a wooden staircase to the beach, and you continue your walk there. In addition to the coastal vistas from the bluffs, there are many colorful patches of ice plant and cypress trees, as well as several benches and overlooks (accessible via short spurs off the main trail)—places where you can find a spot to call your own. We watched a winter squall come in from one of these overlooks; it was sudden, dramatic, and beautiful. Right below Leffingwell Landing are fine tidepools to be explored. Keep on the lookout for passing whales in the winter.

**User Groups:** Hikers and dogs. No horses or mountain bikes. No wheelchair facilities.

**Permits:** No permits are required. Parking and access are free.

**Maps:** For a topographic map, ask the USGS for Cambria.

**Directions:** From north of Templeton on U.S. 101, take the Highway 46 West/Cambria/Hearst Castle exit. Drive west on Highway 46 for 22 miles to Highway 1; continue three miles north on Highway 1, past Cambria, to Moonstone Beach Drive. Turn left on Moonstone Beach Drive and park at Leffingwell Landing.

**Contact:** San Simeon State Beach, San Simeon District, 750 Hearst Castle Road, San Simeon, CA 93452, 805/927-2020 or 805/927-2068, website: www.parks.ca.gov.

## ❹ CERRO ALTO SUMMIT
**4.0 mi / 2.0 hrs**

**off Highway 41, east of Morro Bay**

> **Map 13.2, page 610**

We hope you like to climb, because that's what you do on Cerro Alto Trail to the summit of Cerro Alto, elevation 2,620 feet. The 1,600-foot climb is divided over two miles of steep terrain, much of which burned in a 1994 arson fire, but the reward for your exertion is one of the finest views of the Central Coast—a panoramic vista of the Pacific Ocean, Whale Rock Reservoir, Morro Bay, Piedras Blancas Lighthouse, and the Santa Lucia Mountains. From the trailhead along the camp road south of the parking area, you cross Morro Creek on a bridge, enter a bay and live oak forest, then leave it and head for chaparral country. After .75 mile, bear left, and shortly thereafter bear right. After a series of switchbacks and some rocky sections of trail, you reach the road to the peak, at 1.7 miles. Turn left and circle the peak as you climb another .25 mile to the summit.

Note that if you want to take an easier grade to the summit or if you want to turn this into a loop trip, you can begin hiking from the hiker's parking lot at campsite No. 19. This route takes three miles to reach Cerro Alto's summit instead of two. It joins the shorter route for the final 1.2 miles to the summit. Also note that in recent years, the trails to Cerro Alto have become extremely popular with mountain bikers. If you don't like sharing the trail with bikes, visit on a weekday.

**User Groups:** Hikers, dogs, horses, and mountain bikes. No wheelchair facilities.

**Permits:** No permits are required. A national forest recreation pass is required for each vehicle; fees are $5 for one day or $30 for a year.

**Maps:** For a map, ask the U.S. Forest Service for Los Padres National Forest. For a topographic map, ask the USGS for Atascadero.

**Directions:** From Atascadero on U.S. 101, take the Highway 41 West/Morro Bay exit. Drive eight miles west on Highway 41 to Cerro Alto Campground, on the left, midway between Atascadero and Morro Bay. Park in the signed hikers' parking lot near the camp host's residence at the far end of the campground. Walk back down the camp road to the trailhead by the footbridge.

**Contact:** Los Padres National Forest, Santa Lucia Ranger District, 1616 North Carlotti Drive, Santa Maria, CA 93454, 805/925-9538, website: www.fs.fed.us/r5/lospadres.

# ⑤ CERRO ALTO LOOP
## 2.5 mi / 1.0 hr

**off Highway 41, east of Morro Bay**

Map 13.2, page 610

Not everybody is up for the dry, steep hike to the top of Cerro Alto Peak, and if you're in that camp, you can take another hike, one that offers many of its own rewards. Since some of this area burned in a 1994 fire, you'll see much evidence of regrowth, as well as many blackened trees still standing. Take the trail from the far end of Cerro Alto Campground; you'll return on the trail by the bridge at the lower end of the camp. It's an up-and-down kind of deal, with not too much up or too much down. The first .5 mile is in a forest of oaks, bays, and madrones, with many ferns growing at your feet. As the trail climbs, the terrain changes to chaparral, and at one mile, you reach an old road junction. Turn right, and in less than a mile, the path meets Cerro Alto Trail to the summit. Keep following the old road and switchback to the west. Then make a one-mile descent back to the camp.

**User Groups:** Hikers, dogs, horses, and mountain bikes. No wheelchair facilities.

**Permits:** No permits are required. A national forest recreation pass is required for each vehicle; fees are $5 for one day or $30 for a year.

**Maps:** For a map, ask the U.S. Forest Service for Los Padres National Forest. For a topographic map, ask the USGS for Atascadero.

**Directions:** From Atascadero on U.S. 101, take the Highway 41 West/Morro Bay exit. Drive eight miles west on Highway 41 to Cerro Alto Campground on the left, midway between Atascadero and Morro Bay. Park in the signed hikers' parking lot near the camp host's residence, at the far end of the campground. Start hiking on the signed Cerro Alto Trail from there.

**Contact:** Los Padres National Forest, Santa Lucia Ranger District, 1616 North Carlotti Drive, Santa Maria, CA 93454, 805/925-9538, website: www.fs.fed.us/r5/lospadres.

## 6 CABRILLO PEAK
3.0 mi / 1.5 hrs

**in Morro Bay State Park near Morro Bay**

Map 13.2, page 610

You hardly realize you're in a state park when you reach the trailhead for Cabrillo Peak, which is just a small dirt parking lot alongside a busy road. Where's the entrance kiosk? What about the state park entrance fee? Where are all the campgrounds and restrooms? None of that applies here at Morro Bay State Park's Cabrillo Peak, which is a quiet refuge from the hustle and bustle of Morro Bay tourism. Cabrillo Peak is one of nine "morros"—small volcanic peaks that lie in a loose chain along the central coast. (Morro Rock is another of these and is the most famous of the group.) Although no trail goes to the top of Cabrillo Peak, you can hike on the peak's lower reaches on Quarry Trail and Park Ridge Trail. Both are accessible from two small parking areas off South Bay Boulevard; if you miss the first one, just take the second. The Park Ridge Trail goes straight up, then veers left and joins Quarry Trail. The Cabrillo Peak area contains a variety of native plants and grasslands, including these spring bloomers: bird's eye gilia, brodiea, and mariposa lilies. On the sunniest slopes, coastal sage scrub grows, including black sage and bush monkeyflower. Translation? No shade. That makes the views of Morro Bay and Morro Rock first class, but it also means you'd better carry water.

**User Groups:** Hikers, horses, and mountain bikes. No dogs. No wheelchair facilities.

**Permits:** No permits are required. Parking and access are free.

**Maps:** A map of Morro Bay State Park is available at the main park entrance on State Park Road. For a topographic map, ask the USGS for Morro Bay South.

**Directions:** From San Luis Obispo, take Highway 1 northwest for 11 miles to Morro Bay. Take the Morro Bay State Park exit and continue on South Bay Boulevard. In .75 mile,

take the left fork (do not head for the main part of the park) and drive another .5 mile to the Cabrillo Peak dirt parking lot, on the left side of the road. The first parking lot is for the Quarry Trail; another parking lot shortly following it is for the Park Ridge Trail. Park at either; the two trails join.

**Contact:** Morro Bay State Park, State Park Road, Morro Bay, CA 93442, 805/772-7434; San Luis Obispo Coast State Parks, 805/549-3312, website: www.parks.ca.gov.

## 7 MONTAÑA DE ORO BLUFFS TRAIL
3.0 mi / 1.5 hrs

**in Montaña de Oro State Park west of San Luis Obispo**

Map 13.2, page 610

How can a park this good be free of charge? We can't figure it out, but we're glad it is. The Bluffs Trail at Montaña de Oro State Park is one of the finest coast walks in Central and Southern California, blissfully free of the blight of human development and loaded with classic oceanside beauty. The flat trail winds along the top of Montaña de Oro's shale and sediment bluffs, with nonstop views of rocky offshore outcrops, colorful rock cliffs and arches, and the big blue Pacific. Wooden railings keep hikers from leaning too far over the edge of the constantly eroding bluffs. In addition to all the coastal vistas, the grasses alongside the trail explode in a display of orange poppies and other wildflowers in February, March, and April. The trail ends at a barbed-wire fence and PG&E property lined with huge cacti to keep people out. Just follow the tiny loop and retrace your steps on the trail. A good side trip is to explore the beach right across from the visitors center turnoff, near where you left your car.

**User Groups:** Hikers and mountain bikes. No dogs or horses. No wheelchair facilities.

**Permits:** No permits are required. Parking and access are free.

**Maps:** A map of Montaña de Oro State Park is

available at the park entrance, visitors center, or at Morro Bay State Park. For a topographic map, ask the USGS for Morro Bay South.

**Directions:** From U.S. 101 in San Luis Obispo, take the Los Osos exit and head west on Los Osos Valley Road. Drive 12 miles on Los Osos Valley Road to the Montaña de Oro entrance. Continue 2.5 miles to the small parking area on the right side of the road, 100 yards beyond the left turnoff for the visitors center. The signed Bluffs Trail begins there.

**Contact:** Montaña de Oro State Park, 3550 Pecho Valley Road, Los Osos, CA 93402, 805/528-0513; Morro Bay State Park, 805/772-7434; San Luis Obispo Coast State Parks, 805/549-3312, website: www.parks.ca.gov.

## 8 VALENCIA AND OATS PEAKS
### 7.0 mi / 3.5 hrs

**in Montaña de Oro State Park west of San Luis Obispo**

Map 13.2, page 610

With a cool ocean breeze keeping you comfortable, this seven-mile round-trip hike to two coastal peaks is a spectacular day trip. If you forget to carry water and/or hike in the heat of high noon, it can be a nightmare, so get prepared. The Valencia Peak Trail begins in Montaña de Oro State Park. The wide route heads briefly south and then turns inland for a gradual ascent through grasslands and wildflowers, chaparral, and scrub. There are several junctions; all are well marked.

In two miles and with an elevation gain of 1,100 feet, you arrive at the top of Valencia Peak, elevation 1,347 feet. On a clear day you can see all the way from Point Sal, in the south, to Piedras Blancas, in the north. From there, you must descend for a mile (losing nearly 500 feet) to join a road that connects to Oats Peak Trail, then hike upward once again on Oats Peak Trail. (Sorry, but there's no other way to do it from the top of Valencia Peak.)

Oats Peak is more easily gained (in 1.2 miles), and a survey marker tells you when you reach its summit, at 1,373 feet. From there, you can

walk along the ridge for a while to enjoy more of the spectacular views of the ocean, Morro Rock, and the inland mountains, or you can head back downhill. Keep to Oats Peak Trail for your descent. If you take Oats Peak Trail all the way back, you'll have a 10-minute walk on the park road to get back to your car. One more thing to think about: If you can possibly visit from February to April, you get a good chance at crystal-clear vistas and the best chance of seeing Montaña de Oro's signature wildflower display. These hills are "mountains of gold" in season; hence the park's name.

**User Groups:** Hikers and horses. No dogs or mountain bikes. No wheelchair facilities.

**Permits:** No permits are required. Parking and access are free.

**Maps:** A map of Montaña de Oro State Park is available at the park entrance, visitors center, or at Morro Bay State Park. For a topographic map, ask the USGS for Morro Bay South.

**Directions:** From U.S. 101 in San Luis Obispo, take the Los Osos exit and head west on Los Osos Valley Road. Drive 12 miles on Los Osos Valley Road to the Montaña de Oro entrance. Continue 2.5 miles to the small parking area on the right side of the road, 100 yards beyond the left turnoff for the visitors center. The Valencia Peak Trail begins on the left side of the road.

**Contact:** Montaña de Oro State Park, 3550 Pecho Valley Road, Los Osos, CA 93402, 805/528-0513; Morro Bay State Park, 805/772-7434; San Luis Obispo Coast State Parks, 805/549-3312, website: www.parks.ca.gov.

## 9 LOS OSOS OAKS RESERVE
### 2.0 mi / 1.0 hr

**west of San Luis Obispo in Los Osos**

Map 13.2, page 610

It's hard to believe that a bunch of old oak trees right alongside a busy road could make for such great walking, but they do. The hike is an odd mix of elements, since you hear road noise much of the time, but the forest still seems peaceful. The venerable old oaks in Los Osos Oaks Reserve are as old as 800 years, and they can be visited by wandering on any of three short, flat trails. It's easy to walk a brief stretch on all of them. The Chumash Loop, Oak View Trail, and Los Osos Creek Trail all lead from the parking lot and split off from each other. Oak View is just a short out-and-back trip through the trees and provides the best look at the reserve's highlights; Chumash Loop is a little longer and loops around the reserve. The Los Osos Creek Trail is the least impressive of the three, showing off the fewest fine tree specimens and following a marshy stretch of creek. The oak forest is a mix of very large, old trees with moss hanging from their branches, and tiny, dwarfed ones. Some of the oaks' trunks and branches are so twisted, gnarled, and wrinkled that they look like a tangled web of elephants' trunks. If you're into photography, this is the kind of place that is best captured in black and white. And, if the coast is foggy, this hike is ideal, because all the beauty of the forest is close enough to touch.

**User Groups:** Hikers only. No dogs, horses, or mountain bikes. No wheelchair facilities.

**Permits:** No permits are required. Parking and access are free.

**Maps:** For a topographic map, ask the USGS for Morro Bay South.

**Directions:** From U.S. 101 in San Luis Obispo, take the Los Osos exit and head west on Los Osos Valley Road. Drive 8.5 miles on Los Osos Valley Road to the Los Osos Oaks Reserve, on the left side of the road, which is marked by a small sign. The reserve is exactly one mile east of 10th Street, in Los Osos, and just west of the bear statue on the road. There is a small parking area by the trailhead, just off Los Osos Valley Road.

**Contact:** Los Osos Oaks Reserve, c/o Morro Bay State Park, State Park Road, Morro Bay, CA 93442, 805/772-7434; San Luis Obispo Coast State Parks, 805/549-3312, website: www.parks.ca.gov.

## 10 BIG FALLS
**3.0 mi / 1.5 hrs**

**in the Santa Lucia Wilderness near Arroyo Grande**

Map 13.2, page 610

The journey to Big Falls in the Santa Lucia Wilderness is a wacky, water-filled adventure. Even as late as June, the drive to the trailhead can require dozens of crossings of Lopez Creek. In some places, the stream simply becomes the road. In comparison to the drive, the hike is surprisingly easy and fast. You walk through a fern- and flower-filled sycamore and oak forest to the first waterfall, only .5 mile in. This is not actually Big Falls; it's a smaller waterfall, although plenty of people mistake it for Big Falls. This waterfall is only about 30 feet high, with many small trout swimming in its lower pool and a much deeper pool just above its lip. Sunbathers enjoy the rocky pools upstream. You can continue hiking beyond this cataract to the real Big Falls, another mile farther. Spring wildflowers are excellent along the route. The terrain gets drier and rockier as you climb up out of the canyon to Big Falls, and you'll find different types of flowers and foliage on this upper part of the trail. Big Falls is about 80 feet tall, but it's only impressive early in the year. By June it has much less flow than the smaller waterfall downstream. Note that if you want to hike more, the trail continues beyond Big Falls for another mile, making an exposed and steep ascent to Hi Mountain Road.

**User Groups:** Hikers, dogs, and horses. No mountain bikes. No wheelchair facilities.

**Permits:** No day-use permits are required. A national forest recreation pass is required for each vehicle; fees are $5 for one day or $30 for a year.

**Maps:** For a map, ask the U.S. Forest Service for Los Padres National Forest. For a topographic map, ask the USGS for Tar Spring Ridge.

**Directions:** From San Luis Obispo, drive 15 miles south on U.S. 101 to Arroyo Grande and the Highway 227/Lopez Lake exit. Head east on Highway 227 and turn right on Lopez Drive, following the signs toward Lopez Lake for 10.3 miles. Turn right on Hi Mountain Road (before Lopez Lake's entrance station). Drive .8 mile, turn left on Upper Lopez Canyon Road, and drive 6.3 miles, passing a Scout Camp, and turn right. In .1 mile, the pavement ends. Continue for 3.5 miles on the dirt road, crossing Lopez Creek numerous times in the wet season, to the Big Falls trailhead. The trailhead is not usually marked, so set your odometer and look for a small waterfall on the left side of the road. The trail leads from the right side of the road. Note: Four-wheel-drive vehicles are recommended.

**Contact:** Los Padres National Forest, Santa Lucia Ranger District, 1616 North Carlotti Drive, Santa Maria, CA 93454, 805/925-9538, website: www.fs.fed.us/r5/lospadres.

## 11 LITTLE FALLS
### 1.0 mi / 0.5 hr

**in the Santa Lucia Wilderness near Arroyo Grande**

Map 13.2, page 610

Little Falls is just as pretty as its neighbor Big Falls (see previous listing), and getting to it requires the same wet and rugged drive—but less of it. If your car isn't up to the 3.5 miles of rocky road and stream crossings that it takes to get to Big Falls, maybe you can convince it to go only 1.6 miles to Little Falls. If even that's too much, you can always park where the pavement ends and walk to Little Falls, adding 3.2 miles round-trip to the mileage shown above. It's still a pretty easy hike, with plenty of lovely scenery. You hike from the trailhead along Little Falls Creek—a cool, shady stream that is teeming with small trout and lined with oaks, sycamores, bays, and maples. Maidenhair and giant woodwardia ferns line its rocky pools. After only 15 minutes of hiking (less than .5 mile), you'll see a spur trail heading off to the left, which you can follow upstream for a few hundred feet to Little Falls, a 50-foot limestone waterfall. The main trail

continues beyond this spur to many fine, water-carved pools, perfect for wading into. The trail eventually climbs out of the canyon to Hi Mountain Road.

**User Groups:** Hikers, dogs, and horses. No mountain bikes. No wheelchair facilities.

**Permits:** No day-use permits are required. A national forest recreation pass is required for each vehicle; fees are $5 for one day or $30 for a year.

**Maps:** For a map, ask the U.S. Forest Service for Los Padres National Forest. For a topographic map, ask the USGS for Tar Spring Ridge.

**Directions:** From San Luis Obispo, drive 15 miles south on U.S. 101 to Arroyo Grande and the Highway 227/Lopez Lake exit. Head east on Highway 227; turn right on Lopez Drive, following the signs toward Lopez Lake for 10.3 miles. Turn right on Hi Mountain Road (before Lopez Lake's entrance station). Drive .8 mile and turn left on Upper Lopez Canyon Road. Drive 6.3 miles, passing a Scout Camp, and then turn right. The pavement ends .1 mile farther on. Continue for 1.6 miles on the dirt road, crossing Lopez Creek numerous times in the wet season, to the Little Falls trailhead. The trail leads from the right side of the road. Note: Four-wheel-drive vehicles are recommended.

**Contact:** Los Padres National Forest, Santa Lucia Ranger District, 1616 North Carlotti Drive, Santa Maria, CA 93454, 805/925-9538, website: www.fs.fed.us/r5/lospadres.

## 12 DUNA VISTA AND TWO WATERS TRAILS
### 2.2–6.8 mi / 1.0–3.0 hrs

**at Lopez Lake east of Arroyo Grande**

Map 13.2, page 610

Most people on the Central Coast know that Lopez Lake is completely set up for water recreation—boating, waterskiing, windsurfing, fishing, you name it—but not everyone knows that the park is also great for hiking, especially in springtime. The best path in the park,

Duna Vista Trail, is accessible via either a long hike or a short hike and a boat ride. The latter option works out great for people who want to go hiking while their loved ones go fishing; they can be dropped off and picked up later. If you're going by boat, there are two trailheads (docks) for the Two Waters Trail, one on the Lopez arm of the lake, and one on the Wittenberg arm. You can start from either trailhead, or arrange a shuttle pickup with a friend so that you can start at one end and finish at the other. From either trailhead, the Two Waters Trail runs for .6 mile to the Duna Vista Trail, which you follow uphill for .5 mile. California fuschias bloom along the trail, mixed in among the sage and chaparral. After a 600-foot climb, you're rewarded with views of the Santa Lucia Wilderness, the Pacific Ocean, and Pismo Dunes. (Oh yeah, Duna Vista—now we get it.) If you can't arrange a boat ride, you can hike to the start of the Two Waters Trail. Start walking from the end of the park road on the Wittenberg Trail, connect with the Tuouski Trail by Camp French (a Scout Camp), and follow Tuouski Trail to its junction with the east end of the Two Waters Trail. Keep in mind that this changes a 2.2-mile round-trip into a 6.8-mile round-trip.

**User Groups:** Hikers, horses, dogs, and mountain bikes. No wheelchair facilities.

**Permits:** No permits are required. A $6 day-use fee is charged per vehicle.

**Maps:** A map of Lopez Lake Recreation Area is available at the ranger station. For a topographic map, ask the USGS for Tar Spring Ridge.

**Directions:** From San Luis Obispo, drive 15 miles south on U.S. 101 to Arroyo Grande and the Highway 227/Lopez Lake exit. Head east on Highway 227 and turn right on Lopez Drive, following the signs to Lopez Lake for 10.4 miles. To reach the Two Waters trailhead, you can take a boat ride up the Wittenberg or Lopez arms of the lake, or add four miles to your trip by hiking from the Wittenberg trailhead. To reach the latter, drive 1.5 miles past the park entrance station to the parking area near where the park road is gated off.

**Contact:** Lopez Lake Recreation Area, 6800 Lopez Drive, Arroyo Grande, CA 93420, 805/788-2381, website: www.slocountyparks.com.

## 13 BLACKBERRY SPRINGS AND HIGH RIDGE LOOP
### 2.0 mi / 1.0 hr

**at Lopez Lake east of Arroyo Grande**

Map 13.2, page 610

Great views of the grassy hills and blue water of Lopez Lake are yours for the taking on High Ridge Trail. Start from the Blackberry Springs trailhead at Squirrel Campground. Follow the interpretive signs and learn all about the Chumash Indians who once lived here as you hike uphill through a foliage-rich creek canyon. Watch for fruit-covered blackberry bushes in early summer. Many other plants along the trail are also edible and were used by the Chumash. The trail steepens as it climbs to connect with High Ridge Trail at .75 mile, where you turn left and wander along a firebreak, which offers wide-open views. It's hot and sunny up here, so that may dictate how far you wander, but the trail goes 2.2 miles before it drops down to the Wittenberg arm of the lake. Might as well just head out for .5 mile or so, enjoy the views of the Santa Lucia Wilderness and the coast, and then turn around and head back. Another option is to turn right instead of left on the High Ridge Trail, walk .5 mile, and connect with the Turkey Ridge Trail. Take the Turkey Ridge Trail back to the parking lot by Squirrel Campground for a nice two-mile loop trip.

**User Groups:** Hikers and dogs. No horses or mountain bikes. No wheelchair facilities.

**Permits:** No permits are required. A $6 day-use fee is charged per vehicle.

**Maps:** A map of Lopez Lake Recreation Area is available at the ranger station. For a topographic map, ask the USGS for Tar Spring Ridge.

**Directions:** From San Luis Obispo, drive 15 miles south on U.S. 101 to Arroyo Grande and the Highway 227/Lopez Lake exit. Head east on Highway 227 and turn right on Lopez Drive, following the signs to Lopez Lake for 10.4 miles. Continue past the entrance station to Squirrel Campground and the trailhead for the Blackberry Springs Trail.

**Contact:** Lopez Lake Recreation Area, 6800 Lopez Drive, Arroyo Grande, CA 93420, 805/788-2381, website: www.slocountyparks.com.

## 14 OSO FLACO LAKE
**3.0 mi / 1.5 hrs**

**southwest of Arroyo Grande**

**Map 13.2, page 610**

Oso Flaco Lake and its environs were the site of an extensive dune restoration and native plant revegetation project in the 1980s. The result is an 800-acre natural area that is the perfect place to view coastal wildflowers and wildlife. The trail to Oso Flaco Lake starts out on a gravel causeway for .3 mile, then cuts off to the left on a wooden boardwalk and footbridge that bisects the small lake, one of the few remaining freshwater dune lakes. Immediately you are in the good company of shorebirds and waterfowl, including ducks that play hide-and-seek in the islands of reeds. The boardwalk extends beyond the lake's border and over a series of sand dunes. It serves the dual purpose of making the trail suitable for wheelchairs and protecting the dunes' fragile plant life, which includes several threatened species. (Wheelchair users note: After heavy rains, the boardwalk may be partially submerged under a few inches of water. Call the park to check on trail conditions before planning a visit in winter or spring.) Where the boardwalk ends, you can continue walking on the dunes or head to the beach on your right. By the way, what does Oso Flaco mean? Skinny bear. But it's been a long time since they've seen one of those around here.

**User Groups:** Hikers and wheelchairs. No dogs, horses, or mountain bikes.

**Permits:** No permits are required. A $4 day-use fee is charged per vehicle.

**Maps:** For a topographic map, ask the USGS for Oceano.

**Directions:** From Santa Maria on U.S. 101, take the Highway 166/Guadalupe exit, drive nine miles west, and then turn north on Highway 1 at Guadalupe. Drive 3.6 miles to Oso Flaco Lake Road, turn left, and drive three miles to the trailhead, at the end of the road.

**Contact:** Oceano Dunes State Vehicular Recreation Area, 928 Pacific Boulevard, Oceano, CA 93445, 805/473-7230 or 805/473-7223, website: www.parks.ca.gov.

## 15 LAS ZANJAS AND EL CAMINO LOOP
**2.5 mi / 1.25 hrs**

**at La Purisima Mission north of Lompoc**

**Map 13.3, page 611**

If you came to La Purisima Mission seeking heavenly sanctuary but instead found a bunch of screaming school kids, you can still find your heaven in the hills surrounding the mission. There's a surprising number of good hiking trails here, considering this is a state historic park and not a recreation park. The best place to start is on a level loop trail around the mission. Set out on Las Zanjas Trail (also spelled Las Zonas on some signs), a wide ranch road that leads behind the mission buildings. If you like, take the short cutoff on the right to the large cross on the hill (the trail is signed as Vista de la Cruz). A steep climb gives you wide views of the mission area and the Pacific Coast. Then continue on Las Zanjas to the park boundary, where you can loop back on El Camino Real, an old paved park road. Along the way, you'll be accompanied by cool ocean breezes, blooming buckeye trees and bush monkeyflower, and green grasslands in springtime. Be sure to take a tour of the mission before or after your hike.

**User Groups:** Hikers, dogs, horses, and mountain bikes. No wheelchair facilities.

**Permits:** No permits are required. A $4 day-use fee is charged per vehicle.

**Maps:** A map of La Purisima Mission State Historic Park is available at the entrance station or visitors center. For a topographic map, ask the USGS for Los Alamos.

**Directions:** From Buellton on U.S. 101, take the Solvang/Lompoc/Highway 246 exit, drive west 13.2 miles, and turn right on Purisima Road. The park entrance is one mile down the road, on the right. The trailhead is at the far end of the parking lot, near the visitors center.

**Contact:** La Purisima Mission State Historic Park, 2295 Purisima Road, Lompoc, CA 93436, 805/733-3713, website: www.lapurisimamission.org.

## 16 GAVIOTA OVERLOOK
### 3.0 mi / 1.5 hrs

**in Gaviota State Park near Gaviota**

Map 13.3, page 611

If you don't mind a little climbing to get a great coastal view, Gaviota Overlook Trail will suit you just fine. The trail (really a ranch road) is completely out in the open as it climbs from U.S. 101 to the top of the ridge above Gaviota Beach, but as long as the weather is cool, it's an easy ascent. There are two main trail forks; bear left at both. Since this is coastal grasslands territory, wildflowers are prolific in springtime, but things get kind of arid-looking by late summer. No matter; the view from the top is priceless—miles of open ocean on the one side (including the Channel Islands), and miles of grasslands and chaparral on the other side. Hey, where are all the condominiums? Just kidding. The trail ends at some microwave towers below the highest point on the ridge, but the views are just fine from where you are. The only catch on this trail is that the trailhead is darn near impossible to find, so follow directions precisely.

**User Groups:** Hikers, horses, and mountain bikes. No dogs. No wheelchair facilities.

**Permits:** No permits are required. Parking and access are free.

**Maps:** For topographic maps, ask the USGS for Solvang and Gaviota.

**Directions:** Drive south from Buellton on U.S. 101 for 10 miles to just north of Gaviota Pass, to the blue sign that reads Rest Area 1 Mile, Tourist Information. Immediately beyond it you'll drive over a concrete bridge and must quickly turn right into the very small parking area just beyond the bridge. It's easy to miss. If you reach the rest area, you've gone past it. (Coming from Santa Barbara and points south on U.S. 101, you must exit at Highway 1/Lompoc, then get back on the freeway heading south.)

**Contact:** Gaviota State Park, c/o Refugio State Beach, 10 Refugio Beach Road, Goleta, CA 93117, 805/968-1033 or 805/899-1400, website: www.parks.ca.gov.

## 17 GAVIOTA HOT SPRINGS
### 1.0 mi / 0.5 hr

**in Gaviota State Park near Gaviota**

Map 13.3, page 611

Gaviota State Park got smart and started charging a few bucks for people to park at this trailhead, since hot springs always draw a crowd. Still, if you show up first thing in the morning or anytime during the week, you can most likely soak all by yourself in one of the two small pools here. They're not very big or very deep or very hot either, but, hey— whaddya want for a couple bucks? The pools are a quick-to-reach destination, requiring a short but steep climb from the trailhead, mostly on a fire road. The smell of sulfur and the sway of the palm tree above the upper pool will lull you into believing you're at your own private spa. The upper pool is also the hotter of the two, nearly at bathtub temperature. If you look closely, you can see little bubbles coming up from the ground under the pool— geology in action. If you want to hike more, you can combine this trip with the trek to Gaviota Peak (see next listing).

**User Groups:** Hikers, horses, and mountain bikes. No dogs. No wheelchair facilities.

**Permits:** No permits are required. A $4 day-use fee is charged per vehicle.

**Maps:** For a topographic map, ask the USGS for Gaviota.

**Directions:** From Santa Barbara, drive north on U.S. 101 for 35 miles, pass through the tunnel at Gaviota Pass, and take the first exit after the tunnel, which is signed as Highway 1/Lompoc/Vandenburg Air Force Base. At the stop sign, turn right and head south on the frontage road that parallels the freeway. (Don't bear left on Highway 1.) The frontage road ends in .25 mile at the trailhead parking area.

**Contact:** Gaviota State Park, c/o Refugio State Beach, 10 Refugio Beach Road, Goleta, CA 93117, 805/968-1033 or 805/899-1400, website: www.parks.ca.gov.

## 18 GAVIOTA PEAK
### 6.4 mi / 3.5 hrs

**in Gaviota State Park near Gaviota**

> **Map 13.3, page 611**

The best hike for a good workout in Gaviota State Park is the trail to Gaviota Peak. Start from the Gaviota Hot Springs trailhead, but instead of taking the short spur trail to Gaviota Hot Springs, head left on Gaviota Peak Trail and begin your assault on Gaviota Hill—oops, that's Gaviota Peak, elevation 2,450 feet. The climb isn't too bad (2,000 feet in 3.2 miles), but geez, it can get hot here without much shade. The trail is a dirt road (plus a few single-track sections) that climbs a series of knolls on its way to Gaviota Peak. Technically the peak is actually in Los Padres National Forest, not in the state park. Once you're there, you'll find the views are downright awesome. What can you see? Point Conception, the Pacific, the Channel Islands, Lompoc Valley, and Gaviota Pass at your feet. Hope you picked a day when the fog wasn't visiting.

**User Groups:** Hikers, horses, and mountain bikes. No dogs. No wheelchair facilities.

**Permits:** No permits are required. A $4 day-use fee is charged per vehicle.

**Maps:** For a topographic map, ask the USGS for Gaviota.

**Directions:** Drive north from Santa Barbara on U.S. 101 for 35 miles, pass through the tunnel at Gaviota Pass, and take the first exit after the tunnel, which is signed as Highway 1/Lompoc/Vandenburg Air Force Base. Turn right at the stop sign and head south on the frontage road that parallels the freeway. (Don't bear left on to Highway 1.) The frontage road ends in .25 mile at the trailhead parking area.

**Contact:** Gaviota State Park, c/o Refugio State Beach, 10 Refugio Beach Road, Goleta, CA 93117, 805/968-1033 or 805/899-1400, website: www.parks.ca.gov.

## 19 NOJOQUI FALLS
### 0.5 mi / 0.5 hr

**near Gaviota**

> **Map 13.3, page 611**

A favorite spot of Santa Barbarans cruising upcoast on U.S. 101, Nojoqui Falls County Park has plenty of picnic areas, sports fields, and the like, but only one hiking trail. It's a great, short stroll from the parking area to impressive Nojoqui Falls, which drops 80 feet over a sandstone cliff that is almost completely covered with delicate Venus maidenhair ferns. The hike is good no matter how much or how little the falls are flowing—it's an easy walk through a cooling canopy of oaks and laurels, with Nojoqui Creek babbling alongside the trail. Check out the interesting rocks along the route. They're made of shale, while the waterfall cliff is made of sandstone. You'll see the difference. There's a stair-stepped rock perch right by the waterfall's pool, where you can sit in the shade of big-leaf maples and admire the scene. By the way, how do you pronounce the name of this waterfall and park? It's "no-HO-wee." Not "no-HO-kee" or, heaven forbid, "no-JOKE-ee."

**User Groups:** Hikers and dogs. No horses or mountain bikes. No wheelchair facilities.

**Permits:** No permits are required. Parking and access are free.

**Maps:** For a topographic map, ask the USGS for Solvang.

**Directions:** From Santa Barbara, drive 40 miles north on U.S. 101 to the signed turnoff for Nojoqui Park, north of Gaviota State Beach. Drive one mile on the Old Coast Highway and turn east on Alisal Road. Drive .8 mile to the park entrance on your right. Drive .25 mile down the park access road to the parking lot and trailhead. The trail starts from the far end of the parking lot loop.

**Contact:** Nojoqui Falls County Park, 805/688-4217; Santa Barbara County Parks and Recreation, 300 Goodwin Road, Santa Maria, CA 93455, 805/934-6123 or 805/568-2461, website: www.sbparks.com.

## 20 McPHERSON PEAK TRAIL
### 10.0 mi / 2.0 days

**in the San Rafael Wilderness**

Map 13.4, page 612

McPherson Peak, elevation 5,747 feet, is just on the edge of the spectacular San Rafael Wilderness, a land of condors and steep canyons. Although the trail is steep and can be hot in summer, it gives hikers outstanding views of the wilderness and the desertlike lands of Cuyama to the northeast. From Aliso Park Campground, you start hiking on the dirt road that is signed for Hog Pen Spring Campground, quickly saying good-bye to the shady canyon. Reach the camp in 1.5 miles (there's a spring nearby if you need water); then pick up a trail that continues climbing, now more steeply, to Sierra Madre Road, on the wilderness boundary. Turn right on the dirt road and hike another 2.5 miles through chaparral to McPherson Peak, passing McPherson Camp along the way. The camp has a spring and is an excellent place to spend the night. You can watch the sunset from McPherson Peak and then crawl into your sleeping bag and watch the stars.

**User Groups:** Hikers, dogs, horses, and mountain bikes (mountain bikes may not go past the wilderness boundary). No wheelchair facilities.

**Permits:** A free California campfire permit is required for building a fire or using a backpacking stove; permits are available at the Santa Maria Ranger Station. A national forest recreation pass is required for each vehicle; fees are $5 for one day or $30 for a year.

**Maps:** For a map, ask the U.S. Forest Service for Los Padres National Forest. For a topographic map, ask the USGS for Peak Mountain.

**Directions:** From Santa Maria on U.S. 101, take Highway 166 east for 48 miles to just west of New Cuyama. Turn right (south) on Aliso Canyon Road and follow it for six miles to Aliso Park Campground. The dirt road can be very rough; high-clearance vehicles are recommended. If you are coming from Ventura or Ojai, take Highway 33 north to Highway 166, then go west past New Cuyama.

**Contact:** Los Padres National Forest, Santa Lucia Ranger District, 1616 North Carlotti Drive, Santa Maria, CA 93454, 805/925-9538, website: www.fs.fed.us/r5/lospadres.

## 21 UPPER MANZANA CREEK TRAIL
### 13.0 mi / 1.0–2.0 days

**in San Rafael Wilderness**

Map 13.4, page 612

From Nira Campground, a major entry point into the San Rafael Wilderness, you can hike east or west along Manzana Creek. In spring, the creek is popular with anglers, who come here to catch the resident trout in Manzana Creek. (Some trout are stocked by the campground.) Hikers and backpackers can take Upper Manzana Creek Trail to the east and stop at any one of several excellent campsites, including Manzana (six miles out) and Manzana Narrows (seven miles out). Both have swimming holes. The trail climbs gently from the campground, sometimes switchbacking away from the creek but always returning. There is a modicum of shade from blue oaks and gray pines, mixed in among the low-lying chaparral and manzanita. Note that the creek gets low and is less attractive by midsummer but that winter hiking can be dangerous if the stream level is too high. March through May is the best time to visit.

**User Groups:** Hikers, dogs, and horses. No mountain bikes. No wheelchair facilities.

**Permits:** A free California campfire permit is required for building a fire or using a backpacking stove; permits are available at the Santa Maria Ranger Station. A national forest recreation pass is required for each vehicle; fees are $5 for one day or $30 for a year.

**Maps:** For a map, ask the U.S. Forest Service for Los Padres National Forest. For a topographic map, ask the USGS for Bald Mountain.

**Directions:** From Santa Barbara on U.S. 101, take Highway 154 north and drive 23 miles, past Lake Cachuma, to Armour Ranch Road. Turn right and drive 1.5 miles to Happy Canyon Road (not suitable for trailers). Turn right and drive 14 miles to Cachuma Saddle and a junction with Figueroa Mountain Road; then continue straight on Sunset Valley Road and follow it for four miles to its end, at Nira Campground. Park in the hikers' parking lot.

**Contact:** Los Padres National Forest, Santa Lucia Ranger District, 1616 North Carlotti Drive, Santa Maria, CA 93454, 805/925-9538, website: www.fs.fed.us/r5/lospadres.

## 22 PIÑO ALTO TRAIL
### 0.5 mi / 0.5 hr

**on Figueroa Mountain**

**Map 13.4, page 612**

You just made the drive to Figueroa Mountain and you're wondering what in the heck this place is all about. The Piño Alto Interpretive Trail can spell it out for you, and besides, the vistas will knock your socks off. From one point on the trail, the Santa Ynez Valley is visible for some 20 miles from the northwest to the southeast. You can see Cuyama, Lake Cachuma, the Santa Ynez Mountains, and sometimes even the Channel Islands far off to sea. The trail is located at 4,600 feet

in elevation, situated among ponderosa and Jeffrey pines and big cone spruce. Conifers? In Santa Barbara? That's right. The paved trail surface makes it suitable for wheelchairs. If you want wider vistas, make sure that you drive .5 mile uphill from the trailhead parking lot to the Figueroa lookout tower site. From there you can survey all the mountains of the San Rafael Wilderness. Note that if you like what you see on Figueroa Mountain, many longer day hikes are possible on the nearby Davy Brown/Fir Canyon Trail, starting at either Davy Brown Campground or at the trailhead on Figueroa Mountain Road.

**User Groups:** Hikers, wheelchairs, and dogs. No horses or mountain bikes.

**Permits:** No permits are required. A national forest recreation pass is required for each vehicle; fees are $5 for one day or $30 for a year.

**Maps:** For a map, ask the U.S. Forest Service for Los Padres National Forest. For a topographic map, ask the USGS for Figueroa Mountain.

**Directions:** From Santa Barbara, drive north on U.S. 101, through Buellton, for 45 miles to the Highway 154 East turnoff. Turn east onto Highway 154 and drive three miles to Los Olivos, then turn north (left) on Figueroa Mountain Road. Drive 13 miles to the fork for Figueroa Mountain Lookout Road (dirt). Bear left and drive two miles to the Piño Alto Picnic Area.

**Contact:** Los Padres National Forest, Santa Lucia Ranger District, 1616 North Carlotti Drive, Santa Maria, CA 93454, 805/925-9538, website: www.fs.fed.us/r5/lospadres.

## 23 SNYDER TRAIL
### 12.0 mi / 7.0 hrs

**near the Santa Ynez Recreation Area**

**Map 13.4, page 612**

While Snyder Trail may start out looking like a plain old fire road at its lower end at Paradise Road, by the time it climbs six miles to East Camino Cielo, it becomes a lovely single-track trail that is bordered by more wildflowers than you can count and has more wide-reaching vistas than you can imagine. Don't bother twisting your neck to catch the views on your way up, because on your return trip downhill, they will be laid out in front of you. The nice thing about the trail is that you start gaining vistas fairly quickly, so if you're tiring of the climb, you can simply find a knoll somewhere, have a seat, and pull out your sandwiches. If you decide to go all the way up, just before the top is a popular side trip to the ruins of Knapp's Castle (see listing in this chapter). Take the gated dirt road on the left, 5.5 miles up. If you hike Snyder Trail's entire length, you'll be tired by the end of the day, but you'll have a whole storehouse of fine memories. One caveat: This trail is also popular with mountain bikers, usually heading in the downhill direction. Watch out for them.

**User Groups:** Hikers, dogs, horses, and mountain bikes. No wheelchair facilities.

**Permits:** No permits are required. A national forest recreation pass is required for each vehicle; fees are $5 for one day or $30 for a year.

**Maps:** For a map, ask the U.S. Forest Service for Los Padres National Forest. For a topographic map, ask the USGS for San Marcos Pass.

**Directions:** From U.S. 101 in Santa Barbara, take the Highway 154/State Street exit and drive north for 11.5 miles. Turn right on Paradise Road and drive 4.2 miles to the trailhead for the Snyder Trail, which is at a locked gate on the right side of the road .25 mile west of the Los Prietos Ranger Station.

**Contact:** Los Padres National Forest, Santa Barbara Ranger District, 3505 Paradise Road, Santa Barbara, CA 93105, 805/967-3481, website: www.fs.fed.us/r5/lospadres.

## 24 ALISO CANYON LOOP TRAIL
**3.5 mi / 2.0 hrs**

**in the Santa Ynez Recreation Area**

Map 13.4, page 612

From the east end of Sage Hill Campground, you can set off on Aliso Canyon Trail and choose between a one-mile interpretive walk or a 3.5-mile loop trail. The former is the first mile of the latter and follows Aliso Creek. Be sure to bring along a trail brochure so you can learn all about how the Chumash Indians lived in this area and what plants they used and ate. In the spring, a wildflower-identification book also may be a good idea, as the variety of flowers along this short route is surprising. At the end of the interpretive trail, you can either turn around and hike back or continue on the longer loop trip. To do so, walk back a few feet to a trail junction and ascend for .5 mile to a meadow on a grassy plateau. From there, you climb rather steeply to the top of the ridge that divides Aliso and Oso Canyons, where there are excellent views of the Santa Ynez Canyon and distant mountains. At the ridge top, turn right (often there is no trail sign), following the ridge's backbone. You'll loop around and soon head back downhill. Note that after winter rains, the sloping trails beyond the interpretive trail are often badly eroded. If you're walking the entire loop, wear some good boots.

**User Groups:** Hikers, dogs, horses, and mountain bikes. No wheelchair facilities.

**Permits:** No permits are required. A national forest recreation pass is required for each vehicle; fees are $5 for one day or $30 for a year.

**Maps:** For a map, ask the U.S. Forest Service for Los Padres National Forest. For a topographic map, ask the USGS for San Marcos Pass.

**Directions:** From U.S. 101 in Santa Barbara, take the Highway 154/State Street exit and drive north for about 11.5 miles. Turn right on Paradise Road and drive 4.5 miles to the ranger station. Turn left at the ranger station and drive one mile to Sage Hill Campground. Proceed to the day-use area at the east end of the camp and the trailhead for the Aliso Canyon Trail.

**Contact:** Los Padres National Forest, Santa Barbara Ranger District, 3505 Paradise Road, Santa Barbara, CA 93105, 805/967-3481, website: www.fs.fed.us/r5/lospadres.

## **25** SANTA CRUZ TRAIL
**4.0 mi / 2.0 hrs**

**in the Santa Ynez Recreation Area**

Map 13.4, page 612

The Santa Cruz Trail is one of the most popular in the Santa Ynez Recreation Area, and it's no wonder. The hiking is easy and the swimming holes along Oso Creek are plentiful. Cooling off in the water is the No. 1 reason that people pay a visit to the Santa Ynez Recreation Area in summertime. The destination on this trip is Nineteen Oaks Camp, a popular picnicking spot near the base of Little Pine Mountain. The trail follows an unattractive dirt road out of Upper Oso Campground, but it becomes lovely single-track trail as it continues into the shady canyon. The sandstone-carved creek pools are lovely to see even when the water level is low, and as you climb a bit, you get views of Little Pine Mountain. A spur trail on the right, at 1.9 miles, leads a few hundred yards to Nineteen Oaks Camp, with shady oaks and a few campsites and picnic tables. Most day hikers end their trip there before the trail begins its hot, exposed switchbacks to the top of Little Pine Mountain, elevation 4,506 feet. Be forewarned: You may see off-road motorcyclists at the trailhead, but don't let them scare you off. They'll be exiting your trail in the first mile.

**User Groups:** Hikers, dogs, horses, and mountain bikes. No wheelchair facilities.

**Permits:** No permits are required. A national forest recreation pass is required for each vehicle; fees are $5 for one day or $30 for a year.

**Maps:** For a map, ask the U.S. Forest Service for Los Padres National Forest. For a topographic map, ask the USGS for San Marcos Pass.

**Directions:** From U.S. 101 in Santa Barbara, take the Highway 154/State Street exit and drive north for 11.5 miles. Turn right on Paradise Road and drive 5.5 miles, past the ranger station, to the left turnoff for Upper Oso Campground. Turn left and drive one mile to the campground.

**Contact:** Los Padres National Forest, Santa Barbara Ranger District, 3505 Paradise Road, Santa Barbara, CA 93105, 805/967-3481, website: www.fs.fed.us/r5/lospadres.

## **26** KNAPP'S CASTLE
**0.8 mi / 0.5 hr**

**north of Santa Barbara**

Map 13.4, page 612

Some hikes are just right for all kinds of hikers, no matter what their abilities or tastes, and the trail to Knapp's Castle is one of those. The tricky part is that Knapp's Castle, or actually the remains of Knapp's Castle, is on a chunk of private property within Los Padres National Forest, and it's only by the good graces of the landowner that the public is allowed to hike there. He's a very nice gentleman, and for years he has allowed Santa Barbara hikers to visit his land, which is well known not just for the castle ruins but also for its memorable vistas. If we all mind our manners, hopefully we can keep this beautiful spot accessible for many years to come. So who was the Knapp of Knapp's Castle? George Knapp was the former chairman of the board of Union Carbide, and he built a five-bedroom sandstone mansion on this site in 1916. Although the building burned down in a canyon fire in 1940, its foundation still stands, and it offers a fine spot to sit and look out over the Santa Ynez River Canyon and distant mountains. You can even see far-off Lake Cachuma. The trail to reach Knapp's Castle is a well-graded dirt road. You hike past the gate that says Private Property Ahead, pass through another gate, staying on the dirt road, and reach the castle remains and its fabulous lookout in less than .5 mile of walking.

Special Note: Because Knapp's Castle is on private property, its accessibility to the public is subject to change at any time. Call the Santa Barbara Ranger District office for an update before visiting.

**User Groups:** Hikers and dogs. No horses or mountain bikes. No wheelchair facilities.

**Permits:** No permits are required. A national forest recreation pass is required for each vehicle; fees are $5 for one day or $30 for a year. **Maps:** For a map, ask the U.S. Forest Service for Los Padres National Forest. For a topographic map, ask the USGS for San Marcos Pass. **Directions:** From U.S. 101 in Santa Barbara, take the Highway 154/State Street exit and drive north for 10.5 miles. Turn right on East Camino Cielo and drive 2.9 miles to the parking pullout on the right, across from a locked gate and dirt road on the left. The gate is signed Private Property Ahead. **Contact:** Los Padres National Forest, Santa Barbara Ranger District, 3505 Paradise Road, Santa Barbara, CA 93105, 805/967-3481, website: www.fs.fed.us/r5/lospadres.

## 27 SEVEN FALLS
### 3.0 mi / 1.5 hrs

**north of Santa Barbara**

Map 13.4, page 612

Seven Falls is a perfect springtime day trip in Santa Barbara, best visited from February to April. It has a little bit of everything: waterfalls, swimming holes, vistas, wildflowers, and good trail. The trail has a lot of unsigned junctions, however, so remember to stay left at all of them until after you cross Mission Creek for the second time. From the end of Tunnel Road, start hiking on the gated continuation of the road, passing a water tank and heading uphill on pavement for .75 mile. In a few minutes of climbing, you'll be able to see all the way out to the ocean. Cross a bridge over Mission Creek and continue hiking straight ahead on the road, which turns to dirt. In a few hundred feet you come to a junction; a sign on your left directs you to Jesusita Trail. Follow it to the left and bear left again as the path cuts down on single-track to Mission Creek, where you'll find many good swimming holes. Cross the creek, but instead of following the continuation of Jesusita Trail, head to your

right, upstream, on a use trail. (Remember, this is the only right turn on the route.) In .25 mile of combined hiking and scrambling, you'll reach the first of the sandstone-carved cascades of Seven Falls. These falls flow with force only immediately after a period of rain, but the sandstone pools and canyon walls are pretty to look at even when the creek is nearly dry. **User Groups:** Hikers, dogs, horses, and mountain bikes. No wheelchair facilities. **Permits:** No permits are required. Parking and access are free. **Maps:** For a map, ask the U.S. Forest Service for Los Padres National Forest. For a topographic map, ask the USGS for Santa Barbara. **Directions:** From U.S. 101 in Santa Barbara, take the Mission Street exit and follow it east for just over a mile, crossing State Street. When Mission Street ends, turn left on Laguna Street and drive past the Santa Barbara Mission, turning right on Los Olivos, directly in front of the mission. Passing the mission, bear left on Mission Canyon Road for .8 mile. Turn right on Foothill Boulevard. In .1 mile, turn left onto the continuation of Mission Canyon Road. Then bear left on Tunnel Road and follow it for 1.1 miles until it ends. Park alongside the road, on the right. **Contact:** Los Padres National Forest, Santa Barbara Ranger District, 3505 Paradise Road, Santa Barbara, CA 93105, 805/967-3481, website: www.fs.fed.us/r5/lospadres.

## 28 INSPIRATION POINT
### 5.0 mi / 2.5 hrs

**north of Santa Barbara**

Map 13.4, page 612

The trail to Inspiration Point is sure to get you inspired if only because it's a great path for year-round exercise in Santa Barbara. Follow Tunnel Road Trail to Jesusita Trail, as if you were going to Seven Falls (see previous listing), but after crossing Mission Creek, keep following the main Jesusita Trail instead. Get ready for a switchbacking climb up to Inspiration

Point, which is only one mile away. The tan-colored rock outcrops you see everywhere are coldwater sandstone; often you'll see hang gliders taking off from some of the highest rocks and gliding, seemingly effortlessly, overhead. When you reach Inspiration Point at 1,750 feet, you are rewarded with sweeping views of the Pacific Coast, Santa Barbara and Goleta, and the Channel Islands.

**User Groups:** Hikers, dogs, horses, and mountain bikes. No wheelchair facilities.

**Permits:** No permits are required. Parking and access are free.

**Maps:** For a map, ask the U.S. Forest Service for Los Padres National Forest. For a topographic map, ask the USGS for Santa Barbara.

**Directions:** From U.S. 101 in Santa Barbara, take the Mission Street exit and follow it east for just over a mile, crossing State Street. When Mission Street ends, turn left on Laguna Street and drive past the Santa Barbara Mission, turning right on Los Olivos, directly in front of the mission. Passing the mission, bear left on Mission Canyon Road for .8 mile. Turn right on Foothill Boulevard. In .1 mile, turn left onto the continuation of Mission Canyon Road. Then bear left on Tunnel Road and follow it for 1.1 miles until it ends. Park alongside the road, on the right.

**Contact:** Los Padres National Forest, Santa Barbara Ranger District, 3505 Paradise Road, Santa Barbara, CA 93105, 805/967-3481, website: www.fs.fed.us/r5/lospadres.

## 29 RATTLESNAKE CANYON
**5.0 mi / 2.5 hrs**

**north of Santa Barbara**

Map 13.4, page 612

Rattlesnake Canyon Trail is probably the most popular canyon trail in Santa Barbara and also one of the prettiest, despite its menacing name. The lower reaches of the trail can look like a parade, especially on weekends, but the higher you go, the fewer folks you see. The path is especially popular with people walking their dogs. Rattlesnake Canyon is a lush riparian environment around a year-round creek; a place where the plant life is so lavish that you may think you're in Mendocino or the northern coast. The trail starts out as a wide dirt path (an old carriage road) but soon narrows to single track. It crosses rocky Rattlesnake Creek many times, tunneling through a forest of oak, bay, and sycamore trees on the lower stretch of the trail. In the spring and summer months, the wildflowers here are as good as you'll find anywhere in Santa Barbara. As you climb out of the canyon, you'll gain increasingly broad views of the Pacific Coast and Channel Islands. Watch for hang gliders soaring overhead. At an intersection with a connector trail to Tunnel Trail at 1.7 miles, bear right to finish the steep climb to Gibraltar Road. Suddenly your surroundings aren't quite so lush anymore, but the coastal views—well, on a clear day, they don't get much better than this.

**User Groups:** Hikers, dogs, and horses. No mountain bikes. No wheelchair facilities.

**Permits:** No permits are required. Parking and access are free.

**Maps:** For a map, ask the U.S. Forest Service for Los Padres National Forest. For a topographic map, ask the USGS for Santa Barbara.

**Directions:** From U.S. 101 in Santa Barbara, take the Mission Street exit and follow it east for just over a mile, crossing State Street. When Mission Street ends, turn left on Laguna Street and drive past the Santa Barbara Mission, turning right on Los Olivos, directly in front of the mission. Passing the mission, bear left on Mission Canyon Road for .8 mile. Turn right on Foothill Boulevard. In .1 mile, turn left onto the continuation of Mission Canyon Road. Drive .4 mile and turn right on Las Conoas Road. Drive 1.2 miles and park on the right side of the road, across from the sign for Skofield Park and Rattlesnake Canyon Wilderness Area.

**Contact:** Los Padres National Forest, Santa Barbara Ranger District, 3505 Paradise Road, Santa Barbara, CA 93105, 805/967-3481, website: www.fs.fed.us/r5/lospadres.

## 30 MONTECITO OVERLOOK
3.0 mi / 1.5 hrs

### in Montecito

**Map 13.4, page 612**

The east fork of Cold Springs is a perfect introductory hike to the Santa Barbara front country. For people who think the mountains in Santa Barbara are all chaparral-covered slopes, this trail is an eye-opener to the lush beauty of the mountain canyons. The climb to Montecito Overlook is a good aerobic workout but not a killer and affords great views of the Santa Barbara coast and Channel Islands. Many people don't go all the way to the overlook; they just hike through the shady forest to a bench that overlooks the confluence of the east and middle forks of Cold Springs Creek and find themselves a cool pool to soak their feet. From the roadside pullout, follow the path through the alders alongside Cold Springs Creek, staying on the creek's right (east) side. After the first mile, you leave the creek and begin to switchback uphill to the overlook—really just a flat semiclearing where the trail intersects a dirt road. Pick any spot amid the invading brush where the views are clear and wide. The best spot is a few hundred feet down the road to your right. Hikers looking for more trail to cover can continue another two miles to Montecito Peak, elevation 3,214 feet. The climb is steep and hot (no shade), but for many it's worth it. In addition to the views of the Santa Barbara coast, you can see all the way to the Santa Monica Mountains.

**User Groups:** Hikers, dogs, horses, and mountain bikes. No wheelchair facilities.

**Permits:** No permits are required. Parking and access are free.

**Maps:** For a map, ask the U.S. Forest Service for Los Padres National Forest. For a topographic map, ask the USGS for Santa Barbara.

**Directions:** From Santa Barbara, drive south on U.S. 101 for four miles and exit on Hot Springs Road. Turn left on Hot Springs Road and drive 2.5 miles to Mountain Drive. Turn left and continue 1.2 miles to the Cold Springs trailhead. Park off the road, near the sharp curve where the creek runs across the road. The trail is marked by a rusty Forest Service sign.

**Contact:** Los Padres National Forest, Santa Barbara Ranger District, 3505 Paradise Road, Santa Barbara, CA 93105, 805/967-3481, website: www.fs.fed.us/r5/lospadres.

## 31 WEST FORK COLD SPRINGS
4.0 mi / 2.0 hrs

### in Montecito

**Map 13.4, page 612**

If you hike the west fork of Cold Springs from its start—where it spurs off East Fork Trail—to its end at Gibraltar Road, you get to see the wide range of terrain that is typical in Santa Barbara. Start hiking on East Fork Cold Springs Trail from the rusty forest service sign near the road. After a .5-mile stretch through shady forest canopy alongside the creek, you'll reach a bench that overlooks the confluence of the east and middle forks of Cold Springs Creek. You'll cross the creek here; look carefully for the trail sign. Soon you leave the dense, shady, fern-laden area surrounding Cold Springs Creek and climb out of the canyon into a drier and more exposed landscape. In early spring, look for spectacular Tangerine Falls up ahead, in the Middle Fork Canyon; the waterfall is clearly visible, although distant, from West Fork Trail. (A use trail cuts off from the main trail to reach it, but it requires good scrambling abilities and an immunity to poison oak.) By the time you climb to the end of West Fork Trail, at Gibraltar Road, you'll be glad to turn around and head back down to the coolness below. The views are excellent from the road, however, and you'll get plenty more views as you walk back down the trail. Be careful going down—West Fork Trail is not as well used as East Fork Trail, and it's steep and eroded in places, especially when wet. But that's a small price to pay for the glorious vistas of the Montecito coast and the relative solitude of this trail compared to its popular neighbor, East Fork Trail.

**User Groups:** Hikers, dogs, horses, and mountain bikes. No wheelchair facilities.

**Permits:** No permits are required. Parking and access are free.

**Maps:** For a map, ask the U.S. Forest Service for Los Padres National Forest. For a topographic map, ask the USGS for Santa Barbara.

**Directions:** From Santa Barbara, drive south on U.S. 101 for four miles and exit on Hot Springs Road. Turn left on Hot Springs Road and drive 2.5 miles to Mountain Drive. Turn left and continue 1.2 miles to the Cold Springs trailhead. Park off the road, near the sharp curve where the creek crosses the road.

**Contact:** Los Padres National Forest, Santa Barbara Ranger District, 3505 Paradise Road, Santa Barbara, CA 93105, 805/967-3481, website: www.fs.fed.us/r5/lospadres.

## 32 SAN YSIDRO TRAIL
### 8.0 mi / 4.5 hrs

**in Montecito**

**Map 13.4, page 612**

If you like running water, San Ysidro Canyon is your chance at seeing some, even long after the last rain. Other streams in the Santa Barbara area are often nearly dry by May, but San Ysidro keeps on flowing year-round. The trail up its canyon offers many possible destinations and stopping points; few hike all the way to its terminus, at East Camino Cielo—it's four miles one-way with a 3,000-foot elevation gain. The rewards are great no matter how far you go, beginning with swimming holes and waterfalls in the first two miles of trail, mostly under the shade of oaks and sycamores. After a rocky section, you climb out of the canyon into chaparral country, entering into a series of steep, exposed switchbacks. Most people give up somewhere along this stretch, but those who continue come out near Cold Spring Saddle on East Camino Cielo, elevation 3,480 feet. From there, you'll feel on top of the world.

**User Groups:** Hikers, dogs, horses, and mountain bikes. No wheelchair facilities.

**Permits:** No permits are required. Parking and access are free.

**Maps:** For a map, ask the U.S. Forest Service for Los Padres National Forest. For a topographic map, ask the USGS for Carpinteria.

**Directions:** From U.S. 101 in Montecito, take the San Ysidro Road exit and head east for one mile to East Valley Road/Highway 192. Turn right on East Valley Road/Highway 192 and travel .9 mile. Turn left on Park Lane and drive .4 mile on Park Lane; then bear left on East Mountain Drive and drive .25 mile to the end of the road. Park alongside the road and walk to the trailhead, on the right.

**Contact:** Los Padres National Forest, Santa Barbara Ranger District, 3505 Paradise Road, Santa Barbara, CA 93105, 805/967-3481, website: www.fs.fed.us/r5/lospadres.

## 33 McMENEMY TRAIL
### 2.5 mi / 1.0 hr

**in Montecito**

**Map 13.4, page 612**

If you only have time for a short hike, this lovely trip in San Ysidro Canyon includes a stint on McMenemy Trail, an old favorite of many Santa Barbara hikers. It has just enough of a climb to make you feel that you did your workout for the day but enough pretty views to make you forget that hiking is actually exercise. Begin your trip on San Ysidro Trail (see previous listing), but bear left at the sign for McMenemy Trail, .5 mile in. Unfortunately, this part of the trail is routed through a construction site on private property near the San Ysidro Ranch and has looked unsightly for the last few years. Until the situation improves, just endure it, because soon, a series of switchbacks brings you to the Colonel's stone bench—Colonel McMenemy, that is—where you have a fine view down into Montecito and out to the coast. It's a good place to catch your breath, read a book, or have a picnic. There is even a horse hitch available, just in case you brought your horse along. If you want to keep hiking, you can make a five-mile loop by continuing on McMenemy Trail to Saddle Rock Trail. Turn right, then right again on the Edison Catwalk to return to San Ysidro Canyon Trail.

**User Groups:** Hikers, dogs, horses, and mountain bikes. No wheelchair facilities.

**Permits:** No permits are required. Parking and access are free.

**Maps:** For a map, ask the U.S. Forest Service for Los Padres National Forest. For a topographic map, ask the USGS for Carpinteria.

**Directions:** From U.S. 101 in Montecito, take the San Ysidro Road exit and head east for one mile to East Valley Road/Highway 192. Turn right on East Valley Road/Highway 192, travel .9 mile, and turn left on Park Lane. Drive .4 mile on Park Lane and bear left on East Mountain Drive. Drive .25 mile to the end of East Mountain Drive and park alongside the road. The trailhead is on the right.

**Contact:** Los Padres National Forest, Santa Barbara Ranger District, 3505 Paradise Road, Santa Barbara, CA 93105, 805/967-3481, website: www.fs.fed.us/r5/lospadres.

## 34 VINCENT TUMAMAIT TRAIL
**5.0 mi / 2.5 hrs**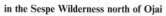

**in the Chumash Wilderness west of Frazier Park**

Map 13.4, page 612

A day hike in the Chumash Wilderness means the possibility of seeing a magnificent condor fly overhead, as well as a visit to Mount Pinos (8,831 feet), the highest point in Los Padres National Forest. This is conifer country, with the peak covered in snow a good part of the year—to the great delight of Southern California cross-country skiers. The Vincent Tumamait Trail begins on the summit of Mount Pinos and runs five miles to Mount Abel, elevation 8,286 feet (also called Mount Cerro Noroeste). If you wish, you can leave a car at Mount Abel and take a one-way shuttle trip between the two impressive peaks. Otherwise

it's great fun just to check out the far-reaching views from the trailhead on Mount Pinos' summit and wander a way on Vincent Tumamait Trail. Head out two miles, downhill at first and then up Sawmill Mountain to the North Fork Trail junction. Bear left at the junction and walk .5 mile to primitive Sheep Camp, a sweet spot in the shade of fir and pine trees, where you can open up your day pack and have lunch. After a rest, you'll be all fueled up for the uphill return trip to the summit. As you hike, keep scanning the skies for those giant condors, many of which nest in the nearby condor sanctuary. By the way, who was Vincent Tumamait? He was a Chumash elder and a beloved storyteller who lived from 1919 to 1992.

**User Groups:** Hikers, dogs, and horses. No mountain bikes. No wheelchair facilities.

**Permits:** No permits are required. A national forest recreation pass is required for each vehicle; fees are $5 for one day or $30 for a year.

**Maps:** For a map, ask the U.S. Forest Service for Los Padres National Forest. For a topographic map, ask the USGS for Sawmill Mountain.

**Directions:** From I-5 near Lebec, take the Frazier Park/Mount Pinos exit and turn west. Drive 12 miles on Frazier Mountain Park Road, which will become Cuddy Valley Road. At 12 miles, bear left on Mount Pinos Highway, and drive nine miles to the dirt road on the left, signed for Mount Pinos Summit. Turn left and drive 1.8 miles to the summit and trailhead. Bear left at the forks.

**Contact:** Los Padres National Forest, Mount Pinos Ranger District, 34580 Lockwood Valley Road, Frazier Park, CA 93225, 661/245-3731, website: www.fs.fed.us/r5/lospadres.

## 35 POTRERO JOHN
**3.2 mi / 1.5 hrs**

**in the Sespe Wilderness north of Ojai**

Map 13.4, page 612

There's nothing nicer than a trail that follows a stream, especially in a place as notoriously dry as Ojai. The Potrero John Trail follows

Potrero John Creek to Potrero John Camp, set at 4,400 feet in elevation. The creek has water most of the year but frequently dries up in the summer, so visit here in winter or spring if possible. From the roadside trailhead, the trail starts out with a brief steep pitch, but it quickly levels off as it ascends the canyon. It follows the canyon floor for 1.5 miles, then crosses the creek on a bridge and enters Portrero Camp. You have a fair chance of having this spot all to yourself, because the trail doesn't go anywhere; it simply ends just beyond the camp. The scenery is typical for this area—chaparral and live oaks—but it's the presence of Potrero John Creek that makes this easy hike so pleasant. So what's a potrero? It's Spanish for meadow.

**User Groups:** Hikers, dogs, and horses. No mountain bikes. No wheelchair facilities.

**Permits:** No permits are required. A national forest recreation pass is required for each vehicle; fees are $5 for one day or $30 for a year.

**Maps:** For a map, ask the U.S. Forest Service for Los Padres National Forest or Sespe Wilderness. A map of the Sespe Wilderness is available from Tom Harrison Maps. For a topographic map, ask the USGS for Lion Canyon.

**Directions:** From Ojai, drive north on Highway 33 for 21 miles to where Potrero John Creek crosses the highway. The trailhead is signed.

**Contact:** Los Padres National Forest, Ojai Ranger District, 1190 East Ojai Avenue, Ojai, CA 93023, 805/646-4348, website: www.fs.fed .us/r5/lospadres.

## 36 CEDAR CREEK AND THE FISHBOWLS
9.0 mi / 4.5 hrs or 2.0 days

**in the Sespe Wilderness northeast of Ojai**

Map 13.4, page 612

Despite the length of this trail, the Fishbowls along Piru Creek are a popular and heavily visited spot, mostly because there is little that is finer in life than a creek with good swimming holes. That and the fact that the trail

has a moderate elevation gain, so even with the nine-mile round-trip, it's a manageable day hike for most people. The Cedar Creek Trail leads uphill from Thorn Meadows Campground (elevation 5,050 feet), first through oaks and then a pretty conifer forest (including the trail's namesake incense cedars). It follows the south fork of Piru Creek much of the way. What starts out as a wide dirt road eventually narrows to a single-track trail. At 3.5 miles in, bear right on Fishbowls Trail, hike along a ridgeline (with lovely views of the forest below), then descend to Fishbowls Camp. Walk upstream from the camp for about 300 yards to reach the Fishbowls, a series of rounded sandstone pools on Piru Creek.

**User Groups:** Hikers, dogs, and horses. No mountain bikes. No wheelchair facilities.

**Permits:** A free California campfire permit is required for building a fire or using a backpacking stove; permits are available at any Southern California Forest Service ranger station. A national forest recreation pass is required for each vehicle; fees are $5 for one day or $30 for a year.

**Maps:** For a map, ask the U.S. Forest Service for Los Padres National Forest. A map of the Sespe Wilderness is available from Tom Harrison Maps. For a topographic map, ask the USGS for Lockwood Valley.

**Directions:** From Ojai, drive 40 miles north on Highway 33 and turn right on Lockwood Valley Road. Drive approximately 15 miles and turn right on Mutau Road. Drive 7.5 miles and turn right on Thorn Meadows Road. Drive .5 mile to the Cedar Creek trailhead.

**Contact:** Los Padres National Forest, Mount Pinos Ranger District, 34580 Lockwood Valley Road, Frazier Park, CA 93225, 661/245-3731, website: www.fs.fed.us/r5/lospadres.

## 37 SESPE HOT SPRINGS
18.0 mi / 2.0 days

**in the Sespe Wilderness northeast of Ojai**

Map 13.4, page 612

Sespe Hot Springs have the hottest natural mineral water in Southern California—as hot as 210 degrees Fahrenheit. This year-round spring heats several pools downstream on Sespe Creek to a temperature warm enough for bathing. This seems like an ideal destination, but don't think about making a summertime trip—the air temperature here is often close to 100 degrees Fahrenheit, and the area around the springs has no vegetation. In fact, it looks something like the surface of the moon. Still, in fall, winter, or spring, this is a wonderful spot. Hike in 1.7 miles on the main wilderness trail to a fork where Little Mutau Creek Trail goes left and Johnson Ridge Trail goes right. Bear right and follow Johnson Ridge Trail, which years ago was open to motorcycle use but is now part of the Sespe Wilderness. It drops steeply to Sespe Creek over the next 6.2 miles, and there is almost no shade along the route. You'll lose 2,500 feet along the way. A final left spur leads you a half mile to the hot spring; you'll probably smell it before you see it. To spend the night, you must hike a mile south from the springs to Sespe Camp. The nearest water is another half mile away in Sespe Creek. It wouldn't hurt to carry some with you as a backup.

**User Groups:** Hikers, dogs, and horses. No mountain bikes. No wheelchair facilities.

**Permits:** A free California campfire permit is required for building a fire or using a backpacking stove; permits are available at any Southern California Forest Service ranger station. A national forest recreation pass is required for each vehicle; fees are $5 for one day or $30 for a year.

**Maps:** For a map, ask the U.S. Forest Service for Los Padres National Forest. A map of the Sespe Wilderness is available from Tom Harrison Maps. For a topographic map, ask the USGS for Lockwood Valley.

**Directions:** From Ojai, drive 40 miles north on Highway 33 and turn right on Lockwood Valley Road. Drive approximately 15 miles and turn right on Mutau Road. Follow Mutau Road to its end (about 10 miles), at the Mutau Flat trailhead.

**Contact:** Los Padres National Forest, Mount Pinos Ranger District, 34580 Lockwood Valley Road, Frazier Park, CA 93225, 661/245-3731, website: www.fs.fed.us/r5/lospadres.

## 38 PIEDRA BLANCA
### 4.0 mi / 2.0 hrs

**in the Rose Valley Recreation Area north of Ojai**

Map 13.4, page 612

Sandstone lovers, this is your spot. Piedra Blanca is a series of huge, rounded sandstone boulders that are somewhat otherworldly looking. If rocks can look sensual, these are. They're set in the Rose Valley Recreation Area, just a short stretch away from Sespe Creek, in what looks a lot like the desert—plenty of sand, desert scrub, and rocks. Start from the gate and hike one mile on the closed road to what was once Lion Campground (it was closed to protect the fragile habitat of local toads and frogs). There you'll cross Sespe Creek's often dry wash and pick up the trail on the far side (head to your left). The rocks of Piedra Blanca are clearly visible, so it's easy to see where you're going. Although the trail continues down the back side of the boulders and beyond, most people just climb to the top of the rocks, then spend some time wandering around and exploring. As you might guess, this is a first-class spot for watching sunsets.

**User Groups:** Hikers, dogs, and horses. No mountain bikes. No wheelchair facilities.

**Permits:** No permits are required. A national forest recreation pass is required for each vehicle; fees are $5 for one day or $30 for a year.

**Maps:** For a map, ask the U.S. Forest Service for Los Padres National Forest. For a topographic map, ask the USGS for Lion Canyon.

**Directions:** From Ojai, drive north on Highway 33 for 15 miles to Sespe Road/Rose Valley Road and the sign for Rose Valley Recreation Area. Turn right and drive 4.8 miles to the parking area by the gated road.

**Contact:** Los Padres National Forest, Ojai Ranger District, 1190 East Ojai Avenue, Ojai,

CA 93023, 805/646-4348, website: www.fs.fed.us/r5/lospadres.

## 39 SESPE RIVER
### 10.0 mi / 1.0–2.0 days

in the Sespe Wilderness north of Ojai

**Map 13.4, page 612**

The Sespe River Trail is an easy way to access the Sespe Wilderness, on a mostly level trail that follows the river. A typical destination on this trail is Bear Creek Camp, at five miles out, but you could hike as much as 27 miles one-way to the Dough Flat trailhead outside of Fillmore. Start your trip at the now-closed road to the old Lion Campground. After a mile of hiking, cross the riverbed and hike downstream on another old road, which was once a four-wheel-drive route to the Sespe Hot Springs. If you're lucky, you'll visit when the creek level is high enough so that there are plenty of deep pools accessible for swimming. In good years, almost every bend in the river offers a tempting pool, but by late summer, the stream can drop to a trickle. Dispersed camping spots are plentiful along this trail. By the way, this is called Sespe River Trail, but on maps, the "river" is called "creek." Generally it looks much more like the latter than the former.

**User Groups:** Hikers, dogs, and horses. No mountain bikes. No wheelchair facilities.

**Permits:** A free California campfire permit is required for building a fire or using a backpacking stove; permits are available at any Southern California Forest Service ranger station. A national forest recreation pass is required for each vehicle; fees are $5 for one day or $30 for a year.

**Maps:** For a map, ask the U.S. Forest Service for Los Padres National Forest or Sespe Wilderness. A map of the Sespe Wilderness is available from Tom Harrison Maps. For a topographic map, ask the USGS for Lion Canyon.

**Directions:** From Ojai, drive north on Highway 33 for 15 miles to Sespe Road/Rose Valley Road and the sign for Rose Valley Recreation Area. Turn right and drive 4.8 miles to the parking area by the gated road.

**Contact:** Los Padres National Forest, Ojai Ranger District, 1190 East Ojai Avenue, Ojai, CA 93023, 805/646-4348, website: www.fs.fed.us/r5/lospadres.

## 40 ROSE VALLEY FALLS
### 0.6 mi / 0.5 hr

in the Rose Valley Recreation Area north of Ojai

**Map 13.4, page 612**

The trip to Rose Valley Falls is an easy walk in the woods to the base of a stunning and unusual sandstone waterfall. If you're making the drive to Rose Valley Recreation Area to camp, fish, or hike, a side trip to Rose Valley Falls is just about mandatory. Start hiking on the signed trail in Rose Valley Campground. The path is bordered on both sides by oaks and fragrant bays, and it parallels Rose Creek. Cross the creek a few times, and as you walk into the canyon, keep looking ahead (up high) for your first glimpse of the 300-foot waterfall. If it has rained lately, you'll see it for sure. In 15 minutes you reach the base of the waterfall, which is glaringly different in appearance from the falls you were just looking at. That's because this is the bottom tier of huge Rose Valley Falls, and you were seeing the upper tier. The lower tier is layered with limestone and sandstone slabs and oozing with wet moss. You can't resist touching it. Some daredevils attempt to climb up and over this lower tier to see more of the upper part of the waterfall, but this should only be attempted by experts with proper climbing equipment.

**User Groups:** Hikers, dogs, horses, and mountain bikes. No wheelchair facilities.

**Permits:** No permits are required. A national forest recreation pass is required for each vehicle; fees are $5 for one day or $30 for a year.

**Maps:** For a map, ask the U.S. Forest Service for Los Padres National Forest. For a topographic map, ask the USGS for Lion Canyon.

**Directions:** From Ojai, drive north on Highway 33 for 15 miles to Sespe Road/Rose Valley Road and the sign for Rose Valley Recreation Area. Turn right, drive three miles, then turn right again on Chief Peak Road, at the sign for Rose Valley Camp. Drive .6 mile to the campground. The trail leads from the far end of the camp.

**Contact:** Los Padres National Forest, Ojai Ranger District, 1190 East Ojai Avenue, Ojai, CA 93023, 805/646-4348, website: www.fs.fed .us/r5/lospadres.

## 41 NORDHOFF PEAK
### 11.6 mi / 6.0 hrs

**east of Ojai**

Map 13.4, page 612

The hike to Nordhoff Peak is a rite of passage for Ojai hikers. After all, journalist Charles Nordhoff was the guy who made Ojai famous. In the late 19th century, he wrote various magazine articles about Ojai Valley's many charms, which encouraged people to move here with the dream of a new life. Nordhoff's summit is at 4,425 feet—high enough to get an occasional few inches of snow—and a hike to the top is a fine way to spend an early spring day in Ojai. That's if you're up to the 5.8-mile, 3,300-foot climb, of course. Forget hiking in the heat of summer; much of the trail is on dusty, open fire roads, with no shade. From the Gridley trailhead, hike up to Gridley Fire Road and turn right, passing by seemingly endless avocado groves. Continuing straight ahead, you'll enter a shadier canyon and pass the primitive camp at Gridley Spring. This is almost the halfway point (2.7 miles); take a breather. Prepare yourself for the next two miles—the steepest on the trip—then begin switchbacking your way up to Nordhoff Fire Road, where you turn left and hike one more mile to the peak. If you think that after all this climbing you ought to get some good views, you won't be disappointed. The last mile of trail offers excellent vistas, and when you reach the old Nordhoff Fire Lookout Tower, you can see all the way to the Pacific Ocean and Channel Islands, Ojai Valley and Lake Casitas closer in, and miles of Los Padres National Forest and its wilderness areas.

**User Groups:** Hikers, dogs, horses, and mountain bikes. No wheelchair facilities.

**Permits:** No permits are required. A national forest recreation pass is required for each vehicle; fees are $5 for one day or $30 for a year.

**Maps:** For a map, ask the U.S. Forest Service for Los Padres National Forest. For a topographic map, ask the USGS for Ojai.

**Directions:** From Ojai at the intersection of Highways 150 and 33, drive east on Highway 150 for two miles and turn left on Gridley Road, .25 mile past the ranger station. Drive 1.5 miles north on Gridley Road until it dead-ends. The trailhead is on the north side of the road.

**Contact:** Los Padres National Forest, Ojai Ranger District, 1190 East Ojai Avenue, Ojai, CA 93023, 805/646-4348, website: www.fs.fed .us/r5/lospadres.

## 42 SANTA PAULA CANYON TO BIG CONE CAMP
### 6.8 mi / 3.5 hrs or 2.0 days

**east of Ojai**

Map 13.4, page 612

What starts out rather pedestrian gets much, much better on Santa Paula Canyon Trail. That's because the first 1.2 miles of the route are mostly on pavement, meandering around the grounds of Thomas Aquinas College and a private ranch and oil-drilling operation, before at last you're on a real trail in the real outdoors. This slow start doesn't keep Santa Paula Canyon Trail from being well loved and frequently used, especially by people looking for an easy overnight backpacking trip, or a place to jump in a swimming hole. You'll find a few people hiking the path even on weekdays. After following the well-signed route to the start of the "real" trail, you'll head deep into Santa Paula Canyon, following the creek and crossing it twice. The trees are dense and wildflowers are sublime. After the second creek crossing at two miles out, get ready for your first real climb on the trail as you follow a wide dirt road up and around Hill 1989. Following the ascent, the trail drops down to a lovely campground in a grassy flat, surrounded by big cone Douglas firs. There are four sites with fire rings at aptly named Big Cone Camp. The trail leads a short distance from the camp steeply down to the main and east forks of Santa Paula Creek, where waterfalls and swimming holes await on a stretch of stream lined with polished rock. Not surprisingly, this area and the campground are quite popular on summer weekends. Those who wish to explore farther can hike another .5 mile to Cross Camp and the edge of the Sespe Wilderness. Just beyond the camp, the stream enters a canyon highlighted by a waterfall called the Punchbowl. In another 1.5 miles is Jackson Hole Camp, and Jackson Falls is a half mile beyond.

**User Groups:** Hikers, dogs, horses, and mountain bikes. No wheelchair facilities.

**Permits:** A free California campfire permit is required for building a fire or using a backpacking stove; permits are available at the Ojai Ranger Station. A national forest recreation pass is required for each vehicle; fees are $5 for one day or $30 for a year.

**Maps:** For a map, ask the U.S. Forest Service for Los Padres National Forest. For a topographic map, ask the USGS for Santa Paula Peak.

**Directions:** From Ojai at the junction of Highways 33 and 150, drive east on Highway 150 for 11.5 miles to Thomas Aquinas College on the left (look for iron gates and stone buildings). Drive 100 yards farther to the parking pullout on the right side of the road, just beyond the highway bridge over Santa Paula Creek. Park there and walk back across the bridge to the paved road on the right side of the college.

**Contact:** Los Padres National Forest, Ojai Ranger District, 1190 East Ojai Avenue, Ojai, CA 93023, 805/646-4348, website: www.fs.fed.us/r5/lospadres.

## 43 McGRATH STATE BEACH NATURE TRAIL
## 0.75 mi / 0.5 hr

**in Oxnard**

Map 13.4, page 612

There's a great little nature trail at McGrath State Beach that offers a far different hike from a walk along the sandy public beach. The trail runs along the Santa Clara Estuary, which is designated as a natural preserve. It's the place where the Santa Clara River joins the Pacific Ocean. In that meeting space, freshwater and saltwater plants and animals intermingle, which means you have the chance to see migrating birds, resident shorebirds, and fish swimming in the estuary. The trail starts out in a shaded willow thicket, a secluded and peaceful change from the hustle and bustle of the beach campground. Watch for the endangered California least tern or Belding's savannah sparrow. When you reach the beach, you can continue hiking along the shoreline, or you can turn around and head back. Note that if you visit in the winter season, this trail is not maintained and can become overgrown.

**User Groups:** Hikers only. No dogs, horses, or mountain bikes. No wheelchair facilities.

**Permits:** No permits are required. An $8 day-use fee is charged per vehicle.

**Maps:** For a topographic map, ask the USGS for Ventura.

**Directions:** From U.S. 101 in Ventura, take the Seaward Avenue exit to Harbor Boulevard. Turn south on Harbor Boulevard and drive four miles to the park entrance. The nature trail begins at the day-use parking lot, a quick right turn after the entrance kiosk. (If you are traveling north on U.S. 101, you must take the Victoria Avenue exit to reach Harbor Boulevard.)

**Contact:** McGrath State Beach, 901 S. San Pedro, Ventura, CA 93001, 805/654-4744, website: www.parks.ca.gov.

## 44 LA JOLLA VALLEY LOOP
### 6.8 mi / 3.5 hrs or 2.0 days

**in Point Mugu State Park south of Oxnard**

Map 13.4, page 612

We rate Point Mugu State Park as the best of all the parks in the Santa Monica Mountains, partly because of its more remote northern location, partly because of its proximity to the ocean, and partly because of its fine hiking trails. One of the best of the latter is this loop trip starting in La Jolla Canyon, which can be an excellent day hike or an easy two-day backpacking trip with an overnight at La Jolla Valley walk-in camp. Follow La Jolla Canyon Trail from the Ray Miller trailhead (that's the wide dirt trail on the left, not the single-track trail on the right) gently uphill. You hike through an open valley that is continually freshened by ocean breezes blowing up the canyon. Pass a small seasonal waterfall, then climb into a rocky area, where hidden among the chaparral are rock caves that were once used by Native Americans. Go right at the first fork and take the left fork at 1.5 miles to La Jolla Valley walk-in camp, situated in a high meadow of native grasses. It's .5 mile farther, shortly beyond a cattail-bordered pond. From the camp, bear left on the dirt road, which narrows to a single track. Continue on La Jolla Valley Loop Trail and circle around, through more native grasses, back to La Jolla Canyon Trail. If you like, you can add on a detour around Mugu Peak on Mugu Peak Trail, which will add two more miles to your roundtrip. Turn right on La Jolla Canyon Trail to head down the canyon to your car. This trip is outstanding in winter or spring, when the hillside grasses are green and the wildflowers bloom.

**User Groups:** Hikers only. No dogs, horses, or mountain bikes. No wheelchair facilities.

**Permits:** No permits are necessary. Backpacking campsites are available on a first-come, first-served basis; backpackers must register at the Sycamore Canyon Campground. A $4 day-use fee is charged per vehicle at the Ray Miller trailhead.

**Maps:** A park map is available from the ranger kiosk at Sycamore Canyon Campground, one mile south on Highway 1. A map of the Santa Monica Mountains is available from Tom Harrison Maps. For a topographic map, ask the USGS for Point Mugu.

**Directions:** From U.S. 101 in Camarillo, take the Las Posas Road exit and drive south through Oxnard. Follow Las Posas Road for eight miles to Highway 1, then turn south on Highway 1. Drive five miles to the La Jolla Canyon trailhead parking area, on the left, across from Thornhill Broome State Beach.

Alternatively, from Highway 1 in Malibu, drive west on Highway 1 for 22 miles to the La Jolla Canyon trailhead parking area, on the right.

**Contact:** Point Mugu State Park, 9000 Pacific Coast Highway, Malibu, CA 90265, 805/488-5223 or 805/488-1827; California State Parks, Angeles District, 1925 Los Virgenes Road, Calabasas, CA 91302, 818/880-0350, website: www.parks.ca.gov.

## 45 BIG SYCAMORE CANYON LOOP
### 9.5 mi / 5.5 hrs

**in Point Mugu State Park south of Oxnard**

Map 13.4, page 612

If you don't mind hiking on fire roads and maybe sharing the trail with mountain bikers and horses, this loop trip in Point Mugu State Park offers a shady stroll in a sycamore-lined canyon, followed by miles and miles of unforgettable coastal views. Start from the gate at the far end of the campground and follow Big Sycamore Canyon Trail as it climbs very gently uphill, paralleling the creek. The sycamore trees here are large and old, and from October to February, you may spot monarch butterflies that cluster among them for the winter. At three miles, bear left on Wood Canyon Trail to reach Deer Camp Junction and picnic area. From there, pick up Overlook Trail for a long, rambling walk back to the trailhead. The Overlook Trail divides Point Mugu's two canyons, Big Sycamore and La Jolla, and is a ridge-top route that offers non-stop views of the coastline to the west and the canyons on either side of you. On a clear day, it's glorious. Note: When you near the end of the trail, you can take the single-track Scenic Trail to return to the trailhead. It shaves off a little distance, and it's more interesting than the final stretch of Overlook Trail.

**User Groups:** Hikers, horses, and mountain bikes. No dogs. No wheelchair facilities.

**Permits:** No permits are required. A $10 day-use fee is charged per vehicle.

**Maps:** A park map is available at the entrance kiosk. A map of the Santa Monica Mountains is available from Tom Harrison Maps. For a topographic map, ask the USGS for Point Mugu.

**Directions:** From U.S. 101 in Camarillo, take the Las Posas Road exit and drive south through Oxnard. Follow Las Posas Road for eight miles to Highway 1, then turn south on Highway 1. Drive seven miles to Sycamore Canyon Campground, on the left.

Alternatively, from Highway 1 in Malibu, drive west on Highway 1 for 20 miles to Sycamore Canyon Campground, on the right.

**Contact:** Point Mugu State Park, 9000 Pacific Coast Highway, Malibu, CA 90265, 805/488-5223 or 805/488-1827; California State Parks, Angeles District, 1925 Los Virgenes Road, Calabasas, CA 91302, 818/880-0350, website: www.parks.ca.gov.

## 46 CALICHE FOREST AND POINT BENNETT

**15.0 mi / 2.0 days**

**on San Miguel Island in Channel Islands National Park**

Channel Islands Detail Map, page 613

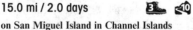

After finding out there's an easy way and a hard way to do something, some people immediately choose the hard way. If you're in that camp, you'll choose San Miguel Island as the Channel Island you want to visit,

instead of Anacapa, Santa Cruz, or any of the other islands. San Miguel Island is 25 miles from the mainland and requires a much-dreaded 3.5-hour boat ride from Ventura, or a slightly longer four-hour boat ride from Santa Barbara. Given that, once you finally get to San Miguel, you'll want to stay for a couple days. To add to the challenge, strong winds and fog are nearly constant on the island, so you must plan accordingly for both hiking and camping. Of course, if you're willing, your reward is having a spectacular island practically all to yourself. No more than 30 campers are allowed on San Miguel Island at one time, and rarely do that many people show up, except on big holiday weekends.

From Cuyler Harbor, where you are dropped off, you hike eastward along the beach for .5 mile, then follow the path another .5 mile over a large sand dune, then up Nidever Canyon. It's a steep stretch, especially if you're carrying a lot of camping gear. When you reach the ridge at the top, you can take a short spur to see a stone monument to Juan Rodriguez Cabrillo, who claimed this island for the Spaniards in 1542, and who may or may not be buried here—nobody's sure. The trail continues to the campground, and then to the remains of the Lester Ranch. The Lester family lived on the island for 12 years and grazed sheep here.

Outside of the Cuyler Harbor/Lester Ranch area, you may hike only in the company of a ranger, in order to protect the island's fragile resources. If you do so, you'll find that the most noticeable wildlife on and around San Miguel Island are pinnipeds—seals and sea lions. Up to five different species and more than 30,000 individuals can be seen at certain times of the year at Point Bennett, a 14-mile round-trip hike from the campground. If you take this hike, plan for a long day and bring lots of water with you. An interesting feature along the way is the Caliche Forest, where the calcium-carbonate sand castings of dead plant roots and trunks stand like frozen statues.

They're a bit like the tufa spires at Mono Lake. Seeing the Caliche Forest requires only a seven-mile round-trip.

Special Note: Truth Aquatics at Sea Landing occasionally runs day trips to San Miguel Island for those who do not wish to camp. This requires leaving Santa Barbara at 3 A.M., arriving at San Miguel Island around 7 A.M., and departing again at 1 P.M. With this schedule, day hikers are usually led to the Caliche Forest and back with a naturalist or ranger. You can sleep on the boat the night before your 3 A.M. departure.

**User Groups:** Hikers only. No dogs, horses, or mountain bikes. No wheelchair facilities.

**Permits:** A camping permit is required (see phone number below). The camping reservation fee is $10. A fee is charged for boat transportation to the island. Call the concessionaires at the numbers below for rates and departure information. The current cost is $90 per person for an overnight trip.

**Maps:** A free map of Channel Islands National Park is available from park headquarters at the address below. A more detailed map is available for a fee from Trails Illustrated. For topographic maps, ask the USGS for San Miguel Island East and San Miguel Island West.

**Directions:** Island Packers provides boat transportation to San Miguel Island from Ventura Harbor. Truth Aquatics at Sea Landing provides boat transportation to San Miguel Island from Santa Barbara Harbor. Reservations are required and should be obtained before you get your camping permit.

**Contact:** Channel Islands National Park, 1901 Spinnaker Drive, Ventura, CA 93001, 805/658-5700 or 805/658-5730, website: www.nps.gov/chis; permits: 800/365-CAMP (800/365-2267); boat trips: Island Packers, 805/642-7688 or 805/642-1393, website: www.islandpackers.com; Truth Aquatics at Sea Landing, 805/963-3564, website: www.truthaquatics.com; maps: Trails Illustrated, 800/962-1643.

# 47 TORREY PINES TRAIL
## 5.0 mi / 2.5 hrs

**on Santa Rosa Island in Channel Islands National Park**

**Channel Islands Detail Map, page 613**

One of the many charms of Santa Rosa Island is that you can fly there in about 20 minutes in a small plane instead of taking the four-hour boat ride from Ventura or Santa Barbara. The National Park Service has allowed one airplane concessionaire in addition to the two boat concessionaires, and this is the island where the plane lands. For people prone to seasickness, this makes Santa Rosa Island the Channel Island of choice. Another of the island's charms is its stand of Torrey pines—yes, the same conifers you see at Torrey Pines State Reserve, in San Diego. These are the only two places in the world where those slow-growing, windswept pines are found, and no one knows why. To see them from the boat pier or the landing strip, follow the main dirt road to the southeast, paralleling the shore. Near the far (southeast) end of the landing strip on the inland side, you'll see a gate and a road that leads uphill to Water Canyon Campground. Pass this gate and continue to the next junction of roads, where you can choose to hike up above the Torrey pines or down below. You can make a loop and circle around the grove if you like, or just take the lower road to stay along the coast and avoid any further climbing. The higher you go, of course, the more outstanding the coastal views.

**User Groups:** Hikers only. No dogs, horses, or mountain bikes. No wheelchair facilities.

**Permits:** If you choose to stay overnight, you must get a camping permit (see phone number, below). The camping reservation fee is $10. A fee is charged for transportation to the island. Call the concessionaires at the numbers below for rates and departure information. The current cost for boat travel is approximately $62 per person for a day trip or $80 per person for an overnight trip. The current cost for air travel is $85 per person for a day trip or $150 per person for an overnight trip.

**Maps:** A free map of Channel Islands National Park is available from park headquarters at the address below. A more detailed map is available from Trails Illustrated. For topographic maps, ask the USGS for Santa Rosa Island North and East.

**Directions:** Island Packers provides boat transportation to Santa Rosa Island from Ventura Harbor; reservations are required. Truth Aquatics at Sea Landing provides boat transportation to Santa Rosa Island from Santa Barbara Harbor. Channel Islands Aviation provides air transportation to Santa Rosa Island from Camarillo Airport.

**Contact:** Channel Islands National Park, 1901 Spinnaker Drive, Ventura, CA 93001, 805/658-5700 or 805/658-5730, website: www.nps.gov/chis; permits: 800/365-CAMP (800/365-2267); maps: Trails Illustrated, 800/962-1643; transport: Island Packers, 805/642-7688 or 805/642-1393, website: www.islandpackers.com; Truth Aquatics at Sea Landing, 805/963-3564, website: www.truthaquatics.com; Channel Islands Aviation, 805/987-1301.

## 48 POTATO HARBOR TRAIL
### 4.4 mi / 2.5 hrs

**on east Santa Cruz Island in Channel Islands National Park**

Channel Islands Detail Map, page 613

Only the eastern quarter of huge Santa Cruz Island belongs to the National Park Service; the other 76 percent of the island is managed by The Nature Conservancy. Although it's possible to hike on The Nature Conservancy's land (call the boat concessionaires listed below for information), you may do so only with a special permit, and usually with a guide. If you prefer to wander on your own or if you want to camp overnight on the island, you need to visit the eastern, national park side of Santa Cruz Island. The boat ride is short enough to make this a day trip, or if you prefer a longer stay, the park service runs a campground in Scorpion Canyon, plus a backcountry camp called Del Norte, 10 miles to the west. You'll

have the luxury of drinking water at Scorpion but not at Del Norte.

The trail to Potato Harbor begins in the campground, which is .5 mile beyond Scorpion Anchorage, where the boat drops you off. Head back into the upper end of the campground (passing the ranch and the first set of campsites) until you see a road veering off to the right, climbing above the canyon. Like almost all of the trails on eastern Santa Cruz Island, this trail is a wide dirt road, best hiked before the end of summer, when it can be dry and dusty. The road climbs steeply for .5 mile, then goes mostly flat, continuing along the bluff tops almost straight west, paralleling the mainland coast. Far ahead you can see a long series of hills and canyons that eventually fade out of view in the haze, and it's easy to assume that these belong to one of the neighboring Channel Islands. Wrong—they are more of the immense bulk of this island—the largest in the chain, at 96 square miles. At two miles out, the trail curves to the southwest, following the line of a fence at the bluff's edge. Look for a spur trail that leads to the edge, and follow it to the obvious view of Potato Harbor—a potato-shaped cove lined with rugged cliffs and filled with deep, clear water.

If you're camping on the island and have more time than the day-trippers, make sure you take the seven-mile round-trip hike to Smuggler's Cove, where there is a lovely cobble beach. A stand of eucalyptus provides a shady picnic area at the edge of the sand.

**User Groups:** Hikers only. No dogs, horses, or mountain bikes. No wheelchair facilities.

**Permits:** If you choose to stay overnight, you must get a camping permit (see phone number, below). The camping reservation fee is $10. A fee is charged for boat transportation to the island. Call the concessionaires at the numbers below for rates and departure information. The current cost is approximately $42 per person for a day trip, or $54 per person for an overnight trip.

**Maps:** A free map of Channel Islands National

Park is available from park headquarters at the address below. A more detailed map is available from Trails Illustrated. For topographic maps, ask the USGS for Santa Cruz Island C and D.

**Directions:** Island Packers provides boat transportation to Santa Cruz Island from Ventura Harbor; reservations are required. Truth Aquatics at Sea Landing provides boat transportation to Santa Cruz Island from Santa Barbara Harbor.

**Contact:** Channel Islands National Park, 1901 Spinnaker Drive, Ventura, CA 93001, 805/658-5700 or 805/658-5730, website: www.nps.gov/chis; permits: 800/365-CAMP (800/365-2267); maps: Trails Illustrated, 800/962-1643; boat trips: Island Packers, 805/642-7688 or 805/642-1393, website: www.islandpackers.com; Truth Aquatics at Sea Landing, 805/963-3564, website: www.truthaquatics.com.

## 49 EAST ANACAPA ISLAND LOOP TRAIL

**2.0 mi / 1.0 hr**

on Anacapa Island in Channel Islands National Park

Channel Islands Detail Map, page 613

Ⓕ Of all the Channel Islands to choose from, why do more people go to Anacapa Island than any other? Because it's easy. At only 12 miles from Port Hueneme, it's the closest island to the mainland. The boat ride doesn't take forever—only about 90 minutes, or as little as 35 minutes on Island Packers' speedy catamaran boat. As you cruise, you're likely to be entertained by dolphins, sea lions, and sometimes even flying fish. The island is actually three tiny islets, and the boat drops you off on the easternmost of the three. If you're feeling the slightest bit seasick, you'll quickly get over it when the boat pulls away and your first task is to climb up the 154 metal steps that cling to the island's cliffs. You'll get plenty of fresh air as you make your way to the island's visitors center, pick up some interpretive information, and set out on this trail, which tours this entire

.3-square-mile islet. The trail's main highlights are two overlooks, at Inspiration Point and Cathedral Cove, where you can look down on seals and sea lions on the rocks below. From Inspiration Point, you can also gaze at the other two Anacapa islets and huge Santa Cruz Island beyond them. Bring your binoculars: There are millions of opportunities for bird-watching, particularly when thousands of western gulls nest in spring and summer. Where you can see over the edge of the rocky cliffs, you'll spot some of the island's 130 sea caves, which make for great kayaking adventures.

Spring wildflowers are superb on Anacapa, including the giant coreopsis, which blooms so brilliantly that its yellow glow can sometimes be seen from the mainland. Note that beaches on East Anacapa are not accessible, because the sea cliffs are hundreds of feet high, but on calm days, you can swim at the landing cove. Bring your snorkeling gear so you can look eye-to-eye with the garibaldis and giant sea kelp. The landing area is inside a 37-acre marine reserve that has been a no-hunting area since 1980. With all the species living protected around the kelp forests and reefs, it makes for a divers' wonderland.

Even though the island is small and its one hiking trail is short, this rates as one of the greatest day trips possible in California. Don't miss it. You can go home from a day here on Anacapa and feel like a different person.

**User Groups:** Hikers only. No dogs, horses, or mountain bikes. No wheelchair facilities.

**Permits:** If you choose to stay overnight, you must get a camping permit (see phone number, below). The camping reservation fee is $10. A fee is charged for boat transportation to the island. Call the concessionaires at the numbers below for rates and departure information. The current cost is $37 per person for a day trip, or $48 per person for an overnight trip.

**Maps:** A free map of Channel Islands National Park is available from park headquarters at the address below. A more detailed map is available from Trails Illustrated. For a topographic map, ask the USGS for Anacapa Island.

**Directions:** Island Packers provides boat transportation to Anacapa Island from Ventura Harbor and Oxnard (Channel Island Harbor); reservations are required. Truth Aquatics at Sea Landing occasionally provides boat transportation to Anacapa Island from Santa Barbara Harbor, although the boat trip is shorter from Ventura.

**Contact:** Channel Islands National Park, 1901 Spinnaker Drive, Ventura, CA 93001, 805/658-5700 or 805/658-5730, website: www.nps.gov/chis; permits: 800/365-CAMP (800/365-2267); maps: Trails Illustrated, 800/962-1643; boat trips: Island Packers, 805/642-7688 or 805/642-1393, website: www.islandpackers.com; Truth Aquatics at Sea Landing, 805/963-3564, website: www.truthaquatics.com.

## 50 SIGNAL PEAK LOOP TRAIL
**3.3 mi / 1.5 hrs**

**on Santa Barbara Island in Channel Islands National Park**

Channel Islands Detail Map, page 613

Santa Barbara Island is the loneliest island in Channel Islands National Park. Located far to the south, it is geographically isolated from the other four islands that make up the national park, being closer in latitude to San Pedro than to Santa Barbara or Ventura. (Yet it's much farther out to sea than developed Catalina Island, which is its closest neighbor.) Getting to Santa Barbara Island requires a 2.5-hour boat ride from Ventura, and the boat concessionaire runs only about a dozen trips to the island each year—much less frequently than to the other islands. And Santa Barbara Island is tiny; at only one square mile, it's the smallest of the Channel Islands. Similar to Anacapa Island in both its size and barren landscape, Santa Barbara Island has 5.5 miles of hiking trails, all of which are worth exploring. One of the best is Signal Peak Trail, which makes a loop over much of the south half of the is-

land, from the landing cove to Signal Peak, which at 634 feet is the highest point on the island. A great feature of this trail is its fine views of Sutil Island, an even smaller island that lies .25 mile southwest of Santa Barbara Island. (Sutil Island is an important seabird rookery; bird-watching is first rate all over Santa Barbara Island.) The trail begins by heading inland from the landing cove. Take the left fork .5 mile out to head south, and curve around the southern end of the island to Signal Peak, on the southwest edge. From the peak, you loop back through the center of the island over gently rolling grasslands.

If you're wondering what season to visit Santa Barbara Island, keep this in mind: As on Anacapa Island, the giant coreopsis blooms its huge yellow flowers here from late March to May.

**User Groups:** Hikers only. No dogs, horses, or mountain bikes. No wheelchair facilities.

**Permits:** If you choose to stay overnight, you must get a camping permit (see phone number, below). The camping reservation fee is $10. A fee is charged for boat transportation to the island. Call the boat concessionaire at the number below for rates and departure information. The current cost is approximately $49 per person for a day trip or $75 per person for an overnight trip.

**Maps:** A free map of Channel Islands National Park is available from park headquarters at the address below. A more detailed map is available from Trails Illustrated. For a topographic map, ask the USGS for Santa Barbara Island.

**Directions:** Island Packers provides boat transportation to Santa Barbara Island from Ventura Harbor; reservations are required.

**Contact:** Channel Islands National Park, 1901 Spinnaker Drive, Ventura, CA 93001, 805/658-5700 or 805/658-5730, website: www.nps.gov/chis; permits: 800/365-CAMP (800/365-2267); maps: Trails Illustrated, 800/962-1643; boat trips: Island Packers, 805/642-7688 or 805/642-1393, website: www.islandpackers.com.

## Chapter 14

© ANN MARIE BROWN

# Los Angeles and Vicinity

# Los Angeles and Vicinity

Islands, mountains, beaches, lakes, deserts—the Los Angeles region offers all this diversity and more. The region is so large, and so varied, it's impossible to describe it without dividing it into smaller pieces.

Two large national forests hold most of the high-country land in the region—Angeles and San Bernardino. The 700,000-acre Angeles National Forest contains the San Gabriel Mountains, which form a high, impenetrable shield that prevents Los Angeles' smog from dissipating. The mountains, which geologists claim are the most fractured and unstable in California (rock slides are an everyday occurrence), sustain a network of more than 500 miles of hiking trails. So close to the freeways, high-rises, and smog of Los Angeles, these high mountains and their clean, sweet air are a hiker's paradise. Sick of the freeway rat race? Head for the trails that grace the slopes of Mount Williamson or Mount Baden-Powell. You can hike all day and be back in L.A. in time for dinner.

A few miles to the east, the San Bernardino Mountains, in San Bernardino National Forest, are one of the highest mountain ranges in California, with peaks that rise to more than 11,000 feet in elevation. The San Bernardinos also contain Southern California's three major recreation lakes: Big Bear, Arrowhead, and Silverwood, plus smaller lakes Gregory and Green Valley. Big Falls, the highest year-round waterfall in Southern California, is located near Big Bear Lake and the San Gorgonio Wilderness. A wealth of hiking trails are found in and around these popular recreation areas.

Yet another mountain range is found in San Bernardino National Forest: the San Jacintos, topped by Mount San Jacinto (at 10,804 feet), which towers over the low desert at Palm Springs. The San Jacintos rise abruptly from the desert floor, completely separated from the other high-elevation ranges of Southern California by low passes and valleys. John Muir called the view from the summit of Mount San Jacinto "one of the most sublime spectacles seen anywhere on Earth." Most recreationists access the San Jacinto range from the resort town of Idyllwild. Destinations like 7,528-foot Suicide Rock and 8,828-foot Tahquitz Peak attract hikers and rock climbers from all over Southern California.

Combined together, these three mountain ranges—San Gabriels, San Bernardinos, and San Jacintos—contain Southern California's great triumvirate of hikeable peaks: Mount San Gorgonio at 11,490 feet, Mount San Jacinto at 10,804 feet, and Mount Baldy at 10,064 feet. Every Los Angeles area hiker worth his or her salt will bag all three summits at some point in his or her career.

One more mountain range is found in the Los Angeles region: the Santa Monica Mountains, a gentler stretch of sloping peaks along the coast. Much of the public land here is part of the Santa Monica Mountains National Recreation Area, but another portion is divided into several state parks: Topanga, Malibu Creek, Leo Carrillo, and Will Rogers. Several smaller parks are managed by the Santa Monica Mountains Conservancy. The trails in the Santa Monica Mountains crisscross chaparral- and sage-covered hillsides, oak woodlands, and native grasslands. Rocky sandstone outcrops poke up here and there, adding variety to the landscape.

If your hiking sensibilities run more toward sunset walks along the coast, hop on a ferry and pay a visit to Catalina Island. Or head to Laguna Beach, where the seaside white sands give way to view-filled coastal hills at Crystal Cove State Park and Laguna Coast Wilderness Park. For wide views of the Malibu coast, check out the trails at Charmlee Wilderness Park. Or, for a true L.A. experience, head for Griffith Park and climb to the top of Mount Hollywood. Who knows, you might just see a movie star on the trail.

# Map 14.1

**Hikes 1–33**
**Pages 652–671**

14.2

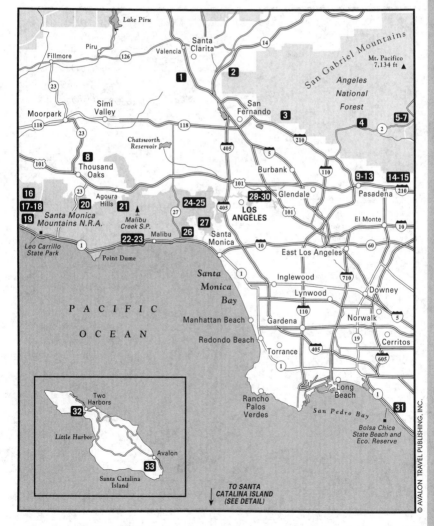

Lake Piru

Fillmore Piru 126 Valencia

Santa Clarita

14

San Gabriel Mountains

Mt. Pacifico 7,134 ft ▲

Angeles National Forest

23

Moorpark

118 23

Simi Valley

San Fernando

**3**

210

**4** 2 **5-7**

101

**8** Thousand Oaks

118

Chatsworth Reservoir

405 5

Burbank

110

**9-13** **14-15**

**16**

23

Agoura Hills

**21**

Malibu Creek S.P.

101

**28-30** Glendale

Pasadena 210

**17-18**

**20**

**24-25**

405

**LOS ANGELES**

El Monte 10

**19**

Santa Monica Mountains N.R.A.

27

**22-23** Malibu

**26**

**27**

Santa Monica

101

10

East Los Angeles

60

Leo Carrillo State Park

1

Point Dume

*Santa Monica Bay*

1

Inglewood

Lynwood

710

Downey

5

P A C I F I C

O C E A N

Manhattan Beach

Redondo Beach

Gardena

110

Torrance

405

1

Norwalk

19

Cerritos

605

Two Harbors

**32**

Little Harbor

Avalon

**33**

Santa Catalina Island

Rancho Palos Verdes

Long Beach

1

*San Pedro Bay*

**31**

*Bolsa Chica State Beach and Eco. Reserve*

**TO SANTA CATALINA ISLAND (SEE DETAIL)**

© AVALON TRAVEL PUBLISHING, INC.

# Map 14.2

**Hikes 34–52**
**Pages 671–683**

# Map 14.3

## Hikes 53–66
## Pages 684–692

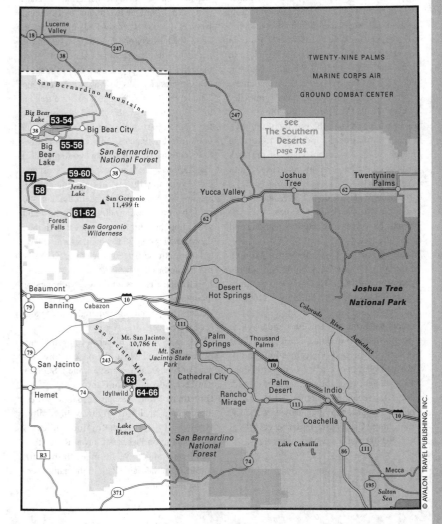

see
The Southern
Deserts
page 724

Lucerne
Valley

18

38

247

San Bernardino Mountains

Big Bear
Lake

53-54

38

Big Bear City

Big
Bear
Lake

55-56

San Bernardino
National Forest

57

59-60

38

58

Jenks
Lake

San Gorgonio
11,499 ft

61-62

Forest
Falls

San Gorgonio
Wilderness

TWENTY-NINE PALMS

MARINE CORPS AIR

GROUND COMBAT CENTER

247

Joshua
Tree

Twentynine
Palms

62

Yucca Valley

62

Beaumont

79

Banning   Cabazon

10

Desert
Hot Springs

Joshua Tree
National Park

Colorado River Aqueduct

111

San Jacinto Mtns.

Mt. San Jacinto
10,786 ft

Palm
Springs

Thousand
Palms

79

243

Mt. San
Jacinto State
Park

10

San Jacinto

63

Cathedral City

Palm
Desert

Indio

Hemet

74

Idyllwild

64-66

Rancho
Mirage

111

10

Lake
Hemet

Coachella

86

111

R3

San Bernardino
National
Forest

Lake Cahuilla

Mecca

74

195

Salton
Sea

371

© AVALON TRAVEL PUBLISHING, INC.

# ◻ CANYON VIEW TRAIL
## 2.0 mi / 1.0 hr

**in Ed Davis Park in Towsley Canyon south of Valencia**

Map 14.1, page 649

Little Ed Davis Park is a part of larger Towsley Canyon, which is a part of the giant Santa Monica Mountains Conservancy parcel of lands. If you visit the park any time except during the sweltering heat of summer, you can walk the two-mile Canyon View Trail and pay a visit to all of Towsley Canyon's major plant communities—grasslands, sage and scrub, riparian, oak woodlands, and just about everything except old-growth redwood forest—in one short trip. How can a park this close to I-5 be this wild looking? We can't figure it out, but it is. The trail begins near the creek, east of the nature center, and ends on Wiley Canyon Trail. (You return via the dirt entrance road.) Despite the brevity of the trail, it has a surprisingly good climb to a ridge where you have excellent views of the rock formations in Towsley Canyon and the Santa Clarita Valley.

**User Groups:** Hikers, dogs, horses, and mountain bikes. No wheelchair facilities.

**Permits:** No permits are required. Parking and access are free.

**Maps:** A free map of the Santa Monica Mountains Conservancy lands is available by contacting the office below. For topographic maps, ask the USGS for Newhall and Oat Mountain.

**Directions:** From the San Fernando Valley, drive north on I-5 to Santa Clarita (five miles north of the I-5 and Highway 14 junction). Take the Calgrove exit, turn left, drive .25 mile, and turn right onto the park entrance road. Park in the second parking lot.

**Contact:** Santa Monica Mountains Conservancy, 5750 Ramirez Canyon Road, Malibu, CA 90265, 310/589-3200, website: www.smmc.ca.gov.

# ◻ PLACERITA CREEK WATERFALL
## 5.5 mi / 2.5 hrs

**in Placerita Canyon County Park southeast of Valencia**

Map 14.1, page 649

Placerita Canyon County Park is a perfect destination for a family outing. It's just far enough out of the Los Angeles Basin to feel like someplace different, and it has trails that are easy enough for hikers of almost any ability. Start your trip at the park nature center, where you should pay a visit to all the taxidermied animals and learn a thing or two about the flora and fauna of the area. Then start hiking on Canyon Trail, which leads from the southeast side of the parking lot and crosses Placerita Creek. Hike through Placerita Canyon, often under the shade of sycamores and oaks, to Walker Ranch Group Campground. At its far side, look for a trail on the right signed as Waterfall Trail, and get ready for the best part of the trip. (Make sure you don't take Los Piñetos Trail, which is just before Waterfall Trail and doesn't go to the falls.) The canyon begins to narrow, and you twist and curve your way through it, crossing and re-crossing the creek a few times. In the final 100 yards before the waterfall, the trail ends, and you simply hike up the streambed. Although the waterfall is only 25 feet high, it forms a lovely little grotto—a perfect place to eat a Power Bar before heading back.

**User Groups:** Hikers and dogs. No horses or mountain bikes. No wheelchair facilities.

**Permits:** No permits are required. Parking and access are free.

**Maps:** Free maps of Placerita Canyon County Park are available at the park nature center. For topographic maps, ask the USGS for San Fernando and Mint Canyon.

**Directions:** From the San Fernando Valley, drive north on I-5 to Highway 14. Follow Highway 14 northeast for four miles to Newhall; exit on Placerita Canyon Road. Turn right (east) and drive 1.5 miles to the park entrance, on the right. Park in the nature center parking lot.

**Contact:** Placerita Canyon County Park, 19152 Placerita Canyon Road, Newhall, CA 91321, 661/259-7721, website: www.placerita.org.

## ❸ TRAIL CANYON TRAIL
### 4.0 mi / 2.0 hrs

**in Angeles National Forest near Sunland**

> **Map 14.1, page 649**

Trail Canyon is located on the western side of the San Gabriel Mountains, an area that is less visited than the more celebrated eastern side. The Trail Canyon Trail (as redundant as that sounds) leads through a shady, stream-carved canyon and up to open slopes, then curves its way to Trail Canyon Falls. The waterfall is so beautiful in winter and early spring that it can take your breath away. The trail begins with a ford and has several more stream crossings along the way, so be prepared for the possibility of wet feet. You walk on a dirt road past a community of cabins and wind around the canyon until, at .75 mile, you spy a single-track trail leading off on the right. Immediately you enter a densely shaded riparian area, thick with sycamores, alders, and cottonwoods. In another .5 mile, you climb out of this canyon and work your way up a slope among spring-blooming chaparral. The path is high above the creek now, and a sharp left curve suddenly reveals the waterfall up ahead about .25 mile. The trail leads to the top of it, where 50-foot Trail Canyon Falls spills over a smooth granite precipice. After admiring the falls, continue a little farther to where the trail crosses the stream. Take a look at the beautiful colors in the rocky streambed. On your return trip downhill, you have lovely canyon vistas to look forward to.

**User Groups:** Hikers, dogs, horses, and mountain bikes. No wheelchair facilities.

**Permits:** No permits are required. A national forest recreation pass is required for each vehicle; fees are $5 for one day or $30 for a year.

**Maps:** For a map, ask the U.S. Forest Service for Angeles National Forest. Maps of the Angeles Front Country and High Country are available from Tom Harrison Maps. For a topographic map, ask the USGS for Sunland.

**Directions:** From I-210 in Sunland, exit on Sunland Boulevard, which becomes Foothill Boulevard. Drive east for one mile to Mount Gleason Avenue. Turn left (north), drive 1.3 miles, and turn right on Big Tujunga Canyon Road. Drive 3.4 miles on Big Tujunga Canyon Road to a sign for Trail Canyon Trail, on the left. Drive .25 mile to a fork, bear right, and drive .25 mile on a rough road to a large parking lot. The trailhead is on the left side of the lot as you drive in.

**Contact:** Angeles National Forest, Los Angeles River Ranger District, 12371 North Little Tujunga Canyon Road, San Fernando, CA 91342, 818/899-1900, website: www.fs.fed.us/r5/angeles.

## ❹ STRAWBERRY PEAK
### 6.4 mi / 3.0 hr

**in Angeles National Forest near Red Box**

> **Map 14.1, page 649**

At 6,164 feet, Strawberry Peak is a San Gabriel Mountain summit that is worth attaining. With a mere 1,500-foot elevation change, the hike is not too strenuous, although it does require some scrambling at the top to bag the summit. It's just enough of an adventure to make you feel like you've done something special with your day. The trail starts out as an abandoned fire road across the highway from Red Box Station Picnic Area; then after .6 mile, it narrows to single-track trail. You switchback your way up a chaparral-covered slope, then lateral around the side of a smaller peak, Mount Lawlor. At 2.2 miles out, the trail drops to a saddle and you begin your summit adventure. Leaving the maintained trail behind, make your way up an obvious brushy path that heads north and then west toward Strawberry Peak's summit. This final mile is much steeper and more difficult than the first two, but press on. Finally you reach the top, which is covered with wind-sculpted coulter pines and big cone spruce.

What's the view like? Strawberry Peak is the highest peak in the front country of the San Gabriels, so it provides a superlative vista of the San Gabriel Valley and Los Angeles Basin, plus many other peaks and ridges of the San Gabriel Mountains.

**User Groups:** Hikers, dogs, horses, and mountain bikes. No wheelchair facilities.

**Permits:** No permits are required. A national forest recreation pass is required for each vehicle; fees are $5 for one day or $30 for a year.

**Maps:** For a map, ask the U.S. Forest Service for Angeles National Forest. Maps of the Angeles Front Country and High Country are available from Tom Harrison Maps. For a topographic map, ask the USGS for Chilao Flat.

**Directions:** From I-210 in La Cañada, take Highway 2 northeast and drive 14 miles to Red Box Station. Turn right and drive to the east end of the parking lot. The trail begins across Highway 2; cross the road carefully and walk 75 yards east (right) to a gated fire road. This is the trailhead.

**Contact:** Angeles National Forest, Los Angeles River Ranger District, 12371 North Little Tujunga Canyon Road, San Fernando, CA 91342, 818/899-1900, website: www.fs.fed .us/r5/angeles.

## 5 VETTER MOUNTAIN LOOKOUT
### 2.2 mi / 1.0 hr

**in Angeles National Forest near Charlton Flat**

Map 14.1, page 649

Vetter Mountain is a San Gabriel summit that even children can attain, via a trail that's only a mile long and gains just 600 feet. The peak was named for Victor Vetter, a forest ranger during the 1920s and 1930s. From the trail sign, follow the path along a small ravine, crossing the forest service road in .5 mile. The trail continues along the ravine, soon leaving the shade of pines and oaks and climbing into yucca and chaparral. You'll huff and puff a bit to gain the ridge top. Turn left on a dirt road, and stroll 150 yards to the fire lookout

tower on Vetter's summit, elevation 5,908 feet. From the tower's perimeter deck, views are extraordinary in all directions, with more than 20 named peaks visible. Bring a map so you can identify them. A historical note: Besides being used to spot fires, the Vetter Lookout was also used to spot enemy aircraft during World War II. Trailhead elevation is 5,500 feet.

**User Groups:** Hikers, dogs, horses, and mountain bikes. No wheelchair facilities.

**Permits:** No permits are required. A national forest recreation pass is required for each vehicle; fees are $5 for one day or $30 for a year.

**Maps:** For a map, ask the U.S. Forest Service for Angeles National Forest. Maps of the Angeles Front Country and High Country are available from Tom Harrison Maps. For a topographic map, ask the USGS for Chilao Flat.

**Directions:** From I-210 in La Cañada, take Highway 2 northeast and drive 23 miles to Charlton Flat. Turn left on the road to Charlton Flat Picnic Area and bear right at the fork. Continue through Charlton Flat for .5 mile to the gate just before the forest service pump house. The Vetter Mountain Trail begins on the left at the wide turnaround area before the gate.

**Contact:** Angeles National Forest, Los Angeles River Ranger District, 12371 North Little Tujunga Canyon Road, San Fernando, CA 91342, 818/899-1900, website: www.fs.fed .us/r5/angeles.

## 6 SILVER MOCCASIN TRAIL TO MOUNT HILLYER
### 6.0 mi / 3.0 hrs

**in Angeles National Forest near the Chilao Visitors Center**

Map 14.1, page 649

The Silver Moccasin Trail is a whopping 53 miles long, running through the San Gabriel Mountains from the Clear Creek trailhead to Mount Baden-Powell. Not many people hike the entire thing,—except the Boy Scouts, who have been doing it since 1942. When they finish, they get the Silver Moccasin Award, which is a much bigger deal than earning a badge for building a campfire. A popular section of the Silver Moccasin Trail is the route to Mount Hillyer, an 1,100-foot climb spread out over three miles. The trail starts in chaparral and occasional gray pines, interspersed with many tall, blooming yucca plants in the spring. The trail surface is a bit sandy but well graded. After a moderate one-mile climb, you tag the edge of Horse Flats Campground, bear left, leave Silver Moccasin Trail, and turn left on Mount Hillyer Trail. The path goes around the camp, then climbs through a steep, rocky area and brings you to Hillyer's summit, which some hikers describe as "just a bump on a hill." On our first trip here, we walked right past the summit without even noticing it. It's the pile of boulders just off the trail to your left. If you find yourself hiking downhill for a while, heading toward looming Mount Pacifico, you've missed the summit. Views of the surrounding mountains are only fair from the summit, but the air is clean and sweet, and the crowds are nonexistent. Mount Hillyer is surrounded by beautiful stands of Jeffrey pines and incense cedars. The sound of the wind in the pines is divine.

**User Groups:** Hikers, dogs, horses, and mountain bikes. No wheelchair facilities.

**Permits:** No permits are required. A national forest recreation pass is required for each vehicle; fees are $5 for one day or $30 for a year.

**Maps:** For a map, ask the U.S. Forest Service for Angeles National Forest. Maps of the Angeles Front Country and High Country are available from Tom Harrison Maps. For a topographic map, ask the USGS for Chilao Flat.

**Directions:** From I-210 in La Cañada, take Highway 2 north and drive 28 miles to the Chilao Visitors Center turnoff, on the left. Turn left and drive .7 mile, past the Chilao and Upper Chilao Picnic Area turnoffs, to a small parking pullout, on the right, for the Silver Moccasin trailhead.

**Contact:** Angeles National Forest, Los Angeles River Ranger District, 12371 North Little Tujunga Canyon Road, San Fernando, CA 91342, 818/899-1900, website: www.fs.fed .us/r5/angeles.

# ⑦ DEVILS CANYON TRAIL
## 10.0 mi / 6.0 hrs or 2.0 days

**in the San Gabriel Wilderness near Mount Waterman**

Map 14.1, page 649

When you've tired of the front country, it's time to make the trip to the rugged San Gabriel Wilderness. Just be prepared to pay for your pleasure, because this is an upside-down hike—down on the way in and up, up, up on the way out. It's a trail of extremes. There's chaparral on some slopes and tall pines and big cone spruce on others. There's sun, then shade. It's dry for the first two miles, and then you reach a tributary creek and follow its meander. The trip down to the Devils Canyon Trail Camp, 3.5 miles in, is usually pretty quick—about an hour and a half for most people. From there, you can make your way downstream along Devils Creek, partly on a trail and partly rock hopping, wading, and scrambling. The canyon gets narrower as you go; willows and alders shade the stream. It's slow travel, but it's immensely enjoyable. Fishing is surprisingly good along the creek, and the highlight of the trip is a 20-foot waterfall dropping over light-colored granite. The fall blocks any farther travel downstream, so at this point, when you've had enough water play, turn around and head back to camp or back to the trailhead. Remember to save plenty of energy and plenty of water for the 3.5-mile trip from the camp back to the trailhead, which has a 2,000-foot elevation gain. It's easy to convince yourself that the miles on the way up are twice as long as they were on the trip down. Trailhead elevation is 5,200 feet.

**User Groups:** Hikers, dogs, and horses. No mountain bikes. No wheelchair facilities.

**Permits:** A free campfire permit is required only for hikers using a camp stove or building a campfire. A national forest recreation pass is required for each vehicle; fees are $5 for one day or $30 for a year.

**Maps:** For a map, ask the U.S. Forest Service for Angeles National Forest. Maps of the

Angeles Front Country and High Country are available from Tom Harrison Maps. For topographic maps, ask the USGS for Chilao Flat and Waterman Mountain.

**Directions:** From I-210 in La Cañada, take Highway 2 north and drive 27 miles to Chilao Campground, on the left. Continue .5 mile beyond the camp on Highway 2 to a parking lot on the left (west) side of the highway. (Go past the Devils Canyon Vista Point.) Park and walk across the road to the trailhead. If you reach the Chilao Visitors Center, you've gone too far.

**Contact:** Angeles National Forest, Los Angeles River Ranger District, 12371 North Little Tujunga Canyon Road, San Fernando, CA 91342, 818/899-1900, website: www.fs.fed .us/r5/angeles.

## 8 WILDWOOD PARK LOOP
**4.0 mi / 2.0 hrs**

in Wildwood Park in Thousand Oaks

Map 14.1, page 649

Wildwood Park is one of the best-kept park secrets in Los Angeles, known mostly to the school kids who come here for outdoor field trips in the spring. From the Arboles trailhead in Thousand Oaks, you can hike downhill into Wildwood Canyon and then stroll along its year-round stream, which produces a stunningly beautiful waterfall when the stream flow is strong. Numerous trails cross and interconnect throughout the park, so you can put together a different loop trip or out-and-back hike every time you visit.

For first timers, a good tour is to hike due west on Mesa Trail for .5 mile to the North Tepee Trail and turn left, dropping down into the canyon. Once there, walk to your right, and then bear left at the next fork, which puts you right at the base of the 70-foot waterfall. Hey, isn't Los Angeles supposed to be a semi-arid desert? Yes, but it's full of surprises. From the falls, you can continue walking downstream and then pick up the Lizard Rock Trail to loop back to Mesa Trail. The presence of year-round

water makes this canyon a haven for wildlife; look for mule deer, rabbits, coyotes, and numerous songbirds and raptors. Interpretive signs teach you to identify various plants and trees along the stream.

**User Groups:** Hikers, dogs, horses, and mountain bikes. No wheelchair facilities.

**Permits:** No permits are required. Parking and access are free.

**Maps:** Park maps are available at the park visitors center. For a topographic map, ask the USGS for Thousand Oaks.

**Directions:** From U.S. 101 in Thousand Oaks, take the Lynn Road exit and head north. Drive 2.5 miles to Avenida de los Arboles, then turn left. Drive .9 mile and make a U-turn into the Arboles parking lot, on the left side of the road.

**Contact:** Conejo Recreation and Park District, 403 West Hillcrest Drive, Thousand Oaks, CA 91360, 805/381-2741 or 805/495-6471, website: www.crpd.org.

## 9 GABRIELINO TRAIL TO BEAR CANYON
**7.0 mi / 4.0 hrs or 2.0 days**

in Angeles National Forest near La Cañada

Map 14.1, page 649

The Gabrielino National Recreation Trail is your ticket to visiting the water slides, minicascades, and pools of spectacular Bear Canyon. Begin hiking into the canyon from the Switzer Picnic Area, which on summer weekends is usually packed with people. Head downstream on the smooth dirt trail through a shady canopy of willows, alders, oaks, and maples. A few creek crossings and one mile of trail bring you to Commodore Switzer Trail Camp, which is comprised of a few primitive sites along the creek—an excellent short and easy backpacking trip. Cross the stream by the camp and head uphill, still on Gabrielino Trail. The trail passes 50-foot Switzer Falls, affording a decent view of it from across the canyon. The stone-building ruins you see are the remains of the Switzer Chapel, where visitors at Switzer's Camp, a popular trail resort in the early 20th century, attended Sunday services above the falls. A few steps farther brings you to a junction where Gabrielino Trail heads right and uphill, and Bear Canyon Trail heads left and downhill. Bear left and descend steeply for a mile, being cautious of the steep drop-offs. When you reach the creek, continue downstream for another mile to Bear Canyon Trail Camp, passing many water slides and crystal-clear pools along the way. Big cone spruce line the cool and shady trail. Trout fishing in the creek is good (best in spring).

**User Groups:** Hikers, dogs, horses, and mountain bikes. No wheelchair facilities.

**Permits:** A free campfire permit is required only for hikers using a camp stove or building a campfire. A national forest recreation pass is required for each vehicle; fees are $5 for one day or $30 for a year.

**Maps:** For a map, ask the U.S. Forest Service for Angeles National Forest. Maps of the Angeles Front Country and High Country are available from Tom Harrison Maps. For topographic maps, ask the USGS for Condor Peak and Pasadena.

**Directions:** From I-210 in La Cañada, take Highway 2 north and drive 9.8 miles to Switzer Picnic Area, on the right. At 9.3 miles, you reach Clear Creek Information Station; bear right. You'll reach Switzer in .5 mile.

**Contact:** Angeles National Forest, Los Angeles River Ranger District, 12371 North Little Tujunga Canyon Road, San Fernando, CA 91342, 818/899-1900, website: www.fs.fed.us/r5/angeles.

## 10 MILLARD FALLS
### 1.0 mi / 0.5 hr

**in Angeles National Forest near Pasadena**

Map 14.1, page 649

If you want to guarantee your kids (or adult friends) a good time, take them to Millard Campground for the short hike and scramble to Millard Falls. In springtime, make sure you're dressed to get wet, because you may have to spend more time in the stream than on a dry trail, especially if it has rained lately. This trip is a perfect easy adventure, suitable for hikers of all abilities. The only minus on the trail is the abundance of carvings found on the smooth-barked alder trees; the carvings desecrate almost every tree, as high as human hands can reach. (Take this opportunity to teach your children never, ever to carve anything on trees.) The route to the falls is a .5-mile walk up the stream canyon, partly in the creek and partly on trail. Start walking at the edge of the camp just beyond the camp host's site, where the trail leads to the right and passes a couple of cabins. Simply head upstream, rock hopping where necessary, until the canyon walls come together at 60-foot Millard Falls. The stream splits in two at the fall's lip, forced to detour around two boulders that are stuck in the waterfall's notch. The two streams rejoin about two-thirds of the way down, creating a tremendous rush of water in springtime. Trailhead elevation is 1,900 feet.

**User Groups:** Hikers and dogs. No horses or mountain bikes. No wheelchair facilities.

**Permits:** No permits are required. A national forest recreation pass is required for each vehicle; fees are $5 for one day or $30 for a year.

**Maps:** For a map, ask the U.S. Forest Service for Angeles National Forest. Maps of the Angeles Front Country and High Country are available from Tom Harrison Maps. For a topographic map, ask the USGS for Pasadena.

**Directions:** From I-210 in Pasadena, exit on Lake Avenue and drive north for 3.5 miles to Loma Alta Drive. Turn west (left) on Loma Alta Drive and drive one mile to Chaney Trail at the flashing yellow light. Turn right and drive 1.5 miles on Chaney Trail, keeping left at the fork, to Millard Campground. Park in the parking lot and follow the fire road on the right (as you drove in) that leads into the campground.

**Contact:** Angeles National Forest, Los Angeles River Ranger District, 12371 North Little Tujunga Canyon Road, San Fernando, CA 91342, 818/899-1900, website: www.fs.fed.us/r5/angeles.

## 11 EATON CANYON
3.0 mi / 1.5 hrs

**in Eaton Canyon Natural Area**

Map 14.1, page 649

Eaton Canyon Natural Area is the kind of place where elementary school groups come in the spring. The buses unload their cargoes of children, who then set off (on what may be their first real hike) through Eaton Canyon's wash. And what a fine introduction to the outdoors— a hike along Eaton Canyon in the good company of cactus, chaparral plants, willows, oaks, and occasionally bunnies and lizards. Start at the park nature center, where you can pick up a free map of the area, then walk to the far end of the parking lot and take the dirt road that leads to the right. Cross the wash, and hike along the wide canyon trail, with the creek on your left. The stream attracts a large variety of wildlife, especially birds that sing all day in this canyon. When you reach a bridge where your trail intersects with the Wilson Toll Road, cross the bridge and take the steep right cutoff on its far side down to the streambed. From there, hike upstream, crossing the creek several times as the canyon narrows on its way to Eaton Canyon Falls. Sadly, the waterfall's cliff has been desecrated by graffiti, but the falls remain a well-loved destination in Eaton Canyon. An odd side note: If you hear the sound of gunfire at the trailhead, don't panic—the local police have a shooting range nearby. As you walk into the canyon, you'll quickly get away from the noise.

**User Groups:** Hikers, dogs, horses, and mountain bikes. No wheelchair facilities.

**Permits:** No permits are required. Parking and access are free.

**Maps:** A free map of Eaton Canyon Natural Area is available at the nature center. For topographic maps, ask the USGS for Pasadena and Mount Wilson.

**Directions:** Heading east from I-210 in Pasadena, take the Sierra Madre Boulevard/Altadena Drive exit and drive north on Altadena Drive for 1.6 miles. Turn right into the entrance for Eaton Canyon Natural Area, which is one block north of New York Drive. If you are heading west on I-210, take the Sierra Madre Boulevard exit and drive north to New York Drive, then turn right on Altadena Drive and continue to the park entrance.

**Contact:** Eaton Canyon Natural Area, 1750 North Altadena Drive, Pasadena, CA 91107, 626/398-5420, website: http://parks.co.la.ca.us.

## 12 BIG SANTA ANITA CANYON
6.0 mi / 3.0 hrs

**in Angeles National Forest near Arcadia**

Map 14.1, page 649

Big Santa Anita Canyon is probably the top easy day hike destination in all of the Arroyo Seco District of Angeles National Forest. It's easy to reach and provides a short, simple, and sweet escape from urban life. The shady, overgrown, magical gulch is just a handful of miles from the Pasadena freeway. Day hikers can't help but covet the adorable summer cabins in the canyon, which you walk past on your way to see 60-foot Sturtevant Falls, the canyon's showpiece. The cabins are what remains of Roberts Camp, a popular weekend resort from the early 20th century. The hike begins at Chantry Flat, elevation 2,200 feet, and you follow Gabrielino National Recreation Trail downhill. It's paved for the first .6 mile heading down into the canyon. When you reach the bottom, you cross Roberts Footbridge and head to the right on the dirt pathway. Traveling under the shade of oaks and alders, and along Big Santa Anita Creek for one mile upstream, leads you to Sturtevant Falls. The artificial waterfalls you see are small check dams, designed (poorly) to keep the creek from flooding. Where Gabrielino Trail forks left and heads uphill, continue straight along the creek, admiring ferns and vines as you walk another .25 mile to Sturtevant Falls. It drops 60 feet over a granite cliff into a perfectly shaped rock bowl. Retrace your steps to the junction and follow Gabrielino Trail uphill. Take the lower trail (the upper trail is safer for horses), which clings to the steep hillsides as it climbs above Sturtevant Falls to Cascade Picnic Area, a shady spot alongside the fern-lined creek. Take a break here before leaving Big Santa Anita Canyon and heading back uphill to the real world.

**User Groups:** Hikers, dogs, horses, and mountain bikes. No wheelchair facilities.

**Permits:** No permits are required. A national forest recreation pass is required for each vehicle; fees are $5 for one day or $30 for a year.

**Maps:** For a map, ask the U.S. Forest Service for Angeles National Forest. Maps of the Angeles Front Country and High Country are available from Tom Harrison Maps. For a topographic map, ask the USGS for Mount Wilson.

**Directions:** From I-210 in Pasadena, drive seven miles east to Arcadia. Exit on Santa Anita Avenue and drive six miles north to the road's end, at Chantry Flat. The trail begins across the road from the first parking area.

**Contact:** Angeles National Forest, Los Angeles River Ranger District, 12371 North Little Tujunga Canyon Road, San Fernando, CA 91342, 818/899-1900, website: www.fs.fed .us/r5/angeles.

## 13 FIRST WATER TRAIL
### 3.0 mi / 1.5 hrs

**in Angeles National Forest near Arcadia**

**Map 14.1, page 649**

You say you flat out refuse to hike on pavement? Then the trip on Gabrielino Trail to Sturtevant Falls might not be right for you, but don't bypass beautiful Big Santa Anita Canyon because of it. An alternate trail drops down into the canyon, but this one is on gorgeous single-track trail all the way, lined with tall oaks and alders, huge chain ferns, slender sword ferns, and a half dozen other fern varieties. The First Water Trail is mostly just a path used by cabin owners in the canyon to reach their homes. That means you'll see far fewer people than on the wide, paved Gabrielino Trail, the main trail into the canyon. You begin at the same trailhead, and the first few hundred yards of the walk are the same, but then you bear off Gabrielino Trail at the sign for First Water Trail and Hermit Falls (on your right). The trail switchbacks gently down into the canyon and then heads south along the north fork of Big Santa Anita Creek. The near-constant shade of the canyon, combined with the presence of a year-round stream, makes it possible for every inch of ground to spring forth plant life. As on Gabrielino Trail, you pass many artificial waterfalls (made by check dams on Santa Anita Creek) that are surprisingly beautiful. The First Water Trail crosses the creek a few times, which can be a little tricky early in the year, and follows the stream on its downstream course. The trail ends at the last cabin in the canyon, just above Hermit Falls. Pick a granite boulder, have a seat, and watch the water flow by.

**User Groups:** Hikers, dogs, horses, and mountain bikes. No wheelchair facilities.

**Permits:** No permits are required. A national forest recreation pass is required for each vehicle; fees are $5 for one day or $30 for a year.

**Maps:** For a map, ask the U.S. Forest Service for Angeles National Forest. Maps of the Angeles Front Country and High Country are available from Tom Harrison Maps. For a topographic map, ask the USGS for Mount Wilson.

**Directions:** From I-210 in Pasadena, drive seven miles east to Arcadia. Exit on Santa Anita Avenue and drive six miles north to the road's end, at Chantry Flat. The trail begins across the road from the first parking area.

**Contact:** Angeles National Forest, Los Angeles River Ranger District, 12371 North Little Tujunga Canyon Road, San Fernando, CA 91342, 818/899-1900, website: www.fs.fed .us/r5/angeles.

## 14 MONROVIA CANYON FALLS
### 1.5–3.4 mi / 1.0–2.0 hrs

in Monrovia Canyon Park

Map 14.1, page 649

Everything about Monrovia Canyon Park is a great experience, including the hike to the park's showpiece: Monrovia Canyon Falls. Three different trailheads allow you to select the distance you wish to hike: Starting at the Bill trailhead by the entrance station, the hike is 3.4 miles round-trip. Starting at the middle parking lot makes a 2.0-mile round-trip. Starting from the trailhead behind the nature center is the easiest, shortest round-trip of 1.5 miles—perfect for families with small children. No matter how you do it, you'll hike through a lush and lovely stream canyon, passing several check dams along the creek. The dense woodland is crowded with oaks, alders, and ferns, creating cool and pleasant shade. When you reach the base of the 50-foot waterfall, you'll find many big rocks that are perfectly situated for gazing in admiration.

Special Note: Check your calendar before you go. Monrovia Canyon Park is closed on Tuesdays. The rest of the week, the park is open only from 8 A.M. to 5 P.M.

**User Groups:** Hikers and dogs. No horses or mountain bikes. No wheelchair facilities.

**Permits:** No permits are required. A $5 day-use fee is charged per vehicle.

**Maps:** A free park map is available at the nature center or entrance station. For a topographic map, ask the USGS for Azusa.

**Directions:** From I-210 in Monrovia, take the Myrtle Avenue exit and drive north through Old Town Monrovia to Foothill Boulevard. Turn right, go through two stoplights to Canyon Boulevard, then turn left and drive north for about 1.5 miles, to the park. (Stay to the right as the road splits.) Park at the far end of the park road, near the picnic area and nature center, for the shortest hike to the falls.

**Contact:** Monrovia Canyon Park, 1200 N. Canyon Boulevard, Monrovia, CA 91016, 626/256-8282, website: www.ci.monrovia.ca.us.

## 15 BEN OVERTURFF TRAIL
### 7.0 mi / 3.5 hrs

in Monrovia Canyon Park

Map 14.1, page 649

Ben Overturff was the man who made Monrovia Canyon a popular recreation area in the early 20th century. He ran a lodge at Deer Park from 1910 to 1945, a wilderness getaway for city dwellers. This trail to the site of Deer Park Lodge was reconstructed in the 1990s and was named in his honor. Start your hike on the Sawpit Canyon Fire Road, passing Sawpit Dam after a steep .4-mile start. The paved fire road is the trail for the initial 1.3 miles to the first Ben Overturff Junction, and it can feel hot and steep at midday. Just grin and bear it until you pass the Boy Scout Trask Camp, where you will be rewarded with the pristine, single-track Ben Overturff Trail. Follow the trail as it winds its way up Sawpit and Sycamore Canyons to the Twin Springs Canyon Junction, at 2.5 miles. If you're getting tired and want to loop back, a trail on the right connects to Sawpit Canyon Fire Road from here. If not, continue past the junction to the Deer Park Cabin site, where you can relax and pull your lunch out of your day pack. At trail's end, you have two options: Retrace your steps on Ben Overturff Trail or take the connector trail to Sawpit Canyon Fire Road and follow the fire road all the way back to the trailhead. A good choice is Ben Overturff Trail, but loop-lovers will probably pick the fire road.

Special Note: Check your calendar before you go. Although the entire park is closed on Tuesdays, Ben Overturff Trail is closed on Tuesdays and Wednesdays. Otherwise, the park is open from 8 A.M. to 5 P.M.

**User Groups:** Hikers and dogs. Horses, mountain bikes, and wheelchairs can use only the fire road portion of the trail.

**Permits:** No permits are required. A $5 day-use fee is charged per vehicle.

**Maps:** A free map/brochure on Ben Overturff Trail is available at the nature center. For a topographic map, ask the USGS for Azusa.

**Directions:** From I-210 in Monrovia, take the Myrtle Avenue exit and drive north through Old Town Monrovia to Foothill Boulevard. Turn right, go through two stoplights to Canyon Boulevard, then turn left and drive north for about 1.5 miles to the park. (Stay to the right.) Park at the first available parking lot below the entrance station; the trail begins at the lower end of the park, by the park toll gate.

**Contact:** Monrovia Canyon Park, 1200 North Canyon Boulevard, Monrovia, CA 91016, 626/256-8282, website: www.ci.monrovia.ca.us.

## 16 SATWIWA LOOP TRAIL AND WATERFALL

**3.0 mi / 1.5 hrs**

**in Santa Monica Mountains National Recreation Area near Newbury Park**

Map 14.1, page 649

You know the hike will be good when at the trailhead parking lot, you're greeted by two friendly roadrunners and a half dozen bunnies. That's how it is here at Rancho Sierra Vista/Satwiwa, a part of Santa Monica Mountains National Recreation Area, near Newbury Park, just a couple miles off U.S. 101. The park's proximity to millions of L.A. commuters makes it a perfect place to show up after work and hike or jog on Satwiwa Loop Trail, and in the rainy season, you can take a side trip to see the waterfall just inside the border of Point Mugu State Park. From the parking lot, walk up the paved Sycamore Canyon Trail for a few hundred yards, then bear left on Satwiwa Loop Trail by the Satwiwa Native American Indian Culture Center. Be sure to take a peek at the dome-shaped stick dwelling, which was reconstructed to show traditional Native American life. Follow the Satwiwa Loop for just under a mile, passing a small pond, a windmill, and grassy hillsides, then connect to Old Boney Trail, on the south side of the loop. Old Boney Trail leads downhill, and where it begins to make a sharp switchback up and out of the canyon, take the left spur up the creek that leads a few hundred feet to Sycamore

Canyon Falls (the sign at this spur trail reads No Horses). The waterfall is a pretty, multi-tiered cascade over sandstone, with a surprising amount of foliage growing around it. Even when the fall is only a trickle, the big-leaf maples and ferns are a delight to visit.

**User Groups:** Hikers and dogs. (Dogs are not allowed past the border of Point Mugu State Park, only on the Satwiwa Loop.) No horses or mountain bikes. No wheelchair facilities.

**Permits:** No permits are required. Parking and access are free.

**Maps:** A free map of Santa Monica Mountains National Recreation Area and a brochure on Rancho Sierra Vista/Satwiwa are available by contacting park headquarters at the address below. A map of the Santa Monica Mountains is available from Tom Harrison Maps. For a topographic map, ask the USGS for Newbury Park.

**Directions:** From U.S. 101 in Thousand Oaks, exit at Lynn Road and head south for 5.5 miles. Turn left at Via Goleta and drive .75 mile to the last parking area. Walk up the trail leading toward the Satwiwa Native American Cultural Center.

**Contact:** Santa Monica Mountains National Recreation Area, 401 West Hillcrest Drive, Thousand Oaks, CA 91360, 805/370-2300, website: www.nps.gov/samo.

## 17 GROTTO TRAIL

**3.5 mi / 2.0 hrs**

**in Santa Monica Mountains National Recreation Area at Circle X Ranch**

Map 14.1, page 649

If you don't mind hiking downhill to your destination and then uphill on your return, Grotto Trail is a fine route for a little excursion in the Santa Monica Mountains. The trail roughly follows the west fork of the Arroyo Sequit on its downhill course to The Grotto, an area of jumbled volcanic boulders, many that are bigger than your average Volkswagen. Hidden among the giant rocks are small caves, pools, and waterfalls. The boulders are great fun to climb around, with millions of possible toe- and fingerholds in the porous rock. Have fun, play around, and enjoy the coolness here, because sooner or later, you have to hike back uphill to the trailhead, covering a 600-foot elevation gain. Note that dogs are allowed on this trail except for the last stretch. Where the trail reaches the stream and the hike continues through the streambed, dogs are not permitted.

**User Groups:** Hikers and dogs. No horses or mountain bikes. No wheelchair facilities.

**Permits:** No permits are required. Parking and access are free.

**Maps:** A free map of the Santa Monica Mountains National Recreation Area and a brochure on Circle X Ranch are available by contacting park headquarters at the address below. A map of the Santa Monica Mountains is available from Tom Harrison Maps. For a topographic map, ask the USGS for Triunfo Pass.

**Directions:** From Malibu, drive west on Highway 1 for 15 miles to Yerba Buena Road, 1.5 miles past Leo Carrillo State Beach. Turn right and drive 5.3 miles up Yerba Buena Road to the entrance to Circle X Ranch, on the right. Park by the ranger station and walk down the road to the group campground, where Grotto Trail begins.

**Contact:** Santa Monica Mountains National Recreation Area, 401 West Hillcrest Drive, Thousand Oaks, CA 91360, 805/370-2300, website: www.nps.gov/samo.

## 18 MISHE MOKWA AND SANDSTONE PEAK LOOP

6.2 mi / 3.0 hrs

**in Santa Monica Mountains National Recreation Area near Circle X Ranch**

Map 14.1, page 649

A great six-mile loop in the Santa Monica Mountains begins a short distance from Circle X Ranch, on Yerba Buena Road. See all those wild-looking volcanic outcrops on the hillsides? That's where you're going. You can hike the loop in either direction, but most people start on Mishe Mokwa Trail.

From the trailhead, hike uphill for .25 mile and take the right fork to access Mishe Mokwa's single track. It's 1.5 gentle miles to Split Rock, a big boulder with a cleft in the middle, where it's an unspoken requirement to walk through the cleft. A picnic area at Split Rock is among the oaks and sycamores, ideally situated for catching some shade. From there, continue on the loop to Backbone Trail (also called Sandstone Peak Trail). Be sure to take the short right spur to Inspiration Point, near Boney Peak, for inspiring views of the coast, and the short right spur to 3,111-foot Sandstone Peak, the highest point in the Santa Monica Mountains. Despite its name, the peak is not made of sandstone; it's volcanic rock. The views are outstanding—you'll think you're on top of the world. Sandstone Peak actually has another name, Mount Allen, so when you reach the top and see the Mount Allen plaque, don't think you're in the wrong place.

**User Groups:** Hikers and dogs. No horses or mountain bikes. No wheelchair facilities.

**Permits:** No permits are required. Parking and access are free.

**Maps:** A free map of Santa Monica Mountains National Recreation Area and a brochure on Circle X Ranch are available by contacting park headquarters at the address below. A map of the Santa Monica Mountains West is available from Tom Harrison Maps. For a topographic map, ask the USGS for Triunfo Pass.

**Directions:** From Malibu, drive west on Highway 1 for 15 miles to Yerba Buena Road, 1.5 miles past Leo Carrillo State Beach. Turn right and drive 6.3 miles up Yerba Buena Road to the Backbone/Sandstone Peak trailhead parking area, on the left side of the road, one mile beyond the entrance to Circle X Ranch, on the right.

**Contact:** Santa Monica Mountains National Recreation Area, 401 West Hillcrest Drive, Thousand Oaks, CA 91360, 805/370-2300, website: www.nps.gov/samo.

## 19 NICHOLAS FLAT TRAIL
### 6.5 mi / 3.0 hrs

**in Leo Carrillo State Park near Malibu**

**Map 14.1, page 649**

Most Southern California state beaches are long stretches of sand with big campgrounds and lots of happy beachgoers, but few have any hiking trails worth writing home about. Leo Carrillo State Park is the exception to the rule, with a couple excellent trails that are far more than just a stroll along the sand. The Nicholas Flat Trail is the park's best path, a fairly steep trail that climbs to a pond at Nicholas Flat, where redwing blackbirds and other songbirds like to spend their days. Start hiking from the Willow Creek/Nicholas Flat trailhead, and at the first junction, bear left. A short but steep climb leads to immediate ocean vistas, and at .75 mile, a spur trail leads to Willow Creek Overlook, a fine viewpoint and an excellent spot to look for passing whales in winter. From the spur trail, you can call it a day and hike back downhill (a short loop is possible from this point—bear right to follow it), or continue uphill to Nicholas Flat. The climb gets steeper from here, and you'll gain 1,000 feet more, but you are rewarded with two more spectacular vista points, plus Nicholas Flat, with its man-made pond and high grasslands. You can loop around Nicholas Flat and choose from myriad good picnicking spots, then head back downhill. When you're finished hiking this trail, make sure you check out the beach across the road (take the pedestrian tunnel under the highway), where you'll find a sea-carved tunnel and many small caves and pocket beaches. Also pay a visit to the visitors center by the beach (open on weekends only), which is housed in a set of trailers painted with dolphins and whales.

**User Groups:** Hikers only. No horses, dogs, or mountain bikes. Wheelchair users have access to the park's "sand wheelchairs" to explore the beach area.

**Permits:** No permits are required. A $10 day-use fee is charged per vehicle.

**Maps:** A map of Leo Carrillo State Park is available at the park entrance station. A map of the Santa Monica Mountains is available from Tom Harrison Maps. For a topographic map, ask the USGS for Triunfo Pass.

**Directions:** From Malibu, drive west on Highway 1 for 13 miles to Leo Carrillo State Park. Turn right into the park entrance. The Nicholas Flat/Willow Creek Trail begins by the entrance kiosk, on the inland side of the highway.

**Contact:** Leo Carrillo State Park, 35000 West Pacific Coast Highway, Malibu, CA 90265, 805/488-5223, 805/488-1827, or 818/880-0350, website: www.parks.ca.gov.

## 20 MEADOW TRAIL AND OCEAN OVERLOOK LOOP
### 3.0 mi / 1.5 hrs

**in Charmlee Wilderness Park near Zuma Beach**

**Map 14.1, page 649**

Maybe you need to change your perspective. If you've been hiking around in the lower canyons of the Santa Monica Mountains, it might be time to get up high and wander around where the wind blows and the vistas are wide. Charmlee Wilderness Park is the place to do it, located four miles up the hill from Zuma Beach. It's high enough so that you don't have to climb anywhere to gain a view; the vistas start right at the trailhead. The park's hiking trails are really fire roads, but that's okay. You can hold hands with your hiking partner while you walk, or carry on a serious discussion about the coastal weather. Walk through the park's picnic area, and follow the dirt road as it leads downhill to a meadow, filled with wildflower blooms in February, March, and April. Follow Meadow Trail to the Ocean Overlook, which is just one of many places where the views of the Malibu coast are excellent. From several points, you have vistas in almost every direction, including up and down the Santa Monica Mountains to the east and west. When you're finished meditating on the scenery, loop back on Meadow Trail to your starting point.

If you want to participate in something special, sign up for one of Charmlee's naturalist-led full-moon hikes. Call the park for dates and to make reservations.

**User Groups:** Hikers, dogs, horses, and mountain bikes. No wheelchair facilities.

**Permits:** No permits are required. A $3 day-use fee is charged per vehicle.

**Maps:** A map of the Santa Monica Mountains is available from Tom Harrison Maps. For topographic maps, ask the USGS for Triunfo and Point Dume.

**Directions:** From Highway 1 in Zuma Beach, drive north on Encinal Canyon Road for four miles to the park entrance on the left. Turn left and drive .4 mile to the parking area near the park office and restrooms.

**Contact:** Charmlee Wilderness Park, 2577 Encinal Canyon Road, Malibu, CA 90265, 310/457-7247 or 310/317-1364, website: www.ci.malibu.ca.us.

## 21 ROCK POOL AND CENTURY LAKE

**4.4 mi / 2.0 hrs**

**in Malibu Creek State Park**

Map 14.1, page 649

The first time you lay eyes on the Rock Pool at Malibu Creek State Park or cross the wide bridge over Malibu Creek or visit pretty blue Century Lake, you may have to ask yourself the question: Where am I? Suddenly it's hard to believe you're in Los Angeles, and just a few miles off the freeway—but you are.

Start hiking from the large main parking area on the flat fire road, called Crags Road, that heads for the visitors center. Continue past the visitors center on a wide bridge, and take the left spur to the Rock Pool, a startlingly beautiful pool in Malibu Creek that is dammed by huge volcanic boulders. Although the pool can nearly dry up in late summer, during the rainy season and shortly thereafter, it is quite dramatic. Retrace your steps to Crags Road (you'll probably pass some rock climbers prac-

ticing their craft on an outcrop along the spur trail), turn left, and continue your park tour by visiting Century Lake, which was dammed in 1901; it's now silting up and slowly becoming a marsh. Walk another .5 mile along Crags Road to the old set of the *M\*A\*S\*H* television series, where you'll find a few obvious props from the show. From there, retrace your steps through the park to the trailhead.

**User Groups:** Hikers, horses, and mountain bikes. No dogs. No wheelchair facilities.

**Permits:** No permits are required. An $8 day-use fee is charged per vehicle.

**Maps:** A map of Malibu Creek State Park is available at the park entrance station. A map of the Santa Monica Mountains is available from Tom Harrison Maps. For a topographic map, ask the USGS for Point Dume.

**Directions:** From Agoura Hills on U.S. 101, take the Las Virgenes exit and drive 3.2 miles south to the entrance to Malibu Creek State Park, on the right. Continue past the entrance kiosk to the day-use parking area.

From Malibu on Highway 1, drive north on Malibu Canyon Road/Las Virgenes Road for six miles to the park entrance, on the left.

**Contact:** Malibu Creek State Park, 1925 Los Virgenes Road, Calabasas, CA 91302, 818/880-0367 or 818/880-0350, website: www.parks.ca.gov.

## 22 ESCONDIDO FALLS

**4.2 mi / 2.0 hrs**

**in Escondido Canyon near Malibu**

Map 14.1, page 649

The first mile of this trail is a bit odd. That's because of an access problem; you have to park in the lot at the start of Winding Way and then walk up the paved road for a mile, past some mammoth Malibu homes, to the actual beginning of Escondido Canyon Trail. Just do it, and don't whine; when you finally reach the canyon, you'll be glad you came.

At the trailhead sign, head to the left, walking upstream. You'll cross the creek a few times on the flat path, which tunnels through shady sections and opens out to grassy flats. About .5 mile from the start of the "real" trail, you'll glimpse a big waterfall up ahead, and in .5 mile more, you're at its base. This is the lower tier of the huge limestone waterfall; the adventurous can take the side trail that leads up and over this 50-foot tier, and climb up to a higher, larger tier. Getting there requires some careful rock scrambling, so be cautious. The upper tier is 150 feet tall, with a deep pool at its base perfect for wading.

**User Groups:** Hikers, dogs, horses, and mountain bikes. No wheelchair facilities.

**Permits:** No permits are required. Parking and access are free.

**Maps:** A free map of the Santa Monica Mountains Conservancy lands is available by contacting the office below. A map of the Santa Monica Mountains is available from Tom Harrison Maps. For a topographic map, ask the USGS for Point Dume.

**Directions:** From Malibu, drive west on Highway 1 for 5.5 miles to Winding Way, on the right, and the large sign for Winding Way Trail. If you reach Kanan Dume Road, you've gone 1.5 miles too far. Turn right, then left immediately into the well-signed parking lot.

**Contact:** Santa Monica Mountains Conservancy, 5750 Ramirez Canyon Road, Malibu, CA 90265, 310/589-3200, website: www.smmc.ca.gov.

## 23 SOLSTICE CANYON TRAIL AND RISING SUN LOOP

**2.8 mi / 1.2 hrs**

**in Santa Monica Mountains National Recreation Area near Malibu**

Map 14.1, page 649

Solstice Canyon has long been a favorite hiking spot for Malibu-area locals, because it's easy to reach, serene, and pretty. This easy loop trip travels along Solstice Canyon Trail (also called Old Sostomo Road) to the Roberts Ranch site and returns via the winding Rising Sun Trail. Although the first mile on Solstice Canyon Trail is on pavement, it parallels Solstice Creek and is a pleasant stroll.

Hike past the restrooms at the parking lot,

then turn right at the T junction and head up the canyon, enjoying the blooming mustard and monkeyflower. Pass by the 1865 Keller House, a lovely stone house that's the oldest in Malibu, and continue to the ruins of Tropical Terrace, at the Roberts Ranch. This once-beautiful home burned in a fire in 1982, but its stone terraces and foundation remain. If you walk around to the far side of the foundation, you'll discover a 30-foot waterfall that drops on Solstice Creek. Enjoy its sweet music and maybe a sandwich from your day pack. Then hike back to the end of Solstice Canyon Trail and pick up Rising Sun Trail, which undulates over the hillsides for 1.7 miles to the space-age-looking TRW buildings. From there you can take the left side of TRW Loop Trail back to the parking lot.

**User Groups:** Hikers, dogs, and horses. Mountain bikes allowed only on Solstice Canyon Trail. No wheelchair facilities.

**Permits:** No permits are required. Parking and access are free.

**Maps:** A free trail map is available at the parking area. A map of Santa Monica Mountains East is available from Tom Harrison Maps. For a topographic map, ask the USGS for Malibu Beach.

**Directions:** From Malibu, drive west on Highway 1 for three miles and turn right on Corral Canyon Road. Drive .2 mile to the park entrance, on the left. Turn left and drive .5 mile to the parking area. Start hiking on the paved road.

**Contact:** Santa Monica Mountains National Recreation Area, 401 West Hillcrest Drive, Thousand Oaks, CA 91360, 805/370-2300, website: www.nps.gov/samo.

## 24 EAGLE ROCK LOOP

**4.5 mi / 2.5 hrs**

**at Trippet Ranch in Topanga State Park**

Map 14.1, page 649

Topanga State Park's most notable feature is sandstone Eagle Rock, and a loop hike from Trippet Ranch can take you to see it. Much of the route travels on a fire road, through grasslands and oaks, with vistas increasing as you ascend. At the main trailhead, a sign announces that Eagle Rock is two miles away. Bear left in a few hundred yards, and climb to a major intersection at 1.4 miles. Take the middle road, signed as North Loop Trail, and climb for .5 mile to Eagle Rock. Leave the trail to explore the tiny caves, hollows, and holes in the smooth sandstone, and to enjoy the 360-degree views from the valley to the ocean. When you've had enough, retrace your steps to the junction, and take the single-track Musch Trail on your right for two miles back to the parking lot. You'll pass a walk-in camp along the way.

Practice naming the chaparral plants as you hike: white sage, chamise, yucca, poison oak, elderberry, and chia, and others. Watch for roadrunners scurrying among them. If you're in a hurry, you can return the way you came instead, following the fire road and shaving .5 mile off the trip.

**User Groups:** Hikers, horses, and mountain bikes. No dogs. No wheelchair facilities.

**Permits:** No permits are required. A $2 day-use fee is charged per vehicle.

**Maps:** A map of the Santa Monica Mountains is available from Tom Harrison Maps. For a topographic map, ask the USGS for Topanga.

**Directions:** From Santa Monica, drive north on Highway 1 and turn right on Topanga Canyon Boulevard. Drive 4.7 miles to Entrada Road, then turn right and drive one mile to the park entrance at Trippet Ranch. The trailhead is at the far side of the parking lot.

**Contact:** Topanga State Park, 20825 Entrada Road, Topanga, CA 90290, 310/455-2465 or 818/880-0350, website: www.parks.ca.gov.

## 25 SANTA YNEZ CANYON
2.4 mi / 1.2 hrs

**in Topanga State Park in Pacific Palisades**

Map 14.1, page 649

Topanga State Park is a park with nebulous borders, a patchwork of wilderness interspersed between continually growing housing developments. The park's Santa Ynez Canyon Trail, for instance, begins in a residential neighborhood where you park your car right along the street. The surprising thing is that once you walk about 50 yards on the trail, you feel as if you've gotten away from it all, especially the sights and sounds of urban living. The canyon bottom makes for flat walking and is pleasantly shaded by oaks, willows, and sycamores. Five-foot-tall tiger lilies grow alongside the trail.

At .5 mile in, cross the creek (don't take the spur trail up its right side), then you'll shortly reach a trail junction, where you should head right. The left fork continues for several miles, all the way to Trippet Ranch and the main section of Topanga State Park. A short walk and stream scramble brings you to the base of Santa Ynez Canyon's 15-foot limestone waterfall, a lovely spot that unfortunately has been defiled by graffiti. Even so, it's worth a look, and the canyon walk is pleasant whether or not the stream is flowing strong.

**User Groups:** Hikers only. No dogs, horses, or mountain bikes. No wheelchair facilities.

**Permits:** No permits are required. Parking and access are free.

**Maps:** A map of the Santa Monica Mountains is available from Tom Harrison Maps. For a topographic map, ask the USGS for Topanga.

**Directions:** From Santa Monica, drive north on Highway 1 and turn right on Sunset Boulevard in Pacific Palisades. Drive .5 mile and turn left on Palisades Drive. Drive 2.4 miles, and then turn left onto Vereda de la Montura. The trailhead is at the intersection of Camino de Yatasto (a private road), and Vereda de la Montura. Park alongside the road.

**Contact:** Topanga State Park, 20825 Entrada Road, Topanga, CA 90290, 310/455-2465 or 818/880-0350, website: www.parks.ca.gov.

## 26 TEMESCAL CANYON AND RIDGE LOOP
### 3.8 mi / 2.0 hrs

**in Temescal Gateway Park in Pacific Palisades**

Map 14.1, page 649

How about a nice loop hike in Temescal Gateway Park and Topanga State Park? Hey, good idea—throw some stuff in the day pack, and let's go. The signed trail leads from the parking lot (it's to the left of the kiosk where you pay your fee) and heads north through a camp and conference center. In .25 mile, you'll reach a junction of three trails. The Temescal Canyon Trail, on the right, is the start of the loop; Temescal Ridge Trail, in the middle, is the return leg of the loop. The Temescal Canyon Trail leads you away from the camp and past a state park boundary sign; then the trail starts to climb. Although the route is bordered by rock walls and dry chaparral, leafy maples and sycamores grow along the stream beside you. At 1.2 miles, you cross a footbridge over a small, seasonal waterfall, then you'll cross over to the west side of the canyon to climb to an intersection with Temescal Ridge Trail. If you like, you can take the right spur trail for .5 mile to Skull Rock, a somewhat spooky-looking sandstone formation, then return to the junction. Finish out the loop by heading downhill on Temescal Ridge Trail, with fine views of the coast entertaining you as you walk.

**User Groups:** Hikers only. No dogs, horses, or mountain bikes. No wheelchair facilities.

**Permits:** No permits are required. A $6 day-use fee is charged per vehicle. Annual passes are available.

**Maps:** A free trail map is available at the Temescal Gateway Park kiosk. A map of the Santa Monica Mountains is available from Tom Harrison Maps. For a topographic map, ask the USGS for Topanga.

**Directions:** From Santa Monica, drive north on Highway 1 to Temescal Canyon Road in Pacific Palisades. Turn right and drive 1.1 miles to the entrance to Temescal Gateway Park.

Cross Sunset Boulevard and continue up the park road for .25 mile to the park office and trail information kiosk.

**Contact:** Temescal Gateway Park, 15601 Sunset Boulevard, Pacific Palisades, CA 90272, 310/454-1395, website: www.smmc.ca.gov.

## 27 INSPIRATION POINT TRAIL
### 2.0 mi / 1.0 hr

**in Will Rogers State Historic Park**

Map 14.1, page 649

Most folks come to Will Rogers State Historic Park to visit the home of the late "cowboy philosopher" and humorist Will Rogers. His humble abode was a gigantic 31-room ranch/mansion. But even if you never heard of the guy and have no interest in cowboy decorating style, the two-mile loop trip to Inspiration Point makes a visit to the park worthwhile. The trail offers superb vistas of the Santa Monica Mountains and Pacific Ocean. Finding the trailhead is a bit tricky; it's behind the Rogers' mansion, at the far edge of the grassy lawn. Cross a tiny footbridge, and you'll see the trailhead sign.

Ignoring all single-track cutoffs, follow the main fire road gently uphill for .75 mile to a major junction with Backbone Trail. Turn right, leaving the fire roads, and head farther uphill for Inspiration Point, a short distance away. A few benches and a horse hitch mark the top, making this a great spot for you and Trigger to gaze out on the scene. Your view includes the Pacific Ocean, the rugged Santa Monica Mountains, the state park below you, and downtown Los Angeles to the southeast. It's hard to believe that the big city is within view of this tranquil place, but there it is. Considering the proportion of your view, it's also hard to believe you're only at 750 feet in elevation. On the clearest days, you can see all the way to Catalina Island, 20-plus miles away. To finish out your hike, return to the junction with Backbone Trail, then turn right and make a loop back downhill. You'll come out near the horse stables, not far from where you parked your car.

**User Groups:** Hikers and horses. No dogs or mountain bikes. No wheelchair facilities.

**Permits:** No permits are required. A $7 day-use fee is charged per vehicle.

**Maps:** A map of Will Rogers State Historic Park is available at the park entrance station. For a topographic map, ask the USGS for Topanga.

**Directions:** From Santa Monica, drive north on Highway 1 to Sunset Boulevard in Pacific Palisades. Turn right on Sunset Boulevard and drive 4.5 miles to Will Rogers State Park Road, then turn left and drive one mile to the park entrance. The trail begins near the Rogers' mansion.

**Contact:** Will Rogers State Historic Park, 1501 Will Rogers State Park Road, Pacific Palisades, CA 90272, 310/454-8212 or 818/880-0350, website: www.parks.ca.gov.

## 28 MAGIC FOREST NATURE TRAIL
### 0.25 mi / 0.25 hr

**in Coldwater Canyon Park**

Map 14.1, page 649

If you have kids and you're anywhere in the vicinity of Coldwater Canyon, bring them to this park for a walk on Magic Forest Nature Trail. The trail, like Coldwater Canyon Park itself, is a delight and is a good source of inspiration for children who are growing up in an urban world. It's also the perfect place for them to learn about the importance of planting trees in urban areas. The organization TreePeople, which is headquartered in this Beverly Hills park, does exactly that in Los Angeles neighborhoods. The trail begins at a small shrine to the rainforest—a coast live oak stump that has been carved into a wood nymph—and continues in an equally charming fashion. Soft wood chips line the path. As you walk, you'll learn all about toyon, coast live oak, chaparral, poison oak, periwinkle, and other common flora. The park isn't exactly wilderness,

but it's a great example of how good a city park can be.

**User Groups:** Hikers and dogs. No horses or mountain bikes. No wheelchair facilities.

**Permits:** No permits are required. Parking and access are free.

**Maps:** A map/brochure of Coldwater Canyon Park is available at the park kiosk. For a topographic map, ask the USGS for Beverly Hills.

**Directions:** From U.S. 101 in Studio City, take the Coldwater Canyon exit and drive south for 2.3 miles, then turn left into the park entrance (at Mulholland). The trail begins by the parking area.

**Contact:** Coldwater Canyon Park, 12601 Mulholland Drive, Beverly Hills, CA 90210, 310/285-2537; TreePeople, 818/753-4600, website: www.treepeople.org.

## 29 HASTAIN TRAIL
### 2.3 mi / 1.5 hrs

**in Franklin Canyon in Santa Monica Mountains National Recreation Area**

Map 14.1, page 649

Unlike nearby Coldwater Canyon Park (see previous listing), here at Franklin Canyon Park, you can't hear the noise of the freeway and the city. That's because you've dropped down into a canyon that is surrounded by open space, insulating it from all urban encroachment. (We were surprised to see a coyote right by the road as we drove in.) A hike on the park's Hastain Trail is an energetic climb on a fire road to an overlook with views of Franklin Canyon, its reservoir, west Los Angeles, and all the way out to the ocean on clear days. After enjoying the view, you can return on a loop by taking the single-track trail on the right down to the Doheny House ranch and picnic area. Walk back on a trail alongside the park road. Before or after your hike, be sure to stop in at the park's Sooky Goldman Nature Center, where you can learn all about the natural history of the Santa Monica Mountains.

**User Groups:** Hikers, dogs, and horses. No mountain bikes. No wheelchair facilities.

**Permits:** No permits are required. Parking and access are free.

**Maps:** A free map of the Santa Monica Mountains National Recreation Area is available by contacting park headquarters at the address below. For a topographic map, ask the USGS for Beverly Hills.

**Directions:** From U.S. 101 in Studio City, take the Coldwater Canyon exit and drive south for 2.3 miles to the intersection of Mulholland Drive and Franklin Canyon Drive. Turn right on Franklin Canyon Drive. Drive 1.5 miles to the fork with Lake Drive, and bear left on Lake Drive. Just beyond the park entrance, look for a parking area and trailhead at a fire road, on the left.

**Contact:** Santa Monica Mountains National Recreation Area, 401 West Hillcrest Drive, Thousand Oaks, CA 91360, 805/370-2300, website: www.nps.gov/samo.

## 30 MOUNT HOLLYWOOD
### 5.0 mi / 2.5 hrs

**in Griffith Park**

Map 14.1, page 649

Griffith Park is as much a part of Los Angeles legend as Mann's Chinese Theater or the Santa Monica Pier. In all of the park's many acres, no trail is more frequently hiked than the trail to the top of Mount Hollywood. Out-of-towners need to be told that this is not the peak that bears the famous "HOLLYWOOD" sign (that's Mount Lee), although you can see that sign from this peak. Actually, people hike to the top of Mount Hollywood for no other reason than that the view from its summit is unforgettable. To see it, start hiking across the street from the Ferndell Museum, heading uphill along the shady trail. About .5 mile out, bear right at the fork and keep climbing, soon leaving the shady, damp canyon and moving into chaparral. There are several well-signed junctions to negotiate, then all of a sudden, voilà—you're at 1,625 feet in elevation on top of Mount Hollywood, the highest point in Hollywood. Check out the view

that stretches from downtown all the way out to the ocean. Oh, and just in case you need to be reminded that you're not really in the wilderness, you'll find water fountains positioned at strategic locations along the trail.

**User Groups:** Hikers, dogs, and horses. No mountain bikes. No wheelchair facilities.

**Permits:** No permits are required. Parking and access are free.

**Maps:** A free map is available at the park ranger station. For a topographic map, ask the USGS for Hollywood.

**Directions:** From I-5 in Hollywood, take the Los Feliz Boulevard west exit and drive three miles to Ferndell Drive. Turn right and drive to the Ferndell Nature Museum.

Alternately, from U.S. 101 in Hollywood, take the Sunset Boulevard exit and drive east one block to Western Avenue. Turn left, go north on Western Avenue, and then bear right on Los Feliz Boulevard. Turn left on Ferndell Drive and park near the Ferndell Nature Museum.

**Contact:** Griffith Park Ranger Station, 4730 Crystal Springs, Los Angeles, CA 90027, 323/913-4688, website: www.ci.la.ca.us/RAP.

## 31 BOLSA CHICA ECOLOGICAL RESERVE
### 1.5 mi / 0.75 hr

**in Huntington Beach**

Map 14.1, page 649

What a dichotomy. From the footbridge over the water at Bolsa Chica Ecological Reserve, you can see mussels, minnows, egrets, cordgrass, pickleweed, and huge flocks of shorebirds swirling in unison over the sparkling waters. But just a few hundred yards away, the state beach is lined with RVs, the oil-drilling grasshoppers are doing their monotonous job, and the traffic is crawling past on Highway 1. Where would you rather be? Right. The 1.5-mile loop trail at Bolsa Chica Ecological Reserve reminds us of what our coastline is supposed to look like and who depends on it the most—the birds on the Pacific Flyway. The 530-acre reserve is a migratory rest stop, and the birds are plentiful and fascinating to watch. The trail runs along the top of a levee, providing a vantage point that's just a few feet above the water's edge. What birds will you see? Brown pelicans, widgeons, pie-billed grebes, mergansers, pintails, and terns. If you're lucky, you may even spot a few endangered species, like the Belding's savannah sparrow (an unusual bird because it can drink seawater) or the California least tern. Consider this: For years, private developers have been trying to pave over this place and build pricey homes and condominiums, but so far, the birds are winning. We're rooting for them.

If you want to hike with a trained naturalist, show up on the first Saturday of any month at 9 A.M. Bring a jacket and binoculars and plan on getting a well-rounded education on bird identification, ecology, and endangered species.

**User Groups:** Hikers only. No dogs, horses, or mountain bikes. No wheelchair facilities.

**Permits:** No permits are required. Parking and access are free.

**Maps:** For a topographic map, ask the USGS for Seal Beach.

**Directions:** From I-405 in Seal Beach, exit at Seal Beach Boulevard and drive west to Highway 1. Turn south on Highway 1 and drive 4.5 miles to the Bolsa Chica Ecological Reserve entrance on the inland side of the highway, across from Bolsa Chica State Beach.

**Contact:** Amigos de Bolsa Chica, 16531 Bolsa Chica Road No. 312, Huntington Beach, CA 92649, 714/840-1575, website: www.amigosde-bolsachica.org.

## 32 TWO HARBORS TO EMERALD BAY
**9.0 mi / 5.0 hrs**

**on Catalina Island**

Map 14.1, page 649

If you want to take a hiking trip to Catalina Island, but you don't want your trip to be complicated or crowded with people, follow this one key instruction: Take the ferry to Two Harbors, not to Avalon. This applies whether you are going for the day or staying overnight. From the ferry drop point at Two Harbors pier, you can pick up your hiking permit and begin hiking right away on the West End Road, a dirt road that is nearly level and sticks close to the shoreline for its entire route. Head west—getting eyefuls of rocky outcrops, steep headlands, beckoning coves, and the beautiful blue Pacific—until at 1.25 miles you reach Cherry Valley and Cherry Cove. The area is named for the native Catalina cherry tree that grows there, which displays beautiful white flowers in the spring. Continue hiking on the flat dirt road, passing Howland Landing at almost four miles out. Stay far away from the plentiful No Trespassing signs there. Remain on the road until you see an obvious cutoff trail on your right leading to beautiful Emerald Bay, at 4.5 miles. Have a picnic on the gorgeous white sand beach and ponder how lucky we are to have this fabulous island so close to Los Angeles.

Although this excursion makes a fine day trip getaway from the mainland, your best bet is to spend the night in Two Harbors (either camping or in more luxurious accommodations), then continue hiking and exploring the next day. If you're on a day trip, you'll have to be back in Two Harbors in time for the boat home.

**User Groups:** Hikers only. No dogs, horses, or mountain bikes. No wheelchair facilities.

**Permits:** A free Santa Catalina Island hiking permit is required and may be obtained on the day of your hike from Two Harbors Visitors Center. Fees are charged for the ferry from the mainland to Two Harbors.

**Maps:** A trail map of Catalina Island is provided when you pick up your hiking permit. For a topographic map, ask the USGS for Santa Catalina West.

**Directions:** Catalina Express provides ferry transportation to Two Harbors from San Pedro.

**Contact:** Two Harbors Visitor Services, P.O. Box 5044, Two Harbors, CA 90704, 310/510-

0303, website: www.catalina.com; Santa Catalina Island Conservancy, 310/510-2595, website: www.catalinaconservancy.org; transport: Catalina Express, 310/519-1212 or 800/481-3470, website: www.catalinaexpress.com.

## 33 EMPIRE LANDING ROAD TRAIL
### 8.3 mi one-way / 4.0 hrs

**on Catalina Island**

**Map 14.1, page 649**

This spectacular one-way hiking trip on Catalina Island requires a bare minimum of planning in exchange for tremendous rewards. First, you have to arrange to take the ferry from the mainland to Avalon, Catalina's "big city." When you arrive, you must pick up your free hiking permit in town and take the shuttle bus from Avalon to Airport in the Sky. That's where your hike on the Empire Landing Road finally begins. Along its 8.3-mile length, you'll travel along the north side of the island on a curvy, up-and-down road that passes by a marble quarry, numerous coves and beaches, and fascinating rock formations. If you're lucky, you'll see an island fox, a huge bison, or maybe even a wild turkey.

When the trail ends at Two Harbors, you have three choices: Take the bus shuttle back to Avalon, camp or stay at the various lodgings in Two Harbors, or take the ferry from Two Harbors back to the mainland. For the latter two possibilities, you must plan in advance. If you want to take the ferry back to the mainland, you need to alert the ferry company that you're going in to Avalon but leaving from Two Harbors. There is no extra fee for this service, but you have to make sure you finish your hike in time to catch the last boat. One more thing to consider: When is the best time of year to visit Catalina? Unquestionably, it's spring or fall, when the weather is good and the summer crowds are nonexistent.

**User Groups:** Hikers only. No dogs, horses, or mountain bikes. No wheelchair facilities.

**Permits:** A free Santa Catalina Island hiking permit is required and may be obtained on the day of your hike from the Santa Catalina Island Conservancy, the Catalina Island Interpretive Center, or at the Catalina Airport. Fees are charged for the ferry from the mainland to Avalon, and for the shuttle bus from Avalon to the airport.

**Maps:** A trail map of Catalina Island is provided when you pick up your hiking permit. For a topographic map, ask the USGS for Santa Catalina.

**Directions:** Several companies, including Catalina Express and Catalina Passenger Service, provide ferry transportation to Avalon from San Pedro, Long Beach, Redondo Beach, and Newport Beach. Transportation is also possible by plane or helicopter through Island Express.

**Contact:** Santa Catalina Island Conservancy, 310/510-2595, website: www.catalinaconservancy.org; Two Harbors Visitor Services, 310/510-0303 (lodging and campgrounds), website: www.catalina.com (general information, permits); boat transport: Catalina Express, 310/519-1212 or 800/481-3470, website: www.catalinaexpress.com; Catalina Passenger Service, 949/673-5245; air transport: Island Express, 310/510-2525; shuttle service: 310/510-0143.

## 34 DEVIL'S PUNCHBOWL LOOP
### 1.0 mi / 0.5 hr

**in the Devil's Punchbowl Natural Area south of Pearblossom**

**Map 14.2, page 650**

The Devil's Punchbowl is visual proof that you're in earthquake country, where faulting and erosion have made bizarre shapes out of ancient sedimentary rocks. They thrust and jut upward, creating vertical walls as high as 300 feet, and they look as if they're about to topple inward on each other. From the viewpoint behind the visitors center, you look down into the land of the devil: the Punchbowl, a giant abyss that is the working of the San Andreas Fault and the result of centuries of stream carving. Juniper, piñon pine, and manzanita manage to eke out a meager living amidst all the sandstone. The park's easy, one-mile loop trail offers fine views into the depths of the Punchbowl. It switchbacks gently downhill to the canyon bottom and then climbs back up, passing by some of the taller rock slabs in the park. Here's a great tip: Park rangers hold full-moon hikes here once a month in the summer. Note: If you find this type of geological action fascinating, you might want to hike the park's longer trail to the dramatic Devil's Chair, a breathtaking overlook above the Punchbowl. Make sure you stop in at the nature center here at Devil's Punchbowl, where you can see its excellent display of wild birds.

**User Groups:** Hikers, dogs, and horses. No mountain bikes are allowed on this trail, although they are allowed on other park trails. No wheelchair facilities.

**Permits:** No permits are required. Parking and access are free.

**Maps:** Free park maps are available at the nature center. For a topographic map, ask the USGS for Valyermo.

**Directions:** From Highway 14 near Palmdale, take the Highway 138 exit east for 16 miles to Pearblossom. Turn right on County Road N-6 (Longview Road) and drive south for eight miles to the Devil's Punchbowl entrance. The trail begins behind the park nature center.

**Contact:** Devil's Punchbowl Natural Area, 28000 Devil's Punchbowl Road, Pearblossom, CA 93553, 661/944-2743, website: http://parks .co.la.ca.us.

## 35 COOPER CANYON FALLS
**4.0 mi / 2.0 hrs**

**in Angeles National Forest near Mount Waterman**

Map 14.2, page 650

After the snow has melted, here's a first-rate reason to make the 34-mile drive to the summit of Mount Waterman: a visit to Cooper Canyon Falls. The best thing about the waterfall—besides the fact that it's set in a gorgeous, 6,000-foot-elevation forest—is that it's just far enough away so that it doesn't get heavily visited. Start

your hike at Buckhorn Campground, at the trailhead for Burkhardt Trail. Although there are small waterfalls and swimming holes along Buckhorn Creek within .25 mile of the camp, the real treasure is two miles away, at Cooper Canyon. The hike is a mostly downhill trip through a dense forest of big firs, cedars, and pines. There's almost no undergrowth in these woods—just conifers and big rocks. It feels as if you're in the southern Sierra Nevada, but, no, this is the San Gabriels. The Burkhardt Trail laterals along the canyon slopes, high above Buckhorn Creek, then makes a left turn into Cooper Canyon and traces a long switchback downhill. At 1.75 miles from the camp, you'll reach a junction with the Pacific Crest Trail and Silver Moccasin Trail. Turn right, toward Burkhardt Saddle and Eagle's Roost. It's only .1 mile to the waterfall, which drops just below the trail's edge. A rope helps you down the steep cliff to its base, where you can stand on an island of boulders and enjoy the falls' noisy, 35-foot drop. Be sure to get here early in the year, when the stream flow is still strong. Trailhead elevation is 6,300 feet.

**User Groups:** Hikers, dogs, horses, and mountain bikes. No wheelchair facilities.

**Permits:** No permits are required. A national forest recreation pass is required for each vehicle; fees are $5 for one day or $30 for a year.

**Maps:** For a map, ask the U.S. Forest Service for Angeles National Forest. Maps of the Angeles Front Country and High Country are available from Tom Harrison Maps. For a topographic map, ask the USGS for Waterman Mountain.

**Directions:** From I-210 in La Cañada, take Highway 2 north and drive 34 miles to Buckhorn Camp, on the left. It's 1.5 miles past the Mount Waterman ski lift, just beyond Cloudburst Summit. The Burkhardt Trail starts at the far end of the camp near the restrooms (bear left at site No. 18).

**Contact:** Angeles National Forest, Los Angeles River Ranger District, 12371 North Little Tujunga Canyon Road, San Fernando, CA 91342, 818/899-1900, website: www.fs.fed .us/r5/angeles.

## 36 MOUNT WATERMAN
**5.8 mi / 3.0 hrs**

**in Angeles National Forest at
Mount Waterman**

Map 14.2, page 650

The peak of Mount Waterman (at 8,038 feet) is a fine destination for a moderate day hike in the San Gabriel Mountains, and the view from the summit is one you won't soon forget. The only problem that awaits is figuring out which peak is really the peak, because the top of Mount Waterman is so wide that there are three summits. From the trailhead (elevation 6,700 feet), bear left off the dirt road and head uphill on remarkably smooth, well-graded single track. The ascent is partially shaded by a mixed pine, cedar, and fir forest. At one mile out, you'll reach a saddle where your views open wide. Climb some more, through long switchbacks, to a junction at two miles out, then go right for the summit. It's an easy .75 mile to the peak, with a total 1,300-foot elevation gain along the entire trail. Keep your eyes peeled for bighorn sheep, which are sometimes seen in the area. Also check out the huge sugar pine cones that are found alongside the trail. When you reach the flat top of Mount Waterman, head off-trail for .25 mile toward the southwest (to your left), where you'll find the highest of Waterman's summits atop a jumble of boulders. Here is the best possible view, looking out over the magnificent San Gabriel Mountains.

**User Groups:** Hikers, dogs, horses, and mountain bikes. No wheelchair facilities.

**Permits:** No permits are required. A national forest recreation pass is required for each vehicle; fees are $5 for one day or $30 for a year.

**Maps:** For a map, ask the U.S. Forest Service for Angeles National Forest. Maps of the Angeles Front Country and High Country are available from Tom Harrison Maps. For a topographic map, ask the USGS for Waterman Mountain.

**Directions:** From I-210 in La Cañada, take Highway 2 north and drive 33 miles to a gated dirt road on the right signed as 3N03 (just west of the Buckhorn Campground sign and one mile east of Cloudburst Summit). Begin hiking on the gated dirt road and bear left in about 50 yards to the single-track Mount Waterman Trail.

**Contact:** Angeles National Forest, Los Angeles River Ranger District, 12371 North Little Tujunga Canyon Road, San Fernando, CA 91342, 818/899-1900, website: www.fs.fed.us/r5/angeles.

## 37 MOUNT WILLIAMSON
**5.0 mi / 3.0 hrs**

**in Angeles National Forest near Islip Saddle**

Map 14.2, page 650

This summit trail feels a bit rougher and more remote than those to many other peaks in the San Gabriel Mountains, and it's famous for its steep drop-offs. But the trail's total elevation gain is only 1,600 feet, and the visual rewards are tremendous. Mount Williamson is on the north side of the Angeles Crest Highway, which means that although you're hiking in a mountain environment, you're on the desert side of the mountain. The forest on this slope is more sparse, the trail is more exposed, and many of the best vistas are of the western Mojave Desert, to the north. Even if you're not in the mood to climb to the 8,214-foot summit, you can hike to a saddle at two miles out, where the Pacific Crest Trail drops down to the west. Views to the south are excellent here, with a big chunk of the San Gabriel Mountains spread out before you. From the saddle, take the summit trail on your right, heading .5 mile farther north on a remarkably steep grade. (A few switchbacks would be convenient here, but there are none.) Although the views have been excellent all along, nothing prepares you for the scene on top of Mount Williamson's narrow ridgeline, where you have dizzying views on both sides: The San Gabriels are on your left; the desert is on your right. Don't turn around at the first pointy summit you reach; follow the backbone trail a bit farther to a second and flatter summit, which is 30 feet higher. The view from here is even more extraordinary—you can look directly down into the Devil's Punchbowl and the San Andreas Fault.

**User Groups:** Hikers, dogs, horses, and mountain bikes. No wheelchair facilities.

**Permits:** No permits are required. A national forest recreation pass is required for each vehicle; fees are $5 for one day or $30 for a year.

**Maps:** For a map, ask the U.S. Forest Service for Angeles National Forest. Maps of the Angeles Front Country and High Country are available from Tom Harrison Maps. For a topographic map, ask the USGS for Crystal Lake.

**Directions:** From I-210 in La Cañada, take Highway 2 northeast and drive 42 miles to Islip Saddle (it's a mile east of the tunnels). Park in the large Pacific Crest Trail parking lot, on the north side of the road; the trail begins on the northwest side. (If you are coming from Highway 138 near Phelan or Piñon Hills, take Highway 2 west for 25 miles to Islip Saddle, 16 miles west of Big Pine.)

**Contact:** Angeles National Forest, Los Angeles River Ranger District, 12371 North Little Tujunga Canyon Road, San Fernando, CA 91342, 818/899-1900, website: www.fs.fed .us/r5/angeles.

## 38 VINCENT GAP TO MOUNT BADEN-POWELL

**8.0 mi / 4.0 hrs**

**in Angeles National Forest near Big Pines**

> **Map 14.2, page 650**

Like the climb to the summit of Mount Baldy, the climb to the summit of Mount Baden-Powell is something of a requirement for Southern California hikers. Luckily, this requirement is a little easier to attain, because the trail up to Mount Baden-Powell is a mere eight-mile round-trip with a 2,800-foot elevation gain. The summit of Baden-Powell is at 9,399 feet and is directly across the San Gabriel Basin from, and slightly north of,

Mount Baldy. As you might guess, the views from the summit are extraordinary. The summit area is also a botanist's delight, as 2,000-year-old limber pines can be found growing there. From the southwest edge of Vincent Gap, the trail leads through open forest—first oak, sugar pine, and Jeffrey pine, and as you climb, mostly lodgepole pine and occasional limber pines. The trail is extremely well maintained, with switchbacks on a moderate grade all the way up to the peak, where you can see more than a vertical mile below you into the canyon of the East Fork San Gabriel River. In addition, your views extend north to the desert and across the canyon to Mount Baldy. In case you haven't heard, the British Lord Baden-Powell, for whom this peak is named, founded the Boy Scouts organization. The Scouts have placed a monument to him at the summit. While you're there, make a vow always to "Be Prepared," just like the Boy Scouts.

**User Groups:** Hikers, dogs, and horses. No mountain bikes. No wheelchair facilities.

**Permits:** No permits are required. A national forest recreation pass is required for each vehicle; fees are $5 for one day or $30 for a year.

**Maps:** For a map, ask the U.S. Forest Service for Angeles National Forest. Maps of the Angeles Front Country and High Country are available from Tom Harrison Maps. For topographic maps, ask the USGS for Crystal Lake and Mount San Antonio.

**Directions:** From I-210 in La Cañada, take Highway 2 northeast and drive 53 miles to Vincent Gap. If you are coming from Highway 138 near Phelan or Piñon Hills, take Highway 2 west for 15 miles to Vincent Gap, which is 5.5 miles west of Big Pines.

**Contact:** Angeles National Forest, Santa Clara/Mojave Rivers Ranger District, 30800 Bouquet Canyon Road, Saugus, CA 91390, 661/296-9710, website: www.fs.fed.us/r5/angeles.

## 39 DEEP CREEK HOT SPRINGS
3.0 mi / 1.5 hrs

**in San Bernardino National Forest
near Hesperia**

Map 14.2, page 650

This trail is not the highlight of this trip, but its destination is. Deep Creek's hot springs are well known, well loved, and heavily visited. Although there are a few ways to hike to them, this route is the most popular simply because it's the shortest. It's called Goat Trail for a reason—this is a no-nonsense path that leads straight down from the trailhead to the creek, and straight up on the return. The total elevation change is only 700 feet, but on a hot day, it's, well . . . hot. Most people visit on cool days in winter and spring. The hot springs consist of three pools alongside the creek; the hottest one is the farthest from the stream's edge. Note that Goat Trail ends on the north side of Deep Creek, and you must ford the creek to reach the hot springs, then hike a short distance downstream. When Deep Creek is running high, this ford can be difficult, so check with the Arrowhead Ranger Station before planning an early spring visit. And keep in mind that although the hot springs are located on public forest service land, the trailhead is not, so you have to pay a fee to park and start your hike here.

**User Groups:** Hikers and dogs. No horses or mountain bikes. No wheelchair facilities.

**Permits:** No permits are required. A toll is charged by Bowens Ranch for crossing over their private land.

**Maps:** For a map, ask the U.S. Forest Service for San Bernardino National Forest. For a topographic map, ask the USGS for Lake Arrowhead.

**Directions:** From Cajon Pass at I-15, drive north for six miles and take the Hesperia exit. Drive east through the town of Hesperia on Main Street and turn left (east) on Rock Springs Road. Follow Rock Springs Road to its end. Turn left on Kiowa Road and drive .5 mile, then turn right on Roundup Way. Follow Roundup Way for 4.4 miles (it turns to dirt),

then turn right on Bowens Ranch Road (dirt). Drive 2.5 miles to a fork, bear right, and drive 3.3 miles farther on Bowens Ranch Road. Stop and register at the ranch house (a toll is charged), then continue to the road's end and the parking area and trailhead.

**Contact:** San Bernardino National Forest, Mountaintop Ranger District, P.O. Box 350, 28104 Highway 18, Skyforest, CA 92385, 909/337-2444, website: www.fs.fed.us/r5/san-bernardino.

## 40 FISH CANYON FALLS
9.4 mi / 5.0 hrs

**in Angeles National Forest near Duarte**

Map 14.2, page 650

If you want to see Fish Canyon Falls, you have to sign up for a difficult hike. Sure, there is a trail that travels all the way to the 90-foot falls, but it has a grade that will leave you begging for mercy. Still, the situation is better now than it was for most of the 1980s and 1990s, when there was no public access at all to the Fish Canyon Falls area. The waterfall lies on Angeles National Forest land, but the trail to reach it was blocked by the expansion of a private quarry. In 1998, a three-mile-long bypass trail was created to solve the problem, but unfortunately, the trail is steep, loose, far too narrow, and riddled with poison oak. So you need to really want this trip in order to sign up for it. The trail begins near the quarry entrance, then ascends steeply for 1.4 miles to Van Tassel Ridge. As if that wasn't punishment enough, next the path abruptly plummets down the other side (don't forget to bring along your hiking poles). Apparently the folks who built this trail never heard of switchbacks. The brutal up-and-down to the ridge must be accomplished in both directions of this trip, and that makes up the majority of the total 3,000-foot elevation gain. At 3.2 miles from the start, the trail joins the old, pleasant Fish Canyon Trail in the canyon bottom. This lovely path meanders gently uphill for 1.5 miles to a high box canyon, where the waterfall is found. If the water flow is high, Fish Canyon Falls is a stunner, dropping 90 feet in four stair-stepped tiers. If you are in good enough physical condition, it's worth seeing at least once in your life.

**User Groups:** Hikers and dogs. No horses or mountain bikes. No wheelchair facilities.

**Permits:** No permits are required. Parking and access are free.

**Maps:** A Fish Canyon trail guide, with a topographical map, is available from the city of Duarte (and is also usually available from a signboard near the trail's start).

**Directions:** From the junction of I-210 and I-605 near Duarte, follow I-605 north to its end, then go right (east) on Huntington Drive. Turn left on Encanto Parkway and drive 1.4 miles northeast to the parking area just before the quarry entrance.

**Contact:** City of Duarte Parks and Recreation Department, 1600 Huntington Drive, Duarte, CA 91010, 626/357-7931, website: www.accessduarte.com.

## 41 SAN ANTONIO FALLS
**1.5 mi / 1.0 hr**

**on Mount Baldy**

Map 14.2, page 650

Mount Baldy is that big mountain that you can see from almost everywhere in the Los Angeles Basin (on a clear day), and if you hike the trail to San Antonio Falls, you'll be able to see almost everywhere in the Los Angeles Basin. Trailhead elevation is 6,160 feet, a fine elevation to start at if you like clean, fresh, mountain air. For the best waterfall show, you've got to time your trip carefully for the first warm days after winter, sometimes as early as March, when the snow melts off the mountain and pours into 80-foot San Antonio Falls. By early summer, the waterfall show is over. The hike to the falls is easy, following the Mount Baldy ski lift maintenance road, which is paved and has only a slight uphill grade. At .7 mile, you round a sharp curve and see the falls, grace-

fully dropping in three tiers. If you wish, you can follow a well-worn path through loose gravel and talus to the waterfall's base, but be careful on the unstable slope. One of the best parts of this trip comes on your return walk to the trailhead. You're witness to lofty views of the far away San Gabriel Basin as you stroll back down the road.

**User Groups:** Hikers, dogs, horses, and mountain bikes. No wheelchair facilities.

**Permits:** No permits are required. A national forest recreation pass is required for each vehicle; fees are $5 for one day or $30 for a year.

**Maps:** For a map, ask the U.S. Forest Service for Angeles National Forest. Maps of the Angeles Front Country and High Country are available from Tom Harrison Maps. For a topographic map, ask the USGS for Mount San Antonio.

**Directions:** From I-10 at Ontario, exit on Mountain Avenue and drive north for six miles until Mountain Avenue joins Shinn Road. Bear left on Shinn Road and continue uphill to Mount Baldy Road. Bear right and drive nine miles north on Mount Baldy Road to Manker Flats Camp and continue .3 mile farther to Falls Road, on the left. Park in the dirt pullouts by Falls Road and begin walking on the gated, paved road.

**Contact:** Angeles National Forest, San Gabriel River Ranger District, 110 North Wabash Avenue, Glendora, CA 91741, 626/335-1251, website: www.fs.fed.us/r5/angeles.

## 42 MOUNT BALDY
**13.5 mi / 8.0 hrs**

**in Angeles National Forest near Upland**

Map 14.2, page 650

You just can't call yourself a Southern California hiker until you've climbed to the top of Mount Baldy (elevation 10,064 feet), the highest peak in the San Gabriel Mountains. The shortest and easiest route (which is neither short nor easy, with a 13.5-mile round-trip and a 3,500-foot elevation gain) starts from San Antonio Falls Road. Follow the trail to San Antonio Falls (see previous listing), but from the waterfall, continue uphill on the road for another 2.5 miles to Mount Baldy Notch. From the top of the ski lift at Baldy Notch, you'll access the infamous Devils Backbone, a sharp and jagged ridge. Prepare to act like a mountaineer, because the going gets a bit dicey on the well-named Devils Backbone, with steep drop-offs on both sides. You have three miles and a 2,200-foot elevation gain to go, and while some of it is in sparse pine and fir forest, most of it is exposed granite country. On your way, you'll pass the south side of Mount Harwood, at 9,552 feet. When you finally reach Baldy's summit, what can you see? Everything—desert, city, ocean, southern Sierra—it's a panoramic view like no other. Note that if you want to cut seven miles and 1,300 feet of elevation gain off your round-trip, you can ride the Mount Baldy ski lift up to Baldy Notch, rather than hiking 3.5 miles up (and then down) San Antonio Falls Road. The ski lift operates only on weekends and holidays during the hiking season, however. By the way, in case you were wondering, Mount Baldy's formal name is Mount San Antonio. "Baldy" has just been its nickname for as long as anybody can remember.

Special Note: Don't try hiking to Baldy's summit in winter, as tempting as the peak looks when covered in snow, because the Devils Backbone section is too treacherous. Try to hike the trail on a spring or early summer day, when there is little visible air pollution in the Los Angeles Basin, so the view from the summit is at its best.

**User Groups:** Hikers and dogs. No horses or mountain bikes. No wheelchair facilities.

**Permits:** A free campfire permit is required only for hikers using a camp stove or building a campfire. A national forest recreation pass is required for each vehicle; fees are $5 for one day or $30 for a year.

**Maps:** For a map, ask the U.S. Forest Service for Angeles National Forest. Maps of the Angeles Front Country and High Country are available from Tom Harrison Maps. For topographic maps, ask the USGS for Mount San Antonio and Telegraph Peak.

**Directions:** From I-10 at Ontario, exit on Mountain Avenue and drive north for six miles until Mountain Avenue joins Shinn Road. Bear left on Shinn Road and continue uphill to Mount Baldy Road. Bear right and drive nine miles north on Mount Baldy Road to Manker Flats Camp, and continue .3 mile farther to Falls Road, on the left. Park in the dirt pullouts by Falls Road and begin walking on the gated, paved road.

**Contact:** Angeles National Forest, San Gabriel River Ranger District, 110 North Wabash Avenue, Glendora, CA 91741, 626/335-1251, website: www.fs.fed.us/r5/angeles.

## 43 ICE HOUSE SADDLE
### 7.2 mi / 4.0 hrs

**in the Cucamonga Wilderness**

Map 14.2, page 650

When it's wintertime in Southern California and you get the itch to throw a few snowballs, where do you go? Ice House Canyon on Mount Baldy, of course. But Ice House Canyon is good in the summer too, especially if you want a hiking escape far from the smog of the Inland Empire. You can go for as long or as short as you like in the canyon—it's a great place to just set out from your car, climb until you're tired, then turn around and head back. If you hike only the first 1.8 miles of trail to the wilderness boundary sign, you don't even need a wilderness permit. When the stream is running in the canyon, many people just go this far and find a spot to sit by the cold, clear water.

If you're looking for a destination, Ice House Saddle (at 7,580 feet) is a good one, perfect for picnicking, with lovely views to the east and west. The saddle is also the site of a major trail junction, where routes lead in four directions, including the famous Three Ts Trail that leads to Timber Mountain, Telegraph Peak, and Thunder Mountain. The Ice House Canyon

Trail begins by passing a few summer cabins, some still in use and others in ruins. It parallels the stunningly clear stream that runs all the way through the canyon. The path is well maintained, and the forest is a lovely mix of oak, big cone spruce, pine, fir, and cedar. At one mile in, you have a choice of taking either Ice House Canyon Trail or Chapman Trail. Both lead to Ice House Saddle, but Ice House Canyon Trail stays along the creek, has a steeper grade, and gets to Ice House Saddle sooner. It's 2.6 miles to the saddle, straight up the canyon, with a total 2,660-foot elevation gain. You'll be huffing and puffing for sure. If you like, you can take the longer Chapman Trail for your return trip, which will add 1.7 miles to the round-trip mileage listed above. (Or hike the loop the other way around.)

**User Groups:** Hikers, dogs, and horses. No mountain bikes. No wheelchair facilities.

**Permits:** A free wilderness permit is required for both day hiking and backpacking in the Cucamonga Wilderness and is available from the San Gabriel River Ranger Station or the Mount Baldy Information Station (open weekends only). A national forest recreation pass is required for each vehicle; fees are $5 for one day or $30 for a year.

**Maps:** For a map, ask the U.S. Forest Service for Angeles National Forest. Maps of the Angeles Front Country and High Country are available from Tom Harrison Maps. For topographic maps, ask the USGS for Cucamonga Peak and Telegraph Peak.

**Directions:** From I-10 at Ontario, exit on Mountain Avenue and drive north for six miles until Mountain Avenue joins Shinn Road. Bear left on Shinn Road and continue uphill to Mount Baldy Road. Bear right and drive 5.5 miles north on Mount Baldy Road to Mount Baldy Village, and continue straight for .25 mile to Icehouse Canyon and the unsigned parking area where the road ends, at an old stone foundation. (Don't take the left fork for Mount Baldy Ski Lift.) The trail begins at the road signed as Private Road, Authorized Vehicles Only.

**Contact:** Angeles National Forest, San Gabriel River Ranger District, 110 North Wabash Avenue, Glendora, CA 91741, 626/335-1251, website: www.fs.fed.us/r5/angeles.

## 44 SEELEY CREEK TRAIL
**2.0 mi / 1.0 hr**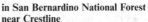

**in San Bernardino National Forest near Crestline**

Map 14.2, page 650

To reach the start of Seeley Creek Trail, you have to drive through a town called Valley of Enchantment, and that should tell you just about all you need to know about the area and the trail. It's beautiful up here—no, let's say it's enchanting—and although the elevation is only 4,000 feet, the conifers grow so big you'll think you're in the southern Sierra. The Seeley Creek Trail is a short and easy walk to a destination called Heart Rock, which during periods of rain or after snowmelt becomes Heart Rock Falls. Heart Rock is a smooth giant boulder in which nature has carved a perfect, heart-shaped bowl, about three feet deep and five feet wide. When Seeley Creek is running strong, a 25-foot waterfall spills into the heart's crown, then flows out the bottom and free falls downward. The stream flows year-round, and Heart Rock is always fascinating to see, but it's most compelling when the waterfall is flowing strong. The trail begins in a rather pedestrian fashion, along a road opposite the buildings of Seeley Camp, a Los Angeles Parks and Recreation camp. But once you walk beyond the camp boundary, the enchantment begins.

**User Groups:** Hikers, dogs, horses, and mountain bikes. No wheelchair facilities.

**Permits:** No permits are required. A national forest recreation pass is required for each vehicle; fees are $5 for one day or $30 for a year.

**Maps:** For a map, ask the U.S. Forest Service for San Bernardino National Forest. For a topographic map, ask the USGS for San Bernardino North.

**Directions:** From I-10 near San Bernardino, take I-215 north five miles to Highway 30 east.

Drive two miles east on Highway 30 and exit on Highway 18/Waterman Avenue. Drive north on Highway 18 for about 20 miles to the junction of Highways 18 and 138. Turn north on Highway 138 and drive 2.5 miles to the sign for Camp Seeley, just past the town of Valley of Enchantment. Turn left at the camp sign on Road 2N03 and take the left fork in the road (don't park in the camp parking lot). Cross the creek, which usually flows over the road, and look for the double-track trail on the right, near a sewer pipeline sign. Park alongside the road. You will be directly across the creek from the main parking lot for Camp Seeley, near the playground area.

**Contact:** San Bernardino National Forest, Mountaintop Ranger District, P.O. Box 350, 28104 Highway 18, Skyforest, CA 92385, 909/337-2444, website: www.fs.fed.us/r5/san-bernardino.

## 45 TELEGRAPH CANYON AND SOUTH RIDGE LOOP

**4.0 mi / 2.0 hrs**

**in Chino Hills State Park near Riverside**

**Map 14.2, page 650**

If you don't mind sharing your walk with equestrians and mountain bikers, this loop trail in Chino Hills State Park may be just what you need to revive yourself from the miles of surrounding freeways and rush-hour traffic. Start walking on the wide Telegraph Canyon Trail from near park headquarters, following a seasonal creek. You'll head out for about two miles and then loop back on South Ridge Trail. If you're in the mood for some single-track hiking, you can always take the right fork one mile out on Hills for Everyone Trail, turning left when it ends and returning to park headquarters on Telegraph Canyon Trail. The park is mostly grasslands and oaks, with a few wet canyon ravines providing homes for sycamore groves and wildlife. Native California walnut trees also grow here. Remember that the best time to visit the park is in winter or spring; if

you come in summer, make it as early in the morning as possible. In addition to the heat, summer brings with it the infamous Inland Empire smog.

**User Groups:** Hikers, horses, and mountain bikes. No dogs. No wheelchair facilities.

**Permits:** No permits are required. A $4 day-use fee is charged per vehicle.

**Maps:** A map of Chino Hills State Park is available at the entrance kiosk. For topographic maps, ask the USGS for Yorba Linda and Prado Dam.

**Directions:** From the junction of Highway 71 and Highway 91 near Corona, drive north on Highway 71 to Soquel Canyon Parkway. Turn left on Soquel Canyon Parkway and drive one mile to Elinvar Avenue. Turn left and drive to the end of Elinvar Avenue, at its intersection with Sapphire Road. Turn left on Sapphire Road and then right immediately at the Chino Hills State Park sign. Continue down the park road to park headquarters and turn into the parking area. The Telegraph Canyon Trail begins just below park headquarters.

**Contact:** Chino Hills State Park, 1879 Jackson Street, Riverside, CA 92504, 909/780-6222, website: www.parks.ca.gov.

## 46 EL MORO CANYON AND RIDGE LOOP

**4.5 mi / 2.0 hrs**

**in Crystal Cove State Park near Laguna Beach**

**Map 14.2, page 650**

El Moro Canyon is on the inland side of Crystal Cove State Park, and when you see how lush and overgrown it is, you'll have a hard time believing that only 12 inches of rain fall here each year. Although El Moro Creek flows only in the wet season, its edges are lined with oaks, sycamores, and willows, and it attracts tons of birds, small mammals, and butterflies. We managed to identify the anise swallowtail butterfly (yellow and black) and the red admiral butterfly (brown, red, and black) on one trip. Unlike the other trails on the inland side of the park, El Moro Canyon Trail is on a gentle grade, which makes it a fine route to take into the park's backcountry. The beginning of the trail is not so great, however, as it starts on a dirt road by the park entrance kiosk and winds behind the back of a trailer park. But in 10 minutes things, start to look up, as you veer left on El Moro Canyon Trail and walk up the shady, tree-lined canyon. At 1.5 miles out, turn right on East Cut Across Trail and make a switchbacking climb to El Moro Ridge. The ascent will get your heart pumping. Turn right on El Moro Ridge Trail and follow it as it rolls along the ridge top, offering many excellent ocean views. The trail leads back down to a single-track trail on the right, which in turn heads back to the trailer park. From there, proceed straight to the park entrance kiosk.

**User Groups:** Hikers, horses, and mountain bikes. No dogs. No wheelchair facilities.

**Permits:** No permits are required. A $10 day-use fee is charged per vehicle.

**Maps:** A trail map of Crystal Cove State Park is available at the visitors center. For a topographic map, ask the USGS for Laguna Beach.

**Directions:** From Corona del Mar, drive south on Highway 1 for three miles to the entrance to Crystal Cove State Park, on the inland side of the highway. Park near the park headquarters building; El Moro Canyon Trail begins down the park road by the entrance kiosk.

**Contact:** Crystal Cove State Park, 8471 Pacific Coast Highway, Laguna Beach, CA 92651, 949/494-3539 or 949/492-0802, website: www.parks.ca.gov.

## 47 BOMMER RIDGE AND BOAT CANYON
**9.6 mi / 5.0 hrs**

**in Laguna Coast Wilderness Park near Laguna Beach**

Map 14.2, page 650

Laguna Coast Wilderness Park is a precious gem, and like most gems, it is closely guarded. Access to the 6,600-acre park is restricted to weekends only, or by special reservation. If

it rains, the park is closed for at least 48 hours afterward. Why all the high security? In a county largely given over to development, this land contains one of the few remaining parcels of coastal sage scrub habitat. You'll smell its wonderful scent almost everywhere you walk. It also holds the only natural lakes in Orange County. What all this means to wildlife is a whole lot of good news.

This view-filled hike starts with a climb up Willow Canyon to Bommer Ridge Trail. The ridge offers expansive vistas of neighboring sage-covered canyons and the wide blue Pacific. Connect to Boat Canyon Trail and head out for more views, now of Emerald Bay, Irvine Cove, and the beaches around Laguna. You'll have to backtrack to find your way back to your car, but who wouldn't want to see this scenery all over again? On the final stretch, you can opt to take Laguna Laurel Canyon Trail instead of Willow Trail. Many interesting rock outcrops can be seen along this stretch, plus wildflowers and plentiful birds. If you're not up for this long hike but would still like to explore Laguna Coast Wilderness Park, a 3.5-mile docent-led hike through Laurel Canyon is offered every Saturday morning. Or just wander on your own; this is one park where it doesn't matter much where you hike. It's all good.

**User Groups:** Hikers, horses, and mountain bikes. No dogs. No wheelchair facilities.

**Permits:** Public access is permitted only on Saturday and Sunday or by special reservation. A $3 day-use fee is charged per vehicle.

**Maps:** A trail map is available at the parking area. For a topographic map, ask the USGS for Laguna Beach.

**Directions:** From I-405 in Irvine, exit south on Laguna Canyon Road. The main park entrance is located .3 mile past the El Toro Road intersection.

**Contact:** Laguna Coast Wilderness Park, 20101 Laguna Canyon Road, Laguna Beach, CA 92651, 949/923-2235, website: www.ocparks.com/lagunacoast.

## 48 HOLY JIM FALLS
**2.5 mi / 1.5 hrs**

in Trabuco Canyon in Cleveland
National Forest

Map 14.2, page 650

It seems that everybody in Orange County knows about and likes to visit Holy Jim Falls. The waterfall and its canyon were named for a beekeeper who lived here in the 1890s—James T. Smith, better known as Cussin' Jim. Apparently he had a temper and a colorful way with language. But conservative map makers who plotted Trabuco Canyon in the early 20th century found Smith's nickname in bad taste, so they changed it to Holy Jim, and it remains. Whether it's because of the interesting history of the area or the beauty that it still exhibits today, the trail to Holy Jim Falls is well known and frequently walked, especially in springtime. The 2.5-mile stroll is in the cool shade along Holy Jim Creek. Start by walking down the dirt road, past some leased cabins, to the signed trailhead. There the trail turns to single track. You're surrounded by a lush canyon filled with oaks, vine maples, wildflowers, and even a few bracken ferns. The trail crosses the creek several times and gently gains some elevation as it heads upstream. Where the trail steepens noticeably as you pass a large, old oak tree on your left, cross the creek one final time. Instead of following the main trail as it switchbacks uphill, you'll head to the right, continuing along the stream. An easy 300-yard stream scramble brings you to the waterfall's base, and if there isn't a scout troop there eating lunch (as there was on our trip), you'll be able to listen to the sweet music of the falls.

**User Groups:** Hikers, dogs, horses, and mountain bikes. No wheelchair facilities.

**Permits:** No permits are required. A national forest recreation pass is required for each vehicle; fees are $5 for one day or $30 for a year.

**Maps:** For a map, ask the U.S. Forest Service for Cleveland National Forest. For a topographic map, ask the USGS for Santiago Peak.

**Directions:** From Laguna Hills (north of San Juan Capistrano) on I-5, exit on El Toro Road and drive east for six miles. Turn right on Live Oak Canyon Road and drive about four miles (two miles past the entrance to O'Neill Regional Park). Turn left on Trabuco Canyon Road, which is an often unsigned, rocky, dirt road just past the paved Rose Canyon Road turnoff. The road is usually suitable for passenger cars. Go five miles on the dirt road to the well-signed parking area for Holy Jim Trail. The trail leads from the left side of the parking lot.

**Contact:** Cleveland National Forest, Trabuco Ranger District, 1147 East Sixth Street, Corona, CA 92879, 909/736-1811, website: www.fs.fed .us/r5/cleveland.

## 49 SAN JUAN LOOP TRAIL
**2.0 mi / 1.0 hr**

in Cleveland National Forest near
Lake Elsinore

Map 14.2, page 650

The San Juan Loop Trail is an easy and informative walk that serves as a good introduction to the Santa Ana Mountains. The only factor you must consider: Don't try to hike here in summer, when these mountains can feel hotter than the desert. The trailhead features a rather negative sign, which explains in doomsday-style terms the dangers of mountain lions, rattlesnakes, poison oak, and rugged terrain. If the sign doesn't convince you to get back in the car and go to Disneyland instead, start hiking on the loop trail, which parallels the road for its first .5 mile. You'll forget about the car noise as you start examining all the plant life along the trail, which includes deep red monkeyflowers, purple nightshade, and tall, spiky yuccas with their silky, milk-white flowers. Lizards dart here and there among the foliage. The terrain is dry and exposed, but thriving nonetheless. A half mile out, you'll pass a railing and overlook above a small seasonal waterfall on San Juan Creek, which has many clear, granite-lined pools. In another .5 mile, you'll pass the turnoff for Chiquito Basin Trail (it's highly recommended for those seeking a longer trip), and then you'll pass through a lovely grove of ancient oaks. The loop trail finishes out by bringing you back to the opposite side of the parking lot.

**User Groups:** Hikers, dogs, horses, and mountain bikes. No wheelchair facilities.

**Permits:** No permits are required. A national forest recreation pass is required for each vehicle; fees are $5 for one day or $30 for a year.

**Maps:** For a map, ask the U.S. Forest Service for Cleveland National Forest. For a topographic map, ask the USGS for Sitton Peak.

**Directions:** From I-5 at San Juan Capistrano, take the Ortega Highway/Highway 74 exit and drive north. In 21 miles, you'll reach the Ortega Oaks store on the right, .75 mile past Upper San Juan Campground. The trailhead is across the road from the store; turn left and park in the large parking lot. Start the loop trail on the right (north) side of the parking lot.

**Contact:** Cleveland National Forest, Trabuco Ranger District, 1147 East Sixth Street, Corona, CA 92879, 909/736-1811, website: www.fs.fed.us/r5/cleveland.

## 50 BEAR CANYON LOOP TRAIL
**6.7 mi / 3.5 hrs**

**in the San Mateo Canyon Wilderness near Lake Elsinore**

Map 14.2, page 650

Is it winter or spring? Is the weather cool and clear? If you've answered yes to both, this is a fine time to take a hike on Bear Canyon Trail—either a little out-and-back trip for as far as you like, or the full 6.7-mile loop which circles a junction called Four Corners. First, stock up on some chocolate from the candy store at the trailhead (this is why it must be a cool day; otherwise, carrying chocolate is out of the question). Set off on the trail adjacent to the store, heading into the San Mateo Canyon Wilderness and climbing gently through chaparral-covered slopes. In spring, many yuccas bloom along this stretch. Take the right fork one mile in, and in another mile, you'll reach the start of the loop; take the right branch to start. The

trail has a mere 700-foot elevation gain, and in places, it offers expansive views of the San Juan Canyon. Pigeon Springs is a popular resting point, where you can find some shade among the oaks. Four Corners is .5 mile beyond Pigeon Springs, and there, you'll turn sharply left to loop back. If you're looking for more of a workout, you can always turn right at Four Corners to head for 3,280-foot Sitton Peak. On the clearest days, you can see up to 50 miles distant from the summit. It looks like you could take a big leap and land on Catalina Island. Sitton Peak is a 9.5-mile round-trip.

**User Groups:** Hikers, dogs, and horses. No mountain bikes. No wheelchair facilities.

**Permits:** No permits are required. A national forest recreation pass is required for each vehicle; fees are $5 for one day or $30 for a year.

**Maps:** For a map, ask the U.S. Forest Service for Cleveland National Forest. For a topographic map, ask the USGS for Sitton Peak.

**Directions:** From I-5 at San Juan Capistrano, take the Ortega Highway/Highway 74 exit and drive north. In 21 miles, you'll reach the Ortega Oaks store on the right, .75 mile past Upper San Juan Campground. The parking area is across the road from the store; turn left and park in the large parking lot. Cross the road to begin hiking on the Bear Canyon Trail, to the right of the store.

**Contact:** Cleveland National Forest, Trabuco Ranger District, 1147 East Sixth Street, Corona, CA 92879, 909/736-1811, website: www.fs.fed.us/r5/cleveland.

## 51 TENAJA FALLS
**1.5 mi / 1.0 hr**

**in the San Mateo Canyon Wilderness near Murrieta**

Map 14.2, page 650

The only hard part about getting to Tenaja Falls is the long drive to the unmarked trailhead. But if you follow the driving directions exactly, even that shouldn't be a problem. Once you've parked, head for the fence that blocks vehicles from the road into the San Mateo

Canyon Wilderness. Cross the creek on a concrete apron, or if the water is too deep, follow a use trail upstream and cross the creek where it's narrower. Just be sure to join up with the main road again; following the streamside use trails is a needlessly difficult way to the falls. (Guess how we know.) On the wide canyon road, you'll hike northward, rising out of the canyon alongside sage- and chaparral-covered hillsides. In a few minutes, you'll round a curve and be treated to a partial view of the waterfall ahead. What a sight—Tenaja Falls is huge compared to other waterfalls in Orange County, dropping 150 feet in five tiers. It's magnificent when flowing full, which is only after a period of rain, usually between December and March. Keep walking toward the waterfall; the trail deposits you at its lip. When the water is low enough, you can cross over the top of the falls to the other side of the creek, but be extremely cautious on the slippery granite if you choose to do so.

**User Groups:** Hikers, dogs, and horses. No mountain bikes. No wheelchair facilities.

**Permits:** No permits are required. A national forest recreation pass is required for each vehicle; fees are $5 for one day or $30 for a year.

**Maps:** For a map, ask the U.S. Forest Service for Cleveland National Forest. For a topographic map, ask the USGS for Sitton Peak.

**Directions:** From Lake Elsinore, drive south on I-15 for about 12 miles to the Clinton Keith Road exit in Murrieta. Drive south on Clinton Keith Road for five miles, which will become Tenaja Road, although you won't see any signs. At a signed intersection with Tenaja Road, turn right and drive west for 4.5 miles. Turn right on Cleveland Forest Road (also known as Rancho California Road), and drive one mile to the Tenaja trailhead. Reset your odometer here and continue 4.4 miles on the dirt road (7S04) to a hairpin turn in the road and the parking area.

**Contact:** Cleveland National Forest, Trabuco Ranger District, 1147 East Sixth Street, Corona, CA 92879, 909/736-1811, website: www.fs.fed .us/r5/cleveland.

## 52 SANTA ROSA PLATEAU ECOLOGICAL RESERVE

**4.5 mi / 2.5 hrs**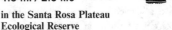

**in the Santa Rosa Plateau Ecological Reserve**

Map 14.2, page 650

Those volcanic-looking rocky mesas you see as you drive through the foothills along Clinton Keith Road are home to some of Southern California's last vernal pools—seasonal ponds that give life to endangered plants and wildflowers and provide a resting place for wintering birds. Whereas these pools are more common in the San Joaquin Valley, here in Southern California, they have all but vanished, which is one reason for the establishment of the Santa Rosa Plateau Ecological Reserve. Another reason is the existence of the rare Engelmann oak, a semideciduous species of oak that only loses its leaves during times of drought. Several fine groves of Engelmann oaks are found within the reserve's border.

If you're visiting in late winter or early spring and you just want to see the vernal pools, you can do so with a one-mile walk on Vernal Pool Trail from a trailhead located two miles west of the reserve visitors center, on Clinton Keith Road. If you're here at any other time of the year, your best bet is to start your trip at the visitors center. If you can, show up on Saturday morning and go on one of the ranger-led interpretive hikes. If you'd rather hike on your own, start out on the left side of Granite Loop Trail. Connect to Vista Grande Trail and head uphill to its junction with Monument Road. You'll pass some lovely Engelmann oaks along the way. Turn right on Monument Road, then take the left spur to the top of Monument Hill (elevation 2,046 feet), the highest point in the reserve. The views of the chaparral- and cactus-covered hills and rolling grasslands are lovely. If you arrive early in the morning before the frequent afternoon haze moves in, you'll be able to pick out classic Southern California landmarks: Mounts San Gorgonio, San Jacinto, and Palomar; Cuyamaca Peak and Mount

Woodson, in San Diego; the high summits of the San Gabriel Mountains; and yes, even the Pacific Ocean. Retrace your steps to head back, or make a semiloop by turning left on Tenaja Truck Trail, then right on Waterline Road.

**User Groups:** Hikers, horses, and mountain bikes. (Horses and mountain bikes allowed only on signed multiuse trails.) No dogs. No wheelchair facilities.

**Permits:** No permits are required. A $2 day-use fee is charged per adult; $1 for children 12 and under.

**Maps:** A trail map is available at the visitors center and at all four trailheads in the reserve. For a topographic map, ask the USGS for Wildomar.

**Directions:** From Lake Elsinore, drive south on I-15 for about 12 miles to the Clinton Keith Road exit in Murrieta. Drive west on Clinton Keith Road for four miles (past Aveneda La Cresta) to the visitors center entrance, on the left. Park near the visitors center.

**Contact:** Santa Rosa Plateau Ecological Reserve, 39400 Clinton Keith Road, Murrieta, CA 92562, 909/677-6951, website: www.santarosaplateau.org.

## 53 COUGAR CREST TRAIL TO BERTHA PEAK

**6.0 mi / 3.0 hrs**

**in San Bernardino National Forest near Big Bear Lake**

Map 14.3, page 651

Put on your hiking boots and prepare to climb. That's what you have to do on Cougar Crest Trail—gain 1,300 feet over three miles to reach Bertha Peak, elevation 8,201 feet. You can see the peak, capped with electronic relay equipment, from the trailhead parking lot. Views of the Big Bear area are spectacular along the route, and the trail is well built, making this an excellent day hike—or running path if you're a jogger. The first mile is on dirt roads in a forest of piñon and Jeffrey pines, but soon the path narrows to single track. The more you climb upward, the more you see; turn around

every now and then to check out the lake and mountain views. Finally, at two miles, you reach the Pacific Crest Trail (PCT), where the grade eases considerably. Turn right and follow the PCT for .5 mile to a dirt road, then turn right again and climb steeply to reach Bertha's summit. Look for old, gnarled juniper trees along the route. The view from the peak includes Big Bear Lake, of course, plus Mount San Gorgonio and other high peaks and ridges, and green Holcomb Valley below you.

**User Groups:** Hikers, dogs, horses, and mountain bikes. No wheelchair facilities.

**Permits:** No permits are required. A national forest recreation pass is required for each vehicle; fees are $5 for one day or $30 for a year.

**Maps:** For a map, ask the U.S. Forest Service for San Bernardino National Forest. For a topographic map, ask the USGS for Fawnskin.

**Directions:** From the town of Big Bear Lake on Highway 18, take the Stanfield cutoff to the north shore of the lake, where it junctions with Highway 38. Turn left and drive 1.3 miles on Highway 38 (.5 mile past the Big Bear Ranger Station) to the Cougar Crest trailhead, on the right side of the road. If you are traveling from Fawnskin, the trailhead is 2.4 miles east of Fawnskin on Highway 38, on the left side of the road.

**Contact:** San Bernardino National Forest, Big Bear Discovery Center, P.O. Box 66, 41397 North Shore Drive, Fawnskin, CA 92333, 909/866-3437, website: www.fs.fed.us/r5/san-bernardino.

## 54 WOODLAND TRAIL

**1.5 mi / 0.75 hr**

**in San Bernardino National Forest near Big Bear Lake**

Map 14.3, page 651

If you're spending the weekend or the week in Big Bear, you'd be well advised to pay a visit to the Big Bear Discovery Center, in Fawnskin. You can get all the information you want about hiking, fishing, and exploring around the Big Bear area from the nice people there. Then take this terrific short walk on Woodland Trail, which starts near the visitors center. You can pick up an interpretive brochure and learn all about serviceberry, yerba santa, Jeffrey and ponderosa pines, indigo bush, and piñon pines. A bonus is that on the return leg of the loop, you get great views of the lake, but you're far enough away that you don't get hit by the wind that often blows on the north side. From high points on the trail, your vista expands all the way across the lake to Big Bear City.

**User Groups:** Hikers, dogs, horses, and mountain bikes. No wheelchair facilities.

**Permits:** No permits are required. A national forest recreation pass is required for each vehicle; fees are $5 for one day or $30 for a year.

**Maps:** For a map, ask the U.S. Forest Service for San Bernardino National Forest. For a topographic map, ask the USGS for Fawnskin.

**Directions:** From the town of Big Bear Lake on Highway 18, take the Stanfield cutoff to the north shore of the lake, where it junctions with Highway 38. Turn left on Highway 38 and drive .5 mile to the Woodland trailhead, on the right side of the road. It's directly across the highway from the East Boat Ramp, or one mile east of the Big Bear Discovery Center.

**Contact:** San Bernardino National Forest, Big Bear Discovery Center, P.O. Box 66, 41397 North Shore Drive, Fawnskin, CA 92333, 909/866-3437, website: www.fs.fed.us/r5/sanbernardino.

## 55 CHAMPION LODGEPOLE PINE
### 1.0 mi / 0.5 hr

**in San Bernardino National Forest near Big Bear Lake**

Map 14.3, page 651

Let's see now. The biggest giant sequoia tree is the General Sherman Tree, in Sequoia National Park. But which is the biggest lodgepole pine tree, and where do you find it? We're delighted you asked. It's the Champion Lodgepole, located only a few miles from Big Bear Lake. The big tree is growing in a grove of world

champions, the largest lodgepole pines around. What's strange is that these big guys are growing at 7,500 feet in elevation, when usually in Southern California, lodgepole pines won't grow at less than 8,000 feet. The Champion is about 400 years old, stands 112 feet tall, and has a circumference of 20 feet. After a long but enjoyable drive on a dirt road to the trailhead, you'll find the trail to the big tree is flat and easy. It follows a small stream to a junction. Turn right and walk the last few yards to the Champion, which is surrounded by a fence and situated at the edge of a pretty meadow.

**User Groups:** Hikers, dogs, horses, and mountain bikes. No wheelchair facilities.

**Permits:** No permits are required. A national forest recreation pass is required for each vehicle; fees are $5 for one day or $30 for a year.

**Maps:** For a map, ask the U.S. Forest Service for San Bernardino National Forest. For a topographic map, ask the USGS for Big Bear Lake.

**Directions:** From the dam on the west end of Big Bear Lake, drive 3.5 miles east on Highway 18/Big Bear Boulevard to Mill Creek Road. Turn right (south) on Mill Creek Road/Forest Service Road 2N10 and follow it for five miles, through several junctions. (The road turns to dirt.) At Forest Service Road 2N11, turn right and drive one mile to the parking area. The route is well signed for the Champion Lodgepole Pine.

**Contact:** San Bernardino National Forest, Big Bear Discovery Center, P.O. Box 66, 41397 North Shore Drive, Fawnskin, CA 92333, 909/866-3437, website: www.fs.fed.us/r5/sanbernardino.

## 56 CASTLE ROCK TRAIL
### 2.0 mi / 1.0 hr

**in San Bernardino National Forest near Big Bear Lake**

Map 14.3, page 651

There are a couple tricky elements about this trail: There's no real parking area, just a pullout along the highway, and although the path to Castle Rock has a mere 700-foot elevation gain, it's compressed into one mile and climbs steeply right from the trailhead. The trail is smooth sand, surrounded by manzanita, big ponderosa pines, and a ton of rocks. It's located by the area of Big Bear Lake called Boulder Bay, a perfectly descriptive name. As you climb, you gain tremendous views of the lake, but you'll miss them completely unless you turn around. In about 20 minutes you'll reach a rocky overlook, which is where many people stop and pull up a granite boulder to sit on. The main trail becomes a spiderweb of trails, as people have chosen all different routes around the rocks. If you continue upward, you'll reach a saddle and then start to descend slightly. Castle Rock, which is easily distinguishable by its shape, is just to the east, off the trail as you head downhill. If you tire out before the saddle, just pick any boulder that's easy to climb and get on top to enjoy the lovely views of the lake. On one trip in late March we were treated to a lovely shower of snow flurries. Isn't Big Bear the greatest? Trailhead elevation is 6,700 feet.

**User Groups:** Hikers, dogs, horses, and mountain bikes. No wheelchair facilities.

**Permits:** No permits are required. A national forest recreation pass is required for each vehicle; fees are $5 for one day or $30 for a year.

**Maps:** For a map, ask the U.S. Forest Service for San Bernardino National Forest. For a topographic map, ask the USGS for Big Bear Lake.

**Directions:** From the dam on the west end of Big Bear Lake, drive one mile east on Highway 18/Big Bear Boulevard to the signed Castle Rock trailhead, on the right (it's by the Big Bear City Limit sign). Park in the turnout on the lake side of Highway 18, about 50 yards farther east, and then walk across the road to the trailhead.

**Contact:** San Bernardino National Forest, Big Bear Discovery Center, P.O. Box 66, 41397 North Shore Drive, Fawnskin, CA 92333, 909/866-3437, website: www.fs.fed.us/r5/san-bernardino.

## 57 PONDEROSA VISTA NATURE TRAIL
### 1.0 mi / 0.5 hr

**in San Bernardino National Forest near Angelus Oaks**

Map 14.3, page 651

The Ponderosa Vista Nature Trail wins hands down for the trail with the most corny interpretive plaques. When you visit, you'll see what we mean. But aside from the overdone prose, everything else on this trail is first-rate, making for a great introduction to the flora and fauna of San Bernardino National Forest. You can choose between the short loop (.3 mile) and the long loop (.6 mile), but why not hike both? You can learn about assorted birds of the forest, such as acorn woodpeckers, redbreasted sapsuckers, and yellow-rumped warblers, as well as various trees—ponderosa pine is the most common conifer in the area, but incense cedars, black oaks, white firs, and piñon pines also grow. The highlight of the trail is an overlook point with a view across the Santa Ana River Canyon. An old photograph at the overlook shows what the canyon used to look like and explains about the building of the Rim of the World Highway in 1935. That was the same year that black bears were introduced to the area. No wonder—with the new highway, they could just get into their RVs and drive in.

**User Groups:** Hikers, dogs, horses, and mountain bikes. No wheelchair facilities.

**Permits:** No permits are required. A national forest recreation pass is required for each vehicle; fees are $5 for one day or $30 for a year.

**Maps:** For a map, ask the U.S. Forest Service for San Bernardino National Forest. For a topographic map, ask the USGS for Big Bear Lake.

**Directions:** From I-10 at Redlands, take the Highway 38 exit and drive northeast for 25 miles to the trailhead for Ponderosa Vista Nature Trail, on the left side of the road. If you reach the Jenks Lake turnoff, you've passed it. Park in the parking lot by the trailhead.

**Contact:** San Bernardino National Forest, Mill Creek Ranger Station, 34701 Mill Creek Road, Mentone, CA 92359, 909/794-1123, website: www.fs.fed.us/r5/sanbernardino.

## 58 WHISPERING PINES TRAIL
### 0.5 mi / 0.5 hr

**in San Bernardino National Forest near Angelus Oaks**

Map 14.3, page 651

Right across the road from Ponderosa Vista Trail is Whispering Pines Trail, another short, easy interpretive trail that is both fun and informative. Time to play Trivial Pursuit: This trail appeared on what television show, filmed in 1969, about a blind girl and a furry dog? If you guessed *Lassie,* you win. In the show, the girl walked this trail and read the braille interpretive displays. Anyway, this nature trail has less of a grade than the one across the highway, although it's not quite as scenic. You will see numerous pines with an incredible amount of holes drilled in them—the work of industrious acorn woodpeckers. A minus is the sound of nearby Highway 38, but the pluses are the sound of the wind in the pines and lots of squirrels and jays.

**User Groups:** Hikers, dogs, horses, and mountain bikes. No wheelchair facilities.

**Permits:** No permits are required. A national forest recreation pass is required for each vehicle; fees are $5 for one day or $30 for a year.

**Maps:** For a map, ask the U.S. Forest Service for San Bernardino National Forest. For a topographic map, ask the USGS for Big Bear Lake.

**Directions:** From I-10 at Redlands, take the Highway 38 exit and drive northeast for 25 miles to the trailhead for Whispering Pines Trail, on the right side of the road. If you reach the Jenks Lake turnoff, you've passed it. Park in the well-signed parking lot by the trailhead.

**Contact:** San Bernardino National Forest, Mill Creek Ranger Station, 34701 Mill Creek Road, Mentone, CA 92359, 909/794-1123, website: www.fs.fed.us/r5/sanbernardino.

## 59 JENKS LAKE
### 1.0 mi / 0.5 hr

**in San Bernardino National Forest near Angelus Oaks**

Map 14.3, page 651

If you can get to Jenks Lake on a weekday when nobody is around, you'll find it's a magical little spot of bright blue water, with Mount San Gorgonio looming in the background. Even in April, the peak can be crested with snow and the wind can whip off the surface of the small lake, creating little whitecaps. If you visit Jenks Lake on a Saturday in July, however, it's another story. The place is likely to be packed with picnicking families, kids from nearby summer camps, and people fishing for largemouth bass, bluegill, and rainbow trout in the stocked lake. No matter when you arrive, you should take the short walk around the perimeter of the lake, then head off on the nature trail that leads behind the picnic area. The south shore of the lake is the quieter side, where no swimming is permitted. After looping around the lake, walk to the back side of the picnic area, where you're likely to be surprised by the view from the trail—the canyon drops off vertically, with sheer cliffs that fall hundreds of feet. Yes, this is the Rim of the World, just like the highway of the same name. Fortunately a railing is in place to keep you from leaning too far over the edge. Note that hikers looking for a longer adventure can set off from either the South Fork or Forsee Creek trailheads (near Jenks Lake) and head into the San Gorgonio Wilderness. If you don't have a permit, you can always walk just to the wilderness boundary and turn around.

**User Groups:** Hikers and dogs. No horses or mountain bikes. Some wheelchair facilities.

**Permits:** No permits are required. A $5 day-use fee is charged per vehicle (the national forest adventure pass does not apply here).

**Maps:** For a map, ask the U.S. Forest Service for San Bernardino National Forest. For a topographic map, ask the USGS for Big Bear Lake.

**Directions:** From I-10 at Redlands, take the Highway 38 exit and drive northeast for 27 miles to the Jenks Lake turnoff on the right. Turn right and follow Jenks Lake Road for two miles to the parking area for the lake. Note that Jenks Lake Road continues and reconnects to Highway 38 a few miles to the east.

**Contact:** San Bernardino National Forest, Mill Creek Ranger Station, 34701 Mill Creek Road, Mentone, CA 92359, 909/794-1123, website: www.fs.fed.us/r5/sanbernardino.

## 60 ASPEN GROVE TRAIL
**5.0 mi / 2.5 hrs**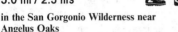

**in the San Gorgonio Wilderness near Angelus Oaks**

Map 14.3, page 651

From the Aspen Grove trailhead, a short walk down a dirt road leads you into a cool and shady grove of aspen trees along Fish Creek, one of only two remaining in San Bernardino National Forest. The grove is small and is continually threatened by nonnative beavers, who chew the aspens down to build dams in Fish Creek. The Department of Fish and Game introduced the beavers in the 1940s, thinking they'd be good for the ecosystem. Now they are trying to remove them, but the little guys with the big teeth are hard to catch. What a dilemma. Anyway, if you're accustomed to the aspen trees of the southern Sierra, you'll notice that these have smaller leaves—an adaptation to the dry climate. One tip: Don't show up in April, when the aspens have no leaves at all. Autumn is the best time to see them, when they are bright gold in color. If you want to do more than hike down the hill and wander among the aspens, you must have a wilderness permit. Once you cross Fish Creek, you're in the San Gorgonio Wilderness. The trail to the right leads to a few more aspens and then peters out. Follow the trail to your left (uphill), heading away from the creek. A pretty walk of less than two miles through a mixed conifer forest will deliver you to two meadows—first, tiny Monkey Flower Flat, and then, after cross-

ing Fish Creek again, Lower Fish Creek Meadow. It's a fine place to lay out a picnic and count the wildflowers. A side note: The drive to and from the Aspen Grove trailhead is awesome, with wide views at every turn in the road.

**User Groups:** Hikers, dogs, and horses. No mountain bikes. No wheelchair facilities.

**Permits:** A free wilderness permit is required for both day hiking and backpacking and is available in advance by mail or fax from the Mill Creek Ranger Station. Permits can also be obtained in person at the Mill Creek Ranger Station or Barton Flats Visitors Center on Highway 38. A national forest recreation pass is required for each vehicle; fees are $5 for one day or $30 for a year.

**Maps:** For a map, ask the U.S. Forest Service for San Bernardino National Forest or San Gorgonio Wilderness. A map of the San Gorgonio Wilderness is available from Tom Harrison Maps. For a topographic map, ask the USGS for Moonridge.

**Directions:** From I-10 at Redlands, take the Highway 38 exit and drive northeast for 32 miles to Forest Service Road 1N02, signed for Heart Bar Campground, Coon Creek, and Fish Creek. Turn right (south) and drive 1.25 miles to Road 1N05, then bear right. Drive 1.5 miles to the Aspen Grove trailhead, on the right.

**Contact:** San Bernardino National Forest, Mill Creek Ranger Station, 34701 Mill Creek Road, Mentone, CA 92359, 909/794-1123, website: www.fs.fed.us/r5/sanbernardino.

## 61 BIG FALLS
**0.6 mi / 0.5 hr**

**in the Falls Recreation Area near Forest Falls**

Map 14.3, page 651

Quick—what's the largest year-round waterfall in Southern California? Big Falls, of course. At 500 feet tall, Big Falls delivers on its name, but unfortunately it's difficult to see the waterfall's full height. That's okay, though, because the Falls Recreation Area is still a great destination, and the short hike to the overlook of Big Falls is a fun and easy walk. The elevation at the trailhead is just over 6,000 feet, which means the air is cool and clear. Begin hiking at the lower parking lot, below the picnic area, and set off on an unsigned path heading downstream along Mill Creek Wash. When you pass a private cabin alongside the wash, look for a good place to cross Mill Creek by rock hopping, and then do so. On the far side of the stream, pick up the trail leading uphill on the right side of Falls Creek, which is a feeder stream to Mill Creek. Hike past a small cascade on the bottom of Falls Creek, and head uphill for about five minutes to the overlook area for Big Falls. What you see is the top 40 to 50 feet of a very Yosemite-like free fall, and then some cascading water below. The huge middle part of the fall is hidden in the rocky canyon. Darn. So where can you get a better view of Big Falls? Actually, the best view is from your car window, as you drive past the last few houses along Valley of the Falls Drive, shortly before entering the Falls Recreation Area. Along this stretch, you can see the full-length vista of Big Falls that usually appears on postcards.

**User Groups:** Hikers, dogs, horses, and mountain bikes. No wheelchair facilities.

**Permits:** No permits are required. A national forest recreation pass is required for each vehicle; fees are $5 for one day or $30 for a year.

**Maps:** For a map, ask the U.S. Forest Service for San Bernardino National Forest. For a topographic map, ask the USGS for Forest Falls.

**Directions:** From I-10 at Redlands, take the Highway 38 exit and drive northeast for approximately 14 miles to the intersection with Forest Home Road. Bear right and continue for 4.5 miles to the Falls Recreation Area, past the town of Forest Falls. (The name of the road changes to Valley of the Falls Drive.) Park in the first parking lot on the left.

**Contact:** San Bernardino National Forest, Mill Creek Ranger Station, 34701 Mill Creek Road, Mentone, CA 92359, 909/794-1123, website: www.fs.fed.us/r5/sanbernardino.

## 62 VIVIAN CREEK TRAIL TO MOUNT SAN GORGONIO

**14.0 mi / 1.0–2.0 days**

in the San Gorgonio Wilderness near Forest Falls

Map 14.3, page 651

There are lots of ways to reach the summit of Mount San Gorgonio, the tallest mountain in Southern California, but the shortest way is on Vivian Creek Trail. That's the good news. The bad news is that it's also the steepest way. The summit of San Gorgonio is at 11,502 feet, and the Vivian Creek trailhead is at 6,100 feet, so you can see what you're in for. Luckily, there are several camps along the way: Vivian Creek Camp at 1.2 miles, Halfway Camp at 2.5 miles (halfway to what, we wonder), and High Creek Camp at 4.8 miles. It's a seven-mile one-way trip to the summit, and although some people hike the round-trip in a day, it's much better to take two or more days so you can enjoy yourself and not have to rush back before dark.

The trail leaves the upper end of Big Falls Picnic Area and crosses Mill Creek Wash, then starts on a steep mile-long climb to the hanging valley of Vivian Creek, where Vivian Creek Falls sometimes fall. Vivian Creek Camp is located here; it's a convenient place to camp if you've gotten a late afternoon start. The trail continues along Vivian Creek, crossing it numerous times under the shade of a mixed conifer forest, to Halfway Camp. A few more switchbacks and you cross High Creek, arriving at High Creek Camp, at 9,000 feet. High Creek Camp is famous for being a cold and windy place to spend the night. At this elevation, only lodgepole pines grow, and as you gain another 2,000 feet in elevation, even these stalwarts give way to granite. At the base of San Gorgonio's summit, you meet up with the trail from Dollar Lake. Turn right, then left at the next junction, and climb to the 11,502-foot summit of Old Greyback, as it's called. Are you exhausted? Join the party—so is everybody else who makes it this far. But what an achievement. Hope you brought a good map so you can identify all the major landmarks of Southern California.

**User Groups:** Hikers, dogs, and horses. No mountain bikes. No wheelchair facilities.

**Permits:** A free wilderness permit is required for both day hiking and backpacking and is available in advance by mail or fax from the Mill Creek Ranger Station. Permits can also be obtained in person at the Mill Creek Ranger Station or Barton Flats Visitors Center on Highway 38. A national forest recreation pass is required for each vehicle; fees are $5 for one day or $30 for a year.

**Maps:** For a map, ask the U.S. Forest Service for San Bernardino National Forest or San Gorgonio Wilderness. A map of the San Gorgonio Wilderness is available from Tom Harrison Maps. For topographic maps, ask the USGS for Forest Falls and San Gorgonio.

**Directions:** From I-10 at Redlands, take the Highway 38 exit and drive northeast for about 14 miles to the intersection with Forest Home Road. Bear right and continue for 4.5 miles to the Falls Recreation Area, past the town of Forest Falls. (The name of the road changes to Valley of the Falls Drive.) Drive to the parking area at the end of the road and walk uphill through the picnic area on the dirt road to reach the trailhead.

**Contact:** San Bernardino National Forest, Mill Creek Ranger Station, 34701 Mill Creek Road, Mentone, CA 92359, 909/794-1123, website: www.fs.fed.us/r5/sanbernardino.

## 63 SEVEN PINES TRAIL
**7.4 mi / 4.0 hrs**

**in the San Jacinto Wilderness near Idyllwild**

Map 14.3, page 651

The best thing about Seven Pines Trail is that you can just wander as far as you please and have a good time. The mileage above reflects hiking 3.7 miles, with a 2,300-foot elevation gain, to the junction with Deer Springs Trail, but even a mile or two on this path is enjoy-

able. The first mile climbs steeply through beautiful conifers and many granite boulders and then joins the beginning of the north fork of the San Jacinto River. Where the path crosses the stream, you enter a gorgeous forest of pines and incense cedars. Hanging out right here might suit you just fine, but if you want more exercise, continue uphill to Deer Springs Junction, which is also the headwaters for the north fork. You'll cross the stream twice more on your way. Trailhead elevation is 6,320 feet.

**User Groups:** Hikers and horses. No dogs or mountain bikes. No wheelchair facilities.

**Permits:** A free wilderness permit is required for day hiking or backpacking and is available in person or in advance by mail from the San Jacinto Ranger District. A national forest recreation pass is required for each vehicle; fees are $5 for one day or $30 for a year.

**Maps:** For a map, ask the U.S. Forest Service for San Bernardino National Forest or San Jacinto Wilderness. A map of the San Jacinto Wilderness is available from Tom Harrison Maps. For a topographic map, ask the USGS for San Jacinto Peak.

**Directions:** From Idyllwild, drive northwest on Highway 243 for 5.5 miles to the right turnoff for Stone Creek, Fern Basin, Marion Mountain, and Dark Canyon Campgrounds. Turn right and drive .2 mile, then bear left, following the signs for Dark Canyon Campground. Continue through the campground and up the hill to reach the Seven Pines trailhead.

**Contact:** San Bernardino National Forest, San Jacinto Ranger District, P.O. Box 518, 54270 Pinecrest, Idyllwild, CA 92549, 909/382-2921, website: www.fs.fed.us/r5/sanbernardino.

## 64 DEER SPRINGS TRAIL TO SUICIDE ROCK
**7.0 mi / 4.0 hrs**

**in the San Jacinto Wilderness near Idyllwild**

Map 14.3, page 651

If you're wondering how to spend a morning or an afternoon in Idyllwild, the hike to Suicide Rock will turn your visit into a trip you'll never forget. Pick up a wilderness permit and head for the trailhead, but be sure to pack some snacks and water for a little celebration at the top. Most of the work is in the first 2.4 miles to Suicide Junction, as you climb up through manzanita, ceanothus, and oaks, heading into the higher country of cedars and pines. At the junction, bear right and leave Deer Springs Trail for the last mile to Suicide Rock, which contours on an easier grade. From the three-mile point onward, your views of Lily Rock and Tahquitz Peak are outstanding, and once you're on Suicide Rock, at 7,528 feet in elevation, you are directly across from Lily Rock's Yosemite-like chunk of white granite. You can watch clouds drift between you and the neighboring peaks, right at eye level. The view below is of the Idyllwild area—there's little in sight besides a few houses and water tanks tucked in among a vast sea of conifers.

**User Groups:** Hikers and horses. No dogs or mountain bikes. No wheelchair facilities.

**Permits:** A free wilderness permit is required for both day hiking and backpacking and is available in person or in advance by mail from the San Jacinto Ranger District. A national forest recreation pass is required for each vehicle; fees are $5 for one day or $30 for a year.

**Maps:** For a map, ask the U.S. Forest Service for San Bernardino National Forest or San Jacinto Wilderness. A map of the San Jacinto Wilderness is available from Tom Harrison Maps. For topographic maps, ask the USGS for San Jacinto Peak and Idyllwild.

**Directions:** From Idyllwild, drive northwest on Highway 243 for one mile to the Deer Springs trailhead on the right side of the road (across the highway from the Idyllwild County Park visitors center parking area).

**Contact:** San Bernardino National Forest, San Jacinto Ranger District, P.O. Box 518, 54270 Pinecrest, Idyllwild, CA 92549, 909/382-2921, website: www.fs.fed.us/r5/sanbernardino.

## 65 ERNIE MAXWELL SCENIC TRAIL
### 5.2 mi / 2.5 hrs

**in San Bernardino National Forest
near Idyllwild**

Map 14.3, page 651

The Ernie Maxwell Scenic Trail is the perfect route for hikers who aren't up to the climbing that is de rigueur for most trails in the Idyllwild area. With only a 600-foot elevation change on an undulating trail, even families with small children could manage this path, which leads through a lovely conifer forest. Keep in mind, however, that since you're not climbing, you will not get the spectacular views that are granted on most other trails in the area; this is a walk that is built for enjoying the close up, rather than the far off. The trail leads downhill from the start, contouring through a forest of Jeffrey, ponderosa, and coulter pines, with scattered firs and incense cedars among them. You can practice your tree identification. The trail's end is a bit of a disappointment; it simply reaches a dirt road where you turn around and hike back. Along the way, you'll see some good views of Suicide Rock and Tahquitz Peak.

**User Groups:** Hikers, dogs, horses, and mountain bikes. No wheelchair facilities.

**Permits:** No permits are required. A national forest recreation pass is required for each vehicle; fees are $5 for one day or $30 for a year.

**Maps:** For a map, ask the U.S. Forest Service for San Bernardino National Forest. For a topographic map, ask the USGS for Idyllwild.

**Directions:** From Idyllwild on Highway 243, turn east on North Circle Drive in downtown, which becomes South Circle Drive, and then becomes Fern Valley Road. Follow Fern Valley Road to Humber Park. You will drive a total of two miles from downtown. The trailhead is on the right, at the lower end of the parking lot.

**Contact:** San Bernardino National Forest, San Jacinto Ranger District, P.O. Box 518, 54270 Pinecrest, Idyllwild, CA 92549, 909/382-2921, website: www.fs.fed.us/r5/sanbernardino.

## 66 DEVILS SLIDE TRAIL TO TAHQUITZ PEAK
**8.4 mi / 4.0 hrs**

**in the San Jacinto Wilderness near Idyllwild**

Map 14.3, page 651

The Devils Slide Trail is the premier hiking trail in the Idyllwild area, with 8,828-foot Tahquitz Peak as the favored destination, especially for hikers from out of town. The best solution to the crowds? Plan a trip before Memorial Day, after Labor Day, or any time during the week. We've hiked the trail in mid-May and saw almost nobody, but then again, it snowed on our trip.

The trail leads from Idyllwild's Humber Park on a steady but manageable uphill climb through the forest to Saddle Junction, 2.5 miles up. Once you reach the junction, head right for Tahquitz Peak. The next mile is loaded with far-reaching views of the desert below and San Jacinto Mountains, seen from an increasingly open lodgepole pine forest. At the next junction, head right again, soon saying good-bye to the trees and hello to a stark landscape of granite. The summit is only .5 mile away. Tahquitz Peak has the only operating fire lookout you can hike to in the San Jacinto Ranger District, and it's staffed by a friendly lookout person. (Two other lookouts in the district are accessible by road, but not by trail.) From the lookout, which was constructed in 1938, you're offered a panoramic view of both the San Jacinto and Santa Rosa Mountains.

Special Note: If you want to hike to Tahquitz Peak via an alternate trail that sees fewer people, take South Ridge Trail instead of Devils Slide Trail. (You still need to pick up a free wilderness permit at the Idyllwild Ranger Station.) It's a 7.2-mile round-trip via South Ridge Trail from the vicinity of Saunders Meadow Road. Be sure to hike early in the day in the summer months—this trail is even more exposed than Devils Slide Trail.

**User Groups:** Hikers, dogs, and horses. No mountain bikes. No wheelchair facilities.

**Permits:** A free wilderness permit is required for both day hiking and backpacking and is available in person or in advance by mail from the San Jacinto Ranger District. A national forest recreation pass is required for each vehicle; fees are $5 for one day or $30 for a year.

**Maps:** For a map, ask the U.S. Forest Service for San Bernardino National Forest or San Jacinto Wilderness. A map of the San Jacinto Wilderness is available from Tom Harrison Maps. For topographic maps, ask the USGS for Idyllwild and San Jacinto Peak.

**Directions:** From Idyllwild on Highway 243, turn east on North Circle Drive in downtown, which becomes South Circle Drive, and then becomes Fern Valley Road. Follow Fern Valley Road to Humber Park. You will drive a total of two miles from downtown. The trailhead is on the right, at the upper end of the parking lot.

**Contact:** San Bernardino National Forest, San Jacinto Ranger District, P.O. Box 518, 54270 Pinecrest, Idyllwild, CA 92549, 909/382-2921, website: www.fs.fed.us/r5/sanbernardino.

## Chapter 15

© ANN MARIE BROWN

# San Diego and Vicinity

# San Diego and Vicinity

San Diego is a sun-drenched region with 76 miles of beaches, two distinct mountain ranges (the Palomar and Laguna-Cuyamaca Mountains) and one giant-sized desert, Anza-Borrego. Blessed with a nearly perfect year-round climate and stunning natural beauty, San Diego is an ideal place for hikers to lace up their boots.

But where to start? The huge county's landscape is so varied that it is best described by splitting it into parts. In few other places of the world can you walk on the beach, hike to a 6,500-foot mountain peak, and admire the stillness of a desert palm grove—all in the same day.

We'll start with the desert. Anza-Borrego Desert State Park encompasses 600,000 acres of palm groves, year-round creeks, slot canyons, and badlands. It is California's largest state park and more than three times the size of Zion National Park. Desert flora runs the gamut from the expected, like barrel cactus and mesquite, to the rare: stands of jumping cholla cactus and aptly named elephant trees. Majestic and endangered bighorn sheep are commonly seen. Hiking trails lead to leafy fan palm groves, cholla cactus gardens, and old homesteading sites. Hikers who show up in spring are treated to an array of desert wildflowers, including the distinctive flaming-red plumes of ocotillos.

Just to the west of this giant desert lie the Laguna and Cuyamaca Mountains. The Cuyamacas are mostly contained within Cuyamaca Rancho State Park, which was badly burned in the major wildfires of 2003. Man and nature are joining together to rebuild this popular park, which, before the great fires, hosted extensive mixed forests of ponderosa and Jeffrey pine, fir, incense cedar, and live and black oak. With elevations ranging from 4,000 to 6,500 feet, the landscape of the Cuyamaca Mountains is a world vastly different from neighboring Anza-Borrego Desert. In a few years, the scars of the great fires will heal, and the park will once again be lush with greenery.

Alongside the Cuyamacas are the Lagunas, which are managed as part of Cleveland National Forest. With a dramatic setting that overlooks the desert thousands of feet below, the Lagunas are easily explored on foot. Hikers can visit a series of waterfalls on Cottonwood Creek or ascend to the summit of 5,900-foot Garnet Peak.

Situated to the north of the Laguna-Cuyamaca range is the smaller Palomar range, which is well known for its Sierra-like landscape. The entire range extends only 25 miles along the northern border of San Diego County, but what it lacks in size it makes up for in beauty. Its 6,000-foot elevation gives rise to dense stands of fir, cedar, spruce, and black oak. Most of the land in the Palomar Mountains is part of Palomar Mountain State Park or Cleveland National Forest. The mountains' most notable man-made feature is the Palomar Observatory, home of the 200-inch Hale telescope, which for many years was the world's largest. You can drive to the observatory site, but it's far more rewarding to hike the trail to it.

If your idea of hiking in San Diego isn't climbing mountains, wandering through conifer forests, or exploring deserts, but rather traipsing alongside the ocean, head for the coastside parks of Torrey Pines State Reserve or Cabrillo National Monument. In addition to providing wide vistas of San Diego's spectacular coastline, both parks offer a close-up look at the meeting place of sand and sea. Explore the wildlife-rich tidepools at Cabrillo or hike through Torrey Pines' sandstone badlands to the beach. A few miles to the north, bird-watchers flock to San Elijo Lagoon, where the oceanside saltwater and freshwater marshes attract a variety of native and migratory species.

Adding up the sum of all these parts begs the question: For hikers who want it all, does San Diego have it all? The answer: Unquestionably, yes.

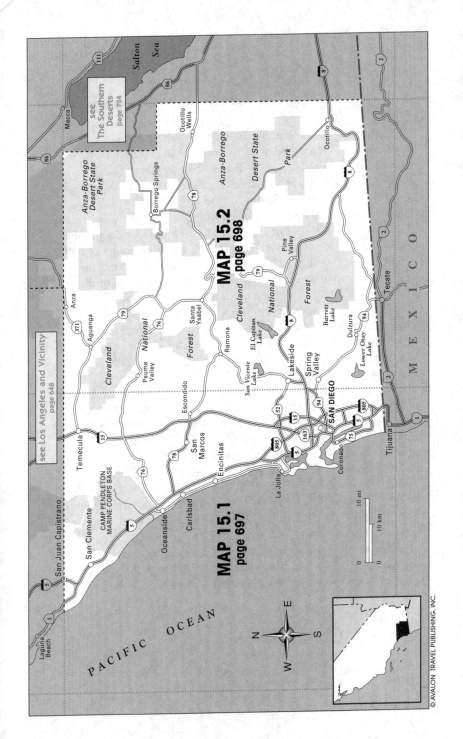

# Map 15.1

**Hikes 1–13**
**Pages 699–705**

15.2

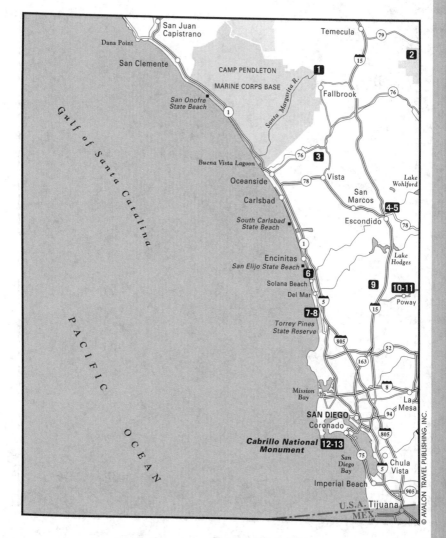

# Map 15.2

**Hikes 14–35**
**Pages 705–718**

© AVALON TRAVEL PUBLISHING, INC.

# 1 SANTA MARGARITA RIVER TRAIL

**5.6 mi / 3.0 hrs**

**in Fallbrook**

**Map 15.1, page 697**

A few miles north of downtown Fallbrook lies the Santa Margarita River, one of the last free-flowing rivers in Southern California. The river forms a native riparian habitat attracting many kinds of wildlife, particularly birds. There are six miles of marked trail, but the most popular walk is a 2.8-mile one-way hike from the Sandia Creek Drive trailhead. It has only a 400-foot elevation gain, so it is suitable for walkers and joggers, as well as people looking for a longer outing. An equestrian trail runs parallel to the hiking trail. There are several places where you can cross the river, but you'll have to get your feet wet; there are no bridges. First-time visitors here are amazed by the beauty of the Santa Margarita River Canyon, with its moss-covered rock outcrops, side canyons that branch off the main river, and dense forest canopy. It's like nothing you'll find anywhere else in San Diego County.

**User Groups:** Hikers, dogs, horses, and mountain bikes. No wheelchair facilities.

**Permits:** No permits are required. Parking and access are free.

**Maps:** For topographic maps, ask the USGS for Temecula and Fallbrook.

**Directions:** From I-15 south of Temecula, take the Mission Road (S13) exit west and drive to De Luz Road in Fallbrook. Turn north on De Luz Road and drive about a mile, then turn right on Sandia Creek Drive. Drive .5 mile to the parking lot on the right, just before the road crosses the river at Rock Mountain Drive.

**Contact:** Fallbrook Land Conservancy, P.O. Box 2701, Fallbrook, CA 92028, 760/728-0889, website: www.sdlcc.org/flc.

# 2 DRIPPING SPRINGS TRAIL

**13.6 mi / 2.0 days**

**in the Aqua Tibia Wilderness**

**Map 15.1, page 697**

At the very northern edge of San Diego County lies the Aqua Tibia Wilderness, a land of extreme summer heat, exposed slopes, no available water sources, and thick chaparral. The place appears suitable for only the most steadfast of hikers. Or so it seems. Actually, if you hike Dripping Springs Trail in the spring, when the temperature is just right, the Aqua Tibia is a pastoral place with blooming shrubs and wildflowers, crystal-clear vistas, and flitting butterflies and bees. (Forget hiking in winter, though; these mountains are often covered in snow.) Trailhead elevation at Dripping Springs Campground is 1,600 feet, and the peak of Aqua Tibia Mountain is at 4,547 feet. The trail leaves the campground, crosses the rocky wash of Arroyo Seco Creek, and starts to climb. In the first three miles of trail, you get views of Vail Lake to the north and the big mountains of Southern California—San Jacinto, San Gorgonio, and San Antonio (Baldy). Another mile passes, and you can see the white dome of Palomar Observatory to the south. The chaparral gets taller as you go, and the trail gets steeper and narrower. When you finally near the peak of Aqua Tibia Mountain, you've climbed out of the chaparral and into oak woodland with a few scattered pines, which means—yes!—shade.

**User Groups:** Hikers, dogs, and horses. No mountain bikes. No wheelchair facilities.

**Permits:** A free wilderness permit is required for overnight stays and can be obtained at the Dripping Springs station near the campground or from the Palomar Ranger District at the address below. Day users should sign the register at the trailhead. A national forest recreation pass is required for each vehicle; fees are $5 for one day or $30 for a year.

**Maps:** For a map, ask the U.S. Forest Service for Cleveland National Forest. For a topographic map, ask the USGS for Vail Lake.

**Directions:** From I-15 in Temecula, take the Highway 79 east exit. Drive 10 miles east on Highway 79 to Dripping Springs Campground, on the right. The trail begins at the south end of the campground.

**Contact:** Cleveland National Forest, Palomar Ranger District, 1634 Black Canyon Road, Ramona, CA 92065, 760/788-0250, website: www.fs.fed.us/r5/cleveland.

## 3 GUAJOME LAKE TRAIL
**2.0 mi / 1.0 hr**

**in Guajome Regional Park near Oceanside**

Map 15.1, page 697

Guajome Regional Park is home to one of the richest riparian areas of any of San Diego County's parks. The big draw is a spring-fed lake and marsh, which have enticed nearly 200 species of birds to visit the park. The waterways are also the happy home of many frogs, which you will hear but probably not see. In fact, "Guajome" means "home of the frog." The park's main hiking trail leads from the parking lot and goes around midsized Guajome Lake, up to the park's wedding gazebo, and alongside Guajome Marsh. Equestrian trails also lead into the drier grassland and chaparral areas of the park, but most hikers stay near the water. An out-and-back trip will cover about two miles, and along the way you might see a few red-winged blackbirds, a white-faced ibis, or even the rare least bell's vireo. Bring your binoculars. Fishing for bullheads, crappie, catfish, and sunfish is also popular at Guajome Lake.

**User Groups:** Hikers, dogs, horses, and mountain bikes. No wheelchair facilities.

**Permits:** No permits are required. A $3 day-use fee is charged per vehicle.

**Maps:** For a topographic map, ask the USGS for San Luis Rey.

**Directions:** From I-5 in Oceanside, take the Mission Avenue and Highway 76 exit, and drive east for seven miles to Guajome Lake Road. Turn right (south) into the park entrance.

**Contact:** Guajome Regional Park, c/o San Diego County Parks and Recreation Department, 2454 Heritage Park Row, San Diego, CA 92110, 858/694-3049, website: www.sd-parks.org.

## 4 JACK CREEK NATURE TRAIL
**1.0 mi / 0.5 hr**

**in the Dixon Lake Recreation Area near Escondido**

Map 15.1, page 697

If you are exceptionally lucky, it will be a rainy year in San Diego, and you will be able to see the waterfall flow along Jack Creek at Dixon Lake Recreation Area. We've only seen it trickle, but we've seen pictures of the 20-foot falls at flood, and it's quite beautiful. Nonetheless, a stroll on the .5-mile Jack Creek Nature Trail is good in any season, although best in winter and spring, when the hills are green and the flowers in bloom. The trail begins by Dixon Lake's entrance station, traveling past a picnic area and along Jack Creek to the lake's edge. You can pick up an interpretive brochure at the trailhead or the park ranger station, or you can just march off boldly without one. Be on the alert: Many cute bunnies are likely to cross your path. (They are western cottontails, to be precise.) If the creek is flowing strong, be sure to take the right spur to the waterfall's base; otherwise, just head straight for the lake. At the water's edge, the trail connects to Shoreline Trail and Grand View Trail, which is useful if you're in the mood to hike more. Many people choose instead to plunk a line in the water and see if they can catch a largemouth bass, rainbow trout, or catfish. If you do so, don't forget your fishing license, and be sure to purchase a Dixon Lake fishing permit.

**User Groups:** Hikers only. No dogs, horses, or mountain bikes. No wheelchair facilities.

**Permits:** No permits are required. A $3 day-use fee is charged per vehicle on weekends only.

**Maps:** For a topographic map, ask the USGS for Valley Center.

**Directions:** From Escondido, drive north on

I-15 and take the El Norte Parkway exit. Drive 3.1 miles east on El Norte Parkway, turn left (north) on La Honda Drive, and drive 1.3 miles to the Dixon Lake entrance, on the right. Turn right, then park at the Jack Creek Picnic Area. **Contact:** Dixon Lake Ranger Station, c/o Escondido Public Works Department, 201 N. Broadway, Escondido, CA 92025, 760/839-4680, website: www.ci.escondido.ca.us.

## 5 CHAPARRAL INTERPRETIVE TRAIL
### 0.6 mi / 0.5 hr

**in the Dixon Lake Recreation Area near Escondido**

Map 15.1, page 697

Short and sweet, Chaparral Interpretive Trail lies on the boundary between Dixon Lake Recreation Area and 3,500-acre Daley Ranch Preserve. The trail is a great place to get an education on San Diego's natural ecology. It travels through four distinct Southern California plant communities—mixed chaparral, oak woodlands, coastal sage scrub, and a mature riparian area. Interpretive signs along the way identify the foliage you see, including Engelmann and coast live oaks, toyon, various sages, and blue-eyed grass. It is not uncommon for hikers to catch sight of a coyote or a bobcat along this trail, especially when hiking early in the morning. In addition to being an easy stroll, much of this trail is under a canopy of shade, making it pleasant for visitors of all ages and most hiking capabilities.

**User Groups:** Hikers only. No dogs, horses, or mountain bikes. No wheelchair facilities.

**Permits:** No permits are required. A $3 day-use fee is charged per vehicle on weekends only.

**Maps:** For a topographic map, ask the USGS for Valley Center.

**Directions:** From Escondido, drive north on I-15 and take the El Norte Parkway exit. Drive 3.1 miles east on El Norte Parkway, turn left (north) on La Honda Drive, and drive 1.3 miles to the Dixon Lake entrance on the right. Turn right, then park at the Jack Creek Picnic Area.

**Contact:** Dixon Lake Ranger Station, c/o Escondido Parks and Recreation, 201 N. Broadway, Escondido, CA 92025, 760/839-4680, website: www.ci.escondido.ca.us.

## 6 SAN ELIJO LAGOON
### 5.0 mi / 2.5 hrs

**in Solana Beach**

Map 15.1, page 697

San Elijo Lagoon Ecological Reserve is bordered by the housing developments and shopping centers of Encinitas, Solana Beach, and Rancho Santa Fe, but the lagoon's multitudes of resident and migratory birds don't seem to mind. When you first see it, you may find it hard to imagine enjoying a nature experience so close to the freeways and roads. Suspend your disbelief for a while and pay a visit to the lagoon, which is a mixture of freshwater from inland creeks and saltwater from the ocean. The south side is a little wilder than the Manchester Avenue side, and the trails are longer, so it's the preferred side for hiking. A gated fire road leads down to the lagoon from the north end of North Rios Avenue, and you can hike either right or left. Birds are abundant, especially great egrets, stilts, gulls, and godwits. Great blue herons occasionally make an appearance, and as you wander inland, you'll see many songbirds among the chaparral.

If you want to educate yourself about what you are seeing, an intelligent series of interpretive signs are displayed on Nature Center Trail, a one-mile loop located on the north side of the lagoon (off Manchester Avenue, in Cardiff). The signs explain about saltwater and freshwater marshes, coastal sage scrub, and the wildlife living in these communities.

**User Groups:** Hikers and dogs. The one-mile Nature Center Trail is wheelchair accessible. No horses or mountain bikes.

**Permits:** No permits are required. Parking and access are free.

**Maps:** For a topographic map, ask the USGS for Encinitas.

**Directions:** From I-5 in Solana Beach, take the Lomas Santa Fe Drive exit and drive west to North Rios Avenue. Turn right and go .8 mile to the end of the road and the trailhead. Park alongside the road.

**Contact:** San Elijo Lagoon Ecological Reserve, San Diego County Parks and Recreation Department, 2454 Heritage Park Row, San Diego, CA 92110, 858/694-3049, website: www.sdparks.org; San Elijo Lagoon Conservancy, 760/436-3944, website: www.sanelijo.org.

## 7 GUY FLEMING LOOP TRAIL
**0.75 mi / 0.5 hr**

**in Torrey Pines State Reserve near Del Mar**

Map 15.1, page 697

Torrey Pines is one of the greatest hiking destinations in San Diego, with several short but sweet trails and enough spectacular scenery to keep you coming back for more. The Guy Fleming Loop Trail is the easiest of the trails in the park, with almost no elevation change, so it's suitable for all levels of hikers. The path has great views of the Pacific Ocean, La Jolla, Del Mar, and Los Peñasquitos Marsh. If you hike the right side of the loop first, you come to the North Overlook, where you can check out the vistas, as well as San Diego's rare tree, the Torrey pine. The trail then loops around to the South Overlook, where you can sometimes see San Clemente and Catalina Islands. People frequently hold weddings at the South Overlook. If they're smart, they plan them for spring, when the wildflowers bloom along the trail.

**User Groups:** Hikers only. No dogs, horses, or mountain bikes. No wheelchair facilities.

**Permits:** No permits are required. A $6 day-use fee is charged per vehicle.

**Maps:** A free map of Torrey Pines State Reserve is available at the park visitors center. For a topographic map, ask the USGS for Del Mar.

**Directions:** From I-5 in Del Mar, take the Carmel Valley Road exit and drive west 1.5 miles. Turn south on Camino del Mar and

drive .7 mile to the reserve entrance. Turn right, drive up the hill .7 mile, and park at the first parking area on the right, signed for Guy Fleming Trail. If this lot is full, you can park farther up the hill, at the visitors center, and walk back down the road.

**Contact:** Torrey Pines State Reserve, c/o San Diego Coast State Parks, 9609 Waples Street, Suite 200, San Diego, CA 92121, 858/755-2063 or 858/642-4200, website: www.parks.ca.gov.

## 8 RAZOR POINT AND BEACH TRAIL LOOP
**2.5 mi / 1.5 hrs**

**in Torrey Pines State Reserve near Del Mar**

Map 15.1, page 697

If you can get a parking spot in the lot by the visitors center at Torrey Pines State Reserve (it's not easy on weekend afternoons), you can start hiking right away on Razor Point Trail, cutting over to Beach Trail from Razor Point and heading to the beach. Razor Point Trail provides dramatic views of the reserve's eroded coastal badlands, which would look like something straight out of the desert if not for the ocean beyond. There's a spiderweb of paths, only some of which are signed, but it's fine to just wander around at random and visit as many of the overlooks as possible. Windswept Torrey pines grace the bluffs, and wildflowers bloom in the sandy soil in springtime. When you're in the mood, head south from Razor Point (paralleling the ocean) until you hook up with Beach Trail, and turn right, squeezing through the narrow, steep sandstone entrance to the beach. It's great fun. A return uphill on Beach Trail makes an excellent loop.

**User Groups:** Hikers only. No dogs, horses, or mountain bikes. No wheelchair facilities.

**Permits:** No permits are required. A $6 day-use fee is charged per vehicle.

**Maps:** A free map of Torrey Pines State Reserve is available at the park visitors center. For a topographic map, ask the USGS for Del Mar.

**Directions:** From I-5 in Del Mar, take the Carmel Valley Road exit and drive west for 1.5 miles. Turn south on Camino del Mar and drive .7 mile to the reserve entrance. Turn right, drive up the hill one mile, and park by the reserve office and visitors center. The trailhead is across the park road from the visitors center.

**Contact:** Torrey Pines State Reserve, c/o San Diego Coast State Parks, 9609 Waples Street, Suite 200, San Diego, CA 92121, 858/755-2063 or 858/642-4200, website: www.parks.ca.gov.

## 9 LOS PEÑASQUITOS CANYON
### 6.5 mi / 3.0 hrs

**in Los Peñasquitos Canyon Preserve**
**near Poway**

Map 15.1, page 697

If it's winter or spring and your thoughts are turning to love, there may be no better spot in San Diego for a first date than Los Peñasquitos Canyon Preserve. The trail that runs from one end of the canyon to the other is wide and level, perfectly built for good conversation and maybe a little hand holding. If the cascades along the creek are flowing, you can find a big volcanic boulder to sit on and watch the reflections of the sky in the water. If not, there are numerous places where you could lay out a picnic under a spreading oak tree. Early in the year, the wildflowers bloom and the grasses become verdant. Can this much beauty be found so close to a large urban area? You bet. Although you can hike the trail starting from either end, the eastern trailhead near Poway is preferred, because that end of the path is more shaded. As you wander, keep watching for mileage marker 3, because soon after it, you'll see a hitching post and bike rack on the right, where you can head off trail and scramble down to the cascades on Los Peñasquitos Creek. Even when the stream is reduced to a trickle, the car-sized boulders in the creek are fascinating to see.

**User Groups:** Hikers, dogs, horses, and mountain bikes. No wheelchair facilities.

**Permits:** No permits are required. Parking and access are free.

**Maps:** For a topographic map, ask the USGS for Poway.

**Directions:** From Escondido, drive south on I-15 for 16 miles to the Mercy Road exit. Turn right (west) on Mercy Road and follow it for one mile, crossing Black Mountain Road, to the trailhead parking area.

**Contact:** Los Peñasquitos Canyon Preserve, c/o San Diego County Parks and Recreation Department, 2454 Heritage Park Row, San Diego, CA 92110, 858/694-3049, website: www.sdparks.org.

## 10 BLUE SKY ECOLOGICAL RESERVE
### 4.0 mi / 2.0 hrs

**in the Blue Sky Ecological Reserve**
**near Poway**

Map 15.1, page 697

The Blue Sky Ecological Reserve provides habitat for several rare and threatened animal and plant species, including harried San Diego humans who desperately need a place to stop and smell the flowers. The reserve is the home of the San Diego horned lizard and a lovely grove of Engelmann oaks. From the trailhead, hike along the wide, flat fire road, ignoring the first two turnoffs. At the third junction, turn right to pay a visit to Lake Poway. The lake is a fine place to catch catfish and trout (they get planted every two weeks) or to rent a rowboat and row your hiking partner around the lake. You can also hike the perimeter of the lake, which will add some climbing and descending to your basically level route. Retrace your steps to the main trail, and head back to the trailhead for a four-mile round-trip. If you want to see more, continue on the main trail to the left fork for Lake Ramona.

If you enjoy hiking with a naturalist, show up at Blue Sky Ecological Reserve on Saturday or Sunday at 9 A.M.; free guided hikes are offered every weekend. The trips are usually only one mile in length—just right for families.

**User Groups:** Hikers, dogs, and horses. No mountain bikes. No wheelchair facilities.

**Permits:** No permits are required. Parking and access are free.

**Maps:** For a topographic map, ask the USGS for Escondido.

**Directions:** From I-15 near Poway, drive north to the Rancho Bernardo Road exit. Drive east for 3.3 miles on Rancho Bernardo Road; the reserve is on the left, at the junction of Rancho Bernardo Road and Espola Road.

**Contact:** Blue Sky Ecological Reserve, 858/679-5469; San Diego County Parks and Recreation Department, 2454 Heritage Park Row, San Diego, CA 92110, 858/694-3049, website: www.sdparks.org.

## 11 MOUNT WOODSON
### 3.6 mi / 2.0 hrs

near Poway

**Map 15.1, page 697**

Mount Woodson is the neighborhood summit to climb for the thousands of people who live in the Poway, Scripps Ranch, and Rancho Bernardo areas. The light-colored, rocky mountain—a favorite playground of rock climbers from all over San Diego—is always there in the background, looming over the suburbs below. If you've never seen Mount Woodson except from the bottom looking up, maybe it's time to lace up your hiking boots. The trail has a 1,500-foot elevation gain to reach the 2,894-foot peak, so you'll get in your workout for the day, but you won't be so wiped out that you can't enjoy the vistas or the fascinating giant boulders you'll see along the trail. Hike on the path south of the fire station, and then follow the paved Mount Woodson Road. You'll reach the top at 1.8 miles, where a ton of electronic equipment is in place. Wander around a bit on the ridge until you find the best spot to look out over the wide blue Pacific, pick out the summit of Mount Baldy, and then congratulate yourself for having bagged Mount Woodson's peak.

**User Groups:** Hikers only. No dogs, horses, or mountain bikes. No wheelchair facilities.

**Permits:** No permits are required. Parking and access are free.

**Maps:** For a topographic map, ask the USGS for San Pasqual.

**Directions:** From Poway, drive east on Poway Road for 3.5 miles and turn north on Highway 67. Drive three miles to the Ramona CDF Fire Station, on the left. The trail begins by the fire station, but you will have to park across the road.

**Contact:** Lake Poway Recreation Area, 858/679-5465; City of Poway Community Services, 858/679-4342.

## 12 BAYSIDE TRAIL
### 2.0 mi / 1.0 hr

in Cabrillo National Monument

**Map 15.1, page 697**

While everybody else at Cabrillo National Monument is visiting the old Point Loma Lighthouse, having their picture taken by the statue of Señor Cabrillo, or checking out the wonderful view of San Diego from the visitors center, you can sneak off for a hike on Bayside Trail and find a surprising amount of solitude. Gorgeous coastal vistas will accompany that solitude, as well as an interesting lesson in native coastal vegetation. This coastal Mediterranean habitat is one of the eight most sensitive in the world.

Take the paved trail from the parking lot to the lighthouse, where you can peer inside at the period furniture and imagine what life was like for the lighthouse keeper and his family at the turn of the century. Then check out the great views from the overlooks on the lighthouse's far side. After this short tour, pick up the paved road on the east side of the lighthouse, signed as Bayside Trail. Take the left fork, which is gravel, and wind gently downhill around Point Loma, occasionally tearing your eyes away from the view so you can read the interpretive signs. If you do, you'll learn all about coastal sage scrub and local and migrating birds. On every step of the trail, the whole of San Diego Bay and the Pacific Ocean are yours to survey. You'll see huge navy ships sailing out to sea, flocks of gulls following the fishing boats back into harbor, sailboats, Jet Skiers, and large offshore kelp beds (it's actually one of the largest kelp forests in the world). The trail ends 400 feet below the statue of Cabrillo, where a sign says Trail Ends—Return by the Same Route. Darn.

**User Groups:** Hikers only. No dogs, horses, or mountain bikes. No wheelchair facilities.

**Permits:** No permits are required. A $5 entrance fee is charged per vehicle, which is good for seven days.

**Maps:** A free map/brochure of Cabrillo National Monument is available at the entrance kiosk or visitors center. For a topographic map, ask the USGS for Point Loma.

**Directions:** From I-5 South in San Diego, take the Rosecrans Street/Highway 209 exit and drive south. Staying on Highway 209, you will turn right on Cañon Street and then left on Catalina Boulevard. The road ends at Cabrillo National Monument. The trail begins by the old lighthouse.

**Contact:** Cabrillo National Monument, 1800 Cabrillo Memorial Drive, San Diego, CA 92106, 619/557-5450, website: www.nps.gov/cabr.

## 13 CABRILLO TIDEPOOLS
### 1.0 mi / 0.5 hr

**in Cabrillo National Monument**

Map 15.1, page 697

We love tidepools, and the ones at Cabrillo National Monument are some of the best in Southern California. You might want to stop in at the Cabrillo National Monument visitors center before you head straight for the tidepools, because the center has a slide program, video, and some great free handouts on how to explore the pools and identify the various creatures who live there. Even more important, you should check your tide table before you visit, or else your hike may be very, very short. A fenced trail leads along the bluff tops

for a few hundred feet, but then you descend to the rocky beach and walk a long stretch. (You have to stop below the coast guard station, as that area is closed to the public for restoration.) What will you see? Most likely, you'll get a peek at mussels, crabs, abalone, barnacles, starfish, anemones, snails, and limpets. If you're lucky, you might see an octopus or a sea urchin. Is it wintertime? Why, we believe a passing gray whale just waved her flipper at you.

**User Groups:** Hikers and dogs. No horses or mountain bikes. No wheelchair facilities.

**Permits:** No permits are required. A $5 entrance fee is charged per vehicle, which is good for seven days.

**Maps:** A free map/brochure of Cabrillo National Monument is available at the entrance kiosk or visitors center. For a topographic map, ask the USGS for Point Loma.

**Directions:** From I-5 South in San Diego, take the Rosecrans Street/Highway 209 exit and drive south. Staying on Highway 209, turn right on Cañon Street, left on Catalina Boulevard, and continue to the monument entrance. After paying the entrance fee at the kiosk, take the right fork (immediately following the kiosk) that is signed as Tidepools Parking Area. Continue down the hill to the parking area.

**Contact:** Cabrillo National Monument, 1800 Cabrillo Memorial Drive, San Diego, CA 92106, 619/557-5450, website: www.nps.gov/cabr.

## 14 WEIR AND LOWER DOANE VALLEY LOOP
### 3.0 mi / 1.5 hrs

**in Palomar Mountain State Park**

Map 15.2, page 698

If you've never visited before, Palomar Mountain State Park is like a shock to your system— a good shock. At 5,500 feet in elevation, the air is cool, the conifers are big, and suburban sprawl seems far, far away. We kept shaking our heads in disbelief at the Sierra Nevada–like feel of the place. A good introduction to the park is this loop hike on three trails: Doane Valley Nature Trail, Weir Trail, and Lower Doane Valley Trail. From the parking area at Doane Pond (which is always busy with children learning to fish), head away from Doane Pond on the trail that crosses the park road. Start your walk on Doane Valley Nature Trail and veer left onto Weir Trail, following pretty Doane Creek under the shade of big pines, firs, and cedars. Cross the creek about one mile out (shortly after the left fork for Baptist Trail), then follow Lower Doane Valley Trail as it loops back around a meadow. You'll probably see deer and mountain quail and hear many birdcalls. You'll certainly see the evidence of resident woodpeckers in the big old trees. When the trail nears Doane Valley Campground, cross the creek again and make a sharp switchback to the right, on Doane Valley Nature Trail. The nature trail will close out your trip, bringing you back to the trailhead in .75 mile. As you pass the giant conifers and grassy meadows along the way, you will ask yourself again and again, "Is this really San Diego?"

**User Groups:** Hikers only. No dogs, horses, or mountain bikes. No wheelchair facilities.

**Permits:** No permits are required. A $6 day-use fee is charged per vehicle.

**Maps:** A map of Palomar Mountain State Park is available at the entrance station or park headquarters. For topographic maps, ask the USGS for Boucher Hill and Palomar Observatory.

**Directions:** From I-15 north of Escondido, drive east on Highway 76 for 21 miles. Turn left (north) on Road S6/South Grade Road and drive 6.5 miles to the junction with Road S7. Turn left on Road S7 and drive three miles into the park. Drive past park headquarters, turn right, and drive to the parking area by Doane Pond and the school camp.

**Contact:** Palomar Mountain State Park, P.O. Box 175, Palomar Mountain, CA 92060, 760/742-3462 or 760/767-5311, website: www.palomar.statepark.org.

## 15 BOUCHER TRAIL AND SCOTT'S CABIN LOOP
### 4.0 mi / 2.0 hrs

**in Palomar Mountain State Park**

**Map 15.2, page 698**

You may be wowed by the view of Pauma Valley from Boucher Lookout (at elevation 5,438 feet), but start walking on Boucher Trail, and you'll be wowed even more. The trail descends from the lookout, passing meadows, oaks, dogwoods, and conifers, and dropping 600 feet as it crosses Nate Harrison Grade (a road) and heads for Cedar Grove Campground. The camp is well named; the cedars are huge and memorable here. You might want to check out the rope swing by the group camp. If not, bear right at the fork by the campground, walk a brief stretch on the camp road, and then cross the park road to pick up Scott's Cabin Trail, which leads to the cabin site of an 1880s homesteader. Only the base of the cabin remains—it's a rather sad-looking pile of sticks and logs. From the site, take the right fork to head back to park headquarters and the Silver Crest Picnic Area. Walk to your right on the park road for a few hundred yards until you can pick up Boucher Trail once more and walk back to the lookout. Here Boucher Trail is the narrow trail that runs between the legs of the driving loop to the lookout. What? You say you forgot your troubles along the way? That's what happens here at Palomar Mountain.

**User Groups:** Hikers only. No dogs, horses, or mountain bikes. No wheelchair facilities.

**Permits:** No permits are required. A $6 day-use fee is charged per vehicle.

**Maps:** A map of Palomar State Park is available at the entrance station or park headquarters. For topographic maps, ask the USGS for Boucher Hill and Palomar Observatory.

**Directions:** From I-15 north of Escondido, drive east on Highway 76 for 21 miles. Turn left (north) on Road S6 (South Grade Road) and drive 6.5 miles to the junction with Road S7. Turn left on Road S7 and drive three miles into the park.

Drive past park headquarters, and bear left at the sign for Boucher Lookout. Park at the lookout and begin hiking on Boucher Trail.

**Contact:** Palomar Mountain State Park, P.O. Box 175, Palomar Mountain, CA 92060, 760/742-3462 or 760/767-5311, website: www.palomar.statepark.org.

## 16 OBSERVATORY TRAIL
**4.4 mi / 2.5 hrs**

**in Cleveland National Forest on Palomar Mountain**

Map 15.2, page 698

The question: Is the Palomar Observatory as great as everybody says? The answer: Yes. And the hike to reach it is far better than the drive to reach it. Even if you have absolutely no interest in astronomy, the National Recreation Trail to Palomar Observatory is just plain fun to hike. From Observatory Campground, the trail is an aerobic uphill climb, but on a well-graded, well-maintained trail with only a 600-foot elevation gain. The shade is dense from oaks and pines, and you'll find many giant-sized pine cones along the trail. At .5 mile, you reach an overlook platform with a lovely view of Mendenhall Valley, and then you head back into the forest to climb some more. The last stretch of trail brings you out to the observatory parking lot, where you turn right, walk through the lot and past the museum, and head straight for the big white golf ball, which is the 200-inch Hale telescope. If you like, hike up the couple flights of stairs to the telescope viewing area and learn all about how the thing works. Think about this: More than 100 billion galaxies like ours are within spotting range of the giant telescope.

**User Groups:** Hikers, dogs, horses, and mountain bikes. No wheelchair facilities.

**Permits:** No permits are required. A national forest recreation pass is required for each vehicle; fees are $5 for one day or $30 for a year.

**Maps:** For a map, ask the U.S. Forest Service for Cleveland National Forest. For a topographic map, ask the USGS for Palomar Observatory.

**Directions:** From I-15 north of Escondido, drive east on Highway 76 for 21 miles. Turn left (north) on Road S6 (South Grade Road) and drive 6.5 miles to the junction with Road S7, and then continue north on Road S6 for three more miles to Observatory Campground, on the right. Drive through the camp to the signed parking area for the amphitheater and trailhead.

**Contact:** Cleveland National Forest, Palomar Ranger District, 1634 Black Canyon Road, Ramona, CA 92065, 760/788-0250, website: www.fs.fed.us/r5/cleveland.

## 17 HOT SPRINGS MOUNTAIN
**5.6 mi / 3.0 hrs**

**on Los Coyotes Indian Reservation near Warner Springs**

Map 15.2, page 698

Most people drive all the way out to Warner Springs and hike to the summit of Hot Springs Mountain (at 6,533 feet) because it's the highest peak in San Diego County—a mere 20 feet taller than Cuyamaca Peak in Rancho Cuyamaca State Park. But if it's April or May, an even better reason to hike here is to see the wildflowers, which are unusually good for this notoriously dry county. Beginning from Nelson's Camp at Los Coyotes Indian Reservation, the first mile of trail is the toughest, with a 550-foot gain on an old jeep trail. At the top, you meet up with a better dirt road that runs up the south slope to Hot Springs Mountain. Turn right (west) on this road and ascend 1.5 miles along a ridgeline. The upper reaches of the mountain are covered in forests of coulter pines and oaks. In between the tree groves, you'll find small meadows peppered with spring flowers. As you near the summit, you'll reach an abandoned fire lookout tower that is showing its age. It has been closed since the mid-1970s. Continue past it on a rough use trail to the highest point on the mountain. Scramble your way up to a concrete platform perched amid brush and boulders, then gaze in wonder at the immensity of the Salton Sea. Total elevation gain on this trip is 1,300 feet.

Note: The reservation is open to the public only on Friday, Saturday, and Sunday. The gate is usually unlocked from 10 A.M. Friday to 5 P.M. Sunday.

**User Groups:** Hikers, dogs, and horses. No mountain bikes. No wheelchair facilities except at the picnic area.

**Permits:** An access permit is required and is available at the entrance gate. A $15 day-use fee is charged per vehicle.

**Maps:** For a map, ask the U.S. Forest Service for Cleveland National Forest. For a topographic map, ask the USGS for Hot Springs Mountain.

**Directions:** From Julian, take Highway 79 north for 20 miles to Warner Springs. Turn east on Camino San Ignacio. Drive .5 mile, then bear right on Los Tules Road and drive 4.5 miles to the reservation entrance gate. Drive six miles beyond the gate (the road turns to dirt), then turn left and drive 2.3 miles farther to Nelson's Camp, on the left.

**Contact:** Los Coyotes Indian Reservation, P.O. Box 189, Warner Springs, CA 92086, 760/782-0711.

## 18 BORREGO PALM CANYON FALLS
**3.0 mi / 1.5 hrs**

**in Anza-Borrego Desert State Park near Borrego Springs**

Map 15.2, page 698

The hike to Borrego Palm Canyon Falls is only 1.5 miles in length, but it feels like a trip from the desert to the tropics. You start out in a sandy, rocky, open plain, sweating it out with the cacti and ocotillo, and you end up in a shady oasis of fan palms, dipping your feet in the pool of a fern-covered waterfall. The trip begins on Borrego Palm Canyon Trail from the state park campground, where you should top off your water bottles and start walking. If you pick up an interpretive brochure at the park visitors center, you can identify the array of desert plants that grow along the trail, including cheesebush, brittle-bush, catclaw (ouch!),

and chuparosa. In .5 mile, when you pass interpretive post 20, you're suddenly surprised by the sight of hundreds of bright green, leafy palm trees up ahead. Borrego Palm Canyon is home to more than 800 mature native palms, the largest of over 25 groves in the park. It's one of the largest oases in the United States. Head toward the palms, and in a few minutes, you'll be nestled in their shade, listening to the desert wind rustle their fronds. Follow the trail a little farther, and you'll reach a 15-foot waterfall that streams over giant boulders and forms a large, sandy pool tucked in among the palms. We saw many maidenhair ferns growing by the water's edge and a tiny hummingbird flitted about the scene. Ah, paradise.

**User Groups:** Hikers only. No dogs, horses, or mountain bikes. No wheelchair facilities.

**Permits:** No permits are required. A $6 day-use fee is charged per vehicle.

**Maps:** A map of Anza-Borrego Desert State Park is available at the park visitors center. For a topographic map, ask the USGS for Borrego Palm Canyon.

**Directions:** From Julian, drive east on Highway 78 for approximately 19 miles to Highway S3/Yaqui Pass Road. Turn left (north) on Highway S3/Yaqui Pass Road and drive 12 miles to Borrego Springs. Turn left on Highway S22/Palm Canyon Drive and drive one mile to the signed junction just before the park visitors center. Turn right and drive one mile to Borrego Palm Canyon Campground. The trailhead is at the west end.

**Contact:** Anza-Borrego Desert State Park, 200 Palm Canyon Drive, Borrego Springs, CA 92004, 760/767-5311, website: www.anzaborrego.statepark.org; visitors center, 760/767-4205.

## 19 MAIDENHAIR FALLS
**5.0 mi / 3.0 hrs**

**in Anza-Borrego Desert State Park near Hellhole Canyon**

Map 15.2, page 698

If you have taken the hike to Borrego Palm Canyon Falls and found that it suited your taste for desert adventure, this trip to Maidenhair Falls is a more challenging path to a slightly bigger and more dramatic desert waterfall. Stop in at the park visitors center before you begin, and pick up a handout with trail directions. Also remember to be prepared for a longer excursion in the desert (bring tons of extra water, and cover your head with a light-colored hat). Your destination is a 20-foot waterfall with a walled backdrop of maidenhair ferns and mosses. The route to reach it travels from Highway S22 south of the visitors center into the mouth of Hellhole Canyon. Begin on California Riding and Hiking Trail for the first 200 yards and turn right. You'll pass a few fan palms, myriad cacti, some odd-shaped rocks, and Native American grinding holes along the route. Cottonwoods grow in places along the stream. Maidenhair Falls is a bit tricky to find, tucked into a narrow canyon corner, but with luck, there will be enough water running in the stream to clue you in to its location.

**User Groups:** Hikers only. No dogs, horses, or mountain bikes. No wheelchair facilities.

**Permits:** No permits are required. Parking and access are free.

**Maps:** A map of Anza-Borrego Desert State Park is available at the park visitors center. For a topographic map, ask the USGS for Tubb Canyon.

**Directions:** From Julian, drive east on Highway 78 for approximately 19 miles to Highway S3/Yaqui Pass Road. Turn left (north) on Highway S3/Yaqui Pass Road and drive for 12 miles to Borrego Springs. Turn left on Highway S22/Palm Canyon Drive and drive one mile to the signed junction just before the park visitors center. Turn left and drive .75 mile to the large parking lot on the west side of the road.

**Contact:** Anza-Borrego Desert State Park, 200 Palm Canyon Drive, Borrego Springs, CA 92004, 760/767-5311; visitors center, 760/767-4205, website: www.anzaborrego.statepark.org.

## 20 INAJA MEMORIAL TRAIL
**0.5 mi / 0.5 hr**

in Cleveland National Forest near Santa Ysabel

Map 15.2, page 698

At 3,200 feet in elevation, you can look down a long way into the steep canyon of the San Diego River. That's what you get here on Inaja Memorial National Recreation Trail, a short but interesting trail that begins at the Inaja Picnic Area. There are steps built in places along the trail as the path undulates along the canyon edge amid various types of chaparral. If you pick up an interpretive brochure at the trailhead, you can learn about live oaks, scrub oaks, wild lilac, toyon, manzanita, and chamise, as well as the granitic rocks of this area. The trail's highlights are the views of both the Santa Ysabel Valley and the Volcan Mountains near Julian. The picnic area and trail have an interesting history: They were named to honor the 11 firefighters who lost their lives in the 60,000-acre Inaja forest fire of 1956.

**User Groups:** Hikers and dogs. No horses or mountain bikes. No wheelchair facilities except at the picnic area.

**Permits:** No permits are required. A national forest recreation pass is required for each vehicle; fees are $5 for one day or $30 for a year.

**Maps:** For a map, ask the U.S. Forest Service for Cleveland National Forest. For a topographic map, ask the USGS for Santa Ysabel.

**Directions:** From Julian, drive northwest on Highway 78/79 for six miles (to one mile south of Santa Ysabel). The Inaja Picnic Area and trailhead are on the south (left) side of the road.

**Contact:** Cleveland National Forest, Palomar Ranger District, 1634 Black Canyon Road, Ramona, CA 92065, 760/788-0250, website: www.fs.fed.us/r5/cleveland.

## 21 DESERT VIEW AND CANYON OAK LOOP
### 3.5 mi / 2.0 hrs

**in William Heise County Park near Julian**

**Map 15.2, page 698**

William Heise County Park, a favorite of San Diego hikers, was nearly obliterated in the Cedar Fire of October 2003, but already as of June 2004, the park's campground and its neighboring nature trail, the Desert View and Canyon Oak Loop, are reopened to visitors. The park is located near Julian, at 4,000 feet in elevation, and was well known for its dense, shady oak woodland. The good news is that many of those oaks still stand, although they do show evidence of having been burned. The Desert View and Canyon Oak Loop provides hikers with a great opportunity to view the process of fire ecology close up, as across the park new shoots are popping up from the ground and the land is turning green once again. From the trailhead, start hiking through the oaks. You'll leave Nature Trail to join Canyon Oak Trail in .25 mile. Bear left on the loop, then bear left on Desert View Trail. The route is steep, but in .1 mile, you reach an overlook with an expansive view of the Cuyamaca and Laguna Mountains. The trail continues upward for another .75 mile to a spur trail leading to a higher overlook—Glen's View. Since the fire, the vista here is better than it has been for years. You'll spy the Anza-Borrego Desert, the Salton Sea, and even the Pacific Ocean. A makeshift scope on top of a stone monument at Glen's View helps you identify all of San Diego County's best features. Hope you picked a clear day.

**User Groups:** Hikers, horses, and mountain bikes. No dogs. No wheelchair facilities.

**Permits:** No permits are required. A $2 day-use fee is charged per vehicle.

**Maps:** A free map of William Heise County Park is available at the entrance station. For a topographic map, ask the USGS for Julian.

**Directions:** From Julian, drive two miles west on Highway 78/79 and turn left (south) on Pine Hills Road. Drive two miles, turn left on Frisius Drive, and drive two more miles. Frisius Drive turns into Heise Park Road and enters the park. From the park entrance kiosk, continue straight on the park road and drive to near its end, at the Area 1 group camp, on the left (also called the Youth Area). Park above campsite No. 64 and then walk back down to the trailhead, signed as Nature Trail and Canyon Oak Trail.

**Contact:** William Heise County Park, 760/765-0650; San Diego County Parks and Recreation Department, 2454 Heritage Park Row, San Diego, CA 92110, 858/694-3049, website: www.sdparks.org.

## 22 CACTUS LOOP AND YAQUI WELL
### 2.75 mi / 1.5 hrs

**in Anza-Borrego Desert State Park near Tamarisk Grove**

**Map 15.2, page 698**

The Cactus Loop and Yaqui Well Trails are two separate nature trails at Anza-Borrego Desert State Park, but since they're right beside each other, you might as well hike both. The Cactus Loop Trail is a .75-mile loop, and more hilly than you might expect from a nature trail. It shows off seven kinds of cacti, including barrel, hedgehog, fishhook, beavertail, and cholla. Visitors often spot chuckwallas and other lizards scurrying among the spiny plants. The Yaqui Well Trail climbs for one mile among cacti, ocotillo, and cholla to a mesquite grove and then reaches Yaqui Well. In a small circle around this seep, a tremendous variety of greenery grows, including mesquite and false desert willow, given life by the year-round presence of water. Desert birds show up here, particularly colorful hummingbirds. If you're in the mood for more desert education, drive five miles east of Tamarisk Grove to the short little loop trail at the Narrows. It's packed with a lot of geologic punch; you'll get a big lesson in geological processes, from faulting and landslides to erosion and earthquakes.

**User Groups:** Hikers only. No dogs, horses, or mountain bikes. No wheelchair facilities.

**Permits:** No permits are required. Parking and access are free.

**Maps:** A map of Anza-Borrego Desert State Park is available at the park visitors center. For a topographic map, ask the USGS for Borrego Sink.

**Directions:** From Julian, drive east on Highway 78 for 19 miles to Tamarisk Grove Campground at Road S3. The trailheads for the Cactus Loop and Yaqui Well Trails are opposite the camp entrance off Road S3.

**Contact:** Anza-Borrego Desert State Park, 200 Palm Canyon Drive, Borrego Springs, CA 92004, 760/767-5311; visitors center, 760/767-4205, website: www.anzaborrego.statepark.org.

## 23 GHOST MOUNTAIN TRAIL
**2.0 mi / 1.0 hr**

**in Anza-Borrego Desert State Park near Blair Valley**

Map 15.2, page 698

When most people imagine a life of living off the land, they instinctively think of doing so in a place where water is plentiful. Not so with Marshal South, who in the 1930s chose Ghost Mountain, in the Anza-Borrego Desert. South and his wife built an adobe home atop the mountain and lived there with their children for more than 15 years. The family tried to live simply, attempting to survive in the spartan style of early Native Americans. Sadly, South's wife eventually tired of the rugged desert life and her husband's odd idealism, and the family split up.

The Ghost Mountain Trail climbs through a series of switchbacks to the remains of the South homesite, which includes a few partial walls, an old mattress frame, and some assorted cisterns and barrels used for storing precious water. The destination is worthwhile not just because the sight of it sparks your imagination, but also because of the lovely, 360-degree desert views you gain as you ascend Ghost Mountain. When you stand on the top on a

clear, cool day, you can almost imagine why South chose this remote homesite.

Remember that Blair Valley and Ghost Mountain are higher in elevation than other parts of the park. Not only does this make them cooler spots for hiking, but it also means that a wide variety of desert plant life grows here. The ocotillos and yuccas put on a spectacular show in early spring.

**User Groups:** Hikers only. No dogs, horses, or mountain bikes. No wheelchair facilities.

**Permits:** No permits are required. Parking and access are free.

**Maps:** A map of Anza-Borrego Desert State Park is available at the park visitors center. For a topographic map, ask the USGS for Earthquake Valley.

**Directions:** From Julian, drive east on Highway 78 for 12 miles to Road S2, turn south, and drive six miles to the left turnoff for Blair Valley Camp. Turn left (east), drive 1.4 miles on a dirt road, and then bear right at the fork. Drive another 1.6 miles, bear right again, and drive .5 mile to the Ghost Mountain/Marshal South Home trailhead.

**Contact:** Anza-Borrego Desert State Park, 200 Palm Canyon Drive, Borrego Springs, CA 92004, 760/767-5311; visitors center, 760/767-4205, website: www.anzaborrego.statepark.org.

## 24 PICTOGRAPH TRAIL
**2.0 mi / 1.0 hr**

**in Anza-Borrego Desert State Park near Blair Valley**

Map 15.2, page 698

Although a Native American rock-art site is the destination of this trip, Pictograph Trail comes with a bonus: an inspiring overlook of the Vallecito Mountains from the brink of a dry waterfall. It's a desert vista that's hard to forget. The path begins at the Pictograph trailhead and wanders through huge granite boulders. First you head through a dry wash and then climb up a ridge. At .5 mile out, you begin to descend. At .75 mile, you'll find some pictographs, painted in red and yellow pigments by the nomadic Kumeyaay Indians. (Look for the pictographs on the side of a boulder on the right side of the canyon.) The slightly faded geometric designs were made with natural pigments and are estimated to be 2,000 years old. Continue farther on the trail, and the canyon narrows dramatically until its walls come together at the brink of a dry waterfall more than 150 feet tall. From its edge the panoramic view is stunning, both of the steep drop-off and the far-off mountains and valley.

**User Groups:** Hikers only. No dogs, horses, or mountain bikes. No wheelchair facilities.

**Permits:** No permits are required. Parking and access are free.

**Maps:** A map of Anza-Borrego Desert State Park is available at the park visitors center. For a topographic map, ask the USGS for Earthquake Valley.

**Directions:** From Julian, drive east on Highway 78 for 12 miles to Road S2, turn south, and drive six miles to the left turnoff for Blair Valley Camp. Turn left (east), drive 1.4 miles on a dirt road, and then bear right at the fork. Drive another 1.6 miles and bear left at the next fork. In .25 mile, bear left again. Continue two more miles to the end of the road, at the Pictograph trailhead.

**Contact:** Anza-Borrego Desert State Park, 200 Palm Canyon Drive, Borrego Springs, CA 92004, 760/767-5311; visitors center, 760/767-4205, website: www.anzaborrego.statepark.org.

## 25 ELEPHANT TREE TRAIL
### 1.5 mi / 1.0 hr

**in Anza-Borrego Desert State Park near Split Mountain**

Map 15.2, page 698

It's not just the odd-looking elephant tree that you get to see on this trail, but also many of the common flora of Anza-Borrego Desert—creosote bush, burroweed, indigo bush, barrel cactus, ocotillo, catclaw, cholla, smoke tree. . . . There's enough desert-plant identification to do to keep you quizzing your hiking partner all day. But it's the single elephant tree on the loop that steals the show, with its crinkled, folded "skin" on its trunk. The tree is an odd patchwork of colors: yellowish bark, blue berries, and orange twigs; and its bark has a very evocative odor, something like a spicy air freshener. The Elephant Tree Trail used to feature several elephant trees, but all but this one lone specimen have died. It is located near the end of the loop. If possible, time your trip for early spring, when the ocotillos sprout brilliant red plumes and the pink sand verbenas bloom.

**User Groups:** Hikers only. No dogs, horses, or mountain bikes. No wheelchair facilities.

**Permits:** No permits are required. Parking and access are free.

**Maps:** A map of Anza-Borrego Desert State Park is available at the park visitors center. For a topographic map, ask the USGS for Harper Canyon.

**Directions:** From Julian, drive east on Highway 78 for 35 miles to Ocotillo Wells. Turn south on Split Mountain Road and drive 5.8 miles to the right turnoff that is signed for Elephant Trees. Turn right and drive .8 mile on a dirt road to the trailhead.

**Contact:** Anza-Borrego Desert State Park, 200 Palm Canyon Drive, Borrego Springs, CA 92004, 760/767-5311; visitors center, 760/767-4205, website: www.anzaborrego.statepark.org.

## 26 COWLES MOUNTAIN
### 3.0 mi / 1.5 hrs

**in Mission Trails Regional Park**

Map 15.2, page 698

The wildfires of October 2003 burned more than 2,800 acres in the East and West Fortuna areas of Mission Trails Regional Park, but almost all of the 40-plus miles of trails have been reopened, and park structures have been rebuilt. The park is a playland for outdoor lovers; the visitors center alone provides enough entertainment to fill an entire afternoon. It's a huge, architecturally unique building with state-of-the-art displays, and it's better designed than many museums. If you only have time to hike one trail in the park, you might as well go for the summit of Cowles Mountain, a 1,591-foot peak with a 360-degree view of the city. They say Cowles Mountain is the highest point in San Diego, but they mean the city, not the county. Pick a cool day, because the trail is sunny and exposed, ascending through chaparral and sage scrub, and with a 951-foot elevation gain to the summit. When you reach the top and look out at the city below, consider the temporary state of all you survey compared to the rock you're standing on, which is nearly 150 million years old. If you feel like hiking some more, you can continue another 1.5 miles from Cowles Mountain Summit to Pyles Peak Summit. If you want to take a somewhat mellower grade to Cowles Mountain, you can start at the trailhead at Mesa Road. From there, it's 2.2 miles to the top.

**User Groups:** Hikers and dogs. No mountain bikes or horses. No wheelchair facilities.

**Permits:** No permits are required. Parking and access are free.

**Maps:** A free map of Mission Trails Regional Park is available at the visitors center. For a topographic map, ask the USGS for La Mesa.

**Directions:** From I-15 south of Poway, take Highway 52 east and exit at Mast Boulevard. Turn left on Mast Boulevard and then right on West Hills Parkway. Turn right on Mission Gorge Road, drive two miles, and then turn left on Golfcrest Drive. Follow Golfcrest Drive to its intersection with Navajo Road, where the trailhead for Cowles Mountain trailhead is located, on the left. If you wish to go to the park visitors center first, continue past Golfcrest Drive on Mission Gorge Road and turn right at the park entrance.

**Contact:** Mission Trails Regional Park, 1 Father Junipero Serra Trail, San Diego, CA 92119, 619/668-3275, website: www.mtrp.org.

## 27 SILVERWOOD WILDLIFE SANCTUARY

**1.5 mi / 1.0 hr**

**in the Silverwood Wildlife Sanctuary near Lakeside**

**Map 15.2, page 698**

The Silverwood Wildlife Sanctuary, a favorite spot of San Diego bird-watchers, was badly burned in the Cedar Fire of October 2003, but it has been reopened to visitors for guided walks on Sundays. Tour groups are limited to 10 people and are quite popular, so be sure to phone in advance. As of June 2004, new growth is already a foot high at the base of the chaparral, and green leaves are appearing on the oak trees. Wildflowers should be spectacular over the next couple springs as the earth recovers from the fire. Along with the flowers, the butterflies and the birds will return, and the latter have always been the main attraction at Silverwood. More than 160 bird species have been sighted at this sanctuary, including Costas hummingbirds, various woodpeckers, flycatchers, towhees, and an abundance of songbirds. The Audubon Society naturalists who lead the hikes here are incredibly knowledgeable about both birds and fire ecology, and they tailor the walk to the ability of the people who attend. This is a wonderful, educational trip for bird-watchers and non-bird-watchers alike.

Special Note: The Silverwood Wildlife Sanctuary is open to the public only on Sundays by guided tour. Call well in advance to sign up for a tour.

**User Groups:** Hikers only. No dogs, horses, or mountain bikes. No wheelchair facilities.

**Permits:** Hikers must sign in at the trailhead register. Parking and access are free, but donations are gratefully accepted.

**Maps:** Sanctuary maps are available at the trailhead register. For a topographic map, ask the USGS for San Vicente Reservoir.

**Directions:** From I-8 in San Diego, drive east to Highway 67 near El Cajon. Drive north on Highway 67 to Lakeside, where you turn right on Mapleview Street. Drive a short distance, turn left on Ashwood Street (which becomes Wildcat Canyon Road), and drive 4.8 miles to 13003 Wildcat Canyon Road.

**Contact:** Silverwood Wildlife Sanctuary, 13003 Wildcat Canyon Road, Lakeside, CA 92040, 619/682-7200, website: www.sandiegoaudubon.org.

## 28 STONEWALL PEAK TRAIL
**4.0 mi / 2.0 hrs**

**in Cuyamaca Rancho State Park**

Map 15.2, page 698

The Cedar Fire of October 2003 obliterated more than 90 percent of Cuyamaca Rancho State Park. Although this seems like a great tragedy for San Diego hikers, fire is a normal and necessary part of the ecosystem here, and the landscape recovers remarkably quickly. Although it will be decades until the dense forests of Cuyamaca Rancho return to their previous splendor, many of the lower growing plants and shrubs are already green and growing. Hikers can look forward to spectacular wildflower displays in the next few years. Although the park was almost completely shut down for several months after the fire, one of the first trails to reopen was the much-loved Stonewall Peak Trail across from Paso Picacho Campground. Although slightly dwarfed by neighboring Cuyamaca Peak, Stonewall Peak is no slouch in the summit department: its peak towers at 5,730 feet in elevation. Stonewall Peak overlooks the site of the turn-of-the-century Stonewall Mine, as well as a large chunk of the Cuyamaca Mountains and Anza-Borrego Desert. The trail has only a 900-foot elevation gain and is remarkably well graded. A series of multiple switchbacks whisk you to the summit on a well graded path. Since the fire raced through here, the trail doesn't have much shade any more, so don't forget your water bottle. The final 50 yards of trail are cut into an exposed stone ridge; granite stairs and a handrail keep you from going over the edge. The view is grand, taking in all of the park, Lake Cuyamaca, and the desert far to the east.

Squint hard and you can see the Palomar Observatory, Mount San Gorgonio, Mount San Jacinto, and the Salton Sea.

Special Note: For more details on trail rebuilding and reopenings at Cuyamaca Rancho State Park, see the website www.cuyamaca.us.

**User Groups:** Hikers only. No dogs, horses, or mountain bikes. No wheelchair facilities.

**Permits:** No permits are required. A $6 day-use fee is charged per vehicle.

**Maps:** A map of Cuyamaca Rancho State Park is available at the entrance kiosk. A more detailed map is available from Tom Harrison Maps. For a topographic map, ask the USGS for Cuyamaca.

**Directions:** From San Diego, drive east on I-8 for 40 miles to the Highway 79 exit. Drive north on Highway 79 for 11 miles and look for Paso Picacho Campground, on the left. The trail begins across the highway from the campground; turn into the camp entrance, and park at the picnic area parking lot.

**Contact:** Cuyamaca Rancho State Park, 12551 Highway 79, Descanso, CA 91916, 760/765-0755, websites: www.cuyamaca.statepark.org or www.cuyamaca.us.

## 29 GREEN VALLEY FALLS
**0.5–3.0 mi / 0.5–1.5 hrs**

**in Cuyamaca Rancho State Park**

Map 15.2, page 698

The Green Valley area in the southern region of Cuyamaca Rancho State Park was one small section of this vast parkland that was spared in the fires of 2003. As the rest of the park heals from the fire and begins the process of regrowth, Green Valley remains a lush, cool oasis for visitors. A trip to Green Valley Falls is an easy walk with a good payoff on a warm day. From the picnic area parking lot at Green Valley Campground, follow the wide fire road along the Sweetwater River to the cutoff for the falls, then hike downhill to your left. By summer, the river's cascades aren't terribly dramatic, but there are still many cool pools where you can soak your toes, as well as wide granite ledges where you can lay out a towel and lounge around on the rocks. If you feel like logging a few more miles, you can continue past the falls cutoff to the fire road's junction with South Boundary Fire Road. Turn right and loop back via South Boundary and Arroyo Seco Fire Roads, making a three-mile round-trip.

Special Note: For more details on trail rebuilding and reopenings at Cuyamaca Rancho State Park, see the website www.cuyamaca.us.
**User Groups:** Hikers, horses, and mountain bikes. No dogs. No wheelchair facilities.
**Permits:** No permits are required. A $6 day-use fee is charged per vehicle.
**Maps:** A map of Cuyamaca Rancho State Park is available at the entrance kiosk. A more detailed map is available from Tom Harrison Maps. For a topographic map, ask the USGS for Cuyamaca.
**Directions:** From San Diego, drive east on I-8 for 40 miles to the Highway 79 exit. Drive north on Highway 79 for seven miles and turn left (west) at the sign for Green Valley Campground. Follow the signs to the picnic area. One sign points either straight ahead or to the left for the picnic area; continue straight to reach the trailhead.
**Contact:** Cuyamaca Rancho State Park, 12551 Highway 79, Descanso, CA 91916, 760/765-0755, websites: www.cuyamaca.statepark.org, www.cuyamaca.us.

## 30 GARNET PEAK
**4.4 mi / 2.5 hrs**

**in the Laguna Mountain Recreation Area**

Map 15.2, page 698

The route to Garnet Peak begins on the Pacific Crest Trail at the Penny Pines trailhead, where you can see the list of names of the good people who have donated funds to California's national forests for reforestation. Part of this trail was singed in the wildfires of October 2003, but the forest service reopened the trail quickly, and the trip to Garnet Peak remains a favorite of San Diego hikers. Follow the well-graded Pacific Crest Trail (PCT) to the north (left). The trail has pleasantly little elevation gain, and it hugs the Laguna Mountain rim, offering nearly continual views of Storm Canyon and the Anza-Borrego Desert. You won't see any trail signs directing you to the peak. Ignore the first two right turnoffs at 1.5 miles out (they lead to expansive overlooks, but they won't take you to the summit). Instead, turn right at the third right turnoff. The Garnet Peak Trail is rocky and uphill, but in less than a mile, you reach the jagged, 5,900-foot summit. There you're rewarded with mind-boggling views of the Anza-Borrego Desert, Palomar Observatory, Mount San Jacinto and Mount San Gorgonio, the Laguna and Cuyamaca Mountains, and on and on. On a crisp January day, we were able to spot snow-covered Mount Baldy, 90 miles to the northwest, as well. Most remarkable is that the desert floor is 5,000 feet below you, and it appears to be straight down. This summit vista can boggle your mind. Total elevation gain on the trail? A mere 500 feet. Judging by the popularity of this trail on the weekends, it might just be too easy.
**User Groups:** Hikers, dogs, and horses. No mountain bikes. No wheelchair facilities.
**Permits:** No permits are required. A national forest recreation pass is required for each vehicle; fees are $5 for one day or $30 for a year.
**Maps:** For a map, ask the U.S. Forest Service for Cleveland National Forest. A map of the Laguna Mountain Recreation Area is available from the Descanso Ranger District or the Laguna Mountain Visitors Center. For a topographic map, ask the USGS for Monument Peak.
**Directions:** From Julian, drive south on Highway 79 to the left fork for Road S1/Sunrise Scenic Byway. Bear left and drive south for about 12 miles to the Penny Pines Plantation, between mile markers 27.5 and 27.0. Park along the road.
**Contact:** Cleveland National Forest, Descanso Ranger District, 3348 Alpine Boulevard, Alpine, CA 91901, 619/445-6235, website: www.fs.fed.us/r5/cleveland.

## 31 LIGHTNING RIDGE TRAIL
### 1.5 mi / 1.0 hr
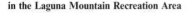

**in the Laguna Mountain Recreation Area**

Map 15.2, page 698

The Lightning Ridge Trail is one of the show-and-tell trails of the Laguna Mountain Recreation Area, where you can get up high and get a clear view of how beautiful and unusual this tall, cool mountain on the edge of the desert really is. The trail is easy enough for almost any hiker to accomplish, with only 250 feet of elevation gain. It begins at a small stone monument at Laguna Campground's amphitheater parking lot and follows the edge of a meadow, making several long, sweeping switchbacks uphill through pines and oaks. Kick a few pine cones as you walk. The trail tops out at a water tank at the top of the ridge. The cement tank is uninspiring, but the view is sweet: Laguna Meadow lies directly below, a beautiful, green expanse in spring. If you time your trip for after a good season of rain, you may see a rare sight: Little Laguna Lake, in the middle of the meadow. This is the secret vanishing lake of the Laguna Mountains.

What's the best time to hike this trail? Unquestionably it's winter or spring—by Memorial Day, the meadow grasses are often dry and brown. If you're lucky, you can walk this trail on a clear winter day, when it's covered with a few inches of snow.

**User Groups:** Hikers, dogs, horses, and mountain bikes. No wheelchair facilities.

**Permits:** No permits are required. A national forest recreation pass is required for each vehicle; fees are $5 for one day or $30 for a year.

**Maps:** For a map, ask the U.S. Forest Service for Cleveland National Forest. A map of the Laguna Mountain Recreation Area is available from the Descanso Ranger District or the Laguna Mountain Visitors Center. For a topographic map, ask the USGS for Monument Peak.

**Directions:** From Julian, drive south on Highway 79 to the left fork for Road S1/Sunrise Scenic Byway. Bear left and drive south for approximately 13 miles to Laguna Campground, on the right, between mile markers 26.5 and 26.0. Turn right on the camp road, and drive .75 mile to the amphitheater parking lot. Park there and then look for the small stone monument just beyond the restrooms, on the northeast side of the parking lot. The trail begins there.

**Contact:** Cleveland National Forest, Descanso Ranger District, 3348 Alpine Boulevard, Alpine, CA 91901, 619/445-6235, website: www.fs.fed.us/r5/cleveland.

## 32 COTTONWOOD CREEK FALLS
### 2.0 mi / 1.0 hr

**in the Laguna Mountain Recreation Area**

Map 15.2, page 698

If you don't have the time for the day hike to spectacular Kitchen Creek Falls, this shorter trip to nearby Cottonwood Creek Falls is a close second choice for scenic beauty. With only a one-mile downhill walk, you'll quickly be exploring the many small waterfalls and big pools along Cottonwood Creek, or happily counting the bright pink flowers on the streamside cacti. The trail is unsigned at its start, and it usually appears overgrown with brush, but after about 100 yards, the path widens, and the downhill grade becomes less steep. When you reach the canyon bottom, which takes about 15 minutes, turn sharply left and walk alongside Cottonwood Creek, heading upstream. In just a few minutes, you'll reach the first of several cascades, each about 12 feet high. Hike as far as you like, pick your favorite waterfall or pool, and have a seat alongside it.

**User Groups:** Hikers, dogs, horses, and mountain bikes. No wheelchair facilities.

**Permits:** No permits are required. A national forest recreation pass is required for each vehicle; fees are $5 for one day or $30 for a year.

**Maps:** For a map, ask the U.S. Forest Service for Cleveland National Forest. A map of the Laguna Mountain Recreation Area is available

from the Descanso Ranger District or the Laguna Mountain Visitors Center. For a topographic map, ask the USGS for Mount Laguna.
**Directions:** From San Diego, drive east on I-8 for 47 miles to the Highway S1/Sunrise Scenic Byway turnoff. Drive north on Highway S1 for about two miles to the large pullout, on the west side of the road (it has an obvious, graffiti-covered rock wall), between mile markers 15.0 and 15.5. Cross the road on foot and locate the unmarked trail at the north end of the guardrail.
**Contact:** Cleveland National Forest, Descanso Ranger District, 3348 Alpine Boulevard, Alpine, CA 91901, 619/445-6235, website: www.fs.fed.us/r5/cleveland.

## 33 DESERT VIEW NATURE TRAIL
### 1.2–3.0 mi / 1.0–2.0 hrs

**in the Laguna Mountain Recreation Area**

Map 15.2, page 698

Wow, what a view. If you've never before stood on a conifer-covered mountain and looked down on the vastness of the desert, your first time is something you'll always remember. That's what you get on Desert View Nature Trail, near the summit of Laguna Mountain. Start hiking from Burnt Rancheria Campground, heading east to meet the Pacific Crest Trail. Turn north (left) on the PCT, hiking along the mountain rim. The trail hugs the rim, which is perched on the edge of Anza-Borrego Desert, providing fine views of the desert floor 4,000 feet below you. On a clear day you can see all the way to Salton Sea shimmering in the distance, and to the odd-looking smokestacks of Plaster City. The trail continues north to the Desert View Picnic Area and returns via a loop through a shady forest of pines and oaks. When you reach a clearing .5 mile out, you'll find a water fountain with a plaque commemorating the great outdoors. Take the spur trail here for the best view of the day, heading east and uphill for a short distance. If you hike the nature trail loop only, you'll have a 1.2-mile round-trip, but most peo-

ple get so captivated by the views that they wind up walking a bit farther on the Pacific Crest Trail to the north. It's so compelling, it's hard to stop.
**User Groups:** Hikers and dogs. No horses or mountain bikes. No wheelchair facilities.
**Permits:** No permits are required. A national forest recreation pass is required for each vehicle; fees are $5 for one day or $30 for a year.
**Maps:** For a map, ask the U.S. Forest Service for Cleveland National Forest. A map of the Laguna Mountain Recreation Area is available from the Descanso Ranger District or the Laguna Mountain Visitors Center. For a topographic map, ask the USGS for Mount Laguna.
**Directions:** From San Diego, drive east on I-8 for 47 miles to the Highway S1/Sunrise Scenic Byway turnoff. Drive north on Highway S1 for about 10 miles to Burnt Rancheria Campground, on the right, between mile markers 22.5 and 23.0 (near the town of Mount Laguna). Park by the amphitheater at Burnt Rancheria Campground, where the trail begins.
**Contact:** Cleveland National Forest, Descanso Ranger District, 3348 Alpine Boulevard, Alpine, CA 91901, 619/445-6235, website: www.fs.fed.us/r5/cleveland.

## 34 KITCHEN CREEK FALLS
### 4.5 mi / 2.5 hrs

**in Cleveland National Forest near Pine Valley**

Map 15.2, page 698

Kitchen Creek Falls is the most beautiful waterfall in San Diego, a visually stunning 150-foot drop that is hidden just a few hundred yards off the Pacific Crest Trail. Thousands of PCT hikers go right past it without even knowing it's there, although they may shake their heads and wonder where all those day hikers are heading. The hike to reach the general vicinity of the falls is quite easy, since it follows the well-graded Pacific Crest Trail from Boulder Oaks, which crosses underneath I-8 and then climbs uphill. The total gain is only about 500 feet. The tricky part comes in finding the unmarked cutoff for Kitchen Creek Falls and then scrambling your way down steep slopes to reach its base. Here's how you do it: After 45 to 50 minutes of hiking, start looking carefully to your left for a narrow spur trail. You'll reach it at exactly two miles up, which for most people is about an hour of trail time. Turn left on the spur and hike a short distance to see if you're looking down on Kitchen Creek—a fairly flat stream with many good-looking pools. If you are, you're also right above the waterfall, and to reach it, you must cut down the hillside on one of many use trails, heading downstream. (Keep the creek on your right; don't cross it.) Use great caution in getting to the waterfall's base—stay on the dirt trails, and stay off the polished granite, even when it's dry. Get yourself safely to a spot where you can look up and admire the gorgeous falls, which are a series of tiered cascades that twist and turn over rounded ledges in the bedrock. Plan on staying a while.

**User Groups:** Hikers, dogs, and horses. No mountain bikes. No wheelchair facilities.

**Permits:** No permits are required. A national forest recreation pass is required for each vehicle; fees are $5 for one day or $30 for a year.

**Maps:** For a map, ask the U.S. Forest Service for Cleveland National Forest. For a topographic map, ask the USGS for Live Oak Springs.

**Directions:** From San Diego, drive east on I-8 for 50 miles to the Buckman Springs Road turnoff. Drive south on the frontage road (old Highway 8) for 2.3 miles to the Boulder Oaks Campground. Stay on the frontage road; do not turn onto Buckman Springs Road. Park at the campground, at the signed trailhead for the Pacific Crest Trail.

**Contact:** Cleveland National Forest, Descanso Ranger District, 3348 Alpine Boulevard, Alpine, CA 91901, 619/445-6235, website: www.fs.fed.us/r5/cleveland.

## 35 MOUNTAIN PALM SPRINGS CANYON

**2.6 mi / 2.0 hrs**

in Anza-Borrego Desert State Park near Bow Willow

Map 15.2, page 698

Although the groves of fan palms in Mountain Palm Springs Canyon are not as large as in Borrego Palm Canyon, they're still beautiful and popular with park visitors. The palm oases, fed by underground springs and shaded by the magnificent fan palms, create a haven for plants and wildlife, as well as for hikers looking for a cool and pleasant place to spend the day. Six distinct palm groves grow in Mountain Palm Springs Canyon, as well as occasional elephant trees; you can visit all of the groves in one walk. The trail doesn't look like much to start, just a rocky arroyo, but it gets more trail-like in short order. The first grove of trees, Pygmy Grove, has been burned. The second grove, Southwest Grove, is larger and prettier. Take the right fork just before you enter Southwest Grove and head uphill to an elephant tree and the one-mile path to the Surprise Canyon Grove. From Surprise Canyon, you can turn left to see Palm Grove Bowl—it's a natural bowl that is ringed with more than 100 palm trees. Return to Surprise Canyon and loop back to your starting point, passing by North Grove on the way. Or retrace your steps to Southwest Grove and take the short spur to the southwest to see Torote Bowl. There are some good elephant tree specimens there. If you visit in early winter when the palms bear their fruit (dates), you may find so many birds singing in the palm trees that you can hardly hear yourself think. Look for the pretty hooded oriole in particular, which builds its nest on the underside of palm fronds.

**User Groups:** Hikers only. No dogs, horses, or mountain bikes. No wheelchair facilities.

**Permits:** No permits are required. Parking and access are free.

**Maps:** A map of Anza-Borrego Desert State

Park is available at the park visitors center. For a topographic map, ask the USGS for Sweeney Pass.

**Directions:** From Julian, drive east on Highway 78 for 12 miles to Road S2, turn south, and drive 29 miles to the Mountain Palm Springs Campground entrance road, on the right. Turn right and drive straight for .6 mile (don't take any of the campsite turnoffs) to the parking area by a stone marker for Mountain Palm Springs Canyon.

**Contact:** Anza-Borrego Desert State Park, 200 Palm Canyon Drive, Borrego Springs, CA 92004, 760/767-5311, website: www.anzaborrego.statepark.org; visitors center, 760/767-4205.

## Chapter 16

© ANN MARIE BROWN

# The Southern Deserts

# The Southern Deserts

The Southern Deserts region encompasses a series of state and regional parks located in the western Mojave—a transitional area between the mountains, valleys, and cities of greater Los Angeles and the more remote eastern Mojave. It also contains two of California's most spectacular national parks, Joshua Tree and Mojave, plus the world famous oasis of Palm Springs and its surrounding desert canyons. Connoisseurs of barrel cactus, Joshua trees, palm groves, and other desert flora will find those treasures here. Come armed with a big hat and a plentiful supply of water, and you can help yourself to an abundance of options for desert hiking.

The western Mojave parks are surprisingly close to home for many thousands of Southern Californians, but their wildness is a world apart. The trails in Vasquez Rocks, Saddleback Butte, Red Rock Canyon, and other nearby parks show off red-colored desert cliffs, tilted sandstone slabs, grassy knolls covered with California poppies, and forests of Joshua trees. These scenic parklands are a stark contrast to the proliferation of 7-Elevens and Wal-Marts located only a few miles west and south.

Although both Joshua Tree National Park and Mojave National Preserve are considered "desert parks," each is distinctly different. Joshua Tree is best known for its wide desert plains covered with strange-looking Joshua trees, amazing rock formations and boulder piles, rugged mountains, and gold-mining ruins. The park is situated where the high Mojave Desert meets the low Colorado Desert, producing a wide variety of desert flora. Much of the park is higher than 4,000 feet in elevation. The most comfortable weather usually occurs from October to May; summer temperatures frequently soar past 100 degrees. Hiking trails in Joshua Tree are plentiful and varied; destinations include gold-mine stamp mills, old homesteads, mountain summits, and fan palm oases.

Only 50 miles to the north, Mojave National Preserve is where the Mojave, Great Basin, and Sonoran Deserts join. As a result of this convergence, Mojave contains a wide diversity of plant and animal life, as well as interesting geological features. Hiking trails lead to the summit of Cima Dome, a granite batholith covered with a dense forest of Joshua trees, and through the volcanic rock cliffs of Hole-in-the-Wall. The 500-foot-tall Kelso Dunes, second highest in California, are another of the preserve's attractions. No official trails lead to the top of the dunes because of the constantly swirling desert sands; hikers simply pick a route and start climbing.

Like Joshua Tree, Mojave National Preserve is mostly high desert terrain, with elevations ranging from 2,000 to 5,000 feet. Although summers can be hot, December to February is frequently windy and cold; higher elevations of the park are sometimes dusted in snow. No services are found anywhere in the park; hikers must come prepared to be self-reliant.

The desert's most famous city, Palm Springs, is also located in the Southern Deserts region. This oasis was originally the home of the Agua Caliente band of the Cahuilla Indians, who still own major portions of the town's land. Not unlike today's Palm Springs visitors, the Agua Caliente worshipped the pure water flowing down the desert canyons, the natural hot springs, and the wind-sheltering curve of the San Jacinto Mountains. Hikers should pay a visit to Agua Caliente Indian Canyons for a real taste of the Palm Springs desert. You won't find manicured golf courses or trendy nightclubs in the Indian Canyons, but you will find lush stands of palms, mesquite, and creosote, as well as the magical silence of the desert.

If the heat in Palm Springs starts to wear you down, you can always buy a ticket for the Aerial Tramway and be whisked from the desert floor to Mount San Jacinto State Park and Wilderness, at 8,516 feet in elevation. In a few short minutes, you'll travel from palms to pines, where the air temperature is usually 40 degrees cooler. At the tram's upper terminus, you can choose from a few short, scenic trails or take the longer trek to the summit of 10,834-foot San Jacinto Peak. Perhaps the Aerial Tramway is final proof that in Palm Springs, a hiker really can have it all.

MAP 16.1 page 725

see
Sequoia and
Kings Canyon
page 508

MAP 16.2 page 726

MAP 16.3 page 727

MAP 16.4 page 728

No Hikes

MAP 16.5 page 729

MAP 16.6 page 730

MAP 16.7 page 731

MAP 16.8 page 732

No Hikes

MAP 16.9 page 733

MAP 16.10 page 734

No Hikes

No Hikes

see
Los Angeles
and Vicinity
page 648

see
San Diego
and Vicinity
page 696

see
San Joaquin
Valley
page 422

see
Santa Barbara
and Vicinity
page 608

Death Valley N.P.

Telescope Pk. ▲ 11,049 ft

Mojave National Preserve

Joshua Tree N.P.

Channel Islands National Park

PACIFIC OCEAN

MEXICO

Las Vegas

Lake Mead National Rec. Area

Colorado River

Needles

Vidal Junction

Blythe

Calipatria

Salton Sea

Palm Springs

Twentynine Palms

Yucca Valley

Ludlow

Baker

Kelso

Tecopa

Shoshone

Inyokern

Four Corners

Barstow

Mojave

Pyramid Lake

Bakersfield

Cuyama

Ventura

Santa Barbara

Santa Rosa Island

Santa Cruz Island

San Clemente Island

Santa Catalina Island

Avalon

Long Beach

LOS ANGELES

Anaheim

SAN DIEGO

Tijuana

NV
CA

AZ

AZ
CA

N
W    E
S

20 mi

20 km

© AVALON TRAVEL PUBLISHING, INC.

# Map 16.1

## Hikes 1–2
## Page 735

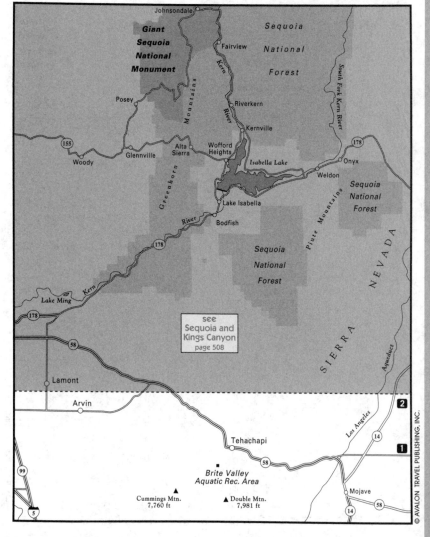

# Map 16.2

**Hikes 3–4**
**Page 736**

© AVALON TRAVEL PUBLISHING, INC.

# Map 16.3

**Hike 5**
**Page 736**

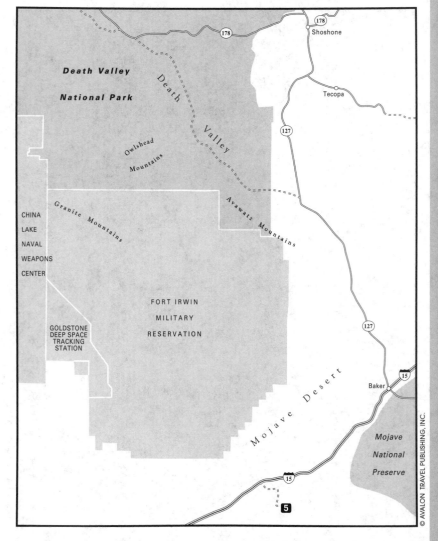

© AVALON TRAVEL PUBLISHING, INC.

# Map 16.4

**Hike 6**
**Page 737**

© AVALON TRAVEL PUBLISHING, INC.

# Map 16.5

**Hikes 7–8**
**Page 738**

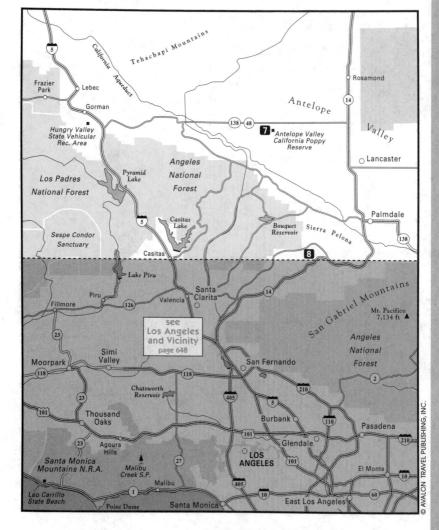

# Map 16.6

**Hikes 9–10**
**Page 739**

© AVALON TRAVEL PUBLISHING, INC.

# Map 16.7

**Hikes 11–15**
**Pages 740–742**

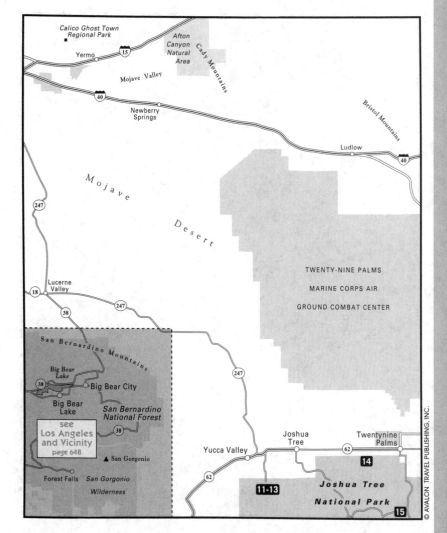

Calico Ghost Town
Regional Park

Afton
Canyon
Natural
Area

Cady Mountains

Yermo

**15**

Mojave Valley

**40**

Newberry
Springs

Bristol Mountains

Ludlow

**40**

**247**

Mojave

Desert

TWENTY-NINE PALMS

MARINE CORPS AIR

GROUND COMBAT CENTER

Lucerne
Valley

**18**

**38**

**247**

**247**

San Bernardino Mountains

Big Bear
Lake

**38**

Big Bear City

Big Bear
Lake

San Bernardino
National Forest

**38**

see
Los Angeles
and Vicinity
page 648

▲ San Gorgonio

Joshua
Tree

Twentynine
Palms

**62**

**14**

Yucca Valley

Forest Falls

San Gorgonio

Wilderness

**62**

**11-13**

*Joshua Tree*

*National Park*

**15**

© AVALON TRAVEL PUBLISHING, INC.

# Map 16.8

**Hikes 16–17**
**Page 743**

Kelso Dunes

**16**

KELBAKER RD

Providence
Mtns. State
Rec. Area

Providence Mountains

**17**

Mitchell
Caverns

*Mojave*
*National*
*Preserve*

Granite Mountains

Fenner

**40**

ESSEX RD

Essex

Clipper Mountains

*B r i s t o l*

*M o u n t a i n s*

**40**

Marble Mountains

Piute Mountains

Old Woman Mountains

Chambless

Amboy

TWENTY-NINE
PALMS
MARINE CORPS
AIR GROUND
COMBAT CENTER

Bristol
Lake

Ship Mtns.

Bullion Mountains

Cadiz Lake

Danby Lake

**62**

*Joshua Tree*

**177**

*National Park*

© AVALON TRAVEL PUBLISHING, INC.

16.4

16.7

16.10

1 2 3 4

5 6 7 8

9 10

# Map 16.9

## Hikes 18–25
## Pages 744–749

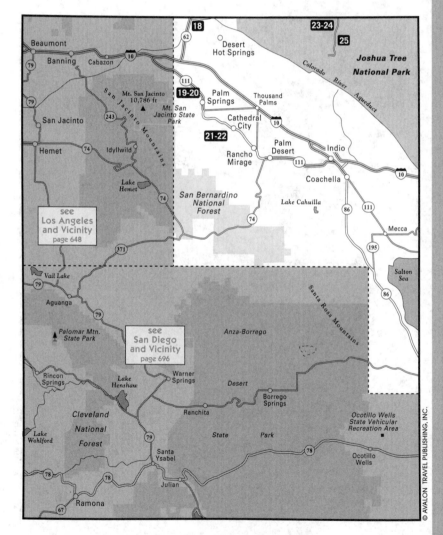

© AVALON TRAVEL PUBLISHING, INC.

# Map 16.10

**Hikes 26–29**
**Pages 749–751**

Joshua Tree

National Park

Eagle Mountains

Coxcomb Mountains

Granite Mountains

Aqueduct

Colorado

River

177

Palen Mountains

Desert Center

26-27

10

Chiriaco Summit
1,710 ft

Chuckwalla Mountains

10

Orocopia Mountains

North Shore

Salton Sea
State Rec. Area

Chocolate Mountains

111

Salton

Sea

Bombay
Beach

CHOCOLATE MOUNTAINS

GUNNERY RANGE

86

Salton
City

Salton Sea National
Wildlife Refuge

Niland

28

111

Calipatria

78

78

86

EL CENTRO
NAVAL AIR
FACILITY

Westmorland

115

29 Glamis

78

© AVALON TRAVEL PUBLISHING, INC.

## 1 DESERT TORTOISE DISCOVERY LOOP

**2.0 mi / 1.0 hr**

off Highway 14 near California City

Map 16.1, page 725

Ⓕ The Desert Tortoise Natural Area features an easy interpretive trail that teaches visitors all about *Gopherus agassizi*, better known as the desert tortoise, California's state reptile. Don't get your heart set on seeing one, though, as the creatures are rather shy. You have to look for them, and you have to get lucky. At the preserve, you can also learn all about other desert reptiles and desert plants. A few very short interpretive trails are worth strolling, but the two-mile Discovery Trail offers the best chance of seeing tortoises. Look for their burrows underneath creosote bushes, and keep your fingers crossed that one decides to pop his or her head out. Spring (usually from early March to late May) is the best time for tortoise sightings, when the wildflowers are in bloom. The tortoises like to eat them. The best tortoise fact we learned on our trip? During a sudden rainstorm, a tortoise may emerge from its burrow and drink enough water to last a full year.

**User Groups:** Hikers and wheelchairs. No dogs, horses, or mountain bikes.

**Permits:** No permits are required. Parking and access are free.

**Maps:** A free map to the Desert Tortoise Natural Area is available at the trailhead. For topographic maps, ask the USGS for California City North and Galileo Hill.

**Directions:** From Mojave, at the junction of Highways 58 and 14, drive northeast on Highway 14 for 4.5 miles to California City Boulevard. Drive east on California City Boulevard for nine miles to 20 Mule Team Parkway. Go east on the parkway and continue driving 1.3 miles to Randsburg-Mojave Road. Turn left (northeast) on Randsburg-Mojave Road and drive four miles to the signed parking area.

**Contact:** Bureau of Land Management, Ridge-crest Field Office, 300 South Richmond Road, Ridgecrest, CA 93555, 760/384-5400, website: www.ca.blm.gov/ridgecrest.

## 2 RED CLIFFS

**2.0 mi / 1.0 hr**

in Red Rock Canyon State Park off Highway 14 north of Mojave

Map 16.1, page 725

Red Cliffs Natural Preserve is a hikers-only section of Red Rock Canyon State Park, where you can walk along and view close-up the reddish columns of 300-foot desert cliffs. The color is caused by iron oxide, or rust, but the myriad creases and folds in the cliffs have been formed by a combination of fire and water—volcanic action and the course of streams and rivers. You hike on old jeep tracks, not a formal trail, passing occasional Joshua trees as you go and gaining views of El Paso Mountains. It's hard to believe that this wilderness-like desert is so close to urban Los Angeles, because when you're out here, you feel like you're really far away. At the preserve boundary .75 mile from the trailhead, you can continue on the old jeep road into the Scenic Cliffs Preserve or turn around and retrace your steps. The Scenic Cliffs area is closed each year from February to May, the nesting season for various birds of prey. If you really want to be wowed, take this hike at sunset, spend the night in the state park campground, and see the stars as you've never seen them before.

**User Groups:** Hikers and horses. No dogs or mountain bikes. No wheelchair facilities.

**Permits:** No permits are required. A $5 day-use fee is charged per vehicle.

**Maps:** For a topographic map, ask the USGS for Cantil.

**Directions:** From Mojave, at the junction of Highways 58 and 14, drive northeast on Highway 14 for 25 miles to the Red Cliffs parking area, on the right (east) side of the road.

**Contact:** Red Rock Canyon State Park, c/o Mojave Desert Information Center, 43779 15th Street West, Lancaster, CA 93534, 661/942-0662, website: www.calparksmojave.com.

## 3 FOSSIL FALLS
### 1.0 mi / 0.5 hr

**off U.S. 395 north of the Highway 178 and Highway 14 junction**

Map 16.2, page 726

Now don't get your hopes up and think you're going to find a waterfall way out here in the desert east of U.S. 395. There's no water to be found anywhere at Fossil Falls, but there's an excellent hike to an ancient lava field where you'll find polished and sculptured rock formations. The trail is well maintained, flat, and easy enough for children, although you don't want to hike it at high noon on a hot day. The falls look more like a giant pit or crevice in the ground, carved with beautiful wind-sculpted lava formations, which were polished in the last ice age. If you know what to look for, you'll also find Native American artifacts in the area, including petroglyphs and rock rings built by the Paiute Indians. If you're the kind of person who likes the weird-looking tufa formations at Mono Lake (we are), you'll enjoy this trail.

**User Groups:** Hikers, dogs, horses, and mountain bikes. No wheelchair facilities.

**Permits:** No permits are required. Parking and access are free.

**Maps:** For a topographic map, ask the USGS for Little Lake.

**Directions:** From the junction of Highway 14 and U.S. 395 near Inyokern, drive north on U.S. 395 for 20 miles to just north of Little Lake, and turn east on Cinder Road. Drive .6 mile, bear right at the fork, and drive another .6 mile to the Fossil Falls trailhead.

**Contact:** Bureau of Land Management, Ridgecrest Field Office, 300 South Richmond Road, Ridgecrest, CA 93555, 760/384-5400, website: www.ca.blm.gov/ridgecrest.

## 4 TRONA PINNACLES
### 0.5 mi / 0.5 hr

**east of Ridgecrest and south of Trona**

Map 16.2, page 726

If the Trona Pinnacles were miniaturized, they'd look like oblong-shaped lumps of modeling clay ready to be turned on a potter's wheel. They're actually tufa spires made of calcium carbonate, and the Trona Pinnacles National Natural Landmark features more than 500 of them, some as high as 140 feet. Like the tufa spires at Mono Lake, the Trona Pinnacles were formed underwater from calcium-rich springs in the days when giant Searles Lake still had water in it—probably 50,000 years ago. Now the lake bed is dry, so the tufa spires jut upward from a flat, dry plain. Yes, they're weird looking, but in a good way. A .5-mile loop trail leads through the pinnacles, but most people just wander around at random, gazing at the strange, giant tufa spires. Wear sturdy hiking shoes—the tufa is quite sharp.

**User Groups:** Hikers and dogs. No horses or mountain bikes. No wheelchair facilities.

**Permits:** No permits are required. Parking and access are free.

**Maps:** A free brochure on Trona Pinnacles is available from the Bureau of Land Management at the address below. For a topographic map, ask the USGS for Searles Lake.

**Directions:** From Ridgecrest, drive east on Highway 178 for 20 miles to the junction with Trona-Red Mountain Road. Continue on Highway 178 for 7.7 more miles to the signed right turnoff for the trailhead. (High-clearance vehicles are recommended.)

**Contact:** Bureau of Land Management, Ridgecrest Field Office, 300 South Richmond Road, Ridgecrest, CA 93555, 760/384-5400, website: www.ca.blm.gov/ridgecrest.

## 5 AFTON CANYON
### 3.0 mi / 1.5 hrs

**east of Barstow**

Map 16.3, page 727

They call Afton Canyon "the Grand Canyon of the Mojave," and although its proportions may be smaller than the other Grand Canyon, Afton is no slacker in terms of desert drama. Sheer walls of pink and red rock rise straight up, 300 feet above the Mojave River, where a thin strip of water flows almost year-round. From the campground, follow the trail east along the river, amid a surprising amount of foliage. Saltcedar trees thrive along the stream, as well as planted cottonwoods and willows, creating a protective habitat for birds and other wildlife. As you travel farther, the canyon gets more interesting. Its walls tower above you, beautifully carved and sculpted by the Mojave River in the days when it was a much bigger waterway—probably 50,000 years ago. Hike as far as you like into the canyon, then turn around and head back. A good side trip is a visit to Pyramid Canyon, one of Afton's side canyons. Start from the campground and cross the river under the first set of railroad trestles, then head south into Pyramid Canyon. The walls slowly narrow until it becomes a classic slot canyon. In the first .25 mile, you can see why they call it Pyramid Canyon.

**User Groups:** Hikers, dogs, horses, and mountain bikes. No wheelchair facilities.

**Permits:** No permits are required. Parking and access are free.

**Maps:** For topographic maps, ask the USGS for Cave Mountain and Dunn.

**Directions:** From Barstow, drive 36 miles east on I-15 and take the Afton Road exit. Drive 3.5 miles southwest to Afton Campground (the dirt road is well graded). Park near the railroad trestles.

**Contact:** Bureau of Land Management, Barstow District Office, 2601 Barstow Road, Barstow, CA 92311, 760/252-6000, website: www.ca.blm.gov/barstow.

# 6 TEUTONIA PEAK
**4.0 mi / 2.0 hrs**

**in the Mojave National Preserve east of Barstow**

Map 16.4, page 728

Teutonia Peak on Cima Dome is the perfect summit for geometry enthusiasts. Cima Dome's big claim to fame is that it's the most symmetrical dome of its type in the United States.

It rises 1,500 feet above the surrounding landscape, and it covers almost 70 square miles. In fact, the dome is so massive that when you're on top of it, you can't see it.

However, when you're on top of Teutonia Peak, you definitely know you're on it. The peak is at 5,755 feet, and you hike to it via a two-mile trail that leads uphill to head-swiveling desert vistas. The first mile of trail is flat and pleasant, leading through cacti, piñon pines, Joshua trees, and cattle grazing lands. Some of the Joshua trees are as tall as 25 feet. (They're a different variety from the kind found in Joshua Tree National Park.) You can clearly see your destination, Teutonia Peak, as well as the rugged-looking New York Mountains in the distance. At 1.5 miles, you start your ascent up the peak. At 1.9 miles, you reach a saddle just shy of Teutonia's summit, where you have panoramic desert views. Scramble the last short stretch to reach the summit and catch your breath, enjoying the far-reaching vistas. In winter, you might not stay long, because the wind can howl up here. As you look around, chew on this: The flatlands below are all a part of massive Cima Dome.

**User Groups:** Hikers, dogs, and horses. No mountain bikes. No wheelchair facilities.

**Permits:** No permits are required. Parking and access are free.

**Maps:** A map of Mojave National Preserve is available at the park visitors center. A more detailed map is available from Tom Harrison Maps. For a topographic map, ask the USGS for Cima Dome.

**Directions:** From Baker, take I-15 east for approximately 25 miles to Cima Road. Turn right (south) on Cima Road and drive 12 miles to the trailhead, on the right side of the road.

**Contact:** Mojave National Preserve, P.O. Box 241, Baker, CA 92309, 760/733-4040, website: www.nps.gov/moja.

## ◼ 7 ANTELOPE VALLEY POPPY RESERVE LOOP
### 2.0 mi / 1.0 hr

west of Lancaster and Highway 14

Map 16.5, page 729

Our first trip to the Antelope Valley California Poppy Reserve was a wee bit disappointing. We showed up in late March, expecting to see the hillsides completely covered in bright orange flowers, but only a few straggler poppies were left, dry and shriveled from the desert wind. It was our own darn fault for poor planning. If you want to see the magic poppy show at Antelope Valley, you simply must time your trip perfectly. The best way to do it is to call the park starting in late February; they'll tell you exactly when the bloom is at its best. It can be anywhere from late February to May, and it's different every year. There are several possible loop trips in the park, but the best one for poppy-watching is the North and South Poppy Loop, a combined two-mile loop that leads from the west side of the visitors center. Wheelchairs can access a short section of this trail. On either leg of the loop, be sure to take the cutoff trail that leads to the Tehachapi Vista Point, where you can get up high and take a look around.

**User Groups:** Hikers and wheelchairs. No dogs, horses, or mountain bikes.

**Permits:** No permits are required. A $5 day-use fee is charged per vehicle.

**Maps:** For a topographic map, ask the USGS for Del Sur.

**Directions:** From Lancaster on Highway 14, take the Avenue I exit and turn west on Avenue I, which becomes Lancaster Road. Drive 14 miles to the entrance to Antelope Valley California Poppy Reserve, on the right. The trail begins by the visitors center.

**Contact:** Antelope Valley California Poppy Reserve, 15101 West Lancaster Road, Lancaster, CA 93536, 661/724-1180 or 661/942-0662, website: www.calparksmojave.com.

## ◼ 8 VASQUEZ ROCKS
### 3.0 mi / 1.5 hrs

in Agua Dulce

Map 16.5, page 729

In case you're wondering whether there is any "country" left near the city of Los Angeles, the park office at Vasquez Rocks Natural Area should convince you. It's a barn, complete with hay and horses. After stopping by and picking up a trail map, take a walk on Foot Trail and get a close-up look at the bizarre tilted rock slabs that have made this place famous. (The park has been used in various TV and movie productions.) The largest rock slabs are nearly 150 feet high, and they are tilted as much as 50 degrees, jutting out at various angles toward the sky. The geologic wonders are a result of continuing earth movement along the Elkhorn Fault, which has compressed, folded, and tilted the underlying sandstone rock layers. If you think about it too much, you won't want to stand still in one place for too long. From the parking area, begin hiking on Foot Trail through the colorful sandstone slabs, then loop back on Pacific Crest Trail (a dirt road), which returns to the other side of the parking area.

**User Groups:** Hikers, dogs, horses, and mountain bikes. No wheelchair facilities.

**Permits:** No permits are required. Parking and access are free.

**Maps:** Free trail maps are available at the park office. For a topographic map, ask the USGS for Agua Dulce.

**Directions:** From the junction of I-5 and Highway 14, drive northeast on Highway 14 for 15 miles to Agua Dulce. Take the Vasquez Rocks/Escondido Canyon exit and drive north on Escondido Canyon Road for 2.2 miles to the park entrance. Continue down the dirt road to the large parking lot and picnic area, and begin hiking on the Foot Trail.

**Contact:** Vasquez Rocks Natural Area, 10700 West Escondido Canyon Road, Agua Dulce, CA 91390, 661/268-0840, website: http://parks.co.la.ca.us.

# 9 SADDLEBACK BUTTE
3.2 mi / 2.0 hrs

east of Lancaster and Highway 14

Map 16.6, page 730

Saddleback Butte State Park is a 3,000-acre Joshua tree woodland, but if those funny-looking trees aren't enough to inspire you to make the trip, this hike to the summit of Saddleback Butte should do it. After a 1,000-foot climb to the 3,651-foot summit, you're rewarded with sweeping vistas of Antelope Valley, the San Gabriel Mountains, the Tehachapi Mountains, and the Mojave Desert. Make sure you've picked a cool day, then start hiking from the park campground through sand and plentiful Joshua trees, heading directly for the clearly visible peak. The first stretch of trail is nearly flat. At one mile out, a trail leads off to the left to Little Butte; ignore it, and continue straight for granite Saddleback Butte. The last .5 mile of trail is remarkably steep and rocky. A saddle near the summit provides excellent views. Keep going to the very top, where you can fully survey the strange surrounding landscape—the meeting place of the western Mojave Desert and the high San Gabriel Mountains.

**User Groups:** Hikers only. No dogs, horses, or mountain bikes. No wheelchair facilities.

**Permits:** No permits are required. A $5 day-use fee is charged per vehicle.

**Maps:** For a topographic map, ask the USGS for Hi Vista.

**Directions:** From Lancaster on Highway 14, take the 20th Street exit. Drive north on 20th Street for less than .5 mile, then turn right (east) on Avenue J. Drive 19 miles on Avenue J to 170th Street East. Turn right, drive one mile, and turn left on Avenue K, at the sign for the state park campground.

**Contact:** Saddleback Butte State Park, 17102 East Avenue J, Lancaster, CA 93535, 661/727-9899 or 661/942-0662, website:www.calparks mojave.com.

# 10 OWL CANYON/ RAINBOW BASIN
4.0 mi / 2.0 hrs

northwest of Barstow

Map 16.6, page 730

You just never know what kind of good stuff you'll find when you travel around the state, and that's certainly true when you reach the Rainbow Basin area north of Barstow. From the Bureau of Land Mangament's (BLM's) Owl Canyon Campground, you can take a four-mile round-trip hike into some colorful desert country. The well-named Rainbow Basin is made from a cornucopia of colorful sediments—deposits that were formed in lake beds 20 million years ago. The most colorful areas can be seen by taking an auto tour around the basin, but before or after you do so, you should take this hike in Owl Canyon.

The trail begins at Owl Canyon Campground in an ordinary looking dirt-and-gravel wash. Within minutes, the canyon walls get narrower and rockier, and various colorful sediments begin to show themselves in the rock. There's so much to look at and photograph, and so many boulders and obstacles to climb over and around, that you won't be moving very fast. At .6 mile, look for a cave entrance on your right. If you have a flashlight, you can tunnel through it and enter a small side canyon. If you keep traveling in the main canyon, you can hike a total of two miles out. The trail ends near the base of Velvet Peak (a granite ridge), in a colorful rock bowl.

**User Groups:** Hikers and dogs. No horses or mountain bikes. No wheelchair facilities.

**Permits:** No permits are required. Parking and access are free.

**Maps:** For a topographic map, ask the USGS for Mud Hills.

**Directions:** From I-15 at Barstow, take the Barstow Road exit and drive north .8 mile. Turn left on Main Street, drive .2 mile, then turn right on First Avenue. Drive one mile, and you will cross over two bridges; just after the second bridge is Irwin Road. Turn left on Irwin Road and drive 5.6 miles. Turn left on Fossil Beds Road (a gravel road), and drive 2.9 miles to the access road for Owl Canyon Campground. Turn right, drive .3 mile, then turn right again and drive 1.6 miles to the family campground (go past the group camp). The trail begins by campsite No. 11.

**Contact:** Bureau of Land Management, Barstow District Office, 2601 Barstow Road, Barstow, CA 92311, 760/252-6000, website: www.ca.blm.gov/barstow.

## 11 HIGH VIEW NATURE TRAIL
### 1.3 mi / 1.0 hr

**in Joshua Tree National Park near Yucca Valley**

**Map 16.7, page 731**

You're unlikely to have much company on this trail. This lack of popularity, along with its fine vistas and easy grade, is one of its best selling points. The trail is a loop that begins and ends at a parking area near Black Rock Canyon Campground. If you pick up an interpretive brochure at the Black Rock Canyon Nature Center (you'll pass it as you drive in), you can get a brief education on desert plants and animals as you walk. The trail undulates along, climbing a total of only 350 feet, until it reaches a high point with a lovely view of 11,502-foot Mount San Gorgonio and a less-inspiring view of the sprawling desert towns of Yucca Valley and Joshua Tree. A bench marks the spot, and there's a trail register where you can record your comments. The loop back downhill is longer and flatter than the way up. This trail is perfect for a clear winter morning's hike. Note that the loop can also be accessed from the campground and nature center via a .5-mile spur trail that begins just west of the nature center.

**User Groups:** Hikers only. No dogs, horses, or mountain bikes. No wheelchair facilities.

**Permits:** No permits are required. Parking and access are free in the Black Rock Canyon area of Joshua Tree National Park.

**Maps:** Free park maps are available at park entrance stations. A more detailed map is available from Tom Harrison Maps. For a topographic map, ask the USGS for Yucca Valley South.

**Directions:** From Banning, drive east on I-10 for 16 miles to the Highway 62 exit. Turn north on Highway 62 and drive 24 miles to the town of Yucca Valley. Turn right on Joshua Lane (signed for Black Rock Canyon) and drive five miles to the entrance to Black Rock Canyon Campground. Just before the entrance, turn right on a dirt road signed for South Park Parking Area and follow it to its end at the trailhead. The parking area is just outside of the national park boundary, but the trail is inside the park.

**Contact:** Joshua Tree National Park, 74485 National Park Drive, Twentynine Palms, CA 92277, 760/367-5500, website: www.nps.gov/jotr.

## 12 WARREN PEAK
### 5.6 mi / 3.0 hrs

**in Joshua Tree National Park near Yucca Valley**

**Map 16.7, page 731**

If you seek a less tame adventure than you get on many short trails in Joshua Tree National Park, the trip to Warren Peak might suit you well. Located in the far northwest corner of the park, the trail and its 5,103-foot summit destination feel surprisingly remote. The peak provides a terrific view of Southern California's tallest mountains, which are crowned with a mantle of snow in winter and early spring. The trail out of Black Rock Canyon Campground starts in a desert wash, with plenty of Joshua trees, piñon pines, and cholla cacti keeping you company. Keep your eyes on the trail signs, which funnel you into the correct forks in the canyon. (There are several critical turns to make.) The sandy wash narrows to a walled canyon, then broadens again. As you climb gently but steadily, you'll see junipers, oaks, and piñon pines replacing some of the lower desert flora. At about two miles out, you'll spy Warren Peak's pointy fractured rock ahead and to the right. The trail gets a bit hard to discern in places, but watch for trail ducks, and keep your eye on Warren Peak. The last .25 mile to the summit is steep and requires some scrambling but is easily accomplished. If it's not too windy, you'll want to stay on top of the pointy, conical peak for a while, and not just so you can read the summit register. Views of Mount San Gorgonio, Mount San Jacinto, San Gorgonio Pass, and the Mojave Desert will make your heart pound. To the southwest are Palm Springs and the Morongo and Coachella Valleys.

**User Groups:** Hikers only. No dogs, horses, or mountain bikes. No wheelchair facilities.

**Permits:** No permits are required. Parking and access are free in the Black Rock Canyon area of Joshua Tree National Park.

**Maps:** Free park maps are available at park entrance stations. A more detailed map is available from Tom Harrison Maps. For a topographic map, ask the USGS for Yucca Valley South.

**Directions:** From Banning, drive east on I-10 for 16 miles to the Highway 62 exit. Turn north on Highway 62 and drive 24 miles to the town of Yucca Valley. Turn right on Joshua Lane (signed for Black Rock Canyon) and drive five miles to the Black Rock Canyon Nature Center. Park and then walk uphill to the Black Rock Canyon trailhead, at the upper end of the campground.

**Contact:** Joshua Tree National Park, 74485 National Park Drive, Twentynine Palms, CA 92277, 760/367-5500, website: www.nps.gov/jotr.

##  EUREKA PEAK
**10.8 mi / 6.0 hrs**

in Joshua Tree National Park near Yucca Valley

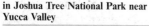
Map 16.7, page 731

The total elevation gain on this trip is only 1,500 feet to reach the summit of Eureka Peak (at 5,518 feet), but it feels more difficult than that. The problem is sand and rocks—lots of them—and the fact that the trail is hard to dis-

cern in places. However, if you're willing to put in some effort, your reward is a commanding view of the western edge of Joshua Tree National Park, as well as Mount San Jacinto and Mount San Gorgonio. Sand and snow—you see it all from here. Begin hiking on California Riding and Hiking Trail, which you'll follow for two miles until you come to a major wash. This is where things start to get tricky; keep looking for trail markers signed as EP (for Eureka Peak) to keep you on track. Take the right fork in the wash, leaving California Riding and Hiking Trail. In another .5 mile, take the next right fork into another wash. Hike through this wash for 1.7 miles to its end. A trail marker directs you to your left, heading up and over a ridge. At the top, turn right (south), hike up to a saddle, and then continue on to the south side of Eureka Peak, where there's a short path to the summit. When you get to the top, what's the only downer? You find that plenty of people have driven their cars up to the peak via a dirt road from Covington Flat. No fair. An option is to follow this road back downhill for one mile to California Riding and Hiking Trail, turn left, and follow the trail back to your starting point. It makes a good loop trip and only adds one mile to your total distance.

**User Groups:** Hikers only. No dogs, horses, or mountain bikes. No wheelchair facilities.

**Permits:** No permits are required. Parking and access are free in the Black Rock Canyon area of Joshua Tree National Park.

**Maps:** Free park maps are available at park entrance stations. A more detailed map is available from Tom Harrison Maps. For topographic maps, ask the USGS for Yucca Valley South and Joshua Tree South.

**Directions:** From Banning, drive east on I-10 for 16 miles to the Highway 62 exit. Turn north on Highway 62 and drive 24 miles to the town of Yucca Valley. Turn right on Joshua Lane (signed for Black Rock Canyon) and drive five miles to the Black Rock Canyon Nature Center. Park at the nature center and then walk uphill to California Riding and Hiking Trail trailhead, on the left (east) side of the campground entrance.

**Contact:** Joshua Tree National Park, 74485 National Park Drive, Twentynine Palms, CA 92277, 760/367-5500, website: www.nps.gov/jotr.

## 14 FORTYNINE PALMS OASIS
**3.0 mi / 1.5 hrs**

**in Joshua Tree National Park near Twentynine Palms**

**Map 16.7, page 731**

The biggest surprise on Fortynine Palms Oasis Trail is not the large and lovely grove of palm trees at the trail's end. It's that there are no Joshua trees to be found anywhere along the trail. What? No Joshua trees in this part of Joshua Tree National Park? It's true—the elevation is a bit too low for them here. Taking their place are the namesake 49 palms, of course, and lovely spring wildflowers, including some orchids growing near the pools in the oasis. Try to hike here in April or May, when the red barrel cacti are in bloom.

The trail is an old Native American pathway, and it's well maintained and easy to follow. It winds around, climbs up and over a small ridge, and then curves around to the palm grove. First you'll see a cluster of 10 palms, and then a larger grouping a short distance away. Although you can see and hear Highway 62 and its sprawling suburban towns as you hike, once you reach the palm grove, all traces of civilization are left behind. Have a seat on a boulder to listen and watch for birds. Orioles, finches, and hummingbirds congregate here for both the trickling spring water and the palm fruits. This is a lush, green, vibrant spot, and it is critically important as a watering hole for bighorn sheep and coyotes. The only downer: Some of the beautiful palm trunks have been carved with people's initials.

**User Groups:** Hikers only. No dogs, horses, or mountain bikes. No wheelchair facilities.

**Permits:** No permits are required. Parking and access are free in this area of Joshua Tree National Park.

**Maps:** Free park maps are available at park entrance stations. A more detailed map is available from Tom Harrison Maps. For a topographic map, ask the USGS for Queen Mountain.

**Directions:** From Banning, drive east on I-10 for 16 miles to the Highway 62 exit. Turn north on Highway 62 and drive 29 miles to the town of Joshua Tree. Continue east on Highway 62 for 10 miles to just west of the town of Twentynine Palms. Turn right (south) on Canyon Road, located by the High Desert Animal Hospital. Drive 1.7 miles on Canyon Road; bear left where the road forks. The pavement ends at the Fortynine Palms Oasis trailhead.

**Contact:** Joshua Tree National Park, 74485 National Park Drive, Twentynine Palms, CA 92277, 760/367-5500, website: www.nps.gov/jotr.

## 15 BARKER DAM LOOP
**1.5 mi / 1.0 hr**

**in Joshua Tree National Park near Twentynine Palms**

**Map 16.7, page 731**

There's a lake in the desert (well, in wet years, anyway), and it's hidden in a magical place called the Wonderland of Rocks. You can't water-ski or fish there, but you can enjoy birdwatching and photograph the reflections of odd-shaped boulders in the water's surface. The lake was last seen in 1998, before a series of dry years hit Southern California, but with a few good winter rains, it will be back. When it exists, the lake is formed by Barker Dam, built at the beginning of the 20th century to improve upon a natural boulder dam that captured rain runoff in this basin. Even if the lake is only a mirage when you visit, this short loop is still a great walk, as it also leads past many of the unique granite boulders of the Wonderland of Rocks. Rock climbers can often be seen strutting their stuff here. The trail loops back past some petroglyphs (take the short spur trail) and Indian grinding holes. If the petroglyphs seem remarkably visible and clear to you, it's because years ago a movie crew painted over them to make them more visible to the camera. For this tragic reason, the park calls these paintings the "Disney petroglyphs."

**User Groups:** Hikers only. No dogs, horses, or mountain bikes. No wheelchair facilities.

**Permits:** No permits are required. There is a $10 entrance fee per vehicle at Joshua Tree National Park, good for seven days.

**Maps:** Free park maps are available at park entrance stations. A more detailed map is available from Tom Harrison Maps. For a topographic map, ask the USGS for Indian Cove.

**Directions:** From Banning, drive east on I-10 for 16 miles to the Highway 62 exit. Turn north on Highway 62 and drive 29 miles to the town of Joshua Tree. Turn right on Park Boulevard and drive 14 miles to Hidden Valley Campground, on the left. Follow the signs for Barker Dam.

**Contact:** Joshua Tree National Park, 74485 National Park Drive, Twentynine Palms, CA 92277, 760/367-5500, website: www.nps.gov/jotr.

## 16 KELSO DUNES
### 3.0 mi / 1.5 hrs

**in the Mojave National Preserve southeast of Barstow**

Map 16.8, page 732

What's the most popular place in Mojave National Preserve to watch the sun set? Unquestionably it's Kelso Dunes. Kelso Dunes are the second-highest sand dunes in California. (Eureka Dunes in Death Valley are the highest.) The dune complex covers 50 square miles, and the dunes reach a height of 700 feet. In a wet spring, desert wildflowers bloom on and around the dunes, adding brighter colors to the gold and pink sand.

Read the interesting interpretive signs at the Kelso Dunes trailhead, then walk a short distance toward the closest dunes, which are plainly visible. Constantly moving sand makes a formal trail impossible. If you climb high enough in the sand, you are rewarded with views of the surrounding desert, including the Granite and Providence Mountains. Many people don't bother to climb to the top, though. They just plop

themselves down and make sand angels or roll around on the dunes' silky surface. Another popular activity is trying to cause small sand avalanches that sometimes produce harmonic booming sounds. For this to occur, the sand must be extremely dry. Some desert lovers swear by the healing power of these vibrating noises.

**User Groups:** Hikers and dogs. No horses or mountain bikes. No wheelchair facilities.

**Permits:** No permits are required. Parking and access are free.

**Maps:** A map of Mojave National Preserve is available at the park visitors center. A more detailed map is available from Tom Harrison Maps. For a topographic map, ask the USGS for Kelso Dunes.

**Directions:** From Barstow, take I-15 east for approximately 60 miles to Baker, then turn south on Kelbaker Road and drive 42 miles, past Kelso, to the signed road on the right for Kelso Dunes. Turn right (west) and drive three miles to the dunes parking area.

If you are coming from the south on I-40, take the Kelso/Amboy exit and drive 14 miles north on Kelbaker Road to the signed road on the left for Kelso Dunes.

**Contact:** Mojave National Preserve, P.O. Box 241, Baker, CA 92309, 760/733-4040, website: www.nps.gov/moja.

## 17 CRYSTAL SPRINGS TRAIL
### 2.0 mi / 1.0 hr

**in the Providence Mountains State Recreation Area southeast of Barstow**

Map 16.8, page 732

The big draw at Providence Mountains State Recreation Area is touring Mitchell Caverns with a park ranger, so a lot of people miss out on the excellent do-it-yourself hiking trails in the area. Crystal Springs Trail is the best of those, leading from the visitors center uphill to a rocky overlook in the Providence Mountains. Trailhead elevation is 4,300 feet. The trail is moderately steep and feels surprisingly remote compared to the parking lot full of people waiting to tour the caverns.

You hike upward through Crystal Canyon, where bighorn sheep are sometimes seen by lucky hikers. Rocky outcrops shoot up from both sides of the trail. You'll witness a remarkable variety of high desert foliage: piñon pines, junipers, and prickly plants galore—chollas, barrel cactus, catclaw, cliff rose, and the like. As you climb, keep turning around to check out the increasingly widening vistas. The trail ends near Crystal Springs, where you get a fine view of the surrounding desert and mountains. Then just turn around and head back downhill.

A good side trip is to add a jaunt in the opposite direction from the visitors center. Follow Niña Mora Overlook Trail from the park campground for .25 mile to an overlook of the Marble Mountains and Clipper Valley. And, of course, if you've driven all the way out here, you should sign up for a tour of Mitchell Caverns. The limestone caverns and their stalagmites, stalactites, and helictites are fascinating to see. Tours are held at 1:30 P.M. daily from September through May, and more frequently on weekends. In summer, tours are offered only on weekends.

**User Groups:** Hikers only. No dogs, horses, or mountain bikes. No wheelchair facilities.

**Permits:** No permits are required. Parking and access are free. A $4 fee is charged per adult for a tour of the park's caverns ($2 for children 16 and under).

**Maps:** A park map is available at the visitors center. For a topographic map, ask the USGS for Fountain Peak.

**Directions:** From Barstow, take I-40 east for approximately 90 miles to the exit for Essex Road, Mitchell Caverns, and Providence Mountains State Recreation Area near the town of Essex. Turn north on Essex Road and drive 15.5 miles to the Providence Mountains visitors center.

**Contact:** Providence Mountains State Recreation Area, P.O. Box 1, Essex, CA 92332, 760/928-2586 or 661/942-0662, website: www.cal-parksmojave.com.

## 18 BIG MORONGO CANYON LOOP

**1.5 mi / 1.0 hr**

**in the Big Morongo Canyon Preserve north of Palm Springs**

Map 16.9, page 733

Big Morongo Canyon Preserve is a bird-watcher's place, plain and simple. In fact, if you're not carrying binoculars and a field book when you visit, you'll feel like a real outsider. Fortunately, you don't have to know anything about birds to have a good time. We examined the interpretive exhibit at the trailhead kiosk, and in a few minutes of hiking, we were able to spot and identify a pair of western tanagers. (And usually we can't tell a blue jay from a blue grouse.) The best bird-watching seasons are spring and fall, so time your trip for those times if possible.

Start this loop from the kiosk by bearing left to connect to Desert Willow Trail, an exposed pathway through a desert wash, then in .4 mile turn left again on Yucca Ridge Trail. As you climb Yucca Ridge, you'll gain panoramic views of Big Morongo Canyon, and the San Jacinto and San Gorgonio Mountains. Note the gneiss and schist rock formations along the trail; they are some of the oldest rocks in California—one to two billion years old. In .7 mile, connect to the more shaded Mesquite Trail and enjoy a streamside walk under a canopy of Fremont cottonwoods and red willows. You may smell the distinct scent of sulfur from underground springs. Finally you'll join Marsh Trail for the final stint back to the trailhead, following a boardwalk made of recycled plastic milk containers. If you haven't added a few species to your bird list by this point in the hike, you will now. More than 1,400 pairs of birds per square kilometer nest here annually, making Marsh Trail a bird-watcher's paradise.

**User Groups:** Hikers only. No dogs, horses, or mountain bikes. Wheelchair users can follow the fully accessible Marsh Trail.

**Permits:** No permits are required. Parking and access are free.

**Maps:** For a topographic map, ask the USGS for Morongo Valley.

**Directions:** From Banning, drive east on I-10 for 16 miles to the Highway 62 exit. Turn north on Highway 62 and drive 11 miles to Morongo Valley. Look for a sign on the right for the Big Morongo Canyon Preserve (at East Drive); turn right and drive 200 yards to the preserve entrance, on the left. Trails begin at the kiosk/information center.

**Contact:** Big Morongo Canyon Preserve, P.O. Box 780, Morongo Valley, CA 92256, 760/363-7190, website: www.bigmorongo.org.

## 19 AERIAL TRAMWAY TO DESERT VIEW TRAIL

**2.0 mi / 1.0 hr**

**in Mount San Jacinto State Park and Wilderness**

Map 16.9, page 733

The first time you ride the Palm Springs Aerial Tramway, you realize that human beings are capable of creating miracles. In just a few minutes (which you spend gaping out the big windows at the view), you are whooshed from the desert floor, at 2,643 feet in elevation, to the Mount San Jacinto State Park and Wilderness, at 8,516 feet. From cacti to clouds, from palms to pines, and in our case, from desert heat to snow flurries. There are dozens of possible hikes from the top of the tramway, but the easiest of them all is on Desert View Trail. Since the trail is in the state park but not in the state wilderness, you don't even need a permit—just get off the tram and start hiking. Where else for so little effort can you get expansive views of the desert and high mountain country? Not too many places.

To reach Desert View Trail, follow the park's nature trail to the left from the back of the tram station; it joins Desert View. The vistas are awesome every step of the way, especially looking out over Palm Springs and the Indian Canyons. As you walk, be on the lookout for Cooper's hawks and yellow-rumped warblers. Here's an insider's tip for planning your trip: The best deal on the Palm Springs Aerial Tramway is to buy the Ride and Dine Ticket (available after 3 P.M.). For just a couple of extra bucks, you get a huge buffet din-

ner to go with your tram ride and day of exploring on the mountain. It's an incredible experience to spend the afternoon hiking, have dinner in the huge dining room as the sun goes down, and then ride the tram back downhill in the darkness.

**User Groups:** Hikers only. No dogs, horses, or mountain bikes. No wheelchair facilities.

**Permits:** No permits are required. The Palm Springs Aerial Tramway charges $20.80 per adult and $13.80 per child under 12 for a round-trip ticket to Mountain Station. Contact the Palm Springs Aerial Tramway for information about schedules, fees and special programs.

**Maps:** A hiking trail map of Mount San Jacinto State Park and Wilderness is available at the offices listed below. For a topographic map, ask the USGS for San Jacinto Peak.

**Directions:** From Banning, drive 12 miles east on I-10 and take the Highway 111/Palm Springs exit. Drive nine miles south on Highway 111 to Tramway Road, then turn right and drive 3.5 miles to the tramway parking area. Walk to the tram station, buy your ticket, and ride the tram to its end at Mountain Station. Walk out the back side of Mountain Station, follow the paved path downhill, and walk to your left for Desert View Trail.

**Contact:** Mount San Jacinto State Park and Wilderness, P.O. Box 308, 25905 Highway 243, Idyllwild, CA 92549, 909/659-2607, website: www.sanjac.statepark.org; Palm Springs Aerial Tramway, 760/325-1391, website: www.ps tramway.com.

## 20 AERIAL TRAMWAY TO SAN JACINTO PEAK

**11.6 mi / 6.6 hrs**

**in Mount San Jacinto State Park and Wilderness**

Map 16.9, page 733

You could hike to 10,834-foot San Jacinto Peak the hard way, upward from Idyllwild on one of several possible trails, but then you'd miss out on the many delights of the Palm Springs Aerial Tramway and hiking through Long and Round Valleys. So take the tram instead, get your wilderness permit at the ranger station, and begin hiking on Round Valley Trail. It switchbacks gently uphill through the pines and firs, most of the time following a creek laden with corn lilies, to reach beautiful Round Valley, at 9,100 feet. At the west end of Round Valley, you reach a Y in the trail, near the seasonal ranger station. Take the left fork heading toward Wellmans Divide, with a short, steep ascent just before you reach it. The views to the north and east are inspiring, including jagged Tahquitz Peak and Red Tahquitz—a bit of foreshadowing of things to come.

At the divide, turn right on Deer Springs Trail. You have 2.6 miles to go, and the views stay with you the whole way. Climb northward on the granite slopes of Miller Peak, make a sharp left switchback, and head southwest to the spur trail for San Jacinto Peak, on the right. Once you're on the spur, it's only a few hundred yards to the peak, where the views are truly breathtaking. You can see just about all of Southern California, even into Mexico and Nevada, and out to the Pacific Ocean. John Muir said that the vista from San Jacinto was "one of the most sublime spectacles seen anywhere on earth," and he was a guy who saw a lot of vistas. Total elevation gain is 2,300 feet.

**User Groups:** Hikers only. No dogs, horses, or mountain bikes. No wheelchair facilities.

**Permits:** A free wilderness permit is required for day hiking or backpacking in the San Jacinto Wilderness and is available from the ranger station at Mountain Station. Backpackers should obtain a permit in advance by mail from Mount San Jacinto State Park and Wilderness at the address below. The Palm Springs Aerial Tramway charges $21 per adult and $14 per child under 12 for a round-trip ticket to Mountain Station. Contact the Palm Springs Aerial Tramway for information about schedules, fees, and special programs.

**Maps:** A hiking trail map of Mount San Jacinto State Park and Wilderness is available at the offices listed below. A map of the San Jacinto Wilderness is available from Tom Harrison Maps. For a topographic map, ask the USGS for San Jacinto Peak.

**Directions:** From Banning, drive 12 miles east on I-10 and take the Highway 111/Palm Springs exit. Drive nine miles south on Highway 111 to Tramway Road, then turn right and drive 3.5 miles to the tramway parking area. Walk to the tram station, buy your ticket, and ride the tram to its end, at Mountain Station. Walk out the back side of Mountain Station, follow the paved path downhill, and head right (west) for a few hundred yards to the ranger station. Get a day hiking permit and continue hiking on the well-signed trail heading for Round Valley.

**Contact:** Mount San Jacinto State Park and Wilderness, P.O. Box 308, 25905 Highway 243, Idyllwild, CA 92549, 909/659-2607, website: www.sanjac.statepark.org; Palm Springs Aerial Tramway, 760/325-1391, website: www.ps tramway.com.

## 21 MURRAY CANYON TRAIL
**4.0 mi / 2.0 hrs**

on the Agua Caliente Indian Reservation in Palm Springs

Map 16.9, page 733

If you think Palm Springs is all tennis courts, golf courses, and beauty parlors, you haven't been to the Indian Canyons off South Palm Canyon Drive. The Indian Canyons—Palm, Andreas, and Murray—are what's left of the old Palm Springs. They're wide-open stretches of desert, with red rock, fan palms, sulfur streams, barrel cactus, bighorn sheep, and broad vistas of surprising color and beauty. The Murray Canyon Trail is an excellent exploration of this area, beginning at the picnic grounds between Murray and Andreas Canyons. The trail is well-packed sand and is clearly marked along the way. After an initial wide-open desert stretch, you enter Murray Canyon, which narrows and twists and turns, so you never see where you're going until you come around the next bend. The stream you've been following begins to exhibit a stronger flow, and the streamside reeds, grasses, palm trees, and wild grape intensify their growth accordingly. If you're a fan of red rock, you'll love the 100-foot-tall slanted rock outcrops and cliffs. After passing a left fork for Kaufmann Trail, climb up and over a small waterfall in Murray Canyon, staying on the left side of the stream. In another .25 mile, you'll reach a larger set of falls. These falls block any possible further progress but provide many good pools for swimming and granite shelves for picnicking.

One thing to keep in mind when you visit Murray Canyon, or any of the Indian Canyons: Make sure you check what time the park gates are closing for the day, and then make sure you finish your hike so your car is out of the parking lot by closing time. Show up 15 minutes late, and you can have a real problem on your hands. (Guess how we know.)

**User Groups:** Hikers and horses. No dogs or mountain bikes. No wheelchair facilities.

**Permits:** No permits are required. A $6 day-use fee is charged per adult; $2 for children 6 to 12.

**Maps:** A free map/brochure is available at the entrance kiosk. For topographic maps, ask the USGS for Palm Springs and Cathedral City.

**Directions:** From Palm Springs, drive south through the center of town on Highway 111/Palm Canyon Drive and take the right fork signed for South Palm Canyon Drive. Drive 2.8 miles, bearing right at the sign for Palm Canyon/Andreas Canyon. Stop at the entrance kiosk, drive about 200 yards, and turn right for Murray Canyon. Drive past the Andreas Canyon trailhead and continue to the Murray Canyon Picnic Area, a mile from the entrance kiosk.

**Contact:** Agua Caliente Band of Cahuilla Indians, Indian Canyons Visitors Center, 2777 North Palm Canyon Drive, Palm Springs, CA 92256, 760/325-3400 or 800/790-3398, website: www.indian-canyons.com.

## 22 TAHQUITZ CANYON
**2.0 mi / 1.0 hr**

**on the Agua Caliente Indian Reservation in Palm Springs**

Map 16.9, page 733

Ⓕ Just about everything in Palm Springs has a legend behind it, and Tahquitz Canyon (pronounced TAW-kits) is no excep-

tion. Named for an Agua Caliente Indian shaman who abused his powers and was banished from his tribe, Tahquitz Canyon is a spectacular outdoor museum of desert flora and fauna. Yet the curse of Tahquitz remains so powerful that even today, some local tribe members refuse to venture into the evil shaman's rock-studded canyon.

Not so for the thousands of Palm Springs visitors who have hiked here since Tahquitz Canyon's public reopening in 1999. After years of abuse by raucous, partying crowds in the 1960s and 1970s, the canyon was closed to public access for more than two decades. The Agua Caliente Indians, owners of this land, took great pains to clean out all the garbage, graffiti, and debris and to restore this desert canyon to its native state. Now, each day, preserve rangers lead groups on an easy, two-mile hike through the canyon to the base of its 60-foot waterfall. Movie buffs will recognize the showering falls as the entrance to the land of Shangri-La in Frank Capra's 1937 film *Lost Horizon.* Tahquitz's other treasures include plentiful bird life, Indian rock art, and lush stands of desert lavender, mesquite, and creosote. Don't miss a trip to this unique place; it is sure to be the highlight of your visit to Palm Springs.

**User Groups:** Hikers only. No dogs, horses, or mountain bikes. No wheelchair facilities.

**Permits:** Advance reservations are required. Fees are $12.50 per adult and $6.50 for children 12 and under.

**Maps:** For topographic maps, ask the USGS for Palm Springs and Cathedral City.

**Directions:** From Palm Springs, drive south through the center of town on Highway 111/Palm Canyon Drive and turn right on Mesquite Avenue. Drive .5 mile to the Tahquitz Canyon visitors center. The guided hike begins here.

**Contact:** Agua Caliente Band of Cahuilla Indians, Tahquitz Canyon Visitors Center, 500 West Mesquite Avenue, Palm Springs, CA 92256, 760/416-7044 or 760/325-3400, website: www.tahquitzcanyon.com.

## 23 RYAN MOUNTAIN TRAIL
**3.0 mi / 2.0 hrs**

**in Joshua Tree National Park near Twentynine Palms**

Map 16.9, page 733

If you hike only one trail in Joshua Tree National Park, this should be the one. Ryan Mountain (at 5,470 feet) provides what many insist is the best view in the park. You can see the Queen Valley, Wonderland of Rocks, Lost Horse Valley, Pleasant Valley, and the far-off mountains, San Gorgonio and San Jacinto. It's a complete panorama. The route travels through boulders and Joshua trees—no surprises here—on a well-maintained and easy-to-follow trail. The ascent is a bit steep—a 1,000-foot elevation gain over only 1.5 miles—but it's over with quickly, so just sweat it out. Be sure to sign the summit register and then have a seat on one of the rocks of Ryan Mountain to enjoy the view. The peak's boulders are estimated to be several hundred million years old, which gives you something to think about while you admire the vista.

**User Groups:** Hikers only. No dogs, horses, or mountain bikes. No wheelchair facilities.

**Permits:** No permits are required. There is a $10 entrance fee per vehicle at Joshua Tree National Park, good for seven days.

**Maps:** Free park maps are available at park entrance stations. A more detailed map is available from Tom Harrison Maps. For a topographic map, ask the USGS for Keys View.

**Directions:** From Banning, drive east on I-10 for 16 miles to the Highway 62 exit. Turn north on Highway 62 and drive 45 miles to Twentynine Palms and the park visitors center. Turn right on Utah Trail Road and drive eight miles to a Y junction. Bear right and continue for nine miles, past Sheep Pass Campground to the trailhead parking area, on the south side of the road. You can also reach the trailhead via Park Boulevard out of the town of Joshua Tree, turning left at Cap Rock Junction and continuing 2.5 miles to the trailhead.

**Contact:** Joshua Tree National Park, 74485 National Park Drive, Twentynine Palms, CA 92277, 760/367-5500, website: www.nps.gov/jotr.

## 24 SKULL ROCK NATURE TRAIL
**1.7 mi / 1.0 hr**

**in Joshua Tree National Park near Twentynine Palms**

Map 16.9, page 733

Joshua Tree National Park is probably just as famous for rock formations as it is for Joshua trees. If you want a close look at some of the park's weird and wonderful hunks of quartz monzonite, Skull Rock Trail will provide it. The official trail is only .25 mile long, but if you're okay with doing a little cross-country hiking, you can easily turn it into a 1.7-mile loop. The trail provides a quick education: Interpretive signs point out paper-bag bush, turbinella oak, cholla cactus, and other desert flora. The path runs between the Skull Rock parking area and Loop E in Jumbo Rocks Campground, so you can start at either place. It winds among giant, rounded rock formations and passes by its namesake, Skull Rock. The big boulder looks loosely like what its name implies. A spiderweb of paths leads around Skull Rock; this is where everyone abandons the formal trail and starts climbing around on the smooth, rounded rock surfaces. To complete the longer loop, you must cross the park road twice, navigate an unmaintained stretch on the north side of the road, and walk a .5-mile stretch of the Jumbo Rocks Campground entrance road. It sounds complicated, but it's quite doable.

**User Groups:** Hikers only. No dogs, horses, or mountain bikes. No wheelchair facilities.

**Permits:** No permits are required. There is a $10 entrance fee per vehicle at Joshua Tree National Park, good for seven days.

**Maps:** Free park maps are available at park entrance stations. A more detailed map is available from Tom Harrison Maps. For a topographic map, ask the USGS for Malapai Hill.

**Directions:** From Banning, drive east on I-10 for 16 miles to the Highway 62 exit. Turn north on Highway 62 and drive 45 miles to Twentynine Palms and the park visitors center. Turn right on Utah Trail Road and drive eight miles to a Y junction. Bear right and continue four miles to the trailhead parking area alongside the road shortly before the entrance to Jumbo Rocks Campground. Begin hiking on the left (south) side of the road. If you are camping at Jumbo Rocks, you can start hiking from the entrance to Loop E.

**Contact:** Joshua Tree National Park, 74485 National Park Drive, Twentynine Palms, CA 92277, 760/367-5500, website: www.nps.gov/jotr.

## 25 LOST HORSE MINE
**4.2 mi / 2.0 hrs**

**in Joshua Tree National Park near Twentynine Palms**

Map 16.9, page 733

You get the full desert experience on the Lost Horse Mine Trail, including spectacular mountain and valley vistas, high desert flora, and a visit to an old gold mine. The trail (really an old road) leads uphill for 1.8 miles to Lost Horse Mine. The mine produced a gold profit at the turn of the century—9,000 ounces of gold—and is the best preserved of all the mines in the national park. Still standing are the mine's stamp mill, old building foundations, and a few open mine shafts. Continue from the mine another .3 mile up the old road, climbing more steeply up the ridge to wide overlooks of the Queen Valley, Lost Horse Valley, Pleasant Valley, and the eastern stretch of the national park. The summit here is 5,278 feet; turn around and retrace your steps before the trail begins to descend.

**User Groups:** Hikers only. No dogs, horses, or mountain bikes. No wheelchair facilities.

**Permits:** No permits are required. There is a $10 entrance fee per vehicle at Joshua Tree National Park, good for seven days.

**Maps:** Free park maps are available at park entrance stations. A more detailed map is available from Tom Harrison Maps. For a topographic map, ask the USGS for Keys View.

**Directions:** From Banning, drive east on I-10 for 16 miles to the Highway 62 exit. Turn north on Highway 62 and drive 29 miles to the town of Joshua Tree and Park Boulevard. Turn right on Park Boulevard and drive 15.8 miles to Cap Rock junction. Bear right and drive 2.4 miles to the dirt road on the left that is signed for Lost Horse Mine. Turn left and follow the dirt road to the trailhead parking area.

**Contact:** Joshua Tree National Park, 74485 National Park Drive, Twentynine Palms, CA 92277, 760/367-5500, website: www.nps.gov/jotr.

## 26 MASTODON PEAK
**3.0 mi / 1.5 hrs**

**in southern Joshua Tree National Park near Cottonwood Spring**

Map 16.10, page 734

The Mastodon Peak Trail begins at Cottonwood Spring Oasis, a little slice of watery paradise for birds and wildlife. After a short paved section, the trail sets off in the desert sand, and after .5 mile, you take the left fork for Mastodon Peak. Shortly you'll pass another trail junction with the path to Cottonwood Spring Campground; stay right. The route has almost no elevation change along its route to the base of the peak. It's a pleasant, easy stroll among tall ocotillos, yucca, and smaller cacti. At the Mastodon's base, you must choose whether or not to scramble to the top; the going is steep but short. Although it's a nice trip just to hike to the peak's base and try to imagine the Mastodon's profile, it's recommended you go for the summit. The easiest route is around the back of the Mastodon, on its east side. In a few minutes you are at the top, admiring the surprisingly wide view: Not only do you see a great expanse of Joshua Tree's desert and the Eagle Mountains, but also snowcapped Mount San Jacinto and the miragelike Salton Sea shimmering in the distance some 30 miles away.

If you want to add some history to your hike, retrace your steps to the junction with the trail to Cottonwood Spring Camp. Turn right there and hike past the Mastodon Gold Mine and the Winona Mill Site. The mine was worked in the 1920s with a modicum of success. From the mill site, you don't need to backtrack to the main trail; the path loops back to the Cottonwood Spring parking area.

**User Groups:** Hikers only. No dogs, horses, or mountain bikes. No wheelchair facilities.

**Permits:** No permits are required. There is a $10 entrance fee per vehicle at Joshua Tree National Park, good for seven days.

**Maps:** Free park maps are available at park entrance stations. A more detailed map is available from Tom Harrison Maps. For a topographic map, ask the USGS for Cottonwood Spring.

**Directions:** From Indio, drive east on I-10 for approximately 25 miles. Turn north on Cottonwood Spring Road and drive seven miles to Cottonwood Spring visitors center. Turn right and drive another mile, passing the campground entrance, to the day-use parking area at Cottonwood Spring Oasis.

**Contact:** Joshua Tree National Park, 74485 National Park Drive, Twentynine Palms, CA 92277, 760/367-5500, website: www.nps.gov/jotr.

## 27 LOST PALMS OASIS
**7.5 mi / 3.5 hrs**

**in southern Joshua Tree National Park near Cottonwood Spring**

Map 16.10, page 734

If the weather is cool and accommodating and you're in the mood for a longer hike in southern Joshua Tree National Park, Lost Palms Oasis Trail comes highly recommended. Many consider Lost Palms Oasis to be the best palm grove in Joshua Tree, and the hike to reach it has little elevation change. The trail begins at Cottonwood Spring Oasis and for the first .5 mile follows the same path as Mastodon Peak Trail. Stay straight at the junction with the trail to Mastodon Peak; continue straight through a series of washes and low ridges covered with various low-elevation desert cacti. There is no indication of the huge palm oasis until you are almost on top of it, at slight-

ly more than three miles out. The main trail brings you to an overlook point above the palms, and a steep use trail descends .25 mile into the grove. Make the rugged 200-foot descent to the canyon bottom; the remoteness of the area and the lush atmosphere of the leafy palm grove make it worth the effort. The Lost Palms Oasis grove contains more than 100 palms in its main canyon. In the upper end of the canyon is a side canyon with more palms, although these are more difficult to reach.

**User Groups:** Hikers only. No dogs, horses, or mountain bikes. No wheelchair facilities.

**Permits:** No permits are required. There is a $10 entrance fee per vehicle at Joshua Tree National Park, good for seven days.

**Maps:** Free park maps are available at park entrance stations. A more detailed map is available from Tom Harrison Maps. For a topographic map, ask the USGS for Cottonwood Spring.

**Directions:** From Indio, drive east on I-10 for approximately 25 miles. Turn north on Cottonwood Spring Road and drive seven miles to Cottonwood Spring visitors center. Turn right and drive a mile, past the campground entrance, to the day-use parking area at Cottonwood Spring Oasis.

**Contact:** Joshua Tree National Park, 74485 National Park Drive, Twentynine Palms, CA 92277, 760/367-5500, website: www.nps.gov/jotr.

## 28 ROCK HILL TRAIL
**2.0 mi / 1.5 hrs**

**on the east shore of the Salton Sea near Calipatria**

Map 16.10, page 734

If it's wintertime—anywhere from December to February—it's a good time to pay a visit to the Salton Sea National Wildlife Refuge (now called the Sonny Bono Salton Sea National Wildlife Refuge, after the 1970s singer-turned-politician), one of the lowest places in the United States, at 228 feet below sea level. Winter is the only season when the area isn't blistering hot, and it's also the time that peak populations of birds are gathered at the refuge.

The place has one hiking trail, called Rock Hill Trail, which gets hiked by approximately 40,000 bird-watchers a year. From the observation platform behind the visitors center, the path heads out along a levee and then abruptly climbs to a hill above the Salton Sea. It's a great place to watch the pelicans dive and to shake your head in wonder at the immense size of the saline Salton Sea. The sea was formed from 1905 to 1907, when a series of manmade dams on the Colorado River burst their seams. Its water has become increasingly saline over the years due to agricultural runoff, evaporation, and the lack of a replenishing freshwater supply.

Although fish do not fare well in the changing waters of the Salton Sea, bird lovers find plenty to cheer about. In addition to seeing the plentiful waterfowl that spend the winter in the saltwater and freshwater marshes—geese of many kinds, mergansers, widgeons, and teals—hikers might spot an endangered species such as the Yuma clapper rail or peregrine falcon. Migrating snow geese and Ross geese are also big attractions along this trail. They are seen in great numbers every December.

**User Groups:** Hikers only. No dogs, horses, or mountain bikes. No wheelchair facilities.

**Permits:** No permits are required. Parking and access are free.

**Maps:** A free map of the refuge is available at the visitors center. For a topographic map, ask the USGS for Niland.

**Directions:** From Indio, drive south on Highway 111 for approximately 50 miles to the turnoff for Sinclair Road, which is four miles south of Niland. (If you reach Calipatria, you've gone too far.) Turn right on Sinclair Road and drive six miles to the Salton Sea National Wildlife Refuge visitors center, located at the intersection of Sinclair Road and Gentry Road.

**Contact:** Sonny Bono Salton Sea National Wildlife Refuge, 906 West Sinclair Road, Calipatria, CA 92233, 760/348-5278, website: http://pacific.fws.gov/salton.

## 29 NORTH ALGODONES DUNES WILDERNESS

1.0 mi / 1.0 hr

**east of Brawley and south of the Salton Sea**

**Map 16.10, page 734**

The Algodones Dunes could best be described as an ocean of sand. They are located in the far southeast corner of California, amid a whole lot of . . . well, to be honest, nothing. Still, this is a unique and fragile place, where a massive dune system covers more than 1,000 square miles. In between the dunes lie flat basins in which desert willow, smoke trees, and mesquite flourish. Rare reptiles, such as the desert tortoise and fringe-toed lizard, make their homes here. The only time to visit the dunes is between October and April, because it is as hot as Hades the rest of the year. Summer days are typically over 120 degrees. The dunes rise to heights of 350 feet and stretch over a five-mile-wide expanse. You can wander around as much as you like, but since walking in sand is a trying experience, you probably won't wander very far. (There are no formal trails across the dunes because of the continually shifting sands.) Mostly, this is a place to come to when you just want to find some solitude, and/or gain a glimpse into a rare, special world comprised entirely of sand and sky.

**User Groups:** Hikers and dogs. No horses or mountain bikes. No wheelchair facilities.

**Permits:** No permits are required. Parking and access are free.

**Maps:** A map/brochure is available from the Bureau of Land Management (BLM) office below. For a topographic map, ask the USGS for Niland.

**Directions:** From Brawley, drive east on Highway 78 for 26 miles. The wilderness area lies on the north side of the highway. Just pull off the road and park; the dunes are clearly visible.

**Contact:** Bureau of Land Management (BLM), El Centro Field Office, 1661 South Fourth Street, El Centro, CA 92243, 760/337-4400, website: www.ca.blm.gov/elcentro.

© ANN MARIE BROWN

# Resources

## National Forests

Many Forest Service trailheads are quite remote and have no drinking water. Parking and access are often free. For overnight use, campfire permits or wilderness permits are usually required. Dogs are usually permitted in national forests with no extra charge and no hassle. Leashes are required for all dogs in some places. Always carry documentation of current vaccinations.

### National Forest Adventure Pass

Angeles, Cleveland, Los Padres, and San Bernardino National Forests require an Adventure Pass for each parked vehicle. Daily passes cost $5; annual passes are available for $30. You can buy Adventure Passes at national forest offices in Southern California and dozens of retail outlets and online vendors. The new charges are use fees, not entrance fees. Holders of Golden Age and Golden Access (not Golden Eagle) cards can buy the Adventure Pass at a 50 percent discount at national forest offices only, or at retail outlets for the retail price. A free annual Adventure Pass can be obtained when buying a Golden Eagle passport at participating forest service offices.

When you buy an annual Adventure Pass, you can also buy an additional annual Adventure Pass for $5 per family vehicle. Major credit cards are accepted at most retail and online outlets, and at some forest service offices. Adventure Passes can be purchased by telephone at 909/382-2622, or by mail at San Bernardino National Forest, Fee Project Headquarters, 1824 S. Commercenter Circle, San Bernardino, CA 92408-3430. Checks should be made payable to USDA Forest Service.

You will not need an Adventure Pass while traveling through these forests, nor when you've paid other types of fees such as camping or ski pass fees. However, if you are camping in these forests and you leave the campground in your vehicle and park outside the campground for recreation purposes, such as at a trailhead, day-use area, near a fishing stream, etc., you will need an Adventure Pass for your vehicle. You also need an Adventure Pass if camping at a no-fee campground. More information about the Adventure Pass program, including a listing of retail and online vendors, can be obtained by website: www.fsadventurepass.org.

### National Forest Maps

National Forest maps are among the best you can get for the price. They detail all backcountry streams, lakes, hiking trails, and logging roads for access. They cost $6 or more, and they can be obtained in person at Forest Service offices or by contacting U.S. Forest Service, Attn: Map Sales, P.O. Box 9035, Prescott, AZ 86313, 928/443-8285, fax 928/443-8207, website: www.fs.fed.us/nationalforeststore. Major credit cards are accepted if ordering by telephone.

### Forest Service Information

Forest Service personnel are most helpful for obtaining camping or hiking trail information. Unless you are buying a map or Adventure Pass, it is advisable to phone in advance to get the best service. For specific information on a national forest, contact the following offices:

**USDA Forest Service**
Pacific Southwest Region
1323 Club Dr.
Vallejo, CA 94592
707/562-USFS (707/562-8737)
fax 707/562-9130
website: www.fs.fed.us/r5

**Angeles National Forest**
701 N. Santa Anita Ave.
Arcadia, CA 91006
626/574-1613
fax 626/574-5233
website: www.fs.fed.us/r5/angeles

**Cleveland National Forest**
10845 Rancho Bernardo Rd., #200
San Diego, CA 92127-2107
858/673-6180
fax 858/673-6192
website: www.fs.fed.us/r5/cleveland

**Eldorado National Forest**
100 Forni Rd.
Placerville, CA 95667
530/622-5061
fax 530/621-5297
website: www.fs.fed.us/r5/eldorado

**Humboldt-Toiyabe National Forest**
1200 Franklin Way
Sparks, NV 89431
775/331-6444
fax 775/355-5399
website: www.fs.fed.us/r4/htnf

**Inyo National Forest**
351 Pacu Lane, Ste. 200
Bishop, CA 93514
760/873-2400
fax 760/873-2458
website: www.fs.fed.us/r5/inyo

**Klamath National Forest**
1312 Fairlane Rd.
Yreka, CA 96097-9549

530/842-6131
fax 530/841-4571
website: www.fs.fed.us/r5/klamath

**Lake Tahoe Basin Management Unit**
35 College Drive
South Lake Tahoe, CA 96150
530/543-2600
fax 530/543-2693
website: www.fs.fed.us/r5/ltbmu

**Lassen National Forest**
2550 Riverside Drive
Susanville, CA 96130
530/257-2151
fax 530/252-6448
website: www.r5.fs.fed.us/lassen

**Los Padres National Forest**
6755 Hollister Ave., Ste. 150
Goleta, CA 93117
805/968-6640
fax 805/961-5729
website: www.fs.fed.us/r5/lospadres

**Mendocino National Forest**
825 N. Humboldt Ave.
Willows, CA 95988
530/934-3316
fax 530/934-7384
website: www.fs.fed.us/r5/mendocino

**Modoc National Forest**
800 W. 12th St.
Alturas, CA 96101
530/233-5811
fax 530/233-8709
website: www.fs.fed.us/r5/modoc

**Plumas National Forest**
P.O. Box 11500
159 Lawrence St.
Quincy, CA 95971
530/283-2050
fax 530/283-7746
website: www.fs.fed.us/r5/plumas

**San Bernardino National Forest**
1824 South Commercenter Circle
San Bernardino, CA 92408-3430
909/382-2600
fax 909/383-5770
website: www.fs.fed.us/r5/sanbernardino

**Sequoia National Forest**
Giant Sequoia National Monument
900 W. Grand Ave.
Porterville, CA 93257
559/784-1500
fax 559/781-4744
website: www.fs.fed.us/r5/sequoia

**Shasta-Trinity National Forest**
3644 Avtech Parkway
Redding, CA 96002
530/226-2500
fax 530/226-2470
website: www.fs.fed.us/r5/shastatrinity

**Sierra National Forest**
1600 Tollhouse Rd.
Clovis, CA 93611

559/297-0706
fax 559/294-4809
website: www.fs.fed.us/r5/sierra

**Six Rivers National Forest**
1330 Bayshore Way
Eureka, CA 95501
707/442-1721
fax 707/442-9242
website: www.fs.fed.us/r5/sixrivers

**Stanislaus National Forest**
19777 Greenley Rd.
Sonora, CA 95370
209/532-3671
fax 209/533-1890
website: www.fs.fed.us/r5/stanislaus

**Tahoe National Forest**
631 Coyote St.
Nevada City, CA 95959
530/265-4531
fax 530/478-6109
website: www.fs.fed.us/r5/tahoe

# State Parks

The California State Parks system provides many popular hiking trails in spectacular settings. For camping, reservations are often necessary during the summer. Although many parks are well known, there are still some little-known gems in the state parks system where campers can enjoy seclusion, even in the summer.

State park fees have increased significantly since 2002, but camping in a state park is still a good deal. Many of the campgrounds along the California coastline are particularly popular in summer and require advance planning to secure a campsite.

For general information about California State Parks, contact:

**California Department of**
**Parks and Recreation**
Communications Office
P.O. Box 942896
Sacramento, CA 94296
916/653-6995
fax 916/657-3903
website: www.parks.ca.gov

# National Parks

California's national parks are natural wonders, ranging from the spectacular yet crowded Yosemite Valley to the remote and rugged Lava Beds National Monument. Expect to pay a park entrance fee ranging $10–20 per vehicle, or as low as $5 per person for hike-in/bike-in (you can buy a Golden Eagle annual pass that waives entrance fees). This entrance fee is valid for seven days. Various discounts are available for holders of Golden Age and Golden Access passports, including a 50 percent reduction of camping fees (group camps not included) and a waiver of park entrance fees.

**National Park Service**
Pacific West Region
One Jackson Center
1111 Jackson St., Ste. 700
Oakland, CA 94607
510/419-0197
fax 510/817-1300
website: www.nps.gov

**Cabrillo National Monument**
1800 Cabrillo Memorial Dr.
San Diego, CA 92106-3601
619/557-5450
website: www.nps.gov/cabr

**Channel Islands National Park**
1901 Spinnaker Dr.
Ventura, CA 93001
805/658-5730
fax 805/658-5799
website: www.nps.gov/chis

**Death Valley National Park**
P.O. Box 579
Death Valley, CA 92328-0579
760/786-3200
fax 760/786-3283
website: www.nps.gov/deva

**Devils Postpile National Monument**
P.O. Box 3999
Mammoth Lakes, CA 93546
760/934-2289 (summer only)
fax 760/934-8896 (summer only)
website: www.nps.gov/depo
For year-round information, contact Sequoia and Kings Canyon National Parks (see listing)

**Golden Gate National Recreation Area**
Fort Mason, Bldg. 201
San Francisco, CA 94123-0022
415/561-4700
fax 415/561-4750
website: www.nps.gov/goga

**Joshua Tree National Park**
74485 National Park Dr.
Twentynine Palms, CA 92277-3597
760/367-5500
fax 760/367-6392
website: www.nps.gov/jotr

**Lassen Volcanic National Park**
P.O. Box 100
Mineral, CA 96063-0100
530/595-4444
fax 530/595-3262
website: www.nps.gov/lavo

**Lava Beds National Monument**
#1 Indian Well Headquarters
Tulelake, CA 96134
530/667-2282
fax 530/667-2737
website: www.nps.gov/labe

**Mojave National Preserve**
222 East Main St., Ste. 202
Barstow, CA 92311
760/733-4040 (information)
fax 760/255-8809
website: www.nps.gov/moja

**Pinnacles National Monument**
5000 Hwy. 146
Paicines, CA 95043
831/389-4485
fax 831/389-4489
website: www.nps.gov/pinn

**Point Reyes National Seashore**
Point Reyes Station, CA 94956-9799
415/464-5100
fax 415/464-5149
website: www.nps.gov/pore

**Redwood National and State Parks**
1111 2nd St.
Crescent City, CA 95531
707/464-6101
fax 707/464-1812
website: www.nps.gov/redw/

**Santa Monica Mountains**
**National Recreation Area**
401 W. Hillcrest Dr.
Thousand Oaks, CA 91360
805/370-2301
fax 805/370-1850
website: www.nps.gov/samo

**Sequoia and Kings Canyon National Parks**
47050 Generals Hwy.
Three Rivers, CA 93271-9651
559/565-3341 or 559/335-2856
website: www.nps.gov/seki

**Smith River National Recreation Area**
P.O. Box 228
Gasquet, CA 95543
707/457-3131
fax 707/457-3794
website: www.fs.fed.us/r5/sixrivers

**Whiskeytown National Recreation Area**
P.O. Box 188
Whiskeytown, CA 96095
530/246-1225 or 530/242-3400
fax 530/246-5154
website: www.nps.gov/whis

**Yosemite National Park**
P.O. Box 577
Yosemite National Park, CA 95389
209/372-0200 for 24-hour recorded message or
209/372-0265
website: www.nps.gov/yose

# U.S. Army Corps of Engineers

**San Francisco District**
333 Market St.
San Francisco, CA 94105
415/977-8272
website: www.spn.usace.army.mil

**Sacramento District**
1325 "J" St.
Sacramento, CA 95814
916/557-8658
website: www.spk.usace.army.mil

**Los Angeles District**
915 Wilshire Blvd.
Los Angeles, CA 90017-3401
213/452-3908
fax 213/452-4191
website: www.spl.usace.army.mil

# Bureau of Land Management

Most of the areas managed by the BLM are primitive and in remote areas. Parking and access are usually free. Holders of Golden Age or Golden Access passports receive a 50 percent discount, except for group camps, at BLM fee campgrounds.

**Bureau of Land Management**
California State Office
2800 Cottage Way, Ste. W-1834
Sacramento, CA 95825-1886
916/978-4400
fax 916/978-4416
website: www.ca.blm.gov

**California Desert District Office**
22835 Calle San Juan de los Lagos
Moreno Valley, CA 92553
951/697-5200
fax 951/697-5299
website: www.ca.blm.gov/cdd

**Alturas Field Office**
708 W. 12th St.
Alturas, CA 96101
530/233-4666
fax 530/233-5696
website: www.ca.blm.gov/alturas

**Arcata Field Office**
1695 Heindon Rd.
Arcata, CA 95521-4573
707/825-2300
fax 707/825-2301
website: www.ca.blm.gov/arcata

**Bakersfield Field Office**
3801 Pegasus Dr.
Bakersfield, CA 93308
661/391-6000
fax 661/391-6040
website: www.ca.blm.gov/bakersfield

**Barstow Field Office**
2601 Barstow Rd.
Barstow, CA 92311
760/252-6000
fax 760/252-6099
website: www.ca.blm.gov/barstow

**Bishop Field Office**
351 Pacu Lane, Ste. 100
Bishop, CA 93514-2471
760/872-4881
fax 760/872-5050
website: www.ca.blm.gov/bishop

**Eagle Lake Field Office**
2950 Riverside Dr.
Susanville, CA 96130
530/257-0456
fax 530/257-4831
website: www.ca.blm.gov/eaglelake

**El Centro Field Office**
1661 S. 4th St.
El Centro, CA 92243
760/337-4400
fax 760/257-4831
website: www.ca.blm.gov/elcentro

**Folsom Field Office**
63 Natoma St.
Folsom, CA 95630
916/985-4474
fax 916/985-3259
website: www.ca.blm.gov/folsom

**Hollister Field Office**
20 Hamilton Ct.
Hollister, CA 95023
831/630-5000
fax 831/630-5055
website: www.ca.blm.gov/hollister

**Palm Springs/South Coast Field Office**
P.O. Box 581260
North Palm Springs, CA 92258-1260
760/251-4800
fax 760/251-4899
website: www.ca.blm.gov/palmsprings

**Redding Field Office**
355 Hemsted Dr.
Redding, CA 96002
530/224-2100
fax 530/224-2172
website: www.ca.blm.gov/redding

**Ridgecrest Field Office**
300 S. Richmond Rd.
Ridgecrest, CA 93555

760/384-5400
fax 760/384-5499
website: www.ca.blm.gov/ridgecrest

**Ukiah Field Office**
2550 N. State St.
Ukiah, CA 95482
707/468-4000
fax 707/468-4027
website: www.ca.blm.gov/ukiah

# Other Valuable Resources

## State Forests
**Jackson Demonstration State Forest**
802 N. Main St.
Fort Bragg, CA 95437
707/964-5674
fax 707/964-0941

**Mountain Home Demonstration State Forest**
P.O. Box 517
Springville, CA 93265
559/539-2321 (summer)
559/539-2855 (winter)

## County/Regional Park Departments
**Del Norte County Parks**
840 9th Street, Ste. 11
Crescent City, CA 95531
707/464-7230
fax 707/464-5824
website: www.co.del-norte.ca.us

**East Bay Regional Park District**
P.O. Box 5381
Oakland, CA 94605-0381
510/562-PARK/7275 or 510/544-2200
fax 510/635-3478
website: www.ebparks.org

**Humboldt County Parks**
1106 2nd St.
Eureka, CA 95501
707/445-7651

fax 707/445-7409
website: www.co.humboldt.ca.us/

**Marin Municipal Water District**
220 Nellen Ave.
Corte Madera, CA 94925
415/945-1455
fax 415/927-4953
website: www.marinwater.org

**Midpeninsula Regional Open Space District**
330 Distel Circle
Los Altos, CA 94022-1404
650/691-1200
fax 650/691-0485
website: www.openspace.org

**Pacific Gas and Electric Company**
FERC/Land Projects
2730 Gateway Oaks, Ste. 220
Sacramento, CA 95833
916/386-5164
fax 916/923-7044
website: www.pge.com/recreation

**Sacramento County Parks and Recreation Division**
3711 Branch Center Road
Sacramento, CA 95827
916/875-6961
fax 916/875-6050
website: www.sacparks.net

San Diego County Parks and
Recreation Department
2454 Heritage Park Row
San Diego, CA 92110
858/694-3049
fax 619/260-6492
website: www.co.san-diego.ca.us/parks

San Luis Obispo County Parks Department
1087 Santa Rosa St.
San Luis Obispo, CA 93408
805/781-5930
fax 805/781-1102
website: www.slocountyparks.org

San Mateo County Parks and
Recreation Department
455 County Center, 4th floor
Redwood City, CA 94063-1646
650/363-4020
fax 650/599-1721
website: www.eparks.net

Santa Barbara County Parks and
Recreation Department
610 Mission Canyon Rd.
Santa Barbara, CA 93105
805/568-2461
fax 805/568-2459
website: www.sbparks.com

Santa Clara County Parks and Recreation
298 Garden Hill Dr.
Los Gatos, CA 95032-7669
408/355-2200
fax 408/355-2290
website: www.parkhere.org

Sonoma County Regional Parks
2300 County Center Dr., Ste. 120-A
Santa Rosa, CA 95404
707/565-2041
fax 707/579-8247
website: www.sonoma-county.org/parks

## State and Federal Offices
**U.S. Fish and Wildlife Service**
1849 "C" St. NW
Washington, DC 20240
website: www.fws.gov

**U.S. Geological Survey**
Branch of Information Services
P.O. Box 25286, Federal Center
Denver, CO 80225
888/ASK-USGS (888/275-8747) or
303/202-4700
website: www.usgs.gov

**California Department of Fish and Game**
1416 9th St., 12th floor
Sacramento, CA 95814
916/445-0411
fax 916/653-1856
website: www.dfg.ca.gov

## Information Services
**Lake County Visitor Information Center**
P.O. Box 1025
6110 East Highway 20
Lucerne, CA 95458
800/525-3743 or 707/274-5652
fax 707/274-5664
website: www.lakecounty.com

**Mammoth Lakes Visitors Bureau**
P.O. Box 48
437 Old Mammoth Rd., Ste. Y
Mammoth Lakes, CA 93546
888/GO-MAMMOTH or 888/466-2666
fax 760/934-7066
website: www.visitmammoth.com

**Mt. Shasta Visitors Bureau**
300 Pine St.
Mt. Shasta, CA 96067
800/926-4865 or 530/926-4865
fax 530/926-0976
website: www.mtshasta.chamber.com

**The Nature Conservancy of California**
201 Mission St., 4th floor
San Francisco, CA 94105-1832
415/777-0487
fax 415/777-0244
website: http://nature.org/wherewework/
northamerica/states/california/

**Plumas County Visitors Bureau**
550 Crescent St.
P.O. Box 4120
Quincy, CA 95971
800/326-2247 or 530/283-6345
fax 530/283-5465
website: www.plumascounty.org

**Shasta-Cascade Wonderland Association**
1699 Hwy. 273
Anderson, CA 96007
800/474-2782 or 530/365-7500
fax 530/365-1258
website: www.shastacascade.com

## Map Companies
**Earthwalk Press**
5432 La Jolla Hermosa Ave.
La Jolla, CA 92037
800/828-MAPS (800/828-6277)

**Map Center**
1995 University Ave., Ste. 117
Berkeley, CA 94704
510/841-6277
fax 510/841-0858

**Map Link**
30 S. La Patera Lane, Unit 5
Goleta, CA 93117
805/692-6777
fax 800/627-7768 or 805/692-6787
website: www.maplink.com

**Olmsted & Bros. Map Company**
P.O. Box 5351
Berkeley, CA 94705
tel./fax 510/658-6534

**Tom Harrison Maps**
2 Falmouth Cove
San Rafael, CA 94901-4465
tel./fax 800/265-9090 or 415/456-7940
website: www.tomharrisonmaps.com

**U.S. Forest Service**
Attn: Map Sales
P.O. Box 9035
Prescott, AZ 86313
928/443-8285
fax 928/443-9035
website: www.fs.fed.us/recreation/
nationalforeststore

**U.S. Geological Survey**
Branch of Information Services
P.O. Box 25286, Federal Center
Denver, CO 80225
888/ASK-USGS (888/275-8747) or
303/202-4700
fax 303/202-4693
website: www.usgs.gov

# Acknowledgments

## U.S. Forest Service

Debe Arndt, High Sierra Ranger District, Sierra National Forest
Mary August, Feather River Ranger District, Plumas National Forest
Paul Bailey, Devil's Garden Ranger District, Modoc National Forest
Cheryl Balle and Ann Wiltshire, Cannell Meadow Ranger District, Sequoia National Forest
Jim Barnhardt, Hat Creek Work Center, Lassen National Forest
Al Buchter, Salmon River Ranger District, Klamath National Forest
Kathy Burnett, Summit Ranger District, Stanislaus National Forest
Anne Carey, Descanso Ranger District, Cleveland National Forest
Joe Chavez, Downieville Ranger District, Tahoe National Forest
Maxine Chittender, Hume Lake Ranger District, Sequoia National Forest
Scott Clemons, Bridgeport Ranger District, Humboldt-Toiyabe National Forest
Jim Fedderly, Calaveras Ranger District, Stanislaus National Forest
Anna Fiorella, Corning Work Center, Mendocino National Forest
Pat Garrahan, Happy Camp Ranger District, Klamath National Forest
Sharon Graham, Covelo Ranger District, Mendocino National Forest
Ken Graves, Hayfork Office, Shasta-Trinity National Forest
Steve Hale, Carson Ranger District, Humboldt-Toiyabe National Forest
Bob Hemus, Orleans Ranger District, Klamath National Forest
Bob Hemus, Six Rivers National Forest
Charlie Kraus, Scott River Ranger District, Klamath National Forest
Ron Lawson, San Jacinto Ranger District, San Bernardino National Forest
Don Lee, Mount Shasta Ranger District, Shasta-Trinity National Forest
Mike LeFevre, Bass Lake Ranger Station, Sierra National Forest
Dean Lutz, Truckee Ranger District, Tahoe National Forest
Patty Mahaffey, Nevada City Ranger District, Tahoe National Forest
Matt Mathes, Pacific Region Headquarters
Geneva May, Sierraville Ranger District, Tahoe National Forest
Marilyn Muse Meyer, Amador Ranger District, Eldorado National Forest
Joe Miranda, Stonyford Ranger Station, Mendocino National Forest
Deborah Nearing, Foresthill Ranger District, Tahoe National Forest
Liz Nelson, Mount Whitney Ranger Station, Inyo National Forest
Barbara Paolinetti, McCloud Ranger District, Shasta-Trinity National Forest
Del Pengilly, Tule River/Hot Springs Ranger District, Sequoia National Forest
Joyce Platt, Information Center, Eldorado National Forest
Robin Renteria, Lake Tahoe Basin Management Unit
John Sandstrom, Big Bar Ranger Station, Shasta-Trinity National Forest
Lisa Sedlacek, Almanor Ranger District, Lassen National Forest
Joseph Signorino, Ojai Ranger District, Los Padres National Forest
Cathy Southwick, Shasta Lake Ranger District, Shasta-Trinity National Forest
Jim Stout, Goosenest Ranger District, Klamath National Forest
Dustin Swan, Bridgeport Ranger District, Humboldt-Toiyabe National Forest
Pandora Valle, Beckwourth Ranger District, Plumas National Forest

Beverly Way, Warner Mountain Ranger District, Modoc National Forest
Charlotte Wheeland, San Gabriel River Ranger District
Lorraine Worley, Doublehead Ranger District, Modoc National Forest
Alfredo Zarate Jr., Mill Creek Ranger Station, San Bernardino National Forest

## National Parks

Nancy Bailey and Karen Haner, Lassen Volcanic National Park
Richard Banuelos, Pinnacles National Monument
Phil Bono and Don Pass, Smith River National Recreation Area
Charlie Calligan, Death Valley National Park
Cathy Cook, Redwood National and State Parks
Tom Dore, Channel Islands National Park
Kris Fister, Sequoia and Kings Canyon National Parks
Trisha Ford, Whiskeytown National Recreation Area
Scott Gediman, Yosemite National Park
Ruby Newton, Mojave National Preserve
Barney Stoffel, Lava Beds National Monument
Charles Taylor, Santa Monica Mountains National Recreation Area
Cindy VonHalle, Joshua Tree National Park

## U.S. Army Corps of Engineers

Mary Ann Deeming, Black Butte Lake
Greg Volkman, Eastman Lake
Angie Wulsow, Lake Sonoma

## Bureau of Land Management

Larry Ames, Ukiah Field Office
Stan Bell, Eagle Lake Field Office
Jenny Weiss, Arcata Field Office

## State Parks

Greg Ahayes, Silverado District
Garratt Aitchison, Sugar Pine Point State Park
Jill Alford, Mendocino District
Jo Ann Allison, Big Sur Station (Big Sur state parks)
Kim Anbrychowicz, Prairie Creek Redwoods State Park
Jim Baird, Patrick's Point State Park
Katie Bernarding, Tomales Bay State Park
Becky Bradford, Butano State Park
Barry Breckling, Henry W. Coe State Park
James Burke and Tom Cline, Cuyamaca Rancho State Park
Brian Cahill, Colorado Desert District
Lori Castro, Castle Crags State Park
Sharon Galligan, Henry Cowell Redwoods State Park
Chuck Grennell, Calaveras Big Trees State Park
Bill Grummer, Bothe-Napa Valley State Park

Mike Hanes, Samuel P. Taylor State Park
David Horvitz, Sonoma Coast State Beach
Fred Jee, Anza Borrego Desert State Park
Allyn Kaye, Torrey Pines State Reserve
John Kolsrud, Armstrong Redwoods State Reserve
Bill Lindemann, Sierra District
John McGee, Point Lobos State Reserve
Susan McLaughlin, Richardson Grove State Park
Bill Mentzer, Mount Tamalpais State Park
Lynn Mochizuki, Leo Carrillo State Park and Malibu Creek State Park
William Moffat, Tule Elk State Reserve
Ken Morse, Jedediah Smith Redwoods State Park
Roger Nelson, Half Moon Bay State Beach
Dean Oertly, Plumas-Eureka State Park
John O'Rourke, Humboldt Redwoods State Park
Alex Ott, Fremont Peak State Park
Paula Pennington, Grover Hot Spring State Park
Shannon Pulce, Chino Hills State Park
Kay Robinson, Henry W. Coe State Park
Kelly Setters, Auburn State Recreation Area
John Trammer, Morro Bay State Park
Andrew Urlie, McArthur–Burney Falls State Park
Suzanne Westover, Salt Point State Park
Dan Winkelman, Angel Island State Park
Bill Wisehard, North Coast Redwoods District
Andy Zilke, Oceana Dunes State Vehicular Recreation Area

## Other Parks and Preserves
Mark Andre, City of Arcata
Edward Arcetta, Santa Clara County Parks Department
Maryanne Bache, San Elijo Lagoon Conservancy
David Brooks, Loch Lomond Recreation Area
Linda Chaplin, Sequoya Challenge
Joe DiDonato, East Bay Regional Parks District
Kay Elliott, Santa Barbara County Parks and Recreation
Paula Forgi, Pacific Gas & Electric Company
John Fulton, San Luis National Wildlife Refuge Complex
Matt Gilbert, Jackson Demonstration State Forest
Bill Hogan, Marin Open Space District
Denise Homer, Arcata Marsh Interpretive Center
Ed Hulme, Marin Municipal Water District
Paul Kilburg, Mission Trails Regional Park
Glenn Kinney, Wildwood Park, Conejo Rec. & Park District
Ken Klis, Lopez Lake Recreation Area
Donna LaGraffe, County of Sonoma
Nola Lamken, Silverwood Wildlife Sanctuary

Irene Lindsey, Kaweah Oaks Preserve
Barbara Lockwood, Dixon Lake/Escondido Parks and Recreation
Dave Lydick, County of Sacramento
Ned MacKay, East Bay Regional Parks District
Nancy McKay, East Bay Regional Parks District
Emily Messenger, TreePeople
Doug Miller, Toro County Park
David Numer, Devil's Punchbowl Natural Area
Olley Olsen, Santa Catalina Island Company
Dennis Parker, San Diego County Parks and Recreation
Sylvia Pelizza, Sonny Bono Salton Sea National Wildlife Refuge
Frances Scalvini, City of Ferndale
Kevin Smith, Santa Rosa Plateau Ecological Reserve
Darrell Wanner, Placerita Canyon County Park
Roger Wilbur, Los Banos Wildlife Area
Jeff Wilson, Tilden Regional Park
Betty Zeller, Big Morongo Canyon Preserve

## Field Scouts Providing Personal Updates

David Dayton, Phil Ford, Michael Furniss, John Hamilton, Jeremy Keyston, Kris Keyston, John King, Doug McConnell, Jim McDaniel, Paul McHugh, John Reginato, Paul and Patty Sakuma, George Seifert, Bob Simms, Marisa Solís, Bob and Eleanor Stienstra, Robert Stienstra Jr., John Thomas, Larry Yant.

# Index

# Notes

# Notes

## ALSO FROM
# AVALON TRAVEL PUBLISHING

### MOON HANDBOOKS®
THE CURE FOR THE COMMON TRIP

With expert authors covering the U.S., Canada, Mexico, Central and South America, and Asia and the Pacific, Moon ensures that travelers have an uncommon experience—and a few new stories to tell.

**www.moon.com**

### MOON METRO
UNFOLD THE CITY

Covering every major city in the world, Metro takes travel to a new level with its innovative fusion of discreet maps and insider advice.

**www.moon.com**

*Rick Steves*

**More *Savvy*. More *Surprising*. More *Fun*.**

Experience everything the *real* Europe has to offer with Rick Steves' best-selling guidebooks, phrase books, videos, and DVDs. As the #1 authority on European travel, Rick gives you inside information on what to visit, where to stay, and how to get there—economically and hassle-free.

**www.ricksteves.com**

www.travelmatters.com

AVALON TRAVEL PUBLISHING GUIDES ARE AVAILABLE
AT YOUR FAVORITE BOOK OR TRAVEL STORE

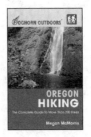

# ⒻOGHORN OUTDOORS®

## YOUR ADVENTURE STARTS HERE

Foghorn authors are recreation gurus who have hiked and biked the trails, fished the rivers, and pitched their tents to provide readers with the most up-to-date information on enjoying the outdoors. **www.foghorn.com**

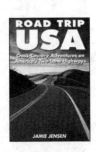

# ROAD TRIP USA

## OPEN ROAD. ENDLESS POSSIBILITIES.

See what the interstates have left behind. **ROAD TRIP USA** takes you off the beaten path, onto classic blacktop, and into the soul of America. **www.roadtripusa.com**

**The Inside Scoop on Where to Take Your Dog**

A special breed of guidebook for travelers and residents who don't want to leave their canine pals behind.

WWW.DOGLOVERSCOMPANION.COM

# LIVING ABROAD

## DREAM. PLAN. MAKE IT HAPPEN.

With authors who have made the move themselves, these guides show readers how to make their dream of living in another country a reality. **www.travelmatters.com**